Introduction to Psychology

Exploration and Application

Introduction to Psychology

Exploration and Application

Third Edition

Dennis Coon
Department of Psychology
Santa Barbara City College, California

West Publishing Company
St. Paul   New York   Los Angeles   San Francisco

About the cover In the background are several contributors to psychology's colorful history; from left to right they are, Sigmund Freud, Abraham Maslow, Wilhelm Wundt, John B. Watson, Karen Horney, and William James. In the foreground is Sarah chimpanzee. Under the guidance of psychologist David Premack, Sarah has participated in a fascinating series of experiments in human-animal communication. Conversations with Sarah are held by placing plastic symbols on a magnetic board. The board on the cover reads, "Sarah give name of book." Accordingly, Sarah is reaching for the Greek letter psi, which is widely used as a symbol for psychology. (For more information about Sarah, and related research, see Chapter 11 of this text.)

A study guide has been developed to assist you in mastering the concepts presented in this text. The study guide clarifies concepts by presenting them in concise, condensed form. It reinforces your understanding of terms, concepts, and individuals and also provides a programmed review and self-test questions. The study guide is available from your local bookstore under the title, *Study Guide to Accompany Introduction to Psychology: Exploration and Application,* prepared by Faren Akins.

A *Mastery Study Guide* written by Tom Bond also is available to accompany this book. The *Mastery Study Guide* is specially designed for self-paced, or PSI, courses. It is also highly appropriate for any course in which true mastery of concepts is the goal.

If you cannot locate either of these books in the bookstore, ask your bookstore manager to order them for you.

Design: Janet Bollow
Text illustrations: Brenda Booth, Sue Sellars, John Foster, Connie Warton, Heather Preston.
Color anatomical illustrations: Marsha Dohrmann
Cover and part opening art: Patrick Maloney
Copy editing: Stuart Kenter
Production Coordination: Janet Bollow Associates
Composition: Typothetae

Library of Congress Cataloging in Publication Data

Coon, Dennis.
    Introduction to psychology, exploration and application.

    Bibliography: p.
    Includes index.
    1. Psychology.   I. Title.
BF121.C625   1983   150   82–21769
ISBN 0–314–69642–3   INTL ED. ISBN 0–314–68853–6
    1st reprint 1983   1st reprint 1983

Acknowledgments The author is indebted to the following for permission to reproduce copyrighted materials.

Fig. 1-1 (*upper right*) © Keith Gunnar, Photo Researchers, Inc.; (*upper left*) © Frank Siteman, EKM-Nepenthe; (*lower right*) Cary Wolinsky, Stock, Boston; (*lower left*) Robert Eckert, EKM-Nepenthe.
Fig. 1-3 Photograph courtesy of the *Los Angeles Times* and Francine Patterson.
Fig. 1-4 Brown Brothers.
Fig. 1-5 Brown Brothers.
Fig. 1-6 Brown Brothers.
Fig. 1-7 United Press International
Fig. 1-8 The Bettmann Archive
Fig. 1-9 © Ted Polumbaum
pp. 28–29 Ulrich, R. E., Stachnik, T. J., and Stainton, N. R. Student acceptance of generalized personality interpretations. PSYCHOLOGICAL REPORTS, 1963, 13, 831–834.
p. 33 van Lawick-Goodall, Jane. *In The Shadow of Man.* Houghton Mifflin Co., 1971. World Rights: William Collins Sons & Co. Ltd., London.
Fig. 2-1 © 1973. Van Bucher, Photo Researchers, Inc.
Fig. 2-2 National Geographic Society Magazine. Photo by Baron Hugo van Lawick.
p. 60 Gazzaniga, M. S. *The Bisected Brain.* Plenum Publishing Co., 1970.
p. 61 Ornstein, R. E. *The Psychology of Consciousness.* W. H. Freeman & Co., 1972.

Fig. 3-15 Courtesy Circus World Museum, Baraboo, Wisconsin.
p. 77 Excerpted from *The Story of My Life,* by Helen Keller. Copyright 1902, 1903 and 1905 by Helen Keller. Copyright © 1955 by Doubleday & Company, Inc. Reprinted by permission of Doubleday & Company, Inc.
p. 94 Anastasi, Ann. *Fields of Applied Psychology,* McGraw-Hill, 1964. Reprinted by permission.
Fig. 4-18 The Bettmann Archive.
Fig. 5-4 © Allan D. Cruickshank, Photo Researchers, Inc.
Fig. 5-7 Albert Fenn, Life Magazine © Time, Inc.
Fig. 5-9 B. Julesz. *Foundations of Cyclopean Perception.* Copyright © 1971, University of Chicago Press.
Fig. 5-15 M. C. Escher "Still Life and Street" © BEELDRECHT, Amsterdam/VAGA, New York Collection Haags Gemeentemuseum—The Hague.
Fig. 5-16 From "Pictorial Perception and Culture" by J. B. Deregowski. Copyright © 1972 by *Scientific American,* Inc. All rights reserved.
Fig. 5-19 Baron Wolman
Fig. 5-20 © 1976 F. B. Grunzweig, Photo Researchers, Inc.
Fig. 5-25 Erdelyi, M. H. and A. G. Appelbaum, "Cognitive Masking: The Disruptive Effect of an Emotional Stimulus Upon the Perception of Contiguous Neutral Items." *Bulletin of the Psychonomic Society.* 1973, 1, 59–61.
p. 125 Kapleau, Philip. *The Three Pillars of Zen,* Harper & Row, 1966.
Fig. 6-2 Marge Agin.
Table 6-1 Stanford Hypnotic Scale, adapted from Weitzenhofler and Hilgard. Stanford University Press, 1959.

Fig. 6-3 Spectrum and Continuum of Drugs, Dr. Robert W. Earle, University of California, Irvine.

Fig. 6-4 Blood Alcohol Content Chart, courtesy of Jozef Cohen.

pp. 136–137 Facts About Drugs from *The Resource Book for Drug Abuse Education*. National Education Association, 1969.

Fig. 6-5 "Beware Marijuana" Poster courtesy of Dr. Lester Grinspoon, Harvard Medical School.

p. 146 Rahula, W. *What the Buddha Taught*. Reprinted by permission of Grove Press, Inc. Copyright © 1959 by W. Rahula, Second and enlarged edition. Copyright © 1974 by W. Rahula. All Rights Reserved.

p. 147 H. Benson. "Systematic Hypertension and The Relaxation Response." Reprinted by permission from *The New England Journal of Medicine*, Vol. 296, pp. 1152–1156, 1977.

Fig. 7-2 Yale Joel, © Life Magazine.

Fig. 7-3 © 1980 Bruce Kliewe, Jeroboam, Inc.

Fig. 7-5 Wide World Photos.

p. 166 *Gestalt Therapy Verbatim* by F. Pearls. Copyright © 1969 Real People Press. Reprinted by permission.

Fig. 8-7 Elliott Erwitt, Magnum Photos.

pp. 192–193 "Twin Oaks: On to Walden Two" Copyright 1971 Time Inc. All rights reserved. Reprinted by permission from TIME.

Fig. 9-1 Ira Kirschenbaum, Stock, Boston.

Fig. 9-4 Chimp-O-Mat. Yerkes Regional Primate Research Center, Emory University.

Fig. 9-8 "Effects of Punishment on Extinction." Chart from B. F. Skinner, *The Behavior of Organism*, 1938. Permission from Prentice-Hall, Inc.

Fig. 9-6 Fred Kaplan, Black Star.

Fig. 9-10 Nursery School Children, Dr. Albert Bandura, Stanford University.

p. 207 Cartoon reproduced courtesy of the Edmonton Journal.

Fig. 9-11 NIA Gerontology Photo.

Fig. 9-12 © Ben Rose, The Image Bank West.

Fig. 10-3 Penfield, W. *The Excitable Cortex in Conscious Man*, 1958. Courtesy of Charles C Thomas Publisher, Springfield, Illinois.

Fig. 10-6 Marge Agin.

Fig. 11-5 Osgood, C. E. "The Nature and Measurement of Meaning." *Psychological Bulletin*, 49, Copyright, 1952 by The American Psychological Association. Reprinted by permission.

Fig. 11-6 © Tom Hollyman, Photo Researchers, Inc.

Fig. 11-7 From "Teaching Language to An Ape." by Ann Premack and David Premack. Copyright © 1972 by *Scientific American*, Inc. All rights reserved.

Fig. 11-12 U.S. Patent No. 556,248. From *Absolutely Mad Inventions* by A. E. Brown and H. A. Jeffcott, Jr. Dover, 1970.

Fig. 12-1 Peeter Vilms, © Jeroboam, Inc.

Fig. 12-4 Hyperphagic Rat courtesy of Dr. Neal E. Miller, Rockefeller University.

Fig. 12-5 "Monkeys and Locks." Harry F. Harlow, University of Wisconsin Primate Laboratory.

Fig. 12-6 Berlyne, D. E. "Curiosity and Exploration." *Science*, Vol. 153, pp. 25–33, Figure 4, 1 July, 1966, Copyright 1966 by the American Assocaition For the Advancement of Science.

p. 279 Zuckerman, M. *Manual and Research Report for the Sensation-Seeking Scale (SSS)*. Mimeograph, University of Delaware, Newark, Delaware, April, 1972. Reproduced by permission.

Fig. 12-8 (*left*) © Mike Harker, The Image Bank, West; (*right*) © P. Rogers, The Image Bank West.

Fig. 12-9 Jerry Berndt, Stock, Boston.

p. 282 Horner, M. S. "The Psychological Significance of Success in Competitive Achievement Situations: A Threat As Well As A Promise." In Day, H. I, D. E. Berlyne and D. E. Hunt (eds) *Intrinsic Motivation: A New Direction In Education*. New York: Holt, Rinehart & Winston, 1971.

Fig. 12-11 Photograph courtesy of Rebecca Skelton.

Figs. 13-1, 13-8 Courtesy of The Record, Hackensack, New Jersey.

Fig. 13-4 Robert Eckert, EKM-Nepenthe.

Fig. 13-5 Photo courtesy of the Stoelting Company, Chicago, Illinois.

Fig. 13-6 Bridges, K. M. B. "Emotional Development in Early Infancy." *Child Development*, 3, 324–341. Figure 1, p. 340. Copyright, 1932.

Fig. 13-7 Ron Garrison, San Diego Zoo Photo.

Fig. 13-9 Susan Miller.

p. 310 The Danger Signals of Depression, National Association of Mental Health.

Table 14-2 Friedman, M. and R. Roseman. *Type A Behavior and Your Heart*, Alfred A. Knopf, Inc. 1974. Reprinted by permission.

Table 14-3 Reprinted with permission from the *Journal of Psychosomatic Research* Vol. 11. T. H. Holmes and R. H. Rahe. "Social Readjustment Rating Scale," 1957, Pergamon Press, Ltd.

Fig. 14-5 Executive Monkey photograph courtesy of Dr. Joseph V. Bradey, the Johns Hopkins University School of Medicine.

Fig. 14-6 The General Adaptation Syndrome graph from *The Stress of Life* by Hans Selye. Copyright © 1956, 1976 by Hans Selye. Used by permission of McGraw-Hill Book Company.

p. 316 The Better Half by Barnes, reprinted courtesy of Register and Tribune Syndicate, Inc.

p. 316 Associated Press news article courtesy of the Associated Press.

Fig. 15-1 "Imitation of Facial and Manual Gestures by Human Neonates." by A. N. Meltzoff and M. K. Moore. *Science*, vol. 198, pp. 75–78, Fig. 1, October 7, 1977. Copyright 1977 by The American Association for the Advancement of Science.

Fig. 15-2 From "The Origin of Form Perception." by Robert L. Fantz. Copyright © 1961 by Scientific American, Inc. All rights reserved. Photograph of Fantz's Looking Chamber by David Linton.

p. 345 Huxley, A. "Human Potentialities." In R. E. Farson (ed.) *Science and Human Affairs*. Palo Alto, California: Science and Behavior Books, 1965.

p. 355 Associated Press newsarticle courtesy of the Associated Press.

Fig. 15-3 Betsy Cole, Stock, Boston.

Fig. 15-5 Ruth Silverman, Stock, Boston.

Fig. 15-6 Photograph courtesy of H. Harlow University of Wisconsin Primate Laboratory.

p. 362 Hayakawa, S. I. "The Use and Misuse of Language." In R. E. Farson (ed.) *Science and Human Affairs*. Palo Alto, California: Science and Behavior Books, 1965.

Fig. 15-7 Thomas McAvoy, Life Magzine © 1955 Time, Inc.

Fig. 15-9 Marge Agin.

Fig. 16-1 © 1979 Optic Nerve, Jeroboam, Inc.

p. 370 *Psychology and Effective Behavior* by James C. Coleman. Copyright © 1969 by Scott, Foresman and Company. Reprinted by permission.

p. 372 Dooley's World © Roger Bradfield.

Fig. 16-2 From "Growing Up" by J. M. Tanner. Copyright © September, 1973 by *Scientific American*, Inc. All rights reserved.

Fig. 16-3 Wayne Miller, Magnum Photos.

Fig. 16-4 Photo Courtesy of Benhaven.

Fig. 16-5 Bill Stanton, Magnum Photos.

p. 383 Ehrenburg, I. "A Last Memoir" In Cousins, N. (ed.) *What I Have Learned*. Saturday Review, 1968.

p. 387 Ginott, H. *Between Parent and Child*. 1965. Reprinted by permission of Dr. Alice Ginott.

Table 17-1 Terman, L. and M. Merrill, *Stanford-Binet Intelligence Scale*. 1937 (Revised ed. 1960b). Houghton Mifflin Co.

Table 17-2 Wechsler Scale, The Psychological Corporation, 1958.

Contents in Brief

Contents

10
Memory 219

11
Thinking, Problem Solving, and Creativity 243

Part IV
Actions and Reactions   267

12
Motivation   269

13
Emotion   292

19
Theories of Personality   435

Part VI
Abnormal Behavior and Psychotherapy   457

20
Deviance and Disorder: The Unhealthy
Personality   459

21
Psychosis 480

22
Insight Therapy 500

23
Behavior Modification 518

Part VII
Self and Others   535

24
Human Sexuality   537

25
Social Psychology I   559

26
Social Psychology II   584

Preface to the Third Edition

To the Student

Having recently completed another excursion through the colorful realm of psychology, I am awed and humbled by the breadth and diversity of knowledge to be found there (not to mention the rate at which it is growing). It is no small wonder to me that first-time visitors are routinely able to digest the contents of a book such as this. Perhaps it is because psychology is naturally interesting and immediately useful; perhaps because it is ultimately about each of us. In any case, I sincerely hope that you will find psychology as fascinating as I have. In this text, I have done everything I could imagine to make your first encounter with psychology meaningful, enjoyable, and worthwhile.

To get off to a good start, and to learn why this book is organized as it is, you should begin by reading the Introduction ("The Psychology of Studying Psychology"), which follows this Preface. In it you will learn skills to help you get the most out of this text, class lectures, and your psychology course as a whole. In the remaining chapters, I hope that some of the delight I have found in my own students' curiosity, insight, imagination, and interest will be apparent. Please view this book as a long letter from me to you. It is, in a very real sense, written about you, for you, and to you.

To the Instructor

This book differs from traditional texts in a number of important ways. If you are already familiar with its format, a description of Third Edition changes follows shortly. If the text is unfamiliar, a brief discussion of its design and underlying philosophy is in order.

A Book for Students   As an instructor I have learned that selection of a textbook is half the battle in teaching a course. A good text does much of the work of conveying information to the students. This leaves class time free for discussion, and it leaves students asking for more. When a book overwhelms students or cools their interest, teaching becomes an uphill battle. For this reason, I have worked hard to make this a readable, comprehensible, and interesting text.

This book is a complete but non-encyclopedic introduction to psychology. I believe an important question to ask of the introductory course is, "What will students remember next year, or in ten years?" Like a good painting, an effective text must be highly selective: What is left out is often as important as what is included. Consequently, I have tried to give students a clear grasp of major concepts, rather than bury them in details of interest only to professionals. In the same sense, a good text must be balanced. I have, therefore, tried to show the value of many theoretical perspectives to foster an appreciation for the contributions of each. I think students will find this book full of intellectual challenge, and teachers will find traditional topics covered to their satisfaction. In addition, I have made a special effort to relate psychology to common experiences and to practical problems of daily life.

A major feature of this book is the series of "Applications" found near the end of each chapter. These sections bridge the gap between psychological theory and practical application. I believe students have every right to ask, "Does this mean anything to me? Can I use it? Why should I learn it if I can't?" No matter how interesting or intellectually stimulating, a text that fails to show the practical consequence of adopting new ideas is irrelevant in a very basic sense. The Applications sections therefore spell out how students can make use of the principles of psychology. In doing so, they breathe life into its concepts.

At the end of each chapter you will find a separate "Exploration." These sections cover current issues, topics from psychology's frontiers, or subjects likely to promote thought and discussion. In essence, they serve as "mini-articles" to provide a taste of the changing issues and ideas that make psychology exciting. Traditionally, such material might appear in "boxes" within a chapter. However, I believe that placement of Explorations at the end of chapters allows greater flexibility. Because of their location, they are easy to assign or delete—something difficult to do with scattered "boxes."

A Format for Learning   Before this book first appeared, psychology texts made surprisingly little use of learning principles to teach psychology. The extensive use of learning aids herein is based on my belief that students can be guided into more effective study and reading habits while simultaneously learning course content. Basically each chapter is built around the well-known SQ3R study-reading formula. Thus, in addition to helping students learn psychology, the chapter format encourages the development of valuable study skills. Student response to this feature of the text has been overwhelmingly positive, with many students reporting that they transfer the SQ3R technique to their other texts.

Each chapter is divided into seven parts: a Chapter Preview, Resources, Resources Summary, Applications, Exploration, Questions for Discussion, and Suggestions for Further Reading. Chapter Previews are used to arouse reader interest, to give an overview of the chapter, and to focus attention on the task at hand. Each Preview concludes with a series of "Survey Questions," to further orient the reader and aid the survey step of the SQ3R method. The Resources section that follows presents major concepts of the chapter. Next, the Resources Summary reviews key ideas, and the Applications section shows how they can be applied. The final sections round out the chapter, expand student horizons, and provide a basis for thought and discussion.

Throughout each chapter "guide questions" are used to maintain reader attention, and to make reading an active learning experience. Despite its appearance, this is not just a question-and-answer format. Rather, it takes the form of a dialogue in which student questions and reactions are anticipated. Guide questions cue students to look for important points in the paragraphs that follow, thus fulfilling the *question* part of SQ3R. And, significantly, they also allow clarification of difficult points through a lively give-and-take between questions and responses.

If you glance through the text you will immediately notice the "Learning Checks" interspersed throughout. These are short, noncomprehensive quizzes that allow readers to gauge recall and comprehension of preceding material. When they cannot answer Learning Check questions, students are directed to review the previous section before reading more. Completing Learning Checks also serves as a form of recitation (the fourth step in SQ3R) to enhance learning. The last SQ3R step (review) is aided by a detailed, point-by-point Resources Summary.

As a supplement to its SQ3R format, *Introduction to Psychology: Exploration and Application* includes a full array of traditional learning aids. These include: boldface type and phonetic pronunciations for important terms, an extensive glossary, summary tables, multi-level subheadings, discussion questions, a detailed index, suggested readings, and a robust illustration program. Moreover, chapters have been kept short so that each can be read in a single session. This brevity provides for flexibility in ordering chapters, and it gives students a sense of closure or completion at the end of each assignment. Finally, and perhaps most importantly, the readability of each chapter has been carefully controlled for maximum student involvement and comprehension.

Third Edition Changes   Three years ago I would have scoffed at the idea of revising this text as extensively as I have for this edition. Without doubt, psychology is a fast-moving field. But is a three-year revision cycle really necessary? After a year and a half of almost continuous work I am forced to conclude that the answer is yes. Like so many other fields, psychology is caught up in an information explosion. Some of the ideas I held true only three years ago now look absolutely wrong in view of recent research. To keep a text current and accurate in psychology is a never-ending task. (Or, to put it another way, the myth of Sisyphus has recently taken on a new poignancy for me!) With this in mind, I am fortunate to be able to note that many of the changes in this edition were suggested by current users. Without their generous sharing of expertise and ideas this revision would have been impossible.

This new edition represents a substantial updating. Virtually every chapter has been rewritten, reorganized, or improved, with much new information evident at every turn of a page. I have drawn upon over three hundred new references (many as recent as 1982) to produce four new or revised Previews, eleven new or revised Applications, five new Explorations, and many, many additions to the Resources sections. Some chapters, such as three and ten, have been heavily revised. A very exciting change that will be readily apparent is the dramatic upgrading of figures, graphs, and illustrations. Two small changes have served to further strengthen the chapter format. By user request, Previews now end with a series of Survey Questions relevant to the chapter. Also by request, Applications sections now include a final Learning Check. The glossary is larger and has pronunciations for difficult terms. The Instructor's Manual has been greatly enlarged and updated. A separate Test Bank, with over 2500 questions revised by Kathryn Schwarz, is now available. In short, this has been anything but a "change-the-second-color" revision.

The changes in this edition are far too numerous to list here. I would, nevertheless, like to at least list new or enlarged Applications and Explorations. In the Applications you will find new sections on: understanding handedness and brain dominance (Chapter 3), pain control (Chapter 4), increasing perceptual accuracy (Chapter 5), lucid dreaming (Chapter 7), breaking bad habits (Chapter 9), coping with death, depression, and bereavement (Chapter 13), stress management (Chapter 14), parenting and child abuse (Chapter 16), understanding shyness (Chapter 18), suicide prevention (Chapter 20), and assertiveness training (Chapter 25). New or enlarged Explorations topics include: synesthesia and the unity of the senses (Chapter 5), operant communities (Chapter 8), pluralistic IQ testing (Chapter 17), the insanity defense (Chapter 20), and attribution theory (Chapter 26). All of the remaining Applications and Explorations remain intact.

A few other additions that cannot go without mention are new discussions of: procrastination, the correlational method, deafness, sensory gating, pain, caffeine and nicotine, sleep apnea and sudden infant death, two-factor learning, motor skills learning, current memory research, mental imagery and creativity, opponent-process theory, primary emotions, stress inoculation, prelanguage communication, learning disabilities, cognitive therapy, self-disclosure, and "jigsaw" classrooms. This, in fact, is really just a sample of the new information to be found in this edition.

Two excellent and completely revised study guides will again be available with this edition. Faren Akins' *Study Guide* offers students a way of structuring learning outside the classroom. Each chapter in the *Study Guide* includes a list of important terms and individuals, a programmed review, and a self-test of multiple choice and true-false questions. Instructors who use a mastery-based approach (including P.S.I.), or who would like to try it, may want to use Tom Bond's *Mastery Study Guide*. Tom's *Mastery Study Guide* is ideal for self-paced courses, but it is highly appropriate for traditional courses as well. Each chapter includes: learning objectives, two objective tests ("Do You

Know the Material," "Can You Apply the Material"), and a fill-in-the-blanks chapter review. Tom has also prepared a special instructor's manual containing multiple test forms, short answer questions (with answers) and an introduction to P.S.I. to make mastery-based teaching both practical and enjoyable.

I sincerely hope that teachers and students will consider this book and its supporting materials a refreshing change from the ordinary. Writing and revising it has been quite an adventure. In the pages that follow, I think the reader will find an attractive blend of the theoretical and practical, the esoteric and the commonplace, plus many of the most exciting topics in psychology.

The enterprise of psychology is a cooperative effort requiring the talents and energies of an entire community of scholars, teachers, researchers, and students. As with the original version of this text, this edition has combined the efforts of a large number of people. I would like to thank first the many students who sent comments, suggestions, and encouragement. To the professional users/reviewers who gave their time and expertise I extend my sincere thanks. I deeply appreciate the efforts of the following people:

Lynn Anderson
Wayne State University, Michigan

Frank Barbehenn
Bucks County Community College, Pennsylvania

Tom Bond
Thomas Nelson College, Virginia

John Boswell
University of Missouri, St. Louis, Missouri

Chris Cozby
California State University, Fullerton, California

Bill Dwyer
Memphis State University, Tennessee

David Edwards
Iowa State University, Iowa

David Gershaw
Arizona Western College, Arizona

Fran O'Keefe
Tidewater Community College, Virginia

Darlene Pacheco
Moorpark College, California

Mark Vernoy
Palomar College, California

Otto Zinser
East Tennessee State College, Tennessee

I would also like to thank Kathryn Schwarz for her excellent work in revising test questions, along with Charles Croll and Linda Kovaacs for sharing their diagnostic reading test with others, via the instructor's manual for this text.

Getting a text into print is an arduous undertaking. With this fact in mind, I would like to express my gratitude to: Stuart Kenter for his thoughtful and conscientious editing; Patrick Maloney for his inimitable cover art; Brenda Booth and Marsha Dohrmann for their excellent interior artwork; Carole Grumney for her work on the Test Bank; Bill Stryker for his on-going advice and support; Tim Danielson for his patience; and Jeanne Hoene for preparing the brochure for this edition. To these individuals goes much of the credit for the successful completion of this project.

Finally, I would like to express my deep appreciation to Clyde H. Perlee, Jr., Editor-in-Chief of West's College Department for helping, inch by inch, row by row, to make my garden grow. This text has benefitted greatly from his guidance and support, as have I. I am equally indebted to Janet Bollow, not simply for designing and assembling this book, or for doing it under trying circumstances, or for humanizing a trying period of my life, but also for introducing me to Sylvia. Last of all, I would like to thank my wife and co-conspirator, Sevren, whose help made this book possible.

Dennis Coon

Introduction to Psychology

Exploration and Application

The Psychology of Studying Psychology

How to Communicate with Your Textbook

In the chapters that follow, you will learn about personality, emotion, creativity, abnormal behavior, and a host of other interesting and useful topics. Since this book is your link to this information, a few words follow about how to make best use of it.

SQ3R The chapters of this text are designed to help you use the **SQ3R method**—a valuable study-reading technique introduced over 40 years ago by Dr. Francis P. Robinson. The SQ3R approach is designed to help you (1) select what is important, (2) understand these ideas quickly, (3) remember what you have read, and (4) review effectively for tests (Robinson, 1941). The symbols SQ3R stand for important steps in effective study reading:

Step One: *Survey* = Look over the title and main headings in each chapter before reading in detail. Read captions under any pictures or illustrations. Read any summary statement or review if the chapter has one. This step should be a quick survey, taking no more than two minutes. It gives you an overall picture of what is in the chapter.

Step Two: *Question* = In order to concentrate on the content of a chapter, turn each topic heading into one or more questions. This will increase your interest in what you read, and it forces you to concentrate on ideas and information. The result is an increase in your comprehension.

Step Three: *Read* = The first R in SQ3R refers to *read*. As you read, try to answer the questions you asked. Read only from *one topic heading* to the next, then stop. Don't go on to another heading.

Step Four: *Recite* = The second R stands for *recite*. After you have turned a heading into questions and read only to the next heading, you should stop and recite; that is, try to answer your questions and summarize what you've read in your own words. If you can't answer your questions or summarize main ideas, scan back over the section until you can. It can be helpful at this point to jot down important terms and ideas in a brief set of notes that includes the questions you asked. After you have completed one section in this way, turn the next topic heading into a question and then read to the following heading. Again, you should look for answers as you read, and you should recite before moving on. Repeat this process until the entire chapter is read.

Step Five: *Review* = When the chapter has been read completely, look over your notes and check your memory by reciting the answers to questions again. Or better yet, get someone to ask you questions about each topic to see if you can answer in your own words.

Question: Does this method really work?

Experiments show that using the SQ3R method improves reading comprehension and efficiency (Boker, 1974). Students who haven't learned a reading strategy tend to read straight through an entire chapter and try to remember everything. This approach is only slightly better than not reading at all! It is not wise to read a textbook as you would a novel. You must actively "dig out" information and give yourself a chance to pause and digest what you are learning. A **survey** prepares you to read effectively by giving you an overview. **Questioning** maintains your concentration on the subject, and it allows you to **read** in short "bites." **Recitation** of what you've read allows you to actively participate in and check up on your learning. Finally, **review** of the

1

whole chapter ties together what you have learned and increases your understanding.

Have you ever had the experience of passing your eyes over several pages of a textbook, only to discover that you couldn't remember anything? More than anything else the SQ3R method helps avoid this. That's why it's important that you *not* keep reading an assignment, but that you stop periodically, recite by taking brief notes in your own words, and review immediately after the entire chapter has been read.

Question: You said earlier that the chapters of this book are set up according to the SQ3R study formula. Can you explain that?

The SQ3R method can be used with any text. However, if you glance through this text you will see that it is designed to help you use it. Look also at the end of this introduction, where you will find a sample chapter. Notice how the steps of the SQ3R method are a part of the format. The opening of each chapter is a preview, followed by survey questions for the chapter. Chapters are further broken up by questions which are answered in the material that follows. Recent research shows that this arrangement leads to improved learning and memory (Boker, 1974; Melton, 1978).

Periodically, there are "Learning Checks" so you can make certain that you understand the most important points. Toward the end of each chapter there is a short review, followed by two sections (called "Applications" and "Explorations") to extend your understanding. After the last chapter in the book, you will find a **glossary,** or "mini-dictionary" of psychological terms. However, to aid your studying, new terms are defined whenever they first appear in the text. As you read, notice also that key terms are printed in **boldface type.** *Italic type* is used to highlight additional ideas of importance, and to provide special emphasis. Pronunciations for unusual or unfamiliar terms are provided along with the term itself. For example, the word *somesthetic* (SOH-mes-THET-ik) is pronounced like the phonetic spelling in parentheses—capital letters indicate accented syllables. Together these features are designed to make learning psychology enjoyable and effective, but there are still some things you must do on your own.

Effective Note-taking

Question: The SQ3R may be good for study-reading, but what about taking notes in class when it's difficult to know what's important?

Effective note-taking requires active listening. **Active listeners** have a plan to follow. They know that they'll "drift away" on other thoughts if they do not control their attention. Here's a listening-note-taking plan that works for many students. The important steps are summarized by the letters in the word **LISAN,** pronounced LISTEN (Carman and Adams, 1972).

L = *Lead. Don't follow.* Try to anticipate what the instructor may be going to say. As in SQ3R, try to set up questions as guides. Questions can come from the instructor's study guides or the reading assignments.

I = *Ideas.* Every lecture will be based around a core of important ideas. Usually an idea is introduced and examples or explanations are given. Ask questions such as: What is the main idea of this lecture? What important ideas will help support this?

S = *Signal words.* Listen for words that tell you the direction the instructor is taking. For instance, here are some groups of signal words:

There are three reasons why . . .	Here come ideas
Most important is . . .	Main ideas
On the contrary . . .	Opposite idea
As an example . . .	Support for main idea
Therefore . . .	Conclusion

A = *Actively listen.* Sit where you can hear and where you can be seen if you need to ask a question. Be on time. Look at the instructor while he or she talks. Bring questions from the last lecture or from your reading you want answered. Raise your hand at the beginning of class or approach your instructor before the lecture begins. Do anything that helps you to be active.

N = *Note-taking.* As you listen, write down only key points. Listen to everything, but be selective and don't try to write everything down. If you're too busy writing, you may miss important parts of the lecture.

There is something more you should know about note-taking: In a recent study, psychologists Robin Palkovitz and Richard Lore (1980) found that most students take reasonably good notes—and then fail to use them! Palkovitz and Lore discovered that students who missed questions on tests could later find the answers in their own notes. Apparently, most students waited until just before an exam to look at their notes. By then the notes were so old they had lost much of their meaning. If you don't want your notes to seem like hieroglyphics, it pays to review them *on a regular basis.* And remember, whenever it is important to listen effectively, the letters LISAN are a guide to better comprehension.

Taking Tests

Question: If I have read effectively and listened effectively in lecture, is there anything else I can do to improve my study skills?

One area that often gives students difficulty is test-taking. Learning the material in a course is only a first step. You must then be able to show what you have learned on a test. Here are some guidelines for test-taking you might consider.

Objective Tests   Objective tests (multiple-choice and true-false items) are often reading tests. They check on your ability to recognize a correct statement among wrong answers or a correct statement against a false one. If you are taking an objective test, try this:

1. Read the directions carefully. Don't assume that because the question has a T or F to circle, or four or five items to select from, that you know what to do. The directions may give you good advice or clues for the test. If the directions are not clear, ask the instructor to clarify them.
2. Read each statement or question carefully. If you have several choices for each item, read them *all* before deciding the correct answer. You may mark one you think is correct only to find the last choice says "both a and d," yet you only marked "a" as the answer.
3. Skip items you are not certain about. Go through the test answering the ones you do know. If there is time left, go back to the ones you skipped.
4. Eliminate certain alternatives. With a four choice per item multiple-choice test, the odds are one in four that you could guess right. If you can eliminate one of the alternatives, your odds are one in three. If you can eliminate two alternatives your guessing odds are one in two, or 50–50. Those are better odds than pure guessing.
5. There is a bit of folk wisdom that says, "Don't change your answers on a multiple-choice test. Your first choice is usually right." Careful study of this idea has shown it to be *false.* Students who switch answers are more likely to change from wrong to right than the reverse (Davis, 1975;

Edwards and Marshall, 1977). This is especially true if you feel *very* uncertain of your first answer. When you have strong doubts, your second answer is more likely to be correct (Johnson, 1975).

Essay Tests   Essay questions are often a student's weak spot simply because of poor organization, poor or no support of main ideas, or not writing directly to the question. When you take essay exams try the following:

1. Read the question carefully. Make sure that you note key words, such as *compare, contrast, discuss, evaluate, analyze,* or *describe.* These words all demand a certain emphasis in your answer.
2. Think about your answer before putting words on paper. It's a good idea to make a brief list of the points you want to make in your answer. Just list them as they pop into your head. Then rearrange your points so that you have them organized in the order you want to write them.
3. Don't beat around the bush or pad your answer. Be direct. Make a point and support it. Get your list of ideas into words.
4. Look over your essay for spelling errors, sentence errors, and grammatical errors. Save this for last. Your ideas are more important than misspelled words or poor sentence structure. You can work on such problems separately if they affect your grades.

Self-Testing and Overlearning   Many students overlook one of the most direct approaches for improving test scores: When studying, you can arrange to take several "practice tests" before a real one is given in class. In other words, studying should include **self-testing** by use of flashcards, "learning checks," a study guide, or questions you have written for yourself. When you study you should say to yourself, "What could I be asked about this?" Ask as many questions as you can and be sure you can answer them. Studying without testing yourself is like practicing for a basketball game without shooting any baskets.

When you prepare for exams, there is something else to keep in mind: Many students *underprepare* for exams, and most *overestimate* how well they will do on exams before taking them (Murray, 1980). A solution to both problems is **overlearning.** In overlearning, study or practice continues beyond "bare mastery" of a topic. This means that you should give yourself enough time for added study and review *after* you think you are prepared for an exam.

The tips on learning skills given here are just to get you

off to a good start. Additional help is available in the books listed at the end of this section. You may also want to look ahead to the discussion on improving memory at the end of Chapter 10.

Procrastination

Whether you're on probation or on the dean's list, a tendency to procrastinate is almost universal among college students. Even when procrastination doesn't lead to failure or lowered grades, it can cause much suffering. Procrastinators put off work until the last possible moment, work only when under pressure, stay away from classes and avoid professors, fabricate reasons for late work, and feel ashamed of the last-minute work they do (Burka and Yuen, 1981).

Question: Why do so many students procrastinate?

College work revolves around deadlines and long-range assignments. A tendency to put off work under these circumstances is fairly natural and not limited to school. However, there are some special reasons for student procrastination. Psychologists Jane Burka and Lenora Yuen, who have worked with procrastinators, observe that many students seem to believe the following equation: *self-worth = ability = performance.* That is, students often equate performance in school with their personal worth. By procrastinating, students can blame poor work on their late start, rather than a lack of ability—after all, it wasn't their best effort, was it?

Perfectionism is a related problem. Students who have very high standards or expectations for themselves may find it hard to start an assignment. Such students seem to expect the impossible from themselves and end up with all-or-nothing work habits (Burka and Yuen, 1981). If you tend to procrastinate, you might find it interesting to list the excuses you've used to avoid studying, and then examine what the excuses tell about your attitudes toward schoolwork.

Time Management   Burka and Yuen supervise an eight-week program for procrastinators at the University of California, Berkeley. Eventually, they say, most procrastinators must face the self-worth conflict; but useful progress can be made by learning better study skills and effective time management. Since we have already discussed study skills, let's consider time management.

A **formal time schedule** can do much to prevent procrastination and maintain motivation in school. To prepare your schedule, make a chart showing all of the hours in each day of the week. Then fill in times that are already committed: sleep, meals, classes, work, team practices, lessons, appointments, and so forth. Next, fill in times when you will study for various classes, and label them. Finally, label the remaining hours as "open" or "free" times. The beauty of keeping such a schedule is that you *know* you are making an honest effort to do well in your classes. Not only will you get more done, you will also avoid the trap of thinking about playing when you are trying to work, and worrying about working while you are trying to play. The key to time management is to treat your study times as serious commitments, like class meetings or a job, and to respect your free times as well. By doing so, you will avoid the feeling that you are working all the time, when in reality you are worrying all the time, but accomplishing little.

Motivation

Question: All these study techniques are fine, but what if I'm just not interested in some of the courses I have to take?

It is important to realize that virtually every topic is interesting to someone, somewhere. Although I may not be interested in the sex life of the South American tree frog, a biologist might be fascinated. If you wait for your teachers to "make" their courses interesting, you are missing the point. Interest is a matter of *your attitude.* No teacher can "make" a course interesting without your help. In fact, many students find that their interest in a subject develops only after they have made an effort to master basic ideas. If you bring an inquiring mind and a positive attitude to your studies, you will find learning exciting, challenging, and interesting. If you wait passively to be entertained, you will find learning a chore. Students and teachers *together* make a class interesting.

A Final Word   There is a distinction made in Zen between "live words" and "dead words." Live words come from personal experience; dead words are "about" a subject. This book can only be a collection of dead words without your personal involvement. It is designed to help you learn psychology, but it cannot do it for you. You will find many helpful, useful, and exciting ideas in the pages that follow. To make them yours, you must set out to learn *actively* as much as you can. We think it will be worth the effort. Good luck!

Suggestions for Further Reading

Brown, Charles, and W. Royce Adams. *How to Read the Social Sciences.* Scott, Foresman, 1968.

Burns, D. D. "The Perfectionist's Script for Self-Defeat," *Psychology Today,* November, 1980, pp. 34–52.

Carman, Robert A., and W. Royce Adams. *Study Skills: A Student's Guide for Survival.* Wiley, 1972.

Ellis, A., and W. J. Knaus. *Overcoming Procrastination.* Rational Living, 1977.

Pauk, W. *How to Study in College,* 2nd ed. Houghton Mifflin, 1974.

Chapter Format

Each chapter begins with a preview of topics to be covered:

Chapter Preview

A Living Nightmare and Life Beyond Time

In January 1959, a New York disc jockey named Peter Tripp staged a "waka-thon" in Times Square. Tripp went without sleep for 200 hours. Tripp's fight to stay awake was difficult from the beginning. After 100 hours, he began to have visual hallucinations. He saw cobwebs in his shoes, and a doctor's tweed coat became a suit of furry worms . . .

These previews end with a series of questions to guide your survey of the chapter:

Survey Questions: How much sleep do we need? What are the effects of sleep loss or changes in sleep patterns? Are there different stages of sleep? How does dream sleep differ from . . .

Next comes the main body of the chapter, the "Resources" section:

Resources

Sleep—A Nice Place to Visit

Each of us will spend some 25 years of life in a strange state of semiconsciousness called sleep. Sleep is unique in many ways. It is not totally unconscious because dreams are often remembered . . .

Throughout each chapter, you will find questions to focus your reading:

Question: How long could a person go without sleep?

Sleep Deprivation With few exceptions, four days or more without sleep becomes hell for anyone, but longer sleepless periods are possible. The world record for continuous wakefulness is held by Randy Gardner—who, at age seventeen, went 268 hours (11 days) without sleep. It might seem that a person would sleep for days after such a marathon. But Randy needed only 14 hours of sleep to recover (Dement, 1972). Surprisingly, it is not necessary to completely replace lost sleep. Most symptoms of sleep deprivation are removed by a single night's rest.

Later, a "Learning Check" gives you an opportunity to test your memory and comprehension:

--- **Learning Check** ---

1. A momentary shift in brain activity to a pattern characteristic of sleep is referred to as:

    a. delta sleep   *b.* light sleep   *c.* microsleep   *d.* deprivation sleep

2. Delusions and hallucinations may continue for several days after a sleep-deprived individual returns to normal sleep. T or F?

(Answers follow each "Learning Check.")

At the end of the "Resources" section, a summary restates important ideas:

--- Resources Summary ---

● Although there is much individual variation in sleep needs, sleep is an innate *biological rhythm* essential for survival. Higher animals and people deprived of sleep experience involuntary *microsleeps.*

● Moderate sleep loss mainly affects vigilance and performance on routine or boring tasks. Extended sleep loss can (somewhat rarely) produce a temporary *sleep deprivation psychosis.* It is not necessary to make up for lost sleep.

Following the "Resources" is a brief discussion on how to apply psychological principles in everyday life. For instance, the "Applications" for the chapter sampled here is on dream recording and dream interpretation. Each chapter concludes with an "Exploration" into a topic of high interest, a controversial issue, or a frontier area of psychology, in this case, dream control. "Explorations" are followed by a series of questions for discussion, and a list of suggested readings.

Contents

Part I

Introduction
to
Psychology

1

An Introduction to Psychology and Psychologists

Chapter Preview

Why Study Psychology?

You are a universe, a collection of worlds within worlds. Your brain is possibly the most complicated and amazing device in existence. Through the action of its 100 billion nerve cells you are capable of art, music, science, philosophy, and war. Your capacities for compassion, affection, and dedication coexist with your capacities for aggression, hatred, and . . . murder? You are the most frustrating riddle ever written, a mystery at times even to yourself. You are at one and the same time a unique event in human history and like everyone who has ever lived. Your thoughts, emotions, and actions, your behavior and conscious experience are the subject of this book.

Perhaps the simplest reason for studying psychology is that we are in the midst of a psychological revolution. Aldous Huxley has said:

> We have had religious revolutions, we have had political, industrial, economic, and nationalistic revolutions. All of them, as our descendents will discover, were trivial by comparison with the psychological revolution toward which we are rapidly moving (Huxley, 1971).

Look around you. Newspapers, magazines, radio, and television abound with psychological information. Psychology is discussed in homes, schools, businesses, and bars. Psychology is an explosive, exciting, and ever-changing panorama of people and ideas. You can hardly consider yourself "educated" without knowing something about it.

There is another reason for studying psychology. Socrates said, "Know thyself," and although we must envy those who have set foot on the moon, looked into an atom, or experienced firsthand the dreamlike landscapes of the ocean's depths, the ultimate frontier still lies close to home. Psychologist D. O. Hebb put it this way: "What is psychology all about? . . . Psychology is about the mind: the central issue, the great mystery, the toughest problem of all" (Hebb, 1974).

Psychology is a journey into inner space. This book is a travel guide. Psychologists can't claim to have "the answers" to all of your questions, but they can show you the contours of the landscape already explored. More importantly, you may find skills in psychology that will aid you in your own search for answers. Ultimately the answers must be your own, but studying psychology is a rich starting point. In this chapter you will find a definition of psychology, a description of various kinds of psychologists and what they do, and a brief history of ideas in psychology.

Resources

"The elephant," said the blind man as he felt the elephant's leg, "is very much like a tree."

"Why how foolish!" said a second blind man (who had hold of the elephant's tail). "The elephant is like a rope."

The third blind man, having encountered the beast's trunk, said, "You're both wrong, the elephant is like a snake."

Psychology: Psyche = Mind; Logos = Knowledge or Study

Question: What is psychology?

Psychology is: memory, stress, psychotherapy, love, persuasion, hypnosis, perception, death, conformity, creativity, conditioning, personality, aging, intelligence, sexuality, emotion, and so much more that a brief description will doubtless leave you in a position similar to that of the blind men. Psychology has become such an enormous and colorful beast that no short description can do it justice.

It is important, then, to be open-minded as you begin the study of psychology. Consider it an adventure, and judge after you have seen what psychology has to offer. By the time you have read this entire book you will begin to have an overall picture of what psychology is, and what psychologists do. For now, let's just say that **psychology** *is the scientific study of the behavior of organisms.* Its goals are to **describe, understand, predict,** and **control** behavior.

Question: What does "behavior" refer to in the definition of psychology?

Behavior is anything you do. Eating, sleeping, talking, thinking, and sneezing are "behaviors." So are dreaming, gambling, taking drugs, watching TV, learning Spanish, basket weaving, and reading this book. Notice that behaviors can be *overt* (visible) or *covert* (private or internal, such as thinking). Much of what we do (overt behavior) can be studied by direct observation. But how do we study thinking, daydreaming, or memory? In such cases we must *infer* what is happening "internally" from what we can observe externally. For example, try answering these questions: "Is a horse bigger than a mouse?"; "Is a collie bigger than a German shepard?" If you are like most people, you answered the first question faster than the second. Why? Most people say they form mental images of the animals to compare their size, and that comparing images close in size is more difficult (Moyer and Bayer, 1976). Although we couldn't directly observe thinking, we were able to learn something interesting about it just the same.

Question: It seems from this example that psychologists try to be objective in their observations. Is that correct?

Yes. Psychologists have a special respect for **empirical evidence.** That is, information gained by direct observation and measurement, rather than through opinion, argument, or citing an authority. Would you say it's true, for instance, that "you can't teach an old dog new tricks"? Why argue about it? A psychologist would get 10 "new" dogs, 10 "used" dogs, and 10 "old" dogs and then try to teach them all new tricks to find out!

Whenever possible, psychologists settle differences by direct investigation. As self-evident as this approach may seem in fields like biology or physics, we are still often tempted in psychology to accept what seems plausible or sensible, rather than what *is.* For example, see how many of these questions you can answer correctly on the basis of personal experience, reasoning, or common sense, and then we will compare your answers to those found scientifically or empirically.

1. Owls can see in complete darkness.   T or F?

2. The higher a person's IQ, the greater the chance of mental illness. (Genius is next to insanity.)   T or F?

3. The image of the moon is magnified by the atmosphere when the moon is low in the sky.   T or F?

4. Those who threaten suicide rarely actually commit suicide.   T or F?

5. When hypnotized, people can be made to perform feats of strength that would ordinarily be impossible.   T or F?

6. Intelligence is completely inherited from one's parents. T or F?

7. If your car breaks down, you are more likely to get help from a passerby on a busy highway than on a lightly traveled country road.   T or F?

8. Punishment is the most effective way to reinforce the learning of new habits.   T or F?

9. Drug addiction is one of the major causes of murder and other violent crimes.   T or F?

10. A one-eyed man could not land an airplane.   T or F?

Scoring this quiz is easy since all of the statements are F, false. If you missed some, don't despair, because the point is simply this: Psychology became a science when psychologists began to perform experiments, make observations, and seek evidence, and you will become a better observer of human behavior to the extent that you do the same.

Question: I've heard that psychology isn't scientific. You have said it is. Is it?

Fig. 1-1 *The variety and complexity of human behavior make psychological investigation challenging.*

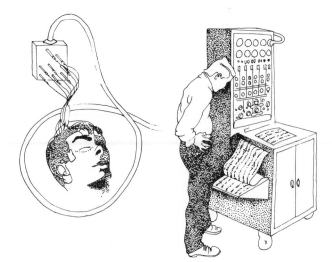

Fig. 1-2 *The scientific study of dreaming has been made possible by use of the EEG, a device that records the tiny electrical potentials generated by the brain of a sleeping subject. It converts these electrical potentials to a written record of brain activity.*

Science Psychology has been described by some as the "almost science" because scientific study of some topics is not yet possible. Sometimes questions go unanswered because of moral or practical limitations. What would happen if a child were placed in a soundproof, lightproof box for the first five years of life? This question will probably never be directly answered. (However, many times an indirect answer can be obtained by studying animals.) Sometimes research must await a receptive social climate. Very little was known about human sexual response until William Masters, a gynecologist, and Virginia Johnson, a psychologist, pioneered direct recording of bodily responses to sexual intercourse. Such research would have been impossible to carry out and publish 30 years ago.

More frequently, psychological questions remain unanswered for lack of a suitable *method*. For years the subjective reports of people who said they never dream had to be considered accurate. But with an advance in technology, the EEG (electroencephalograph or brainwave machine) was developed. It then became possible to tell objectively when a person is dreaming. People who "never dream," it turns out, dream frequently and remember their dreams when awakened during one. Through use of the EEG, the study of dreaming is becoming quite scientific.

Animals Notice that our definition of psychology says, "the study of the behavior of *organisms*." As a group, psy-

chologists are interested in natural laws governing the behavior of *any* living creature—from flatworms to people. Specialists known as **comparative** psychologists (who *compare* the behavior of different species) may spend their entire careers studying rats, cats, dogs, turtles, or chimpanzees (Fig. 1-3). In doing so, they must be very careful to avoid the **anthropomorphic fallacy** (AN-thro-po-MORE-fik: attributing human thoughts, feelings, or motives to animals). The temptation to assume that an animal is "angry," "jealous," "bored," or "guilty" can be strong, but it often leads to false conclusions. As an example, let's say I observe gorillas in the wild (where food is plentiful) and conclude that by nature gorillas are not very "greedy." On the other hand, you place two hungry gorillas in a cage with a banana, stand back to watch the action, and conclude that gorillas are in fact *very* "greedy." Actually, all we have observed is that competition for food is related to the availability of food. Allowing the human concept of greed into the picture just clouds our understanding of gorilla behavior.

Question: You mentioned studying rats. What is a "rat psychologist?"

A good number of psychologists use laboratory rats for research, and some apply their findings to human behavior. Critic Arthur Koestler has accused such psychologists of reversing the anthropomorphic error by treating humans like rats: "For the anthropomorphic view of the rat, American psychology has traded in a rattomorphic view of man" (Koestler, 1964). Elsewhere Koestler charges: "The 'cynical onlooker' might now ask . . . what is there left for the psychologist to study? The short answer is: rats" (Koestler, 1968).

But don't be too hasty in rejecting the efforts of "rat psychologists." In the same way that physicians test a new drug on animals before trying it on humans, psychologists often discover principles in simplified animal experiments that prove useful in solving human problems. Studies of topics as diverse as obesity, memory, and stress have used rats as subjects. More importantly, some principles learned from animals cannot be tested directly on humans. In such instances, animals serve as **models** and provide the only information available on a particular subject. For example, the majority of what is known about the human brain is based on research with animals. You just can't go around destroying parts of human brains to see how they work. (The author, at any rate, has had a hard time finding volunteers.)

Goals To conclude this discussion, let's return for a moment to the goals of psychology. What do they mean in practice? Assume that we would like to answer these questions: What happens when a person has an injury on the right side of the brain? Is there more than one type of memory? How does creative problem-solving differ from routine thought? Do autistic children react differently to their parents than they do to other adults? The answer to each question would require a careful **description** of behavior, the first goal of psychology.

Question: But a description doesn't explain anything, does it?

Right. Useful knowledge in psychology begins with accurate description, but description fails to answer the important "why" questions. *Why* do more women attempt suicide, and why do more men succeed at it? *Why* does frustration encourage aggression? *Why* are bystanders often unwilling to help in an emergency?

Psychology's second goal, **understanding** behavior, is satisfied when we can explain why a phenomenon occurs or exists. Take the last question as an example. Research on "bystander apathy" has shown that people often fail to help when *other* potential helpers are present. This causes a "diffusion of responsibility" so no single bystander feels obligated to help. Generally, the more potential helpers present, the less likely it is that help will be given (Darley and Latane, 1968) (see Chapter 26 for more information).

Psychology's third goal is **prediction.** Notice that the explanation for bystander apathy makes a prediction about the chances of getting help. Anyone who has been stranded by car trouble on a busy freeway will recognize the accuracy of this prediction. Prediction is possible whenever there is a degree of consistency to behavior. As an illustration, quickly jot down the first word that occurs to you when you read the following words:

dark _____ man _____

fast _____ long _____.

Consistent patterns in the use of language make it a good bet that you wrote at least two of these words: *light, woman, slow, short.* Of course, prediction in psychology is rarely as precise as it is in "hard sciences" like physics or chemistry. Just the same, psychological predictions are often quite useful. In a specialty called **psychometrics,** psychological tests are used to predict such things as success in school, work, or career. As another example, psychological theory predicted that students high in test-taking anxiety would show improved performance if given reassurance and advice during testing, a prediction that proved true when tried (Sarason, 1975).

Fig. 1-3 *Some of the most interesting research with animals has focused on attempts to teach primates to communicate with sign language. Here Koko, a lowland gorilla, "discusses" photographs in a book with psychologist Francine Patterson. (See Chapter 11 for more information.)*

Question: Description, explanation, and prediction seem reasonable, but is control a valid goal for psychology?

Control is a frequently questioned and misunderstood goal of psychology, probably because it sounds like a threat to personal freedom. B. F. Skinner, a well-known psychologist, caused a turmoil by publishing a book a few years ago entitled *Beyond Freedom and Dignity.* In it, Skinner advocated the use of more control, in the form of rewards, as a substitute for society's heavy reliance on punishment as a way of controlling behavior. Skinner's call for more "control" was misunderstood by many, who felt it implied manipulation by the government, educators, scientists, or other authorities.

The issue of control is controversial even among psychologists, many of whom strongly disagree with Skinner's views. It should be realized, however, that to most psychologists "control" simply means altering conditions that influence behavior in predictable ways. For example, if a psychologist suggests changes in classroom procedures so children learn more effectively, the psychologist has exercised control. If the psychologist uses conditioning principles to help a person overcome a crippling fear of heights, control is involved. Control is also present if psychological research is used to design an instrument panel that reduces pilot errors in airliners.

To summarize, psychological investigation can provide the means for changing behavior, but it does not say what changes should be made. As is the case with knowledge in other areas, psychological knowledge must be used wisely and humanely. Even Skinner has said, "We shouldn't try to change people. We should change the world in which people live."

Learning Check

To improve your memory of this chapter, see if you can answer these questions. If you miss any, skim over the preceding material before continuing to make sure you understand what you just read.

1. Psychology is the _____ study of the _____ of organisms.

2. Information gained through direct observation and measurement is called _____ evidence.

3. The _____ fallacy involves attributing human feelings and motives to animals.

4. Which of the following questions relates most directly to the goal of *understanding* behavior?

    a. Do men and women differ in intellectual abilities?
    b. Why does a blow to the head cause memory loss?
    c. Will productivity in a business office increase if room temperature is raised or lowered?
    d. How can test anxiety be prevented?

Answers: 4. b   3. anthropomorphic   2. empirical   1. scientific, behavior

A Brief History of Psychology's Brief History

Psychology, it is said, has a long past but a short history. Psychology's past is centuries old because it includes **philosophy,** the study of knowledge, reality, and human nature. In contrast, psychology's history began only about 100 years ago. As sciences go, psychology is the new kid on the block: Easily 9 out of 10 persons to ever work in the field are alive today. Those who dislike history may be tempted to view psychology's past as "Not short enough!" Yet, the ideas in psychology's past are intimately tied to the present. To understand where psychology is now, let's take a brief look at its short history.

Into the Laboratory   Psychology's history began in the year 1879 at Leipzig, Germany. There, the "father of psychology," **Wilhelm Wundt** (VILL-helm Voont), established the first psychological laboratory. Wundt wanted to explore the mind more directly than philosophers had done from their "armchairs." Wundt defined the new science of psychology as the study of *conscious experience*. How, he asked, are sensations, images, and feelings formed? To find out, Wundt combined careful *measurement* with **introspection,** or "looking inward." Wundt called this approach **experimental self-observation** (Blumenthal, 1979).

Experimental self-observation was a highly developed skill, much like that needed to be a professional wine taster. Wundt's subjects had to make at least 10,000 practice observations before they were allowed to describe their sensations in a real experiment (Lieberman, 1979).

Wundt's laboratory was a wonder of gadgets, timers, recorders, and other instruments for presenting stimuli[*] and for measuring or recording responses. His earliest experiments concerned sensation and perception, especially vision, hearing, taste, and touch. Later, he got interested in reaction time, memory, time perception, feelings, and a host of other topics. In all of his work, Wundt emphasized gaining information from *observable* and *measurable* events. Truly, psychology was off to a good start.

Structuralism   Wundt's ideas were carried to the United States by one of his students, a psychologist named E. B. Titchener. There, Titchener and others launched a school of thought called **structuralism.** The structuralists hoped to develop a sort of "mental chemistry" by *analyzing* experience into basic "elements" or building blocks.

Question: How could they do that? You can't analyze experience like you can a chemical compound.

Perhaps not, but the structuralists tried. The structuralists dropped much of Wundt's emphasis on measurement, and used introspection very freely. In this approach, an introspectionist might heft an apple, and then decide that he or

[*] Singular: stimulus; plural: stimuli (STIM-you-lie).

she had experienced the elements "hue" (color), "roundness," and "weight." Another example of the kind of question that might have interested a structuralist is this: What elemental tastes mix together to create complex flavors as different as liver, lime, bacon, or burnt-almond fudge?

Ultimately, introspection left much to be desired as a way of answering psychological questions. The most troublesome problem was simply this: Introspectionists frequently *disagreed*. If two structuralists came up with different lists of elementary taste sensations, who was to say which was right? Despite such limitations, "looking inward" is still a part of modern psychology. The study of hypnosis, meditation, drug effects, problem solving, and many other topics would be incomplete without reports of subjective experiences.

Functionalism   William James, an American psychologist, agreed with Wundt and the structuralists that psychologists should study the mind. However, he broadened the scope of psychology to include animal behavior, religious experience, abnormal behavior, and a number of other interesting topics.

Question: Did James use introspection?

James and other **functionalists** were willing to use several methods to study mental life. These ranged from introspection to experimentation, and included a dash of armchair philosophizing as well. Personally, James preferred ideas to lab work, and he highly valued practical information. In fact, the term functionalism comes from James' interest in how the mind *functions* to adapt us to a changing environment. To James, consciousness was an ever-changing *stream* or *flow* of images and sensations, not a collection of lifeless building blocks as the structuralists claimed.

The functionalists were strongly influenced by Charles Darwin. According to Darwin, organisms evolve, through **natural selection,** in directions that favor their survival. This means that features that help adapt animals to their environment are retained in evolution. Similarly, the functionalists wanted to learn how thought, perception, habits, and emotions aid human adaptation. In short, they wanted to study the mind *in use*.

Question: What effect did functionalism have on modern psychology?

Functionalism brought the study of animals into psychology by linking human and animal adaptation. It also encouraged the development of **educational psychology.** Functionalists such as John Dewey were impressed by the way education improves personal functioning. Accordingly, Dewey urged psychologists to help improve education. Today, modern educational psychologists develop tests, and conduct research on classroom dynamics, teaching styles, and learning. Functionalism also spurred the development of **industrial psychology,** a specialty involving the study and improvement of work environments.

Behaviorism: Stimulus-Response Psychology
Functionalism was soon challenged by a new school of thought called **behaviorism.** Behaviorist John B. Watson

Fig. 1-4   *Wilhelm Wundt, 1832–1920.*   **Fig. 1-5**   *William James, 1842–1910.*   **Fig. 1-6**   *John B. Watson, 1878–1958.*

objected to defining psychology as the study of the "mind" or "conscious experience." In 1913, he made a plea for a truly objective science of psychology on a par with biology, chemistry, or physics. Watson considered introspection unscientific, and rejected mentalistic terms, such as "image," "mind," "consciousness," and so on. Watson found he could study animals quite effectively even though he couldn't ask them questions, or know what they were thinking. He simply observed the relationship between **stimuli** (events in the environment) and an animal's **responses** to them. Why not, he argued, apply the same objectivity to the study of humans?

Watson soon adopted Russian physiologist Ivan Pavlov's **conditioned response** concept as a way of explaining most behavior. (A conditioned response is a learned reaction to a particular stimulus.) Watson's enthusiasm for conditioning theory had obviously reached extremes when he proclaimed:

> Give me a dozen healthy infants, well-formed, and my own special world to bring them up in and I'll guarantee to take any one at random and train him to become any type of specialist I might select—doctor, lawyer, artist, merchant-chief, and yes, beggarman and thief (Watson, 1913).

Question: Would most psychologists agree with Watson's claim about the "dozen healthy infants"?

Behaviorism has had a profound effect on modern psychological thought. One of the best-known and most influential modern behaviorists, B. F. Skinner has said:

> The environment is the key causal matrix. . . . In order to understand human behavior we must take into account what the environment does to an organism before and after it responds. Behavior is shaped and maintained by its consequences (Skinner, 1971).

Many psychologists consider Skinner's brand of behaviorism extreme. Skinner's emphasis on stimulus-response relationships, and his tendency to ignore thought and subjective experience, has led some observers to charge that Skinnerian psychology has "lost consciousness." Despite such criticisms, a majority of psychologists would probably agree that most human behavior is influenced in one way or another by learning.

The behavioristic approach is responsible for much of what we know today about learning, memory, conditioning, and the effective use of reward and punishment. A very direct descendant of behavioristic thought is a type of therapy known as **behavior modification.** In behavior modification, conditioning principles are used to treat problems, such as overeating, phobias, and childhood misbehavior. (See Chapter 23 for more information.)

Gestalt Psychology   The German word *Gestalt* (geh-SHTALT) means form, pattern, or whole. The **Gestalt** school of thought, founded by the German psychologist Max Wertheimer (VERT-heimer), held that it is a mistake to try to analyze psychological events into pieces like "elementary sensations" or stimuli and responses. Unlike other schools of thought, the Gestaltists tried to study experiences as *wholes.* Their slogan was, "The whole exceeds the sum of its parts."

Question: What did they mean by that?

Consider the example of a melody. If the notes from a familiar tune, such as "Yankee Doodle," are played in quick succession, the result is a melody recognizable on any instrument. Next, we could use a new set of notes much higher or lower than the original set. Even if none of the original sounds are used, the melody will still be recognizable—*if* the *relationship* between notes is the same. Now, what if the original notes were played in the correct order, but at a rate of one per hour? What would we have? Nothing. The individual notes would no longer be a melody. The melody is somehow more than the sum of its parts. This may be why "a picture is worth a thousand words," or why a thousand words are still not enough to capture a symphony or a sunset.

The Gestaltists were also fascinated by perceptual illusions. One such illusion is known as the **phi phenomenon,** which you have probably seen in action. In the phi phenomenon, two small light bulbs are placed side-by-side and a few inches apart in a darkened room. If the left bulb is lighted and then turned off just as the right bulb is turned on, a single light appears to come on and *move* from left to right. There is no true motion, but the illusion of movement is strong. This principle underlies the apparent "follow the leader" movement of stationary lights around the edge of theatre signs.

Like a melody or the phi phenomenon, many experiences resist analysis that divides them into separate "pieces." For this reason, the Gestalt viewpoint remains influential in the study of perception. Likewise, many personality theorists consider it important to understand the "whole person," instead of studying thinking, emotion, intelligence, learning, or motivation in isolation.

Psychoanalytic Psychology   As the mainstream of psychology was becoming more objective, scientific, and

Fig. 1-7   *Max Wertheimer, 1880–1941.*   Fig. 1-8   *Sigmund Freud, 1856–1939.*   Fig. 1-9   *Abraham Maslow, 1908–1970.*

experimental, another school of thought was developing on a foundation of clinical insight. By working with troubled patients, an Austrian physician, Sigmund Freud, developed a theory of personality that stood in sharp contrast to laboratory-based theories.

Freud's point of departure was his belief that human mental life is like an iceberg, only part is exposed to view. According to Freud, there are vast areas of **unconscious** thoughts, impulses, and desires which cannot be experienced directly, but which continue to influence our behavior. Freud theorized that these unconscious thoughts are often of a sexual or aggressive nature. Hence, they are threatening and are *repressed* (actively held out of consciousness). Sometimes, he said, they are revealed in dreams, conflicts, and slips of the tongue ("Freudian slips"). Although Freud was not the first to discuss the unconscious, he did much to popularize belief in its existence. In doing so, he added a new dimension not only to psychology, but to art, literature, and history as well.

Also notable was Freud's insistence that all thoughts, emotions, and actions are *determined* (nothing is an accident); his emphasis on the importance of childhood in later personality development ("the child is father to the man"); and his development of a method of psychotherapy called **psychoanalysis.** Each had an impact on psychological thought or practice. Today many theorists, referred to as **neo-Freudians,** have enlarged, altered, and adapted Freud's original ideas. Others have abandoned them entirely. Although Freud's influence has faded in recent years, his presence is still felt in psychology. For example,

some types of psychotherapy continue to emphasize psychodynamics (the internal dynamics of personality) much as Freud did.

Humanistic Psychology   A fairly recent development in psychology is a point of view known as **humanism.** Humanism is sometimes called the "third force" in psychology. (Psychoanalytic psychology and behaviorism are the other two.)

Question: How is the humanistic approach different?

Psychologists Carl Rogers, Abraham Maslow, and others developed the humanistic viewpoint to counter the negativity they saw in behaviorism and psychoanalysis. Humanists reject the Freudian idea that personality is ruled by unconscious forces and the behavioristic idea that we are controlled by the environment. Although humanists admit that one's past affects personality, they emphasize the importance of **free will,** the human ability to make choices.

The humanists have also made psychologists aware of the importance of psychological needs for love, self-esteem, belonging, self-expression, and creativity. According to the humanists, such needs are as important as biological needs for food and water. For example, newborn infants who are deprived of human love and warmth may die just as surely as they would if deprived of food.

Question: How scientific is the humanistic approach?

Humanists collect data and seek evidence to support their ideas, but for the most part they tend to be less interested in attempts to treat psychology as a science. Since they are basically interested in solving human problems, humanists show less interest in research with animals or laboratory studies of behavior. Instead, they emphasize the importance of such *subjective* factors as one's **self-image, self-evaluation,** and **frame of reference.** It is possible, however, to apply scientific knowledge to humanistic goals, and some humanists do so.

One of the most distinctive contributions of the humanistic approach is Maslow's identification of the human need for **self-actualization.** Self-actualization is the need to develop one's potential fully, to lead a rich and meaningful life, and to become the best person one can become. According to the humanists, everyone has this potential. The humanists seek ways to allow it to emerge.

Psychology Today   In recent years, there has been an explosive growth in approaches to psychology. One particularly important addition is **cognitive* psychology,** which studies thinking, language, problem solving, consciousness, creativity, and other "internal" processes. Some of these topics were neglected for many years after the rise of behaviorism, so it may be fair to say that psychology has recently "regained consciousness."

*Cognition refers to thinking or knowing.

At one time, schools of thought functioned almost like political parties in the profession of psychology. Loyalty to a particular viewpoint was often fierce, and clashes between schools were common. Today, most of the traditional schools of thought have given way to a blending of ideas and perspectives. Although loyalties and specialties still exist, many psychologists can be described as **eclectic** (ek-LEK-tik: drawing from many sources) in their approach. Even "pure" behaviorism has evolved into "cognitive behaviorism" for many. Cognitive behaviorists still focus on conditioning, learning, and effects of the environment, but they include images, expectations, and perceptions in their explanations of behavior.

A distinction between **scientific** and **nonscientific** approaches is perhaps the most meaningful division running through psychology today. Nonscientific approaches tend to be based on personal insights, value judgments, subjective experiences, and philosophical searching. Many worthwhile ideas have entered psychology by this route, especially in the areas of personality theory and psychotherapy. Scientific approaches include any and all topics, but always require that an idea be tested empirically. The most powerful principles in psychology are usually those that have survived such rigorous testing. However, science and intuition, creativity and discipline, insight and observation all have a place in modern psychology.

___

Learning Check

See if you can correctly match the following before reading further.

____ 1.	Philosophy	**A.**	Against analysis; studied whole experiences
____ 2.	Wundt	**B.**	"Mental chemistry" and introspection
____ 3.	Structuralism	**C.**	Emphasizes self-actualization and personal growth
____ 4.	Functionalism	**D.**	Interested in unconscious causes of behavior
____ 5.	Behaviorism	**E.**	Gave rise to educational and industrial psychology
____ 6.	Gestalt	**F.**	Studied stimuli and responses, conditioning
____ 7.	Psychoanalytic	**G.**	Part of psychology's "long past"
____ 8.	Humanistic	**H.**	Concerned with thinking, language, problem solving
____ 9.	Cognitive	**I.**	Used "experimental self-observation"
		J.	Also known as engineering psychology

Answers: 1. G 2. I 3. B 4. E 5. F 6. A 7. D 8. C 9. H

Psychologists—Guaranteed Not to Shrink

Question: What is the difference between a psychologist and a psychiatrist? Answer: About $20 an hour. (And going up.)

Confusion often exists about the differences among **psychologists, psychiatrists, psychoanalysts, counselors,** and other mental health professionals. Although many people lump all these together as "shrinks," there are distinct differences in training and emphasis among them.

A psychologist usually has a master's degree or a doctorate in psychology; that is, from three to eight years of specialized postgraduate training in psychological theory and research methods. Depending on their interests, psychologists may teach, do research, administer psychological tests, or serve as consultants to business, industry, government, or the military. (This statement applies to psychiatrists and psychoanalysts too.) Psychologists interested in human emotional problems and their treatment specialize in **clinical** or **counseling psychology** (see Table 1–1).

To enter the profession of psychology today, you would probably find it necessary to have the doctorate (Ph.D., Psy.D., or Ed.D.) in order to be licensed, or to qualify or compete for positions. Most clinical psychologists now have the Ph.D. degree, which requires advanced training in research and clinical skills, plus an added one-year internship in a mental health facility. Others have begun to seek the Psy.D. (Doctor of Psychology). This newly created degree places more emphasis on practical clinical skills rather than on research. It too concludes with a one-year internship (McNett, 1982).

Like clinical psychologists, psychiatrists are also interested in treating human problems, but they are trained differently. A psychiatrist is a medical doctor. After training in general medicine, a psychiatrist specializes in personality, abnormal behavior, and psychotherapy. Psychiatrists often become "talking doctors," meaning that they make little direct use of their medical training. Instead, they spend much of their time doing psychotherapy. In practice, then, the major difference between a psychologist who is doing psychotherapy and a psychiatrist is this: As an M.D., a psychiatrist is trained to recognize and treat physical causes of psychological difficulties, and he or she can prescribe drugs.

To be a psychoanalyst, you must have a moustache and goatee, spectacles, a German accent, and a well-padded couch, or so the TV and movie stereotype goes. Actually, to become an analyst, you must have an M.D. or Ph.D.

degree and then receive specialized training in the theory and practice of Freudian psychoanalysis. In other words, either a psychologist or a psychiatrist may become an analyst by completing additional training. Analysts typically undergo psychoanalysis themselves before applying the method to others.

Question: Is psychoanalysis widely used?

In practice, many psychotherapists find that a flexible and eclectic approach is most effective. This, plus the fact that traditional Freudian analysis is expensive and time-consuming, is gradually making psychoanalysts something of a rare breed. Nowadays, few psychologists or psychiatrists become analysts, and fewer clients seek analysis. As an interesting demonstration of this fact, get a telephone book and compare the number of psychologists, psychiatrists, and psychoanalysts listed in your area.

In many states, counselors (such as marriage and family counselors, child counselors, or school counselors) also do mental health work. To be a licensed counselor typically requires a master's degree plus one or two years of full-time supervised counseling experience. Almost all of a counselor's postgraduate education is directly related to practical counseling skills, with little emphasis on research. The practice of counseling is usually limited to adjustment problems not involving serious mental disorder.

Question: I've heard of something called a Gestalt therapist. What is that?

There are dozens of approaches to psychotherapy. Discussion of Gestalt therapy and a number of other techniques must be deferred to a later chapter (Chapter 22), but this question does raise an interesting issue. Before the American Psychological Association (APA) began a push for licensing and certification of psychologists, it was possible in many states for virtually anyone to purchase an inexpensive license and "hang out a shingle" as a "psychologist." To be legally called a psychologist, a person must now meet a rigorous set of educational requirements. To work as a clinical or counseling psychologist, he or she must have a license issued by a state examining board. However, the law does not prohibit you from calling yourself anything else you choose—Gestalt therapist, primal feeling facilitator, cosmic aura therapist, or Rolfer—or from selling your "services" to anyone willing to pay. Beware of people advertising under such self-proclaimed titles. Even if their intentions are honorable, the training of such individuals is often limited or nonexistent. A fully trained, certified psychologist who chooses to use a particular type of therapy is not the same as someone "trained" only in that technique.

Unfortunately, psychology, like medicine, has attracted a fringe of opportunists, quacks, and charlatans who seek to profit by taking advantage of human needs, fears, and suffering. When the escapades of these "not-really psychologists" make the news, or when a friend or relative has a bad experience with one, psychologists often pay the price in negative public attitudes toward psychology in general. This is indeed unfortunate since psychologists adhere to a professional code established by the APA which stresses: (1) accurate representation of one's professional qualifications; (2) confidentiality in handling of personal information in teaching, practice, or research; and above all, (3) protection of the client's welfare. The APA also encourages psychologists to make their services available to anyone who seeks them, regardless of social considerations or ability to pay.

How to Be a Psychologist— Let Us Count the Ways

Question: Do all psychologists do therapy and treat abnormal behavior?

Even when combined, clinical and counseling psychology account for only about 40 percent of psychologists. The rest divide themselves among the 34 specialties currently recognized by the APA. Some of the major specialties are listed in Table 1-1. (Also see Fig. 1-10.) Over 50 percent of psychologists are employed full time by educational institutions. In this setting, they teach, and may also do research, consultation, or therapy. Those engaged in research may do **"pure" research,** seeking knowledge for the sake of knowledge, or **"applied" research,** in which immediate uses are planned for the information gained.

Table 1-1   Kinds of Psychologists and What They Do

Specialty		Typical Activities
Clinical and counseling psychologists	A*	Does psychotherapy and personal counseling, helps with emotional and behavioral problems, researches clinical problems, is involved in community mental health.
Industrial psychologist	A	Selects job applicants, does skills analysis, evaluates on-job training, improves work environments and human relations in work setting.
Educational psychologist	A	Conducts research on classroom dynamics, teaching styles, and learning variables. Develops educational tests, evaluates educational programs, acts as consultant for schools.
Consumer psychologist	A	Researches and tests packaging, advertising, and marketing methods; determines characteristics of product users, conducts public opinion polling.
School psychologist	A	Does psychological testing, emotional and vocational counseling of students; detects and treats learning disabilities; improves learning and motivation in the classroom.
Developmental psychologist	B	Carries out pure and applied research on child development, adult developmental trends, and aging; does clinical work with disturbed children; acts as consultant to preschools, programs for the aged, and so forth.
Engineering psychologist	A	Does applied research on design of machinery, controls, airplanes, automobiles, and so on for business, industry, and the military.
Medical psychologist	A	Studies the relationship between stress, personality, and disease (heart attacks, high blood pressure, ulcers); manages emotional problems associated with illness or disability.
Environmental psychologist	B	Studies the effects of urban noise pollution, crowding, attitudes toward environment, and human use of space; acts as consultant for design of industrial environments, schools, housing for elderly, and urban architecture.
Forensic psychologist	A	Studies problems of crime and crime prevention, rehabilitation programs in prisons, courtroom dynamics, psychology and law; selects candidates for police work.
Experimental psychologist	P	Applies scientific research methods to study of human and animal behavior; may conduct research in the areas of comparative animal behavior, learning, sensation/perception, personality, physiology, motivation/emotion, social behavior, or cognition.

*Research is typically: applied (A); pure (P); or both (B).

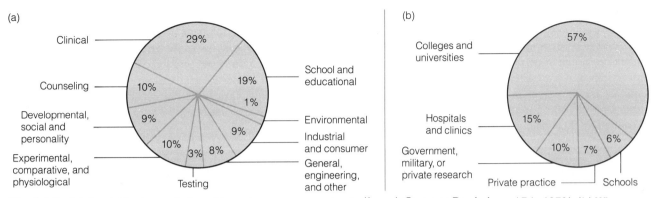

Fig. 1-10 *(a) Specialties in psychology. Percentages are approximate (from* A Career in Psychology, *APA, 1970); (b) Where psychologists work (from Boneau and Cuca, 1974).*

Question: What kinds of things would a typical psychologist at a university do research on?

Here is a sampling of representative research topics.

Comparative "I have always been interested in basic questions about animal behavior, but my current research is applied. I am investigating ways of preventing abnormalities that result when an animal is kept in social isolation for extended periods of time. My goal is to help the space program. If I can provide a way to keep animals 'mentally' healthy while in space, the effects of prolonged weightlessness can be studied."

Developmental "I am interested in development. I am trying to learn how people grow and change over time. My interests stretch from prenatal life to death, but I am especially interested in early childhood. My colleagues and I seek the principles whereby a child develops the ability to think, speak, perceive, and act. Broadly speaking, I am interested in how adult personality and skills emerge from childhood, but my current research is more limited. I am studying the effects of stimulating childhood environments on the development of intelligence."

Learning "I'm also interested in how people get to be the way they are, but in a much more abstract sense. I feel that most human behavior is learned. At any given moment I would describe your behavior as the result of your personal learning history. By studying various kinds of learning, conditioning, and memory in humans and animals, I am helping to construct theories about how learning occurs and what factors affect it. My doctoral dissertation was on avoidance learning. I had rats learn to press a bar in order to avoid receiving an electric shock which followed the onset of a signal light. Right now I'm studying the effects of patterns of reinforcement on learning in pigeons."

Personality "In many ways my area is both the most rewarding and the most frustrating. Personality theorists draw on the findings of all other research areas as well as their own in an effort to create as total a picture and understanding of human personality as possible. I concern myself with the structure and dynamics of personality, motivation, and individual differences. I am studying the personality profiles of college students who score high on tests of creativity."

Sensation and Perception "How do we come to know the world? How does information 'get into' our nervous systems? How is it processed and given pattern and meaning? These are my concerns. I am using an information-processing theory called signal detection to study the visual perception of random shapes."

Physiological Psychology "The brain and nervous system are my meat . . . so to speak. It is my belief that ultimately all other areas in psychology—learning, perception, even personality—will be explained by reference to the action of nerve cells or parts of the brain. I have been doing some exciting research on the role of the hypothalamus in hunger. I find that if I destroy part of the hypothalamus in the brain of a rat, he will eat and gain weight until he looks like a furry water balloon. If I destroy an area just a few millimeters away, he will starve to death while sitting on a pile of food."

Social Psychology   "I study people in a group setting, or under any circumstance in which social factors play a part. Social psychologists in general are interested in attitudes, social influence, riots, conformity, leadership, racism, friendship, and a growing list of other topics. My personal interest is interpersonal attraction. I place two strangers together in a room for a short time and investigate factors which affect their ratings of attraction toward each other."

This small sample should give you some idea of the diversity of psychological research. It also gives you a hint of some of the kinds of information covered later in this book. After you have completed the next Learning Check, be sure to read the "Applications" and "Exploration" that follow the summary. These sections help complete our introductory discussion of the field of psychology.

Learning Check

See if you can answer these questions before continuing.

1. Which of the following can prescribe drugs? Psychologist, psychiatrist, psychoanalyst, counselor?

2. A psychologist who specializes in treating human emotional difficulties is called a _____ psychologist.

3. Roughly 40 percent of psychologists specialize in counseling psychology.   T or F?

4. Seeking knowledge for the sake of knowledge is called _____ research.

Match the following research areas with the topic they cover.

____ 5.   Developmental   **A.**   Attitudes, groups, leadership

____ 6.   Learning   **B.**   Conditioning, memory

____ 7.   Personality   **C.**   The psychology of law

____ 8.   Sensation and perception   **D.**   Brain and nervous system

____ 9.   Physiological psychology   **E.**   Child psychology

____ 10.   Social psychology   **F.**   Individual differences, motivation

____ 11.   Comparative   **G.**   Animal behavior

                                    H.   Information processing

12. Who among the following would most likely be involved in the detection and treatment of learning disabilities?

    a. Consumer psychologist   *b.* Forensic psychologist
    c. Experimental psychologist   *d.* School psychologist

Answers: 1. psychiatrist   2. clinical or counseling   3. F   4. pure   5. E   6. B   7. F   8. H   9. D   10. A   11. G   12. d

Resources Summary

● Psychology is the scientific study of the behavior of organisms. Its stated goals are to describe, understand, predict, and in some cases control behavior.
● Whenever possible, psychologists seek *empirical,* or objective and observable evidence.
● Not all psychological questions are answerable, usually because of moral, practical, technological, or methodological limitations.

● Psychologists study animals as well as people, either out of interest in animals themselves, or to use animals as models for human behavior. One danger in studying animals is the *anthropomorphic fallacy,* the tendency to treat animals as if they had human characteristics. A second danger is the so-called "*rattomorphic fallacy,*" the tendency to treat humans like rats.
● Accurate description is one goal of psychology, but

understanding and the ability to predict and control behavior are also sought. Psychologists engage in control when they alter conditions that affect behavior in predictable ways.

● The history of psychology begins with *philosophy,* an "armchair" approach to understanding human behavior.

● The first psychological laboratory was established in Germany by Wilhelm Wundt, who tried to apply scientific methods to the study of conscious experience.

● The first school of thought in American psychology was *structuralism,* which was a kind of "mental chemistry" based on the method of *introspection.*

● Structuralism was followed by *functionalism, behaviorism,* and *Gestalt* psychology. The *psychoanalytic* approach, which emphasizes unconscious determinants of behavior, developed separately. A more recent development is *humanistic* psychology.

● Three main streams of thought that can still be seen in modern psychology are behaviorism, humanism, and the psychoanalytic approach, but there is a stro. toward blending the best features of many viewpo. Behaviorism in particular has been influenced by the *cognitive* viewpoint, which emphasizes thinking, knowing, and other internal events.

● *Psychologists, psychiatrists, psychoanalysts,* and *counselors* work in the field of mental health, although their training and methods differ considerably.

● *Clinical* and *counseling* psychologists, who do psychotherapy, represent only one of dozens of specialties in psychology. Other representative areas of specialization are: *industrial, educational, consumer, school, developmental, engineering, medical, environmental, forensic,* and *experimental.*

● Psychological research may be *pure* or *applied.* Some common research specialties are: comparative, learning, sensation, perception, personality, physiology, motivation and emotion, social, cognitive, and developmental.

Psychology and Personal Growth— An Introduction to Applications

Question: What can I learn from psychology that will benefit me personally?

The famous physicist Sir Isaac Newton once remarked, "If I have seen farther than others, it is because I have stood on the shoulders of giants." He was referring, of course, to the thinkers who preceded him. In psychology, the "giants" you will encounter are *ideas.* Like Newton's "giants," they are capable of helping you to "see farther." A unique quality of psychology is that its concepts are available to everyone. As former APA president George Miller has said:

> The secrets of our trade need not be reserved for highly trained specialists. Psychological facts should be passed out freely to all who need and can use them . . . There simply are not enough psychologists to meet every need for psychological services. The people at large will have to be their own psychologists, and make their own applications of established principles (Miller, 1969).

Ten years after making this statement Miller (1980) remains convinced that psychologists should "give psychology away," and that's exactly what this book is intended to do.

Psychology is surely one of the most relevant courses you will take. When the topic is human behavior, it's hard not to be interested. But as Miller points out, interest alone is not enough. To ensure that you derive the greatest personal benefit from learning psychology, each chapter in this text has an "Applications" section. Here, information and ideas of immediate usefulness to you will be discussed. In this first "Applications," Maslow's concept of *self-actualization,* mentioned earlier in this chapter, will be expanded upon.

Self-Actualization— Let Your Reach Exceed Your Grasp

Psychologists have had a tendency to study human problems more than human strengths. A notable exception to this can be found in Abraham Maslow's studies of people living unusually effective lives. Maslow became interested in people who seemed to be using almost all of their talents and potentials. How were they different from the average person? To find an answer, Maslow began by studying the lives of great men and women: Albert Einstein, William James, Jane Adams, Eleanor Roosevelt, Abraham Lincoln, John Muir, Walt Whitman, and others. From there, he moved on to direct studies of artists, writers, poets, and other creative individuals.

Along the way, Maslow's thinking changed radically. At first, he studied only people of obvious creativity or high achievement. Eventually, however, it became clear that a housewife, carpenter, clerk, or student could live creatively and make full use of his or her potentials. Maslow referred to this tendency as *self-actualization* (Maslow, 1954).

As he continued his studies, Maslow found that **self-actualizers** shared a great number of similarities. It made little difference if they were famous or unknown, academically distinguished or uneducated, rich or poor—self-actualizers tended to fit this profile:

Some Characteristics of Self-Actualizers

1. Efficient perceptions of reality. Subjects were able to judge situations correctly and honestly and were very sensitive to the fake and dishonest.

2. Comfortable acceptance of self, others, nature. Subjects were able to accept their own human nature with all its shortcomings. The shortcomings of others and the contradictions of the human condition were also accepted with humor and tolerance.

3. Spontaneity. Maslow's subjects extended their creativity into everyday activities. They tended to be unusually alive, engaged, and spontaneous.

4. Task-centering. Most subjects had a mission to fulfill in life or some task or problem outside of themselves to pursue. Humanitarians, such as Albert Schweitzer or Mother Teresa, represent good examples of this quality.

5. Autonomy. Subjects were free from dependence on external authority or other people. They tended to be resourceful and independent.

Applications

6. Continued freshness of appreciation. The self-actualizer seems to constantly renew appreciation of life's basic goods. A sunset or a flower will be experienced as intensely the one-thousandth time as it was the first. There is an "innocence of vision," like that of an artist or a child.

7. Fellowship with humanity. Maslow's subjects felt a deep identification with others and the human situation in general.

8. Profound interpersonal relationships. The interpersonal relationships of self-actualizers are marked by deep, loving bonds.

9. Unhostile sense of humor. This refers to the wonderful capacity to laugh at oneself. It also refers to the kind of humor a man like Abraham Lincoln had. Lincoln probably never made a joke that hurt anybody. His wry comments were a gentle prodding at human shortcomings.

10. Peak experiences. All of Maslow's subjects reported the frequent occurrence of "peak" experiences. These were marked by feelings of ecstasy, harmony, and deep meaning. Subjects reported feeling at one with the universe, stronger and calmer than ever before, filled with light, beautiful and good, etc.

In short, self-actualizers feel safe and unanxious, accepted, loved, loving, and alive.

Question: Maslow's list seems pretty subjective. Is it really a fair description of self-actualization?

You have noticed that Maslow tried to investigate self-actualization empirically, but his choice of people for study was subjective. Undoubtedly there are many ways to reach full development of personal potential. Maslow's primary contribution was to draw attention to the *possibility* of continued personal growth. Maslow considered self-actualization an on-going process, not a simple end point to be attained only once.

In later "Applications" sections you will find information on effective learning, childrearing, stress management, improving memory, changing bad habits, suicide prevention, understanding dreams, sexual adjustment, counseling others, and a host of other highly useful topics. In this first "Applications" section, we would like to issue a challenge to you to make your excursion into psychology a means of advancing your personal growth. The information and insights you will obtain from this book, your instructor, and your fellow students represent a tremendous opportunity to progress toward full use of your unique potential.

Learning Check

1. After careful study, psychologist George Miller has concluded that psychological information is best left in the hands of experts.   T or F?
2. Maslow's early conception of self-actualization was based on studying the lives of highly successful men and women in business, industry, and the military.   T or F?
3. According to Maslow, self-actualizers typically place great importance on external authorities or other people.   T or F?
4. Maslow considered spontaneity, task-centering, and peak experiences characteristic of his self-actualizing subjects.   T or F?

Answers   1. F 2. F 3. F 4. T

=== Exploration ===

Pseudo-Psychologies—P. T. Barnum Would Be Proud

Astrology Pseudo-psychologies (*pseudo* means false) are dubious and unfounded systems superficially resembling psychology. Astrology—probably the most popular pseudo-psychology—is based on the assumption that the position of the stars and planets at a person's birth determines personality characteristics and affects behavior. Like other pseudo-psychologies, astrology has a highly developed system that gives it the appearance of science, but it has repeatedly been shown to have no scientific validity (Jerome, 1975). Astrologers have yet to explain why the moment of birth should be more important than the moment of conception for determining personality. Nor have they revised their system despite its being based on inaccurate descriptions of planetary movement made before the development of modern astronomy.

Question: Then why does astrology seem to work?

Let's return to that question after considering some of the less convincing pseudo-psychologies.

Palmistry Palmistry claims that lines in the hand are indicators of personality and a person's future. Lines that are longer or shorter, more or less bent, clear or distinct, supposedly predict destiny, fortune, length of life, occupation, and health. The fact that palmistry assumes that the hands tell the story of the whole body is hard enough to swallow, but ignoring the effects of dishwater, manual labor, or hand lotion is inexcusable.

Phrenology During the nineteenth century, a German anatomy teacher, Franz Gall, popularized the theory that personality is revealed by the skull. Phrenologists assumed that parts of the brain responsible for various "mental faculties" cause bumps on the head. By feeling these bumps, the phrenologist claimed to read a person's abilities. Phrenology faded rapidly when greater understanding of the brain showed that this is impossible. For instance, the area of the brain which controls hearing was listed on phrenologists' charts as the center for "combativeness" and "destructiveness"!

Graphology Graphologists believe that personality is revealed by handwriting. Graphology is only moderately

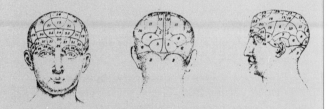

Fig. 1-11   *Phrenology was an attempt to assess characteristics of various areas of the skull. Phrenologists used charts such as the one shown here as guides.*

popular in the United States, although at least 500 companies in this country use handwriting analysis as a tool for evaluating job applicants. In European countries, graphology is widely used for job placement and advancement. These uses are somewhat distressing to psychologists because studies show that graphologists score close to zero on careful tests of accuracy in rating personality (Guilford, 1959). (The failure of graphology as a means of personality evaluation should be distinguished from its proven value for the detection of forgeries.)

Question: If the pseudo-psychologies have no scientific basis, how do they survive and why are they popular?

There are several reasons, all of which can be demonstrated with astrology.

Uncritical Acceptance If you have ever had your astrological chart done, perhaps you have been impressed with its seeming accuracy. Careful reading shows many such charts to be made up of a preponderance of flattering traits. Naturally when your personality is described in *desirable* terms it is hard to deny that the description has the "ring of truth." How much acceptance would astrology receive if the characteristics of a birth sign read like this:

> **Virgo:** You are the logical type and hate disorder. Your nit-picking is unbearable to your friends. You are cold, unemotional, and usually fall asleep while making love. Virgos make good doorstops.

Positive Instances Even when an astrological description of personality contains a mixture of desirable and

Exploration

undesirable traits it may seem accurate. To find out why, read the following personality description.

> You have a strong need for other people to like you and for them to admire you. You have a tendency to be critical of yourself. You have a great deal of unused energy which you have not turned to your advantage. While you have some personality weaknesses, you are generally able to compensate for them. Your sexual adjustment has presented some problems for you. Disciplined and controlled on the outside, you tend to be worrisome and insecure inside. At times you have serious doubts as to whether you have made the right decision or done the right thing. You prefer a certain amount of change and variety and become dissatisfied when hemmed-in by restrictions and limitations. You pride yourself on being an independent thinker and do not accept other opinions without satisfactory proof. You have found it unwise to be too frank in revealing yourself to others. At times you are extroverted, affable, sociable, while at other times you are introverted, wary, and reserved. Some of your aspirations tend to be pretty unrealistic.*

Does this describe your personality? A psychologist read this summary individually to college students who had taken a personality test. Twenty-nine said it was an "excellent" description of their personality; 30 said it was "good"; 15 said it was "average"; and 5 said it was "poor." Thus, only 5 students out of 79 felt that the description failed to adequately capture their personality.

Reread this description and you will see that it contains both sides of several personality dimensions ("At times you are extroverted . . . while at other times you are introverted.") Its apparent accuracy is an illusion based upon the **fallacy of positive instances** in which a person remembers or notices things that confirm his or her expectations and forgets the rest. The pseudo-psychologies thrive on this effect. For example, you can always find "Leo characteristics" in a Leo. If you looked, however, you could also find "Gemini characteristics," "Scorpio characteristics," or whatever.

The P. T. Barnum Effect   P. T. Barnum, the famed circus showman, had a formula for success: "Always have a little something for everybody." Like the personality description above, palm readings, fortunes, horoscopes, and other products of pseudo-psychology are stated in such *general* terms that they can hardly miss. There is always "a little something for everybody." If you doubt this, read *all 12* of the daily horoscopes found in newspapers for several days. You will find that predictions for other signs fit events as well as those for your own sign do.

Question: Couldn't that be because commercial horoscopes don't take into account a person's specific time of birth?

If they did they would probably not be any more accurate, just more convincing. In a recent experiment people were given standardized horoscopes. Some had provided only their sign, others the year, month, and day of their birth. All received the same personality description but those who had provided more detailed information considered their horoscope more accurate (Snyder and Schenkel, 1975). Thus, the more "hocus pocus" a fortune teller, palmist, or astrologer goes through, the more believable are the results.

A Final Note   This "Exploration" is definitely *not* intended as a "put down" of those who believe in astrology. For most people, astrology is a harmless and entertaining pastime. The goal has been to make you a more critical observer of human behavior, and to clarify what is, and is not, psychology. In Chapter 2, you will get a chance to further sharpen your critical skills as we investigate the research methods used in psychology. In the meantime, here is what the stars say about your future.

> Emphasis now on education and personal improvement. Learning experience of lasting value awaits you. Take care of scholastic responsibilities before recreation. Research new possibility. The number "2" figures prominently in efforts.

*Reprinted with permission of author and publisher from: R. E. Ulrich, T. J. Stachnik, and N. R. Stainton, "Student acceptance of generalized personality interpretations," *Psychological Reports*, 1963, **13**, 831–834.

Questions for Discussion

1. The goals of psychology are a refinement of things we do *every* day. Can you relate instances in which you have sought to describe, predict, understand, and control behavior? Do you consider control of behavior an acceptable goal for psychology? Why or why not?

2. Should psychologists study animals? Most people anthropomorphize pets. How could this be a problem in the objective study of animals? In your opinion, can we learn anything about humans by studying animals?

3. In what ways is your behavior controlled by the environment? Do you feel that you have free will? Is there any way to tell if a "free choice" is really determined by your past?

4. How did you picture psychology and psychologists before reading this chapter? Has your image changed? How accurate are television and movie portrayals of psychologists? What psychological specialty do you consider most interesting at this point?

5. Have you ever had a "peak experience"? What was it like? How did it affect you? Does Maslow's view of self-actualization match your own conception of a fully function-ing person? Does Maslow place too much emphasis on impulsiveness and subjectivity?

6. Can you name additional systems of thought that you suspect are pseudo-psychologies? What are their claims? Can you use the points made in the "Exploration" section to explain their attraction for believers?

7. Return to the quiz at the beginning of the chapter (p. 12). Why are all the statements false? Explain those that you can.

8. Discuss the limitations of the following widely used "psychological" terms and "insights" (dubbed "psychobabble" by one critic):

I "flashed on" what he meant and really felt like we were "getting into each other's heads." She's really "together," you know, really "laid back." "I hear you." He gives me "good vibes," he's really "high energy," and you can always tell where he's "coming from." You gotta "go with your feelings" and "let it happen" if you don't want to be "uptight." We give each other the "space" to be our "true selves."

Suggestions for Further Reading

American Psychological Association. *Careers in Psychology.* APA, 1976. (Address: APA, 1200 Seventeenth Street, N.W., Washington, D.C. 20036) Write for free student copy.

Atkinson, R. C. "Reflections on Psychology's Past and Concerns About Its Future," *American Psychologist,* 1977, **32,** 205–210.

Evans, R. I. *The Making of Psychology: Discussions With Creative Contributors.* Alfred A. Knopf, 1976.

Hebb, D. O. "What Psychology Is About," *American Psychologist,* 1974, **29,** 71–79.

Jerome, L. E. "Astrology—Magic or Science?" In: *Objections to Astrology,* Prometheus Books, 1975.

Marks, R. W. (ed.). *Great Ideas in Psychology.* Bantam, 1966.

Psychology Today Magazine. CRM. Available monthly.

Super, D. E., and C. M. Super. *Opportunities in Psychology Careers Today,* 3rd ed. Vocational Guidance Manuals, 1976. (Address: 620 South 5th Street, Louisville, Ky. 40202)

Wertheimer, M. *A Brief History of Psychology.* Holt, 1972.

Woods, P. J. (ed.). *Career Opportunites for Psychologists: Expanding and Emerging Areas.* American Psychological Association, 1976.

Woods, P. J. (ed.) *The Psychology Major: Training and Employment Strategies.* American Psychological Association, 1979.

2

Research Methods in Psychology

From Common Sense to Controlled Observation

Comment overheard on campus: "I don't know why he bothers taking psychology classes. Psychology is just common sense." Is psychology common sense? Is common sense a good source of information?

Consider some "commonsense" statements: Let's say that your grandfather has gone back to college. What do people say? "Ahh . . . never too old to learn." And what do they say when he loses interest and quits? "Well, you can't teach an old dog new tricks." Let's examine another commonsense statement. It is frequently said that "absence makes the heart grow fonder." Those of us separated from friends and lovers can take comfort in this knowledge—until we remember that it's also "Out of sight, out of mind!" Much of what passes for common sense is equally vague and inconsistent. Notice also that these B. S. statements* work best after the fact.

Common sense can be a set of blinders that prevents us from seeking better information or seeing the truth. Einstein reportedly said, "Common sense is the layer of prejudice laid down in our minds before we are 18." In the early stages of the scientific revolution, people laughed at the idea that the world is round. Anyone with eyes could see that it wasn't. They laughed at Pasteur when he proposed that microorganisms cause disease. How could creatures too small to be seen kill a healthy human? Certainly ideas such as these contradicted the common sense of their time. Now few people argue with the findings of established sciences such as chemistry, physics, or medicine, but many still write off psychology as "just common sense."

Jab a hat pin into your finger. The nerve impulse carrying the sensation of pain to your brain seems instantaneous. We can go no further using personal observation. However, by using an electrical stimulus and electronic recorders to measure nerve impulses directly, psychologists have found their top speed to be 120 meters per second, one-third the speed of sound. This is fast, but certainly not instantaneous. We have come a long way from our original observation. Research psychologists use careful measurement and a number of specialized approaches to improve upon and extend observation and to avoid the pitfalls of "common sense." Their techniques are the topic of this chapter.

Survey Questions: How do psychologists gather information? What are the advantages and disadvantages of each approach? How is an experiment performed? How accurate is psychological information found in the popular press? What ethical questions does psychological research raise?

---

*B.S., of course, stands for *Before Science.*

━━━━━━━━━━━━━━━━━━━━━━━━━ Resources ━━━━━━━━━━━━

Scientific Method— Can a Horse Add?

In the United States today it is still possible to find people who believe that the earth is flat. To the "flat-earther" the earth is disc-shaped, with the North Pole at the center and the South Pole ringing the outer edge.

Question: How could anyone believe such a thing after seeing the astronauts' photographs of the earth?

Flat-earthers point out that the opposite side of large lakes can be seen through binoculars; therefore, the earth must be a flat surface. Also, a person who jumps up in the air for one second does not come down 190 miles away. Surely, they say, this fact proves that the earth cannot be a rotating globe (McCain and Segal, 1969).

Obviously, the flat-earthers have made the wrong observations, in the wrong way, and for the wrong reasons—*if* they are interested in the truth. In many ways, psychologists in search of accurate information must avoid the same trap of faulty observation. To do so, they use the **scientific method,** which is based on the collection of solid, observable evidence, accurate description and measurement, precise definition, controlled observation, and consistent results. In its ideal form, the scientific method has five steps:

1. **Observation**
2. **Defining a problem**
3. **Proposing a hypothesis**
4. **Experimentation**
5. **Theory formulation**

Question: What is a hypothesis?

A **hypothesis** is a tentative explanation of an event or a behavior. In common terms, a hypothesis is a clearly stated and *testable* "hunch," or "educated guess." For example, here are some hypotheses discussed in later chapters: "Aggression is encouraged by frustration." "Intellectual development in infancy is altered by parenting styles." "Forgetting is caused by loss of memory traces." Forming a hypothesis and other steps in the scientific method can be illustrated with the story of Clever Hans, a "wonder horse" (Rosenthal, 1965).

Clever Hans, a horse owned by a mathematics instructor, seemed to solve difficult math problems, which he answered by tapping his foot. If you asked Hans, "What is 12 times 2, minus 18," Hans would tap his foot six times. Hans

was so astonishing that he eventually attracted the attention of an inquiring scientist who discovered how Hans was able to perform. Assume that you are the scientist and that you are just itching to find out how Hans *really* does his trick.

Your investigation of Hans' mathematical abilities would probably begin with careful **observation** of both horse and owner while Hans was performing. If these observations fail to reveal any obvious deception, the *problem* becomes more clearly **defined:** What signals Hans to start and stop tapping his foot? Your first **hypothesis** might be that the owner is giving Hans a signal. Your proposed test (an **experiment** of sorts) would be to make the owner leave the room, and then have someone else ask Hans questions. Your proposed test would either confirm or deny this possibility and thereby support or eliminate the hypothesis. By changing the conditions under which you observe Hans, you have **controlled** the situation to gain more information from your observations.

Incidentally, Hans could still answer when his owner was out of the room. But a brilliant series of controlled observations revealed Hans' secret. If Hans couldn't see the questioner, he couldn't answer. It seems that questioners always *lowered their heads* (to look at Hans' foot) after asking a question. This was Hans' cue to start tapping. When Hans had tapped the correct number, a questioner would always *look up* to see if Hans was going to stop. This was Hans' cue to stop tapping!

Question: What about theory formulation?

Since Clever Hans' ability to do math was an isolated problem, no theorizing was involved. However, in actual psychological research, **theory formulation** is quite important. Theories allow the results of a large number of observations to be summarized in a way that accounts for existing data, predicts new observations, and guides further research. Theories of forgetting, personality, mental illness, and the like, are valuable products of psychological research. Without them, psychologists would drown in a sea of seemingly disconnected facts.

In their search for accurate information and useful theories, psychologists study behavior in many ways: They observe behavior as it unfolds in natural settings (**naturalistic observation**); they use statistics and measurement to discover relationships between events (**correlational method**); they use the powerful technique of controlled experimentation (**experimental method**); they study unique problems and therapeutic solutions in the psychological clinic (**clini-**

Fig. 2-1 *This woman is monitoring a reaction-time experiment. A subject in a separate darkened room has been presented with a visual stimulus. This device records the subject's brain waves and eye movements in response to the stimulus.*

cal method); and they use questionnaires and surveys to poll large numbers of people **(survey method)**. Let's see how each of these is used to advance psychological knowledge.

Naturalistic Observation— Psychology Steps Out!

Instead of waiting to encounter haphazardly whatever they are interested in, psychologists may set out to **actively observe** subjects in a **natural setting.** A good example of this style of research is the work of Jane van Lawick-Goodall. She and her staff have been observing chimpanzees in Tanzania since 1960. A quote from her book *In the Shadow of Man* captures the excitement of a scientific discovery:

> Quickly focusing my binoculars, I saw that it was a single chimpanzee, and just then he turned my direction. . . . Cautiously I moved around so that I could see what he was doing. He was squatting beside the red earth mound of a termite nest, and as I watched I saw him carefully push a long grass stem into a hole in the mound. After a moment he withdrew it and picked something from the end with his mouth. I was too far away to make out what he was eating, but it was obvious that he was actually using a grass stem as a tool (Goodall, 1971).

Notice that naturalistic observation only provides *descriptions* of behavior, not explanations. Just the same, this de-

scription forced many scientists to change their view of chimps, because humans had been regarded as the only toolmaking animals.

Question: Chimpanzees in zoos use objects as tools. Doesn't that prove the same thing?

Not necessarily. One of the advantages of naturalistic observation is that the behavior being studied has not been tampered with by outside influences. Only by observing chimps in their natural environment can we tell if they use tools without human interference.

Question: But doesn't the presence of human observers in an animal colony affect their behavior?

Effects of the Observer   Yes. The presence of an observer may change the behavior of the observed. Naturalists studying animal colonies must be very careful to keep their distance and to avoid the temptation to "make friends" with the animals. Likewise, if you are interested in student-teacher interactions in an elementary school classroom, it would hardly do for you to simply walk in and begin taking notes. A stranger in the room would undoubtedly affect both the students and the teacher. When possible, this problem is minimized by **concealing the observer.** For example, Arnold Gesell and his associates (1940) were able to determine at what age children develop the ability to sit up, walk, talk, and so forth, by observing preschoolers through one-way vision screens.

Fig. 2-2 *A special moment in Jane van Lawick-Goodall's naturalistic study of chimpanzees. (Photo by Baron Hugo van Lawick. © National Geographic Society.)*

A closely related problem in naturalistic studies is **observer bias,** in which observers see what they *expect* to see, or record only selected details. Teachers in one study were told to watch elementary school children who had been labeled as either learning-disabled, mentally retarded, emotionally disturbed, or normal. The ratings teachers gave the children differed markedly, depending on the label applied to the child (Foster and Ysseldyke, 1976).

Question: Then should naturalistic observation be used at all?

Psychologists doing naturalistic studies make a special effort to know their biases and to keep **careful records** of observations to minimize such errors. In the final analysis, naturalistic observation can be very valuable (Sommer, 1977). It provides a large amount of information in a relatively short time, raises interesting questions, defines new problems for study, and suggests initial hypotheses. In any scientific investigation, it is an excellent starting point.

Correlational Studies—In Search of the Perfect Relationship

Let's say that a psychologist notes a similarity between the IQs of children and their parents, between physical beauty and social popularity, anxiety and test scores, or even between riots and weather conditions. In each instance, we are dealing with the fact that two observations or events are **co-relating** (varying together in some orderly fashion). A **correlational study** is one that determines the degree of correlation, or relationship, between two traits, behaviors, or events (Myers, 1980). Unlike naturalistic observation, correlational studies can be done either in the lab or in the natural environment. In this approach, two factors of interest are measured, and then a statistical technique is used to determine their degree of correlation. (See Appendix for more information.) For example, we could find the correlation between horsepower and gas mileage in automobiles to see if the two are related. If the correlation is large, knowing horsepower would allow us to predict gas mileage with some accuracy.

Question: How is the degree of correlation expressed?

Correlations can be expressed as a **coefficient of correlation,** which is simply a number falling somewhere between +1.00 and −1.00. If the number is zero, or close to zero, it indicates a weak or nonexistent relationship. For example, the correlation between shoe size and intelligence is zero. (Sorry, size 12 readers.) If the correlation coefficient is +1.00, a **perfect positive relationship** exists; if it is −1.00, a **perfect negative relationship** has been discovered.

Correlations in psychology are rarely perfect. Most fall somewhere between zero and plus or minus one. The closer the correlation coefficient is to +1.00 or −1.00, the stronger the relationship. For example, identical twins are likely to have almost identical IQs, whereas parents and their children have IQs that are only generally similar. The correlation between IQs of parents and children is 0.4; that between identical twins is 0.9.

Question: What do the terms "positive" and "negative" correlation mean?

In a positive correlation, increases in one measure are matched by increases in the other (or decreases are accompanied by decreases). For example, there is a positive relationship between high school grades and college grades; students who do better in high school tend to do better in college (and the reverse). In a negative correlation, *increases* in the first measure are associated with *decreases* in the second. We might observe, for instance, that the higher the air temperature, the lower the activity level of animals in a zoo.

Question: Would that show that air temperature causes changes in activity level?

It might seem so, but we cannot be sure of it without performing an experiment. Correlational studies help us discover relationships and make useful predictions, but correlation *does not demonstrate causation.* The animals' activity might be affected by seasonal changes in weight, hormone levels, or even the feeding schedule used by the zoo. Consider another example of mistaking correlation for causation: What if a psychologist detected a certain chemical in the blood of schizophrenic patients not found in the blood of people functioning normally? Would this demonstrate that the chemical *causes* schizophrenia? This may seem to be the case, but schizophrenia could cause the chemical to form. Or, both schizophrenia and the chemical might be caused by some unknown third factor. Just because one thing *appears* to cause another does not *confirm* that it does. This fact becomes especially clear in the case of obviously noncausal relationships. For example, there is a correlation between the number of storks nesting in English villages and the number of births in those same towns. Does this mean that storks bring babies? Or could it mean that babies attract storks? Obviously, neither. Here's another: There is a relationship between the number of churches in American cities and the number of bars; the more churches, the more bars. Does this mean that drinking makes you religious? Does it mean that religion makes you thirsty? No one, of course, would leap to the conclusion that any one of these events *caused* the other, but, in more realistic situations, to do so is always a temptation.

Exactly nine months after a major power failure in New York State, doctors and nurses in New York hospitals noticed a sharp rise in the birthrate. News reports of this event assumed that when the lights and TVs went off, people had nothing better to do, and the result was a "baby boom" nine months later. A closer look at the birthrate would show that it fluctuates up and down all year. The "baby boom" was but one of dozens of small peaks, and therefore not necessarily linked to the power failure at all. The only way to be absolutely certain that a cause-effect relationship exists is to perform a controlled experiment. You'll learn how in the next section.

Learning Check

Before reading on, answer the following questions about what you just read.

1. Most of psychology can rightfully be called "common sense" because psychologists prefer naturalistic observation to controlled observation.   T or F?

2. A "hypothesis" is any careful observation made in a controlled experiment.   T or F?

3. Two problems in naturalistic observation are:
    a. getting subjects to cooperate and identifying correlations
    b. defining a problem and proposing a hypothesis
    c. effects of the observer and observer bias
    d. running the experiment and making careful records

4. Correlation does not demonstrate causation.   T or F?

5. Which correlation coefficient represents the strongest relationship?
    a. −0.86   b. +0.66   c. +0.10   d. +0.09

Answers: 1. F 2. F 3. c 4. T 5. a

The Experimental Method—Untangling Cause and Effect

One of the most powerful research tools available is the **experiment.** Research psychologists carefully control conditions in an experiment to gain reliable information and to identify cause-effect relationships. An experiment contains three essential elements:

1. **Independent variables,** which are conditions manipulated, applied, or changed in known ways by the experimenter.

2. Dependent variables, which are measures of the outcome of the experiment.

3. Extraneous variables, which are not allowed to affect the experiment's outcome.

The simplest psychological experiment is based on creation of two groups of **subjects** (animals or people). One group is called the **experimental group,** the other is called the **control group.**

Question: How do these groups differ?

The control group and the experimental group are treated exactly alike except for one condition, the **independent variable.** (For the moment, just think of a "variable" as anything that can change or vary, and which might affect the outcome of the experiment.) Suppose you notice that you study better with background music on. This suggests the hypothesis that music improves learning. We could test this hypothesis experimentally by forming two groups of people. One group studies with music on, and the other studies without music. Then we could compare their scores on a test. The group exposed to music is the experimental group because the independent variable (music) is present. The group not exposed to music is the control group.

Fig. 2-3 *Elements of a simple psychological experiment to assess the effects of music during study on test scores.*

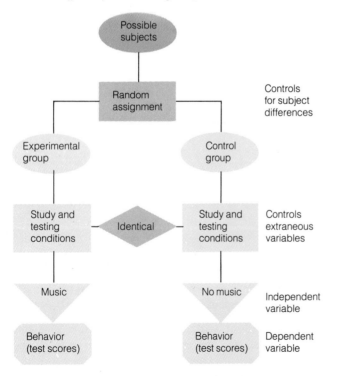

Question: Is a control group really needed? Can't people just study with music on to see if they do better?

Without a control group it would be impossible to tell if music had any effect on learning. The control group provides a *point of reference* to which scores of the experimental group can be compared. If the average test score of the experimental group is higher than that of the control group, it can be concluded that music improves learning efficiency. If the average is lower than the control group, we will know that music hampers learning. If there is no difference, we know that the independent variable had no effect on learning. In this experiment, the "amount learned" (indicated by scores on the test) is the **dependent variable.** In an experiment, we are asking the question, "Does the independent variable *affect* or influence the dependent variable?" (Does music affect or influence learning?) Another way to think of this is that the dependent variable in an experiment *depends on* the independent variable. (The amount learned depends on whether or not music accompanied study.)

Question: How do we know that people in one of the groups aren't more intelligent than those in the other group?

Differences in personal characteristics of subjects that might influence the outcome of an experiment can be eliminated by *randomly* assigning subjects to the two groups. **Random assignment** means that a subject has an equal chance of being a member of either the experimental group or the control group. Even in fairly small groups, this results in few differences in the number of people in each group who are geniuses or dunces, hungry, hungover, Democrat, Republican, tall, music lovers, or whatever.

Other **extraneous,** or outside variables—such as the amount of study time, sex of the subject, the temperature of the room, the time of day, the amount of light, and so forth—can be prevented from affecting the outcome of an experiment by making all conditions except the independent variable *exactly the same* for both the experimental group and the control group. If every possible condition is exactly the same for subjects in the experimental group and the control group except the presence or absence of music during study, and if there is a difference between the two groups in the amount learned, then that difference *must* be caused by the music (Fig. 2-3).

Now let's summarize more formally. In a psychological experiment, two or more groups of subjects are treated differently with respect to the independent variable. In all other ways they are treated the same. That is, extraneous variables are controlled by equalizing or removing them for all groups in the experiment. The impact of the independent variable (or variables) on some behavior (the dependent variable) is then measured. In a carefully controlled experiment, changes in the independent variable can be the only possible **cause** for a change in the dependent variable. This allows clear cause and effect connections to be identified.

Question: Experiments seem to set up artificial situations. Do experimental findings have anything to do with the real world?

There are many advantages to being able to "custom design" conditions in a laboratory experiment, but there is also a degree of artificiality. An alternative is the **field experiment,** which uses the "real world" as a laboratory. Here is an illustration:

One Good Flat Deserves Another

James Bryan and Mary Test (1971) were interested in whether people are more likely to help a person in distress when they have recently seen someone else being helpful. To find out, a Ford Mustang with a flat tire was parked at curbside on a busy street. An inflated tire leaned against the car, and a female college student stood nearby. Of 2000 cars that passed, only 35 stopped in this control condition. In the experimental condition, a second car was parked one-quarter mile back from the test car. The second automobile was raised on a jack and a woman stood watching a man change a tire. Of 2000 vehicles that first passed this staged helping scene, 58 stopped to help the woman in the test car.

Such "real life" experiments are becoming increasingly popular among psychologists as a way of bridging the gap between laboratory studies and everyday life. You may have even participated in an experiment without knowing about it!

Placebo Effects: Sugar Pills and Salt Water   Assume that we want to perform an experiment to see if Dexedrine (a powerful central nervous system stimulant) affects learning. An accurate test of the drug would *not* occur if, before studying, members of the experimental group were given a Dexedrine pill and the control group got nothing.

Question: Why not? The experimental group gets the drug and the control group doesn't. If there is a difference in learning scores, it must be due to the action of the drug. Right?

No, because an error has been made: The experimental group and the control group have been treated differently with respect to more than just the presence or absence of the drug. Members of the experimental group swallowed a pill, and control subjects did not. Without using a **placebo** (plah-SEE-bo), it is impossible to tell if the drug has affected learning, or if just swallowing a pill did.

Question: What is a placebo?

A placebo is a fake pill or injection. A placebo's beneficial effects come from what it suggests rather than from what it contains. Sugar pills and saline (saltwater) injections are common placebos.

Although they have little or no direct chemical effect, placebos can have a tremendous *psychological* impact. As an example of how powerful the **placebo effect** can be, one study showed that an injection of saline solution was 70 percent as effective as morphine in reducing pain for hospital patients (Beecher, 1959). This fact is well known to physicians, who for years have prescribed placebos for complaints they feel have no physical basis (Jospe, 1978). Exactly how placebos relieve pain is not fully understood, but recent experiments suggest that they trigger the release of brain chemicals called **endorphins** (Cohen, 1977; Levine *et al.,* 1979). Endorphins are similar to pain-killing opiate drugs, such as morphine. Thus, the placebo effect is not imaginary.

To control for placebo effects, a psychologist doing drug research could use a **single-blind** arrangement. In this approach, *all* subjects get a pill or injection. The experimental group gets the real drug and the control group gets a placebo. Thus, subjects are *blind* as to whether or not they received the drug. But this is not enough. Experimenters must also be blind as to whether they are giving a drug or a placebo to a particular subject. The **double-blind** arrangement, as this is called, prevents the experimenter from unconsciously influencing subject's reactions.

Question: How could the experimenter influence the subject?

The Experimenter Effect   Psychological researchers face an interesting problem not shared by physicists and chemists. Human subjects are very sensitive to hints from an experimenter about what is expected of them. The **experimenter effect,** as this is called, can cause a powerful influence on a subject's behavior (Rosenthal, 1976). This effect holds true even when animals are used as subjects.

Twelve experimenters (psychology graduate students) were each given five rats to run through a maze. Half of the experimenters were told that they were receiving "maze-bright" rats and half believed that their rats were "maze-dull."

Question: What is a maze-bright rat?

Maze-bright and maze-dull rats have been specially bred to be either brilliant at learning mazes or very slow at it.

> At the end of the experiment it was found that the "maze-bright" rats showed superior learning compared to the "maze-dull" rats in spite of the fact that the rats were actually all of the same variety (Rosenthal and Fode, 1963a).

There was no difference between the rats! But they performed as if they really were bright or slow. The source of the difference was the expectations of the experimenters. Those who thought they had maze-bright rats, named them, handled them frequently, and fed them choice tidbits between learning trials. Experimenters who thought they had stupid rats carried them by the tail and handled them as little as possible. These handling differences affected the way the rats performed in the maze.

The experimenter effect also applies outside the laboratory, where expectations can influence people in interesting ways. Psychologist Robert Rosenthal (1973) reports a typical example: At the U.S. Air Force Academy Preparatory School, 100 airmen were randomly assigned to one of five math classes. Their teachers were unaware of this random assignment. Instead, the teachers were told that their students were selected for high or low levels of ability. Students in the supposed "high-ability" classes improved substantially more in math scores than those in "low-ability" classes. Yet, at first, the classes were all of equal ability. Apparently, the teachers' expectations created a **self-fulfilling prophecy** that affected students' performance.

Learning Check

1. To understand cause and effect, a simple psychological experiment is based on creation of two groups: the

    _____ group and the _____ group.

2. Anything that can change (vary) and that might affect the behavior of subjects is called a _____.

3. There are three types of variables to consider in an experiment: an _____ variable; a

    _____ variable; and _____ variables.

4. A researcher performs an experiment to learn if room temperature affects the amount of aggression displayed by college students under crowded conditions in a simulated prison environment. In this experiment, the independent variable is (circle): room temperature, the amount of aggression, crowding, the simulated prison environment.

5. A procedure used to control both the placebo effect and the experimenter effect in drug experiments is the:
    - a. correlation method
    - b. extraneous prophecy
    - c. double-blind technique
    - d. random assignment of subjects

Answers: 1. experimental, control   2. variable   3. independent, dependent, extraneous   4. room temperature   5. c

---

The Clinical Method— Information by the Case

Many experiments that might prove informative or revealing are impractical, immoral, or impossible to perform. In instances such as these, information may be gained from **case studies.** A case study is an in-depth focus on all aspects of a single subject. Case studies are used heavily by clinical psychologists.

Case studies may sometimes be thought of as **natural experiments.** Gunshot wounds, brain tumors, accidental poisonings, and similar disasters have provided much information on the functioning of the human brain. One remarkable case from the history of psychology is reported by

Dr. J. M. Harlow (1868). Phineas Gage, a young foreman on a work crew, had a 13-pound steel rod blown through the front of his brain by the premature explosion of an excavating charge. Amazingly, he survived the accident, but not without undergoing a profound personality change. Dr. Harlow carefully recorded all the details of what was perhaps the first well-done case study of an accidental *frontal lobotomy* (the destruction of front brain matter).

Over 120 years later, a Los Angeles carpenter named Michael Melnick was the victim of a similar freak accident. Melnick fell from the second story of a house under construction and impaled his head on a steel reinforcing rod. Incredibly, he recovered completely, with no sign of lasting ill-effects (*Los Angeles Times*, 1981). Melnick's very different reaction to a similar injury shows why psychologists prefer controlled experiments, and often use lab animals for studies of the brain. But when a purely psychological problem is under study, the clinical method may be the *only* source of information.

A classic psychological case study is *The Three Faces of Eve* (Thigpen and Cleckley, 1957). Eve White was a mild, restrained, suburban housewife who in the course of psychiatric treatment revealed the existence of a second separate personality. This second personality, Eve Black, was the antithesis of Eve White. Eve Black was childish, mischievous, and erotically flirtatious. Eve Black knew about Eve White and openly talked about the times she had disobeyed her parents or gotten drunk and then "went in" to Eve White. After Eve Black's escapades, Eve White faced her punishment or bore her hangover with bewilderment because she did not know of Eve Black's existence. Eventually, this duality was resolved when a third personality— who called herself Jane—emerged. Jane ultimately separated from Eve White's husband and began a relatively stable new life marked by the slow development of a progression of other personalities.

Now in her fifties, this woman has manifested 21 different personalities over the years. The careful recording of all pertinent facts in cases such as this one is essential to psychology. *Multiple personality* is a rare event, and there are no experimental means for producing it. (Multiple personality is discussed further in Chapter 20.)

Survey Method— Sampling Information

Sometimes psychologists would like to ask everyone in the world a few well-chosen questions: "Have you ever smoked marijuana?" "Have you engaged in premarital sexual intercourse?" "What is your marital status now, and were your parents ever separated or divorced?" "Do you favor abortion?" The answers to questions such as these can reveal much about significant psychological events in the lives of large groups of people. But since it is impractical to question *everyone*, psychologists use the **survey method.** In a survey, people in a **representative sample**[*] are asked a carefully worded series of questions. A careful survey can provide an accurate picture of how large seg-

*A representative sample includes the same proportion of men, women, white-collar workers, Republicans, Democrats, blacks, and so on, as found in the population as a whole.

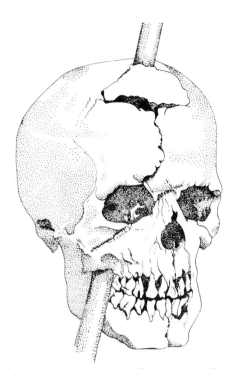

Fig. 2-4 *Some of the earliest information on the effects of damage to frontal areas in the brain came from a case study of the accidental injury of Phineas Gage.*

ments of the general population feel about current issues, even though only a small percentage of people are polled.[†]

Question: How accurate is the survey method?

Modern surveys like the Gallup and Harris polls are quite accurate. The Gallup poll has erred in its election predictions by only 1.5 percent since 1954. This level of accuracy has not always been the case. During the 1936 presidential election, a well-known magazine, the *Literary Digest*, predicted that Alfred Landon would defeat Franklin Roosevelt by a landslide. Roosevelt defeated Landon by about 11 million votes!

Question: How could the poll have been so wrong?

The answer lies in the way that the sample was taken. Most people in the poll were contacted *by telephone*. In 1936, during the Depression, people who had phones were much

†Some psychologists have questioned—tongue in cheek—psychology's claim that its conclusions apply to people in general. The distinguished psychologist Edward Tolman once noted how much of American psychology is based on two sets of subjects: rats and college sophomores. Tolman urged his colleagues to remember that rats certainly are not people and that college sophomores *may not be!*

more wealthy than average, and the wealthy favored Landon. The sample was biased rather than representative. Even when questions are carefully stated and the sample is representative, a survey may be limited by another problem. If a psychologist asked you detailed questions about your sexual history and current sexual activities, how accurate would your replies be? Would you be embarrassed and not completely frank? Or might you have a tendency to exaggerate your sexual experience? Replies to survey questions are not always *accurate or truthful*. Despite such problems, surveys frequently produce useful information. For example, in recent years working women have complained of sexual harassment while at their jobs. How serious or widespread is this problem? A recent survey of working men and women conducted by psychologist Barbara Gutek sheds some light on the question. Gutek

(1981) found that 53 percent of women, but only 37 percent of men, had experienced some form of sexual harassment at work. Gutek also found that women were about twice as likely as men to be the target of sexual comments, gestures, or touching, which they considered to be harassment. Does such information solve the problem of sexual harassment? Obviously not, but it is a first step toward understanding it and remedying it.

A Look Ahead To complete our discussion, this chapter's "Applications" offers a critical look at psychological information reported in the popular press. Following that is an "Exploration" on the ethics of psychological research. You should find these topics an interesting way to conclude our look at research in psychology.

Learning Check

1. Case studies can often be thought of as natural experiments and are used frequently by clinical psychologists. T or F?

2. For the survey method to be valid, a representative sample of people must be polled. T or F?

3. The phenomenon of multiple personality would most likely be investigated by use of:

   a. a representative sample *b.* field experiments *c.* the double-blind procedure *d.* case studies

4. A problem with the survey method is that answers to questions may not always be _____

   or _____.

Answers: 1. T 2. T 3. d 4. accurate or truthful

Resources Summary

Many of the important ideas in this chapter are summarized in the comparison chart you see here. A few additional points to remember follow it.

	Advantages	Disadvantages
Naturalistic observation	Behavior is observed in a natural setting; much information is obtained and hypotheses and questions for additional research are formed.	Little or no control is possible; observed behavior may be altered; observations may be biased; causes cannot be conclusively identified.
Correlational method	Demonstrates the existence of relationships; allows prediction; can be used in lab, clinic, or natural settings.	Little or no control is possible; relationships may be coincidental; cannot confirm cause-effect relationships.
Experimental method	Clear cause-effect relationships can be identified; powerful controlled observations can be staged; no need to wait for natural event.	May be somewhat artificial; some natural behavior not easily studied in laboratory (field experiments may avoid these objections).
Clinical method	Takes advantage of "natural experiments" and allows investigation of rare or unusual problems or events.	Little control is possible; subjective interpretation is often necessary; a single case may be misleading or unrepresentative.
Survey method	Allows information about large numbers of people to be gathered; can address questions not answered by other approaches.	Representative sample is critical and can be difficult to obtain; answers may be inaccurate; people may not do what they say or say what they do.

● The *scientific method* is used to improve upon common sense and to avoid the pitfalls of casual observation. Important steps in scientific investigation usually include: *observing, defining a problem, proposing a hypothesis, experimenting,* and *forming a theory.*

● *Naturalistic observation* is a starting place in many investigations. Three problems with this approach involve: the effects of the observer on the observed, observer bias, and an inability to explain observed behavior.

● In the *correlational method,* relationships between two traits, responses, or events are examined by measuring each factor and calculating a *correlation coefficient.* Correlations allow prediction, but they are insufficient to demonstrate cause and effect connections.

● Cause-effect relationships are identified by *controlled experiments.* In an experiment, two or more groups of *subjects* are formed. These groups differ only with regard to the *independent variable* or condition of interest as a cause in the experiment. Differences in the *dependent variable* (the effect) are then measured while all other conditions (*extraneous variables*) are held constant.

● In experiments testing drugs, a *placebo* (a fake pill or injection) must be used to control psychological expectations associated with taking a drug. Drug research also frequently employs a *double-blind* procedure so that neither subjects nor experimenters know who is receiving a drug.

● A related problem is the *experimenter effect,* the tendency of an experimenter to subtly and unconsciously influence the outcome of an experiment. Expectations can create a *self-fulfilling prophecy,* in which a person changes in the direction of the expectation.

● The *clinical method* employs *case studies,* which are in-depth records of a single subject. Case studies provide important information on topics that would not be studied any other way.

● In the *survey method,* people in a *representative sample* are asked a carefully worded series of questions. Responses to these questions provide information on the attitudes and psychological functioning of large groups of people.

Psychology in the News—Notes on Reading the Popular Press

Question: Is so much emphasis on "research" really necessary in psychology?

In a word, yes. As we have seen, "science" is a powerful way of asking questions about the world; a way of getting trustworthy answers. More importantly, we might ask, "What is the alternative to using the scientific method?" In most areas of knowledge, including psychology, wiping out scientific advances would mean a return to the Dark Ages. Awareness of this fact, along with your understanding of psychological research methods, should do much to make you a more critical observer of human behavior. Below are some additional pointers to sharpen your skills.

Notes on Reading the Popular Press

The tremendous popularity of psychology has spurred extensive coverage of psychological research and theories in popular magazines and daily newspapers. Unfortunately, much of what is covered is based on wishful thinking rather than science. Here are some suggestions for telling the difference.

Suggestion 1   Be skeptical. Psychological reports in the popular press tend to be made uncritically and with a definite bias toward the reporting of "sensational" findings.

Example: A few years ago stories appeared in the press reporting research in the Soviet Union and the United States on "dermo-optical perception." According to these stories, people had been found who could identify colors and read print (even under glass) while blindfolded. These feats were supposedly performed using the fingertips and were given as an indication of the existence of a "sixth sense," or "X-ray eyes." Martin Gardner, a scientist whose hobby is magic, suggests that such "abilities" are based on what professional performers call a "nose peek." Gardner says that it is impossible to prepare a blindfold (without doing damage to the eyes) that does not leave a tiny space on each side of the nose through which a person can peek. In accordance with Gardner's criticism, the phenomenal ability of individuals who performed in the first dermo-optical perception experiments disappeared each time the opportunity to peek was more controlled (Gardner, 1966).

Here is another indication of the need to be critical or skeptical. Psychologist Philip Zimbardo tells with amusement about his mentioning to an inquiring reporter that in the back wards of two mental hospitals in which he had worked women patients seemed to use a greater number of obscenities than male patients. Zimbardo emphasizes that this was nothing more than a casual statement and that it was not based on data of any kind, but when it was reported in *The New York Times* it became an "observation" that he had "noted" over a long period of time. When *Newsweek* reported the *Times* article to its readers, the relationship that was "noted" became one that had been "found." Ultimately, *Playboy's* version stated that "a number of psychologists, *The New York Times* reports, have found that women of every social level have become increasingly uninhibited in their use of obscene language" (*Playboy,* 1969). Zimbardo notes that the only authority mentioned to confirm this "fact" was himself (Ruch and Zimbardo, 1971)!

Suggestion 2   Consider the source of information. It should come as no surprise that information given by an individual or a company intent on selling a product often reflects the profit motive more than it does objective truth. Here is a typical advertising claim: "Government tests have proven that no pain reliever is stronger or more effective than Brand X aspirin." A statement like this usually means that there was *no difference* between the product and others tested in speed or effectiveness of pain relief. No other pain reliever was stronger or more effective, but none was weaker either. Keep the source in mind when reading the claims of makers of home biofeedback machines, sleep learning devices, and the like. Remember also that psychological services may be merchandised as well. Expensive courses that promise instant mental health and happiness, increased efficiency, memory, ESP or psychic ability, control of the unconscious mind, an end to the smoking habit, and so on, are usually supported by a few testimonials and many unproved claims.

Applications

An area of psychological interest that must be viewed with special caution is that of "psychic" phenomena. Stage mentalists make their living by deceiving the public and understandably promote belief in their nonexistent powers. Psychic phenomena when (and if) they do occur are quite fragile and unpredictable. It would be impossible for a mentalist to do three shows a night, six nights a week without consistently using deception.

Question: I've seen some amazing things on TV. Could you give an example of how I may have been fooled?

Here is a typical stage mentalist's routine. The mentalist picks a member of the audience "at random" and begins telling him personal things that "he could not possibly know." How does he do it? Easy! One of his many assistants stood in line outside the theater and eavesdropped on the person's conversations before the show. The assistant then made careful note of where the person was seated and passed on the location and information to the mentalist. The mentalist then announces, "You have an aunt . . . Aunt Bessy . . . she has been very ill . . . you were thinking about her earlier this evening . . . you had a flat tire on the way here this evening."

Suggestion 3 Ask yourself, "Was there a control group?" The essential importance of a control group in any experiment is frequently overlooked by the psychologically unsophisticated—an error to which you are no longer susceptible! The popular press is full of reports of "experiments" performed without control groups: "Talking to Plants Speeds Growth"; "Special Diet Controls Hyperactivity in Children"; "Food Shows Less Spoilage in Pyramid Chamber"; "Theater Reports Increased Beverage Sales during Showing of *Lawrence of Arabia.*"

Consider the last example for a moment. Almost every year it seems a theatre somewhere will claim that a movie has had an unusual effect on viewers. If the showing of *Lawrence of Arabia* were accompanied by increased beverage sales, would this indicate that viewers had been influenced by the desert scenery? Actually, they may have been influenced, but since there is no control group (people who watch another movie under identical conditions), it is impossible to tell if the temperature in the theatre, the time of year, the kind of crowd attracted, or the movie itself affected beverage consumption.

Suggestion 4 Look for errors in distinguishing between correlation and causation. An earlier discussion should make it clear that it is dangerous to presume that one thing has *caused* another on the basis of correlation. In spite of this, you will encounter numerous claims based on questionable correlations. Law enforcement agencies like to point out that most heroin addicts have used marijuana. This is an interesting observation, but it does not justify the conclusion that marijuana use "causes" addiction to hard drugs. Most heroin addicts have also used milk. Lack of proof for a causal link to hard drugs is also not an endorsement of marijuana use, but it does point out how muddled thinking on important issues can become.

Here's another example of mistaking correlation for causation. Jeanne Dixon, a popular astrologer, once answered a group of prominent scientists who had declared that there is no scientific foundation for believing in astrology by saying: "They would do well to check the records at their local police stations, where they will learn that the rate of violent crime rises and falls with lunar cycles" (Dixon, 1975). Dixon, of course, is implying that the moon affects human behavior.

Question: If it is true that violent crime is more frequent at certain times of the month, doesn't it prove her point?

Far from it; increased crime could be due to darker nights, the fact that bills fall due at the first of the month, or any number of similar factors.

Suggestion 5 Be sure to distinguish between observation and inference. If you see a person *crying,* is it correct to assume that he or she is *sad?* Although it seems reasonable to make this assumption, it is actually quite risky. We can observe objectively that the person is crying, but to *infer* sadness may be in error. It could be that the individual has just peeled five pounds of onions or just won the Irish sweepstakes, or is trying on contact lenses for the first time. Psychologists, politicians, physicians, scientists, and other experts often go far beyond the available facts in their claims. This does not mean that their inferences, opinions, and interpretations have no value; the opinion of an expert on the causes of mental illness, criminal behavior, learning problems, or whatever can be very revealing. But be careful to distinguish be-

Applications

tween fact and opinion. Here is an example that illustrates why this is important.

> A 54-year-old schizophrenic patient was rewarded for holding a broom that was given to her by a ward attendant. If she held the broom after it was handed to her, she was given a cigarette by another attendant. The purpose of this experiment was to determine if rewards should be used to alter the patient's rather listless behavior (she had been hospitalized for 23 years and refused to do anything on the ward). Soon the patient spent much of her time holding the broom. At this point, two psychiatrists were invited to observe the patient through a one-way mirror. One psychiatrist's interpretation of the "broom-holding behavior" was that it was a symbolic expression of deep-seated unfulfilled desires. According to him, the broom could be a symbol for:
>
> 1. "a child that gives her love and she gives him in return her devotion.
> 2. a phallic symbol.
> 3. the sceptre of an omnipotent queen" (Ayllon *et al.,* 1965).

The psychiatrist *observed* that the patient spent much of her time holding a broom. He *inferred* that this behavior had deep psychological meaning, when in fact she held the broom for one reason: She received cigarettes for doing so!

Suggestion 6 Beware of over-simplifications, especially those motivated by monetary gain. Courses or programs that offer a "new personality in three sessions," "six steps to love and fulfillment in marriage," or newly discovered "secrets of unlocking the powers of the mind," should be immediately suspect. An excellent example of oversimplification is provided by a brochure entitled, "Dr. Joyce Brothers Asks: How Do You Rate as a

'Superwoman'?" Dr. Brothers, a "media" psychologist who has no private practice and is not known for research, wrote the brochure as a consultant for the Aerosol Packaging Council of the Chemical Specialties Manufacturers Association. A typical suggestion in this brochure tells how to enhance a marriage: "Sweep him off to a weekend hideaway. Tip: When he's not looking spray a touch of your favorite *aerosol* cologne mist on the bedsheets and pillows" (italics added). Sure, Joyce . . .

Suggestion 7 Remember, "for example" is no proof. After reading this chapter you should be sensitive to the danger of selecting single examples. If you read that, "Law student passes state bar exam using sleep-learning device," don't rush out to buy one. Systematic research has shown that these devices are of little or no value (Koukkou and Lehmann, 1968). A corollary to this suggestion is to ask, "Are the reported observations important or widely applicable?"

Summary Journalist Alvin Toffler and others have suggested that we are in the midst of an "information explosion." Indeed, we are all bombarded daily with such a mass of new information that it is difficult to adequately absorb it. The available knowledge, even in a limited area like psychology, biology, medicine, or contemporary rock music, is so vast that no single person can completely know and comprehend it. With this situation in mind, it becomes increasingly important that you become a critical, selective, and informed consumer of information. And if you think the value of scientific thought is restricted to the laboratory, remember the words of Oliver Wendell Holmes: "All life is an experiment."

Learning Check

1. Newspaper accounts of dermo-optical perception have generally reported only the results of carefully designed psychological experiments. T or F?
2. Stage mentalists and psychics often use deception in their acts. T or F?
3. Blaming variations in the rate of violent crime on changes in the lunar cycle is an example of mistaking correlation for causation. T or F?
4. Psychiatric interpretations of a patient's "broom-holding behavior" (described in Suggestion 5) show the importance of using a control group in experiments. T or F?

Answers: 1. F 2. T 3. T 4. F

Smile, You're on Candid Camera!—
The Ethics of Psychological Research

A few years ago, social psychologist Philip Zimbardo and his associates set up a simulated prison at Stanford University to investigate the effects of imprisonment on otherwise healthy individuals. Students were recruited to play the roles of prisoners and guards. Much to everyone's surprise, the experiment had to be called off soon after it began. The "guards" had become so sadistic that four of the ten "prisoners" suffered emotional reactions ranging from crying and depression to acute anxiety and rage (Zimbardo, Haney, and Banks, 1973). This experiment is discussed further in Chapter 26.

The Stanford prison experiment is only one of several that have raised questions about the ethics of psychological research. Were the participants permanently harmed? Did the information gained justify the emotional costs? Are such experiments dehumanizing? In response to such questions the American Psychological Association has adopted guidelines that state in part:

> Having made the decision to conduct research, psychologists must carry out investigations with respect for the people who participate and with concern for their dignity and welfare.

In addition, most college psychology departments have ethics committees that oversee proposed research. Three areas psychological researchers must be particularly sensitive to are: use of deception, invasion of privacy, and lasting harm. As a basis for thought and discussion, review the following three experiments. See if you think they are ethical.

Deception   In many experiments the true interests of a researcher are concealed by deception. This approach is often considered necessary to create a realistic situation and to obtain genuine reactions. For example, a researcher interested in guilt once led subjects to believe that they had broken an expensive piece of machinery. The experimenter had told subjects ahead of time, "All my research money is tied up in this contraption and I'll never get my master's degree if it doesn't function properly."

During the experiment, the machine suddenly popped loudly, released a plume of smoke, and sputtered to a stop. As embarrassed subjects were about to leave, after having "broken" the machine, the experimenter asked if they would sign a petition he was circulating. The petition called for a doubling of tuition fees at the school, something control subjects almost universally refused to endorse. Because of their guilt, more than 50 percent of the experimental subjects signed (reported by Rubin, 1970). Was deception really necessary to answer the researcher's questions about guilt?

Invasion of Privacy   A second area of debate concerns the extent to which invasions of privacy should be allowed in psychological research. One study that has been both criticized and defended involved secret observation of men urinating in a restroom. Psychologist Eric Knowles was interested in the stress caused by "personal space" invasions. An observer concealed himself in a toilet stall in a public restroom and used a hidden periscope to monitor activity at the urinals. As predicted, urination took longer to begin when an assistant occupied a urinal adjacent to the unsuspecting subject (Middlemist, Knowles, and Matter, 1976; Koocher, 1977). This finding is interesting, but does it justify the invasion of privacy used to obtain it?

Lasting Harm   Do psychological experiments ever do lasting harm to participants? This is perhaps the most serious ethical question of all. Zimbardo's Stanford prison study is not the only one that has raised such considerations. For example, in a study of obedience to authority, Stanley Milgram (1974) led subjects to believe they were inflicting painful and dangerous electrical shocks on another person (no shocks were actually given—see Chapter 25). Belief that they were hurting someone proved extremely stressful for most subjects; many left the experiment shaken and upset. As one of Milgram's assistants reported, "I observed an initially poised businessman enter the laboratory smiling and confident. Within 20 minutes

Exploration

he was reduced to a twitching, stuttering wreck, who was rapidly approaching nervous collapse.''

This experiment may sound clearly unethical, but both Milgram (1974) and Zimbardo (1974) did follow-up studies on participants in their experiments. Most felt positive about their experiences and claimed they were glad they had participated. Many added that they had learned something of value about themselves. But what about the few who felt otherwise?

As in medical research, no easy answers exist to the ethical questions raised by psychology. Most students find the studies just described interesting and informative. How can the search for knowledge be properly balanced with human rights? How does the stress produced in an experiment compare to that caused by such routine procedures as classroom tests? How do *you* think a psychologist should decide if his or her research is ethical?

Questions for Discussion

1. Can you think of some "commonsense" statements (other than those already mentioned) that contradict each other? Why do you think such contradictions go unnoticed?

2. Let's say you are interested in investigating the unspoken rules that govern the spacing of people in public places. What research techniques would you use? Can you propose some field experiments that might be performed?

3. What type of correlation would you expect to find between noise levels and productivity in an office? Between income and education? Between physical attractiveness and frequency of dating? Between class attendance and grades? Between use of alcohol by parents and their children? How would you prove a causal link in any of these cases?

4. Regarding self-fulfilling prophecies, how have the expectations of teachers, parents, or friends affected your expectations for yourself? If you have attended a school with slow, normal, and accelerated classes, what advantages and disadvantages do you see in such a system?

5. In your opinion, is it dishonest or unethical for a physician to administer placebos to patients? Why or why not?

6. Have you ever taken part in a survey? On the basis of your participation, how accurate do you think surveys are? What are the flaws of typical "person on the street" surveys often done by local newspapers?

7. Compared to things done regularly by the government, the military, business, and educational institutions, most psychology experiments are pretty tame. With this point in mind, what is your position on the ethical questions raised in the "Exploration" section?

8. Do you consider the experiments described in the "Exploration" section ethical? Why or why not? What changes would you make if you were repeating the experiments?

9. There is a loophole in the statement, "I've been taking vitamin C tablets, and I haven't had a cold all year." What is it?

Suggestions for Further Reading

Anderson, B. D. *The Psychology Experiment,* 2nd ed. Brooks/Cole, 1971.

Galston, A. W., and C. L. Slayman. "The Not-So-Secret Life of Plants," *American Scientist,* May–June, 1979, 337–344.

Gardner, M. *Fads and Fallacies in the Name of Science.* Dover, 1975.

Hays, W. L. "The Measurement of Psychological Entities," Chapter 1 in *Quantification in Psychology.* Wadsworth, 1967.

McCain, G., and E. M. Segal. *The Game of Science.* Brooks/Cole, 1969.

Monte, C. F. *Psychology's Scientific Endeavor.* Praeger, 1975.

Contents

Part II

Foundations
of
Human
Consciousness

3

The Biology of Behavior and Conscious Experience

======= Chapter Preview =======

Worlds within Worlds within Worlds

Imagine yourself smaller than the period at the end of this sentence. Then join me as we enter a microscopic world as bizarre as any found in science fiction: Surrounding us is a thicket of tubelike branches, delicate fibers, and transparent globes. As we watch, pulsing waves of electrical energy flash through the tubes and branches, arriving and scattering in a thousand directions. Wave after wave arrives, each leaving new storms of activity in its wake. Meanwhile, all is bathed in a swirling sea of exotic chemicals and charged ions. We are indeed in a strange realm. Yet there is beauty here, and mind-bending complexity—for we have just stepped into that most amazing of all computers: the human brain.

Once we crack open the fragile shell of the skull, we find in the truest sense "worlds within worlds within worlds." The human brain is a mass of spongy tissue about the size of a large grapefruit. Weighing a little over three pounds, it consists of some 100 billion nerve cells called **neurons.** *All human behavior can ultimately be traced to the activity of these tiny cells. Each neuron in this "enchanted loom" is connected to many others, oftentimes as many as 10,000. This arrangement provides an exceptionally large capacity for combining and storing information. It is estimated that the number of possible interconnections between neurons in a single human brain exceeds the number of atomic particles in the entire universe!*

Question: Then is it true that humans use only a small amount of the brain?

This is not strictly true because every cell in the brain (if it is not dead) is active at all times. However, it is true in the sense that we only store a fraction of the information the brain could hold. Also, there is a large amount of duplication in the brain. Were it not for this, we could not afford to lose thousands of neurons every day through aging.

Scientists have long known that the brain is the organ of consciousness and the origin of action. But only in recent years has it become possible to demonstrate this directly. To prove the point, researcher José Delgado once entered a bullring with a cape and a radio transmitter. The bull charged. Delgado retreated. At the last possible instant, the speeding bull stopped short. Why?

Because Delgado used the radio transmitter to activate electrodes implanted in "control centers" of the bull's brain (more on this in this chapter's "Exploration").

Physiological psychology *is the study of the way in which the brain and nervous system allow us to respond to the world. The physiological psychologist occupies an exotic midground between mind and brain, biology and psychology. Let us enter this fascinating realm for a closer look at our biological heritage and our human potential.*

Survey Questions: How do neurons operate and communicate? What are the functions of major parts of the nervous system? What happens when the brain is injured? How does the glandular system relate to the nervous system? How do right- and left-handed individuals differ? Can the brain be controlled electrically?

Resources

Neurons—"Atoms" of the Nervous System

As physiological psychologist Paul MacLean once remarked, "The towering question before the world concerns whether man can master his brain and behavior before he has blown himself to smithereens through his mastery of physics and chemistry." One of the most powerful keys to understanding the brain is the study of individual nerve cells. Unlike other cells in the body, neurons are specially designed to carry information. They are the basic units of the human "biocomputer."

Question: How do neurons carry information?

Parts of a Neuron   If we think of the nervous system as long "chains" of communicating cells, then neurons are the links. No two neurons are exactly alike in size or shape, but most have four basic parts (Fig. 3-1). The **dendrites,** which look like the roots of a tree, serve as a receiving area for information from other neurons. The cell body, or **soma,** also receives incoming information, which it collects and combines. Periodically, the soma sends nerve impulses down a long, thin fiber called the **axon.** Some axons are only about one-tenth millimeter long, but others may stretch up to a meter through the nervous system of an adult. Axons act like miniature cables carrying messages from the sensory organs to the brain, from the brain to muscles or glands, or simply from one nerve cell to the next. Most axons branch at their ends to form an array of **axon terminals.** These branches connect the neuron to the dendrites and somas of other nerve cells.

The Nerve Impulse   Each neuron can be thought of as a tiny biological battery. Nerve cells are filled with, and surrounded by, electrically charged molecules called **ions,** especially sodium and potassium ions (Fig. 3-2). Differing numbers of these ions are found inside and outside the cell. As a result, a tiny difference in electrical charge exists across the cell membrane (or "skin"). In humans, this charge, called a **resting potential,** is about minus 70 millivolts (a millivolt is one-thousandth of a volt). Messages arriving from other neurons move the resting potential toward a critical level or **threshold** of about minus 50 millivolts. When the neuron's electrical charge reaches the threshold, a nerve impulse is triggered. The nerve impulse, or **action potential,** then sweeps down the axon.

The existence of a threshold for firing makes the action potential an **all-or-nothing** event; it occurs completely or not at all. You might find it helpful to picture the axon as a fuse that is lit at the soma and that burns rapidly to the axon terminals. After an action potential occurs, the cell's voltage briefly drops below its resting level. This drop is called a **negative after-potential.** It occurs while the neuron is recharging. During an action potential, a neuron cannot be made to fire again; this is known as the **absolute refractory period.** While the neuron is recharging, there is a **relative refractory period,** in which nerve impulses are harder to trigger. All of these events occur in about one-thousandth of a second, so the highest firing rate for a neuron is roughly 1000 times per second. Firing rates of one to several hundred per second are more typical (Stevens, 1979).

Question: How fast does the nerve impulse travel?

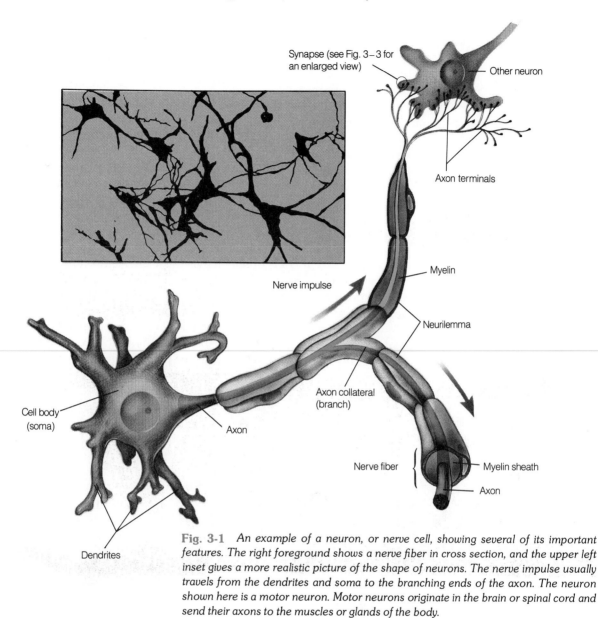

Fig. 3-1 *An example of a neuron, or nerve cell, showing several of its important features. The right foreground shows a nerve fiber in cross section, and the upper left inset gives a more realistic picture of the shape of neurons. The nerve impulse usually travels from the dendrites and soma to the branching ends of the axon. The neuron shown here is a motor neuron. Motor neurons originate in the brain or spinal cord and send their axons to the muscles or glands of the body.*

Fig. 3-2 *Electrochemical changes in a nerve cell generate an action potential when sodium (Na+) ions rush into the cell. After the action potential, an outward flow of potassium (K+) ions restores the resting potential. (See text for further explanation.)*

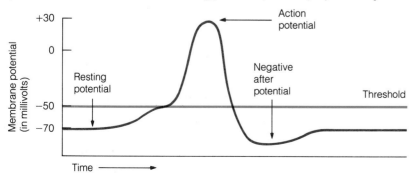

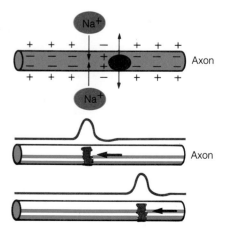

The speed of an action potential depends on a number of things, including the size of the axon. Very thin axons may carry a nerve impulse at a rate of 2.5 meters (about 8 feet) per second, or less. Longer and larger axons that connect the body to the brain average roughly 100 meters per second (about 225 miles per hour). If someone steps on your toes, your brain gets the message in one-fiftieth of a second! The speed of nerve impulses also increases when **myelin** (MY-eh-lin) is present. Myelin forms a layer of fatty insulation around some axons. Myelin typically has small gaps every millimeter or so, which allow nerve impulses to move faster by jumping from gap to gap.

Question: How is information carried from one neuron to another?

Neurotransmitters   We have seen that the nerve impulse is primarily electrical. In contrast, neurons "talk" to one another chemically. When a nerve impulse reaches the tips of the axon terminals, it causes a release of **neurotransmitters.** These potent chemicals cross the tiny space, or **synapse** (SIN-aps), between two neurons. Transmitter molecules then attach to special **receptor sites** on the

Fig. 3-3 *A highly magnified view of the synapse shown in Fig. 3-2. Transmitter chemicals cross the synaptic gap to affect the next neuron. The size of the gap is exaggerated here; it is actually only about one-millionth of an inch. Transmitter chemicals vary in their effect: Some excite the next neuron, and some inhibit its activity.*

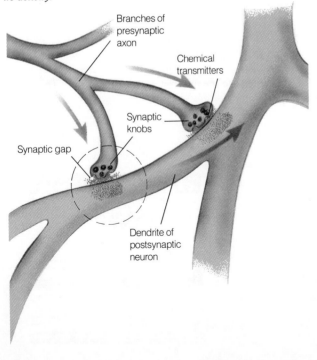

Branches of presynaptic axon

Chemical transmitters

Synaptic knobs

Synaptic gap

Dendrite of postsynaptic neuron

dendrites and soma of the second neuron (Fig. 3-3). (This is also how muscles and glands are activated.)

Question: Does the arrival of a neurotransmitter trigger an action potential in the next neuron?

Not always. Neurotransmitters may *excite* the next neuron (move it closer to firing), or *inhibit* it (make it less likely to discharge). Each neuron is bombarded by messages from hundreds or thousands of other neurons. If a number of excitatory messages arrive at the same time or in quick succession, the neuron reaches its threshold for firing. You may recall that a nerve impulse is an all-or-nothing, yes-or-no event. In contrast, messages received from other cells are combined or *averaged* before a neuron "decides" to send the message on. Multiply these events by 100 billion neurons and 100 trillion synapses and you have a computer of astounding capacity—all fit into a space one-half the size of a shoe box.

There are now some 30 known or suspected neurotransmitters in the brain. Among the more important "chemical messengers" are acetylcholine, adrenaline, noradrenaline, serotonin, dopamine, and histamine. The large variety of transmitter chemicals is one reason why there are thousands of drugs that affect the brain or the nervous system. Many of these drugs operate by imitating, duplicating, or canceling neurotransmitters. For example, the transmitter **acetylcholine** (AS-ih-til-KOH-leen) normally activates muscles. The drug **curare** (cue-RAH-ree), however, blocks the action of acetylcholine at the neuron-muscle junction (Evarts, 1979). As a result, a person or animal given curare will be paralyzed—a fact known to South American Indians of the Amazon River Basin, who use curare as an arrow poison. The mind-altering drug mescaline, which is similar to noradrenaline, is an example of a drug that imitates a brain transmitter; the drugs LSD and psilocybin ("magic mushrooms") do the same (Iversen, 1979).

A stunning series of recent discoveries has revealed a new class of brain transmitters called **neuropeptides** or simply brain peptides. These important chemicals seem to serve as *regulators* of memory, pain, emotion, pleasure, mood, sexual behavior, and other basic processes. An example of a brain peptide in action is shown in Fig. 3-4. As you can see in the drawing, some neurons have specific receptor sites for opiate drugs, such as morphine.

Question: Why would the brain have opiate receptors? After all, the human body isn't born with opium in it.

This is exactly the question that led to a search for natural opiatelike chemicals in the brain. Scientists found that the body produces natural opiates called **enkephalins** (en-KEF-ah-lins) to relieve pain and stress (Iversen, 1979). It now appears that mysteries such as "runner's high," the placebo effect, and acupuncture may be explained by the action of enkephalins. (See Chapter 4 for more information.) Ultimately, an understanding of brain peptides may help explain depression, schizophrenia, drug addiction, and other puzzling problems.

General Neuroanatomy— Wired for Action

Picture two people playing catch with a Frisbee. To an outside observer, this appears to be an interesting but certainly not amazing activity. But consider what is going on inside the body. To launch the Frisbee on its flight or to anticipate its path for a catch, an incredible amount of information must be sensed, interpreted, and directed to countless muscle fibers. The neural circuits of the body are ablaze with activity. Let us consider in more detail the "wiring diagram" that makes this possible.

Neurons and Nerves

Question: Are neurons the same as nerves?

No. Nerves, which can be seen with the unaided eye, are not single cells; rather, they are bundles of nerve fibers (axons and dendrites). Many nerves have a whitish color because they are made up mainly of axons having a coating of myelin. Most nerve fibers outside of the brain and spinal cord also have a thin layer of living cells called the **neurilemma** (NEW-rih-LEM-ah) wrapped around them. (See Fig. 3-1.)

The neurilemma is important because it provides a "tunnel" through which damaged nerve fibers can grow when repairing themselves. If you were to accidentally sever a finger, or even an arm, and if it were sewn back on, there is a good chance the nerves would regenerate. In fact, you could expect feeling to return at a rate of about 1 millimeter per day. Neurons in the brain and spinal cord generally *cannot* be replaced, so they must last a lifetime. This is why spinal injuries are so devastating. If the spinal cord is torn, cut, or crushed, a person may permanently lose use of the body below the point of injury. Also, if the cell body of a neuron is destroyed anywhere in the nervous system, the damage cannot be reversed. For example, this is the cause of polio, a crippling disease in which the cell bodies of neurons controlling muscles are destroyed.

The Nervous System

Taken as a whole, the nervous system is a single unified structure, but it may be divided into smaller parts to make

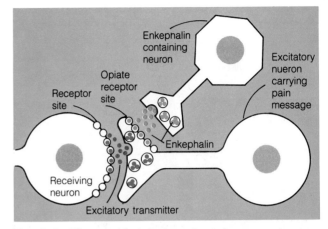

Fig. 3-4   *This simplified diagram shows how natural opiates may operate in the brain to relieve pain. Neurons carrying pain messages appear to have receptor sites for opiatelike transmitters called* enkephalins. *Release of enkephalins by "regulator" neurons suppresses activity in pain-carrying neurons. This suppression blocks or reduces the flow of pain messages. (Adapted from Iversen, 1979.)*

it easier to understand. As seen in Fig. 3-5 and Fig. 3-6, a distinction can be made between the **central** and the **peripheral** nervous systems. The central nervous system (CNS) consists of all nervous tissue encased by bone, or more simply, it includes the brain and spinal cord. If you

Fig. 3-5   *Subparts of the nervous system.*

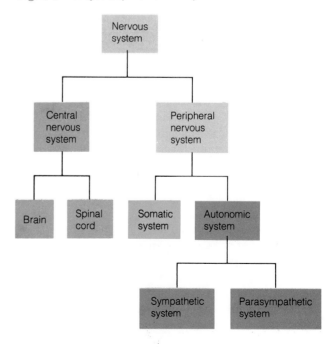

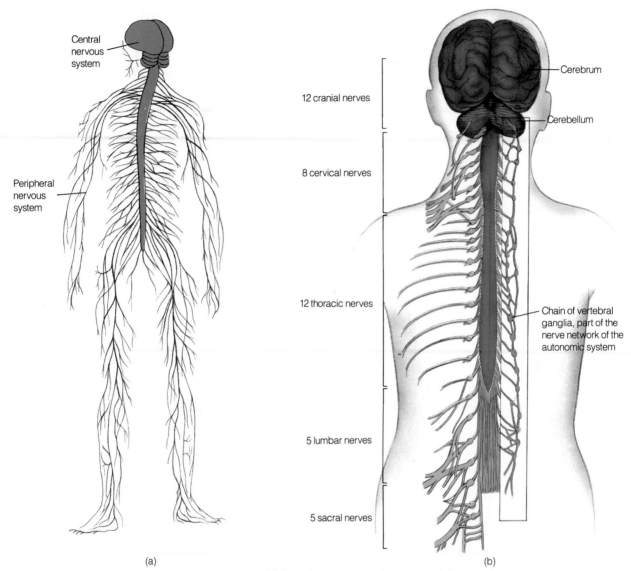

Fig. 3-6 (a) *Central and peripheral nervous systems;* (b) *Spinal nerves, cranial nerves, and the autonomic nervous system.*

touch the back of your head and run your fingers down your spine, you will feel the protective layer of bone around the CNS, the **cranium** for the brain, and the **vertebral column** for the spinal cord.

Question: How are the CNS and the peripheral nervous system related?

The Peripheral Nervous System The peripheral system consists of nerves that carry information to and from the CNS. The peripheral system is divided into two subparts: (1) the **somatic** system, which carries messages to and from the sense organs and the skeletal muscles; and (2) the **autonomic** system, which serves the internal organs and glands of the body. The autonomic nervous system

(ANS) can be further divided into the **sympathetic** and **parasympathetic** branches. Both branches of the ANS are important in the control of emotional response (Fig. 3-7). The ANS, along with the somatic system, coordinates the inner and outer worlds of the body. If a large and angry-looking dog lunges at you unexpectedly, the somatic system will help coordinate the muscles for running, while the autonomic system arranges a rise in blood pressure, quickening of the heart, and so forth.

Question: How do the branches of the autonomic system differ?

The two branches of the ANS have very different functions. The sympathetic branch responds during times of emergency or emotion to prepare the body for "fight or flight." In essence, it mobilizes the body's resources for action. The parasympathetic branch, on the other hand, is most active immediately *after* a stressful or emotional event. Its role is to quiet the body and return it to a lower level of arousal. It also helps maintain vital functions, such as heart rate, breathing, and digestion at moderate levels. (See Chapter 13 for more information on the autonomic system.)

The Spinal Cord   The spinal cord is an especially important part of the nervous system because it acts like a cable connecting the brain to other parts of the body. If you were to cut through the spinal cord, you would see columns of **white matter**—nervous tissue made up of axons that leave the spinal cord at various points to form peripheral nerves. As you can see in Fig. 3-6(b), there are 30 pairs of **spinal nerves** leaving the spinal cord and 1 pair leaving the bottom tip. The 31 pairs, together with an extra 12 nerves that leave the brain directly (the **cranial nerves**), place the entire body in sensory and motor communication with the brain.

Question: How is the spinal cord related to behavior?

Within the spinal cord itself, the simplest behavior pattern (a **reflex arc**) can be carried out without any direct help from the brain (see Fig. 3-8). Imagine that one of our Fris-

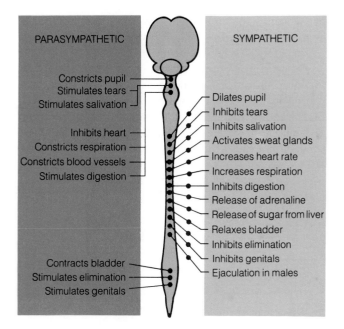

Fig. 3-7 *Sympathetic and parasympathetic branches of the autonomic nervous system. Both branches control involuntary functions. The sympathetic system generally activates the body; whereas the parasympathetic system generally quiets it. The sympathetic branch relays through a chain of ganglia (clusters of cell bodies) outside the spinal cord.*

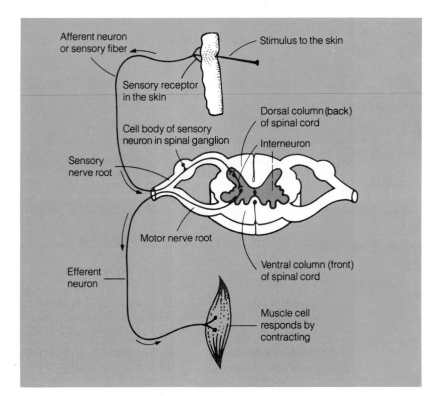

Fig. 3-8 *A simple sensory-motor (reflex) arc. A simple reflex is set in motion by a stimulus to the skin (or other part of the body). The nerve impulse travels to the spinal cord and then back out to a muscle, which contracts. Reflexes provide an "automatic" protective device for the body.*

bee players steps on a thorn. This is detected in the foot by a **sensory neuron** and a message (in the form of an action potential) is fired off to the spinal cord.

The sensory neuron synapses with a **connector neuron** (or **interneuron**) inside the spinal cord. The connector neuron in turn activates another connector cell (in this case, a **motor neuron**) that leads back to muscle fibers. The muscle fibers are made up of **effector cells,** which contract and cause the foot to withdraw. Note that brain activity was not required for a reflex arc. It could even take place in a decapitated animal (or a headless Frisbee player for that matter)!

In reality, more complex activity usually accompanies even a simple reflex. For example, muscles of the limb on the opposite side of the body must contract in order to support the body when its weight is shifted. Even this can be carried out by the spinal cord, but it takes many more cells and several levels of the spinal nerves. Perhaps you have already realized how adaptive it is to have a spinal cord capable of responding on its own. Such automatic responses leave the brain of our Frisbee ace free to deal with more important information—such as the whereabouts of trees, lampposts, and attractive onlookers—as he or she makes a grandstand catch.

Learning Check

Before reading further, see if you can answer these questions.

1. The _____ and _____ are receiving areas where information from other neurons is accepted.

2. Nerve impulses are carried down the _____ .

3. The point of interchange between two neurons is called a myelin.   T or F?

4. The _____ potential becomes an _____ potential when a neuron passes the threshold for firing.

5. Neuropeptides are a newly discovered class of transmitter substances that include naturally occurring opiatelike chemicals called enkephalins.   T or F?

6. The somatic and autonomic systems are part of the _____ nervous system.

7. Sodium and potassium ions cross the synapse to trigger a nerve impulse in the receiving neuron.   T or F?

8. The simplest behavior sequence is a _____ .

9. The parasympathetic nervous system is most active during times of high emotion.   T or F?

Answers: 1. dendrites, soma 2. axon 3. F 4. resting, action 5. T 6. peripheral 7. F 8. reflex arc 9. F

The Cerebral Cortex— My, What a Big Brain You Have!

In many respects, humans are pretty unimpressive creatures. Fragile, weak, born naked and helpless, humans are excelled by animals in almost every category of strength, speed, and sensory sensitivity. The one area in which humans excel is intelligence.

Question: Do humans have the largest brain?

Surprisingly, no. Elephant brains weigh about 13 pounds, and whale brains, 19 pounds. At 3 pounds, the human brain seems puny—until we figure the proportion of brain weight to body weight. We then find that an elephant's brain is one-thousandth of its weight; the ratio for sperm whales

is 1 to 10,000. The ratio for humans is 1 to 60 (Cohen, 1974). If someone tells you that you have a "whale of a brain" be sure to find out if they mean size or ratio!

Question: What about dolphins?

The only other creatures that compare well to humans in both brain size and brain-body ratio are porpoises (dolphins are a type of porpoise). Some are no larger than humans, but have brains 20 percent larger than the average person. It is possible, although not established, that porpoises may be as intelligent (or more so) than humans. Researchers have already shown that these animals communicate with a system of sounds as complex as our own (Wursig, 1979). On the other hand, whales and elephants use large portions of their giant brains to coordinate the basic machinery of their massive bodies. It may be that porpoises also use large portions of their brains for "lower" sensory and motor functions.

So, relatively speaking, humans have very highly developed brains. More importantly, as we move from lower to higher animals, there is an ever-increasing portion of brain tissue devoted to the **cerebral cortex** (seh-REE-brel or ser-EH-brel). (See Fig. 3-9.) In humans, the cerebral cortex accounts for no less than 70 percent of the neurons in the central nervous system.

Corticalization   The cortex covers most of the visible part of the brain with a mantle of **grey matter** (spongy tissue made up mostly of cell bodies and looking a little like a giant walnut). The cortex in lower animals is small and smooth; in humans it is the largest brain structure. Human intellectual superiority appears to be related to this **corticalization** (KORE-tih-kal-ih-ZAY-shun), or increase in the size and wrinkling of the cortex. Also important is the fact that the human brain has larger cortical *association areas* (more on this later). These areas seem to be directly related to higher mental abilities like thinking, language, memory, and problem solving.

Cerebral Hemispheres   The cortex is composed of two sides, or **hemispheres.** At first glance, the hemispheres appear to be mirror images of each other, but they actually differ slightly in shape and wrinkling (Corballis, 1980). The two hemispheres are connected by a thick band of fibers called the **corpus callosum** (KORE-pus kah-LOH-sum). Surprisingly, the two halves control opposite sides of the body. The left side of the brain mainly controls the right side of the body, and the right half of the brain mainly controls left-side body areas. Thus, if a person has an injury

Fig. 3-9   *An illustration showing the increased size of the human cerebral cortex, a significant factor in human adaptability and intelligence.*

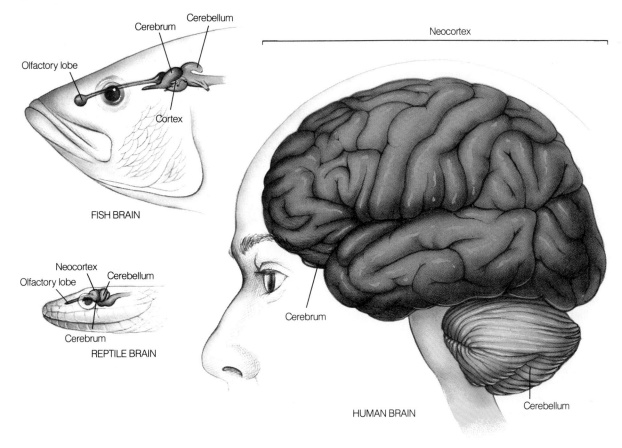

Cerebellum
Cerebrum
Olfactory lobe
Cortex
FISH BRAIN

Neocortex
Olfactory lobe
Cerebellum
Cerebrum
REPTILE BRAIN

Neocortex
Cerebrum
HUMAN BRAIN
Cerebellum

or a stroke that damages the right hemisphere, we can expect parts of the left side of the body to be paralyzed or lose sensation.

Hemispheric Specialization

We turn now to a look at some very remarkable findings. In 1981, Roger Sperry of the California Institute of Technology won a Nobel Prize for his work on the special abilities of the cerebral hemispheres. Sperry and other psychologists have shown that the right and left sides of the brain perform differently on tests of language, perception, music, and other capabilities.

Question: How is it possible to test only one side of the brain?

One way is to work with people who have had a radical form of brain surgery that *disconnects* the hemispheres. The result of these **"split-brain"** operations is essentially a person with two brains in one body (Sperry, 1968). After the surgery, it is a simple matter to route information to one hemisphere or the other.

"Split Brains" Communication between hemispheres normally allows each side of the brain to use information or skills located on the other side. However, in a person with epilepsy, a disturbance on one side of the brain may spread to the other side as well. Thus, in cases of severe epilepsy, the corpus callosum is sometimes cut to control seizures.

In both animals and humans, separation of the hemispheres consistently results in a doubling of consciousness. As Sperry says:

> In other words, each hemisphere seems to have its own separate and private sensations; its own perceptions; its own concepts; and its own impulses to act. . . . Following the surgery, each hemisphere also has thereafter its own chain of memories that are rendered inaccessible to the recall processes of the other (Sperry, 1968).

Question: How does a split-brain person function after the operation?

On occasion, having two "brains" in one body creates quite a dilemma. Another researcher, Michael Gazzaniga, recounts that one of his split-brain patients would:

> . . . sometimes find himself pulling his pants down with one hand and pulling them up with the other. Once, he grabbed his wife with his left hand and shook her violently, while with the right trying to come to his wife's aid in bringing the belligerent left hand under control.*

*Michael S. Gazzaniga, *The Bisected Brain,* Plenum, 1970, p. 107.

Generally, however, split-brain individuals act normally in most situations. This is true because both halves of the brain have about the same experience at the same time. Also, if any conflict arises, one hemisphere tends to override the other. (To find out which of your brain hemispheres is dominant, see the "Applications" section of this chapter.) Split-brain effects become most apparent in specialized testing. For example, a square can be flashed to the right brain and a circle to the left brain (see Fig. 3-10). If the person is asked to draw what she saw using the left hand (out of sight), she will draw the square. If she is then asked to point with her right hand to a picture of what her left hand drew, she will point to a circle (Sperry, 1968). In short, one hemisphere does not know what is happening in the other. In other experiments, monkeys with split brains have been taught to perform two separate and conflicting tasks, one task being performed by each hand-eye-brain unit (Sperry, 1964). This has to be the ultimate case of the "right hand not knowing what the left hand is doing"!

Question: Earlier it was stated that the hemispheres differ in abilities; in what ways do they differ?

Right Brain/Left Brain The brain divides its work up in interesting ways. For example, language is a specialty of the left hemisphere. Roughly 95 percent of all adults use the left side of the brain for speaking, writing, and comprehending language. In addition, the left hemisphere is better at math, judging time and rhythm, and at coordinating complex movements (especially those needed for speech) (Corballis, 1980). In contrast, the right hemisphere can only respond to very simple language, and it cannot speak. Working with the right hemisphere is a little like talking to a child who only knows a dozen words or so. To express itself, the right hemisphere must point to objects or make other nonverbal responses.

At one time, the right brain was regarded as the "minor" hemisphere because it lacked language; however, we now know that it has talents of its own. The right hemisphere is superior at perceptual skills, such as recognizing visual patterns, faces, and melodies, and it is involved in the recognition and expression of emotion (Geschwind, 1979). The right brain is also better at tasks requiring visualization, and "manipulo-spatial" skills, such as arranging blocks to match a sample pattern, putting together a puzzle, or drawing a picture (Gazzaniga and Le Doux, 1978).

The superiority of the right hemisphere at spatial tasks leads to another intriguing observation. A common test of spatial ability involves solving a geometric puzzle. On this test, the split-brain patient's left hand can typically perform

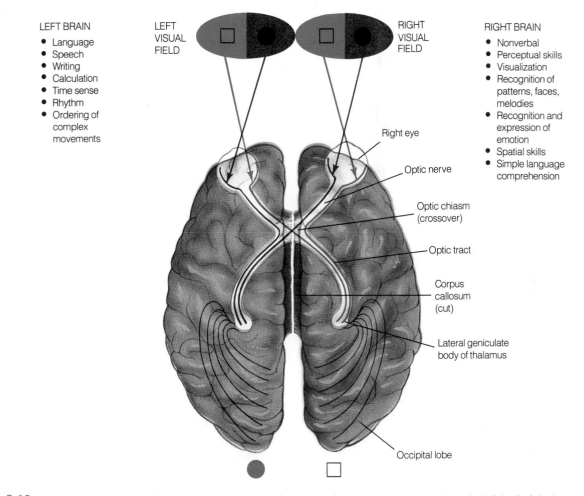

LEFT BRAIN
- Language
- Speech
- Writing
- Calculation
- Time sense
- Rhythm
- Ordering of complex movements

RIGHT BRAIN
- Nonverbal
- Perceptual skills
- Visualization
- Recognition of patterns, faces, melodies
- Recognition and expression of emotion
- Spatial skills
- Simple language comprehension

LEFT VISUAL FIELD

RIGHT VISUAL FIELD

Right eye

Optic nerve

Optic chiasm (crossover)

Optic tract

Corpus callosum (cut)

Lateral geniculate body of thalamus

Occipital lobe

Fig. 3-10 *Basic nerve pathways of vision. Notice that the left portion of each eye connects only to the left half of the brain; likewise, the right portion of each eye connects to the right brain. When the corpus callosum is cut, a "split brain" results, and visual information can be directed to one hemisphere or the other. Separate testing of each side of the brain reveals distinct specializations, as listed.*

quite well, but the right cannot. Robert Ornstein reports that:

> Professor Sperry often shows an interesting film clip of the right hand attempting to solve the problem and failing, whereupon the patient's left hand cannot restrain itself and "corrects" the right—as when you know the answer to a problem and watch me making mistakes, and cannot refrain from telling me the answer (Ornstein, 1972).

Question: Do people with normal brains tend to use one hemisphere more than the other?

It does appear possible to use mainly one hemisphere or the other for some tasks. For example, nonmusicians show increased activity in the right hemisphere when they are asked to whistle a song. But when trained musicians whistle, the left hemisphere is most active (Davidson and Schwartz, 1977). This probably means that music is under the control of speech centers in trained musicians, but remains a nonverbal skill for nonmusicians. Observations like this one suggest that people such as artists, potters, or dancers may be "right-brained," whereas scholars, mathematicians, or lawyers might be "left-brained" (Ornstein, 1972). However, recent studies of lawyers, sculptors, ceramicists, and psychology graduate students found no differences in right and left hemisphere activity (Ornstein and Galin, 1976; Arndt and Berger, 1978). It appears that the skills of both hemispheres are combined in most of the things we do (see Fig. 3-11).

Mind and Brain   Split-brain research is interesting in its own right. But more importantly, it seems to resolve some age-old questions about what the "mind" is, or where it is

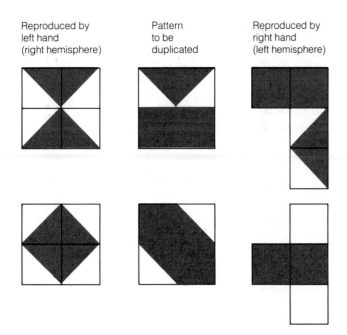

Reproduced by
left hand
(right hemisphere)

Pattern
to be
duplicated

Reproduced by
right hand
(left hemisphere)

Fig. 3-11 *Results from tests of pattern reproduction in a "split-brain" human. Examples of errors made by each hand-hemisphere combination are shown. Notice that both hemispheres made errors and that the types of errors differ. Apparently, both hemispheres contribute to successful completion of most tasks, even those that are primarily "nonverbal." (Adapted from Geschwind, 1979, p. 181.)*

to be found. We have seen that dividing the brain produces two separate "minds," or spheres of consciousness—each with its own special abilities. It follows that consciousness is nothing more or less than the electrical and chemical activity of the brain. In humans, the terms "mind," "brain activity," and "consciousness" are simply different ways of describing the same set of events.

Does this diminish the almost miraculous nature of human consciousness? On the contrary, this view elevates the silent labor of billions of neurons to a level of respect usually reserved for the more spectacular wonders of nature. How does it feel to have the Eighth Wonder of the World inside your head?

Cerebral Maps of Reality

In addition to hemispheres, the cerebral cortex can be divided into several other areas called **lobes** (see Fig. 3-12).

Question: What is known about the function of the lobes?

The functions of various areas in each of the lobes have been "mapped" by clinical and experimental studies. Ex-

perimentally, the surface of the cortex can be activated by touching it with a small electrified needle or wire called an **electrode.** When this is done to a patient undergoing brain surgery (using only local painkillers), the patient can report what effect the stimulation had. The functions of the cortex have also been identified by clinical studies of changes in personality, behavior, or sensory capacity caused by diseases or injury of the brain. Let's consider the outcome of such studies.

The Occipital Lobes The occipital lobes (ok-SIP-ih-tal), which are located at the back of the brain, are the primary **visual area** of the cortex. Patients with *tumors* (cell growths that interfere with brain activity) in the occipital lobes experience blind spots in areas of the visual field.

Question: Do the visual areas of the cortex correspond directly to what is seen?

Visual images are mapped onto the surface of the cortex, but not in a one-to-one fashion. The map is distorted as if it were printed on a sheet of rubber and stretched (Carlson, 1981). It is therefore important to avoid thinking of the visual area as being like a little TV screen in the brain. Visual information creates patterns of activity in nerve cells; it does *not* make a TV-like image. Even if we were tempted to visualize this activity as a "picture," we would still have to ask, "Who's watching the TV?" It is a classic error to think of the brain in terms of some **homunculus** (huh-MUN-cue-lus: "little man") that makes decisions, or watches incoming information.

The Parietal Lobes The parietal lobes (puh-RYE-ih-tal) are located just above the occipital lobes. Touch, temperature, pressure, and other bodily sensations are channeled to the **somatosensory area** (SO-mat-oh-SEN-so-ree) on the parietal lobes. The correspondence between areas of the parietal lobes and parts of the body is not a perfect one. The distorted body in Fig. 3-12 shows that as a map of the body the cortex represents the *sensitivity* of areas, not their size. For example, the lips are large in the illustration because of their great sensitivity, while the back and trunk, which are less sensitive, are much smaller. Notice also that the body is "upside down" on the cortex: Sensations from the foot register at the top followed downward by the leg, hip, trunk, shoulder, neck, arm, hand, fingers, face, lips, and tongue.

The Temporal Lobes The temporal lobes are located on each side of the brain and extend below to the underside of the cortex. Auditory information projects directly to the temporal lobes, making them the site where hearing registers. If we were to stimulate the **primary auditory area** of a temporal lobe, our subject would "hear" a series of sounds. These sounds would increase in pitch as we moved from the top to the bottom; stimulating in another direction, we would find that sound sensations would undergo an orderly change in loudness (Carlson, 1981). This indicates that sound qualities are precisely mapped out on the surface of the brain.

An area called the **hippocampus,** located within the temporal lobes, appears to be important for the storage of long-term memories. Stimulation of the temporal lobe in humans produces memorylike or dreamlike experiences. (See Chapter 10 for more information on this point.) Tumors in the temporal lobes can cause seizures, disordered use of language, memory disturbances, and unusual dream states.

The Frontal Lobes   The frontal lobes perform a mixture of functions. For one thing, **olfactory** (smell) information registers on the underside of the frontal lobes. Another important area is the **motor cortex,** an arch of tissue running roughly ear-to-ear over the top of the brain. This area directs the body's muscles. If the motor cortex is stimulated with a brief electrical current, muscular twitches will be observed in various parts of the body. By increasing the voltage or duration of current, larger groups of muscles can be made to contract, and movements such as rotation of the forearm or clenching of the fist will take place. Like the somatosensory area, the motor cortex corresponds to the importance of bodily areas, not to their size. The hands, for example, get more area than the feet (see Fig. 3-12).

Also related to the frontal lobes are behavioral functions of a more complex nature. When areas of the frontal lobes other than motor cortex are removed, animals lose the ability to judge the passage of time, to hold the solution to a problem in mind, or to respond to emotionally unpleasant situations. Damage to the frontal lobes in humans tends to decrease emotionality and ability to perform tasks requiring thinking, reasoning, or planning (Thompson, 1967).

Question: The sensory and motor areas leave a lot of the cortex unaccounted for. What do the remaining areas do?

Associative Areas   In the human brain, areas that are specifically sensory or motor in function make up only a small part of the cerebral cortex. All other areas (including parts of all the lobes previously described) have been called

the **association cortex.** The association cortex seems to process and combine information from the various senses. When stimulated, it yields responses more complex than simple sensations or movements. The loss of thinking skills after damage to the frontal lobes is an excellent example. Additional clues to the workings of the association cortex come from studies of humans with brain injuries.

Brain Injuries

As you might imagine, damage to the right brain often leaves the left side of the body paralyzed; this is reversed for damage to the left brain. More importantly, the special abilities of the left and right hemispheres may also be affected. A person with left-brain damage may lose the ability to speak, read, write, or spell while remaining able to draw or hum with skill. Persons with right-brain damage may be unable to dress themselves properly, or may get lost while driving, but they can speak and read as before (Gardner, 1975). To make another comparison, a person with left-brain damage may not understand what you say, but he or she will pick up your emotional tone. With right-hemisphere damage, the person can understand what is said, but fails to recognize if it is spoken in an angry or humorous way (Geschwind, 1975).

Question: Is it fair to say that damage to the left hemisphere is usually more serious?

Generally it is, because speech and language are so essential. But Robert Ornstein has suggested that we label the left hemisphere "major" because we tend to place a high value on language skills in our culture (Ornstein, 1972). If you are an artist, the right brain may be the "major hemisphere" from your point of view. It has been observed, for instance, that painters can still do art after left-brain damage. But an artist with right-brain damage may neglect the left side of the canvas, distort outlines, or portray bizarre and repulsive subject matter (Gardner, 1975).

Aphasia   Two areas of the cortex are particularly related to language. One, called **Broca's area** (BRO-cahs), lies on the left frontal lobe. The second, known as **Wernicke's area** (VER-nick-ees) is found on the left temporal lobe (see Fig. 3-12). Injury to either area can cause **aphasia** (ah-FAZE-yah), meaning an impaired ability to use language.

Question: What kinds of impairment take place?

Persons with damage in Broca's area can read and understand the speech of others, but they have great difficulty speaking or writing. Typically, their *grammar,* pronuncia-

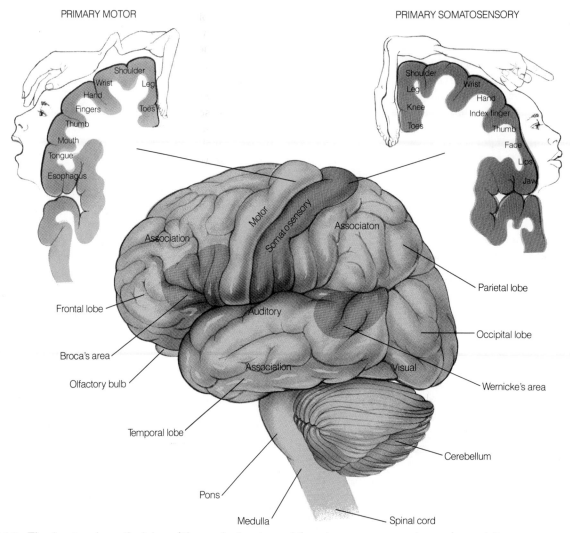

PRIMARY MOTOR

PRIMARY SOMATOSENSORY

Fig. 3-12 *The drawing shows the lobes of the cerebral cortex and the primary sensory, motor, and association areas on each. The top diagrams show (in cross section) the relative amounts of cortex "assigned" to the sensory and motor control of various parts of the body.*

tion, and *speech* are poor. For example, the person may say "bife" for bike, "seep" for sleep, or "zokaid" for zodiac. Generally, the person knows what he or she wants to say, but can't seem to get it into words. For example, one Broca's patient replied with great difficulty when asked about a dental appointment: "Yes . . . Monday . . . Dad and Dick . . . Wednesday . . . doctors . . . and . . . teeth." (Geschwind, 1979).

In Wernicke's aphasia, grammar is normal and pronunciation is correct, but the person has problems with *meaning*. Whereas someone with Broca's aphasia might say "tssair" when shown a picture of a chair, a Wernicke's patient might say "stool." People with injuries to Wernicke's area often speak in incredibly roundabout ways to avoid using certain nouns. While discussing her son's career, one patient said: "Well he was two years away, away down for nothing. He didn't do it and got out and said I want to go over there and . . . how to do things, what he's doing now." (Goodglass, 1980). It is obvious that both Broca's area and Wernicke's area are crucial for normal language use. It is not surprising that they are interconnected in the brain.

Mindblindness One of the most fascinating results of brain injury is **agnosia** (ah-KNOW-zyah). This condition is sometimes referred to as "mindblindness" because it involves an inability to identify seen objects. If shown a candle, for instance, someone with agnosia might describe it as a long narrow object tapering at the top, or draw it accurately, and yet fail to name it. However, if the person is permitted to feel the candle, he or she will name it immediately (Benton, 1980).

Question: Are agnosias limited to objects?

No. A fascinating form of mindblindness is **facial agnosia,** the inability to identify familiar persons. For instance, one patient with facial agnosia was unable to recognize her husband or mother when they visited her in the hospital, and she could not identify pictures of her children. However, as soon as visitors spoke she knew them immediately

from their voices (Benton, 1980). Study of facial agnosias shows that a brain area devoted to recognizing others is located on the underside of the occipital lobes. These areas appear to have no other function. Why would part of the brain be set aside solely for recognizing faces? From an evolutionary standpoint, it is not really so surprising. After all, we are social animals, for whom facial recognition is very important (Geschwind, 1979). This specialization is an additional example of what a marvelous organ of consciousness we possess.

Learning Check

See if you can successfully match the following.

_____	1.	Corpus callosum	**A.** Visual area
_____	2.	Occipital lobes	**B.** Language, speech, writing
_____	3.	Parietal lobes	**C.** Motor cortex and abstract thinking
_____	4.	Temporal lobes	**D.** Spatial skills, visualization, pattern recognition
_____	5.	Frontal lobes	**E.** Speech disturbances
_____	6.	Association cortex	**F.** Causes sleep
_____	7.	Aphasias	**G.** Increased ratio of cortex in brain
_____	8.	Corticalization	**H.** Bodily sensations
_____	9.	Left hemisphere	**I.** Treatment for severe epilepsy
_____	10.	Right hemisphere	**J.** Inability to identify seen objects
_____	11.	"Split brain"	**K.** Fibers connecting the cerebral hemispheres
_____	12.	Agnosia	**L.** Cortex that is not sensory or motor in function
			M. Hearing

Answers: 1. K 2. A 3. H 4. M 5. C 6. L 7. E 8. G 9. B 10. D 11. I 12. J

The Subcortex—
At the Core of the (Brain) Matter

Question: What do brain areas below the cortex do?

A person can lose large portions of the cerebrum and still survive. As a matter of fact, if damage is limited to the less crucial areas of the cortex, little visible change may take place. Not so with the brain areas below the cortex. Most of these are so basic to normal functioning that damage may endanger a person's life. You may have read that in the tragic assassination of Senator Robert Kennedy the fatal bullet entered the lower part of his brain. As a result, Kennedy was unconscious throughout the period between

the shooting and his death, and he had to be maintained on artificial respiration.

Question: Why are the lower brain areas so important?

Below the cerebral cortex and completely covered by it are structures that are termed the **subcortex.** The subcortex can be divided into three general areas called the **brainstem** (or **hindbrain**), the **midbrain,** and the **forebrain.*** For the purpose of this discussion, the midbrain can be viewed primarily as a link between brain areas above and below it. Therefore, let us focus on the forebrain and

*The forebrain also includes the cerebral cortex, which was discussed separately because of its size and importance.

the hindbrain to more fully appreciate their importance (see Fig. 3-13).

The Hindbrain

As the spinal cord enters the skull to join the brain, it widens into the brainstem, consisting principally of the **medulla** (meh-DUL-ah) and the **cerebellum** (ser-ah-BEL-uhm). The *medulla* contains centers important for the reflex control of vital life functions, including heart rate, breathing, swallowing, and the like. For example, the medulla receives information about the carbon dioxide content of the blood and the tension of the muscles that expand the chest for breathing. Combining this information, the medulla *excites* the muscles so that you will inhale, then *inhibits* this excitement to cause exhalation. You can, of course, override this reflex by voluntarily holding your breath; but if you hold your breath long enough to pass out, the higher brain centers relinquish control, and you will once again begin reflex breathing. Various drugs, diseases, or injuries (a gunshot wound in Senator Kennedy's case) can interrupt the vital functions of the medulla enough to end or endanger life.

Also part of the hindbrain is the *cerebellum,* which looks like a smaller version of the cerebral cortex, and lies at the base of the brain. The cerebellum is closely connected to many areas in the brain and spinal cord, and functions primarily to regulate posture, muscle tone, and muscular coordination.

Question: What happens if the cerebellum is injured?

Without the cerebellum, seemingly simple tasks like walking, running, or playing catch would be impossible. The importance of the cerebellum is indicated by the effects of a crippling disease called *spinocerebellar degeneration.* The first symptoms of this disease include tremor, dizziness, and muscular weakness. The disease then rapidly progresses to a point where affected persons underreach or overreach for objects and have difficulty standing, walking, or even feeding themselves.

Reticular Formation   In a space within the medulla and brainstem, is a *network* of fibers and cell bodies called the **reticular** (reh-TICK-you-ler) **formation** (RF).

Question: What does the reticular formation do?

The RF is important for several reasons. First, it acts as a kind of central clearinghouse for most of the information coming to and from the brain. The RF helps direct incoming messages to the appropriate parts of the brain and

outgoing messages to the appropriate parts of the body. Secondly, the reticular formation gives priority to some incoming messages, while excluding others. This is basically what we mean by *attention.* Without the RF, we would be overwhelmed with useless information from the environment. Thirdly, and perhaps most importantly, the reticular formation is responsible for alertness and wakefulness. Incoming impulses from the sense organs branch into the reticular formation, where they form a **reticular activating system** (RAS). The RAS bombards the cortex with stimulation, keeping it active and vigilant (Malmo, 1975). The sleepy driver who snaps to attention when an animal appears in the middle of the road can thank the RAS for arousing the rest of the brain.

Studies of the RF originally indicated that destruction of the upper portions caused animals to enter a permanent coma resembling sleep. It was also observed that electrical stimulation of the same area would instantly awaken a sleeping animal (Moruzzi and Magoun, 1949; Lindsley, Bowden, and Magoun, 1949). Later studies have shown that when an animal is awake, stimulation of the reticular formation causes increased alertness, arousal, and scanning of the environment.

The Forebrain

Like gemstones of nerve tissue, two of the most important parts of the body lie buried deep within the center of the brain. The **thalamus,** and an area just below it called the **hypothalamus,** are part of the forebrain (see Fig. 3-13).

Question: How could these be any more important than other areas already described?

The thalamus is a football-shaped structure that acts as a *final* "switching station" for sensory information on its way to the cortex. Not only does visual, auditory, taste, and touch information relay through the thalamus, it undergoes preliminary processing and analysis there as well. Injury to even small areas of the thalamus could cause deafness, blindness, or loss of any of the other senses, except smell.

The hypothalamus, which in the human is about the size of a thumbnail, has been implicated in the control of behaviors as diverse as sex, rage, temperature control, hormone release, eating and drinking, sleep, waking, and emotion. The hypothalamus is a sort of "crossroads" that connects with many other areas of the cortex and subcortex. As such, it acts as a "final path" for many kinds of behavior leaving the brain. You might think of the hypothalamus as the last area in the brain where behaviors are organized or "decided on." (See Chapter 12 for a discussion of the role of the hypothalamus in hunger and thirst.)

The Limbic System The hypothalamus, parts of the thalamus, and several structures buried within the cortex have been collectively labeled the **limbic system.** Although the specific function of some parts of the limbic system is unclear, as a group they share an unmistakable role in the production of *emotion* and motivated behavior. Rage, fear, sexual response, and other instances of intense arousal have all been obtained from various points in the limbic system. In each case, the response includes not only the internal bodily changes associated with the emotion, but also a complete set of visible behaviors. For example, cats

made aggressive by electrical stimulation of the limbic system will crouch, hiss, expose their claws, lean forward, and tense their muscles—all characteristic of defense or attack. (See this chapter's "Exploration.")

One of the most exciting discoveries in physiological psychology occurred when it was found that animals could be trained to press a lever in order to deliver an electrical stimulation to the limbic system as a reward (Olds and Milner, 1954). Since the original discovery, many additional areas of the limbic system have been shown to act as reward or "pleasure" centers in the brain. Many are found in the hypothalamus, where they overlap with areas associated with drives such as thirst, sex, and hunger (Olds, 1977). (See Chapter 9 for more information.) In addition,

Fig. 3-13   *This simplified drawing shows the main structures of the human brain and describes some of their most important functions.*

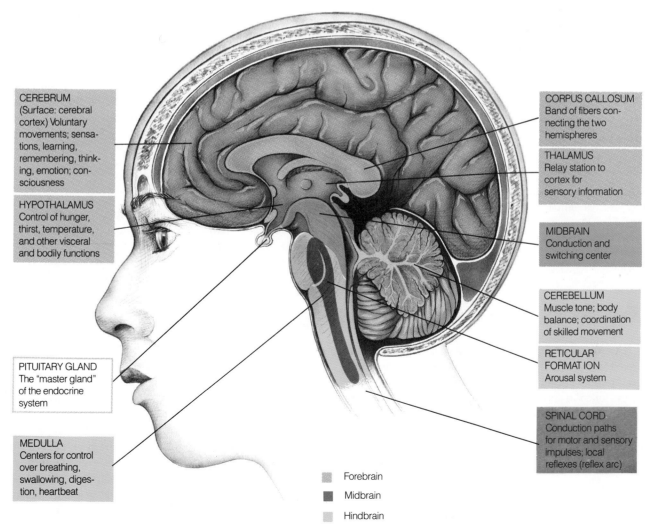

CEREBRUM
(Surface: cerebral cortex) Voluntary movements; sensations, learning, remembering, thinking, emotion; consciousness

HYPOTHALAMUS
Control of hunger, thirst, temperature, and other visceral and bodily functions

PITUITARY GLAND
The "master gland" of the endocrine system

MEDULLA
Centers for control over breathing, swallowing, digestion, heartbeat

CORPUS CALLOSUM
Band of fibers connecting the two hemispheres

THALAMUS
Relay station to cortex for sensory information

MIDBRAIN
Conduction and switching center

CEREBELLUM
Muscle tone; body balance; coordination of skilled movement

RETICULAR FORMATION
Arousal system

SPINAL CORD
Conduction paths for motor and sensory impulses; local reflexes (reflex arc)

Forebrain

Midbrain

Hindbrain

punishment, or "aversive" areas have also been found. When these areas are stimulated, animals show discomfort and will work to turn off the stimulation. Since a great deal of human and animal behavior is directed by the pursuit of pleasure and avoidance of pain, these discoveries continue to fascinate psychologists.

The Brain in Perspective— Beyond the Biocomputer

We have seen that the human brain is an impressive assembly of billions of sensitive cells and nerve fibers. The brain controls vital bodily functions, keeps track of the external world, issues commands to the muscles and glands, generates complex responses in the light of current needs and past experience, creates the magic of consciousness, and regulates its own behavior—*all* at the same time. Each of these basic needs is met by the action of one or more of the three main brain divisions: Control of vital bodily functions is carried out by the hindbrain (with some assistance from the hypothalamus in the forebrain); gathering sensory information and issuing motor commands takes place at all three levels of the brain; response selection, learning, memory, and higher thought processes are controlled by the forebrain, particularly the cortex and association areas.

Redundancy   A final note of caution is now in order. For the sake of simplicity we have assigned functions to each "part" of the brain as if it were a computer. This is only a half-truth. In reality, the brain always functions as a unit. Incoming information scatters to structures all over the brain and converges again as it goes out to muscles and glands. The overall system acts in ways that go far beyond any view that considers only "parts" or "brain centers" (Nauta and Fiertag, 1979). To say the least, the brain is much, much more complicated than implied here.

One reason for the brain's great complexity is the fact that it shows tremendous **redundancy,** or duplication, throughout. The brain may use dozens of areas to carry out a function that any one of the areas could manage alone. Due to this redundancy, the brain demonstrates an impressive capacity for reorganization and recovery after injury.

Question: Does it make any difference at what age a person experiences a brain injury?

Plasticity   Yes. In response to brain damage, children usually show greater **plasticity** (or flexibility) of brain or-

ganization than adults. Even when there is severe damage to the left hemisphere, children under the age of seven can usually shift language processing to the right brain. In fact, people have been located who were born without corpus callosums, having in effect "natural" split brains. As adults, these people can answer questions from both hemispheres, write with both hands, draw with both hands, and solve block-design puzzles with both hands (Sperry, 1974). After age ten, such plasticity becomes rare.

Much of the plasticity of early childhood derives from rapid growth and development of the brain during this period. For the same reason, the brain is more subject to damage of another type at this time. Recent animal research (Lewin, 1975) indicates that **malnutrition** can reduce the number of brain cells in the cerebellum (causing clumsiness), diminish the size of axons, and lower the number of synapses in the cortex by 40 percent. This fact is well worth remembering, since chronically malnourished children show a variety of physical and intellectual losses which researchers have had little success in reversing.

Potential   In the final analysis, the brain is both highly vulnerable and amazingly resilient. In one astounding case, a child had the entire left hemisphere of his brain removed at age five. As an adult, he was paralyzed on the right side and blind in his right visual field. But he was able to speak, read, write, and comprehend so well that he maintained a double major in college and has an above average IQ (Smith and Sugar, 1975).

Cases such as the one just described lead to a realization that full use of the brain's potential may not yet have been reached. At the same time that such injuries contribute to our understanding of the brain's limitations, they raise questions about fuller use of the undamaged brain. Perhaps the future will see breakthroughs in enhancement of memory, intelligence, or recovery from brain damage. For now, it is exciting to think that the human brain hasn't yet yielded all its secrets.

The Glandular System— Slow but Sure Messenger Service

The nervous system is not the only communication network in the body. The **endocrine system** is made up of a number of glands that pour chemicals directly into the bloodstream (see Fig. 3-14). These chemicals, called **hormones,** are carried throughout the body, where they affect bodily functioning and behavior.

Question: How do hormones affect behavior?

The effects can be quite subtle. For instance, during a woman's menstrual period, the body is almost totally lacking in hormones normally released by the ovaries. This causes a small but measurable reduction in women's hearing, smell, taste, and touch sensitivity (Beach, 1975). Because they experience a monthly reproductive cycle, women may be more aware of the influence of hormones than men. But both sexes are affected. In humans, the size of the endocrine glands varies from person to person by a factor of about 3. In addition, the glands sometimes malfunction because of disease or injury. For such reasons, hormone output may vary considerably. In fact, it is the occasional extremes that most dramatically illustrate the importance of the glandular system. To more fully answer the question, let's briefly consider some effects the more important glands have on the body and behavior.

The **pituitary** is a small grape-sized structure hanging from the base of the brain (see Fig. 3-13). One of the more important roles of the pituitary is control of bodily growth. As a child's body grows, the pituitary secretes a hormone that regulates the rate of development. If too little **growth hormone** is released, a person may suffer a growth failure called **dwarfism.** Too much growth hormone causes **giantism** (see Fig. 3-15). Secretion of too much growth hormone toward the end of the growth period causes excessive growth of the arms, hands, feet, and facial bones. This condition, called **acromegaly** (AK-row-MEG-uh-lee), causes a distortion in appearance that some people have used as a basis for successful careers as sideshow entertainers, wrestlers, and the like.

The pituitary also regulates the functioning of other glands (especially the thyroid, adrenal glands, and ovaries or testes). These glands in turn regulate such bodily processes as reproduction, metabolism, and responses to stress. In women, the pituitary also controls the production of milk during pregnancy. Because of its many effects, the pituitary is often called the "master gland." But the master has a master: The hypothalamus, which lies directly above the pituitary in the brain, directs the activity of the pituitary and hence glands throughout the body. This then is the major link between the brain and the glandular system (Schally *et al.*, 1977).

The **thyroid gland** consists of tissue found in the neck, on each side of the windpipe. The thyroid regulates **metabolism**—the rate of energy production and use in the body. As a consequence, it can have a sizable effect on personality. A person with an overactive thyroid (termed **hyperthyroidism**) tends to be thin, tense, excitable, and nervous. An underactive thyroid (**hypothyroidism**) in an adult can cause inactivity, sleepiness, slowness, and overweight. In infancy, hypothyroidism limits development of the nervous

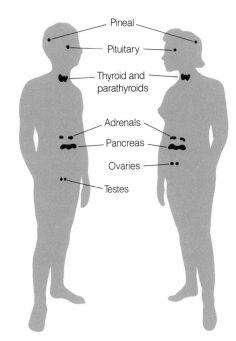

Fig. 3-14   *Locations of the endocrine glands in the male and female.*

Fig. 3-15   *Underactivity of the pituitary gland may produce a dwarf; overactivity, a giant.*

system, and can bring about severe mental retardation (see Chapter 17).

When you are frightened or angry, a number of important changes take place in your body to prepare it for action: Your heartbeat and blood pressure are raised; stored sugar is released into the bloodstream for quick energy; the muscles tense and receive more blood; and the blood is prepared to clot more quickly in the event of injury. These changes are brought about by the hormones **adrenaline** and **noradrenaline,** which are produced by the **adrenal glands.**

The adrenal glands are located just under the back of the ribcage, atop the kidneys. The **adrenal medulla,** or inner core of the adrenal glands, is the source of adrenaline and noradrenaline. The **adrenal cortex,** or outer "bark" of the adrenal glands, produces a second set of important hormones called **corticoids.** One of their jobs is to regulate salt balance in the body. A deficiency of certain corticoids can evoke a powerful craving for the taste of salt in humans (Beach, 1975). The corticoids also help the body adjust to stress, and they are a secondary source of sex hormones. (For a full discussion of the role of sex glands in development, see Chapter 24.) Perhaps you have heard about the use of "anabolic steroids" by athletes who want to "bulk up," or promote muscle growth to increase strength. These drugs are a synthetic version of one of the male corticoids. Like all of the corticoids, they are quite powerful, and therefore dangerous. There is no evidence that they improve performance, and they may cause voice-deepening or baldness in women, and shrinkage of the testicles or breast enlargement in men (*Sexual Medicine,* April, 1980).

An oversecretion of the cortical sex hormones can cause **virilism,** in which a woman grows a beard, or a man's voice becomes so low it is difficult to understand. Oversecretion in children may cause **premature puberty,** resulting in full sexual development. One of the most remarkable cases on record is that of a five-year-old Peruvian girl who gave birth to a son (Strange, 1965).

In this brief discussion of the endocrine system, we have considered only a few of the more important glands. Nevertheless, this should give you an appreciation of how completely your behavior and personality are tied to the ebb and flow of hormones in the body. In the upcoming "Applications" section we move outside the body to see how being right- or left-handed relates to the brain, and in the "Exploration" we will examine the fascinating effects of stimulating the brain electrically.

Learning Check

Here is a chance to check your memory of the preceding discussions.

1. Three major divisions of the brain are the brainstem, or _____, the _____, and the _____.

2. Reflex centers for heartbeat and respiration are found in the (circle):
    cerebellum   thalamus   medulla   RF

3. A portion of the reticular formation, known as the RAS, serves as an _____ system in the brain.

    a. activating   *b.* adrenal   *c.* adjustment   *d.* aversive

4. The _____ is a final relay or "switching station" for sensory information on its way to the cortex.

5. "Reward" and "punishment" areas are found throughout the _____ system, which is also related to emotion.

6. Redundancy and early plasticity underlie the brain's surprising capacity for recovery from some types of brain injuries in early childhood.   T or F?

7. Undersecretion from the thyroid can cause (circle):
    dwarfism   giantism   overweight   mental retardation

8. The body's ability to resist stress is related to the action of the adrenal _____.

Answers: 1. hindbrain, midbrain, forebrain 2. medulla 3. a 4. thalamus 5. limbic 6. T 7. overweight, mental retardation (in infancy) 8. cortex

Resources Summary

● The brain and nervous system are made up of inter-connected individual nerve cells called *neurons*. Neurons are arranged in long chains and dense networks. They pass information from one to another through *synapses*.

● The basic conducting structures of neurons are *axons,* but *dendrites* (a receiving area), the *soma* (the cell body and also a receiving area), and the *axon terminals* (the branching ends of an axon) are also involved in communication.

● The firing of an *action potential* (nerve impulse) is basically electrical, whereas communication between neurons is chemical. Neurons release chemicals called *neurotransmitters* at the synapse, and these cross to *receptor sites* on the receiving cell, causing it to be excited or inhibited.

● *Nerves* are made of axons and associated tissues. Neurons and nerves in the peripheral nervous system can often regenerate; damage in the central nervous system is permanent.

● The nervous system can be divided into the *central nervous system* (the brain and spinal cord) and the *peripheral nervous system,* which includes the *somatic* (bodily) and *autonomic* (involuntary) nervous systems. The autonomic system has two divisions: the *sympathetic* (activating); and the *parasympathetic* (conserving) branches.

● The human brain is marked by advanced *corticalization,* or enlargement and development of the *cerebral cortex.* The left cerebral hemisphere contains speech or language "centers" in most people. It also specializes in the functions of writing, calculation, judging time and rhythm, and ordering or coordinating complex movements. The right hemisphere is largely nonverbal and excels at spatial and perceptual skills, visualization, and recognition of patterns, faces, or melodies.

● *"Split brains"* have been created experimentally in animals, and for medical reasons in humans by cutting the *corpus callosum.* The split-brain individual shows a remarkable degree of independence between the right and left hemispheres. Under some circumstances, the hemispheres function as separate brain units.

● The most basic functions of the *lobes* of the cerebral cortex are as follows: *occipital* lobes—vision; *parietal* lobes—bodily sensation; *temporal* lobes—hearing, language, and memory; *frontal* lobes—olfaction, motor control, speech, and abstract thought.

● There are a number of *association* areas on the cortex that are neither sensory nor motor in function. These are related to more complex skills, such as language, memory, recognition, and problem solving. Damage to either *Broca's area* or *Wernicke's area* causes speech and language problems known as *aphasias.* Damage in other areas may cause *agnosia,* the inability to identify objects by sight.

● The brain as a whole can be subdivided into three general areas: the *forebrain, midbrain,* and *hindbrain.*

● The *subcortex* includes several crucial brain structures. The *medulla* contains centers essential for reflex control of heart rate, breathing, and other "vegetative" functions. The *cerebellum* maintains coordination, posture, and muscle tone. The *reticular formation* directs sensory and motor messages, and part of it, known as the *RAS,* acts as an activating system for the brain. The *thalamus* carries sensory information to the cortex. The *hypothalamus* exerts powerful control over eating, drinking, sleep cycles, body temperature, and a number of other basic motives and behaviors. The *limbic system,* which is made up of several structures, serves as an emotional system in the brain. It also contains distinct reward and punishment areas.

● The *endocrine system* serves as a *chemical* communication system in the body through the release of *hormones* into the bloodstream. Many of the endocrine glands are influenced by the *pituitary* (the "master gland"), which is in turn influenced by the hypothalamus. The endocrine glands influence behavior, body configuration, and even personality.

Handedness—What's Left Is Not Always Right

In the English language, "what's right is right," but what's left may be wrong. We have left-handed compliments, left-overs, people with "two left feet," those who are left behind, left out, and . . . left-handed. Indeed, the Old English word "lyft" means weak or broken. On the other hand (so to speak), we have the right way, the right whale, the right angle, the "right-hand man" (or woman), righteousness, and . . . the right hand.

The Sinister Hand   Left-handedness has a long and undeserved bad reputation. Southpaws have been accused of being clumsy, stubborn (for refusing to use their right hand), and maladjusted. One psychologist of the 1930s described the left-handed as, "Awkward in the house, and clumsy in their games, they are fumblers and bunglers at whatever they do." But as any lefty will tell you, and modern psychology has confirmed, none of this is true. The supposed clumsiness of lefties is merely a consequence of living in a right-handed world: If it can be gripped, turned, folded, held, or pulled, it's probably designed for the right hand. Even toilet handles are on the right side.

What causes handedness? Why are there more right-handed than left-handed people? How do left-handed and right-handed people differ? Does being left-handed really create problems? Are there any benefits to being left-handed? The answers to most of these questions lead us back to the brain, where handedness begins. Let's see what recent research has revealed about handedness, the brain, and you.

Hand Dominance   To begin with, you might find it interesting to compare your hands by copying the design you see here on a piece of paper, once with your right hand and once with your left. You should notice a definite superiority when your dominant hand is used. The interesting thing about this exercise is that there's no real difference in the strength or dexterity of the hands themselves. The agility of the dominant hand is an outward expression of superior motor control on one side of the brain (Herron, 1980).

Question: If a person is left-handed, does that mean the right hemisphere is dominant?

Not necessarily. It's true that the right hemisphere controls the left hand, but a left-handed person's dominant, language-producing hemisphere may be on the opposite side of the brain.

Brain Dominance   About 97 percent of right-handers process speech in the left hemisphere and are left-brain dominant. A good 60 percent of left-handers produce speech from the left hemisphere, just as right-handed people do. About a quarter of all lefties, and 3 percent of righties, use their right brain for language. And approximately 15 percent of left-handers use *both* sides of the brain for language processing (Corballis, 1980; Herron, 1980).

Question: Is there any way for a person to tell which of his or her hemispheres is dominant?

For a time, some psychologists believed that hemispheric dominance could be revealed by eye movements. But recent experiments offer little support for this idea (Erlichman and Weinberger, 1978). A better approach is based on the way you write. Right-handed individuals who write with a straight hand, and lefties who write with a hooked hand, are left-brain dominant for language. Left-handed people who write with their hand below the line, and righties who use a hooked position, are right-brain dominant (Levy and Redd, 1976; Pines, 1980). Are your friends right-brained or left-brained? (See Fig. 3-16.)

Question: How common is left-handedness, and what causes it?

Handedness   Animals such as monkeys show definite hand preferences. However, in most animal groups there is a 50-50 split of right and left "handedness." Among

Applications

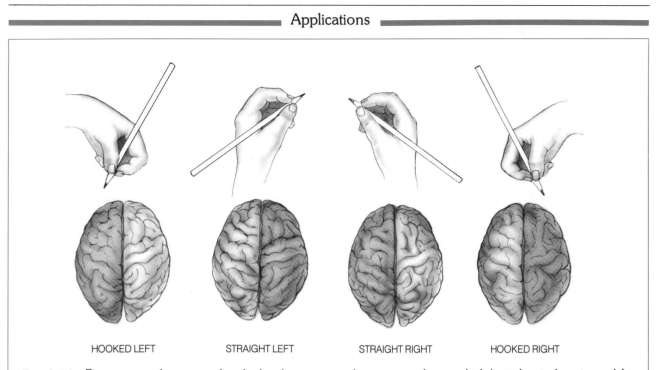

HOOKED LEFT   STRAIGHT LEFT   STRAIGHT RIGHT   HOOKED RIGHT

Fig. 3-16   *Recent research suggests that the hand position used in writing indicates which brain hemisphere is used for language. (Redrawn from an illustration by M. E. Challinor.)*

humans, the split is about 90-10, with right-handedness being most common. The prevalence of right-handedness in humans probably reflects the left brain's specialization for language production (Corballis, 1980). Evidence exists that the majority of humans have been right-handed for at least 50 centuries (Coren and Porac, 1977).

In general, children don't begin to express clear-cut handedness until they are four or five. This delay reflects the early plasticity of the brain (mentioned earlier in the chapter). But brain plasticity does not mean hand preference can be dictated. Parents should never try to force a left-handed child to use the right hand. To do so may invite speech or reading problems; handedness is *hereditary* (Herron, 1980).

Question: Are there any drawbacks to being left-handed?

Other than the fact that lefties must live in a right-handed world, there seem to be none. A recent large-scale study of high school students in California found no differences in school achievement between left- and right-handers, and no physical or mental defects associated with left-handedness (Hardyck *et al.,* 1976). In fact, there may actually be some advantages to being left-handed.

Advantage Left   Throughout history, a notable number of artists have been lefties: from Leonardo da Vinci and Michelangelo, to Pablo Picasso and M. C. Escher. Conceivably, since the right hemisphere is superior at imagery and visual abilities, there is some advantage to using the left hand for drawing or painting (Pines, 1980). Whether this is true or not, the left-handed do seem better at putting together verbal and pictorial symbols or ideas, which may be why there are more left-handed architects than would be expected (Herron, 1980).

One striking feature of lefties is that they are generally less **lateralized** than the right-handed. This means that there is less distinct specialization in the two sides of their brains. In fact, even the physical size and shape of the cerebral hemispheres is more identical in left-handed persons. If you are a lefty, you can take pride in the fact that your brain is less lopsided than the brains of your right-handed friends (Corballis, 1980)! In general, left-handers are more symmetrical on almost everything, including eye dominance, fingerprints—even foot size (Corballis, 1980).

In some situations, less lateralization may be a real advantage. For instance, individuals who are moderately left-handed or ambidextrous seem to have better than

Applications

average pitch memory, which is a basic musical skill (Deutsch, 1978). Correspondingly, more musicians are ambidextrous than would normally be expected. It's not clear, however, if those who are musically gifted were initially less lateralized, or if playing music develops both hands, or possibly both sides of the brain (Pines, 1980).

The clearest advantage of being left-handed shows up when there is a brain injury. Due to their milder lateralization, left-handed individuals typically experience less language loss after damage to either brain hemisphere, and they recover more easily (Geschwind, 1979). Maybe having "two left feet" isn't so bad after all.

Learning Check

1. About 97 percent of left-handed people process language on the left side of the brain, the same as right-handed people do.   T or F?
2. Left-handed individuals who write with their hand below the line are right-brain dominant.   T or F?
3. Most animals, like most humans, show a preference for the right limb.   T or F?
4. In general, left-handed individuals show less lateralization in the brain and, in fact, throughout the body.   T or F?
5. A recent study of high school students demonstrated that left-handed individuals are superior in school achievement.   T or F?

Answers: 1. F   2. T   3. F   4. T   5. F

Exploration

ESB—The Promise and Peril of Brain Control

Question: What is ESB and how is it done?

ESB refers to **Electrical Stimulation** of the **Brain,** a technique that has made direct control over the machinery of the brain a reality. In some instances, ESB is capable of calling forth animal and human behavior with almost robotlike precision. ESB begins with **brain implantation:** the placing of electrical stimulating devices in strategic areas of the brain. Usually, these are fine steel or platinum electrodes (thin wires or needles) inserted through the skull, run under the scalp, and collected at a single external socket. By this means, as many as two dozen or more separate brain sites can be electrically stimulated on command.

Advances in electronics have made it possible for such electrodes to be activated at a distance by use of radio transmitters and receivers. Further developments promise increasingly smaller receivers and stimulating devices, eventually the size of a postage stamp or less. In addition to removing any outward signs of ESB implants, miniaturization may eventually allow placement of a microcomputer in the brain, perhaps as a means of controlling epileptic seizures, or of artificially increasing intelligence.

Question: How is ESB used now?

ESB is used extensively in animal research as a means of exploring brain-behavior connections. An important advantage of ESB is that it allows an animal (or person) to function normally, with the brain intact, while the experimenter turns various brain areas on and off. An early experiment by W. R. Hess demonstrated that full-blown rage could be elicited from cats by ESB. Since then, ESB has proven capable of putting animals and humans through the paces of most basic behaviors. Stimulation applied to the proper brain area can instantly bring about terror, anxiety, rage, sexual desire, aggression, alertness, escape, eating, drinking, sleeping, movement of limbs, euphoria, memories, speech, tears, and more.

Question: How do humans respond to ESB?

ESB experiments with humans have understandably been limited to situations involving extraordinary medical need. For example, ESB may be used to identify brain areas that are triggering violent outbursts so that they may be removed surgically. When tested by ESB, one patient reacted with a sudden outburst of anger upon stimulation of the amygdala (a part of the limbic system) saying, ''I feel like I want to get up from this chair! Please don't let me do it! Don't do this to me. I don't want to be mean!'' When asked by the interviewer if she would like to hit him, she said, ''Yeah I want to hit something. I want to get something and just tear it up!'' The patient was then given a stack of paper, which she tore to shreds (King, 1961). Later, she explained that she had not really been angry at the interviewer, but that she had an overwhelming desire to hit or destroy anything and everything.

Electrodes at other locations produce decidedly different reactions. Upon stimulation of electrodes in the temporal lobe, one patient giggled and made funny comments, saying she enjoyed the stimulation very much. Repetition of the stimulation made the patient flirtatious and forward, and she ended by openly expressing her desire to marry the therapist. When stimulation ceased she again became quiet, reserved, and proper, without familiarity or excessive friendliness.

Question: Could ESB be used to control a person completely against his or her will?

José Delgado of Yale University, who has done some of the most advanced work with ESB, believes it could not. As evidence, he cites research on stimulated aggression in animal colonies. Monkeys receiving ESB become aggressive in direct proportion to their rank in the ''pecking order'' of the colony. When they are at the bottom of the pecking order, stimulation causes few attacks on other monkeys. When they are near the top, aggressive outbursts and attacks are easily triggered. Thus, to the question, ''Could a ruthless dictator stand at a master radio transmitter and stimulate the brains of a mass of hopelessly enslaved people?'' Delgado replies, ''Fortunately it is beyond the theoretical and practical limits of ESB.''

So at this point in its development, ESB cannot really cause a person to behave like a robot. It is true, as we have seen, that a person's emotional reactivity can be influenced, making the person more aggressive or amorous,

Exploration

for instance. But in most cases, the behavioral details of these feelings are modified by the individual's personality and by the situation.

What then, does the future hold for ESB? Will it provide a way to overcome epileptic seizures, end uncontrollable violence, reverse some forms of mental retardation, or link the brain to a computer? Or, will doing "just what the doctor ordered" take on a sinister new meaning? What are the ethical implications of present ESB research? Will more precise brain control become possible? Will Delgado's belief that mass control is unfeasible evaporate? What impact does ESB research have on your conceptions of personality, mind, and free will?

Sources:

José Delgado. *Physical Control of the Mind.* Harper and Row, 1969

_____. "ESB," *Psychology Today,* May, 1970.

Perry London. *Behavior Control.* Harper and Row, 1971.

Questions for Discussion

1. If you could change the brain or nervous system in any way to improve them, how would you do it, and why?

2. What effect would you expect a drug to have if it raised the firing threshold for neurons? If it blocked passage of neurotransmitters across the synapse? If it mimicked the effect of a neurotransmitter? If it stimulated the RF? If it suppressed activity in the medulla?

3. Have you known someone who has had a stroke or other brain injury? What were the effects? How did the person cope with the injury?

4. A member of your family has been having outbursts of hostile and aggressive behavior. In the past year, they have become virtually uncontrollable. ESB has been recommended as the only remaining possible treatment. Would you condone its use? What limitations (if any) do you think should be imposed on ESB procedures?

5. Do you think the distinction between right- and left-hemisphere function is valid? For example, are there verbal skills involved in music, dance, or art?

6. Robert Ornstein has urged us to recognize that full use of human potentials should take advantage of the specialized skills of both cerebral hemispheres. Roger Sperry has charged that "our educational system . . . tends to neglect the non-verbal form of intellect. What it comes down to is that modern society discriminates against the right hemisphere." Do you agree? What changes would you make in educational systems if you do?

7. What would be some of the possible advantages and disadvantages to having a "split brain"?

8. If a person were kept alive with only the spinal cord intact, what kinds of responses would be possible? What if both the spinal cord and medulla were functioning? The spinal cord, medulla, and cerebellum? The spinal cord, medulla, cerebellum, and subcortex? All brain areas except the association cortex?

9. If your brain were removed, replaced by another, and moved to a new body, which would you consider to be yourself, your old body with the new brain, or your new body with the old brain?

10. Can the brain ever expect to understand itself completely? Or, is the brain studying the brain like trying to lift yourself by your "bootstraps"?

Suggestions for Further Reading

Corballis, M. C. "Laterality and Myth," *American Psychologist,* March, 1980, 284–295.

Delgado, J. *Physical Control of the Mind: Toward a Psychocivilized Society.* Harper and Row, 1969.

Eccles, S. J. C. (ed.). *Brain and Conscious Experience.* Springer-Verlag, 1966.

Gazzaniga, M. S. *The Bisected Brain.* Plenum, 1970.

Gazzaniga, M. S. and S. E. LeDoux. *The Integrated Mind.* Plenum, 1978.

Groch, J. *You and Your Brain.* Harper and Row, 1963.

Kinsbourne, M. "Why Is the Brain Biased?" *Psychology Today,* May, 1979.

Morgan, C. *Physiological Psychology,* 4th ed. McGraw-Hill, 1970.

Penfield, W., and T. Rasmussen. *The Cerebral Cortex of Man.* Macmillan, 1950.

Scientific American, September, 1979. (This entire issue is devoted to the brain.)

Wooldridge, D. E. *The Machinery of the Brain.* McGraw-Hill, 1963.

4

The Sensory World and Reality

Sensation and Reality

*Beyond your skin a swirling flow of energy crackles and buzzes. Bombarded by light, heat, pressure, vibrations, molecules, radiation, and mechanical forces, you are immersed in a kaleidoscope of stimulation. All of this would be lost—replaced by darkness and silence—were it not for the existence of the senses. The next time you drink in the beauty of a sunset, a flower, or a friend, remember this: **Sensation** makes it all possible.*

It is apparent that the world as we know it is created from sensory impressions. Less obvious is that what passes for "reality" is shaped by the way sensory systems operate. Our sensory organs can detect only a limited range of physical energies. As a result, events go unrecorded when the senses are not attuned to them. We have, for instance, no receptors for atomic radiation, X-rays, or microwaves; so it is possible to be injured by each of these without knowing it.

What would the world be like if new senses could be added—if we could "see" gamma rays, "hear" changes in barometric pressure, or "taste" light? We can only guess. It is far easier to imagine the loss of a sensory system. The excerpt that follows is from the autobiography of Helen Keller, who was blind and deaf from early infancy. This statement is a vivid reminder of the central role sensation plays in each of our lives:

> Sometimes it is true, a sense of isolation enfolds me like a cold mist as I sit alone and wait at life's shut gate. Beyond there is light, and music, and sweet companionship; but I may not enter. Fate, silent, pitiless, bars the way. . . . Silence sits immense upon my soul. Then comes hope with a smile and whispers, "There is joy in self-forgetfulness." So I try to make the light in others' eyes my sun, the music in others' ears my symphony, the smile on others' lips my happiness (Keller, 1955).

Yellow Is Amazing but Red Is Best   *Now contrast Helen Keller's words with those of Bob Edens, who had his sight restored at age fifty-one after being blind since birth:*

> I never would have dreamed that yellow is so . . . so yellow. I don't have the words, I'm amazed by yellow. But red is my favorite color. I just can't believe red. I can't wait to get up each day to see what I can see. And at night I look at the stars in the sky and the flashing lights. You could never know how wonderful

everything is. I saw some bees the other day, and they were magnificent. I saw a truck drive by in the rain and throw a spray in the air. It was marvelous. And did I mention, I saw a falling leaf just drifting through the air?

If you are ever tempted to take everyday sensory impressions for granted, remember Helen Keller and Bob Edens. As their words show, sensation is our "window on the world." All our meaningful behavior, our awareness of reality, and our ideas about the universe ultimately spring from the senses. It may be no exaggeration to claim that our topic for this chapter is quite, . . . "sensational."

Survey Questions   In general, how do sensory systems function? How do each of the major senses work, and what causes common sensory problems, such as deafness or color blindness? What are the limits of our sensory sensitivity? Why are we more aware of some sensations than others? How can pain be reduced or controlled in everyday situations? What happens when a person is deprived of normal sensory input?

Resources

The Sensory Receptors— What You See Is What You Get

We begin with a paradox. On one hand, we have the magnificent sensitivity of the senses. In one instant you can view a star light-years away, and in the next, you can look into the microcosmic universe of a dewdrop. Yet vision, like each of the other senses, is carefully limited in sensitivity so that it acts as a **data reduction system:** the senses routinely "boil down" floods of information into a select stream of useful data. Such selection can be seen in the fact that "light" is only a small slice of a broader range of energies. In addition to visible light, the **electromagnetic spectrum** includes infrared and ultraviolet light, radio frequencies, TV broadcasts, gamma rays, and other energies (see Fig. 4-14 in color section). If the eyes were not limited to "light" sensitivity, "seeing" would be like getting hundreds of different "channels" at once. Imagine turning on 10 radios tuned to different stations, 10 TVs, a light show, CB, emergency, and amateur radio broadcasts, and trying to make sense of it all. The confusion would be overwhelming. Obviously, *selection* of information is as important as sensitivity to a broad range of stimulation.

Question: How are selection and data reduction accomplished?

Some selection occurs simply because sensory receptors act as biological *transducers*. A **transducer** is a device that converts one kind of energy into another. For exam-

ple, a phonograph needle, which converts vibrations into electrical signals, is a familiar transducer. If you blow on a phonograph needle, or scrape it with your fingertip, you will hear a sound coming from the speakers (and possibly from the owner if it's not your stereo). But if you shine a light on the needle, or put it in cold water, nothing will happen. The needle can only transduce vibration. Similarly, each sensory receptor is designed to convert only certain kinds of energy into nerve impulses. Moreover, many sensory systems **analyze** the environment into important features *before* sending nerve impulses to the brain. For example, Jerome Lettvin (1961) has shown that a frog's eye basically produces only four kinds of "messages." The frog's eye seems to have detectors for stationary edges, moving edges, overall dimming, and small, dark moving spots. Lettvin calls the last message a "bug-detector." It seems that the frog's eye is "wired" to be especially sensitive to bugs flying nearby—usually a real advantage in survival. Humans, of course, are less rigidly programmed, and thus more adaptable. A frog may starve to death surrounded by dead flies!

In addition to selection and analysis, sensory systems **code** important features of the world into messages understood by the brain. As you know, the nervous system can use only a yes-or-no, on-or-off code for its messages. Consequently, sensory codes are based on rates and timing of nerve impulses, the number and types of cells activated, pathways used, and the final place of arrival in the brain. All are needed to sort raw stimulation into usable sensations (Hubel and Wiesel, 1979).

To see coding at work, try this simple experiment:

Close your eyes for a moment. Then take your fingertips and press firmly on your eyelids. Apply enough pressure to "squash" your eyes slightly. Do this for about 30 seconds and see what happens.*

If you tried the experiment, you probably saw stars, checkerboards, and flashes of color called **phosphenes** (FOSS-feens). The reason for this is that the receptor cells at the back of the eye, which normally respond to light, are also sensitive to pressure. Notice though, that the eye is only prepared to code stimulation, including pressure, into *visual* features. As a result you experience *light* sensations, not pressure. Also important in producing this effect is **localization of function** in the brain.

Question: What does localization of function mean?

It means that specific brain areas receive messages from the various sense organs. Thus, the sensation you experience ultimately depends on the area of the brain activated. For example, neurosurgeon Wilder Penfield has electrically stimulated the **visual area** in the brain of conscious human subjects. One subject described his response to such stimulation as: "flickering lights," "colors," "a long, white mark," and other basic visual sensations (Penfield and Roberts, 1959).

Question: What is the point of this?

One practical implication is that it may be possible someday to artificially route visual information to the brain, thus restoring sight in the blind. Researchers are already working on such a system. It uses miniature television cameras to generate electrical signals, which are carried directly to the visual cortex of the brain (Dobelle *et al.,* 1974). (See Fig. 4-1.)

A second implication is that "seeing" does not take place in the eyes, nor "hearing" in the ears, "smelling" in the nose, "taste" in the tongue, nor "touch" in the skin. In seeing, for instance, the eye is only one step in a long chain of events eventually activating populations of cells in the brain. In other words, seeing involves the entire eye-brain system, not the eye alone. The philosophical upshot is that the senses do not operate like copying machines sending back "pictures" of the world. Rather, they are more like scouts sent from the command center we call the brain to the frontiers of the body. There they collect, transduce, analyze, code, and transmit a never-ending flow of data to an information-hungry brain. This incoming flow of information is what we refer to as **sensa-**

*Readers with eye problems should not try this.

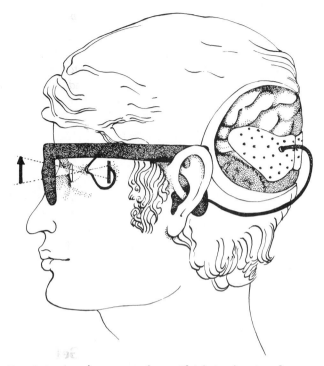

Fig. 4-1 *Artist's concept of an artificial visual system. Images received by an artificial eye would be transmitted to electrodes placed in the visual area of the brain (shown in cut-away view). The artificial eye, which operates like a television camera, might be placed in the eye socket as shown in the drawing. A major barrier to such systems is the brain's tendency to reject implanted electrodes.*

tion. (When the brain organizes sensations into meaningful patterns, we speak of *perception,* which is the topic of Chapter 5.) Let us turn now to a look at the amazing structures that connect us to the world of physical energies.

The Somesthetic Senses— Flying by the Seat of Your Pants

The old barnstorming pilots of the circus era were famous for "flying by the seat of their pants." In other words, for relying on touch, body position, and balance, rather than on instruments, to fly. Likewise, a gymnast launching herself through a routine on the uneven bars may rely as much on the **somesthetic senses** as on vision. Even the most routine activities, such as walking, running, or passing a sobriety test, would be impossible without somesthetic information from the body.

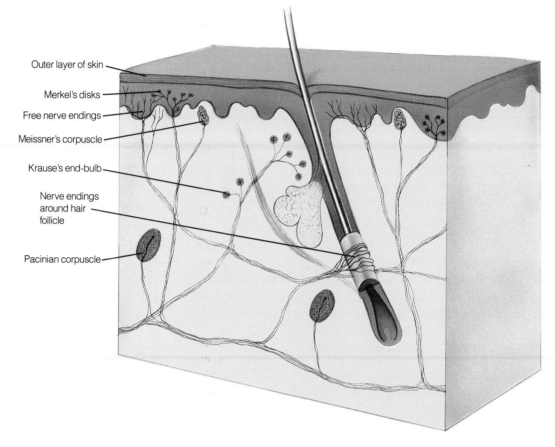

Outer layer of skin
Merkel's disks
Free nerve endings
Meissner's corpuscle
Krause's end-bulb
Nerve endings around hair follicle
Pacinian corpuscle

Fig. 4-2 *The skin senses include touch, pressure, pain, cold, and warmth. This drawing shows different forms the skin receptors can take. Other shapes were once recognized, but most turned out to be variations of the shapes shown. The only clearly specialized receptor is the Pacinian corpuscle, which is highly sensitive to pressure. Free nerve endings are receptors for pain and any of the other sensations. For reasons that are not clear, cold is sensed near the surface of the skin, and warmth is sensed deeper. (Carlson, 1981.)*

Question: What are the somesthetic senses?

The somesthetic senses (*soma:* body, *esthetic:* feel) include the **skin senses** (touch), the **kinesthetic senses** (receptors in the muscles and joints that relay information on body position and movement), and the **vestibular senses** (receptors in the inner ear that signal balance—and cause motion sickness). Because of their importance, let us focus on the skin senses.

   Skin receptors produce at least five different sensations: *light touch, pressure, pain, cold,* and *warmth.* Receptors may specialize somewhat in various sensations (see Fig. 4-2). The surface of the *eye,* however, which has only free nerve endings, produces all five sensations, so receptor shape is not critical (Carlson, 1981). Altogether, the

skin has about 200,000 nerve endings for temperature, 500,000 for touch and pressure, and 3 million for pain.

Question: Does the number of receptors in an area of skin relate to its sensitivity?

Yes. Your skin could be "mapped" by applying heat, cold, touch, pressure, or pain to various points on your body. This procedure would show that the skin receptors are found in varying concentrations, and that sensitivity corresponds roughly to the number of receptors in a given area. As a rough-and-ready illustration, try this two-point touch test:

   The density of touch receptors on various body areas can be checked by having a friend apply two pencil points to the skin with varying distances between them. Without looking, you should respond "one" or "two" each time. Record the distance between the pencils each time you feel two points.

You should find that two points are recognizable when they are one-tenth of an inch apart on the fingertips, one-quarter of an inch on the nose, and three inches at the middle of the back. Generally speaking, important areas such as the lips, tongue, face, hands, and genitals have higher concentrations of receptors.

Question: There are many more pain receptors than other kinds. Why is pain so heavily represented, and does the concentration of pain receptors also vary?

Like the other skin senses, pain receptors vary in their distribution. There are an average of about 232 pain points per square centimeter behind the knee, 184 per centimeter on the buttocks (an area preferred by many parents for "spankings"), 60 on the pad of the thumb, and 44 on the tip of the nose (Geldard, 1972). (Is it better then, to be pinched on the nose than behind the knee? It depends on what you like!) Pain receptors in the internal organs are very scattered and loosely organized. As a result, internal pain is often "referred" to other areas of the body. One very common example of **referred pain** is the angina pain caused by reduced blood flow to the heart, which is usually felt in the left shoulder or arm, rather than the chest. Another is pains from the uterus, which are often felt in the lower back during labor and childbirth.

Just as pain varies in parts of the body, so does it vary from person to person. Occasionally an individual is born with a complete insensitivity to pain. The history of one such individual, a 22-year-old female college student, is typical. Since early childhood, she experienced extensive burns, frostbite, deep cuts, and other serious tissue damage without feeling a thing (McMurray, 1950). This points out the positive side of pain. Pain is usually a signal that the body has been, or is being, damaged. Without pain, we would be unable to detect or prevent injury (Melzack and Dennis, 1978).

You may have noticed that there are really two kinds of pain. Pain carried by *large* nerve fibers is sharp, bright, fast, and associated with specific body areas. This is the body's **warning system.** Give yourself a small jab with a pin, and you will feel this type of pain. Notice as you do that warning pain quickly disappears. A second type of pain is carried by *small* nerve fibers. It is slower, nagging, aching, widespread, and very unpleasant. It gets worse if the pain stimulus is repeated. This is the body's **reminding**

system (Melzack and Dennis, 1978). A sad thing about the reminding system is that it often produces agony even when the reminder is useless, as in terminal cancer, or when pain continues after an injury has healed. Later in the chapter we will return to pain to learn how it can be controlled. If you got carried away with the pin demonstration, maybe you should read ahead now . . .

Smell and Taste— The Nose Knows When the Tongue Can't Tell

Unless you are a wine taster, a perfume blender, chef, or gourmet, you may think of **olfaction** (smell) and **gustation** (taste) as least important among the senses. Certainly a person could survive without these two **chemical senses.** The same cannot be said for animals, however. For many animals, smell is as important as vision, because it reveals the presence of predators, prey, mates, or rivals over long distances, around corners, or otherwise out of sight. Animals are also often more dependent on taste, using it in combination with smell to determine if a food is edible.

Question: How do smell and taste take place?

Smell and taste are closely related experiences. Let's consider each separately before returning to their combined effects.

The Sense of Smell The receptors for smell respond primarily to gaseous molecules carried in the air. As air enters the nose, it passes over millions of nerve fibers embedded in the lining of the upper nasal passages. Airborne molecules passing over the exposed fibers trigger nerve signals that are sent to the brain (see Fig. 4-3).

Question: How are different odors produced?

This is still something of a mystery. One hint comes from the fact that it is possible to develop a sort of "smell blindness" for only one type of odor. This loss, called an **anosmia** (an-NOSE-me-ah) suggests that there are specific receptors for different odors. Indeed, scientists have noticed that molecules having a particular odor are quite similar in shape. Specific shapes have been identified for floral, camphoric (camphor-like), musky, minty, and etherish (ether-like) odors. It is currently believed that there are different shaped "holes" or depressions on the odor receptors. Like a piece fit in a puzzle, a molecule produces

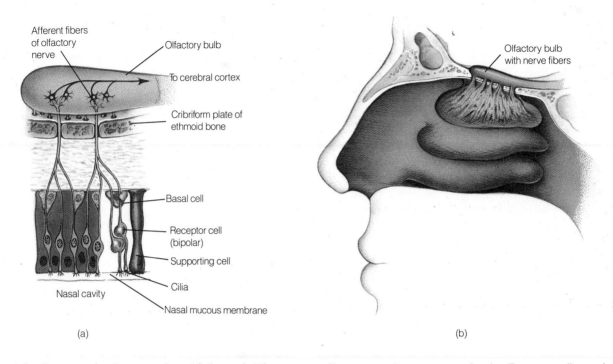

Fig. 4-3 *Receptors for the sense of smell (olfaction). Olfactory nerve fibers respond to gaseous molecules. Receptor cells are shown in cross section at left of part (a).*

an odor when it matches up with a hole of the same shape. This is called the **lock and key theory.** Although there are some exceptions, this theory seems to explain many odors.

Taste   There are at least four basic taste sensations: sweet, salt, sour, and bitter. We are most sensitive to bitter, next to sour, less sensitive to salt, and least sensitive to sweet. This order would seem to have aided survival in the past by preventing poisonings when most humans foraged for food. Now taste adds a joyous (if less essential) dimension to the universal pastime of eating.

Question: If there are only four tastes, how can there be so many foods with different flavors?

Flavors seem more varied than suggested by the four taste qualities because we tend to include sensations of texture, temperature, smell, and even pain along with taste. Notice, for instance, that "hot" is not one of the taste qualities. If you like chilies or other "hot" foods, what you are actually enjoying is *pain* added to taste.

Smell is particularly important in determining flavor. Small bits of apple, potato, and onion "taste" almost exactly alike when the nose is plugged. It is probably no

exaggeration to say that subjective flavor is one-half smell. This is why food loses its "taste" when you have a cold.

The four primary tastes are detected by **taste buds** located mainly on the top of the tongue, but also at other points inside the mouth (see Fig. 4-4). As food is chewed, it dissolves and enters the taste bud, where it sets off a nerve impulse to the brain. Like the skin senses, taste receptors are not equally distributed. Look at Fig. 4-4, and you will see that some areas of the tongue are more sensitive to each of the tastes than others.

Question: People seem to have very different tastes. Why is that?

Some differences are genetic. The chemical phenylthio-carbamine (PTC) tastes bitter to about 70 percent of those tested, and has no taste for the other 30 percent. The sense of taste also varies with age. Taste cells have a life of only several days. With aging, cell replacement slows down, so the sense of taste diminishes (Beidler, 1963). This is why many foods you disliked in childhood have become acceptable to you as an adult. Children who will not eat vegetables, spinach, liver, and so on may be having a very different taste experience than the adult urging the child to eat. Aside from this fact however, most taste preferences are

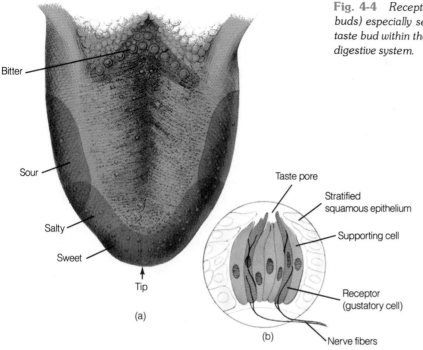

Fig. 4-4 *Receptors for taste: (a) Position of receptors (taste buds) especially sensitive to four taste qualities; (b) Detail of a taste bud within the tongue. The buds occur in other parts of the digestive system.*

Bitter

Sour

Salty

Sweet

Tip

(a)

Taste pore

Stratified squamous epithelium

Supporting cell

Receptor (gustatory cell)

(b)

Nerve fibers

acquired. Would you eat the coagulated secretion of the modified skin glands of a cow after it had undergone bacterial decomposition? If you would, you are a *cheese fancier* (Matthews and Knight, 1963)!

Hearing—Good Vibrations

Rock, classical, jazz, country, pop—whatever your musical taste, you have probably been transported at one time or another by the riches of sound. Hearing provides the brain with a wealth of information not available through the other senses, such as the approach of an unseen car, or the information conveyed by spoken language. Hearing is highly developed even at birth. A newborn baby will consistently look in the direction of a metal "cricket" snapped at various locations around the room.

Question: What is the stimulus for hearing?

If you throw a stone into a quiet pond, a circle of waves will spread from it in all directions. In much the same way, sound travels as a series of invisible waves of **compression** (peaks) and **rarefaction** (RARE-eh-fak-shun, valleys) in the air. Any object set in motion—a tuning fork, the string of a musical instrument, or the vocal cords—will produce **sound waves** as it vibrates. The **frequency** of sound waves (the number of waves per second) corresponds to the

pitch of a sound. The **amplitude,** or "height," of a sound wave tells how much energy it contains, so amplitude corresponds to **loudness** (see Fig. 4-5).

Question: How are sounds transduced?

What we call the "ear" is only the **pinna** (PIN-ah), or visible external part of the ear. The pinna acts like a funnel to

Fig. 4-5 *The stimulus for hearing is waves of compression in the air or, more simply, vibrations. The frequency of sound waves determines their pitch. The amplitude determines loudness.*

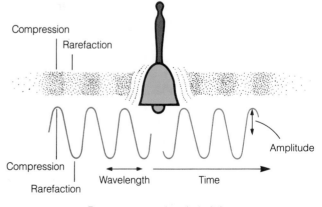

Compression

Rarefaction

Compression

Rarefaction

Wavelength

Time

Amplitude

Frequency = wavelengths/unit time

concentrate sounds. To exaggerate this effect, cup your hands in front of your ears and notice how hearing improves. Animals use the pinna to great advantage by swiveling their ears toward sounds to improve hearing. Humans also have muscles attached to the pinna, but few can wiggle their ears. We generally make do by turning the head to catch faint sounds.

As they spread through the air, sound waves are funneled into the ear where they collide with the **eardrum,** which is like a tight drumhead within the ear canal. The sound waves set the eardrum in motion, which in turn causes three small bones called the **auditory ossicles** to vibrate (see Fig. 4-6). The third ossicle is attached to a second membrane or drumhead called the **oval window.** As the oval window moves back and forth, it sets up waves in a fluid within the canals of the **cochlea** (KOCK-lee-ah).

The cochlea is a small tubular structure resembling a snail shell, and is divided into an upper and lower chamber. In it are the ultimate receptors for hearing.

Approximately 15,000 tiny **hair cells** are found in each ear. These are moved by waves in the canals of the cochlea. When the hair cells are bent, nerve impulses are sent to the brain. This incredible series of events takes place so quickly that when sounds arrive at the ears as little as 0.0001 second apart, it is possible to tell from which side the sound came (Rosenzweig, 1961). Our amazing sensitivity to such differences is the basis for modern stereophonic sound systems.

The ears are amazingly sensitive in another way. The loudest sound the ears can stand is over a *trillion* times more powerful than the quietest they can detect. If the quietest sound is likened to the weight of a feather, then

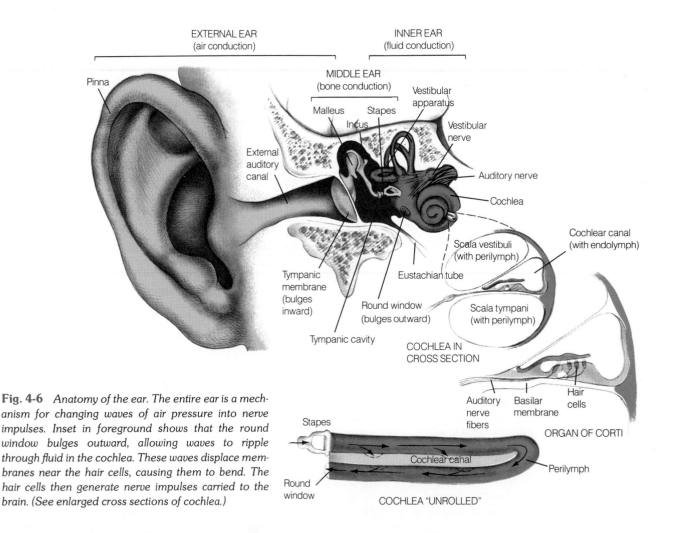

Fig. 4-6 *Anatomy of the ear. The entire ear is a mechanism for changing waves of air pressure into nerve impulses. Inset in foreground shows that the round window bulges outward, allowing waves to ripple through fluid in the cochlea. These waves displace membranes near the hair cells, causing them to bend. The hair cells then generate nerve impulses carried to the brain. (See enlarged cross sections of cochlea.)*

normal conversation weighs like a car, and the loudest sounds, like a battleship. To measure such a large loudness range, psychologists use a unit called the **decibel** (dB). Figure 4-7 gives decibel ratings for various sounds. But don't be fooled by the drawing. Decibels have an exponential relationship to one another. That is, an increase of 10 dBs multiplies sound intensity by 10. A 40-dB increase in loudness represents 10,000 times more sound energy (White, 1981). Keep this in mind when you read about deafness below.

Question: What causes deafness?

Deafness   There are three principal types of deafness. **Conduction deafness** occurs when the eardrums or ossicles are damaged or immobilized by disease or injury. Such damage reduces the transfer of sounds to the inner ear. In many cases, conduction deafness can be overcome with the use of a hearing aid, which makes sounds louder and clearer. **Nerve deafness** is a hearing loss resulting from damage to the hair cells or auditory nerve. Hearing aids are of no help to a person with nerve deafness. In this case, auditory messages cannot reach the brain no matter how loud the sound. **Stimulation deafness** is of special interest because many jobs, hobbies, and pastimes can cause it. Stimulation deafness is caused by exposure to very loud sounds. If you work in a noisy environment, enjoy loud music, motorcycling, snowmobiling, hunting, or other pursuits that expose you to loud sounds, then you may be subject to stimulation deafness.

Question: How loud must a sound be to pose a hazard to hearing?

The danger of hearing loss depends on both the loudness of sound and the length of exposure. An extremely loud sound may rupture the eardrum. Yet a child's cap pistol, which can produce a 155-dB sound, does little damage because it lasts for only one ten-thousandth of a second. But hair cells, which are about as wide as a cobweb, are very fragile. Daily exposure to 85 decibels or more may cause permanent hearing loss. Short periods of exposure to 120 decibels (a rock concert) may cause temporary deafness. Even brief exposures to 150 decibels (jet airplane nearby) can cause permanent deafness (Apfel, 1977; Lipscomb, 1974). Notice that music, as well as noise, can do damage. People who sit directly in front of the speaker columns at highly amplified musical concerts run a high risk of hearing loss. The late Jimi Hendrix was known to have suffered from partial deafness as a consequence of his high-powered musical performances.

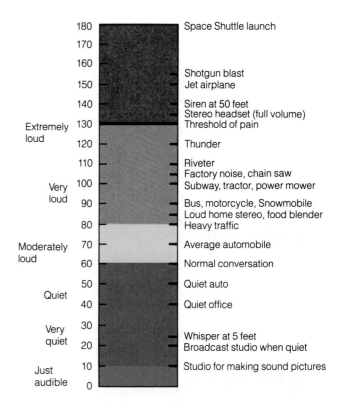

Fig. 4-7 *The loudness of sound is measured in decibels. Zero decibels is the faintest sound most people can hear. Sound in the range of 110 decibels is uncomfortably loud. Prolonged exposure to sounds above 85 decibels may damage the inner ear. Rock music, which may rate 120 decibels, is known to have caused hearing loss in musicians and may affect audiences as well. Sounds of 130 decibels pose an immediate danger to hearing.*

You might find it interesting to check the decibel ratings of some of your activities (Fig. 4-7) as a way of estimating their hearing risks. You should be particularly wary of any activity that causes what is known as a **temporary threshold shift,** or temporary loss of hearing. Another warning is **tinnitus** (tin-NYE-tus), a whistling, or ringing sensation in the ears. Almost everyone experiences tinnitus at times. But if a ringing sensation follows exposure to loud sounds, chances are that hair cells have been damaged (Dunkle, 1982). After repeated exposure to sounds that produce such warnings, you can expect to become permanently hard-of-hearing (Apfel, 1977). The next time you are exposed to an excessively loud sound, remember Helen Keller's words, "Silence sits immense upon my soul," and take precautions against damage. (Fingers are still the best earplugs.)

Learning Check

Before proceeding, let's stop for a quick check on the ideas we have covered.

1. Sensory receptors are biological _____, or devices for converting one type of energy to another.

2. Lettvin found that the frog's eye is especially sensitive to four features of the environment: unmoving edges, moving edges, overall dimming, and small moving spots.   T or F?

3. Important features of the environment are transmitted to the brain through a process known as:

   a. phosphenation   *b.* coding   *c.* detection   *d.* programming

4. Which of the following is not a somesthetic sense?

   a. gustation   *b.* the vestibular sense   *c.* kinesthesis   *d.* olfaction

5. It is now believed that angina pain and labor pains are referred to other parts of the body because there are no pain receptors in the internal organs.   T or F?

6. Olfaction appears to be at least partially explained by the _____ theory of molecule shapes and receptor sites.

7. From the standpoint of survival, we are fortunate that bitter tastes register primarily on the front tip of the tongue.   T or F?

8. Which of the following is *not* an important element in the transduction of sound? (circle)
   pinna   ossicles   phosphenes   oval window   hair cells

9. Daily exposure to sounds with a loudness of _____ decibels or more may cause permanent hearing loss.

Answers: 1. transducers 2. T 3. b 4. both a and d 5. F 6. lock and key 7. F 8. phosphenes 9. 85

Vision—Catching Some Rays

Question: Which of the senses is most essential?

There really isn't an answer to this question. Nevertheless, one fact stands out clearly: Roughly 70 percent of the information reaching the brain comes from vision. For most people, loss of vision is the single most devastating sensory disability. Vision can even dominate other senses. A number "2" traced on your forehead will seem backward, whereas one traced on the back of your head will seem normal. The "2" on the back of your head feels right because it faces forward, as do your eyes. Variations of this effect are known as **visual capture** (vision "captures" other sensations).

Because of its tremendous importance, we will explore vision in more detail than the other senses. Let's begin with the basic dimensions of light and vision.

Dimensions of Vision   Recall that the room in which you are sitting is filled with **electromagnetic radiation,** including light and other energies. The **visible spectrum** is made up of light with various wavelengths. The spectrum starts at wavelengths of 400 nanometers (nan-OM-et-ers;

a nanometer, abbreviated nm, is one-billionth of a meter). Wavelengths at this end of the spectrum produce sensations of purple or violet. Longer wavelengths of light produce sensations of blue, green, yellow, and orange, until red, with a wavelength of 700 nm is reached.

This physical property of light, its *wavelength,* corresponds to the psychological experience of **hue,** or the specific color of a stimulus. White light is made up of a mixture of frequencies from the entire spectrum. Colors produced by a very *narrow band* of wavelengths are said to be very **saturated,** or "pure." A third dimension of vision, **brightness,** corresponds roughly to the *amplitude* (or "height") of light waves; light of greater amplitude carries more energy and appears brighter.

Structure of the Eye

Question: Is it true that the eye is like a camera?

If we were willing to push the issue a bit, the eye could be used as a camera. When the light-sensitive surface at the back of the eye is bathed in alum solution, the last image to strike it will appear like a tiny picture. This fact might make for a great murder mystery, but it's obviously not

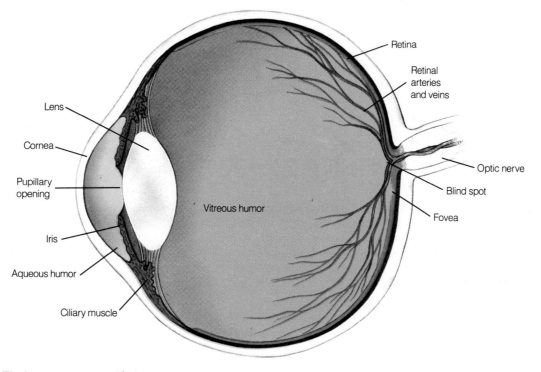

Fig. 4-8 *The human eye, a simplified view.*

much of a way to take a photograph. Besides, people had eyes before there were cameras, so it may be better to say that the camera is like an eye. In any case, several of the basic elements are similar. Both the eye and a camera have a **lens** that focuses an image on a light-sensitive layer at the back of a closed space. In a camera, this layer is the film; in the eye, it is a layer of **photoreceptors** (light-sensitive cells) about the size and thickness of a postage stamp, called the **retina** (see Fig. 4-8).

Question: How does the eye focus?

Focusing   The front of the eye has a clear covering called the **cornea.** The curvature of this transparent "window" bends light rays inward. But the cornea can't change shape to adjust for different viewing conditions. Additional focusing must be carried out by the lens, which is quite elastic. The lens is normally stretched out flat to focus distant objects. When the fibers holding the lens relax, it "fattens" or becomes more rounded. This change focuses the eye for viewing nearby objects. The process of bending, fattening, and stretching the lens is called **accommodation.** In cameras focusing is done more simply—by changing the distance between the lens and the film. If someone

tries to sell you a camera with an elastic lens, tell them you "can't accommodate the offer."

Visual Problems   The overall shape of the eye also affects focusing. If the eye is too short, nearby objects cannot be focused, but distant objects are clear. This is *farsightedness,* or **hyperopia.** If the eyeball is too long, the image falls short of the retina, and objects in the distance cannot be focused. This condition results in *near-sightedness* **(myopia).** When either the cornea or the lens is misshapen, some of the visual field will be focused and some will be fuzzy, a problem called **astigmatism.** All three visual problems can be corrected by placing glasses, or contact lenses, in front of the eye. These added lenses change the path of incoming light to restore crisp focusing (see Fig. 4-9).

Sometimes with age, the lens grows less resilient and less able to accommodate. Since the lens must do its greatest bending to focus objects near the eye, the result is **presbyopia** ("old vision," or farsightedness due to aging). Perhaps you have seen a grandparent or older friend reading a newspaper at arm's length because of presbyopia. A young child can focus as close as 4 inches, a young

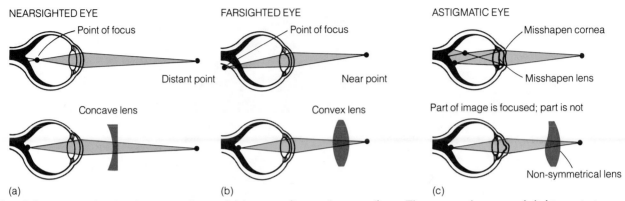

NEARSIGHTED EYE
Point of focus
Distant point

Concave lens

FARSIGHTED EYE
Point of focus
Near point

Convex lens

ASTIGMATIC EYE
Misshapen cornea
Misshapen lens

Part of image is focused; part is not

Non-symmetrical lens

(a)   (b)   (c)

Fig. 4-9 *Visual defects and corrective lenses: (a) A myopic (longer than usual) eye. The concave lens spreads light rays just enough to increase the eye's focal length. (b) A hyperopic (shorter than usual) eye. The convex lens increases refraction (bending), returning the point of focus to the retina. (c) Astigmatic (lens or cornea not symmetrical) eye. In astigmatism, parts of vision are sharp and parts are unfocused. Lenses to correct astigmatism are non-symmetrical.*

adult around 8 inches, and an aging person about 16 inches. If you now wear glasses for nearsightedness, you may have bifocals awaiting you in the future. Bifocal lenses correct near vision *and* distance vision.

Light Control There is one more major similarity between the eye and a camera. In front of the lens in both is a mechanism to control the amount of light entering. This mechanism is the **diaphragm** in a camera; in the eye it is the **iris** (see Fig. 4-10). The iris is a colored circular muscle that expands and contracts to control the size of the **pupil,** or dark opening at the center of the eye. If the eyes are blue, the iris has less pigment than it does for brown eyes, and therefore is less effective in shading the eyes. People with blue eyes, as a result, are more likely to squint in bright light. Albinos, who have no pigmentation in their body or eyes, often find bright light painful and must avoid it.

The iris is extremely important to the normal functioning of the eye. The retina can adapt to changing light conditions, but it does so very slowly. By making rapid adjustments, the iris allows quick movement from a dark-

ened room to bright sunlight. In dim light the pupils *dilate* (enlarge) and in bright light they *constrict* (narrow). At the largest opening of the iris the pupil is 17 times larger than at the smallest. Were this not the case, you would be blinded for quite some time upon walking into a darkened room.

Rods and Cones At this point, our comparison between the eye and a camera breaks down. Beyond its optical parts, the eye becomes a complex device for analyzing information contained in light. Besides, the eye would make a very poor camera. First of all, the eye is equipped with two types of "film," receptor cells called **rods** and **cones.** The rods and cones look different and perform differently. The cones, numbering about 6½ million in each eye, function best in bright light. They also produce *color* sensations and pick up fine details. By contrast, the rods, numbering about 100 million, are incapable of detecting colors. Pure rod vision is black and white. However, the rods are much more sensitive to light than the cones. The rods are therefore mainly responsible for our ability to see in very dim light.

Compared to the film in a camera, the visual receptors are backward: The rods and cones point toward the *back* of the eye, away from incoming light (see Fig. 4-11). In addition, the "film" has a hole in it. Each eye has a **blind spot** because there are no receptors where the optic nerve leaves the eye (see Fig. 4-12). And last, the eye is constantly in motion. This would be disastrous for a camera, but as we shall see later, it is essential for normal vision. In spite of their constant motion, the eyes are a magnificent system, far more impressive than any camera.

Fig. 4-10 *The diaphragm and iris.*

Question: Are there other differences between the rods and cones?

Visual Acuity   The cones are found mainly at the center of the eye. In fact, there is a small cup-shaped depression in the middle of the retina called the **fovea** (FOE-vee-ah) that is packed with about 50,000 cones. If you look at your thumbnail at arm's length, its image just about covers the fovea. Like a newspaper photograph made up of many small dots, the large number of cones in the fovea produces the greatest visual **acuity,** or sharpness. Figure 4-13 describes a widely used rating system for acuity. If vision can be corrected to no better than 20/200 acuity, a person is considered "legally blind." With 20/200 vision the world is seen as nothing but a blur.

Visual acuity is best when an image falls on the fovea. It then steadily decreases as images are moved to the edge of the retina. If you pick a letter on this page and stare at it, you will notice that you cannot read letters a few inches to either side without moving your eyes. This happens because the number of cones trails off rapidly as we move away from the fovea.

Question: What is the purpose of the rest of the retina?

Peripheral Vision   The eyes constantly move to keep images focused on the fovea. Large movements called **saccades** (sack-AIDS) shift the eyes from one fixation point to the next. If you are staring at something and your eyes start to drift, a smaller **microsaccadic** (MY-cro-SACK-aid-ik) movement flicks the eyes back. Nevertheless, areas surrounding the fovea also get light. This creates a large region of **peripheral** (side) **vision.** Compared to cones, the rods reach their greatest numbers about 20 degrees to each side of the fovea, so much peripheral vision is rod vision. In addition, the rods are unusually

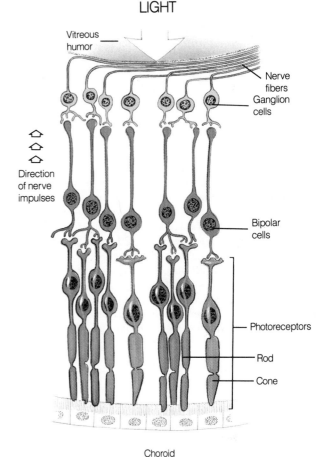

Fig. 4-11 *Anatomy of the retina, light-sensitive element of the eye. Note that light does not fall directly on the rods and cones. It must first pass through the outer layers of the retina. Only about one-half of the light falling on the front of the eye reaches the rods and cones—testimony to the eye's amazing light sensitivity.*

Fig. 4-12 *Experiencing the blind spot. (a) With the right eye closed, stare at the upper right cross. Hold the book about one foot from your eye and slowly move it back and forth. You should be able to locate a position that causes the black spot to disappear. When it does, it has fallen on the blind spot. (b) Repeat the procedure described but stare at the lower cross. When the white space falls on the blind spot, the black line will appear to be continuous. This may help you understand why you do not usually experience a blind spot in your visual field.*

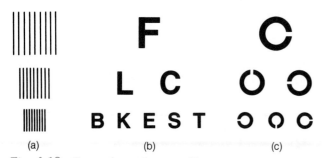

Fig. 4-13 *Tests of visual acuity. Above are some common tests of visual acuity. In (a) sharpness is indicated by the smallest grating still seen as individual lines. Part (b) requires that you read rows of letters of diminishing size until you can no longer distinguish them. The Landolt rings (c) require no familiarity with letters. All that is required is a report of which side has a break in it. Normal acuity is designated as 20/20 vision: At 20 feet in distance you can distinguish what the average person can see at 20 feet. If your vision is 20/40, you can see only at 20 feet what the average person can see at 40 feet. If your vision is 20/200, you need glasses! Vision that is 20/12 would mean that you can see at 20 feet what the average person must be eight feet nearer to see, indicating better than average acuity. American astronaut Gordon Cooper, who claimed to see railroad lines in northern India from 100 miles above, had 20/12 acuity.*

sensitive to *movement.* Thus, while the eye gives its best acuity to the center of vision, it maintains a radarlike scan for movement in peripheral vision. Seeing "out of the corner of the eye" is, of course, very important for sports, driving, and walking down dark alleys. Those who have lost peripheral vision are said to have **tunnel vision,** a condition much like wearing blinders.

Sailors, aviators, astronomers, and night spotters in the military have long made use of an additional aspect of peripheral vision. Although less sensitive to detail, the rods are many times more responsive to light than are the cones. Since there are no rods in the fovea, and their greatest numbers are found 20 degrees to each side, the best night vision is obtained by looking to one side or the other of an object. With a little effort this can be demonstrated:

> On a dark, moonless night, allow your eyes to slowly scan the sky until you find a star off toward the edge of your vision that is so dim that you can just barely see it. Now, if you look directly at the star (so that its image falls on the cones of the fovea), it should appear even dimmer and may actually disappear.

Under ideal conditions, you may be detecting as few as seven photons of light, from a star at the edge of our galaxy, crash-landing on the retina, in the twinkle of an eye.

Color Vision—There's More to It than Meets the Eye

What would you say is the brightest color? Red? Yellow? Blue? Actually, there are two answers to this question, depending on whether we are referring to the rods or the cones. The differing *maximal color sensitivity* of the rods and cones has important practical implications. The cones are most sensitive to wavelengths in the *yellowish-green* region of the spectrum. In other words, if all colors are tested in daylight (with each reflecting the same total amount of light) then yellowish-green appears *brightest.* In recognition of this fact, you may have seen a "day-glow" yellow firetruck, and vests of this color are increasingly worn by roadside work crews.

Question: Then why do hunters usually wear red vests?

The brightest color will not be most visible unless it contrasts with the background. Wearing yellow-green in the forest might camouflage a hunter and encourage an accident.

Question: To what color are the rods most sensitive?

Remember first that the rods do not produce color. If very dim colored lights are used, no color will be seen, but one of the colored lights will appear brighter than the others. When tested this way, the rods are most sensitive to *blue-green* lights. Thus, at night and under other conditions of dim light when rod vision predominates, the brightest-colored light will be one that is blue or blue-green. For this reason, police and highway patrol cars in many states now have blue emergency lights for nighttime work. Also, you may have wondered why the taxiway lights at most airports are blue. It seems like a poor choice, but blue is actually the most visible color to pilots.

Color Theories

Question: How do the cones record color sensations?

No short answer can do justice to the complexities of color vision, but briefly, here is the best current explanation. The **trichromatic** (or three-color) **theory** of color vision holds that there are three types of cones, each with a heightened sensitivity to a specific color: red, green, or blue. Other colors are assumed to result from a combination of these three, whereas black and white sensations are produced by the rods. A basic problem with this theory is that four colors seem psychologically primary: red, green, blue, and yellow. A second view, known as the **opponent-process theory,** was developed to explain why you can't have a reddish-green or a yellowish-blue. According to this theory, the visual system analyzes information into "either-or" color messages. It is assumed that the visual system can produce messages for either red or green, yellow or blue, black or white. Coding one color in a pair (red for instance) seems to block the opposite message (green), so a reddish-green is impossible, but a yellowish-red (orange) can occur. According to the theory, fatigue caused by making one response causes an **afterimage** of the opposite color as the system recovers. To experience an afterimage of this type, turn to the flag picture on the colored pages of this chapter and follow the instructions given there.

Question: Which color theory is correct?

Both and neither! The three-color theory seems to work at the level of the retina, where three types of visual pigments with sensitivity peaks in the red, green, and blue regions have been found. The opponent-process theory seems to apply to events recorded in the optic pathways after information leaves the retina. So both may be correct at a particular level in the visual system. Unfortunately, Edwin Land, inventor of the Polaroid camera, has scrambled this apparently tidy explanation. Land (1977) has been able to get color sensations from two specially prepared black and white slides of the same scene. One slide is projected with red light, and the second is projected with white light and superimposed on the first. Everything should be pinkish, but soft colors appear. What does this mean? It means we do not yet fully understand how color sensations are produced!

Question: What is it like to be color blind? What causes color blindness?

Color Blindness and Color Weakness   A person who is completely **color blind** sees the world as if it were a black and white movie. How do we know? In a few rare cases, people have been color blind in only one eye and can compare (Hsia and Graham, 1965). Two colors of equal brightness look exactly alike to the color-blind individual. The color-blind person either lacks cones or has cones that do not function normally. Complete color blindness is frequently accompanied by visual **nystagmus** (nis-TAG-mus). This is a jerking eye movement that serves to repeatedly move the visual image off the inoperative fovea (Rushton, 1975).

Total color blindness is rare. **Color weakness,** or partial color blindness, is more common. Approximately 8 percent of the male population (but less than 1 percent of women) are red-green color blind. (Another form of color weakness, involving yellow and blue, is extremely rare.) Red-green color blindness is a recessive, sex-linked trait. This

means that it is carried on the X, or female chromosome. Women have two X chromosomes, so if they receive an X with a defective color gene, they get a second chance. This is why red-green color blindness is rare in women. Color-blind men inherit the trait from their mothers (who are usually not color blind themselves). Color blindness is often passed from maternal grandfather to grandson, but it may also skip several generations. The red-green color-blind individual perceives both reds and greens as the same color, usually a yellowish-brown (Rushton, 1975).

Question: Then how can color-blind individuals drive? Don't they have trouble with traffic lights?

Red-green color-blind individuals have normal color vision for yellow and blue, and their acuity is normal. Their main problem while driving is to tell red lights from green. In practice, this is not difficult. In the United States, the red light is always on top, and the green light is brighter than the red. Also, in recognition of this problem, most modern traffic signals have a "red" light that has a background of yellow light mixed with it, and a "green" light that is really blue-green.

Question: How can a person tell if he or she is color blind?

A common test for color blindness and weakness is the **Ishihara** test, which was developed by a Japanese scientist. In the test, numbers and other designs made up of dots are superimposed on a background also made of dots. The background and the numbers are of different colors (red and green, for example). A person who is color blind sees only a collection of dots. The person with normal color vision can detect the presence of the numbers or designs. Figure 4-15 in the color section is a replica of the Ishihara test. You should not consider Fig. 4-15 a true test of color vision, but it may give you some idea of whether or not you are color blind.

Dark Adaptation—
Let There Be Light!

Question: What happens to the eyes when they adapt to a dark room?

Dark adaptation, the increase in sensitivity to light that occurs when one spends time in the dark, is a striking event. Consider walking into a theater. If you enter from a brightly lighted lobby, you practically have to be led to your seat. After a short time, however, you can see the entire room in perfect detail (including the couple kissing over in the corner). Studies of dark adaptation show us that it takes about 35 minutes of complete darkness to reach maximum visual sensitivity. When dark adaptation is complete, the eye can detect lights 10,000 times weaker than those to which it was originally sensitive.

Question: What causes dark adaptation?

Both the rods and cones contain light-sensitive chemicals known as **visual pigments.** When struck by light these compounds bleach* (break down chemically). This process is what causes the rods and cones to generate nerve impulses. To prepare the rods and cones for further sensitivity to light, the visual pigments must recombine. This recombining takes place most quickly and most completely in darkness. When completely dark-adapted, the human eye is almost as sensitive to light as the eye of an owl. Most of the eye's increased sensitivity comes from the rods, which contain a pigment called visual purple, or **rhodopsin** (row-DOP-sin). Increased concentrations of rhodopsin correspond directly to improved night vision.

Before artificial illumination, changing from cone vision to the more sensitive rod vision occurred primarily at sunset, and gradual adaptation was adequate. Now we are often caught in states of temporary semiblindness. Usually this poses no danger, but it can. It takes a long time to dark adapt, but the process can be completely wiped out by just a few seconds exposure to bright light. Try this demonstration:

Find a very dark room and spend 15 or 20 minutes in it. At the end of this time, you should be able to see clearly.

*The afterimages caused by flashbulbs and other bright lights are a direct result of the bleaching process.

Now, close your left eye and cover it tightly with your hand. Turn on a bright light for one or two seconds and look at it with your right eye. With the light off again, compare the vision in your two eyes, first opening one and then the other. You will be completely blinded in your right eye.

This experience should be more than enough to convince you of the wisdom of the oft-repeated warning to avoid looking at the headlights of approaching cars during night driving. Under normal conditions, glare recovery takes about 20 seconds, plenty of time for an accident. After a few drinks, it may take 30 to 50 percent longer.

Question: Is there any way to speed up dark adaptation?

The rods are insensitive to extremely red light. Submarines and airplane cockpits are illuminated with red light. So are the "ready rooms" for fighter pilots and ground crews. In each case this allows the people involved to perform their duties, to read, play cards, or whatever, and still be able to go out into the dark without the usual adaptation time. Since the red light doesn't stimulate the rods, it is as if they had already spent time in the dark.

Question: Can eating carrots really improve vision?

One of the "ingredients" of rhodopsin is **retinal,** which the body makes from vitamin A. When too little vitamin A is available, rhodopsin production declines. Thus, a person suffering from vitamin A deficiency may develop **night blindness.** In night blindness, the person sees normally in bright light while using the cones, but becomes totally blind at night when the rods must function. Since carrots are an excellent source of vitamin A, they could improve night vision for someone suffering a deficiency, but not the vision of anyone with an adequate diet (Carlson, 1981).

Learning Check

After such an extended discussion of vision you may find it helpful to review the questions below.

1. The _____ _____ is made up of electromagnetic radiation with wavelengths between 400 and 700 nm.

2. Match:

____ Myopia   **A.** Farsightedness

____ Hyperopia   **B.** Elongated eye

____ Presbyopia   **C.** Farsightedness due to aging

____ Astigmatism   **D.** Lack of cones in fovea

                   E. Misshapen cornea or lens

3. In dim light, vision depends mainly on the _____; color and fine detail are produced by the _____.

4. The fovea has the greatest visual acuity due to the large concentration of rods found there.   T or F?

5. The term 20/20 vision means that a person can see at 20 feet what can normally be seen from 20 feet.   T or F?

6. When using the cones, the most visible color is (circle):
    reddish-orange   blue-green   yellow-orange   yellowish-green

7. The opponent-process theory of color vision tries to explain why we cannot see a reddish-green or a yellowish-blue.   T or F?

8. The eyes become more sensitive to light at night due to a process known as _____ _____.

Answers: 1. visible spectrum   2. B, A, C, E   3. rods, cones   4. F   5. T   6. yellowish-green   7. T   8. dark adaptation

Psychophysics—Testing the Limits

Question: What is the quietest sound that can be heard? The weakest light that can be seen? The lightest touch that can be felt?

We have seen what magnificent instruments the sense organs are for linking us to the world of stimulation. What are their limits? An area of psychology known as **psychophysics** attempts to answer such questions by relating changes in *physical* stimuli to *psychological* responses. A basic question posed by psychophysics is, "What is the absolute minimum amount of stimulation necessary for a sensation to occur?" The answer defines the **absolute threshold** for a sensory system. For example, at maximum sensitivity, vibrations of the eardrum as small as one-billionth of a centimeter (one-tenth the diameter of a hydrogen atom) can be heard (Békésy, 1957a). If your ears were more sensitive to sounds, they would be less sensitive! That is, if your ears were more sensitive, they would convert the random movement of air molecules into a constant roaring or hissing noise like that heard when a large seashell is held to the ear.

The absolute threshold for vision is equally spectacular. A photon of light is the smallest possible particle or "package" of light energy, yet it only takes *three* photons of light striking the retina to produce a sensation. This is the equivalent of being able to see a single candle flame 30 miles away! Table 4-1 gives the approximate absolute thresholds for the five major senses.

It is interesting to note that some sensory systems have upper limits as well as lower ones. Humans can hear sounds ranging in pitch from 20 cycles (vibrations) per second, to about 20,000 cycles per second. This is an impressive range, from the lowest ground-shaking rumble of a pipe organ to the highest squeak of a stereo "tweeter." In comparison, a piano produces sounds from about 30 *hertz* (another term for cycles per second) to 4,600 hertz, and the human voice, from bass to soprano, only covers a range of 80 to 1,100 hertz. The 20,000-hertz maximum for humans seems high, but dogs, bats, cats, and other animals can hear sounds of much higher frequencies. Perhaps you have seen a "silent" dog whistle. These devices produce sounds above the limits of human sensitivity, but still within a dog's range, which may go as high as 40,000 or 50,000 hertz. A sound is actually present, but as far as a human is concerned, it doesn't exist.

Perceptual Defense and Subliminal Perception

Question: Wouldn't the absolute threshold be different for different people?

Absolute thresholds not only vary from person to person, they also vary from time to time for a single person. The nature of the stimulus, the state of one's nervous system, and the costs of false "detections"—all affect the absolute threshold. The threshold can be raised (**perceptual de-**

Table 4-1   Absolute Thresholds

Sensory modality	Absolute threshold
Vision	Candle flame seen at 30 miles on a clear dark night
Hearing	Tick of a watch under quiet conditions at 20 feet
Taste	1 teaspoon of sugar in 2 gallons of water
Smell	1 drop of perfume diffused into the entire volume of a three-room apartment.
Touch	A wing of a bee falling on your cheek from a distance of 1 centimeter.

(from Galanter, 1962)

fense) or lowered (perceptual vigilance) by any of these factors. For example, perceptual defense was isolated in a series of experiments performed on the recognition of "dirty" and "clean" words (McGinnies, 1949). So-called dirty words such as "whore," "rape," "bitch," and "penis" were briefly flashed on a screen. It was found that these words took longer than "clean" words such as "wharf," "rope," "batch," and "pencil" to be recognized correctly.

Question: Couldn't it be that people wanted to be really sure they had seen a word like "penis" before saying it?

Yes. For a number of years researchers worried about this and other flaws in the original experiment. But more recent research using careful procedures to rule out such objections suggests that perceptual defense does take place (Erdelyi, 1974). It is apparently possible to process information on more than one level, and to resist perceiving information that causes anxiety, discomfort, or embarrassment (Dember and Warm, 1979).

Question: Is this "subliminal" perception?

Basically yes. Anytime information is processed below the normal limen (LIE-men: threshold or limit) for awareness it is subliminal. In the late 1950s, the public was alarmed at reports of an "experiment" conducted by a commercial firm in a New Jersey motion-picture theater. During the showing of a regular movie, the words "Eat popcorn" and "Drink Coca-Cola" were flashed on the screen for 1/3000 second every five seconds. Since the words were presented so briefly, these "ads" were subliminal (below the normal threshold for vision). During the six weeks that the messages were flashed on the screen, the firm recorded an increase of 57.5 percent in popcorn sales and an 18.1 percent increase in Coca-Cola sales. In the uproar that followed, some states rushed to pass laws forbidding the "invisible sell." But since then, subliminal advertising has been shown to be ineffective, and no laws were actually ever passed (Anastasi, 1964). The original "experiment" failed to take into account such factors as weather conditions, the time of year, the particular films shown, the makeup of the audience, or display procedures at the snack bar. To appreciate the importance of such factors, think of the effect the movie *The Sahara Desert* could have on beverage sales!

Well-controlled laboratory experiments have shown that subliminal stimuli are basically weak stimuli. An advertiser would be better off using the loudest, clearest, most attention-demanding stimulus available—as most do. As psychologist Anne Anastasi puts it:

So far there is no evidence that weak stimuli exert more influence on behavior than do strong stimuli. . . . When weak stimuli are employed . . . the probability of *misperception* increases. The advertiser who hopefully flashes the words "Buy Tasty Tea" on a motion picture screen may find that many subjects actually perceive "Burn Trashy Ties"—a suggestion they may feel strongly tempted to accept when opening Christmas packages (Anastasi, 1964).

Difference Thresholds

Another kind of threshold studied in psychophysics is the difference threshold. Here we are asking the question, "How much must a stimulus *change* (increase or decrease) before it becomes *just noticeably different?*" The study of just noticeable differences (JNDs) led to the discovery of one of psychology's first natural "laws." Called *Weber's Law,* it can be roughly stated as: The amount of change in a stimulus needed to produce a JND is a constant *proportion* of the original stimulus intensity.

Question: What does this mean in practice?

Let's take an example. Pretend that you are sitting in a room in which there are 10 candles burning. Ten candles is the original stimulus intensity. Let's say that we begin lighting candles until the room becomes just noticeably brighter. If this takes 3 more candles, how many additional candles will we have to light in a room in which 20 candles are burning in order to cause a just noticeable increase in brightness? Your first guess may be 3, but remember, the JND is a *proportion.* We will have to light 6 candles if we start with 20; 9 if we start with 30; and 12 if we start with 40. Here are Weber's proportions for some common judgments:

Pitch	1/333 (one-third of 1 percent)
Weight	1/50
Loudness	1/10
Taste	1/5

Notice the big difference in auditory sensitivity (pitch and loudness) compared to taste. Very small changes in hearing are easy to detect. A voice or a musical instrument that is off pitch one-third of 1 percent will be noticeable. For taste, we find that a 20 percent change is necessary to produce a JND. If a cup of coffee has five teaspoons of sugar in it, one more (one-fifth of five) will have to be added before there is a noticeable increase in sweetness. It takes a lot of cooks to spoil the broth.

Weber's Law is really just an approximation because it applies mainly to stimuli in the midrange. For other than pure sensory judgments, it is even more approximate. In spite of this, there is a lesson to be learned from it. Consider judgments of money, for instance. If you discovered that you had been overcharged $5 on the purchase of a shirt, would you return to demand your money? If you discovered that you had been overcharged $5 on the purchase of an automobile, would you return to demand your money? If your answer to the first question is yes, then rationally your answer to the second should be too. It may not be, however, since the larger base price of a car makes $5 seem a very small difference.

Adaptation, Attention, and Gating— Tuning In and Tuning Out

Many sensory events never reach conscious awareness. One reason for this is *sensory adaptation*, a second is *selective attention*, and a third is *sensory gating*. Let's see how some information gets filtered out by these processes.

Sensory Adaptation   Think about walking into a house where fried fish, sauerkraut, and head cheese were prepared for dinner. (Some dinner!) You would probably pass out at the door, yet people who have been in the house for some time will be unaware of the food odors due to **sensory adaptation.** Sensory adaptation refers to a decrease in sensory response that accompanies a constant or unchanging stimulus. Fortunately, the olfactory (smell) receptors are among the most quickly adapting. When exposed to a constant odor, they send fewer and fewer nerve impulses to the brain until the odor is no longer noticed. Adaptation to sensations of pressure from a wristwatch, bra, waistband, or glasses is based on the same principle. Sensory receptors generally respond best to *changes* in stimulation. As neurobiologist David Hubel says, "We need above all to know about changes; no one wants or needs to be reminded 16 hours a day that his shoes are on." (Hubel, 1979).

Question: If change is necessary to prevent sensory adaptation, why doesn't vision undergo adaptation like the sense of smell does? If you stare at something, it certainly doesn't go away.

The rods and cones, like other receptor cells, would respond less to a constant stimulus were it not for the fact that the eye normally makes thousands of tiny movements every minute. These movements are caused by tremors in the eye muscles known as **physiological nystagmus.** Although they are too small to be seen, these movements shift visual images from one receptor cell to another. Constant shifting ensures that images always fall on fresh, unfatigued receptors. Evidence for this comes from experiments in which subjects are fitted with a special contact lens that has a miniature slide projector attached to it (see Fig. 4-16). Since

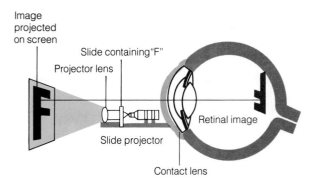

Fig. 4-16   *Stabilized image. Miniature slide projector attached to contact lens moves each time the eye moves. As a result, the projected image always falls on the same area of the retina. Under these conditions, the image disappears after a few seconds. (After Cornsweet, 1970.)*

the projector follows the exact movements of the eye, an image can be stabilized on the retina. When this is done, projected geometric designs fade from view within a few seconds (Pritchard, 1961).

Selective Attention   Also dependent on the functioning of sensory systems is the so-called seat-of-your-pants phenomenon. As you sit reading this chapter, receptors for touch and pressure in the seat of your pants are sending nerve impulses to your brain. Even though these sensations have been present all along, you were probably not aware of them until just now. The seat-of-your-pants phenomenon is an example of **selective attention.** We are able to "tune in on" any of the many sensory messages bombarding us while excluding others. Another familiar example of this is the "cocktail party effect." When you are in a group of people, surrounded by voices, you can still select out and attend to the voice of the person with whom you are conversing; or if that person gets dull, you can eavesdrop on conversations all over the room. (Be sure to smile and nod your head occasionally!)

Question: What makes this possible?

Selective attention appears to be based on a *central* (brain-centered) process of selecting sensory messages. But what about messages on their way to the brain? Is it possible that some are blocked, while others are allowed to pass? Recent evidence suggests there are **sensory gates** that control the flow of incoming nerve impulses in just this way.

Sensory Gating   A fascinating example of sensory gating is provided by the work of Ronald Melzack and Patrick Wall, who are studying "pain gates" in the spinal cord (Melzack and Dennis, 1978; Wall, 1976). Melzack and Wall noticed, as you may have, that one type of pain will sometimes block another. This suggests that pain messages from different nerve fibers pass through the same neurological "gate" in the spinal cord. If the gate is "closed" by one pain message, other messages may not be able to pass through.

Question: How is the gate closed?

Messages carried by large, fast nerve fibers seem to close the gate directly. In so doing, they prevent slower, "reminding system" pain from reaching the brain. Pain clinics use this effect by applying a mild electrical current to the skin. Such stimulation, at or just below the threshold of pain, can greatly reduce more agonizing pain (Melzack and Dennis, 1978).

Messages from small, slow fibers seem to take a different route. After going through the pain gate, they pass on to a "central biasing system" in the brain. Under some circumstances, the brain then sends a message back down the spinal cord, closing the pain gates (Melzack and Dennis, 1978). (See Fig. 4-17.) Melzack and Wall believe this type of

Fig. 4-17 *Diagram of a sensory gate for pain. A series of pain impulses going through the gate may prevent other pain messages from passing through. Or, pain messages may relay through a "central biasing mechanism" that exerts control over the gate, closing it to other impulses.*

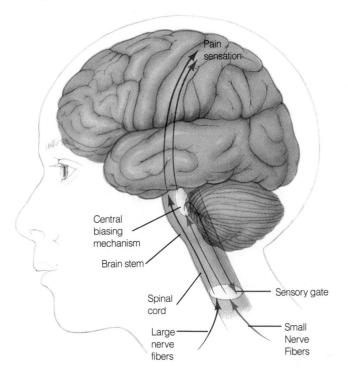

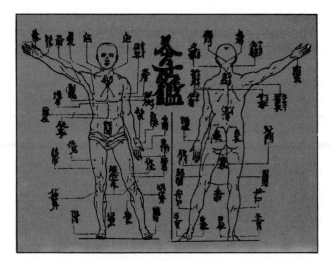

Fig. 4-18 *An acupuncturist's chart. Modern research has begun to explain the pain-killing effects of acupuncture. (See text.)*

gating explains the pain-killing effects of **acupuncture.** As the acupuncturist's needles are twirled, heated, or electrified, they activate small pain fibers. These relay through the biasing system to close the gates to intense or chronic pain.

Acupuncture has an interesting side effect not predicted by sensory gating. People undergoing acupuncture often report feelings of light-headedness, relaxation, or euphoria. How are these feelings explained? The answer seems to lie in the body's newly discovered ability to produce opiatelike chemicals. To combat pain, the brain releases a chemical called **beta-endorphin**[*] which is similar to morphine (Snyder and Childers, 1979). Both acupuncture and electrical stimulation cause a buildup of endorphins in the brain. In other words, the nervous system makes its own "drugs" to block pain. Actually, this ties in nicely with the idea of pain gates. The central biasing system, which closes pain gates in the spinal cord, is highly sensitive to morphine and other opiate pain killers (Melzack and Dennis, 1978).

The discovery of endorphins and their pain-killing effect has caused quite a stir in psychology. At long last, it appears possible to explain a number of puzzling phenomena, including runner's "high," masochism, acupuncture, and the euphoria sometimes associated with childbirth and painful initiation rites in primitive cultures. In each instance, there is reason to believe that pain and stress cause the brain to release endorphins. These, in turn, induce feelings of pleasure or euphoria similar to morphine intoxication (Cannon

[*]Endorphins belong to a larger class of brain chemicals known as *enkephalins.* Enkephalins are discussed in Chapter 3.

et al., 1978). The "high" often felt by long-distance runners serves as a good example of this effect. In one experiment, subjects were tested for pain tolerance. After running one mile, each was tested again. In the second test, all could withstand pain about 70 percent longer than before. The runners were then given naloxone, a drug that blocks the effects of endorphins. Following another mile run, the subjects were tested again. This time, they had lost their earlier protection from pain (Haier *et al.,* 1981). People who say they are "addicted" to running may be closer to the truth than they realize. And more importantly, we may at last have an explanation for those hardy souls who take hot saunas followed by cold showers!

Since you may not want to try acupuncture or electrical stimulation to control everyday pain, the "Applications" section that follows describes some practical ways of reducing pain. Before we turn to this useful topic, here's a "Learning Check."

_____ **Learning Check** _____

1. The minimum amount of stimulation necessary for a sensation to occur defines the _____

   _____.

2. A stimulus that causes discomfort or embarrassment may have to be viewed longer before it is perceived because of

   _____ _____.

3. Subliminal stimuli have been shown to have a powerful effect on the behavior of viewers, especially when embedded in movies.   T or F?

4. Sensory adaptation refers to an increase in sensory response that accompanies a constant or unchanging stimulus.   T or F?

5. The brain-centered ability to influence what sensations we will receive is called (circle):
   sensory gating   central adaptation   selective attention   sensory biasing

6. The pain-killing effects of acupuncture appear to result from sensory gating and the brain's production of beta-

   _____.

Answers: 1. absolute threshold   2. perceptual defense   3. F   4. F   5. selective attention   6. endorphin

_____ Resources Summary _____

● Sensory organs *transduce* physical energies into nerve impulses. Due to their limited responsiveness, selectivity, and *coding* patterns, the senses act as *data reduction systems.* Sensory response can be partially understood in terms of *localization of function* in the brain.

● The *somesthetic* senses include the *skin senses, vestibular senses,* and *kinesthetic senses.* The skin senses include touch, pressure, pain, cold, and warmth. Sensitivity to each is related to the number of receptors present.

● *Olfaction* (smell) and *gustation* (taste) are *chemical* senses responsive to airborne or liquified molecules. The *lock and key* theory partially explains smell. Specific areas on the tongue are more responsive to sweet, salty, sour, and bitter tastes.

● *Sound waves* are the stimulus for hearing. They are transduced by the *eardrum, auditory ossicles, oval window, cochlea,* and ultimately, the *hair cells.* Three basic types of deafness are: *nerve deafness, conduction deafness,* and *stimulation deafness.*

● Vision is such a dominant sense that it often *captures* other sensations. The *visible spectrum* consists of electromagnetic radiation in a narrow range. The eye is in some ways like a camera, but ultimately it is a visual system, not a photographic one.

● Four common visual defects, correctable with glasses, are *myopia* (nearsightedness), *hyperopia* (farsightedness), *presbyopia* (loss of accommodation), and *astigmatism.*

● The *rods* and *cones* are *photoreceptors* making up the *retina* of the eye. The rods specialize in night vision, black and white reception, and motion detection. The cones, found exclusively in the *fovea* and otherwise toward the middle of the eye, specialize in color vision, *acuity* or perception of fine detail, and daylight vision. Much *peripheral vision* is supplied by the rods.

● The rods and cones differ in color sensitivity. Yellowish-green is brightest for the cones; blue-green for the rods (although they will *see* it as colorless).

● Two major theories of color vision are the *trichromatic theory* which proposes three types of cones, and the *opponent-process theory,* which says there are three paired systems: red-green, yellow-blue, and black-white. There is evidence to support both theories, and evidence contradicting both.

● Total color blindness is rare, but 8 percent of males and 1 percent of females are red-green color blind or color weak. Color blindness is a sex-linked trait carried on the X chromosome. It is often passed from maternal grandfather to grandson by a mother who has normal color vision. Color blindness is revealed by the Ishihara test.

● *Dark adaptation,* an increase in sensitivity to light, is caused by increased concentration of visual pigments in both the rods and the cones, but mainly by recombination of *rhodopsin* in the rods. Vitamin A deficiencies may cause *night blindness.*

● The minimum amount of physical energy necessary to produce a sensation defines the *absolute threshold.* The amount of change necessary to produce a *just noticeable difference* in a stimulus defines a *difference threshold.* The study of thresholds and related topics is called *psychophysics.*

● Stimuli below the level of conscious awareness are said to be *subliminal.* Subliminal advertising is basically ineffective. Threatening or anxiety-provoking stimuli may raise the threshold for recognition, an effect called *perceptual defense; perceptual vigilance* may lower the threshold for recognition.

● Incoming sensations are affected by *sensory adaptation* (a reduction in the number of nerve impulses sent), by *selective attention* (selection and diversion of messages in the brain), and by *sensory gating* (blocking or modulation of messages flowing toward the brain). Selective gating of pain messages may take place in the spinal cord. Pain also is controlled by the brain's release of morphinelike chemicals called *endorphins.*

Applications

Controlling Pain

The "Resources" section of this chapter deals with useful information about several of the senses, particularly vision. Because so many applications have already been discussed, this will be a short section. Let's see if we can extend several of the ideas advanced in the chapter into an area of considerable interest: pain and its control.

There are many indications that pain may be controlled by psychological means. To treat incurable headaches, East African bush doctors perform an operation that would be unbearable for most of us. In this operation, the skull is exposed and scraped with a large knife—with no signs of pain from the patient. In India, fakirs pierce their cheeks with needles or sit on beds of spikes. In the South Seas, fire-walkers cross pits of hot coals barefoot. How is such insensitivity to pain achieved? There is no evidence that these people are lacking in pain responsiveness. Very likely the answer lies in four factors that can be used by anyone to influence the amount of pain produced by a particular stimulus. These are: (1) **anxiety;** (2) **attention;** (3) **control;** (4) **interpretation.**

Anxiety   The sensory message of pain can be separated from the emotional elements of pain (Melzack and Dennis, 1978). A consistent finding in studies of pain is that fear or high overall levels of anxiety increase pain (Barber, 1959). A dramatic reversal of this effect is the surprising insensitivity to pain displayed by soldiers wounded in battle. Being excused from further combat produces such relief that it leaves them insensitive to wounds that would agonize a civilian (Melzack, 1974).

Attention   Distraction can radically reduce pain. Think for instance of Joe Namath, former quarterback for the New York Jets, or Jerry West, one of the best shooters in professional basketball history. Both frequently performed with injuries that tormented them in daily life. Nevertheless, when they stepped into a game, pain faded from awareness as they were swept up in the action (Bresler and Trubo, 1979).

Pain, although it is an unusually persistent sensation, can be selectively "tuned out" (at least partially) just like any other sensation. Subjects in one experiment who were exposed to intense pain experienced the greatest pain

relief when they were distracted by the task of viewing color slides and describing them aloud. They experienced the most pain when they paid careful attention to the pain stimulus and described their moment-to-moment reactions to it (Kanfer and Goldfoot, 1966).

Control   Pain over which a person has no control is particularly upsetting. Loss of control seems to increase pain by increasing anxiety and emotional distress. People who are allowed to regulate, avoid, or control a painful stimulus suffer less (Craig, 1978). In general, the more control one *feels* over a painful stimulus, the less pain experienced (Staub *et al.,* 1971).

Interpretation   The meaning or interpretation given a painful stimulus also affects pain. For example, if you give a child a swat on the behind while playing, you'll probably get a burst of laughter. Yet the same swat given as punishment may bring tears. Childbirth provides a similar example. In some cultures, birth is considered a relatively painless natural event—which it usually is for women reared in such cultures. In our culture, childbirth tends to be associated with fear and stress (Bresler and Trubo, 1979). It's not surprising then, that painkillers are often required by women giving birth in the United States. The effects of interpretation have also been demonstrated in the lab. In one experiment, it was found that thinking of pain as pleasurable (denying the pain) greatly increased pain tolerance (Neufeld, 1970).

Pain Relief

Question: How can these facts be applied?

In a sense, they have already been applied to childbirth. "Natural" childbirth training, which emphasizes birth without drugs or painkillers, utilizes all four factors. In preparation for natural childbirth, the prospective mother learns in great detail what to expect at each stage of labor. This alleviates her fears and anxieties tremendously. During labor, she pays attention to important sensations indicating the progress of labor and adjusts her breathing accordingly. Her attention is directed to sensations other than pain. If she has learned a positive attitude toward all the

Applications

sensations of the birth, pain takes on a more positive meaning. Finally, because of her months of preparation and exercise and because of her active participation in the birth process, she feels *in control* of the situation.

Reduced anxiety, redirected attention, and added control can be applied to other painful circumstances. In any situation where pain can be anticipated (a trip to the doctor, dentist, and so on), lowered anxiety may be achieved by making sure that you are *fully informed.* Be sure that everything that will happen or could happen to you is explained, and fully discuss any fears you have. If you are physically tense, the use of relaxation exercises can help lower your level of arousal. (Relaxation techniques are described in detail in the Chapter 23 "Applications" section. The desensitization procedure described in the same chapter may also help reduce anxiety.)

Distraction   Some dentists are now equipped to help you shift attention away from pain. Patients are actively distracted with video games and headphones carrying music or "white" noise.* Some even put a clothespin on the patient's ear as a pain aid. In other situations, shifting attention away from pain can be aided by focusing on some external object. Pick a tree outside a window, a design on the wall, or some other stimulus and examine it in great detail. Prior practice in meditation can be a tremendous aid to such attention shifts. (Meditation techniques are described in Chapter 6.)

Cognitive Strategies   One way to make use of interpretation to lessen pain is to alter the way you think about painful experiences. Research shows that more pain can be tolerated when a person imagines pleasant events during the experience. Another strategy that works for some people, is to interpret a mildly painful event as a new and interesting experience. A third approach is to imagine

*"White" noise is made up of many frequencies. It sounds similar to a waterfall.

that the affected part of your body is numb or detached (Chaves and Barber, 1974).

Question: Is there any way to increase control over a painful stimulus?

Counterirritation   Practically speaking, the possibilities may be limited. You may be able to arrange a signal with a doctor or dentist that will give you control over whether a painful procedure will continue. A second possibility is more unusual. Ronald Melzack's gate-control theory of pain (mentioned earlier) suggests that sending *mild* pain messages to the spinal cord and brain may effectively close the neurological gates to more severe or unpredictable pain. Medical texts have long recognized this effect. Physicians have found that intense surface stimulation of the skin can control pain from other parts of the body, and that a brief, mildly painful stimulus can relieve more severe pain. Such procedures, known as **counterirritation,** are evident in some of the oldest techniques used to control pain: applying ice packs, hot-water bottles, or mustard packs to other parts of the body (Melzack, 1974).

This suggests a possibility for pain control that is based on increased control, counterirritation, and production of endorphins. If you pinch yourself, you can easily *create and endure* pain equal to that produced by many medical procedures (receiving an injection, having a tooth drilled, and so on). The pain doesn't seem too bad because you have control over it, and it is predictable. This fact might be used to *mask* one pain with a second painful stimulus that is under your control. For instance, if you are having a tooth filled, try pinching yourself, or digging a fingernail into a knuckle while the dentist is working. Focus your attention on the pain you are creating and increase its intensity anytime the dentist's work becomes more painful. This suggestion may not work for you, but casual observation suggests that it can be a useful technique for controlling pain in some circumstances. Generations of children have used it to take the edge off of a spanking.

Learning Check

1.   Like heightened anxiety, increased control has a tendency to increase subjective pain.   T or F?
2.   In one experiment, subjects given the task of viewing color slides and describing them aloud experienced less pain than subjects who paid attention to a pain stimulus.   T or F?
3.   Imagining a pleasant experience can be an effective way of reducing pain in some situations.   T or F?
4.   The concept of counterirritation holds that relaxation and desensitization are key elements of pain control.   T or F?

Answers: 1. F   2. T   3. T   4. F

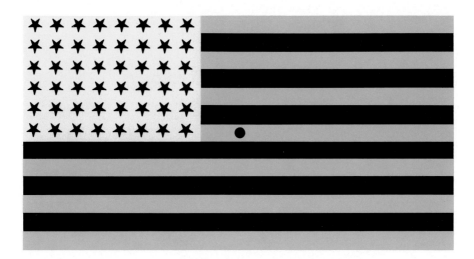

NEGATIVE AFTERIMAGES   Stare at the dot near the middle of the flag for at least 30 seconds. Then look immediately at the dot in the white space below the flag. You will see the American flag in its normal colors. Reduced sensitivity in yellow, green, and black receptors in the eye caused by prolonged staring results in the appearance of complementary colors. Project the afterimage of the flag on other (colored) surfaces to get additional effects.

●

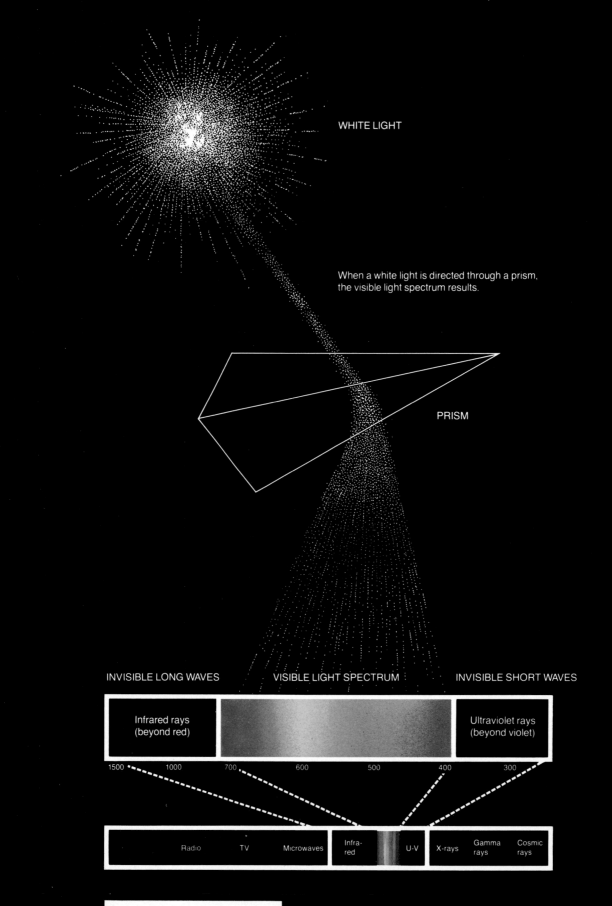

WHITE LIGHT

When a white light is directed through a prism, the visible light spectrum results.

PRISM

INVISIBLE LONG WAVES   VISIBLE LIGHT SPECTRUM   INVISIBLE SHORT WAVES

Infrared rays
(beyond red)

Ultraviolet rays
(beyond violet)

1500   1000   700   600   500   400   300

Radio   TV   Microwaves   Infra-red   U-V   X-rays   Gamma rays   Cosmic rays

Fig. 4-14 *The visible spectrum.*

ARE YOU COLOR BLIND?

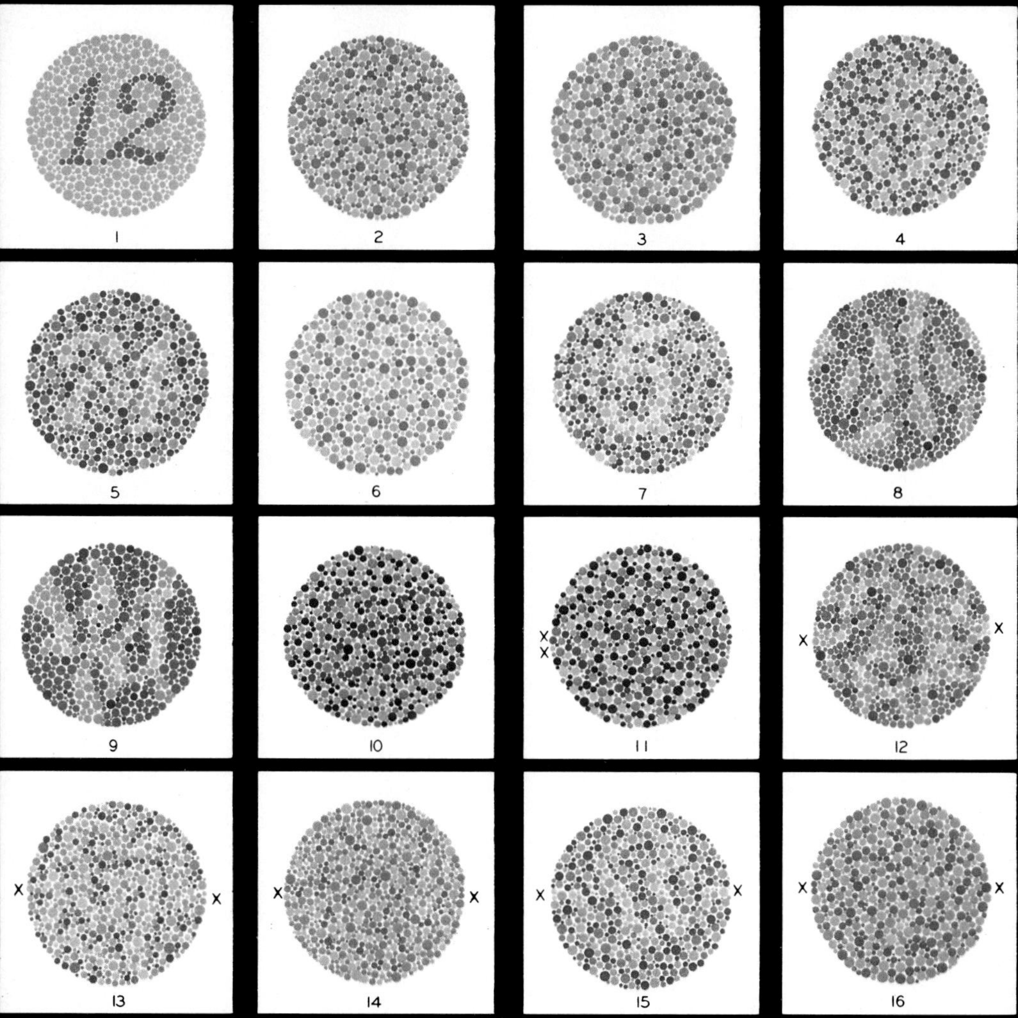

NO.	NORMAL EYE	COLOR BLIND EYE	NO.	NORMAL EYE	COLOR BLIND EYE
1	12	12	9	NOTHING	45
2	8	3	10	26	2 OR 6
3	29	70	11	2 LINES X TO X	LINE X TO X
4	5	2	12	NOTHING	LINE X TO X
5	74	21	13	LINE X TO X	NOTHING
6	45	NOTHING	14	LINE X TO X	NOTHING
7	5	NOTHING	15	LINE X TO X	NOTHING
8	NOTHING	5	16	LINE X TO X	LINE X TO X

Fig. 4-15 *Replica of a test for color blindness.*

SIMULTANEOUS CONTRAST   The blue areas in this figure are printed with the same color ink, but contrasting backgrounds make them look like different shades. (Inmont Corporation.)

RETINAL INTERACTIONS   You will see flickering gray spots between the blocks of this pattern. This is caused by the influence of activity in surrounding areas of the retina. (Inmont Corporation.)

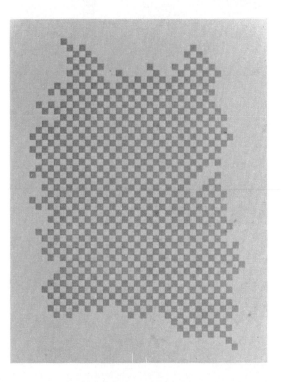

ADDITIVE FUSION OF COLOR   At normal reading distance, alternating squares of yellow and blue are seen. When viewed at a distance of 25 feet or more, the squares are fused into a uniform gray. This principle is sometimes used to blend colors in printing by mixing smaller dots of color. (Inmont Corporation.)

═══════ Exploration ═══════

Sensory Deprivation—Life on a Sensory Diet

Question: What would happen if sensations were prevented from reaching the brain?

A hint comes from reports by prisoners in solitary confinement, arctic explorers, high-altitude pilots, truck drivers, and radar operators. Under conditions of reduced or monotonous stimulation, these people have at times gone "stir crazy," showing dangerous lapses in awareness, bizarre sensations, and perceptual distortions. To find out why, D. O. Hebb and his associates paid volunteers $20 a day to undergo **sensory deprivation.** Subjects spent several days in a small cubicle. They wore goggles to prevent vision, gloves and cuffs to restrict touch, and listened to a constant "white" noise. Few endured more than two or three days of reduced stimulation without "pushing the panic button." Subjects lost track of time, had difficulty concentrating, and underwent a variety of perceptual changes (Heron, 1957).

Question: What sort of changes took place?

The most consistent disturbances after sensory deprivation are distortions in the appearance of colors, accentuation of visual illusions, slower reactions, and a brief warping of lines and space. On the positive side, hearing and touch sensitivity temporarily increase (Zubek, 1969b). (Wearing earplugs for a day might be an interesting prelude to attending a musical concert.)

A dramatic effect reported in early experiments was the occurrence of hallucinations. Subjects described seeing such things as cartoon characters and miniature spaceships in the isolation room. A subject in one experiment screamed in panic, "There is an animal having a long slender body with many legs. It's on the screen, crawling in back of me!" (Heron, 1957). Spurred by such reports, researchers by the score constructed an ingenious array of sensory deprivation environments and volunteers flocked to experiments in hopes of discovering a drugless "trip." Most were disappointed. We now know that true hallucinations rarely take place during sensory deprivation (Zubek, 1969b).

Question: But what about John Lilly's experiments?

The "Womb Tank"   John Lilly, M.D., who is better known for his work on communication with dolphins, pioneered the use of an unusual sensory deprivation environment. Subjects in Lilly's experiments wore a face mask with darkened goggles and floated naked in a tank of body-temperature water. As they drifted weightlessly in this womblike, "hypodynamic" environment, subjects were effectively cut off from smell, touch, vision, hearing, and taste sensations. Under these conditions—with essentially no sensations coming in—subjects often have vivid mental images. However, these are basically **hypnogogic images** (hip-no-GAH-jik), similar to those that occur when one is falling asleep, rather than hallucinations (Zubek, 1969b).

There is a certain fascination attached to sensory deprivation, perhaps because it promises to reveal something about the nature of "reality." Lilly and others have set up isolation tanks at their homes and a large number of people have taken their turn dissolving into "nothingness." For some, the experience is profound; others find it meaningless and boring. For his own part, Lilly has reported fantastic voyages in which he left his body, visited other dimensions, and was counseled by "beings of higher intelligence" (Lilly, 1972). His conclusion after years of work in the isolation tank is that: "What one believes to be true, either is true or becomes true in one's mind." Lilly found that each time he challenged or transcended his prior "programming" his tank experiences expanded into new mental realms.

Studies of sensory deprivation are helping psychologists understand brainwashing techniques, isolation at remote weather outposts, the after-effects of eye surgery, and problems of extended space flight. There may also be commonplace applications. For example, Peter Suedfeld at the University of British Columbia has found that sensory deprivation can help people who want to quit smoking. Those who begin with a sensory isolation session are much more likely to succeed. Suedfeld speculates that

---

Exploration

this procedure removes all cues for smoking and makes for a "clean break" with the habit (Suedfeld, 1980).

For our purposes, sensory deprivation experiments demonstrate again that sensation provides an essential link to the external world and a necessary basis for separating shared reality from internal images. Few people endure more than 10 hours in Lilly's isolation tank. How would it be to spend a lifetime on a "sensory diet"?

Questions for Discussion

1. Is your brain sitting on a laboratory table somewhere? It is theoretically possible that your brain was donated to science some time ago. Let's say that it was preserved and recently reactivated and that a sophisticated computer is artificially generating patterns of nerve activity in the cortex by mimicking normal sensory messages in the nerves. These messages duplicate all of the sights, sounds, odors, and sensations of sitting and reading a book. If this were happening—right now—could you tell? Would you be able to discover you had no body? Defend your answer.

2. William James once said, "If a master surgeon were to cross the auditory and optic nerves, then we would hear lightning and see thunder." Can you explain what James meant?

3. Let's say that you would like to design a system that uses touch to convey "images" to a blind person. How would you proceed? What would be the advantages and disadvantages of using various body areas (hands, back, forehead, and so on)?

4. What changes would be likely to take place if the absolute thresholds for vision and hearing were changed so that we could see infrared and ultraviolet light and hear sounds up to 50,000 cycles per second? (Consider lighting systems, the design of stereo equipment, and so forth.)

5. In Zen Buddhism there is a familiar *koan*, or riddle, that says, "Last night I dreamt I was a butterfly. How do I know today that I am not a butterfly dreaming I am a man?" Can you relate this to the idea that we construct a version of reality out of the more basic world of physical energies surrounding us?

6. Why do you think your voice sounds so different when you hear a tape recording of yourself speaking? (Hint: How else might vibrations from the voice reach the cochlea?)

Suggestions for Further Reading

Case, J. *Sensory Mechanisms.* Macmillan, 1967.
Casey, K. L. "Pain: A Current View of Neural Mechanisms," *American Scientist,* **61,** March-April, 1973.
Cornsweet, T. N. *Visual Perception.* Academic Press, 1970.
Geldard, R. F. *The Human Senses,* 2nd ed. Wiley, 1972.
Keller, H. *Story of My Life.* Airmont, 1970.
Lilly, J. C. *The Deep Self.* Warner Books, 1977.
Melzack, R. *The Puzzle of Pain.* Basic Books, 1973.
Mueller, C. G. *Sensory Psychology.* Prentice-Hall, 1965.
Senden, M. V. *Space and Sight.* Free Press, 1960.

5

Perception

━━━━━━━━━━ Chapter Preview ━━━━━━━━━━

Murder!

The following is a true account. Only the degree of exaggeration has been changed for educational purposes.

I was in a supermarket when a girl suddenly came running around a corner. She looked back and screamed, "Stop! Stop! You're killing him! You're killing my father!" Naturally I was interested! I dropped my things and hurried in the direction from which the girl had come. As I turned the corner, I was greeted by a grisly scene. There was a man stretched out on the floor with another on top of him. The guy on top was huge, at 6 feet 6 inches tall and 300 pounds, he looked only half human. He had his victim by the throat and was beating his head against the floor. There was blood everywhere. I decided to do the right thing. I ran . . . .

By the time the store manager and I returned to the "scene of the crime," the police were just arriving. It took quite a while to straighten things out, but here are the facts that emerged: The "guy on the bottom," had passed out and hit his head as he went down. This caused the cut (actually quite minor) that accounted for the "blood everywhere." The "guy on top" had seen the first man fall and was trying to prevent him from further injuring himself while unconscious. He was also loosening the man's collar.

If I had never returned, I would have sworn in court that I had seen a murder. This perhaps is understandable. But what I will never forget is the shock I felt when I met the "murderer"—the man I had seen a few moments before, in broad daylight, as a huge, vicious, horrible-looking creature. The man was not a stranger. He was a neighbor of mine. I had seen him dozens of times before. I know him by name. He is a rather small man.

Perception *is the process of assembling sensations into a usable mental representation of the world—something done so automatically we are rarely aware of it. It may, in fact, take misperceptions as drastic as that just described to call attention to this marvelous process. Perception creates faces, melodies, works of art, illusions, and on occasion, "murders" out of the raw material of sensation. Let us see how this is accomplished.*

Survey Questions   What are perceptual constancies and what is their role in perception? What basic principles do we use to group sensations into meaningful patterns? How is it possible to see depth and judge distance? What effect does learning have on perception? How is perception altered by motives, values, and expectations? How reliable are eyewitness reports? What is synesthesia?

Perceptual Constancies— Taming an Unruly World

What would it be like to have your vision restored after a lifetime of blindness? Would you weep for joy at the wondrous beauty around you? In reality, a first look at the world can be disappointing. Usually nothing more than a blur is seen.

A newly sighted person must *learn* to identify objects, to read clocks, numbers, and letters, and to judge sizes and distances (Senden, 1960). Indeed, learning to "*see*" can be quite frustrating. Richard Gregory (1970) has described the experiences of Mr. S. B., a 52-year-old cataract patient who had been blind since birth. After an operation restored his sight, Mr. S. B. struggled to make use of his vision. At first, for instance, he could only judge distance in situations already familiar to him. One day, he was found crawling out of his hospital room window to get a closer look at the automobile traffic on the street. His curiosity is understandable, but he had to be restrained. His room was on the fourth floor!

Question: How could Mr. S. B. try to crawl out of a fourth-story window? Couldn't he at least tell distance from the size of the cars?

No, because using size to judge distance requires familiarity with the usual appearance of objects. Try holding your left hand a few inches in front of your eyes and your right hand at arm's length. The image of your right hand should be about half the size of your left hand. Still, because of the countless times you have viewed your hands from different distances, you know your right hand has not shrunk. This is called **size constancy:** The perceived size of an object remains the same even though the size of its retinal image changes.

In order to perceive your hand accurately, you had to draw on past experience. Some perceptions—like seeing a line on a piece of paper—are so basic they seem to be **native** (inborn). But much perception is **empirical,** or based on prior experience (Julesz, 1975). For example, Turnbull (1961) tells of the time he brought a Pygmy from the dense rain forests of Africa to the vast African plains. The Pygmy had no past experience with seeing objects at great distance. Hence, the first time he saw a herd of buffalo in the distance, he thought they were a swarm of insects. When he was told that they were buffalo he was insulted. "Do you think that I am ignorant?" he asked. Imagine his confusion when he was then driven toward the animals. He concluded that witchcraft was being used to fool him because the "insects" seemed to grow into buffalo before his eyes. Perhaps you have also experienced the failure of size constancy in unfamiliar situations. When viewed from an airplane, cars, houses, and people no longer seem normal in size and tend to take on a "cardboard-figure" quality.

A second important constancy is **shape constancy.** Shape constancy can be demonstrated by looking at this page from directly overhead and then from an angle. Obviously, the page is rectangular, but most of the time the image actually reaching your eye is distorted. In spite of this, there is no tendency for you to assume the book changes shape when the image does. (For additional examples see Fig. 5-1.) If you sit front row, far left, in a movie theater, images on the screen will appear quite distorted. However, after a few minutes shape constancy returns and things look normal again. If you try this, note that human faces, in particular, would be almost unrecognizable were it not for shape constancy.

Let's say that you are outside in bright sunlight with a friend who is wearing a white blouse. Suddenly a cloud shades the sun. It might seem that the blouse would grow dimmer, but it still appears bright white. This happens because the blouse continues to reflect a larger *proportion* of light than surrounding objects. The principle of **brightness constancy** states that the apparent brightness of an object stays the same under changing lighting conditions. Brightness constancy applies only when objects are illuminated by the same amount of light. If a piece of gray paper is placed in bright sunlight, and a piece of white paper is placed beside it in deep shadow, the gray paper will look white, and the white paper will look gray. Try it!

To summarize, the energy patterns reaching our senses are constantly changing, even when they come from the same object. Size, shape, and brightness constancy rescue us from a potentially confusing world in which objects would seem to shrink and grow, change shape as if they were made of rubber, and light up or fade like neon lamps. It is no coincidence that this describes the perceptions of people who have been subjected to sensory deprivation, have recently had their sight restored, or have taken drugs like LSD or mescaline. For different reasons, each of these interrupts normal perceptual constancy. Establishing these constancies was only one of the hurdles Mr. S. B. faced in learning to "see." In the next section, we will consider some others.

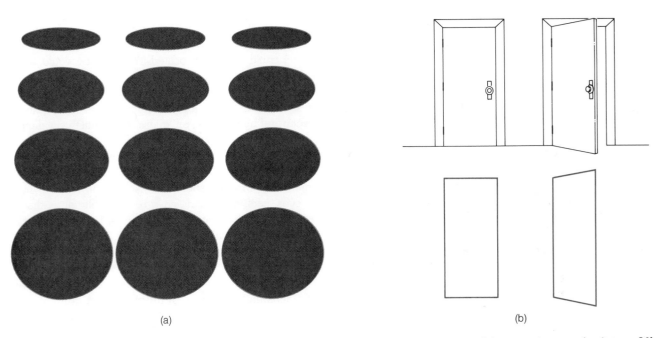

(a)

(b)

Fig. 5-1 *Shape constancy. (a) Do you see a flat design made up of different shapes, or a series of discs receding into the distance? If depth prevails, you have maintained shape constancy. (b) When the door is open, its image actually forms a trapezoid. It is perceived as a rectangle, anyway.*

Perceptual Grouping— Bringing Order to Chaos

William James said that "to the infant the world is just a big, booming, buzzing confusion." Like an infant, Mr. S. B. had to find meaning in his visual sensations. He was soon able to tell time from a large wall clock and to recognize block letters he had previously known only from touch. However, handwriting meant nothing to him for more than a year after his sight was restored. At a zoo he recognized an elephant from descriptions he had heard. But the first time he saw a lathe (a tool he was interested in) he was only able to identify a handle on the front, and then only when he had touched it.

Question: How are sensations organized into meaningful perceptions?

The simplest organization is to group sensations into an object or "figure" that stands out on a plainer background. **Figure-ground** organization is probably inborn, since it is the first perceptual ability to appear when a cataract patient regains sight (Hebb, 1949). In normal figure-ground perceptions, only one figure is seen. However, some patterns are reversible. In Fig. 5-2, it is equally possible to see either a wine glass figure on a dark background or two face pro-

files on a white background. As you shift from one possibility to the other, you should get a clear sense of what figure-ground organization means.

Question: What causes the formation of a "figure"?

The Gestalt psychologists studied this question in detail. Even if you were seeing for the first time, they concluded, the following factors would bring some order to your perceptions (see Fig. 5-3).

1. Nearness. Stimuli that are near each other tend to be grouped together (see Fig. 5-3a).

2. Similarity. "Birds of a feather flock together," and stimuli that are similar in size, shape, color, or form tend to be grouped together (see Fig. 5-3b).

3. Continuation, or continuity. Perceptions tend toward simplicity and continuity. In Fig. 5-3c it is easier to visualize a wavy line on a squared-off line than it is to see a complex row of shapes.

4. Closure. Closure refers to the tendency to *complete* a figure, so that it has a consistent overall form. Each of the drawings in Fig. 5-3d has one or more "gaps," yet each is perceived as a recognizable figure.

5. Contiguity. A principle that can't be shown in Fig. 5-3 is contiguity, or nearness in time *and* space. Contiguity is often responsible for the perception that one thing has

Fig. 5-2 *A reversible figure-ground design. Do you see two faces in profile or a wine glass?*

caused another (Michotte, 1963). A psychologist friend of the author's demonstrates this principle in class by knocking on his head with one hand while knocking on a wooden table (out of sight) with the other. The knocking sound is perfectly timed with the movements of his visible hand. This leads to the irresistible perception that his head is made of wood.

In addition to these principles, learning and past experience greatly affect perceptual organization. Contrast Mr. S. B.'s immediate recognition of letters to his inability to

read handwriting. Also, take a moment and look for the animal pictured in Fig. 5-4. If you had never seen the animal before, could you have located it? Mr. S. B. would have been at a total loss to find meaning in such a picture.

In a way, we are all detectives, seeking patterns in what we see. In this sense, a meaningful pattern represents a **perceptual hypothesis,** or "guess" held until the evidence contradicts it. Have you ever seen a "friend" in the distance, only to have the friend turn into a stranger as you drew closer? The fact that we usually guess right is due to a large *redundancy,* or duplication of sensory information. When the eyes, ears, nose, and sense of touch all tell us that a certain object or event exists, we can be fairly certain of it (Marks, 1978). Recall that when Mr. S. B. was unsure that he was seeing a "handle," his sense of touch removed all doubt.

The active nature of perceptual organization is perhaps most apparent in the case of **ambiguous stimuli** (stimuli allowing more than one interpretation). If you look at a cloud, you may discover dozens of ways to organize its contours into fanciful shapes and scenes. Even clearly defined stimuli may permit more than one interpretation. Stare at the design in Fig. 5-5 if you doubt the active and fluctuating nature of perception. Some designs present conflicting information, and thus defy consistent organization altogether. The tendency to make a three-dimensional object out of a drawing is frustrated by the "three-pronged widget" (Fig. 5-6), an **impossible figure.**

One of the most amazing feats of perceptual organization deserves a separate discussion. Our capacity to create three-dimensional space from two-dimensional images is explored in the next section.

Learning Check

Try these questions before reading more.

1.   Which of the following are subject to basic perceptual constancy? (circle)

figure-ground   size   ambiguity   brightness   continuity   closure   shape   nearness

2.   The first and most basic perceptual organization to emerge when sight is restored to a blind person is:

    a. continuity   *b.* nearness constancy
    c. recognition of numbers and letters   *d.* figure-ground

3.   At times, meaningful perceptual organization represents a _____ or "guess" held until the evidence contradicts it.

4.   Ambiguous figures have more than one meaningful organization.   T or F?

5.   The design known as Necker's cubes is a good example of an impossible figure.   T or F?

Answers: 1. size, brightness, shape 2. *d* 3. hypothesis 4. T 5. F

(a) *Principle of nearness.* Notice how differently a group of six can be perceptually organized, depending upon their spacing.

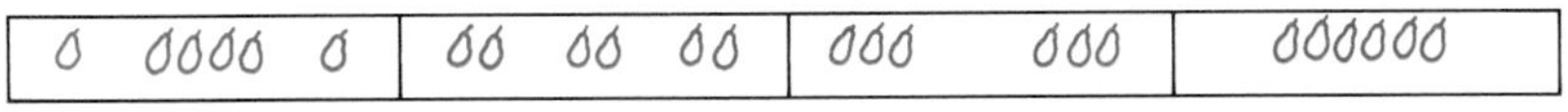

(b) *Principle of similarity.* In these examples, organization depends on similarity of form.

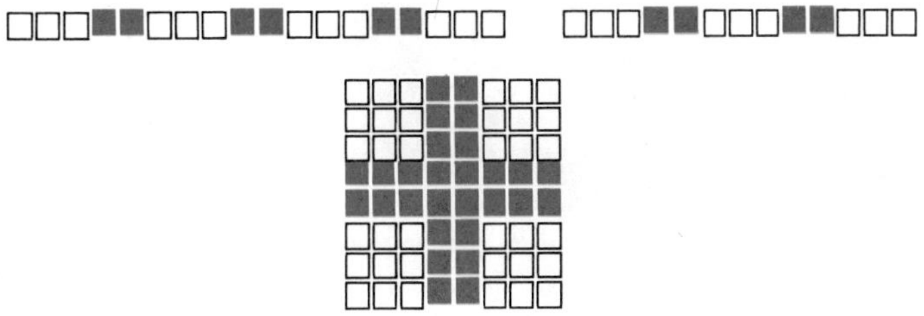

Similarity and nearness can be combined to produce new organization.

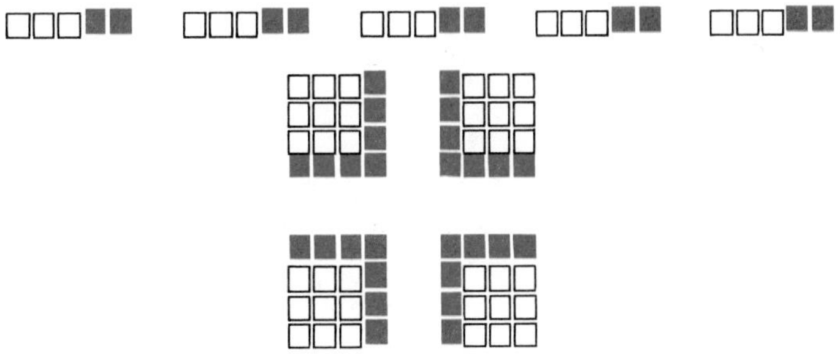

(c) *Principle of continuity.*

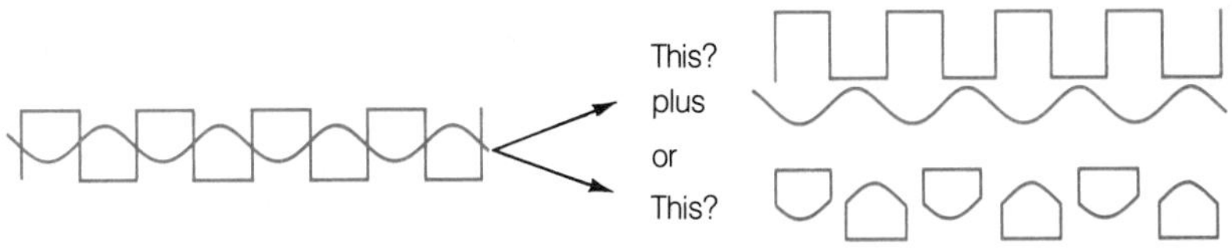

This?
plus
or
This?

(d) *Principle of closure*

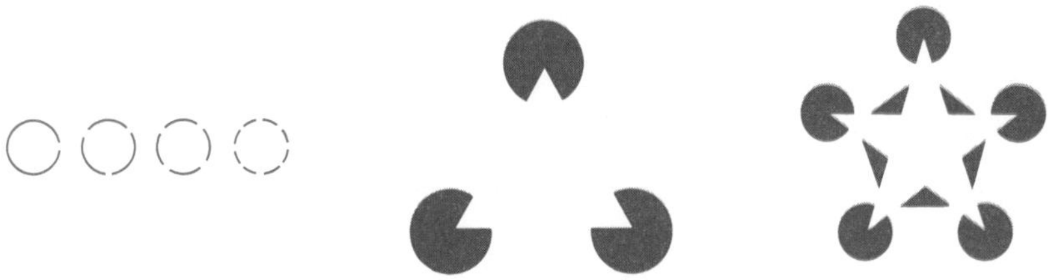

Fig. 5-3   *Perceptual grouping illustrations.*

Fig. 5-4 *An example of perceptual organization. Once the camouflaged animal becomes visible, it is almost impossible to view the picture again without seeing it.*

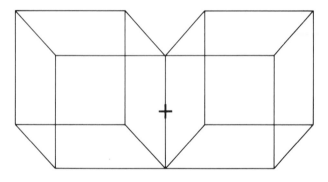

Fig. 5-5 *Necker's cubes. Visualize these as wire boxes. If you stare at the small cross, the cubes will change, sometimes projecting downward, then projecting upward.*

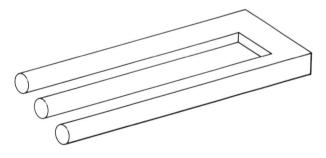

Fig. 5-6 *An impossible figure—the "three-pronged widget."*

Depth Perception— What If the World Were Flat?

Depth perception is the ability to see three-dimensional space and to accurately estimate distances. Without depth perception, you would be unable to successfully drive a car or ride a bicycle, play catch, shoot baskets, thread a needle, or simply navigate around a room. The world would look like a flat surface.

Question: Mr. S. B. had trouble with depth perception after his sight was restored. Does this mean that depth perception is learned?

Some psychologists ("nativists") hold that depth perception is inborn. Others (the "empiricists") view it as learned. Most likely, depth perception is partly learned and partly innate. Evidence of innate depth perception comes from work with the **visual cliff** (see Fig. 5-7). The visual cliff is basically a table covered with glass. On one side, there is a black- and red-checked surface directly beneath the glass. On the other side, the checked surface is 4 feet below. This makes the glass look like a tabletop on one side and a cliff, or drop-off, on the other.

To test for depth perception, six- to fourteen-month-old infants were placed in the middle of the visual cliff. This gave each baby a choice of crawling to the "shallow" side or the "deep" side. (The glass prevented them from falling if they chose the deep side.) The majority of infants chose the shallow side. In fact, most refused the deep side even when their mothers tried to call them toward it (Gibson and Walk, 1960). These results suggest that depth perception is inborn, but there is a catch. In order to be tested, infants must first be able to crawl. By the time they can, they may have *learned* to perceive depth. But other experiments with baby chicks, goats, and lambs—each of which can walk almost immediately—suggest that some depth perception is innate.

Question: Then why do some babies crawl off of tables or beds?

Being able to perceive depth and learning to fear it seem to be different things. Psychologist Joseph Campos reports that two- to five-month-old babies show no signs of fear when placed on the deep side of a visual cliff. However, as soon as infants become active crawlers they refuse to cross the deep side (Campos *et al.*, 1978). Undoubtedly, minor "crash-landings" add to the speed with which a fear of depth is learned.

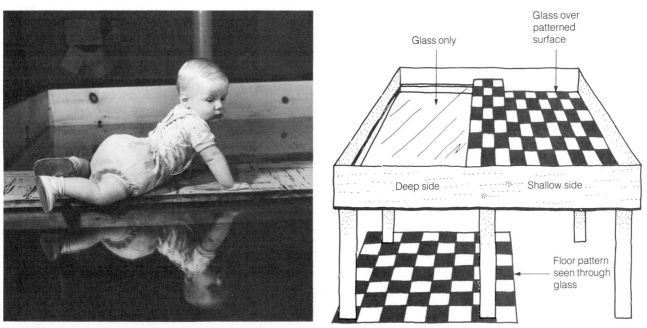

Fig. 5-7 *Human infants and newborn animals refuse to go over the edge of the visual cliff.*

Question: What factors allow us to see depth?

A number of **depth cues** combine to produce the experience of three-dimensional space. Some will work with just one eye **(monocular cues)**, while others require two eyes **(binocular cues).**

Bodily Cues   As their name implies, bodily cues are "built into" the visual system. One such cue is **accommodation.** You may recall from Chapter 4 that the lens in each eye must bend or bulge to focus nearby objects. In contrast, the lens relaxes for viewing distant objects. This process of accommodation takes place in both eyes, but it is actually a monocular depth cue. That is, a person with only one eye can use accommodation to judge depth. But how? Sensations coming from the muscles that support the lens are channeled back to the brain. Differences in these sensations help us to judge distances that fall within about 4 feet of the eyes. Beyond 4 feet, accommodation contributes little to depth perception. Obviously, accommodation is more important to a watchmaker and a person trying to thread a needle than it would be to a basketball player or an airline pilot.

A second bodily source of depth is **convergence,** a binocular cue. When you look at a distant object, the lines of vision from your eyes are parallel. When you look at some-thing 50 feet or less in distance, your eyes must converge (turn in) to focus the object (see Fig. 5-8).

You are probably not aware of it, but whenever you estimate a distance under 50 feet (as when you approach a stop sign, play catch, toss horseshoes, and so forth), you are using convergence. How? Again there is a relationship between muscle sensations and distance. Convergence is controlled by a group of muscles attached to the eyeball. These feed information on *eye position* to the brain to aid it in judging distance. You can feel convergence by exag-

Fig. 5-8   *The eyes must converge or turn in toward the nose to focus close objects.*

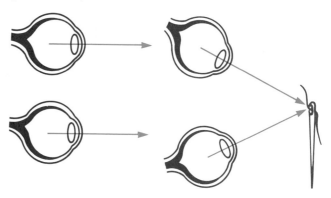

Fig. 5-9 *(a) Stereoscopic vision. (b) The photographs show what the right and left eye would see when viewing a vase. Hold a file card or small piece of paper (four or five inches tall) vertically between the two photos. Place the bridge of your nose on the card so that each eye sees only one photo. Relax your eyes until the vase fuses into one image. The third dimension appears like magic. (c) Now do the same with the random dot stereogram, but with your eyes eight or ten inches from the page. With luck you will see a diamond shape hovering over the background. (See text for explanation.) Some readers will not be able to get the effect without using a prism to perfectly fuse the right and left dot squares. (Julesz, 1971; reprinted by permission of the University of Chicago Press.)*

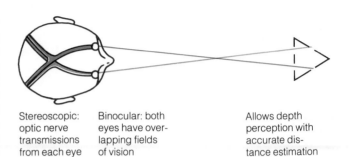

Stereoscopic: optic nerve transmissions from each eye are relayed to both sides of brain

Binocular: both eyes have over-lapping fields of vision

Allows depth perception with accurate dis-tance estimation

(a)

(b)   (c)

gerating it: Focus on your fingertip and bring it toward your eyes until they almost cross. At this point, you can feel sensations from the muscles that control eye movement.

The most important source of depth perception is **retinal disparity,** also a binocular cue. Retinal disparity is based upon the simple fact that the eyes are about two and one-half inches apart. Because of this, each eye receives a slightly different view of the world. When the resulting two images are *fused* into one overall visual image, a powerful sensation of depth occurs (see Fig. 5-9). Retinal disparity can be used to produce 3-D movies by filming with two cameras separated by several inches. The resulting images are simultaneously projected on a screen. The audience then wears glasses that filter out one of the images to each eye. Since each eye gets a separate image, normal **stereoscopic vision** is duplicated. Try this demonstration of retinal disparity and fusion:

Roll a piece of paper into a tube. Close your left eye. Hold the tube to your right eye like a telescope. Look through the tube at some object in the distance. Place your left hand against the tube halfway down its length and in front of your left eye. Now open your left eye. You should see a "hole" in your hand. You couldn't expect a professional photographer to do a better job of blending the two images than your visual system does automatically.

Question: How does retinal disparity produce depth?

Visual space represents more than a blending of two images. In Fig. 5-9c, you will find two squares of random dots, free of lines, contours, or patterns. When these "random dot stereograms" are properly viewed (one to each eye), a center area seems to float above the background. Researcher Bela Julesz created the designs to show that the brain is very sensitive to any **mismatch** of information from the eyes. In this situation, depth comes from shifting dots in one square so the center areas of the squares do not quite match (Julesz, 1971; Ross, 1976). To a large extent then, three-dimensional space is woven from countless tiny differences between what the right and left eyes see.

Seeing in "stereo" also has other advantages. For example, our sensitivity to disparity can be used to detect counterfeit money. A fake bill, especially a good one, is more easily detected when it is viewed by one eye and fused with the image of a real bill. This sets up a "rivalry" between the two images that is easily noticed. Similarly, stereoscopic aerial photos reveal camouflaged areas that would be invisible in a single photograph (Bloomer, 1976).

Question: If disparity is so important, can a person with one eye perceive depth?

A one-eyed person lacks convergence and retinal disparity, and accommodation is only helpful for judging small distances. This means that a person with only one eye will have restricted depth perception. Try driving a car or riding a bicycle some time with one eye closed. You will find yourself braking too soon or too late, and you will have difficulty estimating your speed. In spite of this, you will be able to drive, although with greater difficulty than usual. A person with one eye can even successfully land an airplane—a task strongly dependent on depth perception.

Pictorial Cues for Depth— Three Dimensions from Two

A good movie, painting, or photograph can give a convincing sensation of depth where none exists, and as noted, a one-eyed person can learn to accurately gauge depth.

Question: How is the illusion of depth created on a two-dimensional surface, and how is it possible to judge depth with one eye?

The answer in each case lies in the **pictorial depth cues,** all of which are monocular. The reason the cues work is that they contain much of the information present when a person looks at a real three-dimensional scene (Haber, 1980). To understand how pictorial cues create an illusion of depth, imagine that you are looking outdoors through a window. If you traced everything you saw through the window onto the glass, you would have an excellent drawing, with a convincing sense of depth. If we then analyzed what was on the glass, we would find the following features.

Pictorial Depth Cues

1.   Linear perspective. This refers to the apparent convergence of parallel lines in the environment. If you stand between two railroad tracks, they appear to come together in the distance. Since you know they are parallel, this implies great depth (see Fig. 5-10).

2.   Relative size. If an artist wishes to depict two objects of the same size at different distances, the artist makes the more distant object smaller (see Fig. 5-11). The movies *2001* and *Star Wars* created sensational feelings of depth through rapid changes in the images of planets, space stations, and starships.

3.   Light and shadow. Most objects in the environment are lighted in such a way as to create definite patterns of light and shadow. Appropriate distribution of light and shadow can give a two-dimensional design a three-dimensional feeling (see Fig. 5-12).

4.   Overlap. Overlap (also known as interposition) describes a depth cue caused by one object partially blocking the view of another. Hold your hands up and have a friend try to tell from across the room which is nearer. Relative size will give him the answer if the difference between the two hands is large. But if one is only slightly closer to him than the other, he may have difficulty—until you slide one hand in front of the other. Overlap then removes any doubt (see Fig. 5-13).

5.   Texture gradients. Changes in texture also contribute to depth perception. If you are standing in the middle of a cobblestone street, the street looks coarse near your feet, but the texture of the stones gets smaller and finer as you look off into the distance (see Fig. 5-14). To enhance the perception of speed and depth, highway engineers sometimes paint stripes across freeway offramps and on the roadway in front of toll booths.

6.   Aerial perspective. Smog, fog, dust, and haze add to the apparent distance of an object. Objects seen at great distance tend to be hazy, a washed-out color, and lacking in detail due to aerial perspective. This is true even in clear air but is increasingly the case in our industrialized society. As a matter of fact, aerial haze is often most noticeable when it is missing. If you have traveled the wide open spaces of states such as Colorado or Wyoming, you may have seen mountain ranges that looked only a few miles away, and then were shocked to find that you were actually viewing them through 50 miles of crystal-clear air.

7.   Relative motion. Relative motion, also known as *motion parallax,* can be seen by looking out a window and moving your head from side to side. You will notice that objects near you appear to move a sizable distance as your

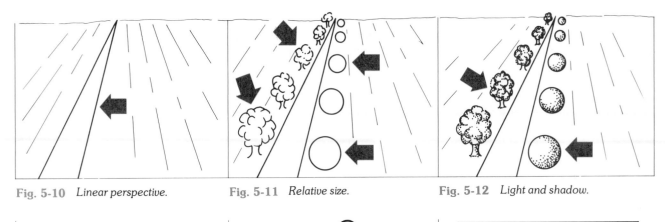

Fig. 5-10 *Linear perspective.*   Fig. 5-11 *Relative size.*   Fig. 5-12 *Light and shadow.*

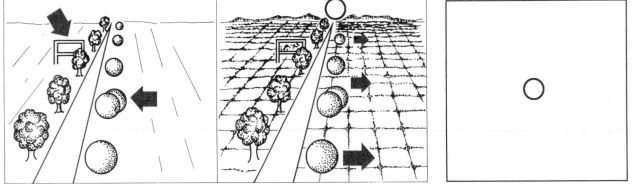

Fig. 5-13 *Overlap.*   Fig. 5-14 *Texture gradients.*

head moves. Trees, houses, and telephone poles at a greater distance appear to move slightly in relation to the background, and distant objects like hills, mountains, or clouds don't seem to move at all. When you are riding in a car, motion parallax takes another form: The next time you drive, notice that objects near the roadside appear to sweep backward, whereas distant mountains or hills appear to move forward with you.

When combined, pictorial cues can create a powerful illusion of depth (see Fig. 5-15).

Question: Is motion parallax really a "pictorial" cue?

Strictly speaking it is not (except in the case of movies, television, and cartoons) because it requires movement. However, when it is present, depth almost always prevails. Much of the realistic depth in a good movie comes from motion parallax captured by the camera and transferred to the screen. People who have lost vision in one eye depend heavily on motion parallax to improve their remaining depth perception. Often, they adopt more frequent head and eye movements to maximize relative motion. Cartoon

animators must also be concerned with motion parallax. Animations like the Disney classic, *Bambi,* used several "layers" of background scenery shifted at different rates during filming.

An ability to use pictorial depth cues would seem so natural as to require no prior learning. This is not entirely the case, however. Studies of people in various cultures show differences in the way pictures are interpreted (Deregowski, 1972). Researcher William Hudson has tested members of remote tribes who are completely unfamiliar with pictorial cues for depth. These people see simplified drawings as two-dimensional designs (see Fig. 5-16).

Question: How do the depth perception cues relate to daily experience?

The Moon Illusion   Like the bodily depth cues, you constantly use the pictorial cues to gauge depth and judge distances. This can be seen through an intriguing illusion. When the moon is on the horizon, it tends to look as large as a silver dollar. When it is directly overhead, it looks like a dime, very much smaller than it did earlier the same eve-

Fig. 5-15 *Pictorial depth. Look closely! How has the artist used cues to imply depth and to fool the eye? M. C. Escher,* Still Life and Street. *© Beeldrecht, Amsterdam/VAGA, New York, 1981. Collection Haags, Gemeentemuseum—The Hague. Reproduced by permission.*

Fig. 5-16 *A Hudson test picture. Two-dimensional perceivers assume the hunter is trying to spear the distant elephant rather than the nearby antelope. Some acquaintance with conventions for representing depth in pictures and photographs seems necessary. (From "Pictorial Perception and Culture" by J. B. Deregowski. Copyright © 1972 by Scientific American, Inc. All rights reserved.)*

ning. Contrary to what some people believe, the moon's image is not magnified. If you take a photograph of the moon and measure its image, you will find that it does not change size on the horizon. But the moon *looks* larger when it's low in the sky. This is because the **apparent distance** of the moon is greater when it is on the horizon than when it is overhead.

Question: But if it seems farther away shouldn't it appear smaller?

No, the idea is that there is an absence of depth cues when the moon is overhead. In contrast, the moon is seen behind houses, trees, telephone poles, and mountains when it is on the horizon. These objects add numerous depth cues, which cause the horizon to seem more distant than the sky overhead (Dember and Warm, 1979).

Size-Distance Invariance   To better understand the moon illusion, picture two balloons, one 10 feet away, and the second, 20 feet away. Suppose the more distant bal-

loon is inflated until its image matches that of the nearer balloon. How do we know the more distant balloon is larger? Because it makes the same size image as a balloon that is obviously closer. Formally, this relationship is known as **size-distance invariance:** If two objects form identical images, but one is more distant, the more distant object must be larger.

The preceding ideas apply to the moon illusion in this way: The moon makes the same size image on the horizon as it does overhead. But the horizon seems more distant. Consequently, the horizon moon must be perceived as larger (Rock, 1962). You can prove this to yourself by removing the normal depth cues present when you look at a "harvest moon." Try looking at the moon through a rolled-up paper tube, or make your hands into a "telescope" and look at the next large moon you see. It will immediately "shrink" when viewed without depth cues. To a degree, the moon illusion can even occur in a drawing. Return to Fig. 5-14 and compare the moon in the drawing with the circle to its right. Both circles are the same size, but the "moon" viewed with depth cues should look slightly larger.

Learning Check

If you have difficulty with any of these questions, skim back over the previous material.

1. The visual cliff uses random dot stereograms to test for depth perception.   T or F?

2. Write a "B" or an "M" after each of the following to indicate if it is a binocular or monocular depth cue.
    accommodation _____   convergence _____
    retinal disparity _____   linear perspective _____
    motion parallax _____

3. List one bodily cue for depth perception: _____

4. Depth can be seen in the absence of distinct lines, contours, or patterns if a mismatch of images to the two eyes is arranged.
    T or F?

5. Interpretation of pictorial depth cues requires little or no prior experience.   T or F?

6. The moon's image is greatly magnified by the atmosphere near the horizon.   T or F?

Answers: 1. F   2. accommodation (M), convergence (B), retinal disparity (B), linear perspective (M), motion parallax (M)   3. accommodation, convergence, or retinal disparity   4. T   5. F   6. F

Perceptual Learning— What If the World Were Upside Down?

There is a story, perhaps fictional, about a visit to the London symphony made by a diplomat from India. According to the story, the diplomat, to his great embarrassment, began clapping loudly after the orchestra finished tuning up. The point of this anecdote is that learning has a powerful impact on perception, something we have already seen in several ways.

Question: How does learning affect perception?

Perceptual Habits   One way is through established patterns of organization and attention, referred to as **perceptual habits.** Stop for a moment and read aloud the short phrase in Fig. 5-17. Did you read "Paris in the spring"? If so, look again. The word "the" appears twice in the phrase. Because of past experience with the English language, the repeated word is frequently overlooked. Language experi-

ence also affects organization of the design pictured in Fig. 5-18. Notice as well that:

It is quite difficult to read inverted print after years of practice reading words in their proper orientation.

An experienced printer would probably have less trouble reading the inverted lines than you did.

Magicians make use of perceptual habits when they use sleight of hand to distract an observer while performing a trick. Another kind of "magic" is related to consistency in the environment. It is usually safe to assume that the overall shape of a room is approximately that of a simple box. This need not be true, however. A decidedly lopsided room can be made to appear square by carefully distorting the proportions of the walls, floor, ceiling, and windows. One such room, called an **Ames room** after the man who designed it, presents a unique problem for the perceptual habits and organization of an observer.

Since the left corner of the Ames room is farther from

Fig. 5-17

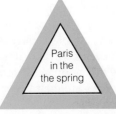

Fig. 5-18   *What do you see here?*

Fig. 5-19 *The Ames room. From the front, the room looks normal; actually, the right-hand corner is very short, and the left-hand corner is very tall. In addition, the left side of the room slants away from viewers. The diagram shows the shape of the room and reveals why people appear to get bigger as they cross the room toward the nearer, shorter right corner.*

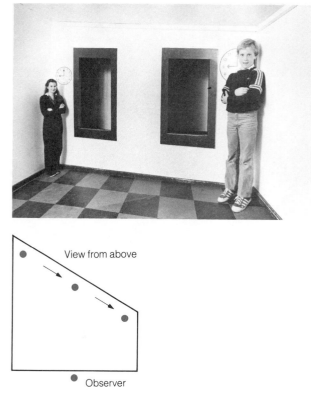

a viewer than the right, a person standing in that corner looks very small, whereas one standing in the right corner looks very large (see Fig. 5-19). If a person walks from the left corner of the room to the right, an observer is faced with maintaining shape constancy by perceiving the room as square, or maintaining size constancy by refusing to see the person "grow." Most people choose shape constancy and see people "shrink" and "grow" before their eyes.

Perceptual learning seems to program the brain for sensitivity to important **features** of the environment. Colin Blakemore and Graham Cooper of Cambridge University raised kittens in rooms with only vertical stripes or horizontal stripes on the walls. When returned to normal environments, the "horizontal" cats could easily jump onto a chair; but when walking on the floor they repeatedly bumped into chair legs. "Vertical" cats, on the other hand, had no difficulty avoiding chair legs, but they missed when trying to jump to horizontal surfaces. The cats reared with vertical stripes were "blind" to horizontal lines, and the "horizontal" cats acted as if vertical lines were invisible (Lewin, 1974). Other experiments show that there is a decrease in brain cells tuned to the missing features (Grobstein and Chow, 1975).

Question: Would it be possible, then, for an adult to adapt to a completely new perceptual world?

Inverted Vision   An answer is offered by experiments in which people have worn lenses that invert visual images. In one such experiment, a subject donned goggles that turned the world upside down and reversed objects from right to left. At first, even the simplest tasks—walking, eating, and so forth—became incredibly difficult. Imagine trying to reach for a door handle and watching your hand shoot off in the wrong direction.

Subjects also reported that head movements made the world swing violently through space, causing severe headaches and nausea. Yet, incredible as it may seem, they eventually adapted to inverted vision. Their success is related to superior human learning abilities. When the eyes of goldfish are surgically turned upside down, the fish swim in circles and rarely adapt (Sperry, 1956).

Question: Did everything turn upright again for the humans?

No. Their visual images remained inverted, but subjects regained ability to perform most routine activities, and their

Fig. 5-20 *Inverted vision. Adaptation to complete inversion of the visual world is possible, but challenging.*

Fig. 5-21 *Are the center dots in both figures the same?*

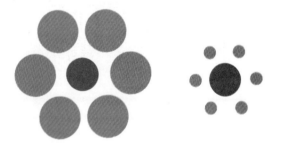

Fig. 5-22 *Context alters the meaning of the middle figure.*

A
12 13 14
C

upside-down world began to seem normal. In fact, when the goggles were removed they became completely disoriented again (Stratton, 1897).

In more recent experiments, subjects wearing inverting lenses have successfully driven cars, and one subject even flew an airplane after a few weeks of adaptation (Kohler, 1962). These feats are the equivalent of driving or flying upside down and backwards. Some ride! **Active movement** in a new visual world seems to be a key element in these adaptations. In one experiment, people wore prismatic glasses that grossly distort vision. Those who walked on their own adapted more quickly than subjects pushed around in a wheeled cart (Held, 1971). Other research shows that at least some adaptation occurs no matter how greatly vision is distorted (Welch, 1978). Such findings are a powerful indication of our capacity for perceptual learning.

Adaptation Level An important factor affecting perception is the **context** in which a stimulus is judged. For example, a man 6 feet in height will look "tall" when surrounded by others of average height, and "short" among a group of professional basketball players. In Fig. 5-21, the center circle is the same size in both designs, but like the man in different company, the circle takes on a different apparent size depending on context. The importance of context is also shown by Fig. 5-22. What do you see in the middle? If you read across, context causes it to be organized as a "13." Reading down makes it a "B."

In addition to external contexts, we all have internal **frames of reference,** or standards by which stimuli are judged. If you were asked to lift a 10-pound weight, would you label it "light," "medium," or "heavy"? The answer to this question depends on what Harry Helson (1964) calls your **adaptation level.** This is your own personal "medium point," or frame of reference. Each person's adaptation level is constantly modified by experience. If most of the weights you lift in day-to-day life *average* around 10 pounds, you will call a 10-pound weight "medium." If you are a watchmaker and spend your days lifting tiny watch parts, you will probably call a 10-pound weight "heavy." If you work as a furniture mover, your adaptation level will exceed 10 pounds, and you will call a 10-pound weight "light."

An indication of how broadly one's frame of reference affects judgments can be found in a study that asked people: "What is middle age?" A group of 10-year-olds said that "middle age" is 36. Adults in their early twenties set "middle age" at 42, and a group of 70-year-olds said 52 (Rethlingshafer and Hinckley, 1963)! Which is closest to your adaptation level?

Illusions   Perceptual learning is responsible for a number of **illusions.** In an illusion, length, position, motion, curvature, or direction is consistently misjudged (Gillam, 1980). Illusions differ from **hallucinations** in that illusions distort stimuli that actually exist. People who are hallucinating perceive objects or events that have no external reality (for example, they hear "voices" that are not there). If you think you see a 3-foot-tall butterfly, you can confirm you are hallucinating by trying to touch its wings. To detect an illusion, it is often necessary to measure a drawing or apply a straight-edge to it.

Illusions offer a fascinating challenge to our understanding of perception. On occasion, they also have practical significance. An illusion called **stroboscopic movement** is responsible for putting the "motion" in motion pictures. The strobe lights sometimes used on dance floors reverse this illusion. Each time the strobe flashes a dancer is "frozen" in a particular position. However, if the flashes are speeded up sufficiently, normal motion is seen. In a similar way, movies project a series of rapid "snap-shots" on the screen, so the gaps in motion are imperceptible.

Question: Can other illusions be explained?

Not in all cases, or to everyone's satisfaction. Generally speaking, size and shape constancy, habitual eye movements, continuity, and perceptual habits combine in various ways to produce the illusions in Fig. 5-23. Rather than attempt to explain all of the pictured illusions, let's focus on one "simple" example. The **Müller-Lyer illusion** (illusion *a*) causes the horizontal line with "arrowheads" to appear shorter than the line with "Vs" on each end. A quick measurement will show that they are the same length. How can we explain this illusion? Evidence suggests it is based upon a lifetime of experience with the edges and corners of rooms and buildings. Richard Gregory (1977) believes you see the horizontal line with the "Vs" as if it were the corner of a room viewed from inside. (See illustration.) The line with "arrowheads," on the other hand, suggests the corner of a room or building seen from outside (see Fig. 5-24).

Earlier, we used size-distance invariance to explain the moon illusion. Gregory believes the same concept explains the Müller-Lyer illusion. Thus, if the V-tipped line looks farther away than the arrowhead-tipped line, you must compensate by seeing the V-tipped line as larger. This explanation of the Müller-Lyer illusion presumes that you have had years of experience with straight lines, sharp edges, and corners—a pretty safe assumption in our culture.

Question: Is there any way to show that past experience causes this illusion?

If we could test someone who saw only curves and wavy lines as a child, we would know if experience with a "square"

Fig. 5-23   *Some interesting perceptual illusions.*

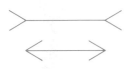

(a) Which of the horizontal lines is longer

(b) Is the diagonal line straight? Check it with a ruler.

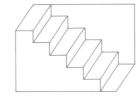

(c) Is this a drawing of a staircase descending from upper left to lower right . . . or is it the view of the underneath of a staircase from lower right to upper left?

(d) Are these lines parallel? Cover some of the slash marks to see.

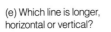

(e) Which line is longer, horizontal or vertical?

(f) Notice how the background distorts the square.

(g) Which quadrilateral is larger?

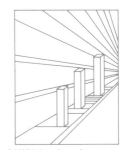

(h) Which column is shortest? Which is longest.

Fig. 5-24 *Why does line (b) in the Müller-Lyer illusion look longer than line (a)? Probably because it looks more like a distant corner than a nearer one. Since the vertical lines form images of the same length, the more "distant" line must be perceived as larger.*

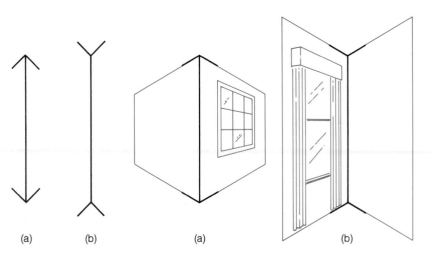

(a)   (b)   (a)   (b)

culture is important. Fortunately, in South Africa there is a tribe of people, the Zulus, who live in a "round" culture. In their daily lives, Zulus rarely encounter a straight line: Huts are shaped like rounded mounds and arranged in a circle, fields are plowed in curved lines, tools and toys lack straight edges, and there are no straight roads, square buildings, or edges.

Question: What happens if a Zulu looks at the Müller-Lyer design?

The typical Zulu does not experience the illusion. At most, he or she sees the V-shaped line as *slightly* longer than the other. This confirms the importance of past experience and perceptual habits in determining our view of the world.

Learning Check

1. Perceptual habits may become so ingrained that they lead us to distort or misperceive a stimulus.   T or F?

2. Perceptual learning seems to program the brain for sensitivity to important _____ of the environment.

3. The Ames room is used to test for adaptation to inverted vision.   T or F?

4. An important factor in adaptation to inverted vision is:

   a. learning new categories   b. active movement
   c. overcoming illusions   d. the stroboscopic movement effect

5. Size-distance relationships appear to underlie the _____ illusion.

   a. stroboscopic b. stair case c. horizontal-vertical d. Müller-Lyer

6. An adaptation level represents a personal "medium point" or internal _____ .

Answers: 1. T 2. features 3. F 4. b 5. d 6. frame of reference

Motives and Perception— May I Have Your . . . Attention!

You are being bombarded by sights, sounds, odors, tastes, and tactile sensations. Which are you aware of? The first stage of perception is *attention*—selection of incoming messages.

Attention Very *intense* stimuli are attention-getting. Stimuli that are brighter, louder, or larger tend to capture attention: A gunshot in a library would be hard to ignore. Big, bright cars probably get more tickets than small, dull ones. Sportscaster Howard Cosell has made a career out of the first principle of attention.

Repetitious stimuli, repetitious stimuli, repetitious stimuli, repetitious stimuli, repetitious stimuli, repetitious stimuli are also attention-getting. A dripping faucet at night makes little noise by normal standards, but because of repetition it may become as attention-getting as a single sound many times louder.

ATTENTION IS ALSO FREQUENTLY RELATED TO *contrast* OR *change* IN STIMULATION. Change is perhaps the most basic source of attention. We quickly **habituate** (respond less) to an unchanging stimulus.

Question: How does habituation differ from sensory adaptation?

Habituation   As described in Chapter 4, *adaptation* decreases the actual number of sensory messages sent to the brain. Messages that reach the brain are selected by attention. Next, the body makes a sort of "What is it?" reaction known as the **orientation response** (OR). An OR is characterized by enlarged pupils, brain-wave changes, a short pause in breathing, increased blood flow to the head, and turning to face the stimulus (Dember and Warm, 1979). If you have ever seen someone do a "double-take," you have observed an orientation response. Now, think about what happens when you buy a new record album. At first, the album holds your attention all the way through. But when the album becomes "old," a whole side may play without your really hearing it. When a stimulus is repeated without change, the OR **habituates,** or decreases. Perhaps you have also noticed that you habituate to scenery along a familiar drive to work or school. Only when a house is painted, a tree removed, or a billboard changed is attention aroused again (Ornstein, 1972).

Motives   Motives also play a role in attention. If you are riding in a car and are hungry, you will notice restaurants and billboards picturing food. If you are running low on gas, your attention will shift to gas stations. Advertisers, of course, know that their pitch will be more effective if it gets your attention. Ads are therefore loud, repetitious, and intentionally irritating. They are also designed to take advantage of two motives that are widespread in our society: *anxiety* and *sex*. Everything from mouth wash to automobile tires is merchandised using sex as a source of attention. For instance, a recent ad for Triple Sec liqueur ran in national magazines under the heading "Sec's Appeal." Another liquor ad shows a woman in a seductive velvet dress and says, "Feel the velvet." And what could be more obvious than ads for designer jeans that feature a shapely posterior pointed at the camera? Other ads combine sex with anxiety. Mouth wash, deodorant, soaps, toothpaste, and countless other articles are pushed in ads that play on desires to be attractive, or have "sex appeal," and to avoid embarrassment.

In addition to directing attention, motives may alter what is perceived:

As part of a supposed study of "the dating practices of college students," male volunteers were told they would be going on a blind date with a female student. Each subject was shown a picture of his date and asked to give a first impression of how attractive she was. Before making these ratings, each subject read a short written passage. (This was done in a way that made the reading seem unrelated to rating the photographs.) Subjects read one of two passages; one was sexually arousing, and the other was not. The important finding was that subjects who read the more arousing passage rated the female as more attractive (Stephan, Bersheid, and Walster, 1971).

This result may come as no surprise to you if you have ever been infatuated with someone and then "fallen out of love." A person who once seemed highly attractive may look quite different when your feelings change.

Here is another example of motives affecting perception, familiar to every sports fan:

Students from Dartmouth and Princeton colleges watched films of a rough game in which a popular Princeton player was injured. Princeton students saw the game as "rough and dirty" and 90 percent believed the other side started the rough play. Dartmouth students agreed that the game was rough but saw both sides as equally to blame. Princeton students believed the other team had committed twice as many penalties as their own team. Dartmouth students saw both teams as guilty of an equal number of penalties (Hastorf and Cantril, 1954).

Question: How could students differ so much in the number of penalties they saw when watching the same film?

The emotionally charged events of the game probably served to distract the Dartmouth students. An interesting recent experiment demonstrates that an "emotional" stimulus can shift attention away from other information. In this experiment, members of a Jewish organization watched as pictures like Fig. 5-25 were flashed on a screen for a split-

Fig. 5-25 *Emotionally significant stimuli influence attention. (Erdelyi and Appelbaum, 1973, p. 50. Reprinted by permission.)*

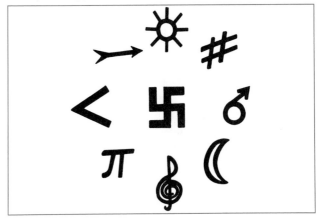

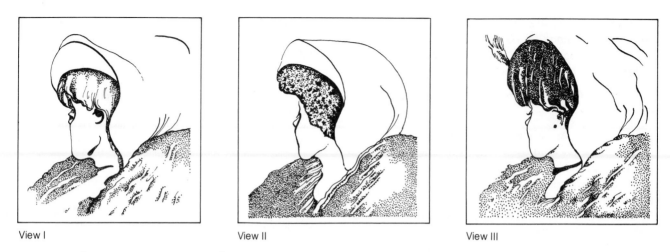

View I   View II   View III

Fig. 5-26 *"Young woman/old woman" illustrations. As an interesting demonstration of perceptual expectancy, show some of your friends View I and some View II (cover all other views). Next show your friends View III and ask them what they see. Those who saw View I should see the old woman in View III; those who saw View II should see the young woman in View III. Can you see both? (After Leeper, 1935.)*

second. Their recognition for symbols at the edge of the figure was impaired when the central item was an emotional symbol like the pictured swastika (Erdelyi and Appelbaum, 1973).

Perceptual Expectancies— On Your Mark, Get Set

Question: What is a perceptual expectancy?

A runner in the starting blocks at a track meet is **set** to respond in a certain way. In perception, past experience, motives, context, or suggestion may create a **perceptual expectancy** that sets you to perceive in a certain way. If a car backfires, runners at a track meet may "jump the gun." As a matter of fact, we all frequently "jump the gun" when perceiving. We respond according to perceptual set by seeing what we expect to see. For example, let's say you are driving across the desert. You are very low on gas. Finally you see a sign approaching. On it are the words "FUEL AHEAD." You relax, knowing you will not be stranded. But as you draw nearer, the words on the sign become "FOOD AHEAD." Most people have had similar experiences in which expectations altered their perceptions. To observe perceptual expectancies firsthand, perform the experiment described in Fig. 5-26.

Many perceptual expectancies are created by *suggestion.* This is especially true when one is perceiving other

people. For example, a psychology professor once arranged an experiment in which a guest lecturer taught his class. Half the students in the class were given a page of notes that described the lecturer as a "rather *cold* person, industrious, critical, practical, and determined." The other students received notes describing him as a "rather *warm* person, industrious, critical, practical, and determined" (Kelley, 1950; italics added). Students who received the "cold" description perceived the lecturer as unhappy and irritable and didn't volunteer in class discussion. Those who got the "warm" description saw the lecturer as happy and good-natured, and they actively took part in discussion with him.

Perhaps you have had a similar experience. If a friend introduces you to a person he or she has always described as "shy," "weird," or "super-friendly," your first impression will probably be influenced by what you have been led to expect. Expectancies may even explain why celebrities and persons of high status can seem "larger than life." In one experiment, an individual was introduced to students as either a student, an assistant, a lecturer, or a professor at a prestigious university. When asked to estimate his height, students judged him to be progressively taller as his status increased (Wilson, 1968). Short people take note! Forget the high heels and get an education!

Categories Have you ever seen playing cards with a *red* ace of spades or a *black* four of hearts? Psychologist Jerome Bruner used a *tachistoscope* (a device for projecting pictures for very short periods) to flash pictures of cards on a screen. He found that subjects misperceived cards that did not fit their expectations. For instance, a *red* six of spades would be misperceived as a normal six of hearts (Bruner and Postman, 1949). Bruner believes that perceptual learning builds up a set of mental **categories.** Experiences are then "sorted" into categories somewhat as if they were slots or "pigeonholes." Since subjects had no category for a red six of spades, they saw it as a six of hearts. Categories such as "punk," "mental patient," "queer," "honky," "bitch," and so on, are particularly likely to distort perception.

Question: Those are extremes; does it really make that much difference what you call someone, or something?

The effect of labels on perception can be seen very clearly in a study in which subjects were briefly shown a series of ambiguous figures (see Fig. 5-27). Each figure was given one of two labels. For half the subjects, the figures were described with the words in List I. Other subjects were given words in List II to describe the same figures. Later, subjects were asked to draw what they had seen. Compare their reproductions, and you will see that labels greatly affected what subjects "saw" and remembered. Perceptual categories, especially those defined by words, do make a difference.

Perceptual categories have a strong impact on our perceptions of others. Even trained psychologists may be influenced by labels and categories. For example, in one study psychotherapists were shown a 15-minute videotaped interview. Half of the therapists were told that the man being interviewed was applying for a job. The rest were told the man was a mental patient. Therapists who thought the man was a job applicant perceived him as "realistic," "sin-

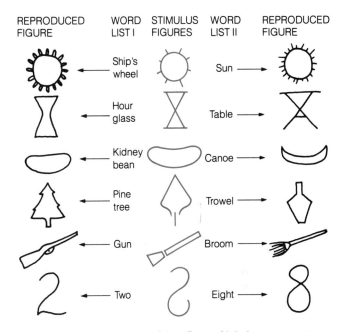

Fig. 5-27 *An illustration of the effects of labels on perception. Stimulus figures were presented along with the descriptions in either Word List I or Word List II. Note the differences in the reproduced figures. (Carmichael, Hogan, and Walter, 1932.)*

cere," and "pleasant." Those who thought he was a patient perceived him as "defensive," "dependent," and "impulsive" (Langer and Abelson, 1974).

In this chapter we have moved from basic perceptions of form to the complexities of perceiving people and events. In the "Applications" section, we will continue this progression with a look at "objectivity" and eyewitness testimony. Before we continue, here's a "Learning Check."

Learning Check

1. Attention is elicited by all but one of the following. Which does not fit?

    a. habituation   *b.* repetition   *c.* change   *d.* intensity

2. The presence of an orientation response shows that habituation is complete.   T or F?

3. Changes in brain waves and increased blood flow to the head are part of an OR.   T or F?

4. Research shows that heightened sexual arousal can cause a person of the opposite sex to appear more physically attractive. T or F?

5. When a person is prepared to perceive events in a particular way, it is said that a perceptual expectancy or _____ has been created.

Answers: 1. a 2. F 3. T 4. T 5. set

Resources Summary

- *Perception* is the process of assembling sensations into a usable mental representation of the world.
- In vision, the image projected on the retina is constantly changing, but the external world appears stable and undistorted because of *size, shape,* and *brightness constancy.*
- The most basic organization of sensations is a division into *figure* and *ground* (object and background). A number of factors contribute to the organization of sensations. These are: *nearness, similarity, continuity, closure,* and *combinations* of the preceding.
- A perceptual organization may be thought of as a *hypothesis* held until evidence contradicts it, but because of a *redundancy* of perceptual information, organization is usually accurate. Exceptions are *ambiguous stimuli* (which have more than one possible organization) and *impossible figures* (which resist stable organization).
- *Depth perception* (the ability to perceive three-dimensional space and judge distances) is present in rudimentary form at or soon after birth (as shown by testing on the *visual cliff*).
- Depth perception depends upon the *bodily cues of accommodation* (bending of the lens), *convergence* (inward movement of the eyes), and *retinal disparity* (the difference in images received by each eye).
- *Stereoscopic vision* (relay of overlapping visual images to both sides of the brain) creates depth by comparing *mismatches* or disparities in what the two eyes see.
- A number of *pictorial cues* also contribute to depth perception. These are: *linear perspective, relative size, light and shadow, overlap, texture gradients, aerial haze,* and *relative motion* (motion parallax). All are monocular depth cues.
- The *moon illusion* is at least partially explained by the greater number of depth cues present when the moon is on the horizon. Another way of saying this is that a *size-distance invariance* underlies the moon illusion.
- The organization and interpretation of sensations is greatly influenced by the development of *perceptual habits.* Studies of *inverted vision* show that even the most basic organization is subject to change.
- Perceptual judgments are not made in a vacuum. They are almost always related to *context* or to an internal frame of reference called the *adaptation level.*
- One of the most familiar of all perceptual illusions, the *Müller-Lyer illusion,* seems to be related to perceptual learning, linear perspective, and the size-distance invariance relationship.
- Attention is closely related to *stimulus intensity, repetition, contrast,* or *change.* Attention is accompanied by an *orientation response.* When a stimulus is repeated without change, the orientation response undergoes *habituation.*
- Personal motives and values often alter perceptions by changing the evaluation of what is seen, or by altering attention to specific details.
- Attention, prior experience, suggestion, and motives combine in various ways to create perceptual *sets,* or *expectancies.* These prepare a person to perceive, or misperceive, in a particular way. *Categories* and *labels* have a strong impact on perceptions.

================= Applications =================

Perception and Objectivity—Believing Is Seeing

Have you ever seen the sun set? An odd question perhaps, since we see the sun ''go down'' every day. Yet, in reality we know that the sun does not ''set.'' Instead, our viewing angle changes as the earth turns until the sun is obscured by the horizon. Want to try the alternative? This evening stand facing the west. With practice, you can learn to feel yourself being swept backward on the rotating surface of the earth—as you watch an unmoving sun recede in the distance (Fuller, 1969).

This radical shift in perspective illustrates the limitations of ''objective'' observation. As with most other perceptions, seeing a ''sunset'' is an active and creative **reconstruction** of events. As we have seen, perception reflects the needs, expectations, attitudes, values, and beliefs of the perceiver. In this light, the phrase ''Seeing is believing,'' must be modified. Clearly, we *see what we believe,* as well as believe what we see. Art teachers know that if beginning students copy a figure drawing upside down their drawings will be more accurate than drawings made right side up. Students working with an inverted drawing must treat it as an abstract design, whereas those working right side up project their own images of the human body into their drawings (Arneheim, 1974).

Question: That's an interesting effect, but of what importance is it?

In some cases, the highly subjective quality of perception contributes to the uniquely personal vision valued in art, music, poetry, and scientific research. Too often, though, it is a real liability.

Eyewitness In the courtroom, eyewitness testimony can be a key element in establishing guilt or innocence. The claim, ''I saw it with my own eyes,'' carries a lot of weight with a jury. But to put it bluntly, eyewitness testimony is frequently wrong.

Psychologists interested in perception are gradually convincing lawyers, judges, and police officers of the limits of eyewitness testimony (Loftus and Monahan, 1980). To illustrate, psychologist Gordon Allport once showed subjects a picture of two men on a streetcar, one white, the other black. The men appeared to be arguing, and the white man was clearly shown holding a weapon (a straight razor). After briefly viewing this picture, subjects were asked to describe what they had seen. About half the white subjects made a crucial change. In their perceptions, the razor somehow moved from the hand of the white man to that of the black man.

Inaccuracies of this kind are not confined to the psychology lab. In one recent court case, a police officer testified that he saw the defendant, a black man, shoot the victim as both stood in a doorway 120 feet away. Measurements made by a psychologist showed that, at that distance, light from the dimly lit doorway was extremely weak—less than a fifth of that from a candle. To further show that identification was improbable, a black juror stood in the doorway under identical lighting conditions. None of the other jurors could identify him. The defendant was acquitted (Buckhout, 1974).

Unfortunately, perception rarely provides an ''instant replay'' of events. Even in broad daylight, eyewitness testimony is untrustworthy. After a disastrous DC-10 airliner crash in Chicago in 1979, 84 *pilots* who saw the accident were interviewed. Forty-two said the DC-10's landing gear was up, and 42 said it was down! As one investigator commented, the best witness may be a ''kid under twelve years old who doesn't have his parents around'' (McKean, 1982). Adults, it seems, are easily swayed by their expectations.

Perceptions formed when a person is surprised, threatened, or under stress are especially prone to distortion. This is why witnesses to crimes so often disagree. As a dramatic demonstration of this problem, an assault was staged on a college campus in which a professor was attacked by an actor. Immediately after the event, 141 witnesses were questioned in detail. Their descriptions were then compared to a videotape made of the staged ''crime.'' The total accuracy score for the group (on features such as appearance, age, weight, and height of the assailant) was only *25 percent* of the maximum possible (Buckhout, 1974).

In many crimes, victims also fall prey to the phenom-

Applications

enon of **weapon focus.** Understandably, victims often fix their entire attention on the knife, gun, or other weapon used by an attacker. In doing so, they fail to perceive details of appearance, dress, or other clues to identity (Loftus, 1979).

Implications   How often are everyday perceptions as inaccurate or distorted as those of an emotionally distraught eyewitness? The answer we have been moving toward is, "very frequently." Bearing this in mind may help you develop tolerance for the views of others and to be more cautious about the "objectivity" of your own perceptions. It may also encourage more frequent reality testing on your part.

Question: What do you mean by "reality testing"?

Reality Testing   In any situation having an element of doubt or uncertainty, reality testing involves obtaining additional information as a check on perceptions. Even simple designs like those in Fig. 5-28 are easily misperceived. One of the designs in the drawing is a continuous line; the other is not. Most people cannot perceive this difference spontaneously. Instead, they must carefully trace and compare the two designs as a check on pure perception (Julesz, 1975).

Psychologist Sidney Jourard offers a more applied example of reality testing. One of Jourard's students believed her roommate was stealing from her. The student gradually became convinced of her roommate's guilt, but said nothing. As her distrust and anger grew, their relationship turned cold and distant. Finally, at Jourard's urging, she confronted her roommate. The roommate cleared herself immediately, and expressed relief when the puzzl-

Fig. 5-28   *Limits of pure perception. (Adapted from patterns devised by Marvin L. Minsky and Seymour A. Papert.)*

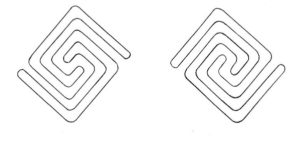

ing change in their relationship was explained (Jourard, 1974). With their friendship reestablished, the true culprit was soon caught. (The cleaning woman did it!)

If you have ever concluded that someone was angry, upset, or unfriendly without checking the accuracy of your perceptions, you have fallen into a subtle trap. Personal objectivity is an elusive quality, requiring frequent reality testing to maintain. At the very least, it pays to ask a person what he or she is feeling when you are in doubt. Undoubtedly, most of us could learn to be better "eyewitnesses" to daily events.

Question: Do some people perceive things more accurately than others?

Perceptual Awareness   Humanistic psychologist Abraham Maslow (1969) felt that some people are unusually accurate in perceptions of themselves and of others. Maslow characterized these people as especially alive, open, aware, and mentally healthy. He found their perceptual styles were marked by: immersion in the present, a lack of self-consciousness, freedom from selecting, criticizing, or evaluating, and a general "surrender" to experience. The kind of perception Maslow described is like that of a mother with her newborn infant, a child at Christmas, or two people in love.

Other researchers have tested Zen masters for signs of enhanced perception. One set of tests focused on habituation to repeated stimuli. The results indicate that Zen masters fail to show the expected habituation (Kasamatsu and Hirai, 1966). This finding lends some credibility to claims that Zen masters perceive a tree as vividly after seeing it 500 times as they did the first time.

Attention   Whereas the average person has not reached perceptual restriction of the "If you've seen one tree, you've seen them all" variety, the fact remains that most of us tend to look at a tree and classify it into the perceptual category of "trees in general" without really appreciating the miracle standing before us. How then can we bring about a **dishabituation** of perception (without going through years of meditative discipline as a Zen master does)? The deceptively simple answer is: *pay attention.*

Applications

The following quote summarizes the importance of attention:

One day a man of the people said to Zen Master Ikkyu: "Master, will you please write for me some maxims of the highest wisdom?"

Ikkyu immediately took his brush and wrote the word "Attention."

"Is that all?" asked the man. "Will you not add something more?"

Ikkyu then wrote twice running: "Attention. Attention."

"Well," remarked the man rather irritably, "I really don't see much depth or subtlety in what you have just written."

Then Ikkyu wrote the same word three times running: "Attention. Attention. Attention."

Half angered, the man demanded "What does that word 'Attention' mean anyway?"

And Ikkyu answered gently: "Attention means attention" (Kapleau, 1966).

To this we can add only one thought, provided by the words of poet William Blake: "If the doors of perception were cleansed, man would see everything as it is, infinite."

Learning Check

1. Most perceptions can be described as active reconstructions of external reality.   T or F?
2. Inaccuracies in eyewitness perceptions obviously occur in "real life," but they cannot be reproduced in psychology experiments.   T or F?
3. Accuracy scores for facts provided by witnesses to staged crimes may be as low as 25 percent correct.   T or F?
4. "Reality testing" is another term for dishabituation.   T or F?

Answers: 1. T 2. F 3. T 4. F

Synesthesia—Hearing Rainbows, Tasting Light

Have you ever seen a laser light show? These productions feature an audio-visual feast of brightly colored lights pulsing to the rhythm of amplified music. Remarkably, some people find such shows uninteresting—not because they dislike the music, or the swirling colors, but because they experience a personal "light show" every day. These people are **synesthetes** (sin-es-THETS), the small minority of people who experience a curious sensory blending called synesthesia. In **synesthesia** (sin-es-THEE-zyah), stimulation of one sense arouses sensations in another. To the synesthetic individual, hearing a voice may induce a burst of colors and tastes as well as sounds (Marks, 1978).

Question: How many people experience synesthesia?

Lawrence Marks, a psychologist who has studied synesthesia in a large number of people, believes that less than 10 percent of the population is regularly synesthetic (Marks, 1975b). However, most people have at least an occasional brush with synesthesia. This, perhaps, is why most of us understand terms such as a "cold" blue, a "bright" sound, or a "smooth" taste.

Color Hearing It's not uncommon to say, "I see what you are saying," but for synesthetes it may be literally true. The most common form of synesthesia is **color hearing,** in which colored visual images are aroused by sounds. These images have vivid motion, depth, transparency, and shape. Speech sounds are most likely to produce the effect, but music is a close runner-up (Marks, 1978, 1975b). Visual images produced by taste are the second most common form of synesthesia. Other pairings, such as "taste hearing" or "smell vision" are more unusual. Synesthetic blending usually occurs in only one direction. That is, if vision produces tastes, tastes probably will not arouse visual images.

Question: How consistent are the colors in color hearing?

For music there is much variation. A tone that is red for one individual might be blue for the next. However, for almost all synesthetes higher notes produce brighter colors. In other words, if middle C on a piano produces

red images, then a high C will be a brighter red (Marks, 1978). Despite music-color differences, there are some core similarities in color hearing. The clearest patterns involve colors aroused by speech sounds, especially vowels. Research with over 400 people shows the following connections are most common (Marks, 1978; 1975b):

a— red and blue color sensations

e— yellow and white

i— yellow and white

o— red and black

u— deep blue, brown, black

In general, high-pitched vowels like *e* and *i* most often produce bright colors, such as white and yellow. The low-pitched vowels *o* and *u* produce the darkest colors. In addition, thunder, drums, deep voices, and other low-pitched sounds are perceived as longer, smoother, darker, and bulkier images. Squeaks, violins, soprano voices, and other high-pitched sounds arouse smaller, thinner, brighter, more angular images (Marks, 1975b).

Unity of the Senses Synesthesia was once thought to have little bearing on normal perception. Thanks to the work of Lawrence Marks this no longer seems true. Marks urges us to think of synesthesia as a vivid example of something more common in perception: the unity of the senses. By the **unity of the senses** Marks means two things. First, the senses obey similar laws of intensity, size, and quality in producing perceptions. In other words, a bright sound and a bright light have much in common, as do a rough surface and a rough sound.

Marks' second point is that the senses normally assist one another in perception—especially when one sense impression helps to confirm another. Certainly, the senses disagree at times. But in general, their unity helps hold together our knowledge of the world. Fortunately, we do not live in separate and conflicting worlds of vision, hearing, taste, and so forth. Instead, we experience one unified perceptual world: a world of sunsets and trees and ice cream cones and thunderstorms (Marks, 1978).

Exploration

The unity of the senses is quite evident in childhood, when perception is simple and direct. In fact, most early perception probably includes some synesthesia. But for most of us, synesthesia is later masked by perceptual learning (Marks, 1975a). Nevertheless, Marks believes synesthesia lies just below the surface of adult perception. Evidence for this is found in the fact that some drugs induce synesthesia in almost everyone who takes them. Marks speculates that a part of the brain normally interrelates the senses, and that it can be "amplified" by certain drugs.

Perceptual Poetry   The poet Rudyard Kipling wrote, "the dawn comes up like thunder." This memorable line is understood by anyone who has heard a thunderclap or watched dawn roll across the landscape. The unity of the senses is of obvious importance in art, music, and poetry. Yet, ultimately, we all use the unity of the senses to enrich perceptions and our descriptions of them. This is why Anglo-Americans, Navajos, and Japanese all agree that *heavy* is "down," "thick," and "dark"; that *white* is "thin," and "calm"; and that *fast* is "thin," "bright," and "diffuse" (Osgood, 1962). It is also why we might hope to help a blind person understand colors somewhat by describing yellow as being like the warmth of the sun or blue like the coolness of water splashing in a fountain. Ultimately, we might envy those synesthetic individuals who experience the actual images such words describe. For all of us, perception is the best show in town—and synesthetes, it would seem, have a ringside seat.

Questions for Discussion

1. Return for a moment to the incident described in the "Chapter Preview." What perceptual factors were involved in the first version of the "murder"? How did the girl affect what was seen?

2. Do you think your perceptions of an argument or fight with a friend, parent, spouse, or lover are accurate? What perceptual factors might affect your viewpoint?

3. Motorcyclists often complain that automobile drivers act as if cyclists are invisible. What perceptual factors might cause drivers to "look right at" motorcyclists without seeing them?

4. A professional basketball player is at the freethrow line for the last shot in a tied championship game. What depth cues are available to him? A professional golfer is making the last putt for a $10,000 prize; what depth cues is she using? A pilot is landing at an unfamiliar airport; what cues

are available to her or him? You are looking through a microscope with one eye; what depth cues can you use?

5. Describe a situation you have misperceived. What influenced your perceptions?

6. What role might habituation play in industrial accidents (especially on production lines) and in driving on arrow-straight superhighways? What changes would you make in work procedures or highway design to combat habituation?

7. In view of the "Chapter Preview" and "Applications," how dependable do you think eyewitness testimony is in a courtroom? What factors other than accuracy of original perceptions might contribute to inaccuracies in testimony?

8. In what ways might synesthesia be useful in perception? How might it be a problem?

Suggestions for Further Reading

Bloomer, C. M. *Principles of Visual Perception.* Van Nostrand Reinhold, 1976.

Carraher, R. G., and J. B. Thurston. *Optical Illusions and the Visual Arts.* Van Nostrand Reinhold, 1968.

Forgus, R. L. *Perception.* McGraw-Hill, 1966.

Gregory, R. L. *Eye and Brain.* McGraw-Hill, 1977.

————. *The Intelligent Eye.* McGraw-Hill, 1970.

Hochberg, J. *Perception.* Prentice-Hall, 1964.

Locher, J. L. (ed.). *The World of M. C. Escher.* Abrams, 1971.

6

Altered States of Consciousness

━━━ Chapter Preview ━━━

Do You Believe in Magic?

In the quiet laboratories of Stanford Research Institute, one of America's largest think tanks, Uri Geller, a self-proclaimed "psychic," has agreed to demonstrate his claimed abilities to communicate by mental telepathy, to detect hidden objects, and to bend metal with "psychic energy." In the course of his testing, Geller was reportedly able to:

Select from a row of ten film canisters, the one which contained an object.
Deflect a sensitive laboratory balance sealed inside a jar by passing his hand over it.
Correctly guess the number that would come up on a die shaken in a closed box eight out of eight times.
Reproduce drawings sealed in opaque envelopes.

Question: Was Geller cheating? Was he using some form of energy or some form of awareness beyond normal consciousness?

There is now little doubt that Geller was cheating (Randi, 1980). But how? You'll find out shortly in a discussion of extrasensory perception (ESP) and other paranormal events. ESP is one of several topics related to altered states of consciousness, the focus of this chapter. But before we delve into this intriguing subject, a word on normal consciousness is in order.

Consciousness William James described consciousness as a "stream"— an everchanging flow of awareness. When you are awake, consciousness includes a mixture of sensations from the external world, sensations from your body, memories of the past, images and daydreams, and expectations about the future. But as James also noted:

Our normal waking consciousness, rational consciousness as we call it, is but one special type of consciousness, whilst all about it, parted from it by the filmiest of screens, there lie potential forms of consciousness entirely different (James, 1958).

States of consciousness related to fatigue, delirium, hypnosis, meditation, drugs, and ecstasy differ significantly from what might be considered "normal" awareness. The sections that follow examine the nature and possible use or abuse of several of the most powerful altered states of consciousness.

Survey Questions   What are psi phenomena and what is the evidence for their existence? What is hypnosis like, and what are its limitations? What are the effects of the most commonly used psychoactive drugs? How is meditation done, and what are its benefits? Why is drug abuse so widespread in our culture?

═══════════ Resources ═══════════

Altered States of Consciousness

Just about everyone distinguishes ordinary waking consciousness from at least a few altered states, such as dreaming, dreamless sleep, and daydreaming. Depending on personal experience and cultural training, a person may add drunkenness, drug "highs," meditation, and the like, to his or her personal list of states of consciousness.

Question: There must be many altered states of consciousness; how are they distinguished from normal consciousness?

An **altered state of consciousness** (ASC) represents a distinct change in the *quality* and *pattern* of mental functioning. ASCs typically differ from normal waking consciousness with regard to: sense impressions, body image, intensity of emotion, memory (gaps, loss, or enhancement), time sense, feeling of personal identity, patterns of thought, feelings of self-control, suggestibility, and the meaning attached to events (Tart, 1975). Definitions aside, most people have little difficulty recognizing that they have experienced an ASC.

Question: Aside from drugs, what causes ASCs?

The list of causes is practically endless. In addition to drugs, sleep, dreaming, and meditation, we could add: sensory overload (for example, a light show, Mardi Gras crowd, or disco), monotonous stimulation ("highway hypnotism" on long drives is a good example), religious and mystical experiences (revivals and religious conversions), unusual physical conditions (high fever, hyperventilation, dehydration, sleep deprivation), long-distance running, music, and too many other possibilities to mention.

To get right to the questions raised by the "Chapter Preview," let's begin with psychic phenomena, including ESP, which is the most controversial of the altered states.

Psychic Phenomena— Beyond Normal Awareness?

Parapsychology is the study of *psychic* phenomena (also known as **psi** phenomena). Psi events are those that lie outside normal experience and seem to defy accepted scientific laws. Modern parapsychologists are seeking answers to the questions raised by psi phenomena. Four major areas of investigation are:

1. **Clairvoyance.** The ability to perceive events or gain information in ways that appear unaffected by distance or normal physical barriers.
2. **Telepathy.** Extrasensory perception of another person's thoughts, or more simply, an ability to read someone else's mind.
3. **Precognition.** The ability to perceive or accurately predict future events. Precognition may take the form of *prophetic dreams* that foretell the future.
4. **Psychokinesis.** The ability to exert influence over inanimate objects by will power ("mind over matter"). If you are able to influence which face of a flipped coin comes up or move an object without touching it, then you have demonstrated psychokinesis.

Question: Do psychologists believe in ESP?

American psychologists as a group remain skeptical about ESP and other psi abilities, a skepticism not fully shared by the general public. A recent Gallup poll found that about half of those interviewed believe in ESP. If you are in the half that doubts ESP, then you should know that there have been some carefully run experiments supporting its existence. If you are among those who believe in ESP, then you should know why the scientific community doubts its existence!

Coincidence   Anyone who has ever had a clairvoyant or telepathic experience will find it hard to question the existence of ESP. But the difficulty of excluding *coincidence* makes natural ESP occurrences less conclusive than they might seem. For example, consider this typical psychic experience: During the middle of the night, a woman away for a weekend visit suddenly had a strong impulse to return home. When she arrived she found the house on fire with her husband asleep inside (Rhine, 1953). An experience like this is striking, but it does not *prove* the existence of ESP. If, by coincidence, a "hunch" turns out to be correct, it may be *reinterpreted* as a premonition or case of clairvoyance (Marks and Kammann, 1979). If it is not confirmed, it will simply be forgotten.[*]

The formal study of psi events owes much to the late J. B. Rhine. Rhine established the first parapsychological laboratory at Duke University and spent the rest of his life

---

[*]A related error in logic (no offense, dolphin-lovers) is the conclusion that dolphins try to save drowning humans. We can never be sure about this because it is not too likely that we will ever hear from drowning swimmers who get carried out to sea by "helpful" dolphins.

Fig. 6-1 *ESP cards used by J. B. Rhine, an early experimenter in parapsychology.*

trying to document ESP. To avoid problems of coincidence and after-the-fact interpretation of "natural" ESP events, Rhine tried to study ESP more objectively. Many of his early experiments made use of the **Zener cards** (see Fig. 6-1). In a typical clairvoyance test, subjects tried to guess the symbols on the cards as they were turned up from a shuffled deck. Pure guessing in this test will produce an average score of 5 "hits" out of 25 cards. A person who consistently scores above this chance level is credited with ESP. Telepathy is tested when one person (the "sender") concentrates on a card and another person (the "receiver") tries to "read the mind" of the sender.

Unfortunately, some of Rhine's most dramatic early experiments used badly printed Zener cards on which a faint outline of the symbol showed through the back. In other experiments, there is evidence that the experimenter knew which card was correct, and unconsciously gave subjects cues with his eyes, facial gestures, or lip movements.

Modern parapsychologists are now well aware of the need for double-blind experiments, maximum security and accuracy in record-keeping, meticulous experimental control, and repeatability of experiments (Rhine, 1974a). In the last 10 years, hundreds of experiments have been reported in parapsychological journals. Many appear to support the existence of psi abilities. Parapsychologist John Palmer recently analyzed over 700 such reports and found that spontaneous guessing, a good emotional adjustment, a positive attitude toward ESP, and altered states of consciousness all improved ESP scores (Hyman, 1979).

Question: Then why do most psychologists remain skeptical about psi abilities?

Statistics and Chance   Most criticisms of psychic research focus on the inconsistency of psi abilities. For every study with positive results, there are others that fail (Hansel, 1980). It is rare for a subject to maintain psi ability over any sustained period of time (Schmeidler, 1977). ESP researchers consider this fact an indication that parapsychological skills are very fragile and unpredictable (Rhine, 1977). But critics argue that subjects who only temporarily score above chance have just received credit for a **run of luck**. When the run is over, it is not fair to assume that ESP is temporarily gone. We must count *all* attempts.

Question: What if a researcher does count all attempts, and finds that the results could occur by chance only one time in a million?

Just such results are reported in many parapsychology experiments. They are, however, still open to the run-of-luck criticism. Suppose an experimenter tests 100 students for psi abilities and finds one who scores well above chance on 200 trials of card-guessing. Even if the experimenter includes all "trial runs," "days when the subject couldn't concentrate," and the scores of the other 99 subjects, a true estimate of the odds against the "psychic" subject's score have not been figured. Why? Because the experimenter can never include all the thousands of trials run in hundreds of other experiments, trials that were *never reported* because no psi effect was found.

Research Methods   Unfortunately, the most spectacular findings in parapsychology are those least often repeated (Gardner, 1977; Hyman, 1977). More importantly, improvements in research methods usually result in fewer positive results. But believers in ESP, such as ex-astronaut Edgar Mitchell, believe other factors explain negative results in ESP tests: "The scientist has to recognize that his own mental processes may influence the phenomenon he's observing. If he's really a total skeptic, the scientist may well turn off the psychic subject" (*Newsweek,* March 4, 1974).

Skeptics and serious researchers in ESP both agree on one point. If psychic phenomena do occur, they cannot be controlled well enough to be used by entertainers. Stage ESP (like stage magic) is based upon a combination of sleight of hand, deception, and patented gadgets. A case in point is Uri Geller, a former nightclub magician who "astounded" audiences from coast to coast with apparent feats of telepathy, psychokinesis, and precognition. Geller's performance in tests at Stanford Research Institute is described in the preview of this chapter. Not mentioned is what University of Oregon Professor Ray Hyman calls an "incredible sloppiness" in performance of these tests. As one example, it has since been shown that needles and laboratory scales placed in jars can be deflected by static electricity transferred to the jar by the "psychic's" hands (Balanovski and Taylor, 1978). Geller's reproductions of sealed drawings, it turns out, were done in a room next to the one where the drawings were made. Original reports of Geller's alleged "ability" failed to mention that there was a hole in the wall between the two rooms. Also unreported in the "die in the box" tests was the fact that Geller was allowed to hold the box and shake it. He is even reported to have been the one to open the box (Wilhelm, 1976; Randi, 1980).

It is important to recognize that criticism of psi research runs deeper than unmasking frauds such as Geller. A first-hand look at psi experiments often reveals serious problems (Marks and Kammann, 1979). For example, parapsychologists Russell Targ and Harold Puthoff (1977) reported a seemingly sensational experiment in "remote viewing." In the experiment, a psychic remained in the lab, while a "sender" went to remote locations. At each location, the sender gave his or her impressions of the spot, which were tape-recorded. At the same time, the psychic taped the impressions he was receiving from the sender. Later, judges tried to match transcripts from the sender and the psychic. Targ and Puthoff claim that an independent judge matched the descriptions at far above chance level. However, critics later discovered that the list of targets was arranged in the order of the visits, and that the judge knew it. Also, the sender's descriptions contained all sorts of clues to targets already visited and the number of tests already performed (Randi, 1980). Thus, *any* judge could easily match targets with the psychic's descriptions from the clues they contained. In fact, when these clues were removed from the transcripts, other judges were unable to successfully match them (Marks and Kammann, 1979).

A good summary of the overall status of parapsychological research is provided by the remarks of Wayne Sage (1972): "Forty years of experiments in the telepathic, clairvoyant, and precognitive capacities of the human mind have left us no more certain, or uncertain, that such abilities even exist." Perhaps exciting discoveries in this realm of consciousness still await us. But, for now, it would seem that the best attitude toward ESP is to maintain an open mind while being carefully skeptical of evidence reported in the popular press or by researchers who are "true believers."

Learning Check

Before reading on, answer the following questions about what you just read.

1. List four major types of psychic phenomena under investigation by parapsychologists.

   _____   _____

   _____   _____

2. Dreaming and dreamless sleep are considered ASCs. T or F?

3. The _____ cards were used as an early test of ESP.

   a. Rhine *b.* Zener *c.* Geller *d.* psi

4. Critics attribute positive results in psi experiments to statistical runs of luck. T or F?

Answers: 1. clairvoyance, telepathy, precognition, psychokinesis 2. T 3. b 4. T

Hypnotism—Look into My Eyes

"Your body is becoming heavy. Your eyes are so tired you can barely keep them open. You feel warm and relaxed and very heavy. You are so tired you can't move. Relax. Sleep, sleep, sleep." These are the last words a book should ever say to you, and the first a professional hypnotist might say.

Hypnotism, like ESP, has a certain aura of mystery surrounding it. Yet unlike ESP, hypnosis is accepted by most psychologists as scientifically valid. Most would agree that **hypnosis** is a *trancelike, altered state of consciousness, characterized by narrowed attention and an increased openness to suggestion.*

Interest in hypnosis began in the 1700s with Franz Mesmer (whose name is the basis for the term **mesmerize**).

Mesmer, an Austrian physician, believed that he could cure diseases by passing magnets over the body of an afflicted person. For a time, mesmerism enjoyed quite a following. In the end, however, Mesmer's theories of "animal magnetism" were rejected by the medical profession, and he was branded a quack and a fraud. The term *hypnotism* was coined later by a respected English surgeon named James Braid. The Greek work *hypnos* means "sleep," and Braid used it to describe the hypnotic trance. Today we recognize that hypnosis is *not* sleep, since EEG (brain-wave) recordings made during hypnosis are similar to those obtained when a person is awake. Confusion about this point remains because many hypnotists give the suggestion, "Sleep, sleep." All things considered, hypnotism, as it is shown in movies and on TV, bears little resemblance to the real thing.

Question: Can anyone be hypnotized?

Approximately 8 people out of 10 can be hypnotized, but only 4 out of 10 will be good hypnotic subjects. If you are willing to be hypnotized, chances are good that you could be. Hypnotic susceptibility can be measured by making a

Table 6-1   Stanford Hypnotic Susceptibility Scale

Suggested Behavior	Criterion of Passing (yielding score of +)
1. Postural sway	Falls without forcing.
2. Eye closure	Closes eyes without forcing.
3. Hand lowering (left)	Lowers at least 6 in. by end of 10 secs.
4. Immobilization (right arm)	Arm rises less than 1 in. in 10 secs.
5. Finger lock	Incomplete separation of fingers at end of 10 secs.
6. Arm rigidity (left arm)	Less than 2 in. of arm bending in 10 secs.
7. Hands moving together	Hands at least as close as 6 in. after 10 secs.
8. Verbal inhibition (name)	Name unspoken in 10 secs.
9. Hallucination (fly)	Any movement, grimacing, acknowledgement of effect.
10. Eye catalepsy	Eyes remain closed at end of 10 secs.
11. Posthypnotic (changes chairs)	Any partial movement response.
12. Amnesia test	Three or fewer items recalled.

(Adapted from Weitzenhoffer and Hilgard, 1959)

series of suggestions to a person and recording the number of suggestions to which he or she responds. A typical hypnotic test is the **Stanford Hypnotic Susceptibility Scale** shown in Table 6-1.

Question: How is hypnosis done? Could anyone be hypnotized against his or her will?

There are as many different hypnotic routines as there are hypnotists. The actual method of hypnotic induction doesn't seem to be too important. Common factors in all techniques are that they encourage a person: (1) to focus attention on what is being said; (2) to relax and feel tired; (3) to "let go" and accept suggestions easily; and (4) to use vivid imagination (Tart, 1975).

In advanced states of hypnosis, "reality testing" may be relaxed so that a partial suspension of normal "will power" is achieved. But at first, one must cooperate willingly in order to become hypnotized. Many theorists feel that all hypnosis is really **self-hypnosis** and that the hypnotist simply serves as a guide to help the subject achieve an altered state of awareness that could be achieved alone.

Question: What does it feel like to be hypnotized?

You might be surprised at some of the actions you performed during hypnosis, and you might experience mild feelings of floating, sinking, anesthesia, or separation from your body. Personal experiences vary widely. However, in all but the deepest stages of hypnosis, people remain aware of what is going on. Here is one subject's description of his hypnotic session:

> I felt lethargic, my eyes going out of focus and wanting to close. My hands felt real light. . . . I felt I was sinking deeper into the chair. . . . I felt like I wanted to relax more and more. . . . My responses were more automatic. I didn't have to *wish* to do things so much or *want* to do them. . . . I just did them. . . . I felt floating . . . very close to sleep (Hilgard, 1968).

Hypnosis often causes a *dissociation,* or "split," in awareness. To illustrate, researcher Ernest Hilgard asks hypnotized subjects to plunge their hand into a painful bath of ice water. Those subjects told to feel no pain say they feel none. The same subjects are then asked if there is any part of their mind that does feel pain. Many write, "It hurts," or, "Stop it, you're hurting me," but continue to act as if they are completely comfortable (Hilgard, 1977, 1978). One part of the hypnotized person says there is no pain and acts as if there is none. Another part, which Hilgard calls the **hidden observer** is aware of the pain, but remains in the background.

Question: Could someone be made to perform an immoral act while hypnotized?

Generally speaking, a person will not do something when hypnotized that he or she would not normally do. However, a person who would not undress in public *might* undress if given the suggestion that he or she is at home alone and that it is bedtime (Eysenck, 1957). Also, hypnosis may *disinhibit* a person by providing an excuse to engage in prohibited behavior. If you were hypnotized and told to throw a cream pie in your teacher's face, you would probably comply because you could not be held responsible. After all, you were hypnotized, weren't you?

Question: What can be achieved with hypnosis?

A vast array of abilities has been tested for responsiveness to hypnotic suggestion. In some cases, the evidence is incomplete or contradictory, but the following conclusions seem reasonably justified (Barber, 1970):

1. Superhuman acts of strength. Hypnosis has no more effect on physical strength than instructions that encourage a subject to make his or her best effort.
2. Memory. Memory per se cannot be improved through hypnosis, but motivation and attention in learning may be. In other words, you might be convinced through hypnosis that you are *extremely interested* in learning history, chemistry, or whatever so that your studying would be improved.
3. Amnesia. Hypnotic subjects can be instructed to forget what occurred during the trance. It is not clear, however, if they do forget or just can't or won't say what happened because of the suggestion that they would forget.
4. Pain relief. Hypnosis can relieve pain. Therefore, it can be especially useful in situations where chemical painkillers cannot be used, or are ineffective. One such situation is control of *phantom limb* pain. (Phantom limb pains are recurring pains that amputees sometimes feel coming from the missing limb.)
5. Age regression. Through hypnosis, subjects have been "regressed" to childhood. Some theorists feel that regressed subjects are only acting childlike and that nothing more than role playing is involved.
6. Sensory changes. Hypnotic suggestions concerning sensations seem to be among the most effective. Given the proper instructions, a person can be made to smell a small bottle of ammonia and respond as if it were a wonderful perfume.

Generally, hypnosis seems to have greatest value as a tool for inducing relaxation, as a means of controlling pain (in dentistry and childbirth, for example), as an aid to maintaining motivation (to study, diet, quit smoking, and so forth), and as an adjunct to other forms of psychological therapy and counseling. The effects that can be obtained with hypnosis are useful, but seldom "amazing" (Hilgard, 1974; Williams, 1974; Rieger, 1976).

Stage Hypnotism

On stage the hypnotist intones, "When I count to three, you will imagine that you are on a train to Disneyland, and growing younger and younger as the train approaches . . ." Responding to these suggestions, grown men and women begin to giggle and squirm like children on their way to a circus.

Question: How do entertainers use hypnosis on stage to get people to do strange things?

They don't. Little or no hypnosis is necessary to do a good stage hypnosis act. T. X. Barber, an authority on hypnosis, says that stage hypnotists make use of several characteristics of the stage setting to perform their act (Barber, 1970).

1. Waking suggestibility. We are all more or less open to suggestion, but on stage people are unusually cooperative because they don't want to "ruin the act." As a result, they will readily follow almost any instruction given by the entertainer.
2. Selection of responsive subjects. Participants in stage hypnotism must *volunteer* to come on stage. This alone ensures that participants are relatively uninhibited and ready to participate. Next the group is "hypnotized" *en masse* and anyone who doesn't succumb (go along) is eliminated.
3. The hypnosis label disinhibits. As we noted before, once a person has been labeled "hypnotized," he or she can sing, dance, act silly, or whatever without fear of embarrassment because being "hypnotized" takes away all personal responsibility for one's actions.
4. The hypnotist as a "director." After participants loosen up and respond to a few suggestions, they find that they are suddenly the star of the show. Audience response to the antics on stage brings out the "ham" in many participants so that all the "hypnotist" need do is direct the action.
5. The stage hypnotist uses tricks. Stage hypnosis is about 50 percent taking advantage of the situation and 50 percent deception. Here is a common deception:

> One of the more impressive stage tricks is to rigidly suspend a person between two chairs and then to stand on the person's chest. This is astounding only because the

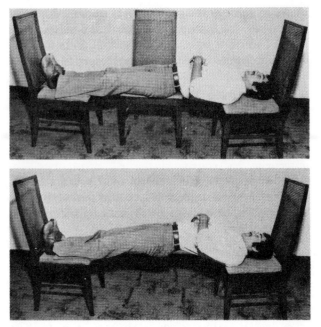

Fig. 6-2 *Arrange three chairs as shown. Have someone recline as shown. Ask him to lift slightly and remove the middle chair. Accept the applause gracefully!*

audience does not question it. Anyone can do it as is demonstrated in the photographs and instructions in Fig. 6-2. Try it!

Question: If entertainers don't hypnotize people, why do those who have been on stage say they were hypnotized?

Some may have been hypnotized, but since most people don't know what it feels like to be hypnotized, the combination of bright lights, nervousness, and the things they did convince them they were. A prime example occurred when the "Amazing Kreskin," a stage mentalist, told talk show host Johnny Carson he could be hypnotized without knowing it. Kreskin suspended Carson between two chairs and asked singer Bette Midler to sit on Carson's stomach. And what was Carson's response to this? "You've proved your point," he said. "I'm wide awake, but I must be hypnotized because I feel as comfortable as a duck in a pond" (Weisinger, 1977).

To summarize, hypnosis is real and is capable of causing a significant change in conscious experience. It is a useful tool that has been effectively applied in a variety of settings. The TV or nightclub stage, however, is not one of these settings. Stage "hypnotists" entertain; they rarely hypnotize.

Learning Check

Here are a few questions to test your memory of our discussion of hypnosis.

1. The term hypnotism was coined by a British surgeon named:

    a. Franz Mesmer   *b.* James Stanford   *c.* T. A. Kreskin   *d.* James Braid

2. Only 4 out of 10 people can be hypnotized. T or F?

3. Which of the following can most definitely be achieved with hypnosis?

    a. superhuman acts of strength   *b.* pain relief   *c.* memory loss   *d.* sleeplike brain waves

4. Could someone be made to perform an immoral act while hypnotized? Yes / No

Answers: 1. d   2. F   3. b   4. Generally no; however, hypnosis may provide an excuse to engage in prohibited behavior.

Drug-Altered Consciousness— The High and Low of It

Alcohol, heroin, amphetamines, barbiturates, marijuana, cocaine, LSD, caffeine, nicotine. . . . The list of consciousness-altering drugs—legal and illegal—available to anyone motivated enough to seek them out is extensive. The surest way to alter human consciousness is to administer a **psychoactive drug.** A psychoactive drug is a substance capable of altering attention, memory, judgment, time sense, feeling of control over one's actions, emotional

mood or expression, and perception (by exaggerating sensations or causing hallucinations) (Ludwig, 1966).

Facts about Drugs   Most psychoactive drugs can be placed on a scale ranging from **stimulation** to **depression.** Figure 6-3 shows the approximate relationships among various drugs and their effects on the central nervous system. A more complete summary of the most frequently abused psychoactive drugs is given in Table 6-2 (pp. 136–137).

Drug dependence falls into two broad categories. When

a person compulsively uses a drug to maintain bodily comfort, a **physical dependence** exists. Physical dependence, commonly referred to as **addiction,** occurs most often with drugs that cause **withdrawal symptoms** (painful or even agonizing reactions that take place when the drug is withheld). Addiction is often accompanied by a **drug tolerance,** in which the user must take larger and larger doses to achieve the desired effect. When a person develops a **psychological dependence,** he or she feels a drug is necessary to maintain emotional or psychological well-being. No withdrawal symptoms or physical cravings are involved, and yet psychological dependence may affect a drug user as powerfully as physical dependence does.

Note in Table 6-2 that the drugs most associated with physical dependence are: heroin, morphine, codeine, methadone, barbiturates, alcohol, amphetamines, and tobacco. *All* of the drugs listed can lead to psychological dependence. Some drugs, of course, have a higher potential for abuse than others. However, it is as useful to classify drug-taking behavior as it is to classify drugs. For example, some people remain social drinkers for a lifetime, whereas others become alcoholics within weeks of taking their first drink. In this sense, drug use can be classified as **experimental** (short-term use motivated by curiosity), **recreational** (occasional social use considered pleasurable by participants), **situational** (use to cope with a specific problem, such as boredom or staying awake for night work), **intensive** (daily use having elements of dependence), or **compulsive** (intense use and extreme dependence) (National Commission on Marihuana and Drug Abuse, 1973). The last three categories of drug-taking tend to be damaging no matter what drug is used. The discussion that follows will focus on the drugs most frequently abused by college students.

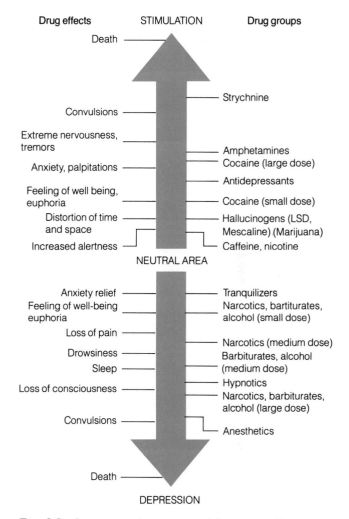

Fig. 6-3 *Spectrum and continuum of drug action. Drugs can be placed on a continuum of stimulation-depression according to their effect on the central nervous system.*

Uppers—Amphetamines, Cocaine, Caffeine, Nicotine

Amphetamines form a large group of synthetic stimulants. Drugs commonly available in this group are *Dexedrine, Methedrine,* and *Benzedrine.* Amphetamines were once widely prescribed by doctors to aid weight loss or to combat mild depression. Both practices are now discouraged because patients frequently become dependent on their "legal" amphetamines. The only fully legitimate medical uses of amphetamines are to treat narcolepsy (sleep attacks) and to counteract overdoses of depressant drugs. In view of this, it must be concluded that the *12 billion* doses of "diet pills" made in the United States each year are in large

measure used for nonmedical purposes (Meyers *et al.,* 1972). Illicit use of amphetamines is widespread among individuals seeking an easy way to stay awake or to temporarily improve mental or physical performance. Truck drivers, athletes, factory workers, and students cramming for exams frequently abuse amphetamines for these purposes.

Amphetamines rapidly produce a drug tolerance. Most abusers begin with one or two pills a day and soon progress to dozens a day to get the same effect. At this point the habitual user may take amphetamines in large doses, or may switch to injecting Methedrine ("speed") directly into the bloodstream to produce euphoria, alertness, and a heightened sense of mental and physical energy and well-being. The true "speed-freak" typically goes on binges

Table 6-2   Comparison of Psychoactive Drugs

Name	Classification	Medical Use	Usual Dose	Duration of Effect	Effects Sought
Heroin	Narcotic	Pain relief	Varies	4 hr	Euphoria, prevent withdrawal discomfort
Morphine	Narcotic	Pain relief	15 milligrams	6 hr	Euphoria, prevent withdrawal discomfort
Codeine	Narcotic	Ease pain and coughing	30 milligrams	4 hr	Euphoria, prevent withdrawal discomfort
Methadone	Narcotic	Pain relief	10 milligrams	4–6 hr	Prevent withdrawal discomfort
Cocaine	Stimulant, local anesthesia	Local anesthesia	Varies	Varied, brief periods	Excitation, talkativeness
Marijuana (THC)	Relaxant, euphoriant; in high doses, hallucinogen	Treatment of glaucoma	1–2 cigarettes	4 hr	Relaxation; increased euphoria, perceptions, sociability
Barbiturates	Sedative–hypnotic	Sedation, relief of high blood pressure, hyperthyroidism	50–100 milligrams	4 hr	Anxiety reduction, euphoria
Amphetamines	Stimulant	Relief of mild depression, control of appetite and narcolepsy	2.5–5 milligrams	4 hr	Alertness, activeness
LSD	Hallucinogen	Experimental study of mental function, alcoholism	100–500 micrograms	10 hr	Insightful experiences, exhilaration, distortion of senses
Mescaline	Hallucinogen	None	350 micrograms	12 hr	Insightful experiences, exhilaration, distortion of senses
Psilocybin	Hallucinogen	None	25 milligrams	6–8 hours	Insightful experiences, exhilaration, distortion of senses
Alcohol	Sedative-hypnotic	Solvent, antiseptic	Varies	1–4 hr	Sense alteration, anxiety reduction, sociability
Tobacco (Nicotine)	Stimulant	Emetic (nicotine)	Varies	Varies	Alertness, calmness, sociability
Caffeine	Stimulant	Counteract depressant drugs, treatment of migrainefflheadaches	Varies	Varies	Wakefulness, alertness

(Question marks indicate conflict of opinion. It should be noted that illicit drugs are frequently adulterated and thus pose unknown hazards to the user.)

*Persons who inject drugs under nonsterile conditions run a high risk of contracting hepatitis, abscesses, or circulatory disorders.

Long-Term Symptoms	Physical Dependence Potential	Psychological Dependence Potential	Organic Damage Potential
Addiction, constipation, loss of appetite	Yes	Yes	No*
Addiction, constipation, loss of appetite	Yes	Yes	No*
Addiction, constipation, loss of appetite	Yes	Yes	No
Addiction, constipation, loss of appetite	Yes	Yes	No
Depression, convulsions	No	Yes	Yes?
Possible lung cancer, other health risks	No	Yes	Yes
Addiction with severe withdrawal symptoms, possible convulsions, toxic psychosis, addiction	Yes	Yes	Yes
Loss of appetite, delusions, hallucinations, toxic psychosis	Yes	Yes	Yes
May intensify existing psychosis, panic reactions	No	No?	No?
May intensify existing psychosis, panic reactions	No	No?	No?
May intensify existing psychosis, panic reactions	No	No?	No?
Cirrhosis, toxic psychosis, neurologic damage, addiction	Yes	Yes	Yes
Emphysema, lung cancer, mouth and throat cancer, cardiovascular damage, loss of appetite	Yes	Yes	Yes
Insomnia, heart arrhythmias, high blood pressure	No	Yes	Yes

Adapted and updated from: *Resource Book for Drug Abuse Education.* NEA, 1969.

lasting several days after which he or she "crashes" from lack of sleep and food.

Question: How dangerous are amphetamines?

The dangers of amphetamine usage are multiple. To stay "high," the speed-freak must inject more and more of the drug as the body's tolerance increases. The American Medical Association (1968) emphasizes that amphetamines speed the expenditure of bodily resources; they do not magically supply energy. Hence, the aftereffects of an amphetamine high can be quite dangerous and uncomfortable. Possible effects include fatigue, depression, terrifying nightmares, confusion, and uncontrolled irritability and aggression. Repeatedly overextending one's body by speeding may lead to:

> considerable weight loss, sores and non-healing ulcers, brittle fingernails, tooth grinding, chronic chest infections, liver disease, a variety of hypertensive disorders, and in some cases cerebral hemorrhage (Canadian Government's Commission of Inquiry, 1971).

Question: What is the meaning of the phrase "speed kills!"?

It should be obvious that amphetamines are dangerous drugs. Withdrawal from amphetamine addiction can be extremely painful (Grinspoon and Hedblom, 1972). But painful as withdrawal may be, it is not usually fatal.

The real meaning of "speed kills" lies in the fact that amphetamines can cause a loss of contact with reality, known as **amphetamine psychosis.** Amphetamine psychosis is similar to extreme paranoia. Affected persons feel threatened and suffer from delusions that someone is out to get them. Acting on these delusions, the speed-freak may become violent, resulting in self-injury or injury to others. At least one drug authority (Snyder, 1972) believes that it is in this sense that the slogan "speed kills," is most accurate: More persons die from amphetamine-caused violence than from overdoses of the drug itself.

Cocaine is a powerful central nervous system stimulant derived from the leaves of the coca plant. It has been used for centuries by natives of the Andes Mountains to suppress appetite, and increase energy or endurance. Its subjective effects are sensations of alertness, euphoria, well-being, power, boundless energy, or exhilaration. Also common is a blurring or fuzziness of vision, ringing in the ears, and a "wired" feeling leading to insomnia. There is often an increase in talkativeness, restlessness, and excitement, but there is no loss of thinking abilities or motor coordination. Hence a cocaine "high" is not easily detected by others (Spotts and Shontz, 1980).

Cocaine has a long history of use and misuse in the United States. At the turn of the century, dozens of nonprescription potions and cure-alls containing cocaine were sold. It was during this time that Coca-Cola was indeed the "real thing." From 1886, when it was first concocted, until 1906 when the Pure Food and Drug Act was passed, Coca-Cola contained cocaine (which has since been replaced with caffeine) (Grinspoon and Bakalar, 1977). In the 1930s, the popularity of cocaine declined when the cheaper synthetic amphetamines became available. This trend was reversed in the 1960s when a federal crackdown on amphetamine sales made this drug less available and more expensive. Today, cocaine is becoming one of the most widely abused drugs.

Question: How does cocaine differ from amphetamines?

The two are very much alike in their effect on the central nervous system, so much so that when experienced users are given both they can't tell the difference. With mild doses subjects could not distinguish cocaine from a placebo, and with moderate doses the effects were more like those of caffeine than amphetamine (Resnick *et al.,* 1977). At high dosages the main difference is that amphetamine effects may last several hours; cocaine is quickly metabolized, so its effects last only about 15 to 30 minutes.

Question: How dangerous is cocaine?

Cocaine is not physically addicting and shows little evidence of tolerance, so increased dosages are not necessary to produce the same effect. The only reported deaths caused by cocaine appear to have involved allergic reactions to the drug. The dangers it holds are related to the period of emotional and physical depression (similar to an amphetamine letdown) that follows a "high." To combat depression, the user often takes another dose, which is

followed by another letdown and another dose. After repeating this cycle regularly, heavy users often suffer chronic nervousness, irritability, and paranoia. In a few extreme cases they experience "cocaine bugs," disturbing sensations like bugs crawling under the skin. Since cocaine is usually inhaled, or "snorted," nasal damage is also possible, although rare (*Science News,* 1977). Research is underway to determine other long-term effects of cocaine use.

Cocaine has acquired quite a reputation as an "elite" or "glamorous" drug because of its use by entertainers, the wealthy, and the privileged. Its danger for abuse may ultimately be limited by its absurdly high price. At the time this was written cocaine was selling on the street for more than $100 a gram, or about $3,000 an ounce. The status conferred by cocaine use may have more to do with its popularity than its chemical effect. Since street drugs are greatly reduced in purity and potency, the effects of cocaine might be more inexpensively duplicated by drinking a half-dozen cups of coffee.

Caffeine Caffeine is the most frequently used psychoactive drug in the United States. Caffeine stimulates the brain by blocking chemicals that normally inhibit or slow nerve activity (Julien, 1978). Its effects become apparent with doses as small as 100 to 200 milligrams (mg), which is the amount found in about two cups of brewed coffee.

Caffeine has various effects on the body: It speeds the heart, promotes the release of stomach acid, and increases urine production; also, it dilates some blood vessels while narrowing others. In large amounts, caffeine may cause convulsions, but this is highly unlikely. It takes about 10 grams of caffeine, the equivalent of 100 cups of coffee, to run a serious risk of death (Julien, 1978). Psychologically, caffeine suppresses fatigue or drowsiness, and increases feelings of alertness; some people have a hard time starting a day without it.

How much caffeine did you consume today? It is common to think of coffee as the major source of caffeine, but there are many others. Caffeine is found in tea, many soft drinks (especially colas), chocolate, and cocoa. Over 2000 nonprescription drugs also contain caffeine, including stay-awake pills, cold remedies, and many name-brand aspirin products. Table 6-3 gives the approximate caffeine content of several foods.

Question: Are there any serious drawbacks to using caffeine?

Many people develop a mild dependence on caffeine. You may have seen evidence of this in yourself, or among your

---

Table 6-3 Average Caffeine Content of Various Foods

Instant coffee (5 oz), 64 mg
Percolated coffee (5 oz), 108 mg
Drip coffee (5 oz), 145 mg
Decaffeinated coffee (5 oz), 3 mg
Black tea (5 oz), 42 mg
Canned ice tea (17 oz), 30 mg
Cocoa drink (6 oz), 8 mg
Chocolate drink (8 oz), 14 mg
Sweet chocolate (1 oz), 20 mg
Colas (12 oz), 50 mg
Soft drinks (12 oz), 0–52 mg

friends or family. Often, when a person stops drinking coffee or tea (to cut down on caffeine), his or her consumption of colas and soft drinks increases. People who think they have given up caffeine are often unaware that they are still consuming it in this way. Soft drinks and colas also start many children on caffeine early in their lives—again frequently without awareness on the part of parents or the child.

Serious abuse of caffeine may result in an unhealthy dependence, known as **caffeinism** (Levitt, 1977). People with caffeinism suffer from insomnia, irritability, loss of appetite, chills, racing heart, and elevated body temperature. It is not uncommon to find that such individuals are consuming 15 or 20 cups of coffee a day. Even in the absence of caffeinism there are some caffeine-related health risks. Caffeine encourages the development of breast cysts in women, and it may contribute to insomnia, stomach problems, heart problems, and high blood pressure in both men and women. Many drug experts recommend that women restrict their caffeine intake during the first three months of pregnancy. It is customary in our culture to think of caffeine as a nondrug. But as this discussion shows, it is wise to remember that caffeine *is* a drug and should be used in moderation.

Nicotine   Nicotine is a natural stimulant found mainly in tobacco. Next to caffeine, it is the most widely used psychoactive drug (Julien, 1978).

Question: How does nicotine compare to other stimulants?

Nicotine is a potent drug. In large doses it causes stomach pain, vomiting and diarrhea, cold sweats, dizziness, confusion, and tremors. In very large doses, nicotine may cause convulsions, respiratory failure, and death (Levitt, 1977). For a nonsmoker, 50–75 milligrams of nicotine could be lethal (smoking about 17 to 25 cigarettes will produce this dosage). Most beginning smokers get sick on one or two cigarettes. In contrast, a heavy smoker may consume 40 cigarettes a day without feeling ill. This difference indicates that regular smokers build a tolerance for nicotine (Levitt, 1977).

Question: Is it true that nicotine can be addicting?

There is growing evidence that for some smokers nicotine is addicting. For many, withdrawal from nicotine causes headache, sweating, cramps, insomnia, digestive upset, irritability, and a sharp craving for cigarettes (Shiffman, 1980).

Question: How serious are the health risks of smoking?

A burning cigarette releases more than 6800 different chemicals. Many of these are potent **carcinogens** (cancer-causing substances). In addition, nicotine itself may be cancer-causing (Bock, 1980). Lung cancer and other cancers caused by smoking are now considered the single most preventable cause of death in the United States. Among men, 97 percent of lung cancers are due to smoking. For women, 74 percent of all lung cancers are due to smoking, a rate that has risen sharply in recent years. Altogether, smoking is responsible for about 30 percent of all cancer deaths in the United States (Reif, 1981). If you think smoking is harmless, or the link between smoking and cancer is unproven, you're kidding yourself. As one expert says, "The scientific link between tobacco smoking and cancer is now as firmly established as any link between cause and effect in a human disease is likely to be" (Reif, 1981). As if this weren't enough, smoking is also linked to heart disease, emphysema, and birth defects (Schwartz *et al.*, 1980). An estimated 340,000 Americans die yearly of smoking-related diseases.

Smokers, unless they have a death wish, must be getting something out of smoking. Most claim that smoking helps them concentrate, makes them feel sociable, or that it calms them. However, psychologist Stanley Schachter asserts, "The heavy smoker gets nothing out of smoking. He smokes only to prevent withdrawal" (Schachter, 1978). Undoubtedly, people smoke for many reasons. But Schachter has shown that smoking does not improve the mood or the performance of heavy smokers in comparison to nonsmokers. On the other hand, heavy smokers who are *deprived* of nicotine feel worse and perform worse than nonsmokers. Schachter has also shown that heavy smokers adjust their smoking to keep bodily levels of nicotine constant. Thus, when smokers are given lighter cigarettes, they smoke more. Also, if they are under stress (which speeds the removal of nicotine from the body), they smoke more (Schachter, 1978). The connection between stress and nicotine probably explains why students smoke more during stressful periods, such as final exams, or at parties, which are also quite stressful.

Question: Is it better for a person to quit smoking abruptly, or taper down gradually?

Many authorities recommend cutting down gradually or at least switching to a low-tar cigarette. But Schachter and others believe it is better to quit "cold-turkey" rather than to merely cut down or smoke lighter cigarettes. Schachter's work shows that smokers who cut down are in a constant state of withdrawal. This causes irritability and discomfort without really ending smoking. Smokers who switch to lighter cigarettes often end up smoking more to get the same total nicotine input. In doing so, they may expose themselves to more cancer-causing substances than before (Schachter, 1978; Shiffman, 1980). Whichever approach is taken, quitting smoking is not easy. Yet tens of millions of people have quit.

Question: How do downers differ from the stimulant drugs?

Downers—Barbiturates and Alcohol

The two most widely used "downers," or depressant drugs, are alcohol and barbiturates. These drugs are so much alike in their effects that barbiturates are sometimes referred to as "solid alcohol." Let's examine the properties of each.

Barbiturates

Barbiturates are **sedative** drugs that produce a general depression of activity in the brain. They are used medically to calm patients or to induce sleep. In mild doses, barbiturates have an effect similar to alcohol intoxication, but an overdose can cause coma or death. Barbiturates combined with alcohol are particularly dangerous as the combined effects of the two drugs are multiplied by a **drug interaction** (one drug enhances the effect of another). Barbiturates are often taken in excessive amounts because a first dose may be followed by a second or third as the user becomes uninhibited or forgetful. Marilyn Monroe, Judy Garland, and a number of other well-known personalities have died of barbiturate overdoses. An overdose of barbiturates first causes unconsciousness and then so severely depresses activity in brain centers controlling heartbeat and respiration that death results.

Abuse   The most frequently abused downers are the newer short-acting barbiturates such as *Seconal* and *Tuinal.* Closely related to these (and to alcohol) is the nonbarbiturate drug *Methaqualone (Quaalude, Sopor,* and *Parest* are its trade names). These drugs seem to be preferred because they take effect quickly, and the "rush" of intoxication only lasts from two to four hours. Like the other depressants, repeated use can cause a physical dependence and emotional depression. Freddie Prinze, a popular television comedian, was on Quaaludes before he committed suicide.

All too often, the short-acting depressants are gulped down with alcohol or added in uncounted quantities to a "spiked" punch bowl. This is the combination that left Karen Ann Quinlan in a permanent coma. It is no exaggeration to restate that mixing barbiturates with alcohol can be fatal.

Alcohol

Contrary to popular belief, alcohol is not a stimulant. The apparent gaiety at drinking parties is due to alcohol's effect as a central nervous system **depressant.** As Fig. 6-4 shows, small amounts of alcohol reduce inhibition and produce feelings of relaxation and euphoria. Greater amounts of alcohol cause progressively more dangerous impairment of brain function until the drinker loses consciousness. Alcohol is also not an aphrodisiac. It usually impairs sexual performance, particularly in males. As William Shakespeare observed long ago, drink "provokes the desire, but it takes away the performance."

Abuse   Alcohol, America's favorite depressant, generates this country's biggest drug problem. Over 100 million Americans use alcohol, and an estimated 10 to 13 million of these have a serious drinking problem. A particularly alarming trend is a recent dramatic increase in alcohol abuse among adolescents and young adults. It is estimated that 20 percent of youths between the ages of fourteen and seventeen are problem drinkers (Chafetz, 1979). The costs of alcohol abuse are high. Of all drivers involved in traffic accidents resulting in death or bodily injury, 73 percent have blood alcohol levels of 0.2 percent or more (Cohen, 1970). It is probably no exaggeration to say of alcohol that:

> Its abuse has killed more people, sent more victims to hospitals, generated more police arrests, broken up more marriages and homes, and cost industry more money than has the abuse of heroin, amphetamines, barbiturates and marijuana combined (Bengelsdorf, 1970).

Questions: What are the signs of alcohol abuse?

Recognizing Problem Drinking   Because alcohol abuse is such a common problem, it is important to recognize the danger signals of alcoholism. Progression from a "social drinker" to a problem drinker to an alcoholic is often subtle. Coleman and Hammen (1974) and Jellinek (1960) have detailed steps in the development of a drinking problem:

1. **Initial phase.** Initially, the social drinker begins to turn more frequently to alcohol to relieve tension or to feel

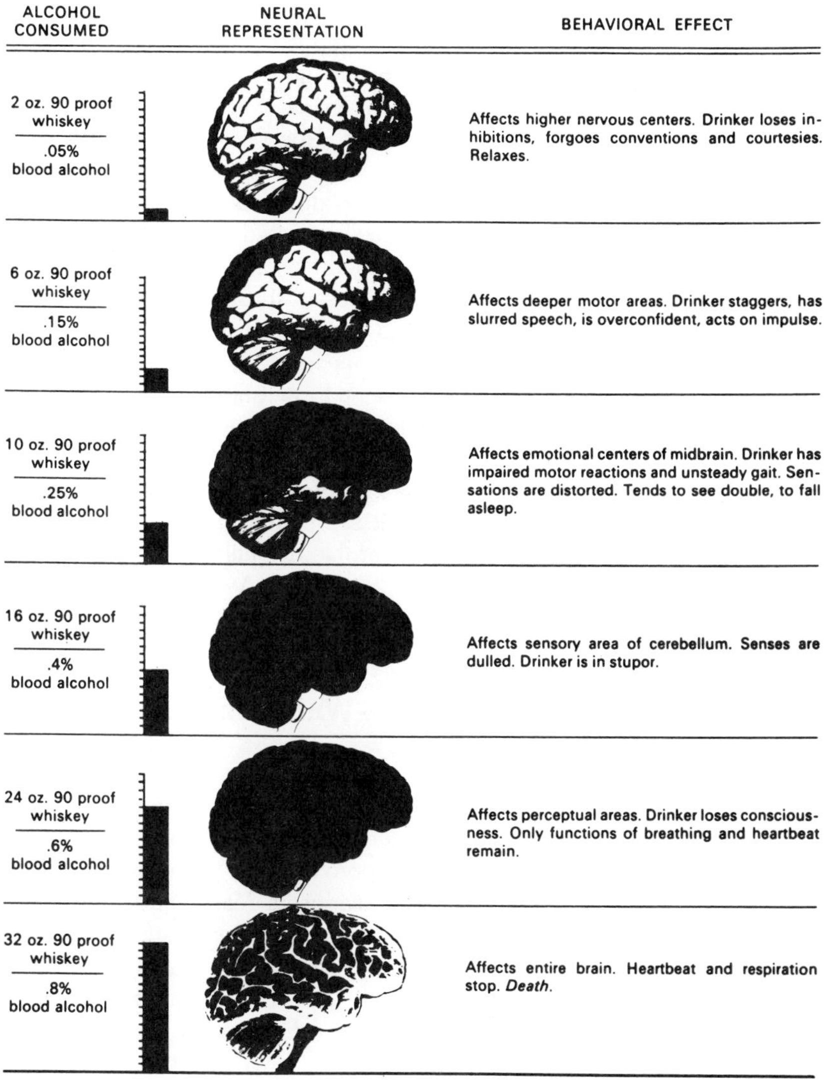

ALCOHOL CONSUMED	NEURAL REPRESENTATION	BEHAVIORAL EFFECT
2 oz. 90 proof whiskey / .05% blood alcohol		Affects higher nervous centers. Drinker loses inhibitions, forgoes conventions and courtesies. Relaxes.
6 oz. 90 proof whiskey / .15% blood alcohol		Affects deeper motor areas. Drinker staggers, has slurred speech, is overconfident, acts on impulse.
10 oz. 90 proof whiskey / .25% blood alcohol		Affects emotional centers of midbrain. Drinker has impaired motor reactions and unsteady gait. Sensations are distorted. Tends to see double, to fall asleep.
16 oz. 90 proof whiskey / .4% blood alcohol		Affects sensory area of cerebellum. Senses are dulled. Drinker is in stupor.
24 oz. 90 proof whiskey / .6% blood alcohol		Affects perceptual areas. Drinker loses consciousness. Only functions of breathing and heartbeat remain.
32 oz. 90 proof whiskey / .8% blood alcohol		Affects entire brain. Heartbeat and respiration stop. *Death.*

Fig. 6-4 The behavioral effects of alcohol are related to blood alcohol content and the resulting suppression of higher mental function. (From Jozef Cohen, Eyewitness Series in Psychology, *p. 44. Copyright © by Rand McNally and Company. Reprinted by permission.)*

good. Four danger signals in this period that signal excessive dependence on alcohol are:

Increasing consumption The individual drinks more and more and may begin to worry about his drinking.

Morning drinking Morning drinking is a dangerous sign particularly when it is used to combat a hangover or to "get through the day."

Regretted behavior The individual engages in extreme behavior while drunk that leaves him feeling guilty or embarrassed.

Blackouts Excessive drinking may be accompanied by an inability to remember what happened during intoxication.

2. Crucial phase. A crucial turning point comes as the person begins to lose control over his drinking. At this stage, there is usually control over when and where a first drink is taken, but one drink starts a chain reaction leading to a second and a third, and so on.

3. Chronic phase. At this point, alcoholics drink compulsively and continuously. They eat infrequently, become intoxicated from far less alcohol than before, and feel a powerful need for alcohol when deprived of it. Work, family ties, and social life all deteriorate. Their self-drugging is usually so compulsive that when given the choice, the bottle comes before friends, relatives, employment, and self-esteem. The alcoholic is an addict.

One of the major stumbling blocks to early detection of an alcohol problem is our society's dual attitude toward

Box 6-1

The Development of a Drinking Problem

Early Warnings

You are beginning to feel guilty about your drinking.

You drink more than you used to and tend to gulp your drinks.

You try to have a few extra drinks before or after drinking with others.

You have begun to drink at certain times or to get through certain situations.

You drink to relieve feelings of boredom, depression, anxiety, or inadequacy.

You are sensitive when others mention your drinking.

You have had memory blackouts or have passed out while drinking.

Signals Not to Be Ignored

There are times when you *need* a drink.

You drink in the morning to overcome a hangover from previous drinking.

You promise to drink less and are lying about your drinking.

You often regret what you have said or done while drinking.

You have begun to drink alone.

You have weekend drinking bouts and Monday hangovers.

You have lost time at work or school due to drinking.

You are noticeably drunk on important occasions.

Your relationship to family and friends has changed due to your drinking.

drinking. Drinking is promoted, approved, and encouraged as an escape from problems, a means of relaxing, and as a source of entertainment at social gatherings. But this approval suddenly turns to rejection when the drinker has had too much or drinks too often—"too much," however, is a hazy and undefined standard (Chafetz, 1979). Box 6-1 may help you form a clearer picture of the development of a drinking problem.

Treatment for alcoholism begins by sobering the person up and cutting off the supply. This procedure is referred to as **detoxification.** It frequently produces all the symptoms

of drug withdrawal and can be excruciatingly unpleasant for the alcoholic. The next step is to try to restore the alcoholic's physical health. Continued heavy use of alcohol usually causes severe damage to the body and nervous system. Food, vitamins, and medical care cannot fully reverse this damage, but a reasonable state of health can be obtained. When they have "dried out" and health has been restored, alcoholics may be treated with tranquilizers, antidepressants, or psychotherapy.

Unfortunately, the success of these procedures has been limited. One lay-group approach that has been fairly successful is Alcoholics Anonymous (AA), which functions on the premise that it takes a former alcoholic to understand and help a current alcoholic. AA's success rate may simply reflect the fact that members participate voluntarily, meaning they have admitted to themselves that they have a serious problem. Sadly, it seems that problem drinkers will often not admit their problems until they have really "hit bottom," but if they are willing, AA presents a practical approach to the problem.

Marijuana—What's in the Pot?

If you pick any 20 college students at random, approximately 8 or 10 will have tried marijuana. A government survey recently estimated that 40 to 50 million Americans have tried marijuana, and approximately 15 million people regard themselves as regular users. Marijuana can no longer be considered a counter-culture drug; it is used by professionals, elected officials, business people, and suburbanites (Carr and Meyers, 1980). As a government commission on drug use concluded, there are now three principal recreational drugs in this country: alcohol, tobacco, and marijuana (Shafer, 1972).

Marijuana and **hashish** are derived from the hemp plant **cannabis sativa.** The main active chemical in cannabis is tetrahydrocannabinol, or **THC** for short. THC is a mild **hallucinogen**—a substance that alters sensory impressions. The range between a psychoactive dose and a toxic dose of THC is enormous. There have been no overdose deaths from marijuana use reported in the United States (Carr and Meyers, 1980). However, enough is now known about the effects of marijuana to make it clear that it cannot be considered harmless. Particularly worrisome is the fact that THC accumulates in the body's fatty tissues, especially in the brain and reproductive organs. A water-soluble drug, such as alcohol, is flushed out of the body in a matter of hours. But THC lingers for two or more weeks. Even if a person smokes marijuana just once a week, the body is never entirely free of THC (Nahas, 1979a).

Question: Does marijuana produce physical dependence?

Some signs of withdrawal symptoms have been observed in volunteers given large doses of THC in clinical settings. However, studies of long-term heavy users of marijuana in Jamaica, Greece, and Costa Rica failed to find any physical dependence (Rubin and Comitas, 1975; Stefanis *et al.,* 1977; Carter, 1980). Marijuana's potential for abuse lies primarily in the realm of psychological dependence, not addiction.

Immediate Effects of Marijuana The physical effects of marijuana usage involve mild stimulation of various pathways in the brain, slower reflexes, bloodshot eyes, increased appetite, and increased heart rate (Grinspoon, 1972). A variety of studies agree that the drug's typical psychological effects are: a sense of euphoria or well-being, relaxation, altered time sense, and perceptual distortions (Carr and Meyers, 1980). Being "stoned" on marijuana impairs short-term memory and slows learning. Lists of words and numbers learned when a person is intoxicated are forgotten when he or she is sober again (Nahas, 1979b). Marijuana's interference with learning can become a serious problem for frequent users.

All considered, marijuana intoxication is relatively subtle by comparison to a drug such as alcohol (Carter, 1980). It may even be necessary for marijuana users to learn to experience an alteration of consciousness. At low dosages, inexperienced users often report that they feel no effect at all (Carr and Meyers, 1980). Very large dosages can cause hallucinations, and some first-time users of larger amounts have feelings of "losing control," or panic. However, most marijuana smokers gauge their intake so that the "high" attained remains pleasurable and controlled. Despite this, it is now well established that driving a car or operating machinery while high on marijuana can be extremely hazardous (Carr and Meyers, 1980). As a matter of fact, driving under the influence of any intoxicating drug is dangerous.

Question: There have been very alarming reports in the press about the dangers of marijuana. Are they accurate?

General Risks of Marijuana Use As one pharmacologist put it, "Those reading only *Good Housekeeping* would have to believe that marijuana is considerably more dangerous than the black plague." Unfortunately, the debate about marijuana's risks has been clouded by both sides: Those who oppose its use on moral, emotional, or personal grounds have exaggerated its dangers; and those who use it regularly have downplayed evidence against it. Let's see if we can strike a balance between these extremes.

In the early 1970s, it was widely reported that marijuana causes brain damage, genetic damage, loss of motivation, and a reduction in the body's natural immunity to diseases.

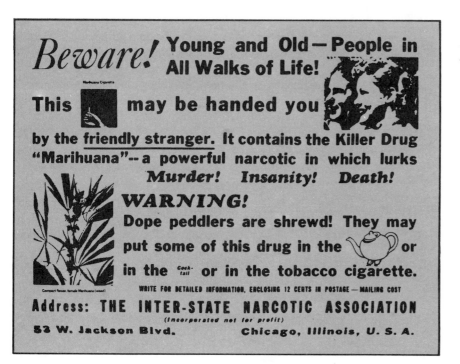

Fig. 6-5 *An outdated antimarijuana poster demonstrates the kind of misinformation that has long been attached to this drug. Research is beginning to sort out what risks are associated with continued use of marijuana.*

These are serious charges, but each has been criticized for being based on poorly done or inconclusive research (Brecher, 1975a; Zinberg, 1976; NIDA, 1976; Julien, 1978). In addition, recent studies in Jamaica, Greece, and Costa Rica failed to find any serious health problems or mental impairment in long-term marijuana smokers (Rubin and Comitas, 1975; Stefanis *et al.*, 1977; Carter, 1980). Does this mean that marijuana gets a clean bill of health? Not really. As is true of alcohol, some adults become highly dependent on marijuana. Frequent use of *any* drug to escape life's problems impedes emotional growth in much the same way that alcoholism does (Cohen, 1969). Also, marijuana smoking can become as persistent as cigarette smoking, and much more expensive.

Virtually everyone involved in the marijuana debate agrees on one point. The use of any drug, including marijuana, can seriously impair the mental, physical, and emotional development of children and adolescents (Zinberg, 1976; Nahas, 1979b). From a practical standpoint it may not matter if a youngster is an alcoholic or a "potaholic." Both problems range from serious, to disastrous.

Another legitimate concern is the possible adulteration of street drugs. For example, Mexican-grown marijuana has in recent years frequently been laced with the dangerous herbicide *Paraquat*. On occasion, street marijuana has also been found to have PCP ("angel dust") or strychnine in it; both are *very* dangerous substances.

One more point to consider is that the possession and use of marijuana is still illegal. True, some states have undertaken a **decriminalization** of marijuana laws. In these states possession brings a citation and a fine comparable to a traffic ticket. In most states, however, possession of any amount of marijuana is a misdemeanor, and in all states, a person caught with larger amounts may be charged with a *felony*. In the sense that the punishment often does more damage than the crime, marijuana laws may not be very realistic. But unless the laws change, marijuana usage can be costly in terms of a career or future employability.

Health Risks   After many years of conflicting and inadequate information, some of marijuana's potential health hazards have been clarified. After an extensive review of research, the National Academy of Sciences concluded in 1982 that marijuana's long-term effects include several health risks.

1. Marijuana smoke is quite irritating to the lungs. In regular users it causes chronic bronchitis and precancerous changes in lung cells. At present, no direct link between marijuana and lung cancer has been established, but it is suspected. Some doctors estimate that smoking several "joints" a week is the equivalent of smoking a dozen cigarettes a day. Medical researcher Gabriel Nahas (1979a) suggests that too little time has passed for the long-term effects of marijuana to show up. It took 60 years of steady cigarette smoking in the United States before the link between cigarettes and lung cancer could be demonstrated. Nahas predicts that evidence of marijuana's damaging effects on the lungs will begin showing up in the mid-1980s.

2. Marijuana temporarily lowers sperm production in males, and some studies show more abnormal sperm in men who use it. This could be a problem for a man who is marginally fertile and wants to have a family.

3. In experiments with female monkeys, THC causes abnormal menstrual cycles and disrupts ovulation. It is not known if the same applies to human females. Other animal studies show that THC causes a higher rate of miscarriages, and that it can reach the developing fetus (Nahas, 1979a). As is true for so many other drugs, it appears that marijuana should be avoided during pregnancy.

When the preceding findings are compared with those from studies of veteran marijuana users in other countries, it is clear that no one can say with complete certainty that marijuana is extremely harmful or completely safe. At present, it appears to be in a class with tobacco and alcohol, but much is still unknown (Carter, 1980). Only future research will tell for sure "what's in the pot."

Learning Check

1. Circle the letters of all the drugs listed below that are capable of causing a physical dependence:

   a. heroin   *b.* morphine   *c.* codeine   *d.* methadone
   e. barbiturates   *f.* alcohol   *g.* caffeine   *h.* amphetamines

2. Amphetamine psychosis is similar to extreme _____ in which the individual feels threatened and suffers from delusions.

3. Cocaine is very similar to _____ in its effects on the central nervous system.

   a. Quaaludes   *b.* codeine   *c.* Cannabis   *d.* amphetamine

4. The combination of _____ and alcohol can be fatal.

5. One drink starts a chain reaction leading to a second and a third in the crucial phase of problem drinking. T or F?

6. This country's biggest drug problem centers on abuse of:

    a. marijuana   *b.* alcohol   *c.* tobacco   *d.* cocaine

7. Most experts now acknowledge that marijuana is physically addicting. T or F?

Answers: 1. all but g   2. paranoia   3. amphetamine   4. barbiturates   5. T   6. b   7. F

Resources Summary

● States of awareness that differ significantly from normal, alert, waking consciousness are called *altered states of consciousness* (ASCs). Altered states are particularly associated with ESP, hypnosis, psychoactive drugs, and meditation.

● *Parapsychology* is the study of ESP and other *psi* (psychic) abilities and paranormal events. Four basic psi phenomena are: *clairvoyance, telepathy, precognition,* and *psychokinesis.*

● The existence of psi phenomena is still debated because coincidence, inconsistency, statistical problems, deception, and sloppy research have invalidated many "proofs." At the same time, a sizable research literature supporting the existence of psi events exists. The debate continues. Stage mentalists do not use ESP to do their acts.

● *Hypnotism* is an altered state characterized by narrowed attention, increased suggestibility, and a dissociation or split in awareness. Many effects of hypnosis are in doubt, but it seems definitely capable of producing relaxation, controlling pain, maintaining motivation, and altering perceptions.

● *Stage hypnotism* makes use of deception and several characteristics of the stage setting to simulate hypnosis. These include: waking suggestibility, selection of responsive subjects, disinhibition, giving stage directions, and simple parlor tricks.

● A *psychoactive* drug is a substance capable of altering functioning of the brain and nervous system in ways that alter consciousness. Most psychoactive drugs can be placed on a scale ranging from *stimulation* to *depression.*

● Drugs may cause a *physical dependence* (addiction) or a *psychological dependence,* or both. The physically addicting drugs are: heroin, morphine, codeine, methadone, barbiturates, alcohol, amphetamines, and tobacco. All psychoactive drugs can lead to psychological dependence.

● Drug use can be classified as *experimental, recreational, situational, intensive,* and *compulsive.* Drug abuse is most often associated with the last three.

● *Amphetamines* are powerful stimulants. They are subject to drug tolerance and can be very destructive to physical health. Heavy use is associated with paranoid delusions (*amphetamine psychosis*) and outbursts of violence.

● *Cocaine* is a stimulant similar to caffeine in effect at low dosages, and almost identical to amphetamine at higher doses. It differs from amphetamine in that no tolerance develops and it has a briefer time-course of action. It is not addicting but has a high dependence potential.

● *Caffeine* is a relatively mild CNS stimulant found in many foods and drug preparations. Caffeine's abuse potential is relatively low, but *caffeinism* sometimes occurs. Excessive caffeine consumption is unhealthy.

● *Nicotine* is a powerful stimulant. There is evidence that heavy smokers develop a tolerance to nicotine and undergo withdrawal if they stop smoking. Heavy users smoke mainly to regulate internal nicotine levels. Smoking causes lung cancer and other health problems.

● *Barbiturates* are depressant drugs sometimes referred to as "solid alcohol" because their action is similar to alcohol intoxication. The overdose level for barbiturates is quite close to the intoxication dosage, making them dangerous drugs. Mixing barbiturates and alcohol may be fatal.

● *Alcohol* is, in terms of potency and sheer numbers of people affected, the most dangerous and heavily abused drug in common use today. The development of a drinking problem is usually marked by an *initial phase* of increasing consumption, a *crucial phase,* in which a single drink can set off a chain reaction, and a *chronic phase,* in which a person lives to drink and drinks to live.

● The immediate effects of *marijuana* include relaxation, sensory distortions, and euphoria. Marijuana is subject to an abuse pattern similar to alcoholism, although large numbers of people use it recreationally without evidence of serious problems. Studies of long-term users have failed to find any drastic health changes due to marijuana. However, animal studies and laboratory studies have implicated marijuana as a possible source of lung cancer and other health risks. Like alcohol and tobacco use, marijuana use involves potential costs, which, for many, outweigh its attraction.

Alternative to Drugs—Meditation

One of the most popular forms of consciousness alteration has been reserved for the "Applications" section of this chapter because of its high degree of usefulness. Transcendental meditation (TM for short) is a simple exercise capable of producing a highly relaxed, although wakeful, condition. Trained meditators claim that improved energy, concentration, memory, sexual response, and alertness come from regular meditation. Others refer to it as the "drugless high" (Campbell, 1974) because it makes them feel relaxed and "at peace." Claims such as these may be exaggerated, but the fact remains that TM has no harmful effects and can be beneficial.

In a study of the bodily changes that occur during TM, Wallace and Benson (1972) found that less oxygen is consumed, the heartbeat slows, respiration is reduced, and brain waves show a marked increase in alpha frequencies. These physiological changes are the *reverse* of what is observed when the body is subjected to stress. Hence it is believed that TM can be a highly valuable means of combating the stress of modern life.

Question: How is meditation done?

Transcendental meditation is the simplest of several styles of meditation. Because of its simplicity, it is easily learned. In one experiment (Maupin, 1965), college students were simply instructed to concentrate on breathing:

> While you are sitting let your breath become relaxed and natural. Let it set its own pace and depth if you can. Then focus your attention on your own breathing: the movements of your belly, not your nose and throat. Do not allow extraneous thoughts or stimuli to pull your attention away from your breathing. This may be hard to do at first, but keep directing your attention back to it. Turn everything else aside if it comes up (Maupin, 1965).

Not all subjects responded to this exercise, but at the end of a two-week period those who did reported that they had experienced deeply satisfying changes in consciousness. Their experiences included intense concentration, pleasant bodily sensations, and extreme detachment from outside worries and distractions.

If you would like to try the meditation exercise just described, set aside a few minutes twice each day. Begin by assuming a sitting or kneeling position on the floor. Keep your back straight and let your head tilt forward slightly. This position should be comfortable enough to allow relaxation without permitting sleep. What you are aiming for is summarized by Walpola Rahula:

> At the beginning, you will find it extremely difficult to bring your mind to concentrate on your breathing. You will be astonished how your mind runs away. It does not stay. You begin to think of various things. You hear sounds outside. Your mind is disturbed and distracted. You may be dismayed and disappointed. But if you continue to practice this exercise twice a day, morning and evening, for about five or ten minutes at a time, you will gradually, by and by, begin to concentrate your mind on your breathing. After a certain period you will experience just that split second when your mind is fully concentrated on your breathing, when you will not hear even sounds nearby, when no external world exists for you (Rahula, 1959).

An alternative form of meditation you may want to try involves the use of a **mantra.** Mantras are smooth, flowing words that are easily repeated. Instead of focusing on breathing, you can silently chant a mantra. Two widely used mantras are "Om" and "Om mani padme hum." A mantra may be chanted anywhere, and like breathing, it is basically used as a focus for attention. If other thoughts arise during meditation, one should return attention to the mantra as often as necessary to maintain meditation.

The Relaxation Response   A principal claim of commercial meditation courses is that they offer a mantra tailored to the needs of each individual. Teachers of TM associated with these courses warn against learning meditation from a book or without proper personal guidance. But medical researcher Herbert Benson of Harvard Medical School has demonstrated that the physical benefits of meditation are the same no matter what word is used for a mantra. Benson believes that the core of meditation is production of the **relaxation response,** an innate physiological pattern that opposes the stressful activation of the body's fight-or-flight mechanisms. Benson feels, quite simply, that most of us have forgotten how to achieve pro-

Applications

found relaxation. Subjects in his experiments have had considerable success in producing the relaxation response by following these instructions:

> Sit quietly in a comfortable position. Close your eyes. Deeply relax all your muscles, beginning at your feet and progressing up to your face. Keep them deeply relaxed.
>
> Breathe through your nose. Become aware of your breathing. As you breathe out, say the word "one" silently to yourself.
>
> Do not worry about whether you are successful in achieving a deep level of relaxation. Maintain a passive attitude and permit relaxation to occur at its own pace. Expect distracting thoughts. When these distracting thoughts occur, ignore them and continue repeating "one." (Adapted from Benson, 1977).

Meditation probably has its greatest value as a means of lowering stress in the body. But it has the added value of allowing a short "mental vacation" from the jarring clamor of the world and from the normal competition of thoughts and worries. Its simplicity is deceptive, and its benefits may take time to become noticeable. Meditation deserves a fair trial. Many people are finding it helpful, and you may too.

Learning Check

1. During meditation there is a marked decrease in alpha-frequency brain waves. T or F?
2. Mantras are words said silently to oneself to end a session of meditation. T or F?
3. Research conducted by Herbert Benson indicates that careful selection of a mantra is necessary to obtain the physical benefits of meditation. T or F?
4. The most immediate benefit of meditation appears to be its capacity for producing a relaxation response. T or F?

Answers: 1. F   2. F   3. F   4. T

Exploration

Perspectives on Drug Abuse

Drug Abuse—Many Questions, Few Answers

Question: Why do people use drugs?

People seek drug experiences for a variety of reasons, ranging from curiosity and a desire to belong to a group to a search for meaning or an escape from feelings of inadequacy (Lipinski and Lipinski, 1970). Some observers believe that drug use is so deeply ingrained in modern society that "We are addicted to addiction. This is to say that, with few exceptions we subscribe to the premise . . . that life cannot be lived without drugs." We are so used to having our own way that we have come to believe "that we should be able to will ourselves to be calm, cheerful, thin, industrious, creative—and moreover, to have a good night's sleep" (Farber, 1966). Farber believes that the medical profession, well meaning but misguided, has accepted these premises wholeheartedly, and unnecessarily encourages drug use. Indeed, one psychologist has observed:

> Depression, social inadequacy, anxiety, apathy, marital discord, children's misbehavior, and other psychological and social problems of living are now being redefined as medical problems, to be solved by physicians with prescription pads (Rogers, 1971).

Perhaps physicians and laymen alike can be partially excused for placing undue faith in the value of drugs because each is the target of multimillion-dollar advertising campaigns aimed at encouraging drug use. Even the lowly aspirin is now pushed as a means of relieving "nervous tension." Advertisements directed at physicians encourage overuse of drugs even more blatantly. An ad pictures a distraught mother with a child and asks, "Her kind of pressures last all day . . . shouldn't her tranquilizer?" Another reads:

> School, the dark, separation, dental visits, monsters. The everyday anxiety of children sometimes gets out of hand.
>
> A child can usually deal with his anxieties. But sometimes the anxieties overpower the child. Then he needs your help. Your help may include Vistaril (Rogers, 1971).

Drugs, of course, have legitimate uses, and have alleviated much unnecessary suffering. The problem is that drugs strong enough to ease pain, induce sleep, end depression, or otherwise alter consciousness have a high potential for abuse.

Drug abuse in the United States has reached epidemic proportions in recent years. Problems once restricted to drug-related subcultures and the urban disadvantaged are now seen regularly among high school and college students, and among the vast middle classes (McGlothlin, 1975). One recent study of *junior high* students found that almost one-quarter claimed to have used illicit drugs (Anhalt and Klein, 1976). A few years ago, country western singer Charlie Pride was proclaiming in song that, "We don't smoke marijuana in Muskogee." But recent information indicates that rural areas and smaller towns have been absorbed into the national drug culture. Only extremely small towns of less than 2500 population still report relatively low rates of drug use (Bowker, 1976). Also giving cause for concern is a strong trend toward multidrug use, often involving use of drugs in combination (Gould, 1977).

Question: What, if anything, should be done about drug abuse?

Prevention   Traditional approaches have emphasized limiting drug supplies, strict law enforcement, and legal penalties. Limiting supplies has been relatively successful in the case of some drugs. But drug abuse and the legality of a drug are two relatively independent issues. This distinction becomes clear when it is recognized that one of the most potent, destructive, and potentially dangerous drugs available is alcohol. Another indication of the overuse of legally manufactured drugs can be found in the 12 billion amphetamine tablets produced each year by American drug companies. This volume is enough to supply every living American with 35 to 50 tablets (Grinspoon and Hedblom, 1972).

Facts such as these have led some observers to conclude that anyone who seeks drug-induced consciousness alteration will find a drug, legal or illegal, to achieve

Exploration

it. Psychiatrist Thomas Szasz (1972) believes that it is therefore futile for the government to attempt to "legislate morality" by regulating what drugs a person chooses to put into his or her body. Szasz suggests that current drug regulations have an effect similar to that produced by the prohibition of alcohol; that is, they encourage a black market, organized crime, disrespect for the law, and occasional poisonings from adulterated drugs.

After an extensive review of research on drugs, drug abuse, and drug laws *Consumer Reports* magazine drew the same conclusion and added these recommendations (Brecher, 1972):

> Stop publicizing the horrors of the "drug menace." Scare publicity has functioned not as warnings, but to popularize drugs and as a lure to recreational drug use.

> Stop misclassifying drugs. Our current legal classification system treats alcohol and nicotine—two of the most harmful drugs—essentially as nondrugs, while marijuana is equated with heroin—a shocking and harmful bit of foolishness. A scientifically based legal system must replace the current politically based one.

Whereas it is true that drug *use* is essentially a "victimless crime," the fact remains that *abuse* of drugs—legal or illegal—represents a serious loss in terms of the productivity and mental health of self-drugged citizens. The point of view expressed by Szasz is obviously controversial. Many, in fact, believe that the answer to drug problems is to be found in stricter penalties and law enforcement. And yet, a sober look at drug abuse makes it clear that some psychoactive drugs are almost always available. In general, Americans tend to overlook the frequency of abuse of legal drugs, such as tranquilizers or alcohol, and overestimate the misuse of illegal drugs (Drug Abuse Council, 1980). Although millions of dollars have been spent on drug enforcement since 1970, there has been virtually no change in the overall level of drug abuse in the United States. Given this fact, some experts believe prevention through education and early intervention is the answer to drug problems. What do you think?

Questions for Discussion

1. Do you agree or disagree with the idea that prohibition of drug use leads to adulteration, black markets, organized crime, unwillingness of abusers to seek help, and greater injury through imprisonment than is caused by the drugs themselves? What arguments can you give to support your position?

2. Why do you think there is such a contrast in the laws regulating cocaine and marijuana in contrast to alcohol and tobacco?

3. In the novel *Brave New World* Aldous Huxley described an imaginary drug called *soma* which made people feel continuously happy and cooperative. If such a drug existed, what controls would you impose on its use? Why? If a drug that could enhance creativity were discovered, what use would you allow for it? What about a drug to improve memory?

4. If you have ever seen a stage hypnotist or participated in a hypnosis demonstration, how did your experience compare with Barber's analysis of stage hypnosis?

5. Television "mentalists" sometimes claim to fix watches, toasters, or clocks over the airwaves. Can you explain why they might appear to succeed?

6. Describe an ESP experience you have had. What alternate explanations can you offer for it? Why do you suppose there is a recent renewed interest in paranormal events, mysticism, and the occult?

7. What rationale can you provide for alcohol becoming the drug of choice for so many adolescents and young adults?

8. If you had a totally free hand, how would you handle this country's drug abuse problem?

Suggestions for Further Reading

Altered States of Awareness. Freeman, 1972.

Barber, T. *LSD, Marijuana, Yoga, and Hypnosis.* Aldine, Modern Applications of Psychology Series, 1970.

Castaneda, C. *The Teachings of Don Juan: A Yaqui Way of Knowledge.* Ballantine, 1971.

———. *A Separate Reality.* Simon and Schuster, 1971.

———. *Journey to Ixtlan.* Simon and Schuster, 1972.

———. *Tales of Power.* Simon and Schuster, 1974.

Diaconis, P. "Statistical problems in ESP research," *Science,* **201,** 1978, 131–136.

Frazier, K. "Science and the parascience cults," *Science News,* **109,** May 29, 1976.

Gibson, H. B. *Hypnosis: Its Nature and Therapeutic Uses.* Taplinger, 1977.

Hansel, C. E. M. *ESP: A Scientific Evaluation.* Prometheus Books, 1980.

Huxley, A. *The Doors of Perception.* Harper and Row, 1970.

Ornstein, R. E. *The Psychology of Consciousness.* Freeman, 1972.

———, and C. Naranjo. *On the Psychology of Meditation.* Viking, 1971.

Randi, J. *Flim Flam!* Lippincott & Crowell, 1980.

Tart, C. T. *Altered States of Consciousness.* Doubleday, Anchor Books, 1969.

Vogler, R. E., and W. R. Bartz. *The Better Way to Drink.* Simon and Schuster, 1983.

7

Sleep and Dreaming

A Living Nightmare and Life Beyond Time

In January 1959, a New York disc jockey named Peter Tripp staged a "waka-thon" in Times Square. Tripp went without sleep for 200 hours. Tripp's fight to stay awake was difficult from the beginning. After 100 hours, he began to have visual hallucinations. He saw cobwebs in his shoes, and a doctor's tweed coat became a suit of furry worms. When he crossed the street to a hotel to change clothes, a dresser drawer seemed to burst into flames. Tripp was con-vinced that the doctors monitoring his health were trying to "test" him by staging these strange occurrences.

After 170 hours, Tripp's agony had become almost unbearable. He struggled with the simplest thought and reasoning problems. His memory became quite poor. His brain-wave patterns looked like those of sleep. He was no longer sure he was himself and finally became convinced that the doctors were trying to send him to jail. By the end of 200 hours, Tripp was no longer able to dis-tinguish between his waking nightmares, hallucination, and reality (Luce, 1965).

In a scene that could hardly be more removed from Peter Tripp's ordeal in Times Square, French scientist Michel Siffre entered Midnight Cave near Del Rio, Texas, on February 14, 1972 (Siffre, 1975). A small nylon tent deep within the cave became Siffre's home for the next six months.

Living alone within the unchanging depths of the cave, Siffre was completely isolated from clocks, calendars, the sun, the moon, and other reminders of time's passing. Siffre's ordeal—equal in many respects to Tripp's—was under-taken to find what effect such isolation would have on the natural rhythms of human life.

While in the cave, Siffre lived by "cycles" rather than by days. A cycle was counted as the time from one awakening to the next. After each period of sleep, Siffre's "day" began with a call to members of an above-ground support crew. They in turn switched on the lights that illuminated Siffre's living area until he was again ready to sleep. When he felt that a "day" had passed, Siffre called the monitoring crew and had the lights turned off.

In addition to the scientific interest of Siffre's experience, there are practical concerns. For example, if two days could be perceived as one, the emotional strain associated with space flight, or the lengthy isolation of nuclear sub-marines, or a lonely radar outpost could be eased considerably.

In partial support of such possibilities, many of Siffre's days lasted well over 24 hours. At first he stayed very close to a 24-hour cycle, and overall his "days" averaged only 28 hours. But at several points, Siffre's "days"—which seemed completely normal to him—lasted 35, 40, or even 50 hours. Siffre's longest cycle lasted an incredible 51 + hours—about 18 hours of sleep and 33 awake.

Both of these men are voyagers into a realm that is at one and the same time familiar to us all and a source of great mystery. This chapter is a further investigation into sleep, dreaming, and points beyond.

Survey Questions   How much sleep do we need? What are the effects of sleep loss or changes in sleep patterns? Are there different stages of sleep? How does dream sleep differ from dreamless sleep? What are the causes of sleep disorders and unusual sleep events? Do dreams have meaning? Can dreams be used to promote self-understanding?

Resources

Sleep—A Nice Place to Visit

Each of us will spend some 25 years of life in a strange state of semiconsciousness called sleep. Sleep is unique in many ways. It is not totally unconscious because dreams are often remembered, and thinking or problem solving may take place in dreams. Sleep is not planless; some people can "set themselves" to awaken at a particular time. During sleep, we are not totally unresponsive to our surroundings. Experiments show that you are more likely to awaken if your own name is spoken, instead of another (Webb, 1978). Likewise, a sleeping mother may ignore a jet rumbling by overhead, but wake at the slightest whimper of her child. In fact, some people can even do simple tasks while asleep. In one experiment, subjects learned to avoid an electric shock by touching a switch each time a tone sounded. After some practice, all were able to do this throughout the night without awakening. Turning off an alarm clock without waking up is a similar response. Of course, there are limits to our responsiveness while asleep. There is no evidence, for instance, that a person can learn math, a foreign language, or other complex skills while asleep (Aarons, 1976).

Because of its many contradictions, sleep has always aroused curiosity. What do we know about this daily retreat from the world?

Question: How strong is the need for sleep?

Sleep expert Wilse Webb (1975) describes sleep as a "gentle tyrant." Webb considers sleep an innate biological rhythm that can never be entirely side-stepped. But sleep is tolerant. If flexibility is needed, sleep will give way. There is a good reason for this. If a person or an animal is in great danger, it would be disastrous to fall asleep. As comedian Woody Allen put it, "The lion and the lamb shall lie down together, but the lamb will not be very sleepy." You could choose, then, to stay awake for an extended period. But there *are* limits. Animals that have had brain operations that prevent sleep fall into a coma and die after several days (Kleitman, 1963).

Early in his career, Webb tried, in every way he could imagine, to teach animals to do without sleep. For example, in one experiment, rats were placed on a treadmill above a tank of water. To avoid being dunked in the water, the rats had to keep walking on the treadmill. If they fell asleep the water immediately woke them. Even so, sleep won out. The animals soon began to engage in repeated microsleeps (Goleman, 1982). A **microsleep** is a brief shift in brain activity to patterns normally found in sleep. Microsleeps also occur in humans. Perhaps you have realized during a monotonous late night drive that several seconds passed since you were last conscious of your surroundings. Many automobile accidents occur during such momentary lapses in awareness caused by a microsleep.

Question: How long could a person go without sleep?

Sleep Deprivation   With few exceptions, four days or more without sleep becomes hell for anyone, but longer sleepless periods are possible. The world record for continuous wakefulness is held by Randy Gardner—who at age seventeen went 268 hours (11 days) without sleep. It might seem that a person would sleep for days after such a marathon. But Randy needed only 14 hours of sleep to recover (Dement, 1972). Surprisingly, it is not necessary to completely replace lost sleep. Most symptoms of sleep deprivation are removed by a single night's rest.

What are the costs of sleep loss? Age and personality make a big difference. Due in part to his youth, Randy Gardner remained coherent to the end of his vigil, whereas Peter Tripp's behavior became quite bizarre. In general, the effects of losing only a night or two of sleep are moderate. In one experiment, young volunteers were kept awake 48 hours at a time. Most showed no impairment on complex mental tasks after two days without sleep. But most grew irritable, and their ability to pay attention, remain vigilant, and follow simple routine declined (Webb, 1978). The volunteers, it seems, could rouse themselves for more complex, engaging, or challenging tasks. What suffered most was low-level, boring, self-motivated tasks. As Wilse Webb says, "It's not your thinking or memory that goes, it's your will to continue; you would prefer to be asleep" (Goleman, 1982).

Longer periods without sleep occasionally produce a temporary **sleep-deprivation psychosis** like that experienced by Peter Tripp. Common elements of this reaction are confusion and disorientation, delusions (false or distorted beliefs), and hallucinations. Hallucinations may be visual, like Tripp's "coat of furry worms," or tactile, such as feeling cobwebs on the face. Fortunately, such "crazy" behavior is less common than once thought. Hallucinations and delusions, if they occur at all, are never evident before 60 hours of sleep loss. The most common reactions to extended sleep loss are inattention, staring, fine hand tremor, drooping eyelids, and an increased sensitivity to pain (Webb, 1978).

Question: What is the normal range of sleep needs?

Sleep Needs and Patterns   According to medical records, there is a man in England who gets by on only 15 minutes to an hour of sleep each night—and feels perfectly fine. However, this is quite a rarity. Only 8 percent of the population averages five hours of sleep or less per night. The majority sleep on a familiar seven- to eight-hour per night schedule. Yet in the same way that individual needs for food differ, there is considerable variation around the eight-hour average for sleep. It is quite normal to sleep as little as five hours per night, or as much as eleven. Urging everyone to sleep eight hours a night would be like advising everyone to wear medium-size shoes.

Question: Do elderly people need more sleep?

They may need it, but they seldom get it! Increasing age usually brings a *reduction* in sleep time. People over the age of fifty average only six hours of sleep a night. In con-

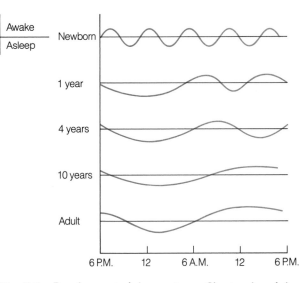

Fig. 7-1   *Development of sleep patterns. Short cycles of sleep and waking gradually become the night-day cycle of an adult. (After Williams, 1964)*

trast, infants spend up to 20 hours a day sleeping, usually in two- or four-hour cycles. This pattern suggests theirs is a "wakefulness of necessity" brought about mainly by needs for food and changing. With increasing age, most children go through a "nap" stage and eventually settle into a steady cycle of sleeping once a day (see Fig. 7-1). Some people, of course, maintain the afternoon "siesta" as an adult pattern.

There is a great temptation to try to reduce sleep time. Buckminster Fuller, inventor of the geodesic dome, claims to have gone for long periods of time sleeping only two hours a day. Fuller noticed that when a dog gets tired it simply lies down and sleeps. Fuller began sleeping whenever he felt like it. For him, this worked out to a half hour every six. Before you try the same thing, you should know that such schedules are usually less efficient than sleeping once a day. Why should this be true? As long as a person gets eight or nine hours of sleep a day, what difference would it make? The problem is that people on shortened cycles—for example, three hours of sleep to six hours awake—often can't get to sleep when the cycle calls for it (Webb, 1978). This is why American astronauts continue to sleep on their normal earth schedule once in space (Goleman, 1982). There is another reason for not shortening sleep schedules. Evidence suggests that we do not now get as much sleep as people living in previous centuries. Thus, we may already be chronically "sleep starved" (Webb et al., 1975).

Most studies of **sleep patterns** show a consistent ratio of *two to one* between time awake and time asleep. This opens a more realistic possibility for altering sleep habits. As Michel Siffre (the temporary cave dweller) found, humans may be able to adapt to longer "days" than those typically imposed by the cycles of the sun. Other experiments (Kleitman and Kleitman, 1953), in which 28-hour days were set up, indicate that younger subjects find it easier to adapt to longer cycles of sleep and waking, presumably because their sleep habits are less firmly established. However, on very long 36-hour cycles (24 awake and 12 asleep) subjects did poorly. Most simply couldn't use the entire 12-hour sleep period, so they lost sleep over several cycles (Webb, 1978). As with sleep needs, we see again that sleep is a "gentle tyrant." Sleep patterns may be bent and stretched, but they rarely yield entirely to human whims.

Stages of Sleep—
The Nightly Roller-Coaster Ride

Question: What causes sleep?

Early conceptions of sleep linked it to fatigue. It was thought that some substance caused by fatigue must accumulate in the bloodstream and cause sleep. But studies of Siamese twins (individuals whose bodies are joined at

Fig. 7-2 *These Siamese twins share the same blood supply, yet one head sleeps while the other is awake. (Photo by Yale Joel,* Life Magazine. © *1954 Time, Inc.)*

birth) show this is false. One twin can frequently be observed sleeping while the second is awake (see Fig. 7-2). During extended wakefulness, a sleep-promoting chemical collects in the brain and spinal cord, *not* in the blood. If this substance is extracted from one animal and injected into another, the second animal will fall asleep (Pappenheimer, 1976). Notice, however, that this experiment does not fully explain sleep. For example, how do we account for the well-rested student who must fight to stay awake during a boring lecture?

All that can be said with certainty is that sleep is *actively* generated by several important structures in the brain: the hypothalamus, reticular formation, and a "sleep center" in the brainstem. Rather than "shutting down" during sleep, the brain changes the *pattern* of its activity, not the amount.

Question: Why should the brain be programmed so that we regularly become unconscious?

No one really knows, but there are some hints. Folk wisdom says that sleep is a time when mental and physical "housekeeping," or restoration, takes place. Indeed, there is a lowering of body temperature and metabolism during sleep—changes that may conserve energy and lengthen life. For example, shrews have a high metabolic rate and rarely sleep. By contrast, bats sleep up to 20 hours a day. The life span of the shrew is about 2 years, whereas bats of the same size live up to 18 years. Thus the bat's ability to "turn itself off" may result in a ninefold increase in life span (Allison and Van Twyver, 1970). During the course of evolution, natural selection may have also favored sleep. Those animals who did not retire to burrow, tree, cave, or hollow had a higher chance of going out at night and getting into trouble, or of being killed (Greenberg, 1978). (No doubt they had more fun, though.)

Question: What happens when you fall asleep?

The Stages of Sleep   The changes that come with sleep can be measured through use of the **EEG (electroencephalograph,** or brain-wave machine). The brain gives off tiny electrical signals that can be amplified and recorded. When a person is awake and alert the EEG shows a pattern of small fast waves called **beta** (see Fig. 7-3). Immediately before sleep the EEG shifts to a different pattern of larger and slower waves called **alpha.** (Alpha waves also occur at other times when one is relaxed and thoughts are allowed to drift.) As the eyes close, breathing becomes slow and regular, the pulse rate slows, and body temperature drops.

Stage 1   As the person loses consciousness and enters **light sleep,** the heart rate slows even more. Breathing

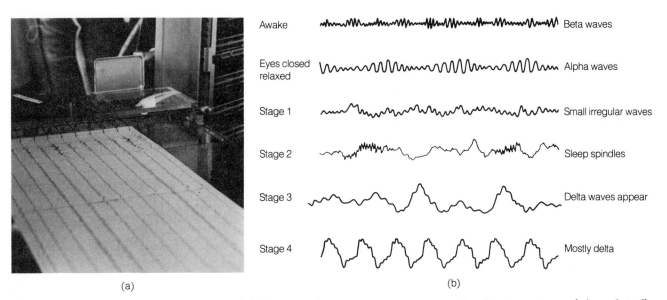

Fig. 7-3 (a) Photograph of an EEG tracing. (b) Changes in brain-wave patterns associated with various stages of sleep. Actually, most wave types are present at all times, but they occur more or less frequently in various sleep stages.

becomes more irregular; the muscles of the body relax. This sometimes triggers a reflex muscle contraction called **myoclonus** (MY-oh-KLOE-nus), which is quite normal. In Stage 1 sleep, the EEG is made up mainly of small, irregular waves with some alpha.

Stage 2 As sleep deepens, the EEG begins to show short bursts of activity called **"sleep spindles"** (see Fig. 7-3).

Stage 3 In Stage 3, a new brain wave called **delta** begins to appear. Delta waves are very large and slow. Delta waves signal deeper sleep and a further loss of consciousness.

Stage 4 About an hour after sleep begins **deep sleep** is reached. In Stage 4 the brain-wave pattern becomes almost pure delta waves, and the sleeper is in a state of nearly complete oblivion. If a loud noise is sounded

during Stage 4, the sleeper will awaken in confusion and may not remember the noise.

After spending some time in Stage 4, the sleeper returns (through Stages 3 and 2) to Stage 1. This cycle of changes between deep sleep and light sleep is repeated four or five times per night (see Fig. 7-4).

Two States of Sleep Along with the discovery of sleep stages, it was noticed that at various times the eyes of a sleeper make rapid movements. These rapid eye movements (or **REMs**) are strongly associated with dreaming. Roughly 85 percent of awakenings made when REMs are present produce reports of dreams (Cartwright, 1978). REMs usually occur in Stage 1 sleep. An exception is the Stage 1 period that occurs as you are falling asleep, which is usually free of REMs and dreams. **REM sleep** can be

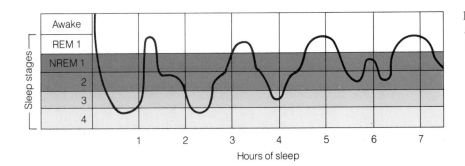

Fig. 7-4 Typical changes in stages of sleep during the night. (After Van de Castle, 1971)

readily observed in animals found around the house, such as dogs and cats. Watch for movement of the eyes under the eyelids, and for facial movements and irregular breathing. In addition to twitching ears, whiskers, and paws, cats and dogs may also move their legs in synchrony, as if they were trying to run.

The two most basic states of sleep now appear to be REM sleep, with its associated dreaming, and **non-REM (NREM)** sleep, which occurs during Stages 2, 3, and 4 (Cartwright, 1978). NREM sleep is dream-free about 90 percent of the time. People awakened during NREM sleep occasionally say they were "dreaming," but most report that something more like thinking was taking place (Van de Castle, 1971). NREM sleep seems to help us recover from fatigue built up during the day. It increases with exercise or physical exertion. In comparison, REM sleep increases when a person is subjected to added daytime stress. Although REM sleep totals only about one and one-half hours per night (about the same as a feature movie), its connection with dreaming makes it as important as NREM sleep. REM sleep may become pronounced when there is a death in the family, a major occupational change, marital conflict, or other emotionally charged event (Hartmann, 1973).

Learning Check

See if you can answer these questions before reading on.

1. A momentary shift in brain activity to a pattern characteristic of sleep is referred to as:

    a. delta sleep   *b.* light sleep   *c.* microsleep   *d.* deprivation sleep

2. Delusions and hallucinations may continue for several days after a sleep-deprived individual returns to normal sleep.   T or F?

3. Older adults, and particularly the elderly, sleep more than children because they are more easily fatigued.   T or F?

4. Most studies of sleep patterns show a consistent ratio two to one between time awake and time asleep.   T or F?

5. Rapid eye movements (REMs) indicate a person is in deep sleep.   T or F?

6. Match the following:

    _____ Awake, relaxed   **A.** Sleep spindles

    _____ Stage 2   **B.** Dreaming

                                  C. Myoclonus

    _____ Stage 4   **D.** Delta waves

    _____ Stage 1, REM   **E.** Alpha waves

Answers: 1. c   2. F   3. F   4. T   5. F   6. E,A,D,B

REM Sleep and Dreaming— Night Mysteries

When researchers Nathaniel Kleitman and Eugene Aserinsky discovered REM sleep in 1952, they ushered in a "Golden Era" of dream inquiry that has allowed us to answer some age-old questions. Let us consider some of the most interesting.

Question: Does everyone dream? Do dreams occur in an instant?

Most people dream four or five times a night, but not all people remember their dreams. "Nondreamers" are often shocked by the vividness of their dreams when first awakened during REM sleep. Dreams are usually spaced about 90 minutes apart, with each succeeding dream lasting a little longer. The first dream lasts only about 10 minutes; the last averages 30 minutes and may run as long as 50. Dreams, therefore, occur in real time, not as a "flash" (Dement, 1960; Cartwright, 1978).

Question: What happens to the body when a person dreams?

REM Sleep   As discussed before, the brain returns to light sleep and rapid eye movements begin. Some eye movements correspond to dream activity: Dream that you are watching a tennis match, and you will probably roll your eyes from side to side (Dement and Kleitman, 1957). Because there is a return to Stage 1, dreaming has been called **paradoxical sleep.** It looks like the sleeper is about to awaken, but he or she is actually harder to arouse. This may be partially explained by the fact that noises and other stimuli are often incorporated into dreams. (Have you ever made your alarm clock into a "telephone call" in a dream?) In one experiment subjects displaying REMs were sprayed with droplets of water. Of these subjects, 42 percent reported dreams of rain, Niagara Falls, and so forth (Dement and Wolpert, 1958).

REM sleep is a time of high emotion. The heart beats irregularly, and blood pressure and breathing fluctuate. Both males and females appear to be sexually aroused: Males usually have an erection, and genital blood flow increases in women. This occurs for all REM sleep, so it is not strictly related to erotic dreams. When an erotic dream does occur, evidence of sexual arousal becomes more pronounced (Cartwright, 1978). With all this emotional activity, it might be expected that muscles would be tense during dreaming. The reverse is true, however. Except for the eyes, the body becomes quite still during REM sleep. It is as if the person is paralyzed. If we imagine the results of acting out dreams, it seems that REM-sleep paralysis prevents some hilarious nighttime escapades. Fortunately, changing positions and other large movements take place *between* REM periods.

Question: How important are dreams? Are they essential for normal functioning?

Dreams   To answer these questions, dream researcher William Dement awakened subjects each time they entered REM sleep. People prevented from dreaming several nights in a row showed an increased tendency to dream. By the fifth night, 20 or 30 awakenings were often necessary to prevent dreaming. When they were finally allowed to sleep without interruption, subjects dreamed extra amounts. This is called the **REM rebound** effect (Dement, 1960). It explains why alcoholics often have horrible nightmares after they quit drinking. Alcohol suppresses REM sleep and sets up a powerful rebound effect when it is withdrawn.

While they were deprived of dream sleep, Dement's subjects complained of memory lapses, difficulty in concentrating, and feelings of anxiety during the day. For a time, this result led to widespread belief that a person would go crazy if kept from dreaming. But sleep researchers now refer to this as the "REM myth." Recent experiments indicate that missing out on *any* particular sleep stage can cause a rebound for that stage. More importantly, daytime

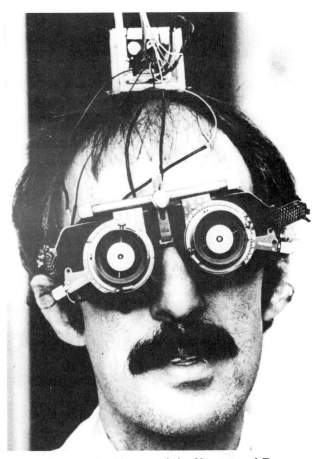

Fig. 7-5 *Dr. John Herman of the University of Texas may look like he just stepped out of the movie* Star Wars, *but he is actually involved in dream research. Dr. Herman is wearing goggles that electronically monitor eye movements during sleep. Use of such devices has greatly extended our understanding of dreaming.*

disturbances are generally related to the total *amount* of sleep lost, not the type of sleep lost (Johnson *et al.,* 1972; Cartwright, 1978).

Just the same, some tantalizing connections between dreaming and mental health remain. One researcher has used the REM rebound effect to link dreaming to schizophrenia. Schizophrenic patients deprived of REM sleep fail to show the rebound effect. This observation suggests they may be discharging dream activity while awake. Perhaps the bizarre behavior of some disturbed individuals can be understood as a blending of dreams with normal daytime experiences (Zarcone, 1971). Going without dreams at night apparently won't make you crazy, but dreaming while awake certainly might.

Question: What is the purpose of REM sleep in normal individuals?

There are several interesting possibilities. It may be that dream sleep provides stimulation needed for developing the brain. Newborn babies spend about 50 percent of their sleeping time in REM sleep. This amounts to a hearty eight or nine hours a day of dream time. Premature babies get even more REM sleep (up to 75 percent). By age five, when the nervous system is more mature, REM time drops to 20 percent, about the same as for an adult (Feinberg and Carlson, 1967; Allison and Van Twyer, 1970). In adulthood, REM sleep may serve other purposes. These include restoring the brain's chemical balance, integrating and storing information learned during the day, preventing sensory deprivation during sleep, and processing emotional events. Although we have much to learn, it seems clear that REM sleep and dreaming are valuable for keeping the brain in good working order.

Sleep Disturbances— Showing Nightly: Sleep Wars!

In the last 10 years, a new kind of treatment center appeared in hospitals. *Sleep clinics,* as they are called, now treat thousands of people who suffer from sleep disorders or complaints. Let's see what has been learned about a few of the most common problems.

Sleepwalking and Sleeptalking   Like many sleep disturbances, sleepwalking is an eerie and fascinating phe-

nomenon. **Somnambulists** (som-NAM-bue-lists) negotiate obstacles, descend stairways, climb trees, and on rare occasions may step out of windows or in front of automobiles. The sleepwalker's eyes are usually open, and he or she is able to respond to commands or questions. Sleepwalkers move as if they can see, but a blank face, lack of recognition, and shuffling feet show they are still asleep.

Question: Does sleepwalking occur during dreaming?

It was long supposed that sleepwalkers are acting out dream events, but EEG studies have shown that somnambulism occurs during Stages 3 and 4. **Sleeptalking** also occurs in NREM stages of sleep and appears to be a completely normal outlet for NREM "thinking." The association of sleepwalking and sleeptalking with the deeper stages of sleep seems to explain why sleeptalking makes little sense and why a sleepwalker who is awakened is confused and remembers little (Jacobson *et al.,* 1965; Luce, 1974). Remember, too, that a person is paralyzed during REM sleep, so vigorous actions cannot occur.

Nightmares and Night Terrors   Stage 4 sleep is also the source of night terrors, severely frightening experiences that can be distinguished from the normal nightmare (see Table 7-1). A **nightmare** is simply a bad dream that takes place during REM sleep. Nightmares are usually brief. The person awakens and remembers the dream in complete detail. During Stage 4 night terrors, a person experiences blind panic, and may hallucinate frightening dream images into the room itself. The attack may last 15 or 20 minutes. When it is over, the person awakens drenched in perspiration, but has only a vague memory of the terror itself. Since night terrors occur during NREM sleep when the body is not immobilized, the victim may sit up, get out of bed, or run around the room. Night terrors are most

---

Table 7-1   Was It a Nightmare or a Night Terror?

	Nightmare	Night Terror
Stage of sleep	☐ REM	☐ NREM
Activity	☐ Slight or no movement	☐ Violent body movement, sits up, cries out, may run
Emotion	☐ Fear or anxiety	☐ Terror and disorganizing panic
Mental state when awakened	☐ Can be calmed, coherent	☐ Incoherent, cannot be calmed, disoriented, may be hallucinating
Physiological changes	☐ No perspiration	☐ Perspires heavily
Recall	☐ Dream activity usually remembered	☐ Amnesia for episode

(Adapted from Woods and Greenhouse, 1974.)

common in childhood, but continue to plague some adults throughout their lives (Kanner, 1957; Kales and Kales, 1973).

Narcolepsy   One of the most dramatic sleep problems is **narcolepsy.** Narcolepsy is characterized by sudden, repeated, and irresistible "sleep attacks." These last anywhere from a few minutes to a half hour. They are so overpowering that victims fall asleep while standing, talking, or even driving. Most victims also suffer from **cataplexy,** a sudden temporary paralysis of the muscles leading to complete body collapse.

Question: What causes such drastic reactions?

When monitored on an EEG, narcoleptics tend to fall directly into REM sleep. (Recall that the first REM period normally occurs about 90 minutes after sleep begins.) The narcoleptic's sleep attacks and muscle paralysis apparently result from an intrusion of REM into the waking state. Fortunately, narcolepsy is quite rare. It tends to run in families, which suggests it is hereditary. This has been confirmed by breeding several generations of narcoleptic dogs (Guilleminault *et al.,* 1976). (These dogs, by the way, are simply outstanding at learning the trick, "Roll over and play dead.") For humans, there is no known cure for narcolepsy, but stimulant drugs may cut down the frequency of attacks.

Insomnia   While some people sleep when they don't want to, a far greater number have trouble getting enough sleep. An estimated 40 million Americans suffer from chronic insomnia (Kripke and Simons, 1976). **Insomnia** includes difficulty in going to sleep, frequent nighttime awakenings, waking too early, or any combination of these. Almost everyone has had an occasional bout of insomnia.

Americans spend more than one-half billion dollars each year on drugs to help them sleep. There is real irony in this expenditure. Nonprescription sleeping pills such as *Sominex, Nytol,* and *Sleep-eze* have little or no sleep-inducing effect (Kales and Kales, 1973). Even worse are prescription *sedatives.* These drugs (usually barbiturates) decrease both Stage 4 and REM sleep, and thereby drastically reduce sleep quality. In addition, a drug tolerance rapidly builds so that the initial dosage becomes ineffective. Many users become "sleeping-pill junkies" as an ever greater number of pills is required to produce sleep. The resulting **drug-dependency insomnia** is a serious problem. Victims must be painstakingly withdrawn from all sleeping medications. Otherwise, terrible nightmares and sleep disturbances drive them back to drug use.

Question: If sleeping pills are a poor way to treat insomnia, what can be done?

Temporary insomnia caused by worry, stress, or excitement usually sets up a cycle in which heightened physical arousal interferes with sleep, then frustration and anger resulting from inability to sleep causes more arousal, which further interferes with sleep, which causes more frustration, and so on. This cycle suggests that one of the best ways to beat temporary insomnia is to avoid fighting it. It is usually best to get up and do something useful or satisfying when you have difficulty sleeping (reading a textbook might not be a bad choice of useful activities). Some insomniacs have been found to have a drop in blood sugar during the night. The restlessness and hunger this causes can be avoided by having a small snack before sleeping. Also, it has been discovered that the amino acid **tryptophan** (TRIP-toe-fan) helps put people to sleep. Interestingly, tryptophan can be found in a glass of milk (Arehart-Treichel, 1977). So grandma was right after all! But she apparently didn't know that an egg-tuna-soybean-cashew-chicken-turkey-cottage cheese sandwich would be even better for inducing sleep. All of the listed foods are also high in tryptophan (Hartmann, 1978).

Question: What about more serious cases of insomnia?

EEG studies of chronic insomniacs show they have very erratic sleep patterns rather than the regular 90 minute cycle of stages (Monroe, 1967). They also show heightened arousal before sleep and throughout the night. Treatment for **chronic insomnia** usually begins with training in relaxation techniques to lower arousal before sleep. (See Chapter 23 "Applications" for more about relaxation.) "Stimulus control" procedures are also helpful. For example, patients are told to strictly avoid doing anything but sleeping in bed. They are not to study, eat, watch TV, read, or even think in bed. In this way, only sleeping becomes associated with retiring (Bootzin, 1973). One of the most helpful techniques for combating insomnia is also the simplest. Many insomniacs have scattered sleep habits. For these people, adopting a regular schedule (getting up and going to sleep at exactly the same time each day) helps establish a firm body rhythm and greatly improves sleep.

Sleep Apnea   If your family tree is like most, it probably includes at least one outrageous snorer. Nightly "wood sawing" is often harmless, but it can signal a serious problem. A person who snores loudly, with short silences and loud gasps or snorts, may suffer from **sleep apnea** (ap-

NEE-uh). In sleep apnea, breathing stops for periods of 20 seconds to two minutes. As the need for oxygen becomes intense, the person wakes a little and gulps in air. He or she then settles back to sleep; but soon, breathing stops again. This cycle is repeated hundreds of times a night (Guillemi-nault, 1979). Understandably, apnea victims complain of insomnia, morning headaches, or daytime sleepiness.

Question: What causes sleep apnea?

Some apnea occurs because the brain stops sending signals to the diaphragm to maintain breathing. Another cause is blockage of the upper-air passages. In either case, the person can breathe normally during the day, so he or she may be unaware of the problem. Apnea becomes more common after age sixty, but it should be suspected any time very loud snoring is present. In addition to causing much misery, apnea seriously endangers health. Persons who suspect they are apneic should seek treatment at a sleep clinic (Hales, 1980).

Sleep apnea is especially dangerous in infancy, when it is suspected as one cause of **Sudden Infant Death Syn-** **drome** (SIDS), or "crib death." SIDS is the most frequent cause of death between the ages of one month and one year (Naeye, 1980). In the "typical" crib death, a slightly premature or small baby with some signs of a cold or cough is put to bed. A short time later, when parents return to the crib, the child is dead. An autopsy usually shows the infant was in good health, with a mild cold or infection at most.

Some doctors think that SIDS is caused by apnea due to immaturity of breathing centers in the brainstem (Hales, 1980). Others suspect direct blockage of the nose is responsible. Most infants will cry, flail, and kick if the nose is blocked for a few seconds—responses that can save them if they roll face-down. But some babies remain passive when breathing is blocked. These infants run a much higher risk of crib death (Lipsett, 1980). Such babies must be carefully watched for the first six or seven months of life. To aid parents in this task, a special monitor may be used to sound an alarm when breathing becomes weak (Naeye, 1980).

Learning Check

Match the following:

A. REM sleep   **B.** NREM sleep

_____ **1.** Paradoxical sleep   _____ **5.** Sleeptalking

_____ **2.** Nightmares   _____ **6.** Emotion and sexual arousal

_____ **3.** Night terrors   _____ **7.** Relaxed muscles, little movement

_____ **4.** Sleepwalking   _____ **8.** Narcolepsy

9. Adults generally spend more time in REM sleep than do children.   T or F?

10. Somnambulists usually also suffer from cataplexy.   T or F?

11. Sleep apnea is suspected as a major cause of SIDS.   T or F?

Answers: 1. A   2. A   3. B   4. B   5. B   6. A   7. A   8. A   9. F   10. F   11. T

Dreams and Beyond—A Separate Reality

Question: What do people usually dream about?

Calvin Hall, a noted authority on dreams, has collected and analyzed over 10,000 dreams. Hall (1966) found that most dreams are extensions of everyday experience. The favorite dream setting is familiar rooms in a house. Action usually takes place between the dreamer and two or three other people with whom the dreamer is emotionally involved— friends, enemies, parents, or employers. Actions in dreams are also predominantly familiar: running, jumping, riding, sitting, talking, and watching. About half of the recorded dreams had sexual elements. Dreams of flying, floating, and falling occur less frequently. Hall also found that if you're dreaming more now, you may be enjoying it less. Unpleasant emotions such as fear, anger, and sadness are more frequent in dreams than pleasant emotions.

Question: Do the dreams of men and women differ?

The dreams of men and women (in our culture) seem to reflect traditional sex roles. Compared to men, women's dreams are more emotional, less aggressive, less focused on sexual themes, more often indoors, and more often about home and family. Male characters appear more in the dreams of both men and women; but in men's dreams they are more likely to be rivals or antagonists. In describing dreams, men use more action words, such as run, hit, or drive; women use more words of feeling or emotion. Women are more often pursued or endangered in their dreams (Winget and Kramer, 1979).

Since many of the elements of dreams are familiar, it might seem that they are woven directly from sensory images experienced each day. However, accident victims confined to wheelchairs continue to have dreams in which they walk or run (as well as dreams in which they are in the chair) (Dement, 1972). There is also evidence that earlier dreams involve recent events, whereas those occurring toward morning draw more on past events, including childhood memories.

Question: How meaningful are dreams?

Interpreting Dreams

Most theorists agree that dreams reflect our waking personalities. For one thing, dreams are similar in many ways to daytime fantasies and thoughts (Winget and Kramer, 1979). Also, a large body of research shows that dream content reflects waking emotional concerns and styles (Cartwright, 1978). Thus, a better question might be, "How deep should we dig in interpreting dreams?" Some theorists believe that dreams have deeply hidden meanings. Others feel dreams are a fairly simple extension of waking thought. Let's examine both views.

Psychodynamic Dream Theory Sigmund Freud's book *The Interpretation of Dreams* (1900) opened a whole new world of psychological investigation. Prior to Freud, most psychologists considered dreams a meaningless carry-over of waking thoughts or the result of indigestion. Upon analyzing his own dreams, Freud felt that many represented **wish fulfillment**. Thus, a student who is angry at a teacher may dream of successfully embarrassing the

teacher in class; a lonely person may dream of romance; or a hungry child may dream of food. Although Freud's view of dreaming is attractive, there is evidence against it. For example, volunteers in a study of the effects of prolonged starvation showed no particular increase in dreams about food and eating (Keys, 1950).

Freud's response to this result probably would have been that not all wish fulfillment is so direct. He believed that the conscience relaxes during sleep, allowing dreams to express *repressed* or *unconscious* desires and conflicts. Many such desires are so threatening that they must be represented in disguised form so as not to directly arouse the person's conscience. A woman sexually attracted to her best friend's husband might dream of stealing her friend's wedding ring and placing it on her own hand, an indirect symbol of her true desires. (For a discussion of dream analysis in psychotherapy see Chapter 22.)

To unlock dreams, Freud identified four **dream processes** that help disguise the hidden meaning of a consciously remembered dream. The first process is called **condensation.** Through condensation a single character in a dream may represent several people at once. A character in a dream that looks like a teacher, acts like your father, talks like your mother, and is dressed like your employer might be a condensation of prominent authority figures in your life. (It might also be someone on the way to a masquerade party!) A second means of disguising dream content is **displacement.** Through displacement the most important emotions of a dream may be redirected toward "safe" or seemingly unimportant images. A student angry at his parents might dream of accidentally wrecking their car instead of directly attacking them.

A third dream process is **symbolization.** This is one of the most controversial of Freud's ideas. Freud believed that dreams are usually expressed in images that are symbolic rather than literal in their meaning. The list in Box 7-1 summarizes some common Freudian interpretations of dream symbols. You will notice that the interpretations strongly emphasize sexual motives and tend to be highly imaginative. Many psychologists reject such interpretations as misleading.

A process called **secondary elaboration** is the fourth method by which the meaning of dreams is disguised. Secondary elaboration is the tendency to reorganize a dream when remembering it. The story line of the dream is made more logical, and additional details are added to connect the jumbled dream images.

Question: Do all dreams have hidden meanings?

Box 7-1

Common Freudian Dream Interpretations and Their Symbols:

1. Parents—emperors, empresses, kings, queens
2. Children (brothers and sisters)—small animals
3. Birth—water
4. Death—journey
5. Nakedness—clothes, uniforms
6. Male genitals—sticks, umbrellas, poles, trees, anything elongated, pointed weapons of all sorts
7. Erection—balloons, airplanes, zeppelins, dreamer himself flying
8. Male sexual symbols—reptiles, fishes, serpent, hand or foot
9. Female genitalia—pits, hollow caves, jars, bottles, doors, ships, chests
10. Breasts—apples, peaches, other fruit
11. Intercourse—mounting a ladder or stairs, entering a room, walking down a hall or into a tunnel, horseback riding, and so forth.

Probably not. Even Freud realized that some dreams are trivial or unimportant "day residues," or carry-overs from ordinary waking events. Also, you may be relieved to learn that Freud's is not the only approach to dream interpretation. For example, Carl Jung, a rebellious student of Freud's, came to believe that, "There are no fixed symbolic meanings." Jung considered it important to learn a person's own symbolic language by studying a *series* of dreams. At the same time, he emphasized the presence of universal images, or **archetypes,** in dreams. Let us say, for instance, that a man dreams of dancing with his sister. To Freud this would probably be a sign of hidden incestuous feelings. For Jung the sister might represent an unexpressed feminine side of the man's personality; or if especially vivid, the dream could symbolize the cosmic dance that intertwines "maleness" and "femaleness" in all lives.

The Activation-Synthesis Hypothesis   A radically different view of dreaming is offered by scientists Allan Hobson and Robert McCarley (1977). After some 15 years of studying REM sleep in cats, Hobson and McCarley believe that dreams are made in this way: Cells in a "sleep center" in the brainstem are activated during REM sleep. These, in turn, arouse nearby cells that control eye movements, bal-

ance, and actions, such as walking, stepping, or running. However, messages from the cells are blocked from actually reaching the body, so no movement occurs. But the cells continue to tell higher brain areas of their activities. Struggling to come up with a reasonable interpretation of this information, the brain searches through stored memories and manufactures a dream. Hobson and McCarley call this explanation of dreaming the **activation-synthesis hypothesis.**

Question: How does this help explain dream content?

Let's use the classic chase dream as an example. In such dreams, we feel we are running, but not going anywhere as a pursuer bears down on us. Hobson and McCarley suggest that in such dreams the brain is being told the body is running, but it gets no feedback from the motionless body to confirm it. As it tries to make sense of this information the brain creates a chase drama. Similarly, sensations of flying or floating may occur as the brain receives information on eye movement and balance, and interprets it as flying.

A Look Ahead   The activation-synthesis hypothesis certainly seems to explain some dream experiences. Most psychologists, however, continue to believe that dreams have deeper meaning. Consider, for example, a recently divorced woman who kept dreaming that she was being swallowed by a giant wave. Dream theorist Rosalind Cartwright (1978) suggested to the woman that the dream meant she felt overwhelmed by life and couldn't cope. Cartwright asked the woman to try swimming the next time the wave engulfed her. She did, with great determination, and the nightmare lost its terror. More importantly, her new dream gave her a sense that she could cope with life again.

There seems little doubt that dreams can make a difference in our lives: Pioneering sleep researcher William Dement once dreamed that he had lung cancer. In the dream a doctor told Dement he would die soon. At the time, Dement was smoking two packs of cigarettes a day. He says, "I will never forget the surprise, joy, and exquisite relief of waking up. I felt reborn." Dement quit smoking the following day (Hales, 1980).

In recent years the idea that dreams can only be interpreted by a professional has given way to an appreciation of the personal nature of dream meanings. As a result, many psychologists now urge people to collect and interpret their own dreams. The "Applications" section that follows offers some practical suggestions for doing just that.

Learning Check

1. Dreams occurring toward morning draw more heavily upon:

    a. recent daytime experiences   b. colored images
    c. symbolization   d. past events and stored images

2. Unpleasant emotions such as fear, anger, and sadness are more frequent in dreams than pleasant emotions.   T or F?

3. Dream content typically reflects one's waking personality and roles.   T or F?

4. In secondary elaboration, a single dream character stands for several others.   T or F?

5. List four dream processes identified by Freud.

    _____   _____

    _____   _____

6. According to the activation-synthesis model of dreaming, dreams are constructed from _____ to explain messages received from nerve cells controlling eye movement, balance, and bodily activity.

Answers: 1. d   2. T   3. T   4. F   5. condensation, displacement, symbolization, secondary elaboration   6. memories

---

Resources Summary

● Although there is much individual variation in sleep needs, sleep is an innate *biological rhythm* essential for survival. Higher animals and people deprived of sleep experience involuntary *microsleeps.*

● Moderate sleep loss mainly affects vigilance and performance on routine or boring tasks. Extended sleep loss can (somewhat rarely) produce a temporary *sleep deprivation psychosis.* It is not necessary to make up for lost sleep.

● *Sleep patterns* show some flexibility, but seven to eight hours remains the average under most conditions. The amount of daily sleep decreases steadily from birth to old age. Once-a-day sleep schedules, with a two-to-one ratio of waking and sleep, are most efficient for most people.

● The brain is as active during sleep as at other times. The *pattern* of activity changes rather than the amount. Sleep is actively generated by brain structures, and is not directly caused by fatigue. A sleep-inducing chemical has been found in the brain and spinal cord.

● Sleep occurs in four *stages.* Stage 1 is *light sleep,* and Stage 4 is *deep sleep.* The sleeper alternates between Stages 1 and 4 (passing through 2 and 3) several times each night.

● There are two basic sleep states, *rapid eye movement* (REM) sleep, and *non-REM* (NREM) sleep. REM sleep is much more strongly associated with dreaming than is non-REM sleep.

● Dreaming and REMs occur mainly during Stage 1. Everyone dreams, and four to five dreams per night is typical. Dreaming is accompanied by emotional arousal, but relaxation of the skeletal muscles. REM sleep is often referred to as *paradoxical* sleep.

● People deprived of dream sleep show a *REM rebound* when allowed to sleep without interruption. Consistent loss of any sleep stage can be disruptive, but total sleep loss seems to be the most important factor.

● *Somnambulism* (sleepwalking) and *sleeptalking* occur during NREM sleep. Except in rare instances neither is dangerous or particularly significant.

● *Nightmares* are brief and upsetting REM dreams. *Night terrors* occur in NREM sleep and produce a panic-like terror.

● *Narcolepsy* (sleep attacks) is apparently caused by the sudden occurrence of Stage 1 REM patterns during normal waking hours. Narcolepsy is frequently accompanied by *cataplexy* (paralysis). A genetic or hereditary basis for narcolepsy is indicated by studies of animals.

● *Insomnia* may be temporary or chronic. When it is treated through use of drugs sleep quality is lowered and *drug-dependency insomnia* often develops.

● One source of insomnia or daytime exhaustion is *sleep apnea.* Individuals suffering from apnea repeatedly stop breathing while asleep, and snore loudly. Apnea is suspected as a major cause of *Sudden Infant Death Syndrome.*

● Most dreams are about familiar settings, people, and actions. Dreams appear to reflect waking personality and roles, but they also include events and images from the past. Negative emotions are more common in dreams than are positive emotions. The night's first dreams involve recent events, whereas later dreams draw on earlier experiences.

● The Freudian, or *psychodynamic,* view is that dreams express unconscious wishes, impulses, or emotions. Freud held that the meaning of dreams is hidden by *condensation, displacement, symbolization,* and *secondary elaboration.* Many theorists have questioned Freud's view of dreams. For example, the *activation-synthesis model* portrays dreaming as a physiological process. Even Freud's former student, Carl Jung, held opposing views. Jung saw many dream images as universal symbols called *archetypes.*

Exploring Your Dreams

An uninterpreted dream is like an unopened letter.
—The Talmud

Dreams can hold an intensity of pain and pleasure sometimes greater than that of the waking world. Yet, if Freudian dream interpretation were the only approach to understanding dreams, there would be little hope of learning from them. As we have seen, Freud considered the meaning of dreams to be deeply hidden. But there are other points of view. Dream theorist Calvin Hall (1966, 1974) prefers to think of dreams as plays and the dreamer as a playwright. Hall does admit that the images and ideas in dreams tend to be more *primitive* than those experienced when one is awake. Nevertheless, much can be learned by simply considering the **setting, cast** of characters, **plot,** and **emotions** portrayed in a dream.

Another dream researcher, Rosalind Cartwright (1969, 1978) suggests that dreams be considered primarily as feeling statements. The overall **emotional tone** of a dream is a major clue to its meaning. Is the dream comical, threatening, joyous, or depressing? Were you lonely, jealous, frightened, in love, or angry? Cartwright encourages use of everyday dream life as a source of varied experience and personal enrichment, and considers dream explorations an avenue for personal growth.

Dream theorist Ann Faraday (1972) also believes in the value of studying one's own dreams. Faraday considers dreams a message *from* yourself *to* yourself. Thus, the way to understand dreams is to remember them, write them down, look for the message they contain, and become deeply acquainted with *your* own symbol system. Here's how:

How to Catch a Dream

1. Before retiring, plan to remember your dreams. Keep a pen and paper or a tape recorder beside your bed.
2. If possible, arrange to awaken gradually without an alarm. Natural awakening is almost always from a REM period.
3. If you rarely remember your dreams, you may want to set an alarm clock to go off two hours after you go to sleep,

or for an hour before you usually awaken. Although less desirable than awakening naturally, this method may let you catch a dream.
4. Upon awakening, lie still and review the dream images with your eyes closed. Try to recall as many details as possible.
5. If you can, make your first dream record (whether by writing or by tape) with your eyes closed. Opening your eyes will disrupt dream recall.
6. Review the dream again and record as many additional details as you can remember. Dream memories disappear quickly. Be sure to describe feelings as well as the plot, characters, and actions of the dream.
7. Put your dreams into a permanent "dream diary." Keep dreams in chronological order and review them periodically. This procedure will reveal recurrent themes, conflicts, and emotions. It almost always produces valuable insights.
8. Remember, a number of drugs suppress dreaming (see Table 7-2).

Since each dream has several possible meanings or levels of meaning, there is no fixed way to work with it. Telling the dream to others and discussing its meaning can be a good start. Describing it may help you relive some of the feelings in the dream and family or friends may be able to offer interpretations you would be blind to yourself. Watch for verbal or visual puns and other playful elements in dreams. If, for example, you dream that you

Table 7-2   Effects of Selected Drugs on Dreaming

Drug	Effect on REM Sleep
Alcohol	Decrease
Amphetamines	Decrease
Barbiturates	Decrease
Caffeine	None
Cocaine	Unknown
LSD	Slight increase
Marijuana	Slight decrease or no effect

Applications

are in a wrestling match and your arm is pinned behind your back, it may mean that you feel someone is "twisting your arm" in real life. Some people find it revealing to enact the dream as a play, or to draw, paint, or dance a dream.

The meaning of most dreams will yield to careful scrutiny and a little detective work. If you still have trouble seeing the meaning of a dream, you may find it helpful to use a technique developed by Fritz Perls. Perls, the originator of gestalt therapy, considered most dreams a special message about what's missing in our lives, what we avoid doing, or feelings that need to be "reowned." Perls felt that dreams are a way of filling in gaps in personal experience (Perls, 1969). An approach that Perls found quite helpful in understanding a dream is to "take the part of" or "speak for" each of the characters and objects in the dream. This process of role playing may be clarified by the following excerpts from one of Perls' dream-work seminars. Linda, one of the participants, has just described dream images of a lake drying up and the animals in it dying. At the bottom of the lake, she expects to find some treasure, but when she looks all she can find is an old license plate. Perls begins by asking her to play the license plate.

> I am an old license plate, thrown in the bottom of a lake. I have no use because I'm of no value—although I'm not rusted—I'm outdated, so I can't be used as a license plate.

Perls urges her to continue:

> Useless, outdated . . . the use of a license plate is to allow—give a car permission to go . . . and I can't give anyone permission to do anything because I'm outdated.

Next, Linda is asked to play the lake.

> I'm a lake . . . I'm drying up, and disappearing, soaking into the earth . . . (with a touch of surprise) *dying*. . . . But when I soak into the earth, I become a part of the earth—so maybe I water the surrounding area, so . . . even in the lake, even in my bed, flowers can grow (sighs). . . . New life can grow . . . from me (cries) (excerpted from Perls, 1969, pp. 86–87).

Thus, we see that Linda's dream has expressed her fears of dying and being unwanted. Perls urges her to recognize that she can express the creative feelings in the dream and that she doesn't need a "license" to do so. It is obvi-

ous that she has learned something about herself through this exercise.

A particularly interesting dream exercise is to continue a dream as waking fantasy so that it may be concluded or carried on to a more meaningful ending. It is also revealing to set up dialogues between people or objects in the dream, especially those that stand in opposition to one another. Speak for them both and you will perhaps discover conflicting aspects of yourself. As the world of dreams and your personal dream language become more familiar, you will doubtless find many answers, paradoxes, intuitions, and insights into your own behavior.

Using Your Dreams

History is full of cases where dreams have been a pathway to creativity and discovery. One of the most celebrated examples of this kind involved chemist Friedrich Kekule who discovered that the molecules in the chemical benzene are arranged in a ring. His discovery came when he was awakened by a dream of a snake eating its own tail:

> The atoms were juggling before my eyes . . . everything was moving in a snakelike and twisting manner. . . . Suddenly, one of the snakes got hold of its own tail and the whole structure was mockingly twisted before my eyes. . . .

As soon as Kekule woke from his dream, he knew the mystery of benzene's structure had been solved. The circle formed by the image of the snake had suggested to him that benzene was shaped like a ring.

Another scientist who had a dream breakthrough is Nobel Prize winner, Dr. Otto Loewi. Loewi had spent years on research relating to the chemical transmission of nerve impulses. A tremendous breakthrough in his research came when he dreamed of an experiment three nights in a row. The first two nights he woke up and scribbled the experiment on a pad, but the next morning he was unable to tell what the notes meant. On the third night, he got up after having the dream, and instead of making notes went straight to his laboratory and performed the crucial experiment. Loewi later commented that if the experiment had occurred to him while awake he would have rejected it.

Loewi's experience gives some insight into the poten-

Applications

tial value of dreams for the production of creative solutions. The dream state is one of reduced inhibition and may be especially useful in solving problems that require a fresh point of view.

The likelihood of being able to take advantage of dreams for problem solving is improved if you "set" yourself before retiring by thinking intently about a problem you wish to solve. Try to steep yourself in the problem by stating it clearly and reviewing all relevant information. Then use the suggestions listed in the previous section to catch your dreams. While this cannot be guaranteed to produce a novel problem solution or a new insight, it is certain to be an adventure.

Lucid Dreaming   If you would like to press further into the territory of dreams you may want to learn "lucid dreaming." During a **lucid dream,** the dreamer "wakes" within an ordinary dream and feels capable of normal thought and action. Lucid dreamers know they are dreaming, but they feel fully conscious within the dream world (La Berg et al., 1981a).

Stephen La Berge and his colleagues at the Stanford University Sleep Research Center have used a unique approach to show lucid dreams are real, and that they occur during REM sleep. In the sleep lab, lucid dreamers agree to make prearranged signals when they become aware they are dreaming. One such signal is to look up abruptly in a dream, causing a distinct upward eye movement. Another signal is to clench the right and left fists (in the dream) in a prearranged pattern. Corresponding

muscle changes in the wrists can then be recorded electrically. Such signals show very clearly that lucid dreaming and voluntary action in dreams are possible (La Berge et al., 1981a; La Berge, 1981b).

Question: How would a person go about learning to have lucid dreams?

La Berge (1980) found he could greatly increase lucid dreaming by following this simple routine: When you awaken spontaneously from a dream, take a few minutes to try to memorize it. Next, engage in 10 to 15 minutes of reading or any other activity requiring full wakefulness. Then while lying in bed and returning to sleep, say to yourself, "Next time I'm dreaming, I want to remember I'm dreaming." Finally, visualize yourself lying in bed asleep, while in the dream just rehearsed. At the same time, picture yourself realizing that you are dreaming. Follow this routine each time you awaken (substitute a dream memory from another occasion if you don't awaken from a dream).

Question: Why would anyone want to have more lucid dreams?

Researchers are interested in lucid dreams because they provide a new tool for understanding dreaming. Using subjects who can signal while they are dreaming may make it possible to explore dreams with first-hand data from the dreamer's world itself (La Berge, 1981b). On a more personal level, lucid dreaming can convert dreams into a nightly "workshop" for emotional growth. The "Exploration" that follows describes how.

Learning Check

1. Calvin Hall's approach to dream interpretation emphasizes the setting, cast, plot, and emotions portrayed in a dream.   T or F?
2. Rosalind Cartwright stresses that dreaming is a relatively mechanical process having little personal meaning. T or F?
3. Both alcohol and LSD cause a slight increase in dreaming.   T or F?
4. "Taking the part of" or "speaking for" dream elements is a dream interpretation technique originated by Fritz Perls.   T or F?
5. Recent research shows that lucid dreaming occurs primarily during NREM sleep or microawakenings.   T or F?

Answers: 1. T   2. F   3. F   4. T   5. F

Controlling Dreams—A Lesson from the Dream People

"Tonight I'm going to fly in my dreams. Tonight I'm going to fly." A growing number of people make pronouncements like this part of their daily thoughts in an attempt to control the content of their dreams. How many know that much of the current interest in dream control began with study of the Senoi, an isolated tribe of people in Malaysia?

In 1954, Australian anthropologist Kilton Stewart published accounts of a group of people who made dreams the heart of their culture. Stewart was amazed at the smoothness with which Senoi culture functioned, seemingly without need of a police force, jails, or psychiatric hospitals. He was further astonished by the Senoi claim that there had not been a violent crime or an intercommunity clash for 200 or 300 years. Both Stewart and the Senoi attributed this situation to the daily practice of a type of dream therapy.

Dream interpretation is a core feature of child education and is common knowledge among all Senoi adults. Each day, breakfast in Senoi homes is like a dream clinic, with adults listening to and analyzing the dreams of children, or discussing the messages held in their own dreams. Like Western dream theorists, the Senoi believe beings in the dream universe represent facets of the dreamer's own psyche coming forth in disguised form. But, unlike traditional dream theorists, the Senoi believe that every person should become master of his or her own dream world. As a result, Senoi children rapidly become lucid dreamers. Thus, if a child reports a frightening falling dream, he or she is encouraged by an adult to redream the episode and to change it into a pleasant flying or soaring dream. Adults are encouraged to continue their dreams until they arrive at resolution. For example, sexual dreams should always move through orgasm, and the dreamer should ask his or her dream lover for a poem, song, dance, or useful knowledge to be shared with the group. If a Senoi dreamer has an argument with an acquaintance or injures him in a dream, the dreamer must apologize to the acquaintance in real life (Stewart, 1969).

After studying dream techniques of the Senoi and other lucid dreamers, American psychologist Patricia Garfield is convinced that we should not only record and probe our dreams, but gain control over them as well. Garfield teaches people to choose the subject of their dreams, to determine the plot, and to use dream events to resolve daytime conflicts. Here are techniques she suggests for achieving dream control (Garfield, 1974):

1. Convince yourself that dreams are important and shaping dreams possible.
2. Form a clear-cut intention to dream of a particular topic. It may help to repeat the intention throughout the day.
3. Accept and cultivate dream personages as "dream friends" or "allies."
4. Confront, challenge, or conquer threatening dream figures and situations.

Garfield offers an example of the last point. She had been troubled by a recurring nightmare in which she was chased by rapists. Although still very frightened, she was determined to end the dream. So she stopped running and faced her attackers. This time a can of chemical spray appeared in her hand, and she dispatched her pursuers from her dream life forever (Kiester, 1975).

Dream control and lucid dreaming can take months to achieve. Is it worth the effort? Garfield feels that dream events such as her nightmare encounter enhance waking self-confidence. Furthermore, becoming conscious in a dream allows the dreamer to expand dream experiences in directions he or she chooses. In this way the vivid flow of dream images can be used to create solutions to problems that will not yield to waking thought.

Can we agree then with Kilton Stewart that, "In the West the thinking we do while asleep usually remains on a muddled, childish, or psychotic level . . ."? Or is dream control a psychological fad? Perhaps time will tell.

Questions for Discussion

1. How would your life change if you had to sleep 15 hours per day? How would it change if you only needed two hours a day?

2. Would you give up sleep if you could?

3. Have you ever gone without sleep for an extended period, or have you had to adapt to an unusual sleep schedule? If so, what were your reactions? Your greatest difficulties?

4. Describe a recent dream you have had. How does it relate to your daytime experiences and feelings? What additional meanings can you find in it?

5. How important are your dreams to you? What value do they have? Do you think recording your dreams would be a worthwhile practice?

6. Have you ever solved a problem in your dreams? How much control do you have over what you dream?

7. You have a friend who claims never to dream. How could you realistically prove to your friend that he or she does dream?

8. Respond to this statement: "The REM state is not sleep at all; during REM we are paralyzed and hallucinating." Do you agree?

9. If you were dreaming right now, how could you prove it?

Suggestions for Further Reading

Berger, R. J. "Morpheus Descending," *Psychology Today,* June, 1970.

Cartwright, R. D. "Happy Endings for our Dreams," *Psychology Today,* December, 1978.

Faraday, A. *Dream Power.* Coward, McCann, and Geoghegan, 1972.

Freud, S. *Interpretation of Dreams.* Hogarth, 1953.

Hales, D. *The Complete Book of Sleep.* Addison-Wesley Publishing Co., 1980.

Hall, C. *The Meaning of Dreams.* McGraw-Hill, 1966.

Kramer, M. (ed.). *Dream Psychology and the New Biology of Dreaming.* Charles C Thomas, 1969.

Luce, G. G., and J. Segal. *Sleep.* Coward-McCann, 1966.

Mitler, M. M., *et al.* "Sleeplessness, Sleep Attacks and Things That Go Wrong in the Night," *Psychology Today,* December, 1975.

Naeye, R. L. "Sudden Infant Death," *Scientific American,* **242**(4) 1980, 56–62.

Webb, W. B. *Sleep, the Gentle Tyrant.* Prentice-Hall, 1975.

Contents

Part III

Learning,
Memory,
and
Thinking

8

Conditioning and Learning I

===== Chapter Preview =====

What Did You Learn in School Today?

When the author was in college, students discovered an interesting "game" that could be played with the plumbing in the dorms. If a toilet was flushed while someone was taking a shower, the cold-water pressure dropped so much that it caused the shower suddenly to become scalding hot. Naturally, the shower victim screamed in terror as his reflexes caused him to leap back in pain. Soon it was further discovered that if several students flushed all the toilets at once, the effects were multiplied many times over!

A flushing toilet has to be one of the world's most uninspiring stimuli. But for a time there was a whole crop of University of California, Riverside, students who jumped involuntarily whenever they heard a toilet flush. Their reaction was the result of a special form of learning called classical conditioning. *Details of how and why classical conditioning occurs are explored in this chapter.*

Consider another learning situation. Let's say that you are at school and that you are "starving to death." Locating a vending machine, you deposit your last quarter to buy a candy bar. Your stomach growls in anticipation as you press the button, and . . . nothing happens. Being civilized and in complete control, you press the other buttons, try the coin return, and look for an attendant. Still nothing. Your stomach growls again. Being no longer either civilized or self-controlled, you give the machine a little kick (just to let it know how you feel). Then, as you turn away, the machine begins to whirr and out pops a candy bar plus 15 cents change. Once this happens, the chances are that you will repeat the "kicking process" in the future. If it pays off several times more, it may become a rather permanent habit. In this case, learning is based on instrumental conditioning *(also called* operant conditioning*).*

Classical and instrumental conditioning underlie much human learning. In fact, conditioning reaches into every corner of our lives. You should certainly find it useful to learn more about it. Are you ready to learn more about learning? If so, read on! This chapter and the next explore conditioning and other forms of learning.

Survey Questions   How is learning defined? What is classical conditioning, and what is its role in human learning? What kinds of factors affect classical conditioning? What is instrumental conditioning? What kinds of factors affect it? In what ways are classical and instrumental conditioning alike? In what ways are they different? How are conditioning principles applied to practical problems?

Resources

What Is Learning— Does Practice Make Perfect?

The weaver bird is a curious little creature. In the spring, it builds a complex nest out of grass and twigs. To hold its creation together, the weaver bird ties a special knot with the grass. How does it learn to tie such a knot? It doesn't! In laboratory studies, weaver birds have been raised in total isolation for several generations. They still tie the knot at their first opportunity to build a nest.

Knot-tying in the weaver bird is a **fixed action pattern (FAP).** A fixed action pattern is an instinctual chain of movements found in all members of a species. Like other **innate** (inborn) **behaviors,** fixed action patterns prepare animals to meet major needs in their lives. A simpler innate behavior is a **reflex.** More complicated behaviors, such as the maternal instinct in lower animals, combine both fixed action patterns and reflexes.

Question: Do humans have instincts?

Humans have reflexes, but most psychologists reject the idea that people have instincts. To qualify as instinctual, a behavior must be complex, unlearned, and "species specific." (**Species specific behaviors** are those that occur uniformly in all members of a species.) Actually, it is fortunate that we are not as rigidly programmed as many animals are. Although it is usually helpful, such programming is also very limiting. If a spider begins spinning a cocoon and its silk glands are removed, it will continue to make all 6400 spinning movements to complete the job. Then it will lay eggs in the nonexistent cocoon (Eibl-Eibesfeldt, 1970)!

Learning Vs. Instinct   What humans lack in instinctual "programming" is more than made up for in learning capacity. Our ability to learn is so advanced that the majority of our daily activities are either wholly learned, or at least greatly affected by learning. Imagine what you would be like if you suddenly lost everything you had ever learned. What could you do? You would be unable to read, write, or speak. You couldn't walk, feed yourself, find your way home, drive a car, or "boogie." Needless to say you would be totally incapacitated. (Dull too!)

Question: Learning is obviously important. What's a formal definition of learning?

Learning is a *relatively permanent change in behavior due to past experience.* Notice that this definition *excludes* temporary changes caused by motivation, fatigue, maturation, disease, injury, or drugs. Each of these can change behavior, but none constitutes learning.

Question: Isn't learning the result of practice?

It depends on what you mean by practice. Merely repeating a response may not produce learning. In conditioning, some type of *reinforcement* must be present. **Reinforcement** refers to any procedure which increases the chances that a particular response will be made. If I want to teach a dog to sit up on command, I could use food to reinforce the response of sitting up to a selected stimulus (the command). Actually, there are several ways in which reinforcement of learning can occur. As a starting point, let's see how responses are learned in classical conditioning.

Classical Conditioning— Does the Name Pavlov Ring a Bell?

Question: How was classical conditioning discovered?

At the beginning of the twentieth century, something happened in the lab of the Russian physiologist **Ivan Pavlov** that raised him to a position of international recognition. What happened was so unastounding that a lesser man might have ignored it: Pavlov's experimental subjects drooled at him.

Actually, Pavlov was studying the digestive process. In order to study and measure salivation, a part of the digestive process, he placed meat powder or some tidbit on a dog's tongue. After a time, Pavlov noticed that his animals were salivating *before* the food was placed in their mouths. Later, the dogs even began to salivate at the mere sight of Pavlov entering the room. Pavlov recognized that this was something more than misplaced affection. Salivation is normally a reflex (automatic, unlearned) response. Some form of learning had to be taking place in order for the animals to be salivating at the sight of food. Pavlov called this form of learning **conditioning.** Because of its importance in psychology's history, it is now called **classical conditioning** (also known as **respondent conditioning**). Although the term *conditioning* has filtered into most peo-

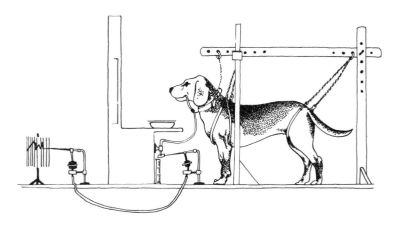

Fig. 8-1 *Pavlov's conditioning apparatus. In Pavlov's early experiments, a tube carried saliva from the dog's mouth to a lever that activated a recording device (far left). The placing of a dish of food in front of the dog was paired with various other stimuli for conditioning.*

ple's vocabularies, few people really understand the process. Compare your understanding with the information that follows.

Question: How did Pavlov study conditioning?

In Pavlov's classic experiments, a bell was rung immediately before meat powder was placed on a dog's tongue. The meat powder caused reflex salivation to occur. Time after time, Pavlov rang the bell and immediately gave the dog meat powder. Eventually, the bell alone began to produce salivation (see Fig. 8-1). (This was shown by sometimes omitting the meat powder after ringing the bell.) Psychologists use several special terms to describe these events. The bell in Pavlov's experiment is a **conditioned** (learned) **stimulus (CS).** The meat powder is an **unconditioned stimulus (US)** (because the dog does not have to learn to respond to it). Unconditioned stimuli typically produce reflex responses. Since a reflex is "built in," it is called an **unconditioned** (not learned) **response (UR).** In Pavlov's experiment, salivation was the UR. When the bell alone causes salivation, the response can no longer be called a simple reflex. Instead, it is a **conditioned** (learned) **response (CR)** (Fig. 8-2).

Question: Are all these terms and code letters really necessary?

In a word, yes, because they help us recognize similarities in various instances of classical conditioning. As an example, see if you can apply the terms to explain the effects of the shower and flushing toilet described in the chapter "Preview."

1. What is the unconditioned (the unlearned) response?
_____

2. What is the unconditioned stimulus that causes the response? _____
3. What is the conditioned stimulus? _____

Now let's see if you understand the terms. The unconditioned, or unlearned, response was a reflex jump from the hot water. The unconditioned stimulus was the hot

Fig. 8-2 *The conditioning procedure.*

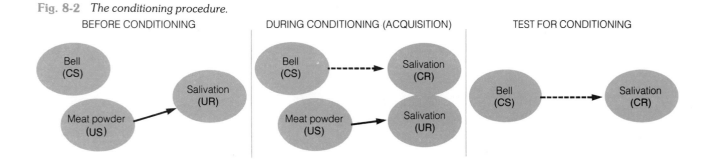

water, or more specifically, the pain caused by the hot water. The conditioned stimulus, that is, the stimulus that was conditioned to cause the person to jump, was the sound of a flushing toilet.

Elements of Classical Conditioning—
Teach Your Little Brother to Salivate

A number of interesting events occur during classical conditioning. To observe them, you could ring a bell, squirt lemon juice in a child's mouth, and establish conditioned salivation to the bell. The child's reactions might then be used to demonstrate additional facets of conditioning.

Acquisition   During **acquisition,** or training, a conditioned response must be **reinforced** (see Fig. 8-3). In classical conditioning, reinforcement occurs when the CS is followed by, or paired with, an unconditioned stimulus (US). In the case of the salivating child, the bell is the CS; salivating is the CR; and the US is the sour lemon juice. To reinforce salivation to the bell, we must pair the bell with lemon juice. For the most rapid conditioning, the US should follow the CS by about one-half second. In this way, the bell is consistently associated with salivation.

Question: After conditioning has occurred, what would happen if the US no longer followed the bell?

Extinction and Spontaneous Recovery   If the lemon juice (US) is briefly omitted and the child salivates to the bell (CS), we have merely demonstrated the presence of conditioning. However, if the US never again follows the CS, a conditioned response will be **extinguished.** If the bell (in our example) is rung repeatedly, and not followed

by lemon juice, the child's tendency to salivate at the ringing of the bell will be *inhibited.* This is called **extinction.** Thus, we see that classical conditioning can be reversed.

Question: If conditioning takes a while to build up, shouldn't it take time to reverse?

Yes. After one session in which the bell is rung until the child quits responding, we might assume that extinction is complete. However, the next day, if the bell is rung, we might initially get a response, a reaction called **spontaneous recovery.** Because of it, several extinction sessions may be necessary to completely reverse conditioning. The author once helped with a horse that had been in an automobile accident while in its horse trailer. Many careful trips around the block were required to extinguish the horse's fear of trailers, because the horse showed spontaneous recovery of its fear after a few days away from the trailer.

Generalization and Discrimination   Once a person or an animal has been conditioned to respond to a particular CS, other stimuli *similar* to the CS may elicit (bring forth) a response. For example, we might expect the child in our conditioning experiment to salivate to sounds like the ringing of a telephone or doorbell. This effect is called **stimulus generalization.** It has been demonstrated many times in experiments involving humans and animals (Kimble, 1961).

It is easy to see that stimulus generalization plays an important role in conditioning. Consider, for instance, the child who accidentally burns a finger while playing with matches. Conditioning principles predict that the sight of a lighted match will become a conditioned stimulus for fear. But will the child's fear be limited only to matches? Because of stimulus generalization, we would also expect the child to show a healthy fear of flames produced by lighters,

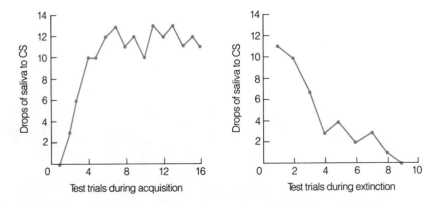

Fig. 8-3 *Acquisition and extinction of a conditioned response. (After Pavlov, 1927)*

fireplaces, stoves, and so forth. Fortunately, generalization tends to extend the effects of learning to new situations and similar circumstances. Were it not for this, we would be far less adaptable creatures than we are.

An important point to keep in mind about stimulus generalization is that it does have limits. Experiments show that there is a gradual decrease in generalization as test stimuli become less like the original CS (Siegel *et al.,* 1968). In other words, if you condition a child to salivate each time you play a particular note on a piano, the child will salivate less when you play higher or lower notes. If the notes are *much* higher or lower, the child will not respond at all (Fig. 8-4).

Let's consider one more possibility with our salivating child (who by this time must be ready to hide in the closet). Suppose that the child is again being conditioned with a bell as the CS. As an experiment, we occasionally sound a buzzer instead of the bell, but never follow it with the US (lemon juice). At first the buzzer produces salivation (due to generalization). But after the buzzer has been presented several times more, the child ceases to respond to it. The child has now learned to *discriminate,* or respond differently to, the bell and the buzzer. In essence, the child's generalized response to the buzzer has extinguished.

Stimulus discrimination is an important element of learning. As an example, you might remember the feelings of anxiety or fear you had as a child when your mother's or father's voice changed to its you're-about-to-get-swatted tone. Most children quickly learn to discriminate voice qualities associated with pain from voice qualities associated with praise or affection.

Classical Conditioning in Humans— An Emotional Topic

Question: How much human learning is based on classical conditioning?

In its simplest form, classical conditioning depends on the existence of reflex responses. A *reflex* is a dependable, inborn stimulus-response connection. For example, pain causes a reflex action in parts of the body. The reflex of the eye to bright lights is the narrowing of the pupil. A puff of air to the eye causes an eye blink. Various foods cause salivation. It is entirely possible that humans can be conditioned to connect any of these reflex responses to a new stimulus. At the very least, you have probably had the experience of having your mouth water upon seeing or smelling a bakery, and you may have even salivated in response

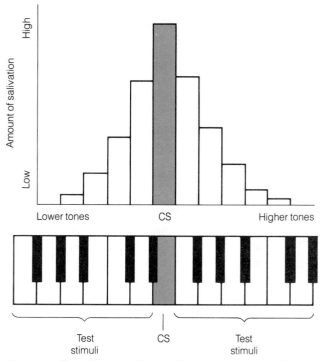

Fig. 8-4   *Stimulus generalization. Stimuli similar to the CS also elicit a response.*

to pictures of food (a picture of a lemon is great for this). However, in practice, simple conditioning of human reflexes doesn't happen very often.

Question: Then why bother talking about it?

Because more *subtle* kinds of conditioning greatly affect human behavior. In addition to simple reflexes, more complex *emotional* or "gut" responses may be conditioned to new stimuli. If your face reddened as part of your emotional reaction to being punished as a child, you may blush now as an adult when you are embarrassed or ashamed.

Another common example of such conditioning is a **phobia.** A phobia is fear that persists even when no realistic danger exists. People who fear animals, water, heights, thunder, automobiles, or bugs, can often trace their fear to a few unfortunate experiences in which they were frightened, injured, upset emotionally, or subjected to pain in the presence of the feared object or stimulus. Reactions of this type, called **conditioned emotional responses (CERs),** play an important part in daily psychological functioning. This is particularly true because CERs may be broadened into phobias by stimulus generalization (see Fig. 8-5). Fortunately, phobias that cause serious prob-

Fig. 8-5 *Hypothetical example of a CER becoming a phobia. Child approaches dog (a) and is frightened by it (b). Fear generalizes to other household pets (c) and later to virtually all furry animals (d).*

(a)   (b)

(c)   (d)

lems can be extinguished. In a therapy technique called **desensitization,** learning principles are used to counter-condition fears, anxieties, or phobias. (Desensitization is described in detail in Chapter 23.)

Vicarious, or Secondhand, Conditioning The importance of conditioned emotional responses is extended by the fact that they can be learned indirectly. One experiment, for example, showed that people could be conditioned to give an emotional response to a light, merely by watching another person get an electric shock each time the light came on. Even though subjects never directly received a shock, they developed a conditioned emotional response to seeing the light come on (Bandura and Rosenthal, 1966). Children who learn to fear thunder by watching their parents have undergone similar conditioning.

Vicarious classical conditioning, as it is called, prob-

ably plays a part in emotional reactions to many situations. For example, the film *Jaws* made ocean swimming a conditioned fear stimulus for many viewers. If movies can affect us, we might expect the impact of the emotional reactions of parents, friends, and relatives to be even stronger. How, for instance, does a city child learn to fear snakes and to respond emotionally to mere pictures of them? Perhaps, the child has been told that "snakes are dangerous," but the child's *emotional* response has probably been learned by observing the negative reactions of others to snakes.

The emotional attitudes we have developed toward certain types of food, political parties, minority groups, escalators—whatever—are probably not only conditioned by direct experience but vicariously as well. Parents may do well to look in a mirror if they wonder how or where a child has "picked up" a particular fear or emotional attitude.

Learning Check

Make certain you can answer these questions before continuing.

1. Complex responses known as _____ help many animals adapt to their environment.

    a. generalizations *b.* unconditioned discriminations
    c. fixed action patterns *d.* releasers

2. Classical conditioning, studied by the Russian physiologist _____, is also referred to as _____ conditioning.

3. Classical conditioning is strengthened or reinforced when the _____ follows the _____.

   a. CS, US   b. US, CS   c. UR, CR   d. CS, CR

4. Training that inhibits, or causes the loss of a conditioned response is called _____.

5. When a conditioned response is elicited by stimuli similar to the CS, stimulus generalization has occurred.   T or F?

6. Phobias may begin with CERs.   T or F?

7. Conditioning brought about by observing pain, joy, or fear of others is called _____ conditioning.

8. A dependable inborn stimulus-response connection is called a/an:

   a. unconditioned stimulus   b. CER   c. reflex   d. reinforcer

Answers: 1. c   2. Pavlov, respondent   3. b   4. extinction   5. T   6. T   7. vicarious   8. c

Instrumental Conditioning— Survival of the Fittest . . . Response

Question: What is instrumental conditioning, and how is it different from classical conditioning?

In classical conditioning, all the "action" happens *before* a response is made. The important question is, "How does one stimulus (the CS) come to act like another (the US)?" In **instrumental conditioning** we are interested in what happens *after* responses are made. Here we ask, "What is the consequence of making a response?" Is the response followed by reward, punishment, or nothing? The basic principle of instrumental conditioning is quite simple: Acts that are *instrumental* in producing reward tend to be repeated. Think of the earlier example of the vending machine. Because kicking the machine was followed by reward, the odds of repeating the "kicking response" were increased.

The idea that reward affects a response is certainly nothing new to parents (and other trainers of small animals). However, parents, as well as teachers, politicians, businesspeople, supervisors, and others, may use reward in ways that are haphazard, inexact, misguided, or superstitious. A case in point is the very term "reward." To be correct, it is better to say "reinforcer." Why? Because "rewards" do not always increase responding. If you try to give licorice candy to a child as a "reward" for good behavior, it will work only if the child likes licorice. As a practical "rule of thumb," psychologists therefore define an **instrumental reinforcer** as any object or event that increases the probability of a response. For convenience, we will use the term "reward" in this chapter, but keep in mind that rewards are not always reinforcers.

Instrumental training is often done in separate **learning trials.** For example, a rat could be tested for its ability to learn a maze. On each trial the rat would be placed in the maze, where it gets a chance to find food. Finding the food ends the trial. An alternative to learning trials is to let subjects respond freely, at their own pace. This approach, developed by B. F. Skinner, is called **operant conditioning.** In operant conditioning a reinforcer is given any time a correct response is made, so no learning trials are needed. Examples of operant responses are waving your hand to get attention in class, or a dog sitting up for a bone. In this chapter, the terms "instrumental" and "operant" will be used interchangeably to refer to the learning of *voluntary* responses. In classical conditioning, responses are *not voluntary,* they are passive, learned reflexes.

Acquisition of an Operant Response   Most laboratory research on operant learning takes place in some form of **conditioning chamber** (also called a "Skinner box," after B. F. Skinner, who invented it for experiments in operant conditioning). (See Fig. 8-6.) A look into a typical Skinner box will clarify the process of operant conditioning.

The Adventures of Mickey Rat

A hungry rat is placed in a small cagelike chamber. The walls are bare except for a metal lever and a tray from which food pellets may be dispensed (see Fig. 8-6).

Frankly, there's not much to do in a Skinner box. This situation increases the chances that our subject will make the response we are interested in rewarding. Hunger also ensures that the animal will be actively *emitting,* or giving off, a variety of responses.

Now let's take another look at our subject.

The Further Adventures of Mickey Rat

For a while our subject walks around, grooms, sniffs at the corners, or stands on his hind legs—all typical "rat behaviors." Then it happens. He places his paw on the lever to get a better view of the top of the cage. *Click!* The lever depresses, and a food pellet drops into the tray. Investigating the tray, he eats the pellet and then grooms himself. Up and exploring the cage again, he leans on the lever. *Click!* After a trip to the food tray, he returns to the bar and sniffs it, then puts his foot on it. *Click!* Soon the rat's behavior has settled into a smooth pattern of frequent bar pressing.

Notice that the rat did not acquire a new skill in this situation. He already had the responses necessary to depress the bar. Reward only alters how *frequently* he presses the bar. In operant conditioning, **reinforcement** is used to alter the frequency of responses, or to assemble them into new patterns or habits.

Shaping   Even with a simple response like bar pressing, it might be a long time before the rat accidentally made the response so that it could be reinforced. We might wait forever for more complicated responses to occur. For example, you would have to wait a long time for a duck to accidentally walk out of its cage, turn on a light, play "Yankee Doodle" on a toy piano, turn off the light, and walk back to its cage. If this is what you wanted to reward, you would never get the chance.

Question: Then how are the animals on TV and at amusement parks taught to perform complicated tricks?

The answer lies in **shaping.** Let's look again at our subject, Mickey Rat.

Fig. 8-6   *The Skinner box. This simple device, invented by B. F. Skinner, allows careful study of operant conditioning. When the rat presses the bar, a pellet of food or a drop of water is automatically released.*

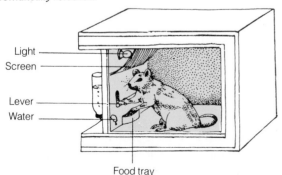

Light
Screen
Lever
Water
Food tray

Mickey Rat Shapes Up

Assume that the rat has not yet learned to press the bar. He also shows no signs of interest in the bar. Instead of waiting for the first accidental bar press, we can shape his behavior patterns. At first, we settle for just getting him to face the bar. Anytime he turns toward the bar, he is rewarded with a bit of food. Soon Mickey spends much of his time facing the bar. Next, we reward him every time he takes a step toward the bar. When he turns toward the bar, then walks away, nothing happens. But when he faces the bar and takes a step forward, *click!* His reponses are being shaped.

By changing the "rules" regarding what makes a successful response, the rat can gradually be trained to approach the bar and to press it. We can reward responses that come closer and closer to the final desired pattern until it occurs. The basic principle of shaping, then, is that gradual or *successive approximations* to the desired response are rewarded. Eventually, a long, complicated chain of responses can be maintained by one small reward at the end of the performance being taught. B. F. Skinner once taught two pigeons to play Ping-Pong in this way.

Extinction   You might expect that a rat's bar-pressing would immediately stop if food delivery ceased. Actually, the rat would stop pressing the bar, but not immediately. Just as acquiring an operant response takes time, so does extinction. If a learned response is not reinforced, it gradually drops out of an organism's behavior. Extinction, therefore, refers to the same general phenomenon it did in classical conditioning.

Extinction may take a long time. In some cases animals will respond thousands of times without reward before giving up. Even after extinction seems complete, there may be a return of the previously rewarded habit. If a rat is removed from a Skinner box after extinction and given a short rest, he will begin pressing the bar when returned to the Skinner box.

Question: Does extinction take as long the second time?

If reward is still withheld, bar-pressing will extinguish again, usually more quickly. The brief return of an operant response following extinction is another example of *spontaneous recovery* (mentioned earlier regarding respondent conditioning). Spontaneous recovery seems to be very adaptive. The rat responds again in a situation that produced food in the past: "Just checking to see if the rules have changed!"

Learning Check

1. Responses in operant conditioning are _____ whereas those in classical or respondent conditioning are passive _____ responses.

2. Changing the rules so that an animal (or person) is gradually trained to respond as you want it to is called _____.

3. Extinction in operant conditioning is also subject to _____ of a response.

   a. successive approximations   *b.* shaping   *c.* automation   *d.* spontaneous recovery

4. Reinforcement in operant conditioning refers to the consequences of a response, or what happens after it is made.   T or F?

Answers: 1. voluntary or emitted, reflex   2. shaping   3. d   4. T

Stimulus Control— Putting Habits on a Leash

We have seen that a response followed by reward will be repeated. A second major principle of operant conditioning is that responses that are rewarded in a particular situation tend to come under the control of stimuli present in that situation. This is called **stimulus control.** Notice how this works with our friend Mickey Rat.

The Return of Mickey Rat

While learning the bar-pressing response, Mickey has been in a Skinner box illuminated by a bright light. During several training sessions, the light is alternately turned on and off. When the light is on, a bar press will produce food. When the light is off, bar-pressing goes unrewarded. We soon observe that the rat presses vigorously when the light is on and ignores the bar when the light is off.

In this example, the light signals what consequences will follow if a response is made. A similar situation would be a child learning to ask for candy when her mother is in a good mood, but not asking at other times. In operant conditioning, stimuli that precede a rewarded response tend to influence *when* and *where* the response will occur. Evidence for stimulus control could be shown in the example above by turning the food delivery *on* when the light is *off*. A well-trained rat would never discover that the rules had changed.

Generalization   Two important aspects of stimulus control are **generalization** and **discrimination.** Let's return to the example of the vending machine to illustrate these concepts. First, generalization.

Question: Is generalization the same in operant conditioning as it is in classical conditioning?

Basically, yes. Responses followed by reward tend to be made again when the stimuli that preceded them are present. As a result, similar stimuli also tend to bring forth a response. Assume, for instance, that you have been consistently rewarded for kicking one particular vending machine. Your "kicking response" tends to occur in the presence of that machine. It has come under stimulus control. Now let's say that there are three other machines on campus identical to the one that pays off. Because they are similar to the machine associated with reward, your kicking response will very likely transfer to them. If each of these machines has the same defect as the original and pays off in response to a kick, your kicking response may *generalize* to other machines on campus bearing only slight similarity to the original.

A good example of generalization is the way children use new words. One child studied by psychologist Melissa Bowerman (1977) first used the word *snow* while handling snow outdoors. For a while, however, the child also called each of the following "snow": the white tail of a toy horse, a white toy boat, a white flannel blanket, and spilled milk on the floor. Similar generalization explains why children may temporarily call all men "daddy"—much to the embarrassment of their parents.

Discrimination   Meanwhile, back at the vending machine. . . . As stated earlier with respect to classical conditioning, to discriminate means to respond differently to different stimuli. Because one vending machine reinforced your kicking response, you began kicking similar machines (generalization). Because these also paid off, you began kicking different machines (more generalization). If kicking these new machines has no effect, the kicking response that generalized to them will extinguish due to nonreward. Thus, your response to machines of a particular size and color is consistently rewarded, whereas the same response to different machines is extinguished. You have learned to discriminate between stimuli that signal reward and non-reward. Your response pattern will shift appropriately in the presence of these **discriminative stimuli.** Stimulus discrimination is also illustrated by the "sniffer" dogs used at airports and border stations to locate drugs and explosives. These dogs are taught to recognize contraband by instrumental discrimination training. During training, the dogs are reinforced only for approaching containers baited with drugs or explosives.

Partial Reinforcement— Las Vegas, a Human Skinner Box?

SERENDIPITY (*n*): to discover one thing while looking for another.

B. F. Skinner, so the story goes, was studying operant conditioning when he ran short of food pellets. In order to continue, he arranged for a pellet to reward every other response. Thus began the formal study of **schedules of reinforcement.** Until now we have treated reward in operant conditioning as if it were continuous. **Continuous reinforcement** means that reward follows every response. This is fine for the laboratory, but has little to do with the real world where successful responses are more inconsistently and unpredictably rewarded. **Partial reinforcement** (reward that does not follow every response) may be administered in a number of patterns. Each has a characteristic effect on the rate at which a response is performed. In addition to these specific effects (to be explored in a moment), there is a general effect that accompanies any schedule of partial reinforcement: *Partial reinforcement while acquiring a response makes the response very resistant to extinction.* This is called the **partial reinforcement effect.** It applies to both classical and instrumental conditioning.

Question: How does getting rewarded part of the time make a habit stronger?

If you have ever visited Las Vegas or a similar gambling mecca, you have probably been amused by the sight of row

Fig. 8-7 *The one-armed bandit (slot machine) is a dispenser of partial reinforcement.*

after row of people pulling slot machine handles. To get the flavor of what's happening here and to gain insight into partial reinforcement effects, imagine that you are making your first visit to Las Vegas and that you know nothing about slot machines. You put a nickel in a slot machine and pull the handle. Twenty-five cents in nickels spills into the tray. Taking one of your newly won nickels, you pull the handle again, and again there is a small payoff. Let's say this continues for 15 minutes. Every pull is followed by a pay-off. Then someone notices the machine is defective, and without your knowing it turns off the payoff mechanism. Suddenly each pull of the handle is followed by nothing. Obviously you would pull several times more before giving up. However, when continuous reinforcement is followed by extinction, the message soon becomes clear enough: No more payoffs.

Contrast this with partial reinforcement. You begin by placing five nickels in the machine without a payoff. You are just about to decide that slot machines are not your game, but you have one more nickel. You stick it in, pull the handle, and . . . bingo! It returns $2 in change. After this, payoffs continue on a partial schedule; some are large, and some are small. All are unpredictable. Sometimes you hit 2 in a row, and sometimes 20 or 30 pulls go unrewarded. Now let's say the machine malfunctions, and, unknown to you, it will never pay off again. How many times do you think you would pull the handle this time before "handle pulling" is extinguished? Since you have developed the expectation that any play may be "the one," it will be hard to resist just one more play . . . and one more . . . and one more. Also, since acquisition on a schedule of partial reward includes long periods of nonreward, it will be harder to discriminate between conditions of reward and extinction.

Question: Do gamblers know about partial reinforcement?

Gambling odds are carefully selected so that in the long run, the "house" always wins. If you play long enough, chance factors ensure that your losses will exceed your winnings. If one chooses to gamble, a sensible approach would be to decide how much you are willing to lose for "entertainment," and then quit when it is gone (or when you are ahead by some modest, predetermined amount). In practice, however, few people do quit, because before they reach their loss limit they have "won" several times on a schedule of partial reward. It is no exaggeration to say that the partial reinforcement effect has left many people penniless.

Schedules of Partial Reinforcement

The patterns in which partial reward could be given are limitless. We will consider only the four most obvious possibilities.

Fixed Ratio (FR)   During continuous reinforcement, every response is followed by reward. A simple variation would be to follow every other response with a reward. Likewise, we could follow every third, fourth, fifth, or nth response with a reward. Each of these possibilities is a **fixed ratio (FR) schedule.** The ratio of rewards to responses is fixed: FR-2 means every other response is rewarded; FR-3 means every third response is rewarded, and so forth.

Question: What effect does an FR schedule have?

The most prominent characteristics of fixed ratio schedules is that they produce *extremely high rates of response* (Fig. 8-8). A hungry rat on an FR-10 schedule will run off 10 responses as fast as he can, pause to eat his reward, and then will run off 10 more. A similar situation occurs when factory or farm workers are paid on a piece-work basis. When a fixed number of items must be produced for a set amount of pay, work output is high.

Fig. 8-8 *Typical response patterns for reinforcement schedules. Results such as these are obtained when a cumulative recorder is connected to a Skinner box. The device consists of a moving strip of paper and a mechanical pen that jumps upward each time a response is made. Rapid responding causes the pen to draw a steep line; a horizontal line indicates no response. Small tick marks on the lines show when a reinforcer was given.*

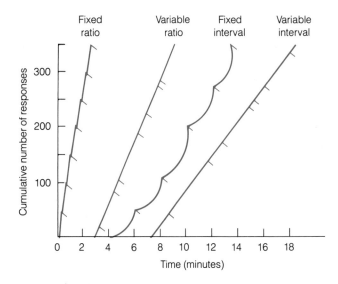

Variable Ratio (VR)   A **variable ratio (VR) schedule** is a slight variation on fixed ratio. Instead of rewarding, for example, every fourth response (FR-4), an organism on a VR-4 schedule gets rewarded on the average every fourth response. Sometimes a response must be made two times for a reward, sometimes five times, sometimes four, and so on. The actual number of responses necessary to produce reward varies, but it averages out to four (in this example). Variable ratio schedules also produce high response rates, although not quite as high as FR. Since reward is less predictable, VR schedules produce slightly greater resistance to extinction than fixed ratio schedules. Playing a slot machine is an example of behavior maintained by a variable ratio schedule of reward. Another would be a child asking for a "treat" at the supermarket. The number of times the child must ask varies from time to time, so the child becomes quite persistent.

Fixed Interval (FI)   Another way of giving partial rewards is to reward only the first response that occurs after the passage of a fixed amount of time. In other words, a rat on a FI-30 sec. schedule must wait 30 seconds after his last rewarded response before a bar press will pay off again. He can press the bar as often as he wants during the interval, but he will not be rewarded. **FI schedules** produce *moderate response rates* punctuated by spurts of activity mixed with periods of inactivity. Animals working on an FI schedule seem to develop a keen sense of the passage of time. For example:

Mickey Rat—Again?

Mickey Rat, trained on a FI-60 sec. schedule, has just been rewarded for a bar press. What does he do? He saunters around the cage, grooms himself, hums, whistles, reads magazines, and polishes his nails. After 50 seconds, he walks to the bar and gives it a press—just testing. After 55 seconds have passed, he gives it two or three presses. Fifty-eight seconds, and he settles down to rapid press-

ing, 59 seconds, 60 seconds, and he hits the rewarded press. After one or two more presses (unrewarded), he wanders off again for the next interval.

Question: Are there human examples of FI schedules?

Clear examples of fixed interval schedules are somewhat rare, but some situations come close. Imagine working at a factory where the supervisor comes by almost exactly every 15 minutes. Your work output would likely rise and fall on a regular 15-minute cycle. Another close parallel would be having a paper due in a class every two weeks. Immediately after turning in a paper, your work probably drops to zero for a week or more, until the next due date draws near.

Variable Interval (VI)   **VI schedules** are the logical variation of fixed interval. Here, reward is given for the first response made after a variable amount of time has passed. A VI-30 sec. schedule means that reward follows an interval that *averages* 30-seconds duration. VI schedules produce *slow, steady rates* of response and tremendous resistance to extinction. When you dial a phone number and get a busy signal, reward (getting through) is on a VI schedule. You may have to wait 30 seconds or 30 minutes. If you are like most people you will doggedly dial over and over again until you get a connection.

Conditioning in Perspective— Great Expectations

An ice cream truck approaches with its bell ringing continuously. A boy runs to the truck, buys an ice cream, and eats it, salivating as he does. What kind of learning is involved? If you are in doubt, look at Table 8-1, which sum-

Table 8-1   Comparison of Classical Conditioning and Operant Conditioning

	Classical Conditioning	Operant Conditioning
Nature of response	Involuntary, reflex	Spontaneous, voluntary
Reinforcement	Occurs *before* response (Conditioned stimulus paired with reinforcing stimulus)	Occurs *after* response (Response is followed by reinforcing stimulus or event)
Role of subject	Passive (Response is *elicited*)	Active (Response is *emitted*)

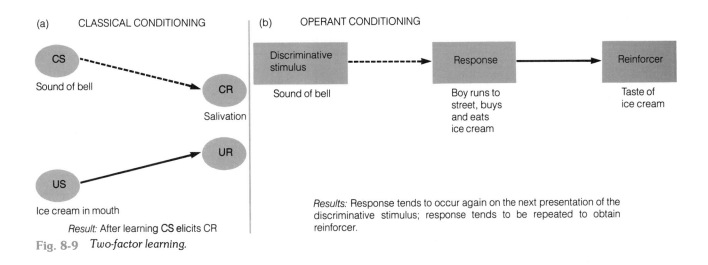

Fig. 8-9   *Two-factor learning.*

marizes differences between classical and operant conditioning. If it seems to you that both kinds of conditioning are present in this example, you are right.

Two-Factor Learning   In the "real world," classical and operant conditioning are often intertwined. As you can see in Fig. 8-9, the boy's behavior reflects both kinds of learning. Each time the ice cream truck approaches, the boy will salivate when he hears the bell (classical conditioning). Also, the bell is a discriminative stimulus signaling that reward is available if certain responses are made. When he hears the bell, the boy will tend to run to the truck, buy, and eat an ice cream (operant conditioning). The boy's involuntary responses are altered by classical conditioning while his voluntary behavior is shaped by operant conditioning.

Question: Other than the fact that they often occur together, do operant and classical conditioning have anything in common?

Information   At one time, psychologists considered conditioning a mechanical "stamping in" of responses. Now many think of learning in terms of "information processing." According to this **informational view,** learning creates mental **expectancies** (or expectations) about events. Once acquired, these expectancies alter behavior. For example, researcher Robert Rescorla (1980) explains classical conditioning this way: Because the CS consistently precedes the US, it *predicts* the US. When the CS is present

the brain *expects* the US to follow. Therefore, the brain prepares the body to respond to the US. In our example, whenever the boy hears the bell, or sees the truck, his mouth waters to prepare for the eating of ice cream. Similarly, when you hear a dentist's drill, your muscles tighten and there is a "catch" in your breathing as your body prepares for discomfort.

If you think about it, instrumental learning also provides information. In operant conditioning, we learn to *expect* that a certain response will have a certain effect at certain times (Bolles, 1979). From this point of view, reward tells a person or an animal which response was "right." Likewise, stimuli preceding an action tell what response to make to get a reinforcer. Thus, when the boy hears the bell, he *expects* that running to the ice cream truck and paying for the ice cream will lead to eating it. If his expectation changes, his behavior will too (after, let's say, the ice cream truck changes its route and he runs out several times and finds instead a garbage truck with its safety bell ringing).

Coming Attractions   Some of the examples in this chapter are simplified and perhaps a little unrealistic. They were selected to clearly express the basic principles of conditioning. To complete our discussion, the upcoming "Applications" section covers more realistic examples of human and animal learning. After that, an "Exploration" examines some of the limits of conditioning and some fascinating experiments in "operant" living. Don't miss these "coming attractions"!

--- **Learning Check** ---

1. Two aspects of stimulus control are _____ and _____.

2. Responding tends to occur in the presence of discriminative stimuli associated with reinforcement and tends not to occur in the presence of discriminative stimuli associated with nonreinforcement.   T or F?

3. When stimuli similar to those that preceded reward also bring forth a response, we call this stimulus generalization.   T or F?

4. When a reward follows every response, it is called:

   a. continuous reinforcement   b. fixed reinforcement
   c. ratio reinforcement   d. controlled reinforcement

5. Partial reinforcement tends to produce slower responding and reduced resistance to extinction.   T or F?

6. The schedule of reward associated with playing slot machines and other types of gambling is:

   a. fixed ratio   b. variable ratio   c. fixed interval   d. variable interval

7. According to the informational view of learning, both classical and operant conditioning create expectancies about events in the environment.   T or F?

Answers: 1. generalization and discrimination   2. T   3. T   4. a   5. F   6. b   7. T

--- **Resources Summary** ---

● *Classical* or *respondent* conditioning and *instrumental* or *operant* conditioning are two basic types of learning. In classical conditioning, an existing reflex response becomes attached to a previously neutral stimulus. In operant conditioning, the frequency and pattern of voluntary responses is altered by reward.

● Many animals are born with *innate* behavior patterns far more complex than *reflexes*. These are organized into *fixed action patterns* (FAPs), stereotyped, or *species specific* behaviors.

● *Learning* is a relatively permanent change in behavior due to past experience. Advanced learning capacity contributes greatly to human adaptability since humans lack instincts.

● A basic type of learning known as conditioning depends on the presence of *reinforcement*. Reinforcement increases the probability that a particular response will occur.

● Classical conditioning, studied by Pavlov, occurs when an *unconditioned stimulus* (US) is preceded by a *conditioned stimulus* (CS). The US causes a reflex called the *unconditioned response* (UR). If the CS is consistently paired with the US, then the CS begins to produce a response by itself. This is called a *conditioned* (learned) *response* (CR).

● When the conditioned stimulus is followed by the unconditioned stimulus, conditioning is *reinforced* (strengthened). When the CS is presented alone, conditioning is *extinguished* (weakened or inhibited). Temporary reappearance of a conditioned response after extinction seems to be complete is called *spontaneous recovery.*

● Through the process of *stimulus generalization,* stimuli, objects, or situations similar to the conditioned stimulus will also produce a response. Generalization gives way to *stimulus discrimination* when an organism learns to respond to one stimulus, but not to similar stimuli.

● Conditioning applies to visceral or emotional responses as well as simple reflexes. As a result *conditioned emotional responses* (CERs) also occur. Irrational fears called *phobias* may be learned CERs. Conditioning of emotional responses can occur *vicariously* (secondhand) as well as directly.

● Instrumental or operant conditioning occurs when a voluntary action is followed by a *reinforcer*. Reinforcement in operant conditioning increases the frequency or probability of a response.

● Complicated operant responses can be taught by rewarding *successive approximations* to a final desired response. This is called *shaping.* It is particularly useful in training animals.

● If an operant response is not followed by reward, it may *extinguish* (disappear). But after extinction seems complete, it may temporarily reappear (*spontaneous recovery*).

● Stimuli that precede a rewarded response tend to control the response on future occasions (*stimulus control*). Two aspects of stimulus control are *generalization* and *discrimination*. In generalization, an operant response is given in situations or to stimuli similar to those associated with reward. In discrimination, responses are given in the presence of stimuli associated with reward, and withheld to stimuli associated with nonreward.

● Reward or reinforcement may be given *continuously* (after every response), or on a *schedule of partial rein-*forcement. Partial reinforcement produces greater resistance to extinction. Four of the most basic schedules of reinforcement are: *fixed ratio, variable ratio, fixed interval,* and *variable interval.*

● Many "real world" situations involve *two-factor learning*—a combination of classical conditioning and operant conditioning.

● According to the *informational view,* conditioning creates *expectancies,* which alter response patterns. In classical conditioning, the CS creates an expectancy that the US will be presented. Learning in operant conditioning is based on the expectation that a response will have a particular effect.

Conditioning in Everyday Situations

A technology of behavior is emerging. A later chapter of this book (Chapter 23) is devoted entirely to the application of conditioning principles to human problems. Conditioning principles are finding their way into business, education, industry, and the home. If you understand these principles, you will find frequent uses for them. It is impossible to detail all the possibilities, but a number of examples should extend your understanding.

Conditioning Pets

One of the most common mistakes people make with pets (especially dogs) is beating them if they do not come immediately when called. Calling the animal then becomes a conditioned stimulus for fear and withdrawal. No wonder it disobeys when summoned on future occasions.

Question: How can conditioning be used to correct this?

Obviously the situation needs to be reversed. A "stop" command can be used to control an animal when it is running away, and return on command can be rewarded. A stop command can be used in conditioning a dog by attaching a 15- to 20-foot-long rope to the dog's collar. During training, if the dog walks or bolts beyond a radius of about 5 or 10 feet, take a firm grip on the rope, give the stop command, and begin walking away from the dog. When the dog hits the end of the rope, it gives him a jolt (this will not hurt him and is not cruel). Very soon, the stop command will bring the dog up short. The rope then becomes unnecessary.

An excellent way to train an animal to come on command is to give a distinctive call or whistle daily during feeding. This makes the signal a discriminative stimulus for reward (food). Effectiveness of the signal is greatly enhanced if it is also used at other times and in other settings and is followed first always, then frequently, then occasionally, with a little food. Ultimately, very few "bribes" will be necessary to maintain the effectiveness of the signal if it is conditioned on a partial schedule of reward. Later, petting and praise can be substituted for food.

Question: What can be done about an animal that begs at the table?

Pets beg at the table for only one reason: They have been rewarded occasionally for doing so. The problem is usually that the owner finds begging bothersome most of the time and seeks to discourage it by not rewarding it with food. But there is always that time when Fido is just too cute to resist. If the owner gives in then, begging has been rewarded on a partial schedule, which makes it very resistant to extinction. Also, persistence has been rewarded. If you don't want your pets to beg, never give in and reward them. If you want them to beg quietly, reward them after a period of silence, not after a particularly sorrowful plea, and then gradually extend the length of the silent period.

Conditioning in Industry

Dr. Thomas Verhave, a psychopharmacologist at a major drug company, once initiated a program to teach pigeons to remove defective, dented, or double-capped capsules from an assembly line (Verhave, 1966). After watching a line of 70 women employees at the monotonous task of sorting capsules from a moving belt, Verhave was reminded of an experiment B. F. Skinner had carried out during World War II with pigeons. Skinner designed a guidance system for air-to-ground missiles that was run by "feathered kamikazes." Using operant conditioning and discrimination training, Skinner taught pigeons to peck at targets projected on a screen (see Fig. 8-10). Three chambers, each housing a screen and one bird, comprised Skinner's "pigeon air guidance system." Pecks on the target were translated into mechanical guidance commands to the missile (Skinner, 1960). Skinner's system worked but was never adopted by the military. But Verhave was convinced that pigeons could be taught to be effective pill inspectors. He developed a device that rewarded pigeons for accepting good capsules and for rejecting defective capsules. Incorrect pecks at an illuminated screen received no reinforcement. Verhave's pi-

Applications

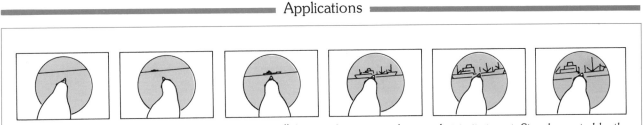

Fig. 8-10 *Target practice for "feathered kamikazes." A trained pigeon guides a rocket to its target. Signals created by the pigeon's pecks modify the direction of the rocket until it is on target.*

geons were performing at a 99 percent level of accuracy after only one week of training, but they were never put into full-time service because company executives feared that the public would not trust medicine inspected by pigeons. Maybe he should have used hawks?!

Conditioning in Business

Perhaps the use of animals in industry will become more prevalent when it is recognized that they are often better capable of working in boring situations than are people. At the moment, most business and industrial applications of reinforcement principles focus on the effects of various bonuses, payment schedules, incentives, commissions, and profit-sharing plans on overall productivity. Before this trend, most people worked for either a straight salary or for an hourly wage. A straight salary can be thought of as a fixed interval schedule of reward. There is little relationship between the amount of effort expended from one paycheck to the next and the amount of pay. This is also partially true of an hourly wage. While it is true that more hours worked mean a larger paycheck, an employee gets paid the same amount for an hour of productive work as he or she does for an hour of goofing off. It can be very demoralizing to see others do less work and receive the same pay.

With these facts in mind, industrial psychologists have sought to make pay relate more directly to work output. The simplest alternative to hourly wages or salary is payment on a piecework (fixed ratio) basis. If an individual is paid a small amount for each item handled, pound picked, shirt sewed, or whatever, work output tends to be high because more items mean more pay. Piecework pay has something of a bad reputation because some employers pay so little on a per-item basis that tremendous amounts of work are necessary to earn a reasonable wage. But this need not be the case. For example, employees of a

small leather factory in Los Angeles are paid for making a prearranged number of items per week (billfold backs, handbag handles, and so on). Employees are allowed to work as many or as few hours per day as they choose, and they can work at any rate. This allows great flexibility for the workers. If they feel tired or want to chat, they work slowly. If they want a three- or four-day weekend, they work faster and longer. The company pays only for the work it gets, and the workers are paid fairly and have an unusually high level of freedom and responsibility.

The most widely used business adaptation of schedules of reinforcement is a combination of hourly wages and incentives for extra effort. Fixed interval rewards (hourly wage or salary) guarantee a good overall level of productivity and give workers a secure base pay, whereas fixed ratio rewards (incentives, bonuses, commissions, or profit sharing) tie extra effort to increased pay.

Conditioning and Children

Children seem to have an almost endless craving for attention. This makes attention and approval from a parent a very powerful reinforcer.

Question: How does this affect a child?

Parents often unknowingly reinforce *negative attention-seeking* in children. Generally, children are *ignored* when they are quiet or are playing constructively. They get attention as they get louder and louder, when they yell "Hey Mom!" at the top of their lungs, when they throw a tantrum, or "show off," or when they break something. Granted the attention they get is often a scolding, but it is still attention, and it still rewards negative attention-seeking. To avoid this, parents could ignore children when they seek attention this way. However, if attention-seeking declines because it is not rewarded, some other behavior must be rewarded to take its place. Parents report dra-

Applications

matic changes in their children's behavior when they make a special effort to actively praise, attend to, or spend time with their children when they are quiet or playing constructively.

Question: What can be done about a child who throws tantrums in a store if she isn't allowed to buy candy?

Children are realists. If you say, "No, you may not buy candy" and stick to it, the child will get the message. Children can discriminate between what is said in a situation and the *actual* possibility of a reward. Children learn to throw tantrums with one parent but not the other; they learn to discriminate between parents' and grandparents' susceptibility to their requests; and they discriminate between a casual no and an angry no. The problem is that no occasionally becomes, "OK, but shut up!" If so, whining or crying has been rewarded on a partial schedule, and it will occur even more frequently in the future. Consistency is the key. If tantrums *never* pay off, they will be abandoned.

Question: But what if the tantrum is really embarrassing? Sometimes parents are willing to do anything to quiet the child.

Beginning a program of nonreward for tantrums may require considerable courage, but it does work. If you don't mind the idea of buying a treat, but dislike the tantrum, try requiring the child to "help" you in some (quiet) way as a condition for receiving the treat. If necessary, walk away from the child and return only when the child has quieted down; or leave the store with the child when a tantrum starts and allow a return to the store only when the child has quieted down.

Conditioning Other Adults

Students seldom realize how much power they have over their teachers. Even tough-skinned veteran teachers are (believe it or not) still human and therefore sensitive to whether or not they are succeeding in class and being accepted by students. This fact can be used in a demonstration of the effects of reward on human behavior.

Shaping a Teacher

For this demonstration, approximately one-half (or more) of the students in a classroom must participate. First, a

target behavior should be selected. This should be something like "lecturing from the right side of the room." (Keep it simple; teachers aren't too clever.) Begin training in this way: Each time the instructor turns toward the right side of the room or takes a step in that direction, participating students should look *really* interested. Also, smile, ask questions, lean forward, and make eye contact. If the teacher turns to the left or takes a step in that direction, participating students should lean back, yawn, check out their split ends, close their eyes, or generally look bored. Soon, without being aware of why, the instructor should be spending most of his or her time each class period lecturing from the right side of the classroom.

This little trick has been a favorite of psychology graduate students for decades. For a time, one of the author's professors delivered all of his lectures from the right side of the room while toying with the venetian-blind cords. (We added the cords the second week!)

As was pointed out in the discussion of reinforcement with children, attention and approval are powerful rewards for human behavior. This is something to keep in mind when interacting with others.

Question: But how can this be applied?

An excellent example is provided by the work of two educators, Paul S. Graubard and Harry Rosenberg, who taught "incorrigible," "deviant," and "socially outcast" students to use reinforcement on classmates. They cite the example of Peggy, an attractive, intelligent student who was unable to make friends. Peggy encountered so much hostility that she was miserable and unhappy, and because of this did poorly in school.

When asked to name three other students she would like to have as friends, Peggy named three students who frequently insulted her. Here is how Peggy began to put into effect the reinforcement principles she had learned: She began by ignoring Doris if she said anything bad to her. When Doris said anything nice, Peggy complimented her, or sat down and asked Doris to join her. Doris soon began to say nice things about Peggy, to sit by her in class, and for the first time ever, they were able to ride on the bus together without fighting.

Peggy dealt with another student's hostility in the same way. Whenever Elwyn said something bad to her, she turned her back on him. But the first time he walked past her without saying something bad, she gave him a

---

Applications

big smile and said, "Hi, Elwyn, how are you today?" The authors add that after Elwyn recovered from his initial shock, he grew to be Peggy's best friend (Graubard and Rosenberg, 1974).

The examples cited above should give you an idea of the value of understanding conditioning and of applying conditioning principles to everyday problems. Their successful use requires practice, but your efforts are sure to foster a deeper appreciation for their application. Give them a try!

Learning Check

1. Pets who beg for food are often very persistent because they have been rewarded on a schedule of partial reinforcement.   T or F?
2. The attempt of a drug company to use pigeons as pill inspectors had to be abandoned because the pigeons could not achieve an acceptable level of accuracy.   T or F?
3. A straight salary can be thought of as fixed interval reinforcement, whereas "piecework" pay is a fixed ratio schedule.   T or F?
4. Negative attention-seeking refers to the idea that parents tend to reward negative attention from their children.   T or F?
5. Compliments, attention, and approval can serve as powerful reinforcers of human behavior.   T or F?

Answers: 1. T   2. F   3. T   4. F   5. T

The "Misbehavior of Organisms"—Conditioning Beyond the Learning Lab

Applying conditioning principles beyond the learning lab is rarely as neat or simple as a textbook discussion tends to imply. The complexities of human and animal behavior are a challenge under the best of circumstances. Let's look at two examples of the kinds of difficulties encountered.

The Reluctant Raccoon A number of years ago two noted psychologists, Keller and Marion Breland, went into business training animals for television shows, zoo displays, and amusement parks. Along with their many successes came some revealing failures:

Raccoons condition readily, have good appetites, and this one was quite tame and an eager subject. We anticipated no trouble. Conditioning him to pick up the first coin was simple. We started out by reinforcing him for picking up a single coin. Then the metal container was introduced, with the requirement that he drop the coin into the container. Here we ran into the first bit of difficulty: he seemed to have a great deal of trouble letting go of the coin. He would rub it up against the inside of the container, pull it back out, and clutch it firmly for several seconds. However, he would finally turn it loose and receive his food reinforcement. Then the final contingency: we put him on a ratio of 2, requiring that he pick up both coins and put them in the container.

Now the raccoon really had problems (and so did we). Not only could he not let go of the coins, but he spent seconds, even minutes, rubbing them together (in a most miserly fashion), and dipping them into the container. He carried on the behavior to such an extent that the practical demonstration we had in mind—a display featuring a raccoon putting money in a piggy bank—simply was not feasible. The rubbing behavior became worse and worse as time went on, in spite of nonreinforcement (Breland and Breland, 1961).

The Brelands ran into similar difficulties with other animals. In each case an innate behavior pattern intruded on learned responses. They called this problem **instinctive drift:** learned responses tend to "drift" toward innate ones. The "miserly" behavior of the raccoon, then, was simply an innate food-washing response.

This and similar quirks in conditioning show that there

are a number of **biological constraints,** or limits, to animal learning. Another example is the honey bee's ability to learn where its hive is. Recent research shows that bees must relearn the location of their hives on their first flight out each morning. At no other time will this information register in the bee's brain. As beekeepers have known for centuries, moving a hive during the day completely confuses the bees; if the hive is moved at night, the bees come and go effortlessly the next day (Gould and Gould, 1981). It is wise to remember that the laws of learning operate within a framework of biological limits and possibilities (Adams, 1980).

An Operant Commune?

Humans, of course, are not subject to instinctive drift. They are, however, notoriously independent creatures. In 1948 B. F. Skinner published *Walden Two,* a utopian novel about a model community run on operant conditioning principles. For years, the pros and cons of such a community were debated, with many skeptics claiming that people would never accept Skinner's vision of **behavioral engineering.** Now, someone has tried it. At Twin Oaks, a farm commune in the Virginia hills, a group of adventuresome souls put some of Skinner's ideas to a test. *Time* magazine (Sept. 20, 1971) reports on their successes and difficulties:

Behavioral engineering goes on every minute of the day. A member who gets angry, who makes demands or who gives ultimatums is simply not "reinforced," to use the behavioral term. He is ignored. What is considered appropriate behavior—cooperating, showing affection, turning the other cheek and working diligently—is, on the other hand, applauded, or "reinforced," by the group. Members are singled out for compliments if they do a job well; signs are put up telling who cleaned a room, for example.

Turnover last year was close to 70 percent. The ones who leave first, in fact, are often the most competent members, who still expect special recognition for their talents. "Competent people are hard to get along with," says Richard Stutsman, one of Twin Oaks' trained psychologists. "They tend to make demands, not requests. We cannot

Exploration

afford to reinforce ultimatum behavior, although we recognize our need for their competence. So, often we give in to them on little things, and then when a big demand arises we have to deny them."

Twin Oaks has also had problems with interpersonal conflicts. The need to criticize some members, disruptive love relationships (especially "love triangles"), and child-adult problems have been especially difficult (Kinkade, 1973).

Experimental Living   Many of the problems at Twin Oaks may have little to do with its operant qualities. In fact, another "operant community" at the University of Kansas has been quite successful. Here, college students have taken part in an Experimental Living Project in which 30 men and women share a large house (Miller, 1976). In this "community" work, leadership, and self-government are tied directly to behavioral principles.

Worksharing provides a good example of the Project's approach. Basic jobs, such as preparing food and cleaning, are divided into approximately 100 tasks. Each task is described in terms of its expected end result. Residents perform all of these tasks themselves, and one community member checks daily to see that each job was completed. (This role is rotated periodically.) To maintain job performance, credits are assigned for each of the tasks. At the end of the month, residents who have collected 400 credits get a sizable rent reduction. This system has been very effective in maintaining day-to-day work habits. As anyone who has shared living quarters knows, good intentions are no guarantee that the chores will get done. More importantly, residents rated the Project as superior to dormitory living and similar alternatives. Most were highly satisfied with the system (Miller, 1976).

Twin Oaks and the Experimental Living Project are good examples of the possibilities and complexities of applying conditioning principles to human behavior. They are, to say the least, fascinating experiments, and they raise an interesting question: How would you feel about living in a behaviorally engineered community?

Questions for Discussion

1. Lately you have been getting a shock of static electricity every time you touch a door handle. You begin to notice a hesitation in your door-opening movements. Can you analyze this situation in terms of classical conditioning?

2. Over the years, balloons have occasionally popped in your face when you were blowing them up. Now you squint and feel tense whenever you blow up a balloon. What kind of conditioning is this? What schedule of reinforcement has contributed to the conditioning? How could you extinguish the response?

3. You are in charge of a group of fifth-grade children that meets regularly for recreation. Other members of the group have excluded a younger girl and a very shy boy from activities. How could you use reinforcement principles to improve this situation? (Include techniques aimed at both the excluded children and the group.)

4. What role has reinforcement played in your selection of a major? Friends? A job? The clothes you wore to school today?

5. From your point of view, what would be the ideal way to be paid at a job? Should pay be weekly, hourly, daily? Should it be tied to work output? Should rewards other than money be offered? If you owned a business what would you consider the ideal way to pay your employees?

6. How many situations can you list in which rewards are haphazardly or inefficiently applied (for example, tax breaks for people who have children instead of those who don't; better seats for those who take "cuts" in line, etc.)? How would you feel about applying a behavioral engineering approach to such problems?

7. How might operant conditioning principles be used to encourage people to pick up litter (what rewards could be offered, and how might the cost of rewards be kept low)?

8. In what ways would instinctive drift be adaptive for an animal? In what ways would it be maladaptive?

9. Can you use operant principles to explain why the more competent members of the Twin Oaks community tended to be the ones to leave?

Suggestions for Further Reading

Farnum, G., and P. S. Graubard. "Little Brother Is Changing You," *Psychology Today,* March, 1974.

Pavlov, I. *Conditioned Reflexes.* Clarendon Press, 1927.

Powers, R. B., and J. G. Osborne. *Fundamentals of Behavior.* West, 1976.

Reynolds, G. S. *A Primer of Operant Conditioning.* Scott, Foresman, 1975.

Skinner, B. F. *Behavior of Organisms.* Wiley, 1938.

————. *Walden Two.* Macmillan, 1960.

————. "The Ethics of Helping People," *The Humanist,* January/February, 1976.

9

Conditioning and Learning II

═══ Chapter Preview ═══

Any subject can be taught effectively in some intellectually honest form to any child at any stage of development.

Jerome Bruner

Dr. Moore's "Learning Machine"

Teaching two- to five-year-olds to read, write, type, and compose stories may sound like an impossible task. However, if the proper conditions of learning are created, it can become a reality. In the early 1960s, Dr. Omar Khayyam Moore of Yale University designed a "responsive learning environment" to take full advantage of children's intellectual curiosity and creativity. In his lab, children "play" with a "talking typewriter." An encounter with the talking typewriter begins the first time a child presses a key. Immediately a letter appears on the paper and a voice names it through a loudspeaker. Surprised by this response, the child tries other keys. Soon the machine captures the child's complete attention, and the connection between keys and letters begins to form.

After a number of sessions in which typing is fairly random, a new game begins. Whenever the child's attention starts to wander, a curtain is removed from a screen above the machine. A single letter appears and the letter is named over the loudspeaker. Children who return to random key pressing suddenly find that the keys no longer work—until they press the key corresponding to the letter on the screen. When a child finds the right key, the correct letter is printed and a voice names it again. Then a new letter appears on the screen. Later words appear. If the key for the first letter is pressed, a pointer moves to the second letter. When a child has correctly typed all three letters of a word, such as "dog," the machine pronounces the word, and a new word appears. Children rapidly go from random typing to reading and writing, and then they compose their own sentences and stories—all before the age of five! (Pines, 1963.)

In comparison to popular video games like Space Invaders or Pac Man, Dr. Moore's talking typewriter looks pretty tame. Just the same, children in Moore's lab learn rapidly and become completely lost in the joy of discovery, simply because the environment is responsive to their actions. As these children show, an ability to learn is every human's birthright. This chapter extends the discussion of learning principles begun in Chapter 8.

195

Survey Questions   How do reinforcers alter behavior? What are the effects of punishment, and what are its advantages and disadvantages? What is cognitive learning? Does imitation have any effect on learning? How does biofeedback relate to learning? What are motor skills and how are they best learned? How would I go about breaking a bad habit? How serious is the impact of television violence?

===== Resources =====

Reinforcement Revisited— What's Your Pleasure?

Learning is the key to adaptability in an ever-changing environment. And, as we saw in Chapter 8, reinforcement is a key element in learning. Reinforcers clearly have a large impact on our daily lives. Let's examine the reinforcement of instrumental behavior in more detail.

Fig. 9-1 *Mean number of innings pitched by major league baseball players before and after signing long-term guaranteed contracts. The performance of 38 pitchers who signed multi-year contracts for over $100,000 per season is shown. When salary was no longer contingent upon good performance, there was a rapid decline in innings pitched and in the number of wins. During the same six-year period, the performance of pitchers on one-year contracts remained fairly steady. (Data from O'Brian et al., 1981)*

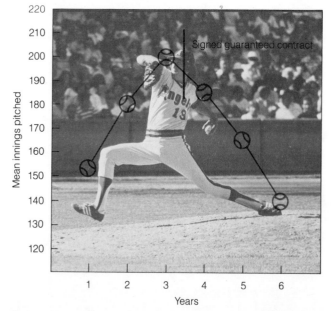

Generally speaking, reinforcement is associated with pleasure, comfort, rewards, or an end to discomfort. Many of the most obvious reinforcers reduce pressing biological drives. Food, water, sex, and removal of pain are all naturally reinforcing. Whatever form reinforcement takes, to be effective it must be **response contingent.** That is, getting a reinforcer is *contingent on* (or depends on) making a response. Contingent reinforcement also affects the *performance* of responses already learned. This is evident in situations ranging from animal training to job performance and pay (see Fig. 9-1).

Reinforcers operate in two basic ways. **Positive reinforcement** takes place when a reward or pleasant event follows an action. An example would be giving a dog a food treat, or a pat on the head when it sits up. **Negative reinforcement** also increases responding, but it does so by ending discomfort. If you have a headache and take an aspirin, your aspirin-taking will be reinforced if the headache stops. Likewise, a rat could be taught to press a bar by giving it a food pellet for each bar press (positive reinforcement); or, the rat could be shocked mildly through the bottom of the cage until it pressed the bar and turned off the shock (negative reinforcement). Often, positive and negative reinforcement combine. If you are uncomfortably hungry, eating a meal is reinforced by the good-tasting food (positive reinforcement) and by an end to hunger (negative reinforcement).

Negative reinforcement is often mistaken for punishment. However, **punishment** is "any event that follows a response and *decreases* its likelihood of occurring again" (Adams, 1980). As noted, negative reinforcement *increases* responding. The difference can be seen in the case of a drug addict undergoing withdrawal. Drug-taking is negatively reinforced because it temporarily lessens the pain of withdrawal. If the drug intensified the pain (punishment), the addict would quickly stop taking it.

Question: Isn't it also punishing to have privileges, money, or other positive things taken away?

Yes. Punishment is either the presentation of an aversive (painful or disliked) event, or the removal of a positive event. Parents who "ground" their teenage children for misbehavior are using the second kind of punishment. Because of its importance, we will return to punishment after a further look at reinforcement. For your convenience, Fig. 9-2 summarizes what we have covered so far.

When dealing with humans, an effective reinforcer may be anything from an M&M to a pat on the back. In categorizing reinforcers, useful distinctions can be made among *primary reinforcers, secondary reinforcers, generalized reinforcers,* and *feedback.*

Primary Reinforcement

Primary reinforcers are "natural," or unlearned, and apply almost universally to a species. They are usually biological in nature and produce comfort, end discomfort, or fill an immediate physical need. Several things already mentioned —food, water, and sex—are primary reinforcers. Everytime you open the refrigerator, walk to a drinking fountain, turn up the heat, or make a trip to an ice cream parlor, your actions reflect the effect of primary reinforcement.

In addition to the most obvious examples, there are other less "natural" primary reinforcers. One of the most unusual (and powerful) involves direct stimulation of "pleasure centers" in the brain (Olds, 1975). (See Fig. 9-3.)

Wiring a Rat for Pleasure

Use of brain stimulation for reward requires the permanent implantation of tiny electrodes in specific areas of the brain. A rat "wired for pleasure" can be trained to press the bar in a Skinner box to deliver electrical stimulation to its own brain. A rat will press the bar thousands of times per hour if each bar press is rewarded by brain stimulation. After 15 or 20 hours of constant pressing, animals sometimes collapse from exhaustion. When they revive, they begin pressing again. If the reward circuit is not turned off, an animal will ignore food, water, and sex in favor of bar-pressing.

One shudders to think what might happen if brain implants were easy and practical to do. (They are not.) Every company from *Playboy* to General Motors would have a device on the market, and we would have to keep a closer watch on politicians than usual!

Secondary Reinforcement

In some primitive societies, habits may still be acquired and maintained mainly by primary reinforcement. Most of us, however, respond to a much broader range of rewards.

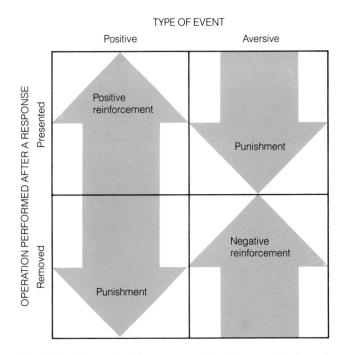

Fig. 9-2 *Types of reinforcement and punishment. The impact of an event depends upon whether it is presented or removed after a response is made. Each square defines one possibility: Arrows pointing upward indicate that responding is increased; downward-pointing arrows indicate that responding is decreased. (Adapted from Kazdin, 1975)*

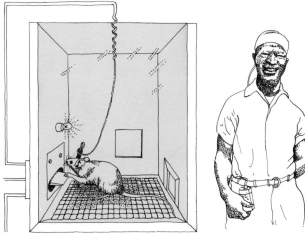

Fig. 9-3 *In the apparatus shown in (a), the rat can press a bar to deliver mild electric stimulation to a "pleasure center" in the brain. Humans also have been "wired" for brain stimulation, as shown in (b).*

Money, praise, attention, approval, success, affection, and grades all serve as *learned,* or **secondary reinforcers,** in modern society. An indication of how subtly secondary reinforcers may affect us comes from an experiment in which a psychologist asked subjects to say aloud all the words they could think of. As each subject spoke, the psychologist said "mm-hmm" after every plural noun. Soon subjects began to say more plural nouns to win the psychologist's approval (Greenspoon, 1955).

Question: How does a secondary reinforcer gain its ability to reward responding?

A secondary reinforcer may simply be associated with a primary reinforcer. This can be demonstrated experimentally in this way:

Son of Mickey Rat

A rat caged in a Skinner box has learned through operant conditioning to press the bar for food pellets. Each rewarded bar press is also followed by a brief auditory tone. After a period of training in which bar-pressing, food, and the tone are associated, the rat is moved to a new cage. This cage has no bar, but it does have a button mounted on the wall. If the rat pushes the button, the tone sounds, but no food is delivered. Even though primary

reinforcement in the form of food is missing, the rat learns to press the button to turn on the tone. Because of its prior association with food, the tone has become a secondary reinforcer.

Tokens   Secondary reinforcers may also gain their value more directly when they can be *exchanged* for primary rewards. Printed money obviously has little or no value on its own. You can't eat it, drink it, or sleep with it. However, it can be exchanged for food, water, lodging, and other . . . necessities.

In a series of classic experiments, chimpanzees were taught to work for *tokens.*

Chimps were first trained to put poker chips into a "Chimp-O-Mat" vending machine which dispensed a few grapes or raisins for each chip. Once the animals had learned to exchange tokens for food, they would learn new tasks to earn the chips and would also operate a device that required lifting a heavy weight to obtain them. Value of the tokens was maintained by occasionally allowing the chimps to use the "Chimp-O-Mat" to exchange chips for food (Wolfe, 1936; Cowles, 1937). (See Fig. 9-4.)

One problem with primary reinforcers is that people and animals receiving them may *satiate* quickly (Kazdin, 1975). (To be satiated means to be fully satisfied or to have reduced desire.) If, for example, you wanted to use candy to reward a retarded child for correctly naming things, the child might only show interest while still hungry. A major advantage of tokens is that they do not lose their reinforcing value as quickly as do primary reinforcers. This is why tokens (plastic chips, gold stars, and the like) have been quite useful in work with troubled children, adolescents, adults in special programs, and in education of the mentally retarded. Tokens are even used at times in ordinary elementary school classrooms. In each case, the goal is to provide an immediate tangible reward as an incentive for learning. Typically, tokens may be exchanged for food, desired goods, special privileges, or trips to movies, amusement parks, and so forth. (For more information on this interesting application of secondary reinforcement, see Chapter 23.)

Question: People sometimes hoard money even when all their needs are taken care of. Why is that?

Generalized Reinforcers   Interestingly, the chimps working for tokens also tended to hoard them, even when hungry. This and similar observations suggest that money may become a **generalized reinforcer.** That is, a secondary reinforcer that has become independent of its connec-

Fig. 9-4 *Poker chips normally have little or no value for chimpanzees, but this chimp will work hard to earn them once he learns that the "Chimp-O-Mat" will dispense food in exchange for them.*

tion with primary reward. Not only can money be exchanged for primary rewards, it may also form an avenue to other secondary reinforcers, such as prestige, attention, approval, status, or power. This property makes its value so general in our society that people sometimes pursue and hoard money just for the sake of having it.

Prepotent Responses Discovering what will serve as a reinforcer can sometimes be a problem. Praise, candy, or a pat on the back may be reinforcing for one person but not another. One way out of this dilemma is to apply the **Premack principle.** The idea, advanced by David Premack (1965), is that any high-frequency (or "prepotent") response can be used to reinforce a low-frequency response. Let's say you love to watch television and do so frequently. In contrast, you hate to take out the trash and rarely do it. If this were the case, TV-watching could be used to reinforce taking out the trash. By requiring yourself to take out the trash before turning on the TV you would increase the occurrence of the low-frequency response. If you are interested in applying reinforcement to change your own behavior (your study habits, for instance), remember that anything you do frequently (watching television, talking with friends, reading magazines, listening to music) can serve as a reinforcer.

Delay of Reinforcement

Reinforcement usually has its greatest effect on learning when the time lapse between a response and the reward that follows is short. This point can be demonstrated in a simple experiment.

Mickey Rat II and Friends Get Delayed

Several groups of rats are trained to press the bar in a Skinner box for a food reward. For some of the animals, a bar press is followed immediately by a food pellet. Other animals are trained with ever-greater amounts of delay between a bar press and a reward. When the delay reaches about 50 seconds, very little learning occurs. If delivery of the food pellet follows a bar press by more than about a minute and a half, no learning occurs (Perin, 1943). (See Fig. 9-5.)

If you wish to reward either an animal or a child for a correct response, reward will be most effective if it is given *immediately* after the response. This effect is also true of punishment. If you discover that your dog dug up and ate a tree in the yard while you were gone, it will do little good to punish him hours later. Likewise, the commonly heard childhood threat of "Wait 'til your father comes home, then

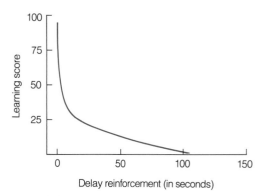

Fig. 9-5 *The effect of delay of reinforcement. Notice how rapidly the learning score drops when reward is delayed. Animals learning to press a bar in a Skinner box showed no signs of learning if food reward followed a bar press by more than 100 seconds. (Perin, 1943)*

you'll be sorry" does more to make Father an ogre than it does to effectively punish an undesirable response.

Question: Let's say I work hard all semester in a class to get an "A." Wouldn't the delay in reinforcement keep me from learning anything?

No, for several reasons. First, as a human you can anticipate future reward. Second, you get rewarded throughout the semester by grades and feedback (more on this in a moment). Third, a single reward can often maintain a long *chain* of responses. A simple example of **response chaining** is provided by Barnabus, a rat trained by psychologists at Brown University.

The Great Barnabus

By carefully working backwards from the last response to the first, Barnabus was trained to make an ever-longer chain of responses to obtain a single food pellet. When in top form, Barnabus was able to: climb a spiral staircase, cross a narrow bridge, climb a ladder, pull a toy car with a chain, get into the car, pedal it to a second staircase, climb the staircase, wriggle through a tube, climb onto an elevator and descend to a platform, press a lever to receive a food pellet, and . . . start over! (Pierrel and Sherman, 1963.)

Many of the things we do every day involve similar response chains; the long sequence of events necessary to prepare a meal, for instance, is rewarded by the final eating. A violin maker may spend three months carrying out thousands of operations for the final reward of hearing the first note from an instrument. Tying a shoe is a short but familiar response chain.

Superstitious Behavior   A reward will reinforce not only the last response that precedes it, but also other responses occurring shortly before the reward is given. This helps account for the learning of many human superstitions. If a golfer taps his club on the ground three times and then hits an unusually fine shot, the success of the shot rewards not only the correct swing but also the three taps. Animals undergoing operant conditioning often develop similar unnecessary habits. If a rat scratches its ear just before its first accidental bar press, it may continue to scratch its ear before each subsequent bar press. All the animal actually has to do to receive a food pellet is press the bar, but it may continue "superstitiously" to scratch its ear each time as if this were necessary.

Question: But if the superstitious behavior is unnecessary why does it continue?

Superstitious acts probably *appear* to pay off to the person or animal. For example:

Son of Mickey Rat in which Jonathan Livingston Pigeon Makes a Guest Appearance

A pigeon has been placed in a Skinner box. When it pecks at a lighted key, the pigeon is rewarded by food that drops into a feeder. The pigeon is allowed to peck at the key three times to obtain food. Then the key is disconnected from the food-delivery mechanism. At random intervals food falls into the tray as the pigeon continues pecking. *There is no connection between pecking and food,* but there *appears* to be. During 20 testing periods, 20 minutes in length, the pigeon made an average of 2700 "superstitious" pecks (Neuringer, 1970).

Many human superstitions seem to be based on the same phenomenon. If you get the large half of a wishbone and have good fortune soon thereafter, you may credit the wishbone for your luck. If you walk under a ladder and then break a leg, you may avoid ladders in the future. Each time you avoid a ladder and nothing unusually bad occurs, your superstitious response is reinforced. Belief in magic can also be interpreted along these lines. Primitive rituals to produce rain, ward off illness, or produce abundant crops very likely earned the faith of participants by occasionally appearing to succeed. Besides, better safe than sorry!

Feedback

Imagine that you are given the task of throwing darts at a target. The dart must be thrown over a screen, which prevents you from telling if you have hit the target. If you were allowed to throw 1000 darts over the screen, we would expect little improvement in your performance, because no feedback is provided. Feedback (information about what effect a response has had) plays a particularly important role in human learning. You may recall that O. K. Moore's "learning machine" does not specifically reward children for correct responses, but since it provides feedback, tremendous amounts of learning take place.

The value of feedback (also called **knowledge of results,** or **KR**) is one of the most useful lessons to be derived from psychological studies of learning. One can almost always increase the amount of feedback in a learning situation, and more feedback generally means faster learning or improved performance.

Question: How can feedback be applied to human learning?

There are numerous possibilities, many already in widespread use. In learning to play a musical instrument, to sing, speak a foreign language, or deliver a speech, a tape recorder can be invaluable. In sports, videotape is being used to improve everything from tennis form to a pitcher's "pick-off move."

Feedback is valuable academically too. If you were to receive only a single grade in a course, you would have little way of knowing how you were doing. Most teachers use tests, quizzes, reports and other assignments throughout a semester so students can judge their progress. You can add to this feedback on your own. When studying, you can arrange to "take" a test several times before taking it officially in class. In other words, self-testing by use of flash cards, workbooks, reviews, "learning checks," answering questions following chapters—all will help you to correct errors and speed learning *before* the actual test in class. Make your errors before they count: Studying for a test without feedback is like practicing for a basketball game by shooting baskets blindfolded.

Learning Aids   In recent years three interesting and specialized applications of feedback have been developed. These are *programmed instruction, computer-assisted instruction,* and *biofeedback.* Biofeedback is of such interest that we will devote an upcoming section to it.

Question: How do programmed instruction and computer-assisted instruction make use of the feedback principle?

For feedback to be most effective, it should be *immediate* and *detailed.* **Programmed instruction** gives information to students in a format that requires precise answers about information as it is presented. This approach breaks learning into a series of small steps, and provides constant feedback to correct errors. It also minimizes incorrect responses. Entire courses may be programmed, in which case each student can proceed at his or her own pace. The "learning check" that follows this discussion is done in a programmed format so that you can see what one looks like.

In **computer-assisted instruction (CAI)** students work at individual computer terminals. As the computer transmits lessons to a display screen, the student responds by typing answers on a keyboard or by touching the display screen with an electronic "pencil" (Fig. 9-6). In addition to providing immediate feedback on the screen and over earphones, the computer can *analyze each answer*. This allows use of a **branching program** in which additional information and questions are given when an error is made. Elementary school children seem to do especially well with a "computer tutor" due to the immediate feedback and individualized pacing. Computer-assisted instruction has been impressively successful in teaching reading; CAI students usually advance far more rapidly than is typical for traditional reading instruction (Atkinson, 1968).

Fig. 9-6 *Computer-assisted instruction. CAI provides immediate feedback and additional exercises when needed.*

Learning Check

To give you a feeling for what programmed instruction is like, this learning check is presented in a programmed format. To use it, you should cover the answers on the left, uncovering each after you have filled in a blank.

reinforcer	A _____ is any object or event that increases the probability of a response. Reinforcement affects both the learning and
performance	the _____ of behaviors. Reinforcers are most effective when they are
contingent	_____ on making a particular
Positive	response. _____ reinforcement takes place when a reward or pleasant event follows
reinforcement	an action. Negative _____ rewards a response by bringing an end to discomfort. Punishment refers to discomfort that is initiated by a response, or to the
removal	_____ of positive events. Primary reinforcers are natural physiological or biological rewards. Direct stimulation of "pleasure centers" in the brain may also
primary	serve as _____ reinforcement.
secondary	Learned reinforcers are called _____ reinforcers. As a secondary reinforcer, money
generalized	has such universal value that it may be thought of as a _____ reinforcer.
responses	Prepotent _____ can also reinforce less frequently occurring responses.
long	Delay of reinforcement reduces its impact. If the delay is _____, no learning at all will take place.
knowledge	Nevertheless, long chains of behavior may be maintained by a single reinforcer. For humans, much learning
of	is based upon informational feedback about the effects of a response. Feedback is also known as KR, or
results	_____ _____ _____ .

Punishment—Spare the Rod!

At this point we have considered only the role of reinforcement in learning. No account of learning can be complete without also discussing the effects of punishment. For better or worse, punishment is one of the most popular ways to influence behavior in our society. Spankings, reprimands, loss of privileges, fines, jail sentences, firings, failing grades, and the like all reflect a widespread reliance on punishment (Fig. 9-7).

Question: Reinforcement strengthens a response. Does punishment weaken a response?

Edict of Louis XI, King of France A.D. 1481

"Anyone who sells butter containing stones or other things (to add to the weight) will be put into our pillory, then said butter will be placed on his head until entirely melted by the sun. Dogs may lick him and people offend him with whatever defamatory epithets they please without offense to God or King. If the sun is not warm enough, the accused will be exposed in the great hall of the gaol in front of a roaring fire, where everyone will see him."

Fig. 9-7 *Punishment has long been used to suppress undesirable behavior.*

Common sense tells us that punishment abolishes undesired behavior. Is this always true? The effectiveness of punishment depends greatly on its *timing, consistency,* and *intensity.* Punishment works best when it occurs while a response is being made, or *immediately* afterward (timing), and when it is given *each time* a response occurs (consistency). Thus, a dog that has developed a habit of constantly barking can be effectively (and humanely) punished by spraying water on its nose each time it barks. Ten to fifteen such treatments are usually enough to greatly reduce barking. This would not be the case if punishment were applied occasionally or long after the barking took place.

Severe punishment can be extremely effective in stopping behavior. If a child sticks a finger in a light socket and gets shocked, it may be the last time the child *ever* tries it. More often, however, punishment only temporarily *suppresses* a response. If the response is still reinforced, punishment may be particularly ineffective. Responses suppressed by **mild punishment** usually reappear later. If a child sneaks a snack from the refrigerator before dinner and is punished for it, the child may pass up snacks for a short time. But since "snack-sneaking" was also rewarded by the sneaked snack, the child will probably try again at a later date.

This fact has been demonstrated experimentally by arranging for rats to be slapped on the paw when pressing the bar in a Skinner box. Two groups of well-trained rats were placed on extinction. One group was punished with a slap for each bar press, while the other was not. It might be expected that the slap would cause bar-pressing to extinguish more quickly. This was not the case, however, as can be seen in Fig. 9-8. Punishment temporarily slowed responding, but did not cause more rapid extinction. Slapping the paws of rats or children has little permanent effect on the strength of a response. However, it is worth stating again, intense punishment may permanently suppress a response. Experiments show that even something as basic as eating can be suppressed. Animals severely punished while eating may never eat again (Bertsch, 1976).

Question: Then should punishment be used in the learning process?

Using Punishment Wisely Parents, educators, animal trainers, and the like have three basic tools available to

Fig. 9-8 *The effect of punishment on extinction. Immediately after punishment, the rate of bar pressing is suppressed, but by the end of the second day, the effects of punishment had disappeared. (After B. F. Skinner, The Behavior of Organisms. © 1938. D. Appleton-Century Co., Inc. Reprinted by permission of Prentice-Hall, Inc.)*

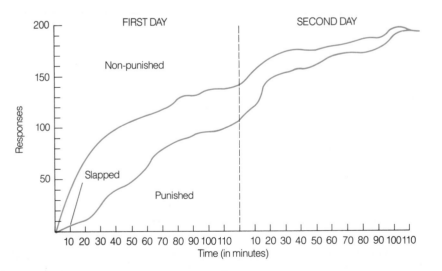

control simple learning: (1) *reinforcement* (or reward) strengthens a response; (2) *nonreinforcement* causes a response to extinguish; (3) *punishment* suppresses a response. These tools work best in combination. When punishment is mild, as it should be, its effect may be limited if reinforcers are still available in the situation. If you choose to use punishment, it is best to also reward an alternate, desirable response. Used alone, punishment tells a person or animal that a response was "wrong," but provides no alternative. If reinforcement is missing from the formula, punishment becomes less effective.

In a situation that poses immediate danger, such as when a child reaches for the top of a stove or a dog runs into the street, mild punishment may prevent disaster. Punishment in such cases is most effective when it produces responses *incompatible* with the undesired response. Let's say a child reaches toward a stove burner. Would a swat on the bottom serve as effective punishment? Probably so. It would be better, however, to slap the child's outstretched hand so it will be withdrawn in the presence of the stove.

Question: Are there drawbacks to the use of punishment?

Yes, several. Let's consider the case against punishment.

Side Effects of Punishment

The basic problem with punishment is that it is usually *aversive* (painful or uncomfortable). As a result, people and situations associated with punishment tend, through classical conditioning, to also become aversive (feared, resented, or disliked). This association, perhaps, is why children so often choose school windows to break when others are available. The aversive qualities of punishment make it especially inappropriate for teaching children to eat politely, or for toilet training.

Escape and Avoidance   A second major problem is that aversive stimuli usually encourage **escape** and **avoidance learning.** Escape learning simply reflects the operation of negative reinforcement:

A dog is placed in a two-compartment cage called a shuttle box. If it is shocked in one of the compartments, it will quickly learn to jump to the second compartment to *escape* the shock. If a buzzer is sounded 10 seconds before the shock is turned on, the dog will soon learn to associate the buzzer with shock. It will then *avoid* pain by jumping *before* the shock begins (Solomon and Wynne, 1953).

Psychologists have theorized that avoidance involves two-factor learning (described in Chapter 8). An animal first

learns, through classical conditioning, to feel fear in the presence of the buzzer. Then, leaping from the compartment is rewarded by negative reinforcement in the form of a reduction in fear (this is instrumental learning).

Once avoidance is learned it is very persistent. The shock can be turned off, and the dog will continue to leap from the compartment at each sounding of the buzzer. But if the buzzer is never followed by shock, why doesn't fear of the buzzer extinguish? One possibility is that only a small amount of fear is needed to reward avoidance. Consequently, the full fear response does not occur and is not extinguished (Adams, 1980).

Question: How are escape and avoidance learning related to punishment?

Escape and avoidance learning are a regular part of daily experience. For instance, if you work with a loud and obnoxious person, you may initially escape from conversations with him; later you may learn to avoid him altogether. In any situation involving frequent punishment, similar desires to escape and avoid are activated. For example, children who run away from punishing parents (escape), may soon learn to lie about their behavior (avoidance), or to spend as much time away from home as possible (also an avoidance response).

Aggression   A third problem with punishment is that it can greatly increase *aggression*. Researchers have shown that animals consistently react to pain by attacking whomever or whatever else is around (Azrin *et al.,* 1965). A common example of this effect is the faithful dog that nips its owner while undergoing a painful procedure at a veterinarian's office.

We also know that one of the most common responses to frustration is aggression. Generally speaking, punishment is painful, frustrating, or both. Punishment, therefore, sets up a powerful learning environment for the promotion of aggression. When a child is spanked, the child becomes angry, frustrated, and feels aggressive. What if the child then goes outside and hits a brother, sister, or a neighbor? The danger is that it may feel good because it releases anger and frustration. If so, aggression has been rewarded and will tend to occur again in other frustrating situations. One study found that overly aggressive adolescent boys had been severely punished for aggression at home. Since aggression was suppressed at home, parents were frequently surprised to learn that their "good boys" were in trouble at school for fighting and other forms of aggression (Bandura and Walters, 1959).

To summarize, the most common error in the use of

punishment is to rely on it exclusively as a means of training or discipline. The overall emotional adjustment of a child or pet disciplined mainly by reward is usually superior to one disciplined mainly by punishment. Frequent punishment makes a person or an animal unhappy, confused, anxious, aggressive, and fearful of the source of punishment. Children who receive a lot of punishment from parents or teachers learn not only to dislike parents and teachers, but also to dislike and to avoid the activities associated with punishment (schoolwork or household chores, for instance) (Munn, 1969). It is not entirely unreasonable with three-to-five-year-old children to occasionally use mild physical punishment. (See Chapter 16 "Applications".) Otherwise, it would seem that the adage, "Spare the rod and spoil the child" should at least be changed to, "Use the rod sparingly or spoil the child," and perhaps to simply, "Spare the rod."

Cognitive Learning—Beyond Conditioning

Question: Is all learning just a connection between a stimulus and a response?

Some learning can be thought of this way. But, as we saw in the last chapter, even basic conditioning may have "mental" elements to it. To further illustrate, assume that you have been conditioned—by pairing a light with shock—to feel fear each time the light comes on. If the shock is then turned off, and the light presented many times, we can expect a gradual extinction of your fear response. But what if you were simply *told* that shock would not follow the light again? The surprising finding is that your fear would disappear almost immediately. (Grings and Lockhart, 1963; Wickens *et al.,* 1963). As a human, you can anticipate future reward or punishment and react accordingly, even to the point of overriding a conditioned response.[*]

There is no doubt that human learning includes a large *cognitive,* or mental, dimension. As humans, we are greatly affected by information, expectations, perceptions, mental images, and the like. Loosely speaking, **cognitive learning** refers to understanding, knowing, anticipating, or otherwise making use of higher mental processes. Cognitive learning extends into the realms of memory, thinking, problem solving, and the use of concepts and language. Since these topics are covered in later chapters, our discussion here is restricted to an initial look at learning "beyond conditioning."

[*]You may be wondering why this doesn't seem to work when a doctor or dentist says, "This won't hurt a bit." Here's why: They lie!

How do you navigate around the town you live in? Is it fair to assume that you have simply learned to make a series of right and left turns to get from one point to another? Actually, if you are in a new town, finding your way around may be temporarily done in this way. Soon, however, you develop an overall mental picture of how the town is laid out. This **cognitive map** (internal representation of relationships) acts as a guide even when you must detour or take a new route.

Question: Are animals capable of cognitive learning?

A little psychological "monkey business" shows that they are. In one experiment, chimpanzees were carried around a field by one psychologist, while another hid 18 pieces of fruit in various locations. Each chimp was returned to its cage and then released into the field. Chimps who watched the hiding of the fruit found about a dozen pieces each. Control chimps averaged only one find per test—mainly because they followed monkeys who were "in the know" (and got in on the fruits of their labors) (Menzel, 1978). Actually, it's not surprising that higher animals are capable of cognitive learning. Yet even the lowly rat—not exactly a mental giant—learns *where* food is found in a maze, not just which turns to make to reach the food (Tolman, 1946).

Latent Learning   Cognitive learning is closely related to another phenomenon known as **latent** (hidden) **learning.** Learning sometimes occurs with no obvious reinforcement at all.

Mickey Rat II Learns Where the Action Is

Two groups of rats are allowed to explore a maze. Rats in one group find food at the far end of the maze and soon learn to make their way rapidly through the maze when released. Rats in the second group are unrewarded and show no signs of learning. But later, when these rats are given food, they run the maze as well as the rewarded group (Tolman and Honzik, 1930).

Although there was no outward sign of it, the unrewarded rats were learning their way around the maze.

Question: How did they learn if there was no reinforcement?

Many experiments have demonstrated that curiosity is a strong drive in animals, as well as in people. Monkeys have been known to solve puzzles after hours of playing with them simply to satisfy curiosity or end boredom (Harlow and Harlow, 1962). Apparently, the satisfaction of exploring the environment can be enough to reward learning. In humans, latent learning is probably related to higher level abilities, such as anticipation of future reward. If you give an attractive classmate a ride home, you may make mental notes about how to get to his or her house even if a date only seems to be a remote future possibility.

Learning to Learn   *Learning to learn* is another interesting cognitive effect. It too can be demonstrated by an animal experiment. A monkey is given the problem of picking which of two objects has a raisin under it. On the first trial a raisin is placed under a cup; to the right of it is a box with nothing underneath. The monkey chooses the cup and gets the raisin. On the next trial the position of the objects is reversed, but the cup still has the raisin. This time the monkey chooses the box, apparently selecting by position, not by object. After a large number of trials the monkey learns that the treat is always found under the cup, regardless of position. Then a new problem is presented, this time using a dish and a toy car. Again, the monkey's learning is gradual. However, after several hundred trials and many new problems, the monkey will have developed a **learning set**, or preparedness for further learning. Given a new problem, it gets it right on the first or second trial (Harlow, 1949). Humans given similar problems catch on immediately. Perhaps it could be said that persistence is the monkey's forte, and learning to learn, the human's.

Much of what is meant by cognitive learning is summarized by the word *understanding*. Psychologists long ago discarded the idea that education is some kind of exercise for the mind that strengthens "reason," "concentration," "thinking," or *mental faculties*. Rather, specific skills are learned that can be applied to new situations or problems. In gaining such skills, Jerome Bruner (1968) has emphasized the value of **discovery learning**. In discovery learning, skills are acquired by insight and understanding instead of by *rote* (repetition and memorization of facts or rules).

Question: As long as learning occurs what difference does it make?

Figure 9-9 illustrates the difference. Two groups of students were taught to calculate the area of a parallelogram. Some were encouraged to see that a "piece" of a parallelogram could be "moved" to create a rectangle. These students were better able to solve unusual problems than were students who simply memorized a rule (Wertheimer, 1959). Although rote learning is valuable, it is worthwhile in education to take the extra steps needed to encourage understanding as well.

Modeling—Do As I Do, Not As I Say

The class watches intently as a skilled potter centers a ball of clay on the wheel and deftly pulls it up into a vase form. There is little doubt that many skills are learned by what Albert Bandura (1971) calls observational learning, **modeling**, or, simply, imitation. The efficiency of learning by observation is obvious: A seemingly simple skill, such as throwing a small pot, could take pages and pages to describe in words, and a beginner would likely still not know how to proceed. Whereas we clearly place great faith in *verbal instruction*, learning by observation fills an important need. Many responses simply cannot be effectively passed on by verbal instruction. Imagine trying to *tell* someone how to tie a shoe, do a dance step, or crochet.

Question: It seems obvious that we learn by observation, but how does this occur?

By observing a **model** (someone who serves as an example) a person may: (1) learn new responses; (2) learn to

Fig. 9-9 *Learning by understanding and by rote. For some types of learning, understanding may be superior, although both types of learning are useful. (After Wertheimer, 1959)*

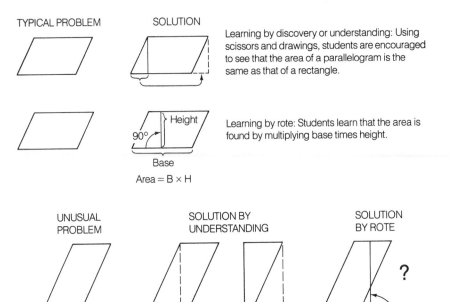

TYPICAL PROBLEM

SOLUTION

Learning by discovery or understanding: Using scissors and drawings, students are encouraged to see that the area of a parallelogram is the same as that of a rectangle.

Height

90°

Base

Area = B × H

Learning by rote: Students learn that the area is found by multiplying base times height.

UNUSUAL PROBLEM

SOLUTION BY UNDERSTANDING

SOLUTION BY ROTE

?

90°

carry out or avoid previously learned responses, depending on what happens to the model for doing the same thing; or, (3) learn a general rule that can be applied to various situations (Rosenthal and Zimmerman, 1978).

For observational learning to occur several things must take place. The learner must pay *attention* to the model and *remember* what was done. (A beginning auto mechanic might be interested enough to watch an entire tune-up, but unable to remember all the steps.) The learner must be able to *reproduce* the learned behavior. (Sometimes this is a matter of practice, but it may be that the learner will never be able to perform the behavior. I may admire the feats of world-class gymnasts, but with no amount of practice could I ever reproduce them.) If a model is *successful* or *rewarded,* the learner is more likely to imitate the behavior.

This is also the case for models who are attractive, rewarding, admired, or high in status (Bandura and Walters, 1963). Once a new response is tried, normal *reinforcement determines if it will be repeated* thereafter.

Modeling has a powerful effect on behavior. In a classic experiment, children watched an adult attack a large blow-up "Bo-Bo" doll. Some children saw an adult sit on the doll, punch it, hit it with a hammer, and kick it around the room (Fig. 9-10). Others saw a color movie of these actions, and a third group saw a cartoon version of the aggression. Later, the children were frustrated (by having some attractive toys taken away from them) and then allowed to play with the Bo-Bo doll. Most imitated the attack they had seen the adult perform. Some even added new aggressive acts of their own! The cartoon was only slightly

Fig. 9-10 *A nursery-school child imitates the aggressive behavior of an adult model he has just seen in a movie. (Photo courtesy of Albert Bandura)*

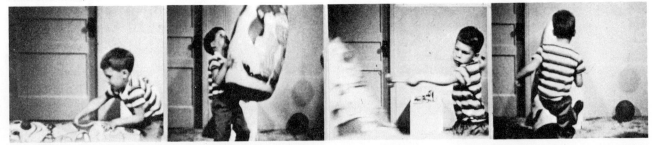

No Comment Necessary

Television as a model:
TV violence during an average week
During an average week, TV programs contain over 600 acts of violence.

Ninety-five percent of televised cartoons contained violence.

In TV plays more than one-half of the major characters were responsible for inflicting violence on someone.

Foreigners and nonwhites are more likely to die on TV than are whites.

Forty percent of TV "lawmen" initiated violence, and 70 percent contributed to it. (U.S. National Commission on the Causes and Prevention of Violence, 1970.)

"He said his first words today—'Bang you're dead.'"

less effective in encouraging aggression than the live adult model and the filmed model (Bandura, Ross, and Ross, 1963).

Question: Then do children blindly imitate adults?

No. Remember that observational learning equips a person to duplicate a response, but whether it is actually imitated depends on whether the model was rewarded or punished for what was done. Nevertheless, research shows that when parents tell a child to do one thing, but model a completely different response, children are inclined to imitate what the parents *do,* and *not* what they *say* (Bryan and Walbek, 1970). Thus, through modeling, children learn not only attitudes, gestures, emotions, and personality traits, but fears, anxieties, and bad habits as well.

Consider a typical situation. Little Shawn-Erin-Ringo-Jeremy Jones has just been interrupted at play by his little brother. Angry and frustrated, he hits his little brother. This behavior interrupts his father's TV program. Father promptly spanks little Shawn-Erin-Ringo-Jeremy, saying, "This will teach you to hit your little brother." And it will. Because of modeling effects, it is unrealistic to expect a

child to "Do as I say, not as I do." The message the father has given the child is clear: "You have frustrated me; therefore, I will hit you." Is it any wonder that the child does the same when he is frustrated?

Question: Can television serve as a model for observational learning?

There is reason to believe that it can. As a convicted criminal once told *TV Guide* magazine, "TV taught me how to steal cars, how to break into establishments, how to go about robbing people, even how to roll a drunk. Once after having watched *Hawaii Five-O,* I robbed a gas station. The show showed me how to do it." The rash of "repeat performances" that followed TV coverage of the first successful airliner hijackings also demonstrates the power of TV as a model. Many psychologists have been particularly concerned about the effects of televised criminal activity and violence (see inset). Given the influence of television in our culture, TV's impact as a model deserves further examination—something we will undertake in this chapter's "Exploration."

Learning Check

1. Three factors that greatly influence the effects of punishment are timing, consistency, and _____.

2. Mild punishment tends to only temporarily _____ a response that is also reinforced. (circle)

   enhance   aggravate   replace   suppress

3. Three undesired side effects of punishment are: (1) conditioning of fear and resentment, (2) encouragement of aggression, and (3) the learning of escape or _____ responses.

4. In humans, extinction of a conditioned response can be influenced by expectation.   T or F?

5. An internal representation of relationships is referred to as a _____ _____ .

6. Learning that suddenly appears when a reward or incentive for performance is given, is called:
    a. discovery learning   b. latent learning   c. rote learning   d. reminiscence

7. Albert Bandura uses the term _____ to describe observational learning.

8. If a model is successful, rewarded, attractive, or high in status, his or her behavior is:
    a. difficult to reproduce   b. less likely to be attended to   c. more likely to be imitated   d. subject to positive transfer

9. Children who observed a live adult behave aggressively became more aggressive; those who observed movie and cartoon aggression did not.   T or F?

Answers: 1. intensity 2. suppress 3. avoidance 4. T 5. cognitive map 6. b 7. modeling 8. c 9. F

Learning Principles in Action— Biofeedback

An exciting recent psychological discovery is that humans can learn to control bodily activities formerly believed to be involuntary. For years, yoga and Zen masters have demonstrated extraordinary control over "involuntary" functions like heart rate, blood pressure, oxygen consumption, and temperature of parts of the body. Now, Western technology is showing that under the proper conditions anyone can learn to duplicate these "impossible" effects.

Question: How is this possible?

Electronic Yoga?   By applying the general principle of feedback to the control of bodily responses, we arrive at **biofeedback.** If I were to say to you, "Raise the temperature of your right hand," you probably couldn't because you wouldn't know when you were succeeding. However, your task could be made easier by attaching a sensitive thermometer to your hand. If the thermometer were wired so that an increase in temperature would activate a signal light, all you would have to do is try to keep the light on as much as possible. With practice you could then learn to raise your hand temperature at will.

Question: How does the light help?

Yoga and Zen masters use *meditation* to achieve this kind of control. Meditation makes the mind and body very "quiet" and allows a person to focus on tiny changes in bodily functioning. Biofeedback accomplishes the same thing by making bodily activities "louder." Bodily processes are monitored (usually electronically) and converted into a signal that provides the person with clear feedback about what the body is doing.

Question: If you succeed at raising hand temperatures, what are you actually doing?

Biofeedback also involves cognitive learning. If asked to describe what you had done, you might say, "I thought warm thoughts," or, "I just had a feeling when the light was on and I kept trying to recapture that feeling." The point is, when you are given feedback, you can repeat whatever it was that you were doing, even if it was a very subtle mental state.

Neal Miller and his research associates have found that almost any bodily function can be voluntarily controlled if feedback or reward follows change in the function. In one typical experiment, Miller taught rats to change the speed of their heart rate.

> Rats were temporarily paralyzed with the drug curare and maintained on artificial respiration. While paralyzed they were given rewards in the form of electrical stimulation to "pleasure centers" in the brain. The animals showed a 20 percent jump in heart rate during training when small increases in heart rate were followed by reward. Rats rewarded for decreasing their heart rate showed a 20 percent drop (Miller and DiCara, 1967).

Miller initially thought the animals were directly speeding and slowing their hearts. But later experiments suggest the animals were not completely paralyzed, allowing them to affect heart rate by moving voluntary muscles (Miller and Dworkin, 1974). In any case, Miller and others have shown that rats can also learn to change their blood pressure, the blood flow to their stomach or kidneys, and the frequency of stomach contractions. They can even increase blood flow in one ear without affecting the other (Miller, 1969). Can you "blush" in your left ear?

Question: Of what value is this?

Applications of Biofeedback

Research with animals has spurred application of biofeedback for the treatment of psychosomatic problems (illnesses caused mainly by stress or psychological factors). For example, Dr. Elmer and Alyce Green have had success in training people to prevent migraine headaches. Patients begin training with one temperature-sensitive electrode taped to a finger and another to the forehead. Patients learn to move the needle on a dial that registers the difference between hand and forehead temperature. This teaches them to redirect blood flow away from the head to their extremities. Since migraine headaches are caused by excessive blood flow to the head, biofeedback training equips patients to short-circuit headaches before they develop (Luce and Peper, 1971).

Early successes led many to predict that biofeedback would offer a cure for psychosomatic illnesses, anxiety, phobias, drug abuse, and a long list of other problems. In reality, biofeedback has proven helpful, but not an instant cure. Biofeedback can definitely relieve muscle-tension headaches and migraine headaches (Budzynski, 1977; Adler and Adler, 1976). It shows promise for lowering blood pressure and alleviating irregular heart rhythms (Kristt and Engel, 1975). (See Fig. 9-5.) Some control of the digestive system seems possible through biofeedback, which may be helpful for ulcer patients. Biofeedback has even been used with some success to control epileptic seizures (Sterman, 1977). But questions about the value of biofeedback remain. Many of the benefits reported may simply reflect *general relaxation* (Blanchard and Epstein, 1978).

Question: Does biofeedback apply to brain waves?

Alpha Control   Alpha waves are one of several distinctive patterns of brain activity that can be recorded with the EEG (electroencephalograph, or brain-wave machine). Several years ago psychologist Joseph Kamiya developed a technique whereby subjects are signaled by a tone or light whenever they produce alpha waves (Kamiya, 1968). Subjects in alpha-control experiments report that high levels of alpha are accompanied by sensations of pleasure, relaxation, "passive alertness," or peaceful images. Some people have looked upon these findings as a potential avenue to "instant

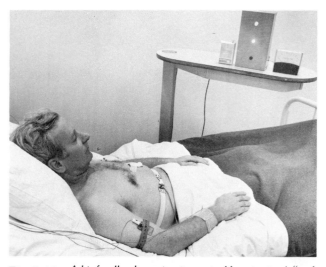

Fig. 9-11   *A biofeedback session to control heart rate. A "traffic signal" (center box) of red, green, and yellow lights tells the patient to speed or slow his heartbeat. A buzzer sounds when the desired heart-rate change takes place.*

bliss," but evidence on the overall value of alpha training is still contradictory. Simple relaxation may once again be implicated. It seems that the age of "electronic yoga" is not yet quite with us.

Learning Principles in Action— Learning Skills Skillfully

A **motor skill** is a series of actions molded into a smooth and efficient performance. Typing, walking, pole-vaulting, shooting baskets, playing golf, driving a car, and skiing are all examples. How do we learn such skills? Many begin as simple response chains. At first, sensations from one response act as a cue to produce the next response, which becomes a cue for the next, and so on. However, as skills improve, we typically develop **motor programs** for them (Blumenthal, 1977). Motor programs are mental plans or models of what a skilled movement should be like. A good example of this kind of learning is provided by a guitarist friend of the author's. The guitarist once cut the first finger of his right hand before a performance. Normally, he did his "finger-picking" with his thumb and first two fingers. How could he perform with an injured finger? No problem! He used the second and third fingers instead. His musical skills were in his head (as a motor program), not in his fingers.

Fig. 9-12   *Strobe-light photograph of a motor skill. Multiple exposures reveal the complexity of skilled movement. Motor skills are guided by mental plans or programs.*

Question: How do motor programs guide movement?

Consider walking as an example. In order to walk, we use feedback from the body and senses to compare our actions to an internal standard or program. Any difference between this feedback and the "walking program" tells us to make a correction. Such monitoring, plus rapid corrections, is what allows us to walk on ice, sand, rocks, and stairs with no loss of skill. Motor programs also underlie many sports skills. A basketball player, for instance, may never make exactly the same shot twice in a game. This makes it almost impossible to practice *every* shot that might occur. Instead, the skilled athlete learns a variety of general programs, not a collection of set responses (Klausmeir and Goodwin, 1975).

New skills usually require conscious guidance. Think of when you learned to drive a car. Initially, almost all of your attention was focused on steering, signaling, accelerating, and braking; holding a conversation or tuning the radio was probably out of the question. However, as motor programs develop we can pay less attention to movements. Eventually, skills become *automated,* or practically automatic. This frees higher brain centers to make decisions and attend to other information (Singer, 1978). Thus, a basketball player who can dribble without thinking about it is free to plan his or her next move. Likewise, a skilled skier can enjoy the scenery on a downhill run, or a driver can think about things other than driving.

Question: Are motor skills easily lost?

A concert pianist or a ballet dancer may require constant practice to maintain performance. On the other hand, you have probably observed that you were able to type, roller-skate, swim, ride a bicycle, and so forth after years without practice. Perhaps it is not surprising that such everyday skills resist loss. Most are tremendously **overlearned** (practiced far beyond basic mastery of the skill). But what about skills somewhere between typing and ballet? How well are they retained? For instance, can we expect astronauts to retain landing skills at the end of long space flights? Or might they become dangerously "rusty" without practice? Figure 9-13 suggests an answer.

Figure 9-13 shows how much learning is retained after varying amounts of time. People who learned a new motor pattern (keeping a pointer on a rotating target) showed little loss of skill after 10 weeks without practice. Those who learned a list of nonsense syllables (meaningless three-letter words) remembered very few at the end of the same period. This and a large number of similar studies show that *well-practiced motor skills are very resistant to loss* (Annett, 1979). The astronauts we left hanging in space a moment ago should have no trouble landing.

Question: Does Figure 9-13 also show that motor skills are retained better than words?

It is almost impossible to answer this question because there is no way to equate motor tasks and verbal tasks. It is true that verbal learning is often rapidly lost (think about how much you remember from classes taken last semester). Still, some verbal learning—a song or a poem, for example —may be retained for life. One reason for the rapid forgetting of words is that new learning often conflicts with old. (See the discussion of "interference" in Chapter 10.) In contrast, motor skills seem relatively free of such conflicts. Ultimately, all that can be said with certainty is that motor skills are quite lasting. It's a good thing they are too. Imagine leaving your car at a garage and returning in two weeks— only to find your driving skills so shot that you are a menace to society on the way home!

Becoming Skilled

Question: Why is there a jump in the motor skill curve after practice has stopped?

Improved performance of a motor skill *after* practice is called **reminiscence.** Reminiscence is explained in this way: Learning increases during practice, but so does fatigue, boredom, and loss of motivation. These negative factors lower *performance* toward the end of a practice session even though *learning* continues. Later, when a rest period removes fatigue, performance rises sharply (Drowatzky, 1975).

Figure 9-14 gives another example of reminiscence, and shows a related effect. Improvement in the performance of a motor skill is most rapid when short practice sessions are alternated with rest periods. This pattern, which is called **spaced practice,** helps keep fatigue and boredom to a minimum. It can also prevent the learner from practicing errors while tired. The opposite of spaced practice is

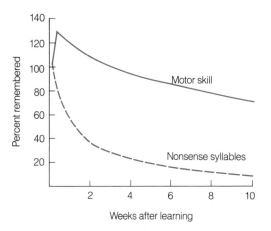

Fig. 9-13 *The curves of forgetting for a simple motor skill and simple verbal learning. Notice that there is less rapid forgetting of the motor skill and that there is actually an improvement shortly after practice has ended. (After Leavitt and Scholsberg, 1944)*

massed practice, in which little or no rest is given between learning sessions. Notice in Fig. 9-14 that massed practice lowers performance.

After a short rest, it can be seen that massed and spaced practice produce similar amounts of learning. But what about later, after a month or more has passed? Are both practice patterns equally effective? There is evidence that, in the long run, new skills learned with spaced practice are retained better than those learned by massed practice (Drowatzky, 1975). This suggests that you should keep practice sessions short and well spaced if you are learning

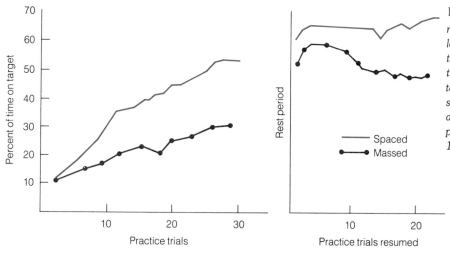

Fig. 9-14 *Performance curves for massed and spaced practice. Subjects learned to keep a pointer on a moving target. During the first learning session, the spaced practice group performed better. After a rest period, performance was similar for both groups, but further trials again lowered performance in the massed practice group. (From Jones and Ellis, 1962)*

to type, play a musical instrument, juggle, or master some other motor skill.

Skillful Learning   The points that follow should also be kept in mind for optimal skill learning. (Sources: Drowatzky, 1975; Gagne and Fleishman, 1959; Klausmeir, 1975; Meichenbaum, 1977; Singer, 1978.)

1. Begin by observing and imitating a skilled model. Modeling provides a good mental picture of the skill. At this point, try simply to grasp a visual image of the skilled movement.
2. Learn *verbal rules* to back up motor learning. "In golf, the feet should be at a right angle to the hole when putting"; "To turn right when skiing, shift your weight to the left foot." Such rules are usually most helpful in the early phases of skill learning. As a skill becomes more automated, internal speech may actually interfere. When first learning cross-country skiing, for example, it is helpful to say "left arm, right foot, right arm, left foot." But soon, such verbalizations get in the way.
3. Practice should be as *lifelike* as possible, so that artificial cues and responses do not become a part of the skill. A competitive diver should practice on the board, not on a trampoline. If you want to learn to ski, try to practice on snow, not straw.
4. Get feedback from a mirror, videotape, coach, or observer. Knowledge of results is one of the most powerful factors controlling learning of motor skills. Whenever possible, someone experienced in the skill should direct attention to *correct responses* when they occur.
5. When possible, it is better to practice *natural units* rather than break the task into artificial parts. When learning to type, it is better to start with real words rather than exercises or nonsense syllables.
6. Learn to evaluate and analyze your own performance. Remember you are trying to learn a motor program, not just train your muscles. Motor skills are actually very "mental."

The last point leads to one more suggestion. Research has shown that merely "thinking about" or imagining a skilled performance can aid learning (Annett, 1979). This technique is called **mental practice.** It seems to help by refining motor programs. The more familiar you are with a skill, the more mental rehearsal helps (Meichenbaum, 1977; Drowatzky, 1975). When you begin to get really good at a skill you are interested in, give mental practice a try. You may be surprised at how effective it can be.

Transfer of Training   Most skiing enthusiasts are familiar with a learning approach known as the *graduated length method.* In this approach the beginning skier learns on short, easily managed skis, and moves to progressively longer skis as skill is developed. This technique is an intuitive application of the principle of **positive transfer.** Positive transfer is said to have taken place when mastery of one task aids mastery of a second task. Another example would be learning to balance and turn on a bicycle before learning to ride a motorcycle or Moped.

Question: Is there such a thing as "negative transfer"?

There is indeed. In **negative transfer,** skills developed in one situation conflict with those required for mastery of a new task. Learning to back a car with a trailer attached is a good example. Normally, when you are backing a car, the steering wheel is turned in the direction you want to go, the same as when moving forward. However, with a trailer attached, the steering wheel must be turned *opposite* from the direction you want the trailer to go. This situation results in negative transfer, and regularly creates comical scenes at campgrounds and boat launching ramps. On a more serious note, similar problems eventually led to standardization of airplane cockpits after many tragic crashes caused by negative transfer. Fortunately, negative transfer occurs less often than positive transfer, and it is usually brief (Drowatzky, 1975). Negative transfer is most likely to occur when a new response must be made to an old stimulus. If you have ever encountered a "pull" type handle on a door that must be pushed open, you will appreciate this final point.

_____ **Learning Check** _____

1. Biofeedback is a type of meditation in which the body is made very quiet so that bodily functioning can be detected.   T or F?

2. Rats given electrical brain stimulation as a reward can be made to alter such bodily functions as heart rate, blood pressure, and stomach contractions.   T or F?

3. Biofeedback can definitely relieve:
    a. depression   *b.* diabetes   *c.* stomach ulcers   *d.* muscle-tension headaches

4. Joseph Kamiya developed a technique whereby subjects can gain control over the brain's production of

5. An important step in the mastery of many motor skills is achieved when the skill becomes
    a. reversible   *b.* automated   *c.* graduated   *d.* fixed

6. Mental models, called _____ _____ appear to underlie well-learned motor skills.

7. In motor skill learning, massed practice generally produces performance that is superior to spaced practice.   T or F?

8. Learning verbal rules to back up motor learning is usually most helpful in the early stages of acquiring a skill.   T or F?

Answers: 1. F   2. T   3. d   4. alpha waves   5. b   6. motor programs   7. F   8. T

Resources Summary

● *Reinforcers* increase the probability of responses they follow. In *positive reinforcement,* reward or a pleasant event follows a response. In *negative reinforcement,* a response ends discomfort, and is therefore repeated. Punishment decreases responding. *Punishment* is either the presentation of an *aversive event,* or the removal of a *positive event* after a response is made.

● *Primary reinforcers* are "natural," physiologically based rewards. Electrical stimulation of "pleasure centers" in the brain can also serve as a primary reinforcer.

● *Secondary reinforcers* are learned rewards. They typically gain their reinforcing value by direct association with primary reinforcers, or by being subject to exchange for primary reinforcers. *Tokens* and money gain their reinforcing value in this way. Money may be exchanged for so many other reinforcers, both primary and secondary, that it sometimes becomes a *generalized reinforcer* (a secondary reinforcer that has become independent of its association with primary reinforcement). *Prepotent,* or high-probability responses, can be used to reinforce low-frequency responses.

● *Delay* of reinforcement greatly reduces its effectiveness, but long *chains* of responses may be built up in which a single reinforcer rewards many responses. *Superstitious behaviors* often become part of response chains because they appear to be associated with reinforcement.

● *Feedback* or *knowledge of results* aids learning and improves performance. It is most effective when it is *immediate* and *detailed.* Feedback has been applied to learning in *programmed instruction.* Programmed instruction breaks learning into a series of small steps and provides immediate feedback. *Computer assisted instruction* (CAI) does the same, but has the added advantage of being able to provide alternate exercises and information when needed.

● *Punishment* is most effective when it is *immediate, consistent,* and *intense.* Mild punishment tends to only temporarily suppress a response if it is also reinforced, or was acquired by reinforcement.

● The undesirable side effects of punishment include: conditioning of *fear* to punishing agents, and situations or activities associated with punishment; the learning of *escape* and *avoidance* responses; and the encouragement of *aggression.*

● *Cognitive learning* involves higher mental processes, such as understanding, knowing, or anticipating. In simple learning situations, both animals and people seem to form *cognitive maps* (internal representations of relationships). In *latent learning,* learning remains internal and unseen until a reward or incentive for performance is offered. *Learning to learn* is revealed by progressive improvements in the ability to solve similar problems. *Discovery learning* emphasizes insight and understanding, in contrast to *rote learning.*

● Much human learning is achieved through observation or *modeling.* Modeling (or observational learning) is influenced by many factors, especially the personal characteristics of the model and the success or failure of the model's behavior. Studies have shown that aggression is readily learned and released by modeling.

● In *biofeedback* training, bodily processes are monitored and converted to a signal that indicates what the body is doing. With practice, biofeedback allows alteration of many bodily activities. It shows promise for the alleviation of some stress-related illnesses. Its long term effectiveness is still being evaluated. The usefulness of *alpha control* (voluntary control of brain waves) is also debated.

● *Motor skills* are nonverbal response chains assembled into a smooth performance. Motor skills are guided by internal mental models called *motor programs.* Motor skills are resistant to forgetting and often show improvement *after* practice (reminiscence). Motor skill learning is usually best when practice is *spaced,* rather than *massed.* Depending on the relationship between prior learning and a new task, motor skills may show *positive* or *negative transfer* (carry-over to a new situation).

Applications

Everybody Has Them—Breaking Bad Habits

Question: How can I use learning principles to break a bad habit?

The following techniques offer some helpful possibilities.

1. Try to discover what is reinforcing a habit and *remove, avoid,* or *delay* the *reinforcement.*

Example: A student who developed a habit of taking longer and longer "breaks" when studying realized that the breaks usually were lengthened by TV watching. A chance to watch TV was also reinforcing more frequent "break-taking."

Comment: To improve study habits, the student should either resolve to stay out of the room where the TV is located until work is done, or else require two hours of study for one-half hour of TV watching.

Example: Pam has a slightly different problem. While reading in the evening her periods of concentration last only about 15 minutes. They are usually followed by a trip to the kitchen for a snack. In addition to falling behind in her reading, she is gaining weight.

Comment: Snacking is rewarding her impulse to avoid reading. She should do her reading at school or at a library, so that there is a delay between the impulse to eat and the reward of snacking. At home, she should keep only foods that must be prepared to eat, or keep only staples on hand, so that a separate trip to a store is required for "goodies." Requiring a walk around the block before eating a snack would also help (Ferster *et al.,* 1962).

2. Try to get the *same reinforcement with new responses.*

Example: A young mother realized she was yelling at her children more often than she would like. This habit seemed to be reinforced by the periods of relative quiet that followed when she raised her voice.

Comment: To avoid this habit, she should (as much as possible) ignore her children when they are noisy and should make a special effort to praise them, show approval, and pay attention to them when they are playing quietly and constructively.

Example: Frank has been drinking increasing amounts of beer after getting home from work in the evening. He usually feels more relaxed but often drinks too much and gets into arguments with other family members.

Comment: Frank's need to "unwind" and dissipate the frustrations of the workday might be better achieved by participation in an athletic activity, such as jogging, swimming, bowling, handball, and so forth. An organized team sport might ensure that he will actually stick with his substitute activity.

3. *Avoid* or *narrow down cues* that elicit the bad habit.

Example: A student has begun to notice how much impulse-buying he does at the grocery store. As a first step in avoiding this habit, he has begun to shop after he has had a meal because he has observed that hunger is a cue for his food-buying.

Comment: He should also make a shopping list and stick to it so that he only looks at items he intends to buy.

Example: A father has noticed that he nags and criticizes his four-year-old son almost nightly because the boy pours ketchup all over his dinner. He is upset about this and other daily instances of criticizing the boy.

Comment: The father has identified one cue for his excessive criticizing. It could be avoided by giving the boy a small bowl of ketchup to prevent the regular dinner battle. Other cues for nagging can be avoided in similar ways as they are identified (Schmidt, 1976).

Example: Raul is not ready to give up smoking, but would like to cut down. He has taken many smoking cues out of his daily routine by removing ashtrays, matches, and extra cigarettes from his house, car, and office. He also has been making an effort to avoid situations in which most of his smoking occurs by staying away from other smokers, taking a walk after meals (leaving his cigarettes at home), and putting a piece of gum in his mouth when he feels nervous.

Comment: To improve his control of smoking, Raul should try narrowing cues. He could begin by smoking only inside buildings, never outside or in his car. He

Applications

could then limit his smoking to home. Then to only one room at home. Then to one chair at home. If he succeeds in getting this far, he may want to limit his smoking to only one uninteresting place: a bathroom, basement, or garage, for example (Goldiamond, 1971).

4. Make an *incompatible response* in the presence of stimuli that usually precede the bad habit.

Example: A sprinter has developed a habit of "jumping the gun" at track meets and is frequently disqualified.

Comment: The sprinter should prepare for meets by remaining in the blocks while his coach fires the starter's pistol several times.

Example: A child has developed the habit of throwing her coat on the floor after coming in the front door. After being scolded, she would hang it up.

Comment: The parents should recognize that scolding has become the cue for hanging the coat up. The girl should not just be scolded, but should put her coat on again, go outside, come in the door, and hang her coat up. Soon, coming in the door will become the cue for hanging the coat up.

Example: June bites her nails so much they are painful and unsightly. She has identified several situations in which she is most likely to bite her nails and would like to break the connection between these and her habit.

Comment: June should make a list of incompatible behaviors she can engage in when she has the urge to bite her nails. These might include: putting her hands in her pockets, taking notes in class, sketching pictures, crossing her arms, leaning against something with her hands, chewing gum, playing a musical instrument, or combing her hair (Perkins and Perkins, 1976).

5. Use *negative practice* to associate a bad habit with discomfort.

Example: Rick has a facial tic that appears when he is nervous or tired. The tic looks like a wink made with his right eye.

Comment: In negative practice, a response is repeated until it becomes boring, painful, or produces fatigue.

This increases awareness of the habit and tends to discourage its recurrence. Rick should stand in front of a mirror and repeat the tic until the muscles used become quite uncomfortable. Similarly, if you have a habit of saying "you know" or "uh" too often when speaking, set aside 15 minutes a day and repeat the error over and over while thinking, "I hate the way this sounds when someone else says it."

6. Utilizing *feedback* is one of the most direct of all approaches to changing bad habits.

Example: Four college students who are renting a house together are concerned about their high utility bills. Also, they would like to make an effort to conserve energy. To date, however, their good intentions have not lowered their electric bill.

Comment: The roommates should keep a daily record of their energy consumption by writing down and posting the numbers shown on their electric meter. A study of families given this kind of daily feedback showed that their energy use was greatly reduced (Palmer *et al.,* 1977).

The last technique described is worth emphasizing. Almost any habit will benefit from simply keeping score. Keep track of the number of times daily that you arrive late to class, smoke a cigarette, watch an hour of TV, drink a cup of coffee, bite your fingernails, swear, or whatever other response you are interested in changing. A simple tally on a piece of paper will do, or you can get a small mechanical counter like those used to keep golf scores or to count calories.

Throughout this chapter, we have tried to emphasize the practical applications of learning theories to everyday problems. Many simple difficulties can be handled effectively without special training. If you have a really troublesome habit, such as overeating, excessive use of alcohol, cigarettes, or marijuana, you may find it most expedient to consult a professional counselor. Additional learning techniques for overcoming mild difficulties can be found in Chapter 23, "Behavior Modification," Chapter 12, "Motivation," and Chapter 8, "Conditioning."

Applications

_____ **Learning Check** _____

1. Removing or avoiding reinforcement of a bad habit can help eliminate it, but delaying reinforcement has no effect. T or F?
2. A mother who praises her children when they are quiet instead of yelling at them when they are noisy has received the same reinforcement for an alternate response. T or F?
3. Restricting smoking to only one room in a house is an example of using feedback to alter a bad habit. T or F?
4. To break the link between an undesired response and various situations in which it occurs, it can be helpful to practice making an incompatible response in the same situations. T or F?
5. In negative practice, we learn to avoid or narrow down cues that elicit a bad habit. T or F?

Answers: 1. F 2. T 3. F 4. T 5. F

Modeling and Television—The "Tube" As Teacher

Did you know that the world is populated primarily by males, professionals, whites, and members of the middle class? Did you know that women make up only 28 percent of the population; that one-half of all women are teenagers or in their early twenties; that more than one-third are unemployed or have no identifiable purpose beyond offering emotional support to men, or serving as objects of sexual desire? That minorities are generally service workers, criminals, victims, or students? That the elderly are usually infirm, senile, or helpless? If you watch much TV these are the impressions you get daily on the "tube" (U.S. Commission on Civil Rights, 1977).

Are the distortions and stereotypes of "TV land" cause for concern? It would seem so. Television is a major influence in the lives of most children and many adults (Comstock *et al.*, 1978). In over 71 million homes (99 percent of all United States households) TV is practically a "member of the family."

Televised Violence An indication of the potential impact of TV can be found in these figures: By the time the average person has graduated from high school, he or she will have viewed some 15,000 hours of TV, compared to only 11,000 hours of formal classroom instruction. In that time, such viewers will have seen some 18,000 murders, and countless acts of robbery, arson, bombing, torture, and beatings. About 80 percent of all TV programs contain acts of violence, and the typical Saturday morning cartoon averages one violent or aggressive act *per minute* (cartoons are six times more violent per hour than the average adult program) (Rothenberg, 1975).

Question: Earlier, the effects of observational learning were described. Do they apply to TV violence?

Where the effects of TV violence on children are concerned the answer appears to be "yes." At this point, hundreds of studies, involving well over 10,000 children, from every conceivable background, have been completed. The vast majority point to the same conclusion: "If large groups of children watch a great deal of televised violence they will be more prone to behave aggressively"

(Rubinstein, 1978; Comstock *et al.*, 1978; Liebert *et al.*, 1973).

Question: How does TV violence affect children?

As Albert Bandura showed in his "Bo-Bo doll" study, children may learn new aggressive actions by watching violent or aggressive behavior, or they may learn that violence is "OK." Either way, they are more likely to act aggressively. Also, remember that the children in Bandura's study imitated a cartoon almost as much as they did live human models. The claim that cartoons are "harmless," or "all in fun" becomes questionable in this light. Some TV stations now refuse to carry "Tom and Jerry," "Bugs Bunny," and "Roadrunner" cartoons because their violence levels are so high.

In addition to encouraging imitation of aggression, TV violence tends to lower sensitivity to violent acts. As anyone who has seen a street fight or a mugging can tell you, TV violence is sanitized and unrealistic. The real thing is gross, ugly, and gut-wrenching. Even when it is graphic, TV violence is viewed in the relaxed and familiar setting of the home. For at least some viewers, this combination diminishes emotional reactions to violent scenes. Perhaps you have seen the brutal and bloody fight scene in the classic boxing film *Champion*. Victor Cline and his associates showed it to groups of boys and monitored their heart rate, respiration, and perspiration as they watched. They found that heavy TV viewers (averaging 42 hours a week) showed much less emotion than those who watched little or no TV (Cline *et al.*, 1972). Television, in other words, can cause a *desensitization* to violence (see Chapter 23 for more on desensitization).

Question: Couldn't TV's impact also be used constructively?

TV as a Positive Model There is no denying TV's tremendous power to inform and to entertain. When these features are combined, as they have been in specials such as "Roots" or "Holocaust," the effect can be quite constructive. Perhaps the best examples of TV as a positive social force are the educational programs "Sesame

Exploration

Street'' and ''The Electric Company.'' Over 150 research reports have dealt with the impact of these programs. An overwhelming majority of these evaluations are positive. Clearly, television can teach children while holding their voluntary interest and attention (Rubenstein, 1978).

As a model for ''prosocial'' attitudes and responses, TV could be used to promote helping, cooperation, charity, and brotherhood in the same way that it has tended to stereotype and encourage aggression. To illustrate, children in one experiment watched a TV program that emphasized helping (a ''Lassie'' episode). Later these children were more willing than others to help a puppy in distress even when it meant skipping a chance to win prizes (Rubinstein *et al.,* 1974).

Almost since the first TVs blinked to life in living rooms across the country, television has been damned and defended, praised and put down. In view of our discussion, you might want to think about these questions: Why is so much violence shown on TV? Do you think your views or behavior have been influenced by TV? Given what you know about modeling, what changes would you make in TV programming? Would others watch the programs you propose? Would you? (Additional questions follow.)

Questions for Discussion

1. Can you think of anything you do that is not affected in some way by learning?

2. How could you include more feedback (or more immediate feedback) in your study habits?

3. Make a list of the reinforcers that have the greatest effect on your behavior. Which seem to exert the greatest influence, primary or secondary reinforcers?

4. How have your feelings and attitudes toward money been shaped by its status as a "generalized reinforcer"?

5. Do you consider classroom grades reinforcers or a form of threatened punishment (or both)? What change (if any) would you like to see in reinforcers available in the classroom?

6. Describe a superstitious behavior or ritual you have engaged in and explain how it might have been learned.

7. How would your life change if motor skills were highly subject to loss?

8. Choose a bad habit you would like to break. How could you apply the principles discussed in this chapter to breaking this habit?

9. In your opinion, should TV programs come with a "violence rating scale," like the ratings of tar and nicotine on cigarette packages, or a rating system, such as that used for movies? What, if anything, would you suggest be done about the quality of TV programming and the amount of TV violence?

Suggestions for Further Reading

Comstock, G. S., Chaffee, S., Katzman, N., McCombs, M., and Roberts, D. *Television and Human Behavior.* Columbia University Press, 1978.

Drowatzky, J. N. *Motor Learning: Principles and Practices.* Burgess, 1975.

Hilgard, E. R., and G. H. Bower. *Theories of Learning,* 4th ed. Prentice-Hall, 1975.

Hill, W. F. *Learning,* 3rd ed. Chandler, 1980.

Kazdin, A. E. *Behavior Modification in Applied Settings.* Dorsey Press, 1975.

Pew, T. W., Jr. "Biofeedback Seeks New Medical Uses for Concept of Yoga," *Smithsonian,* December, 1979.

Rubinstein, E. A. "Television and the Young Viewer," *American Scientist,* November-December, 1978.

Stern, R. M., and W. J. Ray. *Biofeedback: How to Control Your Body, Improve Your Health, and Increase Your Effectiveness.* Dow Jones-Irwin, 1977.

Whaley, D., *et al. Contingency Management.* Behaviordelia, P.O. Box 1044, Kalamazoo, MI.

10

Memory

━━━━━ Chapter Preview ━━━━━

"What the Hell's Going On Here?"

February, 1978. Steven Kubacki is cross-country skiing on the ice of Lake Michigan. He stops for a moment, takes off his skis and drops his backpack, pausing to enjoy the winter solitude. It's cold; colder in fact than he had realized. Steven decides to turn back. In a few minutes comes a new realization: He is lost. Wandering on the ice, he grows numb and very, very tired.

Put yourself in Steven Kubacki's shoes, and you will appreciate the shock of what happened next. Steven clearly recalls wandering lost and alone on the ice. Immediately after that, he remembers waking up in a field. But as he looked around, Steven knew something was wrong. It was spring! The backpack beside him contained running shoes, swimming goggles, and a pair of glasses— all unfamiliar. As he looked at his clothing—also unfamiliar—Steven thought to himself, "What the hell's going on here?" Fourteen months had passed since he left to go skiing (Loftus, 1980). How did he get to the field? Where did the strange gear come from? Steven couldn't say. He had lost over a year of his life to total amnesia.

As Steven Kubacki's amnesia vividly shows, life without memory would be meaningless. Imagine the terror and confusion of having all of your memories wiped out, from birth to the present. You would have no identity, no knowledge, no life history, no recognition of friends or family. Your past would be a total blank. In a very real sense, we are our memories.

This chapter discusses memory, forgetting, and factors affecting both. As an inquiring person, you should find this information interesting. Also included is a large section on improving memory skills. As a student, you should find this discussion particularly helpful. Almost anyone (including you) can learn to use his or her memory more effectively.

Survey Questions   How do we store information in memory? Is there more than one type of memory? How are memories organized? How are they measured? What are "photographic" memories like? What causes forgetting? How accurate are everyday memories? How can memory be improved?

Resources

Stages of Memory—Do You Have a Mind Like a Steel Trap? Or a Sieve?

"A dusty storehouse of facts." That's how many people think of memory. In reality, **memory** is an *active system* that receives, stores, organizes, alters, and recovers information. In some ways, memory acts like a computer (Fig. 10-1). Information to be recorded is first **encoded,** or changed into a usable form. This step is like punching data onto cards before feeding it into a computer. Next, information is **stored,** or held in the system. As we will see in a moment, human memory has three different storage systems. If you put information into a computer, or merely a filing cabinet, it has to be available when you need it. Likewise, memories must be **retrieved,** or taken out of storage to be useful. In order to "remember" something, encoding, storage, and retrieval must all take place.

Memory is highly selective. Many of the things we need to remember for a short time—shopping lists, telephone numbers, appointments, trivia—would only clutter up our "memory files" if stored forever. Memory keeps the files neat by rapidly "dumping out" information needed only briefly. Even so, your memory may record one quadrillion separate bits of information in a lifetime (Asimov, 1967). How is it possible, then, to quickly find specific memories? The answer is that memories seem to be arranged in an orderly fashion. As one psychologist put it, "Somewhere in each person's brain lives a superb librarian" (Loftus, 1980). Each person's "memory index" is highly organized and "cross-referenced."

Question: What are the "three separate memory systems" mentioned a moment ago?

Psychologists have identified three distinct stages of memory. To be stored for a long period of time, information must pass through all three stages. (Please refer to Fig. 10-2.)

Sensory Memory   Let's say a friend asks you to pick up several things for her at a market. Your friend reads aloud from her shopping list. How do you remember it? Incoming information first enters **sensory memory** (also called the **sensory register**). Sensory memory holds an exact copy of what is seen or heard. If the information is seen, an **icon** (EYE-kon), or image, persists for about one-half second afterward (Klatzky, 1980). To witness an icon, close your eyes for a moment. Hold your hand in front of your face and blink your eyes rapidly open and closed again. You will continue to see a fleeting image of your hand for a split second after closing your eyes.

Question: What about hearing?

Hearing is held as a brief **echo** in sensory memory. There is some evidence that echos last longer than icons, perhaps as long as two seconds (Klatzky, 1980). As your friend reads her shopping list, you briefly store each item as an echo. In general, sensory memory holds information just long enough to transfer it to the second memory system.

Short-Term Memory   Not everything seen or heard is kept in memory. Let's say a radio is playing in the background as your friend reads her shopping list. Do you remember what the announcer says too? Probably not. *Selective attention* (discussed in Chapter 4) determines what information moves from sensory memory into a second system called **short-term memory (STM).** Short-term memories are also brief, but longer than sensory memories. By attending to your friend's words, you will place the shopping list in short-term memory.

Fig. 10-1   *In some ways a computer acts like a mechanical memory system. Both systems process information, and both allow encoding, storage, and retrieval of data.*

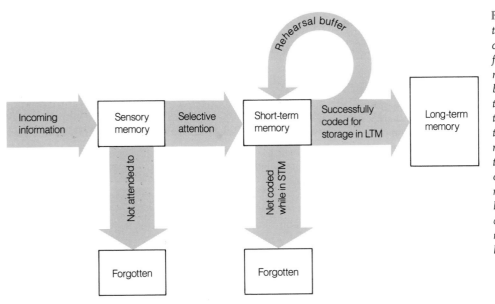

Fig. 10-2 *Memory is thought to involve at least three steps. Incoming information is first held for a second or two by sensory memory. Information selected by attention is then transferred to temporary storage in short-term memory. If new information is not rapidly encoded, or rehearsed, it is forgotten. If it is transferred to long-term memory, it becomes relatively permanent, although retrieving it may be a problem. The preceding is a useful* model *of memory; it may not be literally true of what happens in the brain.*

Question: How are short-term memories encoded?

Short-term memories can be stored as images. But more often, they are encoded by *sound*, especially in remembering words and letters. Assume, for example, you memorize a list of letters. When tested, you are more likely to mistakenly put a "B" where a "V" belongs than, say, a "U" (Klatzky, 1980). The "U" may look like a "V," but "B" *sounds like* "V." Similarly, if you are introduced to Tim at a party and you forget his name, you are more likely to call him Jim than Bob. Your friend with the list will be lucky if you don't bring home peas instead of cheese and soap instead of soup!

Short-term memory acts as a *temporary* storehouse for *small amounts* of information. Unless the information is important, it is quickly removed from STM and forever lost. Short-term memory prevents our minds from being cluttered with names, dates, telephone numbers, and other trivia (Miller, 1964). At the same time, it provides a **working memory,** where we do much of our thinking. Dialing a phone number, mental arithmetic, remembering a shopping list, and the like all rely on STM (Atkinson and Shriffrin, 1971).

As you may have noticed when dialing a phone number, STM is severely affected by any *interruption* or *interference* (Adams, 1967). You've probably had this experience with STM. You look up a telephone number and walk to the phone, repeating the number to yourself. You dial the number and get a busy signal. Returning a few minutes later, you find that you must look up the number again. This

time as you are about to dial, someone asks you a question. You answer, turn to the phone, and find that you have forgotten the number.

We have seen that short-term memory is brief, easily interrupted, and limited in "size." How, then, do we remember for greater lengths of time?

Long-Term Memory   Information that is important or meaningful is transferred to the third memory system, called *long-term memory*. In contrast to STM, **long-term memory (LTM)** acts as a permanent storehouse for information. LTM contains everything you know about the world. That's *everything*, from aardvark to zucchini, math to Monopoly, facts to fantasy. And yet, there appears to be no danger of running out of room in LTM. LTM has an almost limitless capacity to store information (Klatzky, 1980).

Question: Are long-term memories also encoded as sounds?

Information in LTM is stored on the basis of *meaning* and importance, not by sound, as in STM. If you are recalling information from LTM and make an error, it will probably be related to meaning. For example, let's say you memorize a list of words. Two weeks later you try to remember the list. If one of the words was *barn,* and you can't remember it, you are more likely to say *shed* or *farm* than *born*.

When new information enters STM, it is compared to knowledge stored in LTM. This gives the new information meaning and makes it easier to store it in LTM. As an example, try to memorize this story:

With hocked gems financing him, our hero bravely defied all scournful laughter that tried to prevent his scheme. "Your eyes deceive," he had said, "An egg, not a table, correctly typifies this unexplored planet." Now three sturdy sisters sought proof. Forging along, sometimes through calm vastness, yet more often over turbulent peaks and valleys, days became weeks as many doubters spread fearful rumors about the edge. At last from nowhere welcome winged creatures appeared, signifying momentous success. (Dooling and Lachman, 1971)

This story emphasizes the importance of meaning in forming lasting memories. People given the title of the story were able to remember it far better than those not given a title. See if the title helps you as much as it did them. The title is, "Columbus Discovers America."

Dual Memory   Most of our daily memory chores are handled by STM and LTM. To summarize their connection, picture short-term memory as a small desk at the front of an immense warehouse full of filing cabinets (LTM). As information is brought into the warehouse, it is first placed on the desk. Since the desk is small, it must be quickly cleared off to make room for new information. Some items are simply tossed away because they are unimportant. Meaningful or important information is placed in the permanent files (LTM). When we want to use knowledge from LTM to answer a question, the information is returned to STM. Or, in the analogy, a copy is taken out of the files (LTM) and moved to the desk (STM), where it can be used.

Question: What would happen if new information came in while STM is being used for thinking or answering a question?

There would be less room for the new information. If a person is asked to do mental work, such as solving a simple word problem while trying to remember a short list, memory for the list suffers (Baddeley and Hitch, 1974). In other words, thinking competes for "space" in STM.

Now that you have a general picture of STM and LTM, it is time to explore both in more detail. The discussions that follow should add to your understanding.

Learning Check

Match: **A.** Sensory memory   **B.** STM   **C.** LTM

1. _____ Working memory

2. _____ Holds information for two seconds or less

3. _____ Stores icon or echo

4. _____ Permanent, unlimited capacity

5. _____ Temporarily holds small amounts of information

6. _____ Encoded largely in terms of meaning

7. Words and letters are encoded mainly by sound in STM. T or F?

Answers: 1. B   2. A   3. A   4. C   5. B   6. C   7. T

Short-Term Memory—
What's Your Magic Number?

Question: How much information can be held in short-term memory?

For an answer, read the following numbers once. Then close the book and write as many as you can in the correct order.

8 5 1 7 4 9 3

This is called a **digit-span test.** If you were able to correctly repeat this series of seven digits, you have an average short-term memory.

Now try to memorize the following list of digits, reading them only once.

7 1 8 3 5 4 2 9 1 6 3

This series was probably beyond your short-term memory capacity. Psychologist George Miller has shown that short-term memory is limited to what he calls the "magic number" **seven** (plus or minus two) **bits** of information (Miller, 1956). It is as if short-term memory has seven "slots" or "bins" into which separate items can be placed. Immediate memory is usually perfect as long as seven items or less are involved. But as more are added, errors start showing up.

When all of the "slots" in STM are filled, there is no room for new information (Klatzky, 1980). If more is added, both the original items and the new items may be lost. You have probably encountered this effect at a party. Let's say your hostess begins calling out names, introducing everyone who is there, "Ted, Barbara, Donna, Roseanna, Wayne, Shawn, Linda . . ." "Stop," you think to yourself after

Linda is introduced. But the hostess continues, "Eddie, Jay, Gordon, Frank, Marietta, Dan, Patty, Glen, Ricky." The hostess leaves, satisfied that you have met everyone. And you spend the evening talking with Ted, Barbara, and Ricky, the only people whose names you remember!

Recoding   Before we continue, try your short-term memory again, this time on letters instead of digits. Study the following letters for about 30 seconds. Then close the book and try to reproduce the entire letter square.

```
S  A  V  A  O
R  E  E  E  G
U  R  S  Y  A
O  O  D  N  S
F  C  N  E  R
```

Notice that the square contains 25 letters, or separate "bits" of information. It is well beyond the seven-item limit of STM. Nevertheless, students are often able to memorize it. Those who succeed usually change the 25 separate bits into five **chunks** of information. This can be done by making each line of letters into a nonsense word: *savao, reeeg, ursya, oodns,* and *fcner.* If you saw this possibility, you were probably able to memorize the letter square. Look at the square again and notice that it can even be organized into *one* chunk, easily remembered by anyone. If you read *up* the columns, starting in the lower left corner, you will find the chunk: "Four score and seven years ago."

Question: How does chunking help?

STM seems to be able to hold about seven of whatever units we are using, be they numbers, letters, words, phrases, or familiar sentences (Klatzky, 1980). Picture STM as a small desk again. Through chunking, we combine several individual items into one "stack" of information. This allows us to place seven stacks on the desk where before there was only room for seven separate items.

Chunking **recodes** information into larger units. But how does it do so? Most recoding takes advantage of units that already have meaning in LTM. In one memory experiment, a list of letters was read this way: TVF . . . BIJF . . . KY . . . MCA. Memory for this series was much lower than when the same letters were read as: TV . . . FBI . . . JFK . . . YMCA (Bower and Springston, 1970). The phrase mentioned earlier, "Four score and seven years ago," acts as a single chunk because it is already stored in LTM.

Question: How long do short-term memories last?

Rehearsal   Short-term memories appear to weaken and disappear very rapidly. However, a short-term memory can be prolonged quite easily by silently repeating it until it is needed. Each time the information is repeated it is "recycled" in STM, or given a fresh start. Remembering a telephone number you intend to use only once is often done this way.

Keeping a short-term memory alive by silently repeating it is called **rehearsal.** The longer a short-term memory is rehearsed, the greater its chances of being stored in LTM. What if rehearsal is prevented, so a memory cannot be recycled or moved to LTM? Without rehearsal, STM is incredibly short.

In one experiment subjects heard meaningless syllables like XAR followed by a number like 67. As soon as subjects heard the number they began counting backwards by threes. (This counting prevented them from repeating the syllable.) Subjects were stopped after different lengths of time and tested for memory of the last syllable they had heard. After only 18 seconds of delay, memory scores fell to zero (Peterson and Peterson, 1959).

After *18 seconds* without rehearsal, the short-term memory was gone forever! Keep this in mind when you get only one chance to hear information you want to remember. For example, if you are introduced to someone and his or her name slips out of STM, there is no way to retrieve it. To escape this awkward situation you might try saying something like, "I'm curious, how do you spell your name?" But unfortunately, the response to this strategy is too often an icy reply like, "B-O-B S-M-I-T-H, it's really not too difficult." To avoid embarrassment, pay careful attention to the name, repeat it to yourself several times, and try to use it in the next sentence or two—before you lose it.

Long-Term Memory— Where the Past Lives

An electrode was placed at location number 11 on the patient's brain. She immediately said, "Yes, sir, I think I heard a mother calling her little boy somewhere. It seemed to be something happening years ago. . . . It was somebody in the neighborhood where I live." A short time later, the electrode was applied to the same spot. Again the patient said, "Yes, I hear the same familiar sounds, it seems to be a woman calling, the same lady" (Penfield, 1958). These statements were made by a woman undergoing brain surgery for epilepsy. Only local anesthetics were used, so the patient was awake as her brain was electrically stimulated

(Fig. 10-3). When activated, some brain areas seemed to produce vivid memories of long-forgotten events.

Question: Does this mean that every experience a person has ever had is recorded in memory?

Permanence   Results like those described led neurosurgeon Wilder Penfield to claim that the brain records the past like a "continuous strip of movie film, complete with sound track" (Penfield, 1957). But as you now know, this is an exaggeration. Many events never get past short-term memory. More importantly, there is reason to doubt Penfield's conclusion. In only about 3 percent of cases does brain stimulation produce memorylike experiences. Most reports resemble dreams more than memories, and many are clearly fictional. Memory experts Elizabeth and Geoffrey Loftus have carefully examined Penfield's work and other

Fig. 10-3 Exposed cerebral cortex of a patient undergoing brain surgery. Numbers represent points that reportedly produced "memories" when electrically stimulated. A critical evaluation of such reports suggests that they are more like dreams than memories. This fact raises questions about claims that long-term memories are permanent. (From Wilder Penfield, The Excitable Cortex in Conscious Man, 1958. Courtesy of the author and Charles C Thomas, Publisher, Springfield, Illinois.)

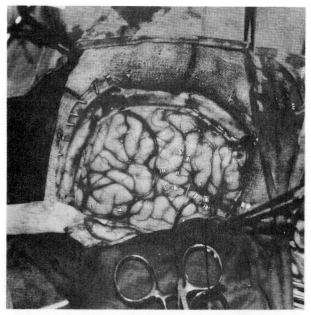

research on "truth serums" and hypnosis. They conclude there is little evidence that long-term memories are absolutely permanent (Loftus and Loftus, 1980). It is probably most accurate to say that long-term memories are *relatively* permanent, or long-lasting.

Question: Isn't it true, though, that some things are remembered for a lifetime?

Yes. So the question is, which memories last a lifetime and which are more often forgotten? A partial answer emerges if we consider two types of long-term memories: *semantic* and *episodic* (Tulving, 1972).

Semantic and Episodic Memory   Most of our basic *factual knowledge* about the world is almost totally immune to forgetting. The names of objects, the days of the week or months of the year, simple math skills, the seasons, words and language, and other general facts are all quite lasting. Such facts make up a part of LTM called **semantic memory.** Semantic memory serves as a mental dictionary or encyclopedia of basic knowledge.

Semantic memory has no connection to times or places. It would be rare, for instance, to remember when and where you first learned the names of the seasons. In contrast, **episodic memory** (ep-ih-SOD-ik) is "autobiographical." It records life events (or "episodes") day after day, year after year: Can you remember your seventh birthday; your first date; an accident you witnessed; the first day of college; ideas you have read in this text; what you had for breakfast three days ago? All are episodic memories.

Question: Are episodic memories as lasting as semantic memories?

In general, episodic memories are more easily forgotten than semantic memories. This is because new information constantly pours into episodic memory. Stop for a moment and remember what you did last summer. That was an episodic memory. Notice that you now remember that you just remembered something. You have a new episodic memory in which you remember that you remembered while reading this text! It's easy to see how much we ask of our memory system.

Constructing Memories   As new episodic memories are formed, older memories are often updated, changed, lost, or *revised* (Cofer, 1975). Consider this illustration: Loftus and Palmer (1974) showed subjects a filmed automobile accident. Afterward, some subjects were asked to estimate how fast the cars were going when they "smashed" into each other. For others, the words *bumped, contacted,* or *hit* replaced *smashed.* One week later, subjects were asked, "Did you see any broken glass?" Those asked earlier about the cars that "smashed" into each other were more likely to say "yes." (No broken glass was shown in the film.) The new information ("smashed") was included in subjects' memories and altered them.

Updating memories is called **constructive processing.** Recent research, particularly that done by Elizabeth Loftus (1975, 1977, 1980), shows that memory does not act like a movie camera or videotape machine. Gaps in memory, which are common, may be filled in by logic or inference. As memories fade, they are especially likely to be altered by new information. Indeed, it is possible to have "memories" for things that never happened (such as remembering broken glass at an accident when there was none). People in Loftus' experiments who had these **pseudo-memories** (false memories) were often highly confident they were accurate. When they saw the accident film again, many were quite upset about the false "testimony" they gave (Loftus, 1980).

The updating of episodic memory is a common problem in police work. For example, a witness may select a photo of a suspect from police files, or see a photo in the news. Later, the witness identifies the suspect in person (in a lineup or in court). Has the witness really remembered the person who committed a crime? Or is it the recently seen photograph that is remembered? Even if the suspect is innocent, he or she may be "remembered" as the criminal. It is quite possible for a photo to update or blend with the original memory. Many tragic cases of mistaken identity have occurred in this way.

Organization If you were asked to give the names of as many of your relatives as you could remember, would you list them in random order? It's highly unlikely. Most people first name close family (parents, brothers, and sisters), then grandparents, aunts, uncles, cousins, and so forth. As mentioned earlier, long-term memories appear to be highly organized (Lindsay and Norman, 1977). What is the **structure** of this organization? Could it be, for instance, that LTM is arranged alphabetically like a dictionary? Not a chance! If I ask you to name a black and white animal that lives on ice, is related to a chicken, and cannot fly, you do not have to go from aardvark to zebra to find the answer. You need only search through birds, not all animals. In fact, you probably think only of black and white birds living in the arctic. Which of these cannot fly? *Voila,* the answer is Penguin.

The arrangement of information in LTM may be based on rules, images, categories, symbols, similarity, formal meaning or personal meaning (Atkinson and Shiffrin, 1971). In the last 10 years, psychologists have begun to develop a picture of the structure of memory, especially semantic memory. Most of their findings are beyond the scope of this book. One example, however, will serve to illustrate this line of research.

You are given the following two statements, to which you must answer yes or no: *A canary is an animal. A canary is a bird.* Which do you answer more quickly? Collins and Quillian (1969) found that *A canary is a bird* produced a faster "yes" than *A canary is an animal.* Why should this be so? Collins and Quillian believe a **network model** of LTM explains why. According to them, LTM is organized as a network of linked ideas (see Fig. 10-4). When ideas are farther apart, it takes a longer chain of associations to connect them. The more two items are separated, the longer it takes to answer. In other words, *canary* is probably close to *bird* in your "mental dictionary." *Animal* and *canary* are farther apart. Remember though, this has nothing to do with alphabetical order. We are talking about organization based on meaning.

Simple memory networks seem to be combined into higher-order structures. An example is a mental **script** (Schank and Abelson, 1977). Scripts are like plot summaries, or outlines, of everyday events. Most of us, for example, have a mental "restaurant script," a "going to the market script," a "laundromat script," and so on. A "restaurant script" might include the players: customer, waiter, cook, cashier; the props: table, menu, food, bill, money; and expected events: entering, being seated, given a menu, placing an order, and so forth. Scripts allow us to easily understand and remember events. Say a friend tells you, "The check-out counter was crowded so I moved to another line and the waiter came with a menu to put the clothes in an empty dryer." This sounds like nonsense because it combines parts of three different scripts. It is also harder to remember than sentences matching a script.

Psychologists still have much to learn about the nature of long-term memory. For now, one thing stands out clearly: People who have "good memories" excel at organizing information and making it meaningful (Mandler, 1968). In the "Exploration" for this chapter, we will investigate ways to use organization and meaning to improve memory.

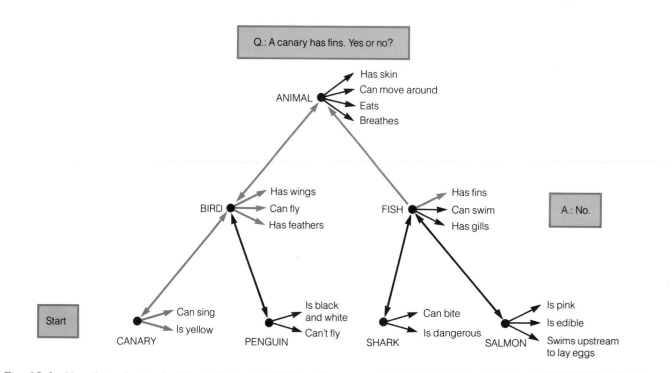

Fig. 10-4 *Hypothetical network of facts about animals shows what is meant by the structure of memory. Small networks of ideas such as this are probably organized into larger and larger units and higher levels of meaning. (Adapted from Collins and Quillian, 1969)*

Learning Check

1. The digit-span test is commonly used to measure LTM.   T or F?

2. There is evidence that STM lasts about 18 seconds without rehearsal.   T or F?

3. Information can be held indefinitely in STM by (circle):
chunking   recoding   networking   rehearsal

4. Semantic memories are quite lasting and stable, whereas _____ memories are more subject to updating and loss.

5. Constructive processing is often responsible for creating pseudo-memories.   T or F?

6. Electrical stimulation of the brain has shown conclusively that all memories are stored permanently, but not all memories can be retrieved.   T or F?

7. Association networks and _____ are examples of the structure or organization found in LTM.

Answers: 1. F 2. T 3. rehearsal 4. episodic 5. T 6. F 7. scripts

---

Measuring Memory— "The Answer Is on the Tip of My Tongue"

Initially, it might seem that you either remember something or you don't. But a moment of thought should convince you that this is not always true. While driving, have you ever found your way to a place to which you could not have given directions? Have you ever recognized someone you had only seen once before and thought was completely forgotten? In either case, you have used a form of partial memory called *recognition*. Partial memory is also demonstrated by the **tip-of-the-tongue phenomenon**. This is the experience of having an answer or a memory just out of reach—on the "tip of your tongue."

In one study of partial memory, university students were asked to read the definitions of words, such as *sextant, sampan,* and *ambergris.* When asked to give the defined words, students often drew a blank because these were words they had seen but rarely used. When students couldn't give the word, they provided whatever other information they could about it. It was found that students could often accurately guess the first and last letter and even the number of syllables of the word they were seeking. They were also able to give words that sounded like or meant the same as the defined word (Brown and McNeill, 1966).

Because memory is not an all-or-nothing event, there are several ways of measuring it. Three commonly used **memory tasks** are *recall, recognition,* and *relearning.* Let's see how they differ.

Recall   What is the name of the first song on your favorite record album? Who won the World Series last year? Who wrote the *Gettysburg Address?* If you can answer these questions, you have demonstrated recall. To **recall** means to supply or reproduce important facts or information. Tests of recall often require *verbatim* (word-for-word) memory. If you study a poem or a speech until you can recite it without looking, you will have recalled it. Recall is also used when you take an *essay* exam and provide facts and ideas without prompting. Students often consider essay tests the most difficult. One reason for this is that essay tests, like most recall tests, offer few cues to aid memory.

The order in which information is memorized has an interesting effect on recall. To experience it, try to memorize this list, reading through it once: BREAD, APPLES, SODA, HAM, LETTUCE, MUSTARD, COOKIES, RICE, CHEESE, ICE CREAM, BEETS, ORANGES, CRACKERS, FLOUR, EGGS. Now look away and write as many of the words as you can. What do you notice about the results? Most people write the last few items first, then the first items, and finally the middle items (if they are remembered at all). Figure 10-5 shows the results of a similar test. Notice that the greatest number of errors is found for the middle items on a list. This is called the **serial position effect.** The last items in a list appear to be remembered best because they are still in STM. The first items are also remembered because they entered an "empty" short-term memory where they could be rehearsed (Tarpy and Mayer, 1978). The middle items are neither held in STM nor transferred to LTM, so they are often lost.

Recognition   If you were asked to write down all the facts you could remember from a class taken last year, it might be concluded that you remembered very little. However, a more sensitive testing procedure based on **recognition** could be used. For instance, you could be given a *multiple-choice* test covering the facts and ideas from the course. Since multiple-choice tests only require you to recognize the correct answer, you would probably find evidence that considerable learning had carried over. Similarly, if you were asked to describe the people you went to school with in the sixth grade, or to recall their names, you could probably remember only a few. But if you were shown pictures or names of former classmates mixed with strangers, you would accurately *recognize* many more.

Recognition memory can be amazingly accurate for pictures, photographs, or other visual input. One investigator showed subjects 2560 photographic slides at a rate of one every 10 seconds. Subjects were then shown 280 pairs of photographs. One in each pair was from the first set of photos and the other was similar but "new." Subjects could tell with 85 to 95 percent accuracy which photograph they had seen before (Haber, 1970). This finding may explain why people so often say, "I may forget a name, but I never forget a face."

Recognition is usually superior to recall. This is why police departments use photographs or a lineup to identify

Fig. 10-5   *The serial position effect. Graph shows the percentage of subjects correctly recalling each item in a 15-item list. Recall is best for the first and last items. (Data from Craik, 1970)*

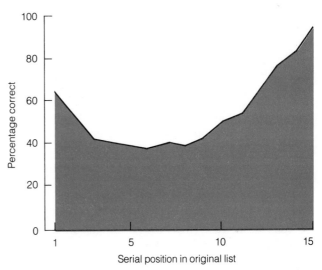

Fig. 10-6 *Test-taking typically requires recall or recognition memory.*

criminal suspects. Witnesses who disagree in their recall of a suspect's height, weight, age, or eye color often agree completely when recognition is all that is required.

Question: Is recognition always superior?

It depends greatly on the kind of **distractors** used. These are false items included along with an item to be recognized. If the distractors are very similar to the correct item, memory may be poor. A reverse problem sometimes occurs when only one choice looks like it could be correct. This can produce a **false positive,** or false sense of recognition. For example, there have been instances in which witnesses described a criminal as black, tall, or young. Then a lineup was held in which a suspect was the only black among whites, the only tall suspect, or the only young person (Loftus, 1980). Under such circumstances a false identification is very likely.

Relearning   In a classic experiment on memory, a psychologist read a short passage in Greek to his son. This was done daily when the boy was between fifteen months and three years of age. At age eight, the boy was asked if he remembered the Greek passage. He showed no evidence of recall. He was then given selections from the passage he heard and selections from other Greek passages. Could he recognize the one he heard? "It's all Greek to me!" he said, indicating there was no recognition (and drawing a frown from everyone in the room). Had the psychologist stopped here, he might have concluded that no memory remained. However, the child was then asked to

memorize the original quotation and others of equal difficulty. This time, his earlier learning became evident. The boy memorized the passage he had heard in childhood 25 percent faster than the others (Burtt, 1941). As this experiment suggests, relearning is typically the most sensitive measure of memory.

When a person is tested by **relearning,** how do we know a memory still exists? As with the boy described, relearning is measured by a **savings score.** Let's say you learn all the names in a telephone book to give your memory some exercise. It takes you one hour of study to recall the names perfectly. (You have a *great* memory, or it's a small town!) Two years later you are asked to recall the names. You remember none. Then you attempt to relearn the names. This time, you master them in 45 minutes. You have saved 15 minutes in study time. Thus, your savings is 25 percent (15 divided by 60 times 100).

Reduced study time in relearning is a good reason for taking a wide range of classes in school. It may seem that time spent studying algebra, history, or a foreign language is wasted because so little is remembered a year or two later. But if you ever need such information, you will find you can relearn it in far less time than it took at first.

Redintegration   There is a fourth way in which memories may be retrieved. Imagine finding a picture taken on your sixth birthday or tenth Christmas. As you look at the photo, one memory leads to another, which leads to another and another. Soon you have unleashed a flood of seemingly forgotten details. This process is called **redintegration** (ruh-DIN-tuh-GRAY-shun). Many people find that such memories are also touched off by distinctive odors out of the past, from a farm visited in childhood, Grandma's kitchen, the seashore, a doctor's office, the perfume or after-shave of a former lover, and so on. The key idea in redintegration is that one memory serves as a cue to trigger another. As a result, an entire past experience may be reconstructed from one small recollection. Such memories usually involve personal experience rather than formal learning.

Eidetic Imagery—Picture This!

Question: What is a "photographic memory"? How is it different from the types of memory already described?

Eidetic (eye-DET-ik) **imagery,** known informally as photograhic memory, occurs when a person has visual images clear enough to be "scanned" or retained for at least 30 seconds. Eidetic imagery is most often observed in childhood. About eight children out of one hundred can give detailed descriptions and can answer questions about pictures they have viewed for only a few seconds. Their images are quite clear and last up to four minutes (Haber, 1969).

In one series of tests, children were shown a picture from *Alice in Wonderland* (Fig. 10-7). To test your eidetic imagery, look at the picture and read the instructions there. Now, let's see how much you remember. Can you say (without looking again) which of Alice's apron strings is longer? Are the cat's front paws crossed? How many stripes are on the cat's tail? After the picture was removed from view, one ten-year-old boy was asked what he saw. He replied, "I see the tree, gray tree with three limbs. I see the cat with stripes around its tail." Asked to count the stripes, the boy replied, "There are about sixteen," (a correct count!). The boy then went on to describe the remainder of the picture in striking detail (Haber, 1969).

Don't be disappointed if you didn't do too well when you tried your eidetic skills. Most eidetic imagery disappears during adolescence and becomes quite rare by adulthood (Haber, 1974). Because of this loss, some psychologists suggest that we all have "photographic memory" to a degree, but we trade it in for memorizing more through language as we get older. If this is true, it may not be too much of a loss. After their images faded, eidetic children were no better able to describe the picture than were noneidetic children. The majority of eidetic memorizers have no better long-term memory than average.

Internal Images   Eidetic images are projected on a surface out in front of a person. Many psychologists feel that a second type of imagery is also used in memory. Can you remember how many doors there are in your house or apartment? To answer a question like this many people form **internal images** of each room and count the doorways they "see."

Kosslyn, Ball, and Reisler (1978) found an interesting way to show that memories do exist as images. Subjects first memorized a sort of "treasure map" similar to the one shown in Fig. 10-8a. They were then asked to visualize one object on the map, such as the tree at the lower right. Next they were asked to picture a black dot moving from the first object to another, such as the "hut" at the top of the island. Were subjects really "seeing" an image as they performed this task? It seems they were. As shown in Fig. 10-8b, the time it took to "move" the dot was directly related to actual distances on the map.

Some people have internal images so vivid they may also be said to have a "photographic memory." A notable

Fig. 10-7   *Test picture used to identify children with eidetic imagery. To test your eidetic imagery, look at the picture for 30 seconds. Then look at a blank surface and try to "project" the picture on it. If you have good eidetic imagery, you will be able to see the picture in detail. Return now to the text and try to answer the questions there. (Redrawn from an illustration in Lewis Carroll's* Alice in Wonderland*)*

example of such memory was reported by A. R. Luria (1968) in his book, *The Mind of a Mnemonist.* Luria studied a man (Mr. S) who had practically unlimited memory for visual images. Mr. S could remember almost everything that ever happened to him with incredible accuracy. When Luria tried to test Mr. S's memory by using longer and longer lists of words or numbers, he discovered that no matter how long the list Mr. S was able to reproduce it without error. Even when tested 15 years later, Mr. S was still able to remember these lists. As fantastic as this might sound to a struggling student, Mr. S's memory caused great difficulty. He remembered so much that he could not separate what was important from the trivial. For instance,

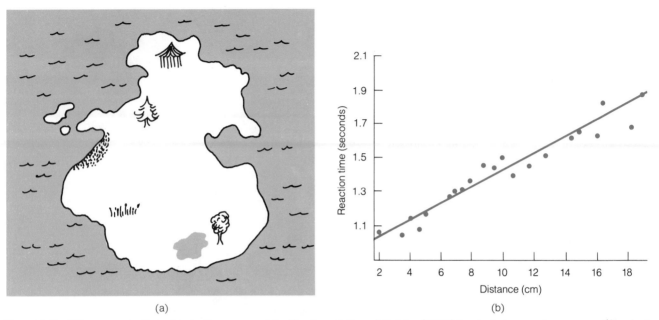

(a)   (b)

Fig. 10-8 *"Treasure map" similar to the one used by Kosslyn, Ball, and Reisler (1978) to study images in memory. (See text for explanation.)*

if he were tested on the contents of this chapter after reading it, he would remember not only every word, but all the images each word made him think of and all the sights, sounds, and feelings that occurred as he was reading. Finding the answer for one specific question, writing a logical essay, or even understanding a single sentence, therefore, became very difficult for him.

Learning Check

Unless you have a memory like Mr. S's, it might be a good idea to see if you can answer these questions before reading on.

1. Four common techniques for measuring or demonstrating memory are

_____, _____, _____,

and _____.

2. Multiple choice tests primarily require _____ memory.

3. Essay tests require _____ of facts or ideas.

4. The measure of memory revealed by a "savings" score is: (circle)
   retrieval   eidetic recognition   relearning   reconstruction

5. Children with eidetic imagery typically have no better than average long-term memory.   T or F?

Answers: 1. recall, recognition, relearning, redintegration   2. recognition   3. recall   4. relearning   5. T

Why We, Uh, Let's See; Why, We, Uh . . . Forget!

Question: Why are some memories lost so quickly? For example, why is it hard to remember information a week or two after taking a test in class?

Generally speaking, most forgetting occurs immediately after memorization. In a famous set of experiments, **Herman Ebbinghaus** (1885) tested his own memory at various times after learning. Ebbinghaus wanted to be sure he would not be swayed by prior learning, so he memorized **nonsense syllables.** These are meaningless three-letter words, such as GEX, CEF, or WOL. The importance of using meaningless words is shown by the fact that VEL, FAB, and DUZ are no longer used on memory tests. Subjects who recognize these words as detergent names find them very easy to remember.

By waiting various lengths of time before testing himself, Ebbinghaus constructed a **curve of forgetting** (see Fig. 10-9). Owing to the great care Ebbinghaus took in his work, these findings remain valid today. Notice that forgetting is rapid at first and is followed by a slow decline. As a student, you should see that the less time there is between review for a test and the taking of the test, the less forgetting will occur. However, don't misinterpret this as a reason for cramming. The error most students make is to cram *only*. If you cram, you don't have to remember for very long, but you may not learn enough in the first place.

If you space your practice (see Chapter 9) by using short, daily study sessions and, in addition, cram or review before a test, you will get the benefit of good preparation and a minimum time lapse. A study on retention done by H. F. Spitzer (1939) demonstrated the value of spaced review or periodic studying. Students reviewed immediately after studying and then reviewed again several days later and a third time 63 days later. These students remembered over 30 percent more than students who did not review what they had learned.

"I'll never forget old, old . . . oh what's his name?" Forgetting is both frustrating and embarrassing. Why *do* we forget? The Ebbinghaus curve gives a general picture of forgetting, but it doesn't explain it. For explanations, we must search further.

Encoding Failure

Whose head is on a United States penny? Which way is it facing? What is written on the top side of a penny? Can you accurately draw and label a penny? In a recent experiment, Nickerson and Adams (1979) asked a large group of students to draw a penny. Few could. Well then, could the students at least recognize a drawing of a real penny among fakes? (See Fig. 10-10.) Again, few could. About the only students who did well on either test were coin collectors.

The most obvious reason for forgetting is also the most commonly overlooked. In many cases, we "forget" because a memory was never formed in the first place. To use pennies, all we must be able to do is recognize them by comparison to nickels, dimes, quarters, and half-dollars. It's not necessary to learn their details. No doubt you could memorize a coin in a moment. But few of us ever encode the details of a penny because we don't need them. If you are bothered by frequent forgetting it is wise to ask yourself, "Have I been storing the information in the first place?"

Decay

One view of forgetting says that **memory traces** (changes in nerve cells or brain activity) fade or **decay** over a period of time. Decay seems to be a definite factor in the loss of sensory memories. Such fading also applies to STM. Information stored in STM seems to initiate a brief flurry of activity in the brain that quickly dies out (Shiffrin and Cook, 1978). Short-term memory therefore operates like a "leaky bucket": New information constantly pours in, but it rapidly

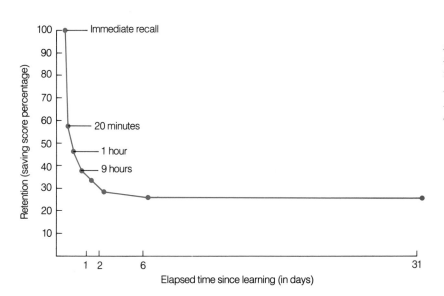

Fig. 10-9 *The curve of forgetting. This graph shows the amount remembered (measured by relearning) after varying lengths of time. Notice how rapidly forgetting occurs. Material learned was nonsense syllables. Meaningful information is not forgotten so quickly. (After Ebbinghaus, 1885)*

Fig. 10-10 *Some of the distractor items used in a study of recognition memory and encoding failure. Penny A is correct, but was seldom recognized. Pennies G and J were popular wrong answers. (Adapted from Nickerson and Adams, 1979)*

fades and is replaced by still newer information (Miller, 1956).

Disuse The decay of memory traces also has appeal as an explanation for long-term forgetting. Perhaps long-term memory traces fade from **disuse** and eventually become so weak they can no longer be retrieved. There is no sure way to prove or disprove this possibility, but reasons exist to question it. One already mentioned is the recovery of seemingly forgotten memories through redintegration. Another is that disuse fails to explain why some unused memories fade and others are carried for life. A third contradiction will be recognized by anyone who has spent time with the elderly. People growing senile may become so forgetful that they can't remember what happened a week ago. Yet at the same time your Uncle Oscar's recent memories are fading, he may have vivid memories of trivial and long-forgotten events from the past. "Why I remember it as clearly as if it were yesterday," he will say, forgetting that the story he is about to tell is the same one he told earlier the same day.

Question: If decay and disuse don't fully explain forgetting, what does?

There are several additional possibilities. Let's briefly consider each.

Cue-Dependent Forgetting

Often memories appear to be *available,* but not accessible. An example is having an answer on the "tip of your tongue." You know the answer is there but can't quite "get a handle" on it. This situation indicates that many memories are "forgotten" because **cues** present at the time of learning are absent when the time comes to retrieve information. For example, if you were asked, "What were you doing

on Monday afternoon of the third week in September two years ago?" your reply might be, "Come on. How should I know?" However, if you were reminded, "That was the day the courthouse burned," or, "That was the day Mary had her automobile accident," you might remember immediately.

An interesting implication of cue-dependent forgetting is that you should, when possible, study in the same room in which you will be tested. If this is not practical, you should at least *review* in the classroom. The room itself, and the objects in it will then become cues to aid your recall.

Interference

Further understanding of forgetting comes from an experiment in which college students learned lists of nonsense syllables. After studying, one group of students slept for eight hours and were then tested for memory of the lists. A second group remained awake for eight hours and went about their business as usual. When the second group was tested, they remembered *less* than the group that slept (see Fig. 10-11). This difference is based on the fact that new learning can **interfere** with previous learning (Shiffrin, 1970). Interference applies to both short-term and long-term memories (Klatzky, 1980).

It is not completely clear if new memories alter existing memory traces, or if they make it harder to "locate" (retrieve) earlier memories. In either case, there is no doubt that interference is a major cause of forgetting. In one series of studies, college students were asked to memorize lists of words. Each day they learned a new list to be remembered only until the next day. Students who learned only one list recalled about 80 percent. Those who learned 20 lists (one each day) were only able to recall 15 percent of the last list one day later (Underwood, 1957). (See Fig. 10-12.)

Question: If interference has such an effect on memory, what would happen if a person were placed in "suspended animation" immediately after learning?

Theoretically, any length of time could pass without the memory being lost. Without new memories to cause interference, it would be as if no time at all had passed. Of course, this experiment has not been performed with humans, but something similar has been done with a rather interesting experimental subject, the common cockroach. If a cockroach is placed in a cold, dark place, it enters a state resembling hibernation. This effect was used in a study in which two groups of cockroaches learned their way through a maze. One group was then allowed to wander around in a lighted cage doing all the things cockroaches normally do. The second group was placed in a darkened refrigerator. As predicted, the refrigerated cockroaches showed significantly better memory when they were later tested in the maze (Minami and Dallenbach, 1946).

Inhibition   Both the sleeping college students and the refrigerated cockroaches remembered more because **retroactive** (RET-ro-AK-tiv) **inhibition** was held to a minimum. Retroactive inhibition refers to the tendency for new learning to interfere with old learning. Avoiding new learning prevents retroactive inhibition from occurring. This fact doesn't exactly mean you should sleep in your refrigerator after you study for an exam, but it does suggest you should avoid studying for other classes until the exam.

Sleeping after study can improve your memory, and reading, writing, or even watching TV may cause interference.

Retroactive inhibition is easily demonstrated in the laboratory by this arrangement:

Experimental group:	**Learn A**	**Learn B**	**Test A**
Control group:	**Learn A**	**Rest**	**Test A**

Imagine yourself as a member of the experimental group. In Task A, you learn a list of telephone numbers. In Task B, you learn a list of social security numbers. How do you do on a test of Task A (the telephone numbers)? If you do not remember as much as the control group that *only* learns Task A, retroactive inhibition has occurred. The second thing learned interfered with memory of the first thing learned; the interference went "backward" or was "retroactive" (see Fig. 10-13).

A second basic type of interference is **proactive** (pro-AK-tiv) **inhibition.** Proactive inhibition occurs when prior learning interferes with later learning. A test for proactive inhibition would take this form:

Experimental group:	**Learn A**	**Learn B**	**Test B**
Control group:	**Rest**	**Learn B**	**Test B**

If the experimental group remembers less than the control group on a test of Task B, then learning Task A interfered with memory of Task B.

Question: Then proactive interference goes "forward"?

Yes. For instance, if you cram for a psychology exam and then later the same night cram for a history exam, your

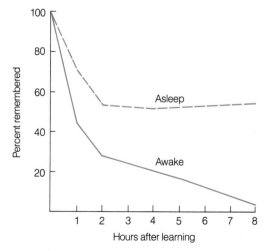

Fig. 10-11   *The amount of forgetting after sleep or waking activity. Notice that sleep causes less memory loss than waking. (After Jenkins and Dallenbach, 1924)*

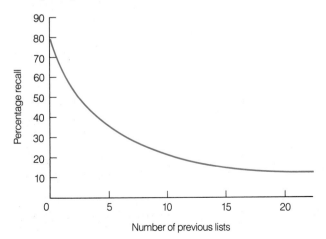

Fig. 10-12   *Effects of interference on memory. A graph of the approximate relationship between percentage recalled and number of different word lists memorized. (Adapted from Underwood, 1957)*

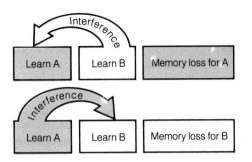

Fig. 10-13 *Proactive and retroactive inhibition. The order of learning and testing shows whether interference is proactive (forward) or retroactive (backward).*

memory for the second subject studied (history) will be less accurate than it would have been had you studied only history. (Due to retroactive inhibition your memory for psychology would probably also suffer.) The moral is, of course, don't procrastinate in preparing for exams.

Repression

Take a moment from reading and scan over the events of the last few years of your life. What kinds of things most easily come to mind? This is a question that interested psychologist Marigold Linton. Linton (1979) kept a careful record of everything that happened to her over a six-year period and compared her memories to it. Linton found that she tended to remember happy, positive events better than disappointments and irritations. A clinical psychologist would call this tendency **repression,** or motivated forgetting. Through repression, painful, threatening, or embarrassing memories are held out of consciousness by forces within one's personality. The forgetting of past failures, traumatic childhood events, the names of persons you dislike, or appointments you don't want to keep, may indicate repression.

Question: If I try to forget a test I have failed, am I repressing it?

No. Repression can be distinguished from **suppression,** an active attempt to put something out of mind. By not thinking about the test, you have merely suppressed a memory. If you choose to, you can remember the test. Clinicians consider true repression an *unconscious* event. When a memory is repressed, we are unaware that forgetting has even occurred. Interestingly, repression probably explains why most people think of themselves as more honest than

average, better drivers than average, better than average friends, and so on. We can't all be better than average, but by repressing our shortcomings, we can maintain the illusion we are (Loftus, 1980). (See Chapter 14 for more information on repression.)

Although repression is difficult to demonstrate experimentally, we have much evidence of its existence. An unanswered question, however, is why some traumatic events are vividly remembered whereas others are repressed. Psychologists Roger Brown and James Kulik (1977) use the term "flashbulb memories" to describe lasting images that are often frozen in memory at times of personal tragedy, accident, or loss. One reason such memories can be so vivid is that the hormone ACTH is secreted at times of stress. ACTH has been shown to enhance memory formation, possibly by sharpening attention (Sandman *et al.,* 1975).

Memory Formation— Some "Shocking" Findings

One possibility overlooked in our discussion of forgetting is that memories may be lost as they are being formed. For example, a head injury may cause a "gap" in memories preceding the accident. **Retrograde amnesia,** as it is called, can be understood by assuming that transferring memories from temporary storage to long-term memory takes a certain amount of time. The forming of a long-term memory is called **consolidation** (John, 1967). You can think of consolidation as being somewhat like writing your name in wet concrete. Once the concrete is set, the information (your name) is fairly lasting, but while it is setting it can be wiped out (amnesia) or scribbled over (interference).

In one experiment on consolidation, a rat was placed on a small platform. Eventually the rat stepped down to the floor. When it did, it received a painful electric shock. After one shock, the rat can be returned to the platform repeatedly, but it will not step down. Obviously, the shock has been remembered. But what would happen if we prevented the memory of the shock from being stored? Interestingly, one means of preventing consolidation is to give the rat a different kind of shock called **electroconvulsive shock (ECS)** immediately after each learning experience (Jarvik, 1964). ECS is a mild electric shock to the brain. It does not harm the animal and is not painful, but it does destroy any memory that is being formed. If each painful shock (the one the animal remembers) is followed by ECS (which destroys memories during consolidation), the rat will step down from the platform over and over, each time getting shocked and then receiving ECS to erase the memory of the shocks. (ECS has been employed as a psychiatric treatment for severe depression in humans. Used in this way, "electroshock therapy" also causes memory loss. (See Chapter 21 for details.)

Question: What would happen if the ECS were given several hours after the learning?

If enough time is allowed to pass between learning and the ECS, the memory is unaffected because consolidation has been completed. This is why people with head injuries usually only lose memories from immediately before the accident while older memories remain intact (Baddeley, 1976). Likewise, you would forget more if you followed a study session with eight hours of waking activity and then eight hours of sleep than you would if you studied, slept eight hours, and then were awake for eight hours. In both cases 16 hours have passed, but in the second instance forgetting is reduced because more consolidation has taken place before interference begins.

Question: What part of the brain causes consolidation?

Actually, many areas of the brain are responsible for memory, but of particular importance is the **hippocampus.** This structure, buried deep within the temporal lobes at each side of the brain, has recently been connected to long-term memory formation.

Humans who have had the hippocampus damaged show a striking inability to store new memories. A patient described by Brenda Milner is typical. Two years after an operation that affected the hippocampus, a 29-year-old patient continued to give his age as 27 and reported that it seemed that the operation had just taken place (Milner, 1965). His memory of events before the operation remained clear, but he found new learning almost impossible. When his parents moved to a new house a few blocks away on the same street, he could not remember the new address, and he was observed to read the same magazines over and over again without finding their contents familiar. If you were to meet this man he would seem fairly normal since he still has short-term memory. But if you were to leave the room and return 15 minutes later, he would act as if he had never seen you before (Milner, 1965). Years ago his favorite uncle died, but he suffers the same grief anew each time he is told of the death. Lacking the ability to form memories, he lives eternally in the present.

The Chemistry of Memory— Will We Eat College Professors?

Question: Can memory be improved with drugs?

The possibility of chemically improving memory has long intrigued both psychologists and the general public. We have known for some time that various stimulating drugs speed up consolidation if given just after learning. Note, however, that this only reduces the time during which interference can take place; it does not directly increase memory. Also, the drugs involved (metrazol, strychnine, nicotine, caffeine, and amphetamine) must be given in carefully controlled dosages, because at higher levels they *disrupt* memory, or are poisonous (McGaugh, 1970).

Question: What effect does alcohol have on memory?

Memory losses are common when a person overindulges in alcohol. A person suffering an alcohol blackout may lose anywhere from a few minutes to several hours of memory. Such losses appear to result because alcohol impairs encoding or consolidation of memories. If a person studies while drunk and is tested later, memory suffers. In contrast, if a person is sober while studying but drunk when tested, little forgetting occurs (Birnbaum *et al.*, 1978). Alcohol blackouts are most likely when a person (1) gulps a large amount of alcohol very quickly, (2) is very tired, or (3) has also taken a tranquilizer or sedative (Loftus, 1980).

Studies of **RNA** (ribonucleic acid) launched much of the current interest in artificially improving memory. Since RNA is involved in protein production and other cell functions, changes in RNA can alter the activity of individual nerve cells. To many researchers this suggested that **engrams,** or memory traces, might be directly related to changes in RNA. Are brain chemicals such as RNA responsible for memory? An interesting early test of the idea involved teaching planaria (flatworms—see Fig. 10-14) to

Fig. 10-14 *A flatworm like those used in studies of "cannibal" worms and memory.*

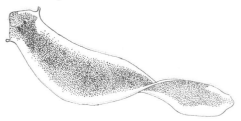

remember a simple response. The "trained" planaria were then chopped up and fed to "untrained" planaria. When this experiment was first performed, the "cannibal worms" supposedly showed evidence of learning* (McConnell, 1962). Later experiments used rats, mice, gerbils, or hamsters as subjects. In these experiments, RNA was extracted from the brains of trained animals and injected into untrained animals.

Question: Could RNA be used to transfer memories from one person to another?

It's highly unlikely. The results of memory transfer experiments have been very inconsistent (John, 1967). For every experiment showing memory transfer, there are others that flatly deny it. At present, researchers are a long way from isolating a "memory molecule," if one even exists. The value of the RNA experiments is that they started a line of inquiry that may eventually unlock the secrets of memory. Scientists are now investigating a bewildering array of chemicals and brain processes that affect memory (McGaugh, 1973). Will this research ever produce a "memory pill" or injection? Some neuroscientists are confident that memory can be and will be artificially enhanced. At present, however, the possibility of something like a "chemistry pill" or a "math pill" seems especially remote.

Learning Check

1. According to the Ebbinghaus "curve of forgetting," we forget slowly at first and then a rapid decline occurs.   T or F?

2. Which explanation seems to account for loss of short-term memories? (circle)
   decay   disuse   repression   interference

3. When memories are available but not accessible, forgetting may be cue-dependent.   T or F?

4. When learning one thing makes it more difficult to recall another, forgetting may be caused by
   _____.

5. You are asked to memorize long lists of telephone numbers. You learn a new list each day for 10 days. When tested on list 3 you remember less than a person who only learned the first three lists. Your larger memory loss is probably due to: (circle)
   disuse   retroactive inhibition   regression   proactive inhibition

6. Repression is thought of as a type of motivated forgetting.   T or F?

7. Retrograde amnesia results when consolidation is speeded up.   T or F?

8. Studies have conclusively shown that engrams are actually changes in RNA in the brain.   T or F?

Answers: 1. F   2. both decay and interference   3. T   4. interference or inhibition   5. retroactive inhibition   6. T   7. F   8. F

Resources Summary

● *Memory* is an active, computerlike system that *encodes, stores,* and *retrieves* information.

● A widely accepted model of memory proposes three separate but interrelated memory systems. These are: *sensory memory, short-term memory* (also called *working memory*), and *long-term memory.*

● Sensory memory is *exact,* but very brief. Visual *icons* last less than 0.5 second and auditory *echoes* less than 2 seconds. Through *selective attention,* some information is transferred to STM.

*For a time this led to the tongue-in-cheek suggestion that we may be wasting a great natural resource: We should grind up the brains of retired college professors and feed them to promising young students!

● STM has a capacity of about *seven bits* of information, but this can be extended by *chunking* or *recoding.* Short-term memories are often encoded by sound. They are very sensitive to interruption or interference. STM may last only 18 seconds without *rehearsal.* New information seems to rapidly displace old in STM, and memories lost from STM are gone forever.

● LTM functions as a general storehouse of information, especially meaningful information. Long-term memories are *relatively* permanent, or lasting. LTM seems to have an almost unlimited storage capacity.

● LTM can be subdivided into *semantic memory* (basic facts and meanings) and *episodic memory* (personal learning and experiences). Episodic memory is subject to *constructive processing,* or on-going revision and updating. LTM, especially semantic memory, is highly *organized* to allow retrieval of needed information. The pattern, or *structure,* of this organization is the subject of current memory research.

● The *tip-of-the-tongue phenomenon* shows that memory is not an all-or-nothing event. Memories may therefore be revealed by *recall, recognition, relearning,* or *redintegration.*

● In recall, memory proceeds *without explicit cues* or stimuli, as in an *essay exam.* A common test of recognition is the *multiple-choice* question, which requires selection of a correct answer. In relearning, "forgotten" material is learned again. Memory is indicated by any *savings* in time or effort necessary to remaster the material. In redintegration, memories are *reconstructed,* as one memory serves as a cue to trigger another, and another.

● *Eidetic imagery* (photographic memory) occurs when a person is able to project an image onto a blank surface. Such images allow nearly complete recall in some children, although the *effect* is brief. Eidetic imagery is rarely found in adults. However, many adults have *internal memory images.* When these images are very vivid an astounding memory for detail may be observed.

● Forgetting and memory were extensively studied by pioneer researcher *Herman Ebbinghaus.* His *curve of forgetting* shows that memory loss is most rapid immediately after learning. This is one reason why *periodic review* can be helpful in studying.

● *Failure to encode* information is a common cause of "forgetting." Forgetting in sensory memory and STM probably reflects *decay* of *memory traces* in the nervous system. Decay or *disuse* of memories may also account for LTM loss, but much forgetting cannot be explained in this way.

● Often forgetting is *cue-dependent.* That is, information is stored and *available,* but is not *accessible,* because the cues necessary to retrieve it are not present.

● Much forgetting in both STM and LTM can be attributed to *interference* of memories with one another. When recent learning interferes with memory of prior learning, *retroactive inhibition* has occurred. If old learning interferes with new learning, *proactive inhibition* has occurred. Interference is reduced when study is followed by sleep, rather than by additional learning or activity.

● *Repression* is the forgetting of painful, embarrassing, or traumatic memories. Repression is thought to be unconscious, in contrast to *suppression,* in which one consciously tries to avoid thinking of something.

● *Retrograde amnesia* and the effects of electroconvulsive shock (*ECS*) may be explained by the concept of *consolidation.* Consolidation theory holds that *engrams* (permanent memory traces) are formed during a critical period after learning. Until they are consolidated, long-term memories are easily destroyed. The *hippocampus* is a brain area that has been connected to consolidation of memories. Stimulant drugs can speed up consolidation, but disruption of memory will occur if the dosage is too large.

● Early research on the chemistry of memory focused on *RNA* as a likely basis for memory storage. Research on storage and transfer of memory in planaria has given way to similar studies in higher animals, and interest has shifted to other chemicals and brain mechanisms. Future artificial enhancement of memory is a possible outcome of such research.

How to Improve Your Memory

While you are waiting around for the development of a memory pill. let's focus on some ways of improving your memory right now.

Question: How much can memory be improved? What if I have a very poor memory?

No matter how good (or bad) your basic memory is, you could probably make much better use of the capacity you do have. As James Weinland (1957) has said, ''A person is entitled to say that he has a poor memory only if he forgets many things that deeply interest him and that he has made an effort to remember.'' Weinland's point is aptly illustrated by the student who complains he can't remember facts in his classes, but who can remember the names of every part in an automobile, the names of all the players in the National Football League, and the cubic displacement and horsepower of every motorcycle sold in the United States.

In this and previous chapters, many factors affecting learning and memory have been mentioned. The list below summarizes these factors and some not previously discussed. You can improve your memory and study efficiency by controlling as many of these factors as possible.

Knowledge of Results   Learning proceeds most effectively when feedback or knowledge of results allows you to check to see if you are learning. Feedback also helps you identify material that needs extra practice, and it can be rewarding to know that you have remembered or answered correctly. A prime means of providing feedback for yourself when studying is *recitation.*

Recitation   Recitation means repeating to yourself what you have learned. If you are going to remember something, eventually you will have to retrieve it. Recitation forces you to practice retrieving information as you are learning. When you are reading a text, you should stop frequently and try to remember what you have just read by summarizing it aloud. In one experiment, the best memory score of all was earned by a group of students who spent 80 percent of their time reciting and only 20 percent reading (Gates, 1958). Maybe students who talk to themselves aren't crazy after all!

Overlearning   Numerous studies have shown that memory is greatly improved when study is continued beyond ''bare mastery.'' In other words, after you have learned material well enough to remember it once without error, you should continue studying. Overlearning is your best insurance against ''going blank'' on a test because of nervousness or anxiety.

Selection   The Dutch scholar Erasmus said that a good memory should be like a fisherman's net: It should keep all the big fish and let the little ones escape. If you boil down the paragraphs in most textbooks to one or two important terms or ideas, you will find your memorization chores more manageable and will probably remember more than you would if you tried to retain everything. Practice careful and selective marking in your texts and use marginal notes to further summarize ideas. Most students mark their texts too much instead of too little. If everything is underlined, you haven't been selective.

Spaced Practice   Spaced practice is generally superior to massed practice. By improving concentration, three 20-minute study sessions can produce more learning than one hour of continuous study. Perhaps the best way to make use of this principle is to *schedule* your time. If most students were to keep a totally honest record of their weekly activities, they would probably find that very few hours were spent really studying. To make an effective schedule, designate times during the week before, after, and between classes when you will study particular subjects. Then treat these times just as if they were classes you had to attend.

Organize   Assume that you must memorize the following list of words: *north, man, red, spring, woman, east, autumn, yellow, summer, boy, blue, west, winter, girl, green, south.* This rather difficult list could be reorganized as follows: *north, east, south, west, spring, summer, au-*

Applications

tumn, winter, red, yellow, green, blue, man, woman, boy, girl. This simple reordering made the second list much easier to learn when college students were tested on both lists (Deese and Hulse, 1967). In another experiment, students who made up stories using long lists of words to be memorized learned the lists better than those who didn't (Bower and Clark, 1969). Organizing class notes and outlining chapters can be helpful when studying. It may even be helpful to outline your outlines, so that the overall organization of ideas becomes clearer and simpler.

Whole versus Part Learning If you had to memorize a speech, would it be better to try to learn it from beginning to end or in smaller parts like paragraphs? Generally it is better to practice whole packages of information rather than smaller parts. This is especially true for fairly short, organized information. An exception is that learning parts may be better for extremely long, complicated information. Try to study the largest *meaningful* amount of information possible at one time.

For very long or complex material, try the *progressive part method.* In this approach, you break a learning task into short sections. At first, you study part "A" until it is mastered. Next, you study parts "A" and "B"; then "A," "B," and "C"; and so forth. This is a good way to learn the lines of a play, a long piece of music, or a poem. After the material is learned, you should also practice it by starting at points other than "A" (at "C," "D," or "B," for example). This helps prevent getting "lost," or going blank in the middle of a performance.

Serial Position Whenever you must learn something in *order,* you should be aware of the *serial position effect.* As you will recall, this describes a tendency to make the most errors in remembering the middle of a list. If you are introduced to a long line of people, the names you are likely to forget will be those in the middle, so you should make an extra effort to attend to them. The middle of a list, poem, or speech should also be given special attention and extra practice.

Sleep Remember that sleeping after study produces the least interference. Since you obviously can't sleep after every study session, or can't study everything just before you sleep, your study schedule (see the "Spaced Practice" section) should include ample breaks between subjects. Using your breaks and free time in a schedule is as important as living up to your study periods.

Review If you have spaced your practice and overlearned, review will be like icing on your study cake. Review shortly before an exam cuts down the time during which you must remember details that may be important for the test, but not otherwise meaningful to you. When reviewing, hold the amount of new information you try to memorize to a minimum. It may be realistic to take what you have actually learned and add a little more to it at the last minute by cramming, but remember that more than a little new learning will confuse you and interfere with what you already know.

If you consistently use the principles reviewed here, you should get grades at least one step higher without increasing your study time, or you should get the same grades after spending less time. Give this an honest try, and we can almost guarantee these results. Besides, if you haven't adopted the SQ3R and LISAN techniques described in "The Psychology of Studying Psychology" in the beginning of this book, it might be time to give them a try.

Learning Check

1. To improve memory, it is reasonable to spend as much or more time reciting as reading. T or F?
2. Organizing information while studying has little effect on memory because semantic memory is already highly organized. T or F?
3. The progressive part method of study is best suited to long and complex learning tasks. T or F?
4. Sleeping immediately after studying is highly disruptive to the consolidation of memories. T or F?

Answers: 1. T 2. F 3. T 4. F

Exploration

Mnemonics—Memory Magic

Question:　Some stage performers use memory as part of their acts. Do they have eidetic imagery?

Various "memory experts" entertain by giving demonstrations in which they memorize the names of everyone at a banquet, the order of all the cards in a deck, long lists of disconnected words, or other seemingly impossible amounts of information. These tricks are performed through the use of **mnemonics** (nee-MON-iks). A mnemonic is any kind of memory system or aid.

Some mnemonic systems have become so common that almost everyone knows them. If you are trying to remember how many days there are in a month, you may find the answer by reciting, "Thirty days hath September. . . ." Physics teachers often help their students remember the colors of the spectrum by giving them the mnemonic "Roy G. Biv": *red, orange, yellow, green, blue, indigo, violet*. The budding sailor who has trouble telling port from starboard may remember that port and left both have four letters or may remind himself, "I *left* port." And what beginning musician hasn't remembered the notes represented by the lines and spaces of the musical staff by learning "face" and "*every good boy does fine*."

Mnemonic techniques are ways of avoiding *rote* learning (learning by simple repetition). The superiority of mnemonic learning as opposed to rote learning has been demonstrated many times. For example, Bower (1973) asked college students to study 5 different lists of 20 unrelated words. At the end of a short study session, subjects were asked to recall all 100 items. Subjects using mnemonics remembered an average of 72 items, whereas a control group using simple, or rote, learning remembered an average of 28.

Stage performers rarely have a naturally superior memory. Instead, they make extensive use of memory systems to perform their feats. Few of these systems are of practical value to the student, but the principles underlying mnemonics are. By practicing mnemonics you should be able to greatly improve your memory with little effort.

The basic principles of mnemonics are:

1. Use mental pictures. There are at least two kinds of memory, *visual* and *verbal*. Visual pictures or images are generally easier to remember than words. Turning information into mental pictures is therefore very helpful (Paivio, 1969).

2. Make things meaningful. Transfer of information from short-term to long-term memory is aided by making it meaningful. If you encounter technical terms that have little or no immediate meaning for you, *give* them meaning, even if you have to stretch the term to do so. (This point is clarified by the examples below.)

3. Make information familiar. Connect it to what you already know. Another way to get information into long-term memory is to connect it to information already stored there. If some facts or ideas in a chapter seem to stay in your memory easily, associate other more difficult facts with them.

4. Form bizarre, unusual, or exaggerated mental associations. When associating two ideas, terms, or especially mental images, you will find that the more outrageous and exaggerated the association, the more likely you are to remember it later.

A sampling of typical applications of mnemonics should make these four points clear to you.

Example 1　Let's say you have 30 new vocabulary words to memorize in Spanish. You can proceed by rote memorization (repeat them over and over until you begin to get them) or you can learn them with little effort through mnemonics. To remember that the word *pájaro* (pronounced pa-ha-ro) means bird, you can give the word familiar meaning and use mental images. *Pájaro* (to me) sounds like "parked car-o." To remember that *pájaro* means bird, I will visualize a parked car jam-packed full of birds. I will try to make this image as vivid and exaggerated as possible. I will picture the birds flapping and chirping and feathers flying everywhere. Perhaps I will also visualize my own car parked with a giant bird peeking out from inside. If you form similar images for the rest of the words on the list, you may not remember them all, but you will get most without any further practice. As a matter of fact, if you have formed the *pájaro* images just now, it is going to be almost impossible for you to ever see the word *pájaro* again without remembering that it means bird.

Exploration

Question: What if I think pájaro *means "parked car" when I take my Spanish test?*

This is why you should form one or two extra images so that the important feature (bird, in this case) is repeated.

Example 2 Let's say you have to learn the names of all the bones and muscles in the human body for biology. You are trying to remember that the jawbone is the *mandible.* This one is easy because you can associate it to a *man nibbling,* or maybe you can picture a *man dribbling* a basketball with his jaw (make this image as ridiculous as possible). If the muscle name *latissimus dorsi* gives you trouble, familiarize it by turning it into *"the ladder misses the door, sigh."* Then picture a ladder glued to your back where the muscle is found. Picture the ladder leading up to a small door at your shoulder. Picture the ladder missing the door. Picture the ladder sighing like an animated character in a cartoon.

Question: This seems like more to remember, not less; and it seems like it would cause you to misspell things.

Mnemonics are not a complete substitute for normal memory; they are an aid to normal memory. Mnemonics are not likely to be helpful unless you make extensive use of *images.* Your mental pictures will come back to you easily. As for misspellings, mnemonics can be thought of as a built-in hint in your memory. Often, when taking a test, you will find that the slightest hint is all you need to remember correctly. A mnemonic image is like having someone leaning over your shoulder who says, "Psst, the name of that muscle sounds like 'ladder misses the door, sigh.'"

Here are two more examples to help you appreciate the flexibility of a mnemonic approach to studying.

Example 3 Your art history teacher expects you to be able to name the artist when you are shown slides as part of exams. Many of the slides you have only seen once before in class. How will you remember them? As the slides are shown in class, make each artist's name into an object or image. Then picture the object *in* paintings done by the artist. For example, Van Gogh you can picture as a *van* (automobile) *going* through the middle of each Van Gogh painting. Picture the van running over things and knocking things over. Or, if you remember that Van Gogh cut off his ear, picture a giant bloody ear in each of his paintings.

Example 4 If you have trouble remembering history, try to avoid thinking of it as something from the dim past. Picture each historical personality as a person you know right now (a friend, teacher, parent, and so on). Then picture these people doing whatever the historical figures did. Also try visualizing battles or other events as if they were happening in your town or make parks and schools into countries. Use your imagination.

Question: How can mnemonics be used to remember things in order?

Here are three techniques that are helpful.

1. Form a chain. To remember lists of ideas, objects, or words in order, try forming an exaggerated association (mental image) connecting the first item to the second, then the second to the third, and so on. To remember the following short list in order: *elephant, doorknob, string, watch, rifle, oranges,* picture a full-sized *elephant* balanced on a *doorknob* playing with a *string* tied to him. Picture a *watch* tied to the string, and a *rifle* shooting *oranges* at the watch. This technique can be used quite successfully for lists of 20 or more items. Try it next time you go shopping and leave your list at home.

2. Take a mental walk. Mnemonics were well known to ancient Greek orators, who would take a mental walk along a familiar path to associate ideas they wanted to cover in a speech to the images of statues found along the walk. You can do the same thing by "placing" objects or ideas along the way as you mentally take a familiar walk.

3. Use a system. Many times the first letter or syllables of words or ideas can be formed into another word that will serve as a reminder of order. "Roy G. Biv," just cited, is an example. As an alternative, learn the following: 1 is a bun, 2 is a shoe, 3 is a tree, 4 is a door, 5 is a hive, 6 is sticks, 7 is heaven, 8 is a gate, 9 is a line, 10 is a hen. To remember in order, form an association between bun and the first item on your list, then form an association between shoe and the second item, and so on.

If you have never used mnemonics, you may still be skeptical, but give this approach a fair trial. Most people find they can greatly extend their memory through the use of mnemonics. You may want to discuss these ideas further with your instructor and classmates.

Questions for Discussion

1. What type of classroom testing do you prefer? Why? What would you consider an ideal way to be tested? ("Never" does not count as an answer!)

2. Would you like to have a memory like the man studied by A. R. Luria? What would be the advantages and disadvantages of such a memory? If, as an adult, you retained eidetic memory, how would you use it?

3. If you were forced to give up either STM or LTM, which would you choose? Think carefully about your answer.

4. We have seen that there are several reasons for forgetting. Which does the use of mnemonics most directly combat? How would you minimize the other major causes of forgetting?

5. You must study French, Spanish, psychology, and biology in one evening, and you have little time for breaks. What do you think would be the best ordering of subjects to minimize interference? Why?

6. If scientists perfect a drug that improves memory do you think it should be widely available? Would you want to try it? If a drug were perfected that could cause selective forgetting of memories, would you support its use for victims of rape, assault, disaster, or a horrifying accident?

7. What mnemonic strategies have you used in studying? Which have been most helpful? How could a person with poor mental imagery use mnemonics?

8. What will you do to cope with remembering longer zip codes?

9. Describe a case of mistaken identity you have seen in the news. What aspects of memory contributed to the mistake?

Suggestions for Further Reading

Bower, G. H. "Mood and Memory," *American Psychologist*, 1981, **36,** pp. 129–148.

Cermack, L. S. *Improving Your Memory*. McGraw-Hill, 1976.

Haber, R. N. "How We Remember What We See," *Scientific American,* May, 1970, pp. 104–112.

Klatzky, R. *Human Memory: Structures and Processes,* 2nd ed. Freeman, 1980.

Lindsay, P., and D. Norman. *Human Information Processing.* Academic, 1977.

Linton, M. "I Remember It Well," *Psychology Today,* July, 1979, pp. 81–86.

Loftus, E. *Memory.* Addison-Wesley, 1980.

Luria, A. R. *The Mind of a Mnemonist.* Basic Books, 1968.

11

Thinking, Problem Solving, and Creativity

Chapter Preview

Chess Anyone?

David Levy was in trouble. It was the fourth game of a six-game chess match and Levy was trying a new strategy. If he lost the match, Levy would forfeit $2500 of his own money. Game one was a tie. Levy won games two and three. Now, in game four, he was locked in a sharp tactical battle, and he was losing. What was wrong? In the earlier games Levy relied on the kind of wide-open maneuvering that had made him an International Master. In contrast, his opponent's strength was a powerful short-term, or tactical, style of play. Maybe "powerful" isn't the right word. Unbeatable is closer to the truth, as Levy soon learned. For the moment David Levy had met his match. He watched silently as the robot arm of Chess 4.7 *made its final move, winning game four.*

Chess 4.7 is a computer program designed by David Slate and other systems analysts at Northwestern University. In 1977 it won the Minnesota Open Chess Tournament—against humans. However, David Levy, the reigning Scottish champion, proved to be a tougher opponent. After losing game four, Levy quickly returned to his original style of play—and won the match (Ehara, 1980). For all their raw power, computers are only able to plan five or six chess moves in advance (by considering over one billion possibilities). They don't make mistakes in the short run, but they can be beaten by strategy and foresight.

David Levy's victory symbolizes one of the most unique of all human capacities: the ability to think intelligently and creatively. We know how computers "think" because they are our own creation. But how do we explain David Levy's creativity and problem-solving ability? Or yours? Thinking, problem solving, and creativity are the challenging topics of this chapter.

Survey Questions   What is the nature of thought? What basic units are used in thinking, and how do they differ? How do concepts and language influence thought? Can animals think? Can they be taught to use human languages? What do we know about effective problem solving and creativity? Can creativity be learned?

What Is Thinking?—It's All in Your Head!

Thinking refers to many things: daydreaming, fantasy, problem solving, reasoning, free association, and dreaming (to name but a few). During most of your waking hours, you are engaged in some form of thought. Stated more formally, **thinking** or **cognition** refers to the mental manipulation and combination of images, concepts, words, rules, symbols, and precepts. Although thinking is not a uniquely human activity, you might imagine trying to teach an animal to duplicate the feats of someone like Hans Eberstark, who is a "lightning calculator." Eberstark can multiply two 12-digit numbers in his head, supplying the correct answer in about two minutes!

Fig. 11-1 *Psychologist Wolfgang Köhler felt that solution of a multiple-stick problem revealed a capacity for insight.*

Question: To what extent are animals capable of thought?

Most pet owners can readily supply stories about apparent thinking in animals. A friend might say, "Wow, you should have seen Studebaker figure out how to get into the closet where I hid the dog food." Are animals actually thinking in situations such as this? In a rudimentary sense they are. At its most basic, thinking is the **internal representation** of a problem or situation. (Picture a chess player who mentally "tries out" several possible moves before actually touching a chesspiece.) Animals demonstrate internal representation in **delayed response problems.** For example, a hungry animal might be allowed to watch as a light is turned on over one of three goal boxes. The animal has previously learned that the lighted box contains food. The light is turned off, and after a delay, the animal is released. Can it select the correct box? If the delay is brief, the answer is yes (Hunter, 1913). When tested under similar circumstances, most animals can maintain, or *re-create,* some kind of mental image long enough to make a correct choice.

Animals also show evidence of problem-solving ability far exceeding that just described. In fact, German psychologist Wolfgang Köhler felt that higher animals such as chimpanzees show a capacity for insight. **Insight** is a sudden reorganization of the elements of a problem whereby the solution becomes evident. One of Köhler's brightest subjects, a chimp named Sultan, was able to solve problems with such ease that Köhler challenged him with a **multiple-stick problem.** In this problem several sticks of increasing length were arranged between the cage and a banana (see Fig. 11-1). To reach the banana, Sultan had to use the first stick to retrieve the second stick (which was longer than the first). The second stick could then be used to retrieve an even longer stick, which could then be used to reach the banana (Köhler, 1925).

When confronted with this problem, Sultan made a few futile attempts to reach through the bars to get the banana. Then he noticed the sticks. Sultan looked at the banana then at the sticks . . . then at the banana. Picking up the first stick, Sultan smoothly and without further hesitation solved the problem and raked in the banana. Of course, it is possible that Sultan was only using **implicit** (unseen) **trial and error** to solve the problem. In other words, he may have been trying alternatives internally, so that all but the correct response was discarded before he acted. But Köhler felt Sultan had actually perceived the relationship between elements of the problem (the shorter and longer sticks and the banana) and that his solutions were insightful.

Basic Units of Thought   In the "Chapter Preview" we used chess playing as an example of human thought. Let's briefly consider another chess example. Miguel Najdorf of Argentina is a Grandmaster chess player. In an exhibition, Najdorf once simultaneously played 45 chess games, while *blindfolded.* It is estimated that over 3600 different positions arose during the evening of the exhibition (Hearst, 1969). How did Najdorf perform this feat? Like most people, he used several basic types of internal representation. The *basic units of thought* include: (1) **images,** (2) **muscular responses,** (3) **concepts,** and (4) **language** or **symbols.** All four units are usually combined in situations requiring complex thought and internal representation. Indeed, in some situations people need all the help they can get. To accomplish their seemingly impossible mental feats, blindfolded chess players report that they use a combination of visual images, muscular sensations involving "lines of force," concepts ("Game 2 is an English opening"), and the special notational system or "language" used by chess players (Hearst, 1969). Because of their obvious importance, each of the units of thought is discussed in greater detail in the following sections.

Mental Imagery—In the Mind's Eye

A survey of 500 people found that 97 percent have visual imagery and 92 percent auditory imagery. Over 50 percent had imagery that included movement, touch, taste, smell, and pain (McKellar, 1965). When we speak of images, we are usually referring to a mental "picture." But as you can see, images may involve the other senses as well. For example, your image of a bakery may include its delicious odor, as well as its appearance. Some people tend to use more imagery of one kind than another. An artist might rely heavily on visual imagery; a musician, on auditory imagery; and an acrobat, on kinesthetic imagery. As you may recall from an earlier "Exploration" (Chapter 5), some people have a rare form of imagery called **synesthesia.** For these people, images cross normal sensory barriers, as when sounds are experienced as colors. Despite such variations, it is generally accepted that most people use images as a means of thinking and solving problems (Fig. 11-2).

Question: How are images used to solve problems?

Stored images can be used to bring prior experience to bear on problem solving. If you were given the question, "How many uses can you think of for an old automobile tire?" you might begin by picturing all the uses you have already seen: as a swing, as a boat bumper on a pier, as soles for sandals, and so on.

To generate more original solutions, **created images** may be used. Thus, an artist may completely picture a proposed sculpture before beginning work. Even in abstract subjects, such as science and mathematics, creative thought may rely on the use of imagery. Albert Einstein once reported that the basis for his thought was a kind of mental play in which muscular and visual images were associated and combined. Only in the later stages of his thought process were the results translated into language or mathematical symbols.

Does the "size" of a mental image make any difference? To find out, first picture a cat sitting beside a housefly. Now try to "zoom in" on the cat's ears so you see them clearly. Next, picture a rabbit sitting beside an elephant. How quickly can you "see" the rabbit's front feet? Did it take longer than picturing the cat's ears? When a rabbit is pictured with an elephant, the rabbit's image must be small because the elephant is large. Using such tasks, Stephen Kosslyn (1975) found that the smaller an image is, the harder it is to "see" its details. To put this finding to use, try

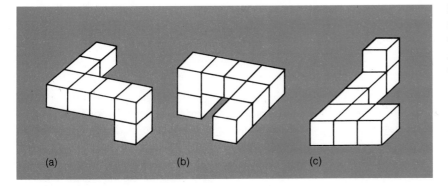

(a)   (b)   (c)

Fig. 11-2 Imagery in thinking. Subjects were shown a drawing similar to (a) and drawings of how (a) would look in other positions, such as (b) and (c). Subjects could recognize (a) after it had been "rotated" from its original position. However, the more (a) was rotated in space, the longer it took to recognize it. This result suggests that subjects actually formed a three-dimensional image of (a) and rotated the image to see if it matched. (Shepard, 1975)

forming over-sized images of things you want to think about. For example, to understand electricity, picture the wires as large pipes with electrons the size of golf balls moving through them; to understand the human ear, explore it (in your mind's eye) like a large cave; and so forth.

Muscular Imagery—A Moving Experience?

Question: How do muscular responses relate to thinking?

It is somewhat surprising to recognize that we think with our bodies as well as our heads. Jerome Bruner (1966) believes that we often represent things in a kind of **muscular imagery** created by actions or *implicit actions*. For example, people who "talk" with their hands are using gestures to help themselves think as well as to communicate. A great deal of information is contained in *kinesthetic sensations* (feelings from the muscles and joints). As one talks, these sensations help structure the flow of ideas. A good way to see this happening is to ask a friend who has participated in a sporting event to describe what took place. Along with a verbal description, you will probably get an "instant replay" of many of the actions. Partially acting-out the "big plays" helps the person to think about and recapture the order of important events (Horowitz, 1970).

Question: A person can think while sitting perfectly still. Is any muscular imagery used under these circumstances?

Yes. One of the reasons thinking can be hard work is that it is accompanied by an undercurrent of muscular tension and **micromovements** throughout the body. In one classic study, a subject was asked to imagine that he was hitting a nail with a hammer. As he did, there was a clearly recorded burst of activity in the muscles of his unmoving arm (Jacobson, 1932). Another study of muscular imagery employed deaf-mutes who were accustomed to using sign language for communication. When these subjects were asked to multiply and divide numbers in their heads, 80 percent showed increased muscular activity in their hands. Only 30 percent of a group of speaking subjects showed similar increases (Max, 1937).

Question: Is it possible to think without using muscle responses?

Apparently it is. An investigator once had himself injected with curare, a drug that paralyzes all the voluntary musculature. While he was paralyzed, he was asked to solve a number of problems and to answer questions. When the drug wore off, he gave his answers to the questions and reported that he had been completely capable of thought while immobilized (Smith *et al.*, 1947).

Learning Check

1. A _____ _____ problem can be used to show that animals are capable of representative thought.

2. Chimpanzees who appear to achieve insightful solutions to problems may only be using implicit trial and error. T or F?

3. List four basic units of thought:

   _____, _____

   _____, _____

4. Synesthesia is the use of kinesthetic sensations as a vehicle for thought. T or F?

5. Our reliance on muscular imagery and micromovements in thinking means that problem solving is impaired by drugs that cause paralysis. T or F?

Answers: 1. delayed response 2. T 3. images, muscular responses, concepts, and language or symbols 4. F 5. F

Concepts—"A Rose Is a Rose Is a Rose"

A **concept** is a word or idea that represents a class of objects or events. Concepts provide a powerful tool for thought because they allow us to function on an *abstract* level, free from distracting details. In addition, concepts allow the meaning carried by familiar words to be transferred to less familiar words or situations. For example: The mysterious sounding word *podbromhidrosis* simply means smelly feet; *galeanthropy* is the delusion that one has become a cat; and a *ballhooter* is a lumberjack who rolls logs down a hill! Transfer of conceptual meaning is the basis for most formal education. We are fortunate to be free of the inefficiency that would result if the meaning of a concept such as "schizophrenia" had to be established by bringing dozens of disturbed persons to psychology class.

Question: How are concepts learned?

Concept formation is the process whereby we classify information into meaningful categories. In early childhood, much concept formation simply involves experience with **positive** and **negative instances** of the concept. This is not as simple as it might seem: Imagine a child learning the concept of "dog."

Dog Daze

A child and her father go for a walk. At a neighbor's house, they see a medium-sized dog. The father says, "See the *dog.*" As they pass the next yard, the child sees a cat and says, "Dog!" Her father corrects her, "No, that's a *cat.*" The child now thinks, "Aha, dogs are large and cats are small." In the next yard, she sees a Pekingese and says, "Cat!" "No, that's a dog," replies her father.

The child's confusion is understandable. However, with continued exposure to positive and negative instances, the child will eventually recognize Great Danes and Chihuahuas as examples of the same category—dogs. As adults, we are more likely to acquire concepts by learning or formulating **rules.** For example, a "triangle" must be a closed shape with three sides made of straight lines. Rule learning is generally more efficient than exposure to examples, but examples remain important (Rosenthal and Zimmerman, 1978). It is unlikely that memorizing a series of rules would allow an uninitiated listener to accurately categorize "punk," "new wave," "fusion," "salsa," and "reggae" music.

When you think of the concept "bird," do you picture a list of features that birds have? Probably not. Most people tend to think of concepts in terms of **prototypes,** or ideal models (Rosch, 1977). A robin, for instance, is a model bird, whereas an ostrich is not. What this tells us is that not all instances of a concept are considered equally representative. Identifying an ostrich is largely a matter of noticing how it differs from a "model" bird. Concept identification becomes difficult when we cannot come up with any prototype relevant to what we see. What, for example, are the objects shown in Fig. 11-3?

Question: Are there different kinds of concepts?

Several general types of concepts have been identified. A **conjunctive concept** refers to a class of objects having one or more features in common. Conjunctive concepts are sometimes referred to as "and" concepts: To belong to the

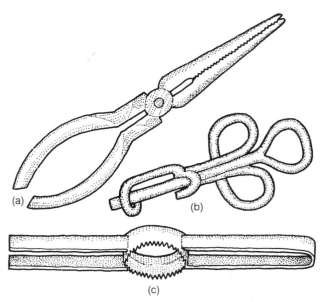

Fig. 11-3 *Use of prototypes in concept identification. Even though its shape is unusual, item (a) can be related to a model (an ordinary set of pliers) and thus recognized. But what are items (b) and (c)? If you don't recognize them, look ahead to Fig. 11-4. (After Bransford and McCarrell, 1977)*

concept class, an item must have "this feature, *and* this feature, *and* this feature." For example, a "motorcycle" must have two wheels, *and* an engine, *and* a seat, *and* handle bars. **Relational concepts** classify objects on the basis of their relationship to something else, or by the relationship between features of an object. "Large," "above," "left," "north," and "upside down" are all relational concepts. **Disjunctive concepts** refer to objects that have at least one of several possible features. These are "either-or" concepts. To belong, an item must have "this feature *or* that feature, *or* another feature." For example, in the game of baseball, a "strike" is *either* a swing *or* a miss, *or* a pitch down the middle, *or* a foul ball. A "barn" is either a place where crops and feed are stored, or a building for animals, or both. The "either-or" quality of disjunctive concepts makes them difficult to learn.

Generally speaking, concepts have two types of meaning. The **denotative meaning** of a word or concept is its explicit definition. The **connotative meaning** is its emotional or personal meaning. For example, the denotative meaning of the word *naked* (having no clothes) is the same for a nudist as it is for a movie censor, but we could expect their connotations to differ.

Fig. 11-4 *Context can substitute for a lack of appropriate prototypes in concept identification.*

Question: Can you give a clearer statement of what a connotative meaning is?

Researcher Charles Osgood (1952) used a method called the **semantic differential** to measure connotative meaning (see Fig. 11-5). Osgood found that when words or concepts are rated on a series of scales, most of their connotative meaning boils down to the dimensions: *good-bad, strong-weak,* and *active-passive.* Because concepts vary on these dimensions, words or phrases having approximately the same denotative meaning may be substituted to imply different connotations. For example, I am *conscientious;* you are *careful;* and he is *nit-picking!*

Language—What's in a Word?

As we have seen, thinking sometimes takes place without language. Everyone has had the experience of searching for a word to express an idea that exists as a vague image or feeling. Nevertheless, most thought leans heavily on language, because it allows the world to be **encoded** into symbols that are easily manipulated. Language is also important to thought because it makes the accumulated knowledge of human experience available to present and future generations.

Study of the meaning of words and language is called **semantics.** It is here that the connection between language and thought becomes most evident. Suppose, on an intelligence test, you were asked to circle the word that does not belong in this series:

SKYSCRAPER   CATHEDRAL   TEMPLE   PRAYER

If you circled PRAYER you answered as most people do. Now try another problem, again circling the odd item:

CATHEDRAL   PRAYER   TEMPLE   SKYSCRAPER

Had you seen only this question you probably would have circled SKYSCRAPER. There is a subtle change in meaning caused by re-ordering the words (Judson and Cofer, 1956, cited by Mayer, 1977).

Semantic problems often arise when a word has multiple, or unclear meaning: If you overhear someone saying that you are a "heavy" person, should you be insulted or flattered? Does the sentence, "They are eating apples," mean that apples are being eaten, or that the apples are edible? Choice of words may directly influence thinking about important events by shifting meaning: Has one country's army "invaded" another? Or "effected a protective incursion"? Is the city reservoir "half full," or "half empty"? Would you rather eat "prime beef" or "dead cow"?!

Question: Could a person's native language affect his or her thought patterns?

Let's explore this question. How many words do you know for the term *camel?* In Arabic, there are over 6000 variations of the word *camel,* but the only other English term is *dromedary.* How many other words do you know for the term *snow?* If you are a skier, you may be able to add *hard pack, powder, kernel,* and perhaps a few more, but this exhausts most of the possibilities. By contrast, Eskimos have no single word for snow; their language includes close to 30 terms for various kinds of snow and ice (Whorf, 1940). On the basis of such differences, linguist Benjamin Whorf has proposed the theory of **linguistic determinism.**

The idea of linguistic determinism is simple but intriguing. Whorf feels that language is not only an instrument for reproducing ideas, but also a *shaper* of ideas. Each culture prepares its members to think about particular topics by providing words with which to categorize experience. If you were to watch a parade of 30 camels and were questioned afterward about what you saw, you could be forgiven if you were only able to say "a bunch of camels." The English language does not equip you to easily encode the details of what you saw. In our culture, the automobile has about the same importance that camels once had in Arabic culture. It would be rare for a person in our culture to look at 30 cars and not be able to remember the make, model, and special features of many of them. This reflects not only the importance attached to cars, but also the language available to think about them.

Other differences in the way languages divide up experience make for some interesting comparisons. The Hopi have only one word referring to the concepts "insect," "airplane," and "aviator." The Navajos have only one word for "flint," "metal," and "knife." If these groupings seem strange, remember that it seems just as strange to an Eskimo when we call "snow" what they call *quali, kimoaqruk,* and *pukak!* Clearly, thought is intimately tied to and influenced by language.

Question: What does it take to make a language?

The Structure of Language   First of all, a language must provide *symbols* that can be used to stand for objects and ideas. The symbols we call words are built out of **phonemes** (basic speech sounds) and **morphemes** (speech sounds collected into meaningful units). The units of speech can be arranged into countless combinations. Consider the possibilities in just four morphemes: "reach," "to," "able," "un." From these, we can make: "able to," "unable to," "reach to," "to reach," "able to reach," "unable to reach," "reachable," "unreachable," "reachable to," "unreachable to," "unto," "unto Able."

The second requirement of language is that it have a **grammar,** or set of rules for the combination of sounds into words and words into sentences. One part of grammar is known as **syntax,** or rules pertaining to word order in sentences. Syntax is very important in communication through language. Rearranging words almost always changes the meaning of a sentence: "Dog bites man" versus "Man bites dog." In addition to having their words in

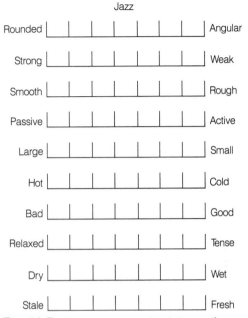

Jazz

Rounded								Angular
Strong								Weak
Smooth								Rough
Passive								Active
Large								Small
Hot								Cold
Bad								Good
Relaxed								Tense
Dry								Wet
Stale								Fresh

Fig. 11-5   *This is an example of Osgood's semantic differential. Connotative meaning of the word "jazz" can be established by rating it on the scales. Mark your own rating by placing dots or X's in the spaces. Connect the marks with a line; then have a friend rate the word and compare your responses. It might be interesting to do the same for "rock and roll," "disco," and "classical." You also might want to try the word "psychology." (From C. E. Osgood. Copyright © 1952 American Psychological Association. Reprinted by permission.)*

Fig. 11-6   *Human thought and the use of language are intimately interrelated.*

the proper order, spoken sentences must be *short*. In normal conversation, most sentences last less than *three seconds*. Psychologist James Deese (1978) believes this is true because of the limits of short-term memory. In order to speak, we must keep track of what has been said and what remains to be said. Similarly, listeners must remember the first words of a sentence to understand the last.

Traditional grammar has been concerned with "surface" language—the actual sentences spoken. More recently, American linguist Noam Chomsky has drawn attention to the rules used to change core ideas into a variety of sentences. Chomsky (1968) argues that we do not learn all the sentences we might ever utter. Rather we actively and creatively *generate* them by applying **transformation rules.** For example, the core sentence, "Dog bites man," can be transformed to:

Past: The dog bit the man.

Passive: The man was bitten by the dog.

Negative: The dog did not bite the man.

Question: Did the dog bite the man?

Children show evidence of applying transformation rules when they form sentences such as, "I runned home." The child has applied the past tense rule to the irregular English verb "to run."

The third, and perhaps most essential, characteristic of language is that it is **productive.** The great strength of any true language is that it can be used to produce new possibilities or to generate new ideas. Since words do not resemble the things they represent, they can be rearranged to produce an infinite variety of meaningful sentences (Bruner, 1966). Some are silly: "Please don't feed me to the goldfish." Some are profound: "We hold these truths to be self-evident, that all men are created equal. . . ." In either case, it is the productive quality of language that makes it such a powerful tool for thought.

Question: Do animals use language?

Animals do communicate. The cries, gestures, and mating calls of various animals have broad meanings immediately understood by other animals of the same species. For the most part, however, natural animal communication is quite limited. For example, most primates (apes and monkeys) make only a few dozen distinct cries. These have meanings that might be translated as messages such as "attack," "flee," or "food here." In the wild, animal communication appears to lack the productive quality of human language. However, recent attempts to teach language to chimpanzees have raised intriguing questions about their thinking and language abilities.

Talking Chimps   Early experiments involving attempts to teach chimps to **talk were** a dismal failure. The world record for talking **was** held by Viki, a chimp who could say only four words *(mama, papa, cup,* and *up)* after six years of intensive training (Fleming, 1974; Hayes, 1951). Then there was a breakthrough. Beatrice Gardner and Allen Gardner of the University of Reno, Nevada, used a combination of operant conditioning and imitation to teach a female chimp named Washoe to use **American Sign Language (ASL).** ASL is a set of hand gestures used by the deaf (each gesture stands for a word).

Washoe's communication skills blossomed rapidly as her "vocabulary" grew. Soon she began to put together primitive sentence strings like: "Come-gimme sweet," "Out please," "Gimme tickle," and "Open food drink." She now has a vocabulary of about 240 signs, and can construct six-word sentences. She has even tried to communicate with other chimpanzees through use of sign language (Gardner and Gardner, 1969).

Some critics are skeptical about Washoe's achievements, since her arrangement of "words" is somewhat haphazard. Children quickly learn the difference between word orders like "Give me candy" and "Me give candy." An answer to this criticism has come from the work of David Premack (1970), who taught a female chimp named Sarah to use 130 "words" consisting of plastic chips arranged on a magnetized board (see Fig. 11-7).

Since the beginning of her training, Sarah has been required to use proper word order. She has learned to answer questions, to label things "same" or "different," to classify things by color, shape, and size, and to construct compound sentences. One of her most outstanding achievements is use of sentences involving **conditional relationships:** "If Sarah take apple, then Mary give Sarah chocolate": "If Sarah take banana, then Mary no give Sarah chocolate."

Question: Can it be said with certainty that the chimps understand such interchanges?

Most researchers working with chimps feel that they have indeed communicated with them. Especially convincing are spontaneous responses made by the chimps. Washoe once "wet" on psychologist Roger Fouts' back while riding on his shoulders. When Fouts asked, with some annoyance, why she had done it, Washoe signed, "It's funny!"

Lana is another language-using chimp, trained by Duane M. Rumbaugh and his associates at the Yerkes Primate Research Center in Atlanta. Lana communicates by pressing buttons on a computer keyboard that requires her to use proper word order to be understood or rewarded. The keyboard also allows Lana to ask questions. When shown a new object Lana immediately asks, "What name of this?"

Some of the most convincing evidence on animal intelligence has come from recent work by Penny Patterson. Patterson has trained a young gorilla named Koko to use over 300 signs (which shows gorillas are as capable of learning as are chimps). Patterson considers conversations held about *past events* and *feelings* a strong indication of Koko's comprehension. For example, three days after Koko bit Patterson, the following conversation took place:

Me: "What did you do to Penny?"

Koko: "Bite."

Me: "You admit it?"

Koko: "Sorry bite scratch. Wrong bite."

Me: "Why bite?"

Koko: "Because mad."

Me: "Why mad?"

Koko: "Don't know."

(Adapted from Patterson, 1978, p. 459.)

Such interchanges may seem convincing. But communication and actual language use are two different things. Several psychologists have recently expressed doubt that apes can really use language. For one thing, the chimps rarely "speak" without prompting. Many of their seemingly original sentences turn out to be responses to questions or imitations of signs made by the teacher. Also, it often appears that the apes are simply performing *instrumental responses* to get food or other "goodies" (Savage-Rumbaugh *et al.,* 1980; Seidenberg and Petitto, 1979; Terrace, 1979). By using such responses, the apes then manipulate their trainers to get what they want. You might say that the critics believe the apes have made monkeys out

Fig. 11-7 *After reading the message, "Sarah insert apple pail banana dish" on the magnetic board, Sarah performed the actions as directed. (From "Teaching Language to an Ape" by Ann J. Premack and David Premack. Copyright © 1972 by Scientific American, Inc. All rights reserved.)*

of their trainers. Although the debate is far from resolved, such research promises to unravel some of the mysteries of language learning. In fact, it has already proven helpful for teaching language to aphasic children (children with serious language impairment) (Huges, 1974).

Learning Check

Before you read more, it might be a good idea to see if you can answer these questions.

1. A "xog" is defined as anything that is small, blue, and hairy. "Xog" is a _____ concept.

2. The connotative meaning of the word *naked* is "having no clothes."   T or F?

3. True languages are _____ because they can be used to generate new possibilities.

4. The basic speech sounds are called _____; the smallest meaningful units of speech are called

    _____.

5. One of the chimpanzee Sarah's most outstanding achievements has been the construction of sentences involving: (circle)
    negation   adult grammar   unprompted questions   conditional relationships

6. Critics consider "sentences" constructed by apes to be simple _____ responses having little meaning
    to the animal.

Answers: 1. conjunctive 2. F 3. productive 4. phonemes, morphemes 5. conditional relationships 6. instrumental

Problem Solving—
Getting an Answer in Sight

A good way to start off a discussion of problem solving is to solve a problem. Give this one a try.

> A famous ocean liner (the *Queen Ralph*) is steaming toward port at 20 miles per hour. It is 50 miles from shore when a seagull takes off from its deck and flies toward port. At the same instant, a speedboat leaves port at 30 miles per hour. The bird flies back and forth between the speedboat and the *Queen Ralph* at a speed of 40 miles per hour. How far will the bird have flown when the two boats pass?

If you don't immediately see the answer to this problem, read it again. (The answer is revealed in the "Solution by Insight" section that follows.)

We all do a tremendous amount of problem solving every day. Problem solving can be as commonplace as figuring out how to make a nonpoisonous meal out of the leftovers in the refrigerator, or as significant as developing a cure for cancer. In either case, we begin with an awareness that an answer probably exists and that by proper manipulation of the elements of thought a solution can be found. A number of different approaches to thinking and reasoning in problem solving can be identified.

Mechanical Solutions   **Mechanical solutions** may be achieved by *trial and error* or by *rote*. If I have forgotten the combination to my bike lock, I may be able to discover it by trial and error. In an era of high-speed computers, many trial and error solutions are best left to machines. A computer could generate all possible combinations of the five numbers on my lock in a split second.

Mechanical problem solving is quite inefficient when more than a few alternative solutions exist. As nearly everyone knows, if given enough time, a roomful of monkeys randomly pounding on typewriters would eventually produce all the great works of literature. However, a tireless staff of inspectors would be needed to watch for the gems

in all the gibberish. It is easy to imagine the experiment running for years before the inspector at post 15 caught the line, "To be or not to be, that is the *gesornenplatz.*" (From a skit by Bob Newhart, reported by Bennett, 1977.)

When a solution is achieved by rote, we mean that thinking has proceeded according to a learned set of rules. If you have a good background in mathematics, you may have solved the problem of the bird and the boats by rote. (I hope you didn't. There is an easier solution.)

Solutions by Understanding   Many problems are unsolvable by mechanical means or by the use of habitual modes of thought. In this case, a higher level of thinking based on *understanding* is necessary. A classic series of studies on this type of thinking has been performed by German psychologist Karl Duncker (1945). Duncker gave college students this problem:

> Given an inoperable stomach tumor and rays which at high intensity will destroy tissue (both healthy and diseased), how can the tumor be destroyed without damaging surrounding tissue? (Students were also shown the sketch in Fig. 11-8.)

Question: What did this problem show about problem solving?

Duncker asked the students to think aloud so that he could follow the course of their thinking. He found that there were two phases to successful problem solving. First, the student had to discover the **general properties** of a correct solution. This discovery was usually accomplished gradually, beginning with suggestions to desensitize surrounding tissue, to move the tumor toward the exterior, and so on. As soon as a student came to the realization that the intensity of the rays had to be lowered on their way to the tumor, a number of **functional** (workable) **solutions** could be proposed. This marked the second stage of problem solving, during which a specific solution was selected. (The correct solution, of course, is to focus weak rays from several sources on the tumor or to rotate the person's body so that the exposure of healthy tissue is minimized.)

Solution by Insight   You will recall that Köhler's apes sometimes showed *insight* in their problem solving. With humans, we say that insight has occurred when an answer suddenly appears after a period of unsuccessful thought. An insight is usually so rapid and clear that one often wonders how such an "obvious" solution could have been missed. Perhaps you experienced insight when trying to solve the problem of the boats and the bird. Since the boats will cover the 50-mile distance in exactly one hour

Fig. 11-8 *A schematic representation of Duncker's tumor problem. The dark spot represents a tumor surrounded by healthy tissue. How can the tumor be destroyed without injuring surrounding tissue? (After Duncker, 1945)*

and since the bird flies 40 miles per hour, the bird will have flown 40 miles when the boats meet. No math is necessary if you have insight into this problem. We will return to the topic of insight in a moment. Let us turn now to consideration of factors that influence problem solving.

Functional Fixedness   The ease with which a solution is achieved in problem solving is related to a variety of factors. These include complexity of the problem, novelty of the answer, motivation of the thinker, and prior experience with similar problems. In addition to these, there is a very important barrier to problem solving called **fixation**. Fixation is the tendency to get "hung up" on wrong solutions, or to become blind to other alternatives. A prime example of fixation is **functional fixedness.** Functional fixedness is the inability to see new uses (functions) for familiar objects, or for objects that have been used in a particular way.

Question: How does functional fixedness affect problem solving?

Karl Duncker, who originated the concept of functional fixedness, performed a clever study to demonstrate its operation. Duncker challenged students to mount a candle on a vertical board so that it could burn in the normal way. Duncker gave each student three candles, some matches, some cardboard boxes, some thumbtacks, and other items. Half of Duncker's subjects received these items *inside* the cardboard boxes. The others received all the items, including the boxes, laid out on a tabletop. Duncker found that when the items were in the boxes, solution of the problem was very difficult. This is because the boxes were seen as *containers,* not as items that might be part of the solution. (If you haven't guessed the solution, check Fig. 11-9.)

Functional fixedness is just one example of the mental blocks that prevent creative thinking. Here's another: How would you remove a five dollar bill placed below a stack of precariously balanced objects (without touching or moving the objects)? A good answer is to split the bill at the edge and tear it in half, gently pulling from opposite ends. Many people fail to see this solution because they have learned not to destroy things of value. In a book entitled *Conceptual Blockbusting,* James Adams (1974) lists several other barriers to creative thought (see box above).

Adams' last point requires an example. Adams says that years were wasted in unsuccessful attempts to develop a mechanical tomato picker that didn't smash tomatoes. Eventually design specialists realized they were focusing on the wrong part of the problem. The result? A new plant was developed with tougher skinned fruit that could withstand rough handling.

Common Barriers to Creative Thinking

1.   Emotional barriers: Inhibition and fear of making a fool of oneself, fear of making a mistake, inability to tolerate ambiguity, excessive self-criticism.

2.   Cultural barriers: Values which hold that fantasy is a waste of time, playfulness is for children only; reason, logic, and numbers are good; feelings, intuitions, pleasure, and humor are bad or have no place in the serious business of problem solving.

3.   Learned barriers: Conventions about uses (functional fixedness), meanings, possibilities, taboos.

4.   Perceptual barriers: Habits leading to a failure to identify important elements of a problem.

Creative Thinking— Fluency, Flexibility, and Originality

Question: What distinguishes creative thinking from more routine problem solving?

As we have noted, problem solving may be the result of thinking that is mechanical, insightful, or based on understanding. To this we can add that thought may be **inductive** (going from specific facts or observations to general principles) or **deductive** (going from general principles to specific situations). Thinking may also be **logical** (proceeding from given information to new conclusions on the basis

Fig. 11-9   *Materials for solving the candle problem were given to subjects in boxes (a) or separately (b). Functional fixedness caused by condition (a) interfered with solving the problem. The solution to the problem is shown in (c).*

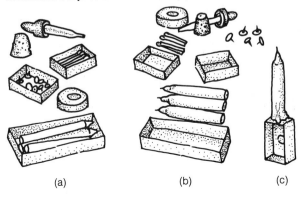

(a)   (b)   (c)

of explicit rules) or **illogical** (intuitive, associative, or personal).

Creative thinking involves all these styles of thought (in varying combinations) *plus* fluency, flexibility, and originality (Guilford, 1950). The meaning of these terms can be illustrated by returning to an earlier example. Let's say that you would like to find a creative use (or uses) for the millions of automobile tires discarded each year. The creativity of your suggestions could be rated in this way: **Fluency** is defined as the total number of suggestions you are able to make. **Flexibility** is defined as the number of times you shift from one class of possible uses to another. **Originality** refers to how novel or unusual your suggestions are. By totaling the number of times you showed fluency, flexibility, and originality, we could rate the creativity of your thinking on this problem. Speaking more generally, we would be rating your capacity for **divergent thinking.**

Divergent thinking is the most widely used measure of creative problem solving. In routine problem solving or thinking, there is one correct answer, and the problem is to find it. This leads to **convergent thought** (lines of thought converge on the correct answer). Divergent thinking is the

reverse, in which many possibilities are developed from one starting place.

There are several tests of divergent thinking. In the **Unusual Uses Test,** a person is asked to think of as many uses for an object (such as the tires just mentioned) as possible. In the **Consequences Test,** the object is to answer a question such as, "What would be the results if everyone suddenly lost the sense of balance and were unable to stay in an upright position?" Subjects try to list as many reactions as possible. In the **Anagrams Test** subjects are given a word such as *creativity* and asked to make as many new words as possible by rearranging the letters. Each of these tests can be scored for fluency, flexibility, and originality. (For an example of other tests of divergent thought, see Fig. 11-10.)

Question: Isn't creativity more than divergent thought? What if a person comes up with a large number of useless answers to a problem?

A good question. Divergent thought is definitely an important part of creative thinking, but there is more to it. To be creative, the solution to a problem must be more than

Fig. 11-10   *Some tests of divergent thinking. Creative responses are more original and more complex.* [(a) *After Wallach and Kogan, 1965;* (b) *after Barron, 1958.*]

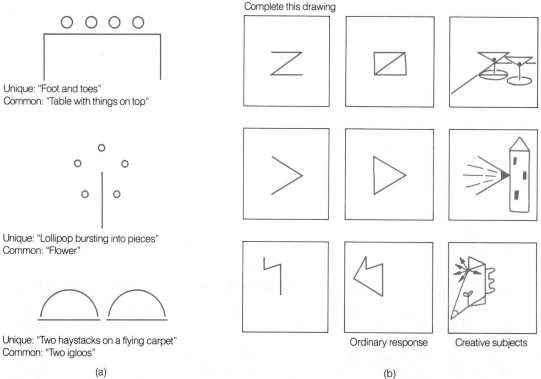

Unique: "Foot and toes"
Common: "Table with things on top"

Unique: "Lollipop bursting into pieces"
Common: "Flower"

Unique: "Two haystacks on a flying carpet"
Common: "Two igloos"

(a)

Complete this drawing

Ordinary response   Creative subjects

(b)

novel, unusual, or original. It must also be useful or meaningful, and it must meet the demands of the problem (MacKinnon, 1962). This is the dividing line between a "harebrained scheme" and a "stroke of genius." (See Figs. 11-11 and 11-12.)

Question: Is there any pattern to creative thinking?

Stages of Creative Thought   The best summary of the sequence of events in creative thinking proposes five stages that usually occur:

1. Orientation. As a first step, the problem must be defined, and important dimensions identified.
2. Preparation. In the second stage, creative thinkers saturate themselves with as much information pertaining to the problem as possible.
3. Incubation. Most major problems produce a period during which all attempted solutions will have proved futile. At this point, problem solving may proceed on a subconscious level: While the problem seems to have been set aside, it is still "cooking" in the background.
4. Illumination. The stage of incubation is often ended by a rapid insight or series of insights. These produce the "Aha!" experience, often depicted in cartoons as a light bulb appearing over the thinker's head.
5. Verification. The final step is to test and critically evaluate the solution obtained during the stage of illumination. If the solution proves faulty, the thinker reverts to the stage of incubation.

Of course, creative thought is not always so neat. After studying Beethoven's notebooks, renowned conductor Leonard Bernstein had this to say about them: ". . . Beethoven struggled with all his force. The man rejected, rewrote, scratched out, tore up, and sometimes altered a passage as many as twenty times. . . . Beethoven's manuscript looks like a bloody record of a tremendous inner battle" (Pronko, 1969). Nevertheless, the stages listed are a good summary of the most typical sequence of events.

You may find it helpful to attach the stages to the following more or less true story. Legend has it that the king of Syracuse (a city in ancient Greece) once suspected that his goldsmith had substituted cheaper metals for some of the gold in a crown and had pocketed the difference. Archimedes, a famous mathematician and thinker, was presented with the problem of discovering whether or not the king had been cheated.

Archimedes began by defining the problem (orientation): "How can I determine what metals have been used in the crown without damaging it?" He then investigated

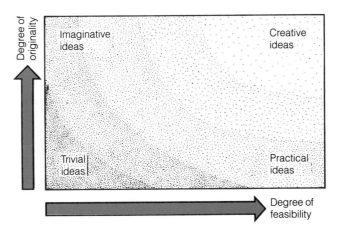

Fig. 11-11 *Creative ideas combine originality with feasibility. (Adapted from McMullan and Stocking, 1978)*

all known methods of analyzing metals (preparation). All involved cutting or melting the crown, so Archimedes was forced to temporarily set the problem aside (incubation). Then one day as he stepped into his bath, Archimedes suddenly knew he had the solution (illumination). He was so excited he is said to have run naked through the streets

Fig. 11-12 *Hat-tipping device. According to the patent, it is for "automatically effecting polite salutations by the elevation and rotation of the hat on the head of the saluting party when said person bows to the person or persons saluted." In addition to being original or novel, a creative solution must fit the demands of the problem. Is this a creative solution to the "problem" of hat-tipping?*

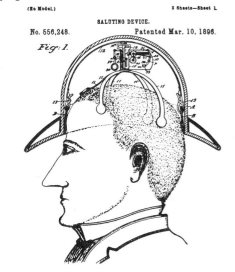

Creativity Profile

The following qualities have repeatedly been found to characterize creative individuals:

1. An unusual awareness of people, events, and problems.
2. A high degree of verbal fluency.
3. Flexibility with numbers, concepts, media; flexibility in social situations.
4. Originality of ideas and expressions, a sense of humor.
5. An ability to abstract, organize, and synthesize.
6. A high energy/activity level.
7. Persistence at tasks of interest.
8. Impatience with routine or repetitive tasks.
9. A willingness to take risks.
10. A vivid and spontaneous imagination; this may take the form of "fibbing" or imaginary companions in childhood.

(Source: Meeker, 1978.)

shouting "Eureka, eureka!" (I have found it, I have found it!). On observing his own body floating in the bath, Archimedes realized that different metals would displace different amounts of water. All that remained was to test the solution (verification). Archimedes placed an amount of gold (equal in weight to that given the goldsmith) in a tub of water. He marked the water level and removed the gold. He then placed the crown in the water. If it were pure gold, the crown would raise the water to exactly the same level. Unfortunately, the purity of the crown and the fate of the goldsmith are to this day unknown!

Question: What makes a person creative?

The Creative Personality   According to the popular stereotype, highly creative people are eccentric in thought and appearance, introverted, neurotic, socially inept, unbalanced in their interests, and frequently, on the edge of madness. Although some well-known artists and musicians cultivate a public image to fit the stereotype, there is little truth in it. Studies by psychologist Donald MacKinnon paint a very different picture of the creative person. After extensive interviews and testing of creative writers, archi-

tects, mathematicians, and scientists, MacKinnon (1968) drew these conclusions:

1. Although most of the people studied were above average in intelligence, there was no difference in average IQ between highly creative, and less creative people in the same field. Others have drawn the same conclusion. A certain minimum level of intelligence may be necessary for successful work in a particular field, but at any given level of IQ, some people are creative and some are not. There is little correlation between creativity and high IQ (Taylor, 1978; Nelson and Crutchfield, 1970).

2. Creative people usually have a greater than average range of knowledge and interests, and they are more fluent in combining ideas from various sources. In a sense, the creative person approaches problems with the stage of preparation partially completed. It is inaccurate to describe creative persons as narrow or unbalanced.

3. The creative person has an openness to experience. Creative males are able to give more expression to the "feminine" side of their personality; creative females can be "masculine" as well as "feminine." The creative person accepts irrational thought and even encourages it as a source of novelty and originality. Creative people show a relative lack of inhibition about their thoughts, feelings, and fantasies.

4. MacKinnon's subjects enjoyed symbolic thought, ideas, concepts, and possibilities. At work, they combined dedication and productivity with a playful attitude. They tended to be interested in truth, form, and beauty, rather than in recognition or success. Their creative work was an end in itself.

5. Highly creative people value independence and have a preference for complexity. They delight in the challenge of an unfinished or unresolved problem. They are unconventional and nonconforming primarily in their work; otherwise they do not have particularly unusual, outlandish, or bizarre personalities. Indeed, most creative personalities resemble the profile in the accompanying box.

Question: Can creativity be learned?

Most of what we know about creativity remains preliminary, despite much research on the topic. Nevertheless, it is beginning to look as if some of the thinking skills that contribute to creative problem solving can be taught. In the "Applications" section of this chapter you will find a brief discussion of some helpful strategies.

Learning Check

1. Insight refers to rote, or deductive, problem solving.   T or F?

2. The first phase in problem solving by understanding is to discover the general properties of a correct solution.   T or F?

3. The term *fixation* refers to the point at which a helpful insight becomes fixed in one's thinking.   T or F?

4. Functional fixedness is usually an aid to problem solving.   T or F?

5. Fluency, flexibility, and originality are characteristics of:

    a. convergent thought   *b.* deductive thinking
    c. creative thought   *d.* trial and error solutions

6. List the stages of creative thinking in the correct order:

    _____ , _____ ,

    _____ , _____ ,

    _____ .

7. An ability to organize, abstract, and synthesize ideas blocks creativity; these are noncreative qualities.   T or F?

8. To be creative, an original idea must also be practical or feasible.   T or F?

Answers: **1.** F **2.** T **3.** F **4.** F **5.** c **6.** orientation, preparation, incubation, illumination, verification **7.** F **8.** T

Resources Summary

● Thinking is the manipulation and combination of *internal representations* of external stimuli or situations.
● Animals reveal a capacity for thought when they solve *delayed response problems,* and in some cases, problems requiring *insight* or *implicit trial and error.*
● Four basic units of thought are *images, concepts, muscular responses,* and *language.*
● Most people have internal images of one kind or another. Images may be *stored* or *created.* Sometimes they cross normal sense boundaries in a type of imagery called *synesthesia.* Images used in problem solving may be three-dimensional, and their size may change.
● Muscular images are created by memory of actions or by *implicit actions. Kinesthetic sensations* and *micromovements* seem to help structure the flow of thought for many people.
● A *concept* is a generalized idea of a class of objects or events. *Concept formation* is often based on *positive and negative instances* and on *rule learning.* In practice, concept identification frequently makes use of *prototypes,* or general models of the concept class. Concepts may be classified as *conjunctive* ("and" concepts), *disjunctive* ("either-or" concepts), or *relational.*

● The *denotative* meaning of a word or concept is its dictionary definition. *Connotative* meaning is personal or emotional. Connotative meaning can be measured with the *semantic differential.*
● Language allows events to be *encoded* into *symbols* for easy mental manipulation. Thinking in language is influenced by meaning. The study of meaning is called *semantics.* The idea that language can shape thinking is known as *linguistic determinism.*
● Language carries meaning by combining a set of symbols according to a set of rules (*grammar*), which includes rules about word order (*syntax*). A true language is *productive,* and can be used to generate new ideas or possibilities.
● Animal communication is relatively limited because it lacks symbols that can be rearranged easily. Attempts to teach chimpanzees systems such as *American Sign Language* suggest to some that primates are capable of language use. Others question this conclusion.
● The solution to a problem may be arrived at *mechanically* (by trial and error, or by rote application of rules), but mechanical solutions are frequently inefficient or ineffective except where aided by computer.

● Solutions by *understanding* usually begin with discovery of the *general properties* of an answer. Next comes proposal of a number of *functional solutions.*

● When understanding leads to a rapid reorganization of a problem whereby the solution becomes obvious it is said that *insight* has occurred. Insight and other problem solving can be blocked by *fixation. Functional fixedness* is a common fixation, but *emotional blocks, cultural values, learned conventions,* and *perceptual habits* are also a problem.

● Creative thinking requires *divergent* thought, characterized by *fluency, flexibility,* and *originality.* To be creative a solution must be useful or meaningful as well as original.

● Five stages often seen in creative problem solving are *orientation, preparation, incubation, illumination,* and *verification.* Not all creative thinking fits this pattern.

● Studies suggest the *creative personality* has a number of identifiable characteristics, most of which contradict popular stereotypes. There appears to be little or no correlation between IQ and creativity.

━━━━━ Applications ━━━━━

Difficulties in Thinking and Problem Solving

We all at one time or another experience difficulties in thinking and problem solving. The following should alert you to some of the more common problems.

Rigid Mental Set Try the problems pictured in Fig. 11-13. If you have difficulty, try asking yourself what *assumptions* you are making. The problems are designed to demonstrate the limiting effects of a mental set. (The answers to these problems, along with an explanation of the sets which prevent their solution, are found on page 261.) In addition to the assumptions and mental sets we bring to a problem, problems themselves may produce a disruptive set. A simple example is the following: The name "Polk" is pronounced "poke," the word "folk" is pronounced "foke," and the white of an egg is pronounced _____? Here is another example. See if you can unscramble each set of letters to make a word that uses all the letters:

MEST _____,
LFAE_____,
DUB _____,
STKAL _____,
OTOR _____,
LTEPA _____.

Now try a new list:

FINEK _____,
OPONS_____,
KROF _____,
PUC _____,
SDIH _____,
LTEPA _____.

Did you notice that the last problem was the same in each case? Many people don't, and end up solving the problem twice. To complete the first list *(stem, leaf, bud, stalk, root)*, the item LTEPA is usually unscrambled as PETAL. In the second list *(knife, spoon, fork, cup, dish)* LTEPA becomes PLATE for many people.

Now that you have been forewarned about the danger of faulty assumptions see if you can correctly answer the following questions.

1. Argentinians do not have a fourth of July.   T or F?
2. How many birthdays does the average person have?
3. A farmer had nineteen sheep. All but nine died. How many sheep did he have left?
4. It is not unlawful for a man living in Winston-Salem, North Carolina, to be buried west of the Mississippi River. T or F?
5. Some months have 30 days, some have 31. How many months have 28 days?

6. I have two coins that together total 55 cents. One of the coins is not a nickel. What are the two coins?
7. It would be far better to have an elephant eat you than a gorilla.   T or F?

These questions are designed to cause thinking errors. Here are the answers:

1. F. Of course they have a fourth of July. What would they do, go from the third to the fifth?   **2.** One, celebrated each year.   **3.** Nineteen—nine alive and ten dead.   **4.** F. It is against the law to bury a living man anywhere.   **5.** All of them.   **6.** A half-dollar and a nickel. One of the coins is not a nickel, but the other one is!   **7.** F. It would be better to have the elephant eat the gorilla. (Read it again.)

If you got caught on any of the questions, consider it an additional reminder of the value of actively challenging the assumptions you are making in any instance of problem solving.

Problems with Logic A major thinking difficulty centers on the process of *logical reasoning*. Simple sequences of logical thought can be arranged as a set of *premises* (assumptions) and a *conclusion*. This format is called a **syllogism.** A syllogism can be evaluated for the *validity* of its reasoning and for the *truth* of its *conclusion*. It is entirely possible to draw true conclusions using faulty

Fig. 11-13 (a) *Nine dots are arranged in a square. Can you connect them by drawing four continuous straight lines (without lifting your pencil from the paper)?* (b) *Six matches must be arranged to make four triangles. The triangles must be the same size, with each side equal to the length of one match. (The solutions to these problems appear on page 261.)*

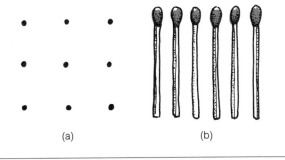

(a)   (b)

Applications

logic, or to draw false conclusions using valid logic. The examples below show how this is possible.

Syllogism I
    All humans are mortal.
    (Major premise)
    All women are humans.
    (Minor premise)
    Therefore, all women are mortal.
    (Conclusion)

Comment: As you can see from the diagram in Fig. 11-14, the logic of this syllogism is valid. Since our premises are true, this means the conclusion is true. The diagram shows all women included within the boundaries of mortals.

Syllogism II
    All women are humans.
    All humans are mortal.
    Therefore, all mortals are women.

Comment: In this example the conclusion drawn is false, because the reasoning is invalid. The diagram for Syllogism I shows that all mortals are not women. Notice how little the syllogism has to be changed to produce a false conclusion. Now consider Syllogism III.

Syllogism III
    All psychologists are weird.
    Mary is a psychologist.
    Therefore, Mary is weird.

Comment: In this case the reasoning is valid, but the conclusion is false, because the first premise is false. All psychologists are *not* weird. (Honest!) Now let's consider one more syllogism.

Syllogism IV
    All ducks have wings.
    All birds have wings.
    Therefore, all ducks are birds.

Comment: This syllogism shows the importance of paying close attention to logic. The reasoning appears to be valid since the conclusion is true, but substitute ''bats,'' or ''airplanes,'' for ''ducks'' and see how the conclusion reads. It is a good idea to get in the habit of questioning the logic used by politicians, and advertisers . . . and psychologists, for that matter!

Fig. 11-14

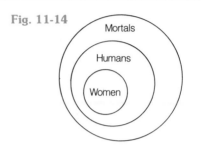

Oversimplification It may be an oversimplification to say so, but oversimplification is another basic source of thinking errors. There are two types of oversimplification that are particularly troublesome. The first is **all-or-nothing thinking.** Classifying things as absolutely right or wrong, good or bad, acceptable or unacceptable, or honest or dishonest prevents appreciation of the complexity of most life problems. The second problem is thinking in terms of **stereotypes.** Stereotypes are particularly troublesome when human relationships are involved. An overly simplified, inaccurate, or rigid picture of men, blacks, women, Republicans, liberals, police officers, or any other group of people leads to muddled thinking about individual members of the group. Try to look for this and the other errors in your own thinking habits.

Enhancing Creativity—Brainstorms

Thomas Edison once explained his creative accomplishments by saying, ''Genius is 1 percent inspiration and 99 percent perspiration.'' Many studies of creativity show that ''genius'' owes as much to persistence and dedication as it does to inspiration (Pronko, 1969). Once it is recognized that ''creativity'' can be hard work, then something can be done to enhance it. Here are some suggestions on how to begin (from Hayes, 1978, and indicated sources).

1. Define the problem broadly. Whenever possible, enlarge the definition of problems for which you seek creative solutions. For instance, assume your problem is defined as, ''Design a better doorway.'' This is likely to lead to ordinary solutions. Why not change the problem to, ''Design a better way to get through a wall''? Now your solutions will be more original. Best of all might be to state the problem as, ''Find a better way to define separate areas for living and working.'' This could lead to truly creative solutions (Adams, 1974).

Let's say that you are the leader of a group interested in designing a new can opener. Wisely, you ask the group to

---

Applications

think about *opening* in general, rather than about can openers. This was just the approach used in developing the pop-top can. As the design group discussed the concept of opening, one member suggested that nature has its own openers, like the soft seam on a pea pod. Instead of a new can-opening tool, the group invented the self-opening can (Fig. 11-16) (Stein, 1974).

2. Create the right atmosphere. A variety of experiments show that people make more original, spontaneous, and imaginative responses when exposed to others (models) doing the same (Rosenthal and Zimmerman, 1978). If you want to become more creative, spend time around creative people. This is the premise underlying much education in art, theater, dance, and music.

3. Allow time for incubation. Trying to hurry, or to force a problem's solution, may simply encourage fixation on a deadend. In one representative experiment, subjects were asked to state as many consequences as possible that would follow if people no longer needed to eat. Most subjects rapidly produced several ideas and then ran dry. After working for a time, some subjects were interrupted and required to do another task for 20 minutes. Then they returned to the original question. The interruption produced an improvement in their score, even though they worked no longer than the control group (Fulgosi and Guilford, 1968).

4. Seek varied input. Remember, creativity requires divergent thinking. Rather than digging deeper with logic, you are attempting to shift your mental "prospecting" to new areas. The author knows a poet who cuts newspapers into small pieces and scatters them on the floor. He then rearranges pieces that have fallen next to each other, until interesting ideas begin to emerge.

Edward de Bono (1970) suggests a similar technique for breaking mental sets when you are stuck on a problem. De Bono recommends that you randomly look up words in the dictionary and relate each to the problem. Often this activity will trigger a fresh perspective or open a new avenue. For instance, let's say you are asked to come up with new ways to clean oil off a beach, and you draw a blank. Following de Bono's suggestion, you would read the following randomly selected words, relate each to the problem, and see what thoughts are triggered: *weed, rust, poor, magnify, foam, gold, frame, hole, diagonal, vacuum, tribe, puppet, nose, link, drift, portrait, cheese, coal.*

5. Look for analogies. Many "new" problems are really old problems in new clothing. Representing a problem in

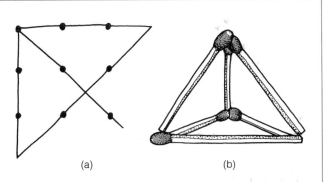

Fig. 11-15 *Problem solutions.* (a) *The dot problem can be solved by extending the lines beyond the square formed by the dots. Most people assume incorrectly that they may not do this.* (b) *The match problem can be solved by building a three-dimensional pyramid. Most people assume that the matches must be arranged on a flat surface.*

a variety of ways is often the key to solution. Most problems become easier to solve when they are effectively represented. For example consider this problem:

Two backpackers start up a steep trail at 6 A.M. They hike all day, resting occasionally, and arrive at the top at 6 P.M. The next day they start back down the trail at 6 A.M. On the way down they stop several times and vary their pace. They arrive back at 6 P.M. On the way down, one of the hikers, who is a mathematician, tells the other that she has realized that they will pass a point on the trail at exactly the same time as they did the day before. Her nonmathematical friend finds this hard to believe, since on both days they have stopped and started many times, and changed their pace. The problem: Is the mathematician right?

Perhaps you will see the answer to this problem immediately. If not, think of it this way: What if there were *two* pairs of backpackers, one going up the trail, the second coming down, and both hiking on the *same day*? It becomes ob-

Fig. 11-16

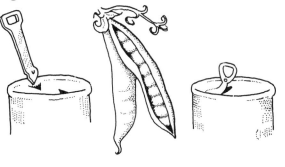

Applications

vious that the two pairs of hikers will pass each other at some point on the trail. Therefore, they will be at the same place at the same time. The mathematician was right (adapted from Hayes, 1978).

An alternative approach to enhancing creativity is called *brainstorming.* Although brainstorming is a group technique, it can be applied to individual problem solving as well.

Question: What is brainstorming? How is it done?

Brainstorming   The essence of brainstorming is that *production* and *criticism* of ideas are kept completely separate. To encourage divergent thinking in group problem solving, participants are encouraged to produce as many ideas as possible without fear of criticism or evaluation. Only *after* a brainstorming session is complete are ideas reconsidered and evaluated (Haefele, 1962). As ideas are freely generated, an interesting **cross-stimulation effect** takes place in which one participant's ideas trigger ideas for others. The four basic rules for successful brainstorming are:

1. Criticism of an idea is absolutely barred. All evaluation is to be deferred until after the session.
2. Modification or combination with other ideas is encouraged. Don't worry about giving credit for ideas or keeping them neat. Mix them up!
3. Quantity of ideas is sought. In the early stages of brainstorming, quantity is more important than quality. Toss out lots of ideas.
4. Unusual, remote, or wild ideas are sought. Let your imagination run amok!

Question: How is brainstorming applied to individual problem solving?

The essential point to remember is to *suspend judgment.* Ideas should first be produced without regard for logic, organization, accuracy, practicality, or any other evaluation. In writing an essay, for instance, you would begin by writing ideas in any order, the more the better, just as they occur to you. Later you would go back and reorganize, rewrite, and criticize your efforts.

As an aid to achieving steps 2, 3, and 4 of the brainstorming method, you might find this checklist helpful for encouraging original thought. It can be used to see if you have overlooked a possible solution (adapted from Parnes, 1967).

Creativity Checklist

1. Consider other uses for all elements of the problem. (This is designed to alert you to fixations that may be blocking creativity.)
2. Adapt. How could other objects, ideas, procedures, or solutions be adapted to this particular problem?
3. Modify. Imagine changing anything and everything that could be changed.
4. Magnify. Exaggerate everything you can think of. Think on a grand scale.
5. Minify. What if everything were scaled down? What if there were no differences between elements of the problem? ''Shrink'' the problem down to size.
6. Substitute. How could one object, idea, or procedure be substituted for another?
7. Rearrange. Break the problem into pieces and shuffle them.
8. Reverse. Consider reverse orders, opposites, and turn things inside out.
9. Combine. This one speaks for itself.

By making a habit of subjecting a problem to each of these procedures, you should be able to greatly reduce the chances that you will overlook a useful, original, or ''creative'' solution.

Learning Check

1. In evaluating a syllogism, it is possible to draw a true conclusion with faulty logic, or a false conclusion with valid logic.   T or F?
2. Stereotyping is an example of oversimplification in thinking.   T or F?
3. Exposure to creative models has been shown to enhance creativity.   T or F?
4. In brainstorming, each idea is critically evaluated as it is generated.   T or F?
5. Defining a problem broadly produces a ''cross-stimulation effect'' that can inhibit creative thinking.   T or F?

Answers: 1. T 2. T 3. T 4. F 5. F

=== Exploration ===

Daydreams and Fantasy—In the Land of Make-Believe

Has your reading of this chapter been interrupted by a daydream? Clinical psychologist Jerome Singer has found that most people daydream sometime each day. Why do we do so? And what do we know about this unique form of thought? Let's see.

Question: What are most daydreams about?

Content One early study of college students found that most daydreams are about vocational success, sex and romance, money and possessions, achievement, or physical attractiveness (Shafer and Shoben, 1956). In another study, Cameron and his associates (1968) found that students attending a lecture spent nearly one-fourth of the lecture time daydreaming, most often about sex. (I'm sure you can guess who got the starring role in these fantasies!) Daydreams, it seems, tend to reflect areas of current interest or concern in one's life.

Two of the most common daydream "plots" are the **conquering hero** and the **suffering martyr** themes. In a conquering hero fantasy, the daydreamer is a famous, rich, or powerful person: a star, athlete, musician, famous surgeon, brilliant lawyer, or magnificent lover. Themes such as these seem to reflect mastery needs and escape from the frustrations and compromises of everyday life. Suffering martyr daydreams are built around feelings of being neglected, hurt, rejected, or unappreciated by others. In suffering martyr fantasies some event occurs that causes others to regret their actions and to realize what a *wonderful person* the daydreamer was all along. At one time or another just about everyone has felt misunderstood or unappreciated. These feelings seem to underlie suffering martyr daydreams.

Question: Do the daydreams of men and women differ?

Not to any great degree, although Singer (1974) has found a small bias along the lines of the traditional sex roles and values of our culture. Women tend slightly toward more personal, emotional themes, and fantasies related to physical attractiveness; men slightly favor active, athletic, achieving, or heroic themes.

Question: Are most daydreams good or bad?

Patterns Singer found three patterns in fantasy, two negative, and one positive. Some people find their daydreams distracting. These people have difficulty concentrating, their mind wanders, and their daydreams often make them anxious. A second pattern is represented by the person who has very negative daydreams filled with unpleasant emotions, guilt, self-torment, fears of failure, hostility, aggression, and self-doubt. Such people definitely do not enjoy their daydreams. The majority of people fall into a third category—the "happy daydreamer." These people have pleasant daydreams and enjoy them, using them for self-amusement, future planning, problem solving, etc.

Question: Why do we daydream?

Benefits Daydreams often fill a need for stimulation when a person must perform a routine or monotonous task. They also improve the ability to delay immediate pleasures so that future goals can be achieved. In this respect, fantasies can help define future plans and aspirations by allowing the daydreamer to try on various roles, lifestyles, and occupations.

Fantasies often act as a substitute source of gratification at times of frustration or deprivation. During World War II, for example, psychologists studied 32 conscientious objectors who had volunteered to go on a semistarvation diet for six months. By the end of the twenty-fifth week, food dominated their thoughts, talk, and daydreams. Some men even hung pictures of hearty meals or tempting desserts on the walls to gaze at and daydream about (Keys *et al.*, 1950).

In everyday terms, fantasy can be a valuable outlet for frustrated impulses. If you have a momentary urge to kill the fool in front of you on the highway, substituting fantasy for action may avert disaster. Laboratory studies confirm that discharging hostility in fantasy can reduce the impulse to behave aggressively (Biblow, 1973).

Perhaps the greatest value of fantasy is its contribution to creativity. In the imaginative realm of fantasy, nothing is impossible—a quality allowing for tremendous fluency and flexibility of thought. Since creativity is a balance between rational and nonrational thought, and since it relies

Exploration

heavily on divergent thinking, fantasy is directly linked to creativity.

Question: Then should fantasy and daydreaming be encouraged?

There are, of course, limits to anything. If you spend so many waking hours in a dream world that you are unable to pass your classes, you are no longer having fantasies—you are being had by your fantasies. More generally, however, fantasy and daydreaming are associated with positive emotional adjustment, lower levels of overt aggression, and greater mental flexibility or creativity (Singer, 1974).

Prospect   In childhood, fantasy and make-believe play are accepted and encouraged. As children grow older they are often expected to "quit daydreaming and pay attention." Whereas it is true that discipline and logic in thought are valuable, it can be argued that something of importance is lost when fantasy is discouraged. Albert Einstein, one of the world's most celebrated thinkers, was—in his own words—"disorderly and a dreamer."

Some psychologists believe we overemphasize convergent thinking, and urge greater use of imagination in education (Jones, 1968). Preliminary work indicates that a simple thing like giving children ambiguous toys leads to a greater variety of play themes and more interesting play (Pulaski, 1973). You might find it interesting to think about how else imagination and creativity might be encouraged in children or adults. Think of the relationship between fantasy and your own moments of creative insight. What suggestions would you make? Use your imagination!

Questions for Discussion

1. If you suddenly lost your ability to internally represent problems, what changes would you have to make?

2. In your opinion, are chimps trained to use hand signs really using language? Why or why not?

3. Describe a time when you have used imagery to solve a problem. What are the advantages and disadvantages of imagery in comparison to other units of thought?

4. How do differences in connotative meaning contribute to arguments and misunderstandings? Do you think connotative meaning could or should be standardized?

5. The text implies that animals communicate, but do not use language in the human sense. Do you agree? Can you give an example of animal communication that qualifies as a language?

6. Think of the most creative person you know. What is that person like? How does he or she differ from your less creative acquaintances?

7. In your opinion, should measures of divergent or creative thinking be used to select students for college admission? Why or why not?

8. What effects would you expect the following to have on fantasy: Television? Highly realistic toys? Free or unstructured time? High levels of stress or anxiety? Skits, role-taking, or acting? Sensory deprivation? Sensory overload?

Suggestions for Further Reading

Adams, J. *Conceptual Blockbusting.* Freeman, 1974.

Bourne, L. E., B. R. Ekstrand, and R. L. Dominowski. *The Psychology of Thinking.* Prentice-Hall, 1971.

De Bono, E. *Lateral Thinking: Creativity Step by Step.* Harper & Row, 1970.

Koberg, D., and J. Bagnall. *The Universal Traveler.* Kaufmann, 1974.

Koestler, A. *The Act of Creation.* Macmillan, 1964.

Mayer, R. E. *Thinking and Problem Solving.* Scott, Foresman & Co., 1977.

Patterson, F., and E. Linden. *The Education of Koko.* Holt, Rinehart and Winston, 1981.

Singer, J. L. *Daydreaming: An Introduction to the Experimental Study of Inner Experience.* Random House, 1966.

Terrace, H. S. *Nim.* Random House, 1979.

Contents

Part IV

Actions
and
Reactions

12

Motivation

Flight of the Gossamer Albatross

What would it feel like to pedal an airplane over the English Channel? In 1979, biologist Bryan Allen found out the hard way by serving as pilot and "engine" for the first human-powered flight over the Channel. Allen pedaled a delicate aircraft, the Gossamer Albatross, *22.5 miles across the Channel in a grueling three-hour flight. For his effort, a team headed by aeronautics engineer Paul MacCready collected a prize of $220,000. But money was the last thing on Allen's mind as he drove himself to the limits of endurance, fighting headwinds, thirst, leg cramps, and exhaustion. The following excerpts are from Allen's (1979) account of the flight.*

6:59 A.M. At last, word comes over the radio . . . "We have France in sight—four miles to go. . . ."

Four miles or four hundred. I'm fading now and know it. Gradually the head winds have been building up . . . I talk to myself . . . Don't give up now, you *can* do it! As I waver between hope and despair, the radio crackles again:

"Altitude six inches, six inches; get it up, you've got to get it up!"

7:29 A.M. One mile. Less distance than I had flown *Gossamer Condor* two years before for the original Kremer prize. Then, however, there were no head winds or turbulence, no thirst, no cramps . . . Despite the cramps, I struggle back up to five feet. "Against all hope," I repeat to myself, "against all hope."

7:36 A.M. Four hundred yards to shore . . . One hundred yards now. I am running on reserves I never knew I had. . . .

Motivation *This chapter is about motivation; about goals, needs, and the dynamics of behavior. Bryan Allen's final burst of effort ("I am running on reserves I never knew I had. . . .") is but one example of highly motivated behavior—behavior ranging from eating and drinking to feats such as Allen's historic flight. How do we explain such diversity? The answer is, by considering a broad sweep of ideas—from "feeding centers" in the brain to Abraham Maslow's concept of self-actualization. The pages that follow are an introduction to some of the most interesting and useful of these ideas.*

Survey Questions Are there different types of motives? What causes hunger? Thirst? Overeating? In what ways are pain avoidance and the sex drive unusual? Is there a connection between arousal and motivation? How are motives learned? Are some motives more basic than others? What is behavioral dieting? Intrinsic motivation? Job enrichment? Is there any truth to biorhythm theory?

===== Resources =====

Motivation—Forces That Push and Pull

We move. Our behavior is directed toward different goals. Some goals are pursued more vigorously than others. The same goal may be pursued for different reasons, or different goals may be pursued for the same reasons. We use the concept of motivation to explain each of these basic aspects of behavior. To be more specific, **motivation** refers to "the dynamics of behavior, the process of initiating, sustaining, and directing activities of the organism" (Goldenson, 1970b).

Question: Can you clarify that?

Yes. Let's relate the concept of motivation to a simple sequence of activity:

> Liz is studying (psychology, of course) in the library. She begins to feel hungry and stops to check her pockets for a piece of gum. She resumes studying, but thoughts of food begin to interrupt her concentration. Her stomach growls. She feels restless and decides to buy an apple from a vending machine. The machine is empty, so she goes to the cafeteria. Closed. She returns to the library, packs up her books, and drives home, where she prepares a meal and eats. At last her hunger is satisfied, and she again resumes studying.

Liz's food seeking was *initiated* by her bodily need for food; it was *sustained* because her need was not immediately met; and her activities were *directed* by possible sources of food. Notice too that her food seeking was *terminated* by achieving her goal.

A Model of Motivation   Many motivated activities can be thought of as beginning with a **need**. The need that initiated Liz's search for food was a depletion of necessary substances within the cells of her body. Needs cause a psychological state or feeling called a **drive** to develop. (The drive is hunger, in Liz's case.) Drives activate a **response** (or a series of actions) designed to attain a **goal** that will relieve the need. Relieving the need temporarily ends the motivational chain of events. Thus, a simple model of motivation can be shown in this way:

$$\text{NEED} \rightarrow \text{DRIVE} \rightarrow \text{RESPONSE} \rightarrow \text{GOAL}$$
$$\text{(NEED REDUCTION)}$$

Question: Why use the terms "need" and "drive"? Aren't they the same thing?

We need both terms to discuss motivation because the strength of needs and of drives may not be the same. If you were to begin fasting, your bodily need for food would increase daily, but you would probably find yourself less "hungry" on the seventh day of fasting than you were on the first. Your need increases, but the hunger drive comes and goes and may disappear at times.

Before we consider the preceding a complete model of motivation, let us observe Liz's eating behavior on another occasion:

> Liz has gone out to dinner at a fine restaurant. There, she consumes soup, salad, a large steak, a large baked potato, one-half of a freshly baked loaf of bread, two pieces of Italian cheesecake, and four cups of coffee. After the meal she remarks about her discomfort from having overeaten. Soon after Liz gets home, her roommate arrives with a strawberry pie. Liz exclaims that strawberry pie is her favorite dessert and proceeds to eat three good-sized pieces and has a cup of coffee to "wash it down."

Is this hunger? Certainly we can believe that Liz's extra-large meal was enough to satisfy her biological needs for food.

Question: What effect does this story have on the model of motivation?

This story illustrates that motivated behavior can be energized by external stimuli, as well as by the "push" of internal needs. The "pull" exerted by a goal is called its **incentive value.** Some goals are so desirable (strawberry pie, for example) that they motivate behavior in the absence of internal need. Other goals are so low in incentive value that they will be rejected even though they might meet the internal need. Fresh, live grubs, for instance, are considered a delicacy in some parts of the world. Grubs are actually an excellent source of protein, but it is doubtful that the average American could eat them no matter how hungry he or she might be.

In most instances, it is helpful to recognize that actions are energized by a combination of internal needs *and* external incentives, and that a strong state of need may make a less attractive incentive into a desirable goal. You may never have eaten a grub, but chances are good that you have eaten some pretty horrible "leftovers" when the refrigerator was bare. Incentives also help account for motives that do not seem to have any identifiable internal need, such as drives for success, status, or approval (see Fig. 12-1).

This discussion may sound a long way from questions such as, "Why do people climb mountains?"; "Why is my aunt so mean?"; or, "Why do people skyjack airplanes?"

(or rob banks, or batter children, or collect stamps). It is. Many of the "motivation" questions put to psychologists are really questions about personality, learning, adjustment, or other psychological processes.

As psychologists have studied it, motivation is a blending of biology and psychology. The psychologist would like to know how biological needs for the likes of food, water, air, or sleep are translated into the drives of hunger, thirst, and so on. Also of interest is the question of how we acquire more subtle needs for things such as friendship, achievement, status, money, or knowledge.

Types of Motives For the purpose of study, motives can be divided into three major categories:

1. Primary motives are based on biological needs that must be met for survival. The most important primary motives are: hunger, thirst, pain avoidance, and needs for air, sleep, elimination of wastes, and regulation of body temperature. Primary motives are unlearned.

2. Stimulus motives also appear to be innate, but they are not necessary for mere survival of the organism. Their purpose seems to be to provide useful information about the environment and stimulation to the nervous system. The stimulus motives include: activity, curiosity, exploration, manipulation, and physical contact.

3. Learned, or secondary, motives account for the great diversity of human activities suggested by the "Chapter Preview." Behavior like Bryan Allen's flight over the English Channel is probably best understood in terms of learned motives or goals. Many secondary motives are related to acquired needs for affiliation (the need to be with others), approval, status, security, and achievement. The important motives of fear and aggression also appear to be subject to learning.

Primary Motives and Homeostasis—Keeping the Home Fires Burning

How important is food in your life? Water? Sleep? Air? Temperature regulation? For most of us, satisfying these biological needs is so habitual there is a tendency to overlook how much of our behavior they actually direct. But exaggerate any of these needs through famine, shipwreck, poverty, near-drowning, or exposure, and their powerful grip on behavior becomes evident. We are, after all, still animals in many ways. As Abraham Maslow pointed out, biological needs tend to be *prepotent* (dominant) over psychological needs or motives. If your survival is threatened by starvation, lack of water, or a need for oxygen,

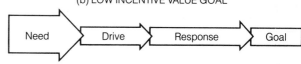

(a) HIGH INCENTIVE VALUE GOAL

Need → Drive → Response → Goal +

(b) LOW INCENTIVE VALUE GOAL

Need → Drive → Response → Goal

Fig. 12-1 *Eating may be motivated by internal needs or external incentives* (top). *Needs and incentives interact to determine drive strength* (bottom). (a) *Moderate need combined with a high-incentive goal produces a strong drive.* (b) *Even when a strong need exists, drive strength may be moderate if a goal's incentive value is low.*

you will probably set aside needs for prestige, achievement, approval, and the like, until your more pressing physical needs are met. (This idea will be discussed at a later point in the chapter.) The biological drives are essential because they maintain **homeostasis** (HOE-me-oh-STAY-sis), or bodily equilibrium (Cannon, 1932).

Question: What is homeostasis?

The term *homeostasis* means standing steady, or steady state. Within the body there are "ideal" levels for body temperature, concentration of various chemicals in the blood, blood pressure, and so forth. When the body deviates from these ideal levels, automatic reactions restore equilibrium. You might find it helpful to think of the homeostatic mechanisms as being similar in operation to a *thermostat* set at a particular temperature.

A (Very) Short Course on Thermostats

If room temperature falls below the level set on a thermostat, the heat is automatically turned on to warm the room. When the heat equals or slightly exceeds the ideal temperature, it is automatically turned off. In this way, room temperature is maintained in a state of equilibrium hovering around the ideal level.

In the human body the first reactions to disequilibrium are also automatic. For example, if you become too hot, blood flow to body surfaces is increased, muscular activity is inhibited, and perspiring begins, thus lowering body temperature. Reactions such as these may take place without any awareness on your part. You become aware of the need to maintain homeostasis only when driven by continued disequilibrium to seek shade, warmth, food, water, and so forth.

Since hunger is one of the most interesting and completely understood of the primary drives, we will examine it in detail before returning to a discussion of biological drives in general. But before reading more, you may find it helpful to complete the learning check that follows.

Learning Check

1. Motives _____, sustain, and _____ activities.

2. Needs provide the _____ of motivation, whereas incentives provide the _____.

   Classify the following needs or motives by placing the correct letter in the blank.

   A. Primary motive   **B.** Stimulus motive   **C.** Secondary motive

3. _____ curiosity   6. _____ thirst

4. _____ status   7. _____ achievement

5. _____ sleep   8. _____ physical contact

9. The maintenance of bodily equilibrium is called thermostasis.   T or F?

10. A goal high in incentive value may create a drive in the absence of any internal need.   T or F?

Answers: 1. initiate, direct   2. push, pull   3. B   4. C   5. A   6. A   7. C   8. B   9. F   10. T

Hunger—Pardon Me, That's Just My Hypothalamus Growling

Question: What causes hunger?

When you feel hungry, you probably associate a desire for food with sensations from your stomach. This, sensibly enough, is where the search for hunger began. In an early study, Cannon and Washburn (1912) decided to see if the contractions of an empty stomach cause hunger. To do this, Washburn trained himself to swallow a toy balloon. Once it was in the stomach, the balloon was inflated through an attached tube so that stomach contractions could be recorded (see Fig. 12-2). Cannon and Washburn observed that when Washburn's stomach contracted, he felt "hunger pangs." They concluded that hunger is nothing more than stomach contractions.

Later research contradicted this conclusion. Perhaps you already guessed that something more than the stomach is involved in hunger. Many people experience hunger as an overall feeling of weakness or "shakiness" that does not seem to be associated with the stomach. While it is certainly true that eating is limited when the stomach is distended (full), it can be shown that the stomach is not essential for experiencing hunger.

Question: How has this fact been demonstrated?

For one thing, cutting the sensory nerves from the stomach (so that stomach sensations can no longer be felt) does not abolish hunger. Even more convincing is the fact that there are a number of people who have had their stomachs removed surgically. These people continue to feel hungry and to eat regularly. It would seem that some *central* factor must be the cause of hunger. One important factor now appears to be the level of sugar in the blood. If blood is

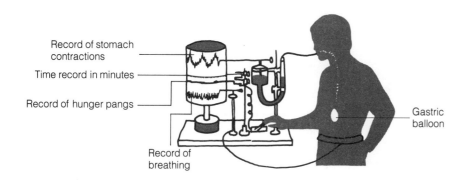

Record of stomach contractions

Time record in minutes

Record of hunger pangs

Record of breathing

Gastric balloon

Fig. 12-2 *In Cannon's early study of hunger, a simple apparatus was used to simultaneously record hunger pangs and stomach contractions. (After Cannon, 1934)*

transferred from a starving dog to one that was recently fed, the second dog will begin eating. The reverse also holds true. If insulin is injected in a human, it produces **hypoglycemia** (HI-po-gly-SEE-me-ah, low blood sugar) and stimulates feelings of hunger and stomach contractions (Cofer and Appely, 1964). Strange as it may seem, the liver may also be responsible for hunger.

Question: The liver?

Yes, the liver. Recent evidence suggests that the liver responds to a lack of bodily "fuel" by sending nerve impulses to the brain, thus triggering eating (Friedman and Stricker, 1976).

Question: What part of the brain controls hunger?

Eating is primarily under the control of the **hypothalamus,** a small structure in the center of the brain (see Fig. 12-3).

Cells in the hypothalamus are sensitive to levels of sugar (and perhaps other substances) in the blood. The hypothalamus also receives messages from the liver and stomach, and these messages combine to produce hunger. One area of the hypothalamus has been identified as a **feeding center.** If the feeding center is electrically stimulated, even a well-fed animal will immediately begin eating; if the feeding center is destroyed, the animal will refuse to eat and will die if not force-fed (Anand and Brobeck, 1951).

A second area of the hypothalamus seems to operate as a **satiety center** (or "stop center") for eating. If the satiety center is destroyed, dramatic overeating results. Rats with damage to this area overeat to the point of total obesity, sometimes getting so large that they can barely move. Some balloon up to weights of 1000 grams or more (see Fig. 12-4). A normal rat weighs about 180 grams. To picture this weight change in human terms, envision someone you know who weighs 180 pounds growing to a weight of 1000 pounds!

It should come as no surprise that there is more to hunger than simple "start" and "stop" systems in the brain. Recent evidence suggests that fat stored in the body also influences hunger. The body acts as if there is a **set-point** for the *proportion* of fat it maintains. That is, the set-point acts like a "thermostat" for body fat. Your personal set-point is the weight you maintain when you are making no effort to gain or lose weight. When an overweight person loses weight, the body goes below the set-point, and the person feels hungry most of the time (Friedman and Stricker, 1976).

Question: Do people have different set-points?

Yes. The set-point appears to be partially inherited and partially determined by early feeding patterns. Persons with overweight parents are many times more likely to be over-

Fig. 12-3 *Location of the hypothalamus in the human brain.*

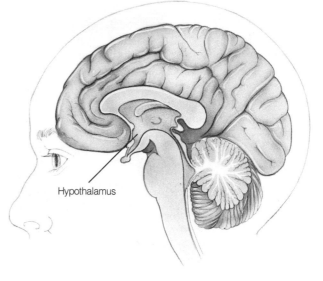

Hypothalamus

Fig. 12-4 *Damage to the hunger-satiety center in the hypothalamus can produce a very fat rat, a condition called hypothalamic hyperphagia (overeating). This rat weighs 1080 grams. (The pointer has gone completely around the dial and beyond.) (Photo courtesy of Neal Miller)*

weight themselves. Also, the set-point may be lastingly altered when a child is overfed. If a weight problem begins in childhood the person will, as an adult, have *more* fat cells and *larger* fat cells in the body. If the person does not become overweight until adulthood, his or her fat cells will be larger, but their number will not increase. Thus, when a weight problem begins in childhood, it is much more difficult to control because there are more fat cells in the body. Parents take note: A fat baby may be headed for a lifelong problem. By one month of age, the average American baby is consuming 135 percent of the calories actually needed.

Obesity   Overweight adults also differ psychologically from slim adults. Psychologists Stanley Schachter (1971) and Judith Rodin (1978) have shown that the overweight are usually sensitive to **external cues** for eating. As Rodin

points out, we are all sensitive to food signs and signals. The sight or aroma of a favorite food, or realization that mealtime has arrived, makes people want to eat, even when they do not feel hungry. Many overweight people, however, are highly, sometimes uncontrollably, sensitive to such food cues (Rodin, 1978).

Many experiments have demonstrated the unusual sensitivity of those who overeat. Since their eating is largely under external control, it is greatly affected by the attractiveness of food or the amount of effort necessary to obtain it (Liebett, 1968; Schachter and Rodin, 1974; Rodin, 1978). Even the time of day can affect eating in the overweight. In one intriguing experiment, subjects were allowed to nibble on some crackers as they waited in a room. On the wall was a clock that could be adjusted to run fast or slow. When obese subjects were led to believe it was closer to mealtime than it actually was (fast clock), they ate more crackers than when they thought dinnertime was farther away than it actually was (slow clock). Subjects of normal weight *decreased* their eating when they thought it was closer to mealtime (Schachter and Gross, 1968). When the clock read five minutes after six, the reaction of fat subjects seems to have been, "Hmm, dinnertime, I must be hungry!"

It is tempting to assume that fatness comes from constant overeating. Actually, this is one of the major myths about obesity. Studies by Albert Stunkard (1980) and Judith Rodin (1978) show that fat people generally eat normal amounts of food. Overeating occurs mainly when a person is gaining weight. Once excess weight is gained, it can be maintained with a normal diet. This fact explains why sensitivity to food cues can be so devastating. Theoretically, it takes only 100 extra calories a day to gain 10 pounds in a year. This amounts to one extra muffin, one pear, one cup of soup, or one small piece of cheese per day (Bennett and Gurin, 1982). Ten years of slight overeating could leave a person 100 pounds overweight.

Question: Is it true that people overeat when they are emotionally upset?

Yes. It has long been recognized that people with weight problems are just as likely to eat when they are anxious, angry, bored, or distressed as when hungry (Bruch, 1961). Add to this the fact that recent experiments show overweight people are generally more emotionally reactive than normal-weight people. Add also the fact that unhappiness frequently accompanies obesity in our fat-conscious culture (Rodin, 1978). The result is a pattern of overeating that leads to emotional distress and still more overeating. When this pattern is coupled with externally cued eating, weight control becomes extremely difficult to achieve. External reminders of food are everywhere, and opportunities to eat are numerous in Western society. Since overeating is a serious problem for many, the "Applications" for this chapter summarizes weight loss techniques developed by psychologists. If you have ever fought the "battle of the bulge," you should find this section interesting.

Other Factors in Hunger

As the research on overeating suggests, "hunger" is affected by a number of factors in addition to actual bodily needs for food. Let us consider some additional topics of interest.

Cultural Factors   Learning to think of some foods as desirable and others as revolting obviously has much to do with eating habits. In America we would never consider eating the eyes out of the steamed head of a monkey, but in Thailand this dish is considered a real delicacy. Many Americans still have trouble getting used to the thought of eating brain, cow's tongue, chocolate-covered grasshoppers, and caviar—all commonly accepted foods in other countries. By the same token, our willingness to consume large quantities of meat, to eat cows, and to cook fish would be considered barbaric in many cultures.

Taste   Even tastes for "normal" foods may vary considerably. In one experiment it was demonstrated that the hungrier a person is, the more "pleasant" a sweet food tastes. However, when subjects were "full," they reversed their judgments and considered sweet foods to be "unpleasant" (Cabanac and Duclaux, 1970). It is also interesting to note that a **taste aversion** can be easily learned if a food causes sickness, or if it simply precedes sickness caused by something else (Nachman, 1970). Not only will such foods be avoided, they can become positively nauseating for the person involved. A friend of the author's, who became ill after eating a cheese Danish (well, actually, *several*), has never again been able to come face to face with this delightful pastry.

Question: If getting sick occurs a long time after eating, how does it become associated with the food eaten?

A good question. Taste aversions are a type of classical conditioning. And, as stated in Chapter 8, a long time-delay normally prevents conditioning. For this reason, it is theorized that there is a *biological tendency* to associate an upset stomach with food eaten earlier. Such learning is

usually protective for both animals and people (Garcia *et al.,* 1974). Yet sadly, many human cancer patients suffer taste aversions long after the nausea of their drug treatments has passed (Bernstein, 1978).

If you like animals, you will be interested in an imaginative approach to an age-old problem. In many parts of the country predators are poisoned, trapped, or shot on sight by owners of livestock. These practices have virtually extinguished the timber wolf, and in some areas, the coyote faces a similar end. How might the coyote be saved, without an unacceptable loss of livestock? In a pioneering experiment, coyotes have been given lamb tainted with lithium chloride. Coyotes who take the bait rapidly become nauseated and vomit. After one or two such treatments they develop **bait shyness**—a lasting distaste for the tainted food (Gustavson and Garcia, 1974). If applied consistently, taste aversion conditioning might solve many predator-livestock problems at less expense than traditional methods. Perhaps this technique could even be used for the protection of roadrunners. . . .

Specific Hungers   Evidence exists that animals and people are able to develop **specific hungers** for nutritional substances lacking in their diet. For example, if animals are made ill by being deprived of vitamin B, they develop a marked preference for foods containing this essential vitamin (Scott and Verrey, 1947).

Question: Is that why pregnant women sometimes crave strange foods?

It is possible that such cravings are a response to added nutritional needs, but it is not too likely. Because of the extra care taken during pregnancy, an expectant mother's diet is usually adequate. Such food cravings are probably better explained by expectations passed on as part of the lore about pregnancy.

Question: Then do humans have specific hungers?

There is some direct evidence of specific hungers occurring in humans, particularly in children. In one classic experiment on **self-selection feeding,** human infants were given a daily "cafeteria" choice of foods. Over a period of several months they selected a balanced diet, and their health and growth were normal (Davis, 1928). In fact, one child who began the study suffering from rickets voluntarily drank large amounts of cod-liver oil, and apparently cured himself of his nutritional disease. In similar fashion, malnourished children have been known to eat plaster from the walls in order to obtain the calcium it contains.

It should be noted, however, that the "wisdom of the body" is actually fairly limited. In the experiment described, the babies could only select from nutritious foods. If candy had been a choice, they might not have done so well. Even by early childhood, learned food preferences tend to override specific hungers, so that poor diets of sweets and "junk-food" are not uncommon in our society.

Primary Motives Revisited— The Strange Case of Sex and Pain

The pattern of factors we have observed in the control of hunger is similar to that found for most of the other primary motives. For example, thirst is only partially related to dryness of the mouth and throat. When drugs are given to persons or animals so that their mouths remain constantly wet or dry, thirst and water intake remain normal. Like hunger, thirst appears to be controlled from the hypothalamus, where separate *thirst* and *thirst-satiety* centers are found. Also like hunger, thirst is strongly affected by individual learning and by cultural factors.

Question: Is there such a thing as a "specific thirst"?

In a sense, there is. Before the body can retain water, minerals lost through perspiration (mainly salt) must be replaced. Animals develop a marked preference for salt water when their salt levels are lowered experimentally (Carlson, 1981). Likewise, when a person is really thirsty, a slightly salty liquid may be more satisfying than plain water. Among some of the nomadic peoples of the Sahara Desert, blood is a highly prized beverage, perhaps because of its saltiness.

The drives for food, water, air, sleep, and elimination are all fairly similar in that they are generated by a combination of activities in the body and the brain, are modified by learning and culture, and are influenced by external factors. Two of the primary drives are unlike the others. These are the drive to avoid pain, and the sex drive. Each differs from the other primary drives in some interesting ways.

Question: How is the drive to avoid pain different?

Pain   Drives such as hunger, thirst, and sleepiness come and go in a fairly regular cycle each day. Pain, by contrast, is an **episodic drive,** since it is aroused only when damage to the tissues of the body takes place. Most of the primary drives cause a person to actively seek a desired goal (food, drink, sleep, and so forth). The pain drive has as its goal the avoidance or elimination of pain.

The desire to end pain seems so basic that it may come as a surprise that avoiding pain appears to be partially learned. This fact was demonstrated by a study in which puppies were raised in total isolation. Each puppy was housed in a cage that prevented exposure to the normal bumps, bites, and other pains of "puppyhood." Later, the isolated dogs were moved to a normal environment for testing. When exposed to pain, the dogs acted strangely. For example, when a lighted match was held near their noses, many pushed toward it as if they felt no pain (Melzack and Scott, 1957). Apparently, the dogs had not learned the meaning of pain, or how to avoid it.

Human pain avoidance is also affected by learning. Some people, for instance, feel they must be "tough" and not show any discomfort; others complain loudly at the smallest ache or pain. As you might expect, the first attitude raises pain tolerance, and the second lowers it (Klienke, 1978). Such attitudes explain why members of some societies endure cutting, burning, whipping, tattooing, and piercing of the skin that would agonize the typical American.

The Sex Drive   Sexual motivation is quite unusual by comparison to other biological motives. In fact, many psychologists do not think of sex as a primary motive because sex (contrary to anything your personal experience might suggest) is not necessary for *individual* survival. It is necessary, of course, for the survival of humans and other creatures as a *group.*

In lower animals the sex drive is directly related to the action of hormones in the body. Females of the lower species are only interested in mating when their fertility cycle is in the stage of **estrus,** or "heat" (caused by secretion of the hormone **estrogen** into the bloodstream). Hormones are important in the male animal as well, and in most lower animals castration will abolish the sex drive. By contrast to the female, however, the normal male animal is always ready to mate. His sex drive is primarily aroused by the behavior of a receptive female. In animals, mating is therefore closely tied to the fertility cycle of the female.

Question: How much do hormones affect the sex drive in humans?

The link between hormones and the sex drive grows weaker as we ascend the biological scale. Hormones do affect the human sex drive, but only to a limited degree. For example, one recent study found no connection between female sexual activity and the monthly menstrual cycle (Udry and Morris, 1977). In humans, mental, cultural, and emotional factors determine sexual expression. However, the liberation from hormones is not total. Human males show a loss of sex drive after castration, and some women lose sexual desire when using birth control pills (McCauley and Ehrhardt, 1976).

Human sexual behavior and attitudes are discussed in detail in Chapter 24. For now, it is enough to note that the sex drive is largely **nonhomeostatic.** In humans, the sex drive can be aroused at virtually any time by almost anything. It therefore shows no clear relationship to deprivation (the amount of time since the drive was last satisfied). True, an increase in desire may occur as time passes. But, on the other hand, recent sexual activity does not prevent sexual desire from occurring again. The sex drive is also unusual in that its arousal is as actively sought as its reduction.

The nonhomeostatic quality of the sex drive can be shown in this way: An animal is allowed to copulate until it seems to have no further interest in sexual behavior. Then, a new sexual partner is provided. Immediately, the animal resumes sexual activity. This pattern is called the *Coolidge Effect* after former United States president Calvin Coolidge. What, you might ask, does Calvin Coolidge have to do with the sex drive? The answer is found in the following story. While touring an experimental farm, Coolidge's wife reportedly asked if a rooster mated just once a day. "No ma'am," she was told, "he mates dozens of times each day." "Tell that to the president," she said, with a far-away look in her eyes. When President Coolidge reached the same part of the tour, his wife's message was given to him. His reaction was to ask if the dozens of matings were with the same hen. No, he was told, different hens were involved. "Tell *that* to Mrs. Coolidge," the president is said to have replied.

Learning Check

1. Systems for the control of hunger and thirst are found in the _____ of the brain.

2. The satiety center signals the body to start eating when it receives signals from the liver or detects changes in blood sugar. T or F?

3. According to Schachter's research, people who suffer from obesity are unusually sensitive to external eating cues.   T or F?

4. Bait shyness occurs when:
   a. a specific hunger develops
   b. the set-point for body fat is altered
   c. the hypothalamus is activated electrically
   d. a taste aversion is formed

5. If an animal is deprived of a necessary food substance, the animal may develop: (circle)
   taste aversion   estrus drive   specific hunger

6. Pain avoidance is an _____ drive.

7. Sexual behavior in animals is largely controlled by estrogen levels in the female and the occurrence of estrus in the male. T or F?

Answers: 1. hypothalamus   2. F   3. T   4. d   5. specific hunger   6. episodic   7. F

Stimulus Needs—Sky Diving, Horror Movies, and the Fun Zone

"Curiosity killed the cat," it is sometimes said, but nothing could be further from the truth. Curiosity plays a very important role in the survival of animals and people. You have surely observed that animals devote large amounts of time and energy to investigating new or unusual objects in the environment. Drives for **exploration, manipulation,** or simply for **curiosity** seem to exist in most animals. As mentioned earlier in this chapter, such drives might be explained by the life-and-death necessity of keeping track of sources of food, danger, and other important details of the environment. However, the curiosity drives seem to go beyond such needs.

Monkey Business

One early researcher (Romanes, 1912) reported that one of his monkeys worked for two hours to open a trunk containing nuts. This activity took place while the monkey was surrounded by nuts left in plain sight. In another experiment, monkeys confined to a dimly lit box learned to perform a simple task in order to open a window that allowed them to view the outside world (Butler and Harlow, 1954). In still another experiment, monkeys quickly learned to solve a mechanical puzzle made up of interlocking metal pins, hooks, and hasps (Butler, 1954). (See Fig. 12-5.)

Fig. 12-5 *Monkeys happily open locks that are placed in their cage. Since no reward is given for this activity, it provides evidence of the existence of stimulus needs. (Photo courtesy of Harry F. Harlow)*

In each of these situations, no reward was offered for exploration or manipulation. The monkeys seemed to be working for the sheer fun of it. An interest in video games, chess, puzzles, Rubick's cube, and the like provides a human parallel. Curiosity, the drive to *know*, also seems to be powerful in humans. Scientific investigation, intellectual

Fig. 12-6 *Berlyne studied curiosity in infants by showing them these designs. Babies looked first at the more complex patterns on the right. (From Science 153: 25–33. Copyright © 1966 by the American Association for the Advancement of Science.)*

curiosity, and other advanced activities may be an extension of this basic drive.

Closely related to the curiosity drive are needs for sensory stimulation. As discussed in Chapter 4, people who have undergone **sensory deprivation** (for example, prisoners, arctic explorers, radar operators, and truck drivers) often report sensory distortions and disturbed thinking. The nervous system seems to require varied, patterned stimulation to respond normally (Suedfeld, 1975). The drive for stimulation can even be observed in infants. When babies are shown patterns of varying complexity (Fig. 12-6), they spend more time looking at complex patterns than at simpler ones (Berlyne, 1966). Indeed, human infants seem to have an almost limitless appetite for stimulation. They spend most of their waking hours tasting, touching, listening to, and visually exploring anything and everything in their immediate surroundings. By the time a child can walk, there are few things in the home that have not been tasted, touched, viewed, handled, or, in the case of toys, destroyed!

Question: Are stimulus needs homeostatic?

Arousal Theory

Some psychologists would argue that they are not. However, by relating drives for stimulation and curiosity to the concept of homeostasis, we get a model of motivation that is very useful for understanding many human activities. This position, called the **arousal theory** of motivation, assumes that there is an ideal level of arousal for various activities and that individuals behave in ways that keep arousal near this ideal level (Hebb, 1966).

Question: What do you mean by "arousal"?

Arousal refers to variations in activation of the body and nervous system. Arousal is zero at death; it is low during sleep; it is moderate during normal daily activities; and it is high at times of excitement, emotion, or panic. Arousal theory assumes that an individual becomes uncomfortable when arousal is too low (as when a person is bored) or when it is too high (as might be the case during intense fear, anxiety, or panic). Curiosity and the drive to seek stimulation can be interpreted as an attempt to raise the level of arousal when it is too low. Most adults seem to vary their activities to maintain a comfortable level of activation. Music, parties, athletics, conversation, sleep, and a wide range of other activities may be mixed to keep arousal at moderate levels, thus preventing both boredom and overstimulation.

Question: Do people vary in their needs for stimulation?

Sensation Seekers The city dweller who visits the country complains that it is "too quiet," and seeks some "action." The country dweller finds the city "hectic," "overwhelming," or "too much," and seeks peace and quiet. The arousal theory of motivation also assumes that the ideal level of arousal varies from one person to the next, and that individuals learn to seek a particular arousal level.

Marvin Zuckerman has devised a test to measure such differences. The *Sensation-Seeking Scale* (SSS), as he calls it, includes statements such as these (from Zuckerman, 1972):

1. A. I would like to sky dive.
   B. Skydiving is too dangerous a sport to try.
2. A. Good music should shock or jolt the senses.
   B. Good music should give one a feeling of peace and security.
3. A. I can't stand to take cold showers.
   B. I am invigorated by a brisk, cold shower.
4. A. When in a restaurant, I would prefer to order dishes I know well.
   B. When in a restaurant, I would prefer to order something I've never had before.
5. A. I don't like the feeling of being high (on alcohol or marijuana).
   B. I often like to get high (on alcohol or marijuana).

It is easy to see that each item offers a choice between seeking new sensations or experiences and avoiding them. People who score high on the full-length version of this test tend to be extroverted, independent individuals who value change. They also report more sexual partners than low scorers; they are more likely to smoke, and prefer spicy, sour, and crunchy foods over blander foods. Low sensation seekers are orderly, nurturant, giving, and like the company of others (Zuckerman, 1972). Which are you? (Most people fall somewhere in between.)

Question: Is there an ideal level of arousal?

Levels of Arousal Discounting individual differences, performance of a task is usually best when arousal is moderate. Let's say that you have to take an essay exam in one of your classes. If you are sleepy or feeling lazy (arousal level too low), your performance will suffer. If you are in a state of anxiety or panic about the test (arousal level too high), you will also perform below par. This relationship between arousal and efficiency of behavior can be symbolized as an **inverted U function** (see Fig. 12-7). At very low levels of arousal the body is not sufficiently energized to perform effectively. With increased arousal, performance continues to improve up to the middle regions of the curve; then it begins to drop off as an individual becomes emotional, frenzied, or disorganized. Such disorganization might occur if you were trying to start a car stalled on a railroad track, with a speeding train bearing down on you.

Question: Is performance always best at moderate levels of arousal?

No, the optimal level of arousal depends on the complexity of the task to be performed. For simple tasks, greater activation runs little risk of disorganizing performance. If a task is relatively *simple,* the optimal level of arousal will be *high.* When a task is *difficult* or *complicated,* the best perfor-

Fig. 12-7 (a) *The general relationship between arousal and efficiency can be described by an "inverted U" curve. The optimal level of arousal or motivation is higher for a simple task* (b) *than for a complex task* (c).

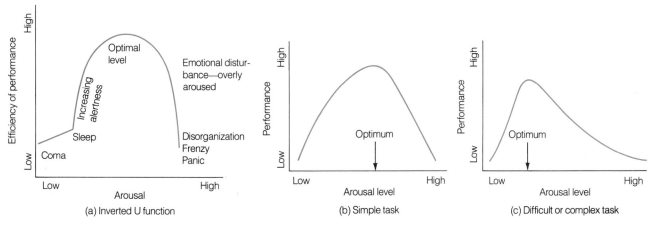

(a) Inverted U function (b) Simple task (c) Difficult or complex task

mance occurs at *low* levels of arousal. This relationship is called the **Yerkes-Dodson law** (see Fig. 12-7). It applies to a wide variety of tasks and to measures of motivation other than arousal.

Some examples of the Yerkes-Dodson law in operation might be helpful. At a track meet it is almost impossible for a sprinter to get too aroused for a race. The task is direct and uncomplicated: Run as fast as you can for a short distance. On the other hand, a golfer making the last putt in an important tournament and a basketball player making a game-deciding free throw face more sensitive and complex tasks. Excessive arousal is almost certain to hurt their performance. In school most students have had experience with "test anxiety" as a familiar example of the effects of excessive arousal on performance.

Question: Then is it true that by learning to calm down a person would do better on tests?

Usually, but not always. Studies of anxious students show that they are typically most anxious when they don't know the material. If this is the case, calming down simply means you will remain calm while failing. One of the best ways to overcome test anxiety is to be overprepared (Spielberger *et al.*, 1976).

Learned Motives—Cheap Thrills and the Pursuit of Excellence

Many motives are acquired rather directly. It is easy enough to see that praise, money, success, pleasure, and similar reinforcers affect our goals and desires. But how do we learn to enjoy activities that are at first painful or frightening? Why do people climb rocks, jump out of airplanes, run marathons, take sauna baths, or swim in frozen lakes? For an answer, let's examine a related situation.

When a person first tries a drug such as heroin, he or she feels a "rush" of pleasure. However, as the drug wears off, a period of discomfort or craving occurs. The easiest way to end the discomfort is to take another dose—as many drug users quickly learn. But in time, habituation takes place; the drug stops producing pleasure, although it will end discomfort. At the same time, the aftereffects of the drug grow more painful. At this point, the drug user has acquired a powerful new motive. In a vicious cycle, heroin relieves discomfort, but it guarantees that withdrawal will occur again in a few hours.

Psychologist Richard L. Solomon (1980) offers an intriguing explanation for drug addiction and other learned motives. According to his **opponent-process theory,** a stimulus that causes strong emotion, such as fear or pleasure, is often followed by an opposite emotion when the stimulus ends. For example, if you are in pain, and the pain ends, you will feel a pleasant sense of relief. If you feel pleasure, as in the case of drug use, and the pleasure ends, it will be followed by craving or discomfort. If you are in love, and feel good when you are with your lover, you will be uncomfortable when he or she is absent.

Question: What happens if the stimulus is repeated?

Solomon assumes that when a stimulus is repeated, our response to it habituates, or gets weaker. First-time skydivers, for instance, are almost always terrified. But with repeated jumps, fear lessens, until finally the skydiver feels a "thrill" instead of terror. In contrast, emotional aftereffects get stronger with repetition. After a first jump, beginning parachutists experience a brief but exhilarating sense of relief. After many such experiences, seasoned skydivers can get a "rush" of euphoria that lasts for hours after a jump (see Fig. 12-8). With repetition, the pleasurable aftereffect gets stronger, and the initial "cost" (pain or fear) gets weaker. The opponent-process theory thus explains how skydiving, rock climbing, ski jumping, and other hazardous pursuits become reinforcing. If you are a fan of horror movies or of carnival rides, your motives may be based on the same effect.

Social Motives

Competition and achievement are highly valued in American culture. In less industrialized nations, the desire to achieve may be minimal. Some of your friends are more interested than others in success, money, possessions, status, love, approval, grades, dominance, power, or belonging to groups. In each case, we are referring to differences in **social motives** or goals. Social motives are acquired in complex ways through socialization and cultural conditioning. The behavior of outstanding artists, scientists, athletes, educators, and leaders is best understood in terms of such learned needs, particularly the need for achievement.

The **need for achievement (nAch)** is certainly not the only social motive of importance, but it is a dominant motive in American culture. To many people, being "motivated" means being interested in achievement. In other chapters we will investigate the motives behind aggression, love affiliation, and approval. For now, let us focus on the need for achievement.

The need for achievement can be defined as a desire to

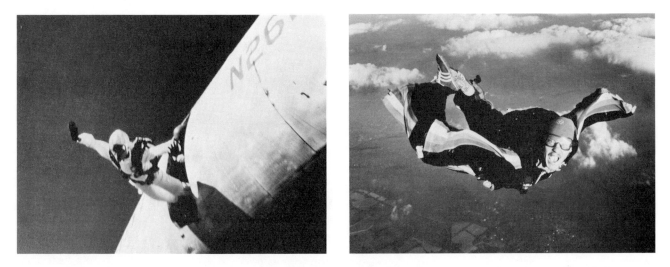

Fig. 12-8 (left) *A terrified sport parachutist takes the plunge. The typical emotional sequence for a first jump is: anxiety before, terror during, and relief after the jump.* (right) *After many jumps, the emotional sequence becomes: eagerness before, a thrill during, and exhilaration after a jump. The new sequence strongly reinforces skydiving.*

meet some *internalized standard of excellence* (McClelland, 1961). The person with high needs for achievement strives to do well in any situation in which evaluation takes place.

Question: Is that like the aggressive business person who strives for success?

Not necessarily. Needs for achievement may lead to material wealth and prestige, but a person who is a high achiever in art, music, science, or amateur athletics may be striving for excellence without concern for material reward. The need for achievement differs from a **need for power,** which is a desire to have *impact,* or control, over others (McClelland, 1975). People who seek power are more interested in prestige than in excellence. For example, male college students who score high in power motivation tend to own prestigious possessions, to read flashy magazines, to enjoy gambling, and to exploit their sexual relationships (Winter, 1973).

David McClelland (1958, 1961) and a number of other psychologists have been interested in the effects of high or low needs for achievement. Using a simple measure of nAch, McClelland found that he could predict the behavior of high and low achievers in many situations. In one study, for example, the occupations of college graduates were compared to scores on a need for achievement test given in their sophomore year. Fourteen years after graduation, those who scored high in nAch were more often found in careers involving an element of risk and responsibility than

were those with low nAch (McClelland, 1965). McClelland has even related the achievement motive to the rise and fall of entire cultures. By studying achievement imagery in the literature of various cultures, he has shown that a rise in the achievement needs of a society precedes periods of growth, expansion, and prosperity, and a decline has been associated with the fall of civilizations (1961).

Characteristics of Achievers   In front of you are five targets placed at various distances from where you are standing. You are given a beanbag to toss at the target of your choice. Target A, anyone can hit; target B, most people can hit; target C, some people can hit; target D, very few people can hit; target E is rarely if ever hit. If you hit A, you will receive $2; B, $4; C, $8; D, $16; and E, $32. You get only one toss. Which one would you choose? McClelland's research suggests that if you have a high need for achievement, you will select C or perhaps D.

Those high in nAch are *moderate* risk-takers. When faced with a problem or challenge, persons high in nAch avoid goals that are too easy because they offer no sense of satisfaction. They also avoid long shots because there is no hope of success or because if success occurs it will be due to luck rather than skill. Persons low in nAch select either sure things or impossible goals. Either way, there is no risk of personal responsibility for failure. Desires for achievement and calculated risk-taking are converted into successful performance of tasks in many situations. People

Fig. 12-9 *Many human motives are acquired.*

high in nAch do better on various tasks in the laboratory. They are more likely to complete difficult tasks, they make better grades in high school and college, and they tend to excel in their chosen occupations. College students high in nAch tend to attribute success to their own ability, and failure to insufficient effort. Students low in nAch are more likely to attribute success to good luck, and failure to bad luck or a lack of ability (Kleinke, 1978). Thus, high nAch students are more likely to keep trying, or to renew their efforts when faced with a poor performance. When the going gets tough, high achievers get going.

Question: Why are some people high in achievement motivation and others low? How do people learn high needs for achievement?

The need for achievement has been related to variables such as social class, ethnic background, and religious affiliation. But the most direct factor in its development seems to be parental attitudes. Studies have shown that the mothers of children with high needs for achievement tend to have higher expectations for their children. They encourage greater independence early in life and tend to be warm, loving, supporting, and nonauthoritarian. The formula for developing achievement seems to be a fairly demanding parent who encourages self-reliance and rewards independent behavior. Simply leaving a child to his or her own ends is not enough (Winterbottom, 1953, 1958).

Fear of Success Have you ever hidden your talents in favor of blending into a group? Have you ever backed off from "winning" in sports or school? Have you ever "played dumb" with friends? Everyone has probably done so at

times. Each of these actions involves an avoidance, or fear, of success (see box on next page). Fearing failure seems natural enough. But why would anyone avoid success? Most often because: (1) success can require a stressful shift in self-concept, (2) many people fear rejection when they stand out in a group, and (3) some people fear the extra demands of being a "successful person" (Tresemer, 1977). All three reasons are illustrated by a secretary who quit when she was offered a job as a supervisor. When asked why she quit, she said it was because she didn't want to be a "career woman," because she feared her former friends in the office would reject her, and because she disliked telling others what to do.

Question: Do fears of success occur mainly in women?

Both men and women are subject to success fears (Wood and Greenfield, 1976). But women in our culture experience an added conflict. Matina Horner, an experimental psychologist, asked bright, successful female students at the University of Michigan to enlarge upon the statement, "After first term finals, Anne finds herself at the top of her medical school class" (Horner, 1971, 1972). Their responses were somewhat shocking:

Anne is an acne-faced bookworm. . . . She studies 12 hours a day and lives at home to save money.

Anne doesn't want to be number one in her class. . . . She feels she shouldn't rank so high because of social reasons. She drops to ninth and then marries the boy who graduates number one.

Although Anne is happy with her success, she fears what will happen to her social life.

Sixty-five percent of the women tested gave similar responses, indicating success fears. Only 9 percent of men gave similar responses to a story about "John." More striking was the fact that women rarely made negative comments when they read the story about John.

Question: What do men say when they read the "Anne" story?

Later studies show that men also ascribe more fear of success to Anne than to John (deCharms and Muir, 1978). Thus, both men and women act as if there is a conflict between success and femininity.

It appears that many women in our society have learned to see achievement and social acceptance as conflicting goals. When does the conflict begin? Probably as soon as children start to learn traditional sex-role behaviors. John Lavach and Hope Lanier (1975) have detected the conflict in girls in the seventh to the tenth grade. By adulthood, some women not only fear success, they also fear they will be considered unfeminine if they excel. Understandably, successful women are most often those who define achievement as an acceptable feminine quality (Kleinke, 1978). Perhaps the women's movement and changing attitudes will help remove this unnecessary stumbling block for future generations of talented and aspiring women.

An Overview of Motivation— Maslow's Hierarchy

As a sidelight to his research on self-actualization* (described in Chapter 1), humanistic psychologist Abraham Maslow proposed that there is a **hierarchy** (or ordering) of human needs. By this he meant that some needs are more basic or powerful than others. Think for a moment about the needs that influence your behavior. Which seem strongest? Which do you spend the most time and energy satisfying? Now look at Maslow's hierarchy (Fig. 12-10).

Note that physiological needs are at the bottom. Since these are necessary for survival, they tend to be dominant over the higher needs. It could be said, for example, that "to a starving person, food is god."

Maslow believed that higher needs are expressed only when the prepotent physiological needs are satisfied. This is also true of needs for safety and security. Until there is a basic amount of order and stability in meeting the lower needs, a person may have little interest in higher pursuits. For this reason, Maslow described the first two levels of the hierarchy as **basic needs.** Higher, or **growth needs,** in-

*Recall that self-actualization means full development of personal potential.

Who's Afraid of a Little Success?

Which of the following statements do you agree with?

1. I am happy only when I am doing better than others.
2. Achievement commands respect.
3. It is extremely important for me to do well in all things that I undertake.
4. Often the cost of success is greater than the reward.
5. I believe that successful people are often sad and lonely.
6. I think "success" has been emphasized too much in our culture.

(Source: Zuckerman and Allison, 1976.)

Agreement with the first three statements shows a positive attitude toward success. People who agree with the last three statements tend to avoid success. It might seem that avoiding success is always undesirable. In reality, an overemphasis on achievement can be as big a handicap as avoidance of success. Our society is notorious for its successful but unhappy workaholics. In the final analysis, a truly successful life strikes a balance between achievement and other needs.

clude love and belonging (family, friendship, caring), needs for esteem and self-esteem (recognition and self-respect), and self-actualization needs (Fig. 12-11). Although Maslow felt that a desire for self-actualization is universal, he placed it at the top of the hierarchy. This placement indicates that he viewed it as fragile and easily interrupted by lower needs.

Fig. 12-10 *Maslow felt that lower needs in the hierarchy are dominant. Basic needs must be satisfied before growth motives are fully expressed. Desires for self-actualization are reflected in various meta-needs (see text).*

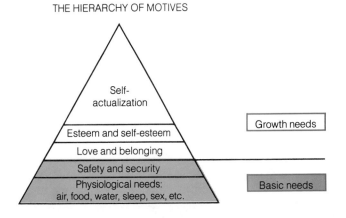

THE HIERARCHY OF MOTIVES

Fig. 12-11 *Wheelchair adventurers end the first day of a demanding backpacking trip. Maslow considered such behavior an expression of needs for self-actualization.*

Table 12-1   Maslow's list of meta-needs
Meta-needs are seen as an expression of tendencies for self-actualization, the full development of personal potential.

1.	Wholeness (unity)	8.	Beauty (rightness of form)
2.	Perfection (balance and harmony)	9.	Goodness (benevolence)
3.	Completion (ending)	10.	Uniqueness (individuality)
4.	Justice (fairness)	11.	Playfulness (ease)
5.	Richness (complexity)	12.	Truth (reality)
6.	Simplicity (essence)	13.	Autonomy (self-sufficiency)
7.	Aliveness (spontaneity)	14.	Meaningfulness (values)

Question: How are needs for self-actualization expressed?

Maslow called the less powerful but humanly important actualization motives, **meta-needs** (Maslow, 1970). These are listed in Table 12-1. According to Maslow, there is a tendency to move up the hierarchy to the meta-needs. A person whose survival needs are met, but whose meta-needs are unfulfilled, falls into a "syndrome of decay" and experiences despair, apathy, and alienation.

Maslow's hierarchy is not well documented by research and questions can be raised about it. How, for instance, do we explain a person who chooses fasting as a means of attaining greater self-awareness? How has the need for self-actualization overcome the need for food? (Perhaps the answer is that fasting is always temporary.) Despite such objections Maslow's views have been widely influential as a way of understanding and appreciating the interplay of human motivation.

Question: Did Maslow believe that many people are motivated by meta-needs?

Maslow estimated that only about one person in ten is primarily motivated by self-actualization needs. Most are more concerned with esteem, love, or security. Perhaps this is because incentives and rewards in our society are slanted to encourage conformity, uniformity, and security in schools, jobs, and relationships. When was the last time you met a meta-need?

Learning Check

1. Drives for exploration, manipulation, and curiosity provide evidence for the existence of _____ _____ needs.

2. People who score high on the SSS tend to be extroverted, independent, and individuals who value change.   T or F?

3. When a task is complex, the ideal level of arousal is _____; when a task is simple, the optimal level of arousal is _____.

4. The overall relationship between arousal and efficiency can be described as:
   a. nonhomeostatic   *b.* a negative correlation
   c. an inverted U function   *d.* an SSS score

5. According to the opponent-process theory, some motives are acquired as a result of the emotional aftereffects of various activities.   T or F?

6. The need for achievement can be described as a desire to meet an internalized _____ of _____.

7. People with high nAch are attracted to "long shots" and "sure things."   T or F?

8. Matina Horner detected a conflict perceived between femininity and achievement in college women.   T or F?

9. According to Maslow, meta-needs are the most basic and prepotent sources of human motivation.   T or F?

Answers: 1. stimulus 2. T 3. low, high 4. c 5. T 6. standard of excellence 7. F 8. T 9. F

Resources Summary

● Motives *initiate, sustain,* and *direct* activities. Motivation typically involves the sequence: *need, drive, goal,* and *goal attainment* (need reduction).

● Behavior can be activated either by *needs* (push) or by *goals* (pull). The attractiveness of a goal and its ability to initiate action are related to its *incentive value.*

● Three principal types of motives are: *primary motives* (based on biological survival needs), *stimulus motives* (which serve needs for activity, exploration, manipulation, and so forth), and *secondary motives* (activated by learned needs and valued goals). Most primary motives operate to maintain *homeostasis.*

● Hunger is influenced by a complex interplay of factors. These include: fullness of the stomach, blood sugar levels, metabolism in the liver, and fat stores in the body. The most direct control of eating is effected by the *hypothalamus,* which has distinct *feeding* and *satiety centers,* or systems.

● Other factors influencing hunger are: learned *taste preferences* or *taste aversions, cultural values,* and sensitivity to *external eating cues.* Obesity has been related to eating that is primarily under external control.

● Lack of nutritional substances in the diet can sometimes produce *specific hungers,* as demonstrated by *self-selection* or "cafeteria" style feeding experiments with animals and infants.

● Like hunger, thirst is affected by a number of bodily factors, but is primarily under the central control of the hypothalamus. There is evidence that *specific thirst* occurs for salty liquids.

● Pain avoidance is an unusual primary drive because it is *episodic* as opposed to *cyclic.* Pain avoidance and pain tolerance are partially learned. The sex drive is also unusual in that it is *nonhomeostatic* (increases in drive level are sought as actively as decreases).

● The stimulus motives include needs for *exploration, manipulation, change,* and *sensory stimulation.* Stimulus motives appear to be innate since they operate independent of other rewards.

● Drives for stimulation are partially explained by the *arousal theory* of motivation, which states that an ideal level of bodily arousal will be maintained if possible. Research suggests that the desired level of arousal or stimulation varies from person to person. Stimulus needs have been measured with the *Sensation Seeking Scale (SSS).*

● Optimal performance on a task usually occurs at moderate levels of arousal. This relationship is described by an *inverted U function.* An added qualification, known as the *Yerkes-Dodson law,* states that for simple tasks the ideal arousal level is higher, and for complex tasks it is lower.

● Learned motives are sometimes acquired by direct reinforcement. The *opponent-process theory* of learned motivation explains how more unusual motives are acquired. *Social motives,* learned through socialization and cultural conditioning, account for much of the diversity of human motivation.

● One of the most prominent and intensely studied social motives is the *need for achievement (nAch).* Achievement striving differs from the *need for power.* High nAch is correlated with success in many situations, and with moderate risk-taking, occupational choice, parental values, and child-rearing styles.

● There is evidence that at times both men and women fear success or high achievement. Women in particular are likely to view high achievement as conflicting with popularity, femininity, or social acceptance.

● Maslow's *hierarchy of motives* categorizes needs as *basic* and *growth-oriented.* Lower needs in the hierarchy are assumed to be *prepotent* (dominant) over higher needs. Self-actualization, the highest and most fragile need, is reflected in what Maslow termed *meta-needs.* Maslow felt that most of us are motivated by lower needs in the hierarchy.

Applications

Managing Motives—The Goal Is Control

Hopefully, the previous discussion has helped you to better understand the operation of a number of basic motives. In this section we will consider two applications of research on motivation. First we will return to the topics of hunger and overeating for a look at psychological techniques for weight control. Then we will investigate the question of how motivation operates in real life settings, such as school, work, and play. Both are interesting topics, and the ideas described may prove useful to you. Let's begin with hunger.

Behavioral Dieting— Kicking the Food Habit

Most people today are aware that obesity may be hazardous to health, yet all around us are people who suffer from being overweight. The overweight run a high risk of developing heart and kidney diseases, of encountering dangerous complications in surgery, and of simply living fewer years than slimmer people. Before you count yourself out of this endangered group of people, consider this: Americans who are only 10 percent overweight eventually run a 20 percent greater risk of dying before their time than do people of normal weight (Lappe, 1971). If you are not now overweight, perhaps you never will be. But in our overfed culture, chances are pretty good that at some point you may need to control your weight.

Question: What can be done to control weight?

The basic approach for years has been to "diet"; that is, to restrict food intake drastically for a brief period. This, of course, is perfectly sensible in theory: You must eat less to lose weight. In practice, however, most people who lose weight by dieting regain it rapidly.

What is really needed if one wishes to control weight is a complete overhaul of *eating habits* and control of the *external cues* for eating. The person who succeeds in changing eating habits can expect a permanent weight reduction. "Behavioral dieting," as this approach has been called, has repeatedly proved superior to simple dieting for weight control. The following list is a collection of many of the behavioral techniques used to aid weight loss

(compiled from Lake, 1973; Kiell, 1973; Mayer, 1968; and Trotter, 1974).

1. *Begin any weight control program with a physical checkup.* About 5 percent of all weight problems are physical.

2. *Learn your eating habits by observing yourself and keeping a "diet diary."* Begin by making a complete record of your eating habits for two weeks. Record where you eat, what you eat, and the feelings and events that occur just before and after eating. How do others around you respond to your eating? Is someone encouraging you to overeat?

3. *Count calories.* The only way to lose is to eat less, and calories allow you to keep an accurate record of your food intake.

4. *Develop techniques to control the act of eating.* Begin by taking smaller portions. Carry only what you plan to eat to the table. Put all other food away before leaving the kitchen. Eat slowly, finish one mouthful before taking another, count your mouthfuls, leave food on your plate, avoid eating alone (you're less likely to overeat in front of others).

5. *Learn to weaken your personal eating cues.* When you have learned when and where you do most of your eating, avoid these situations. Try to restrict your eating to one room, and do not read, watch TV, study, or talk on the phone while eating. Require yourself to interrupt what you are doing in order to eat. Be especially aware of the "night-eating syndrome." Most calories are consumed late in the day or at night. Keep food out of sight and find things to do to keep yourself busy during this dangerous period.

6. *Avoid snacks.* Buy low-calorie foods that require preparation, and fix only a single portion at a time. If you have an impulse to snack, set a timer for 20 minutes and see if you are still hungry then. Delay the impulse to snack several times if possible. Dull your appetite by filling up on raw carrots, bouillon, water, coffee, or tea.

7. *Exercise.* Physical activity burns calories. Stop saving steps and riding elevators. Add activity to your routine in every way you can think of. Contrary to popular opinion, regular exercise does not increase appetite. For reasons

Applications

that are not well understood, exercise lowers the body's set-point for fat storage (Bennett and Gurin, 1982).

8. *Get yourself committed to weight loss.* Involve as many people in your program as you can.

9. *Make a list of rewards you will receive if you change your eating habits and punishments that will occur if you don't.* You may find it helpful to set up specific rewards (see Chapter 23 for more details). Don't reward yourself with food.

10. *Chart your progress daily.* Record your weight, the number of calories eaten, whether you met your daily goal. (Set realistic goals by cutting down calories gradually. About a pound per week weight loss is realistic, but remember, you are changing habits, not just losing weight.) Take pride in your successes. Post your chart in a prominent place. This feedback on your progress is possibly the most important of all the techniques. Be patient with this program. It takes years to develop eating habits. You can expect it to take at least several months to change them. If you are unsuccessful at losing weight with these techniques, you might find it helpful to seek the aid of a psychologist familiar with behavioral weight-loss techniques.

Intrinsic and Extrinsic Motivation—Getting Motivated

Some people cook for a living and consider it hard work. Others cook for pleasure and dream of opening a restaurant. For some people carpentry, gardening, writing, photography, or jewelry-making is fun. For others the same activities are drudgery they must be paid to do. How can the same activity be "work" for one person and "play" for another?

Question: Isn't it basically the difference between wanting to do something and having to do it?

To a large extent it is. More formally, we could say that the difference lies in a distinction between *intrinsic* and *extrinsic motivation.*

When you undertake an activity for enjoyment, to demonstrate competence, or to gain skill, your motivation is usually intrinsic. **Intrinsic motivation** occurs when there is no obvious external reward or ulterior purpose behind your actions. The activity is an end in itself.

Extrinsic motivation stems from obvious external factors, such as pay, grades, rewards, obligations, or approval. Most of the activities we think of as "work" are

extrinsically rewarded. If you are also intrinsically motivated at work, so much the better. But most jobs are not sufficiently self-rewarding to be done without extrinsic motivation.

Play-Into-Work It might seem that increasing extrinsic incentives would strengthen motivation, but this is not always the case. Research with children shows that excessive rewards can undermine spontaneous interest (Ross *et al.,* 1976).

Question: How could rewards lower motivation?

An experiment by David Greene and Mark Lepper (1974) provides a good example. Greene and Lepper gave children Magic-Markers (felt-tip pens) and measured how long they spontaneously played with them. A few days later they asked the children to draw pictures with the pens. Some of the children were lavishly rewarded for drawing. Others drew without reward. After a few more days, the children were again allowed to play with the markers. The children who had been rewarded for using the markers showed much less interest than before. The unrewarded children played with the markers as much as they had the first time. Greene and Lepper conclude that they had turned play into work by *requiring* some of the children to use the markers.

When an activity becomes something that "must" be done, rather than something you choose to do, it usually takes on the complexion of work. You have probably known someone who made a business out of a hobby, only to find that what was once enjoyable became work. Because of the emphasis placed on grades and requirements, schools tend to make work out of the natural and highly enjoyable process of learning. Many hobbies and pastimes involve tremendous amounts of learning and the development of high levels of skill, yet in the absence of extrinsic motivation they are perceived as "fun."

Question: How can the concept of intrinsic motivation be applied?

Balance Motivation can't always be intrinsic. Nor should it be. Not every worthwhile activity is intrinsically satisfying. In addition, extrinsic motivation is often needed if we are to develop a level of skill or knowledge sufficient for an activity to become intrinsically rewarding. Many adults who greatly enjoy playing music were required by their parents to take music lessons when they were children. The same effect can be observed in learning to read,

Applications

to appreciate art or literature, or to enjoy a sport. At first, external encouragement or incentives may be needed to get a person to the level of ability needed for intrinsic motivation to occur.

So, both extrinsic and intrinsic motivation are necessary. But extrinsic motivation should not be overused. Greene and Lepper (1974) summarize: (1) If there is no intrinsic interest in an activity to begin with, there is nothing to lose by using extrinsic rewards; (2) if needed skills are lacking, extrinsic rewards may be necessary to begin; (3) extrinsic rewards may focus attention on an activity so that real interest can develop—this is especially true for motivating learning in children; (4) if extrinsic rewards or incentives are to be used, they should be as small as possible, used only when absolutely necessary, and faded out as soon as possible. By following these rules, you can avoid taking spontaneous interest and satisfaction out of motivation for others, especially children.

Question: How does this apply to adults?

Work For years, in business and industry the trend was to make work more streamlined and efficient, and to tie greater pay to greater productivity. However, in recent years many workers have begun to complain that personal satisfaction and a sense of accomplishment are lacking in their jobs. Far too many jobs are routine, repetitive, boring, and unfulfilling. It's no wonder that extrinsic incentives, such as bonuses and raises, have not always been successful in increasing productivity. Many businesses are finding they cannot simply buy greater commitment to work. An alternative that is finding favor with both employees and employers is a strategy known as **job enrichment.** Job enrichment is basically an attempt to put intrinsic motivation back into work.

Question: How is job enrichment done?

Job enrichment usually involves removing some of the controls and restrictions on employees, giving them greater responsibility, freedom, choice, and authority. Employees also switch to doing a complete cycle of work or completing an entire item or project, instead of doing an isolated part of a larger process. Whenever possible, workers are given feedback about their work or progress. This feedback comes to them directly instead of to a supervisor. Workers are encouraged to learn new and more difficult tasks and to specialize in particular skills. This approach has been used with tremendous success by large corporations such as IBM, Maytag, Western Electric, Chrysler, and Polaroid. It is usually accompanied by lower production costs, increased job satisfaction, reduced boredom, and less absenteeism (Schultz, 1979).

Motivation The distinction between intrinsic and extrinsic motivation is simple but powerful. It can help you understand some of the difficulties of attending school, for instance. Many students taking a course like psychology have read books about psychology on their own, and are personally interested in the subject. But when learning is *required,* as it is in formal courses, natural curiosity may evaporate. This need not be the case. If you find your motivation flagging in school (or work) take your eye off the grade or the paycheck and focus on day-to-day satisfactions and intrinsic rewards. With only a little effort, most of what you learn in school can be related to interests or hobbies, to your personal relationships, and certainly to your future. Don't hesitate to be a ''selfish'' learner. If you are not learning for yourself, who are you learning for? This attitude is beautifully expressed by a student who returned to college after completing a degree in a field his parents wanted him to enter. He hated college the first time through and fought it every step of the way. Upon his return he was interested, alive, highly motivated and had a new major. His explanation for his change in attitude and motivation was, ''This time it's for me.''

Learning Check

1. To change eating habits, it is useful to minimize pleasure by eating as quickly as possible. It also helps to avoid exercise because it increases appetite.   T or F?
2. Intrinsic motivation is often undermined in situations in which obvious external rewards are applied to a naturally enjoyable activity.   T or F?
3. Job enrichment programs basically apply the concept of extrinsic motivation to work environments.   T or F?
4. If a child has no initial interest in an activity, extrinsic rewards may be the best way to increase motivation.   T or F?

Answers: 1. F 2. T 3. F 4. T

Exploration

Body Rhythms and Biorhythms—Fact and Fallacy

Due to its recent popularity, you have probably heard of *biorhythm theory*. Perhaps you have been curious about it. What does biorhythm theory claim? What evidence is there to support it? Is there any value to having your biorhythms charted?

Biorhythm Theory   Biorhythm theory states that we are all subject to three separate cycles: a physical cycle lasting 23 days, an emotional or sensitivity cycle of 28 days, and a 33-day intellectual cycle. The first half of each cycle is supposedly positive (made up of good days) and the second half negative. According to the theory, all three cycles begin at birth and flow in and out of synchronization throughout one's life. When a cycle changes from positive to negative it is termed a "critical day." When all three cycles line up on critical days, the chances for disaster or accident are supposedly quite high.

Although you can easily chart your own biorhythms, an incredible number of commercial charting services would like to do it for you. Most promote themselves with case histories of celebrities who made serious errors, had accidents, or performed exceptionally well when biorhythms were working for or against them. What they usually overlook, however, is all the cases that don't fit. For example, Reggie Jackson, as an outfielder for the New York Yankees, went on an incredible hitting streak to lead his team to victory in the 1977 World Series. And what, we might ask, were Jackson's biorhythms doing at that time? They were all at "rock bottom" (Louis, 1978).

Question: But what about companies that have cut accident rates by charting employees' biorhythms? Doesn't that support the theory?

It might seem so, but there is a catch. Consider an example: When they arrive for work, bus drivers for the Ohmi Railway Company in Japan receive a card that warns them if they are about to have a critical day, as predicted by their biorhythms. Drivers who receive cards are urged to be extra careful for that day. Since this program began there has been a dramatic reduction in accidents. Is this proof of biorhythmic theory? Not at all. What if the drivers were selected *at random* and warned to be extra careful? If they heeded the warnings, we would expect an overall drop in accident rates, even if the warnings had no relationship to biorhythms.

Save Your Money   Some of the logical problems with biorhythm theory may have already occurred to you. Why should the three cycles begin at birth? After all, the fetus is alive before birth. Are we to believe, as well, that a Caesarian birth can change a person's entire life? Or that being born a few days earlier or later can make a lifelong difference? And why should the cycles last exactly 23, 28, and 33 days for everyone on earth?

The strongest evidence against biorhythm theory comes from accident studies and other attempts to match cycles with outcomes. For instance, one researcher compared 100 no-hit baseball games pitched in the major leagues to biorhythm charts for the pitchers. He found no connection between cycles and these performances (Louis, 1978). In Canada, the Workmen's Compensation Board of British Columbia studied over 13,000 occupational accidents. The outcome? Accidents are no more likely to occur on "critical" days than at any other time (Nelson, 1976). Another study found absolutely no correlation between aviation accidents and pilots' biorhythms (Wolcott *et al.,* 1977).

In summary, evidence is rapidly mounting against biorhythm theory. If you fail a test, have an accident, lose a game, insult your boss, or dissolve your marriage, don't look to a biorhythm chart for the explanation.

Body Rhythms   While biorhythm theory has received little scientific support, other bodily rhythms are thoroughly documented. The body operates like a finely tuned instrument, regulated by internal "biological clocks." Every 24 hours the body undergoes a complex cycle of changes. These daily changes are called **circadian** (SUR-kay-dee-AN) **rhythms** (*circa:* about; *diem:* a day). An understanding of circadian rhythms and their effects can be quite useful.

Question: What kind of bodily changes are associated with these rhythms?

Almost a hundred bodily rhythms have been studied. The most important changes are in body temperature, blood

Exploration

pressure, urine volume, amino-acid level, and the activity of the liver and kidneys. These and a number of other bodily activities all reach a peak sometime during the day. Especially important is production of adrenaline, which causes general arousal, and is three to five times greater during the day (Luce, 1971). Most people have much more energy and are more efficient during their personal high point. The terms "day person" and "night person" are familiar references to such differences.

There are two major ways to make use of circadian rhythms. The first is to learn your own personal high and low points. A good way to do this is to keep a log of your mood and energy level for each hour through the day. (See sample.) Do this for two weeks and then average your rating for each hour from early morning until bedtime. This technique is much more meaningful than a commercial biorhythm chart. For increased efficiency, you can use it to then schedule studying, chores, and recreation around your personal rhythms.

A second application is related to what has been called "time-zone fatigue" or "jet lag." It is a well-documented fact that businesspersons, diplomats, athletes, and other time-zone travelers frequently make errors or turn in poorer performances because their body rhythms have been temporarily disrupted. If you travel great distances east or west, the peaks and valleys of your circadian rhythms will be out of phase with the physical environment. "Shift" work has the same effect, causing a loss of efficiency, as well as fatigue, irritability, nervousness, depression, and a decline in mental agility (Taub and Berger, 1974). The best way to deal with such changes is to *pre-adapt* to a new schedule whenever possible. Before traveling, for instance, you should go to sleep one hour later (or earlier) each day until your sleep cycle matches the time at your destination.

Question: What does all of this have to do with those of us who are not world travelers?

Sample Body-Rhythm Log

Rating Scale:

Mood: Very negative 1 2 3 4 5 Very positive
Energy: Very low 1 2 3 4 5 Very high

Time	Mood	Energy level	Two-week average for: Mood	Two-week average for: Energy level
8:00	3	2	3.2	2.5
9:00	3	3	3.0	3.1
10:00	4	3	3.4	3.6
Etc.			Etc.	

There are few college students who have not at one time or another "burned the midnight oil," especially during a final-exam period. (Ah, there's a study in motivation!) During this or any other strenuous period, it is wise to remember the effects of disturbing bodily rhythms. Younger persons, of course, are less affected by disruptions, but everyone is susceptible, and any major deviation from your regular schedule of activities, sleep, and rest is likely to cost more than it's worth. Often, you can accomplish as much during one hour in the morning as you could have in three hours of work after midnight. The two-hours difference in efficiency might as well be spent sleeping. If you feel you must depart from your normal schedule, do it gradually over a period of days. Studies show that most people take over two weeks to establish a new circadian rhythm. If you can anticipate an upcoming body-rhythm change (when traveling, before finals week, or when doing shift work), adapt yourself to your expected schedule beforehand.

Questions for Discussion

1. Which of the primary drives do you consider the strongest? Why? Which occupies the greatest amount of your time and energies? How could the strength of the primary drives be established for animals?

2. Discuss some of the factors that contribute to overeating at Thanksgiving or a similar feast.

3. The sex drive is not essential for individual survival, and it can be easily interrupted by any of the other primary drives. Why do you think so much energy is directed toward sexuality in our culture?

4. In what ways have you observed the stimulus motives at work in human behavior? Does learning contribute to curiosity or needs for stimulation?

5. Does the American emphasis on competition (in your opinion) encourage achievement or discourage it? (Consider the effects, for example, when only one person can be considered the "winner" in many situations.)

6. How could you apply the concept of incentives to improve your motivation to study?

7. Have you experienced a major disruption of your body's circadian rhythms? What effect did this have on your functioning?

8. In *Lady Windermere's Fan,* playwright Oscar Wilde said, "In this world there are only two tragedies. One is not getting what one wants, and the other is getting it. The last is the real tragedy." What do you think Wilde meant? Where does your motivation come from?

9. If you had a guaranteed income would you "work?" What do you think you would spend your time doing? For how long? What, if anything, does this reveal about sources of intrinsic motivation?

Suggestions for Further Reading

Bennett, W., and J. Gurin. *The Dieter's Dilemma.* Basic, 1982.

Berlyne, D. E. *Conflict, Arousal, and Curiosity.* McGraw-Hill, 1960.

Bindra, D., and J. Steward. *Motivation; Selected Readings.* Penguin, 1966.

Bolles, R. C. *Theory of Motivation,* 2nd ed. Harper & Row, 1975.

Lepper, M. R., and D. Greene. *The Hidden Costs of Reward.* Erlbaum, 1978.

McClelland, D. C. *The Achieving Society.* Van Nostrand, 1961.

Orbach, S. *Fat Is a Feminist Issue.* Paddington Press, 1978.

Roberts, W. W., and H. O. Kiess. "Motivational Properties of Hypothalamic Aggression in Cats," *Journal of Comparative and Physiological Psychology,* **54,** 1964, 187–193.

Schachter, S., and J. Rodin. *Obese Humans and Rats.* Lawrence Earlbaum, 1974.

Solomon, R. L. "The Opponent-Process Theory of Acquired Motivation," *American Psychologist,* August, 1980, pp. 691–712.

Time Magazine. "Why You Do What You Do: Sociobiology—A New Theory of Behavior," August 1, 1977.

13

Emotion

Voodoo Death

Few events are more psychologically bizarre than sudden death caused by "voodoo" or "magic." Yet, many explorers and anthropologists have witnessed this strange phenomenon. Here is an account of what happens in one tribe when a man discovers that he has been cursed by an enemy:

> He stands aghast, with his eyes staring at the treacherous pointers, and with his hands lifted as though to ward off the lethal medium, which he imagines is pouring into his body. His cheeks blanch and his eyes become glassy and the expression of his face becomes horribly distorted. . . . His body begins to tremble and the muscles twist involuntarily. He sways backwards and falls to the ground, and after a short time appears to be in a swoon; but soon he writhes as if in mortal agony, and, covering his face with his hands, begins to moan. . . . From this time onwards he sickens and frets, refusing to eat and keeping aloof from the daily affairs of the tribe. Unless help is forthcoming in the shape of a counter-charm death is only a matter of a comparatively short time (Basedow, 1925; cited in Cannon, 1942).

This and other cases of voodoo death are difficult for those of us living in a modern society to believe. At first glance they seem to require a belief in the supernatural powers of magic. Actually, all they require is a belief in emotion. Walter Cannon (1942), a well-known physiologist, studied a large number of voodoo deaths and concluded that they really do occur.

Question: How could a voodoo curse cause death?

Cannon felt these deaths can be explained by changes in the body that accompany strong emotion. Those who have been cursed believe so completely they will die that they become terrified. Cannon believed the fear is so intense and lasting that it causes a heart attack or other bodily disaster.

More recent research suggests that Cannon's explanation was only partially correct. It now appears that such deaths are caused not by fear itself, but by the body's reaction to fear. After a period of strong emotion, the parasympathetic nervous system normally restores balance to the body by reversing many of the changes caused by emotion. For example, during intense fear, heart rate is increased by the sympathetic nervous system; to counteract this, the parasympathetic system later slows the heart. It is now believed that the cursed person's emotional response is so intense that the parasympathetic nervous system overreacts and slows the heart to a stop (Seligman, 1974). There is more to this story (as we will see in a later section of this chapter). For now, it is enough to say that emotions are not only the "spice of life." For some, they may be the spice of death as well.

Survey Questions What are the "parts" of an emotion? How do psychologists explain emotions? What happens to the body during emotion? Can "lie detectors" really detect lies? How do emotions develop? How accurately are they expressed by "body language" and the face? What do we know about coping with threatening situations, helplessness, death, and depression? Do the eyes reveal feelings?

Resources

Dissecting an Emotion—How Do You Feel?

Have you ever seen a pound of anger, a quart of hate, or an ounce of joy? Of course, the question is ridiculous, yet we talk about emotions as if they were real "things." Rage, grief, ecstasy, joy, sadness, boredom—we use these terms so freely it is easy to forget that emotions are often *inferred* from the actions of others; they cannot be directly observed. A person staring off into space might be bored, depressed, in love, or stoned (the last, by the way, is not an emotion). Even relying on others to tell us how they feel can be a problem. Clinical psychologists regularly see clients who mistake anger for fear, guilt for depression, or lust for love. For such reasons, the study of emotion is difficult. The effort is worthwhile, however; emotions separate us from machines, plants, and computers, and add deeper meaning to life.

Have you ever waited until someone was in a good mood to ask them for a favor? If so, you are aware that emotions have a powerful influence on *everyday* behavior. More importantly, emotions underlie such basic **adaptive behaviors** as attack, retreat, seeking comfort, helping others, reproduction, and the like (Plutchik, 1980). At times, human emotions can be disruptive—as in having "stage fright" or "choking up" in an athletic contest—but in general emotions are an aid to survival. This seems to be why emotional reactions were retained in evolution.

Parts of an Emotion

There are a number of facets to any emotional experience. Consider the following vivid description of emotion from Dostoevsky's *Crime and Punishment.* In it, Lizavita Ivanova is about to be murdered by the main character, Raskolnikov:

. . . When she saw him run in, she trembled like a leaf and her face twitched spasmodically; she raised her hand as if to cover her mouth, but no scream came and she backed slowly away from him toward the corner, with her eyes on him in a fixed stare, but still without a sound, as if she had

no breath left with which to cry out. He flung himself forward with the axe; her lips writhed pitifully like those of a young child when it is just beginning to be frightened and stands ready to scream.

Question: What does this tell us about emotion?

Subjective Feelings If you have ever experienced extreme fear like that described by Dostoevsky, you will recognize that **subjective feelings** are one part of any emotional experience. Such feelings vary in terms of *intensity, pleasantness* or *unpleasantness,* and *complexity.* For example, joy is a simple, pleasant, and intense emotion. Jealousy is a complex, unpleasant emotion that may be quite intense. Unfortunately, it is difficult to go beyond such simple classifications because feelings are very difficult to describe. In one rather bizarre study, women were required to crush snails between their fingers and to describe their feelings. The best they could do was to *name* their emotions (Coleman, 1949). Notice that Dostoevsky did not even try to describe the feeling of fear, only the reactions.

Emotional Expressions When a person is afraid, we observe that the hands tremble, the face contorts, and posture becomes tense and defensive. These and other **emotional expressions** are particularly important for the study of emotion in animals, and in the communication of emotion from one person to another (Fig. 13-1). A marked shift in voice tone or modulation is another familiar emotional expression. This vocal change usually is accompanied by verbal expressions of emotion ranging from the nonstop abuse of rage to the surprisingly subdued last words found on flight recorders after air disasters (a common last word is "Damn," spoken calmly).

Physiological Changes Most people closely identify a pounding heart, sweating palms, and "butterflies" in the stomach with the experience of emotion. This observation is valid since **physiological changes** taking place in the body are the core of fear, anger, joy, and other emotions. These changes, which are the third part of an emotion,

Fig. 13-1 *How accurately do facial expressions reveal emotion? After you have guessed what emotion these people are feeling, turn to page 303.*

include alterations in heart rate, blood pressure, perspiration, and other bodily "stirrings." Most of these reactions are caused by release of **adrenaline** (a general bodily stimulant) into the bloodstream and by actions of the nervous system.

Question: Are physical changes in the body different for different emotions?

There are differences, but they are minor. Your heart is as likely to pound during joy as it is during anger. This is why the fourth part of an emotion is important.

Interpretation   Basic to any emotional experience is the **interpretation** placed on it. This may be seen in some interesting ways. One is by the injection of adrenaline into laboratory subjects. This typically produces "cold emotions" in which people feel "as if" they should be fearful, angry, or excited, but experience no real emotion because they know the drug caused these feelings (Marañon, 1924). A second example of the importance of emotional interpretations is provided by this case study:

> Mister J. had recently suffered a divorce, lost his job, and had assumed responsibility for two small children. Mr. J. sought the aid of a psychologist during this stressful period

of his life. The psychologist reports that he would occasionally get a call from Mr. J. asking for an appointment to discuss the onset of a deep depression. More often than not, Mr. J. would call back to cancel the meeting because his feelings of depression were a "false alarm." He had misinterpreted the fatigue and other early signs of a cold or flu as feelings of depression. In the context of his life situation it is easy to see how he might be misled (Downey, 1976).

Classifying Emotions

Question: Are some emotions more basic than others?

It would seem so, but theorists often disagree as to which are the most basic. One of the best lists of **primary emotions** has been compiled by Robert Plutchik (1980). Based on his research, Plutchik lists the following eight primary emotions: **fear, surprise, sadness, disgust, anger, anticipation, joy,** and **acceptance** (receptivity). If it seems that some important emotions are missing, it may be because each listed emotion can vary in *intensity*. Anger, for instance, may vary from rage to simple annoyance; fear, from terror to apprehension; sadness, from grief to moodiness.

Everyone knows that red and blue can be mixed to produce purple. But what emotions would you mix to produce awe, love, or guilt? One of Plutchik's most interesting ideas concerns the mixing of primary emotions (see Fig. 13-2). As shown in Fig. 13-2, adjacent emotions can be mixed to yield a third, more complex emotion. Other mixtures are also possible. For example, a child about to eat a stolen cookie may have the combined emotions of joy and fear. The result? Guilt—as you may recall from your own childhood. Likewise, we could consider feelings of jealousy to be a mixture of love, anger, and fear.

Theories of Emotion— Four Ways to Fear a Bear

Question: What is the typical sequence of events in experiencing an emotion?

There are many theories about what takes place during emotion. Let's take a brief look at four of the most popular viewpoints.

The Commonsense Theory of Emotion   Common sense tells us that we see a bear, feel fear, become aroused, and run (and sweat and yell). For various reasons, psychologists have questioned this ordering of events. The theories of emotion that follow tell why. (Refer to Fig. 13-3.)

The James-Lange Theory (1884–1885) In the 1880s, American psychologist William James (the functionalist) and Danish psychologist Carl Lange proposed a different version of the relationship between emotional feelings and the body. James and Lange suggested that, "We are afraid of a bear because we run, or angry because we strike." In doing so, they turned the tables on our usual view of emotion. According to James and Lange, bodily arousal (such as increased heart rate) does not follow a feeling, such as fear. Instead, they argued, *emotional feelings follow bodily arousal.* Thus, we see a bear, run, are aroused, and *then* feel fear as we become aware of our bodily reactions.

To support this line of thought, James pointed out that we often do not experience an emotion until after reacting. For example, imagine that you are driving and that a car suddenly pulls out in front of you. You swerve and skid to an abrupt halt at the side of the road. Only after you have come to a stop do you notice your pounding heart, rapid breathing, and tense muscles—and recognize your fear.

The James-Lange theory of emotion may help explain an interesting effect you have probably observed. When you are feeling "down" or sad, forcing yourself to smile will sometimes be followed by an actual improvement in your mood (Laird, 1974). Also interesting is the effect of spinal injuries on emotion. Spinal injuries in the area of the neck cut off most sensations from the body. As the James-Lange theory would predict, people with such injuries tend to feel less emotion than before. For example, one man caught in a sinking fishing boat observed, "I knew I was sinking, and I was afraid all right, but somehow I didn't have that feeling of trapped panic that I know I would have had before" (Hohman, 1966).

The Cannon-Bard Theory (1927) American physiologist Walter Cannon and his student Phillip Bard found a number of reasons to question the James-Lange theory. While agreeing that the body becomes stirred up during emotion, Cannon and Bard noted that there are only slight differences in the physiology of various emotions. These differences are just not enough to allow for the rich and varied emotional life that humans experience. Cannon and Bard also pointed out that the viscera and internal organs are relatively insensitive. This too casts doubt on the idea that emotional feelings come mainly from the body.

Question: What does account for the variety of emotions, the body or the brain?

For the reasons just stated, and a number of others, Walter Cannon (1932) proposed that emotional feelings and bod-

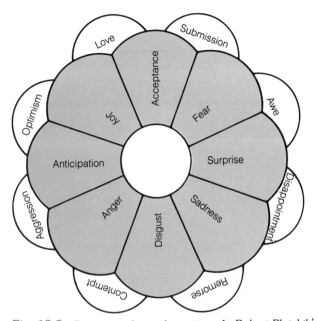

Fig. 13-2 *Primary and mixed emotions. In Robert Plutchik's model, there are eight primary emotions (as shown in the colored areas). Adjacent emotions may combine to give the emotions shown in white areas. Mixtures involving more widely separated emotions are also possible. (Adapted from Plutchik, 1980)*

Fig. 13-3 *Theories of emotion.*

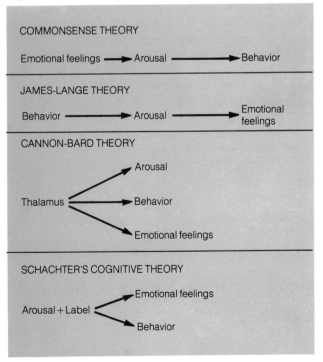

ily arousal are both organized in the brain. In this version, seeing a bear activates the thalamus, which in turn alerts both the cortex and the hypothalamus for action. The cortex is responsible for emotional feelings and emotional behavior, and the hypothalamus is responsible for arousing the body. Thus, if the bear is seen as dangerous, bodily arousal, running, and feelings of fear will all be generated at the same time by brain activity.

Let's summarize: The commonsense theory of emotion is probably wrong. The James-Lange theory says emotion *is* bodily arousal and that the body must be aroused *before* an emotion is experienced. The Cannon-Bard theory moved emotions from the body to the head by saying that emotions are organized in the brain and that emotional feelings and bodily expressions occur simultaneously. There is a fourth possibility.

Schachter's Cognitive Theory of Emotion (1971)

The previous theories are mostly concerned with emotion as a physical response. In Stanley Schachter's view, cognitive (mental) factors also enter into emotion. According to Schachter, emotion occurs when a particular *label* is applied to general physical *arousal*. Schachter assumes that when we are aroused, we have a need to interpret our feelings. Assume, for instance, that someone sneaks up behind you on a dark street and says, "Boo!" No matter who the person is, your body will be aroused (pounding heart, sweating palms, and so on). If the person is a total stranger, you may interpret this arousal as fear; if the person is a close friend, the arousal may be labeled as surprise, or delight. The label (such as anger, fear, or happiness) applied to bodily arousal is influenced by past experience, the situation, and the reactions of others.

To test this theory, Schachter and Singer (1962) injected subjects with the drug adrenaline. (Subjects were unaware of what drug they were receiving.) While the adrenaline was taking effect, each subject was asked to wait in a room with another subject. The second "subject" was really an accomplice who was trained to act very *happy* or very *angry.* As the adrenaline began to take effect, subjects found themselves in a room with someone who was joking, doodling, flying paper airplanes, and generally acting extremely happy *or* with someone who was acting very angry by criticizing the experimental questionnaire, complaining about the wait, and eventually stomping out of the room.

Question: What does this have to do with the person's emotions?

Schachter and Singer were interested in what would happen as subjects began to feel aroused. Would the actions of the other "student" influence the emotions felt by the real subject? They found that if subjects were *correctly informed* about the effects of adrenaline (pounding heart, trembling hands), the antics of the actor had little effect on them. Informed subjects knew the drug had caused their unusual feelings. Those who were *uninformed* or *misinformed* (told that the drug would cause numbness and itching) were highly influenced by the "anger" and "happiness" conditions.*

Faced with a stirred-up body and no explanation for the way they were feeling, subjects became happy or angry in accordance with the situation in which they found themselves. Schachter would predict, then, that if you met a bear, you would be aroused. If the bear seemed unfriendly, you would interpret your arousal as fear, and if the bear was throwing paper airplanes, you would be happy, amazed, and relieved!

Further support for the cognitive theory of emotion comes from an experiment in which subjects watched a slapstick movie (Schachter and Wheeler, 1962). Before viewing the movie, one-third of the subjects received an injection of adrenaline, one-third got a placebo injection, and the remaining subjects were given a tranquilizer. Subjects who received the adrenaline rated the movie funniest and showed the most obvious amusement while watching it. Those given the tranquilizer were least amused, and the placebo group fell in between. Again, the explanation would be that the adrenaline group experienced arousal that was then interpreted as amusement in the context of watching the movie. This and similar experiments make it clear that emotion is much more than just an agitated body. Perception, experience, attitudes, judgment, and many other more clearly "mental" factors also affect emotion.

Attribution   We now move from slapstick movies and fear of bear bodies to appreciation of bare bodies. Stuart Valins (1967) has added an interesting refinement to Schachter's theory of cognitive labeling. According to Valins, perceptions of emotion depend on what feelings of physical arousal are attributed to. To demonstrate **attribution,** Valins (1966) showed undergraduate male students a series of slides of nude females. While watching the slides, subjects heard an amplified heartbeat that they believed was their own. In reality they were listening to a recorded

---

*To be accurate, it must be noted that one recent attempt to repeat the Schachter-Singer study failed to get the same results (Marshall, 1976; Zimbardo, 1977). Remember, however, that a theory is not proved or disproved by a single experiment. A large number of other studies lend support to the cognitive theory of emotion.

heartbeat carefully designed to beat *louder* and *stronger* when some (but not all) of the slides were shown.

After viewing the slides, subjects were asked to rate which they found most attractive. Students exposed to the false heart-rate information consistently rated slides that were paired with a "pounding heart" as the most attractive. In other words, when a subject saw a slide and heard his heartbeat become more pronounced, he attributed his "emotion" to the slide and his interpretation seems to have been, "Now that one I like!"

Question: That seems somewhat artificial. Does it really make any difference what arousal is attributed to?

To further illustrate attribution, imagine yourself in this situation: You are taking (and failing) an important and extremely difficult test. The person giving the test departs for a few minutes, leaving the test answers behind. Do you give in to temptation and cheat? It may depend on how much guilt or fear you feel as you consider cheating. This is the dilemma people faced in an experiment by Dienstbier and Munter (1971). Before beginning the test, each subject took a placebo pill. Some were told to expect reactions from the pill resembling fear. Others thought the pill would cause neutral side effects unrelated to emotion.

Question: Did one group cheat more than the other?

Yes. Subjects who expected fearlike reactions from the pill cheated more than those who expected neutral side effects. The people who cheated apparently blamed the butterflies in their stomach and their pounding heart on the pill, rather than on guilt or fear. As a result of this **misattribution,** they were less inhibited about cheating.

You might still be wondering how attribution works in the "real world." Consider what happens when parents interfere with the budding romance of a son or daughter. Often, trying to break up a young couple's relationship *intensifies* their feelings for one another. Parental interference adds frustration, anger, and fear or excitement (as in seeing each other "on the sly") to the couple's feelings. Since they already care for one another, they are likely to attribute all this added emotion to "true love" (Walster, 1971).

Attribution theory predicts that you are most likely to "love" someone who gets you stirred up emotionally, even when fear, anger, frustration, or rejection is part of the formula. Thus, if you want to successfully propose to someone, take them out to the middle of a narrow, windswept suspension bridge over a deep chasm and look them in the eyes. As their heart pounds wildly (from being on the bridge, not from your irresistible charms), tell them you

Fig. 13-4   *Which theory of emotion best describes the reaction of these people? Given the complexity of emotion, each theory appears to possess an element of truth.*

love them. Attribution theory predicts they will conclude, "Oh wow, I must love you too."

The preceding is not as far-fetched as it may seem. In an ingenious study, a female experimenter interviewed men in a park, some on a swaying suspension bridge 230 feet above a river and others on a solid wooden bridge just 10 feet above the ground. After the interview, each subject was given the experimenter's telephone number, so he could "find out about the results" of the study if he wanted. Men interviewed on the suspension bridge were much more likely to give the "lady from the park" a call (Dutton and Aron, 1974). Apparently, these men experienced heightened arousal, which they interpreted as attraction to the experimenter—a clear case of love at first fright!

Learning Check

Check your comprehension by answering these questions.

1. See if you can list four components of emotion: _____

    _____

2. Injection of the hormone adrenaline in laboratory subjects produces nonemotional physiological changes, described as:

    a. cold emotions   *b.* cognitive emotions   *c.* cognitive arousal   *d.* modulations

3. Awe, remorse, and disappointment are among the primary emotions listed by Robert Plutchik.   T or F?

4. According to the James-Lange theory of emotion, we see a bear, are frightened, and run.   T or F?

5. The Cannon-Bard theory of emotion says that bodily arousal and emotional experience occur _____.

6. According to Schachter's cognitive theory, bodily arousal must be labeled or interpreted for an emotional experience to occur.   T or F?

7. The example of the man who thought he was depressed when he was actually ill demonstrates the concept of attribution.   T or F?

8. Subjects in Valin's false heart-rate study attributed apparent increases in their heart rate to the action of a placebo.   T or F?

Answers: 1. subjective feelings, emotional expressions, physiological arousal, interpretation   2. a   3. F   4. F   5. simultaneously   6. T   7. T   8. F

Physiology and Emotion— Arousal, Sudden Death, and Lying

To a large degree, the physical aspects of emotion are innate or built into the body. The physical reactions of an African Bushman frightened by a wild animal and an urbane city dweller frightened by a prowler are quite similar. Unpleasant emotions produce especially consistent reactions. Among the most frequent are: pounding heart, muscular tenseness, irritability, dryness of the throat and mouth, sweating, butterflies in the stomach, frequent urination, trembling, restlessness, sensitivity to loud noises, and a large number of internal reactions (Shaffer, 1947). The consistency of these reactions is tied to the fact that they are caused by the **autonomic nervous system (ANS).** As you may recall from the discussion in Chapter 3, the reactions of the ANS are *automatic* and not normally under voluntary control. There are two divisions to the ANS, one called the **sympathetic branch,** and the other, the **parasympathetic branch.**

Question: What do these do during emotion?

Fight or Flight   The sympathetic branch prepares the body for emergency action—"fight or flight"—by arousing a number of bodily systems and inhibiting others. (Sympathetic nervous system effects are listed in Table 13-1.) These changes have a purpose. Sugar is released into the bloodstream for quick energy, the heart beats faster to distribute blood to the muscles, the unnecessary process of digestion is temporarily inhibited, blood flow in the skin is restricted to reduce bleeding, and so forth. Most of the sympathetic reactions increase the chances that a person or an animal will survive an emergency.

The actions of the parasympathetic branch generally reverse emotional arousal and calm and relax the body. After a period of high emotion, the heart is slowed, the pupils return to normal size, blood flow shifts away from the muscles and back to the internal organs, and so forth. In addition to restoring balance, the parasympathetic system helps build up and conserve bodily energy.

The parasympathetic system responds much more slowly than the sympathetic. This is why when you experience an emotion, such as fear, increased heart rate, muscular tension, and other signs of arousal do not subside until 20 or 30 minutes after the threat has passed.

Sudden Death   As we noted in the "Chapter Preview," the parasympathetic system may overreact during intense fear and in rare cases cause death. Voodoo curses are not the only cause of such deaths. There is evidence that in times of war the pressures of combat can be so intense that some soldiers literally die of fear (Moritz and Zamchech, 1946). Even in civilian life such deaths are apparently possible. In one case a terrified young woman was admitted to a hospital because she felt she was going to die. A backwoods midwife had predicted that the woman's two sisters would die before their sixteenth and twenty-first birthdays. Both died as predicted. The midwife also predicted that this woman would die before her twenty-third birthday. She was found dead in her hospital bed the day after she was admitted. It was two days before her twenty-third birthday (Zimbardo, 1975). The woman was an apparent victim of her own terror.

Question: Is the parasympathetic nervous system always responsible for such deaths?

Probably not. In the case of older individuals, or people with heart problems, the direct effects of sympathetic activation may be enough to bring about heart attack and collapse. For example, at a memorial concert honoring the late Louis Armstrong, his widow was stricken with a fatal heart attack as she played the final chord of "St. Louis Blues." Psychiatrist George Engel (1977) has studied hundreds of similar deaths. He found that almost half were associated with the extremely traumatic disruption of a close human relationship, or the anniversary of the loss of a loved one. Clearly, relationships are one of the most potent sources of human emotional response.

Lie Detectors   Because bodily changes caused by the autonomic nervous system are good indicators of emotion, several ways of measuring them have been developed. One use of such measures is the "lie detector." If you have not yet done so, chances are good that sooner or later you will take a lie detector test. Of course this doesn't mean you are likely to become a criminal. It simply reflects the fact that a growing number of businesses use lie detectors to screen job applicants and to check the honesty of current employees. These practices must be questioned for two reasons: First, the lie detector's accuracy is doubtful; and second, such testing is often a serious invasion of privacy (Lykken, 1981).

Question: What is a lie detector? Do lie detectors really detect lies?

The lie detector is more accurately referred to as a **polygraph** (Fig. 13-5). A polygraph (the word means "many writings") is a portable device capable of drawing a record of changes in **heart rate, blood pressure, breathing rate,** and the **galvanic skin response (GSR).** (The GSR is recorded from the surface of the hand by electrodes that measure skin conductance or, more simply, sweating.) The polygraph has become popularly known as a lie detector because of its frequent use in criminology and job inter-

Table 13-1   Autonomic Nervous System Effects

Organ	Parasympathetic System	Sympathetic System
Pupil of eyes	Constricts to diminish light	Dilates to increase light
Tear glands Mucous membrane of nose and throat Salivary glands	Stimulate secretion	Inhibit secretion Causes dryness
Heart	Slowing, constriction of blood vessels	Acceleration, dilation of blood vessels to increase blood flow
Lungs, windpipe	Constrict bronchi of lungs to relax breathing	Dilate bronchi to increase breathing
Esophagus Stomach Abdominal blood vessels	Stimulate secretions and movement	Inhibit secretions and movements, diverts blood flow
Liver	Liberates bile	Retains bile
Pancreas	———	Releases blood sugar
Intestines	Stimulate secretion	Inhibit secretion
Rectum Kidney Bladder	Excitation, expulsion of feces and urine	Inhibition, retention of feces and urine
Skin blood vessels	Dilate, increase blood flow	Constrict, skin becomes cold and clammy
Sweat glands	Inhibit	Stimulated to increase perspiration
Hair follicles	Relaxed	Tensed to make hair stand on end (piloerection)

viewing. In reality, the polygraph is not a lie detector at all. As critic David Lykken (1981) points out, there is no unique "lie response" that everyone gives when not telling the truth. The machine only records *general emotional arousal*—it can't tell the difference between fear, anxiety, lying, or excitement.

When attempting to detect a lie, the polygraph operator begins by asking a number of **control** (nonemotional)

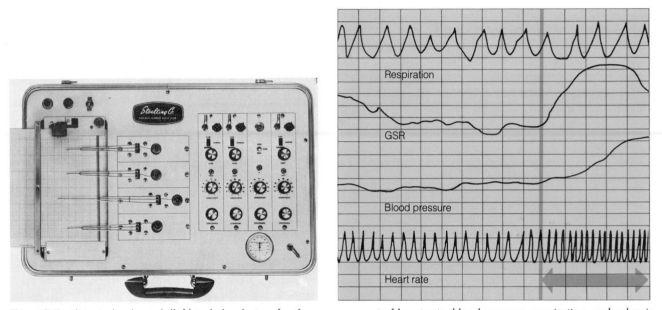

Fig. 13-5 *A typical polygraph* (left) *includes devices for the measurement of heart rate, blood pressure, respiration, and galvanic skin response. Pens mounted on the top of the machine make a record of bodily responses on a moving strip of paper* (right). *Changes in the area marked by the blue arrow indicate emotional arousal. If such responses appear when a person answers a question, he or she may be lying, but other causes of arousal are also possible.*

questions. ("What is your name? What did you have for lunch?" And so forth.) During this procedure a "baseline" or normal emotional responsiveness is established. Then **critical questions** can be asked. ("Have you ever stolen money from an employer?" "Did you murder Hensley?") A person who lies will presumably become anxious or emotional when answering critical questions.

Question: Wouldn't a person be nervous just from being questioned?

Yes, but to minimize this problem, a skilled polygraph examiner asks a *series* of questions with critical items mixed among them. An innocent person may respond emotionally to the whole procedure, but supposedly only a guilty person will show increased response to key questions. For example, a suspected bank robber might be shown a picture and asked, "Was the teller who was robbed this person? Was it this person?" (Lykken, 1974).

Even when questioning is done properly, "lie detection" may be inaccurate. For example, in August, 1978, Floyd Fay was convicted of murdering his friend Fred Ery. To prove his innocence, Fay volunteered to take a lie detector test, which he failed. Fay spent two years in prison before the real killer confessed to the crime (Lykken, 1981). If he was innocent, why did Fay fail the test? Put yourself in his

place, and it's easy to see why. Imagine the examiner asking, "Did you kill Fred?" Since you knew Fred, and you are a suspect, it's no secret that this is a critical question. What would happen to *your* heart rate, blood pressure, breathing, and perspiration under such circumstances?

Proponents of lie detection claim from 90 to 95 percent accuracy. But in one laboratory experiment, accuracy was lowered to 25 percent by subjects who intentionally thought exciting or upsetting thoughts during questioning (Smith, 1971). Similarly, the polygraph may be thrown off by self-inflicted pain, or by people who can lie without anxiety. One recent experiment showed that tranquilizing drugs interfere with the detection of lies (Waid and Orne, 1982). Worst of all, the test's most common error is to label an innocent person guilty, rather than a guilty person innocent (Lykken, 1981). In one series of tests done by police polygraph examiners, 49 percent of truthful subjects were rated as deceptive (Horvath, 1977). A chance level of accuracy would be 50 percent.

Recently, a new "lie detecting" device, called a **voice stress analyzer,** has been developed. This machine operates by picking up tiny modulations or tremors in the voice. Like the polygraph, it really detects stress, nervousness, or emotion rather than lying. Its accuracy is probably even lower than that of the polygraph. Actual tests using criminal subjects (whose guilt or innocence was later established) showed an accuracy rate only slightly above chance (Rice, 1978).

Each year hundreds of thousands of ordinary workers are forced to take polygraph exams. In some cases unsatisfactory results or failure to submit to an exam may lead to demotion, transfer, or outright firing. Growing use of voice stress analyzers may pose an even greater threat to privacy and personal rights. Since no cooperation is required, a voice test can be given without a person knowing it. Interviews or telephone conversations are easily taped for later analysis. Some insurance companies already use voice analyzers in this way to identify possible false claims (Rice, 1978).

In view of what we have said here, it is ironic that only a few states have passed laws requiring operators of lie detection devices to be licensed. True, some states have adopted laws forbidding employers to require job applicants to take polygraph tests, and the federal government is considering a law banning secret use of voice analyzers. The fact remains, however, that there is a good chance you will at some time be given a "lie detector" test. Should this occur, the best advice is to remain calm; then actively challenge the outcome if the machine wrongly questions your honesty.

Learning Check

See if you can correctly answer these questions.

1. Emotional arousal is closely related to activity of the _____ nervous system.

2. The sympathetic system prepares the body for "fight or flight."   T or F?

3. The parasympathetic system inhibits digestion and raises blood pressure and heart rate.   T or F?

4. What bodily changes are measured by a polygraph? _____

   _____

5. The polygraph is really an _____ detector.

Answers: 1. autonomic 2. T 3. F 4. heart rate, blood pressure, breathing rate, galvanic skin response 5. arousal or emotion

---

Development and Expression of Emotions—Feeling Babies and Talking Bodies

Question: How do emotions develop? Are some emotions more basic than others?

From his experiments with infants, John B. Watson identified three emotions that he considered unlearned. These are: **rage,** elicited in an infant by restricting movement; **fear,** elicited by loud noises, loss of support, and sudden shaking; and **joy,** elicited by stroking, tickling, and patting (Watson, 1930). Even the basic reactions of rage, fear, and joy take some time to develop. General **excitement** is the only emotional reponse a newborn infant clearly expresses. However, as any parent can tell you, the emotional life of a baby blossoms rapidly. One researcher (Bridges, 1932) observed a large number of babies and found that all the basic human emotions (including those that are learned and those that are not) appear before age two. Bridges found that there is a consistent order in which emotions appear and that the first basic split is between pleasant and unpleasant emotions (see Fig. 13-6). This is a very important development. Recent research shows that there is a fascinating interplay of emotions between babies and adults. When new parents see and hear a crying baby, they feel annoyed, irritated, disturbed, or unhappy. In addition, their blood pressure and perspiration increase (Frodi *et al.,* 1978). Such reactions encourage parents to tend to a baby's needs, thus increasing its chances for survival.

Question: Does the ordering Bridges observed apply to children of all cultures?

Development of the ability to express emotion is probably related to maturation of the brain, since children of all cultures show a similar pattern. In a recent investigation anthropologist Mel Konner observed the !KungSan of Botswana, Africa. The !KungSan are one of the few remaining hunting-gathering tribes in the world. Although !KungSan children are raised very differently than children in our own culture, Konner observed that their rate of emotional development is the same as our own (Greenberg, 1977). Babies the world over, it seems, rapidly become capable of

Fig. 13-6   *In the human infant, emotions are rapidly differentiated from an initial capacity for excitement. (After K. M. B. Bridges, 1932. Reprinted by permission of The Society for Research in Child Development, Inc.)*

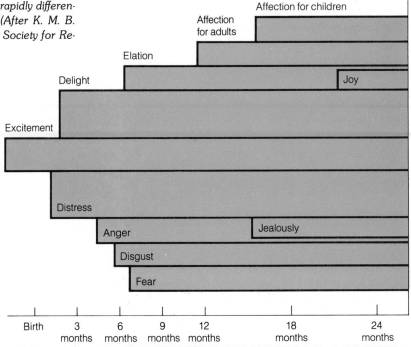

letting others know what they like and dislike. (Prove this to yourself sometime by driving a baby buggy.)

Question: Are children more emotional than adults?

Studies have shown that the occurrence of temper tantrums declines drastically between infancy and adolescence, and that emotional outbursts in general tend to become less intense as people grow older (MacFarlane *et al.*, 1954; Chown and Heron, 1965).

Question: Does this mean that people "mellow" as they age, or do they simply learn to suppress underlying emotions?

The answer is debatable, but some suppression undoubtedly does take place. For example, men and women show a difference in willingness to cry that is obviously learned. A little boy in our culture usually is encouraged to "be a man" by learning not to cry. This is unfortunate. It is pretty generally accepted by psychologists that free expression of emotion is essential for personal development. Many males pay a high price for their "manhood" by denying themselves crying as an emotional outlet. Some observers consider the "inexpressive male" a real tragedy of traditional sex role socialization. The strong, silent, and emotionally inexpressive male has long been glorified in movies, sports, fiction, and on television. Many men have learned

to view expression of their feelings as inconsistent with masculinity. The result is a style of emotional isolation that can undermine relationships with women, family, and other males (Balswick and Peek, 1971).

Emotional Expression

Are human emotional expressions a carry-over from more primitive and animal-like stages of human evolution? Charles Darwin thought so. Darwin (1872) observed that tigers, monkeys, dogs, and human beings all bare their teeth in the same way during rage. Darwin believed that emotional expressions were retained during the course of human evolution because communicating feelings to others is an aid to survival. Animals use a wide range of body movements, vocalizations (barks, screams, grunts, hoots, etc.) and facial gestures to communicate to other members of their species such emotional signals as fear, threats, greeting, danger, pain, hunger, courtship, and other information necessary for the survival of the individual and of the group (Nelson and Jurmain, 1979). (See Fig. 13-7.)

Question: Are emotional expressions the same for all people?

The most basic expressions appear to be fairly universal. Children who are born deaf and blind and who, therefore, have little opportunity to learn emotional expressions from others use the same facial gestures as others to display joy, sadness, disgust, and so on (Knapp, 1978). In fact, the gestures of such children may be one of the few examples of "pure" emotional expression. By adulthood, most people have learned to carefully control facial expression so that many gestures become unique to various cultures. Among the Chinese, for example, sticking out the tongue is a gesture of surprise, not of disrespect or teasing. Despite such differences, facial expressions of *fear, surprise, sadness, disgust, anger,* and *happiness* are recognized by people of all cultures (Ekman, 1980). Notice that this covers most of the primary emotions listed earlier in the chapter. It's also nice to note that a smile is the most universal and easily recognized facial expression of emotion.

Body Language If a friend approached you and said, "Hey, ugly, what are you doing?" would you be offended? Probably not, because such expressions are usually accompanied by a big grin. The facial and bodily gestures of emotion speak a language all their own and add an additional message to what is said verbally. The study of communication through body movement, posture, gestures, and facial expressions is called **kinesics** (informally referred to as "body language").

Question: What kinds of messages are sent with body language?

Most of the popular books on body language (for example, Fast, 1970) tend to list particular meanings for gestures. For instance, a woman who stands rigidly, crosses her arms over her breasts, or sits with her legs tightly crossed is supposedly sending a "hands off" message. But researchers in the field of kinesics emphasize that gestures are rarely this fixed in meaning (Swensen, 1973). The message might simply be, "I'm cold." Being more realistic, we would say that an overall **emotional tone** is usually communicated by "body language."

The most expressive and frequently noticed part of the body is the face. Physiologists estimate that the face is capable of producing some 20,000 different expressions. Most of these are **facial blends,** involving a mixture of two or more basic expressions. Imagine, for example, that you just received an "F" on an unfair test. Quite likely, your eyes, eyebrows, and forehead would show anger, while your mouth would express sadness (Knapp, 1978).

Most of us believe we can fairly accurately tell what others are feeling by observing facial expressions. If thousands of facial blends occur, how do we make such judgments? The answer seems to lie in the fact that facial ex-

Fig. 13-7 *The "yawn" of this baboon is actually a threat. Emotional expressions allow dominance relationships among animals to be maintained with little actual fighting.*

Fig. 13-8 *Facial and bodily gestures do not always allow an observer to accurately "read" emotion. The agonized expression on the face of Frank De Vito is deceptive. Mr. De Vito and his wife have just learned that he has won $1 million in the New Jersey state lottery.*

pressions can be boiled down to basic dimensions of **pleasantness-unpleasantness, attention-rejection,** and **activation** (or arousal) (Schlosberg, 1954). By smiling when giving a friend a "hard time," you add the emotional messages of pleasantness and acceptance to the verbal insult and change its meaning. As they say in movie Westerns, it makes a big difference to "Smile when you say that, pardner."

Other emotional feelings are telegraphed by the body. The most general seem to be **relaxation** or **tension,** and **liking** or **disliking.** Relaxation is expressed by casual positioning of the arms and legs, leaning back (if sitting), and spreading the arms and legs. Liking is expressed mainly by leaning toward a person or object (Mehrabian, 1969) (Fig. 13-9). Thus, body positioning can reveal feelings that would normally be concealed. Who do you "lean toward"?

Question: Does body positioning or movement reveal lying or deception?

If you know a person well, you may be able to detect deception from expressive changes (Ekman and Friesen, 1975). But don't count on it. Most people learn to maintain careful control over their facial expressions. A good

Fig. 13-9 *Emotions are often unconsciously revealed by gestures and body positioning.*

example is smiling to avoid hurting someone's feelings when you receive a disappointing present. Often because of such control, deception is best revealed by the lower body. Tense leg positions, and restless or repetitive foot and leg movements are associated with "fibbing" in most people (Ekman and Friesen, 1975). Even a good "con artist" may be too busy attending to his or her face to exert much control over these cues.

Coping with Emotion— When Is Fear Healthy?

You have been selected to give a speech to 300 people; or, a physician has informed you that you must undergo a dangerous and painful operation; or, the one true love of your life walks out the door. What would your emotional response to these situations be? How do you cope with an emotional threat? According to Richard Lazarus (1968, 1975), there are two important steps in the process of coping with a threatening situation. The first is **primary appraisal,** in which you decide if a situation is threatening or not. Then you make a **secondary appraisal,** during which you choose a means of meeting the threat.

The emotional effects of appraising a threat have been demonstrated in a fascinating experiment performed by Joseph C. Spiesman and his associates (1964). These researchers used a graphic film called *Subincision* to stimulate emotional responses in volunteer subjects. Subincision is a ritual used to initiate adolescent boys into manhood in a primitive Australian tribe. The filmed procedure begins with three or four adults holding a boy down to prevent escape. Then a crude and obviously painful operation is performed in which the adolescent's penis is slit on the underside for its entire length. To add insult to injury, the operation is performed with a sharpened flintstone. Needless to say, American viewers respond emotionally to the gory details of this film.

The film was shown in four different versions to test the emotional effects of different appraisals. The first had no sound track. The second emphasized the painful and traumatic aspects of the operation. The third treated the operation in an intellectual and distant way. The fourth glossed over the threatening aspects of the operation and denied that it was painful.

Question: Did the sound tracks affect emotional reactions?

Recordings of heart rate and GSR showed quite clearly that appraisal of a situation affects emotional response.

The film emphasizing traumatic aspects of the operation produced an increase in emotion over that caused by the silent film. On the other hand, the intellectual and denial sound tracks reduced emotion. The way a situation is "sized up" therefore becomes very important to coping with it. Public speaking, for instance, can be appraised as an intense threat, or as a chance to perform. Emphasizing the threat by imagining failure, rejection, or embarrassment obviously invites disaster. On the other hand, underestimating the threat of a situation can also create problems. The key to effectively appraising a threatening situation seems to be to achieve a *realistic amount of fear*. Either too much or too little reduces one's ability to cope.

Question: How could too little fear be a problem?

Irving Janis (1958) has studied the adjustment of people who must undergo major surgery. He found that *moderate* levels of fear were associated with better adjustment to the pain, helplessness, and vulnerability felt after the operations. People who showed little fear beforehand failed to do the "work of worrying" necessary for anticipating and rehearsing the approaching discomforts. Those who showed extreme fear were adversely affected because they added emotional upheaval to the stress of surgery. Fear appears to be a very useful emotion, but only when it is in proportion to the amount of threat. When fear is moderate and realistic it helps people prepare for stressful or threatening events.

Learned Helplessness—Is There Hope?

Question: What would happen if a person appraised a threatening situation as hopeless?

Bruno Bettelheim (1960), who survived imprisonment in Nazi concentration camps, has described a reaction he calls "give-up-itis." Many of the prisoners felt so helpless that they developed a "zombie-like" detachment that made them into "walking corpses." Martin Seligman (1974) has described a similar reaction in Vietnam prisoner of war camps. Seligman reports the case of a young marine who had adapted unusually well to the stresses of being a POW. His health was apparently related to a promise made by his captors that if he would cooperate he would be released on a certain date. As the date approached, his spirits soared. Then came a devastating blow. He had been deceived. There was never any intention of releasing him. He immediately lapsed into a deep depression, refused to eat or drink, and died shortly thereafter.

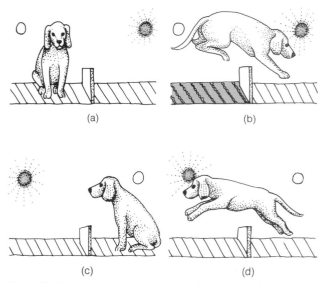

Fig. 13-10 *In the normal course of escape and avoidance learning, a light dims shortly before the floor is electrified* (a). *Since the light does not yet have meaning for the dog, the dog receives a shock (noninjurious, by the way) and leaps the barrier* (b). *Dogs soon learn to watch for the dimming of the light* (c) *and to jump before receiving a shock* (d). *Dogs made to feel "helpless" rarely even learn to escape shock, much less to avoid it.*

Examples such as these are admittedly extreme, but they demonstrate once again the power of emotions. Recent attempts to understand such events have focused on the concept of **learned helplessness.**

Learned helplessness has been demonstrated in the laboratory with animals tested in a shuttle box (Fig. 13-10). If placed in one side of a divided box, dogs will quickly learn to leap to the other side to escape an electric shock. If they are given a warning before the shock occurs (for example, a light dims), most dogs will learn to avoid the shock by leaping the barrier before the shock arrives. This is true of most dogs, but not those who have learned to feel helpless.

Question: How is a dog made to feel helpless?

Before being tested in the shuttle box, some dogs were placed in a harness (from which they could not escape) and were given several painful shocks. The animal was helpless to prevent these shocks (Overmier and Seligman, 1967). When placed in the shuttle box, these dogs reacted to the first shock by crouching, howling, and whining. None tried to escape. They helplessly resigned themselves to their fate—after all, they had already learned that there was nothing they could do about shock.

Question: What does learned helplessness have to do with emotion?

Depression Seligman and his associates have drawn attention to the similarities between learned helplessness and depression. Symptoms that occur in both depression and learned helplessness include: feelings of powerlessness and hopelessness, decreased activity, lowered aggression, loss of sexual drive and appetite, and, in humans, a tendency to see oneself as failing even when this is not the case (Miller, Rossellini, and Seligman, 1977).

Depression is one of the most widespread emotional problems, and it undoubtedly has many causes. However, Seligman has made a good case for learned helplessness as a major factor in many cases of depression and hopelessness. For example, Seligman (1972) describes the fate of Archie, a 15-year-old boy. For Archie, school has been an unending series of shocks and failures. Other students treat him as if he's stupid; in class he rarely answers questions because he doesn't know some of the words. He feels knocked down every direction he turns. These may not be electric shocks, but they are certainly psychological "shocks," and Archie has learned to feel helpless to prevent them. When he leaves school his chances of success will be poor. He has learned to passively endure whatever shocks life has in store for him.

Question: Does Seligman's research give any clues about how to "unlearn" helplessness?

Hope With dogs, the most effective technique has been to forcibly drag them away from the shock into the "safe" compartment. After this is done several times, the animals regain "hope" and feelings of control over the environment. Just how this can be accomplished with humans is a question for further research. It seems obvious, however, that someone like Archie would benefit from an educational program that would allow him to "succeed" repeatedly.

We might even be able to "immunize" people against helplessness and depression by giving them experience at mastering seemingly impossible challenges. The Outward Bound schools, in which people pit themselves against the rigors of mountaineering, white-water canoeing, and wilderness survival, might serve as a model for such a program.

As a final note, the value of hope should not be overlooked. As fragile as this emotion seems to be, it is a powerful antidote to depression and helplessness. As an individual, you may find hope in religion, nature, human companionship, or even technology. Wherever you find it, remember its value: It is among the most important of all human emotions.

Learning Check

1. The first recognizable emotional response in a newborn baby is fear.   T or F?

2. The pattern of emotional development in human infants varies greatly from one culture to another.   T or F?

3. Charles Darwin held that emotional expression aids survival for animals.   T or F?

4. A formal term for "body language" is: _____ .

5. Circle the three dimensions of emotion communicated by facial expressions:

   pleasantness-unpleasantness   curiosity-disinterest   anger
   attention-rejection   complexity   activation

6. Patterns of movement in the lower extremities are often a better indicator of deception than are expressive facial gestures.
   T or F?

7. People seem to best cope with threatening situations when their fear level is lowest.   T or F?

8. Depression in humans is similar to _____ _____ observed in animal experiments.

Answers: 1. F   2. F   3. T   4. kinesics   5. pleasantness-unpleasantness, attention-rejection, activation   6. T   7. F   8. learned helplessness

Resources Summary

● There is evidence that "voodoo" deaths actually occur; they are probably caused by intense and prolonged emotional response. Despite this, emotions were probably retained in evolution because they are linked to many basic *adaptive behaviors.*

● Four major parts of an emotion are: *subjective feelings, emotional expressions, physiological changes* in the body, and *interpretation* of the emotional experience.

● The following are usually considered to be *primary emotions: fear, surprise, sadness, disgust, anger, anticipation, joy,* and *acceptance.* Other emotions seem to represent mixtures of the primaries.

● Because of the complexity of emotions, several theories have been proposed to account for them.

● The *James-Lange theory* says that emotional *experience* follows the bodily reactions of emotion.

● The *Cannon-Bard theory* says that bodily reactions and emotional experience occur at the same time and that emotions are organized in the brain.

● Schachter's *cognitive theory* of emotion emphasizes the importance of labels or interpretations applied to feelings of bodily arousal.

● Closely related to cognitive theory is the process of *attribution.* Attribution refers to the emotional effects of associating bodily arousal with a particular person, object, or situation.

● Physical changes associated with emotion are caused by the action of *adrenaline,* a hormone released into the bloodstream, and by activity in the *autonomic nervous system (ANS).*

● The *sympathetic branch* of the ANS is primarily responsible for arousing the body, the *parasympathetic branch* for quieting it. Sudden death due to prolonged and intense emotion is probably a parasympathetic effect. Heart attacks caused by sudden intense emotion are more likely due to sympathetic arousal.

● The *polygraph* or "lie detector" measures emotional arousal by monitoring *heart rate, blood pressure, breathing rate,* and the *galvanic skin response (GSR).* The accuracy of the lie detector has been challenged by recent research. A new "lie detecting" device called a *voice stress analyzer* appears to be even less accurate.

● Emotions develop from the *generalized excitement* observed in newborn babies. Three of the basic emotions— *fear, rage,* and *joy*—may be unlearned. Basic emotional expressions, such as smiling, frowning, or baring one's teeth when angry, also appear to be unlearned. As a result, some psychologists consider them a carry-over from earlier stages of evolution.

● Body gestures and movements (body language) also express feelings, mainly by communicating *emotional tone* rather than specific messages. Three dimensions of facial gestures are *pleasantness-unpleasantness, attention-rejection,* and *activation.* The formal study of body language is known as *kinesics.*

● The *appraisal* of a situation greatly affects emotional response to it. Fear reactions in particular are related to the appraisal of threat. Accurate appraisal of threat and moderate amounts of fear may be helpful in coping with a stressful situation.

● The concept of *learned helplessness* has been used to explain failure to cope with threatening situations, and as a model for understanding *depression.*

Coping with Death and Depression—Problems for Everyone

DEAR ABBY: Do you think about dying much?
                                        CURIOUS

DEAR CURIOUS: No, it's the last thing I want to do.

There are a number of situations in each person's life that are heavily charged with emotion. The second most difficult to handle is probably the death of a close friend or relative; the first is one's own impending death.

Death is a topic of importance to us all. The statistics on death are very convincing: One out of one dies. In spite of this, there tends to be a conspiracy of silence surrounding the topic of death. Perhaps this is because most of us would rather not be reminded of our ultimate demise. Modern medical practice and the funeral industry have also served to insulate most people from contact with death. As a result, most of us are poorly informed about a process that is as basic as birth.

We have seen in this chapter that it is valuable to understand one's own emotions and those of others. With this in mind, this section begins with an investigation of emotional responses before, during, and after death.

Fears of Death

Fears of death are not so extensive as might be supposed. In a public opinion poll of 1500 adults, only about 4 percent showed evidence of directly fearing their own death (Kastenbaum and Aisenberg, 1972). Those fears that do exist apparently change with age. Hall (1922) found that younger individuals fear the *occurrence* of death, whereas older people fear the *circumstances* of death. In another study, elderly patients were rated for signs of fear before death. It was found that feelings of acceptance, anticipation, and, in some cases, apathy, far outnumbered instances of fear before death.

These findings seem to indicate a general lack of fear about death, but there is another possible interpretation. It may be more accurate to say that they reflect a deeply ingrained tendency to deny the reality of death. The mere fact that death has been something of a taboo subject suggests that underlying fears do exist. When *Psychology*

Today surveyed its readers on the subject of death, it was found that less than one-third of those who replied grew up in families in which death was openly talked about (Schneidman, 1971). The average person's exposure to death unfortunately consists of the artificial and obviously unrealistic portrayals of death on TV. It has been estimated that by the time a person is 14 years old, he or she will have witnessed 18,000 TV deaths. With almost no exceptions these will have been *homicides,* not deaths due to illness or aging (Tobin, 1972).

The Stages of Death

A more direct indication of emotional responses to death comes from the work of Elizabeth Kübler-Ross (1975). Kübler-Ross, a **thanatologist** (one who studies death), has spent hundreds of hours at the bedsides of the terminally ill. She has found that the dying person tends to go through a series of emotional stages in order to prepare for death. The five basic steps are:

1. Denial and isolation. The initial reaction to impending death is an attempt to deny its reality and to isolate oneself from all information confirming that death is really going to occur. Initially the person may be convinced that "It's all a mistake," that lab reports or X-rays have been mixed up, or that a physician is in error. This may proceed to attempts to ignore or avoid any reminder of the situation.

2. Anger. In this stage the dying say, "Why me?" As they face the ultimate frustration of having everything ever valued stripped away, their anger spills over into rage or envy toward those who will continue living. Even good friends may temporarily become enemies because of their health.

3. Bargaining. During this period, the dying bargain with themselves or with God. The dying person says, "Just let me live a little longer and I'll do anything to earn it." Individuals may bargain for time by trying to be "good" ("I'll never smoke again"), by righting past wrongs, or by praying that if they are granted more time they will dedicate themselves to their religion.

Applications

4. Depression. As death draws nearer and the person begins to recognize that it cannot be prevented, feelings of futility, exhaustion, and deep depression set in. The person recognizes that he or she will be separated from friends, loved ones, and the familiar routines of life, and this causes a profound sadness.

5. Acceptance. Assuming that death is not sudden, many people eventually reach a stage during which they calmly accept death. The dying are neither happy nor sad, but are at peace. This is usually a quiet time when the struggle with death has been resolved. The need to talk about death is ended, and silent companionship from others is frequently all that is desired.

Not all terminally ill individuals experience all these stages, and the stages may not always occur in this order. Individual styles of dying vary greatly, according to emotional maturity, religious belief, age, education, the attitudes of relatives, and so forth. Some psychologists feel that Kübler-Ross' description of dying has been taken too literally by the public. It is probably best not to think of the stages as a fixed series to go through, with later stages being ''more advanced.'' Rather, the stages describe typical and appropriate reactions to impending death. In this sense, Kübler-Ross' work is a good summary of emotional reactions to the difficult process of dying.

Question: How can I make use of this information?

This information can be put to use in a number of ways. First of all, it can help both the dying individual and survivors to recognize and to cope with periods of depression, anger, denial, and bargaining. Secondly, it is helpful to realize that close friends or relatives of the dying person may go through many of the same emotional stages before or after the person's death.

Perhaps the most important thing to recognize is that the dying person may have a need to share feelings with others and to discuss death openly. Too often, the dying person feels isolated and separated from others by the wall of silence erected by doctors, nurses, and family members. Adults tend to ''freeze up'' with a dying person, saying things such as, ''I don't know how to deal with this.''

Understanding what the dying person is going through may make it easier for you to offer support at this important time. A simple willingness to be with the person and to honestly share his or her feelings can help bring dignity, acceptance, and meaning to death. (For more information on death see Chapter 16 ''Exploration'': ''Approaching Death—New Pathways.'')

Bereavement   After a friend or relative has died, a period of grief typically follows. Grief is a natural and normal reaction to loss, and most psychologists regard it as an essential part of adjusting to death. In our culture, funeral services frequently serve as useful outlets for grief by encouraging the release of emotions.

Grief usually follows a predictable pattern (Schulz, 1978; Parkes, 1979). Grief normally begins with a period of **shock,** or numbness. For a brief time, the bereaved remain in a dazed state in which they may show little emotion. Most find it extremely difficult to accept the reality of their loss. This phase usually ends by the time of the funeral, which unleashes tears and bottled up feelings of despair.

Initial shock is followed by sharp **pangs of grief.** These are episodes of painful yearning for the dead person, and sometimes, anguished outbursts of anger. During this period the wish to have the dead person back is intense. Often, mourners continue to think of the dead person as alive; they may hear his or her voice, or encounter the deceased in vivid dreams. During this period, agitated distress alternates with silent despair, and suffering is acute.

The first powerful reactions of grief gradually give way to weeks or months of **apathy, dejection,** and **depression.** The person faces a new emotional landscape with a large gap that cannot be filled. Life seems to lose much of its meaning, and a sense of futility dominates the person's outlook. The mourner is usually able to resume work or other activities after two or three weeks, but insomnia, loss of energy and appetite, and similar signs of depression may continue.

Little by little, the bereaved person accepts that which cannot be changed, and makes a new beginning. Pangs of grief may still occur, but they are less severe and less frequent. Memories of the dead person, though still painful, now include positive images and nostalgic pleasure. As was true of approaching death, individual reactions to

Applications

grief vary considerably. In general, however, a month or two typically passes before the more intense stages of grief have run their course.

As you can see, the grief process allows survivors to discharge their anguish and to prepare to go on living. A person who avoids this "grief work" by suppressing feelings may later experience a more severe and lasting depression. Therefore, it is important for people who suffer a loss to accept the need to grieve, and for those around them to support this necessary expression of emotion (Schulz, 1978).

Coping with Depression

Recent studies show that during the school year up to 78 percent of students at American colleges suffer some of the symptoms of depression. At any given time roughly one-quarter of the student population is involved (Beck and Young, 1978). Why should so many students be "blue"? A variety of problems typically contribute to such depressive feelings. Among the most common are:

1. Stresses from the increased difficulty of college work and pressures to make a career choice often leave students feeling that they are missing out on fun or that all their hard work is meaningless.
2. Isolation and loneliness are common when a student leaves his or her support group behind. Formerly, family, a circle of high school friends, and often an intimate boyfriend or girfriend could be counted on for support or encouragement.
3. Problems with studying and grades frequently trigger depression. Many students enter college with high aspirations and little former experience with failure. At the same time, many lack basic skills necessary for academic success.
4. A fourth common cause of college depression is the breakup of an intimate relationship, either with a former boyfriend or girlfriend, or with a newly formed college romance (Beck and Young, 1978).

Recognizing Depression Most people know, obviously enough, when they are "down." Aaron Beck, a nationally recognized authority on depression, suggests you should assume more than a minor fluctuation in mood is involved when five conditions exist:

1. You have a consistently negative opinion of yourself.
2. You engage in frequent self-criticism and self-blame.
3. You place negative interpretations on events that usually wouldn't bother you.
4. The future looks bleak and negative.
5. You feel that your responsibilities are overwhelming.

Question: What can be done to combat depression?

Combating Depression Beck and Greenberg (1974) suggest you should begin by making a *daily schedule* for yourself. Try to schedule activities to fill up every hour during the day. It is best to start with easy activities and progress to more difficult tasks. Check off each activity as it is completed. In this way you will begin to break the self-defeating cycle of feeling helpless and falling further behind (depressed students spend much of their time sleeping). A series of small accomplishments, successes, or pleasures may be all you need to get going again. However, if you are lacking skills needed for success in college ask for help in getting them. Don't remain "helpless."

Beck and Greenberg also believe that feelings of worthlessness and hopelessness are supported by thoughts such as those listed here. They recommend writing down self-critical or negative thoughts as they occur, especially those that immediately precede feelings of sadness. After you have collected these thoughts, write a rational answer to each. For example, the thought, "No one loves me," should be answered with a list of those who do care.

Attacks of the "college blues" are common and should be distinguished from more serious cases of depression. Severe depression is a serious problem that can lead to suicide or a major impairment of emotional functioning.

Question: How can mild depression be distinguished from more serious problems?

This is a rather difficult judgment to make because it is related to many psychological dimensions. Practically speaking, a useful answer can be found in a list of 10 "danger signals" compiled by the National Association for Mental Health to help people distinguish normal depression from reactions that require professional help. Here is the list:

1. A general and lasting feeling of hopelessness and despair.
2. Inability to concentrate, making reading, writing, and

Applications

conversation difficult. Thinking and activity are slowed because the mind is absorbed by inner anguish.

3. Changes in physical activities such as eating, sleeping, and sex. Frequent physical complaints with no evidence of physical illness.

4. Loss of self-esteem, which brings on continual questioning of personal worth.

5. Withdrawal from others due to immense fear of rejection.

6. Threats or attempts to commit suicide, viewed as a way out of a hostile environment and a belief that life is worthless.

7. Hypersensitivity to words and actions of others and general irritability.

8. Misdirected anger and difficulty in handling most feelings. Self-directed anger because of perceived worthlessness may produce general anger directed at others.

9. Feelings of guilt in many situations. A depressed person assumes he or she is wrong or responsible for the unhappiness of others.

10. Extreme dependency on others. Feelings of helplessness and then anger at the helplessness.

No single item (except number 6) necessarily indicates dangerous depression, but if several are observed, it should be assumed that it would be wise to seek professional help.

Learning Check

1. The majority of deaths portrayed on TV involve elderly people who die of some fatal disease.   T or F?
2. In the stage that Kübler-Ross describes as "bargaining," the dying individual asks, "Why me?"   T or F?
3. A dazed state of shock or numbness is typical of the first phase of grief.   T or F?
4. Many authorities stress that suppression of grief often leads to later problems, such as severe depression.   T or F?
5. At any given time, close to one-half of the college student population suffers some of the symptoms of depression.   T or F?
6. To break a cycle of depression and helplessness, Beck and Greenberg suggest it is best to start with easy activities and progress to more difficult tasks.   T or F?

Answers: 1. F   2. F   3. T   4. T   5. F   6. T

Exploration

Emotion—The Eyes Have It. Or Do They?

Question: Is there any truth to the idea that the eyes can reveal emotion?

The eyes have long been considered "windows on the soul" and indicators of emotion. If you doubt someone's word, you may ask them to "look you in the eye," so you can judge their honesty. To express emotion, poets use phrases such as, "her eyes were limpid pools, wide with adoration." Many seasoned poker players claim to have detected a "bluff" by watching the eyes of their opponents. And we often use words, such as *soft, hard, piercing, cold,* or *warm,* to describe a person's eyes. Psychologist Eckhard Hess (1975b) believes that in each instance we are mainly referring to the *size* of a person's *pupils.* As you know, changes in light intensity cause dilation (enlargement) and constriction (narrowing) of the pupils. Hess contends that the pupils also change size in response to emotion.

Question: Can that be demonstrated?

Pupillometrics To study emotion registered by the eyes, Hess uses a technique he calls **pupillometrics.** First he films the eyes as they respond to different visual stimuli. Then he projects the movies on a screen and measures changes in the diameter of the pupils. At first, Hess was convinced that enlargement of the pupils meant a person was experiencing a pleasant emotion, and that constriction indicated unpleasant emotion. For example, male subjects showed dilation when viewing slides of nude women, hungry subjects had dilated pupils when they looked at pictures of food, and people generally showed constriction when shown pictures of human suffering. However, the case for constriction has proved weak (Woodmansee, 1970). Extremely unpleasant pictures (of mutilated corpses, for example) will produce both dilation and constriction in some people. It seems that a person may be "wide-eyed" with terror as well as with pleasure.

Despite such problems, Hess is convinced that pupil response can reveal emotion—even when a person is unaware of it or unwilling to admit it. For example, women in one experiment said they did not find a male pinup photo attractive, but their pupils dilated as they looked at it. Sensing that he had discovered not only a "window on the soul," but also a "door to the pocketbook," Hess sought to apply pupillometrics commercially. The technique of measuring pupil response has been used to pretest the attractiveness of greeting cards, packaging, silverware designs, and advertisements.

Question: Is the technique effective?

Many critics have argued that it is not. At this point, most evidence suggests that changes in pupil size register **arousal, interest,** or **attention,** rather than pleasant or unpleasant emotion. In response to his critics Hess has recently developed what he calls the **total evaluation technique (TET)** (Hess, 1975a). This technique combines galvanic skin response, pupil response, and expressions of liking or disliking to give a fuller measure of emotional reactions to products and advertisements. The TET approach looks promising, but its accuracy and practicality are as yet unproven.

Judging Others Even if the eyes do not send totally reliable messages about emotion, people act as if they do. Most people tend to *interpret* large pupils as a sign of pleasant feelings, and small pupils as a sign of negative feelings. To illustrate, Hess (1975b) showed two photos of an

Fig. 13-11 *Select the face you think looks more attractive, warm, or friendly. Research by Eckhard Hess (1975) suggests you will choose the face on the left because the pupils of the eyes are larger.*

Exploration

attractive young woman to a group of men. The photos were identical, with one exception. In one the woman's pupils had been retouched to make them larger, and in the other they were retouched to make them smaller. The men consistently described the woman with large pupils as "soft," "feminine," or "pretty." The same woman, with small pupils, was described as "hard," "selfish," and "cold" (Fig. 13-11).

The reactions of the men in this experiment may explain why the drug belladonna was once popular among women. When put into the eyes, belladonna (which means "pretty lady") causes the pupils to dilate. Until its use was restricted, many women used it to make themselves more "beautiful." This effect, of course, does not apply only to women. In another experiment subjects were introduced to two individuals of the opposite sex and asked to choose one as a partner for the experiment. One of the potential partners had been given eye drops to dilate his or her pupils, and the other had not. Subjects of both sexes tended to select the person with the larger pupils as their partner. Perhaps at long last we know why the "bad guys" in movies always have beady eyes!

Questions for Discussion

1. Do you consider yourself more or less emotional than average? What role has learning played in the development of your emotional life? (Consider the influence of family, friends, and culture.)

2. In what ways have emotions contributed to your enjoyment of life? In what ways have they caused problems for you?

3. There is an element of truth to each of the theories of emotion. Which seems to apply best to your own emotional experience?

4. What would be the advantages and disadvantages of being emotionless? (You might use Mr. Spock from "Star Trek" as a model for answering this question.)

5. In your opinion, what limits, if any, should be placed on the use of lie detection devices by businesses?

6. How general are the emotional stages of death described by Kübler-Ross? Do they describe the reactions of people you know who have died? Do you think they would apply to other significant losses such as divorce, collapse of a business, loss of health, or death of a friend?

7. Why do you think dying individuals so often feel isolated? How could the emotional needs of dying persons be better served than they are now in hospitals and nursing homes?

8. Did you learn "body language" from your parents? How similar are your facial and hand gestures to theirs?

9. In what ways do schools, parents, and the government encourage feelings of helplessness? In what ways do they (or could they) add to feelings of confidence, competence, or "hope"?

Suggestions for Further Reading

Darwin, C. *The Expression of Emotions in Man and Animals.* Chicago University Press, 1965 (first published in 1872).

Ekman, P., and Friesen, W. V. *Unmasking the Face.* Prentice-Hall, 1975.

Kübler-Ross, E. *On Death and Dying.* Macmillan, 1969.

Lykken, D. T. *A Tremor in the Blood: Uses and Abuses of the Lie Detector.* McGraw-Hill, 1981.

Mark, V. H., and F. R. Ervin. *Violence and the Brain.* Harper & Row, 1970.

McGee, M. G., and M. Snyder. "Attribution and Behavior: Two Field Studies," *Journal of Personality and Social Psychology,* **32,** 1975, pp. 185–190.

Plutchik, R. *Emotion.* Harper & Row, 1980.

Schachter, S., and J. E. Singer. "Cognitive, Social, and Physiological Determinants of the Emotional State," *Psychological Review,* **69,** 1962, pp. 379–399.

Schulz, R. *The Psychology of Death, Dying, and Bereavement.* Addison-Wesley, 1978.

Seligman, M. "Fall into Helplessness," *Psychology Today* (June) 1973, pp. 43–48.

14

Frustration, Conflict, Stress, and Defense

How to Build a Human Time Bomb

When he was arrested, John was sitting atop a three-ton bulldozer staring into space. Behind him lay a mile-long path of destruction, for John had cut a broad, straight path through yards, roads, and fields. Trees and fences fell before his blade. The path led back to his house where the dozer was usually kept. Why did he do it? John explained that his father had denied him use of the family car that morning. Hours later, his anger reached the exploding point. . . .

Question: What would cause someone to react so drastically to a family disagreement?

In John's case, the answer is that he was frustrated—*very frustrated! How does it feel to be frustrated? Try the following and see.*

On a sheet of paper, draw a star similar to that pictured in Fig. 14-1, but four or five inches tall. Place the drawing on a flat surface in front of a mirror, and hold a second piece of paper over the drawing so you can see the star only in the mirror. Then, using only the *mirror image* for a guide, try to trace a pencil line around the border of the star. If you watch only the mirror image of your hand and the star, you will find this task surprisingly frustrating.

If you were temporarily unsuccessful at this task, you will have some idea of what mild frustration feels like.

   Perhaps you have been as frustrated as John must have been when he climbed into the driver's seat. For example, picture yourself looking for a parking

Fig. 14-1

314

place in a crowded lot. Imagine that you are late for a test and have already been delayed by an irritating traffic jam. After 15 minutes of frantic searching, you finally spy an empty space, but as you start toward it, a Volkswagen darts around the corner and into the space. A car behind you begins to honk impatiently. Your car's radiator boils over. In such a situation you might be seized by an overwhelming desire to run over anything in sight—other cars, pedestrians, lampposts, trees, and flower beds. Few people actually carry out such impulses, but the feeling is common. Aggressive urges frequently accompany frustration.

Question: Is frustration the same as anger?

No. **Frustration** *can be defined as a negative emotional state that occurs when one is prevented from reaching a goal. John's desire to use the family car was blocked by his father. You were probably at least temporarily frustrated in your attempt to trace the star, and in the imaginary parking lot, the goal of finding a parking space was blocked by the presence of other cars.*

This chapter will discuss frustration and some of the strategies people adopt to deal with it. We will also discuss some common forms of **conflict.** *Conflicts develop when a person has two or more competing or contradictory motives or goals. Choosing between college and work, marriage and single life, or study and failure are conflicts many students face.*

Frustration and conflict are two principal causes of stress. **Stress** *occurs when demands are placed on an organism to adjust or adapt. Stress is a normal part of life, but when it is severe or continues for long periods, it can do tremendous damage. Therefore, the last section of this chapter focuses on ways for you to avoid or cope with frustration, conflict, and stress.*

Survey Questions   What causes frustration and what are typical reactions to it? When and why do people use psychological defense mechanisms? Are there different types of conflict? How is stress related to health and disease? What can be done to alleviate or manage stress?

Resources

Sources of Frustration—
Blind Alleys and Lead Balloons

Question: What causes frustration?

Obstacles of many kinds cause frustration. A useful distinction can be made between *external* and *personal* sources of frustration. **External frustration** is based on conditions outside of the individual which impede progress toward a goal. All of the following are external frustrations: getting stuck with a flat tire, having a marriage proposal rejected, finding the cupboard bare when you go to get your poor dog a bone, finding the refrigerator bare when you go to get your poor tummy a T-bone, finding the refrigerator gone when you return home, being chased out of the house by your starving dog. In other words, external frustrations are based upon *delay, failure, rejection, loss,* and other direct blocking of motives.

Notice that external obstacles can be either **social** ("slow drivers," "people who talk in theaters," "people who take 'cuts' in line"), or **nonsocial** ("stuck doors," "a dead battery," "rain on the day of the game"). If you ask 10 of your friends what has frustrated them recently, most will probably describe someone's behavior ("My sister wears my clothes without asking," "My supervisor is unfair," "My history teacher grades too hard"). As social animals, we humans are highly sensitive to social sources of frustration.

Frustration usually *increases* as the **strength, urgency,** or **importance** of a blocked motive increases. An escape artist submerged in a tank of water and bound with 200 pounds of chain could be expected to become *quite* frustrated by the jamming of a trick lock. Remember too that motivation becomes stronger as we near a goal. As a result, frustration is more intense when a person encounters an obstacle very close to a goal. If you've ever missed an "A" grade by two points, you were probably very frustrated. If you've missed an "A" by *one* point . . . well, frustration builds character, right?

A final factor typically affecting frustration is summarized by the old phrase, "the straw that broke the camel's back." *Repeated* frustrations can accumulate in their effect until a small irritation unleashes an unexpectedly violent response. The boy who bulldozed the countryside probably had been frustrated many times before by his father.

Personal frustrations are based on an individual's personal characteristics. If you are four feet tall and aspire to be a professional basketball player, you very likely will be frustrated. If you want to go to medical school, but can only earn D grades when working at your fullest capacity, you will likewise be frustrated. In both examples, frustration is ultimately based on personal limitations, although the resulting failures may be *experienced* as externally caused frustration. We will return to this point in the "Applications" section of this chapter. In the meantime, let's look at some typical reactions to frustration.

Reactions to Frustration—Irresistible Force Meets Immovable Object

Question: Does frustration always cause aggression? Aren't there other reactions?

Aggression is one of the most persistent and frequent responses to frustration, a fact documented by much psychological research (Miller, 1941). It is so common, in fact, that experiments are hardly necessary to show it. A glance at almost any newspaper will provide examples such as this one:

Burien, Washington (AP)—Barbara Smith committed the assault, but police aren't likely to press charges. Her victim was a 1964 Oldsmobile which failed once too often to start.

When Officer Jim Fuda arrived at the scene, he found one beat-up car, a broken baseball bat and a satisfied 23-year-old Seattle woman.

"I feel good," Ms. Smith reportedly told the officer. "That car's been giving me misery for years and I killed it."

Aggression is not usually the first reaction to frustration. More often, frustration is met with **persistence** char-

"Bills, bills, bills! I'll remember this when it comes time for your Christmas tip."

acterized by more **vigorous efforts** and more **variable responses.** For example, if you put your last dime in a vending machine and find that pressing the button has no effect, you will probably press harder and faster (vigorous effort) and then you will press all the other buttons (varied response). Persistence may help you to get *around* a barrier and to achieve your goal. However, if the machine *still* refuses to deliver or to return your dime, you may then become aggressive and kick the machine (or at least tell it what you think of it). Notice that many sports are based on the connection between frustration and aggression. For example, football is based on placing a barrier between the ball carrier and a goal. Millions of Americans derive great secondhand joy out of seeing a football player aggressively *break through* the opposing team's line to make the goal.

Increased persistence can be very adaptive. Overcoming a barrier ends the frustration and satisfies the need or motive directed toward the goal. The same is true of aggression that removes or destroys a barrier. Picture a small band of primitive humans, parched with thirst but separated from a waterhole by a menacing animal. It is easy to see that attacking the animal may ensure their survival. In modern society such direct aggression is seldom acceptable. If you encounter a long line at the drinking fountain, aggression is hardly an appropriate response. Since direct aggression is disruptive and generally discouraged, it is frequently *displaced.*

Question: How is aggression displaced? Does displaced aggression occur often?

Direct aggression toward a source of frustration may be impossible or it may be too dangerous. If you are frustrated by your boss at work or by a teacher at school, the cost of direct aggression may be too high (loss of a job or failure of a needed class). Instead, the aggression may be displaced or *redirected* toward whoever or whatever is available.

Targets of displaced aggression tend to be "safer" or less likely to retaliate than the original source of frustration. Attacking the helpless countryside when the real source of frustration is one's father is a clear case of **displaced aggression.** Sometimes long *chains* of displaced aggression can be observed, in which one person displaces aggression to the next. For instance, a businessman who is frustrated by high taxes reprimands an employee, who swallows his anger until he reaches home and then yells at his wife, who in turn yells at the children, who then tease the dog; the dog chases the cat, who later knocks over the canary cage.

Psychologists attribute much of the hostility and destructiveness in our society to displaced aggression. Urban ghetto areas that have been rocked by riots are filled with people who live daily with high levels of frustration brought on by poverty and social inequalities. In many communities across the nation, the result of such long-term frustration has been displaced aggression on a grand scale, with anything and everything serving as potential targets for attack and destruction.

Another form of displaced aggression is **scapegoating.** A scapegoat is a person (or a group of people) toward whom displaced aggression is habitually directed. For example, during and before World War II, Hitler used the Jews in Germany as scapegoats. Hitler blamed Germany's problems on the Jews and encouraged the German people to vent their frustrations through hatred of the Jews. Another disturbing example of displaced aggression on a large scale is the fact that in the United States between 1880 and 1930 there was a strong correlation between the price of cotton and the number of lynchings of blacks in the South. As the price of cotton went down (and frustration increased), the number of lynchings increased (Dollard *et al.*, 1939).

Question: I have a friend who dropped out of school and joined the French foreign legion. He seemed very frustrated before he quit. What type of response to frustration is this?

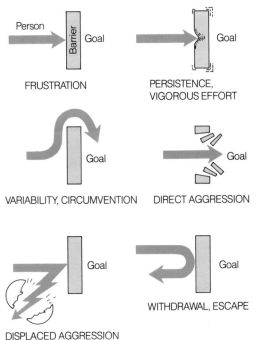

Fig. 14-2 *Frustration, and reactions to it.*

Another major reaction to frustration is **escape** or **withdrawal.** It is unpleasant to be frustrated. If other reactions do not reduce feelings of frustration, a person may try to escape. Escape may mean actually leaving a source of frustration (dropping out of school, quitting a job, leaving an unhappy marriage), or it may mean *psychologically* escaping. Two common forms of psychological escape are *apathy* (pretending not to care) and the *use of drugs* such as alcohol, marijuana, or narcotics. (See Fig. 14-2 for a summary of common reactions to frustration.)

Thus far we have examined only the most obvious responses to frustration. A whole class of *defensive* reactions also exists. Let's see how they operate.

Learning Check

Be sure you can answer these questions before continuing.

1. When progress toward a goal is blocked, the resulting psychological state is called _____.

2. Delays, rejection, and losses may be thought of as what kind of frustration? _____.

3. Which of the following is *not* considered a common reaction to frustration?

   a. ambivalence   *b.* aggression   *c.* displaced aggression   *d.* persistence

4. Scapegoating can be thought of as a type of displaced aggression.   T or F?

5. Sampson Goliath is seven feet tall and weighs 300 pounds. He has failed miserably in his aspirations to become a jockey.
    The source of his frustration is mainly: _____.

6. As a reaction to frustration, apathy may be viewed as a form of _____.

7. Being very close to a goal when a barrier is encountered typically increases the intensity of frustration.   T or F?

Answers: 1. frustration 2. external 3. a 4. T 5. personal 6. escape or withdrawal 7. T

Psychological Defense—Mental Karate?

Situations causing frustration, conflict, or stress are often accompanied by an unpleasant emotional state known as **anxiety.** A person who is anxious becomes tense, uneasy, apprehensive, worried, and feels vaguely threatened. Anxiety is less focused and specific than fear, but like fear it activates the autonomic nervous system. Thus, when you are anxious your heart beats faster, your palms sweat, your breathing accelerates, and your chest feels tight. In fact, your entire body feels "uptight."

Since anxiety is unpleasant and uncomfortable, we are usually motivated to avoid it. Anxiety caused by stressful situations, or by confrontations with our own shortcomings and limitations, frequently leads to use of **psychological defense mechanisms.**

Question: What are psychological defense mechanisms and how do they lessen anxiety?

A defense mechanism is any technique used to avoid, deny, or distort sources of anxiety. Defense mechanisms are also used to maintain an idealized self-image so that we can comfortably live with ourselves. Many of the defenses were first identified by Sigmund Freud, who assumed they operate *unconsciously.* Often, this unconscious quality creates large "blind spots" in awareness, as when an extremely stingy person fails to recognize that he or she is a "tightwad." Everyone has at one time or another used such defenses; let's consider a few of the most common. (A more complete listing is given in Table 14-1. Notice, though, that the defenses are listed alphabetically. Many psychologists consider *repression* the most basic defense, because it contributes to several others.)

Denial   One of the most primitive defense mechanisms is **denial.** Denial means to protect oneself from an unpleasant reality by refusing to accept it or believe it. Denial is closely associated with death, illness, and similar painful and threatening experiences. For instance, if you were informed that you have only three months to live, what would be your first reactions? They would probably include thoughts such as: "Aw, come on, someone must have mixed up the X-rays," or, "The doctor must be mistaken," or simply, "It can't be true!" Similar denial and disbelief

Table 14-1   Psychological Defense Mechanisms

Compensation	Counteracting a real or imagined weakness by emphasizing desirable traits or by seeking to excel in other areas.
Denial	Protecting oneself from an unpleasant reality by refusing to perceive it.
Fantasy	Fulfilling frustrated desires in imaginary achievements or activities.
Intellectualization	Separating emotion from a hurtful, threatening, or anxiety-provoking situation by talking and thinking about it in formal or "intellectual" terms.
Isolation	Separating contradictory thoughts or feelings into "logic-tight compartments" so that no conflict is created.
Projection	Attributing one's own feelings, shortcomings, or unacceptable impulses to others.
Rationalization	Justifying one's own behavior by giving reasonable and "rational" but false reasons for it.
Reaction Formation	Preventing dangerous impulses from being expressed by exaggerating opposite behavior.
Regression	Retreating to an earlier level of development or to earlier, less demanding habits or situations.
Repression	Preventing painful or dangerous thoughts from entering consciousness.
Sublimation	Working off frustrated desires, or unacceptable impulses, in activities that are constructive.

are common reactions to the unexpected death of a friend or relative: "It's just not real. I don't believe it. I just don't believe it!" And, in an all too common example, denial often explains why a person may be the "last to know" when a spouse or lover is "cheating on them." Even when signs of infidelity are clear, the person may fail to perceive them until long after it's obvious to others.

Repression   Freud noticed that his patients had tremendous difficulty recalling shocking or traumatic events from childhood. It seemed that powerful forces were holding these painful memories from awareness. Freud called this **repression.** Apparently, we protect ourselves by repressing thoughts or impulses that are painful or threatening. Feelings of hostility toward a loved one, the names of disliked people, and past failures and embarrassments are common targets of repression.

Repression may seem similar to denial, but there is a difference. Let's say you are often criticized by others for being selfish. If you are aware of the criticism, but refuse to believe that it is meant seriously, you are using denial as a defense. What if, on the other hand, you selectively forget each time your selfishness is mentioned? Such repression would leave you totally unaware of your fault. In the first instance, you are aware of the criticism, but deny its seriousness; in the second, you repress the criticism entirely.

Reaction Formation   **Reaction formation** is a defense in which impulses are not only repressed, they are also held in check by exaggerated opposite behavior. For example, a mother who unconsciously resents her children may, through reaction formation, become overprotective and overindulgent to an exaggerated degree. Her real thoughts of "I hate them" and "I wish they were gone" are replaced by "I love them" and "I don't know what I would do without them." The mother's hostile impulses are traded in for "smother love," so that she will not have to admit her dislike of her children. The basic idea is that an unacceptable feeling or impulse is so threatening that it is not enough simply to repress it. The individual goes overboard to act out a behavior opposite from the real impulse or feeling.

Regression   In its broadest meaning, **regression** refers to any return to earlier, less demanding situations or habits. Most parents who have a second child have had to put up with at least some regression by the older child. Frustrated by a new rival for attention, an older child may regress to childish speech, bed-wetting, or infantile play after the new

baby arrives. However, regression is usually less severe. The child at summer camp who gets homesick and longs for the security of familiar surroundings is undergoing mild regression. An adult who throws a temper tantrum or a married adult who "goes home to mother" is also regressing. Milder forms of regression can be observed on college campuses the last week or so before final exams. Touch football games, Frisbee matches, the throwing of paper airplanes, and other playful activities blossom as students begin to feel the pressure of exams.

Projection   Projection is an unconscious process that protects us from the anxiety caused by traits in ourselves that consciously we would find unacceptable.

Question: How does projection work?

A person who is **projecting** unconsciously transfers his or her own shortcomings or unacceptable impulses to others. By exaggerating these unacceptable traits in others, the individual lessens his or her own failings.

The author once worked for a greedy shop owner who was dedicated to separating every customer from as much money as possible, often by sharp and deceptive practices. This same man considered himself a pillar of the community and a good Christian. How did he justify to himself his greed and dishonesty? He believed that everyone who entered his store was bent on cheating him any way they could. In reality, few, if any, of his customers shared his motives, but he projected his own greed and dishonesty to them.

Rationalization   Every teacher is familiar with a rather amazing phenomenon that occurs whenever a test is scheduled. On the day of the exam, an incredible wave of disasters sweeps through the city. An amazing number of mothers, fathers, sisters, brothers, aunts, uncles, grandparents, friends, relatives, and pets become ill or die. Motors suddenly fall out of automobiles. Books are lost or stolen. Alarm clocks roll over and ring out no more.

The making of excuses comes from a natural tendency to explain one's behavior. When the explanations offered are reasonable, rational, and convincing—but not the real reasons—we say a person is *rationalizing.* **Rationalization** unconsciously provides us with reasons for behavior we ourselves find somewhat questionable. Here is a typical example of rationalization. A student who fails to turn in an assignment made at the beginning of the semester explains:

> My car broke down two days ago and I couldn't get to the library until yesterday. Then I couldn't get all the books I needed because some were checked out, but I wrote what

I could. Then last night, as the last straw, the ribbon in my typewriter broke, and since all the stores were closed I couldn't finish the paper on time.

If asked why he left the assignment until the last minute (the real reason for its being late), the student would probably launch into another set of rationalizations. If these are questioned, the student will probably become emotional as he is forced to see himself without the protection of his rationalizations.

Sour grapes and **sweet lemons** reactions are two familiar variations of rationalization. "Sour grapes" refers to making an unobtainable goal seem less appealing. If you are not invited to a party, you will probably tell yourself, "It would have been dull anyway. I'm not missing anything." If you apply for a job and fail to get it, you may review its "sour" points to soften your disappointment. "Sweet lemons," of course, is the reverse of sour grapes. Here, we convince ourselves that an undesirable situation is really positive. Talk to someone who just bought a gas-guzzling car, paid too much for a house, or accepted an undesirable job. The slightest hint of skepticism on your part will unleash a flood of good points about the car, house, or job that you have "overlooked." By rationalizing, the person tries to justify his or her decision, and lessens the anxiety of thinking, "Oh no, what have I done!"

Question: All of the defense mechanisms described seem pretty undesirable. Do they have a positive side?

When people overuse defense mechanisms they become less adaptable because great amounts of emotional energy are used to control anxiety and to maintain an unrealistic self-image. Defense mechanisms do have their value, however. They may help prevent a person from being overwhelmed by a temporary threat and may provide time to learn to cope with continuing threats or frustrations. If you recognize some of your own behavior in the descriptions here, it is hardly a sign that you are hopelessly defensive. As noted earlier, most people make occasional use of defense mechanisms.

Two defense mechanisms that have a decidedly more positive quality to them are *compensation* and *sublimation*.

Compensation   Compensation is a form of behavior whereby a person tries to make up for some personal defect or fault. **Compensatory reactions** are defenses against feelings of inferiority. A person who has a deficiency or weakness (real or imagined) may go to unusual lengths to overcome the weakness or to compensate for it by excelling in other areas. Two of the better known "muscle men" in America are Jack LaLanne and Charles Atlas. Both made successful careers out of body building, in spite of the fact that they were thin and sickly as young men. Perhaps it would be more accurate to say *because* they were thin and sickly. There are dozens of examples of compensation at work. A childhood stutterer may excel in debate at college. Franklin D. Roosevelt's outstanding achievements in politics came after he was stricken with polio. As a child, Helen Keller was unable to see or hear, but she became an outstanding thinker and writer. Doc Watson, Ray Charles, Stevie Wonder, Ronnie Milsap, and a number of other well-known musicians are blind.

Sublimation   **Sublimation** is defined as working off frustrated desires (especially sexual desires) in substitute activities that are constructive and accepted by society. Freud believed that art, music, dance, poetry, scientific investigation, and most other creative activities represent a rechanneling of sexual energies into productive and acceptable behavior. He believed that almost any strong desire can be sublimated. For example, a very aggressive person may find social acceptance as a professional soldier, boxer, or football player. Greed may be refined into a successful business career. Lying may be sublimated into storytelling, creative writing, or politics.

Sexual motives appear to be the most easily and widely sublimated. Freud would have had a field day with such modern pastimes as surfing, motorcycle riding, drag racing, and dancing to or playing rock music, to name but a few. People enjoy each of these activities for a multitude of reasons, but it is hard to overlook the rich, sexual symbolism possible in each.

Summary   Most psychologists continue to assume, as did Freud, that the defense mechanisms operate unconsciously. However, some would argue that there is no reason why defense mechanisms cannot also be used to consciously control anxiety. Others, if they use the concept of defense at all, prefer to think of defense mechanisms as *learned* strategies. Denial and repression might be learned "not-thinking" responses, for example. In either case, the defense mechanisms provide a good description of common psychological reactions to frustration, stress, and anxiety. If you are unable to see some of the defenses in your own behavior, perhaps you are being too defensive!

Conflict—Yes-No-Yes-No-Yes-No-Yes-No-Yes-No . . . Well, Maybe

Conflict creates a special kind of frustration. When an individual must make a decision between *incompatible* or *contradictory* needs, desires, motives, wishes, or external demands, he or she experiences conflict. There are four basic forms of conflict, each with its own characteristics (Lewin, 1935). (See Fig. 14-3 and Fig. 14-4.)

Approach-Approach Conflicts The simplest conflict comes from having to choose between two *positive* or desirable alternatives. Choosing between tutti-frutti-coco-nut-mocha-champagne-ice and orange-marmalade-peanut-butter-coffee-swirl at the ice-cream parlor may throw you into a temporary conflict, but if you really like both choices, your decision will be quickly made. Even when more important decisions are involved, **approach-approach conflicts** tend to be the easiest to resolve. The old fable about the mule who died of thirst and starvation while standing between a bucket of water and a bucket of oats is obviously unrealistic. When both alternatives are positive, the scales of decision are easily tipped one direction or the other.

Avoidance-Avoidance Conflicts   **Avoidance conflicts** are based on being forced to choose between two *negative,* or undesirable, alternatives. A person in an avoidance conflict is "caught between the devil and the deep blue sea," or "caught between the frying pan and the fire." In real life, avoidance conflicts involve choosing between things like birth control and religious belief, studying and failure, unwanted pregnancy and abortion, the dentist and tooth decay, a monotonous job and poverty.

Question: Suppose I don't object to abortion. Or suppose that I consider any pregnancy sacred and not to be tampered with.

Notice that these examples can only be defined as conflicts on the basis of an individual's own needs and values. If a

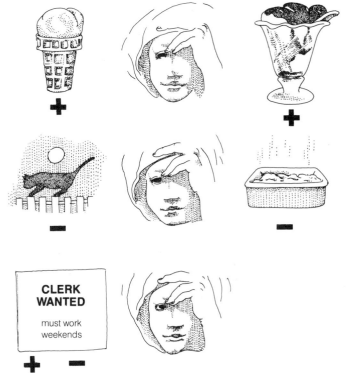

Fig. 14-3   *Three basic forms of conflict.*

woman wants to terminate a pregnancy and has no personal objection to abortion, she experiences no conflict. If she would not consider abortion under any circumstances, there is no conflict.

Avoidance conflicts often have a "damned if you do, damned if you don't" quality. In other words, both choices are negative, but *not choosing* is impossible or equally undesirable. For example, many people complain that in

Fig. 14-4   *Conflict diagrams. As shown by colored areas, the desire to approach or avoid grows stronger near a goal. Dashed lines indicate reactions to each conflict. An approach conflict (left) is easily decided. Moving toward one goal increases its attraction and makes the second alternative more "distant." In an avoidance conflict (center), tendencies to avoid are deadlocked, resulting in inaction. In an approach-avoidance conflict (right), approach proceeds to the point where desires to approach and to avoid cancel each other. (After Miller, 1944)*

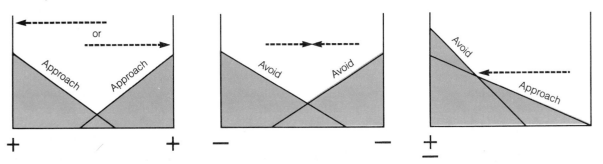

political elections neither candidate is a good choice, but not voting is worse.

A more dramatic example of the unsolvable nature of avoidance conflicts is illustrated by the plight of a person trapped in a hotel fire 20 stories from the ground. Should the person jump from the window and almost surely die on the pavement? Or should he or she try to dash through the flames and almost surely die of smoke inhalation and burns? When faced with a choice such as this it is easy to see why people often *freeze,* finding it impossible to make a decision or to take action. In the hotel room, a trapped individual may first think about the window, approach it, and then back away after looking down 20 stories. Next the person may try the door, and again back away as heat and smoke billow in. In actual disasters of this sort, people are often found dead in their rooms, victims of an inability to take action.

Indecision, inaction, and freezing are not the only reactions to avoidance conflicts. Since avoidance conflicts are stressful and rarely resolved, people sometimes pull out of avoidance situations entirely. This reaction, called *leaving the field,* is another form of escape. In our example of the hotel fire, the individual cannot leave the field (or conflict situation) unless he or she can fly. In many cases, however, escape is possible. The author recently talked to a student who could not attend school unless he worked. However, if he worked he could not earn passing grades. His solution after much conflict and indecision? He joined the navy.

Approach-Avoidance Conflicts   Approach-avoidance conflicts are also difficult to resolve. Since people seldom escape them, they are in some ways more troublesome than avoidance conflicts. A person in an **approach-avoidance conflict** is "caught"—being simultaneously attracted to, and repelled by, the same goal or activity. Attraction keeps the person in the situation, but its negative aspects cause turmoil and distress. For example, a high school student arrives to pick up his date for the first time. He is met at the door by her father who is a professional wrestler—seven feet tall, 300 pounds, and entirely covered with hair. The father gives the boy a crushing handshake and growls that he will break him in half if the girl is not home on time. The student considers the girl attractive and has a good time. But does he ask her out again? It depends on the relative strength of his attraction and his fear. Almost certainly he will feel *ambivalent* about asking her out again, knowing that another encounter with her father is involved.

Ambivalence (mixed positive and negative feelings) is a central characteristic of approach-avoidance conflicts. Ambivalence is usually translated into *partial approach*

(Miller, 1944). Since our student is still attracted to the girl he may spend time with her at school and elsewhere, but may not actually date her again. Some more realistic examples of approach-avoidance conflicts are: planning marriage to someone your parents strongly disapprove of, wanting to be an actor but suffering stage fright, wanting to buy a car but not wanting to be tied to monthly payments, wanting to eat when overweight, and wanting to go to school but hating to study. Many of life's important decisions have approach-avoidance dimensions.

Question: Aren't real life conflicts more complex than the ones described here?

In reality, conflicts are rarely as clear-cut as those described. People in conflict are usually faced with several dilemmas at once, so several types of conflict are superimposed and intermingled. The fourth type of conflict moves us closer to this realistic state of affairs.

Double Approach-Avoidance Conflicts   You are offered two jobs, one with good pay but poor hours and dull work, the second with interesting work and excellent hours, but low pay. Which do you select? This situation is more typical of the choices we must usually make. It offers neither completely positive, nor completely negative, alternatives. It is, in other words, a **double approach-avoidance conflict,** since each alternative has both positive and negative qualities.

When faced with double approach-avoidance conflicts, people tend to **vacillate,** or waver, between the alternatives. Just as you are about to choose one such alternative, its undesirable aspects tend to loom large so you swing back toward the other choice. If you have ever been romantically attracted to two people at once, each having qualities you like and dislike, then you have probably experienced vacillation.

Double approach-avoidance conflicts also tend to occur when you must select one of two good things, *if* choosing one excludes the other. To illustrate, let's say that you have been invited to attend a one-time-only musical concert and a once-a-year party, both on the same night. This might seem like a double approach conflict, but actually it is not. If you go to the concert you must miss the party, so attending the concert is both good (you see a favorite musical group) and bad (you miss the party). The same is true in reverse for attending the party.

On a day-to-day basis, most double approach-avoidance conflicts are little more than an annoyance. When they involve major life decisions, such as choice of a career, school, mate, job, whether to have children, and so forth, they add significantly to the amount of stress experienced.

Learning Check

1. The psychological defense known as denial refers to the natural tendency to explain or justify one's actions.   T or F?

2. Fulfilling frustrated desires in imaginary achievements or activities defines the defense mechanism of:

   a. compensation   *b.* isolation   *c.* fantasy   *d.* sublimation

3. In compensation, one's own undesirable characteristics or motives are attributed to others.   T or F?

4. Of the defense mechanisms, two that are considered relatively constructive are: (circle)

   compensation   denial   isolation   projection   regression   rationalization   sublimation

5. Conflict is related to the presence of contradictory _____ or an attempt to reach contradictory

   _____.

6. The easiest type of conflict to resolve is typically an _____ conflict.

7. Inaction and freezing are most characteristic of avoidance conflicts.   T or F?

8. Approach-avoidance conflicts produce mixed feelings called _____.

Answers: 1. F   2. c   3. F   4. compensation and sublimation   5. motives, goals   6. approach-approach   7. T   8. ambivalence

Stress—Invisible Killer on the Loose

Question: What do hard-driving businesspersons and "executive" monkeys have in common?

Ulcers! In an early study of the effects of stress, pairs of monkeys were subjected to electric shock. One monkey in each pair was made an "executive" who could postpone shocks by pressing a lever every few seconds (Fig. 14-5). In time, the executive monkeys developed stomach ulcers and the nonexecutive monkeys did not.

How could the executives' ulcers be explained if both monkeys received shocks? At first, psychologists assumed it was due to the added stress of their "responsibility" (Brady, 1958). However, recent studies of humans with ulcers contradict this idea. The old stereotype of the over-stressed business executive has all but disappeared. We now know that many jobs are stressful. Ulcers occur as often in bus drivers, farmers, secretaries, teachers, and construction workers as they do in business executives. Also, more recent research has shown that having control over a stressor usually *lowers* the amount of stress experienced.

Why then did the executive monkeys get ulcers? A second look at the experiment tells why: Only the most emotionally responsive monkeys were selected as executives (Seligman, Maier, and Solomon, 1971). This guaranteed that the executives would be motivated to turn off the shocks. However, it also meant the executives were highly stressed regardless of such factors as "responsibility" or control.

It is common to assume that stress is always bad, or

Fig. 14-5 *The "executive" monkey on the left has control over the electrical shocks received by both monkeys. The monkey on the right has no control. Which monkey gets ulcers, and why does it get them? (See text.) (Photo courtesy of Joseph Brady)*

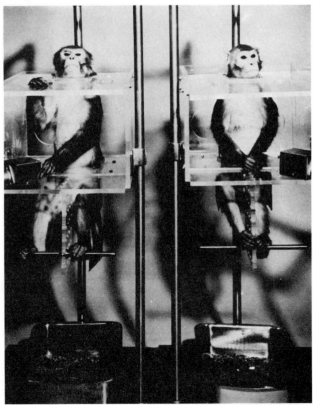

that a complete lack of stress is ideal. However, stress is not always damaging or undesirable. As stress researcher Hans Selye (1976) observes, "To be totally without stress is to be dead." Stress occurs anytime we must adjust or adapt to the environment. Naturally, unpleasant situations such as work pressures, marital problems, or financial troubles produce stress. But so do travel, sports, a new job, ski jumping, dating, and other pleasant activities. Even if you aren't a thrill seeker, a healthy lifestyle may include a fair amount of stress.

Question: Why is stress sometimes damaging and sometimes not?

As was true in the case of the executive monkeys, psychologists are learning that stress reactions in humans are more complex than once thought. Let's examine some of the chief factors that determine whether or not stress is harmful.

When Is Stress a Strain?   It goes almost without saying that some situations are inherently more stressful than others. Police officers, for instance, suffer from an unusually high rate of stress-related diseases. The threat of injury or death, coupled with periodic confrontations with drunk or belligerent citizens takes a toll. A major factor here is the *unpredictable* nature of police work. An officer who stops to issue a traffic ticket never knows if he or she will find a cooperative citizen or an armed criminal waiting in the car.

The effect of unpredictability in creating stress is shown by an interesting lab experiment involving three groups of rats. In the experiment, one group was given shocks preceded by a tone that served as a warning; a second group got shocks without warning; the third group received no shocks, but heard the tone. After a few weeks, an autopsy was performed on the rats. The animals that received no shocks had no stomach ulcers; those receiving unpredictable shocks had severe ulcers; and those given predictable shocks showed little or no ulceration (Weiss, 1972).

Pressure is another element in stress, especially job stress. **Pressure** occurs when activities must be speeded up, when deadlines must be met, when extra work is added unexpectedly, or when a person must work at or near maximum capacity for long periods. Most students who have survived final exams are familiar with the effects of pressure.

Question: Can't boredom also be stressful?

Yes. Surprisingly, an underload on a person's system (as in assembly-line boredom) can be as stressful as an overload. To understand why, it is necessary to examine the role of control in producing stress.

As mentioned earlier, people generally experience more stress in situations over which they have little control. For example, DeGood (1975) subjected male college students to an unpleasant shock-avoidance learning task. Some subjects were allowed to select their own rest periods, while others rested at times selected by the experimenter. Subjects allowed to select their own rest periods showed lower stress levels (as measured by blood pressure) than those given no choice.

Control, or a lack of it, even carries over to the aftereffects of stress. In another experiment, subjects were jolted by an extremely loud and unpleasant noise (a tape recording of a desk calculator, mimeograph, typewriter, and several people speaking different languages, all mixed together). One group was allowed to turn off the noise each time it came on, but they were encouraged not to so their response to the noise could be measured. A second group had no control over the blasts of sound.

Both groups responded to the noise with initial signs of stress, and both gradually adapted to the assault on their senses. Afterward, however, the people who had no control over the noise did more poorly on tests of concentration, and they were more easily frustrated than the people given control (Glass and Singer, 1972). If you have ever worked in a noisy office, factory, childcare center, restaurant, or similar setting, you will recognize this effect.

The evidence we have reviewed indicates that when emotional "shocks" are *intense* or *repeated, unpredictable, uncontrollable,* and linked to *pressure,* stress will be magnified and damage is likely to result. Yet, as important as these factors are, they are not the whole story. You have probably noted, for instance, that some people are stressed by events that others find a stimulating challenge. Ultimately, stress depends on how a situation is perceived. Whenever a stressor is appraised as a *threat,* a powerful stress reaction follows (Lazarus, 1975; Roskies and Lazarus, 1980). Further, stress is increased when a person believes he or she lacks *competence* to meet a particular demand (Bandura, 1977; Woolfolk and Richardson, 1978). Thus, the intensity of the body's stress response often depends on what we think and tell ourselves about stressors.

Psychosomatic Disorders

Chronic or repeated stress can damage physical health, as well as upset emotional well-being (Selye, 1976). Prolonged stress reactions are related to a large number of psychosomatic illnesses. Most people recognize that ulcers are stress-related, but so are many other illnesses. In **psychosomatic disorders** (*psyche:* mind; *soma:* body), psychological and emotional factors are associated with actual damage to tissues of the body. Psychosomatic problems, therefore, are *not* the same as *hypochondria*. **Hypochondriacs** suffer from imaginary diseases. There is nothing imaginary about a bleeding ulcer. A *severe* case could be fatal. The person who says, "Oh, it's *just* psychosomatic," misunderstands the seriousness of stress-related diseases.

Question: What diseases are psychosomatic? Who gets them?

The most common problems are gastrointestinal and respiratory (ulcers and asthma, for example), but there are many others. Included are problems such as eczema (skin rash), hives, migraine headaches, rheumatoid arthritis, hypertension (high blood pressure), colitis (ulceration of the colon), and heart disease. Actually, these represent only the major problems. Lesser health complaints are also frequently stress-related. Typical examples include muscle tension, headaches, neckaches, backaches, indigestion, constipation, fatigue, insomnia, and sexual dysfunction (Hurst, Jenkins, and Rose, 1979; Brown, 1980). It is estimated that one-half or more of all patients who go to see a doctor have a psychosomatic disorder, or have an illness complicated by psychosomatic symptoms.

It would be a mistake to assume that stress is the sole cause of psychosomatic diseases. Usually, several factors combine to produce damage. These include hereditary differences, specific organ weaknesses, and learned tendencies to focus stress on a particular part of the body. Personality also enters the picture. To a degree there are "ulcer personalities," "asthma personalities," and so on. The best documented of such patterns is the "cardiac personality"— an individual prone to heart disease.

Type A   Two noted cardiologists, Meyer Friedman and Ray Rosenman offer a glimpse at how some people create unnecessary stress. On the basis of a long-term study of personality and heart problems, Friedman and Rosenman (1974) classified people into two categories: **Type A** personalities (those who run a high risk of heart attack), and **Type B** personalities (those who are unlikely to have a heart attack). After classifying people as Type A or Type B, Friedman and Rosenman did an eight-year follow-up, finding more than twice the rate of heart disease in Type A's than in Type B's (Rosenman *et al.,* 1975).

Question: What is the Type A personality like?

Type A people are hard-driving, ambitious, highly competitive, achievement oriented, and striving. Type A people believe that with enough effort they can overcome any obstacle and they "push" themselves accordingly. In tests of physical capacity (on a treadmill) Type A's work closer to their actual limits of endurance, but say they are less fatigued than do Type B people (Glass, 1977). Type A's don't know when to quit!

Perhaps the most tell-tale Type A characteristic of all is a *chronic sense of time urgency*. Type A's seem unsatisfied with the normal pace of events. They hurry from one activity to another, racing the clock in self-imposed urgency. The result is a constant sense of tension and frustration as they deny fatigue, strive for control, and drive their stress level to unhealthy heights.

Question: Is there any way to identify Type A people?

A psychological test known as the *Jenkins Activity Survey* can be used to identify Type A persons. Although the test cannot be duplicated here, many of the destructive habits of Type A people are summarized in a shorter self-identification test in Table 14-2. If all or most of the list applies to you, you may be a Type A. Your future plans may also be an indication. When asked what they would do after college, 60 percent of Type A's said "go to graduate or professional school." In contrast, 70 percent of B's said "go to work, get a job" (Glass, 1977).

Since our society places a premium on achievement, competition, and mastery, it is not surprising that many people develop Type A personalities. The best way to avoid the destructive stress this produces is to adopt behavior that is the opposite to that listed in Table 14-2. It is entirely possible to "succeed" without sacrificing your health in the process. (For additional suggestions on combating Type A behavior, consult Friedman and Rosenman, *Type A Behavior and Your Heart.*)

A very basic question remains unanswered in our discussion of stress. How does stress, and our response to it, translate into bodily damage? The answer seems to lie in the body's defenses against stress, a pattern of reactions known as the **general adaptation syndrome.**

The General Adaptation Syndrome   Study of the general adaptation syndrome (G.A.S.) began when Canadian physiologist Hans Selye (1976) noticed that the initial symptoms of almost any disease or trauma (poisoning, infection, injury, or stress) are almost identical. After more research Selye concluded that the body responds in the same way to any stress, be it infection, failure, embarrassment, adjustment to a new job, school difficulties, or a stormy romance.

Question: What pattern does the body's response to stress take?

The G.A.S. consists of three stages: an *alarm reaction,* a *stage of resistance,* and a *stage of exhaustion* (Selye, 1976).

Table 14-2   Characteristics of the Type A Person*

Check the items that apply to you.

Do you:

_____   Have a habit of explosively accentuating various key words in ordinary speech even when there is no need for such accentuation?

_____   Finish other persons' sentences for them?

_____   *Always* move, walk, and eat rapidly?

_____   Quickly skim reading material and prefer summaries or condensations of books?

_____   Become easily angered by slow moving lines or traffic?

_____   Feel an impatience with the rate at which most events take place?

_____   Tend to be unaware of the details or beauty of your surroundings?

_____   Frequently strive to think of or do two or more things simultaneously?

_____   Almost always feel vaguely guilty when you relax, vacation, or do absolutely nothing for several days?

_____   Tend to evaluate your worth in quantitative terms (number of A's earned, amount of income, number of games won, and so forth)?

_____   Have nervous gestures or muscle twitches such as grinding your teeth, clenching your fists, or drumming your fingers?

_____   Attempt to schedule more and more activities into less time, and in doing so make fewer allowances for unforeseen problems?

_____   Frequently think about other things while talking to someone?

_____   Repeatedly take on more responsibilities than you can comfortably handle?

*Shortened and adapted from Meyer Friedman and Ray H. Rosenman, *Type A Behavior and Your Heart.* New York: Alfred A. Knopf, 1974.

In the **alarm reaction,** the body mobilizes its resources to cope with added stress. The pituitary gland secretes a hormone that causes the adrenal glands to step up their output of adrenaline and noradrenaline. As these hormones are dumped into the bloodstream, some bodily processes are speeded up and others are slowed, to concentrate bodily resources where they are needed.

Fig. 14-6   *The General Adaptation Syndrome. During the initial alarm reaction to stress, resistance falls below normal. It rises again as bodily resources are mobilized, and it remains high during the stage of resistance. Eventually, resistance falls again as the stage of exhaustion is reached. (From* The Stress of Life *by Hans Selye. Copyright © 1956, 1976 by Hans Selye. Used by permission of McGraw-Hill Book Company)*

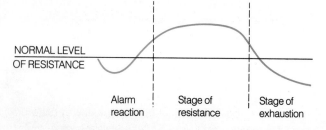

NORMAL LEVEL
OF RESISTANCE

Alarm reaction   Stage of resistance   Stage of exhaustion

In the first phase of the alarm reaction, people have such symptoms as headache, fever, fatigue, sore muscles, shortness of breath, diarrhea, upset stomach, loss of appetite, and lack of energy. Notice that these are also the symptoms of being "sick," of stressful travel, of high altitude sickness, final exams week, and possibly of "falling in love"!

Soon the body's defenses are stabilized and symptoms of the alarm reaction disappear. Physically the body has made adjustments to resist stress. However, the outward appearance of normality is maintained at a high cost. During the **stage of resistance,** the body is better able to cope with the original source of stress (see Fig. 14-6), but resistance to other stresses is lowered. For example, animals placed in an extremely cold environment become more resistant to the cold, but more susceptible to infection. It is during the stage of resistance that the first signs of psychosomatic disorders begin to appear.

If stress continues, the **stage of exhaustion** may be reached. In this stage the body's resources are exhausted and the stress hormones are depleted. Unless a way of alleviating stress is found, a psychosomatic disease, organ failure, serious loss of health or complete collapse results. At work, reaching the stage of exhaustion is commonly referred to as **burn-out.** Job burn-out is not a formal term or a recognized disease, but the concept is widely understood. It refers to chronic fatigue, apathy, and psychosomatic illness due to long-term job stress. In short, the employee who "burns out" is physically, mentally, and emotionally depleted. Burn-out may occur in any job, but it is a special problem in emotionally demanding "helping professions," such as nursing, teaching, and social work.

The stages of the G.A.S. may sound melodramatic if you are young and healthy, or if you have never had a personal encounter with prolonged stress. However, stress is not to be taken lightly. When Selye examined animals in the latter stages of the G.A.S., he found enlargement and discoloration of their adrenal glands, intense shrinkage of the thymus, spleen, and lymph nodes, and deep bleeding stomach ulcers (Cox, 1978). Stress is indeed an "invisible killer." In the "Applications" section that follows we will investigate some techniques for detecting and alleviating stress. In the meantime, take it easy!

Learning Check

1. Ulcers developed by executive monkeys and other subjects of stress experiments are an example of a _____ disorder.

2. Greater control over a source of stress is usually associated with a reduction in the amount of stress experienced.   T or F?

3. People suffering from hypochondria have serious tissue damage caused by stress or prolonged emotion.   T or F?

4. Which of the following is *not* classified as a psychosomatic disorder?

    a. hypertension   *b.* colitis   *c.* eczema   *d.* thymus

5. The first stage of the G.A.S. is called the _____ reaction.

6. Most outward symptoms of stress disappear during the stage of _____.

7. According to Friedman and Rosenman, the Type A personality can relax without guilt and rarely suffers from a sense of time urgency.   T or F?

Answers: 1. psychosomatic 2. T 3. F 4. d 5. alarm 6. resistance 7. F

Resources Summary

● *Frustration* is the negative emotional and behavioral state that occurs when progress toward a goal is blocked. Sources of frustration may be usefully classified as *external* (including both *social* and *nonsocial* obstacles) or *personal.*

● External frustrations are based upon *delay, failure, rejection, loss* and other direct blocking of motives. Personal frustration is related to *personal characteristics* over which one has little control. Frustrations of all types become more intense as the *strength, urgency,* or *importance* of the blocked motive increases. Being near a goal also intensifies frustration.

● Major behavioral reactions to frustration include *persistence, more vigorous responding, circumvention, direct aggression, displaced aggression* (including *scapegoating*), and *escape* or *withdrawal.*

● Frustration and attendant feelings of anxiety or inadequacy frequently lead to use of *psychological defense mechanisms.* A large number of defense mechanisms have been identified, including *compensation, denial, fantasy, intellectualization, isolation, projection, rationalization, reaction formation, regression, repression,* and *sublimation.* Each helps people to deny, avoid, or distort sources of anxiety.

● Conflict occurs when one must choose between contradictory alternatives. Four major types of conflict are: *approach-approach* (choice between two desirable alternatives); *avoidance-avoidance* (both alternatives are negative); *approach-avoidance* (a goal or activity has both positive and negative aspects); and *double approach-avoidance* (both alternatives have advantages and disadvantages).

● Approach-approach conflicts are usually the easiest to resolve. Avoidance conflicts are difficult to resolve, and are characterized by *inaction, indecision, freezing,* and a *desire to escape* (called *leaving the field*). People usually remain in approach-avoidance conflicts, but fail to fully resolve them. Approach-avoidance conflicts are associated with *ambivalence* and *partial approach. Vacillation* (a wavering between alternatives) is probably the most common reaction to double approach-avoidance conflicts.

● *Stress* occurs when demands are placed on an organism to adjust or adapt. When stress is intense or prolonged (especially when associated with prolonged emotional response), it may cause damage in the form of ulcers and other *psychosomatic* problems.

● Stress is more damaging in situations involving *pressure,* a lack of *control, unpredictability* of the stressor, and *intense* or *repeated* emotional shocks. Stress is intensified when a situation is perceived as a *threat,* and when a person does not feel *competent* to cope with it.

● In psychosomatic (mind-body) disorders an interplay of stress, heredity, personality, learning, and specific vulnerability combines to bring about physical illness or bodily damage. Psychosomatic disorders have no connection to *hypochondria,* the tendency to imagine that one has some terrible disease.

● People with *Type A personalities* are aggressively competitive, striving, and have a chronic sense of time urgency. These characteristics combine to double the chances of heart attack.

● The body reacts to stress in a series of stages called the *general adaptation syndrome (G.A.S.).* The stages of the G.A.S. are *alarm, resistance,* and *exhaustion.* The pattern of bodily reactions and changes in resistance observed in the G.A.S. follows closely that observed in the development of a psychosomatic disorder.

============= Applications =============

Stress Management

Question: How do I know if I am subjecting myself to too much stress?

Despite all the research on stress this question remains difficult to answer. We can get some help, however, from research linking stressful events to changes in health.

Dr. Thomas Holmes and his associates at the University of Washington School of Medicine in Seattle have demonstrated something that physicians have suspected for a long time: Stressful events reduce the body's natural defenses against disease and increase the likelihood of illness (Holmes and Masuda, 1972). They found that di-

saster and sorrow often precede illness. More surprising is the finding that almost any major *change* in one's life requires adjustment and increases susceptibility to accident and illness.

Life Change Units Holmes and his associates have developed a rating scale to help determine the potential health hazards faced when stresses accumulate. They call this the **Social Readjustment Rating Scale (SRRS).** It is reprinted in Table 14-3. The effect of life events is expressed in **life change units (LCUs).**

As you read the scale, notice that a positive life event

Table 14-3 Social Readjustment Rating Scale. The Social Readjustment Rating Scale lists significant life events and offers a rating of their contribution to susceptibility to illness.

Rank	Life Event	Life Crisis Units	Rank	Life Event	Life Crisis Units
1	Death of spouse	100	23	Son or daughter leaving home	29
2	Divorce	73	24	Trouble with in-laws	29
3	Marital separation	65	25	Outstanding personal achievement	28
4	Jail term	63	26	Wife begins or stops work	26
5	Death of a close family member	63	27	Begin or end school	26
6	Personal injury or illness	53	28	Change in living conditions	25
7	Marriage	50	29	Revision of personal habits	24
8	Fired at work	47	30	Trouble with boss	23
9	Marital reconciliation	45	31	Change in work hours or conditions	20
10	Retirement	45	32	Change in residence	20
11	Change in health of family member	44	33	Change in school	20
12	Pregnancy	40	34	Change in recreation	19
13	Sex difficulties	39	35	Change in church activities	19
14	Gain of new family member	39	36	Change in social activities	18
15	Business readjustment	39	37	Mortgage or loan less than $10,000	17
16	Change in financial state	38	38	Change in sleeping habits	16
17	Death of close friend	37	39	Change in number of family get-togethers	15
18	Change to different line of work	36	40	Change in eating habits	15
19	Change in number of arguments with spouse	35	41	Vacation	13
20	Mortgage over $10,000	31	42	Christmas	12
21	Foreclosure of mortgage or loan	30	43	Minor violations of the law	11
22	Change in responsibilities at work	29			

Adapted with permission from ''Social Readjustment Rating Scale,'' by T. H. Holmes and R. H. Rahe, *Journal of Psychosomatic Research*, 1957. Reprinted with permission from Pergamon Press, Ltd.

Applications

may be as costly as a disaster. Marriage rates 50 life change units, even though it is usually considered a happy event. Notice also that many items read "Change in. . . ." This means that an improvement in life conditions is as costly as a deterioration.

To use the scale, add up the LCUs for all life events you have experienced during the last year and compare the total to these standards:

0 to 150—No significant problems

150 to 199—Mild life crisis (33 percent chance of illness)

200 to 299—Moderate life crisis (50 percent chance of illness)

300 or over—Major life crisis (80 percent chance of illness)

When the LCU total exceeds 300 points, there is an 80 percent chance of illness or accident in the near future.

A more conservative rating of stress can be obtained by totaling LCU points for events occurring only during the previous six months. Studies of U.S. Navy personnel produced these figures for six-month totals (Rahe, 1972):

LCUs	Average number of illnesses reported for six-month period
0 to 100	1.4
300 to 400	1.9
500 to 600	2.1

Question: Many of the listed life changes don't seem relevant to young adults or college students. Does the SRRS apply to these people?

The SRRS has been criticized for listing only a small number of items to represent a broad range of possible stressful events. It also tends to be more appropriate for older, more "established" adults. However, recent research has shown that the health of college students is also affected by stressful events. When the scale was revised to include items pertinent to students (for example, "entered college," "change in major field of study," "broke or had broken a steady relationship"), elevated LCU scores again correlated with more frequent illness (Martin *et al.,* 1975).

The SRRS is not a foolproof way to rate stress. For one thing, different events are more or less stressful for some individuals than others. Also, stress tolerance varies widely from person to person. In addition, some studies have failed to confirm the link between LCUs and illness (Schless, 1977). Despite such objections, a high LCU score should be taken seriously. It would be a good idea to total your LCUs once or twice a year as a rough index of stress levels. If your score goes much over 300 an adjustment in your activities or lifestyle may be called for. Remember, "To be forewarned is to be forearmed."

Question: What can be done about a high score?

A high LCU score is a signal that additional stress should be avoided. One way to achieve this is to make as few additional changes as is practical. Added responsibilities should be avoided and existing responsibilities reduced if possible. The best response of all is to use **stress management** skills. For serious problems, stress management should be learned directly from a therapist or a stress clinic. When ordinary stresses are involved, there is much you can do on your own. Many elements of stress management are straightforward and easily applied.

Stress Management

The simplest way of coping with stress is to modify or remove its source, by leaving a stressful job, for example. Obviously, this is often impossible, which is why learning to manage stress is so important.

As shown in Fig. 14-7, stress triggers *bodily effects, upsetting thoughts,* and *ineffective behavior.* Also shown is the fact that each element worsens the others in a vicious cycle. Indeed, the basic idea of the "Stress Game" is that once it begins, *you lose*—unless you take action to break the cycle. The information that follows tells how. (Stress management techniques are derived from Davis, McKay, and Eshelman, 1980; Meichenbaum, 1977; Woolfolk and Richardson, 1978, and other sources as indicated.)

Bodily Reactions

Much of the immediate discomfort of stress is caused by the body's fight/flight emotional response. The body is ready to act, with tight muscles and a pounding heart.

Fig. 14-7 *The stress game.* (Adapted from Rosenthal and Rosenthal, 1980.)

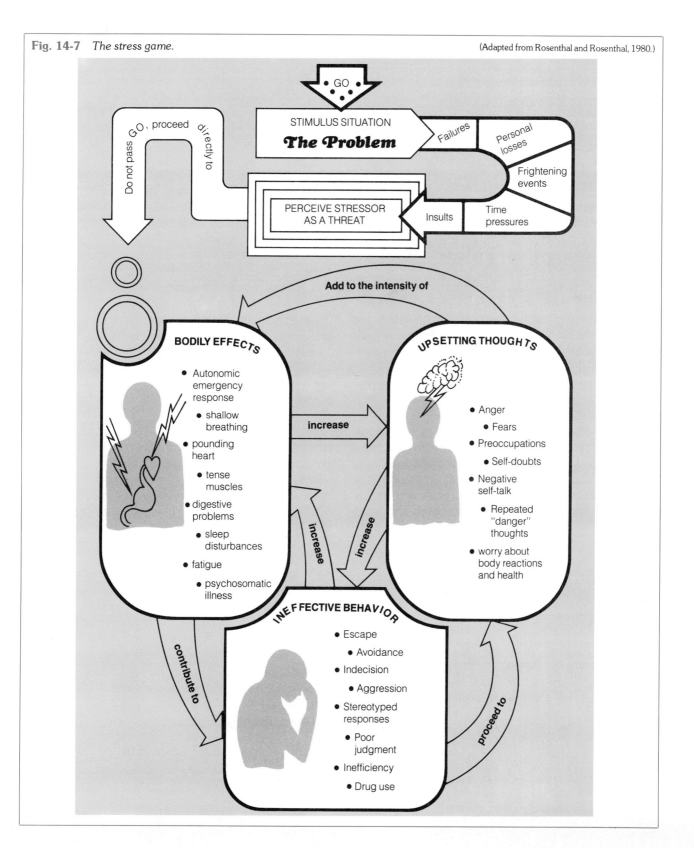

Applications

When action is prevented, we merely remain "up-tight." A sensible remedy is to learn a reliable, drug-free way of relaxing.

Exercise   Because stress prepares the body for action, its effects can be dissipated by using the body. Any full-body exercise can be effective. Swimming, dancing, jumping rope, yoga, most sports, and especially walking, are valuable outlets. Be sure to choose activities that are vigorous enough to relieve tension, yet enjoyable enough to be done repeatedly. Exercising for stress management is most effective when it is done daily.

Meditation   Many stress counselors recommend meditation for quieting the body and promoting relaxation. The meditation technique described in Chapter 6 is a good starting place. Remember, too, that listening to or playing music, nature walks, absorbing hobbies, and the like can be "meditations" of sorts.

Progressive Relaxation   Progressive relaxation refers to a method in which people learn to relax systematically, completely, and by choice. To learn the full technique, consult Chapter 23 of this book. The basic idea is to tighten all the muscles in a given area of the body (the arms for instance) and then voluntarily relax them. By tensing and relaxing each area of the body, it is possible, with practice, to greatly reduce tension.

Ineffective Behavior

Stress is often made worse by our response to it. The following suggestions may help you deal with stress more effectively.

Slow Down   Remember that stress can be self-generated. Try to deliberately do things at a slower pace—especially if your pace has speeded up over the years. Tell yourself, "What counts most is not if I get there first, but if I get there at all." Or, "My goal is distance, not speed."

Organize   Disorganization creates stress. Try to take a fresh look at your situation and get organized. Setting priorities can be a real stress fighter. Ask yourself what's really important and concentrate on the things that count. Learn to let go of trivial but upsetting irritations. And above all, when you are feeling stressed, remember to K.I.S.: *Keep It Simple.*

In problem solving, it pays to be systematic. Try to clearly define the problem and estimate the effects of various actions. Afterward, evaluate the results, so that you can make immediate adjustments or improve future problem solving. Try to plan alternatives or "fall back" plans in the event of disaster.

Strike a Balance   Work, school, family, friends, interests, hobbies, recreation, community, church—there are many important elements in a satisfying life. Damaging stress often comes from letting one element get blown out of proportion, especially work or school. Your goal should be *quality* in life, not quantity. Try to strike a balance between challenging, "good stress" and relaxation. Remember, when you are "doing nothing" you are actually doing something very important: Set aside time for "me-acts," such as loafing, browsing, puttering, playing, napping.

Recognize and Accept Your Limits   Many of us set unrealistic and perfectionistic goals. Given that no one can ever be perfect, this attitude leaves many people feeling inadequate, no matter how well they have performed. Set gradual, achievable goals for yourself. Also, set realistic limits on what you try to do on any given day. Learn to say "no" to added demands or responsibilities.

Seek Social Support   Recent studies have shown that close, positive relationships with others facilitate good health and morale (Cobb, 1976). One reason for this is that support from family and friends serves as a buffer to cushion the impact of stressful events (Paradine *et al.,* 1981). Talking out problems and expressing tensions can be incredibly helpful. If things really get bad, seek help from a therapist, counselor, or clergyman (please note that "bartender" is not on the list).

Upsetting Thoughts

Assume you are taking a test. Suddenly you realize you are running short of time. If you say to yourself, "Oh no, this is terrible, I've blown it now," your body's response

---

Applications

will probably be sweating, tenseness, and a knot in your stomach. On the other hand, if you say, "I should have watched the time, but getting upset won't help now, I'll just take one question at a time," your stress level will be much lower. As stated earlier, stress is greatly affected by the view we take of events. Physical symptoms and a tendency to make poor decisions are increased by negative thoughts, or "self-talk." In many cases what you say to yourself can be the difference between coping and collapsing.

Coping Statements   Donald Meichenbaum (1977) of the University of Waterloo, Canada, has recently popularized a technique called **stress inoculation.** In it, clients learn to fight fear and anxiety with an internal monologue of positive **coping statements.** First, clients learn to identify and monitor **negative self-statements.** They then learn to substitute coping statements from a supplied list. Eventually, they are encouraged to make their own lists.

Question: How are coping statements applied?

Coping statements are used to block out, or counteract, negative self-talk in stressful situations. In giving a short speech for instance, you would replace "I'm scared," "I can't do this," "My mind will go blank and I'll panic," or "I'll sound stupid and boring," with "I'll give my speech on something I like," or "I'll breathe deeply before I start my speech," or "My pounding heart just means I'm psyched up to do my best." Some additional examples of coping statements follow.

Preparing for Stressful Situation

I'll just take things one step at a time.

If I get nervous I'll just pause a moment.

Tomorrow I'll be through it.

I've managed to do this before.

What exactly do I have to do?

I won't let negative thoughts creep in.

I can stay calm if I try.

Confronting the Stressful Situation

Relax now, this can't really hurt me.

Stay organized, focus on the task.

There's no hurry, take it step by step.

Nobody's perfect, I'll just do my best.

This works, I'm doing fine.

This isn't so bad.

It will be over soon, just be calm.

Meichenbaum cautions that saying the "right" things to yourself may not be enough to bring about real improvement in stress tolerance. You must practice this approach in actual stress situations. Also, it is important to develop your own personal list of coping statements by finding what works for you. Ultimately, the value of learning this, and other stress management skills, ties back into the idea that much stress is self-generated. Knowing that you *can* manage a demanding situation is in itself a major antidote for stress.

Coping with Frustration and Conflict

A psychologist studying frustration placed rats on a small platform at the top of a tall pole. Then he forced them to jump off the platform toward two elevated doors, one locked and the other unlocked. If the rat chose the correct door, it swung open and he landed safely on another platform. If he chose the locked door, he bounced off it and fell into a net far below.

The problem of choosing the open door was made unsolvable and very frustrating by randomly alternating which door was locked. After a time, most rats adopted a **stereotyped response.** That is, they chose the same door every time. This door was then *permanently* locked. All the rat had to do was to jump to the other door to avoid a fall, but time after time the rat bounced off the locked door (Maier, 1949).

Question: Isn't this an example of persistence?

No. There are important differences between stereotyped responses to frustration and persistence. Think of the struggle an infant undergoes when learning to walk. For an adult a corresponding amount of frustration would be overwhelming. The typical adult can stand to "fall on his face" just so often. If you were to approach learning a foreign language, or an equally difficult task with a willingness to "fail" as much as a child does when learning to

Applications

walk, you would almost surely be a success. Persistence does pay off. But all too often people are not persistent enough because they fear failure. Fear of failure may *ensure* failure. However, persistence that is not *flexible* can lead to "stupid," stereotyped behavior like that of a rat on a jumping stand. It is important when dealing with frustration to know when to quit and establish a new direction.

Here are some suggestions to help you avoid needless frustration.

1. Try to identify the source of your frustration. Is it internal, external, or personal?

2. Is the source of frustration something that can be changed? How hard would you have to work to change it? Is it under your control at all?

3. If the source of your frustration can be changed or removed, are the necessary efforts worth it?

The answers to these questions help determine if persistence will be futile. There is value in learning to accept gracefully those things which cannot be changed.

It is also important to distinguish between *real* barriers and *imagined* barriers. All too often we create our own imaginary barriers. For example:

> Anita wants a part-time job to earn extra money. At the first place she applied she was told that she didn't have enough "experience." Now she complains of being frustrated because she wants to work but cannot. She needs "experience" to work, but can't get experience without working. She has quit looking for a job.

Is Anita's need for experience a real barrier? Unless she applies for *many* jobs it is impossible to tell if she has overestimated its importance. For her the barrier is real enough to prevent further efforts, but with persistent looking she might locate an "unlocked door." If a reasonable amount of persistence does show that "experience" is essential, it might be obtained in other ways—through temporary volunteer work, for instance.

Question: How can I handle conflicts more effectively?

Most of the suggestions just made also apply to conflict. However, here are some additional things to remember when you are in conflict or must make a difficult decision.

1. Don't be hasty when making important decisions. Take time to collect information and to weigh pros and cons. Hasty decisions are often regretted. Even if you do make a faulty decision, it will trouble you less if you know that you did everything possible to avoid a mistake.

2. Try out important decisions *partially* when possible. If you are thinking about moving to a new town, try to spend a few days there first. If you are choosing between colleges, do the same. If classes are in progress, sit in on some. If you want to learn to skin-dive, rent equipment for a reasonable length of time before buying.

3. Look for workable compromises. Again it is important to get all available information. If you think that you only have one or two alternatives and they are undesirable or unbearable, seek the aid of a teacher, counselor, minister, or social service agency. You may be overlooking possible alternatives these people will know about.

4. When all else fails, make a decision and live with it. Indecision and conflict exact a high cost. Sometimes it is best to select a course of action and stick with it unless it is *very obviously* wrong *after* you have taken it.

In class you may want to describe some of the frustrations and conflicts you have experienced and how you handled them. Prepare to discuss frustrations and conflicts you have resolved unusually effectively or that you could have improved on. Do you have some additional hints to share with other students?

Learning Check

1. Research using the SRRS shows that, like negative life events, positive changes may also be stressful.   T or F?

2. Any score over 100 on the SRRS indicates a significant increase in the chances of illness or accident.   T or F?

3. Exercise, meditation, and progressive relaxation are considered effective ways of countering negative self-statements.   T or F?

4. Research shows that social support from family and friends has little effect on the health consequences of stress. T or F?

5. One element of stress inoculation is training in the use of positive coping statements.   T or F?

6. Stereotyped responding can be particularly troublesome in coping with frustration.   T or F?

Answers: 1. T 2. F 3. F 4. F 5. T 6. T

━━━━━━━━━━━━━━ Exploration ━━━━━━━━━━━━━━

Future Shock—The Only Constant Is Change

Whether we welcome it, shun it, or are merely indifferent to it, the future arrives to greet us each day. It always has. But now, according to journalist Alvin Toffler, the future may be arriving a little too fast for most of us—with potentially dire consequences.

Toffler is the author of *Future Shock,* a book about the physical and psychological damage caused by subjecting people to too much change in too little time. Toffler believes we live in the most rapidly changing environment humans have ever faced. He predicts "shattering stress and disorientation" and "psychological and physical illness on a massive scale" as large numbers of people become casualties of "future shock."

As Thomas Holmes' life change research suggests, change *can* be stressful. Similarly, Toffler's launching point is the observation that sweeping social changes have taken place during the last generation, changes unprecedented in magnitude and swiftness. But the real essence of future shock, according to Toffler, is the idea that the *rate of change is accelerating.* He argues that social, political, economic, technological, cultural, and personal changes now take place at a rate that threatens us with a "massive adaptational breakdown."

Whether you have traveled widely or not, you are probably aware of an effect known as *culture shock.* When thrown into the strange surroundings of a different culture, where all the familiar patterns and psychological landmarks are missing, people often become disoriented and find adapting stressful. Toffler's point is that our own culture is changing so quickly that a kind of "culture shock" occurs in the context of time, not by travel to another country. The present becomes different from the past so quickly that new traditions, values, beliefs, perceptions, and behaviors become obsolete almost as quickly as they are adopted. Toffler analyzes three dimensions of such overly rapid change: *transience, novelty,* and *diversity.*

Transience is reflected in rapid changes of residence, employment, friends, life-styles, media personalities, fads, in the growing emphasis on throwaway products, and in the decline of stable "roots" in home and family.

Novelty is represented by the incredible deluge of scientific and technological innovations we are confronted with: test-tube babies, genetic engineering, farming the ocean floor, breeder reactors, weather control, cloning, and so forth.

Diversity refers to overstimulation brought on by too many choices—by too much too fast. Toffler portrays people in technologically advanced nations as being immersed in a sea of alternatives virtually too vast to cope with. Youth revolution, economic revolution, sexual revolution, racial revolution, technological revolution, cults and subcults, engineered environments, social disarray, the "information explosion," and rapid travel—all these and more contribute, in Toffler's view, to future shock.

Critique Toffler blames such diverse problems as chronic anxiety, senseless violence, apathy, and widespread depression on future shock. He argues that if we do not do something, collectively and individually to slow the pace of change, then large numbers of people will become progressively incompetent to deal rationally with the runaway pace of modern life. How seriously should we take his analysis? Here are some objections that have been raised:

• Toffler's version of events has a "Stop-the-world-I-want-to-get-off" quality that hints at exaggeration and overstatement.
• It has been over 10 years since *Future Shock* was published, yet people seem no worse off now than they did then.
• Toffler seems to forget that each generation has had to bear the burdens of change, and that each has probably assumed that they lived in the most stressful of times, or at least the most rapidly changing.
• Future shock may appeal to our tendency to shift blame to "society" for feelings of disorientation, frustration, or tension.

Even when such criticisms are considered, it seems reasonable to assume that there is such a condition as

Exploration

future shock, and that some of us do or will suffer from it. It is to Toffler's credit that he has prompted us to ponder the role accelerating change has in creating stress.

What Do You Think?   Now that you know some of the pros and cons on future shock, what do you think about it? Is it an overly simplistic and pessimistic view of our ability to adapt? Or is it a valid warning? Give it some thought; the future may depend on it.

Questions for Discussion

1. How could you reduce conflict or avoid an unfortunate decision in the following situations: choosing a school to attend, choosing a major, deciding about marriage, choosing a job, buying a car?

2. Calculate your life-change score. If your score is elevated, what could you do to reduce the chances of illness? If it is low, what could you do to put more excitement in your life?! Can you see any relationship between previous periods of illness and the number of life changes that preceded them?

3. What do you consider the most prominent sources of stress in our society? What do you think should or could be done to combat these stresses? In your view is there any truth to the idea that we are "future-shocked"? What evidence can you give to support your answer?

4. The defense mechanisms listed in this chapter were described in psychodynamic terms; that is, in terms of the balance of forces within the personality. Can you advance a learning-theory explanation for any of the defenses? (Hint: Think in terms of avoidance learning and the rewards connected with defensive responses.)

5. What are the advantages and disadvantages of using defense mechanisms? Do you think it would be possible for a person to be completely free of defense mechanisms?

6. Defend or deny the following statement (attributed to Professor P. T. Barnumandbailey Circuits): "Television is the opiate of the people. If all the TV tubes in the United States suddenly went blank, the mental health of the nation would crumble because people could no longer escape their problems by watching television."

7. How could you best deal with the following sources of frustration: delays, losses, lack of resources, failure, rejection?

8. "Erhard Seminars Training" is a pop psychology organization that teaches "graduates" that "What is, is, and what isn't, isn't." What are the values and limitations of adopting this outlook toward failures and frustrations?

Suggestions for Further Reading

Cherey, L. "The Man Who First Named Stress," *Psychology Today,* March, 1978, p. 64.

Davis, M., McKay, M., and Eshelman, E. R. *The Relaxation and Stress Reduction Workbook.* New Harbiner, 1980.

Dollard, J., *et al. Frustration and Aggression.* Yale University Press, 1939.

Levi, L. *Society, Stress, and Disease.* Oxford University Press, 1971.

Maier, N. R. F. *Frustration.* Ann Arbor Paperbacks, 1961.

Meichenbaum, D. "Stress-Inoculation Training." In: *Cognitive-Behavior Modification.* Plenum, 1977.

Schafer, W. *Stress, Distress, and Growth.* Responsible Action, 1978.

Selye, H. *The Stress of Life.* McGraw-Hill, 1976.

Toffler, A. *Future Shock.* Random House, 1970.

Woolfolk, R., and Richardson, F. *Stress, Sanity, and Survival.* Signet, 1978.

Contents

Part V

Human
Development
and
Personality

15

Human Development

Chapter Preview

Alien Minds

You may not have noticed. Not everyone has. There are alien creatures among us. More arrive daily. They look a lot like you and me . . . but they're smaller . . . and they think differently. They speak in strange patterns and they ask many questions. It's obvious they are trying to understand how we live. Their goal is to inhabit the planet earth in our place. Who are these creatures and where are they from? You need not be alarmed; they come not from outer space, but from inner space. They are the product of a biological union—of life perpetuating life. They are children.

There are a number of reasons for studying children. At a practical level, parents and educators need accurate information to promote full development of a child's potentials. In personal terms, the study of children helps answer the question, "How did I become the person I am today?" At the theoretical level we recognize that adult personality is closely tied to the child in each individual's past.

These facts make the study of children rewarding, but there is another reason: Children are more than just "little adults." Their understanding of the world is qualitatively different from yours and mine. Entry into a child's circle of awareness has much of the intrigue of meeting a person from another culture. It might even be compared to an encounter with an "alien mind." In short, children are extremely interesting creatures, and a tremendous amount of psychological research has focused on them.

Question: What branch of psychology studies children?

*The study of children is the heart of **developmental psychology.** However, you should recognize that developmental psychologists are interested in every stage of life from "the womb to the tomb." Developmental psychology can therefore be described as the study of progressive changes in behavior and abilities from conception to death. With a definition like this it's clear that developmental psychology includes many topics—so many in fact, that some appear in other chapters. In this chapter, you will find a number of general principles of development, including an account of the far-reaching events in the first years of life. Perhaps learning about development will contribute to your own development. Find out by reading more!*

341

Survey Questions What can newborn babies do? How aware are infants of their surroundings? How do heredity and environment affect prenatal development, self-awareness, motor skills, and learning? How important are parenting styles, and a child's emotional attachment to parents? How do children acquire language and thinking abilities? What are the effects of a poor early environment? Can anything be done to enhance early development? What role does genetics play in human development?

================================ Resources ================================

The Newborn Baby— The Basic Model Comes with Options

At birth the human **neonate** (NEE-oh-NATE, *neo:* new; *nate:* born) is completely helpless and will die if not cared for. Newborn babies have only a limited sensitivity to pain. They cannot lift the head, turn over, or feed themselves. Does this mean they are inert and unfeeling? Definitely not! Neonates are more sensitive and responsive than many people realize. They will, in fact, follow a moving object with their eyes and will turn in the direction of sounds.

A number of adaptive *reflexes* can also be observed. An object pressed in the palm will be grasped with surprising strength. Indeed, this **grasping reflex** is so strong that many infants can hang by their hands if lifted. Since this is an inborn response, we might assume that it was acquired through evolution. Charles Darwin surely would have argued that the grasping reflex improves an infant's chances for survival by reducing the possibility of falling. Another adaptive reflex can be demonstrated by touching a baby's cheek. Immediately the baby will turn toward your finger, as if searching for something.

Question: How is this turning adaptive?

The **rooting reflex,** as this is called, helps the infant to find a bottle or breast. Then, when a nipple touches the infant's mouth, the **sucking reflex** helps the baby obtain needed food. At the same time, getting fed rewards nursing, which rapidly increases in vigor during the first days after birth. Thus, we see that learning begins immediately in the newborn.

Also of interest is the **Moro reflex.** If a baby's head is allowed to drop, or if the baby is startled by a loud noise, the infant will make movements similar to an embrace. These movements have been compared to the ones used by baby monkeys to cling to their mother. It is left to the reader's imagination to decide if there is any connection.

It is tempting to think of newborn babies as mere bun-

dles of reflexes. But a number of observations show that infants respond in ways that are more subtle than was once imagined. For example, Andrew Meltzoff and Keith Moore (1977) have found that babies are born mimics. Figure 15-1 shows Dr. Meltzoff as he sticks out his tongue, opens his mouth, and purses his lips at a twenty-day-old girl. Will the baby imitate him? Videotapes made of babies tested in this way confirmed that they consistently imitate adult facial gestures. Such mimicry is obviously an aid to rapid learning in infancy.

Question: How much intelligence does a newborn have?

Child psychologist Jerome Bruner believes babies are smarter than most people think. Bruner cites an experiment in which three- to eight-week-old babies showed signs of understanding that a person's voice and body are connected. If babies heard their mother's voice coming from where she was standing, they remained calm. If her voice came from a loudspeaker several feet away, the babies became agitated and began to cry.

In another experiment, six-week-old infants were placed in a "baby theater," where they were allowed to watch a movie while sucking on a pacifier. The movie was out of focus, but the pacifier controlled the projector. Babies quickly learned to suck faster on the pacifier to bring the movie into clearer focus. The babies seemed to have grasped the significance of their actions. Bruner considers this a sign that the human mind is quite active from birth onward (Pines, 1970).

Another look into the private world of infants can be drawn from tests of their vision.

Question: How is it possible to test a baby's vision?

Working with infants always requires imagination because of their inability to talk. To test infant vision, Robert Fantz (1963) invented a device called a **looking chamber** (Fig. 15-2a). A child is placed on his or her back inside the chamber, facing a lighted area above. Next, two objects

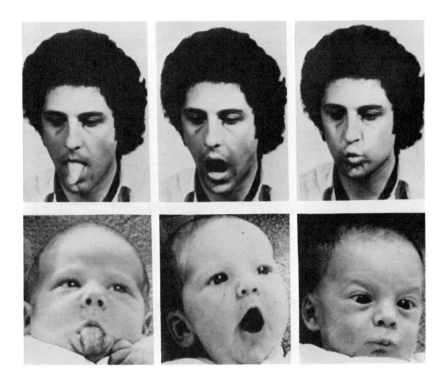

Fig. 15-1 *Infant imitation. In the top row of photos Andrew Meltzoff makes facial gestures at an infant. The bottom row records the infant's responses. Videotapes of Meltzoff and of tested infants helped ensure objectivity. (Photos courtesy of Andrew N. Meltzoff.)*

are placed in the chamber. By observing the movements of the infant's eyes and the images reflected from their surface, it is possible to tell what the infant is looking at.

Fantz found that three-day-old babies prefer complex patterns, such as checkerboards and bull's eyes, to simpler colored rectangles. Other researchers have determined that infants are more excited by circularity and curves, and that they will look longer at red and blue than at other colors (see Fig. 15-2b; Ruff and Birch, 1974; Bornstein, 1975). Findings such as these demonstrate (as a friend of the author's once put it) that, "There really is a person inside that little body."

Of possibly greater interest is the finding that infants spend more time looking at a human face pattern than at a scrambled face or a colored oval (see Fig. 15-2c). When real human faces were used, Fantz found that familiar faces were preferred to unfamiliar faces. However, preference for the familiar reverses at about age two, when unusual objects begin to hold greater interest for the child. For instance, Jerome Kagan (1971) showed three-dimensional face masks to two-year-olds and found they were fascinated by a face with eyes on the chin and a nose in the middle of the forehead. Kagan believes their interest came from a need to understand why the scrambled face differed from what they had come to expect.

To summarize: Bright, complex, circular, curved, red, and blue stimuli first catch an infant's eye; next there is a preference for the familiar; following that is an interest in the unusual. We also know that the infant develops an intense early interest in the human face.

Perhaps the most striking aspect of the human infant is the dazzling speed with which he or she is transformed from a helpless baby to an independent person. Early growth is extremely rapid. By the third year of life, the child stands, walks, talks, explores, and has a unique personality. At no other time after birth does development proceed more rapidly. During this period there is a fascinating interplay of forces shaping the child's development; most importantly, heredity and environment.

Heredity and Environment— The Nature of Nurture and the Nurture of Nature

Question: Which has a greater effect on development, heredity or environment?

For many years psychologists debated—sometimes heatedly—the relative importance of "nature" versus "nurture"

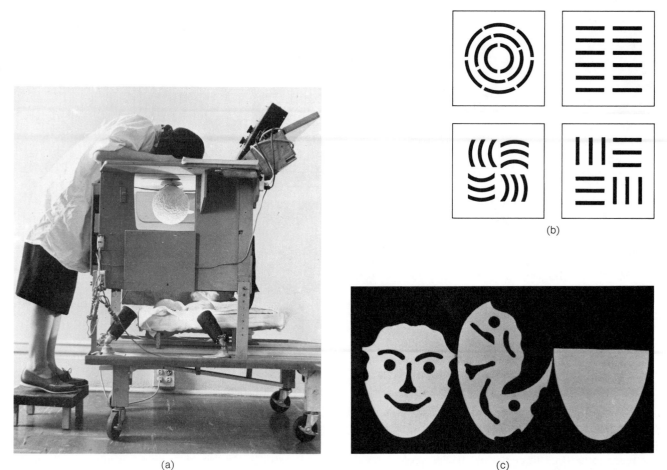

(a)

(b)

(c)

Fig. 15-2   *(a) Eye movements and fixation points of infants are observed in Fantz's "looking chamber." (b) Thirteen-week-old infants preferred concentric and curved patterns like those on the left to nonconcentric and straight-line patterns like those on the right. (c) Infants tested in a looking chamber look at the normal face longer than at the scrambled face and at both faces longer than at the design on the right. (Photo courtesy of David Linton. Drawing from "The Origin of Form Perception" by Robert L. Fantz. Copyright © 1961 by Scientific American, Inc. All rights reserved.)*

in determining behavior. The potent effects of **heredity** ("nature") certainly cannot be denied. At the moment of conception, when a sperm and egg unite to make a new organism, an incredible number of personal characteristics and developmental patterns are determined. For example, there are about one million different species of animals on earth. The mere fact that heredity "programs" a growing bundle of cells to become a fish, a bird, an ape, a hamster, or a person has obvious implications for the course of development.

Each person receives a totally unique biological inheritance from his or her parents. An exception to this statement is the case of **identical twins.** Since they develop from a single fertilized egg, identical twins have identical

heredity. It has been estimated that the genetic information carried in the 46 **chromosomes** of a single human cell would fill thousands of 1000-page books—and that's in fine print!*

Hereditary instructions carried by the chromosomes influence development throughout life by affecting the sequence of growth, the timing of puberty, and the course of aging. The broad outlines of the **human growth sequence** are therefore universal. They extend from conception to senescence and death, as Table 15-1 shows. In addition, heredity determines sex, eye and skin color,

*For more information on heredity and genetics see the "Exploration" at the end of this chapter.

Table 15-1 Human Growth Sequence

Period*	Duration (approximate)	Descriptive Name
Germinal	First two weeks after conception.	Zygote
Embryonic	Two to eight weeks after conception.	Embryo
Fetal	From eight weeks after conception to birth.	Fetus
Neonatal	From birth to a few weeks after birth.	Neonate
Infancy	From a few weeks after birth until child is walking securely. Some children walk securely at less than a year while others may not be able to until age 17–18 months.	Infant
No designated name for this period	From about 15–18 months until about 2–2½ years.	Toddler
No specific name. Sometimes called "run about years"	From age 2–3 to about age 6.	Preschool child
Middle years of childhood	From about age 6 to about age 12.	No specific name
Pubescence	Period of about 2 years before puberty.	No specific name
Puberty	That point of development at which biological changes of pubescence reach a climax marked by sexual maturity.	No specific name
Adolescence	From the beginning of pubescence until full social maturity is reached (difficult to fix duration of this period).	Adolescent
Adulthood	From adolescence to death.	Adult
Young adulthood (19–25)	Sometimes subdivided into other periods as shown at left.	
Adulthood (25–40)		
Maturity (41 plus)		
Senescence	No defined limits which would apply to all people. Extremely variable. Characterized by marked physiological and psychological deterioration.	Adult (senile), "old age"

*Note: There is no exact beginning or ending point for the various growth periods. The ages listed are approximate, and each period may be thought of as shading or blending into the next.
(Table courtesy of Tom Bond.)

the sequence of motor development, and susceptibility to some diseases. Heredity also exerts considerable influence over body size and shape, height, intelligence, athletic potential, and a host of other details (Fig. 15-3). Score "1" for those who favor heredity as the more important factor in development!

Does this mean "nurture" takes a back seat in development? Consider Aldous Huxley's (1965) dramatic summary of the influence of **environment:**

> Anatomically and physiologically man has changed very little during the last 20 or 30 thousand years. The native or genetic capacities of today's bright city child are no better than the native capacities of a bright child born into a family of Upper Paleolithic cave-dwellers. But whereas the contemporary bright baby may grow up to become almost anything—a Presbyterian engineer, for example, a piano-playing Marxist, a professor of biochemistry who is a mystical agnostic and likes to paint in

water-colors—the Paleolithic baby could not possibly have grown into anything except a hunter or food-gatherer.*

Score "1" for the environmentalists!

The outcome of this debate (we have only viewed an opening round) is recognition that *both* heredity and environment are important. The two are, in fact, inseparable. As a person grows, there is a constant interplay, or *interaction,* between the forces of nature and nurture. Heredity shapes development by providing a framework of personal potentials and limitations that are altered by learning, nutrition, disease, culture, and other environmental factors.

Question: How soon after birth do hereditary differences appear?

*From "Human Potentialities" by A. Huxley. In R. E. Farson, ed., *Science and Human Affairs.* Palo Alto, California: Science and Behavior Books, 1965.

Fig. 15-3 *Identical twins. Twins who share identical genes (identical twins) demonstrate the powerful influence of heredity. Even when they are reared apart, identical twins are strikingly alike in motor skills, physical development, and appearance (Horn, Plomin, and Rosenman, 1976).*

They appear immediately. Infants are unique individuals from the time of birth. Jerome Kagan (1969) found that newborn babies differ in activity, irritability, distractibility, and other aspects of **temperament.** Another careful study found that babies could be reliably separated into three categories: *"easy children"* (about 40 percent of those observed); *"difficult children"* (about 10 percent); and *"slow-to-warm-up children"* (about 15 percent). The remaining children did not fit neatly into one category (Thomas *et al.,* 1968).

"Easy children" are those who are relaxed and agreeable. Such children adapt well to their surroundings. "Difficult children" tend to overreact to most situations. They are moody, intense, easily angered or frustrated, and prone to tantrums. By contrast, the "slow-to-warm-up child" is restrained and unexpressive. These children are slow to react and might be described as "shy" or withdrawn. Recent research suggests that such differences are at least partially due to variations in body chemistry that affect brain activity (Sostek and Wyatt, 1981).

Question: Does that mean temperamental differences last throughout a person's life?

Not necessarily. Kagan conducted a follow-up on ten-year-old children who were studied as infants. He found little connection between infancy and later childhood for dimensions such as irritability, activity, or attentiveness (Kagan, 1976).

Question: Then how do temperamental differences influence development?

Because of inborn differences in readiness to smile, cry, vocalize, reach out, or pay attention, babies rapidly become *active participants* in their own development. Growing infants change the environment at the same time they are changed by it. For example, Amy is an "easy" baby who smiles frequently and is easily fed. This encourages touching, feeding, and affection from her mother. The mother's responses, in turn, reward Amy and cause more smiling and other positive reactions. A dynamic *relationship* has been established between mother and child. Of course, this kind of give and take can also work in reverse, as when "difficult" babies anger or frustrate their parents and become *more* difficult due to the parents' reactions.

We might say, then, that three factors combine to determine a person's **developmental level** at any stage of life. These are: *heredity, environment,* and the individual's *own behavior,* each tightly interwoven with the others.

Maturation—Heredity at the Helm

In some areas of development the effects of heredity outweigh those of environment. For example, one classic study concerned this question: "If babies are not allowed to practice crawling or walking early in life, will they walk at the same age as unrestrained children?"

To obtain an answer, Dennis (1940) studied Hopi Indian children who were kept on cradle boards for the first nine months of life. According to tradition, these children were firmly bound to a board for most of each day. As a result, they got little or no practice at sitting, creeping, or walking. Nevertheless, they learned to walk at about the same age (15 months) as unrestrained children. The age at which a child learns to walk is more the result of *maturation* than of learning.

Question: What, specifically, is maturation?

Maturation refers to growth and development of the body; or more specifically, of muscle, bone, and the nervous system. Maturation underlies the *orderly sequence* observed in the unfolding of many basic responses.

While the *rate* of maturation varies from child to child,

the *order* is virtually universal. For instance, the strength and coordination needed for sitting appears before that needed for crawling. Therefore, infants the world over sit before they crawl (and crawl before they stand, stand before they walk, and so on) (see Fig. 15-4). In general, increased muscular control proceeds from *head to toe,* and from the *center* of the body *to the extremities.*

Readiness   Maturation often creates a condition of **readiness** for learning. The principle of readiness (also known as the **principle of motor primacy**) states: "Until the necessary physical structures are mature, no amount of practice will be sufficient to establish a skill." It is impossible, for instance, to teach children to walk or to become toilet trained before they have matured enough to control the necessary muscles. Parents who try to force children to learn skills for which they are not yet ready invite failure and run the risk of needlessly frustrating the child.

Question: Then are there definite ages at which children become ready to learn particular skills?

No. Readiness is not an all-or-nothing effect. Training that comes too early will be unsuccessful; training that is only a little early may succeed, but will be inefficient; and training when a child is maturationally ready produces rapid learning. This progression can be seen in an experiment in which a group of two- and three-year-old children were given 12 weeks of special practice at learning to climb a ladder (to reach a tabletop covered with toys). By the end of the 12-week period, the children had become good climbers. At this point, children in a second group (matched in age with the first group) were given practice at ladder climbing (Hilgard, 1932).

Question: Did it take the second group 12 weeks to learn to climb?

No. The second group caught up to the first after just one week. Even though they missed out on the previous 12 weeks of practice, their bodies had continued to mature. Hence, they learned more rapidly and efficiently when given the chance.

Many parents are anxious to see their children move through the developmental stages, and there is always a temptation to try to "hurry" a child along. However, it is valuable to recognize that much unnecessary grief can be avoided by respecting a child's personal rate of growth. For instance, eager parents who toilet trained an eighteen-month-old child in ten trying weeks of "false alarms" and assorted "accidents," might have done it in two or three weeks by waiting until the child was twenty months old to begin.

Self-Awareness   When you look in a mirror, you recognize the image looking back as your own.* At what age did this sense of recognition first develop? Like many other events in development, **self-awareness** depends on maturation of the nervous system.

Question: How is self-awareness demonstrated in a baby?

In an experiment that certainly must have been fun to do, mothers of children nine to twenty-four months old secretly rubbed a spot of rouge on their child's nose. Each child was then brought in front of a mirror for testing. The question was, "Will the child notice the red spot on his or her nose, indicating recognition of the mirror image?" The probability that children would touch their nose was very low at nine months but jumped dramatically through the second year. In an even stronger test of self-recognition, infants were shown their own videotaped images on a TV screen. Most infants had to be fifteen months old before they could recognize their own images (Lewis and Brooks-Gunn, 1979). Increased self-awareness, then, closely parallels the human growth sequence (Kagan, 1976).

Other Skills   The dramatic effect of maturation on the pace of learning other basic skills is demonstrated by the following experiment (Kellogg and Kellogg, 1933):

Donald's Strange Sister

When Donald was nine months old, his parents brought a seven-month-old chimp home to be raised as one of the family. Every effort was made to treat Donald and Gua (the chimp) like brother and sister. For the next eight months they were treated as much alike as possible and received equally affectionate care and training. During this time, Gua rapidly surpassed Donald in learning many "civilized" acts (such as drinking from a cup, using a spoon, responding to spoken instructions, and maintaining bowel and bladder control). By the time Donald was about 18 months old, however, Gua's superiority came to an end as Donald began to use language. From this time on, he excelled Gua in everything but physical strength.

Gua's early superiority is easily explained. A chimp has only about one-third the life span of a human and matures much more rapidly. Gua's rapid maturation gave her an early "edge" in learning. Notice, however, that her abilities quickly hit a peak, whereas Donald's continued to improve as he matured. Notice also the importance of Donald's inherited potential for learning language.

---

*Except, perhaps, early on Monday mornings.

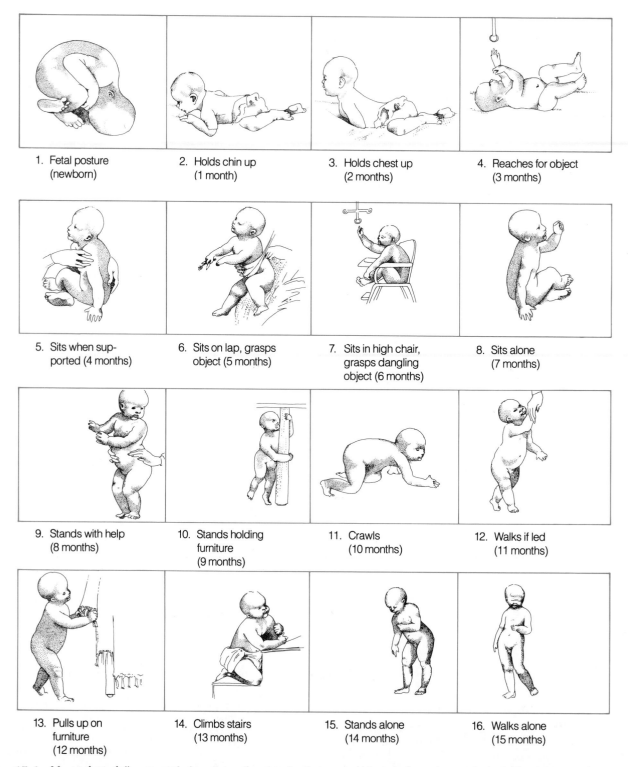

1. Fetal posture (newborn)
2. Holds chin up (1 month)
3. Holds chest up (2 months)
4. Reaches for object (3 months)
5. Sits when supported (4 months)
6. Sits on lap, grasps object (5 months)
7. Sits in high chair, grasps dangling object (6 months)
8. Sits alone (7 months)
9. Stands with help (8 months)
10. Stands holding furniture (9 months)
11. Crawls (10 months)
12. Walks if led (11 months)
13. Pulls up on furniture (12 months)
14. Climbs stairs (13 months)
15. Stands alone (14 months)
16. Walks alone (15 months)

Fig. 15-4 *Most infants follow an orderly pattern of motor development. Although the order in which children progress from one stage to the next is similar, there are large individual differences in the ages at which various stages are reached. The ages listed are averages. (Based on Shirley, 1933 and Frankenburg and Dodds, 1967.)*

Learning Check

1. If an infant is startled it will make movements similar to an embrace, known as the:

    a. grasping reflex   b. rooting reflex   c. Moro reflex   d. adaptive reflex

2. After age two, infants tested in a looking chamber show a marked preference for familiar faces and simpler designs.   T or F?

3. As a child develops there is a continuous _____ between the forces of heredity and environment.

4. Which of the following represents a correct sequence?

    a. zygote, fetus, embryo, neonate, infant   b. zygote, embryo, neonate, fetus, infant
    c. embryo, zygote, fetus, neonate, infant   d. zygote, embryo, fetus, neonate, infant

5. "Slow-to-warm-up" children can be described as restrained, unexpressive, shy, or withdrawn.   T or F?

6. The orderly sequence observed in the unfolding of many basic responses can be attributed to

    _____.

7. Clear signs of self-awareness or self-recognition are evident in most infants by the time they reach eight months of age.   T or F?

8. The principle of motor primacy is also known as _____.

Answers: 1. c   2. F   3. interaction   4. d   5. T   6. maturation   7. F   8. readiness

---

Early Environment—As the Twig Is Bent

Environment obviously begins to modify development immediately after birth, but it may come as a surprise that the prenatal environment is also important. Normally we think of the **intrauterine environment** of the womb as highly protected and stable. In general, it is; but a number of conditions can affect the fetus before birth.

Prenatal Development   During embryonic and fetal development it is quite possible for the effects of environment to reach the seemingly well-protected confines of the womb. If a mother's health or nutrition is poor, if she contracts certain diseases, such as German measles or syphilis, uses drugs, or is exposed to X-rays or atomic radiation, the fetus may be harmed. The resultant damage is referred to as a **congenital problem.** Congenital problems (or "birth defects" as they are sometimes called) are distinct from **genetic problems,** which are inherited. (You will find more information on genetic problems in this chapter's "Exploration.")

Question: How is it possible for the fetus to be harmed?

As you may know, there is no direct intermingling of blood between mother and fetus. Nevertheless, some substances, especially drugs, still reach the fetus. If the mother is addicted to morphine, heroin, or methadone, the infant may be born with a drug addiction. Most common prescription drugs—many of them capable of producing fetal malformations—also reach the fetus.

Even a partial listing of troublesome drugs underscores the need for caution in drug use during pregnancy; potentially damaging substances include: general anesthetics, cortisone, tetracycline, excessive amounts of vitamins A, D, B_6, and K, some barbiturates, opiates, tranquilizers, synthetic sex hormones, and possibly even aspirin (Cox, 1979).

Question: What about alcohol and tobacco?

Repeated heavy drinking by a pregnant woman can produce a pattern known as the **fetal alcohol syndrome.** It includes miscarriage or premature birth, and infants with low birth weight, an underdeveloped head, facial abnormalities, and deformations of the heart, bones, fingers, elbows, or urogenital system (Jones and Smith, 1973). Later in childhood, mental retardation, irritability, poor coordination, or learning disabilities may be observed. With such risks, the safest course during pregnancy is to entirely avoid drinking. The *maximum* amount a pregnant woman should drink on any day is one ounce of hard liquor, or one glass of wine, or two glasses of beer, and even these amounts may damage the fetus.

Smoking also has an adverse effect on prenatal development. Smoking can elevate or lower the heart rate of the unborn child, and a mother who smokes heavily is more likely to miscarry. Heavy smokers run a higher risk of premature birth and tend to give birth to underweight babies. Both premature birth and low birth weight increase the chances of infant sickness and death after birth (Cox, 1979).

Question: Is it true that a mother's emotions can affect the fetus?

Adrenaline produced by the mother's body at times of stress or emotional upset can indeed reach the fetus and increase fetal activity. It is not yet known how much effect this has on the unborn child.

It is known that mothers who are emotionally distraught during pregnancy are more likely to have "colicky" babies. There is no truth, however, to stories about babies acquiring fears, a taste for a particular food, an interest in music, and so on, because the pregnant mother ate the food, listened to music, or was frightened.

Maternal and Paternal Influences   In later years, a child's environment expands to include the effects of culture, subculture, family, school, television, and peers. Im-

Fig. 15-5   *"Fathering" typically makes a contribution to early development differing in emphasis from "mothering."*

mediately after birth and for the first few years, the most important influences come from an infant's caretakers. The quality of "mothering" and "fathering" is therefore of prime importance.

One revealing study of **maternal influences** began with selection of children who were unusually competent (A children), who were above average in ability (B children), or who had a low degree of competence (C children). As increasingly younger children were observed, it became apparent that A and C patterns were already set by age three. To learn how this was possible, children under three and their mothers were observed at home (White and Watts, 1973). On the basis of several years of research, five caretaking styles were identified.

1. "Super mothers" went out of their way to provide educational experiences for their children and allowed the child to initiate some activities. This caretaking style produced an A child, competent in most areas of development.

2. "Smothering mothers" pushed their children and constantly ordered them around. The child's current level of ability was never accepted as adequate. The result was a child of A intellectual ability, but one who was immature and shy.

3. "Almost mothers" waited for their children to lead in most situations and seemed to have difficulty understanding and meeting the child's needs. The typical outcome was a B child of above-average competence who had some difficulty in dealing with the environment.

4. "Overwhelmed mothers" spent little time with their children. This mother's children spent much of their time sitting or doing nothing; some were cared for primarily by brothers or sisters. Overwhelmed mothers appeared to be having difficulty meeting the demands of daily living; the entire home tended to be disorganized. The "overwhelmed" pattern was associated with C children of average or below-average competence.

5. The "zoo-keeper mother" gave her children good physical care, but interacted with them very little. This mother's childcare routines were rigid and highly structured. Her children tended to be of below-average competence and to approach problems inflexibly (Pines, 1969).

Although not yet confirmed by others, these findings support two beliefs long held by developmental psychologists: First, that mothering *does* make a difference; and second, that early development has lasting effects on a person.

Question: Aren't you overlooking the effects of "fathering"?

Yes. Fathers also contribute significantly to an infant's social and intellectual growth. In fact, fathers make a unique contribution to development by interacting with the infant in ways that differ from those typical of mothers.

Recent studies of **paternal influences** have shown that even in nontraditional families fathers spend much less time in active childcare (feeding and changing) than do mothers. Whereas mothers spend an average of one and one-half hours per day feeding their infant, fathers average 15 minutes. Almost one-half of all the fathers surveyed never changed their child's diapers; 75 percent had no *established* duties for the child's care. In most households the father's main role tends to be that of a *playmate* for the infant. Fathers typically spend four or five times as much time playing with their infants as they do in caretaking (Parke and Sawin, 1977).

It might seem that the father's role as a playmate makes him less important in the child's development. Not so. From the birth of the child onward, fathers are more visually attentive to the child than are mothers. They are much more tactile (lifting, tickling, and handling the baby), more physically arousing (engaging in rough-and-tumble play), and more likely to engage in unusual play (imitating baby, for example). Mothers speak to the infant more, play more conventional games (such as peekaboo), and as previously noted, spend more time in caretaking activities. *Both* parents influence intellectual growth with their attitudes toward a child's *investigation,* or exploration, of the world. The child who repeatedly hears, "Don't touch that" (chair, handle, trash, radio, pencil, flower, etc.), or, "I told you not to" (go up there, play with that, leave this spot, get dirty, and so forth), may become passive and intellectually dulled (Carew, Chan, and Halfor, 1976). Placing virtually all common objects off limits for a child is a serious mistake.

In summary, in the average household the father's greatest early contribution to an infant's development comes from the quality of his play with the child; the mother's contribution tends to center on verbal stimulation and the quality of the caretaking she provides (Parke and Sawin, 1977).

Language Development— Fast-Talking Babies

There's something almost miraculous about a baby's first word. As infants, how did we manage this leap into the world of language? What role did maturation play? How did our parents aid the search for that magical first word? In recent years, psychologists have begun to unravel the mysteries of language learning. Before delving into their discoveries, let's survey the typical course of language development.

Language Acquisition   The development of language is closely tied to maturation. As any parent can tell you, babies can cry from birth on. By one month of age, the infant can control crying enough to use it as an attention-getting device, and parents can tell the nature of the infant's needs from the tone of the crying. Around six to eight weeks of age, babies begin **cooing** (the repetition of vowel sounds like "oo" and "ah").

By the time a child is six months old, the nervous system has matured enough to allow the child to grasp objects, to smile, laugh, sit up, and to **babble.** In the babbling stage, consonant sounds are added to produce a continuous outpouring of repeated language sounds. The influence of environment at this stage is indicated by the fact that babbling increases when parents talk to the child (Mussen *et al.,* 1979).

At about one year of age, the child can stand alone for a short time and can respond to words such as "No," or "Hi." Soon afterward, the first connection between words and objects is formed, and children may address their parents as "Mama" or "Dada." Between the ages of one and a half and two years, children become able to stand and walk alone. By this time their vocabulary may include from two dozen to 200 words. At first there is a **single-word stage,** during which the child says things such as "go," "juice," or "up." Next, the child links words in **single-word pairs,** such as "Mommy/Mommy," or "car/ride" (Bloom and Lahey, 1978). Soon after, words are arranged in simple two-word sentences called **telegraphic speech:** "Want Teddy." "Mama gone." From this point on, growth of the child's vocabulary and language skills proceeds at a phenomenal rate. By first grade, the child can understand around 8000 words and use about 4000.

The Roots of Language

In a fascinating study, researchers Louis Sander and William Condon (1974) filmed newborn infants as the babies listened to various sounds. A later frame-by-frame analysis of the films showed something astonishing: Infants move their arms and legs in synchrony to the rhythms of human speech. Random noise, rhythmic tapping, or disconnected vowel sounds will not produce this "language dance." Only the natural rhythms of speech will do.

Why would day-old infants "dance" to speech, but not other sounds? One possibility is that language recognition is innate. Linguist Noam Chomsky (1968, 1975) has long claimed that humans have a **biological predisposition** to develop language. According to Chomsky, language organization is inborn, much like a child's ability to coordinate walking. In Chomsky's view, all that is needed to unlock basic language patterns is for children to hear the speech of adults. If such inborn language recognition does exist, it may explain why children around the world use a limited number of patterns in their first sentences. Typical patterns include (Mussen *et al.,* 1979):

Identification:	See kitty.
Nonexistence:	Allgone milk.
Possession:	My doll.
Agent-Action:	Mama give.
Negation:	Not ball.
Question:	Where doggie?

Question: Does Chomsky's theory explain why language develops so rapidly?

Perhaps. But many psychologists feel that Chomsky underestimates the importance of learning. **Psycholinguists** (specialists in the psychology of language) have recently shown that language is not magically "switched on" by adult speech. Imitation of adults and rewards for correctly using words (as when a child asks for a cookie) are also part of language learning. More importantly, parents and children begin to communicate long before the child can speak. Months of shared effort precede the child's first word (Miller, 1977). From this point of view, the filmed infants' behavior reflects a readiness to interact *socially* with parents, not innate language recognition.

Question: How do parents communicate with infants before they can talk?

Early Communication   Parents go to a great deal of trouble to get babies to smile and vocalize (Fig. 15-6). In doing so, they quickly learn to change their actions to keep the infant's attention, arousal, and activity at optimal levels (Brazelton *et al.,* 1974). A familiar example is the "I'm Going to Get You Game." In it, the adult says, "I'm gonna getcha . . . I'm gonna getcha . . . I'm gonna getcha . . . Gotcha!" Through such games, adults and babies come to share similar rhythms and expectations (Stern, 1982). Soon a system of shared **signals** is created. Touching, vocalizing, gazing, and smiling help lay a foundation for later language use. Specifically, these signals establish a pattern of "conversational" turn-taking (Snow, 1977):

Mother	Ann
	(smiles)
Oh what a nice little smile!	
Yes, isn't that nice?	
There.	
There's a nice little smile.	(burps)
Well, pardon you!	
Yes, that's better, isn't it?	
Yes.	(vocalizes)
Yes.	(smiles)
What's so funny?	

Adult speakers usually want to know if a listener is paying attention. This is why **mutual monitoring** is a basic element of adult conversation. In conversation, you probably watch for head-nodding and check for attention by saying, "Right?" or "O.K.?" Interestingly, parents display a similar pattern when talking to babies. In a typical episode, a parent gets the baby's attention by touching or talking to it. The parent then intensifies the baby's attention with eye contact, touching, talking, or movement. Then, either the parent or baby withdraws by looking away, and a new cycle begins. From the outside, such exchanges may look meaningless. In reality, they represent real communication. A baby's vocalizations and attention provide a way of interacting emotionally with parents (Stern *et al.,* 1975).

Parents as Tutors   Parents help children learn language in more ways than they may suspect. One way is through the use of **caretaker speech,** or "motherese," as it is sometimes called. Caretaker speech may be more familiar to you as Baby Talk. When talking to infants, parents of all cultures raise the tone of their voice, use shorter phrases, repeat themselves more, and slow their rate of speaking, (Parke, 1982). They also simplify pronouns ("Did Jenny eat it?") and pronunciation. In Baby Talk, phrases such as

Fig. 15-6 *Infant engagement scale. These samples from a 90-point scale show various levels of infant engagement, or attention. Babies participate in prelanguage "conversations" with parents by giving and withholding attention, and by smiling, gazing, or vocalizing. (Source: Beebe et al., 1982)*

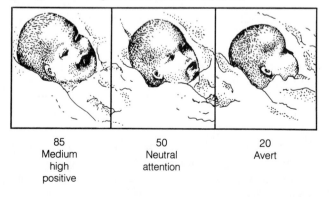

| 85 Medium high positive | 50 Neutral attention | 20 Avert |

"pretty rabbit" become "pwitty wabbit," "skambled eggs" may replace scrambled eggs, and a stomach is a "tummy."

Question: What is the purpose of such changes?

Parents are apparently trying to help their children learn language. When a baby is still babbling, parents tend to use long, adult-style sentences. But as soon as the baby says its first word, they switch to Baby Talk. The changes in pronunciation parents make are probably not very important. But simplification is, because it helps babies learn the basic rules of language (Cherry, 1979). As a child's speaking ability improves, parents tend to adjust their speech to the child's level of language development. Especially from age one-and-a-half to four, parents use strategies to clarify what a child says, and prompt the child to say more. Two typical strategies are (Newman and Newman, 1978):

Expansion: *Child:* Doggie bite.
                  Parent: Yes the dog bit *the toy.*

Prompting: *Child:* Doggie briggle.
                  Parent: What did the doggie do??

In summary, some elements of language may be innate, but a full flowering of speech requires careful cultivation. Now that we have our subjects (babies) walking and talking, let's move on to some other facets of development.

Fig. 15-7 *"Mother" Lorenz leads his charges on a stroll. The goslings have imprinted on Dr. Lorenz because he was the first moving object they saw after they hatched.*

Critical Periods in Development— Mother Goose and Motherless Monkeys

Question: Why do experiences early in life have such lasting effects?

Part of the answer lies in the existence of critical periods for acquiring particular behaviors. A **critical period** is a time when susceptibility to environmental influences (both positive and negative) is increased. Critical periods usually correspond to times of rapid development. For example, the infamous drug thalidomide interferes with limb formation in the developing fetus. Before its use was banned, many mothers in the United States and Europe had the misfortune of taking thalidomide during the period of fetal limb formation (the sixth to eighth week of pregnancy). The result was severe birth defects.

Imprinting Often, certain events must occur during a critical period for a person or an animal to develop normally. To illustrate, Konrad Lorenz, an ethologist who studies animal behavior, once became curious about why baby geese follow their mother. The obvious explanation seemed to be, "It's instinctive," but Lorenz showed otherwise.

Mother Lorenz

Normally the first large moving object a baby goose sees is its mother. Lorenz hatched geese in an incubator so the first moving object they saw was Lorenz. From then on, these baby geese followed Lorenz. They even reacted to his call as if he were their mother (Lorenz, 1937). (Fig. 15-7.)

It can be seen that the response pattern of "mother-goose following" is not automatic. It is established during a critical period by the essential experience of seeing a large moving object. The rapid and early learning of a permanent behavior pattern of this type has been called **imprinting.**

In most birds, the critical period for imprinting is very brief. For instance, Hess (1959) found that if ducklings are not allowed to imprint on their mother or some other object within 30 hours after hatching, they never will.* In many animals, imprinting and other events taking place during critical periods have lifelong consequences (Lorenz, 1962):

*Ducklings have been imprinted on decoys, rubber balls, wooden blocks, and a number of other unlikely objects.

Revenge of the Jackdaw

Imprinting normally serves to attach a young animal to its mother. It also guides the selection of a mate of the same species at sexual maturity. In another of Lorenz's experiments, a jackdaw (European starling) imprinted on him. When the bird reached sexual maturity, Lorenz became the object of its mating ritual. Part of this ritual involves stuffing worms into the mouth of the intended mate—as a surprised Lorenz learned while asleep on the lawn one day. When Lorenz refused its "gift," the jackdaw stuffed a worm in Lorenz's ear (showing, perhaps, that it's not nice to fool Mother Nature)!

Question: Does imprinting occur in humans?

Attachment   True cases of imprinting are limited to birds and other animals (Hess, 1959). However, human infants form an **emotional attachment** to their *primary caretakers* (usually parents), and there is a critical period during which this must occur for healthy development (Bowlby, 1969, 1973). Until babies are about six months old, they show no more attachment to parents than they do to strangers. After this period, they begin to display **stranger anxiety** and show other signs of having learned to fear the unfamiliar (Scott, 1967; Kagan, 1976).

Some researchers have disputed the idea that stranger anxiety is universal, viewing it instead as a limited cultural phenomenon (Klein and Durfee, 1976). There is no question, however, about the existence of another indication of the emotional bond between infant and parent. At around eight to twelve months of age, babies display **separation anxiety** (crying and signs of fear) when their parents leave them alone, or alone with strangers (Kagan, 1976). Separation anxiety disappears later when parting with parents becomes a frequent event (as when the child goes to a preschool or nursery, stays with a baby sitter, or with grandparents).

Question: Does daycare for young children interfere with normal attachment?

Fortunately, it seems that it does not. A recent survey of daycare effects concluded that "*high-quality* nonmaternal care does not appear to have harmful effects on the preschool child's maternal attachment, intellectual development, social-emotional behavior, or physical health" (Etaugh, 1980).

Motherless Monkeys   Research with rhesus monkeys suggests that like imprinting infant attachments can have lasting effects. Harry Harlow (1966, 1967) has shown that baby monkeys separated from their mothers and raised in isolation become troubled adult animals. Among other things, these "motherless monkeys" never develop normal sexual behaviors, and they make very poor mothers if mated. They are coldly rejecting or indifferent to their babies and may brutalize or injure them. It has been suggested that human parents who abuse, reject, or physically injure their children may be displaying a similar pattern. Most abusive parents were themselves rejected or mistreated as children.

Question: Are the effects of early isolation permanent?

For a long time it was believed that such damage was irreversible. However, Suomi and Harlow (1972) have reported that the bizarre and stereotyped behavior of monkeys subjected to six months of isolation can be altered. This was done by placing the abnormal monkeys with younger normal monkeys for a 26-week "therapy" session.

Findings such as these by no means imply that parents can ignore the early experiences of their infants. Meeting a baby's **affectional needs** is every bit as important as meeting more obvious needs for food, water, and physical care. Such findings do show, however, that even with the existence of critical periods, infants display considerable resilience.

All things considered, one of the most important developmental tasks of the first year of life appears to be creation of a bond of trust and affection between the infant and at least one other person. Parents are sometimes afraid of "spoiling" a baby with too much attention, but for the first year or two this is nearly impossible. As a matter of fact, a later capacity to experience warm and loving relationships may depend on it.

Question: Are there other critical periods?

Other Critical Periods   Psychologists are just beginning to explore the full range of critical periods in human development. It is well known, for example, that if a person waits until adulthood to learn a second language, it becomes virtually impossible to achieve an authentic native accent. In general, reaching maximum ability in artistic, athletic, musical, or language skills requires practice that begins at an early age. A case in point is the success of Russian athletes who are selected early and rigorously trained throughout childhood. The work and theories of Japanese music teacher Shinichi Suzuki are also highly suggestive. Using scaled-down instruments, Suzuki has taught children as young as three years old to play the violin. By age six, these children have spent half their lives playing Bach, Handel, Mozart. By age ten, many are so phenomenal that serious adult students envy their ability.

In many ways it would be accurate to say that all of infancy is a *relatively critical period* in development. While we must wait for further research on variables affecting the kinds of skills described here, one area is fairly well understood. The effects of early stimulation and deprivation are discussed in the following section.

Deprivation and Enrichment— A Practical Definition of Tender Loving Care

News item: "Wild Child Raised by Apes Found in Africa." Over the years there have been several reported discoveries of "feral children." These are children who have supposedly grown up in the care of animals and who act like animals when found. Actually, there is little documented evidence that such children have existed, but we needn't go this far afield for proof of the destructive effects of early **deprivation.**

There are numerous confirmed cases of children who have spent the first five or six years of life in closets, attics, and other restricted environments. When discovered, these children are usually mute, severely retarded, and emotionally damaged. Some suffer from **deprivation dwarfism—** stunted growth associated with isolation, rejection, or general deprivation in the home environment. (See inset news excerpt.) Special efforts to teach such children to speak and function normally often meet with limited success.

Question: What aspects of such experiences are responsible for the damage done?

One of the earliest hints came when psychoanalyst René Spitz (1945) compared two groups of infants. One group was made up of healthy and lively babies in an institution Spitz called the "nursery." In the "foundling home" was a second group of babies who suffered from a condition called **hospitalism.** This is a pattern of deep depression marked by weeping and sadness, long periods of immobility or mechanical rocking, and a lack of normal response to other humans. The foundling home also had an unusually high rate of infant deaths, and development of the living babies was severely retarded.

By comparing conditions at the two institutions, Spitz found some striking differences. At the nursery, each baby had a separate attendant; at the foundling home, there were eight babies to a nurse. Spitz considered the "wasting away" of the foundling home babies a result of **anaclitic** (dependency) **depression.** In other words, he emphasized the fact that babies in the nursery had dependable "mother figures," whereas those in the foundling home had one-eighth of a nurse each.

"Closet Child" Now with Loving Parents

LONG BEACH (AP)—Becky's story began to unfold when the Sheriff's Department responded to a tip like hundreds of others. They found Becky in urine-soaked clothes, asleep on a hard cot in her parents' bedroom.

"She was almost like an animal," one of the deputies reported.

Her world then was the bedroom and its closet, in which she was kept for untold hours. Now Becky lives in a spacious foster home.

Since Becky's rescue, she has gained 12 pounds and grown 6 inches. But she is still a mite, for she weighed only 24 pounds and stood only 32 inches tall last April.

When she was found, Becky couldn't even crawl; now she walks. Then, she knew only a few words—now she speaks in sentences. She is, except for the hurt in her eyes, like almost any toddler.

But Rebecca is no toddler. She is nine years old, and her pediatrician says she may never catch up.

Question: In other words, the babies failed to form an attachment to an adult, right?

Yes. Recent work shows that lack of attachment is a major element in early deprivation. For example, making living conditions better for a group of children in a Canadian institution failed to reverse their declining mental health. The children improved only when they were placed with caring foster parents or adoptive parents (Flint, 1978).

A second major factor in many cases of deprivation is a lack of **perceptual stimulation.** All of the "wasted" babies studied by Spitz were well cared for physically. However, they were kept in bare rooms, in cribs with white sheets hung on the sides. The infants could only see the blank ceiling, and their only contact with others came during a few brief periods each day when they were quickly fed or changed. To put it mildly, there was *nothing happening* for these children; no change, no input, no cuddling, no attention, and most of all, no stimulation. This was deprivation in the fullest sense of the word.

Early Stimulation Experiments with animals have confirmed the destructive effects of a lack of stimulation in infancy. For example, monkeys raised in darkness for the first three months of life are unable to use their vision properly when brought into the light (Riesen, 1965).

Also revealing is the research of Harry Harlow. As mentioned earlier, Harlow separated infant rhesus monkeys from their mothers at birth. The real mothers were replaced with "surrogate (artificial) mothers"—essentially dummies of approximately the same size and shape as real monkeys. Some of the surrogates were made of cold, unyielding wire, and others were covered with soft terry cloth (Fig. 15-8). When the infants were given a choice between the two mothers, they consistently chose to spend most of their time clinging to the cuddly terry cloth mother. This was true even when a bottle was mounted in the wire mother, making it the source of food.

The "love" and attachment displayed toward the cloth mothers was identical to that shown toward natural mothers. When frightened by rubber snakes, wind-up toys, and other "fear stimuli," the infant monkeys ran to their cloth mothers and clung to them for security (Harlow and Zimmerman, 1958). Harlow has concluded that one of the most important dimensions of early stimulation is **contact comfort,** supplied by touching, holding, and stroking an infant. Harlow's findings may be inconclusive where humans are concerned, but other findings back them up. For example,

Fig. 15-8 *An infant monkey clings to a cloth-covered surrogate mother. Baby monkeys become attached to the cloth "contact-comfort" mother but not to a similar wire mother. This is true even when the wire mother provides food. (Photo courtesy of Harry Harlow, University of Wisconsin Primate Laboratory.)*

one researcher found that just 20 minutes of extra touching a day could affect the developmental rate of infants in an institution (Casler, 1965).

For many psychologists, the concept of contact comfort has become part of the rationale for advocating breast feeding of infants. Breast feeding almost guarantees a baby will receive an adequate amount of touching and handling. In addition, the breast-feeding mother produces **colostrum** (ko-LOSS-trum) rather than milk for the first few days after birth. Colostrum is a fluid rich in proteins that carries antibodies from the mother to the newborn and helps to prevent certain infectious diseases.

Question: What about the mother who can't breast-feed or who prefers not to?

The advantages of breast feeding are not overriding. If a mother is aware of the importance of touching and cuddling and makes an effort to provide it, bottle feeding is in no way psychologically inferior to breast feeding. In fact, a mother's warmth or coldness, relaxation or tension, and acceptance or rejection have more to do with the effects of feeding than does the choice of breast or bottle (Heinstein, 1963).

Enrichment   If too little stimulation limits development, can an abundance of stimulation enhance it? A number of attempts to answer this question have made use of **enriched environments.** An enriched environment is one that has been deliberately made more novel, complex, and richly stimulating. Enriched environments for infants may be the "soil" from which brighter children grow. To illustrate, let us begin with an experiment in which rats were raised in an enriched environment (Kretch *et al.,* 1962):

Building Bigger and Better Brains

To begin with, infant rats were divided into two groups. One group was raised in *stimulus-poor* conditions. These animals were housed in adequate but unstimulating cages with gray walls that contained nothing to explore or investigate. The second group was housed in a sort of "rat wonderland." The walls of the *stimulus-enriched* environment were decorated with colored patterns, and the cage was filled with platforms, ladders, and cubbyholes to be explored. When the rats reached adulthood, they were tested for ability to learn mazes. The stimulated rats dramatically out-performed their deprived relatives. In addition, later tests showed that the stimulated rats had brains that were larger and heavier with a thicker cortex.

It is a long leap from rats to people, but it is hard to overlook the significance of an increase in brain size caused by sensory stimulation. If stimulation can enhance the "intelligence" of a lowly rat, it is reasonable to assume that human infants also benefit from stimulation.

Question: Is there any evidence that this is actually the case?

As might be expected, it is much harder to prove that such things occur in humans. In Chapter 17 you will find a full discussion of the effects of environment on intelligence. For now, let us examine one case of enrichment applied to humans.

Infants like to reach out and touch things, but normally it takes about five months after birth for this skill to develop. In an experiment conducted at a state hospital, newborn infants were given several kinds of extra stimulation each day for several months (White and Held, 1966):

> Each child in the stimulus enrichment condition was handled an extra 15 minutes daily; each was placed in a position that allowed visual exploration outside the crib; white

crib sheets were replaced by patterned sheets with colorful animal designs; and a collection of bright and colorful objects was hung over each child's crib.

As limited as these changes may seem, they caused **visually directed reaching** to occur an average of a month and a half early. This may not sound like an earth-shaking improvement in adult terms, but to an infant it represents a substantial acceleration of development.

This is only one of many experiments showing a positive relationship between stimulation and improvements in various abilities, particularly those that might be labeled "intellectual." Most people recognize that babies need lots of "tender loving care" where physical needs are concerned. But as the previous discussion shows, a complete definition of tender loving care should include a baby's psychological needs as well. It would be a good idea to place stimulation, affectionate touching, and personal warmth high on any list of infant needs.

Learning Check

The preceding sections of this chapter contain a large amount of information. Check your comprehension by answering the questions below. Skim back over the material if you miss any.

1. A duckling can be imprinted after the critical period has passed if the environment is enriched.   T or F?

2. The development of separation anxiety in an infant corresponds to formation of an attachment to parents.   T or F?

3. A baby's affectional needs can be met by supplying adequate food, water, and physical care.   T or F?

4. Harlow's "motherless monkeys" became attached to the surrogate mother that fed them.   T or F?

5. René Spitz attributed hospitalism to anaclitic depression.   T or F?

6. Bottle feeding prevents a mother from providing an adequate amount of contact comfort for an infant.   T or F?

7. The intrauterine environment has little effect on a person's development.   T or F?

8. The "super mother" goes out of her way to provide educational experience, but accepts the child as he or she is.   T or F?

9. The development of speech and language usually occurs in which order:

    a. crying, cooing, babbling, telegraphic speech   *b.* cooing, crying, babbling, telegraphic speech
    c. babbling, crying, cooing, telegraphic speech   *d.* crying, babbling, cooing, identification

10. The term "caretaker speech" refers to the babbling sounds infants make when paying attention to their parents.   T or F?

Answers: 1. F 2. T 3. F 4. F 5. T 6. F 7. F 8. T 9. a 10. F

Cognitive Growth—
How Do Children Learn to Think?
How Do Children Think to Learn?

Question: How much does a child's intelligence differ from that of an adult?

From the standpoint of maturation, it is estimated that 50 percent of adult intelligence is developed by age four and

80 percent by age eight (Bloom, 1964). These figures are somewhat deceptive because a child's intelligence differs from that of an adult in *quality* as well as quantity. Generally speaking, a child's thinking is *less abstract* than that of an adult. Children use fewer generalizations, categories, or principles and tend to base their understanding of the world on particular examples, tangible sensations, and concrete objects.

An indication of the concrete nature of thinking in very

young children is their failure to recognize the permanence of objects. Older children and adults realize that an object that is out of sight still exists. With a very young child, "out of sight" can literally mean "out of mind." If a ball rolls behind something while a four- or five-month-old child is playing with it, the child behaves as if the ball has ceased to exist and stops looking for it.

Long after children have discovered the permanence of objects, their thinking remains concrete in other ways. For example, before age six or seven, children are unable to make **transformations.** If you show a child a short, wide glass full of milk and a tall, narrow glass (also full), the child will tell you the taller glass contains more milk. Children will tell you this even if you allow them to watch as you pour milk from the short glass into an empty, tall glass. They are not bothered by the apparent transformation of the milk from a smaller to a larger amount (Fig. 15-9). They respond only to the fact that "taller" seems to mean "more." After about age seven, children are no longer fooled by this situation. Perhaps this is why seven has been called the "age of reason." From seven on, we see a definite trend toward more abstract thought (Elkind, 1968).

Question: Is there any pattern to the growth of intellect in childhood?

Fig. 15-9 *Children under age seven intuitively assume that a volume of liquid is increased when it is poured from a short, wide container into a tall, thin one.*

Piaget's Theory of Cognitive Development

According to the late Swiss psychologist and philosopher Jean Piaget (1951, 1952) there is. Piaget (pronounced Pea-ah-JAY) believed all children pass through a series of distinct *stages* in their intellectual development. For most of his life Piaget studied thinking differences between children and adults. Many of his first observations were of his own children.* In various "naturalistic experiments," children were presented with problems to be solved (the milk-glass problem is a good example). Their responses convinced Piaget that intellect grows through what he called "assimilation" and "accommodation."

Assimilation refers to using existing patterns in new situations. Let's say a toy hammer is Benjamin's favorite toy. Benjamin uses the hammer properly, and loves to pound on the blocks that came with it. For his birthday, Benjamin gets a toy wrench and some oversize plastic nuts and bolts. If he uses the wrench for pounding, it has been assimilated to an existing mental structure. In **accommodation,** existing ideas are modified to fit new requirements. For instance, a younger child might think that a dime is worth less than a (larger) nickel. As the child begins to spend money, he or she will be forced to alter ideas about what "more" and "less" mean. Thus, new situations are assimilated to existing ideas, and new ideas are created to accommodate new experiences.

Piaget's theories have had a profound effect on our thinking about children. The following is a brief summary of what he found.

The Sensorimotor Stage (0–2 Years) In the first two years of life, a child's intellectual development is largely *nonverbal.* The child is mainly concerned with learning to coordinate appropriate movements with information from the senses. At first, the infant must rely on reflexes to guide responses, but soon movements become *purposeful.* The infant can voluntarily reach out to touch or grasp an object and begins actively to explore the environment. Also important at this time is gradual emergence of the concept of **object permanence.** At about a year and a half, the child begins to pursue disappearing objects. By age two, the child can anticipate the movement of an object behind a screen. When watching an electric train, for example, the child looks ahead to the end of a tunnel rather than staring at the spot where the train disappeared.

*It is tempting to imagine that Piaget's illustrious career could very well have been launched one day when his wife said to him, "Watch the children for a while, will you, Jean?"

In general, developments in this stage indicate that the child's conceptions are becoming more *stable*. Objects cease to appear and disappear magically, and a more orderly and predictable world replaces the confusing and disconnected sensations of infancy.

The Preoperational Stage (2–7 Years) During the preoperational period, the child is developing an ability to think *symbolically* and to use language. A casual conversation with a child in this stage might leave you impressed by the child's surprisingly grown-up statements. But the child's thinking is still very **intuitive.** (Do you remember thinking as a child that the sun and the moon followed you when you took a walk?) In addition, the child's use of language is not as sophisticated as it might seem. Children have a tendency to confuse words with the objects they represent. If the child calls a toy block a "car" and you use it to make a "train," the child may be upset. To children, the name of an object is as much a part of the object as its size, shape, and color. This seems to underlie a preoccupation with name calling. To the preoperational child, an insulting name may hurt as much as "sticks and stones."*

During the preoperational stage, the child is also quite **egocentric,** or unable to take the viewpoint of other people. The ego seems to stand at the center of his or her world. To illustrate, show a child a two-sided mirror and then hold it between the two of you so the child can see herself in it. If you ask her what she thinks *you* can see, she imagines that you see *her* reflected image instead of your own. The child's limited and egocentric conception of the world is also demonstrated by the following (Laurendeau and Pinard, 1962):

Adult: Why is it dark at night?

Child: Because if you don't sleep, Santa Claus won't give you any toys.

Adult: Where does the dark come from at night?

Child: Well, bandits they take something or mother pulls down the blinds and then it's very dark.

The concept of egocentrism helps us to understand why children can seem exasperatingly selfish or uncooperative at times. A child who blocks your view by standing in front of a television set assumes that you can see if he can. If you ask him to move so you can see, he may move so that he can see better!

*I am reminded of one rather protected youngster who was angered by her older brother. Searching for a way to retaliate against her larger and stronger foe, she settled on, "You panty-girdle!" It was the worst thing she could think of.

Monopoly a la Piaget

Piaget's stages of cognitive development may be easier to remember if we relate them to a single example. What would happen at each stage if we played a game of *Monopoly* with the child?

Sensorimotor stage:	The child puts houses, hotels, and dice in mouth, plays with "Chance" cards.
Preoperational stage:	The child plays *Monopoly* but makes up own rules and cannot understand instructions.
Concrete operational stage:	Children understand basic instructions and will play by the rules, but are not capable of hypothetical transactions dealing with mortgages, loans, and special pacts and bargains with other players.
Formal operations stage:	The child no longer plays game mechanically; complex and hypothetical transactions unique to each game are now possible.

The Concrete Operational Stage (7–11 Years) An important development during this stage is mastery of the concept of **conservation.** Children have learned the concept of conservation when they understand that rolling a ball of clay into a "snake" does not increase the amount of clay and that pouring liquid from a tall, narrow glass into a shallow dish does not reduce the amount of liquid. In each case the volume remains the same despite a change in shape or appearance. The original amount is "conserved."

During the concrete operations stage, a child's thought begins to include the concepts of time, space, and number. Categories and principles are used, and the child can think logically about concrete objects or situations. These abilities explain why children stop believing in Santa Claus when they reach the concrete operations stage. Because of their ability to conserve, they come to realize such things as: Santa's sack couldn't hold that many toys, or that it would be impossible to visit everyone's house in one evening (Fehr, 1976).

Another important development at this time is the ability to reverse thoughts or operations. Lack of *reversibility* is illustrated by this conversation with a four-year-old boy (Phillips, 1969):

"Do you have a brother?"

"Yes."

"What's his name?"

"Jim."

"Does Jim have a brother?"

"No."

Reversibility of thought allows the older child to recognize that if $4 \times 2 = 8$, then 2×4 does, too. Younger children must memorize each relationship separately.

The Formal Operations Stage (11 Years and Up)
Sometime after about the age of 11, the child begins to break away from concrete objects and specific examples. Thinking is based more on **abstract principles.** Children can think about their thoughts and become less egocentric. The older child or adolescent also gradually becomes able to consider **hypothetical possibilities** (see inset on page 359). For example, if you ask a younger child: "What do you think would happen if it suddenly became possible for people to fly?" the child might respond, "But people can't fly." Older children are able to consider the possibilities and to discuss their implications.

The stage of formal operations represents attainment of full adult intellectual ability. The older adolescent is capable of inductive and deductive reasoning and can conceptualize mathematics, physics, philosophy, psychology, and other theoretical and abstract systems. From this point on, improvements in intellectual ability are based on the accumulation of knowledge, experience, and wisdom, rather than on an enlargement of basic thinking capacity.

Learning Check

Match each item with one of these stages:

A. Sensorimotor   B. Preoperational   C. Concrete operations   D. Formal operations

1. _____ egocentric thought

2. _____ abstract or hypothetical thought

3. _____ purposeful movement

4. _____ intuitive thought

5. _____ conservation

6. _____ reversibility

7. _____ object permanence

8. _____ nonverbal development

9. Assimilation refers to applying existing thought patterns or knowledge to new situations.   T or F?

Answers: 1. B 2. D 3. A 4. B 5. C 6. C 7. A 8. A 9. T

Resources Summary

● The human *neonate* has a number of *adaptive reflexes,* including the *grasping, rooting, sucking,* and *Moro* reflexes. Neonates show immediate evidence of learning, and of appreciating the consequences of their actions.

● Tests in a *looking chamber* reveal a number of visual preferences in the newborn. The neonate is drawn to complex, circular, curved, red or blue designs; also preferred are human face patterns, especially familiar faces. In later infancy interest in the unfamiliar emerges.

● The *nature-nurture controversy* concerns the relative contributions to development of *heredity* (nature) and *environment* (nurture). Hereditary instructions are carried by the *chromosomes* in each cell of the body. Heredity influences a large number of personal characteristics and programs the general *human growth sequence.*

● Heredity is also involved in differences in *temperament* present at birth. Most infants reliably fall into one of three temperament categories: *easy* children, *difficult* children, and *slow-to-warm-up* children.

● Most psychologists accept that heredity and environment are inseparable and *interacting* forces. A child's *developmental level* therefore reflects *heredity, environment,* and the effects of the child's *own behavior.*

● *Maturation* of the body and nervous system underlies the orderly *sequence* of motor, cognitive, and language development. The *rate* of maturation, however, varies from individual to individual.

● The development of self-awareness, walking, bowel and bladder control, and many other basic capacities closely parallels maturation. Many early skills are subject to the principle of *readiness* (or *motor primacy*).

● *Prenatal development* is subject to environmental influences in the form of diseases, drugs, radiation, and the mother's diet, health, or emotions. Prenatal damage to the fetus may cause *congenital problems,* or "birth defects."

● Studies of parents and their children suggest that *caretaking styles* have a substantial impact on emotional and intellectual development. Whereas mothers typically emphasize caretaking, fathers tend to function as a playmate for the infant.

● *Language development* proceeds from *control of crying,* to *cooing,* then *babbling,* use of *single words,* then *single-word pairs,* and finally, *telegraphic speech.*

● The underlying patterns of telegraphic speech suggest a *biological predisposition* to acquire language that is augmented by learning. *Prelanguage communication* between parent and child involves *shared rhythms,* "conversational" *turn-taking, mutual monitoring,* and nonverbal *signals,* such as smiling, movement, and gazing. *Caretaker speech* and other parental behavior helps promote language learning.

● A variety of *critical periods* exist throughout development, including periods before birth. Many animals display critical periods in *imprinting.*

● *Emotional attachment* of human infants to their caretakers is a critical early event. Although the effects of early isolation or rejection are not irreversible, emotional damage can be lasting. Infant attachment is reflected by *separation anxiety,* and perhaps by *stranger anxiety.*

● Early *perceptual* and *emotional deprivation* seriously retards development. Even physical growth may be affected as is the case in *deprivation dwarfism.*

● Research on deprivation suggests that perceptual stimulation is essential for normal development. Work with subhuman primates (monkeys) has also pointed to *contact comfort* as an important source of infant stimulation.

● Deliberate *enrichment* of the environment in infancy has a beneficial effect on the development of animals. Research with human infants has also demonstrated the value of enrichment.

● The intellect of a child is *less abstract* than that of an adult. Jean Piaget theorized that intellectual growth occurs through a combination of *assimilation* and *accommodation.* He also held that children go through a fixed series of *cognitive stages.* The stages and their approximate age ranges are: *sensorimotor* (0–2), *preoperational* (2–7), *concrete operations* (7–11), and *formal operations* (11–adult).

Making the Most of a Magic Time of Life

Many applications of the ideas presented in this chapter are self-evident. A few bear additional emphasis or extension.

Maturation It is valuable to remember that individual differences in maturation rates are the rule in human development. Aware parents recognize the difference between the **statistical child** and the **particular child.**

Developmental norms specifying ages at which particular abilities appear are based on *averages.* There is always a wide range of normal variation around each average. Thus, it is reasonable to expect plateaus, reversals, and periods of rapid advancement in the development of a particular child. This applies not only to the appearance of motor skills such as crawling and walking, but also to language development and the stages of cognitive development described by Piaget. In all areas of development the uniqueness of a child should be respected. This means resisting the temptation to compare the child to others, particularly in the child's presence. Each child is an individual and should be judged as such.

Enrichment As we have already emphasized, babies need stimulation. By keeping this need in mind, parents can do much to provide opportunities for varied sensory experience during infancy. A baby should be surrounded by colors, music, people, and things to see, taste, smell, and touch. Babies are not vegetables. It makes perfect sense to talk to infants, to take them outside, to hang mobiles over their cribs, or to rearrange their rooms weekly. Most parents could put far more imagination into attempts to enrich an infant's surroundings than they typically do.

Question: Can enrichment be overdone?

The possibility of providing too much stimulation is remote, unless complex stimulation comes too far in advance of an infant's ability to respond to it. Babies five weeks or less in age may become fussy and irritable in an enriched environment.

Question: Is enrichment useful only during infancy?

Definitely not. Enriching the environment at any stage of childhood appears to be well worth the effort. As a matter of fact, Jerome Kagan has recently reported that stimulation in later childhood can have a greater effect on intellectual development than previously believed possible.

Kagan studied babies who were raised in darkened huts in an isolated Guatemalan village. Without the benefit of even a moderate amount of stimulation, these children were severely retarded by age two. Yet by age eleven they had become beautiful children—gay, alert, and active (Kagan and Klein, 1973). The rich stimulation of village life during later childhood was enough to reverse the effects of early deprivation.

Kagan relates his findings to a serious error he believes we make in this country. He points out that most of our schools tend to decide at an early age that some children have potential and that others do not. Those who seem bright and promising are more often exposed to stimulating and enriching experiences than those who do not. In this way, schools may needlessly perpetuate the effects of a poor start in life.

Question: In general, what kinds of experiences are most likely to encourage intellectual development?

Piaget's theory suggests that the ideal is to provide experiences that are only slightly novel, unusual, or challenging. Remember, a child's intellect develops mainly through accommodation. As old concepts and thinking habits become obsolete they are discarded or adapted to fit new demands.

To stretch a child's intellect, demands must be made, but experiences that are too far beyond the familiar may cause frustration and withdrawal. Therefore, gradually expanding beyond a child's current level of comprehension is usually most productive.

Piaget's work also shows the importance of relating to a child on the right level. If you give a physical explanation when a very young child asks, "Why does the sun come up in the morning?," you may have missed the point. Answering in terms of the child's egocentric viewpoint is more likely to be meaningful. An answer such as, "So

Applications

that you will know it's time to get up'' is completely satisfactory for a young child. Later, explanations can be made increasingly abstract and accurate.

It is also valuable to remember that children are newcomers to language. Many of the ''silly'' things children say have meanings that become apparent only to the adult patient enough to look for them. For example, language expert S. I. Hayakawa (1965)* relates this incident:

> Once when our little girl was three years old, she found the bath too hot and said, ''Make it warmer.'' It took me a moment to figure out that she meant, ''Bring the water more nearly to the condition we call warm.'' It makes perfectly good sense if you look at it that way.

Intellectual growth is encouraged when children feel free to express ideas and feel understood when they do.

Question: Are there any guidelines for relating to children at the right level?

In a delightful book entitled *Using Psychology,* Morris Holland offers some suggestions about how best to relate to children at different stages of intellectual development. The following points are drawn from his discussion (Holland, 1975).

*From ''The Use and Misuse of Language'' by S. I. Hayakawa. In R. E. Farson, ed., *Science and Human Affairs.* Palo Alto, California: Science and Behavior Books, 1965.

1. Sensorimotor stage (0—2). Active play with a child is most effective at this stage. Encourage explorations in touching, smelling, and manipulating objects. ''Peekaboo'' is a good way to establish the permanence of objects.

2. Preoperational stage (2—7). Although children are beginning to talk to themselves and to act out solutions to problems, touching and seeing things will continue to be more useful than verbal explanations. Concrete examples will also have more meaning than generalizations. The child should be encouraged to classify things in different ways. Learning the concept of conservation may be aided by demonstrations involving liquids, beads, clay, and other substances.

3. Concrete operational stage (7—11). Children in this stage are beginning to use generalizations, but they still require specific examples to grasp many ideas. Expect a degree of inconsistency in the child's ability to apply concepts of time, space, quantity, and volume to new situations.

4. Formal operations stage (11—adult). At this point, it becomes more realistic to explain things verbally or symbolically to a child. Helping the child to master general rules and principles now becomes productive. Encourage the child to create hypotheses and to imagine how things ''could be.''

Keeping this general outline in mind should help you adjust to the changing patterns of intellect displayed by developing children.

Learning Check

1. The idea that the particular child is different from the ''statistical child'' applies to language development and cognitive skills, but not to motor development.   T or F?
2. In his study of a Guatemalan village, Kagan found that a stimulating environment can sometimes reverse severe early deprivation.   T or F?
3. To promote accommodation, it is best to provide information or experiences only moderately beyond a child's current level of comprehension.   T or F?
4. Playing ''peekaboo'' is a good way to help the sensorimotor child master the concept of conservation.   T or F?

Answers: 1. F   2. T   3. T   4. F

===== Exploration =====

Heredity—Carry It On

If your family "tree" has a number of illustrious members you may justifiably feel proud. You share many genetic similarities with your parents, grandparents, and more distant relatives. On the other hand, if your family tree is decorated with crooks, deviants, and deadbeats, take heart: Heredity isn't everything! As a matter of fact, it is estimated that at the moment of conception the possible combinations of sperm and ovum could produce billions of *genetically different* children. So from conception on we are each in some ways similar to our relatives and at the same time genetically unique.

Question: How does heredity operate?

Genes and Chromosomes   As mentioned earlier, the nucleus of every cell in the body contains 46 threadlike structures called **chromosomes** that transmit the coded instructions of heredity. Chromosomes are made up of the giant chemical molecule **deoxyribonucleic** (de-OX-see-RYE-bo-new-KLEE-ik) **acid**, or **DNA**. DNA is perhaps best pictured as a rope ladder that is twisted into a spiral. The rungs of this ladder are made up of four possible combinations of chemical bases. The order of bases forms a code carrying genetic information. The language of life and hereditary instructions are thus written in an "alphabet" of only four letters.

The DNA alphabet might not seem like nearly enough to contain all the information necessary to run the body. However, if all the DNA in the human body were unwound and laid end-to-end, it would stretch from the earth to the sun and back—400 times! Along the DNA "ladder," then, lies an astronomical amount of chemically coded information.

Question: What is a gene?

Genes are smaller units of a chromosome, or actually, just an area on the DNA "ladder" containing instructions that affect a particular process or personal characteristic. There are at least 100,000 genes in every human cell, and perhaps more. In some cases a single gene is responsible for a particular inherited characteristic, such as eye color. Most characteristics, however, are **polygenetic,** or determined by many genes working in combination.

Genes may be *dominant* or *recessive.* When a gene is **dominant,** the trait it controls will be present every time the gene is present. When a gene is **recessive,** it must be paired with a second recessive gene before its effect will be expressed. Some examples should make this relationship clearer. We receive one-half of our chromosomes (and genes) from each parent. If you were to get a brown-eye gene from your father and a blue-eye gene from your mother, you would be brown-eyed, because brown-eye genes are dominant.

Question: If brown-eye genes are dominant, how is it that two brown-eyed parents sometimes have a blue-eyed child?

If each parent has two brown-eye genes, the couple's children can only be brown-eyed. But what if each parent has one brown-eye gene and one blue-eye gene? In this case the parents would both have brown eyes, but there is one chance in four that their children will get two blue-eye genes and have blue eyes (see Fig. 15-10).

The sex of a child is also genetically determined, in this case by two specialized chromosomes. When two **"X" chromosomes** are inherited the child will be a female; an "X" chromosome paired with a **"Y" chromosome** yields a male. The woman's ovum always provides an X chromosome since she has two Xs in her own genetic makeup. In contrast, one-half of the male's sperm carry X chromosomes and the other half Ys. This has significance beyond determining sex, since some traits are **sex-linked,** or carried by genes on the X chromosome.* An example is color-blindness, which is carried on an X chromosome and given from mother to son.

Behavioral Genetics   Some breeds of dogs have reputations for being docile or aggressive, intelligent or slow, calm or emotional. Such differences fall in the realm of **behavioral genetics**—the study of inherited *behavioral* characteristics. Just as physical traits can be inherited, many behavioral traits also appear to be genetically transmitted. For instance, selective breeding of animals can

---

*In a few instances, sex-linked traits are carried on a Y chromosome. However, this is exceedingly rare.

Exploration

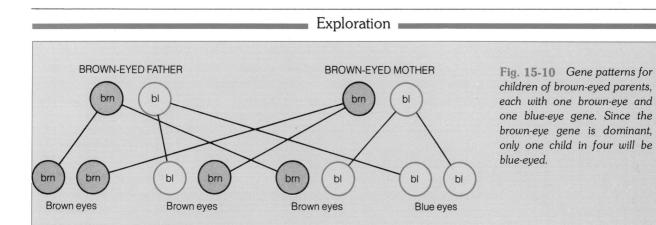

BROWN-EYED FATHER   BROWN-EYED MOTHER

brn   bl   brn   bl

brn   brn   bl   brn   brn   bl   bl   bl

Brown eyes   Brown eyes   Brown eyes   Blue eyes

Fig. 15-10 *Gene patterns for children of brown-eyed parents, each with one brown-eye and one blue-eye gene. Since the brown-eye gene is dominant, only one child in four will be blue-eyed.*

produce striking differences in social behavior, emotionality, learning ability, aggressiveness, activity levels, and other behaviors (Sprott and Staats, 1975).

Question: To what extent do such findings apply to humans?

Researchers working with animals use selective breeding, inbreeding, and careful control of the environment to show genetic effects. In contrast, studies of humans must rely mainly on comparisons of identical twins and other close relatives. Such studies are, of course, less conclusive. Nonetheless, they demonstrate that intelligence, some mental disorders, temperament, and other complex human qualities are directly influenced by heredity. (For specific examples of behavioral genetic research, see Chapters 17 and 21.)

Genetic Counseling Improved understanding of human genetics can be applied to combat troubles that "run in the family." It is now possible to identify a large number of genetic disorders, such as sickle cell anemia, hemophilia, cystic fibrosis, muscular dystrophy, albinism, some forms of mental retardation, and so forth. Prospective parents who suspect that they may be carriers of genetic disorders may seek **genetic counseling.** By examining the family history of each prospective parent, and in some cases by directly mapping chromosomes, the risk of a genetic disorder can be calculated.

Question: What can a couple do if the risk of a genetic defect is high?

Knowing the risks, parents can choose not to have a child, or if the odds are in their favor, they may elect to take the chance. Even when there is a reasonable likelihood of a genetic disorder, some couples elect to have children, but

then have a test performed during pregnancy to detect the presence or absence of the genetic defect. Such prenatal testing is done by **amniocentesis** (AM-nih-oh-SEN-teh-sis), which involves taking a sample of amniotic fluid from the mother's womb. This procedure allows determination of fetal sex and the detection of many genetic defects.

Amniocentesis is usually done at about the fifteenth week of pregnancy. Thus, when a serious genetic defect is detected, couples who do not object to abortion can terminate the pregnancy. Parents who consider abortion unacceptable still have the advantage of forewarning, so they may prepare the best possible care for the child.

The Future

Recent advances in biology, genetics, and the exploding knowledge about how DNA controls heredity will quite likely bring about profound changes in the human condition. Let's sample some of the possibilities.

Eugenics It is probably true that domestic plants and animals have been improved more in the past 50 years than in the previous 5000. This improvement has been accomplished primarily through *eugenics* (you-JEN-iks), or selective breeding for desirable characteristics. Some extremists have already proposed that eugenics be applied to humans. Even if this state of affairs never actually happens (it is loaded with ethical problems), the steady application of genetic counseling could have a eugenic effect on the general population.

Genetic Engineering In the future it may become possible to remove defective genes and replace them with normal ones. Could such genetic engineering also be

Exploration

used to produce beauty, intelligence, resistance to aging, or superhuman athletic potential? In theory yes, but practically speaking, probably not. Literally thousands of genes affect such qualities, not to mention the effects of environment. For this reason, limited genetic engineering involving one or two genes may soon become possible, but tampering with the genes on a major scale is not likely in the near future. **Cloning,** the production of an entire organism from a single cell, is also likely to remain science fiction (where humans are concerned) for the immediate future.

Sex Selection The selection of an infant's sex prior to conception is likely to become possible, and quite soon, too. This will be done by separating X- and Y-bearing sperm and then artificially fertilizing the ovum with all male-producing, or female-producing sperm.

Gene Cards One authority on genetic engineering and genetic defects predicts that ultimately people will carry a "gene identity card," based on blood tests made during childhood. These would show what hereditary diseases a person is predisposed to, or which may be passed on in childbearing when combined with the gene pattern of a mate (Milunsky, 1977).

Many of the ideas reviewed here may seem more like biology than psychology. But rapid advances in our knowledge of heredity have an important place in the understanding of behavior. Moreover, rapid advances in biology and genetics, especially the prospect of genetic engineering, raise a number of important psychological and ethical questions. Some of the most obvious are listed in the "Questions for Discussion" that follow.

Questions for Discussion

1. Should humans try to control their own heredity? Who would decide what characteristics should be developed? Who would get them? For what purpose? Would you endorse use of genetic engineering to delay or prevent aging?

2. If preselection of the sex of a child becomes possible, what effect would you predict on the ratio of males to females born? (Currently 106 males are born for every 100 females.) Why do you make this prediction? What are its implications?

3. In view of the importance of infant attachment and the participation of fathers in child care, what changes would you recommend in maternity and paternity leaves from work? Would you change the traditional division of labor in maternal and paternal roles? Why or why not?

4. What is your reaction to the following statement, made by anthropologist Margaret Mead? "Fathers are a biological necessity but a social accident."

5. In what ways is it accurate to treat children as "little adults"? In what ways is it inaccurate? What is the value of children in society?

6. Do you think an infant would be more or less likely to survive if maturation proceeded from toe to head and from the extremities inward?

7. How many ways can you think of for an infant to reward its mother and for the mother to reward the infant?

8. What types of toys would you select for an infant or young child? Do you think simple toys or elaborate toys would be best? Why? Would your choice change for an older child? Why?

9. How has heredity affected your development? How has environment affected you?

10. How would childrearing be different if parents had to teach children *deliberately* to walk or to talk?

11. If you were the director of an orphanage or a similar institution, what steps would you take to ensure the normal development of infants in your care?

Suggestions for Further Reading

Bartz, W. R., and R. A. Rasor. *Surviving with Kids.* Ballantine, 1980.

Curtiss, S. *Genie: A Psycholinguistic Study of a Modern-Day "Wild Child."* Academic Press, 1977.

Dworetzky, J. P. *Introduction to Child Development.* West, 1981.

Ginsburg, H., and S. Opper. *Piaget's Theory of Intellectual Development.* Prentice-Hall, 1969.

Hanson, R. A., and R. Reynolds. *Child Development.* West, 1980.

Harlow, H. F., and M. K. Harlow. "The Effect of Rearing Conditions on Behavior," *Bulletin of The Menninger Clinic,* September, 1962, pp. 213–224.

Miller, G. A. *Spontaneous Apprentices: Children and Language.* The Seabury Press, 1977.

Pines, M. "Superkids," *Psychology Today,* January, 1979, pp. 53–63.

Valett, R. E. *Developing Cognitive Abilities: Teaching Children to Think.* Mosby, 1978.

Whiting, J., and I. Child. *Child Training and Personality.* Yale University Press, 1953.

16

Challenges of Development: The Cycle of Life

━━━━━━━━━━━━━━━━━━━━━━━━ Chapter Preview ━━━━━━━━━━━━━━━━━━━━━━━━

Life with Billy

By the time he was five, Billy's "record" read like a script of a parent's worst nightmare. Billy threw uncontrollable temper tantrums and never seemed to sleep. At age five Billy had not learned to talk. He got into closets and tore up his mother's evening dresses and urinated on her clothes. He smashed furniture and spread soap powder and breakfast food all over the floors. He tripped the maid at the head of the stairs and then lay on the floor doubled up with laughter. He attacked his mother at every opportunity, once going for her throat with his teeth. He tried to stuff his baby brother in a toy box. When Billy's parents bought him a doll they called by the baby's name, they began finding the doll pushed head down in the toilet bowl. Billy refused to eat anything but cold, greasy hamburgers from a certain drive-in. To get through a week, his parents were forced to buy the hamburgers by the sack and hide them around the house, so Billy wouldn't eat them all at once. When his parents went out driving they had to detour around drive-ins to prevent Billy from frothing at the mouth and trying to jump out the window (Moser, 1965). Billy, you may note, was not an average five-year-old.

Question: What was his problem?

Billy was an autistic child. His problem is rare. Few children get off to as bad a start in life as Billy. Nevertheless, every individual faces certain challenges and problems on the path to healthy development. Some obstacles, such as toilet training or establishing an identity, can be considered universal. Others are specialized problems. In either case, the challenges of development extend far beyond childhood and on into old age. In this chapter we will examine some of the special problems presented by each stage of life. Be alert for information pertinent to your own life. Be alert for Billy, too. You'll meet him again later in the chapter.

Survey Questions   What are the typical tasks and dilemmas of childhood, adolescence, adulthood, and old age? Does the way a baby is born alter the course of development? What are some of the more serious childhood problems? What happens psychologically during adulthood and aging? How do effective parents rear their children? In what ways are attitudes toward death changing?

═══════════════════════════════════ Resources ═══════════════════════════════════

The Cycle of Life—
Rocky Road or Garden Path?

If you pride yourself on being "one of a kind," you have good reason. There is no such thing as a "typical person" or a "typical life." Nevertheless, there are certain broad similarities in the universal **life stages** of infancy, childhood, adolescence, young adulthood, middle adulthood, and old age. Each stage represents a milestone in physical maturation and psychological development, and each confronts a person with a new set of **developmental tasks** to be mastered. These are skills that must be acquired or personal changes that must take place for optimal development.

In an influential book entitled *Childhood and Society* (1963), personality theorist Erik Erikson suggests that we also face a specific **psychosocial dilemma,** or "crisis," at each stage of life. According to Erikson, resolving these crises creates a new balance between a person and the social world. An unfavorable outcome throws us off balance and makes it harder to deal with later crises. A string of "successes" produces healthy development and a satisfying life. Those who are plagued with unfavorable outcomes may experience life as a "rocky road."

Question: What are the major developmental tasks and life crises?

This is a broad question requiring an extended answer. Read on!

Stage One, First Year of Life: Trust versus Mistrust During the first year of life children are completely dependent on others for safety and comfort. Erikson believes that a basic attitude of **trust** or **mistrust** is formed at this time. Trust is established by regular satisfaction of a baby's needs. Babies given adequate warmth, touching, love, and physical care learn to view the world as a safe and dependable place. Mistrust is caused by inadequate or unpredictable care and by parents who are cold, indifferent, or rejecting. Basic mistrust may become the core of later insecurity, suspiciousness, or inability to relate to others.

Stage Two, 1—3 Years: Autonomy versus Shame and Doubt Stage two is the age of exploration. Muscular development allows children to take charge of their own behavior. Growing independence is expressed by climbing, touching, exploring, and a general desire to do things for themselves. Parents help their children develop a sense of **autonomy** by encouraging them to try new skills and by reassuring them if they fail. Consistent *overprotection* may limit development by denying opportunities for self-direction. Teasing and ridicule also create problems. The child's first crude efforts to do things often result in spilling, falling, wetting, and other "accidents." Erikson feels that parents who make fun of their children cause them to feel ashamed of their actions and to doubt their abilities. Thus, feelings of **shame** and **doubt** are the unfavorable outcome of this stage.

Fig. 16-1 According to Erikson, children aged three to five face an important conflict between initiative and guilt.

Stage Three, 3—5 Years: Initiative versus Guilt In stage three the child moves from simple self-control to an ability to take initiative. Through play the child learns to plan, undertake, and carry out a task. Parents reinforce **initiative** by giving freedom to play, to ask questions, to use imagination, and to choose activities. The child may be emotionally handicapped by parents who criticize severely, discourage play, or ridicule questions. In this case, children learn to feel that their play, ideas, or questions are silly or stupid and become *ashamed* of them. They also learn to feel **guilty** about the activities they initiate when these activities seem to be a nuisance to parents.

Stage Four, 6—12 Years: Industry versus Inferiority Many of the events of middle childhood are symbolized by that fateful day when you made your first trip to school. With dizzying speed your world expanded beyond the bounds of the family, and you were confronted with a whole series of new challenges. Erikson describes the elementary school years as the child's "entrance into life." Children begin to learn skills valued by society, and success or failure can have lasting effects on feelings of adequacy. Children learn a sense of **industry** if they win praise for building, painting, cooking, reading, studying, and other productive activities. If a child's accomplishments are regarded as messy, childish, or inadequate, feelings of **inferiority** result. For the first time, teachers, classmates, and adults outside the home become as important as parents in shaping attitudes toward oneself.

Stage Five, Adolescence: Identity versus Role Confusion Adolescence is a turbulent time for many persons in our culture. Caught between childhood and adulthood, the adolescent faces some unique problems. The tasks of this period can be described as:

> Developing a clear sense of identity and self-confidence. Adjusting to body changes. Developing new, more mature relations with age-mates. Achieving emotional independence from parents. Selecting and preparing for an occupation. Achieving mature values and social responsibility. Preparing for marriage and family life. Developing concern beyond self (Coleman, 1969).*

Question: Which of these tasks does Erikson consider most important?

Erikson considers a need to answer the question, "Who am I?" the primary crisis during this stage of life. Mental and physical maturation brings to the individual new feelings,

a new body, and new attitudes (Fig. 16-2). The adolescent must build a consistent **identity** out of self-perceptions and relationships with others. Conflicting experiences as a student, friend, athlete, worker, son or daughter, lover, and so forth, must be integrated into a unified sense of self. According to Erikson, persons failing to develop a sense of identity experience **role confusion,** an uncertainty about who they are and where they are going.

Role confusion may cause a person to seek identity by emulating musicians, athletes, leaders of religious groups, or media heroes. Role confusion may also underlie a tendency to overidentify with a clannish group and to reject anyone who looks or acts different. Despite these excesses, the search for identity is also a basis for healthy explorations in religion, philosophy, psychology, ecology, politics, human rights, and other areas of personal relevance. In many cases, making vocational plans helps a person define an identity.

Stage Six, Young Adulthood: Intimacy versus Isolation Many young adults are deferring marriage in favor of less binding relationships, and those who marry are having fewer children. Communal living, extended educational goals, alternatives to full-time employment, and other variations in life-style undoubtedly generate new developmental challenges. Despite such changes, the psychological crisis pinpointed by Erikson would seem to apply to many people.

Question: What does Erikson consider the major conflict in early adulthood?

Erikson emphasizes the need to achieve an essential quality of **intimacy** in one's life. After establishing a stable identity, a person is prepared to share meaningful love or deep friendship with others. By "intimacy," Erikson means an ability to care about others and a willingness to share experiences with them. Marriage or sexual intimacy is no guarantee that these qualities will be developed. Erikson considers many marriages mere partnerships lacking in true intimacy. Failure to establish intimacy with others leads to a deep sense of **isolation.** The person feels alone and uncared for in life. This circumstance often sets the stage for later difficulties.

Many researchers now believe that personality development continues until at least age fifty. Successful adjustment during middle age centers on a conflict summarized by Erikson's seventh stage of development.

Stage Seven, Middle Adulthood: Generativity versus Stagnation According to Erikson, an interest in guiding the next generation, called **generativity,** is the main source

*From *Psychology and Effective Behavior* by James C. Coleman. Copyright © 1969 by Scott, Foresman and Company. Reprinted by permission.

of balance in mature adulthood. In general, this means caring about oneself, one's children, and the future. Generativity may be achieved by guiding one's own children or by helping other children (as a teacher, clergyman, or coach might do). It may also be achieved through productive or creative work. In any case, a person's concern and energies must be broadened to include the welfare of others and society as a whole. Failure in this is marked by a stagnant concern with one's own needs and comforts. Life loses meaning, and the person feels bitter, dreary, and trapped.

Question: What does Erikson see as the conflicts of old age?

Stage Eight, Late Adulthood: Integrity versus Despair Because old age is a time of reflection, a person must be able to look back over the events of a lifetime with a sense of acceptance and satisfaction. According to Erikson, the previous seven stages of life become the basis for successful aging. The person who has lived richly and responsibly develops a sense of **integrity.** This sense allows aging and death to be faced with dignity. If previous life events are viewed with regret, the elderly person falls into **despair.** In this case, there is a feeling that life has been a series of missed opportunities, that one has failed,

and that it is too late to reverse what has been done. Aging and the threat of death then become a source of fear and depression.

Although Erikson has not specifically discussed it, others believe that preparing for death may be an internal process. This view holds that approaching death causes aged individuals to undertake a **life review** (Butler and Lewis, 1977; Barrow and Smith, 1979). During the life review (which may be a universal process during the last days of life), vivid memories of earlier events bring to the surface unresolved questions, conflicts, and issues. At this time older people reevaluate the meaning of life, and ideally find new meaning that reduces fear and anxiety and prepares them for facing death (Barrow and Smith, 1979).

Countless details must be ignored to condense the events of a lifetime into a few pages. Although much is lost, the net effect is a clearer picture of an entire life cycle. In this brief overview, we have seen that the successful life begins with learning to trust others and ends with trusting and feeling good about one's life: Thus, the circle closes and the cycle is complete.

Evaluation For simplicity, Erikson's dilemmas are stated in either/or terms. However, it would be quite unusual for a person to experience only one side of each conflict. In

Fig. 16-2 *Dramatic differences in physical size and maturity are found in adolescents of the same age. The girls pictured are all 13, the boys 16. Maturation that occurs earlier or later than average undoubtedly affects the "search for identity." (From "Growing Up" by J. M. Tanner. Copyright © September 1973 by Scientific American, Inc. All rights reserved.)*

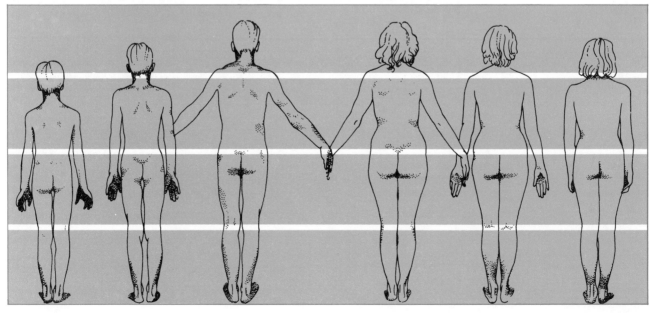

many instances, a mixture of positive and negative effects spills over into later development. It is also important to recognize that Erikson's account of the human life cycle is theoretical; some theorists have emphasized different life events. Is Erikson's description, then, an exact map of your future? Probably not. But it does reflect major psychological events in the lives of many people. It may therefore allow you to anticipate typical trouble spots so that you can prepare for them. You may also be better prepared to understand the problems and feelings of friends and relatives at various stages in their life cycles.

Having completed our whirlwind birth-to-death tour, we will revisit several life stages for a closer look at some of the challenges, landmarks, tasks, and problems of each. Before we begin, it might be a good idea to complete the "Learning Check" that follows.

Learning Check

Since Erikson's eight life stages are scattered through the previous pages you might find it helpful to summarize them. Complete this do-it-yourself summary to check your recall of the stages. Compare your answers to those listed below to make sure you have a correct summary.

Stage	Crisis	Favorable outcome
First year of life	1. _____ vs.	Faith in the environment and in others
	2. _____	
Ages 1–3	Autonomy vs.	Feelings of self-control and adequacy
	3. _____	
Ages 3–5	4. _____ vs. guilt	Ability to begin one's own activities
Ages 6–12	Industry vs.	Confidence in productive skills, learning how to work
	5. _____	
Adolescence (ages 12–18)	6. _____ vs. role confusion	An integrated image of oneself as a unique person
Early adulthood (ages 18–35)	Intimacy vs.	Ability to form bonds of love and friendship with others
	7. _____	
Middle adulthood (ages 35–60)	Generativity vs.	Concern for family, society, and future generations
	8. _____	
Late adulthood	9. _____ vs.	Sense of dignity and fulfillment, willingness to face death
	10. _____	

Answers: 1. trust 2. mistrust 3. shame or doubt 4. initiative 5. inferiority 6. identity 7. isolation 8. stagnation 9. integrity 10. despair

Birth—The First Hurdle

Question: Is it possible for problems in development to begin with birth?

Birth is presumably quite stressful. From the warm and protected confines of the womb, a baby is forcefully thrust into a cold, noisy world. The new arrival is greeted with glaring lights, booming voices, cutting of the umbilical cord, and weighing on a cold scale. According to French obstetrician Frederick Leboyer, these events make birth a needlessly traumatic experience.

In *Birth without Violence* (1975), Leboyer advocates a system that purportedly makes birth pleasant for both mother and baby. Delivery takes place in a silent, dimly lit room. Immediately after birth, the baby is placed on its mother's stomach and gently massaged. After several minutes of soothing, the umbilical cord is cut and the baby is bathed in warm water. Leboyer claims that babies delivered in this way are healthier, happier, and less anxious than those subjected to birth procedures he considers "violent" and "cruel."

From a medical standpoint, many obstetricians have been skeptical of Leboyer's methods, considering some to be actually dangerous.

Question: How could a "gentle birth" be dangerous?

Some doctors working in darkened delivery rooms have had trouble because they couldn't see well enough to detect a "blue baby" or other complications. Leboyer's reason for not cutting the umbilical cord is to provide oxygen to the baby until it is breathing well. But most babies are breathing when their head and shoulders are clear of the birth canal. Moreover, placing the baby on the mother elevates it above the placenta. This arrangement can cause a loss of blood and leave the baby anemic. In addition, studies in England have shown that the temperature of bath water for three-hour-old babies must be the same as that of the mother or the baby may stop breathing.

Still, gentle birth has an intuitive appeal to many parents, and thousands of babies have been delivered by the Leboyer method.

Question: Are babies delivered by the Leboyer method any different from those delivered by standard methods?

Leboyer *claims* that children from gentle births are happier, more relaxed, and more emotionally stable. However, he offers no solid evidence that they are actually any better off than children born other ways (Trotter, 1975). Skeptics argue that parents who choose gentle births are likely to be more loving and attentive after birth. If this is the case,

the emotional health of their infants might have nothing at all to do with the method of delivery. Another cause for skepticism is the fact that most male babies, including those given gentle births, are circumcised. Circumcision is a minor, but painful, operation. If pain and stress are bad during birth, why are they acceptable shortly after? Until more evidence is available, the psychological advantages of gentle births must be considered unproven.

Maternal-Infant Bonding   There is a better case for the value of altering events immediately *after* birth. A series of studies by Marshall Klaus and John Kennel (1976) suggests that optimal development may depend upon close contact between a mother and her infant in the first hours after birth. These researchers believe that mother-child pairs who spend extra time together form a stronger **emotional bond,** which affects the behavior of both mother and child.

Question: What evidence do we have of such bonding?

Klaus and Kennel studied two groups of women and infants. One group had traditional contact with their infants: a glimpse after birth and one-half-hour visits every four hours for feeding. In addition to this contact, mothers in

Fig. 16-3   *Does the manner in which an individual is born have psychological significance?*

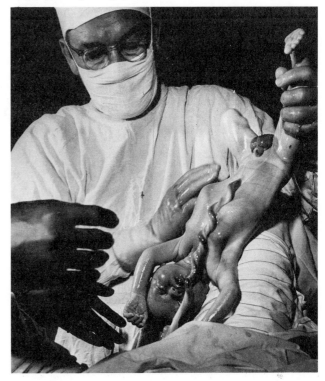

the second, "extended-contact," group were given their babies for one hour during the first three hours after birth and for an extra five hours of contact each afternoon on the first three days after delivery (Trotter, 1975).

Question: Did extra contact make a difference?

Although only 16 hours of extra contact were involved, striking differences in the infants and mothers appeared later. In the first year, the "bonded" babies gained more weight and had fewer infections, and their mothers directed more affection, fondling, and eye contact to the infants.

During a two-year follow-up, the extended-contact mothers spoke to their children in longer sentences, and they asked more questions, used more advanced language, and made fewer commands. Differences such as these might be expected to improve language and intellectual development. Indeed, at five years after birth, the extended-contact children had higher IQs and higher scores on language tests (Klaus and Kennel, 1976).

Question: Then should parents make a special effort to increase contact with their infants shortly after birth?

Some researchers have questioned the findings just described (Brazelton, 1975). However, recent studies in Sweden support the idea that even a small amount of added contact has lasting effects on the mother-infant relationship. Skin-to-skin contact from holding, cuddling, or nursing the baby appears to be particularly effective (De Chateau, 1980). At present, the *potential* value of parent-infant bonding appears attractive, and extra contact can certainly do no harm.

With the preceding in mind, many hospitals now have "birthing rooms" that allow the father to "room-in," so that he may participate in the birth and share in caring for the newborn. Even traditional delivery rooms are allowing fathers to be present during birth to coach the mother through labor. In some cases the father cuts the umbilical cord and gives the infant its first bath. Babies are now less often rushed off to a nursery; in many hospitals the baby spends its first night with the parents in a homelike setting. These changes, plus widespread participation in prepared childbirth (or "natural" childbirth) classes, are making birth a more psychologically rewarding event for mother, father, and baby.

Problems of Childhood—
Why Parents Get Gray Hair

One of the basic assumptions of the Leboyer method of birth seems to be that stress is bad. Is this true? As dis-

cussed in Chapter 14, stress is a normal part of life. But how much stress is normal or healthy during infancy and childhood? Contrary to what common sense might suggest, a moderate amount of stress during infancy may be beneficial.

The Mickey Rat School of Hard Knocks

When baby rats were subjected to handling, mild electric shocks, or frightening rides in a bottle washing machine, they opened their eyes sooner, gained weight faster, and grew larger than their nonstressed littermates (Levine, 1969). The stressed rats were also more active as adults and were less timid and emotional when placed in stressful situations (Dennenberg, 1967).

These effects are apparently due to stimulation of the body's adrenal-pituitary system. As noted in the previous chapter, stimulation during infancy is generally beneficial. The benefits apparently extend to moderately stressful stimulation.

Question: Can we really conclude by observing rats that moderate stress is acceptable for humans?

Perhaps not, but there is evidence of similar effects in humans. One study of several cultures concerned the fate of children subjected to stressful rituals such as piercing of the ears, nose, or lips. It was found that stressed children averaged over two inches taller as adults than those who escaped the rituals (Landuet and Whiting, 1964).

Such observations do not allow us to conclude that all childhood stresses are beneficial. Nor do they mean that parents should go out of their way to stress a child. What they do suggest is that there is no point in trying to completely protect children from stressful stimulation. **Overprotection** (sometimes called "smother love") can be as damaging as overstressing a child. Certainly, the urge to protect a child is difficult to resist at times. However, most children do a good job of keeping stress at comfortable levels when *they* initiate an activity (Murphy and Moriarty, 1976). At a public swimming pool, for instance, some children can be observed making harrowing leaps from the high dive, while others stick close to the wading area. If no immediate danger is present, it is reasonable to let children get stuck in trees, make themselves dizzy, squabble with neighbor children, and so forth. Getting into a few scrapes can help prepare a child to cope with later stresses.

Question: How can you tell if a child is being subjected to too much stress?

Normal Childhood Problems   Child specialists Chess, Thomas, and Birch (1965) have listed a number of difficulties experienced at times by almost every child. These can be considered normal reactions to the unavoidable stress of growing up.

1. All children experience occasional **sleep disturbances,** including wakefulness, frightening dreams, or a desire to get into their parents' bed.
2. **Specific fears** of the dark, dogs, school, or of a particular room or person are also common.
3. Most children will be **overly timid** at times, allowing themselves to be bullied by other children into giving up toys, a place in line, and the like.
4. Temporary periods of **general dissatisfaction** may occur when nothing pleases the child.
5. Children also normally display periods of **general negativism** marked by tantrums, refusal to do anything requested, or a tendency to say no on principle. Negativism is particularly characteristic of two-year-olds, and may be a sign of growing independence.
6. Another normal problem is **clinging,** in which the child refuses to leave the side of his mother or to do anything on his own. Clinging is especially common among three-year-olds.
7. Development does not always advance smoothly. Every child will show occasional **reversals** or **regressions** to more infantile behavior.

Two additional problems common to the elementary school years are **sibling rivalry** and **rebellion.** Where there is more than one child in a family, it is normal for a certain amount of jealousy or rivalry to develop between brothers and sisters. Sibling rivalry can be minimized by parents who avoid "playing favorites" and who resist the temptation to compare one child to another. Most schoolchildren also at times rebel against the rules and limitations of the adult world. For many children, the company of peers offers a chance to "let off steam" by doing some of the things the adult world forbids. Being messy, noisy, hostile, or destructive is normal when engaged in to a moderate degree.

It is important to keep in mind that "normal problems" can signal a more serious disturbance if they are displayed for prolonged periods or if they become exaggerated. Problems of a more serious nature are identified in the following section.

Significant Childhood Problems— Off to a Bad Start

Although severe emotional disturbances affect only a minority of children, the number involved is larger than most people realize. A report of the President's Joint Commission on the Mental Health of Children (1970) estimated that 0.6 percent of our children are psychotic; about 2 or 3 percent are severely disturbed; and an additional 8 to 10 percent are neurotic. These studies mean that 1 child in 10 may have a serious emotional problem.

Question: What is the nature of these problems?

Toilet-Training Disturbances Difficulty sometimes centers on toilet training or bowel and bladder habits. The two most common problems are **enuresis** (EN-you-REE-sis, lack of bladder control) and **encopresis** (EN-coh-PREE-sis, lack of bowel control). Enuresis is more common than soiling and many times more common among males than females. Both wetting and soiling can be a means of expressing pent-up aggression, or a means of retaliating against parental demands considered unfair by the child.

Parents should not be overly alarmed by some delays in toilet training, or by a few "accidents." Male children in particular may be late in achieving control, because male muscular development tends to be slower than female. Even when problems persist, they can have purely physical causes. Many bedwetters, for instance, have difficulty because they become extremely relaxed when asleep. These children can be helped by limiting the amount they drink during the evening. They should also be encouraged to use the toilet before going to bed, and they can be rewarded for "dry" nights. Understanding, sympathy, and tact can do much to alleviate mild disturbances. Where more serious problems are suspected, parents should seek professional help.

Feeding Disturbances Feeding disturbances take a variety of forms. The disturbed child may vomit or refuse food for no reason, or may drastically overeat or undereat. **Overeating** may be encouraged by an overprotective mother who compensates for feeling unloved by showering the child with "love" in the form of food. Some parents may overfeed a child because they consider a fat baby healthy or desirable. Whatever the source, the overfed child develops conflicts that have lifelong consequences. Even by early childhood, obesity may result in exclusion from active social life with playmates. Later, guilt, disappointment, and anxiety are common.

Serious cases of *undereating* are called **anorexia nervosa** (AN-or-EX-yah ner-VOH-sah, nervous loss of appetite). The victims of anorexia nervosa are mostly adolescent females (5 to 10 percent are male). Victims suffer devastating weight loss from self-inflicted starvation, and/or **bulimia** (bue-LIHM-ih-yah). Bulimics gorge on food, then induce vomiting or take laxatives to purge themselves (Vigersky, 1977). In a culture that values slimness, these practices may seem relatively harmless. They are not. Often, they cause serious health problems, including hair loss, muscle spasms, kidney damage, dehydration, erosion of tooth enamel, malnutrition, and even heart attack (Palazolli, 1978).

The causes of self-starvation are not well understood. For younger children it appears to be related to the fact that eating is a social event. That is, refusal to eat can be a way of gaining attention, or of doing battle with parents. During adolescence, undereating may represent conflicts about maturing sexually. Another cause is a distortion of body image in which anorexics see themselves as "fat," when in fact they are wasting away. Very telling is the fact that many anorexics are high achievers with a strong need to please others. Striving for *perfection* can lead them to diet so severely that it disrupts normal appetite.

Another childhood eating difficulty is a condition called **pica** (PIE-ka). Some children go through a period of intense appetite during which they eat or chew on all sorts of inedible substances. Most commonly these are plaster or chalk, but some children displaying pica try to eat things like buttons, rubber bands, mud, or paint flakes. The latter can be quite dangerous because some paint contains lead, which is highly poisonous.

Speech Disturbances   The two most common speech problems are **delayed speech** and **stuttering.** Delayed speech is generally discovered by the time a child starts school. The child may fail to learn language because of a general lack of stimulation. Other possible causes are parents who discourage the child's attempts to grow up, and interference caused by the stress of separation from the mother, hospitalization, or birth of a sibling.

Stuttering was once held to be primarily a psychological disturbance. In recent years most researchers have shifted to the belief that stuttering is usually physical in origin. For example, stuttering is four times more common in males than in females, and there seem to be hereditary factors underlying its occurrence (Sheehan and Costley, 1977). In some instances, stuttering may reflect tension or frustration in the child, or it may merely be a learned response. Whatever the cause of stuttering, parents often react with obvious emotion to the appearance of a "speech disorder." Parental reaction can add considerably to the child's feelings of anxiety or inadequacy and thus perpetuate the problem.

Learning Disorders   Brian was active and cheerful as a preschooler. After entering school, however, he became shy and difficult. What had happened? Brian's teacher suspected a learning disability, and a specialist confirmed it.

Learning disabilities include problems with thinking, perception, language ability, control of attention, or activity levels. Brian's specific problem was **dyslexia** (dis-LEX-yah), an inability to read with understanding. Because of it, he often felt confused and "stupid" in class, although his intelligence was normal. As Brian's case shows, parents should be alert for signs of learning difficulties. Frequent confusion when a child tries to handle information may signal a need for professional help.

One of the most significant learning disorders is **hyperactivity.** The hyperactive child is constantly in motion and cannot concentrate. The child talks rapidly, cannot sit still, rarely finishes work, acts on impulse, and cannot pay attention. These characteristics severely limit the hyperactive child's ability to learn.

Question: What causes hyperactivity?

The causes of hyperactivity are still something of a mystery. Some blame factors as different as fluorescent lighting in the classroom and artificial dyes and flavorings in the diet, but both these explanations have recently been challenged (O'Leary, 1977; Preston, 1977).

The most widely held theory is that hyperactivity is the result of **minimal brain dysfunction (MBD).** Experts who support this theory link hyperactivity to a lag in brain maturation, or to undetected damage to the brain. Those who see hyperactivity as a physical problem typically advocate the use of drugs to control it. The drugs used are usually stimulants such as amphetamine and Ritalin. It might seem strange to give stimulants to hyperactive children but, paradoxically, the drugs calm the children and lengthen their attention span.

A number of scientists have objected to the blanket use of powerful stimulants in the treatment of hyperactive children. Currently, as high as 1 percent of the nation's children between the ages of five and twelve are on Ritalin or amphetamines (Havighurst, 1976)! Many have charged that use of such drugs may be dangerous and unnecessary.

Question: What kind of treatment do they suggest?

Some have gone so far as to suggest that hyperactivity may be normal, or at least that it need not be treated since it usually disappears by adolescence. However, given the serious effects of hyperactivity on family adjustment as well as on the child's feelings of adequacy, some treatment is called for. Some researchers have found **behavior modification** as effective as drug treatment (Wulbert and Dries, 1977; Pelham, 1977). Behavior modification is essentially the application of learning principles to human problems (see Chapter 23 for more information).

Childhood Autism Childhood **autism** is a problem that affects 1 in 2500 children, boys four times more often than girls. Autism is one of the most severe childhood problems. The autistic child is locked into a private world and appears to have no need for affection or contact with others. Autistic children do not even seem to know or care who their parents are.

In addition to being extremely isolated, the autistic child typically has a host of other problems. The child may throw gigantic temper tantrums. Sometimes these include self-destructive behavior such as head banging or biting the shoulders or hands. Language learning is usually so retarded that the child is mute. If they speak at all, autistic children often infuriatingly parrot back everything said, a reaction known as **echolalia** (EK-oh-LAY-li-ah). These children also engage in frequent repetitive actions such as rocking, flapping their arms, or waving their fingers in front of their eyes. Additionally, autistic children may show no response to an extremely loud noise (sensory blocking) or may spend hours watching a water faucet drip (sensory "spin-out") (Ferster, 1968; Rimland, 1978).

Question: Do parents cause autism?

At one time, experts blamed parents for autism. The parents of autistic children were sometimes described as "cold," "distant," or "intellectual" toward their children. Accordingly, autism was viewed as a failure to establish trust and attachment during the child's first months of life. Such beliefs undoubtedly added a painful burden of guilt to the problems already faced by parents. It is now recognized that autism is caused by congenital defects in the nervous system (Schopler, 1978). This is why autistic children often seem different soon after birth. Even as babies, these children are aloof and do not cuddle or mold to their parents' arms. When parents seem distant with an autistic child, it is typically a reaction to the child's lack of response to their affection.

Question: Can anything be done for an autistic child?

Even with help, only about one autistic child in four approaches normalcy. Nevertheless, almost all autistic children can make progress with proper care (Schopler, 1978). Imagine the relief parents feel when an autistic child is taught to talk, or prevented from throwing tantrums. When treatment is begun early, behavior modification has been particularly successful in producing such improvements. Do you remember the child described in the "Chapter Preview"? Billy was one of the first patients in an extraordinary program for the autistic. Billy was selected for the program, designed by Dr. Ivar Lovaas at U.C.L.A., because of his appetite for hamburgers. The process of teaching Billy to talk illustrates one aspect of the program.

Teaching Billy to talk began with his learning to blow out a match—making a sound like "who." Each time he made the "who" sound, Billy was rewarded with a bite of one of his beloved hamburgers. Next he was rewarded for babbling meaningless sounds. If he accidentally said a word, he was rewarded. After several weeks, he was able

Fig. 16-4 *The autistic child seems lost in his own world.*

to say words such as "ball," "milk," "mama," and "me." By a painstaking continuation of this process, Billy was eventually taught to talk. Notice that this process is basically an example of **operant shaping,** discussed in Chapter 8.

In a behavior modification program, each of the autistic child's other maladaptive behaviors is attacked using combinations of reward and punishment. Strangely enough, one of the most disturbing autistic behaviors is the easiest to control. Lovaas and others have found that following actions such as head banging by punishment can bring a swift end to self-destructive behavior (Lovaas, 1965, 1966).

In addition, therapists are finding new ways of rewarding adaptive behavior. For instance, sensory stimulation, such as tickling or music, is often very reinforcing for the autistic child (Rincover *et al.,* 1977).

Autism and other severe childhood problems represent a monumental challenge to the ingenuity of psychologists, educators, and parents. However, great strides have been made in the last few years, and there is reason to believe that in the future even more help will be available to children who get a bad start in life.

Learning Check

See if you can answer these questions before you continue reading.

1. When baby rats are subjected to moderate stress, they lose their appetites and become weak and sickly.   T or F?
2. Children of other cultures who take part in stressful childhood rituals average over two inches taller as adults than children who do not.   T or F?
3. Negativism is especially characteristic of five-year-olds.   T or F?
4. Sleep disturbances and specific fears can be a sign of significant childhood problems when they are prolonged or exaggerated.   T or F?
5. A moderate amount of sibling rivalry is considered normal.   T or F?
6. Encopresis is the formal term for lack of bladder control.   T or F?
7. The hyperactive child is lost in his own private world.   T or F?
8. Research has demonstrated that the Leboyer method of delivery in childbirth promotes superior maternal-infant bonding and emotional adjustment in later childhood.   T or F?

Answers: 1. F 2. T 3. F 4. T 5. T 6. F 7. F 8. F

Challenges of Adulthood— A Second Look at Adult Life Stages

After a "settling down" period somewhere in the twenties, adult development is uniform and uninteresting, right? Wrong! A fairly predictable series of challenges are associated with development from adolescence to old age. At first, there is a struggle for independence as the individual pulls away from parents and moves into adulthood. The twenties are typically devoted to building a workable life in terms of occupation, education, marriage or relationships, life-style, and, for some, having children. For many the thirties are, indeed, a time of settling down, and for some, the stability achieved will carry through the middle years of life. But a recent study suggests that many people go through an upheaval or "midlife crisis" between the ages of 35 to 45 (Levinson, 1978). In later years, aging, the

death of parents, children leaving home, needs for financial security, and other such events spur continued change. Let's take a selective look at some of the major developments in adulthood.

Question: What personality changes and psychological developments can a person look forward to in adulthood?

Recent research has added several important substages to the psychological events discussed by Erikson. One of the most informative accounts is based on the work of Roger Gould, a psychiatrist interested in adult personality. Gould's research (1975) reveals that the most common patterns are as follows.

Ages 16—18: Escape from Dominance   Ages 16 to 18 are marked by a struggle to escape from parental dominance. Efforts to do so cause considerable anxiety about an uncertain future and conflict about continuing dependence on parents.

Ages 18–22: Leaving the Family The majority of people break away from their families in their early twenties. Leaving home is usually associated with building new friendships with other adults. These friends serve as substitutes for the family and as allies in the process of breaking ties.

Ages 22–28: Building a Workable Life The trend in the mid-twenties is to seek mastery of the real world. Two dominant activities are striving for accomplishment (seeking competence) and reaching out to others. Note that the second activity corresponds to Erikson's emphasis on seeking intimacy at this time. Married couples in this age group tend to place a high value on "togetherness."

Ages 29–34: Crisis of Questions Around the age of 30 many people experience a minor life crisis. The heart of this crisis is a serious questioning of what life is all about. Assurance about previous choices and values wavers. Unsettled by these developments, the person actively searches for a style of living that will bring meaning to the second half of life. Marriages are particularly vulnerable during this time of dissatisfaction. Extramarital affairs and divorces are common symptoms of the "crisis of questions."

Ages 35–43: Crisis of Urgency People of ages 35–43 are typically beginning to become more aware of the reality of death. Having a limited number of years to live begins to exert pressure on the individual. Attempts to succeed at a career or to achieve one's life goals become intensified. Generativity, in the form of nurturing, teaching, or serving others, helps alleviate many of the anxieties of this stage.

Ages 43–50: Attaining Stability The urgency of the previous stage gives way to a calmer acceptance of one's fate in the late forties. The predominant feeling is that the die is cast and that former decisions can be lived with. Those who have families begin to appreciate their children as individuals and ease up on their tendency to extend their own goals to their children's behavior.

Age 50 and Up: Mellowing After age 50 a noticeable mellowing occurs. Emphasis is placed on sharing day-to-day joys and sorrows. There is less concern with glamor, wealth, accomplishment, and abstract goals. Many of the tensions of earlier years give way to a desire to savor life and its small pleasures.

Question: Where does the "midlife crisis" fit in?

A Midlife Crisis? Obviously, not everyone has difficulty at the midpoint of life. However, psychologist Daniel J. Levinson, at Yale University, has carried out an in-depth study of lives from early adulthood to later maturity. Levinson (1978) found that most of his subjects went through a period of instability, anxiety, and change between the ages of 37 and 41 (Gould's "crisis of urgency" period).

Roughly one-half of the people studied by Levinson defined the midlife period as a sort of "last chance" to achieve their life goals. Such goals were often stated as a key event; for example, attaining a supervisory position, achieving a certain income, becoming a full professor, shop steward, and so forth. For these individuals the midlife period is stressful, but manageable.

A second pattern involved a serious midlife decline. Sometimes this decline was related to obvious failure or to choice of a deadend job or life-style. In other cases it meant that subjects had experienced external success but felt that what they were doing was pointless.

Levinson characterizes the third pattern as "breaking out" of a seriously flawed life structure. In this case, negative aspects of work, relationships, or life-style that were once accepted had become intolerable, leading to dramatic changes in work, goals, and relationships. Such changes require risk-taking and sacrifice, and for many, they mean literally starting over. In most cases, 8 to 10 years of instability and rebuilding followed the changes of "breaking out."

Thus, it can be seen that the midlife crisis, if it takes place, can be both a danger and an opportunity. Ideally it is a time of reworking old identities, of achieving long-sought goals, of finding one's own truths, and of preparation for later maturity and aging (Barrow and Smith, 1979).

Middle Age After the "deadline decade" of midlife, a new series of issues typically confronts the person, but a new level of stability is also usually achieved. In the forties and fifties, declining strength, physical vigor, and youthfulness make it clear to individuals that more than half of their time is gone. At the same time, greater stability comes from "letting go of the impossible dream" (Sheehy, 1976). That is, there is an increased attempt to be satisfied with the direction one's life has taken and to accept that hoped-for life goals may no longer be possible.

For most women during this era, **menopause** represents the first real encounter with aging. At menopause monthly menstruation ends, and a woman is no longer able to bear children. In menopause, the level of the hormone estrogen drops—sometimes causing drastic changes in mood or appearance, and the occurrence of physical symptoms such as "hot flashes" (a sudden uncomfortable sensation of heat).

Many women find menopause as difficult to adjust to as adolescence, and many experience anxiety, irritability, or depression at this time. Most postmenopausal women, however, report that menopause was not as bad as they expected, and that much of their anxiety came from not knowing what to expect (Mussen *et al.,* 1979). Some women fear that menopause will end their sex life, but in reality, many women report a resurgence of sexual interest after the possibility of pregnancy ends.

Question: Do men go through similar changes?

Males do not undergo any abrupt physical change directly comparable to menopause. Just the same, some authorities now feel that 40- to 60-year-old males often pass through a **climacteric** (kly-MAK-ter-ik) or significant physiological change (Zaludek, 1976). During the climacteric, decreases in male hormone output may cause psychological symptoms similar to those experienced by women in menopause. However, men remain fertile at this time, and many of their symptoms (depression, anxiety, irritability) are more likely related to self-doubts caused by declining vigor and changing physical appearance.

After the late fifties, problems an individual faces in maintaining a healthy and meaningful life are complicated by the inevitable process of aging. How unique are the problems of older people, and how severely do they challenge the need to maintain integrity and personal comfort? We will look at some answers in the next section.

Aging—Will You Still Need Me When I'm Sixty-Four?

In 1978, students at Long Beach City College in California elected Pearl Taylor their spring festival queen. Ms. Taylor had everything necessary to win: looks, intelligence, personality, and campus-wide popularity. At about the same time, citizens of Raleigh, North Carolina, elected Isabella Cannon as their mayor.

Question: What's so remarkable about these events?

Not too much really, except that Pearl was 90 years old when elected, and Isabella was 73 (Barrow and Smith, 1979). Both are part of the "graying of America." In the 1800s the average life expectancy was 36 years. By 1900

it was 49 years. In 1951 the United States average was 69 years, and it is now around 77 years. There is little doubt that future improvements in medical care will bring even longer life spans (Hellman, 1971).

Due to increased life expectancy and a declining birth rate, both the number and the proportion of older people in the United States are growing. Currently, some 21 million Americans are over the age of 65. By the year 2020, some 40 million persons, or *one out of every five,* will be 65 years of age or older. These figures make the aged the fastest growing segment of society. Understandably, psychologists have become increasingly interested in aging.

Question: What is life like for the aged?

There are large variations in aging. Most of us have known elderly individuals at both extremes: Those who are active, healthy, satisfied, and whose minds are clear and alert; and those who are confused, childlike, dependent, or senile. Despite such variations, some generalizations can be made.

Aging   **Biological aging** is a gradual process that begins quite early in life. Peak functioning in most physical capacities reaches a maximum by about 25 to 30 years of age. Thereafter, gradual declines can be observed in muscular strength, flexibility, circulatory efficiency, speed of response, sensory acuity, and other functions.

Question: So people are "over the hill" by 30?

Hardly! Prime abilities come at different ages for different activities. Peak performances for professional football and baseball players usually occur in the mid-twenties; for professional bowlers, the mid-thirties; for artists and musicians, the fifties; and for politicians, philosophers, business or industrial leaders and others, the early sixties. Also, there are large differences in physical decline from one person to the next. Some people are biologically old at 45; others may be fit at 80. In fact, many older people competing in events such as the Senior Olympics are in such good physical shape they put people 30 and 40 years younger to shame (Barrow and Smith, 1979).

For those who are still young, the prospect of aging physically may be the greatest threat of old age. However, it is a misconception to believe that most elderly people are sickly, infirm, or senile. Only about 5 percent of the elderly are in nursing homes. As for the possibility of mental deterioration, Dr. Alex Comfort (1976) comments, "The human brain does not shrink, wilt, perish, or deteriorate with age. It normally continues to function well through as many as nine decades." As a **gerontologist** (jer-ON-TOL-o-jist: one who studies aging), Comfort estimates that only

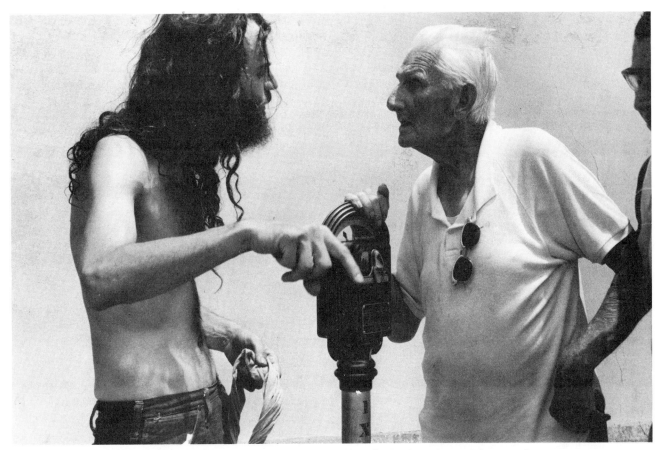

Fig. 16-5   *Is "oldness" a social convention? Do the needs of "old people" differ from those of the young?*

25 percent of the disability of old people is medically based. The remaining 75 percent is social, political, and cultural.

Comfort's view is backed up by studies of the intellectual capacities of aging individuals. Little overall decline occurs in intelligence test scores with aging. Although it is true that "fluid" abilities (those requiring speed or rapid learning) may decline, "crystallized" abilities such as vocabulary and accumulated knowledge actually improve at least into the seventies (Baltes and Schaie, 1974). The general intellectual decline attributed to old age is largely a myth.

The maintenance of intellect, creativity, and productivity is quite likely when aging individuals remain active and suffer no major physical problems. Continued intellectual stimulation, education, and practice of skills are also associated with a delay of age-related declines (Sherman, 1971). This fact is demonstrated by people who have remained productive well into their seventies and eighties, people such as: Pablo Picasso (artist); Margaret Mead (anthro-

pologist); Lillian Carter (nurse in the Peace Corps); Pablo Casals (cellist); Ruth Gordon (actress, writer); Oliver Wendell Holmes (judge); Georgia O'Keeffe (painter), and so on.

Question: What kind of person adjusts most successfully to aging?

Activity and Disengagement   In some cultures the aged are respected and revered. In our culture considerable value is placed on youthfulness. This orientation adds an important psychological dimension to the difficulties of aging. Ilya Ehrenburg (1968) expresses the problem in an examination of his own reactions to aging:

> For the past 15 years or so, I have been learning how to be an old man. This is not nearly as easy as I thought when I was young. I used to think that desires die down along with the possibilities of satisfying them; but then I began to understand that the body ages before the spirit, and that one has to learn to live like an old man.

382 Human Development and Personality

Acceptance of the aging process is just one of the developmental tasks of later life. Others are:

Adjusting to decreasing physical strength. Adjusting to retirement and reduced income. Adjusting to death of spouse and friends. Meeting social and civic obligations within one's ability. Establishing an explicit affiliation with age group. Maintaining interests, concern beyond self (Coleman, 1969).

Two principal theories have been proposed to explain successful adjustment to the physical and social changes of aging. **Disengagement theory** assumes that it is normal and desirable that people will withdraw from society as they age (Cumming and Henry, 1961). According to this theory, elderly persons welcome disengagement since it relieves them of roles and responsibilities they have become less able to fulfill. Likewise, society benefits from disengagement as younger persons with new energy and skills fill positions vacated by aging individuals.

Certainly we have all known people who disengaged from society as they grew older. Nevertheless, the disengagement theory can be criticized for describing successful aging as an "orderly retreat."

Question: What does the second theory say?

A second view of optimal aging is provided by **activity theory,** which assumes that activity is the essence of life for people of all ages. Activity theory predicts that people who remain active physically, mentally, and socially will adjust better to aging (Havighurst, 1961).

Proponents of activity theory believe that aging persons should maintain the activities of their earlier years for as long as possible. If a person is forced to give up particular roles or activities, they recommend that these be replaced with others. In so doing, the aging person is able to maintain a better self-image, greater satisfaction, and more social support—resulting in more successful aging.

Question: Which theory is correct?

The majority of studies conducted on aging support the *activity theory,* although there have been exceptions (Barrow and Smith, 1979). At the same time, some people do seek disengagement, so neither theory is absolutely "correct." Actually, successful aging probably requires a combination of activity and disengagement. For example, one researcher has shown that the elderly tend to disengage from activities that are no longer satisfying while maintaining those that are (Brown, 1974).

Another major factor in successful aging is the person's **self-concept.** Rosow (1963) tells us that there is a dif-

ference between the "young-old" and the "old-old." The young-old recognize that they are aging but do not think of themselves as "old" and do not accept the role of "old person." Old-old persons are resigned to being old, and see themselves as "old." This distinction makes it clear that age in years is not the essence of being "old." Aging is a real event, but "old age" is a social convention. In a very real sense, you are "only as old as you think you are."

Alex Comfort (1976) has charged that the concept of "oldness" is used to expel people from useful work. Comfort believes that retirement, which usually cuts income in half at a set age, is just another name for dismissal and unemployment. Comfort may have best put the problems of aging in perspective by listing the needs of the elderly. He says that as an "old" person you will have four needs: dignity, money, proper medical care, and useful work— exactly the things you have always needed.

Ageism   In one way or another you have encountered ageism. **Ageism** refers to discrimination or prejudice on the basis of age. It applies to people of all ages and can oppress the young as well as the old. For instance, a person applying for a job may just as likely be told, "You're too young," as, "You're too old." Ageism, however, probably has more negative impact on older individuals since it is usually expressed as an aversion, hatred, or rejection of the elderly.

Another facet of ageism is stereotyping of the aged. Popular stereotypes of the "dirty old man," "meddling old woman," "senile old fool" and the like, especially as seen in films and on TV, help perpetuate the myths underlying ageism. Contrast such images to those associated with youthfulness: The young are perceived as fresh, whole, attractive, energetic, active, emerging, appealing, and so forth.

Question: What can be done about ageism?

Despite a tremendous emphasis on youth and "youth culture" many older people are refusing to accept stereotyped images of themselves as lonely, dependent, unattractive, incompetent, and so forth. Organizations such as the Gray Panthers have lobbied for changes in laws that discriminate against older citizens, and they often boycott or challenge organizations that stereotype the elderly.

One of the best ways to combat ageism as it applies to older persons is to counter stereotypes with facts. Bernice Neugarten (1971) has examined the lives of 200 people between the ages of 70 and 79. Neugarten found that 75 percent of these people were satisfied with their lives after retirement. Other myths about aging identified by Neugarten are:

1. Old persons generally do not become isolated and neglected by their families. Most *prefer* to live apart from their children.

2. Old persons are rarely placed in mental hospitals by uncaring children.

3. Old persons who live alone are not necessarily lonely or desolate.

4. Few elderly persons ever show signs of senility or mental decay, and few ever become mentally ill.

In short, most of the elderly studied by Neugarten were integrated, active, and psychologically healthy. Findings such as these call for an end to the forced obsolescence of the elderly. As a group, older people represent a valuable source of skills, knowledge, and energy that we can no longer afford to cast aside. As we face the challenges of this planet's uncertain future, we need all the help we can get!

Learning Check

Check your comprehension with these questions.

1. Building a workable life tends to be the dominant activity during which age range?

   a. 18–22   b. 22–28   c. 29–34   d. 35–43

2. Levinson's description of the "midlife crisis" corresponds roughly to Gould's:

   a. Escape from Dominance   b. Crisis of Questions
   c. Crisis of Urgency   d. Settling Down Period

3. The average male experiences the menopause between the ages of 45 and 50.   T or F?

4. Many indications of biological aging start to become evident as early as the mid-twenties.   T or F?

5. An expert on the problems of aging is called a _____.

6. The activity theory of optimal aging holds that aging individuals should restrict their activities and withdraw from former community activities.   T or F?

7. After age 65, a large proportion of older people show significant signs of senility and most require special care.   T or F?

Answers: 1. b   2. c   3. F   4. T   5. gerontologist   6. F   7. F

Resources Summary

● According to Erikson, each life stage provokes a specific *psychosocial crisis*. In order of occurrence these are: *trust versus mistrust, autonomy versus shame and doubt, initiative versus guilt, industry versus inferiority, identity versus role confusion, intimacy versus isolation, generativity versus stagnation,* and *integrity versus despair.*

● In addition to the dilemmas identified by Erikson, we recognize that each life stage requires successful mastery of certain *developmental tasks.* One such task, occurring shortly before death, may be a *life review.*

● Frederick Leboyer advocates a delivery technique he calls *gentle birth.* Many of the assumptions, and even the safety, of gentle birth have been questioned. The effects of gentle birth on infant development and emotions are as yet unclear.

● There is evidence that a stronger *maternal-infant bond* develops when mothers have added contact with their infants shortly after birth. Bonding may benefit the developing child by way of lasting changes in the mother's behavior. Participation of fathers in the early care of their infants is also considered desirable.

● Evidence exists that a *moderate amount* of stress in childhood is not only normal, but perhaps beneficial to development because it stimulates the body's adrenal-pituitary system.

● Few children grow up without experiencing some of the normal problems of childhood: *negativism, clinging, specific fears, sleep disturbances, general dissatisfaction, regressions, sibling rivalry,* and *rebellion.*

● Significant problems affect about 1 child in 10. Major areas of difficulty are: *toilet training* (including *enuresis* and *encopresis*); *feeding disturbances,* such as *overeating, anorexia nervosa* (self-starvation), *bulimia* (gorging and purging), and *pica* (eating nonfood substances); speech (*delayed speech, stuttering*); and *learning disorders* (*dyslexia, hyperactivity,* and other problems). *Childhood autism* is representative of some of the more severe problems that can occur. Some cases of hyperactivity and autism are being treated successfully with *behavior modification*.

● Certain relatively consistent events mark adult development in our society. These range from escaping parental dominance in the late teens to a noticeable acceptance of one's lot in life during the fifties. Some research indicates that a *midlife crisis* affects many people in the 37–41 age range. Adjustment to later middle age is often complicated for women by *menopause* and for men by a *climacteric*.

● As life span increases and the birthrate decreases, both the *number* and *proportion* of older people in the population has grown. *Biological aging* begins between 25 and 30, but peak performance in a particular pursuit may come at various points throughout life. Intellectual decline is quite limited at least through one's seventies.

● *Gerontologists* have proposed two major theories of successful aging. The *disengagement theory* holds that withdrawal from society is necessary and desirable in old age. The *activity theory* counters that optimal adjustment to aging is tied to continuing activity and involvement. There is an element of truth to each, but the activity theory has received more support.

● *Ageism* refers to prejudice, discrimination, and stereotyping on the basis of age. It affects people of all ages, but is especially damaging to older people. Most ageism is based upon myths and misinformation.

========== Applications ==========

Parenting

Raising children draws many of the problems of development into a single arena. When parenting is effective, both adult and child benefit. When parents fail to give their children a good start in life, everybody suffers—the child, the parents, and society as a whole. What does it take to be a good parent? In the previous chapter, emphasis was placed on promoting a child's intellectual development. This goal is worthwhile, but is it enough? Healthy development requires emotional and social competence as well as intellectual ability. In addition to the skills needed for achievement, effective parents give their children a capacity for love, joy, and fulfillment.

Question: What can parents do to promote healthy development in their children?

Much of the answer can be found in two key areas of parent-child relationships. These are *communication* and *discipline.* In each area parents can set an example of tolerance, understanding, and acceptance that goes beyond their traditional role as mere dispensers of "dos" and "don'ts."

Rearing Children

One of the lasting myths about parenthood is belief that "Love is all a parent has to give a child." No psychologist would deny that love is essential for healthy development, but *discipline* can be of equal importance. Parents with unmanageable, delinquent, or unhappy children often can honestly claim that they have given them lots of love. Yet when parents fail to provide a framework of guidelines for behavior, children become antisocial, aggressive, and insecure. Parents who allow themselves to be dominated or manipulated create lifelong patterns of manipulation and self-serving behavior in the child.

Question: Does this mean that discipline should be strict and unbending?

No. The family need not be made into a military boot camp. Effective discipline can be quite permissive. It is important to remember that rules about the proper time and place to engage in toilet functions, restraints on natural impulses for sex and aggression, and numerous other parental curbs on behavior are frustrating to children. The problem in providing adequate discipline is to socialize a child without undue frustration and without destroying the bond of love and trust between parent and child.

Question: How can a balance be maintained?

Many experts are advocating a new style of childrearing that recognizes a child's psychological needs. The core of this approach is a special form of permissiveness. Dr. Haim G. Ginott (1965) in his highly acclaimed book *Between Parent and Child* explains:

> The essence of permissiveness is the acceptance of children as persons who have a constitutional right to have all kinds of feelings and wishes. . . . All feelings and fantasies, all thoughts and wishes, all dreams and desires, are accepted, respected, and may be permitted expression. . . . Overpermissiveness is the allowing of undesirable acts. Permissiveness brings confidence and an increasing capacity to express feelings and thoughts. Overpermissiveness brings anxiety and increasing demands for privileges that cannot be granted.

In other words, discipline should give children freedom to express their deepest feelings through speech and actions. This does not mean freedom to do entirely as one pleases. It means the child has room to move about freely *within* well-defined limits. Of course, individual parents may choose limits that are more or less "strict." But this choice is less important than the consistency of parental standards. *Consistent* discipline gives a child a sense of security and stability; inconsistency makes the child's world seem unreliable and unpredictable.

Question: How can limits best be maintained?

Parents tend to base discipline on one or more of the following techniques: **power assertion, withdrawal of love,** or **child management** (Coopersmith, 1968; Hoffman, 1970).

"Power assertion" refers to physical punishment or to a show of force in which parents take away toys or privileges. As an alternative, some parents may temporarily withdraw love by refusing to speak to a child, by threatening to leave, by rejecting the child, or by otherwise acting as if the child is temporarily unlovable. Management tech-

Applications

niques combine praise, recognition, approval, rules, reasoning, and the like to encourage desirable behavior. Each of these approaches can effectively control a child's behavior, but their side effects differ considerably.

Question: What are the side effects?

Power-oriented techniques, particularly harsh or severe physical punishment, are associated with fear, hatred of parents, and a lack of spontaneity and warmth. Severely punished children also tend to be defiant, rebellious, and aggressive.

Withdrawal of love, which is a major middle-class mode of discipline, produces children who tend to be self-disciplined. We might say that such children have developed a good conscience. They are often described as "model" children or as unusually "good." But as a side effect, they are also frequently anxious, insecure, and dependent on adults for approval.

Management techniques also have their limitations. Most important is the need to carefully adjust them to a child's level of understanding. Younger children may not always see the connection between rules, explanations, and their own behavior. In spite of this limitation, management techniques receive a big plus in an important area of child development. Psychologist Stanley Coopersmith (1968) has found a direct connection between parental styles of discipline and a child's **self-esteem.**

Question: What is self-esteem?

By "self-esteem" we mean a quiet confidence that comes from regarding oneself as a worthwhile person. Many theorists consider high self-esteem essential for emotional health. Individuals with low self-esteem have a low estimation of their value as people. This attitude has a negative effect on many of their activities and their relationships with others.

Coopersmith divided boys into groups having high or low self-esteem. He then investigated the childrearing attitudes and practices of the boys' parents. He found that low self-esteem was related to the use of physical punishment or withholding of love. High self-esteem, by contrast, was related to management techniques that emphasized strict and consistent discipline coupled with high parental interest and concern for the child. It seems parenting that minimizes physical punishment and avoids unnecessary withdrawal of love is most effective.

Question: Are you saying that physical punishment and withdrawal of love should not be used?

Most parents have used each of the three major types of discipline at one time or another, and each has its place. Coopersmith's findings simply suggest that physical punishment and withdrawal of love should be used with caution. In using these two forms of punishment, the following guidelines should be observed.

1. Separate disapproval of the act from disapproval of the child. Instead of saying, "I'm going to punish you because *you* are bad," say, "I'm upset about *what you did.*"
2. Punishment should never be harsh or injurious to a child. Don't physically punish a child while you are angry. Also remember that giving a child the message "I don't love you right now" can be more painful than any spanking.
3. Punishment is most effective when it is administered immediately. This statement is especially true for younger children.
4. Spanking and other forms of physical punishment are not particularly effective for children under age two. The child will only be confused and frightened. Spankings also become less effective after age five because they tend to humiliate the child and breed resentment.
5. Reserve physical punishment for situations that pose an immediate danger to the younger child, for example, when a child runs into the street.

After age five, management techniques are the most effective form of discipline. At all ages, it is helpful to keep in mind this comparison: **Authoritarian parents** view children as having few rights but adultlike responsibilities; **overly permissive parents** view children as having few responsibilities, but rights similar to adults; **effective parents** balance their own rights with those of their children (Baumrind, 1980). Especially useful in maintaining such a balance are techniques that emphasize communication.

Communication Between Parent and Child

When clear communication is maintained between parent and child, many discipline problems can be avoided before they develop. Dr. Haim Ginott (1965) has suggested that it is essential to make a distinction between a child's feelings and a child's behavior. Since children (and parents, too) do not choose how they will feel, it is

---

Applications

important to allow free expression of feelings.

The child who learns to regard some feelings as "bad," or unacceptable, is being asked to deny a very real part of his experience. Ginott encourages parents to teach their children that all feelings are appropriate, and only actions are subject to disapproval. Many parents are unaware of just how often they block communication and the expression of feelings in their children. Consider this typical conversation excerpted from Ginott's book (1965):

Son: I am stupid, and I know it. Look at my grades in school.

Father: You just have to work harder.

Son: I already work harder and it doesn't help. I have no brains.

Father: You are smart, I know.

Son: I am stupid, I know.

Father: *(loudly)* You are not stupid!

Son: Yes, I am!

Father: You are not stupid. Stupid!

By debating with the child, the father misses the point that his son *feels* stupid. It would be far more helpful for the father to encourage the boy to talk about his feelings.

Question: How could he do that?

He might say, "You really feel that you are not as smart as others, don't you? Do you feel this way often? Are you feeling bad at school?" In this way, the child is given an opportunity to express his emotions, and he feels understood. The father might conclude the conversation by saying, "Look, son, in my eyes you are a fine person. But I understand how you feel. Everyone feels stupid at times."

Communication with a child can also be the basis of effective discipline. Dr. Thomas Gordon (1970), a child psychologist who has developed a program called Parent Effectiveness Training (PET), offers a useful suggestion. Gordon believes that parents should send "I" messages to their children, rather than "you" messages.

Question: What's the difference?

"You" messages take the form of threats, name-calling, accusing, bossing, lecturing, or analyzing. Generally, "you" messages tell children what's "wrong" with them.

An "I" message is a form of communication in which you tell children what effect their behavior has had on you. To illustrate the difference, consider this example.

After a hard day's work, Susan wants to sit down and rest a while. She begins to relax with a newspaper when her five-year-old daughter starts banging loudly on a toy drum. Most parents would respond with a "you" message:

"You go play outside this instant." (bossing)

"Don't ever make such a racket when someone is reading." (lecturing)

"You're really pushing it today, aren't you?" (accusing)

"You're a spoiled brat." (name-calling)

"Do you want me to swat you?" (threatening)

Gordon suggests sending an "I" message such as, "I am very tired, and I would like to read. I feel upset and can't read when you make so much noise." This forces the child to accept responsibility for the effects of her actions. If this doesn't curb misbehavior, the consequences can also be stated as an "I" message: "If you keep banging on that drum, I will have to put it away." If the child makes more noise, then she has caused the toy to be put away. If she takes it outside, then she has decided to do so. Both parent and child have been allowed to maintain a sense of self-respect and self-worth, and a needless clash has been averted.

Only two additional points on communicating with children need be noted. They are: "Listen more than you talk"; and "Live the message you wish to communicate."

Child Abuse

Sadly, no account of parenting would be complete without a brief discussion of child abuse. Much as we might like to believe otherwise, from 200,000 to 400,000 cases of physical child abuse are reported each year in this country. Undoubtedly, many more go unreported (President's Commission on Mental Health, 1978). If sexual abuse, emotional abuse, and neglect are included, an estimated 1 to 2 million instances of child abuse occur each year in the United States (Giovannoni and Becerra, 1979). In about one-third of all cases of physical abuse, the child is seriously injured. Every year hundreds of children are killed by their own parents.

Question: What are abusive parents like?

Characteristics of Abusive Parents Abusive parents are usually young (under 30), and more are from

Applications

lower-income levels. However, professionals working with child abuse see parents of all ages and income levels.

Abusive parents often have a high level of stress and frustration in their lives. Typical problems include loneliness, marital discord, unemployment, drug abuse, divorce, family violence, heavy drinking, and work anxieties (Giovannoni and Becerra, 1979). Nationally, there is evidence that abuse goes up when unemployment rises. Thus, some abuse represents displaced aggression, with the child as its target. Some parents are aware that they are mistreating a child, but they are unable to stop. Other abusive parents literally hate, or are disgusted by, their child. The child's sloppiness, diapers, crying, or needs are unbearable to them. Often, these parents expect the child to love them and make them happy. When the child (who is usually under three years old) cannot meet their unrealistic demands, they react with lethal anger.

As mentioned previously, the core of much child abuse is a "cycle of violence" that flows from one generation to the next. That is, most abusive parents were themselves mistreated as children (Williams and Money, 1980). Many abusive parents simply never learned how to love, communicate with, or discipline a child.

Question: What can be done about child abuse?

Preventing Child Abuse Many public agencies now have teams to identify battered or neglected children. However, legal "cures" for child abuse are not very satisfying. The courts can take custody of a child, or the parents may agree to place the child in a foster home. Foster care can be an improvement, but it may also traumatize the child. In some cases, children are allowed to remain with their parents, but under court supervision. Even then, there is a chance of further injury, unless the parents get help.

Self-help groups staffed by former child abusers and concerned volunteers are a major aid to parents. One such group is Parents Anonymous, a national organization of parents determined to help each other stop abusing children. Local groups set up networks of members that parents can call in an abuse crisis, or when they feel one coming on. Parents Anonymous also offers education on the causes of child abuse. In workshops, parents learn how to curb violent impulses and how to cope with their children. One of the most important aspects of such groups is the mutual support they offer: Parents discover that child abusers are not monsters, and that others share similar problems.

A third way of preventing child abuse is by changing attitudes. Despite newspaper and TV coverage of the problem, many parents believe it is their "right" to slap or hit their children. A recent survey found that corporal punishment is widely accepted in this country. Even hitting a child with a leather strap or a wooden stick was rated as only "moderately serious" (Giovannoni and Becerra, 1979). A child had to be "banged against a wall," or "hit in the face with a fist," before it was considered an act of abuse. As the authors of the survey put it, the public attitude appears to be, "It's all right to hit your child, but not too hard; in fact it's all right to hurt your child—but not too badly."

To face the problem squarely, we must realize that the line between acceptable discipline and child abuse is blurred. As a society, we seem to say, "Violence is O.K. if the child isn't injured; if the child is injured then it's child abuse." Of course, when the child is injured, it's too late to take it back. By condoning punishment that hovers on the threshold of abuse, we greatly raise the chances of injury. The best solution to physical abuse, then, may lie in rethinking our attitudes toward corporal punishment and the rights of children.

Learning Check

1. According to the text, effective discipline gives children freedom within a structure of consistent and well-defined limits.   T or F?
2. Coopersmith found that high self-esteem in childhood is related to discipline based on either management techniques or withdrawal of love.   T or F?
3. Spankings and other physical punishment are most effective for children under the age of two.   T or F?
4. Authoritarian parents view children as having few rights, but many responsibilities.   T or F?
5. Most parents who abuse children were themselves mistreated as children.   T or F?

Answers: 1. T   2. F   3. F   4. T   5. T

Exploration

Approaching Death—New Pathways

In January, 1967, H. Bedford, a psychology professor from Glendale, California, died at the age of 73. His body was immediately frozen—submerged in liquid nitrogen—making him the first person in the United States to try to cheat death by cryonic suspension (Keeffe, 1977). Mr. Bedford's story is only one indication of changing attitudes toward dying.

For some, death is a sudden tragedy; for others, it is a long-wished-for release. Whatever the case, death—the last phase of life—is something we all must face. It therefore behooves each of us to know something about death. In this section we will add to an earlier discussion of death (Chapter 13) by considering four departures from traditional approaches to dying: the hospice movement, passive euthanasia, active euthanasia, and cryonics.

Hospice   At the beginning of this century most people died at home. Of the more than 2 million deaths in the United States in 1977, more than 70 percent took place outside the home, most in either a hospital or a nursing home (Fulton, 1979). Just as some people have begun to question traditional funeral practices (embalming, viewing, elaborate and expensive caskets and ceremonies), many are now beginning to question treatment of the terminally ill. Too often the terminally ill are isolated, frightened, in pain, and stripped of control over their final days of life. The hospice concept was created to counter this situation.

A **hospice** is basically a hospital for the terminally ill, modeled after a pioneering English facility (there are now over 30 hospices in England). The goal of the hospice is to give specialized care to the dying individual and to improve the quality of life in the person's final days. The first hospice was created in recognition of the dying individuals' needs to be included, to know that someone still cares, to maintain control over their lives, and to have a say in their own dying. In operation, hospices present a striking contrast to the grim wards for the terminally ill found in many hospitals.

Question: How is a hospice different?

First, there are lots of people present. A hospice offers support, counseling, guidance, and companionship from volunteers, other patients, staff, clergy, and counselors. Friendship and kindness are expressed toward patients so that when the time comes to die, they know they will be remembered with respect and love.

Secondly, the atmosphere differs markedly from that of a traditional hospital. A hospice attempts to provide pleasant surroundings, an atmosphere of intentional informality, and a sense of continued living for patients. Unlimited, around-the-clock visits are permitted by relatives, friends, children, and even pets. Patients receive constant attention, they play games, make day trips, have predinner cocktails if they choose, entertainment is provided, volunteers visit with the patients—in short, life goes on.

A third aspect of hospice care is the freedom of choice allowed patients. Patients decide about their own diets, about whether or not they will use pain-killing drugs, and about whether or not they want to continue medical care. Patients may also choose freedom from intolerable pain. This is usually achieved by providing patients with Brompton's mixture, a combination of cherry syrup and morphine. The dosage of morphine in a Brompton's "cocktail" is small enough so the person does not become euphoric or groggy; it simply relieves pain.

There are currently several hospices under development in the United States. If their success in England is any indication, hospices here will almost certainly be a welcome addition to many communities.

A Right to Die?   The "right to die" concept might be better stated as a right to "live in peace and comfort until death." Much of the recent interest in this issue has focused on the Karen Ann Quinlan case. At this writing, Karen is still in a coma—as she has been for several years since suffering an overdose of drugs and alcohol. After all chance of recovery was lost, Karen's parents began a legal fight to turn off the respirator and other devices being used to prolong her life. In 1976 the New Jersey Supreme Court issued a landmark decision giving permission to the parents to order removal of Karen's life-support equipment. Doctors predicted Karen would die, but she continued to live.

Is there a right to die? Doctors and other medical personnel are legally and morally bound to prolong and pre-

Exploration

serve life, and in most states relatives and guardians cannot legally give permission for removal of life-supporting equipment. One way out of this dilemma that is gaining support is the **living will** (see address at end of chapter). The intent of a living will is to free the terminally and irreversibly ill from a slow and cruel death, allowing death with dignity. The will is made out when the person is still healthy, and states that, in the event of irreversible illness, the person does not want to have life sustained by medical machines, or heroic measures. A living will is not yet binding in most states, but it does make clear the wishes of terminally ill persons unable to speak for themselves.

Euthanasia   The right to die won for Karen Quinlan by her parents may be thought of as **passive euthanasia** (YOU-tha-NAY-zyah), in which death is allowed to occur but is not actively caused. In **active euthanasia,** steps would be taken at a patient's request to deliberately hasten death, perhaps by administering drugs that induce death painlessly. Proponents of euthanasia see it as a basic human right to die with dignity when all meaning has gone out of further life. Should euthanasia ever become legal (many people find the idea totally unacceptable), it might also become possible for next of kin to request euthanasia for an incapacitated individual.

There are several arguments against euthanasia. The case of Karen Delahanty of Avon, Connecticut, provides a good starting point. After a head-on automobile accident, Karen entered a coma from which doctors predicted she would never recover. One year later she miraculously regained consciousness. What if euthanasia had been carried out?

Other questions that arise, in addition to unexpected recovery, include: What guarantee is there that the choice of euthanasia would be made freely and without pressure? Could family members be trusted to make a correct decision? Would they feel guilt afterward? What about the medical personnel involved; how would they respond emotionally to "mercy killing"? The reader can undoubtedly supply other objections.

Cryonics   To complete our brief sampling of new approaches to dying, let's return to cryonics. Cryonics involves freezing a person's body upon death. The idea is to keep the person frozen until medical science perfects ways to thaw, restore, and revive the person. Those who have been placed in **cryonic suspension** obviously are gambling that if they are revived a cure will exist for whatever killed them.

Question: Does freezing actually work?

Cryonic suspension really must be viewed as a symbolic attempt to cheat death, or perhaps as an emotional hedge against the finality of death. At this point, cryonic suspension is totally impractical because freezing does serious damage to the body. Freezing and unfreezing the brain would almost surely turn it to mush—wiping out most or all of the memories stored there. If a person frozen at death is ever successfully revived, that person would have no identity, and perhaps no understanding of where they were or why they were there. They would, in most cases, be quite old. Whereas it is true that for a few pioneering souls there is clearly "ice after death," immortality, it would seem, does not yet fall within the province of technology.

Questions for Discussion

1. Describe an incident from your own childhood that you consider growth-promoting. Describe an incident that set you back or had a negative effect on you. How do these incidents differ?

2. Were you physically punished as a child? What is your attitude toward physical punishment now? Would you use physical punishment on your own children?

3. In what ways do parents add to the conflicts of young adults who are seeking independence?

4. Do you know a person who seems to have "flunked" one or more of Erikson's developmental stages? What effect has this had on the person's subsequent development?

5. Anthropologist Margaret Mead has charged, "We have become a society of people who neglect our children, are afraid of our children." Do you agree?

6. Do we need a "children's liberation movement" to establish the civil rights of children? (Keep in mind that few parents show their children the courtesy they show strangers.)

7. How common do you think it is to experience a "mid-life crisis"? Would you expect people of other cultures to experience a similar crisis?

8. When and how would you prefer to die? If you had a terminal illness would you want to be told? Do you think sudden death or death with forewarning would be better?

9. Should passive euthanasia be allowed? Should active euthanasia be allowed? What are the arguments for and against each? Do you think a "living will" is a good idea? Why or why not?

10. If you could choose to remain a particular age, which would you choose? Why? What are your attitudes toward aging?

Suggestions for Further Reading

Bartz, W. R., and R. A. Rasor. *Surviving with Kids.* Ballantine, 1980.

Bettelheim, B. *The Empty Fortress: Infantile Autism and the Birth of the Self.* Free Press, 1967.

Chess, S., A. Thomas, and H. G. Birch. *Your Child Is a Person.* Viking, 1965.

Comfort, A. *A Good Age.* Crown, 1976.

Erikson, E. *Childhood and Society.* 2nd ed. Norton, 1963.

Fontana, V. J. *The Maltreated Child.* Thomas, 1974.

Ginott, H. G. *Between Parent and Child.* Macmillan, 1965.

Gordon, T. *P.E.T.: Parent Effectiveness Training.* Wyden, 1970.

Kimmel, D. C. *Adulthood and Aging.* Wiley, 1974.

Palazolli, M. *Self Starvation.* Aronson, 1978.

Siegel, R. K. "The Psychology of Life after Death," *American Psychologist,* October, 1980, pp. 911–931.

Williams, G. J., and J. Money. *Traumatic Abuse and Neglect of Children at Home.* Johns Hopkins University Press, 1980.

Where to Write for Information

Anorexia Nervosa: National Association of Anorexia Nervosa and Associated Disorders, Box 271, Highland Park, Illinois 60035.

Autism: The National Society for Autistic Children, 101 Richmond St., Huntington, West Virginia 25701.

Child Abuse: Parents Anonymous, 22330 Hawthorne Blvd., Torrance, California 90505.

Hospice: The National Hospice Organization, 301 Tower Suite 506, 301 Maple Ave. West, Vienna, Virginia 22180.

Hyperactivity: Department of Health, Education, and Welfare, Office of the Secretary, Secretary's Committee on Mental Retardation, Washington, D.C. 20201.

Learning Disorders: National Association for Children with Learning Disabilities, 5225 Grace St., Pittsburgh, Pennsylvania 15236.

Living Will: Concern for Dying, 250 West 57th St., New York, New York 10019.

17

Intelligence

━━━━━━━━━━━━ Chapter Preview ━━━━━━━━━━━━

What Day Is It?

Ask George in which recent years April 21 fell on a Sunday. Without hesitation he will answer: "1968, 1963, 1957, 1946." Surprisingly, this gives only the slightest hint of his skill. If encouraged, George will go back as far as 1700— with complete accuracy! His "calendar calculations" cover a range of at least 6000 years, extending centuries beyond present perpetual calendars. With equal ease he can identify February 15, 2002, as a Friday or August 28, 1591, as a Wednesday.

Question: Is he a genius?

George's abilities are all the more amazing in view of the fact that he is mentally retarded and cannot add, subtract, multiply, or divide even simple numbers (Horwitz et al., 1965). George is an "idiot savant," a person of subnormal intelligence who shows highly developed mental ability in one or more very limited areas.

Question: How could he be retarded and have this ability both at the same time?

The striking contrast between George's general retardation and incredible mental ability serves as a fitting introduction to the challenge psychologists have faced in their efforts to define and measure intelligence. Quite frankly, we are still searching for definitive answers to questions like these: "Is intelligence a general trait or a specific skill?" "Is intelligence determined by the genetic 'wheel of fortune' or is it nurtured by environment?" "Is it possible to construct an intelligence test that is fair to all people?" "How important is intelligence for 'success'?" Because our understanding of intelligence is undergoing rapid change, we cannot hope to give final answers.

For the sake of clarity, this chapter is divided into two distinct parts. In the "Resources" section we will assume that intelligence can be measured, and we will use measurements as a way of answering a number of questions about intelligence. In the "Applications" section we will consider some of the questions that have been raised about intelligence tests and the meaning of their results.

Survey Questions   How do psychologists define intelligence? What are the qualities of a good psychological test? What are typical IQ tests like? How do IQ scores relate to gender, age, and occupation? What does IQ tell us about "genius"? What causes mental retardation? Does heredity or environment determine intelligence? Are IQ tests fair to all racial and cultural groups?

================= Resources =================

Defining Intelligence—
Intelligence Is . . .
It's . . . You Know, It's . . .

The existence of individual differences is a basic psychological fact. With over 4.7 billion human beings on earth, still no two are exactly alike. Even identical twins have different fingerprints and voiceprints. Many personal qualities might be measured, but one of the most intensely studied has been *intelligence*. Much of the interest in intelligence stems from its seemingly pervasive relationship to ability in many areas.

Like so many important concepts in psychology, intelligence cannot be observed directly: It has no mass, occupies no space, and is invisible. Nevertheless, we feel certain it exists. Consider the following two individuals:

When she was fourteen months old, Anne H. wrote her own name. She taught herself to read at age two. At age five, she astounded her kindergarten teacher by walking into class with a stack of encyclopedias—which she proceeded to read. At ten she breezed through an entire high school algebra course in 12 hours.

At age ten Billy A. can write his name and can count, but he has trouble with simple addition and subtraction problems and finds multiplication impossible. He has been held back in school twice and is still incapable of doing the work his eight-year-old classmates find easy. His teachers have suggested that he be transferred to a special educational program for slow learners.

Anne is considered a genius; Billy, a slow learner. There seems little doubt that they differ in intelligence.

Question: Wait! Anne's ability is obvious, but how do we know that Billy isn't just lazy?

This dilemma is precisely the one that **Alfred Binet** faced in 1904. The minister of education in Paris had given Binet the task of devising a way to distinguish slower students from the more capable (or the capable but lazy). In a flash of brilliance, Binet and an associate assembled a test consisting of "intellectual" questions and problems. Next, they established which questions an "average" child could answer at each age. Children low in intellectual ability were identified by below-par performance on the test.

Binet's approach gave rise to modern intelligence tests and at the same time launched 80 years of debate that has often been heated and at times bitter. Part of the debate is related to the basic difficulty of defining intelligence.

Question: Is there an accepted definition of intelligence?

Most psychologists would probably agree with David Wechsler's general description of **intelligence** as the: *global capacity of the individual to act purposefully, to think rationally, and to deal effectively with the environment.* Beyond this, there is so much disagreement that many psychologists simply accept an **operational definition** of intelligence. (A concept has been defined "operationally" when the procedures used to measure it have been specified.) In other words, by selecting items for an intelligence test, a psychologist is saying in a very direct way: "This is what I mean by intelligence." A test that measures memory, reasoning, and verbal fluency offers a very different definition of intelligence than one that measures strength of grip, length of the nose, or age in days.

Reliability and Validity   Suppose that a famous educator and psychologist, Ike Q. Tester, is dissatisfied with existing intelligence tests and decides to develop his own (the *I. Q. Tester IQ Test*). Professor Tester decides that his test should be extremely efficient, so he limits it to a single question. According to Professor Tester, one's intelligence is revealed by an ability to complete this meaningful series of numbers: 5 5 6 6 8 1 ____. As a concerned citizen, there are two questions you should ask about Professor Tester's test: "Is it *reliable?*" and, "Is it *valid?*"

Question: What does reliability refer to?

A reliable bathroom scale gives the same weight on several successive weighings. For a test to be **reliable** it must yield the same score, or close to the same score, each time it is administered to the same individual. It is quite easy to see that a test has little value if it is unreliable. Imagine a medical test for pregnancy, for instance, that gives positive and negative responses for the same woman on different occasions.

To establish the reliability of the *I. Q. Tester IQ Test,* we could administer it to a large group of people and then test them again at a later date (this procedure is known as "test-retest reliability"). By comparing their scores we find that the *Tester Test* is quite reliable. In fact, the scores are *identical* for both tests: Everyone scores *zero* each time (except Professor Tester, who scores 100 percent and thereby proclaims himself the only human in possession of intelligence). Upon questioning, Tester reveals his secret of success: The series of numbers in the question comes from his Social Security number. Hence, anyone else who answers correctly does so purely by chance!

If Tester had provided a larger number of questions, the reliability of his test could be determined in another way. Reliability is sometimes measured by comparing the score on one-half of the test items to the score on the other half ("split-half reliability"). Likewise, if Tester offered two versions of the test we could compare scores on one to scores on the other for each person ("equivalent forms reliability"). In any case, Tester has shown the scores on his test to be consistent (reliable); but, are they *valid?*

Obviously we have been playing with a silly example; by no stretch of the imagination can the *I. Q. Tester IQ Test* be considered valid. A test has **validity** when it measures what it claims to measure. Like the *I. Q. Tester IQ Test,* many psychological tests you will encounter have little or no validity. This is especially true of "personality" tests found in magazines or offered by commercial "self-improvement" courses.

Question: How is the validity of a test established?

As a starting point a test should include items that look as if they are related to what is supposedly being measured ("face validity"). A test of athletic aptitude would be suspect if it required addition of long columns of numbers, and a test of mathematical aptitude that measured reaction speed would be of questionable validity. A better way of determining validity is to compare test scores to actual performance ("criterion validity"). A test of legal aptitude, for example, might be validated by comparing test scores to grades in law school. If high scores correlate with high grades or other measures of success, the test may be considered valid.

Tester's Last Stand   Let's return to Professor Tester for a final point. Although he admits his test has problems, Professor Tester claims that at least it is *objective.* Is he right? Actually, yes, because a test is said to be **objective** if it gives the same score when different people correct it. Tester's test *is* objective, as are most intelligence tests. However, objectivity is not enough to guarantee a fair test. To be useful, a psychological test must also be *standardized.*

Test **standardization** refers to two things: First, it means that the same procedures are used in giving the test to all people; and second, it means finding the norm, or average score, made by a large group of people like those for whom the test was designed. Without standardization, it would be unfair to compare the scores of people taking a test on different occasions. And without norms, there would be no way to tell if a score is high, low, or average.

Later in this chapter we will address the question of whether intelligence tests are valid. For now, let's take a practical approach, by examining some widely used standardized tests, and the meaning of scores on them.

Testing Intelligence— Making the Invisible Visible

The Stanford-Binet   American psychologists quickly recognized the usefulness of Binet's test. In 1916, **Lewis Terman** and others at Stanford University revised it for use in this country. After several more revisions, the **Stanford-Binet Intelligence Scale** is still widely used. The Stanford-Binet assumes that intellectual ability in childhood improves with increasing age. As a result, the Stanford-Binet is really a set of increasingly difficult tests, one for each age group.

The age-ranked questions of the Stanford-Binet allow a person's **mental age** to be determined. For example, at ages eight or nine, very few children can define the word "connection." At age ten, 10 percent can. At age thirteen, 60 percent can. In other words, the ability to define "connection" indicates mental ability comparable to that of the average thirteen-year-old and gives a mental age of thirteen (on this single item). Table 17-1 is a sample of items that persons of average intelligence can answer at various ages.

Mental age gives a good indication of one's actual abilities, but it says nothing about whether overall intelligence is high or low. To know the meaning of mental age, **chronological age** (age in years) must also be considered. Mental age can then be related to chronological age to yield an **IQ,** or **intelligence quotient.** IQ is defined as mental age (MA) divided by chronological age (CA) and multiplied by 100:

$$\frac{\text{MA}}{\text{CA}} \times 100 = \text{IQ}$$

An advantage of the IQ is that it allows comparison of intelligence among children with different combinations of chronological and mental ages. A ten-year-old child with a mental age of twelve has an IQ of 120:

$$\frac{\text{(MA) } 12}{\text{(CA) } 10} \times 100 = 120 \text{ (IQ)}$$

A second child having a mental age of twelve, but with a chronological age of twelve would have an IQ of 100:

$$\frac{\text{(MA) } 12}{\text{(CA) } 12} \times 100 = 100 \text{ (IQ)}$$

The IQ shows that the younger child is brighter than his twelve-year-old friend, even though their intellectual skills are actually the same. Notice that IQ equals 100 when

MA = CA. An IQ score of 100 is therefore defined as average intelligence.

Question: Then does a person with an IQ score below 100 have "below average intelligence"?

Not unless the IQ is significantly below 100. An IQ of 100 is the *mathematical* average (or mean) for such scores. "Average intelligence" is usually defined as any score from 90 to 109. The important point is to see that IQ scores will be over 100 when mental age is higher than age in years; and that IQ scores below 100 occur when age in years exceeds mental age. An example of the second possibility would be a fifteen-year-old with a MA of twelve:

$$\frac{12}{15} \times 100 = 80 \, (IQ)$$

Question: How old do children have to be before their IQ scores become stable?

Stability of IQ IQ scores are not very dependable until about age six. The correlation between IQ scores obtained at age two and those obtained at age eighteen is only 0.31. (Recall that a correlation of 1.00 indicates a perfect correspondence.) By age six the correlation to IQ at age 18 jumps to 0.61—a close enough correspondence to get an idea of adult IQ from the childhood score (Honzik *et al.,* 1948).

IQ test scores become more reliable with increasing age and there is less change when testing sessions are close together. The average change (median change) in IQ on retesting is roughly five points in either direction. However, during intellectual development children may show small increases, declines, or fluctuations in tested intelligence. No typical pattern exists, and in many cases changes in IQ of 15 points or more may take place from time to time. Overall, though, changes are usually quite small after middle childhood.

Question: How much does aging affect the IQ?

Since IQ reflects education, maturity, and experience as well as native intellectual capacity, studies of IQ change have shown a gradual increase in intellectual ability until somewhere between the ages of twenty and thirty. After age thirty, there is a gradual decline (Wechsler, 1958). Other studies have shown little or no change in intelligence due to aging (Schaie, 1980).

You may recall from the previous chapter that more recent findings on IQ and aging have clarified the contradictory results just mentioned. When general information or comprehension is emphasized, there is little decline in

Table 17-1   Sample Items from the Stanford-Binet Intelligence Scale

Two years old	On a large paper doll, points out the hair, mouth, feet, ear, nose, hands, and eyes.
	When shown a tower built of four blocks, builds one like it.
Three years old	When shown a bridge built of three blocks, builds one like it.
	When shown a drawing of a circle, copies it with a pencil.
Four years old	Fills in the missing word when asked, "Brother is a boy; sister is a ___" and "In daytime it is light; at night it is ___."
	Answers correctly when asked, "Why do we have houses?" "Why do we have books?"
Five years old	Defines *ball, hat,* and *stove.*
	When shown a drawing of a square, copies it with a pencil.
Nine years old	Answers correctly when examiner says, "In an old graveyard in Spain they have discovered a small skull which they believe to be that of Christopher Columbus when he was about ten years old. What is foolish about that?"
	Answers correctly when asked, "Tell me the name of a color that rhymes with head." "Tell me a number that rhymes with tree."
Adult	Can describe the difference between laziness and idleness, poverty and misery, character and reputation.
	Answers correctly when asked, "Which direction would you have to face so your right hand would be toward the north?"

(Terman & Merrill, 1960.)

IQ until advanced age. Tests or test items requiring speed, rapid insight, or perceptual flexibility show earlier losses and a rapid decline after middle age (Baltes and Schaie, 1974). *Overall,* age-related losses are minimal for most healthy, well-educated individuals (Schaie, 1980). Perhaps the most intriguing link between IQ and aging is the observation that impending death may be signaled by significant changes in brain function. Certain intellectual skills have been shown to decline abruptly about five years before death. This **terminal decline** in IQ can be measured even when the person appears to be in good health (Jarvik *et al.,* 1973).

Question: Is the Stanford-Binet *the only intelligence test?*

The Wechsler Test   A widely used alternative to the Stanford-Binet is the **Wechsler Adult Intelligence Scale-Revised,** or **WAIS–R.** This test also has a form adapted for use with children, called the **Wechsler Intelligence Scale for Children–Revised (WISC–R).** The Wechsler tests bear an overall similarity to the Stanford-Binet, but differ in some important respects. The WAIS–R is specifically designed to test adult intelligence, and both the WISC–R and the WAIS–R rate **performance** (nonverbal) intelligence in addition to **verbal** intelligence. The Stanford-Binet only gives one overall IQ, whereas the Wechsler tests can be broken down to reveal strengths and weaknesses in various areas. Overall IQ scores on the WAIS-R and WISC-R are always calculated directly without using the concept of mental age. The intellectual skills revealed by the Wechsler tests and some sample items are listed in Table 17-2.

Group Tests   Both the Stanford-Binet and the Wechsler tests are **individual intelligence tests** that must be administered by a specially trained tester. Other tests of intelligence have been designed for use with large groups of people. **Group intelligence tests** are usually in paper-and-pencil form and require the examinee to read, to follow instructions, and to solve problems of logic, mathematics, or the visual arrangement of figures. The first group intelligence test was the *Army Alpha,* developed for use in classifying World War I military inductees. If you're wondering if you have ever taken an intelligence test, the answer is probably yes. The Scholastic Aptitude Test (SAT), the American College Test (ACT), and the College Qualification Test (CQT) are all group tests that can be used to estimate a person's intelligence as well as his or her chances for college success.

Table 17-2   Sample Items Similar to Those Used on the WAIS-R

Verbal Subtests	Sample Items
Information	How many wings does a bird have? Who wrote *Paradise Lost?*
Digit Span	Repeat from memory a series of digits, such as 3 1 0 6 7 4 2 5, after hearing them once.
General Comprehension	What is the advantage of keeping money in a bank? Why is copper often used in electrical wires?
Arithmetic	Three men divided 18 golf balls equally among themselves. How many golf balls did each man receive? If two apples cost 15¢, what will be the cost of a dozen apples?
Similarities	In what way are a lion and a tiger alike? In what way are a saw and a hammer alike?
Vocabulary	This test consists simply of asking, "what is a _____?" or "what does _____ mean?" The words cover a wide range of difficulty or familiarity.

Performance Subtests	Description of Item
Picture Arrangement	Arrange a series of cartoon panels to make a meaningful story.
Picture Completion	What is missing from these pictures?
Block Design	Copy designs with blocks (as shown at right).
Object Assembly	Put together a jigsaw puzzle.
Digit Symbol	

1	2	3	4
X	III	I	0

Fill in the symbols:

3	4	1	3	4	2	1	2

(Courtesy of The Psychological Corporation.)

Learning Check

Check your comprehension before you continue reading.

1. The first successful intelligence test was developed by _____.

2. If we define intelligence by writing a test, we are using:

   a. a circular definition   b. an abstract definition

   c. an operational definition   d. chronological age as the definition of intelligence

3. Place an "R" or a "V" after each operation to indicate if it would be used to establish the reliability or the validity of a test.

   a. Compare score on one-half of test items to score on the other half.   (   )
   b. Compare scores on test to grades, performance ratings, or other measures.   (   )
   c. Compare scores from the test after administering it on two separate occasions.   (   )
   d. Compare actual content of test items to what is supposedly being measured.   (   )

4. IQ is defined as $\dfrac{(\quad\quad)}{(\quad\quad)} \times 100$.

5. Ability to answer general information and comprehension questions shows the most rapid decline during aging.   T or F?

6. The WAIS–R is a group intelligence test.   T or F?

7. Establishing norms and uniform procedures for administering a test are elements of standardization.   T or F?

Answers: 1. Alfred Binet 2. c 3. a.(R),b.(V),c.(R),d.(V). 4. $\dfrac{MA}{CA} \times 100$ 5. F 6. F 7. T

Variations in Intelligence— The Numbers Game

Based on observations of a large number of randomly selected people, the classifications shown in Table 17-3 have been established for various IQ ranges. A look at the percentages reveals a definite pattern. The distribution of IQs approximates a **normal** (bell-shaped) **curve** in which the majority of scores fall close to the average and relatively few at the extremes. Figure 17-1 graphically shows this characteristic of measured intelligence.

Question: On the average, do males and females differ in intelligence?

Sex IQ does not give a definite answer to this question since intelligence test items are selected to be equally difficult for both sexes. It seems safe to assume that men and women do not differ in overall intelligence, and no significant IQ difference has been found. However, tests like the WAIS–R allow a comparison of the intellectual strengths and weaknesses of men and women. Here a difference does emerge: Women perform better on test items that require verbal ability, vocabulary, and rote learning; men are best at items that require visualization of spatial relationships and arithmetic reasoning (Wechsler, 1958). It is not clear whether these differences are genetic or the result of

differences in experience associated with sex roles. In any case, differences in male and female skills balance out in general intelligence.

Question: How much do variations in IQ scores relate to success in school, jobs, and other undertakings?

School and Occupation IQ differences of a few points tell little about intellectual potential. But when a broader range of scores is considered, meaningful differences emerge. The correlation between IQ and school grades is .50—a sizable association. Furthermore, the average IQ of

Table 17-3   Distribution of Adult IQ Scores on WAIS–R

IQ	Verbal Description	Percent of Adults
Above 130	Very superior	2.2
120–129	Superior	6.7
110–119	Bright normal	16.1
90–109	Average	50.0
80– 89	Dull normal	16.1
70– 79	Borderline	6.7
Below 70	Mentally retarded	2.2

(Wechsler, 1958.)

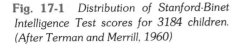

Fig. 17-1 *Distribution of Stanford-Binet Intelligence Test scores for 3184 children. (After Terman and Merrill, 1960)*

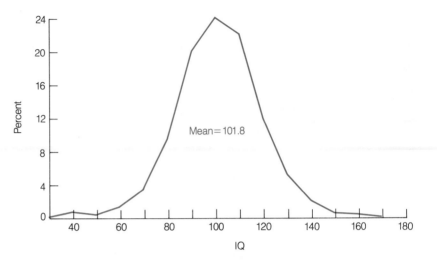

high school graduates is approximately 110; college graduates average 120; and persons who attain the Ph.D. or other advanced degrees average 130 (Cronbach, 1970).

As one might expect, there is also a relationship between IQ and job classification. Persons holding "high-status"* positions average much higher IQs than those in "lower status" occupational settings. For example, accountants average about 120 in IQ and miners about 90 (Anastasi and Foley, 1958). It is important to note, however, that there is a considerable range of IQ scores in all occupations. There are many people of high intelligence who, because of choice or circumstance, will be found in "low-ranking" occupations (Fig. 17-2).

It is tempting to interpret the association between IQ and occupation as evidence that high-status jobs require more intelligence. This interpretation is dangerous because intelligence tests as a rule require the same types of mental gymnastics as are necessary for success in school. Since higher status jobs often require an academic degree, the apparent connection between IQ and job status may be misleading. Selection procedures for professional jobs appear to be biased in favor of a particular type of intelligence; namely, the kind measured by intelligence tests.

When variations in IQ are extreme—below 70 or above 130—influences on adjustment and one's potential for success become unmistakable. Only 4.5 percent of the population score in these ranges, but this translates to about 10 million people in the United States who are exceptional by way of having very high or very low IQs. Discussions of the mentally gifted and the mentally retarded follow.

*The term *high-status* is used to refer to the traditionally higher paid business and professional occupations.

The Mentally Gifted— Is Genius Next to Insanity?

Question: How high is the IQ of a genius?

Only about 1 percent of the population scores above 140 on IQ tests. A person scoring this high is at least "gifted" and, depending on the standards used, may be considered a "genius." (Some psychologists reserve the term *genius* for even higher IQs, or for other qualities.)

Are high IQ scores in childhood associated with later ability? To directly answer this question, Lewis Terman selected 1500 children with IQs of 140 or more. By following the development of this gifted group into adulthood, Terman identified a number of popular misconceptions about genius.

Misconception: The gifted tend to be peculiar, socially backward people.
Fact: On the contrary, Terman's gifted subjects were socially well adjusted and showed above-average leadership capacity.
Misconception: "Early ripe means later rot": The gifted tend to fizzle out as adults.
Fact: This is false. When retested as adults, Terman's subjects again scored in the upper IQ ranges.
Misconception: The very bright are usually physically inferior "eggheads" or weaklings.
Fact: This is also a misconception. As a group, the gifted were above average in height, weight, and physical appearance.
Misconception: The highly intelligent person is more susceptible to mental illness ("Genius is next to insanity").
Fact: Terman demonstrated conclusively that the gifted

have better than average mental health records, indicating a greater *resistance* to mental illness.

Misconception: Intelligence has nothing to do with success, especially in practical matters.

Fact: The later success of Terman's subjects was the most striking finding of the study. As a group, they were considered to be very successful. The number who had completed college, earned advanced degrees, or held professional positions was much higher than average. Many had received special recognition for outstanding achievement such as being listed in *Who's Who* or *American Men and Women of Science*. By average age of forty, the gifted group was responsible for the production of dozens of books, thousands of scientific articles, and hundreds of short stories and other publications (Terman and Oden, 1959).

Question: Were all of the gifted children superior as adults?

No. Remember that high IQ reveals *potential,* not capacity. A high IQ is no guarantee of success. Some of the gifted had committed crimes, were unemployable, or were poorly adjusted. You have probably known people of high intelligence who seemed to be adversely affected by their intellectual gifts. Overall, however, Terman's study makes it clear that the very bright tend to be superior in many ways. (Frustrating, isn't it?)

Question: How did the more successful subjects differ from the less successful?

In a recent follow-up study, psychologists compared 100 of the most successful gifted subjects with 100 of the least successful. The highly successful subjects differed mainly in their greater *persistence* and motivation to succeed (Goleman, 1980). The meaning of this finding is clear: As one educator put it, "No one is paid to sit around being capable of achievement—what you do is always more important than what you should be able to do" (Whimbey, 1980).

Question: How might a parent spot an unusually bright child?

Early signs frequently observed in gifted children include: a tendency to seek out and identify with older children and adults; an early fascination with explanation and problem solving; talking in complete sentences as early as two or three years of age; an unusually good memory; precocious talent in art, music, or numerical skills; an early interest in books, coupled with early reading, often by age three; showing of kindness, understanding, and cooperation toward others.

Notice that this list includes behavior other than straight "academic" intelligence. Children may be gifted in ways other than that reflected by a high IQ score. In fact, if such things as artistic talent, mechanical aptitude, musical aptitude, athletic potential, and so on, are considered, 19 out of 20 children could be labeled "gifted" in some respect (Fig. 17-3) (Feldman and Bratton, 1972).

Being gifted in the sense of having a high IQ is not without its problems, particularly in childhood. The gifted child may rapidly become bored in a classroom designed for average children. Boredom can lead to behavioral problems or clashes with teachers who consider the gifted child a show-off or smart aleck. The extremely bright child may also find the company of his or her classmates less stimulating than that of older children or adults. In recognition of these problems, many school systems now provide special programs and classes for "MGM" children (Mentally Gifted Minors).

Fig. 17-2 *John Kirtley belongs to Mensa, an international organization of exceptionally intelligent people. Although his IQ score is 174, John prefers to do custodial work, feeling that his unusual intellect would be "used" by his employers if he pursued a technical occupation.*

Fig. 17-3 *It is wise to remember that there are many ways in which a child may be "gifted." Many schools now offer gifted and talented education (GATE) programs for students with a variety of special abilities—not just those who score well on IQ tests.*

Mental Retardation— A Difference That Makes a Difference

An individual with intellectual abilities significantly below average is termed **mentally retarded.** An IQ score of 70 or below has traditionally been the dividing line between normal intelligence and retardation. Below an IQ of 70, additional distinctions may be made as shown in Table 17-4.

Question: Are the retarded usually placed in institutions?

No. Total care is only necessary for the **profoundly** retarded. The **severely** and **moderately** retarded are capable of mastering basic language skills and routine self-help

Table 17-4   Levels of Mental Retardation

IQ Range	Degree of Retardation	Educational Classification
68–83	Borderline	Slow learner
52–67	Mild	Educable retarded
36–51	Moderate	Trainable retarded
20–35	Severe	Trainable retarded
Below 20	Profound	Total-care group

(Robinson and Robinson, 1970.)

skills. Many become self-supporting by working in a "sheltered workshop" (a special simplified work environment). The **mildly** retarded benefit from carefully structured and supervised education. As adults, they are capable of living alone and may marry (although they tend to have difficulties with many of the demands of adult life) (Suinn, 1975).

It is important to realize that the mentally retarded have no handicap where feelings are concerned. They are sensitive to rejection and are easily hurt by teasing or ridicule. Likewise, they respond warmly to love and acceptance. Professionals working with the retarded emphasize their rights to self-respect and to a place in the community. This is especially important during childhood, when the support of others adds significantly to the person's chances of becoming a well-adjusted member of society (Fig. 17-4).

Question: What causes mental retardation?

Causes of Retardation

About 25 percent of all cases of mental retardation are *organic,* or related to known physical disorders, including one or more of the following:

1. Birth injuries (such as a lack of oxygen) are a relatively rare but significant problem.

2. **Fetal damage** is a more common problem. Maternal drug abuse, and disease or infection contracted by the mother before birth, or by the child shortly after birth, can cause retardation.

3. **Metabolic disorders,** such as cretinism and phenylketonuria (see next section), are typical organic problems.

4. In some cases, definite **genetic abnormalities** can be identified.

Question: What about the other 75 percent of cases?

In the majority of retardation cases no known biological problem can be identified. In such cases the degree of retardation is usually mild, in the 50 to 70 IQ range, and quite often other family members are also mildly retarded (*DSM-III*, 1980).

Familial retardation, as this is called, occurs most often in very low income or impoverished households. In some such homes nutrition, early stimulation, medical care, and emotional support are inadequate. Yet, even where a child's physical needs are being met, the intellectual and educational level of the home is typically low, making the chances of familial retardation high. The positive side to this picture is that most cases of familial retardation could be prevented by improved nutrition, educational opportunities, and early childhood enrichment programs.

To conclude our discussion, let's briefly return to organic retardation for a look at several interesting and distinctive problems.

Phenylketonuria (PKU)   PKU is a genetically inherited lack of an important enzyme, which causes the buildup of phenylpyruvic acid (a destructive chemical) in the body. PKU is now easily detected in babies by medical testing during the first month of life. It can usually be controlled by a special diet low in foods containing substances the child's body can't handle.

Microcephaly   Microcephaly means small-headedness. The microcephalic suffers a rare abnormality in which the skull is extremely small or fails to grow. The brain is forced to develop in a severely limited space, causing severe retardation that usually requires the individual to be placed in an institution. The microcephalic is typically affectionate, well behaved, and easy to work with.

Hydrocephaly   Hydrocephaly (water on the brain) is caused by a buildup of cerebrospinal fluid within brain

Fig. 17-4   *This youngster is a participant in the Special Olympics—an athletic event for the mentally retarded. It is often said of the Special Olympics that, "Everyone is a winner—participants, coaches, and spectators."*

cavities. Pressure from this fluid can damage the brain, and greatly enlarge the head. Hydrocephaly is not uncommon—about 8000 babies are born with the problem each year in the United States. Thanks to new medical procedures, most of these infants will now lead normal lives. Treatment typically involves surgically implanting a tube that drains fluid from the brain into the abdomen. If this is done within the first three months of life, retardation can usually be avoided.

Cretinism   Cretinism is a form of retardation that develops in infancy due to insufficient secretion of thyroid hormone. In some parts of the world, cretinism is caused by too little iodine in the diet (iodine is necessary for normal thyroid function). Widespread use of iodized salt makes this cause of the condition rare in the United States. Cretinism causes stunted physical and intellectual growth that cannot be corrected unless detected early. Fortunately, it is easily and routinely detected in infancy and may be treated by thyroid hormone replacement.

Down's Syndrome   The disorder known as Down's syndrome causes moderate to severe retardation and a shortened life expectancy (usually around 40 years). Distinctive features of this problem, once known as *mongolism,* are almond-shaped eyes and an overly large, protrud-

ing tongue. It is now known that the Down's child also has an extra chromosome. That is, cells in the child's body have 47 chromosomes, instead of the usual 46. This condition results from flaws in the parents' egg or sperm cells. Thus, while Down's syndrome is *genetic,* it is not *hereditary,* and does not "run in the family."

A very significant factor in Down's syndrome appears to be the age of parents at the time of conception. The reproductive cells of older men and women are more prone to errors during cell division, which raises the odds that an extra chromosome will be present. Mothers in their early twenties have about 1 chance in 2000 of giving birth to a Down's syndrome baby. After age forty, the odds increase to about 1 in 46. In other words, after age forty, a woman runs roughly 50 times greater risk of having a Down's child than she does in her twenties. Recent research has also linked the age of the father to increased risk (Heber, 1970). These rather significant changes in risk should be considered in family planning. There is no "cure" for Down's syndrome. However, these children are usually loving and responsive, and they can make progress in a caring environment. Experts working with Down's syndrome children emphasize that they can do most of the things that other children can do, only slower (Pueschel *et al.,* 1978).

Learning Check

1. The distribution of IQs approximates a _____ (bell-shaped) curve.
2. The association between IQ and "high-status" jobs shows that "high-status" jobs require more intelligence.   T or F?
3. Women tend to excel on test items that require verbal ability, vocabulary, and rote learning.   T or F?
4. Only about 6 percent of the population score above 140 on IQ tests.   T or F?
5. An IQ score below 90 indicates mental retardation.   T or F?
6. Many cases of mental retardation without known organic causes appear to be _____.

Match:

7. ____ PKU
8. ____ Microcephaly
9. ____ Hydrocephaly
10. ____ Cretinism
11. ____ Down's Syndrome

A. Too little thyroid hormone
B. Very small brain
C. 47 chromosomes
D. Lack of an important enzyme
E. Excess of cerebrospinal fluid
F. Caused by a lack of oxygen at birth

Answers: 1. normal 2. F 3. T 4. F 5. F 6. familial 7. D 8. B 9. E 10. A 11. C

Heredity and Environment—
The Nature and Nurture of Intelligence

Question: Is intelligence inherited?

This seemingly simple question is loaded with controversy. Some psychologists believe intelligence is strongly affected by heredity. Many others feel that environment is dominant. Let's examine some of the evidence for each view.

In a classic study of genetic factors in learning, Tryon (1929) managed to breed separate strains of "maze-bright" and "maze-dull" rats. Tryon began by testing a large number of animals in a maze. Rats that performed best were selected and interbred, and the slowest rats were likewise mated. This procedure was continued for several generations, until separate groups of seemingly "bright" and "stupid" rats emerged. At this point, the slowest "super rat" out-performed the best "dull" rat. This and other studies of **eugenics** (selective breeding for desirable characteristics) suggest that some traits are highly influenced by heredity.

Question: That may be true, but is maze-learning really a measure of intelligence?

No, it isn't. The Tryon study seemed to show that intelligence is inherited, but later researchers found the "maze-bright" rats weren't actually *smarter* than "maze-dull" rats. The "bright" rats were simply more motivated by food and less easily distracted during testing (Whimbey, 1980). When they weren't chasing after rat chow, the "bright" rats were no more intelligent than the supposedly dull rats. Because of such problems, animal studies cannot tell us with certainty how heredity and environment affect intelligence. Let's see what human studies reveal.

Most people are aware that there is a rough correspondence between the intelligence of parents and their children, or between brothers and sisters. As Table 17-5 shows, the similarity in IQ scores among relatives grows in proportion to their closeness on the "family tree."

Question: Does that indicate that intelligence is hereditary?

Not necessarily, because brothers, sisters, and parents share similar environments as well as similar heredity. To separate heredity and environment, we need to make some select comparisons.

Twin Studies   Notice, in Table 17-5, that the IQ scores of fraternal twins are more alike than those of ordinary siblings. **Fraternal twins** come from two separate eggs fertilized at the same time. Thus, they are no more genetically

Table 17-5   Approximate Correlations Between IQ Scores for Persons with Varying Degrees of Genetic Similarity

Identical twins reared together	.87
Identical twins reared apart	.75
Fraternal twins reared together	.58
Parents and their children	.40
Siblings reared together	.36
Unrelated children reared together	.30
Unrelated children reared apart	.00

(Estimates based on data from Erlenmeyer-Kimling and Jarvik, 1963; Adams *et al.*, 1976; Horn *et al.*, 1979; and Scarr and Weinberg, 1977.)

alike than ordinary siblings. Why then, should fraternal twins' IQ scores be more similar? The reason is environmental: Parents treat twins more alike than ordinary siblings, which results in a closer match in IQs.

More striking similarities are observed with **identical twins,** who develop from a single egg and have *identical* genes. At the top of Table 17-5, you can see that identical twins who grow up in the same family have highly correlated IQs. This is what we would expect with identical heredity and highly similar environments. Now, let's consider what happens when identical twins are reared apart. As you can see, the correlation drops, but only from 0.87 to 0.75. Psychologists who emphasize genetics believe these figures show that intelligence is 70 to 80 percent hereditary (Eysenck, 1981).

Question: How do environmentalists interpret the figures?

Environmentalists point out that some separated twins differ by as much as 20 IQ points. In every case where this occurs, there are large educational and environmental differences between the twins (Whimbey, 1980). Also, separated twins are almost always placed in homes socially and educationally similar to their biological parents. This fact would tend to inflate apparent genetic effects by making the separated twins' IQs more alike (Kamin, 1981).

The Burt Controversy   For many years, hereditarians replied to the preceding point by citing the work of British psychologist Cyril Burt. Burt claimed to have studied 53 sets of separated identical twins. Their IQs, he said, were highly correlated, even though the twins were placed in homes unrelated in socioeconomic status. Unfortunately, Burt's data are now known to be a product of scholarly fraud. American psychologist Leon Kamin (1974, 1981) noticed that Burt's numbers "looked funny," and later went on to prove that Burt had made up the twins.

It is clear that Burt's twin studies cannot be counted as evidence in favor of a hereditary view of intelligence. However, hereditarians argue that most of Burt's findings have been duplicated by others (Rimland and Musinger, 1977). Be that as it may, the Burt affair has caused some psychologists to revise their thinking on the heritability of intelligence. Many now estimate it at 45 percent, and some even question this figure.

The strongest evidence for an environmental view of intelligence comes from families having one adopted child and one biological child. As Figure 17-5 shows, parents contribute genes *and* environment to their biological child. With an adopted child, they contribute only environment. If intelligence is highly genetic, the IQs of biological children should be more like their parents' IQs than are the IQs of adopted children. However, two recent studies show that children reared by the same mother resemble her in IQ to the same degree. It does not matter whether or not they share her genes (Kamin, 1981; Horn *et al.,* 1979; Scarr and Weinberg, 1977).

Question: *How much can environment alter intelligence?*

IQ and Environment In one study, striking increases in IQ were observed when children were moved from an orphanage to more stimulating environments. Twenty-five children, all considered mentally retarded and unadoptable, were moved to an institution where they received personal attention from adults. Later, these supposedly retarded children were adopted by parents who gave them love, a family, and a stimulating environment. The IQs of the children showed an average gain of 29 points. For one child, the increase was an amazing 58 points. A second group of initially less "retarded" children who remained in the orphanage *lost* an average of 26 IQ points (Skeels, 1966)!

The educational level of parents creates another interesting environmental effect. In a study done in France, IQ scores for 32 adopted children were compared with the scores of brothers and sisters who remained with the bio-

logical parents. In most cases the biological parents were poorly educated and worked in "nonprofessional" jobs. The adopted children had mostly gone to families of higher educational and socioeconomic status. It was found that average IQ scores matched almost perfectly those of children from similar family backgrounds. That is, children who stayed with their biological parents had lower IQs than their adopted brothers and sisters. Basically, the adoptees performed the same as nonadopted upper-middle-class children (Schiff *et al.,* 1978). This and the preceding study are an encouraging indication that intelligence can be raised by an improved environment.

Some environmental effects are more subtle than the previous examples indicate. Robert B. Zajonc (ZYE-onz) has found that IQ decreases as family size grows. The brightest children come from the smallest families, and within a family the brightest children are, on the average, those who are born first (Zajonc, 1975; Zajonc and Markus, 1975). Zajonc believes that each arriving baby temporarily lowers the "average intellectual level" in the family, thus making it a less stimulating environment.

Question: *If I am the last child from a large family how should I take these findings?*

Not too seriously! The average IQ score for the oldest of two children is only 10 points higher than the average for the last of nine children. Differences of this amount may mean little in terms of what a person can actually do. Also, later-born children often excel in other ways (see Chapter 18). Later-borns, for instance, usually have excellent social skills, leading to greater popularity among peers and schoolmates.

Summary In summary, few psychologists seriously believe that heredity is not a factor in intelligence, and all acknowledge that environment affects it. Estimates of the contributions of each factor continue to vary. But ultimately, both camps agree that improving social conditions or education can raise intelligence. There is probably no limit to how far *down* intelligence can go in an impoverished environment, but heredity may impose some limits on how far up IQ can go, even under ideal conditions (Scarr-Salapatek, 1971). It might help, then, to think of inherited intellectual potential as a rubber band that is stretched by outside forces. A long rubber band may be stretched more easily, but a shorter one can be stretched to the same length if enough force is applied (Stern, 1956). Of course a superior genetic "gift" may allow for a higher maximum IQ, but in the final analysis, intelligence reflects development as well as potential, nurture as well as nature.

Fig. 17-5 *Comparison of an adopted child and a biological child reared in the same family. (After Kamin, 1981.)*

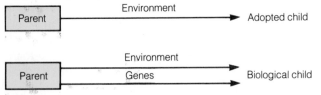

Learning Check

1. Selective breeding for desirable characteristics is called _____.

2. The closest similarity in IQs would be observed for:

   a. parents and their children   b. identical twins reared apart   c. fraternal twins reared together   d. siblings

3. Most psychologists believe that intelligence is 90 percent hereditary.   T or F?

4. Except for slight variations during testing, IQ cannot be changed.   T or F?

5. Environmental effects are probably more capable of lowering IQ than of raising it.   T or F?

6. According to the research of Robert Zajonc, children in large families provide extra stimulation for one another thereby increasing intelligence.   T or F?

Answers: 1. eugenics   2. b   3. F   4. F   5. T   6. F

Resources Summary

● *Intelligence* refers to one's general capacity to act purposefully, think rationally, and deal effectively with the environment. In practice, intelligence is *operationally defined* by the creation of intelligence tests.

● To be of any value, a psychological test must give consistent results. This aspect of a test is known as its *reliability.* A worthwhile test must also have *validity,* meaning that it measures what it claims to measure. Widely used intelligence tests are *objective* (they give the same result when scored by different people) and *standardized* (the same procedures are always used in giving the test, and norms have been established so scores can be interpreted).

● The first practical intelligence test was assembled by Alfred Binet. A modern version of Binet's test is the *Stanford-Binet Intelligence Scale.* A second major intelligence test is the *Wechsler Adult Intelligence Scale–Revised* (WAIS–R). The WAIS–R measures both *verbal* and *performance* intelligence. Intelligence tests have also been produced for use with groups. *Group tests* include the *Army Alpha,* the *SAT,* the *ACT,* and the *CQT.*

● Intelligence is expressed in terms of an *intelligence quotient* (IQ). IQ is defined as *mental age* (MA) divided by *chronological age* (CA) and then multiplied by 100. An "average" IQ of 100 occurs when mental age equals chronological age.

● IQ scores become fairly stable at about age six and they become increasingly reliable thereafter. The peak of intellectual ability typically occurs between twenty and thirty years of age, but intellectual decline is slight for most people until their seventies. Shortly before death a more significant *terminal decline* in intelligence is often observed.

● The distribution of IQ scores approximates a *normal curve.* There are no overall differences between males and females in tested intelligence, but intellectual strengths exist for each. IQ is strongly related to school grades and levels of academic achievement. There is also an association between IQ and job status, but this may be artificial.

● People with IQs in the "gifted" or "genius" range of above 140 tend to be superior in many respects. By criteria other than IQ, a large proportion of children might be considered as "gifted" in one way or another. Intellectually gifted children often have difficulties in average classrooms and benefit from special accelerated programs.

● The term "mentally retarded" is traditionally applied to those whose IQ falls below 70. Further classifications of retardation are: *mild* (52–67), *moderate* (36–51), *severe* (20–35), and *profound* (below 20). Chances for educational success are related to the degree of retardation.

● About 25 percent of the cases of mental retardation are *organic,* being caused by *birth injuries, fetal damage, metabolic disorders,* or *genetic abnormalities.* The remaining 75 percent are of undetermined cause. Many of these cases are thought to be the result of *familial retardation,* a generally low level of educational and intellectual stimulation in the home often coupled with poverty and poor nutrition.

● Five specialized forms of organic retardation are: *phenylketonuria (PKU), microcephaly, hydrocephaly, cretinism,* and *Down's Syndrome.*

● Studies of *eugenics* in animals and familial relationships in humans demonstrate that intelligence is partially determined by heredity. However, environment is also important, as revealed by drastic changes in tested intelligence brought about by stimulating environments. Intelligence reflects the combined effects of both heredity and environment on development of intellectual abilities.

━━━━━━━━━━━━━━━━━ Applications ━━━━━━━━━━━━━━━━━

Intelligence in Perspective—
Are Intelligence Tests Intelligent?

Almost everyone has some curiosity about how they would score on an intelligence test. If you would like to get a rough estimate of your IQ, take the following self-administered test.

Dove Counterbalance Intelligence Test

Time limit: 5 minutes   Circle the correct answer.

1. T-bone Walker got famous for playing what?
   a. trombone   c. T-flute   e. "hambone"
   b. piano   d. guitar

2. A "gas head" is a person who has a _____.
   a. fast-moving car   d. habit of stealing cars
   b. stable of "lace"   e. long jail record for arson
   c. "process"

3. If you throw the dice and 7 is showing on the top, what is facing down?
   a. 7   c. boxcars   e. 11
   b. snake eyes   d. little joes

4. Cheap chitlings (not the kind you purchase at a frozen-food counter) will taste rubbery unless they are cooked long enough. How soon can you quit cooking them to eat and enjoy them?
   a. 45 minutes   d. one week (on a low flame)
   b. two hours   e. one hour
   c. 24 hours

5. Bird or Yardbird was the jacket jazz lovers from coast to coast hung on _____?
   a. Lester Young   d. Charlie Parker
   b. Peggy Lee   e. Birdman of Alcatraz
   c. Benny Goodman

6. A "handkerchief head" is:
   a. a cool cat   c. an Uncle Tom   e. a preacher
   b. porter   d. a hoddi

7. Jet is _____.
   a. an East Oakland motorcycle club
   b. one of the gangs in *West Side Story*
   c. a news and gossip magazine
   d. a way of life for the very rich

8. "Bo Diddly" is a _____.
   a. game for children   d. new dance
   b. down-home cheap wine   e. Moejoe call
   c. down-home singer

9. Which word is most out of place here?
   a. splib   c. gray   e. black
   b. blood   d. spook

10. If a pimp is uptight with a woman who gets state aid, what does he mean when he talks about "Mother's Day"?
   a. second Sunday in May
   b. third Sunday in June
   c. first of every month
   d. none of these
   e. first and fifteenth of every month

11. How much does a "short dog" cost?
   a. 15¢   c. 35¢   e. 86¢ plus tax
   b. $2   d. 5¢

12. Many people say that "Juneteenth" (June 10th) should be made a legal holiday because this was the day when:
   a. the slaves were freed in the United States
   b. the slaves were freed in Texas
   c. the slaves were freed in Jamaica
   d. the slaves were freed in California
   e. Martin Luther King was born
   f. Booker T. Washington died

13. If a man is called a "blood," then he is a _____.
   a. fighter   d. hungry hemophile
   b. Mexican-American   e. red man or Indian
   c. Negro

14. What are the Dixie Hummingbirds?
   a. a part of the KKK
   b. a swamp disease
   c. a modern gospel group
   d. a Mississippi Negro paramilitary strike force
   e. deacons

15. The opposite of square is _____
   a. round   c. down   e. lame
   b. up   d. hip

Applications

If you scored 14 on this exam, your IQ is approximately 100, indicating average intelligence. If you scored 11 or less you are mentally retarded. With luck and the help of a special educational program, we may be able to teach you a few simple skills!

Race and IQ

Question: Isn't this test a little unfair?

No, it is *very* unfair. It was constructed by black sociologist Adrian Dove as "a half serious attempt to show that we're just not talking the same language." Dove tried to slant his test as much in favor of urban black culture as he believes the typical intelligence test is biased toward a white middle-class background.

Dove's test is a thought-provoking reply to the fact that black children in the United States score an average of about 15 points lower on standardized IQ tests than do white children. By reversing the bias Dove has shown that intelligence tests are not equally valid for all groups. As Kagan (1973) has commented, "If the Wechsler and Binet scales were translated into Spanish, Swahili, and Chinese and given to every ten-year-old in Latin America, East Africa, or China, the majority would obtain IQ scores in the mentally retarded range."

Certainly we cannot believe that children of different cultures are all retarded. The fault must lie in the test. In recognition of this problem, some psychologists are trying to develop **culture-fair tests** that will not disadvantage certain groups. (For a sample of culture-fair test items, see Fig. 17-6.)

Biased tests are not the only IQ issue blacks have confronted. Arthur Jensen, writing in the *Harvard Educational Review,* claimed in 1969 that the lower IQ scores of blacks can be primarily attributed to "genetic heritage." Jensen was soon joined by William Shockley, a physicist, who made blatantly racist statements. According to Shockley, "Nature has color-coded groups of individuals" so that their "intellectual adaptability" may be easily recognized (Shockley, 1972).

Before we go any further, it is important to note that few psychologists support either Jensen or Shockley.

Shockley, in fact, may simply be dismissed as highly prejudiced and naive in his confusion of IQ (a score on a test) and intelligence.

Question: What about Jensen's claim?

Soon after Jensen claimed that differences in the average IQ for whites and blacks are genetic, psychologists responded with a number of counterarguments.

First, it is no secret that as a group blacks in the United States are more likely than whites to live in environments that are physically, educationally, and intellectually impoverished.

Second, even if we assume that the gap in IQ between blacks and whites is hereditary, it is small enough to be corrected by environment. Jensen's reply to this claim is that special educational programs such as Head Start have proved incapable of narrowing the IQ gap. But it is essentially ridiculous to expect that a brief summer program or a few hours a day are enough to counteract the differences

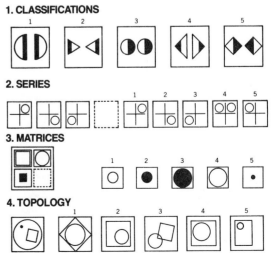

Fig. 17-6 *Sample items from a culture fair test. 1. Which pattern is different from the remaining four? (Number 3.) 2. Which of the five figures on the right would properly continue the three on the left, i.e., fill blank? (Number 5.) 3. Which of the figures on the right should go in the square on the left to make it look right? (Number 2.) 4. At left, the dot is outside the square and inside the circle. In which of the figures on the right could you put a dot outside the square and inside the circle? (Number 3.) (Courtesy of R. B. Cattell.)*

1. CLASSIFICATIONS

2. SERIES

3. MATRICES

4. TOPOLOGY

Applications

in educational and environmental advantages of blacks and whites.

Third, Jensen ignores the point made by the Dove Test. The assumptions, biases, and content of standard IQ tests do not allow meaningful comparisons between ethnic, cultural, or racial groups (Garcia, 1977). As Leon Kamin (1981) says, "The important fact is that we cannot say which sex (or race) might be more intelligent, because we have no way of measuring 'intelligence.' We have only IQ tests." Kamin's point is that the makers of IQ tests decided in advance to use test items that would give men and women equal IQ scores. It would be just as easy to put together an IQ test that would give blacks and whites in this country equal scores. Differences in IQ scores are not a fact of nature, but a decision by the test-makers. This is why whites do better on IQ tests written by whites and blacks do better on IQ tests devised by blacks. Another example of this fact is an intelligence test made up of 100 words selected from the *Dictionary of Afro-American Slang*. Williams (1975) gave the test to 100 black and 100 white high school students in St. Louis and found that the black group averaged 36 points higher than the white group.

Perhaps the most devastating criticism of Jensen is that his logic is faulty. Consider this example: Corn comes in different varieties selectively bred to grow to a certain height. If we plant tall and short varieties side by side in the same field, we will observe a genetically determined difference in their height at maturity. But what if we take corn (all the same variety) and plant half in a fertile field and half in poor soil? Again we observe a difference in maximum height, but this time it is obviously a mistake to assume that it is genetically caused.

Only when black children are raised in exactly the same surroundings as white children can hereditary factors be clearly assessed. Along this line, a recent study looked at the fate of black children adopted by white families. These children had IQ scores averaging 106, which is comparable to the national average for white children (Scarr-Salapatek and Weinberg, 1975). It is not clear if the black children were actually "brighter" as a result of this experience or if they were just better prepared to take a "white" test. The fact remains, however, that when an equal opportunity for intellectual development is capable of closing the IQ gap, then the genetic view of IQ differences must be abandoned.

Questioning the Concept of IQ— Beyond the Numbers Game

Blacks are not the only segment of the population with reason to question the validity of intelligence testing and the role of heredity in determining intelligence. The clarifications won by blacks extend to others as well.

Consider the nine-year-old child confronted with this question on a classroom-administered intelligence test: "Which of the following does not belong with the others? Roller skates, airplane, train, bicycle." If the child misses the question, does this reveal a lack of intelligence? It can be argued that an intelligent choice could be based on any of these alternatives: Roller skates are not typically used for transportation; an airplane is the only non-land item; a train can't be steered; a bicycle is the only item with just two wheels (after Sheils and Monroe, 1976). The parents of a child who misses this question may have reason to be angry since educational systems tend to classify children and then make the classification stick.

Recent court decisions have led some states to outlaw use of intelligence tests in public schools (see "Exploration" section). Criticism of intelligence testing has also come from the academic community. Harvard University psychologist David McClelland (1973) believes IQ is of little value in predicting real competence to deal effectively with the world. McClelland concedes that IQ predicts school performance, but when he compared a group of college students with straight A's to another group with poor grades, he found no differences in later career success.

Standardized Testing In addition to IQ tests, 400 to 500 million standardized multiple-choice tests are given in schools and workplaces around the nation each year. Many, like the Scholastic Aptitude Test (SAT), may determine whether a person is admitted to college. Other tests —for employment, licensing, and certification—directly affect the lives of thousands by qualifying or disqualifying them for jobs.

The power of such tests is revealed by a study of admissions at colleges that claimed to take into account such factors as high school grades, employment, and extracurricular achievements (science projects, awards and prizes in art, music, writing, social service, and so forth). Wing and Wallach (1971) found that even when college admis-

Applications

sions officers said they weighed outside indications of talent, in reality their admissions could be predicted almost perfectly by SAT scores.

Widespread reliance on standardized intelligence tests and aptitude tests raises questions about the relative good and harm they do. On the positive side, tests can open opportunities as well as close them. A high test score may allow a disadvantaged youth to enter college, or it may identify a child who is bright but emotionally disturbed. Test scores may also be fairer and more objective than arbitrary judgments made by admissions officers or employment interviewers. Also, tests *do* accurately predict academic performance. The fact that academic performance *does not* predict later success may call for an overhaul of college course work, not an end to testing.

On the negative side, mass testing frequently excludes people of obvious ability. In one recent case, a student who was seventh in his class at Columbia University, and a member of Phi Beta Kappa, was denied entrance to law school because he had low scores on the Law School Admissions Test (*U.S. News and World Report,* May 14, 1979). Other complaints relate to the frequent appearance of bad or ambiguous questions on standardized tests, overuse of class time to prepare students to do better on the tests, and in the case of intelligence tests, the charge that tests are often biased.

What should we make of the positive and negative aspects of standardized testing? Robert Glaser says we should remember that tests are ''limited tools for limited purposes.'' Glaser (1977) also says that tests are now used primarily to *select* people. In schools they could instead be used to *adapt* instruction to the strengths, weaknesses, and needs of each student—thereby increasing the chances of success.

Conclusion

An application of the preceding discussion to your personal understanding of intelligence can be summarized in this way. Intelligence tests are a two-edged sword; we have learned much from their use, yet they have the potential to do great harm. In the final analysis, it is important to remember that creativity, motivation, physical health, mechanical aptitude, artistic ability, and numerous other qualities not measured by intelligence tests contribute to achievement of life goals. Also remember that *IQ is not intelligence.* IQ is an *index* of intelligence (as defined by a particular test). Change the test and you change the score. An IQ is not some permanent number stamped on the forehead of a child that forever determines potential.

Let us end on an optimistic note. Rather than getting caught in the debate about hereditary and environmental factors in intelligence, or the validity of intelligence tests, some psychologists and educators are seeking ways to teach necessary intellectual skills to all children. In some cases their success has been striking.

One experiment divided 40 children from extremely disadvantaged (slum) families into two groups. Children in the control group received no extra attention or training. Beginning shortly after birth, the experimental group was given a wide variety of stimulation to develop perceptual, motor, and language abilities. At age two, the children were placed in small classes with other children and several teachers. Each child received lots of teacher attention and exposure to a broad range of topics and thinking exercises. When tested at age $5\frac{1}{2}$, the average IQ for the control group was about 95; the average for the experimentals was 124 (reported by Whimbey, 1980). These results should be encouraging to everyone interested in the fulfillment of human potentials.

Learning Check

1. The *WAIS-R, Stanford-Binet,* and *Dove Test* are all culture-fair intelligence scales.   T or F?
2. Jensen's claim that genetics account for racial differences in average IQ ignores environmental differences and the cultural bias inherent in standard IQ tests.   T or F?
3. IQ scores predict school performance.   T or F?
4. IQ is not intelligence, it is an index of intelligence.   T or F?

Answers: 1. F 2. T 3. T 4. T

The Larry P. Case—"Six-Hour Retardates"

The case: Larry P. vs. the California State Superintendent of Education.

The issue: Larry P. is one of six black children who claim that biased IQ test scores were wrongly used to place them in classes for the educable mentally retarded (EMR).

The outcome: In a landmark decision, federal judge Robert Peckham ruled that IQ test scores alone can no longer be used for EMR placement. The ruling has virtually eliminated IQ testing in California schools. It is likely to do the same in many other states.

The bare facts of the Larry P. case only hint at the interesting issues it raised. Testimony during the trial brought out the following:

For Larry P.: All six youngsters suing the state had scored below 75 on standardized IQ tests. But they scored from 17 to 35 points higher when retested by psychologists who used language and examples the children were familiar with.

For the State: Experts admitted that IQ test questions can be easier for some groups than for others. However, they held that IQ tests accurately predict school performance, and are therefore valid.

For Larry P.: Witnesses pointed out that EMR assignments are almost always permanent. They also described the devastating effects of placing a child of normal intelligence in an EMR class. One researcher found that other students commonly refer to EMR students with cruel nicknames. EMR students are not expected to progress beyond the third- to fifth-grade level. Thus, by the time of graduation, a child of normal intelligence would be hopelessly behind other students. After graduation, EMR students find it difficult to get jobs, because they have been labeled "retarded."

For the State: Defense experts claimed that IQ tests help prevent mistakes in EMR assignments—for example, by revealing the true potential of a child who might be considered "slow" by a biased teacher. They also defended the EMR program as an effort to help less able students.

For Larry P.: Roughly twice as many black and Hispanic children are found in EMR classes than would normally be expected—a fact suggesting a defect in the tests, not in the children (Ristow, 1978).

Ignorance vs. Stupidity   In the end, Judge Peckham ruled that IQ tests violate federal antidiscrimination laws. He was convinced, he said, that they are based mainly on verbal tasks that are unfair to children whose home environment does not provide practice in formal English or verbal skills. He further held that, ". . . if tests suggest that a young child is probably going to be a poor student, the school cannot on that basis alone, deny that child the opportunity to develop and improve the academic skills necessary for success in our society" (from *Psychology Today,* February, 1980, p. 120).

During the trial, a substitute judge trying to get his bearings made this comment: The case, he said, seemed to rest on "confusion over the difference between ignorance and stupidity." Although a little blunt, this clearly states the court's final ruling. Supporters of the Larry P. decision believe it affirms the rights of disadvantaged children, whose ignorance—a lack of knowledge—has been mistaken for stupidity—a lack of intelligence. One such supporter is Dr. Jane Mercer, a sociologist who gave key testimony in the case.

Six-hour Retardates   Mercer testified that the more a child's family is like the average white Anglo middle-class norm, the better the child scores on IQ tests. Mercer believes that schools often label children retarded when actually the children only lack culturally tied knowledge (Mercer, 1977). Mercer has found that many black or Hispanic EMR students show abundant signs of normal intelligence. A child who does poorly in the classroom or on an IQ test may function perfectly well at home and in the community. Mercer refers to such children as "six-hour retardates"—youngsters who are "retarded" only during the school day.

Question: If standardized IQ tests cannot be used to assess student abilities, what can?

Exploration

SOMPA Dr. Mercer and her associate June Lewis think they have an answer. They call it *SOMPA*, which stands for *System of Multicultural Pluralistic Assessment.* SOMPA is not a new test. Rather, it's a controversial new way of looking at children. Because it takes cultural differences into account, SOMPA is the only system that currently meets standards established by the Larry P. case.

Question: How does SOMPA differ from standard IQ tests?

SOMPA combines three ways of looking at a child:

A Medical Model SOMPA uses existing tests to determine if a child has any problems with dexterity, vision, hearing, or general health. These tests identify physical problems that may be causing low school performance.

A Social Model Scores on the standard WISC–R are combined with evaluations of the child's behavior outside the classroom. By determining how the child functions with family, friends, and in the community, the school psychologist can avoid the mistake of creating a "six-hour retardate" on the basis of a test score.

A Pluralistic Model SOMPA assumes that when everything else is held constant (educational advantages at home, especially), the child who has learned the most probably has the most "learning potential." Off-campus environments, however, are not equal. SOMPA therefore assumes that true potential can be masked by a child's cultural background. To avoid this problem, SOMPA compares each child's WISC–R score with those of children from similar backgrounds. The result is what Mercer calls a child's Estimated Learning Potential (ELP). Mercer considers ELP a truer measure of a child's intelligence than the standard IQ (Mercer, 1977).

To show how SOMPA works, Mercer offers an example. Maria Gonzales is seven years old. She lives with her mother, father, and five brothers and sisters in an inner city barrio. Maria's mother and father were both reared in rural Mexico, where the mother finished fourth grade and the father, second grade. Maria's family speaks only Spanish. The average score for a child like Maria—with a background so different from core Anglo culture—is about 85. Maria's score on the WISC–R was 114, almost 30 points above this average. Mercer estimates Maria's real learning potential at 133. If her family had been more like the middle-class norm, Maria's score would have remained at 114. Considering her age and background, Maria's performance on the WISC–R is truly outstanding (Mercer, 1977). Maria is probably a gifted child whose potential should not be wasted.

The idea behind SOMPA, then, is to keep average kids out of classes for the mentally retarded, and to identify gifted children who might otherwise be passed over as average. If Mercer is correct in her thinking, SOMPA may launch a new generation of intelligence measures, and spur new ways to meet the educational needs of children from differing backgrounds.

Understandably, both the Larry P. decision and SOMPA are controversial. Some psychologists object to the courts making educational decisions. Others are uncomfortable with the idea of using multiple norms to interpret IQ test scores. If you were Judge Peckham, how would you have ruled? If you were a school psychologist, how would you feel about using SOMPA? In your opinion, what role should IQ tests have in a democratic society?

Questions for Discussion

1. In what ways might our society encourage the development of different intellectual skills in males and females?

2. Do you know your IQ? Would you like to know it? Why?

3. What advantages or disadvantages would you expect to be associated with knowing your own IQ? With having a teacher know your IQ? With your parents knowing your IQ?

4. How might public education be restructured to encourage full intellectual development for all children? How might grading be changed to reflect broader definitions of intelligence?

5. How would you feel about the application of eugenics to human reproduction? Can you think of circumstances under which you would or would not consider it acceptable?

6. The debate over the relative importance of heredity and environment in determining intelligence has raged for decades. Why do you think the debate has lasted so long, and attracted so much interest? If the heritability of IQ could be known with certainty, what difference would it make?

Suggestions for Further Reading

Cronbach, L. *Essentials of Psychological Testing.* 3rd ed. Harper and Row, 1970.

Eysenck, H. J., and L. Kamin. *The Intelligence Controversy.* Wiley, 1981.

Garcia, J. "IQ: The Conspiracy," *Psychology Today* (April), 1972, pp. 40–43.

Goleman, D. "1,528 Little Geniuses and How They Grew." *Psychology Today* (February) 1980, p. 28 ff.

Kamin, L. J. *The Science and Politics of IQ.* Erlbaum/Wiley, 1974.

Pines, M. "Superkids," *Psychology Today* (January) 1979, pp. 53–63.

Rosenthal, R., and L. Jacobson. *Pygmalion in the Classroom.* Holt, 1968.

18

Personality: Traits, Types, and Testing

═════════════ Chapter Preview ═════════════

The Hidden Essence

Rural Colorado. A dirt road as rough, in miniature, as the surrounding peaks. The car lurched and complained as we picked our way through the last few yards of brain-jarring ruts. An ancient farmhouse—obviously a terminal case—stood to one side, a hulking monument to neglect.

Annette was out of the house—hooting and whooping—before we had stopped. If anyone were suited for a move to the "wilds" of Colorado it was Annette, the "terror of Tenth Street." Still, it was difficult to imagine a more radical change. After separating from her husband, she had traded housewifery in the city for survival in the hinterlands. Survival, by the way, is no exaggeration. Annette was working as a ranch hand and as a lumberjack, trying to make it alone through some hard winters.

So radical were the changes in Annette's life, I must confess I expected just as radical a change in her. She was, on the contrary, more her "old self" than ever.

Perhaps you have had a similar experience. After several years of separation it is always intriguing to see an old friend. Often, you will be struck at first by the ways in which the person has changed in appearance, interests, knowledge, and so forth. Soon, however, you will probably be pleased to discover how superficial such changes really are. Under it all there is a core that ties the semistranger before you to the person you once knew. It is exactly this core of consistency that psychologists have in mind when they use the term personality.

The Extra Dimension *Personality touches many aspects of our daily lives. Selecting a mate, choosing friends, getting along with co-workers, voting for a president, and numerous other activities raise questions about personality. And despite our advanced technology, the human dimension still determines success or failure in many situations. Human error contributed significantly to the Three Mile Island Nuclear Power Plant accident. Similarly, it is often said that the most dangerous part of an automobile is "the nut at the wheel." Even when the engineering problems of extended space flight are solved, the human element will remain: Can humans withstand prolonged confinement without serious personality clashes? It is easy to imagine a conversation such as this:*

413

"Mission Control, this is Colonel Willis. Please inform Colonel Rapp that I am beginning a sleep cycle."

"Mission Control, this is Colonel Rapp. Please tell Colonel Willis that if he would work more and sleep less, we would be on schedule."

"Now just a minute Rapp, you're the one who held up the meteorological report, not to mention the . . ."

Clearly, space travelers will have to be selected for maturity, stability, and compatible personalities. But what is personality? How does it differ from temperament, character, or attitudes? How stable are personality characteristics? These and related questions are the concern of this chapter.

Survey Questions   How do psychologists use the term *personality?* Does body build have any connection to personality? Are some personality traits more basic or important than others? Does being a first child, or a later child, have any effect on personality? How do psychologists measure or assess personality? What are the advantages and limitations of each method? What causes shyness? What is psychological androgyny (and is it contagious)?

Resources

Do You Have Personality?

"Jim's not handsome, but he has a great personality." "My father's business friends think he's a nice guy, but they never see him at home where his real personality comes out." "The girls are such a paradox. They have completely different personalities." Statements such as these are made so effortlessly and with such authority that we often believe people know what personality is. But when questioned, many people stammer and finally say something about "charm," "charisma," "character," or simply that some people have "more personality" than others. If you have used the term *personality* in such ways, you have given it a different meaning than a psychologist would. To a psychologist it makes little sense to ask, "Do I have personality?" or to proclaim, "She has lots of personality." In psychological terms, everyone has personality.

Question: Then how do psychologists use the term?

Since personality is a *hypothetical construct,** psychologists give it different meanings. However, most regard **personality** as a person's *unique and enduring behavior patterns.* In other words, personality refers to the consistency in what a person is, has been, and will become. It also refers to the

singular combination of talents, attitudes, values, hopes, loves, hates, and habits that marks each person as unique.

Question: How is psychologists' use of the term different from the way most people use it?

Many people confuse personality with what is technically known as **character.** The term *character* implies that a person has been *evaluated,* not just described. If, by saying someone has "personality," you mean that person is friendly, enthusiastic, moderate, honest, open, or loving, you are really referring to character. By saying someone has "lots of personality," you reveal what you like, not the "amount" of personality possessed. In some cultures, a person with "good character" is fierce, aggressive, and competitive. In other cultures, cooperation, humility, and restraint are valued. Thus, while everyone in a particular culture has personality, not everyone has character—or at least not good character. (Do you know any good characters?)

   An additional distinction can be made between personality and **temperament.** Temperament is the "raw material" from which personality is formed. Temperament refers to the hereditary aspects of one's emotional nature: sensitivity, strength and speed of response, prevailing mood, and fluctuations in mood (Allport, 1961).

   Personality is very difficult to study because it cannot be directly observed. The remainder of this chapter is devoted

---

*An explanatory concept that is not directly observable.

to discussion of techniques and approaches that have helped pin down this elusive concept.

Personality Types—Which Are You?

The study of **personality types** is a natural extension of interest in personality. Informally, we speak of the hot-tempered redhead, the executive type, the athletic type, the motherly type, the strong, silent type, and the like. Informal conceptions of personality types abound.

Question: How valid is it to speak of personality "types"?

Psychologists have been hesitant to adopt most type systems because they oversimplify personality. Consider the idea, first proposed by Swiss psychiatrist Carl Jung, that a person is either an **introvert** (shy, self-centered person) or an **extrovert** (bold, outgoing person). These terms have become so widely accepted that many people think of themselves and their friends as belonging to one category or the other. However, the wildest, wittiest, most party-loving "extrovert" you know is introverted at times, and extremely introverted persons are assertive and sociable in some situations. Rather than classify people, it may make better sense to rate them in degrees of introversion or extroversion. Yet, even if this is done, we will find that most people fall somewhere in the middle, between the extremes.

Another example of a type system is William Sheldon's **constitutional theory** of personality.

Body Build and Personality   In the early 1950s, Sheldon became interested in the possibility that a connection exists between body build and personality. Sheldon (1954) carefully analyzed body dimensions of thousands of male college students and concluded that physique can be described as a combination of three basic components: **endomorphy, mesomorphy,** and **ectomorphy.** Endomorphy is characterized by a fat, soft, round body structure. (Sheldon noted that endomorphs float in water!) Mesomorphy is marked by a robust development of muscles, bones, and ligaments. This gives the body a hard, muscular, or angular appearance. (Mesomorphy is not necessarily an athletic body. A "walking muscle" might be a more apt description.) Ectomorphy is characterized by underdeveloped muscles and bones. The ectomorph is flat-chested, thin, fragile, and linear. (But has a large head!)

Question: How can I tell if I am an endomorph, mesomorph, or ectomorph?

Fig. 18-1   *Does this man have personality? Do you?*

You are probably none of these. "Pure" examples of each physique are rare. The average person's **somatotype** (body type) is a mixture of all three components. In rating body structure, a number from 1 to 7 is assigned to each dimension. The average person is rated around 4 on each (see Fig. 18-2).

Question: What connection did Sheldon find between body type and personality?

Sheldon compared ratings on 60 personality characteristics with the three body types. Three personality types emerged: **viscerotonia, somatotonia,** and **cerebrotonia.**

Viscerotonia combines sociability, tolerance, and goodwill with a love of eating, sleeping, and physical comfort. Somatotonia is characterized by assertiveness, boldness, energy, aggression, a callous attitude toward the feelings of others, and a love of physical exercise. The cerebrotonic individual is self-conscious, shy, sensitive, nervous, and has a need for privacy and intellectual stimulation.

It may come as no surprise to learn that Sheldon found a strong association between endomorphy and viscero-

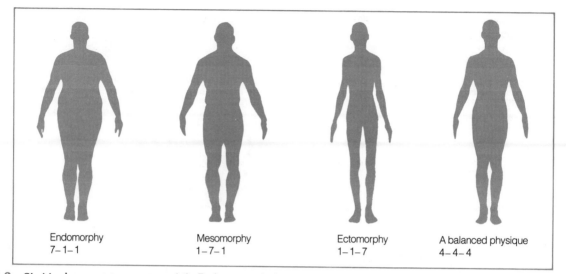

| Endomorphy | Mesomorphy | Ectomorphy | A balanced physique |
| 7–1–1 | 1–7–1 | 1–1–7 | 4–4–4 |

Fig. 18-2   *Sheldon's somatotype system. A 1–7–1 type might be a gymnast or an Olympic weight lifter. Many high-fashion models are 1–1–7 types. A sumo wrestler is typically a 7–1–1 type.*

tonia, mesomorphy and somatotonia, and ectomorphy and cerebrotonia. But before you leap to conclusions about yourself or your friends, remember that most people are a mixture of the three body types. Also, notice that Sheldon's findings reflect *stereotyped* images of fat, muscular, and thin persons. It is very likely that Sheldon was influenced by such stereotypes when he rated the personalities of his subjects.

Question: Then is there a relationship between body type and personality or isn't there?

Current thought recognizes that body types may have some influence on personality. For example, it is possible that people with a particular body type are more likely to succeed at certain activities. The muscular mesomorph's boldness, for instance, could reflect greater success at bullying others (Cortes and Gatti, 1972). In addition, the same cultural stereotypes that influenced Sheldon may also affect personality development. In the final analysis, it seems fair to assume that body type plays a role in personality formation, but rarely is it an overriding factor. It is as big a mistake to judge people by their bodies as it is to judge books by their covers.

Ultimately, most systems of personality "types" oversimplify, and fail to adequately reflect personality differences. A much more effective approach is based on the concept of personality *traits*. If you have resisted the idea of putting yourself in an all-or-nothing category, be it introvert, extrovert, endomorph, or whatever, then you may find the trait approach to personality more satisfying.

The Trait Approach— Personality as Consistency

How many words can you think of to describe the personality of a close friend? You should have little trouble making a long list: Over 18,000 English words refer to personal characteristics (Allport and Odbert, 1936). Many of these words describe personality *traits*. **Traits** are *relatively permanent* and *enduring qualities* that a person shows in most situations. For example, if you are usually optimistic, reserved, or friendly, these qualities might be considered stable traits of your personality.

Question: What if I am sometimes pessimistic, uninhibited, or shy?

The first three characteristics are still traits as long as they are *most typical* of your behavior. Let's say Ima Student approaches most situations with optimism, but has a habit of expecting the worst each time she takes a test. If her pessimism is limited to this situation or to a few others, it is still accurate and useful to describe her as an optimistic person.

In general, the trait approach attempts to specify those traits which best describe a particular individual. Take a moment to check traits in Table 18-1 that you feel are descriptive of your personality. Are the traits you checked of equal importance? Are some stronger or more basic than others? Do any overlap? For example, if you checked "dominant," did you also check "confident" and "bold"? Answers to these questions would interest a **trait theorist.** To understand personality, trait theorists attempt to classify traits and to reduce them to a manageable number by discovering which are most basic.

Question: Are there different kinds of traits?

Classifying Traits Gordon Allport (1961), a psychologist who has written extensively about personality traits, identifies several types of traits. **Common traits** are those shared by most members of a culture. Common traits reveal similarities among people of a particular national origin or linguistic background, but they tell us little about individual members of a culture. Since we know that no two people are exactly alike, we must also consider unique personal characteristics, or **individual traits.**

If the difference between common traits and individual traits is unclear, consider this illustration: Each person's hand is unique in the details of its shape (individual traits), but in an anatomy class we can still describe the characteristics of "hands in general" (common traits). Thus, Allport felt that by studying traits we could discover what is true of personalities in general at the same time that we could improve our understanding of individual personalities. The study of personality in general has been called the *nomothetic approach,* and the detailed study of a single individual, the *idiographic approach.*

Allport also made distinctions among **cardinal traits, central traits,** and **secondary traits.** Cardinal traits are so basic that all of a person's activities can be traced to existence of the trait. It is said, for instance, that an overriding factor in the life of Albert Schweitzer was "reverence for every living thing." Likewise, Abraham Lincoln's personality was dominated by the cardinal trait of honesty. According to Allport, few people have cardinal traits.

Question: How do central and secondary traits differ from cardinal traits?

Central traits are the basic building blocks that make up the core of personality. Allport found that a surprisingly small number of central traits is sufficient to capture the essence of a person. College students asked to write a short description of someone they knew well mentioned an average of only 7.2 central traits (Allport, 1961).

In contrast, secondary traits are less consistent and less important aspects of a person. For this reason, any number of secondary traits could be listed in a personality description. Secondary traits include such things as food preferences, attitudes, political opinions, and reactions to particular situations. In Allport's terms, a personality description might therefore include:

Table 18-1 Adjective Checklist

Check the traits you feel are characteristic of your personality. Are some more basic than others?

aggressive	organized	ambitious
confident	loyal	generous
warm	bold	cautious
sensitive	mature	talented
sociable	busy	funny
dominant	dull	accurate
humble	uninhibited	future-oriented
thoughtful	serious	helpful
orderly	anxious	conforming
liberal	curious	optimistic
meek	neighborly	passionate
kind	compulsive	honest
cheerful	emotional	good-natured
clever	calm	reliable
jealous	religious	nervous

Name: Jane Doe
Age: 22
Cardinal traits: None
Central traits: Possessive, autonomous, artistic, dramatic, self-centered, trusting
Secondary traits: Prefers colorful clothes, likes to work alone, politically liberal, always late, and so forth

Source Traits A second major approach to the study of personality traits is illustrated by the work of Raymond B. Cattell (1965). Cattell was dissatisfied with merely classifying traits. Instead, he wanted to reach deeper into personality to learn how traits are organized and interrelated.

Cattell began by studying characteristics making up the visible portions of personality. He called these **surface traits.** Through use of questionnaires, direct observation, and life records, Cattell assembled data on the surface traits of a large number of people. He then noted that surface traits often appear in *clusters,* or groupings. In fact, some traits appeared together so often they seemed to represent a single more basic trait. Cattell called such underlying personality characteristics **source traits.**

Question: How do source traits differ from Allport's "central traits"?

The main difference is that Allport classified traits subjectively, whereas Cattell used a statistical technique called **factor analysis** to reduce surface traits to source traits. Factor analysis uses groups of correlations to identify traits that are interrelated. With factor analysis Cattell developed a list of 16 underlying source traits. He considers this the number of basic characteristics necessary to adequately describe an individual personality.

Cattell's list of source traits also forms the basis of a personality test called the *Sixteen Personality Factor Questionnaire* (often referred to as the *16 PF*). Like many personality tests of its type, the 16 PF can be used to produce a **trait profile.** A trait profile is a graphic representation of the scores obtained by an individual on each trait. Trait profiles can be very helpful for obtaining a "picture" of an individual personality or for making comparisons between the personalities of two or more persons (see Fig. 18-3).

The Trouble with Traits   Let's say you have observed that a friend seems to be aggressive in many situations. Someone asks why your friend seems so aggressive. You explain that aggressiveness is a trait of his personality. Have you actually explained his behavior? Let's review the logic involved. How do we know your friend has the trait of aggressiveness? Because he acts aggressively. And why does he act aggressively? Because he has the trait of aggres-

siveness. And how do we know he has this trait? Because he acts aggressively. And why does he act aggressively?

Without going any further, the *circularity* of a trait approach to personality can be easily seen. Traits are a good way to describe personality, but they often do little to explain behavior. For this reason, many psychologists have shown interest in developing models or theories of personality. (A discussion of personality theories is found in the next chapter.)

Birth Order—Personality by Position?

Without exception you are one of the following: the oldest or only child in your family, a middle child, or the youngest. If you had it to do over again, which would you choose to be? Your answer could depend on the personality traits you would most like to have. Birth order, or **ordinal position,** in a family can leave a lasting imprint on adult personality.

Question: What traits are associated with birth order?

The clearest differences are between **firstborn** and **later-born** children. The firstborn seem to have a higher chance of achieving eminence than later-born. Freud, Kant,

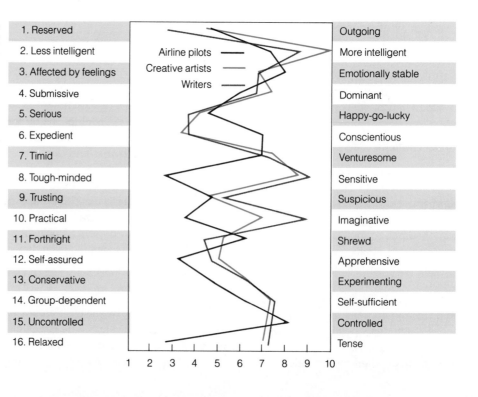

Fig. 18-3 *The 16 source traits measured by Cattell's 16PF are listed on the left. Scores can be graphed as a profile for an individual or a group. Profiles shown are group averages for airline pilots, creative artists, and writers. Notice the similarity between artists and writers and the difference between these two and pilots. (After Cattell, 1973.)*

Beethoven, Dante, Einstein, and a disproportionately large number of other eminent men and women were firstborn children (Harris, 1964). Firstborns have better high school and college grade averages. More firstborns become National Merit Scholars, and more are medical students or graduate students. Of the last 36 presidents, 20 were firstborn, as were most of this country's astronauts. More firstborns are listed in *Who's Who in America* (Harris, 1964; Hilton, 1967). In short, firstborns tend to be high achievers—responsible, hardworking, and self-disciplined.

Before congratulating yourself on being a firstborn or lamenting that you are not, consider this: Firstborns are also shyer, more conforming, and more likely to be anxious under stress than later-born persons (Schachter, 1959).

Question: What are the strengths of later-born persons?

Later-born persons tend to excel in social relationships. They are affectionate, friendly, and at ease with others. Youngest children also tend to be more original and creative than firstborns.

Question: How does birth order influence personality?

Parental Attitudes   The answer seems to lie in the "emotional set" parents bring to each child. Because they are the first on the scene, oldest children often get more attention, praise, and concern than later children. The first child is talked to more, spanked more, and more protected. The firstborn is also more likely to be a planned child, and is breast-fed longer (Sears, Maccoby, and Levin, 1957). This pattern of behavior and attitudes seems to benefit the firstborn, who come to think of themselves as important persons. High parental expectations for the firstborn are then translated into high self-expectations.

A principal disadvantage of being firstborn is that inexperienced parents are more anxious and inconsistent. As a result, firstborns develop higher levels of anxiety and a tendency to conform to adult values. Parents consistently report that they used lighter discipline and were more relaxed with second or later children. The youngest child in a family is particularly prone to be pampered and to have fewer responsibilities than did older brothers and sisters.

At this point it should be emphasized that birth-order effects can be stated only as broad patterns. Being a first or later-born child does not mean that your personality will fit the preceding descriptions. Countless factors, including the number of children in a family, their sex, age differences, and the age of parents, can modify birth-order effects. Nevertheless, when large samples of people are considered, birth-order effects typically emerge (Belmont and Marolla, 1973).

Question: How important are the age and sex of other children in the family?

Sibling Effects   The effect of siblings (brothers and sisters) on one's development is obviously important. In fact, at least one theorist has suggested that siblings are as important as parents in shaping some aspects of personality. Walter Toman (1970) believes brothers and sisters often turn to each other when parents cannot fill all their psychological needs. Thus, your relationship with brothers and sisters may have served as a training ground for adult attitudes and relationships. According to Toman (1970), the following are common patterns:

Oldest Brother of Brother(s) This individual is aggressive, assertive, and a perfectionist. He gets along well with other males and might be described as a "man's man."

Oldest Brother of Sister(s) This person is most at ease with women. He therefore prefers women as friends and work partners. He does not consider himself "one of the boys" or a leader of men.

Oldest Sister of Sister(s) She is a competent and efficient worker who prefers a position of leadership. She may be somewhat dominant or commanding and thus unhappy when not in charge.

Oldest Sister of Brother(s) Men play an important role in her life. She relates easily to her husband if married and enjoys directing and advising children. She is independent, practical, and achieving.

Youngest Brother of Brother(s) He is a great lover of attention. He can be an imaginative and creative worker, but is also erratic and unproductive at times. He is rarely a leader.

Youngest Brother of Sister(s) He seems to have learned how to charm others into catering to his needs. Women adore him.

Youngest Sister of Sister(s) Like the youngest brother of sisters, she is charming, but also more flighty, emotional, and adventurous. Her lack of experience with males may cause difficulties if she marries.

Youngest Sister of Brother(s) She gets along well with males, particularly those who favor a traditionally "feminine" woman. Men consider her a good sport, but women may not always like her.

It is very important for you to remember that the preceding is a *theory*. Like all generalizations, these descriptions apply more to some people than to others. They should not be taken as the gospel; they have been included because they are thought-provoking.

Learning Check

1. _____ is personality evaluated.

2. All people can be classified as either introverts or extroverts.   T or F?

Match in accordance with Sheldon's theory:

3. _____ Endomorphy   **A.** Cerebrotonia

4. _____ Mesomorphy   **B.** Somatotonia

5. _____ Ectomorphy   **C.** Viscerotonia

6. ". . . The hereditary aspects of one's emotional nature: sensitivity, strength and speed of response, and prevailing mood." This statement defines:

   a. personality *b.* character *c.* somatomorphy *d.* temperament

7. According to Allport, few people have _____ traits.

8. Central traits are those shared by most members of a culture.   T or F?

9. Cattell believes that clusters of _____ traits reveal the presence of underlying _____ traits.

   a. common, source *b.* central, secondary *c.* secondary, central *d.* surface, source

10. Cattell's personality questionnaire provides ratings on 16 surface traits.   T or F?

11. Whereas firstborn persons tend to be high achievers, later-born persons tend to excel in social relationships.   T or F?

Answers: 1. Character 2. F 3. C 4. B 5. A 6. d 7. cardinal 8. F 9. surface, source 10. F 11. T

Personality Assessment— Psychological Yardsticks

Earlier we discussed some of the limitations of the trait approach to personality. One of the greatest values of the trait approach is the refinement it has brought to personality measurement and testing. To adequately study traits, psychologists have found it necessary to develop a variety of means for assessing personality. The resulting techniques have been of tremendous value in research, industry, education, and clinical work.

Question: How is personality "assessed"?

Psychologists use **interviews, observation, questionnaires,** and **projective tests** to measure personality. Each is a refinement of more informal ways of judging others.

   At one time or another, you have probably "sized up" a potential date, friend, or employer by engaging in conversation (interview). Perhaps you have asked a friend, "When I am delayed I get angry. Do you?" (questionnaire). Maybe you watch your professors when they are angry or embarrassed to learn what they are "really" like (observation). Or possibly you have noticed that when a person says, "I think people feel . . . ," he may be expressing his own feelings (projection).

It can be seen that everyone engages in personality assessment. If our judgments are important, as in choosing a roommate or a spouse, errors can be costly. As professionals, psychologists also make judgments of personality that are costly when in error. Understandably, they have had an interest in improving the accuracy of personality assessment. Let's see what they have learned.

The Interview

A very direct way to learn about a person's personality is to engage in conversation. An interview is described as **unstructured** if the conversation is informal, and the interviewee is allowed to determine what subjects are discussed. In a **structured** interview information is obtained by asking a series of planned questions.

Question: How are interviews used?

Interviews are used to identify personality disturbances, to select persons for employment, college, or special programs, and for research on the dynamics of personality. Interviews also provide information for counseling or therapy. For instance, a counselor might ask a depressed person, "Have you ever contemplated suicide? What were the circumstances?" The counselor might then follow by asking, "How did you feel about it?" or, "How is what you are now feeling different from what you felt then?"

One advantage of interviewing is that it is flexible, and it uncovers feelings. In addition, it allows observation of a person's tone of voice, hand gestures, posture, and facial expressions. These "body language" cues may add completely new meaning to what is said, as when a person claims to be "completely calm," but trembles uncontrollably.

Limitations   Interviews give rapid insight into personality, but they are subject to certain limitations. For one thing, interviewers can be swayed by preconceptions. A person identified as a "housewife," "college student," "high school athlete," or "ski bum" may be misjudged because of an interviewer's attitudes toward a particular life-style. Secondly, an interviewer's own personality may cause an accentuation or distortion of the interviewee's characteristics. A third problem is the tendency of interviewees to be influenced by actions of the interviewer.

Question: How is that possible?

An interviewer's *approval,* expressed by nodding or smiling, and *disapproval,* expressed by frowning or silence, affects what is said in an interview (Greenspoon, 1955). The situation is complicated by the tendency of interviewers to smile and talk more with persons of the opposite sex. It is also known that younger persons are less likely to say "unacceptable" things to an older interviewer and that blacks tend to give more "proper" responses to white than to black interviewers (Rosenthal, 1969). If you are young, black, and female, your chances of being accurately interviewed by an older white male may be pretty low.

A final problem in interviewing is the **halo effect.** The halo effect is a tendency to generalize a favorable or unfavorable impression to unrelated details of personality. A person who is likable or physically attractive may be rated more mature, intelligent, or adjusted than he or she actually is. The halo effect is something to keep in mind when interviewing for employment. First impressions do make a difference.

Even with their limitations, interviews are a respected method of personality assessment. In many cases, interviews are an essential step to additional personality testing and to counseling or therapy.

Direct Observation and Rating Scales

Are you fascinated by bus depots, airports, subway stations, or other public places? Many people relish a chance to observe the behavior of others. When used as an assessment procedure, direct observation is a simple extension of this natural interest in "people watching." For instance, a psychologist might arrange to observe a disturbed child playing with other children. By careful observation, the psychologist will identify personality characteristics and clarify the nature of the child's problems.

Question: Wouldn't observation be subject to the same problems of misperception as an interview?

Yes. Misperceiving can be a difficulty. Because of it, **rating scales** are sometimes used (see Table 18-2). Rating scales limit the chance that some traits will be overlooked while others are exaggerated. Perhaps they should be standard procedure for choosing a roommate, spouse, or lover!

An alternative to rating scales is to do a **behavioral assessment.** In this case, observers record how often various *actions* occur, not what traits they think a person has. For example, psychologists working with hospitalized mental patients may find it helpful to record the frequency of patients' aggression, self-care, speech, and unusual behaviors (Alevizos and Callahan, 1977).

Situational Testing   A specialized form of direct observation is called **situational testing.** Situational tests are based on the premise that the best way to learn how a person reacts to a certain situation is to simulate that situation. Situational tests expose a person to frustration, temptation, pressure, boredom, or other conditions capable of revealing personality characteristics. One of the most ambitious examples of situational testing was devised by the Office of Strategic Services (OSS) during World War II. The OSS was a forerunner of the CIA, and its agents were involved in dangerous and demanding espionage.

Question: How were OSS candidates tested?

Candidates were tested under conditions requiring the same skills of leadership, tolerance for stress, and ability to cooperate needed for success as a spy. Some of the tests were both diabolical and ingenious. For example:

Lesson 1: Never Trust Another Spy

In one test, a candidate and two "helpers" were required to build a tower out of heavy logs. Soon after the trio started work the candidate's troubles began. One of the helpers knocked down part of the structure; the other followed instructions improperly; both repeatedly insulted the candidate. The whole scene soon began to look like something from a slapstick movie.

What was happening? In reality the "helpers" were *observers* trained to sabotage the efforts of the candidate. The "helpers," of course, recorded each candidate's reactions.

Table 18-2   Sample Rating Scale Items

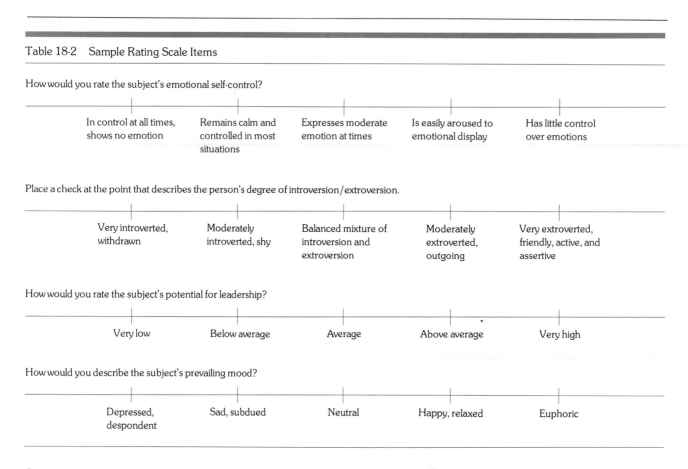

How would you rate the subject's emotional self-control?

| In control at all times, shows no emotion | Remains calm and controlled in most situations | Expresses moderate emotion at times | Is easily aroused to emotional display | Has little control over emotions |

Place a check at the point that describes the person's degree of introversion/extroversion.

| Very introverted, withdrawn | Moderately introverted, shy | Balanced mixture of introversion and extroversion | Moderately extroverted, outgoing | Very extroverted, friendly, active, and assertive |

How would you rate the subject's potential for leadership?

| Very low | Below average | Average | Above average | Very high |

How would you describe the subject's prevailing mood?

| Depressed, despondent | Sad, subdued | Neutral | Happy, relaxed | Euphoric |

Some candidates decided to work alone, or stalked off in disgust. Others patiently attempted to work with the two "clowns" assigned to help.

An interesting current use of situational tests is the "Shoot–Don't Shoot" training now done by many police departments (Fig. 18-4). At times, police officers must make split-second decisions about using their guns. A mistake may be fatal. In the *Shoot–Don't Shoot Test,* actors play the part of armed juveniles or criminals. As various high-risk scenes are acted out live, or on videotape, officers must decide to shoot or hold fire. A newspaper reporter who recently took the test (and failed it) gives this account (Gersh, 1982):

> I judged wrong. I was killed by a man in a closet, a man with a hostage, a woman interrupted when kissing her lover, and a man I thought was cleaning a shotgun. . . . I shot a drunk who reached for a comb, and a teen-ager who pulled out a black water pistol. Looked real to me.

In addition to the training it provides, the *Shoot–Don't Shoot Test* uncovers police cadets who lack the good judgment needed to carry a gun out on the street.

Personality Questionnaires

Most **personality questionnaires** are paper-and-pencil tests requiring people to answer questions about themselves. As measures of personality, questionnaires are more *objective* than interviews or observation. Questions, administration, and scoring are all standardized so that scores are unaffected by the opinions or prejudices of the examiner.

Many personality tests have been developed, including tests such as the *Guilford-Zimmerman Temperament Survey,* the *California Psychological Inventory,* the *Allport-Vernon Study of Values,* the *16 PF,* and many more. One of the best known and most widely used objective tests of personality is the *Minnesota Multiphasic Personality Inventory (MMPI).* The MMPI is composed of 550 items to which a subject must respond "true," "false," or "cannot say." Items include statements such as:

> Everything tastes the same.
> There is something wrong with my mind.
> I enjoy animals.
> Whenever possible I avoid being in a crowd.
> I have never indulged in any unusual sex practices.

Fig. 18-4 *A police officer undergoes a Shoot—Don't Shoot Test. Variations on this situational test are used by a growing number of police departments. All officers must score a passing grade.*

Someone has been trying to poison me.
I daydream often.*

Question: How can these items show anything about personality? For instance, what if a person has a cold so that "everything tastes the same"?

The answer to a single item tells nothing about personality. A person who agrees that "everything tastes the same" might indeed have a cold. It is only through *patterns* of response that personality dimensions are revealed. Items on the MMPI were selected for their ability to correctly identify persons with particular psychiatric problems. If a series of items is consistently answered in a particular way by depressed persons, it is assumed that others who answer the same way are also prone to depression.

Question: What personality dimensions are measured by the MMPI?

The MMPI was designed to measure 10 major aspects of personality. Each is represented by a separate subscale on the test. The subscales and their interpretations are:

1. **Hypochondriasis** (HI-po-kon-DRY-uh-sis). Reflects exaggerated concern about one's physical health.
2. **Depression.** High scorers are marked by feelings of worthlessness, hopelessness, and pessimism.
3. **Hysteria.** Reflects somatic complaints related to psychological disturbances (psychosomatic problems).
4. **Psychopathic deviancy.** Shows a disregard for social and moral standards and emotional shallowness in relationships.
5. **Masculinity/femininity.** Indicates degree of traditional "masculine" aggressiveness or "feminine" sensitivity.
6. **Paranoia.** Indicates extreme suspiciousness and feelings of persecution.
7. **Psychasthenia** (psych-as-THEE-nih-ah). Suggests presence of irrational fears (phobias) and compulsive (ritualistic) actions.
8. **Schizophrenia.** Reflects withdrawal, unusual and bizarre thinking or actions.
9. **Hypomania.** Suggests emotional excitability, manic moods or behavior, and excessive activity.
10. **Social introversion.** High score indicates a tendency to be socially withdrawn.

After the MMPI is scored, results are charted as an MMPI profile (see Fig. 18-5). By comparing a person's profile to scores produced by normal adults, various personality disorders can be identified. The most common interpretation

Fig. 18-5 *An MMPI profile showing hypothetical scores indicating normality (black line), depression (blue line), and psychosis (gray line).*

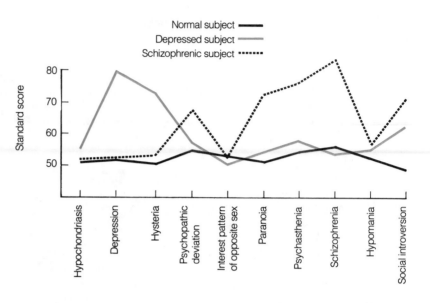

is that neurotics (persons with mild emotional disturbances) score high on scales 1–3; psychotics (severely disturbed persons) score high on scales 6–9; and antisocial or delinquent persons score highest on scale 4.

Question: How accurate is the MMPI?

The accuracy of the MMPI or any other personality questionnaire rests on the assumption that people are willing to tell the truth about themselves.

Because of the importance of this assumption, the MMPI has an additional "Lie Scale" to detect attempts of subjects to make themselves look better (or worse) than they really are. An elevated score on the Lie Scale may cause results on the remainder of the test to be discounted. This supposedly makes the MMPI a difficult test to fake. However, the Lie Scale alone is not enough to ensure accuracy of the results. If MMPI scores were used as the only basis for classifying a person as neurotic, severely depressed, or schizophrenic, a large number of normal people would be incorrectly labeled (Cronbach, 1970). Fortunately, such judgments usually take into account information from interviews or other sources.

Critique Humorist Art Buchwald (1965) once lampooned personality questionnaires by writing his own test. Here is a sample of his items:

Answer, "Yes," "No," or "Don't bother me, I can't cope!"

I would enjoy the work of a chicken flicker.
My eyes are always cold.
Frantic screams make me nervous.

I believe I smell as good as most people.
Most of the time I go to sleep without saying good-bye.
I use shoe polish to excess.
The sight of blood no longer excites me.

Buchwald's questions may seem ridiculous, but they are not very different from the real thing. Psychologist Frank McMahon once described personality test questions as a "smoke screen against logic."

To avoid the problems of traditional tests, McMahon (1964) constructed an "above-board" test in which the meaning of questions is clearly stated. For example, the true-or-false question: "Some people have it in for me" is followed by: "If True, 'I can't seem to get them off my mind,' True or False."

Not all psychologists share McMahon's feelings, and most are well aware of a test's limitations. If psychologists were the only persons giving these tests there would be few problems. However, many organizations, including businesses, routinely use personality tests, and errors or abuses sometimes occur.

Question: What if I am not hired, accepted to a program, or given a promotion because of my score on a personality test?

The U.S. Supreme Court handed down a decision in 1971 limiting the use of tests as conditions of employment or promotion. If you think a test was unfair, you may have a case. More importantly, it should be recognized that errors can occur even when a test is fair and properly administered. The American Psychological Association recommends that an employee or potential employee should have the right to review and appeal personnel decisions in which test results play a part. In short, if you feel you were inaccurately rated by a personality test, you should challenge it.

Projective Tests of Personality— Inkblots and Thematic Plots

Projective tests are a very different approach to personality assessment than the techniques already discussed. Interviews, observation, rating scales, and inventories typically provide information on overt or observable traits. By contrast, projective tests attempt to uncover deep-seated or *unconscious* wishes, thoughts, and needs.

Question: How is a test able to do that?

As a child you may have delighted in finding faces and objects in cloud formations. Or perhaps you have learned something about your friends' personalities from their reactions to movies or paintings. If so, you will have some insight into the rationale for constructing and interpreting projective tests. A **projective test** provides an *ambiguous stimulus* that subjects must describe or about which they must make up a story. Describing an unambiguous stimulus (a picture of an automobile, for example) tells little about your personality. But when you are faced with an unstructured stimulus or situation, you must organize and interpret what is seen in terms of your own life experiences. Everyone sees something different in a projective stimulus, and what is seen presumably reveals inner workings of the personality.

Since projective tests have no right or wrong answers, the ability of subjects to fake or "see through" the test is greatly reduced. Moreover, projective tests can be an unusually rich source of information, since responses are not restricted to simple true/false or yes/no answers.

Question: Is the inkblot test a projective technique?

The Rorschach Inkblot Test The inkblot test, or *Rorschach* (ROR-shock), is one of the oldest and most widely used projective tests. Developed by Swiss psychologist Hermann Rorschach in the 1920s, it consists of a set of 10 standardized inkblots. These vary in color, shading, form, and complexity:

Question: How does testing take place?

First, subjects are shown each blot and asked to describe what they see in it (Fig. 18-6). Later the psychologist may return to a blot, asking a subject to identify specific sections of it, to elaborate on previous descriptions, or to suggest a completely new story about it.

Scoring the Rorschach is complex. A subject's responses are scored in terms of three major categories: (1) *location,* indicating whether a response was to the blot as a whole or to specific parts; (2) *determinants,* indicating whether the subject's response was determined by shape, color, or texture of the blot; and (3) *content,* consisting of the description or story given to the blot. Obvious differences in content such as "blood dripping from a dagger" versus "flowers blooming in a field" are important for identifying a subject's conflicts and fantasies. But, surprisingly, content is considered less important than location, determinants, and organization of responses. These factors allow a

Fig. 18-6   *Inkblots similar to those used on the Rorschach. What do you see?*

psychologist to view the ways in which a subject perceives the world and to detect disorders in personality function.

The Thematic Apperception Test   Another popular projective test is the *Thematic Apperception Test* (TAT) developed by Harvard psychologist and personality theorist Henry Murray.

Question: How does the TAT differ from the Rorschach?

The TAT consists of 20 sketches depicting various scenes and life situations (see Fig. 18-7). The subject is shown each sketch and is asked to make up a story about the people in it. Later the subject is shown each sketch a second

Fig. 18-7   *This is a picture like those used for the Thematic Apperception Test. If you wish to simulate the test, tell a story that explains what led up to the pictured situation, what is happening now, and how the action will end.*

or, perhaps, a third time and asked to elaborate on previous stories or to construct new stories for each.

The term "apperception" means "readiness to perceive"; the word "thematic" refers to the existence of themes or recurring plots. When a subject tells a story about a TAT card, the tester gets a view of deep-rooted fantasies, thoughts, and conflicts by analyzing the themes underlying the subject's perceptions.

Question: How is the TAT scored?

Scoring of the TAT is restricted to analysis of the content of the stories. In particular, the psychologist is concerned with what the basic issues are in each story. Interpretation focuses on how people feel, how they interact, what events led up to the incidents depicted in the sketch, and how the story will end.

A simpler method of interpreting the TAT is to score the frequency with which particular themes, motives, or traits appear in the entire series of stories. Thus, a psychologist might note how often a client mentions marriage problems, unsatisfying relationships with parents, or anxieties about sexual matters. The psychologist might also count the number of times the central figure in each story is angry, overlooked, apathetic, jealous, or threatened.

Question: How accurate are projective tests?

Limitations of Projective Testing   Although projective tests have been popular with clinical psychologists, their *validity* is considered lowest among tests of personality. (Recall that a test is valid when it measures what it claims to measure.) Because of the subjectivity involved in scoring, *objectivity* (consistency) of judgments among different users of the TAT and Rorschach is also low. Note that after the subject interprets an ambiguous stimulus, the scorer must interpret the subject's ambiguous responses. In a sense, the interpretation of a projective test may be a projective test for the scorer! In addition, themes revealed by projective tests are not necessarily courses for action. In fact, they may reflect what subjects have seen in books or movies rather than their own thoughts and motives.

Despite the drawbacks of projective tests, many psychologists attest to their value, especially as part of a **battery** *of tests and interviews*. It is said that in the hands of a skillful and experienced clinician, projective tests are helpful in the detection of major conflicts and in making decisions about the goals of therapy. Moreover, since projective tests are unstructured, they may be more effective for getting clients to talk about anxiety-provoking topics than are the direct questions of inventories and interviews.

Sudden Murderers—A Research Example

Personality studies provide us with clues to some of the most perplexing human events. Consider Fred Cowan, a model student in school and described by those who knew him as quiet, gentle, and a man who loved children. Despite his size (6 feet tall, 250 pounds) Fred was described by a co-worker as "someone you could easily push around."

Fred Cowan is representative of a puzzling phenomenon: The sudden murderer—a gentle, quiet, shy, good-natured person who explodes without warning into violence (Lee et al., 1977). Two weeks after being suspended from his job, Fred returned to work determined to get even with his supervisor. Unable to find the man, he killed four co-workers and a policeman before taking his own life.

Question: Isn't such behavior contrary to the idea of personality traits?

It might seem that sudden murderers are newsworthy simply because they seem such unlikely candidates for violence. On the contrary, research conducted by Melvin Lee, Philip Zimbardo, and Minerva Bertholf suggests that sudden murderers explode into violence *because* they are shy, restrained, and inexpressive, not in spite of it. These researchers studied prisoners at a California prison. Ten were inmates whose homicide was an unexpected first offense; 9 were criminals with a record of habitual violence prior to murder; and 16 were inmates convicted of nonviolent crimes.

Question: Did the inmates differ in personality makeup?

Lee and his associates administered a battery of tests to the inmates. Included were the MMPI, a test measuring shyness, an adjective checklist, and personal interviews with each inmate. As expected, the sudden murderers were passive, shy, and overcontrolled (restrained) individuals. The habitually violent inmates were "masculine" (aggressive), undercontrolled (impulsive), and less likely to view themselves as shy than the average person (Lee et al., 1977).

Interviews and other observations have revealed that quiet, overcontrolled individuals are likely to be especially violent if they ever lose control. Their attacks are usually triggered by a minor irritation or frustration, but the attack reflects years of unexpressed feelings of anger and belittlement. When sudden murderers finally release the strict controls they have maintained on their behavior a furious and frenzied attack ensues. Usually it is totally out of proportion to the offense against them, and often they have amnesia for some or all of their violent actions.

In comparison, the previously violent murderers showed very different reactions. Although they killed, their violence was moderate—usually only enough to do the necessary damage. Typically they felt they had been cheated or betrayed and that they were doing what was necessary to remedy the situation or to maintain their manhood (Lee et al., 1977).

This brief example illustrates how some of the concepts and techniques discussed in this chapter can be applied to further our understanding. The "Applications" and the "Exploration" that follow should add balance to your view of personality. Don't be shy: Read on!

Learning Check

1. Planned questions are used in a _____ interview.

2. The halo effect is the tendency of an interviewer to influence what is said by the interviewee.   T or F?

3. Which of the following is considered the most objective measure of personality (circle):
   rating scales   personality questionnaires   projective tests   the TAT

4. Situational testing allows direct _____ of personality characteristics.

5. Delinquents typically score highest on which MMPI scale (circle):
   depression   hysteria   psychopathic deviancy   hypomania

6. The use of ambiguous stimuli is most characteristic of (circle):
   interviews   projective tests   personality inventories   direct observation

7. The content of one's responses to the MMPI is considered an indication of unconscious wishes, thoughts, and needs.   T or F?

8. OSS candidates were selected through use of situational tests.   T or F?

9. A surprising finding is that sudden murderers are usually overcontrolled, very masculine, and more impulsive than average.   T or F?

Answers: 1. structured   2. F   3. personality questionnaires   4. observation   5. psychopathic deviancy   6. projective tests   7. F   8. T   9. F

Resources Summary

● *Personality* is made up of one's unique and enduring behavior patterns. *Character* is personality evaluated. *Temperament* refers to the hereditary and physiological aspects of one's emotional nature.

● A basic approach to the study of personality is classification into *types*. Jung's concepts of the *introvert* and the *extrovert* are an example of this approach. One well-known type system is Sheldon's *somatotype theory.* Sheldon linked body types to personality types in the following way: *endomorphy-viscerotonia, mesomorphy-somatotonia,* and *ectomorphy-cerebrotonia.* Like most type systems, Sheldon's oversimplifies personality.

● The *trait* approach attempts to specify qualities of personality that are most enduring or characteristic of a person. Allport makes useful distinctions between *common traits* and *individual traits* and among *cardinal, central,* and *secondary traits.*

● A second trait approach, developed by Cattell, attributes visible or *surface traits* to the existence of underlying *source traits.* Cattell identified 16 source traits by use of a statistical method called *factor analysis.*

● Cattell's source traits are measured by the *Sixteen Personality Factor Questionnaire (16 PF).* Like other trait measures, the outcome of the *16 PF* may be graphically presented as a *trait profile.*

● A variety of research suggests that birth order or *ordinal position* in a family can influence personality development. Firstborn and only children tend to be high achievers, but also shyer, more conforming, and more anxious under stress than later-borns. Later-borns are more likely to excel in social skills and tend to be more original and creative than firstborns. Differences of this type may also extend to *sibling effects.*

● Accurate *assessment* of personality is of great importance to psychologists. Techniques typically used to measure personality are: *interviews, observation, questionnaires,* and *projective tests.*

● *Structured* and *unstructured* interviews provide much information, but they are subject to interviewer bias and misperceptions. Expressions of approval and disapproval by the interviewer and the *halo effect* (the tendency to generalize first impressions) may also lower the accuracy of an interview.

● *Direct observation,* sometimes involving *situational tests, behavioral assessment,* or use of *rating scales,* allows evaluation of a person's actual behavior.

● *Personality questionnaires,* such as the *Minnesota Multiphasic Personality Inventory (MMPI),* are quite objective, but their accuracy and validity are open to question.

● *Projective tests* ask a subject to project thoughts or feelings to an ambiguous stimulus or unstructured situation. The *Rorschach,* or *inkblot test,* is a well-known projective technique. A second is the *Thematic Apperception Test (TAT).* The validity and objectivity of projective tests are quite low. Nevertheless, projective techniques are considered useful by many clinicians, particularly as part of a *battery* of tests.

Shrinking Violets and Bashful Beaux—Understanding Shyness

Do you:

Find it hard to talk to strangers?

Lack confidence with people?

Find it difficult to make friends?

Feel awkward in social situations?

Feel nervous with people who are not close friends?

If so, you may be one of the *40 percent* of American college students who currently consider themselves to be shy. If you are shy and wish you weren't, it may help to know that many others are shy too. However, three-fourths of those who are shy, say they don't like it (Zimbardo *et al.,* 1978).

Touch a snail and it retreats into its shell. Speak to a shy person, and he or she may shrink back as if threatened. As a personality trait, **shyness** refers to an avoidance of others, coupled with social inhibition (restraint and signs of strain when socializing) (Buss, 1980). Shy persons fail to make eye contact, retreat when spoken to, speak too quietly, pause too long in conversations, and display little interest or animation.

Question: What causes shyness?

Elements of Shyness   To begin with, shy persons often lack **social skills.** Many simply have not learned how to meet others, how to start a conversation and keep it going, or how to end social encounters. **Social anxiety** is also a factor in shyness. Most people are nervous in some social situations (such as meeting an attractive stranger). Such anxiety is typically a reaction to *evaluation fears* (fears of being embarrassed, ridiculed, rejected, or of seeming inadequate). Such fears occur for both the shy and the nonshy. However, social anxieties are more frequent or intense for shy persons. A third problem for shy persons is a **self-defeating bias** in their thinking. Specifically, shy persons almost always blame themselves when a social encounter doesn't go well (Girodo, 1978).

Immediate Causes of Shyness   Have you ever had to deliver a speech to a group of strangers? If so, you are

probably aware that shyness is most often triggered by *novel* or *unfamiliar* social situations. A person who does fine with family or close friends may become shy and awkward when meeting a stranger. Shyness is also magnified by formality, meeting someone of higher status, being noticeably different from others, or being the focus of attention (as in giving a speech) (Buss, 1980; Pilkonis, 1977).

Question: Don't most people become cautious and inhibited in such circumstances?

Yes. That's why we need to see how the personalities of shy and nonshy persons differ.

Dynamics of the Shy Personality   There is a tendency to think that shy persons are wrapped up in their own feelings and thoughts. In some cases this may be true. But surprisingly, researchers Jonathan Cheek and Arnold Buss (1979) found no connection between shyness and *private* self-consciousness (attention to inner feelings, thoughts, and fantasies). Instead, they discovered that shyness is linked to *public* self-consciousness.

Persons who rate high in **public self-consciousness** are intensely aware of themselves as social objects (Buss, 1980). They are concerned about what others think of them, and feel others are evaluating them. They worry about saying the wrong thing, or appearing foolish. With such concerns, many shy persons feel they are being rejected even when they are not. In public, they may feel ''naked,'' or as if others can ''see through them.'' Such feelings trigger anxiety or outright fear during social encounters, leading to awkwardness and inhibition.

As mentioned, almost everyone feels anxious in at least some social situations. But there is a key difference in the way shy and nonshy persons *label* this anxiety. Shy persons tend to consider their social anxiety a *lasting personality trait.* In contrast, nonshy persons believe that *external events* cause their occasional feelings of shyness. Particular people or situations may trigger anxiety or ''stage fright'' for the nonshy, but this group assumes that

Applications

almost anyone would feel as they do under the same circumstances (Zimbardo *et al.,* 1978).

Why should labeling make such a difference? The answer seems to lie in its effect on *self-esteem.* Nonshy persons tend to have higher self-esteem than shy persons. The greater confidence of the nonshy comes from an ability to benefit more from successful social encounters. Nonshy persons give themselves credit for successes and they recognize failures are often due to circumstances. In contrast, shy people blame themselves for social failures and never give themselves credit for successes. It's no wonder they often have lower self-esteem (Girodo, 1978; Buss, 1980).

Consequences of Shyness   Even when it is mild, shyness can cause problems. Among the the most common are:

1. Difficulties in making new friends or meeting people.
2. Feelings of isolation and loneliness.
3. Misperception by others; a shy person may strike others as vain, bored, unfriendly, or uninterested.
4. A general lack of self-projection and confidence in social settings.

Unless shyness is intense and quite painful, it is a mistake to think of it as a major problem. Yet, as the preceding list shows, shyness does have its costs. As one author notes, people who were once shy look back on the shyness of their youth ''with about the same tenderness that they recall adolescent pimples.''

Question: What can be done to reduce shyness?

Overcoming Shyness

Visitors to China frequently marvel at the almost total lack of shyness among the Chinese. In America, many children seem to ''outgrow'' shyness as they gain social skills and wider social experience. Some adults overcome shyness with the aid of a ''shyness clinic'' or similar program. (Shyness clinics are sometimes offered on college campuses or by private psychologists.) Many previously shy people simply made an effort to learn new social skills and break out of old routines. Each of these observations suggests that shyness is to a large extent learned and open to change. If you are shy and would like to change, the infor-

mation that follows may offer a starting point. Even if you are not shy, you may find some of the ideas useful.

Shy Beliefs   While directing a shyness clinic, Michel Girodo (1978) observed that shyness is often maintained by a number of unrealistic or unproductive beliefs. Here's a sample:

1. *If you wait around long enough at a social gathering, something will happen.*
Comment: This is really a cover-up for fear of initiating conversation. For two people to meet, at least one has to make an effort; it might as well be you.

2. *Other people who are popular are just lucky when it comes to being invited to social events, or asked out.*
Comment: Except for times when a person is formally introduced to new acquaintances, this is false. People who are more active socially typically make an effort to meet and spend time with others: They join clubs, invite others to do things, strike up conversations, and generally leave little to ''luck.''

3. *The odds of meeting someone interested in socializing are always the same, no matter where I am.*
Comment: This is another rationalization for inaction. It pays to seek out settings and events that have a higher probability of leading to social contact. Drama clubs, hiking clubs, sports teams, school events, and so forth often serve as a convenient excuse to bring together people interested in socializing.

4. *If someone doesn't seem to like you right away, they really don't like you and never will.*
Comment: This belief leads to much unnecessary withdrawal and isolation. Even when a person doesn't show immediate interest, it doesn't mean the person dislikes you. Liking takes time and opportunity to develop.

Unproductive beliefs like the preceding can be replaced with statements such as these:

1. I've got to be active in social situations.
2. I can't wait until I'm completely relaxed or comfortable before taking a social risk.
3. I don't need to pretend to be someone I'm not, it just makes me more anxious.
4. I may think other people are harshly evaluating me, but actually I'm being too hard on myself.

Applications

5. I can set reasonable goals for expanding my social experience and skills.

6. Even people who are very socially skillful are never successful 100 percent of the time. I shouldn't get so upset when an encounter goes badly. (Adapted from Girodo, 1978.)

Social Skills Learning to play a musical instrument, ski, or speak a foreign language takes practice. So does the learning of social skills. There is nothing "innate" about knowing how to meet people or enjoy a conversation. There are many ways in which social skills can be directly practiced. It can be helpful, for instance, to get a tape recorder and listen to several of your conversations. You may be surprised by the way you pause, interrupt, miss cues, or seem disinterested. Similarly, it can be useful to look at yourself in a mirror and exaggerate facial expressions of surprise, interest, dislike, pleasure, and so forth. By such methods, most people can learn to put more animation and skill into their self-presentation.

One of the simplest ways to make better conversation is by learning to ask questions. A good series of questions shifts attention to the other person and shows you are interested in her or him. Nothing elaborate is needed. You can do fine with questions such as "Where do you (work, study, live)?" "Do you like (dancing, to travel, music)?" "How long have you (been at this school, worked here, lived here)?" The best questions are often *open-ended* (Girodo, 1978):

"Do you get a chance to travel much?" (as opposed to: "Have you ever been to Florida?").

"What's it like living on the west side?" (as opposed to: "Do you like living on the west side?").

"What kinds of food do you like?" (as opposed to "Do you like Chinese cooking?").

It's easy to see why open-ended questions are helpful. If a question can be answered by one or two words, it takes a large number to keep a conversation alive. Also, in replying to open-ended questions, people often give "free information" about themselves. This extra information can be used to ask other questions or to lead into other topics of conversation.

This brief sampling of ideas is no substitute for actual practice. Overcoming shyness requires a real effort to learn new skills and test old beliefs and attitudes. It may even require the help of a counselor or therapist. At the very least, it requires a willingness to take social risks. Breaking down the barriers of shyness will always include some awkward or unsuccessful encounters. Nevertheless, the rewards are powerful: human companionship and personal freedom.

Learning Check

1. Surveys show that 14 percent of American college students consider themselves to be shy.   T or F?
2. Social anxiety and evaluation fears are seen almost exclusively in shy individuals; the nonshy rarely have such experiences.   T or F?
3. Unfamiliar people and situations most often trigger shyness.   T or F?
4. Public self-consciousness plus a tendency to label oneself as shy are major characteristics of the shy personality. T or F?
5. Misperception by others is a common problem associated with shyness.   T or F?
6. Changing personal beliefs and practicing social skills can be helpful in overcoming shyness.   T or F?

Answers: 1. F   2. F   3. T   4. T   5. T   6. T

Exploration

Check One: □ Masculine, □ Feminine, □ Androgynous

Are you: a leader, aggressive, ambitious, analytical, asser-tive, athletic, competitive, dominant, forceful, indepen-dent, individualistic, decisive, self-reliant, and willing to take risks? If so, you are quite "masculine." Are you: affec-tionate, cheerful, childlike, compassionate, flatterable, gentle, gullible, a lover of children, loyal, sensitive, shy, soft-spoken, sympathetic, tender, understanding, warm, and yielding? If so, then you are quite "feminine."

Question: What if I have characteristics from both lists?

Then you may be **androgynous** (an-DROJ-ih-nus).

   The two lists of traits just given are from the work of Stanford University psychologist Sandra Bem. Bem gave longer lists of traits to students and asked them to classify each trait as more desirable for men or for women. The first list includes traits that got a high "masculine" rating; the second list is made up of favored "feminine" traits.

Masculine, Feminine, Neutral

With these lists in hand, Bem then constructed the **Bem Sex Role Inventory (BSRI),** a list of 20 masculine traits (self-reliant, assertive, and so forth), 20 feminine traits (affectionate, gentle), and 20 neutral traits (truthful, friendly) (see box). Next, Bem and her associates gave the BSRI to thousands of people, asking them to say whether or not each trait applied to them. Fifty percent of those sur-veyed fell into traditional masculine or feminine categories; 15 percent scored higher on traits characteristic of the op-posite gender; and 35 percent were androgynous, getting roughly equal scores on the masculine and feminine items.

Question: You haven't said yet what it means to be an-drogynous. Is it having both male and female traits?

Psychological Androgyny   The word **androgyny** (an-DROJ-ih-nee) literally means "man-woman." Androgyny sounds as if it might have something to do with androids, asexuality, or sex-change operations, but it actually refers to liberation from the constraints of traditional sex roles. A person who is androgynous has both masculine and femi-nine traits.

Androgyny, then, has nothing to do with a reversal of sex roles or the creation of an army of sexless androids. Rather, it emphasizes the shared humanity of both sexes. Bem's interest in androgyny stems from her belief that the complexity of our fast-changing society requires flexibility with respect to sex roles. She believes that it is right, and more than ever necessary, for men to be gentle, compas-sionate, sensitive, and yielding, and for women to be force-ful, self-reliant, independent, and ambitious. In short, Bem feels that people should be androgynous.

   Psychological tests have long assumed that masculinity and femininity are opposites: A high score on one dimen-sion meant a low score on the other. Yet, we have known for years that people who are unusually bright or creative tend to show traits of both sexes on standard personality tests (Maccoby, 1966). The concept of androgyny chal-lenges old assumptions with the idea that it is possible to be *both* "masculine" and "feminine." More importantly, the androgynous individual can be aggressive or yielding, forceful or gentle, sensitive or assertive, *as the situation requires.*

Adaptability   In an interesting series of experiments, Bem and her associates have shown that androgynous in-dividuals are more adaptable: They behave in ways that are appropriate for a given situation unhindered by sex roles or images of what is appropriate "masculine" or "feminine" behavior. For example, androgynous women were more independent and assertive than feminine women when subjected to group pressures; androgynous men were more nurturant than masculine men, comfort-ably holding, touching, and playing with kittens and babies (masculine men were particularly unresponsive in these situations); androgynous men were also better able to show sympathy and to offer support to a troubled student than were the masculine men.

   Bem's conclusion from a number of studies is that rigid sex roles can seriously restrict behavior, especially for men. She believes masculine males have great difficulty expressing warmth, playfulness, and concern—even when these are appropriate—because they view such ac-

Exploration

Masculine, Feminine, and Neutral Items from the BSRI

Masculine items	Feminine items	Neutral items
49. Acts as a leader	11. Affectionate	51. Adaptable
46. Aggressive	5. Cheerful	30. Conceited
58. Ambitious	50. Childlike	9. Conscientious
22. Analytical	32. Compassionate	60. Conventional
13. Assertive	53. Does not use harsh language	45. Friendly
10. Athletic	35. Eager to soothe hurt feelings	15. Happy
55. Competitive	20. Feminine	3. Helpful
4. Defends own beliefs	14. Flatterable	18. Inefficient
37. Dominant	59. Gentle	24. Jealous
19. Forceful	47. Gullible	39. Likable
25. Has leadership abilities	56. Loves children	6. Moody
7. Independent	17. Loyal	21. Reliable
52. Individualistic	26. Sensitive to the needs of others	30. Secretive
31. Makes decisions easily	8. Shy	33. Sincere
40. Masculine	38. Soft-spoken	42. Solemn
1. Self-reliant	23. Sympathetic	57. Tactful
34. Self-sufficient	44. Tender	12. Theatrical
16. Strong personality	29. Understanding	27. Truthful
43. Willing to take a stand	41. Warm	18. Unpredictable
28. Willing to take risks	2. Yielding	54. Unsystematic

Note: The number preceding each item reflects the position of each adjective as it actually appears on the inventory. (Source: Bem, 1977, p. 322.)

tions as "feminine." Likewise, feminine women have trouble being independent and assertive, even when independence and assertiveness are called for. Androgynous subjects in Bem's experiments, however, seemed able to do just about anything the situation called for.

In another experiment, Bem gave people the choice of performing either a masculine activity (oil a hinge, nail boards together, and so forth) or a feminine activity (prepare a baby bottle, wind yarn into a ball, and so on). Masculine men and feminine women consistently chose sex-appropriate activities, even when the opposite choice paid more!

Question: What are people like who score low in both masculinity and femininity on the BSRI?

A good question. Recent research makes it clear that people who are truly androgynous score high in both masculine and feminine traits. Androgyny is *not* an absence of both qualities. People who score low in both masculinity and femininity are more conforming, less playful, and less nurturant than average, and they have lower self-esteem (Spence and Helmreich, 1978).

Summary

To summarize, Bem insists that "Behavior should have no gender." What you do for a living or for entertainment, what you wear, how you express your emotions, or whatever, should have nothing to do with gender. Androgynous individuals can be tender or dominant, nurturing or ambitious, dependent or decisive as needed, and on the basis of their individual humanity or the demands of the situation, not on the basis of gender.

It is clear that Bem thinks of her androgynous subjects as freer, more adaptable, and more emotionally healthy than those maintaining traditional sex roles. Many people, some psychologists included, disagree. How do you feel about androgyny? What are the benefits and costs of both androgyny and traditional sex roles?

Sources: Bem, 1974; Bem, 1975a; Bem, 1975b; O'Leary and Depner, 1976.

Questions for Discussion

1. Are birth-order and sibling effects an example of personality typing? To what extent do they oversimplify matters?

2. Do you know people who seem to fit Toman's theory of sibling effects, or people who seem to contradict the theory? To what extent do Toman's predictions apply to you? Is Toman's theory of sibling effects subject to the fallacy of positive instances? (See Chapter 2.)

3. Have you ever been interviewed or given a personality test? How accurate did you consider the resulting assessment of your personality?

4. Under what circumstances would you consider a personality test an invasion of privacy?

5. If you could select only three personality traits, which would you consider most basic? Why?

6. If you were selecting candidates for an extended space flight, how would you make your choices? What could be done to improve the accuracy of your judgments of candidates' personalities?

7. Do you think there is such a thing as "national character"? That is, do all Germans, all French, all Americans, all Canadians, and so forth, have common traits?

8. Do you know anyone who seems to have a cardinal trait? What do you think are central traits of your personality? Secondary traits?

9. Do you think animals have personalities? Defend your answer.

10. Can you name any public personalities (entertainers, politicians, athletes, artists, musicians) whom you deem to be androgynous? Are any of your friends or acquaintances androgynous? Do you agree or disagree with Bem's assertion that these people are more adaptable?

Suggestions for Further Reading

Aero, R., and E. Weiner. *The Mind Test.* Morrow, 1981.

Allport, G. *Pattern and Growth in Personality.* Holt, 1961.

Bem, S. L. "The Measurement of Psychological Androgyny," *Journal of Consulting and Clinical Psychology,* **42**(1974): 155–162.

_____. "Sex-role Adaptability: One Consequence of Psychological Androgyny," *Journal of Personality and Social Psychology,* **31** (1975a): 634–643.

_____. "Androgyny vs. the Tight Little Lives of Fluffy Women and Chesty Men," *Psychology Today,* September, 1975b, pp. 58–62.

Cattell, R. B. *The Scientific Analysis of Personality.* Penguin, 1965.

Cronbach, L. J. *Essentials of Psychological Testing,* 3rd ed. Harper and Row, 1970.

Girodo, M. *Shy? (You don't have to be!).* Pocket Books, 1978.

Harris, I. D. *The Promised Seed: A Complete Study of Eminent First and Later Sons.* Free Press, 1964.

Olds, L. E. *Fully Human.* Prentice-Hall, 1981.

Pleck, J. H. *The Myth of Masculinity.* MIT Press, 1981.

19

Theories of Personality

═══════ Chapter Preview ═══════

Eels, Cocaine, Hypnosis, and Dreams

One of his earliest scientific discoveries was the location of the testes in a species of eel. Later he made a discovery he believed would ensure his greatness. He obtained some cocaine and began to study its value as a medicine. Soon he was convinced that it was a wonder drug. He proclaimed, "I took coca again and a small dose lifted me to heights in a wonderful fashion. I am just now busy collecting the literature for a song of praise to this magical substance" (Jones, 1953, p. 84). His infatuation with cocaine came to a rapid end when he prescribed it to aid a friend addicted to morphine: The friend developed a double dependency. His next experiment was with hypnosis, but he abandoned it when it did not meet his needs. At age forty-four, rejected by friends, and virtually unknown in intellectual circles, he published his first book, a masterwork entitled The Interpretation of Dreams *(1900). Less than 1000 copies were sold.*

Question: Who are you talking about?

The hero of this little essay is no less than the best known of all personality theorists, Sigmund Freud. Volume after volume followed Freud's initial work until he had built a monumental theory of personality and profoundly influenced the course of modern thought. Other theorists owe a debt to his pioneering efforts.

   As there are literally dozens of personality theories, we cannot hope to do more than introduce the reader to the most influential. For clarity, we will confine ourselves to three broad perspectives: (1) psychodynamic theories; (2) behavioristic theories; and (3) humanistic theories. *Psychodynamic theories focus on the inner workings of personality, especially internal conflicts and struggles. Behavioristic theories place greater importance on the external environment and on the effects of conditioning and learning. Humanistic approaches emphasize individual subjective experience and personal growth.*

Survey Questions   How do psychodynamic theorists explain the workings of personality? What do behaviorists emphasize in their approach to personality? How do the ideas of humanistic psychologists differ from other perspectives? According to each major perspective (psychodynamic, behavioristic, humanistic), what childhood events shape adult personality? What steps can be taken to promote self-actualization? How does moral development relate to personality?

435

━━━━━━━━━━━━━━━━ Resources ━━━━━━━━━━━━━━━━

My life has been aimed at one goal only; to infer or to guess how the mental apparatus is constructed and what forces interplay and counteract in it.

Sigmund Freud

Psychoanalytic Theory— The Battle Within

Psychoanalytic theory, the best-known psychodynamic approach, grew out of the clinical study of disturbed individuals. Sigmund Freud, a Viennese physician, became interested in personality and the treatment of mental disorders when he determined that many of his patients' problems were without physical cause. Starting about 1890 and continuing until he died in 1939, Freud evolved a theory of personality that is more complex than a short description can show. We will consider only its main features.

Question: How did Freud view personality?

The Structure of Personality

Freud conceived of personality as a dynamic system of energies directed by three structures: the **id,** the **ego,** and the **superego.** Each is a complex system in its own right, and behavior in most situations involves the activity of all three.

The Id   The id is made up of inherited biological instincts and urges present at birth. It is self-serving, irrational, impulsive, and totally **unconscious.** The id operates on the **pleasure principle,** meaning that pleasure-seeking impulses of all kinds are freely expressed. If everyone's personality were solely under control of the id, the world would be chaotic beyond belief. Newborn infants are sometimes described as "all id" since they desire immediate satisfaction of their needs.

Freud thought of the id as a wellspring of energy for the entire **psyche,** or personality. This energy, called **libido,** derives from the **life instincts** (called **Eros**), which promote survival and underlie sexual desires. Freud also postulated a **death instinct (Thanatos),** which he deemed responsible for aggressive and destructive urges (Fig. 19-1). Most id energies are directed toward discharge of tensions associated with sex and aggression.

The Ego   The ego, sometimes described as the "executive," draws its energy from the id. The id is like a blind king whose power is awesome but who must rely on others to carry out his orders. The id can only produce mental images of things it desires (called "primary process thinking"). The ego wins power to direct the personality by matching the desires of the id with external reality.

Question: Are there other differences between the ego and the id?

Yes. In contrast to the id, which operates on the pleasure principle, the ego is directed by the **reality principle** (which involves delaying action until it is appropriate). The operation of the reality principle results in "secondary process thinking," which is basically realistic problem solving. The ego is thereby the system of thinking, planning, and deciding. It is in conscious control of the personality.

Question: What is the role of the superego?

The Superego   The superego acts as a judge or censor for the thoughts and actions of the ego. One part of the superego, called the **conscience,** represents all actions for which a person has been punished. When standards of the conscience are not met, you are punished internally by *guilt* feelings. The **ego-ideal** represents all behavior one's parents approved or rewarded. The ego-ideal is a source of goals and aspirations. When its standards are met, *pride* is felt. By these processes, the superego acts as an "internalized parent" to bring behavior under control. In Freudian terms, a person with a poorly developed superego will be a delinquent, criminal, or antisocial personality. In contrast, an overly strict or repressive superego will cause inhibition, rigidity, or intolerable guilt.

The Dynamics of Personality

Question: How do the id, ego, and superego interact?

It is important to recognize that Freud did not envision the id, ego, and superego as parts of the brain, or as "little people" running the human psyche. In reality they are distinct and conflicting psychological processes. Freud theorized a delicate balance of power among the three. For example, the demands of the id for immediate gratification frequently conflict with the superego's moral restrictions. Perhaps the role of each division of the personality can be clarified by an example.

Freud in a Nutshell

Let's say you are sexually attracted to someone. The id clamors for immediate satisfaction of its sexual desires, but is opposed by the superego (which finds the very

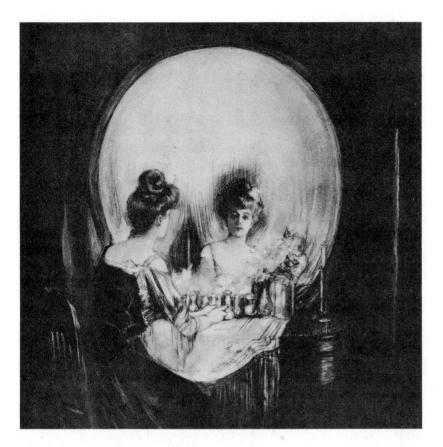

Fig. 19-1   *Freud considered personality an expression of two conflicting forces: life instincts and the death instinct. Both are symbolized in this drawing by Allan Gilbert. (If you don't immediately see the death symbolism, stand farther from the drawing.)*

thought of sexual behavior appalling). The id says, "Now, now, now!" The superego icily responds, "Never!" And what does the ego say? The ego says, "I have a plan!"

To be sure, the oversimplification is drastic, but it captures the essence of Freudian personality dynamics. In its attempts to reduce tension, the ego could initiate actions leading to friendship, romance, courtship, and marriage. If the id is unusually powerful, the ego may direct an attempted seduction. If the superego is dominant, the ego may be forced to *displace* or *sublimate* sexual energies to other activities (sports, music, dancing, pushups, cold showers . . .). According to Freud, similar internal struggles and redirection of energies typify most personality functioning.

Question: Is the ego always caught in the middle?

Basically yes, and the pressures on it can be quite strong. In addition to meeting the conflicting demands of the id and the superego, the overworked ego must deal with external reality. When the ego is threatened or overwhelmed, the person feels anxiety. Impulses from the id that threaten a loss of control cause **neurotic anxiety.** Threats of punishment from the superego cause **moral anxiety.** Each

person develops habitual ways of reducing these anxieties, and many resort to use of *ego-defense mechanisms* to lessen internal conflicts (see Chapter 14).

Levels of Awareness   A major principle of psychoanalytic theory is that behavior is often an expression of unconscious forces within the personality. The unconscious includes repressed memories and emotions as well as the instinctual drives of the id. Although they are below the level of awareness, unconscious thoughts, feelings, or impulses may slip into behavior in disguised or symbolized form. For example, if you meet someone you would like to know better, you may unconsciously leave a book or a jacket at his or her house to ensure another meeting.

Question: Earlier you said the id is completely unconscious. Are the actions of the ego and superego unconscious?

At times, yes, but they also operate on two other levels of awareness, the conscious and the preconscious (Fig. 19-2). The **conscious** level includes everything we are aware of at a given moment: thoughts, perceptions, feelings, and memories. The **preconscious** contains material that can be readily brought to awareness. If you stop to think about a time when you have felt angry or rejected, you will be moving this memory from the preconscious to the conscious level of awareness.

Another illustration of the levels of awareness is found in the operation of the superego. At times we consciously attempt to live up to moral codes or standards; at other times a person may feel guilty without knowing why. Psychoanalytic theory attributes the latter instances to unconscious workings of the superego. In Freudian psychology, events that are truly unconscious cannot be readily brought to awareness or directly known by the individual.

Psychodynamic Theories— Freud's Descendants

Freud's revolutionary ideas quickly attracted a brilliant following. Just as rapidly, Freud's insistence on the importance of instinctual drives and sexuality caused many to disagree with him. Those who stayed close to the core of Freud's thought are now referred to as **neo-Freudians** (*neo:* new). Some of the better known neo-Freudians include: Karen Horney, Anna Freud (Freud's daughter), Otto Rank, and Erich Fromm. Other early followers of Freud broke away more completely and developed their own opposing theories. This group includes people such as Alfred Adler, Harry Sullivan, and Carl Jung.

Question: How did the thinking of these people differ from Freud's ideas?

A complete account of other psychodynamic theories must await your first course in personality. For now, let's sample three alternate views: one representing an early rejection of Freud's thinking (Adler); a second embracing most but not all of Freud's theory (Horney); and the third involving

a carry-over of Freudian ideas into a related but unique theory (Jung).

Alfred Adler (1870–1937)   Adler broke away from Freud because he disagreed with Freud's emphasis on the unconscious, on instinctual drives, and on the importance of sexuality. Adler believed that we are *social* creatures governed by social urges, *not* by biological instincts. In Adler's view, the main driving force in personality is a **striving for superiority.** By this concept he meant a struggle to overcome imperfections, an upward drive for competence, completion, and mastery of limitations.

Question: What motivates "striving for superiority"?

Adler felt that everyone experiences **feelings of inferiority,** mainly because we begin life as small, weak, and relatively powerless children surrounded by larger and more powerful adults. Feelings of inferiority may also come from the inevitable limitations each of us possess. The struggle for superiority arises from such universal feelings.

While everyone strives for superiority, each person tries to **compensate** for different limitations, and each chooses a different pathway to superiority. Adler believed that this situation creates a unique **style of life** (or personality pattern) for each individual. According to Adler the core of each person's style of life is formed by age five.* However, later in his life Adler began to emphasize the existence of a **creative self,** by which he meant that humans continuously create their own personalities through their choices and experiences.

Karen Horney (1885–1952)   Karen Horney (HORN-eye) was a neo-Freudian who remained faithful to most of Freud's ideas, but altered or rejected some, and added many of her own. Like Adler, Horney, also, resisted Freud's more mechanistic, biological, and instinctive ideas.

Question: For example?

As a woman, Horney rejected Freud's claim that "anatomy is destiny." This view, inherent in Freudian psychology, held males to be dominant or superior to females. Horney was among the first to counter the obvious male bias in Freud's thinking.

Horney also disagreed with Freud about the causes of neurosis. Freud held that the neurotic (anxiety-ridden) individual is struggling with forbidden drives that threaten a loss of control. Horney's view was that a core of **basic anxiety** occurs when people feel isolated and helpless in

*According to Adler, valuable clues to a person's style of life are revealed by the earliest memory that can be recalled. You might therefore find it interesting to search back to your earliest memory and contemplate what it tells you.

Fig. 19-2 *The approximate relationship between the id, ego, superego, and levels of awareness.*

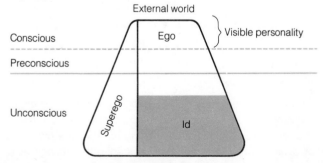

a hostile world—feelings rooted in childhood. Basic anxiety then causes troubled individuals to exaggerate a single mode of interacting with others.

According to Horney each of us can move **toward** others (by depending on them for love, support, or friendship); we can move **away** from others (by withdrawing, acting as a "loner," or by being "strong" and independent); or we can move **against** others (by attacking, competing with, or seeking power over them). Horney felt that emotional health requires a balance in moving toward, away from, and against others. In her view, emotional problems tend to lock people into overuse of only one of the three modes—an insight that remains valuable today.

Carl Jung (1875–1961)   Jung (pronounced Yung) was a student of Freud's, but the two parted ways as Jung began to develop his own ideas. Like Freud, Jung called the conscious part of the personality the ego. In addition, however, he noted that between the ego and the outside world we often find a **persona,** or mask. The persona is the "public self" presented to others when people adopt particular roles, or when they shield their deeper feelings. As mentioned in the previous chapter, actions of the ego may reflect attitudes of **introversion** (in which energy is mainly directed inward), or of **extroversion** (in which energy is mainly directed outward).

Question: Was Jung's view of the unconscious the same as Freud's?

Jung used the term **personal unconscious** to refer to what Freud simply called the unconscious. The personal unconscious is a storehouse for personal experiences, feelings, and memories that are not directly knowable. Departing from Freud, Jung also proposed a deeper **collective unconscious,** shared by all humans. Jung believed that since the beginning of time all humans have had experiences with birth, death, power, god figures, mother and father figures, animals, the earth, energy, evil, rebirth, and so on. According to Jung, such universals create **archetypes** (AR-keh-types: original ideas, patterns, or prototypes). Archetypes, found in the collective unconscious, are unconscious images that cause us to respond emotionally to *symbols* of birth, death, energy, animals, evil, and the like. Jung believed that he detected symbols representing such archetypes in the art, religion, myths, and dreams of every culture and age.

Question: Are some archetypes more important than others?

Two particularly important archetypes are the **anima** (representing the female principle) and the **animus** (represent-

ing the male principle). Each person has both an anima and an animus. For full development, Jung considered it essential that expression be given to both the "masculine" and "feminine" side of personality. Existence of the anima in males and the animus in females also enables us to relate to members of the opposite sex.

Jung considered the **self archetype** the most important of all. The self archetype represents unity. Its existence causes a gradual movement toward balance, integration, and harmony within the personality. Jung felt that we become richer and more completely human when a balance is achieved between conscious and unconscious, anima and animus, thinking and feeling, sensing and intuiting, shadow and ego, introversion and extroversion.

Question: Was Jung talking about self-actualization?

Essentially he was. Jung was the first to use the term "self-actualization" with respect to this striving for completion and unity. He believed that the self archetype is symbolized in every culture by **mandalas** (magic circles) of one kind or another (Fig. 19-3). Jung's theory may not always be "good psychology," but clearly he was a man of genius and vision. If you would like to know more about Jung and his ideas, a good starting place is his autobiography, *Memories, Dreams, Reflections.*

Fig. 19-3   *Jung considered circular designs symbols of the self archetype and representations of unity, balance, and completion within the personality.*

Learning Check

1. List the three divisions of personality postulated by Freud: _____ .

2. Which division is totally unconscious? _____ .

3. Which division is responsible for moral anxiety? _____ .

4. Freud proposed the existence of a death archetype known as Thanatos.   T or F?

Match:

_____ 5. striving for superiority   **A.** Freud

_____ 6. basic anxiety   **B.** Adler

_____ 7. pleasure principle   **C.** Horney

_____ 8. collective unconscious   **D.** Jung

_____ 9. anima

Answers: D '6   D '8   V 'L   Ɔ '9   B 'S   F .4   superego .3   id .2   id, ego, superego .1

Learning Theories of Personality— Habit I Seen You Somewhere Before?

Question: How do behaviorists approach personality?

According to some critics: As if people are robots like R2D2 of *Star Wars* fame. Actually, the behaviorist position is not nearly as mechanistic as some critics would have us believe, and its value is now well established. For one thing, the behaviorists have shown repeatedly that children can *learn* the likes of kindness or hostility, generosity or destructiveness (Bandura and Walters, 1963; Hoffman, 1975). But what does this have to do with personality? Everything, according to the behavioral viewpoint. The behaviorist position is that personality is no more (or less) than a collection of learned behavior patterns. "Personality," like other learned behavior, is acquired through classical and operant conditioning, observational learning, reinforcement, extinction, generalization, and discrimination (Fig. 19-4). When Mother says, "It's not nice to make mud pies with Mommy's blender. If we want to grow up to be a big girl we won't do it again, will we?" she serves as a model, and in other ways shapes her daughter's personality.

In general, learning theorists reject the idea that personality is made up of consistent traits. They would contend, for instance, that there is no such thing as a trait of "honesty" (Bandura, 1973; Mischel, 1968).

Question: Certainly some people are honest while others are not. How can honesty not be considered a trait?

A learning theorist would agree that some people are *more often* honest than others. But knowing this does not allow us to predict whether or not a person will be honest in any specific situation. It would not be unusual, for example, to find that a person honored for returning a lost wallet has cheated on his income tax (or his wife). If you were to ask a learning theorist, "Are you an honest person?" the reply might be, "In what situation?" Yet, in drawing our attention to **situational determinants** of behavior, learning theorists have not entirely removed the "person" from personality. Walter Mischel (1973) acknowledges that some situations are very powerful determiners of behavior (for instance, an escaped lion walks into the supermarket; you accidentally sit on a lighted cigarette; you find your lover in bed with your best friend). Other situations are trivial and have little impact on behavior. Thus, external events interact with each person's unique learning history to produce behavior in any given situation.

Question: How do learning theorists view the structure of personality?

Behavior = Personality   A basic behavioral view of personality, proposed by John Dollard and Neal Miller (1950), holds that **habits** form the structure of personality. As for the dynamics of personality, Dollard and Miller believe habits are governed by four elements of the learning process: **drive, cue, response,** and **reward.** A drive is any stimulus strong enough to goad a person to action (hunger, pain, lust, frustration, fear, and so on). Cues are signals from the environment that guide responses so they are most likely to bring about reinforcement (reward).

Question: I can't see the connection to personality.

An example may clarify this viewpoint. Let's say a child is frustrated by an older brother who takes a toy from him. A number of responses are open to the child. He can throw a temper tantrum, hit the older brother, tell Mother, and so forth. The *response* selected depends on available cues and the previous effects of each response. If telling Mother has paid off in the past, and she is present, this may be the immediate response. If a different set of cues exists (if Mother is absent or if the older brother looks particularly menacing), some other response may be selected. To an outside observer, the child's actions seem to reflect his personality. To the learning theorist, they are a direct reaction to the combined effects of drive, cue, response, and reward.

Question: Doesn't this analysis leave out a lot?

Yes. Learning theorists originally set out to provide a simple, clear model of personality. But in recent years they have had to acknowledge a fact they originally tended to overlook. The fact is: People think. The new breed of behavioral psychologists—who include perception, thinking, and other "mental" events in their view of personality—are called **social learning theorists** (because they also emphasize social relationships and modeling).

Social Learning Theory The "cognitive behaviorism" of social learning theory can be illustrated by three concepts proposed by Julian Rotter (1975). They are: the psychological situation, expectancy, and reinforcement value. Let's examine each.

Someone trips you. How do you respond? Your response probably depends on whether you think it was an accident or intentional. It is not enough to know the setting in which a person responds. We also need to know the person's **psychological situation.** That is, how the person *interprets* or *defines* the situation. Here's another example, let's say you do poorly on an exam. Do you consider it a challenge to work harder, time to drop the class, or an excuse to get drunk? Again, your interpretation is important.

Expectancy refers to anticipation that a response will produce reinforcement. To continue the example, if "working harder" has paid off in the past, it is a likely response to a low test score. But according to Rotter, behavior is not automatic. To predict your response, we would also have to know if you *expect* your efforts to pay off in the present situation. In fact, expected reinforcement may be more important than actual past reinforcement. And what about the *value* you attach to grades, school success, or personal competence? Rotter's third concept, **reinforcement value,** states that, as thinking creatures, humans attach different values to various activities or rewards. This too must be taken into account to understand personality.

One additional idea deserves mention here. We all at

Fig. 19-4 *Freud believed that aggressive urges are "instinctual." In contrast, behavioral theories assume that personal characteristics such as aggressiveness are learned. Is this boy's aggression the result of observational learning, harsh punishment, or prior reinforcement?*

times evaluate our actions and may reward ourselves with special privileges or treats when the evaluation is positive. With this in mind, social learning theory adds the concept of **self-reinforcement** to the behavioristic view. Thus, habits of self-praise or self-reproach become important dimensions of personality. In fact, self-reinforcement might be considered the behaviorist's equivalent of the Freudian superego.

Radical Behaviorism As you have probably noted, social learning theory is only moderately behavioristic. The most extreme view of personality is held by radical behaviorist B. F. Skinner, who has said, "Intelligent people no longer believe that men are possessed by demons . . . but human behavior is still commonly attributed to indwelling agents" (Skinner, 1971). For Skinner, "personality" is a convenient fiction we invent to pretend we have explained behavior that is actually controlled by the environment. Skinner believes that everything a person does is ultimately based on past and present rewards and punishments. Perhaps Skinner's point of view has been shaped by his environment.

Humanistic Theory—New Images

Humanism is a reaction to the pessimism of psychoanalytic theory and the mechanism of learning theory. At its core is a new image of what it means to be human. Humanists reject the Freudian view of personality as a battleground for biological instincts and unconscious forces. They view people as unique and set apart from the rest of the animal kingdom. Humanists also oppose the mechanical, "thing-like" overtones of the behaviorist viewpoint. We are not, they say, merely a bundle of moldable responses; instead, we are creative beings capable of making responsible choices. The humanistic viewpoint leads to a greater emphasis being placed on immediate **subjective experience** than on prior learning.

Humanists tend to be optimistic in their belief that people are motivated not merely to survive, but to strive for *self-actualization* (fulfillment of potential). Humanists feel that personal growth and harmonious functioning occur when people are realistically in touch with themselves and others.

Question: Who are the major humanistic theorists?

There are many psychologists whose theories fall within the humanistic tradition. Of these, the best known are Carl Rogers and Abraham Maslow. Since Maslow's ideas are discussed in earlier chapters, as well as in this chapter's "Applications," let's concentrate on Rogers' view of personality.

Carl Rogers' Self Theory

Carl Rogers is a contemporary psychotherapist who, like Freud, based his theory on clinical experience. Unlike Freud, who portrayed the normal personality as "adjusted" to internal conflict, Rogers sees greater possibility for inner harmony. The **fully functioning person,** he says, is one who has achieved an openness to feelings and experiences and has learned to trust inner urges and intuitions (Rogers, 1961). Rogers feels this attitude is most likely to occur when a person receives ample amounts of love and acceptance from others.

Personality Structure and Dynamics Rogers' theory of personality centers on the concept of the **self,** a flexible and changing perception of personal identity that emerges from the **phenomenal field.**

Question: What is the "phenomenal field"?

The phenomenal field is the person's total *subjective* experience of reality. The self is made up of those experiences identified as "I" or "me" that are separated from

Fig. 19-5 *Humanists consider self-image a central determinant of behavior and personal adjustment.*

"not me" experiences. Much human behavior can be understood as an attempt to maintain consistency between one's **self-image** and actions. For example, individuals who think of themselves as kind and considerate will act accordingly in most situations.

Question: Let's say I know a person who thinks she is kind and considerate, but she really isn't. How does this fit Rogers' theory?

According to Rogers, experiences that match the self-image are **symbolized** (admitted to consciousness) and contribute to gradual changes in the self. Information or feelings inconsistent with the self-image are said to be **incongruent.** It is incongruent, for example, to think of yourself as a considerate person if others frequently mention your rudeness. It is also incongruent to pretend you are kind when you are feeling callous or to say you are not angry when you are seething inside.

Experiences seriously incongruent with the self-image can be threatening, and they are often distorted or denied conscious recognition. Blocking, denying, or distorting experiences prevents the self from changing and creates a gulf between the self-image and reality. As the self-image grows more unrealistic, the **incongruent person** becomes confused, vulnerable, dissatisfied, or seriously maladjusted (see Chapter 20).

When your self-image is consistent with what you really think, feel, do, and experience, you are best able to actualize your potentials. Rogers calls this **congruence.** Instead of becoming a rigid source of threat, the self-image of a **congruent person** is flexible, and it realistically changes as new experiences occur. Rogers also considers it essential to have congruence between the self-image and the **ideal self.** The ideal self is similar to Freud's ego-ideal. It is an image of the person you would most like to be.

Question: Is it really incongruent to not live up to one's ideal self?

Rogers is aware that we never fully attain our ideals, but the greater the gap between the way you see yourself and the way you would like to be, the greater the tension and anxiety experienced. The Rogerian view of personality functioning can therefore be summarized as a process of maximizing potentials by accepting information about oneself as realistically and honestly as possible.

Learning Check

1. Social learning theorists relate personality "traits" to _____.

2. Dollard and Miller consider cues the basic structure of personality.   T or F?

3. Humanists emphasize subjective experience and innate drives for self-actualization.   T or F?

4. A close match between the self-image and the ideal self creates a condition called incongruence.   T or F?

5. Self-reinforcement is to behavioristic theory as superego is to psychoanalytic theory.   T or F?

6. The radical behaviorist view of personality is represented by:

   a. Neal Miller   *b.* B. F. Skinner   *c.* Abraham Maslow   *d.* Carl Rogers

Answers: 1. habits or specific situations   2. F   3. T   4. F   5. T   6. b

---

Personality Development— Three Theories

Every society must bring about the **socialization** of its children by teaching them language, customs, rules, roles, and morals. The job of preparing children for participation in society is typically placed in the hands of parents. This arrangement is convenient and fateful. While socializing children, parents impart something of their own personality to a child.

Question: How does this occur? What factors are most influential in the development of adult personality?

Each theory offers a different version of the important events in personality formation. Let's begin with a look at the psychoanalytic viewpoint.

A Freudian Fable?

Freud theorized that the core of personality is formed before age six in a series of **psychosexual stages.** His account holds that childhood urges for erotic pleasure have lasting effects on development. Freud's emphasis on infantile sexuality is one of the most controversial aspects of his thinking. However, Freud used the term "sex" very broadly to mean any pleasurable activity.

Freud identified four psychosexual stages, the **oral, anal, phallic,** and **genital.** At each stage, a different part of the body becomes an **erogenous zone** (an area capable of producing pleasure). Each then serves as the principal source of pleasure, frustration, and self-expression. Freud believed that many adult personality traits can be traced to **fixations** in one or more of the stages.

Question: What is a fixation?

A fixation is an unresolved conflict or emotional hang-up caused by overindulgence or frustration. A description of the psychosexual stages shows why Freud considered fixations important.

The Oral Stage   During the first year of life, most of the infant's pleasure comes from stimulation of the mouth. If a child is overfed or frustrated, oral traits may be created. Adult expressions of oral needs include gum chewing, nail biting, smoking, kissing, overeating, and alcoholism.

Question: What if there is an oral fixation?

Fixation early in the oral stage produces an **oral-dependent** personality. Oral-dependent persons are gullible (they swallow things easily!), passive, and need lots of attention (they want to be mothered). Frustrations later in the oral stage cause aggression in the form of biting. Fixation here causes **oral-aggressive** adults to be argumentative ("biting sarcasm" is their forte!), cynical, and exploitive of others.

The Anal Stage   Between the ages of one and three, the child's attention shifts to the process of elimination. When parents attempt toilet training, the child can gain approval or express rebellion or aggression by "holding on" or "letting go." Therefore, harsh or indulgent toilet training may establish such responses as personality traits. Freud characterized the **anal-retentive** (holding-on) personality as obstinate, stingy, orderly, and compulsively clean. The **anal-expulsive** (letting-go) personality is disorderly, destructive, cruel, or messy.

The Phallic Stage   Adult characteristics of the **phallic personality** are: vanity, exhibitionism, sensitive pride, and narcissism (self-love). Freud theorized that such traits develop between the ages of three and six. At this time, increased sexual interest causes the child to become physi-

cally attracted to the parent of the opposite sex. In males this attraction generates the **Oedipus conflict.** In it, the boy feels rivalry with his father for the affection of the mother. Freud felt the male child feels threatened by the father (specifically, the boy fears castration). To alleviate his anxieties, the boy must **identify** with the father. Identification causes him to take on the father's values and to form a conscience.

Question: What about the female child?

In a counterpart to the Oedipus conflict called the **Electra conflict,** the girl loves her father and competes with her mother. However, according to Freud, the girl's identification with the mother is more gradual and less effective in creating a conscience. Freud believed that females already feel castrated and so are less driven to identify with their mothers than boys are with their fathers. This particular aspect of Freudian thought has been thoroughly (and rightfully) denounced by modern feminists. It is probably best understood as a reflection of the male-dominated times in which Freud lived.

Latency   According to Freud there is a period of *latency* from age six to puberty. Latency is not actually a stage. Rather, it is a time during which psychosexual development is temporarily interrupted. Freud's contention that psychosexual development is "on hold" at this time is a bit difficult to accept for those who work with children. Nevertheless, Freud saw latency as a relatively quiet time compared to the stormy first six years of life.

The Genital Stage   At puberty a resurgence of sexual energies activates all the unresolved conflicts of earlier years. This resurgence, according to Freud, is the reason why adolescence can be such a trying time, filled with emotion and turmoil. The genital stage begins at puberty and is marked, through adolescence, by a growing capacity for mature and responsible social-sexual relationships. The genital stage culminates in heterosexual love and the attainment of full adult sexuality.

Critical Comments   As bizarre as Freud's developmental theory might seem, it has been influential for several reasons. First, it pioneered the idea that the first years of life help shape adult personality. Second, it identified feeding, toilet training, and early sexual experiences as critical events in personality formation. Third, Freud was among the first to propose that development proceeds through a series of stages. (Erik Erikson's psycho-*social* stages are a modern extension of Freudian thinking.)

445 Theories of Personality

Question: Is the Freudian view of development widely accepted?

Despite its contributions, Freud's theory remains controversial, and few psychologists embrace it without reservation. In some cases Freud was clearly wrong. His portrayal of the elementary school years (latency) as free from sexuality and unimportant for personality development defies belief. His idea of the role of a stern or threatening father in the development of a strong conscience in males has also been challenged. Studies show that an affectionate and accepting father is more likely than a stern one to create a strong conscience in a son (Mussen *et al.,* 1969; Sears *et al.,* 1957). Freud also overemphasized sexuality in personality development; other motives and cognitive factors are of equal importance. Many more criticisms could be listed, but the fact remains that there is an element of truth to much of what Freud said.

Question: How do learning theorists account for personality development?

Behavioristic Views of Development

Many of Freud's major points can be restated in terms of modern learning theory. Miller and Dollard (1950) agree with Freud that the first six years are crucial for personality development, but for different reasons. Rather than thinking in terms of psychosexual urges and fixations, they ask, "What makes early learning experiences so lasting in their effects?" Their answer is that childhood is a time of urgent and tearing drives, powerful rewards and punishments, and crushing frustrations. Also important is **social reinforcement** based on the effects of attention and approval from others. These forces combine to shape the core of personality.

Critical Situations   Miller and Dollard consider four developmental situations to be of critical importance. These are: (1) **feeding;** (2) **toilet** or **cleanliness training;** (3) **sex training;** and (4) learning to express **anger** or **aggression.**

Question: Why are these of special importance?

Feeding serves as an illustration. If children are fed when they cry, they are encouraged to actively manipulate the environment. The child allowed to cry without being fed learns to be passive. Thus, a basic active or passive orientation toward the world may be established by early feeding experiences. Feeding can also affect later social relationships because the child learns to associate satisfaction and

pleasure, or frustration and discomfort, with the presence of others.

Toilet and cleanliness training can be a particularly strong source of emotion for both parents and children. Parents are usually aghast the first time they find a child smearing feces about with gay abandon. Their reaction is often sharp punishment, and that of the child, frustration and confusion. Many attitudes toward cleanliness, conformity, and bodily functions are formed at such times. Studies also show that severe, punishing, or frustrating toilet training can have undesirable effects on personality development (Sears *et al.,* 1957). Toilet and cleanliness training therefore demand patience and a sense of humor.

Question: What about sex and anger?

When, where, and how a child learns to express anger and aggression are of obvious importance. Since many of the most important factors are discussed elsewhere (see Chapter 9), we will focus on sex training.

Becoming Male or Female   From birth onward, children are identified as boys or girls and encouraged to learn sex-appropriate behavior. Two processes that contribute significantly to personality development in general, and particularly to sex training, are *identification* and *imitation.* **Identification** refers to the child's emotional attachment to admired adults, especially to those the child depends on for love and care. Identification typically encourages **imitation,** a desire to be like the valued and admired adult (Fig. 19-6). Many of a child's "male" or "female" traits come from conscious or unconscious attempts to pattern behavior after that of the same-sex parent with which the child identifies.

Question: When children are around parents of both sexes, why don't they imitate behavior typical of the opposite sex as well as the same sex?

You may recall from Chapter 9 that Albert Bandura and others have shown that learning takes place vicariously as well as directly (Bandura, 1965). This means we can learn without direct reward by observing and remembering the actions of others. But imitation of actions depends on their outcome. For example, boys and girls have equal opportunities to observe adults and other children acting aggressively. However, girls are less likely than boys to imitate aggressive behavior because they rarely see female aggression rewarded or approved. Thus, many arbitrary dimensions of "maleness" or "femaleness" are perpetuated at the same time sexual identity is established.

A study of preschool children (Lisa Serbin and Daniel

A Humanistic View of Development

Why do mirrors, photographs, tape recorders, and the reactions of others hold such fascination and threat for most people? Carl Rogers would say it is because they provide information about one's self. The development of a self-image is highly dependent on information from the environment. It begins with a sorting of perceptions and feelings—my body, my toes, my nose, I want, I like, I am, and so on—and soon expands to include self-evaluation: I am a good person, I am bad right now, etc.

Question: How does development of the self contribute to later personality functioning?

Rogers holds that positive and negative evaluations by others cause a child to develop internal standards of evaluation called **conditions of worth.** In other words, we learn that some actions win our parents' love and approval while others are rejected.

Learning to evaluate some experiences or feelings as "good" and others as "bad" is directly related to a later capacity for self-esteem, positive self-evaluation, or **positive self-regard,** to use Rogers' term. To think of yourself as a good, lovable, worthwhile person, your behavior and experiences must match your internalized conditions of worth. The problem is that this can cause incongruence by leading to the denial of many legitimate feelings and experiences.

To put it simply, Rogers sees many adult adjustment problems as an attempt to live by the standards of others. He believes congruence and self-actualization are encouraged by substituting **organismic valuing** for conditions of worth. Organismic valuing is a direct, gut-level response to life experiences that avoids the filtering and distortion of incongruence. It is the ability to trust one's own feelings and perceptions—to become one's own "locus of evaluation." Organismic valuing is most likely to develop, Rogers feels, when children (or adults) receive "unconditional positive regard" from others. That is, when they are "prized" just for being themselves, without any conditions or "strings" attached.

Fig. 19-6 *Adult personality is influenced by identification with parents.*

O'Leary, 1975) found that boys are three times more likely to get teacher attention for aggressive or disruptive behavior than are girls. Boys who hit other students or broke things typically got loud scoldings that drew the attention of the whole class. When teachers responded to disruptive girls, they gave brief, soft rebukes that others couldn't hear. Since we know that attention of almost any kind reinforces children's behavior, it is clear that the boys were being encouraged to be active and aggressive. Serbin and O'Leary found that girls got the most attention when they were within arm's reach, literally or figuratively clinging to the teacher. It's easy to see that the teachers were unwittingly encouraging the girls to be submissive, dependent, and passive.

Learning Check

1. Freud's version of personality development is based on the concept of _____ stages.

2. Arrange these stages in the proper order: phallic, anal, genital, oral. _____

3. Freud considered the anal-retentive personality obstinate and stingy.   T or F?

4. Which of the following is not a critical learning situation in the behaviorist theory of personality formation? (circle correct answer)

    feeding   sex training   language training   anger training

5. Behavioristic theories emphasize identification and _____.

6. Rogers considers acceptance of conditions of _____ a troublesome aspect of development of the self.

Answers: 1. psychosexual   2. oral, anal, phallic, genital   3. T   4. language training   5. imitation   6. worth

Personality Theories—
Overview and Comparison

Question: Which personality theory is right?

Each theory has made significant contributions to our understanding of personality by meaningfully organizing observations of human behavior. Nevertheless, none of the major theories can be fully proved or disproved. (If a theory could be proved true it would no longer be a theory. It would be a law.) At the same time that theories are neither true nor false, their implications or predictions may be. The best way to judge a theory, then, is in terms of its *usefulness* for explaining behavior, for stimulating research, and for suggesting ways of treating psychological disorders. Each theory has fared differently in these areas. A few brief comments follow on the three major perspectives we have considered: psychoanalytic theory, behavioristic theory, and humanistic theory.

Psychoanalytic Theory   By present standards psychoanalytic theory seems to overemphasize sexuality and biological instincts. It also takes an unnecessarily dim view of human potential. To a large extent these distortions have been corrected by the neo-Freudians and other related theorists. Carl Jung, Alfred Adler, Otto Rank, Karen Horney, Erich Fromm, Erik Erikson, and many others have elaborated psychoanalytic theory and have extended it far beyond its original scope.

Freud has been particularly criticized for his preoccupation with conflicts related to sex and aggression. Perhaps he can be excused for this. Freud's views of human nature were highly influenced by the social climate in which he lived. Most of the patients who ended up on his couch had problems directly related to the strict morals and rigid rules of Victorian Vienna. Freud honestly tried to describe what he observed, but what he saw does not fully apply to modern men and women.

Question: What about the theory's value for explanation, research, and treatment?

One of the most telling criticisms of Freudian theory is that it can be used to explain any psychological event *after* it has occurred, but it offers little help in predicting future behavior. For this reason, many psychoanalytic concepts are difficult or impossible to test empirically. Most of the research inspired by psychoanalytic theory has been restricted to case studies and clinical observations.

As previously noted, Freudian theory suggests a treatment procedure for psychological disorders. This is one of the areas in which the theory has been most useful. Freudian concepts of unconscious motivation, repression, ego-defense, and childhood conflicts have found their way into the thinking of many psychotherapists. This aspect of psychoanalytic theory is examined in greater detail in Chapter 22.

Behavioristic Theory   Learning theories have provided a good framework for personality research. Of the three major perspectives, the behaviorists have made the best effort to rigorously test and verify their concepts. Their emphasis on conditions under which behaviors are learned has led to the development of effective methods for modifying maladaptive behavior (see Chapter 23).

Question: What are the criticisms of behavioristic theories?

Learning is obviously important in most areas of human functioning. However, behavioristic theories tend to underestimate the importance of temperamental, emotional, cognitive, and subjective factors in personality. Moreover, proponents of the trait approach have been critical of the tendency of behavioral theories to deny consistencies in behavior. Although many responses are undoubtedly situational, unique and enduring personality traits also seem to exist. Within its scope behavioristic theory is masterfully

Table 19-1   Comparison of Three Views of Personality

	Psychoanalytic Theory	Behavioristic Theory	Humanistic Theory
View of human nature	negative	neutral	positive
Is behavior free or determined?	determined	determined	free choice
Principal motives	sex and aggression	drives of all kinds	self-actualization
Personality structure	id, ego, superego	habits	self
Role of unconscious	maximized	practically nonexistent	minimized
Conception of conscience	superego	self-reinforcement	ideal self, valuing process
Developmental emphasis	psychosexual stages	critical learning situations; identification and imitation	development of self-image
Barriers to personal growth	unconscious conflicts; fixations	maladaptive habits; pathological environment	conditions of worth; incongruence

effective in accounting for human behavior. The most valid criticism that can be raised against it is that it can be a narrow approach to the rich textures of human experience.

Humanistic Theory   A great strength of the humanists has been their willingness to investigate areas of importance ignored by other viewpoints. Their stress on the positive dimensions of human experience has helped restore balance to psychological thought. As Maslow (1968) put it, "Human nature is not nearly as bad as it has been thought to be. . . . It is as if Freud supplied us the sick half of psychology and we must now fill it out with the healthy half."

Question: How does humanistic theory measure up as a basis for research?

The chief criticism of humanistic theory in this respect lies in the impreciseness of its concepts. For example, what

really is "self-actualization"? Can it be measured? Are the characteristics of self-actualizers open to debate? Imprecise concepts have not completely prevented humanists from carrying out research, but their approach generally tends to be more philosophical than empirical. The real strength of this perspective is the encouragement it gives for self-examination and personal growth. The humanistic emphasis on self-awareness, experiencing, and free emotional expression underlies many of the new growth-oriented psychotherapies.

Summary   In the final analysis, we need the concepts of all three perspectives (and those discussed in the previous chapter) to account adequately for the complexities of personality. There is an element of truth to each view, and a balanced picture emerges only when all are considered. Table 19-1 provides a final overview of the three principal theories we have discussed.

Resources Summary

● Freud's psychoanalytic theory emphasizes unconscious forces and conflicts within the personality. In this theory, personality is made up of the *id, ego,* and *superego. Libido,* derived from the life instincts, is the primary energy running the personality. Conflicts within the personality may cause *neurotic anxiety* or *moral anxiety* and motivate use of *ego-defense mechanisms.* The personality operates on three levels, the *conscious, preconscious,* and *unconscious.*

● Some of Freud's followers, known as *neo-Freudians,* altered and updated his theories. Others have developed related but separate *psychodynamic theories.*
● Alfred Adler proposed a more *social* view of personality, emphasizing *feelings of inferiority* and *striving for superiority.* Striving for superiority and *compensation* for limitations creates a unique *style of life,* which is further altered by the *creative self.*

449 Theories of Personality

● Karen Horney countered some of Freud's male-oriented thinking and contended that emotional disturbances are rooted in *basic anxiety*. Basic anxiety can cause an overuse or overdependence on one of three modes of relating to others: moving *toward, away* from, or *against* others.

● Carl Jung broke away from Freud to develop his own theory, which includes a number of unique concepts such as: the *persona, extroversion* and *introversion,* the *personal unconscious,* and the *collective unconscious.* His most controversial ideas pertain to the existence of *archetypes,* such as the *anima* and *animus,* and the *self archetype.*

● Behavioral theories of personality emphasize learning, conditioning, and immediate effects of the environment. Learning theorists generally reject the idea of stable personality "traits," preferring instead to stress the *situational determinants* of behavior.

● Learning theorists John Dollard and Neal Miller consider *habits* the basic core of personality. Habits express the combined effects of *drive, cue, response,* and *reward.*

● *Social learning theory* adds cognitive elements, such as perception, thinking, and understanding to the behavioral view of personality. Such elements are exemplified by Julian Rotter's concepts of the *psychological situation, expectancies,* and *reinforcement value.* Some social learning theorists treat "conscience" as a case of *self-reinforcement.*

● Humanistic theory emphasizes *subjective experience* and needs for *self-actualization.* Carl Rogers' theory views the *self* as an entity that emerges from the *phenomenal field.* Experiences that match the *self-image* are *symbolized* (admitted to consciousness), while those that are *incongruent* are excluded. The *incongruent person* has a highly unrealistic self-image. The *congruent* or *fully functioning person* is flexible and open to experiences and feelings.

● The Freudian view of personality development is based on a series of *psychosexual stages:* the *oral, anal, phallic,* and *genital* stages. *Fixation* at any stage can leave a lasting imprint on personality.

● The behavioristic view of personality development holds that social *reinforcement* in four situations is critical. The situations are: *feeding; toilet* or *cleanliness training; sex training;* and *anger* or *aggression training.* Identification and imitation are of particular importance in sex training.

● In the development of personality, humanists are primarily interested in the emergence of a *self-image* and self-evaluations. As parents apply *conditions of worth* to children's behavior, thoughts, and feelings, children begin to do the same. Internalized conditions of worth then contribute to incongruence and interrupt the *organismic valuing process.*

The Search for Self-Actualization

Some people fear finding themselves alone—and so they don't find themselves at all (André Gide).

What a man can be, he must be. This need we may call self-actualization (Abraham Maslow).

Self-actualization is a concept that has reappeared several times in this book. Perhaps you have been attracted to the promise it holds for personal growth. Self-actualizers lead rich, creative, and fulfilling lives.

Question: What steps can be taken to promote self-actualization?

Promoting self-actualization is more difficult than might be imagined. Many people are caught in a struggle for survival or security and never get a chance to develop their potentials fully. Others show little interest in personal growth or in the qualities Maslow described. Moreover, Maslow made few specific recommendations about how to proceed. Nevertheless, a number of helpful suggestions can be gleaned from his writings (Maslow, 1954, 1967, 1971).

Steps toward Self-Actualization

There is no magic formula for leading a more creative life. Knowing or even imitating the traits of unusually effective people cannot be counted on to promote self-actualization. Self-actualization is primarily a *process,* not a goal or an endpoint. As such, it requires hard work, patience, and commitment. Here are some ways to begin.

Be Willing to Change   Begin by asking yourself, "Am I living in a way that is deeply satisfying to me and which truly expresses me?" If not, be prepared to make changes in your life. Indeed, ask yourself this question often and accept the need for continued change.

Take Responsibility   You can become an architect of self by acting as *if* you are *personally* responsible for every aspect of your life. Shouldering responsibility in this

way is not totally realistic, but it helps end the habit of blaming others for your own shortcomings. This attitude is illustrated by a young woman who realized in a counseling session, "I can't depend on someone else to give me an education. I'll have to get it myself" (Rogers, 1962).

Examine Your Motives   Self-discovery involves an element of risk. To learn your strengths, limitations, and true feelings, you must be willing to go out on a limb, speak your mind, and take some chances. Fears of failure, rejection, loneliness, or disagreement with others are a tremendous barrier to personal change. If most of your behavior seems to be directed by a desire for "safety" or "security," it may be time to test the limits of these needs. Try to make each life decision a choice for growth, not a response to fear or anxiety.

Experience Honestly and Directly   Wishful thinking is another barrier to personal growth. Self-actualizers trust themselves enough to accept all kinds of information without distorting it to fit their fears and desires. Try to see yourself as others do. Be willing to admit, "I was wrong" or, "I failed because I was irresponsible." This basic honesty can be extended to perception in general. Try to experience the world as you did when you were a child: fully, vividly, and directly. Try to see things as they are, not as you would like them to be.

Make Use of Positive Experiences   As a "rule of thumb," growth-promoting activities usually "feel good." Perhaps you have felt unusually alert and alive when expressing yourself through art, music, dance, writing, or athletics. Or perhaps life seems especially rich when you are alone in nature, surrounded by friends, or when you are helping others. Whatever their source, Maslow considered "peak experiences" temporary moments of self-actualization. Therefore, you might actively repeat activities that have caused feelings of awe, amazement, exaltation, renewal, reverence, humility, fulfillment, or joy.

Applications

Be Prepared to Be Different   Maslow felt that everyone has a potential for "greatness," but most fear becoming what they might. Much of this fear is related to the fact that actualizing potentials may place you at odds with cultural expectations or with others who are important in your life. As part of personal growth, be prepared to be unpopular when your views don't agree with others. Trust your own impulses and feelings; don't automatically judge yourself by the standards of others. Accept your uniqueness: As one young woman put it, "I've always tried to be what others thought I should be, but now I'm wondering whether I shouldn't just see that I am what I am" (Rogers, 1962).

Get Involved   Maslow found with few exceptions that self-actualizers tend to have a mission or "calling" in life. For these people "work" is not done just to fill deficiency needs, but to satisfy higher yearnings for truth, beauty, brotherhood, and meaning. Many of the things you do may be motivated by more commonplace needs, but you can add meaning to these activities by endeavoring to work hard at whatever you do. Get personally involved and committed. Turn your attention to problems outside yourself.

Slow Down   Try to avoid hurrying or overscheduling your time. Self-awareness takes time to develop, and a certain amount of leisure is essential for contemplation and self-exploration. Time pressures tend to force a person to rely compulsively on old habits.

Start a Journal   Although this suggestion does not come from Maslow's writings, it is a valuable means of promoting self-awareness. Many people find a journal provides the kind of information necessary to make growth-oriented life changes. A journal should include a description of significant events in your daily life. In addition, thoughts, feelings, fears, wishes, frustrations, and dreams should be recorded. Some find it useful to write dialogues in their journal in which they speak to parents, teachers, lovers, objects, and so forth. Review and reread your journal periodically. You will find it is easier to learn from an event after it has "cooled off" and you can view it objectively.

Assess Your Progress   Since there is no final point at which one becomes self-actualized, it is important frequently to gauge your progress and to renew your efforts. Boredom is a good sign you are in need of change. If you feel bored at school, at a job, or in a relationship, consider it a challenge or an indication that you have not taken responsibility for personal growth. A situation is only as "boring" as you allow it to be. Almost any activity can be used as a chance for self-exploration if it is approached creatively.

What to Expect   As we have already noted, growth-promoting activities are usually personally satisfying.

Question: Are there other signs that one is moving in the right direction?

Yes, there should be a noticeable improvement in the quality of your daily life and a greater acceptance of yourself and of others. You should feel more confident and should carry out daily routines with less strain or conflict. These changes do not happen overnight, and your first steps toward self-actualization may be threatening at the same time they are exhilarating. Positive changes can also be quite subtle. An idea of what to expect is provided by the words of Henry David Thoreau. After he had spent two years in the wilderness at Walden Pond, Thoreau had this to say about his experience:

> I learned this, at least, by my experiment: that as one advances confidently in the direction of his dreams, and endeavors to live the life which he has imagined, he will meet with a success unexpected in common hours. He will put some things behind, will pass an invisible boundary; new universal and more liberal laws will begin to establish themselves around and within him. . . . The laws of the universe will appear less complex, and solitude will not be solitude, nor poverty, poverty, nor weakness, weakness.

Applications

Learning Check

1. In his writings, Maslow emphasized that self-actualization is a process, not a goal or endpoint.   T or F?
2. Making fuller use of personal potentials requires learning to live up to the expectations of others.   T or F?
3. Maslow described peak experiences as temporary moments of self-actualization.   T or F?
4. A major characteristic of self-actualizers is their interest in status and personal recognition.   T or F?
5. According to Maslow, wishful thinking and distorted self-perceptions are barriers to self-actualization.   T or F?

Answers: 1. T   2. F   3. T   4. F   5. T

═══════════ Exploration ═══════════

Moral Development—Values and Personality

A person with a terminal illness is in great pain and pleading for death. Should extraordinary medical procedures be used to keep him alive? If a friend of yours desperately needed to pass a test and asked you to help him cheat, would you do it?

Questions such as these have more to do with personality than you might suspect. We have already seen that personality theories use some concept of conscience in their explanations of behavior. By conscience, we typically mean a system of *moral values* for evaluating one's own behavior. For many, conscience is simply an internal source of reward (pride) and punishment (guilt). But according to researcher Lawrence Kohlberg, conscience is only one of several ways in which moral values are represented in the personality. Kohlberg (1963, 1969) believes there are higher levels of moral development and that these are acquired in a fixed series of stages.

Question: What does he base this belief on?

Moral Dilemmas To study moral development, Kohlberg posed *moral dilemmas* to children of different ages. Here is one of the dilemmas he used (Kohlberg, 1969; adapted):

> A woman was near death from cancer, and there was only one drug that might save her. It was discovered by a druggist who was charging ten times what the drug cost him to make. The sick woman's husband could only get together $1000, which was half of what the drug cost. He asked the druggist to sell it cheaper or to let him pay later. But the druggist said no. So the husband got desperate and broke into the man's store to steal the drug for his wife. Should he have done that? Was it actually wrong or right? Why?

Each child was asked to say what action should be taken by the husband. Choices the children made were interesting, but the reasons they gave to back them up were of greater importance. By classifying the reasons given, Kohlberg identified three levels of moral development.

At the first, or **preconventional level,** moral thinking is determined by the consequences of actions (punishment, reward, or exchange of favors). In the second, or **conventional level** of morality, actions are directed by a desire to conform to the expectations of others or to uphold socially accepted rules and values. The third, or **postconventional level** represents advanced moral development. Behavior at this level is directed by self-accepted moral principles. In addition to the three levels, Kohlberg identified six stages of moral development.

Stages of Moral Development

Preconventional

Stage 1. Punishment orientation. In this stage actions are evaluated in terms of possible punishment, not goodness or badness. Obedience to power is emphasized.

Stage 2. Pleasure-seeking orientation. Right action is determined by one's own needs. Concern for the needs of others is largely a matter of "You scratch my back and I'll scratch yours," not of loyalty, gratitude, or justice.

Conventional

Stage 3. Good boy/good girl orientation. Good behavior is that which pleases others in the immediate group or which brings approval. The emphasis is on being "nice."

Stage 4. Authority orientation. Upholding law, order, and authority, doing one's duty, and following social rules are emphasized.

Postconventional

Stage 5. Social-contract orientation. Support of laws and rules is based on rational analysis and mutual agreement. Rules are recognized as open to question, but are upheld for the good of the community and in the name of democratic values.

Stage 6. Morality of individual principles. Behavior is directed by self-chosen ethical principles that tend to be general, comprehensive, or universal. High value is placed on justice, dignity, and equality.

Examples of Reasoning at Each Stage

Stage 1. "He shouldn't steal the drug because he could get caught and sent to jail" (avoiding punishment).

Exploration

Stage 2. "It won't do him any good to steal the drug because his wife will probably die before he gets out of jail" (self-interest).

Stage 3. "He shouldn't steal the drug because others will think he is a thief. His wife would not want to be saved by thievery" (avoiding disapproval).

Stage 4. "Although his wife needs the drug, he should not break the law to get it. Everyone is equal in the eyes of the law, and his wife's condition does not justify stealing" (traditional morality of authority).

Stage 5. "He should not steal the drug. The druggist's decision is reprehensible, but mutual respect for the rights of others must be maintained" (social contract).

Stage 6. "He should steal the drug and then inform the authorities that he has done so. He will have to face a penalty, but he will have saved a human life" (self-chosen ethical principles).

Question: Does everyone eventually reach Stage 6?

Kohlberg found that people advance through the stages at different rates and that many people fail to reach the "principled" stages of morality. The self-interested stages (1 and 2) are most characteristic of young children and older delinquents. Conventional group-oriented morals of Stages 3 and 4 are characteristic of older children and most of the adult population. Kohlberg estimates that postconventional morality, representing self-direction and higher principles, is characteristic of only about 20 percent of the adult population. Possibly from 5 to 10 percent of the population consistently operates at Stage 6.

Morality in the Real World To illustrate the importance of moral development as a personality character-

istic, let us compare two very different individuals. First let's apply Kohlberg's analysis to statements attributed to Nazi officer Adolf Eichmann, accused of sharing responsibility for the deaths of millions of Jews in Germany during World War II:

> In actual fact, I was merely a little cog in the machinery that carried out the directives of the German Reich [Stage 1]. It was really none of my business [Stage 2]. Yet what is there to "admit"? I carried out my order [Stage 1] (Kohlberg, 1969).

Compare this to the words of Mahatma Gandhi, the famous leader who protested British rule of India. Gandhi once addressed a British court:

> Nonviolence is the first article of my faith. It is also the last article of my creed. But I had to make a choice. I had to either submit to a system which I considered had done irreparable harm to my country, or incur the risk. . . . I am here, therefore, to invite and cheerfully submit to the highest penalty that can be inflicted upon me for what in law is a deliberate crime and what appears to me to be the highest duty of a citizen.

Gandhi, like other great leaders (Lincoln, Martin Luther King), was clearly operating at Stage 6.

Moral development is a promising topic for additional psychological study. Kohlberg has recently embarked on research into the possibility of teaching higher levels of morality. Although Kohlberg's definition of morality is open to debate, his research appears to be a worthwhile endeavor. Many of the problems facing us today—overpopulation, environmental destruction, crime, prejudice—are essentially problems of individual conscience.

Questions for Discussion

1. How did you answer Kohlberg's moral dilemma? Do you think your answer reflects the role of moral reasoning in your personality?

2. Kohlberg says moral reasoning is a stable personality characteristic; social learning theory says honesty is situational. Which do you think is right? Why?

3. Do you think higher levels of moral reasoning can be taught without specifically teaching moral values?

4. What level of moral reasoning is most frequently displayed by the characters in TV dramas, comedies, or commercials?

5. Do you think the "draft dodgers," antiwar activists, or conscientious objectors of the 1960s were acting in self-interest or at higher levels of morality?

6. Can you describe an action you performed recently that seems to represent operation of the id, ego, or super-ego? How would a behaviorist or a humanist interpret the same event?

7. Can you cite a behavior or an experience that seems to support the existence of the unconscious or of unconscious motivation?

8. Can you cite observations that support Freud's scheme of psychosexual stages? Can you cite observations that contradict it?

9. Is "Mr. Clean" an anal-retentive?

10. As a child whom did you identify with? What effect did this have on your personality?

11. Freud thought that adolescent males who clash with adult male authority figures (teachers, ministers, policemen, and so forth) are experiencing a carry-over of the Oedipus conflict. What do you think?

12. What experiences have you had that have contributed to personal growth? What experiences set you back or were otherwise negative in their effects? Which personality theory best explains the differences between these experiences?

13. The film *Close Encounters* culminates with a visit to Earth by a magnificent round spaceship. The ship opens to reveal childlike creatures who have come to take a chosen few to a new life among the stars. What archetypal symbols are represented by these images? Can you think of other films, works of art, or images that seem to symbolize Jungian archetypes?

Suggestions for Further Reading

Adler, A. *The Science of Living*. Doubleday, 1929.

Fadiman, J., and R. Frager. *Personality and Personal Growth*. Harper and Row, 1976.

Freud, S. *An Outline of Psychoanalysis*. Norton, 1949.

Hall, C. S., and G. Lindzey. *Theories of Personality*, 3rd ed. Wiley, 1978.

Jones, E. *The Life and Work of Sigmund Freud* (3 volumes). Basic Books, 1953–1957.

Jung, C. G. *Memories, Dreams, Reflections*. Random House, 1963.

———. *Man and His Symbols*. Doubleday, 1964.

Maddi, S. R. *Personality Theories: A Comparative Analysis*. Dorsey, 1968.

Mahoney, M. J. "Reflections on the Cognitive-Learning Trend in Psychotherapy," *American Psychologist*, 1977, **32**, 5–13.

Mischel, W. *Personality and Assessment*. Wiley, 1968.

Pervin, L. A. *Personality: Theory, Assessment, and Research*. Wiley, 1970.

Rogers, C. R. *On Becoming a Person*. Houghton-Mifflin, 1961.

Time Magazine. "Why You Do What You Do: Sociobiology—A New Theory of Behavior," August 1, 1977, 54–63.

Contents

Part VI

Abnormal
Behavior
and
Psychotherapy

20

Deviance and Disorder: The Unhealthy Personality

Catch-22: A Practical Definition of "Crazy"

"Can't you ground someone who's crazy?"

"Oh, sure, I have to. There's a rule saying I have to ground anyone who's crazy."

"Then why don't you ground me? I'm crazy. Ask Clevinger."

"Clevinger? Where is Clevinger? You find Clevinger and I'll ask him."

"Then ask any of the others. They'll tell you how crazy I am."

"They're crazy."

"Then why don't you ground them?"

"Why don't they ask me to ground them?"

"Because they're crazy, that's why."

"Of course they're crazy," Doc Daneeka replied. "I just told you they're crazy, didn't I? And you can't let crazy people decide whether you're crazy or not, can you?"

Yossarian looked at him soberly and tried another approach. "Is Orr crazy?"

"He sure is," Doc Daneeka said.

"Can you ground him?"

"I sure can. But first he has to ask me to. That's part of the rule."

"Then why doesn't he ask you to?"

"Because he's crazy," Doc Daneeka said. "He has to be crazy to keep flying combat missions after all the close calls he's had. Sure, I can ground Orr. But first he has to ask me to."

"That's all he has to do to be grounded?"

"That's all. Let him ask me."

"And then you can ground him?" Yossarian asked.

"No. Then I can't ground him."

"You mean there's a catch?"

"Sure there's a catch," Doc Daneeka replied. "Catch-22. Anyone who wants to get out of combat duty isn't really crazy."

There was only one catch and that was Catch-22, which specified that a concern for one's own safety in the face of dangers that were real and immediate was the process of a rational mind. Orr was crazy and could be grounded. All he had to do was ask; and as soon as he did, he would no longer be crazy and would have to fly more missions. Orr would be crazy to fly more missions and sane if he didn't, but if he was sane he had to fly them. If he flew them he was crazy and didn't have to; but if he didn't want to he was sane and had to. Yossarian was moved very deeply by the absolute simplicity of this clause of Catch-22 and let out a respectful whistle

"That's some catch, that Catch-22," he observed.

"It's the best there is," Doc Daneeka agreed.[*]

This excerpt from Joseph Heller's novel Catch 22 *captures the ambiguities presented by the classic question, "What is normal?" In the 1800s, doctors and laymen alike used such terms as "crazy," "insane," "cracked," and "lunatic" quite freely. The "insane" were considered bizarre and definitely different from you or me. Today our understanding of "mental illness" or emotional disturbance is becoming increasingly sophisticated. Drawing lines between normal and abnormal and between pathological and healthy can be accomplished only by taking into consideration some complex issues.*

In this chapter and the next we will summarize some of the major psychological disturbances and the characteristics that distinguish them.

Survey Questions   How is normality defined, and what are the major psychological disorders? What is a personality disorder? Is the term "neurosis" still used? To what problems does it refer? Who becomes "neurotic," and why? What are affective disorders? What can be done about them? What causes suicide, and what can be done to prevent it? What role does the concept of insanity play in criminal trials?

Resources

Psychopathology— Defining Major Psychological Problems

When she was found by police, Evelyn Hunter was wandering around a downtown park. She had no purse, no identification, and no idea who she was or where she had come from. Evelyn Hunter is probably not her true name—it is simply the first name she could think of when asked. Since the day she was found her home has been a hospital room.

William Milligan is accused of being the "university rapist" who attacked four women near the Ohio State University campus in 1978. Milligan has been described by psychiatrists as having ten separate personalities. The rapist is assumed to have been a personality identified as an "18-year-old lesbian."

Unlike the *Catch-22* excerpt, the preceding accounts are "nonfiction." They are typical newspaper reports, and they are but one indication of the magnitude of mental health problems in this country. Here are the facts on psychopathology:

[*]*Catch 22,* copyright © 1955, 1961 by Joseph Heller. Reprinted by permission of Simon and Schuster, Inc., a division of Gulf & Western Corporation.

Nearly half of all hospital beds in all types of hospitals are occupied by the mentally ill.

1 out of every 10 children born will experience either a major or a minor mental disorder.

1 out of every 100 persons will become so severely disturbed as to require hospitalization at some point in his or her lifetime.

In 1975, about 30 out of every 1000 people received some form of care at psychiatric hospitals, an increase of 12 percent since 1970.

Each year over 2 million persons are admitted or re-admitted to out-patient services or psychiatric treatment in general hospitals. (*Statistical Abstract of the United States: 1978.*)

A tremendous variety of problems comes under the general heading of *psychopathology.* **Psychopathology** may be defined as the *inability to behave in ways that foster the well-being of the individual and ultimately of society.* This definition covers not only obviously maladaptive behavior such as drug addiction, compulsive gambling, or loss of contact with reality, but also any behavior that interferes with personal growth and self-fulfillment (Coleman *et al.,* 1980).

Psychological problems are grouped into broad categories of maladaptive behavior. The most widely accepted system of classification is found in the *Diagnostic and Statistical Manual of Mental Disorders* (*DSM-III,* 1980). If you were to glance through this manual you would find a wide range of disorders described, including those which follow.

Organic mental disorders are problems caused by brain pathology; that is, by senility, drug damage, diseases of the brain, injuries, the toxic effects of poisons, and so on. Organic disorders are often accompanied by such symptoms as severe emotional disturbances, impairment of thinking, memory loss, personality changes, and delirium.

Substance use disorders are defined as psychological dependence on mood- or behavior-altering drugs: alcohol, barbiturates, opiates, cocaine, amphetamines, hallucinogens, cannabis, tobacco, and others. Problems in this category usually center on impairment of social or occupational functioning and inability to stop use of the drug. (See paintings in color section.)

Psychotic disorders are the most severe type of psychopathology, often requiring hospitalization. In psychosis there is a retreat from reality: The person can no longer tell what is fantasy or hallucination, and what is real. In addition there is usually a major loss of ability to control thoughts and actions (Fig. 20-1).

Affective disorders primarily involve disturbances in mood or emotion (affect: emotion). In an affective disorder individuals may be *manic,* meaning agitated, euphoric, and hyperactive, or they may be *depressed.* In either case, extremes of mood are intense or long lasting. Depressed individuals run a high risk of suicide.

Anxiety disorders may take the form of *phobias* (irrational fears of objects, activities, or situations), *panic* (in which the person suffers sudden unexplainable feelings of total panic), or *generalized anxiety* (chronic and persistent anxiety). Also associated with anxiety disorders is a pattern known as *obsessive-compulsive* behavior (more on this later).

Somatoform disorders are indicated when a person has physical symptoms suggesting physical disease or injury (paralysis, blindness, or chronic pain, for example) for which there is no identifiable cause. The assumption in such cases is that psychological factors underlie the symptoms.

Dissociative disorders include cases of sudden temporary *amnesia* (as experienced by Evelyn Hunter), and instances of *multiple personality* (William Milligan, for example).

Personality disorders are deeply ingrained maladaptive personality patterns. Such patterns are usually recognizable by adolescence and continue throughout most of adult life. They include paranoid (overly-suspicious), narcissistic, dependent, compulsive, aggressive, antisocial, introverted, and other personality types.

Psychosexual disorders include *gender identity* disorders (where sex role or gender identity does not match physical gender), *transsexualism* (a persistent discomfort about one's sex and a desire to change to the opposite sex), and a wide range of deviations in sexual behavior

Fig. 20-1   *Psychosis is a severe mental disorder that frequently requires hospitalization.*

(fetishism, voyeurism, and so on). Also included in this category are a variety of *psychosexual dysfunctions* (problems in sexual desire or sexual response; see Chapter 24).

Question: Shouldn't neurosis be included on the list?

The former *Diagnostic and Statistical Manual (DSM-II)* listed neurosis as a disorder, but the new version (*DSM-III*) does not. Why? Because it was felt that "neurosis" is too vague a term, and that it tends to lump together too many separate problems. Be that as it may, the term "neurosis" is still widely used by mental health professionals, and it is recognized and understood by the public. For this reason we will use it in this chapter as a convenient way of distinguishing milder problems from the highly disruptive symptoms of psychosis.

In general the "neuroses"* are disorders in which high levels of anxiety (basically inappropriate fear) cause personal discomfort and maladaptive behavior patterns. The patterns most often observed in "neurosis" are: *anxiety disorders, somatoform disorders,* and *dissociative disorders.* In contrast to psychosis, there is no major loss of contact with reality in the neurotic disorders. And while the "neurotic" individual is quite incapacitated, hospitalization is rarely required, as it often is in psychosis.

Question: Is psychosis the same as insanity?

No. Psychosis is a *psychiatric* term that describes a particular form of psychopathology. **Insanity** is a *legal* term. Insanity refers to legal responsibility for one's actions or to the legal designation required for involuntary commitment to a mental institution. Insanity is usually established through the testimony of psychiatrists who serve as expert witnesses in a court of law (see this chapter's "Exploration").

Normality—What Is Normal?

Setting aside certain behaviors or certain people as psychologically unhealthy raises the age-old issue of what is normal. Defining normality can be a tricky business. We might begin by saying that **subjective discomfort** is characteristic of psychopathology; that is, the unhealthy personality will be marked by unhappiness, anxiety, depression, or other signs of emotional upset.

Question: But couldn't a person be psychotic without feeling subjective discomfort?

Yes. A problem with this definition is that a person's behavior might be quite maladaptive without producing subjective discomfort. A psychotic displaying obviously bizarre and maladjusted behavior might feel "on top of the world." It could be said, additionally, that a *lack* of discomfort may indicate a problem. If a person were to show no signs of grief or depression in response to the death of a friend or loved one, we would suspect psychopathology just as surely as we might if grief continued for months. In practice, subjective discomfort accounts for most instances in which a person makes a decision to voluntarily seek professional help.

Some psychologists have tried to pin down normality more objectively by using **statistical definitions.** For example, since we know that anxiety is a characteristic of neurosis we could devise a test to learn how many people show low, medium, or high levels of anxiety. Usually the results of such a test will fall into a **normal*** (bell-shaped) **curve** (see Fig. 20-2). Notice that most people's scores are in the center region of such a curve. Those people who deviate from the average by being anxious all the time (high anxiety) might be considered abnormal. Incidentally, a person who never feels anxiety might also be considered abnormal.

Question: Then a statistical definition of abnormality tells us nothing about the meaning of a deviation from the norm?

Right. It is as statistically "abnormal" (unusual) for a person to score above 145 on an IQ test as it is to score below 55, but only in the second case would we consider the score "abnormal" or undesirable.

Another major problem with a statistical definition is the question of *where to draw the line* between normality and abnormality. To take a new example, we could undoubtedly calculate the average frequency of sexual intercourse for persons of a particular age, sex, and marital status. Obviously a person who feels driven to seek sexual release dozens of times a day has a problem. But as we move back toward the norm we face the statistical problem of drawing lines. How often must an otherwise normal behavior occur before it becomes abnormal?

Social nonconformity may also serve as a basis for judgments of normality. Abnormal behavior can sometimes be viewed as a failure in *socialization.* Here we refer to the person who has not adopted the usual minimum rules for social conduct, or who has learned to engage in socially destructive or self-destructive behavior. This form of non-

---

*Neurosis: singular; neuroses: plural

*Normal in this case is a statistical concept referring only to the shape of the curve.

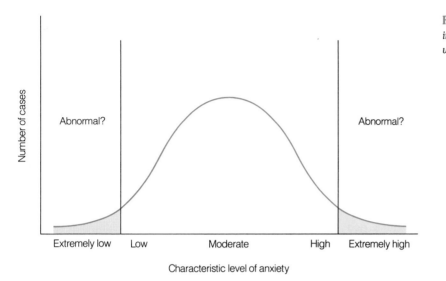

Fig. 20-2 *The number of people displaying a personal characteristic may help define what is statistically abnormal.*

conformity must be carefully distinguished from that of the individual who is nonconforming because of high levels of creativity or a unique life-style. It should be noted also that adherence to social norms is no guarantee of freedom from psychopathology. In some cases neurosis takes the form of rigid conformity.

Before any behavior can be defined as normal or abnormal, we must consider the **context** in which it occurs. Is it abnormal for a grown man to remove his pants and expose himself to another man or woman in a place of business? It depends on whether the other person is a bank clerk or a physician! Almost any imaginable behavior can be considered normal in some context, as the following example indicates:

> In mid-October, 1973, an airplane carrying a rugby team called the "Old Christians" crashed in the snowcapped Andes of South America. Incredibly, 16 of the 45 people who had been aboard at the time of the crash survived 73 days in deep snow and subfreezing temperatures. They were forced to use extremely grim measures to do so— they ate the bodies of those who had died in the crash (adapted from *Time,* Jan. 8, 1973).

One of the most influential contexts in which any behavior is judged is that of culture. In some cultures it is considered normal to believe that plants and trees are inhabited by spirits; or to defecate or urinate in public; or to appear naked in public. In our culture each of these behaviors would be considered unusual or abnormal. Cultural differences can also be more subtle. For example, the Western Apache of Arizona think non-Indians have "an unnatural curiosity" about others; they use names too freely and have

too "vigorous a handshake," which "violates" a person's privacy; they speak too often and ask too many questions, and, by "talking about trouble," they increase its "chance of occurrence." All these behaviors are seen by the Apache as embarrassing and even dangerous (Basso, 1979). By such examples, it can be seen that there is a high degree of **cultural relativity** in perceptions of normality and abnormality. Still, all known cultures classify people as abnormal if they either fail to communicate with others or are consistently unpredictable in their actions.

Question: How much do small differences in appearance affect perceptions of normality?

To answer this question, psychologists Ted Rosenthal and Glenn White (1971) arranged for a person they called "Bill" to visit two psychology classes.

Normality—The Long and Short of It

Bill was introduced to each class as a person who had "spent some time in a psychiatric ward." (Bill was actually a healthy undergraduate who had volunteered to take part in the experiment.) Following this introduction, Bill read "a few facts about himself" to the class. This description was quite neutral and gave no real hint of major psychological problems. Bill then left, and students were asked to rate his "severity of maladjustment" and also to rate the severity of "symptoms" he displayed. Bill's performance was repeated for a morning and an afternoon class. The only difference was that in the morning he had shoulder-length hair and wore jeans and a T-shirt, but in the afternoon he wore slacks and a sport coat (without tie) and had a fresh, short haircut.

Overall, the college students who took part in this experiment judged Bill "sicker" in short hair and sport coat than with long hair and jeans. Students were then put into categories of "hip," "square," or "unclassified" on the basis of their own hair length and style of dress. It was found that "hip" students rated the short-haired Bill as "sicker" and "square" students rated him healthiest! Their judgments were, therefore, connected to their own personal appearance. Even trained psychologists may be affected by such **value differences.** In other experiments, psychologists were given test results of nonexistent persons along with case histories suggesting "lower" or "middle-class" backgrounds. When the test results were attributed to persons with a "lower-class" background, such persons were judged to be more maladjusted (Haase, 1964; Levy and Kahn, 1970).

These studies demonstrate the subtle difficulties of making judgments about normality. They also make it clear that "mental health" must not be too narrowly defined lest it become a form of prejudice in which "abnormal" becomes "anyone not like me."

Question: If abnormality is so hard to define how are judgments of psychopathology made?

It should be clear at this point that all definitions of abnormality are **relative.** Yet, in spite of the great difficulty of formally defining abnormality, we do know that psychological disturbances occur and that they must be identified.

In practice, the judgment that a person needs help usually occurs when the person *does something* (hits a person, hallucinates, stares into space, collects rolls of toilet paper, and so forth) that *annoys* or *gains the attention* of a person in a *position of power* (an employer, teacher, parent, spouse, or the person himself or herself) who then *does something* about it. (A police officer may be called, the person may be urged to see a psychologist, a relative may start commitment proceedings, or the person may voluntarily seek help.)

The sections that follow continue our discussion of normality and psychopathology by describing in greater detail some of the problems already mentioned. You will find short sections on sexual deviance and the antisocial personality, followed by an expanded discussion of "neurotic" and affective disorders. A full discussion of psychotic disorders is reserved for the next chapter. Before you read further, see if you can answer these questions.

Learning Check

1. Approximately what percentage of hospital beds are occupied by the mentally ill? (circle)
   10 percent   25 percent   50 percent   75 percent   90 percent

2. Which among the following are *not* major psychological problems listed in *DSM-III?* (circle)
   psychotic disorders   affective disorders   neurosis
   personality disorders   insanity   anxiety disorders

3. A major difference between psychotic disorders and anxiety disorders (or other "neurotic" problems) is that in psychosis the individual has _____.

4. Statistical definitions of abnormality successfully avoid the limitations of other approaches.   T or F?

5. One of the most powerful contexts in which judgments of normality and abnormality are made is:

   a. the family   *b.* religious systems   *c.* occupational settings   *d.* culture

Answers: 1. 50 percent   2. neurosis, insanity   3. lost contact with reality   4. F   5. d

---

The Antisocial Personality— Rebel Without a Cause

As stated previously, personality disorders involve deeply ingrained maladaptive personality patterns. For example, the paranoid personality is overly suspicious, mistrusting, hypersensitive, guarded, and unsure of the loyalty and honesty of others. Persons having a narcissistic personality pattern are preoccupied with their own self-importance; they need constant attention and admiration, and they are absorbed in fantasies of power, wealth, brilliance, beauty, love, and so forth. The dependent personality involves an extreme lack of self-confidence in which others are allowed to assume responsibility for major areas of the person's life, and the person places his or her own needs second to others. The list of such maladaptive patterns is long, so let us focus on a single frequently misunderstood personality disorder: the antisocial personality.

Question: What are the characteristics of an antisocial personality?

The individual possessing an **antisocial personality** (sometimes referred to as a *sociopath* or *psychopath*) typically has a long history of conflict with society. Antisocial persons are irresponsible, impulsive, selfish, lacking in judgment, unable to feel guilt, emotionally shallow, unable to learn from experience, and lacking in moral values. In childhood, lying, stealing, fighting, truancy, and resisting authority are common signs of a developing antisocial personality. In adolescence, aggressive sexual behavior, excessive drinking, and drug abuse are frequently added. In short, the sociopath is poorly socialized, has a general disregard for the truth, and seems to lack a conscience (*DSM-III*, 1980; Cleckley, 1964).

Question: Are sociopaths dangerous?

Sociopaths are rarely the crazed murderers that have been portrayed on TV and in movies. It is true that many sociopaths are delinquents or criminals who may pose a threat to the general public. But antisocial personalities such as Charles Manson, whose "family" of followers committed the grisly Tate-LaBianca murders, are quite unusual. Most sociopaths create a good first impression and are frequently described as "charming." Their lying, self-serving manipulation, and lack of dependability only gradually become evident to their "friends." As Harold Greenwald comments:

> Usually when we talk about the psychopath we are talking about the *unsuccessful* psychopath. The reason why we generally do not discuss the successful psychopath is because we would then have to discuss many of the rulers of the world. . . . Many of the symptoms . . . such as lack of morals and apparent lack of guilt, exist widely among people of power and influence (Greenwald, 1967; quoted in *Psychosources,* 1973).

Many successful businesspeople, entertainers, politicians, and other "normal" individuals reveal sociopathic leanings in their willingness to use other people coldly for their own ends. Some psychologists believe that the "manipulative personality" may be a better description of the problem as it is encountered in noncriminal individuals (Bursten, 1973).

Question: What causes sociopathy?

People with antisocial personalities usually have a childhood history of emotional deprivation and disregard. This, perhaps, is chiefly responsible for their failure to develop

concern for the feelings of others. In addition, adult sociopaths display some subtle physical differences. For example, they produce unusual brainwave patterns suggesting underarousal of the brain (Hare and Cox, 1978).

A more interesting finding comes from psychological testing in which adult sociopaths must learn to avoid an electric shock. Under these and similar circumstances, they show much less anxiety than normal people (Lykken, 1957; Schachter and Latane, 1969; Hare and Cox, 1978). Those with antisocial personalities might therefore be described as *emotionally cold.* They simply do not feel normal pangs of conscience, guilt, or anxiety. This coldness seems to account for an unusual ability to calmly lie, cheat, steal, or manipulate others.

Question: Can sociopathy be treated?

Antisocial personality disorders are rarely treated with success since sociopaths manipulate therapy as they might any other situation. If it is to their advantage to act "cured," they will do so, but they return to former patterns of behavior at the first opportunity. There is, however, some evidence that antisocial behavior declines somewhat after age thirty.

Sexual Deviance— Trench Coats, Whips, Leathers, and Lace

Sexual deviance, like any form of deviance, implies a departure from accepted standards of proper behavior. By the most strict standards (including the law in some states), any sexual activity other than face-to-face heterosexual intercourse between married adults is "deviant." But public standards and behavior found privately acceptable by consenting adults are often at odds. By private standards, oral-genital contact, masturbation, and premarital sex can no longer be considered sexual deviations.

From a psychological point of view, the mark of true sexual deviations is that they are compulsive, destructive, or bizarre, or they cause guilt, anxiety, or discomfort for one or both participants. Deviations fitting this definition are related to a wide variety of behaviors, including **pedophilia** (sex with children), **bestiality** (sex with animals), **incest** (sex with blood relatives), **fetishism** (sexual arousal associated with inanimate objects), **exhibitionism** (displaying the genitals), **voyeurism** (viewing the genitals of others), **transvestism** (achieving sexual arousal by wearing clothing of the opposite sex), **sadism** (inflicting pain as part of the sex act), and **masochism** (receiving pain as part of the sex act).

Question: Isn't homosexuality a deviation?

Homosexuality   It is correct to say that homosexuality is a deviation from societal norms in the sense that most people are heterosexual. It is important to remember, however, that cultural standards are relative. A recent survey of 76 cultures found that almost two-thirds accept some form of homosexuality (Weinberg and Williams, 1974).

In 1973 the American Psychiatric Association removed male homosexuality and female lesbianism from its list of sexual deviations. This was done mainly in recognition of the fact that few homosexuals are disturbed by their sexual orientation *per se.* If they suffer from any maladjustment, it is usually due to the pressures of rejection by family, employers, or society in general. The gay person is basically comfortable with his or her attraction to members of the same sex. Psychological testing consistently shows no differences between heterosexuals and homosexuals (Marmor, 1980; Bell, Weinberg, and Hammersmith, 1981). According to *DSM-III,* homosexuality can be considered a "disorder" only when it is accompanied by distress, guilt, self-hate, or similar emotional reactions.

Misconceptions   Sexual deviation is a highly emotional subject for many people. As a result, many misconceptions about sexual deviance have developed. Psychologist James Coleman (1972) lists the following as major *misconceptions:*

1. *Sexual offenders are typically homicidal sex fiends.* Actually only about 5 percent of all convicted sex offenders inflict physical injury upon their victims.
2. *Sexual offenders are oversexed from exposure to pornography.* Most offenders are *undersexed*—more inhibited than average and less exposed to pornography.
3. *Sexual offenders suffer from glandular imbalance.* Not so. Human sexual patterns are learned.
4. *Sexual offenders typically progress from minor to more serious sex crimes.* This progression is rare. Usually the person persists in one sexually maladaptive activity.
5. *Sexual offenders are usually repeaters.* Sex offenders have one of the lowest rates of repeated offenses.

The picture of sexual deviance that most often emerges is one of sexual inhibition and immaturity in which some relatively infantile sexual expression (like exhibitionism or pedophilia) is selected as a sexual outlet because it is less threatening than normal sexuality. For example, child molesters are typically married, but have poor marital sexual adjustment. Most are shy and passive and many are religious or puritanical. Contrary to common belief, the majority of child molesters are heterosexuals. Most often their victims are relatives, family friends, or neighbors. Like most other sexual offenders, the child molester is more to be pitied than feared.

Rape   A notable exception to the point just made can be found in the problem of forcible rape. Rapists usually inflict more violence on their victims than is necessary to achieve their goal. Most authorities no longer think of rape as a sexual act. Rather, it is an act of brutality or aggression based on the need to debase others. Many rapists are antisocial personalities who impulsively take what they want without concern for the feelings of the victim or guilt about their deed. Others harbor deep-seated resentment or outright hatred toward women. The goal for these men is not sexual intercourse; it is to attack, subordinate, humiliate, and degrade the victim.

Rape is the fastest growing violent crime in America, and at that, it is likely that only one out of three rapes is reported. The women's movement has recently drawn attention to the fact that, as an act of aggression, rape is a logical extension of sexist attitudes. This is reflected by the difficulty many men have in understanding the emotional impact rape has on women. Typical aftereffects include rage, guilt, depression, loss of self-esteem, shame, and in many cases, a lasting mistrust of male-female relationships.

There is a way, perhaps, for men to understand the seriousness and the damage of rape: The male who doubts the seriousness of rape should imagine himself mistakenly placed in jail where he is violently raped (sodomized) by other inmates. There is no pleasure in rape for victims of either sex. It is truly a despicable crime.

Learning Check

1. Which of the following personality disorders is associated with an inflated sense of self-importance and a constant need for attention and admiration?

    a. narcissistic   *b.* paranoid   *c.* antisocial   *d.* manipulative

2. Almost all persons with antisocial personalities are criminals or delinquents.   T or F?

3. Antisocial personality disorders are difficult to treat but there is typically a decline in antisocial behavior after adolescence.   T or F?

4. The formal term for child molesting (sexual activity involving children) is:

   a. sadism   *b.* bestiality   *c.* pedophilia   *d.* fetishism

5. What percentage of sex offenders inflict physical injury on their victims? _____

6. Rape is primarily an act of brutality or aggression, rather than an exclusively sexual act.   T or F?

Answers: 1. a   2. F   3. F   4. c   5. 5 percent   6. T

Neurosis—When Anxiety Rules

Imagine for a moment the feeling of waiting to take an important test for which you are unprepared; or waiting to give a speech to a large audience of strangers; or waiting for a dentist to start work. You have almost certainly felt **anxiety** in one of these situations. Anxiety is similar to fear except that it is a response to a *nonspecific threat* or an *anticipation of harm.* When people get "stage fright," we say that they are anxious because it is unclear what they fear.

Question: Is it abnormal to feel anxiety?

We all occasionally feel anxiety, and at times of great stress anxiety may be intense, but anxiety that is out of proportion to a given situation may reveal a problem:

> A college student appeared at the counseling center with a complaint that he was deathly afraid of examinations. . . . He had previously been involved in a confrontation with an instructor whom he accused of having administered an unfair test in that there was not enough time to answer all the questions. . . . He soon realized that the time limit had not been long enough because he had wasted most of his time in attempting to control his anxieties. He had already skipped two other examinations by remaining in bed petrified with his fears of failure (adapted from Suinn, 1975).*

Neurosis   This brief excerpt demonstrates many of the characteristics of neurotic anxiety and neurotic behavior. Let us expand our earlier definition of neurosis. (Remember, we are actually referring to a number of more specific problems when we speak of neurosis in general.)

> Neurosis is an emotional disturbance characterized by high levels of anxiety. Also present are feelings of insecurity and inferiority, unhappiness, misery, and dissatisfaction with life. Typically there is a tendency to use elaborate defense mechanisms and avoidance responses to control anxiety and maintain minimal functioning. There is, however, no

gross distortion in perceptions of reality (as in psychosis), and no gross personality distortions (also commonly seen in psychosis).

Some estimates of the frequency of neurosis run as high as 70 percent of the general population, but probably not more than 5 percent *ever* suffer a *severe* neurotic disorder.

Question: Is a neurosis the equivalent of a "nervous breakdown"?

Adjustment Disorders   Neurotic behavior patterns (described in forthcoming sections) are almost always self-defeating. They therefore seriously disrupt people's lives and they almost always cause considerable misery. But neurosis rarely brings about a "breakdown."

Actually, the term "nervous breakdown" has no formal meaning. There is nothing wrong with the nerves of a neurotic individual. Furthermore, the term "nervous breakdown" is applied haphazardly to a variety of problems. What people usually have in mind when they use the term is best described as an *adjustment disorder.* **Adjustment disorders** are the result of obvious environmental stresses that push people beyond their ability to cope effectively. For example, a soldier may suffer **combat exhaustion** after an extended period of stress. Combat exhaustion is characterized by insomnia or repeated nightmares, loss of appetite, extreme sensitivity, unexplained crying, body tremors, hand wringing, and attacks of uncontrollable anxiety (Fig. 20-3).

A similar emotional disturbance can result when a person is faced with sudden disaster, such as a flood, loss of a job, or a serious accident. The civilian equivalent of combat exhaustion is sometimes called a **traumatic neurosis** because of its clear connection to environmental stress. Adjustment disorders are usually successfully treated with rest, sedation, and a chance to "talk through" fears and anxieties.

Question: How is neurosis different from an adjustment disorder?

Adjustment disorders are sometimes called "false neuroses" because they disappear when stress is eased. In a

*From *Fundamentals of Behavior Pathology* by R. M. Suinn. Copyright © 1975. Reprinted by permission of John Wiley & Sons, Inc. Additional Suinn quotes in this chapter and the next are from the same source.

Fig. 20-3 *Combat exhaustion resembles neurosis but is the result of prolonged exposure to stress. Most soldiers recover quickly when returned to a normal environment.*

true neurosis the person's anxiety is a lasting pattern that seems completely out of proportion to the situation. Consider, for example, the following description of Ethel B:

> . . . She was never completely relaxed, and complained of vague feelings of restlessness, and a fear that something was "just around the corner." Although she felt that she had to go to work to help pay the family bills, she could not bring herself to start anything new for fear that something terrible would happen on the job. She had experienced a few extreme anxiety attacks during which she felt "like I couldn't breathe, like I was sealed up in a transparent envelope. I thought I was going to have a heart attack. I couldn't stop shaking" (Suinn, 1975).

Question: Do all neurotics feel like Ethel B?

Anxiety is a key element in the neurotic disorders, but it gives rise to numerous maladaptive patterns of behavior. Each can be understood as an ineffective means of coping with personal discomfort. A description of several major patterns follows.

Anxiety Disorders

The essential feature of the simplest anxiety disorder (known as a **generalized anxiety disorder**) is at least six months of persistent anxiety. Individuals experiencing chronic anxiety typically complain of sweating, racing heart, dizziness, upset stomach, accelerated breathing, and other autonomic nervous system effects. They also continually worry, anticipating disasters such as fainting, losing control, dying, injury or death of close relatives, and so forth.

Question: Was Ethel B's problem a generalized anxiety disorder?

No. The added presence of *anxiety attacks* indicates she suffered from a **panic disorder.**

Panic Disorder In this relatively simple, but very disturbing pattern, continuous tension, worry, and anxiety occasionally explode into sudden episodes of intense panic. During a panic, or anxiety attack, affected individuals experience heart palpitations or chest pain, choking or smothering sensations, vertigo, feelings of unreality, trembling, and fear of dying, going crazy, or doing something uncontrollable during the attack (*DSM-III*, 1980). Many believe that they are having a heart attack, are going insane, or are about to die.

It is sometimes said that such persons suffer from **free-floating anxiety,** since a panic attack can be triggered by almost anything. In addition, they usually suffer from secondary fears about when and where the next panic will occur. Nervousness and apprehension between attacks is therefore further intensified. Needless to say, individuals showing this pattern are unhappy and uncomfortable much of the time.

Phobic Disorder Phobias are irrational fears that persist even when there is no real danger to a person. In a **phobic disorder,** irrational fears, anxiety, and avoidance are focused on specific objects, activities, or situations (Fig. 20-4).

Acrophobia—fear of heights

Agoraphobia—fear of open places

Claustrophobia—fear of closed spaces

Nyctophobia—fear of darkness

Pathophobia—fear of disease

Zoophobia—fear of animals

Fig. 20-4 *For a person with a strong fear of heights (acrophobia), merely looking at the diver in this photograph may be unsettling.*

This list of possibilities is only partial: Phobias may be attached to almost any object or situation.* Almost everyone has a few mild phobias: Fear of heights, closed spaces, or bugs and crawly things are common. A neurotic phobia differs from such garden-variety fears in that it produces overwhelming anxiety that may cause vomiting, wild climbing and running, or fainting. Phobic persons are so threatened that they will go to almost any length to avoid the feared object or situation. A person with a neurotic fear of water and drowning will not only avoid swimming and boats, but in addition, may be unable to visit a beach or take a bath. One individual treated by the author developed such a fear of public rest rooms that he would endure intense discomfort for hours or would travel across town to his home in order to urinate where he felt safe.

Question: Are some phobias more common than others?

The most common and disruptive problem is agoraphobia (ah-go-rah-FOBE-be-ah). One expert estimates that 1 out of every 100 people has agoraphobia severe enough to restrict his or her life to a serious degree (Hardy, 1976). Agoraphobic individuals have an intense fear of leaving the familiar setting of the home. They refuse to walk or travel alone and actively avoid unfamiliar situations. Typically they develop elaborate alibis to avoid areas of insecurity and they depend heavily on others to maintain a semblance of a normal life. Some are literally "housebound" (*DSM-III*, 1980).

Obsessive-Compulsive Disorder   **Obsessions** are images or thoughts that intrude into consciousness against a person's will. You have probably experienced a mild obsessional thought in the form of some song or stupid commercial jingle that is repeated over and over in your mind. This may be irritating, but it is certainly not disturbing in any major sense. True obsessions are so disturbing that they cause anxiety or extreme discomfort. Such obsessions may center on images of one's own violent death, feelings of being "dirty" or "unclean," feelings that one is about to lose control, or similar threatening preoccupations.

Obsessions usually give rise to **compulsions.** These are irrational acts a person feels driven to repeat (Fig. 20-5). Typically the compulsive act helps control or block out anxi-

*Obviously, by combining the appropriate root word with the word *phobia* any number of unlikely fears can be named. Some are: *acarophobia,* a fear of itching; *zemmiphobia,* fear of the great mole rat; *nictophobia,* fear of backing into door knobs; *phobiaphobia,* fear of fear; and *hippopotomonstrosesquipedaliophobia,* fear of long words!

Fig. 20-5 *Is this compulsive behavior? A farmer collected millions of pieces of rope and twine to create this incredible ball.*

ety caused by the obsession. A person who feels guilty or unclean because of a conflict about masturbation might be driven to wash his hands hundreds of times a day. A minister who finds profanities popping into his mind might take up compulsively counting his heartbeat to prevent their appearance. A young mother who repeatedly has an image of a knife plunging into her infant might count all the knives in the house several times a day and insist that they always be locked up.

Of course, not all obsessive-compulsive disorders are so dramatic; many simply involve extreme orderliness and rigid routine. Compulsive attention to detail and rigid adherence to procedures and rules make the highly anxious person feel more secure by keeping activities totally structured and under control.

Question: Earlier it was stated that the woman found wandering in the park had amnesia. How does that relate to anxiety?

Dissociative Disorders

A dissociative reaction is marked by striking episodes of *amnesia, fugue,* or *multiple personality.* **Amnesia** is the inability to recall one's name, address, or past. **Fugue** (sounds like fewg) is physical flight to escape extreme conflict or threat. Fugue and amnesia are sometimes coupled. A person may wander away from work or school only to

later arrive in a strange place with no knowledge of the journey. It can easily be seen that forgetting one's identity or fleeing unpleasant situations is a defense against anxiety that cannot be tolerated.

Multiple personality is a rare condition in which two or more separate personalities exist in an individual. The fictional story of *Dr. Jekyll and Mr. Hyde* is a well-known example of **dual personality.** (Note that dual personality is *not* schizophrenia; schizophrenia is a form of psychosis discussed in the next chapter.) One of the most dramatic examples of multiple personality *ever* recorded is described in the book *Sybil* (Schreiber, 1973). Sybil is a woman who had 16 different personalities. Each personality had a distinct voice, vocabulary, and posture. One personality could play the piano (not Sybil), but the others could not.

When a personality other than Sybil was in control, Sybil experienced a "time lapse" or memory blackout. For example, as a child she once "awoke" as a fifth grader and couldn't understand why she was not in her third-grade classroom. When she was asked to do a multiplication problem, she couldn't begin. Two years of her life were missing, and the personality that had inhabited her body had learned multiplication, but Sybil had not.

Sybil's amnesia and alternate personalities developed during childhood when she was regularly beaten, locked in closets, perversely tortured, and almost killed. Sybil's first dissociations allowed her to escape by creating another person who would suffer torture in her place. Multiple personality often begins with similar unbearable childhood experiences. In later years Sybil continued the pattern by developing additional personalities to defend against new stress. Fortunately, multiple personality is far rarer in real life than it is in TV dramas!

Somatoform Disorders

Perhaps you have known someone, particularly someone prone to anxiety and depression, who seems to suffer from an unending series of physical complaints. Usually such individuals believe they have been "sickly" for much of their lives. Often, they have a complicated medical history, and they have, over the years, consulted numerous physicians, sometimes two or more simultaneously. Life for these people is an endless struggle against headaches, fatigue, fainting, nausea, abdominal problems, allergies, menstrual and sexual difficulties, as well as countless other aches, pains, and "diseases."

Question: Are you describing hypochondria?

Basically, yes. In **hypochondriasis** (HI-po-kon-DRY-uh-sis), the person has multiple physical complaints for which medical attention is sought, but for which no clear physical cause can be found. A rarer form of somatoform disorder (or "body-form" disorder) is called a *conversion reaction*.

Question: How does a conversion reaction differ from hypochondriasis?

Conversion reactions are said to occur when anxiety or severe emotional conflicts are "converted" into physical symptoms resembling disease or disability. Conversion disorders are usually quite dramatic. For instance, a soldier might go deaf or lame, or develop "glove anesthesia" just before a battle.

Question: What is "glove anesthesia"?

"Glove anesthesia" is a loss of sensitivity in the areas of skin that would normally be covered by a glove. Glove anesthesia demonstrates that conversion symptoms often contradict known medical facts. The system of nerves in the hands does not form a glovelike pattern and could not cause the observed symptoms. Conversion reactions are also revealed by a disappearance of symptoms when the "victim" is asleep, hypnotized, or anesthetized (Fig. 20-6).

The physical symptoms of a conversion disorder usually serve to excuse the person from a threatening situation. In one case a college student who had a minor traffic accident awakened the following morning with a numbness in his legs and found himself unable to move them. A conversion reaction was suspected when it was noted that he did not seem at all disturbed by his inability to walk. Investigation revealed that his parents were pressuring him to stay in

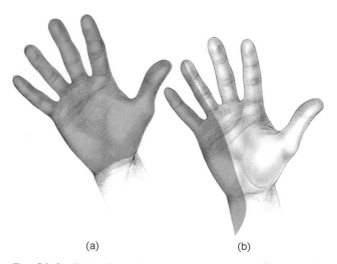

(a)   (b)

Fig. 20-6   *"Glove" anesthesia is a conversion reaction in which the person loses feeling in areas of the hand that would be covered by a glove (a). If anesthesia were physically caused, it would follow the pattern depicted in (b).*

school although he wanted to quit and that he was not prepared for his final exams. If he failed his exams, he expected to be drafted (Suinn, 1975).

A final note of interest: Conversion disorders probably account for many of the so-called miracle cures attributed to faith healers or medical quacks. Persons with conversion symptoms who firmly believe they are being helped may undergo a miraculous cure, but they usually develop new symptoms later.

Learning Check

Under the general label of "neurosis" we have discussed the disorders listed below. See if you can correctly match each with the items on the right by placing letters in the parentheses.

1. Adjustment disorders   (   )

2. Anxiety disorders:
   generalized anxiety disorder   (   )
   panic disorder   (   )
   phobic disorder   (   )
   obsessive-compulsive disorder   (   )

3. Dissociative disorders   (   )

4. Somatoform disorders   (   )

A. Disturbing thoughts, rigid routine, mechanical behavior

B. Hypochondriasis and conversion reactions

C. Free-floating anxiety and anxiety attacks

D. Persistent, specific, irrational fears

E. Not a true neurosis; combat exhaustion and traumatic neurosis

F. Amnesia, fugue, multiple personality

G. Chronic worry, anxiety, nervousness

Answers: 1. E   2. G,C,D,A   3. F   4. B

Theories of Neurosis—
Three Ways to Construct a Neurosis

Question: What causes the problems described in the preceding section?

At least three major perspectives on the causes of neurotic disorders can be identified. These are: (1) the psychodynamic approach; (2) the humanistic-existential approach; and (3) the behavioristic approach.

Psychodynamic Approach   Freud was the first to propose a comprehensive explanation of neurosis. According to Freud, neurosis represents a raging conflict between the three subparts of the personality—the id, ego, and superego. Freud particularly emphasized anxiety caused by forbidden id impulses for sex or aggression which threaten to break through into behavior. Also important in the Freudian view is guilt generated by the superego in response to these impulses. Caught in the middle, the ego is overwhelmed by conflicting demands, and the person must adopt rigid defense mechanisms and inflexible behavior to prevent a disastrous loss of control.

Humanistic-Existential Approaches   Humanistic psychologist Carl Rogers interprets neurosis as the end product of a faulty *self-image* (Rogers, 1959). Rogers feels that neurotic individuals have built up unrealistic pictures of themselves, leaving them vulnerable to contradictory information. Let's say, for example, that an essential part of a particular student's self-image is seeing himself or herself as highly intelligent. If the student does poorly in school, he or she may deny or distort self-perceptions and perceptions of the situation. Rigid defense mechanisms, a conversion reaction, anxiety attacks, or other neurotic symptoms may result from threats to one's self-image. These symptoms in turn become new threats and require further distortions. We have, in other words, a classic example of a vicious cycle of maladjustment that feeds on itself once started.

Some psychologists take a more existential point of view, emphasizing that neurosis reflects a loss of meaning in one's life. According to the existentialists, humans must exercise *courage* and *responsibility* in their choices if life is to have meaning. Too often, they say, we give in to "existential anxiety" and back away from life-enhancing choices. Existential anxiety is the anguish that comes from knowing that we will ultimately die, hence, that we have a crushing responsibility to choose wisely and courageously. From this perspective, people who are unhappy and neurotic are living in "bad faith." That is, they have collapsed in the face of the awesome responsibility of choosing a meaningful existence; they have lost their way in life.

Behavioristic Approach   Behaviorists have generally rejected the previous explanations of neurosis. The behavioristic position is that neurotic "symptoms" are learned just as any other behavior. A sample of behavioristic thinking follows.

One aspect of neurotic behavior all theorists agree upon is that it is ultimately self-defeating. This is largely summarized by the **neurotic paradox.** A paradox is a contradiction. The contradiction in neurotic behavior is that in the long run it makes the person more miserable, but its immediate effect is to make him feel temporarily less anxious.

Question: How does a pattern such as this get started?

The behavioristic explanation is that the neurotic paradox is an example of **avoidance learning.** Avoidance learning was described earlier, in Chapter 9. Here's a quick description to refresh your memory of it:

> An animal is placed in a special cage. After a few minutes a light comes on, followed a moment later by a painful shock. After the shock begins, the animal escapes over a partition into a second chamber. After a few minutes, a light comes on in this chamber, and the shock is repeated. Soon the animal learns to *avoid* the shock by moving *before* the shock occurs. Once an animal learns to avoid the shock, it can be turned off altogether. A well-trained animal may then avoid the nonexistent shock indefinitely.

The same analysis can be applied to neurotic behavior. A behaviorist would say that anxiety has been conditioned to various situations and that the immediate reinforcement of *relief* from anxiety keeps the neurotic pattern alive. This is why neurotic behavior often looks very "stupid" to an outside observer.

There is probably a core of truth to each of the three explanations. Understanding a particular example of neurosis may be aided by combining parts of all three perspectives. Each perspective also suggests a different approach to treatment. Since the possibilities are numerous, discussion of therapy for neurosis and other problems is found later in Chapters 22 and 23.

Affective Disorders—
On the Dark Side of the Mood

Nobody loves you when you're down and out—or so it seems. Psychologists have gradually come to realize that disturbances in mood—the **affective disorders**—are among the most serious of all. In terms of sheer numbers, studies show that in Europe and in the United States between 10 and 20 percent of the adult population has had a major depressive episode at some time (*DSM-III,* 1980). Roughly 25 percent of all cases treated by private psychiatrists and psychologists are for depression (Marmon, 1975).

Question: Don't affective disorders include manic behavior?

Although manic behavior is included, depression is by far the most common problem.

In depressive disorders, sadness and despondency are exaggerated or prolonged for unreasonable lengths of time. Indications of a depressive disorder are: sadness, hopelessness, inability to experience pleasure or to take interest in anything, withdrawal from family and friends, fatigue, limited movement, sleep and eating disturbances, feelings of worthlessness, an extremely negative self-image, and, often, recurrent thoughts of suicide. In severe cases it becomes impossible for depressed persons to function at work or at school, and sometimes they cannot even feed or clothe themselves.

Question: How are depressive disorders different from milder, more normal feelings of depression?

If a loved one dies or a person suffers a major failure or setback, a period of mourning or depression is to be expected. Depression at such times represents an emotional readjustment that is soon completed. When someone is in a continuous or unusually intense state of depression we must look for causes that go beyond the incident that seemed to trigger the depression. In what might be described as **reactive** (or "neurotic") **depression,** we find that the person was unprepared to cope with a major loss because of a long series of former disappointments, or because the person is emotionally dependent or immature. In any case, the triggering incident is merely the "last straw" that reveals an underlying emotional disturbance.

Question: Is there an explanation for severe depression?

Depression and other affective disorders have resisted adequate explanation and treatment. Some investigators are focusing on the biology of mood changes. These researchers are interested in brain chemicals and transmitter substances, electrolytes, serotonin and noradrenaline levels and so forth. Their findings are complex and inconclusive, but progress has been made. For example, the chemical **lithium carbonate** can be effective in treatment of some cases of depression, particularly those also showing manic behavior (Depue and Monroe, 1978).

Others have sought psychological explanations. Psychoanalytic theory, for instance, holds that depression is caused by repressed anger that is displaced and turned inward as self-blame and self-hate (Isenberg and Schatzberg, 1976). As discussed earlier in Chapter 13, behavioral theories of depression emphasize learned helplessness. In some cases, extinction may also be involved. Let's say that many of your attempts to initiate constructive behavior meet with failure or painful results. Soon you might begin feeling "What's the use?" or "It doesn't matter" (Ullmann and Krasner, 1975). If such feelings lead to isolation, withdrawal, or apathy, your chances of being reinforced for "trying" will be further reduced: Depression may thus feed depression.

Adequate understanding and treatment of depression is a challenge to the ingenuity of psychologists, psychiatrists, and other investigators. It is to their credit that this major source of human misery has recently become the target of intensified research. While we await the outcome of their efforts, a problem remains: Thousands of depressed people commit suicide each year. What can be done about it? This chapter's "Applications" section provides some answers.

A Final Note—You're O.K. . . . Really!

It is the author's hope that you will not fall prey to the psychological equivalent of "medical student's disease" after reading this chapter. Medical students, it seems, have a predictable tendency to notice in themselves the symptoms of each dreaded disease they learn about. As a psychology student you may have noticed what seem to be neurotic or other abnormal tendencies in your own behavior. If so, don't panic: This only shows that pathological behavior is an *exaggeration* of normal defenses and reactions, not that your behavior is pathological.

Learning Check

1. The humanistic explanation of neurosis emphasizes the importance of a faulty self-image.   T or F?

2. According to the behavioristic view, the neurotic paradox is explained by _____ learning.

3. The existential explanation of neurosis is based on a conflict between subparts of the personality.   T or F?

4. Learned helplessness and the effects of extinction are emphasized by _____ theories of depression.

   a. humanistic   *b.* behavioristic   *c.* biological   *d.* psychoanalytic

5. The drug lithium carbonate has been shown to be an effective treatment for neurotic disorders.   T or F?

Answers: 1. T   2. avoidance   3. F   4. b   5. F

Resources Summary

● Mental or emotional disturbances are a major health problem. Major categories of *psychopathology* include: *organic mental disorders, substance use disorders, psychotic disorders, affective disorders, anxiety disorders, somatoform disorders, dissociative disorders, personality disorders,* and *psychosexual disorders.*

● Traditionally, a distinction has been made between *neuroses*—milder disorders related to high anxiety—and *psychoses*—problems involving loss of contact with reality. *Insanity* is a legal term defining the ability to know right from wrong and whether or not one may be held responsible for one's actions.

● Formal definitions of normality usually take into account all or most of the following: *subjective discomfort, statistical definitions,* or *norms, social nonconformity, personal values,* and the *cultural* or *situational context* of behavior. There are problems with each definition in that all are *relative* standards. In practice, judgment of normality is a social act influenced by many factors.

● Personality disorders are deeply ingrained maladaptive personality patterns. A frequently misunderstood personality disorder is *sociopathy,* or *antisocial personality.* Antisocial persons seem to lack a *conscience.* They are emotionally unresponsive, manipulative, and have shallow interpersonal relationships. However, few are homicidal and only a small proportion are criminals.

● Sexual deviance may be the most relative disorder of all. Many "sexually deviant" behaviors are acceptable in other cultures. Deviations that often cause difficulty are: *pedophilia, bestiality, incest, fetishism, voyeurism, exhibitionism, transvestism, sadism,* and *masochism.* Homosexuality is not considered a disorder *per se* although homosexual persons may experience adjustment difficulties due to societal rejection. Sex offenders are rarely dangerous; they can best be characterized as sexually inhibited and immature. *Forcible rape* is a violent crime of aggression rather than a sex crime.

● *Neurosis* is characterized by high levels of anxiety, rigid defense mechanisms, and self-defeating behavior patterns.

Several patterns of neurotic behavior have been identified. The term "nervous breakdown" has no formal meaning but "breakdowns" do correspond somewhat to *adjustment disorders* such as *combat exhaustion* and *traumatic neuroses.*

● *Anxiety disorders,* characterized by excessive anxiety or anxiety-based behaviors, include: *generalized anxiety disorder* (chronic anxiety and worry), *panic disorder* (anxiety attacks, panic, free-floating anxiety), *phobic disorder* (specific irrational fears), and *obsessive-compulsive disorders* (obsessions and compulsions).

● *Dissociative disorders* may take the form of *amnesia* (loss of memory and personal identity), *fugue* (flight from familiar surroundings), or *multiple personality* (development of two or more distinct personalities).

● *Somatoform disorders* center on physical complaints that mimic disease or disability. In *hypochondriasis* there are multiple physical complaints for which medical attention is sought. In *conversion disorders* actual symptoms of disease or disability develop but they are psychological in origin.

● Three broad types of explanation for neurosis are: (1) the *psychodynamic* approach emphasizing unconscious conflicts within the personality; (2) the *humanistic* approach emphasizing the effects of a *faulty self-image* and the related *existential* approach emphasizing a loss of *meaning* in one's life; and (3) the *behavioristic* approach which emphasizes the effects of previous learning, particularly *avoidance learning.*

● *Affective disorders* primarily involve disturbances of mood or emotion producing *manic* (agitated, elated, hyperactive) or *depressive* (sad, apathetic, suicidal) states. Depression is the most common affective disorder. "Neurotic," or *reactive depressions,* are often triggered by external events. However, they are more intense or prolonged than normal. Biological, psychoanalytic, and behavioral theories of depression have been proposed. Research on the causes and treatment of depression continues.

========== Applications ==========

Warning: Suicide May Be Hazardous to Your Health

"To be, or not to be? That is the question . . ."

By the time you finish reading this page, someone in the United States will have attempted suicide. Suicide is a very disturbing and widely misunderstood mental health problem. It ranks as the seventh cause of death in the United States, and approximately 1 person out of 100 has attempted suicide at some time in his or her life. Given these figures, it seems likely that you will sooner or later be affected by the suicide attempt of a friend, relative, neighbor, or co-worker. Check your knowledge of suicide against the following information.

Question: What factors affect suicide rates?

Season   Suicide rates vary from city to city and time to time, but some general patterns emerge. Contrary to popular belief, there is little connection between major holidays, such as Christmas, and the suicide rate. For reasons not clearly understood, the peak actually comes in May (Zung and Green, 1974).

Sex   Men have the questionable honor of being better at suicide than women. Three times as many men as women *complete* suicide, but women make more attempts. More men than women succeed at suicide because they typically use a gun or an equally fatal technique. Women most often attempt a drug overdose, a method that leaves greater chance of help arriving before death occurs (Lester, 1972).

Age   Age is also a factor in suicide. More than half of all suicides are committed by individuals over forty-five years old. This may be changing—there has been a recent increase in suicide rates for adolescents and young adults.

Part of this increase comes from the ranks of college students where suicide is the leading cause of death. Contrary to popular belief, the most dangerous time for student suicide is the beginning (first six weeks) of a semester, not during final exams. School is a factor in some suicides, but only in the sense that suicidal students were not living up to their own extremely high standards. Many were good students. Other important factors in student suicide are

chronic health problems (real or imagined) and interpersonal difficulties (some suicides are rejected lovers, but others are simply withdrawn and friendless people) (Seiden, 1966).

Of special concern to psychologists is the recent dramatic increase in adolescent suicides. At present, about 5000 teenagers and young adults commit suicide each year. This rate—about 13 deaths per day—is double the number reported 10 years ago. In some cities, authorities have reported virtual "epidemics" of adolescent suicide. Also distressing is the fact that an increasing number of youth suicides employ such highly lethal methods as shooting themselves.

Income   Some professions, particularly medicine and psychiatry, show higher than average suicide rates. Overall, however, suicide is quite democratic. It is equally a problem of the rich and the poor (Labovity and Hagedorn, 1971).

Marital Status   An additional factor in suicide is marital status. Marriage (when successful) may be the best natural deterrent to suicidal impulses. The highest suicide rates are found among the divorced; the next highest rates occur among the widowed; lower rates are recorded for single persons; and married individuals have the lowest rate of all.

Question: Why do people try to kill themselves?

One theory is that suicide is aggression directed inward. Suicidal people often feel that the world has treated them unfairly. Their growing anger toward situations they cannot change may drive them to show others how badly they have been treated by taking their own lives (Lester, 1968).

French sociologist Emile Durkheim attributed many suicides to what he called *anomie* (ah-no-ME) (Durkheim, 1951). Anomie is a state of *alienation* brought about by rapidly changing social conditions that cause feelings of rootlessness, lack of identity, and unsatisfying personal relationships.

Immediate Causes   The best explanation for suicide may simply come from a look at the conditions that pre-

Applications

cede it. Usually there is a history of interpersonal troubles with family, in-laws, or a lover or spouse. Often there is a drinking problem, sexual adjustment problems, or job difficulties (Humphrey *et al.,* 1972).

A combination of factors such as these lead to severe depression and a preoccupation with death as the "answer" to the person's suffering. There is usually a break in communication with others that causes the person to feel isolated and misunderstood. Self-image becomes very negative. The person feels "worthless" and wants to die (Lester, 1972).

A long history of such conditions is not always necessary to produce a desire for suicide. People who attempt suicide are not necessarily "mentally ill." Anyone may temporarily reach a state of depression severe enough to attempt suicide. Most dangerous for the average person are times of divorce, separation, failure, and bereavement. Each can create what seems like an intolerable situation and motivate an intense desire for escape.

The causes of increased adolescent suicide remain unclear. As with adults, there is often a backdrop of problems with drugs, depression, school, peers, family, divorced parents, or the breakup of a romance. However, many victims come from stable and affluent homes. Some experts suggest that many cases of adolescent suicide result from *unrealistic expectations.* For example, parents may create feelings of despair by pressuring their children to meet impossibly high standards. Even without such pressure, teenagers may expect the impossible of themselves in school, sports, romance, or progress toward a future career. Extremely high expectations can bring self-esteem to rock-bottom over even the smallest "failure." Again, the outcome is feelings of helplessness, hopelessness, and a desire to escape.

Preventing Suicide—You Can Help

Question: Is it true that people who talk about or threaten suicide are rarely the ones who try it?

No. This is one of the major fallacies about suicide. Of every 10 potential suicides, eight give warning beforehand (Schneidman *et al.,* 1965; Rudestam, 1971). A person who threatens suicide should be taken seriously. A potential suicide may say nothing more than, "I feel sometimes like I'd be better off dead." Warnings may also come indirectly. If a friend gives you a favorite ring and says, "Here, I won't be needing this any more," or comments, "I guess I won't get my watch fixed—it doesn't matter anyway," it may be a plea for help.

Question: Is it true that suicide can't be prevented, that the person will find a way to do it anyway?

No. The decision to attempt suicide usually comes when a person is alone, depressed, and unable to view matters objectively. You *should* intervene if someone seems to be threatening suicide.

It is estimated that about two-thirds of all suicide attempts fall in the "to be" category. That is, they are made by people who do not really want to die. Almost a third more are characterized by a "to be or not to be" attitude. These people are ambivalent or undecided about dying. Only about 3 to 5 percent of cases represent individuals who definitely want to die. Most people are, therefore, relieved when someone comes to their aid (Shneidman *et al.,* 1965). Remember that suicide is almost always a cry for help and that you *can* help.

Question: What is the best thing to do if someone hints they are thinking about suicide?

Suicide expert David Lester (1971b) believes that your most important task is to establish *rapport* with the person. You should offer support, acceptance, and legitimate caring. Lester gives some important suggestions about how to handle a potential suicide.

1. A suicidal person feels misunderstood. You should, therefore, try to accept the feelings the person is expressing. Telling suicidal persons they really don't want to kill themselves, or listing reasons why they shouldn't, only adds to feelings that no one understands. This usually makes a bad situation worse. The person needs *acceptance,* not reassurance.

2. Acceptance should extend to the idea of suicide itself. One of the worst things you can do is to say something like, "You're not thinking of doing something drastic, are you?" Hiding from suicide or trying to avoid talking about it makes the person feel wrong, unaccepted, and alone. Don't be afraid to talk about suicide directly. It is completely acceptable to ask, "Are you thinking of suicide?"

Applications

Establishing communication with suicidal persons may be enough to carry them through a difficult time. You may also find it helpful to get day-by-day commitments from them to meet for lunch, to share a ride, and the like. Let the person know you *expect* her or him to be there. Such commitments, even though small, can be enough to tip the scales when a person is alone and thinking about suicide.

Don't end your efforts too soon. One of the most dangerous times for suicide is when a person suddenly seems to get better after a severe depression. Many experts agree that this often means the person has finally made the decision to end it all. The improvement in mood is deceptive because it comes from an anticipation that suffering is at an end (Lester and Lester, 1971).

There are over 200 centers for suicide prevention in the United States, and most sizable cities have mental health "crisis intervention" teams. Both services have staff trained to talk to potential suicides over the phone. Give a person who seems to be suicidal the number of one of these services to place near a phone. Urge the person to call you or the other number if he or she becomes frightened or impulsive.

The preceding applies mainly to persons who are having mild suicidal thoughts. If a person actually threatens suicide, you must act more quickly. Ask how the person plans to carry out the suicide. A person who has a concrete, workable plan should be asked to accompany you to the emergency ward of a hospital. If the person seems on the verge of attempting suicide, don't worry about over-reacting; call the police, crisis intervention, or a rescue unit. Needless to say, you should call immediately if a person is in the act of attempting suicide or if a drug has already been taken. The majority of suicide attempts come at temporary low points in a person's life and may never be repeated. Get involved—save a life!

Suicide—Summary of Misconceptions

The following is a list of misconceptions about suicide.

1. More women than men commit suicide.
2. College students are most likely to attempt suicide during final exam periods.
3. Anyone who would attempt suicide is mentally ill. Suicide is always the act of a psychotic person.
4. Suicide strikes more often among the poor.
5. Once a person becomes suicidal, he or she is suicidal forever (or will be repeatedly).
6. Suicides give no warning.
7. People who talk about suicide are rarely the ones who attempt it.
8. A person who attempts suicide really wants to die.
9. A sudden improvement in mood after a suicidal depression means that the danger has passed.
10. There is nothing that can be done to prevent suicide.

Remember: All these statements are *false*.

Learning Check

1. More women use guns in their suicide attempts than do men.   T or F?
2. While the overall suicide rate has remained about the same, there has been a decrease in adolescent suicides. T or F?
3. Suicide is equally a problem of the rich and the poor.   T or F?
4. The highest suicide rates are found among the divorced.   T or F?
5. The French sociologist Durkheim attributed many suicides to unrealistic expectations.   T or F?
6. The majority (two-thirds) of suicide attempts fall in the "to be" category.   T or F?

Answers: 1. F 2. F 3. T 4. T 5. F 6. T

Exploration

Psychology and the Law—The "Twinkie Defense"

Mark David Chapman claimed devils forced him to kill former Beatle John Lennon. In court, his lawyer asserted that Chapman was "not guilty by reason of insanity." However, at mid-trial Chapman decided to plead guilty to second-degree murder. His reason? He said God had visited him in his cell and told him to confess.

Chapman's case was one of thousands each year that mingle law, psychiatry, psychology, and public opinion. For over 130 years, the **insanity defense** has bedeviled the courts, and raised difficult legal, moral, and psychological questions.

Question: What exactly is the insanity defense?

Insanity   The insanity defense entered Western law as the **M'Naghten rule.** In 1843 the English House of Lords ruled on the case of Daniel M'Naghten, a "madman" who attempted to kill a member of Parliament, but murdered another man instead. The court held that a defendant—in this case M'Naghten—must understand the wrongfulness of his or her actions to be held responsible for them. Persons suffering from "mental disease or other defects" that prevent them from knowing right from wrong are "insane." In our legal system, the taking of life by an insane person is not murder.

Defendants may also claim they knew their act was wrong, but they had an **irresistable impulse** they could not control. An example is the person who finds his or her spouse in a stranger's arms and kills in a jealous rage. A related defense claims **diminished capacity** to control actions, or to know right from wrong. A person who commits a crime while under the influence of drugs might make this plea.

The Twinkie Defense   The problems posed by the insanity defense are vividly shown by three recent cases. In Oakland, California, a jury declared Darlin June Cromer sane in the racial killing of a five-year-old boy. This, despite the fact that one psychiatrist testified that Cromer was "the most psychotic person" he'd ever seen. Cromer was sentenced to life in prison (Einstein, 1981). On the opposite side of San Francisco Bay, ex-city supervisor Dan White

admitted killing San Francisco Mayor George Moscone and Supervisor Harvey Milk. However, White's lawyer convinced the jury that White acted with diminished capacity. The defense claimed, among other things, that White was deranged from eating too much "junk food"—an argument that became known as the Twinkie Defense.* Testimony in the trial established that White planned the murders beforehand and carefully avoided security guards to reach his victims. White received a seven-year jail sentence. The verdict so outraged many citizens that a new law in California now bans claims of "diminished capacity" (Tierney, 1982). In yet another case, "Vampire Killer" Richard Chase was convicted of killing six people and drinking the blood of some of them. Chase was declared sane.

These cases point to the inconsistencies of a system that allows people who appear sane to be judged insane, and apparently insane people to be judged sane.

Question: How is sanity determined?

Expert Testimony   Criminal trials involving insanity have a typical pattern: Defense psychiatrists interview the defendant and then testify that he or she was insane at the time of the crime; prosecution psychiatrists examine the defendant and testify to his or her sanity. After these **expert witnesses** contradict one another's testimony, it's up to the jury to decide who is right.

Opinion Please   The preceding brief discussion raises several interesting questions.

1. The states of Montana and Idaho have banned the insanity plea, but in many states it remains intact. Several other states now allow only a "guilty, but mentally ill" plea. In your opinion, should questions of sanity be considered in criminal trials? Should the insanity defense be allowed? Before you answer, you should know that pleas of insanity are actually relatively rare, being used in only about 1 out of every 500 court cases. In only about 2 percent of these

*For those unschooled in junk food trivia, a "Twinkie" is a small sugary sponge cake with a cream filling.

Exploration

cases does the insanity defense succeed. Nationally, this amounts to about 100 cases a year (Carelli, 1982). More importantly, a verdict of innocence by reason of insanity does not set a person free. In most states it requires automatic commitment to a mental hospital. Thereafter, the law places the burden of proof on patients. To be released, they must show that they are no longer a danger to themselves or others. Moreover, in some cases, persons declared ''insane'' have been hospitalized longer than they would have been imprisoned for a criminal conviction.

2. Should the courts accept pleas of ''diminished capacity''? Before you answer this question, think about the ''guilt'' of a severely retarded person, or someone with a brain tumor who commits a crime.

3. In your opinion, who should decide if a person should be committed? Should it be a judge, jury, psychiatrist, or psychologist? Who should decide when an ''insane'' person can be released? Should a person have the right to refuse treatment? What if the person committed a crime? Before answering these questions, it may be useful to know that psychiatric predictions of violent behavior are largely inaccurate. Follow-ups of arrests and mental hospital records show that from two-thirds to nine-tenths of the time, experts are *wrong* in forecasting violence (Loftus and Monahan, 1980). At present, there is no way to accurately predict which individuals are likely to be dangerous to themselves or to others.

As you can see, there are no easy answers to the preceding questions. Nevertheless, when the issues are ''madness,'' personal freedom, criminal responsibility, and justice, everyone has an opinion. What's yours?

Questions for Discussion

1. What effect might living in different parts of town, membership in an ethnic group, or growing up in a different culture have on perceptions of "normality?"

2. Can you think of a behavior that would be considered "abnormal" under any possible set of circumstances?

3. How would your perception of a person be likely to change if you knew he or she were an "ex-mental patient"?

4. To what extent does "maladjusted" or "sick" mean "different from me"?

5. Are standards of "normality" in our society broad enough to accommodate varying life-styles?

6. In what ways might our ultracompetitive society contribute to the development of a sociopathic personality?

7. How would you explain the increase in youth suicide?

Suggestions for Further Reading

Alvarez, A. *The Savage God: A Study of Suicide*. Bantam, 1973.

Coleman, J. C., *et al. Abnormal Psychology and Modern Life*. Scott, Foresman, 1980.

Dollard, J., and N. E. Miller. *Personality and Psychotherapy*. McGraw-Hill, 1950.

Goldstein, J. J., and J. O. Palmer. *The Experience of Anxiety: A Casebook*. Oxford, 1963.

Lester, G., and D. Lester. *Suicide: The Gamble with Death*. Prentice-Hall, 1971.

McMahon, F. B. *Abnormal Behavior, Psychology's View*. Prentice-Hall, 1976.

Parker, B. A. *Mingled Yarn: Chronicle of a Troubled Family*. Yale, 1972.

Schreiber, F. R. *Sybil*. Regency, 1973.

21

Psychosis

====== Chapter Preview ======

Psychosis—"Losing It"

I'm a man 36 years of age, that in 1956–57 they changed the flag of the United States of America once by adding Alaska as a State to the Union and thus paving the way for Hawaii to become a state in 1959. That of course, gives me the *"capacity of the flag itself"* and therefore like any Congressional Medal of Honor winner, gives me the *"capacity of the President of the United States of America. . . ."*

. . . in 1955–56 civil authorities . . . some "small time" politicians got together on me and sand-bagged me brainwashed me and bugged me with a *"short-wave* Radio grid center, with an ultra-violet cross grid" called a "bug." Its sole purpose is to use a person's senses against himself so as to perjure and distort him to no end of humiliation . . . they vibrate your nerves physically with it and never ceases.

. . . I'd been there several months before they gave me "ground privileges" and once on the grounds they started frequencing my time all the more, vibrating the back of my neck, first flicking it to the front of my face, like a "whip" or a cat of 9 tails (Suinn, 1975).

The excerpts above are taken from a letter written by a man experiencing a psychosis. They demonstrate some of the severe disturbances in thinking, behavior, speech, and emotions that accompany psychosis.

Psychosis also represents a loss of contact with reality. Novelist Joanne Greenberg (1964) describes a split from reality this way:

The walls dissolved and the world became a combination of shadows . . . all direction became a lie. The laws of physics and solid matter were repealed and the experience of a lifetime of tactile sensation, motion, form, gravity, and light were invalidated. She did not know whether she was standing or sitting down, which way was upright, and from where the light, which was a stab as it touched her, was coming. She lost track of the parts of her body; where her arms were and how to move them. As light went spinning erratically away and back she tried to clutch at thoughts only to find that she had lost all memory of the English language.*

What is psychosis really like? What causes it? What can be done about it? For answers to these and related questions, read on.

*From *I Never Promised You a Rose Garden* by Hannah Green (Joanne Greenberg). Copyright © 1964 by Hannah Green. Reprinted by permission of Holt, Rinehart, & Winston, Publishers.

Survey Questions   What are the general characteristics of psychosis? How do paranoid psychosis, schizophrenia, and affective psychosis differ? What causes schizophrenia? How are psychotic disorders treated? Is psychiatric labeling damaging? How do "radical" therapists view psychiatric hospitalization?

Resources

"In that direction," the Cat said, waving its right paw round, "lives a Hatter: and in that direction," waving the other paw, "lives a March Hare. Visit either you like: they're both mad."

   "But I don't want to go among mad people," Alice remarked.

Lewis Carroll, *Alice in Wonderland*

Psychosis— When Things Really Go Wrong

Alice's unwillingness to "go among mad people" is quite understandable. Even close friends and family members may be perplexed, dismayed, and put off by the behavior of a psychotic person—a person who at times may seem a complete stranger to them. **Psychosis**—a major loss of contact with shared reality—ranks among the most serious of all psychopathologies. It can be considered comparable to a life-threatening illness in its capacity to disrupt people's lives.

Question: What is psychosis like?

A person experiencing a psychotic break undergoes a number of important changes. Following are descriptions of some of the major characteristics of psychoses.†

Presence of Delusions   **Delusions** are false beliefs that are held even when the facts contradict them. Individuals with the psychotic delusion that they are Jesus Christ will not be disturbed by an inability to walk on water or to perform miracles. Some common forms of delusion are: (1) *depressive* delusions, in which people feel that they have committed horrible crimes or sinful deeds; (2) *somatic* delusions, such as belief that one's body is "rotting away" or that it is emitting foul odors; (3) delusions of *grandeur,* in which individuals think they are extremely important persons; (4) delusions of *influence,* in which people feel they are being controlled or influenced by others or by unseen forces; (5) delusions of *persecution,* in which people feel

†Psychosis: singular; psychoses: plural.

others are "out to get them"; and (6) delusions of *reference,* in which unrelated events are given personal significance (as when it is assumed that a newspaper article or a television program is giving a special personal message to the person) (*DSM-III,* 1980). If you reread the opening quotation in the "Chapter Preview" you will find evidence of delusions of grandeur, influence, and persecution.

Hallucinations and Sensory Changes   **Hallucinations** are sensory experiences that occur in the absence of a stimulus. The most common psychotic hallucination is hearing voices, which may be familiar, may be answered, and frequently are insulting. Although rarer, psychotic individuals may also feel "insects crawling under the skin," taste "poisons" in their food, or smell "gas" their "enemies" are using to "get" them. Sensory changes may bring about extreme sensitivity to heat, cold, pain, or touch. Anesthesia, a loss of normal sensitivity, is also possible.

Disturbed Emotions   Emotions may swing violently between the extremes of elation and depression, or the psychotic person may be chronically hyperemotional, depressed, emotionally "flat," or apathetic. In **flat affect** there are virtually no signs of emotion. In such cases, the voice is often monotonous and the face frozen.

Personality Disorganization or Disintegration   Major disturbances such as those just described, coupled with additional problems in thought, speech, memory, actions, and attention bring about *personality disintegration* and a break with reality. As a result, significant impairment almost always occurs in work, social relations, and self-care. When psychotic disturbances and personality disintegration are evident for weeks or months (often including a period of deterioration, an active phase, and a residual phase), then the individual is said to have experienced a psychosis (*DSM-III,* 1980).

Question: How could a person function with such problems?

Actually, the preceding description is somewhat exaggerated, since it is rare to find all these changes occurring at once. As a matter of fact, you would probably find a trip to a psychiatric hospital disappointing if you expected to see flamboyant, dramatic, or bizarre behavior. Typically, psychotic behavior occurs in brief *episodes*. The symptoms of psychosis come and go and much of the time may be quite subtle (Fig. 21-1).

Even people who seem to be "out of it" are not necessarily totally unresponsive to their surroundings. In one interesting experiment, psychotics were interviewed in two ways. Some were told that the purpose of the interview was to determine if they were "ready for discharge." In this group, patients who were known to like the hospital acted very bizarre and disturbed during the interviews. A second group was told that the interview was to determine if the patient should be allowed "open ward" privileges. In this case disturbed patients suddenly became amazingly free of symptoms (Braginsky and Braginsky, 1967).

This experiment shows that psychotic symptoms can be considered a primitive form of communication, the message being, "I need help," or, "I can't handle it any more." This explanation becomes particularly evident when it is realized that one of the most universal symptoms of psychosis is difficulty in communicating verbally with others.

Psychotic speech tends to be garbled and chaotic, sometimes sounding like no more than a "word salad."

Question: Are there different types of psychosis?

A psychosis based on known brain pathology related to disease, gunshot wound, accident, or other physical cause is termed an **organic psychosis.** A psychosis based on unknown or psychological factors is called a **functional psychosis.** The possible causes of functional psychoses are explored later in this chapter.

Organic Psychosis   One example of organic psychosis is **general paresis** (pah-REE-sis). General paresis occurs in a small number of cases of untreated syphilis. In advanced stages, syphilis attacks brain cells and gradually brings about a deterioration in behavior. Most characteristic of general paresis is a loss of inhibition leading to shocking profanity and obscenity—the "dirty old man" syndrome.

A second source of organic psychosis that gives special cause for alarm is lead and mercury poisoning (see Fig. 21-2). Although relatively rare, such poisoning is entirely capable of damaging the brain and causing hallucinations, delusions, and a loss of emotional control. A particularly dangerous situation is found in many old houses and apart-

Fig. 21-1   *A scene in a state mental hospital.*

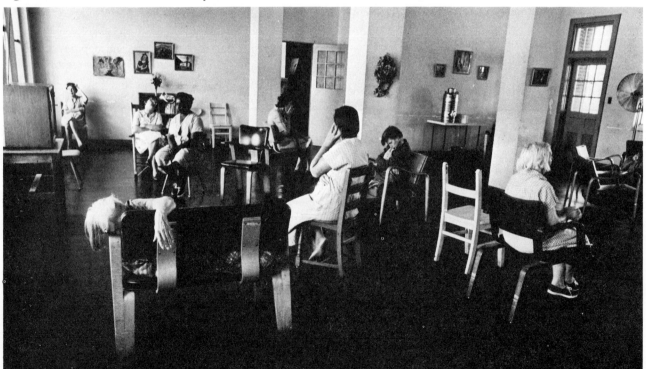

ment buildings, since many are painted with old-style leaded paints. Children who eat this paint may become psychotic or retarded.

Senile psychosis (or **senile dementia**) is probably the most common of organic problems. Senile dementia (duh-MEN-sha) is typically marked by disturbances in memory, abstract reasoning, judgment, impulse control, and personality—a combination that usually leaves the individual confused, suspicious, apathetic, or withdrawn. Senile dementia is closely associated with physical deterioration of the brain brought on by circulatory problems, repeated strokes, or general shrinkage and atrophy of the brain.

The three major types of functional psychoses are *paranoia, schizophrenia,* and *affective psychosis.* Information on each is provided in the following sections.

Paranoid Psychosis— An Enemy Behind Every Tree

Paranoia is a rare form of psychosis. The true paranoid does not suffer from hallucinations, emotional excesses, or personality disintegration. The major characteristic of paranoia is the presence of delusions of grandeur or persecution. Many self-styled reformers, absurdly jealous husbands or wives, crank letter writers, "Communist hunters," and the like, are paranoids.

Most often, paranoid delusions center on feelings of persecution. Paranoid individuals believe they are being cheated, spied upon, followed, poisoned, harassed, or that someone is plotting against them. Paranoids are usually intensely suspicious, believing they must be on guard at all times. The evidence paranoids find to support their beliefs is usually unconvincing to others. Every detail of the paranoid's existence is woven into a personal version of "what's really going on." Buzzing during a telephone conversation may be interpreted as "someone listening," a stranger who comes to the door asking for directions may be seen as "really trying to get information," and so forth.

Fig. 21-2   *The Mad Hatter, from Lewis Carroll's book,* Alice in Wonderland. *History provides numerous examples of psychosis caused by toxic chemicals. Carroll's Mad Hatter character is modeled after an occupational disease of the 18th and 19th century. In that era, hatmakers were heavily exposed to mercury used in the preparation of felt. Consequently, many suffered brain damage and became psychotic, or "mad" (Kety, 1979).*

Paranoids are rarely treated or admitted to mental hospitals because it is almost impossible to suggest to them that they need help. A friend, relative, or psychologist who does so simply becomes part of the "conspiracy" to "persecute" them. Paranoids frequently lead lonely, isolated, and humorless lives marked by constant suspicion and hostility toward others. Paranoids are not necessarily dangerous to others, but they can be. A person who believes that "the Mafia" is slowly closing in on him may be moved to violence by his irrational fears. A person standing at the door with his hand in his coat pocket could become the target of a paranoid attempt at "self-defense."

Because our next topic, schizophrenia, involves several new terms and ideas, let's stop for a quick "Learning Check" before proceeding.

Learning Check

1. A person who wrongly believes that his or her body is "rotting away" is suffering from:

   a. depressive delusions   *b.* delusions of grandeur
   c. somatic delusions   *d.* delusions of persecution

2. Persons suffering from psychoses are totally unresponsive to their surroundings.   T or F?

3. A psychosis caused by lead poisoning would be termed a *functional* disorder.   T or F?

4. Paranoia is the most common form of psychosis.   T or F?

5. In *flat affect,* a sensory experience—such as hearing voices—occurs in the absence of a stimulus.   T or F?

Answers: 1. c   2. F   3. F   4. F   5. F

Schizophrenia—Shattered Reality

Approximately half of all admissions to mental hospitals are diagnosed as *schizophrenic*. **Schizophrenia** (SKIZ-oh-FREE-nih-ah) is a major health problem: 1 person in 100 will become schizophrenic, and one-fourth of all hospital beds in the United States are occupied by schizophrenics. Most schizophrenics are young adults, but schizophrenia can occur at any age.

Question: Does a schizophrenic have two personalities?

"Schizophrenia" does not refer to having more than one personality. You will recall from the previous chapter that multiple personality is a dissociative reaction to neurosis.

The word *schizophrenia* can be interpreted to mean "split-mind," but this refers to a split between thought and emotion. In schizophrenia, emotions may become blunted or "flat," or they may be very inappropriate. For example, a schizophrenic may smile or giggle when told his mother has died, or may describe her death with no visible emotion. In addition, schizophrenia is characterized by: withdrawal

Fig. 21-3 *The hebephrenic schizophrenic's behavior is marked by silliness, laughter, bizarre, and often obscene behavior.*

from contact with others and a loss of interest in external activities; a breakdown of personal habits and ability to deal with daily events; and the delusions, hallucinations, and thought abnormalities found in other types of psychosis. Schizophrenic delusions can be particularly bizarre. They often include the idea that the person's thoughts and actions are being controlled, that his or her thoughts are being broadcast so that others can hear them, that thoughts have been "inserted" into the person's mind, or that thoughts have been removed.

Question: Is there more than one type of schizophrenia?

Schizophrenia may ultimately turn out to be a whole group of related disturbances. For now, we can identify four major subtypes of schizophrenia, and one closely related personality disorder.

Borderline Schizophrenia Problems referred to as *borderline,* or *simple schizophrenia,* develop slowly, usually starting in adolescence. Affected individuals gradually become withdrawn and isolated from their surroundings. They are usually seen as listless and apathetic by others, and they are often considered "odd," "shiftless," or "eccentric." Their behavior may be markedly peculiar (collecting garbage, eating cigarette butts, talking to themselves, etc.) and their emotions are usually dulled. Typically, they seem to prefer to avoid contact and communication with others.

Problems of this type superficially resemble some aspects of schizophrenia. But since borderline schizophrenia is usually a long-term pattern, and the person is not actively psychotic, it is probably best to think of it as a personality disorder (formally called a *schizotypal* personality disorder). Many borderline schizophrenics (or **schizotypal personalities**) go unnoticed and untreated, living out colorless and isolated lives on the fringes of society as vagrants, derelicts, or prostitutes.

Hebephrenic Schizophrenia Hebephrenic (HEE-beh-FREN-ik), or **disorganized schizophrenia,** comes as close as any true psychiatric problem to matching the stereotyped portrayals of "insanity" seen in movies and on television. The hebephrenic's personality disintegration is almost complete. The result is silliness, laughter, bizarre, and often obscene behavior (Fig. 21-3). The following excerpt is from the intake interview of a hebephrenic patient:

Dr. I am Dr. _____. I would like to know something more about you.
Patient You have a nasty mind. Lord!! Lord! Cat's in a cradle.
Dr. Tell me, how do you feel?

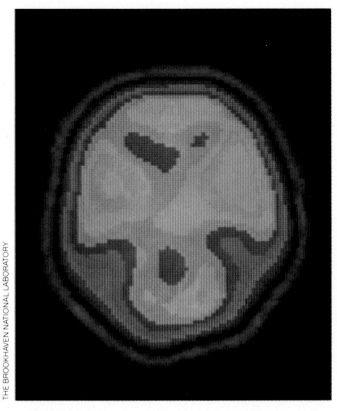

NORMAL

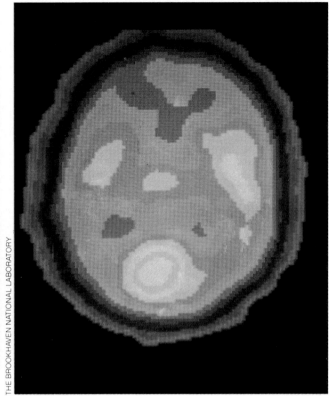

SCHIZOPHRENIC

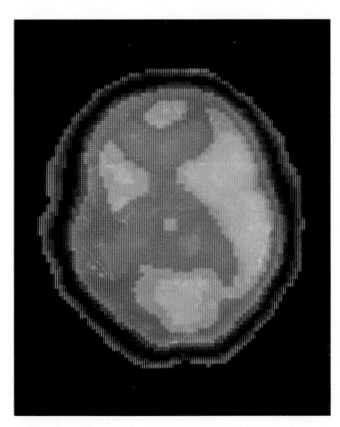

MANIC-DEPRESSIVE

Positron emission tomography produces "PET scans" of the human brain. Colors indicate various levels of activity. Distinctly different patterns of activity are observed in the brains of normal, manic-depressive, and schizophrenic individuals. In the future, such differences may aid diagnosis of mental disorder.

The portraits and self-portraits shown here were painted by Andy Wilf between 1978 and 1981. During that time, Wilf is said to have increasingly abused drugs and alcohol. This dramatic series of images is a record of his self-destructive descent into a private hell. The final painting shows a shrouded skull—and foretells the artist's fate. Wilf died of a drug overdose early in 1982.

Drug abuse is but one of the many psychopathologies, or "problems in living," psychologists seek to alleviate. For a full discussion of abnormal behavior and various therapies, see Chapters 20, 21, 22, and 23.

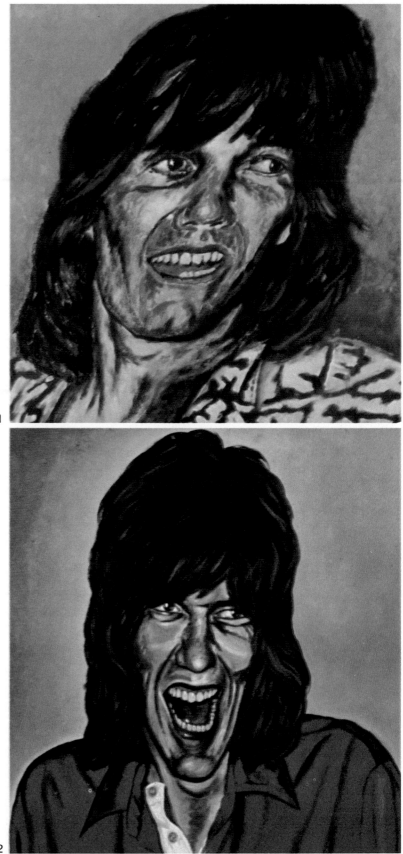

1

2

3

4

Like Andy Wilf's paintings, this series by Louis Wain reflects a troubled personality. Wain was a British illustrator who became schizophrenic in middle age. As Wain's psychosis progressed, his cat paintings became highly abstract and fragmented. In many ways Wain's paintings resemble the perceptual changes caused by psychedelic drugs such as mescaline and LSD. Recent research suggests that psychosis may, in fact, be the result of mind-altering changes in brain chemistry.

Patient London's bell is a long, long dock. Hee! Hee! (Giggles uncontrollably.)

Dr. Do you know where you are now?

Patient D_____n! S_____t on you all who rip into my internals! The grudgerometer will take care of you all! (Shouting) I am the Queen, see my magic, I shall turn you all into smidgelings forever!

Dr. Your husband is concerned about you. Do you know his name?

Patient (Stands, walks to and faces the wall) Who am I, who are we, who are you, who are they, (Turns) I . . . I . . . I . . . I! (Makes grotesque faces)

Edna was placed in the women's ward where she proceeded to masturbate. She always sat in a chosen spot and in a chosen way, with her feet propped under her. Occasionally, she would scream or shout obscenities. At other times she giggled to herself. She was known to attack other patients. She began to complain that her uterus was attached to a "pipeline to the Kremlin" and that she was being "infernally invaded" by Communism (Suinn, 1975).

Hebephrenic schizophrenia typically develops in early adolescence or young adulthood and is often preceded by serious personality disorganization in earlier years. Chances of improvement are limited, and social impairment is usually extreme (*DSM-III*, 1980).

Catatonic Schizophrenia The catatonic seems to be in a state of total panic. This brings about a stuporous condition in which odd positions may be held for hours or even days. Sometimes, a condition called *waxy flexibility* occurs. In this, the catatonic can be arranged into any position like a mannequin. These periods of immobility may be similar to the tendency to "freeze" at times of great emergency or panic. There is evidence that catatonic individuals are struggling desperately to control their inner turmoil because stupor may occasionally give way to outbursts of agitated and sometimes violent behavior. The following excerpt describes a **catatonic episode:**

Manuel appeared to be physically healthy upon examination. Yet he did not regain his awareness of his surroundings. He remained motionless, speechless, and seemingly unconscious. One evening an aide turned him on his side to straighten out the sheet, was called away to tend another patient, and forgot to return. Manuel was found the next morning, still on his side, his arm tucked under his body, as he had been left the night before. His arm was turning blue from lack of circulation but he seemed to be experiencing no discomfort. Further examination confirmed that he was in a state of waxy flexibility (Suinn, 1975).

Notice that in addition to his other problems Manuel was unable to talk. *Mutism* plus a marked decrease in responsiveness to the environment make the catatonic patient difficult to "reach." Fortunately, this bizarre form of schizophrenia has become rare in Europe and North America.

Paranoid Schizophrenia Paranoid schizophrenia is the most common form of schizophrenic disorder. **Paranoid schizophrenia,** like paranoia, centers around delusions of grandeur and persecution, but in paranoid schizophrenia there is personality disintegration that is not evident in paranoia. The paranoid schizophrenic also experiences hallucinations and has delusions that are more fragmented and unconvincing than those of the paranoid. Thinking that their minds are being controlled by the government or "cosmic rays from space," or that someone is trying to poison them, paranoid schizophrenics may feel forced into violence to protect themselves. Some observers believe that Sirhan Sirhan, the assassin of Senator Robert F. Kennedy, was a paranoid schizophrenic who was preoccupied with the delusion that he was the "savior of his people."

The three "types" of schizophrenia described occur most often in textbooks. In reality there is considerable overlap among the types, and a real patient may shift from one pattern of behavior to another at different times during the course of the psychosis. Many are simply classified as suffering from **undifferentiated schizophrenia.**

The diagnosis of schizophrenia is fairly subjective and open to considerable error (see this chapter's "Applications") (McCabe, 1976). Additionally, there is evidence that over one-half of those diagnosed as schizophrenic have learned to fake some of their symptoms or to mask others in order to lengthen or shorten their hospital stay (Martin *et al.,* 1977). All things considered, however, there is no doubt that schizophrenia is "real," or that it is a major challenge to medical and psychological researchers.

Affective Psychosis— Peaks and Valleys

About 14 percent of patients admitted to mental hospitals suffer from an *affective* psychosis.

Question: How does an affective psychosis differ from other types?

In addition to the usual psychological disturbances, **affective psychosis** is marked by persistent and excessive

Fig. 21-4 *In a depressive psychosis, suicidal impulses can be intense and despair total.*

changes in mood or emotion. Afflicted individuals may be continuously loud, inappropriately elated, hyperactive, and energetic **(manic type),** or continuously sad and guilt-ridden **(depressive type),** or they may alternate between the two states **(manic-depressive** or **mixed type)** (*DSM-III, 1980*).

Manic individuals throw themselves into fits of activity characterized by extreme distractibility, rapid shifts in thoughts ("flights of ideas"), constant talking, and restless movement. In advanced stages, manic behavior becomes more and more incoherent, agitated, and out of control. Eating or sleeping may be ignored until individuals push themselves into states of total delirium. This brief excerpt from a case history illustrates manic behavior:

> Her husband had returned home to find her twirling around the living room bizarrely draped in her wedding gown tied with a bathtowel and wearing a lampshade. She gaily greeted him, laughed with an ear-piercing shrillness, and invited him to stay for the exciting "coming-out" party she was giving. Strewn on the table were a thousand handwritten invitations signed with a flourish and addressed to such dignitaries as the President of the United States, the justices of the Supreme Court, the Emperor of Japan. She made incessant noises: singing her own

ballads, shouting mottoes, which she devised, reciting limericks, making rhyming sounds, and yelling obscenities (Suinn, 1970).

Depressive reactions show a reverse pattern in which feelings of failure, sinfulness, worthlessness, and total despair predominate. The individual becomes extremely subdued and withdrawn and frequently becomes intensely suicidal. Depressive reactions pose one of the most serious threats to the survival of a disturbed individual since suicide attempted during a psychotic depression is rarely a "plea for help." The person intends to succeed and may give no prior warning (Fig. 21-4). The excerpt below describes the condition of a woman admitted to a hospital in a psychotic depression.

> Her husband had brought her to the hospital because she had refused to eat for about three days, slept fitfully, and spent long hours staring off into space. She would speak to those around her, but only after more or less continuous coaxing. In very slow, monotonous speech she commented that she was talking to her dead sister who was wearing a white gown, but with a face eaten up by worms and with part of her eye socket missing. This hallucination was intermixed with some discussion between the patient and God that seemed to center around a mixture of pleading with Him to do something about the sister and reprimanding Him for letting her get into that condition (McMahon, 1976).*

Manic and depressive reactions are closely interrelated. When manic behavior occurs, it may still be considered a reaction to depression. The manic individual seeks to escape feelings of worthlessness and depression in an unending rush of activity.

Question: How do affective psychoses differ from the affective disorders described in Chapter 20?

Affective psychosis usually involves more severe mood disorders. Also, of course, psychotic delusions, hallucinations, and the like, are present in addition to emotional excesses. In addition, affective psychosis appears to be **endogenous** (en-DODGE-eh-nus: produced from within) rather than a reaction to external events.

Question: Is it possible to suffer from more than one form of psychosis at a time?

Yes. Psychological problems don't always fit neatly into one category or another. For instance, at times it is difficult to know if a person should be classified as schizophrenic, or

*From *Abnormal Behavior, Psychology's View,* F. B. McMahon. Copyright 1976. Reprinted by permission of Prentice-Hall, Inc., Englewood, Cliffs, N.J.

suffering from a mood disorder. In view of this problem, *DSM-III* lists **schizoaffective psychosis** in a "mixed and/or other" category. Schizoaffective disorders combine schizophrenic thought disturbances with depression or mania. This might sound like "double trouble." But actually, there is a better chance of recovery from schizoaffective psychosis than from schizophrenia accompanied by apathy or blunted emotions.

The Causes of Schizophrenia— An Unsolved Riddle

Former British Prime Minister Winston Churchill once described a question that perplexed him as "a riddle wrapped in a mystery inside an enigma." The same words might be used to describe the causes of schizophrenia, the most common and devastating of the psychoses.

Question: What do we know about the causes of schizophrenia?

Environment   Some psychologists suspect that early **psychological trauma** may contribute to the later devel-

opment of schizophrenia. Case studies of schizophrenia often show its victims were exposed to violence, sexual abuse, death, divorce, or separation in childhood. In general, there seems to be a greater than average degree of stress in the childhood of those who develop schizophrenia. A question that remains unanswered is why childhood trauma leaves some individuals emotionally crippled and others not.

Many psychologists theorize that a **disturbed family environment** is a causal factor in schizophrenia. For example, one intriguing theory is that the schizophrenic is *forced* to escape into psychosis by being placed in what British psychiatrist R. D. Laing calls a *position of checkmate* (1967, 1970). This idea can be illustrated by imagining that someone is standing over you with a large stick. This person gives you these instructions:

> In a moment I'm going to ask you if this stick is real. If you say "yes" I will hit you with it. If you say "no" then I will hit you with it. If you refuse to answer I will hit you with it.

Your reaction to this dilemma might very well be stammering, emotion, and a defensive crouch. To a person outside the situation your reactions might look "crazy" (Fig. 21-5).

Fig. 21-5 *Can the catatonic's rigid postures and stupor be understood in terms of abnormal body chemistry? Environment? Heredity?*

Similarly, Laing feels that the schizophrenic's strange thoughts and behavior are really an adaptation to an impossible environment. Laing and others also believe the families of schizophrenics constantly engage in **double-bind communication.**

A double-bind message is one that places the listener in an unsolvable conflict like that just posed. For example, the mother of a schizophrenic might issue this typical double-bind message, "You don't really love me; you're only pretending you do." This statement asks for a show of love but makes showing love impossible. Anything the person does becomes "wrong."

Gregory Bateson provides another classic double-bind example.

A young man who had fairly well recovered from an acute schizophrenic episode was visited in the hospital by his mother. He was glad to see her and impulsively put his arm around her shoulders whereupon she stiffened. He withdrew his arm and she asked, "Don't you love me anymore?" He then blushed and she said, "Dear, you must not be so easily embarrassed and afraid of your feelings." The patient was able to stay with her only a few minutes more and following her departure he assaulted an aide and was put in the tubs (Bateson *et al.,* 1956).

Although they are attractive, environmental explanations such as these are not enough to account for schizophrenia. This can be seen by comparing children raised in foster homes (with normal parents) to children raised by schizophrenic mothers. When the children of schizophrenic parents are raised away from their chaotic home environment, they are still likely to become psychotic (Page, 1971).

Question: Does that mean that heredity is a factor in schizophrenia?

Heredity It is always difficult to separate the effects of heredity from the effects of environment. Just the same, the evidence for heredity as a factor in schizophrenia has been growing ever stronger in recent years. It now appears that some individuals inherit a *potential* for developing schizophrenia.

Question: How can that be shown?

Here is a prime example: If one *identical* twin becomes schizophrenic (remember, identical twins have identical genes), then the other twin has a *50 percent* chance of also becoming schizophrenic. There is even a case on record of *four* identical quadruplets *all* developing schizophrenia (Rosenthal and Quinn, 1977).

Question: What about other family relationships?

If *both parents* are schizophrenic, a child has a 45 percent chance of developing the disorder; persons with a brother or sister and one parent who are schizophrenic run a 17 percent risk themselves; persons with a schizophrenic brother or sister have a 10 percent chance of also becoming schizophrenic; and for *fraternal* twins the chance of mutual schizophrenia is about 12 percent (Gottesman and Shields, 1972; Gottesman, 1978).

These figures can be compared to the risk of developing schizophrenia for the population in general, which is 1 percent. Comparisons such as these, and a variety of other studies, have shown that schizophrenia is more common among close relatives than distant relatives, and that it tends to run in families (Reiss, 1974).

Question: How could someone inherit a susceptibility to schizophrenia?

Body Chemistry LSD and similar drugs produce effects that partially mimic the symptoms of psychosis. Also, the same drugs (phenothiazines) that are effective in treating an LSD overdose are effective in treatment of schizophrenia (Mandell *et al.,* 1972). Such similarities have suggested to many scientists that psychosis may be based on **biochemical abnormalities** that cause the body to produce some substance similar to a *psychedelic* (mind-altering) drug. At present the most likely candidate is **dopamine** (DOPE-ah-meen), an important chemical messenger in the brain.

Question: How does dopamine fit into the picture?

By far the most exciting discovery in recent years is the close link between dopamine and schizophrenia. Many researchers now believe that schizophrenia is directly related to overactivity in brain dopamine systems (Barchas *et al.,* 1978).

Early hints of a dopamine-psychosis link came when researchers noted that large doses of amphetamines (speed) produce symptoms that are almost identical to paranoid schizophrenia. Amphetamines, it turns out, also raise brain dopamine levels. Another piece of the puzzle fell into place when it was discovered that all major *antipsychotic* drugs *block* the action of dopamine at receptor areas in the brain (Iversen, 1979).

Question: Then is schizophrenia a "dopamine high"?

For a time it seemed so. But no extra or abnormal amounts of dopamine could be found in the brains of schizophrenics (Davis, 1978). So much for the dopamine theory!

But wait. Our story is not over. In a dramatic break-

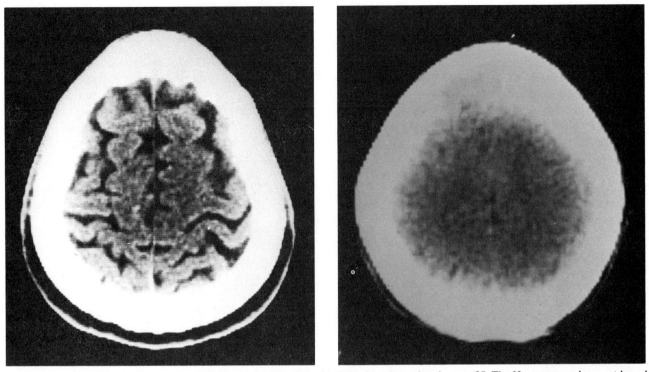

Fig. 21-6 (left) *CT scan of would-be presidential assassin John Hinkley, Jr., taken when he was 25. The X-ray image shows widened fissures in the wrinkled surface of Hinkley's brain* (right). *CT scan of a normal 25-year-old's brain. In most young adults the surface folds of the brain are pressed together too tightly to be seen. As a person ages, surface folds of the brain normally become more visible. Pronounced brain fissuring in young adults may be a sign of schizophrenia, chronic alcoholism, or other problems (McKean, 1982).*

through, a team of researchers at the University of Toronto, Canada, have found nearly *double* the normal number of dopamine receptors in the brains of schizophrenics. These extra receptors exist in especially large numbers in the limbic system (a major emotional system of the brain). Many scientists now believe that dopamine activation triggers a flood of unrelated thoughts, feelings, and perceptions, and directly accounts for the voices, hallucinations, delusions, and other disturbances of schizophrenia (Iversen, 1979). Because of the extra receptors, schizophrenics may get psychedelic effects from normal levels of dopamine in the brain. The implication of this, and related research on other brain chemicals, is that schizophrenics may be on a permanent "drug trip" caused by their own bodies (Hoffer, 1972).

Medical researchers have long hoped for a way to directly observe the schizophrenic brain. Two new medical techniques are now making it possible. One, called a **CT scan,** provides an X-ray picture of the brain. (CT stands for computed tomography, or computer-enhanced X-ray images.) Fig. 21-6 shows a CT scan of John Hinkley Jr.'s brain.

Hinkley, you may recall, shot President Reagan and three other men in 1981. In the ensuing trial, Hinkley was judged insane. As you can see, Hinkley's brain differed from the norm. Specifically, it had wider surface fissuring, and enlarged ventricles (fluid-filled spaces within the brain). Similar changes, which are normal in older people, are found in about 1 out of 10 young schizophrenics. Although the meaning of such changes is still in doubt, the CT scan promises to aid in diagnosing schizophrenia, and to provide new information on its causes (McKean, 1982).

A second new technique, called a **PET scan** provides an image of brain *activity.* (PET stands for positron emission tomography.) To make a PET scan, a radioactive sugar solution is injected into a vein. When the sugar reaches the brain, a device measures how much is used in each area. This information is then translated into a colored map, or scan, of brain activity (see color pages). Researchers are already finding patterns in such scans that are consistently linked with schizophrenia, mood disorders, and other problems. Some researchers believe that in the future PET scans will be routinely used to accurately diagnose schizophrenia (Landis, 1980). For now, PET scans show that there is a clear difference in schizophrenic brain activity.

Summary   In summary, the emerging picture of psychosis takes this general form: *Anyone* subjected to enough stress may be pushed to a psychotic break; but some people inherit a difference in bodily chemistry or brain structure that makes them more susceptible. Thus, the right combination of inherited potential and environmental stress brings

about important changes in brain chemicals, or generates mind-altering substances in the body (McMahon, 1976; Gottesman, 1978).

Ultimately, distinctions between organic and functional psychoses may be dropped, and treatment of major disturbances may become more chemical than psychological. But for now, psychosis remains "a riddle wrapped in a mystery inside an enigma." Let us hope the recent advances that we have so briefly explored are as promising as they appear to be.

Learning Check

Match the following:

_____ 1. Schizotypal personality   A.   Manic or depressive behavior

_____ 2. Hebephrenic schizophrenia   B.   Mutism, odd postures, immobility

_____ 3. Catatonic schizophrenia   C.   Borderline, or simple schizophrenia

_____ 4. Paranoid schizophrenia   D.   Silliness, disorganization, bizarre behavior

_____ 5. Affective psychosis   E.   Delusions of grandeur or persecution

6. Schizophrenics have two or more personalities.   T or F?

7. R. D. Laing attributes psychotic behavior to a "crazy" or impossible environment, often created in the home by:

   a. manic parents   *b.* schizoaffective interactions

   c. psychedelic interactions   *d.* double-bind communication

8. The _____ _____ of a schizophrenic person runs a 50 percent chance of also becoming psychotic.

9. Abnormally high numbers of noradrenaline receptors have been found in the brains of schizophrenics.   T or F?

10. Enlarged surface fissures and ventricles, as revealed by CT scans, are found only in the brains of chronic schizophrenics.   T or F?

Answers: 1. C 2. D 3. B 4. E 5. A 6. F 7. d 8. identical twin 9. F (dopamine receptors) 10. F

Treatment—Medical Approaches

Question: Is psychosis incurable? If a person's symptoms temporarily disappear can an unexpected relapse occur?

An organic psychosis cannot be "cured" in the usual sense, but it may be controlled with drugs and other techniques. With functional psychoses the outlook is still rather negative, but many people are *permanently* cured. It is wrong to fear "former mental patients," or to exclude them from work, friendships, or other social situations. A psychotic episode does not inevitably lead to a lifelong maladjustment, but too often it leads to unnecessary rejection due to the groundless fears of others.

Question: What can be done about psychosis?

Two basic forms of treatment can be distinguished. The first, called **psychotherapy,** can be described as two people talking about one person's problems. Psychotherapy is a special relationship between a counselor or psychologist and a person in trouble. Psychotherapy is applied to everything from a brief crisis to a neurosis or full-scale psychosis. Because approaches currently in use are so varied, a complete discussion of psychotherapy is found in the next two chapters.

A second major approach to treatment is **somatic** (bodily) **therapy.** The principal somatic treatments are *chemotherapy, electroconvulsive therapy,* and *psychosur-*

gery. Somatic therapy is often carried out in the context of psychiatric *hospitalization.* All these approaches have a distinct medical slant, and they are used primarily to treat psychoses. For these reasons, somatic therapy provides an appropriate conclusion to our discussion of psychosis.

Drugs   The atmosphere in mental hospitals changed radically in the mid-1950s with the widespread adoption of chemotherapy (CHEM-oh-therapy). **Chemotherapy** is the use of drugs or chemical substances to alleviate the symptoms of emotional disturbance. Drugs may be used to relieve the anxiety attacks and other discomforts of neurosis, but they are more frequently used to combat psychosis. Drugs such as Thorazine are credited with emptying mental hospitals, reducing the hospital population from a peak of 560,000 to fewer than 200,000 patients in barely a generation.

Question: What types of drugs are used in chemotherapy?

The three major classes of drugs are *minor tranquilizers, major tranquilizers (antipsychotics),* and *energizers.* **Minor tranquilizers** calm anxious or agitated persons; **energizers** improve the mood of those who are depressed; and **antipsychotics** control hallucinations and other symptoms of psychosis.

Question: Are drugs a valid approach to treatment?

Drugs have greatly improved the chances for recovery from a psychiatric disorder. They have shortened the length of hospital stays and have made it possible for more individuals to be returned to the community where they may be treated on an "out-patient" basis.

Few experts would argue for a return to the conditions that existed before chemotherapy became available. But there are some drawbacks. First of all, drugs generally do not *cure* mental illness—they only temporarily relieve symptoms. Such relief may allow patients to benefit more fully from psychotherapy and other attempts to help them, but drugs alone may not remove underlying problems. As a matter of fact, patients may separate temporary improvement caused by a drug from improvement they consider genuine. As one patient told the author, "The drugs made me talk more and seem happy, but I knew I really wasn't."

The extensive use of drugs also raises the issue of balancing benefits against possible adverse side effects. Side effects can range from dry mouth, constipation, and confusion to a major deterioration of behavior or physical health. A particularly disturbing pattern has come to light in recent years with respect to *tardive dyskinesia* (TAR-div dis-cah-KNEE-zih-ah). In this neurological condition patients develop rhythmical facial and mouth movements, as

well as unusual movements of the limbs and other parts of the body. As many as 10 percent of patients taking major tranquilizers for extended periods develop tardive dyskinesia.

Perhaps the most valid criticism of chemotherapy is the simple observation that it is overused. Apparently the temptation to reach for the prescription pad is great. Most observers agree that too many drugs are being given to too many people. Researcher David Rosenhan (see the "Applications" section of this chapter) feels that drugs are no longer being given at therapeutic levels; rather, they are being used to keep patients docile and easy to manage. Many critics feel that the locks that came off the doors of old-style institutions have simply been replaced by "chemical locks." In the long run, concern over side effects and the overuse of drugs may temper the popularity of chemotherapy. But where psychosis is concerned, drugs are usually helpful and will remain a major mode of treatment for some time to come.

Shock   **Electroconvulsive therapy (ECT)** is a rather drastic medical treatment for depression. In the usual ECT session, a 150-volt electrical current is passed through the brain for slightly less than a second (Fig. 21-7). The current triggers a convulsion and causes the patient to lose consciousness for a short time. Muscle relaxants and sedative drugs are given before ECT to soften its impact. Treatments are administered in a series of six to eight sessions spread over three to four weeks. There is some loss of memory for the period of treatments, but memory usually returns within six months.

Question: How does shock help?

Actually, it is the seizure activity that is considered helpful. Proponents of ECT claim that shock-induced seizures alter the biochemical balance in the brain, bringing an end to severe depression and suicidal or self-destructive behavior (Frankl, 1977).

Many people consider ECT a distasteful procedure, and not all professionals support its use. In fact, experts are engaged in a heated debate concerning the effectiveness of ECT and the seriousness of its side effects. Critics claim that memory losses caused by ECT are often permanent and that there is evidence of occasional brain damage from its use (Freidberg, 1977). Others have charged that ECT is no more effective than drugs, and that it is used for all types of problems even though it is effective only in treatment of depression (Costello, 1976; Turek and Hanlon, 1977). Proponents of ECT argue that evidence of damage comes mainly from studies done before sedation, muscle relaxants, and use of oxygen reduced chances of injury. Their

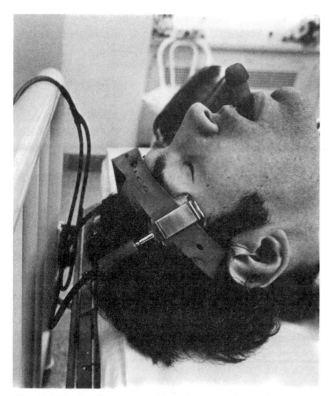

Fig. 21-7 *In electroconvulsive therapy, electrodes are attached to the head, and a brief electrical current is passed through the brain. ECT is used in the treatment of severe depression.*

view is that ECT is like any other medical treatment: It involves calculated risks (Fink, 1977).

As is the case with chemotherapy, the major problem with ECT seems to lie in overuse and misuse. Some patients have had literally hundreds of shock treatments and have suffered damage in the process. In spite of such abuses, ECT, when carefully used, is still considered a valid treatment for selected cases of depression—especially when it brings a rapid end to wildly self-destructive behavior.

Surgery The most extreme biological treatment is **psychosurgery,** a general term applied to any surgical alteration of the brain. The best known psychosurgery is the *prefrontal lobotomy.* In the **prefrontal lobotomy** and related techniques, the frontal lobes are surgically disconnected from other areas of the brain. The original goal of this procedure was to calm a person who had not responded to any other type of treatment.

When the lobotomy was first introduced in the early 1950s, there were enthusiastic claims for its success. But later studies suggest that the effects of a lobotomy are quite

unpredictable. Some patients were calmed, some showed no noticeable change, and some became "vegetables." Lobotomies also produced a high rate of undesirable side effects, such as seizures, extreme lack of emotional response, and even stupor (Barahal, 1958). As such problems became apparent, the lobotomy was abandoned.

Question: To what extent is psychosurgery now used?

Psychosurgery is still considered a valid treatment by many neurosurgeons. However, most now use sophisticated **deep lesioning** techniques. In this approach, small target areas are selected in the brain's interior. Then, an electrified needle is lowered into the target, where it destroys a tiny amount of tissue. The appeal of deep lesioning is that it can have fairly specific effects. For instance, a patient with uncontrollable aggressive impulses may be calmed by psychosurgery.

For the past 5 to 10 years, some 400 patients a year have undergone psychosurgery in the United States. In view of the earlier damage done by lobotomies, this is somewhat surprising. All forms of psychosurgery are *irreversible.* As you may recall from Chapter 3, damage to the brain is permanent. This is one of the reasons that chemotherapy has sharply limited use of psychosurgery. A drug can be given or taken away. You can't take back psychosurgery.

Recently, an 11-member federal commission that began with a severe bias against psychosurgery concluded it is acceptable in carefully selected cases (Culliton, 1976). Many critics disagree—arguing that psychosurgery is a horror that should be banned altogether. Others continue to report success with psychosurgical procedures (Mitchell-Heggs et al., 1976). While refusing to ban psychosurgery, the federal commission recommends stringent control. According to the commission, patients must give voluntary, *informed* consent (they must be told the surgery is "experimental"); courts must be consulted in the case of children, criminals, or the involuntarily confined; and the institution at which surgery is performed must have a surgical review board (Culliton, 1976).

Hospitalization Somatic therapy, psychotherapy, and other techniques may require a special setting or special control for a period of time. Traditionally, this has meant a trip to a psychiatric hospital or state institution. **Hospitalization** by itself may be considered a form of treatment since it removes a troubled individual from situations that may be provoking or maintaining the problem.

At its best, the hospital is a controlled environment in which diagnosis, support, refuge, and psychotherapy are provided. At worst, an institution can be a brutalizing experience that leaves a person less prepared to face the world than before (Fig. 21-8).

In the last 20 years the resident population in large mental hospitals throughout the United States has been reduced by two-thirds. This reduction is largely due to policies designed to improve the odds that hospitalization will be constructive.

Hospitals are ideally used as a last resort after other forms of treatment within the community have been exhausted. Recent research indicates that most psychiatric patients do as well with short-term hospitalization (3 to 4 weeks) as they do with longer (3 to 4 month) periods (Glick *et al.,* 1979). In view of this, hospital stays are now held to a minimum through use of *revolving-door* policies, in which patients are released as soon as possible and readmitted only if necessary. Also, modern hospitals provide recreation and rehabilitation to help end an old problem: Formerly many patients became so "institutionalized" that they had difficulty returning to the community. Also helpful are "halfway houses" and voluntary support groups that ease the patient's return to the community.

Question: How successful have such policies been?

In truth their success has been limited. Many states have welcomed a reduction in mental hospital populations as a way to save money. The upsetting result is that many chronic patients are being discharged to a lonely existence in hostile communities without adequate care.

Large mental hospitals may no longer be warehouses for society's unwanted, but many former patients are no better off consigned to bleak lives in nursing homes, single-room hotels, and "board and care" homes (Bassuk and Gerson, 1978). Ironically, high quality psychological and psychiatric care is available in almost every community. As much as anything, a simple lack of sufficient funding prevents large numbers of people from getting the care they need.

Community Mental Health Programs— Hope and Help for Many

A bright spot in the area of mental health care has been the passage of federal legislation to encourage creation of community mental health centers. **Community mental health centers** attempt to shift emphasis away from institutionalization and hospitalization and seek new answers to mental health problems by providing short-term hospitalization, outpatient care, and special crisis or emergency services (Perlmutter and Silverman, 1972).

If it is like most, the mental health center in your community has two major goals. Its primary aim is to provide direct psychological aid to troubled citizens. The second goal of mental health centers is prevention. Consultation, education, and crisis intervention are used to end or prevent problems before they become serious. Also, some centers attempt to raise the general level of mental health in target areas by combating problems such as unemployment, delinquency, and drug abuse.

Question: How have community mental health centers fared in meeting their goals?

In practice, they have concentrated much more on providing clinical services than they have on prevention (Bloom and Parad, 1977). This situation appears to be primarily the result of wavering government support (translation: money).

Overall, community mental health centers have succeeded in making mental health services more accessible

Fig. 21-8   *Depending on the quality of the institution, hospitalization may be a refuge or a brutalizing experience. Many state "asylums" or mental hospitals are antiquated and in need of drastic improvement.*

than *ever* before. Many of their programs are made possible by **paraprofessionals,** individuals who work under the supervision of more highly trained staff. Some paraprofessionals are ex-addicts, ex-alcoholics, or ex-patients who have "been there." Many more are persons (paid or volunteer) who have skills in tutoring, crafts, counseling, or are simply warm, empathetic, and skilled at communication. There is a severe shortage of people working in mental health care. The contributions of paraprofessionals will undoubtedly continue to grow. A possible career as a paraprofessional should not be overlooked by the student planning to work in the field of mental health.

Learning Check

1. The use of chemotherapy has required longer hospital stays since drugs can only be given under hospital supervision.   T or F?
2. ECT is a modern form of chemotherapy.   T or F?
3. Electroconvulsive therapy is mainly used as a treatment for depression.   T or F?
4. Tardive dyskinesia is a possible complication in long term use of:

    a. major tranquilizers   *b.* minor tranquilizers   *c.* energizers   *d.* ECT

5. Currently, the frontal lobotomy is the most widely used form of psychosurgery.   T or F?
6. Psychosurgery can be reversed if it is unsuccessful.   T or F?
7. Whenever possible, the community mental health movement emphasizes prevention of mental health problems.   T or F?
8. Research indicates that relatively short periods of psychiatric hospitalization are just as beneficial as long-term hospital stays.   T or F?

Answers: 1. F 2. F 3. T 4. a 5. F 6. F 7. T 8. T

Resources Summary

● Psychosis is a break in contact with reality that is marked by *delusions, hallucinations, sensory changes, emotional disturbances,* and in some cases, *personality disintegration.*

● Psychotic symptoms, as well as lesser problems in thought, speech, memory, and attention, tend to be most prominent during short *episodes* of increased disturbance. There is evidence that some such symptoms are partially under voluntary control.

● An *organic psychosis* is based on known injuries or diseases of the brain. Other problems of unknown origin are termed *functional psychoses.* Three common causes of organic psychosis are untreated syphilis (*general paresis*), *poisoning,* and *senile dementia.*

● A diagnosis of *paranoid psychosis* is almost totally based on delusions of grandeur or persecution, and rarely involves personality disintegration. Because they often have intense and irrational delusions of persecution, paranoids may be violent if they believe they are threatened.

● *Schizophrenia* is the most frequently occurring psychosis. It is distinguished by a split between thought and emotion, delusions, hallucinations, and communication difficulties. Several subtypes of schizophrenia have been identified.

● A *schizotypal personality disorder,* sometimes referred to as borderline schizophrenia, involves gradual withdrawal into isolation from others and odd, apathetic behavior.

● *Hebephrenic,* or *disorganized, schizophrenia* shows extreme personality disintegration and silly, bizarre, or obscene behavior. Social impairment is usually extreme.

● *Catatonic schizophrenia* is associated with stupor, mutism, and odd postures. Sometimes violent and agitated behavior also occurs.

● In *paranoid schizophrenia* (the most common subtype), outlandish delusions of grandeur and persecution are coupled with psychotic symptoms and personality breakdown.

● *Affective psychosis* involves extremes of mood coupled with psychotic symptoms. *Manic, depressive,* and *manic-depressive,* or *mixed* types of affective disorders are commonly seen.

● When schizophrenic thought disorders combine with emotional extremes, a person is said to be suffering from a *schizoaffective psychosis.*

● Current explanations of schizophrenia emphasize a combination of *environmental stress, inherited susceptibility,* and *biochemical abnormalities* in the body or brain. One popular environmental theory is that schizophrenics are subjected to unsolvable dilemmas through *double-bind communication*. A better case can be made for the importance of early *traumatic experiences* and *disturbed family environments* as underlying factors in schizophrenia. In addition, studies of twins and other close relatives strongly support a genetic view of schizophrenia. Recent biochemical studies have focused on abnormalities in brain transmitter substances, especially *dopamine* and its receptor sites.

● Three somatic or medical approaches to treatment of psychosis are *chemotherapy* (use of drugs), *electroconvulsive therapy* (*ECT*—brain shock for the treatment of depression), and *psychosurgery* (surgical alteration of the brain). All three techniques are capable of producing seri-

ous side effects, and all are controversial to a degree (due to questions about effectiveness and the cost/benefit ratio).

● *Hospitalization* is often associated with the administration of somatic therapy, and it is also considered a form of treatment. Prolonged hospitalization is now discouraged by *revolving-door* admissions policies, and by an emphasis on providing care within the community.

● A development in mental health care that seeks to avoid or minimize hospitalization is the creation of *community mental health centers*. Community mental health centers also have as their goal the *prevention* of mental health problems through education, consultation, and crisis intervention.

Applications

"On Being Sane in Insane Places"

Question: Suppose someone were committed to a psychiatric hospital by accident. Would the staff notice? Would the person be able to get out?

David Rosenhan of Stanford University set out to answer these questions and another: "How accurately do psychiatric hospitals distinguish between people who are psychotic and those who are healthy?"

To find out, Rosenhan and several colleagues had themselves committed (Rosenhan, 1973). Entrance to mental hospitals was gained by faking only one symptom. Rosenhan and the others complained of hearing voices which said "empty," "hollow," and "thud." In 11 out of 12 tries, they were admitted with a diagnosis of "schizophrenia."

Pseudo-patients   After being admitted, these "pseudo-patients" dropped all pretense of mental illness. Yet, even though they acted completely normal, none of the researchers was ever recognized by hospital *staff* as a phony patient. Other patients were not so easily fooled. It was not unusual for a real patient to say to one of the researchers, "You're not crazy, you're checking up on the hospital!" or "You're a journalist."

Rosenhan and the others spent from one to seven weeks in hospitals before being discharged. The hospitals ranged from very modern and plush to ancient and shoddy. No matter how good the facilities or how good the hospital's reputation, Rosenhan found some disturbing conditions.

Contact between staff and patients was very limited and sometimes marked by fear or hostility. It was found that attendants and staff only spent an average of 11.3 percent of their time out of the "cage," the glassed-in central compartment in the ward.

It was not unusual for the morning attendants to wake patients with a hostile call of: "Come on, you m_____ f_____s, out of bed!" When patients tried to talk with staff, they were often ignored or received strange replies. One pseudo-patient approached a psychiatrist and politely asked when he might get grounds privileges. The doctor's reply was, "Good morning, Dave. How are you today?"

Rosenhan found that therapy other than drugs was very limited. Daily contact of patients with psychiatrists,

psychologists, or physicians averaged about *seven minutes*. On the other hand, the researchers were given a total of 2100 pills to swallow. (Only two of these were actually taken, the rest being pocketed or flushed down the toilet.)

Nonpersons   Patients tended to be treated as nonpersons. A nurse unbuttoned her uniform to adjust her bra in front of a room full of male patients. She was not being sexy; she just didn't consider the patients men. Patients would often be discussed by the staff while the patient was standing nearby. It was as if patients were invisible.

A situation that sums up Rosenhan's findings better than any other is his note-taking. Rosenhan began taking notes by carefully jotting things on a small piece of paper hidden in his hand. He learned quickly that hiding was totally unnecessary. He was soon walking around with a clipboard and note pads, recording observations and collecting data.

No one questioned this behavior. Note-taking was simply seen as a symptom of his "illness." As a matter of fact, Rosenhan found that anything he did was ignored. When a staff member manhandled a patient (as happened occasionally) Rosenhan would be right there—taking notes on the whole incident!

Labels   These observations clarify the failure of staff members to detect the fake patients. Because they were seen in the *context* of a mental ward and because they had been *labeled* schizophrenic, *anything* the pseudo-patients did was seen as a symptom of their "illness."

To return to the original hypothetical question about talking your way out of an accidental commitment, it should be clear that it could be quite futile to say, "Look, this is all a mistake. I'm not crazy. You've got to let me out." The response might very well be, "Have you had these paranoid delusions for long?"

Many mental health professionals found Rosenhan's findings hard to believe. This led to a follow-up study, in which the staff of another hospital was warned that one or more pseudo-patients were going to try to gain admission

Applications

over the next three months. Thus alerted, the staff at this hospital tried to identify fake incoming patients. Among 193 candidates, 41 were labeled fakes by at least one staff member, and 19 more were labeled "suspicious." This only served to confirm Rosenhan's original findings since he never sent *any* patients—fake or otherwise—to this hospital!

It is an important final note that all of the normal people who served as pseudo-patients in the original studies were discharged as schizophrenics "in remission" (temporarily free of symptoms). In other words, the label that prevented hospital staff from seeing the normality of the researchers stayed with them when they left. Psychiatrist Karl Menninger (1964) has commented on a similar situation:

> A label can blight the life of a person even after his recovery from mental illness. A young doctor I knew suffered for a time from some anxiety and indecision. He consulted a psychiatrist and soon recovered. Unfortunately, a "tentative" diagnosis of schizophrenia got abroad—I don't know how—and the young doctor's professional career was seriously impaired. He was injured, not by mental illness but by a word.

Observations such as these are not a total condemnation of psychiatric hospitals. Many of the conditions Rosenhan encountered will be found in *any* hospital or other large institution. But Rosenhan's findings do carry an important message for professionals and nonprofessionals alike: *Labels can be dangerous.* As Stoller (1967, pp. 29–30) has said:

When a person is labeled—neurotic, psychotic, executive, teacher, salesman, psychologist—either by himself or by others, he restricts his behavior to the role and even may rely upon the role for security. This diminishes the kind of experiences he is likely to have. Indeed, it is those groups whose members have shared labels—be it schizophrenic or executive—which are hardest to help move into intimate contact.

Implications The terms reviewed in this and the previous chapter can, and do, aid communication about human problems. But if used carelessly, they may do great damage. Everyone has felt or acted "crazy" during brief periods of stress or high emotion. The person whose adjustment problems extend over a longer period of time is different from you or me only in the severity of his or her difficulty.

It is therefore more productive to label problems than to label people. Think of the difference in impact between saying, "He is experiencing a serious emotional disturbance" and saying, "He is a *psychotic.*" Which statement would you choose to have said about yourself?

It is also important to realize that a severely disturbed person will appreciate being treated normally. Rosenhan's research makes it clear that the person is not helped by being thrust into the role of a "patient." One former patient's comments clarify this last point:

> After I got back from the hospital, my friends tried to *act* like nothing had changed. But I could tell they weren't being honest. For instance, a friend invited me to dinner and everything went fine until I dropped my fork. Both my friend and his wife jumped up and stared at me like they thought I might explode. I was quite embarrassed.

Learning Check

1. In the majority of their attempts, Rosenhan's pseudo-patients were admitted to mental hospitals after complaining only that they were hearing voices.   T or F?
2. Although they were often detected by professional staff members, the normality of the pseudo-patients was never recognized by other patients.   T or F?
3. During a short hospital stay, one pseudo-patient was denied psychiatric drugs even though he requested them.   T or F?
4. Rosenhan found that almost anything pseudo-patients said or did was interpreted as a symptom of their "illness."   T or F?
5. When they were alerted that a number of pseudo-patients might try to gain entry, hospital staff members were able to more accurately detect the fakes.   T or F?

Answers: 1. T 2. F 3. F 4. T 5. F

Exploration

Who Is "Crazy" and What Should Be Done about It?

Two well-known critics of traditional psychiatric treatment for "mental illness" are Thomas Szasz and Ronald D. Laing. Szasz (1966) believes that mental illness is a myth. Szasz charges that traditional medical concepts of disease have been wrongly applied to emotional problems. The "medical model," as this is called, treats such problems as "diseases" with "symptoms" that can be "cured." Szasz and a number of other experts prefer to view emotional disturbances as "problems in living." This view makes the goal of therapy "change" rather than "cure" and changes a "patient" to a "client."

Szasz has also questioned handling of the civil rights of psychiatric "patients." Szasz estimates there are 750,000 persons in mental hospitals, 90 percent of them involuntarily. He sees this as a serious mistake. To commit people because they might be dangerous to themselves is indefensible by Szasz's standards.

According to Szasz, the only legitimate reason for depriving a person of freedom is for being "dangerous to others," but then only if the person has broken the law by committing violence or by threatening to do so. Szasz considers the disturbed no more dangerous than a randomly selected group of citizens. He therefore rejects involuntary commitment as "punishment without trial, imprisonment without limit, and stigmatization without hope of redress" (1969).

Szasz's position seems to be that people have the right to be as "crazy" as they want as long as they hurt no one else and don't break existing laws. Psychiatrist R. D. Laing takes a more extreme position. Laing believes that our world has become so "mad" that anyone adjusted to it is in serious trouble. He claims:

> The experience and behavior that are labeled schizophrenia are a special sort of strategy that a person invents in order to live in an unliveable world (1967).*

Based on his respect for those who are unable or unwilling to "play the game" anymore, Laing set up an "antihospital" in London called Kingsley Hall. In Kingsley Hall, no distinctions were made between patients and staff. Kingsley Hall was run as a self-governing communal arrangement without white coats and "chemical straitjackets."

In Kingsley Hall, "psychotics" were encouraged to explore the limits of their break from reality as a means of establishing a more honest relationship with the world. In this regard Laing has said:

> Madness need not be all breakdown. It may also be breakthrough. It is potentially liberation and renewal as well as enslavement and existential death.

Laing believes schizophrenia is real, but he also thinks it can be good for you. In his view psychosis is similar to a psychedelic "trip"—an ultimate existential confrontation with oneself, one's reality, and the meaning of life.

It is undoubtedly a mistake to assume that the findings of David Rosenhan and the visions of people such as Szasz and Laing justify abandoning the tremendous advances in mental health care represented by current approaches. These people do, however, raise serious questions about the future. In an area as complex as treatment of major emotional disturbances, there is much room for improvement and innovation. In addition, they have focused attention on the important civil rights questions of involuntary commitment. As a final bit of "food for thought," consider the following incident, recorded by a reporter visiting a large state mental hospital:

> A thin man, old and dry, stopped the guide and said, "When the hell you gonna get me a suit and let me outa here? How about it? . . ." The guide said something indefinite and the man walked away, nodding. This was the section for killers, I had been told, so I asked what the thin man had done.
> "He painted a horse."
> "He what?"
> "He painted a horse."
> "What's wrong with that?"
> "It was in a field. A live horse. He was drunk and somebody bet him he couldn't make a horse look like a zebra, I think, so he painted it and they put him here. For being drunk probably."
> "How long has he been in?"
> "Thirty-seven years. By the time they got around to letting him out he really was crazy. . . . For his own good we just can't let him go out of here."*

*From *The Politics of Experience*, R. D. Laing. Copyright © 1967 by R. D. Laing. Reprinted by permission of Penguin Books Ltd.

*Bruce Jackson, "Our Prisons Are Criminal," *New York Times Magazine*, September 22, 1973, pp. 54–57.

Questions for Discussion

1. What positive and negative roles do mental institutions play in society?

2. Is Szasz justified in his appraisal of mental institutions as simply prisons by another name?

3. Do you think Szasz and Laing are unrealistically romantic in their approach to mental illness, or are they the wave of the future?

4. Under what circumstances would you consider it reasonable for a stranger to be involuntarily committed? A friend? A close relative? Yourself?

5. In your opinion how could a person experiencing a severe "problem in living" be most effectively helped?

6. Should a mental patient have the right to:
    a. refuse medication
    b. demand legal counsel and alternative medical opinions
    c. refuse to work in a mental hospital or to choose the work that will be done
    d. communicate by phone, letter, or in person with anyone at any time
    e. keep personal property (including drugs, matches, pocketknives, and other potentially harmful materials)
    f. request an alternative to legal commitment to a mental hospital?

7. In view of what you know about the causes of psychosis, how valid do you consider the "medical model" of mental illness? What are the advantages and disadvantages of such a model? What are the advantages and disadvantages of a "psychological model"?

Suggestions for Further Reading

American Journal of Psychiatry, **134** (9), 1977. A special issue devoted to the pros and cons of ECT.

Arieti, S. *Understanding and Helping the Schizophrenic.* Basic Books, 1979.

Bassuk, E. L., and S. Gerson. "Deinstitutionalization of Mental Health Services," *Scientific American,* February, 1978, pp. 46–53.

Braginsky, B. M., D. Braginsky, and K. Ring. *Methods of Madness: The Mental Hospital as a Last Resort.* Holt, 1969.

Coleman, J. C., *et al. Abnormal Psychology and Modern Life.* Scott, Foresman, 1980.

Goffman, E. *Asylums.* Doubleday, 1961.

Grant, V. *This Is Mental Illness: How It Feels and What It Means.* Beacon, 1963.

Green, H. *I Never Promised You a Rose Garden.* New American Library, 1971.

Kesey, K. *One Flew Over the Cuckoo's Nest.* Viking, 1964.

Laing, R. D. *The Politics of Experience.* Ballantine, 1964.

Rosenhan, D. L. "On Being Sane in Insane Places," *Science,* **179,** 1973, pp. 250–258.

Szasz, T. *The Myth of Mental Illness.* Delta, 1967.

—— T. *The Manufacture of Madness.* Harper and Row, 1970.

22

Insight Therapy

═══════════════════════ Chapter Preview ═══════════════════════

Quiet Terror on a Spring Afternoon

The warm California sun shone brightly. A light breeze danced inland from the ocean. Outside my office window an assortment of small birds sang to a beautiful spring day. I could hear them between Susan's frightened sobs.

As a psychologist I see many students with personal problems. Still, I was somewhat surprised to see Susan standing at my office door. Her excellent work in class and her healthy, casual appearance left me unprepared for her first words. "I feel like I'm losing my mind," she said. "Can I talk to you?"

In the next hour Susan sketched the features of her own personal hell. Her calm exterior hid a world of overwhelming fear, anxiety, and depression. She had lost several part-time jobs because at each one she began to fear her co-workers and the customers so much that she could barely bring herself to speak to them. Her absenteeism and embarrassing interchanges with customers would gradually lead to her dismissal. At school she felt "different" and was sure that other students could tell she was "weird." Several disastrous romances had left her terrified of men. Lately she had become so depressed that she had begun to think frequently of suicide. At times she became so terrified for no apparent reason that her heart pounded wildly and she felt that she was about to lose control of herself completely.

Susan's visit to my office was an important turning point. Emotional conflicts had made her existence a living nightmare. At a time when she was becoming her own worst enemy, Susan had realized that she needed the help and support of another person to overcome her problems. In Susan's case, that person was a talented psychologist to whom I referred her. Combining various forms of psychotherapy, the psychologist was able to help Susan come to grips with her emotions and return a healthy balance to her personality.

This chapter emphasizes psychological *techniques currently used to alleviate problems like Susan's.* Insight *therapies, as these are called, can be distinguished from a special alternative approach called* behavior modification. *Behavior modification is discussed in the next chapter.*

Survey Questions   How did modern psychotherapies develop? Is Freudian psychoanalysis still used? What are the characteristics of client-centered therapy, rational therapy, and existential therapy? Can psychotherapy be done with groups of people? What are group therapies like? What do the various therapies have in common? How would a person go about finding professional help? What can be done to help a troubled friend?

Resources

Humpty-Dumpty sat on a wall.
Humpty-Dumpty had a great fall.
All the King's horses and all the King's men
Couldn't put Humpty together again.

Psychotherapy—
Restoring Psychological Health

In our age of stress, conflict, and anxiety, who will put you together again, and how will they do it? Actually, the odds are that you will *not* experience a life-impairing emotional problem like Susan's, but if you did, what kind of help is available? In most cases, the answer is some form of *psychotherapy.*

Question: What is psychotherapy?

Psychotherapy is any psychological technique designed to facilitate positive changes in a person's personality, behavior, or adjustment. The psychotherapist has many approaches to choose from: psychoanalysis, desensitization, primal therapy, Gestalt therapy, logotherapy, Rogerian therapy, reality therapy, transactional analysis, behavior modification—to name but a few.

Due to a recent explosive growth in the number of therapies, some confusion may exist concerning the differences among various approaches. It may be helpful to recognize that psychological problems are complex, and that the best approach for a particular person or problem will not always be the same. Also, psychotherapies vary considerably in emphasis.

Insight therapies foster a deeper understanding of the assumptions, beliefs, emotions, and conflicts underlying a problem. **Action therapies** focus on directly changing troublesome habits and behavior. In **directive therapies,** the therapist guides the client strongly—giving instructions, offering interpretations, posing solutions, and sometimes even making important decisions for the client. **Nondirective** approaches place responsibility for the course of therapy on the client. In these, it is up to the client to discover his or her own solutions. **Individual therapies** proceed on a one-to-one basis between client and therapist. In **group therapy,** individual problems are resolved by making use of the special characteristics of the group setting. You should realize that psychotherapy need not be undertaken only as a means of solving a deep psychological problem or an immediate crisis. Some therapies are designed to encourage personal growth and enrichment for people who are already functioning effectively.

Psychotherapy—Humble Beginnings

The history of treatment for psychological problems gives ample reason for appreciating the humanity of modern therapies. Archaeological findings dating to the Stone Age suggest that most primitive approaches were marked by fear and superstitious belief in demons, witchcraft, and magic. One of the more dramatic "cures" practiced by primitive "psychotherapists" was a process called **trepanning** (treh-PAN-ing). A hole was bored, chipped, or bashed into the skull of the patient, presumably to relieve pressure or release evil spirits. Actually, trepanning may have simply been an excuse to kill people who were unusual since many of the "patients" didn't survive the "treatment."

During the Middle Ages, treatment for the mentally ill in Europe focused on **demonology.** Abnormal behavior was attributed to supernatural forces such as possession by the devil or the curses of witches and wizards. As treatment, **exorcism** was used to drive out the evil. For the fortunate, exorcism was a religious ritual. More often, it took the form of physical torture to make the body an inhospitable place for the devil to reside (Fig. 22-1).

One explanation for the rise of demonology may lie in a condition called **ergotism** (AIR-got-ism). In the Middle Ages, rye fields were often infested with ergot fungus (Fig. 22-2). Ergot, we now know, is a natural source of LSD and other mind-altering chemicals. Eating bread made from tainted grain can cause symptoms that might easily be interpreted as possession, bewitchment, or madness. Pinching sensations, convulsions, muscle twitches, facial spasms, delirium, and visual hallucinations are all common reactions to ergot poisoning (Matossian, 1982; Kety, 1979). Thus, many of the "patients" of demonology may have been doubly victimized.

The idea that the emotionally disturbed are "mentally ill" and that they should be treated compassionately emerged after 1793. This was the year **Philippe Pinel** changed the Bicêtre Asylum in Paris from a squalid "madhouse" into a mental hospital by personally unchaining the inmates. Although almost 200 years have passed since Pinel began humane treatment for the emotionally disturbed, the process of improving conditions in psychiatric hospitals and of changing public attitudes toward psychotherapy continues today. Increased acceptance of the value of psychotherapy is a positive sign, but public attitudes toward the disturbed still tend to be colored by suspicion and fear. Perhaps as more people take part in psychotherapy as a growth experience, it will become more widely understood.

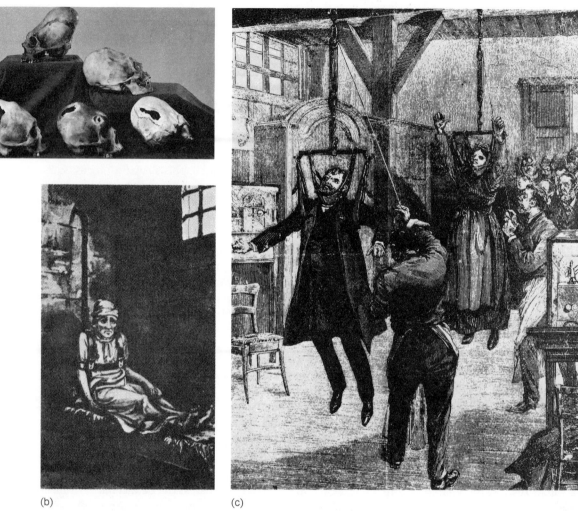

Fig. 22-1 *Early approaches to the treatment of mental illness. (a) Primitive "treatment" for mental disorder sometimes took the form of boring a hole in the skull. (b) Many early asylums were no more than prisons with inmates held in chains. (c) One late nineteenth-century "treatment" was based on swinging the patient in a harness—presumably to calm the patient's nerves.*

Question: When was psychotherapy developed?

The first true psychotherapy was developed around the turn of the century by Sigmund Freud.

As a physician in Vienna, Freud was intrigued by the cases of **hysteria** (physical symptoms such as paralysis or numbness without known physical cause) he encountered.[*] Slowly Freud became convinced that the symptoms of hysteria were only the tip of the iceberg, that deeply hidden unconscious conflicts (frequently sexual in nature) were to blame. Based on this insight, Freud went on to develop his

[*]"Hysterical" symptoms are now referred to as *somatoform disorders.* (See Chapter 20.)

own comprehensive form of therapy. Since **psychoanalysis,** as Freud called his technique, is the "granddaddy" of most modern psychotherapies, let us examine it in some detail.

Psychoanalysis— Expedition into the Unconscious

Question: Isn't psychoanalysis the therapy where the patient lies on a couch?

Freud's patients usually reclined on a couch during therapy, while Freud sat out of sight taking notes and offering interpretations. This arrangement was selected to encourage relaxation and a free flow of thoughts and images from the unconscious (Fig. 22-3). It is the least important of several characteristics of psychoanalysis and has been abandoned by many modern analysts.

Question: How did Freud treat emotional problems?

Freud's theory stressed that repressed memories, motives, and conflicts—particularly those stemming from instinctual drives for sex and aggression—were the cause of neurosis. Although unconscious and repressed, these factors remain active in the personality, forcing the person to develop rigid ego-defense mechanisms and to devote excessive amounts of time and energy to compulsive and self-defeating behavior. Freud relied on four basic techniques to uncover the unconscious roots of neurosis (Freud, 1949).

1. Free association. During psychoanalysis, the patient must say whatever comes to mind without regard for whether it makes sense or is painful or embarrassing. Thoughts are allowed to move freely from one association to the next.

2. Dream analysis. The purpose of free association is to lower defenses so that unconscious material may emerge. Freud considered dreams an unusually good additional means of tapping the unconscious. Freud referred to dreams as "the royal road to the unconscious" because he felt that forbidden desires and unconscious feelings are more freely expressed in dreams. He distinguished between the **manifest** (obvious, visible) **content** and the **latent** (hidden) **content** of dreams.

To appreciate fully the unconscious message of a dream, Freud sought to reveal its latent meaning by interpreting **dream symbols.** Let's say a young husband reports a dream in which he pulls a pistol from his waistband and aims at a target while his wife watches. The pistol repeatedly fails to discharge, and the man's wife laughs at him. Freud might see this as an indication of repressed feelings of sexual impotence, with the gun serving as a disguised image of the penis. (You may wish to refer back to Chapter 7 to review the discussion of Freudian dream interpretation there.)

3. Analysis of resistance. When free associating or describing dreams, the patient may *resist* talking or thinking about certain topics. Such resistances are said to reveal particularly important unconscious conflicts. As the analyst becomes aware of resistances, he or she brings them to the patient's awareness so they can be dealt with realistically.

4. Analysis of transference. The individual undergoing psychoanalysis may transfer feelings to the therapist that relate to important past relationships with others. At times

Fig. 22-2 *Two ears of rye infested with ergot fungus (dark areas). The psychedelic effects of the fungus may explain some cases of "possession" in Medieval Europe and "bewitchment" in colonial New England.*

the analyst may be reacted to as if he or she were a rejecting father, an unloving or overprotective mother, or a former lover. This is considered a prime opportunity to help the patient undergo an emotional reeducation. As the patient reexperiences repressed emotions, the therapist can help the patient recognize and understand them.

Question: Is psychoanalysis still used?

In its original form psychoanalysis called for three to five therapy sessions a week for up to seven years. Because of the huge amounts of time and money this requires, most psychodynamic therapists now substitute more direct interviewing for free association, and the length of therapy has been shortened considerably.

A more important question about psychoanalysis may be: "Does it work?" The development of newer, more streamlined psychotherapies is in part due to questions about the effectiveness of psychoanalysis. One psychologist, H. J. Eysenck (1967), has gone so far as to suggest that psychoanalysis simply takes so long that there is a **spontaneous remission** of symptoms (improvement due to the mere passage of time). To support his argument, Eysenck cites research showing that people placed on *waiting lists* improve at the same rate as those who begin therapy.

Fig. 22-3   *Pioneering psychotherapist, Sigmund Freud, in his office.*

How seriously should Eysenck's criticism be taken? At present his view appears fairly extreme. It is true that problems ranging from hyperactivity to "neurosis" improve with the passage of time. However, more recent work affirms that psychoanalysis is usually better than no treatment at all (Bergin and Suinn, 1975). Undoubtedly, many people have been helped by psychoanalytic therapy. But to the modern therapist questions remain: "When psychoanalysis works, why does it work? What procedures are essential and which are unnecessary?" Based on intuition, personal philosophy, clinical experience, and the personality theory they find most acceptable, modern psychotherapists have posed surprisingly varied answers to these questions. Following sections will acquaint you with some of the therapies currently in use.

Learning Check

See if you can answer the following questions. If you miss any, review the previous sections.

Match

_____ 1.   Directive therapies   **A.**   Change behavior

_____ 2.   Action therapies   **B.**   Place responsibility on client

_____ 3.   Insight therapies   **C.**   The client is guided strongly

_____ 4.   Nondirective therapies   **D.**   Seek understanding

5.   Pinel is famous for his use of exorcism.   T or F?

6.   Freud developed trepanning.   T or F?

7.   A spontaneous remission of symptoms means that psychotherapy has succeeded.   T or F?

8.   In psychoanalysis, an emotional attachment to the therapist by the patient is called:

   a. free association   *b.* resistance   *c.* manifest association   *d.* transference

Answers: 1. C 2. A 3. D 4. B 5. F 6. F 7. F 8. d

Humanistic Therapies—
Restoring Human Potential

The goal of traditional psychoanalysis is adjustment. Freud was actually quite conservative in his claims: Any of his patients, he said, could expect only to change their "hysterical misery into common unhappiness"! The humanistic therapies outlined in upcoming sections are generally more optimistic. Most assume that it is possible for people to live rich and rewarding lives and to make full use of their potentials. Psychotherapy is seen as a means of giving natural tendencies toward mental health a chance to emerge—a chance to enhance mental health as well as to regain it.

Question: What is client-centered therapy? How is it different from psychoanalysis?

Client-Centered Therapy Psychoanalysts delve into childhood, dreams, and the unconscious. Psychologist Carl Rogers has found it more productive to explore *conscious* thoughts and feelings. The psychoanalyst tends to take a position of authority from which he or she offers interpretations of what is "wrong" with the patient or of what dreams or childhood experiences "mean." Rogers believes that what is right or valuable for the therapist may not be right and valuable for the client. (Rogers prefers the term "client" to "patient.") Accordingly, **client-centered therapy** is *nondirective*. The client is the center of the process. He or she determines what will be discussed during each session.

Question: If the client runs things, what does the therapist do?

The therapist's job is to create an "atmosphere of growth" by maintaining four basic conditions.

First, the therapist offers the client **unconditional positive regard.** In other words, the client is accepted *totally*. The therapist refuses to react with shock, dismay, or disapproval to anything the client says or feels. Total acceptance by the therapist is the first step to self-acceptance by the client. Second, the therapist attempts to achieve genuine **empathy** for the client by trying to see the world through the client's eyes and to feel some part of what he or she is feeling. As a third essential condition, the therapist strives to be **authentic** in his or her relationship with clients. The therapist must not hide behind a professional role. Rogers believes that phony fronts and facades destroy the growth atmosphere sought in client-centered therapy. Fourth, the therapist does not make interpretations, pose solutions, or offer advice. Instead, the therapist **reflects** the client's thoughts and feelings. By repeating or restating what the client has said or by telling the client what emotion he or she seems to be displaying, the therapist serves as a psychological "mirror" in which clients learn to see themselves more clearly and realistically. Rogers feels that a person armed with a realistic self-image and with a new level of self-acceptance will gradually discover solutions to life problems.

Rational-Emotive Therapy According to Albert Ellis (1962, 1973), the basic idea of **rational-emotive therapy (RET)** is as easy as A-B-C. Ellis assumes that people become unhappy and develop self-defeating habits because of unrealistic or otherwise faulty *beliefs*.

Question: How are beliefs important?

Ellis analyzes the situation in this way: A stands for the **activating experience,** which the person assumes to be the

Fig. 22-4 *Contemporary psychotherapist, Carl Rogers, originator of client-centered therapy.*

cause of C, the emotional **consequence.** For instance, a person who is rejected (the activating experience) feels depressed, threatened, or hurt (the emotional consequence). Rational-emotive therapy shows the client that the true cause of difficulty is what comes between A and C: Between the activating experience and the emotional consequence stands B, the client's irrational and unrealistic **belief.** In this example, the unrealistic belief leading to unnecessary suffering is: "It is necessary that we be loved and approved by everyone at all times."

Question: Is RET a nondirective therapy?

No. Rational-emotive therapists are very directive in their attempts to change a client's irrational beliefs and "self-talk." The therapist may directly attack clients' logic, challenge their thinking, confront them with evidence contrary to their beliefs, and may even assign "homework" for the clients.

RET has been criticized by some as superficial and argumentative, but Ellis' basic insight has considerable merit. Almost anyone can benefit from learning to recognize self-defeating beliefs. Here are four more **irrational assumptions** to look for in your own thinking: (1) one should be thoroughly competent, adequate, and achieving in all possible respects to be worthwhile; (2) it is awful and catastrophic when things are not the way one would like very much for them to be; (3) one's past history has an all-important effect on present behavior; because something once strongly affected one's life, it will continue to do so indefinitely; and (4) "easy and pleasurable conditions *must* exist in my life."

According to Ellis (1976), RET teaches people how to "dispute and surrender these unrealistic expectations and commands, how to accept themselves and others unconditionally and undamningly, and how to put up with inevitable annoyance and frustrations."

Existential Therapy   According to the existentialists, "being in the world" (existence) creates deep and unavoidable conflicts. Each of us, they say, must deal with the realities of death. We must face the fact that each person creates his or her private world by making choices. We must overcome the isolation of living on a vast and indifferent planet. We must confront feelings of meaninglessness.

Question: What do these concerns have to do with psychotherapy?

Like client-centered therapy, **existential therapy** tries to promote self-knowledge and self-actualization. However, there are important differences. Client-centered therapy seeks to uncover a "true self" hidden behind an artificial screen of defenses. In contrast, existential therapy emphasizes the idea of **free will.** That is, through *choices* one can *become* the person he or she wants to be. Existential therapy attempts to restore meaning and vitality to life so that the individual has the *courage* to make rewarding and socially constructive choices. Typically, existential therapy focuses on the "ultimate concerns" of human existence. These include the inescapable givens of **death, freedom, isolation,** and **meaninglessness** (Yalom, 1980).

Question: What does an existential therapist do?

One example of existential therapy is Victor Frankl's **logotherapy.**

Frankl (1955) developed his approach on the basis of experiences in a Nazi concentration camp. In the camp Frankl observed the breakdown of countless prisoners as they were stripped of all hope and human dignity. Frankl felt that those who survived with their sanity did so because they had managed to hang on to a sense of *meaning* (logos). In some cases this was nothing more than the ultimate human freedom—the freedom to choose one's own attitude in any set of circumstances. Like most existential therapists, Frankl uses a flexible approach centered around **confrontation.** The person is challenged to examine the quality of his or her existence and choices and to *encounter* the unique, intense, here-and-now interaction of two human beings. When existential therapy is successful, it brings about a reappraisal of what's important in life. Indeed, some clients experience an emotional rebirth not unlike that seen in people who have survived a close brush with death.

Learning Check

See if you can answer the following questions.

Match

_____ 1. Client-centered therapy   A. Meaning

_____ 2. Rational therapy   B. Unconditional positive regard

_____ 3. Existential therapy   C. Faulty beliefs

_____ 4. Logotherapy   D. Choice and becoming

5. The rational therapist tries to *reflect* a client's thoughts and feelings.   T or F?

6. Client-centered therapy is directive.   T or F?

7. Confrontation and encounter are concepts of existential therapy.   T or F?

Answers: 1. B 2. C 3. D 4. A 5. F 6. F 7. T

Group Therapy—Give Me Your Huddled Masses Yearning to Be Free

Question: Is group therapy just individual therapy with more than one person?

Most psychotherapies can be adapted for use in groups. Psychologists first tried working with groups as a practical response to the need for more therapists than were available. To their surprise, group therapy not only worked, it also offered some special advantages. In group therapy, a person could *act out,* or directly experience, problems in addition to talking about them, and support was provided by other members who shared similar problems. Groups also helped form a bridge between therapy and real-life problems by providing a more realistic situation than the protected atmosphere of individual therapy. For reasons such as these, a number of specialized group techniques have emerged. Because they range from Alcoholics Anonymous to nude encounter, only a few representative approaches will be sampled here.

Psychodrama   One of the first group approaches was developed by J. L. Moreno (1953) who called his technique **psychodrama.** In psychodrama, an individual **role plays** (acts out) dramatic incidents resembling those that cause problems in real life. For example, a disturbed teenager might act out a typical family fight with the therapist playing his father, and other patients, his mother, brothers, and sisters. Moreno believes that insights and the emotional relearning from these enactments transfer to the real-life situations. Therapists using psychodrama often find **role reversals** especially helpful (Leveton, 1977). For instance, the teenager just described would be asked to role play his father or mother, in order to better understand their feelings.

Gestalt Therapy   The Gestalt therapy approach, which is most often associated with the late Frederick (Fritz) Perls (1969), is built around the idea that perception, or *awareness,* becomes disjointed and incomplete in the maladjusted individual.

Question: What does "Gestalt" mean?

The German word **Gestalt** means *whole,* or complete. The Gestalt therapist seeks to help the individual rebuild thinking, feeling, and acting into connected wholes.

Working in a group setting, the Gestalt therapist encourages the individual to become aware of his or her emotions by observing nonverbal cues such as posture, voice, and eye or hand movements. To accomplish his goals, Fritz Perls used a collection of dramatic techniques with such flamboyant titles as "awareness training," "dream work," the "hot seat," and the "empty chair." In all these techniques as well as in his writings, Perls' one basic message comes through clearly: Emotional health comes from getting in touch with what you *want* to do, not what you *should* do, *ought* to do, or *should want* to do.

Question: How does Gestalt therapy help people discover their real wants?

Above all else, Gestalt therapy emphasizes *present* experience. Clients are urged to focus on awareness of bodily sensations, feelings, perceptions, and other immediate reactions. The goal is to teach people to: live now; live here; stop imagining; experience the real; stop unnecessary thinking; taste and see; express rather than explain, justify, or judge; give in to unpleasantness and pain just as to pleasure; surrender to being as you are (adapted from Naranjo, 1970).

Encounter Groups and Sensitivity Training   Abraham Maslow (1965) observed that the humanistic movement in psychology has led people who are already effective in their behavior to display an interest in psychotherapy. Often their interest is expressed by participation in sensitivity-training or encounter groups (Fig. 22-5). Groups such as these were first developed in 1945 at the National Training Laboratories in Bethel, Maine. At first, they were called "T-groups" (training groups), but soon they took new forms and new names as they were adopted at Esalen and other "growth centers" around the country.

Question: What is the difference between sensitivity and encounter groups?

Sensitivity groups tend to be less confrontive than encounter groups. Participants take part in experiences that gently extend sensitivity to oneself and others. For example, the

Fig. 22-5 *A group therapy session. Sensitivity and encounter groups attempt to strip away superficialities and inhibitions.*

"trust walk," in which blindfolded participants are led about by "guides," is a typical exercise used to develop trust and confidence in others. Experiments in which group members try to communicate nonverbally with hands or eyes may be used to improve awareness of others. Body awareness may be explored through techniques like the "blind mill," in which participants close their eyes and walk about touching each other (in nonsexual ways). Techniques such as these foster personal growth without posing too great a threat to participants.

In **encounter groups** more intense emotion and communication may take place. An encounter group may meet only once or twice, many times, or in a *marathon* lasting 18 hours or more (Stoller, 1972). In any case, the emphasis is on tearing down defenses and facades through discussion that can be brutally honest. Because of the danger of hostile confrontation or psychological damage, encounter-group members are carefully screened for freedom from severe emotional problems, and a trained leader or "facilitator" guides the group through difficult situations.

Question: Are sensitivity and encounter groups really psychotherapies?

Sensitivity and encounter groups can certainly be an exciting and valuable avenue for personal growth. They can also be a disaster if poorly run. Along with problems of poor leadership or group composition, there are additional dangers of disappointment and overreaction to group rejection. Also, the after-effects of rapid intimacy may pose a threat to existing relationships. Kurt Back (1972) may have summarized it best when he said, "Encounter groups may comfort, but they do not cure anything." A troubled individual should approach participation in an encounter group with some caution.

Transactional Analysis— Different Strokes for Different Folks

Transactional Analysis (TA) is a rather unique therapy. TA teaches people a theory of personality to use in becoming more aware of themselves, their interactions with others, and their life patterns or "scripts."

Question: How does TA enhance awareness?

TA is based on a relatively simple scheme proposed by Eric Berne (1961, 1964). Berne says the personality has three basic parts or **ego-states,** known as the *Parent,* the *Adult,* and the *Child.* These can be distinguished from one another by distinct behaviors, words, tones, gestures, attitudes, and expressions.

The **Child** is a carry-over from youth. The Child can be primitive, impulsive, demanding, creative, playful, or manipulative. The Child tends to say things such as: "I want"; "I need"; "I won't"; or, simply, "wow."

In addition to this perpetual Child, Berne says we carry another product of our past in the form of the Parent ego-state. The **Parent** is an internal record of all the messages received from one's parents or other authorities as personality developed. The Parent can be evaluative and restrictive or nurturing and allowing. It is activated whenever you judge or nurture yourself or another person. The Parent makes such statements as: "You should"; "You ought to"; "Why didn't you?"; "That's good"; "You can do it"; "That's bad"; and "Try harder."

According to TA, people get into trouble when they use an inappropriate ego-state. TA teaches people how to develop each ego-state and helps them decide when to use it. The **Adult** is a mature and rational decision-making part of the personality. With the adult in charge an individual can explore alternatives and their consequences and decide which ego-state is needed. TA gives people a thinking strategy to explore alternatives and decide what changes they wish to make, especially in *relationships* with others.

Question: How does the ego-state analysis apply to relationships?

The Parent-Adult-Child analysis can be extended to interactions between two people. That is, a message can be sent from any of the ego-states in one person to any of the ego-states in another. TA holds that trouble comes in relationships when *crossed* or *ulterior transactions* (exchanges) occur. (See Fig. 22-6.) Diagram (*a*) represents an Adult-to-Adult transaction such as, "What time is it?" "It's one o'clock." Communication continues because the expected response was received. But what if the reply is Parent-to-Child, such as, "Why don't you just forget about the time and see if you can get some work done for a change?" Now communication breaks down, or is "crossed" (diagram *b*).

Question: What happens in an ulterior transaction?

In an ulterior transaction the exchange *appears* to take place on one level, but actually takes place on another. For example, the apparent Adult-to-Adult question "Isn't it getting late?" might carry with it an unspoken (ulterior) cue: "Hey, why don't we quit early tonight?" The reply, "Yeah, it's getting late," might have nothing to do with the time, it

may instead be a Child-to-Child reply, "Yeah, let's go play, the supervisor won't know if we leave early."

Ulterior transactions may sound harmless enough, but they form the basis of **games,** which are indirect ways of communicating. For example, one spouse might ask another, "How much money is in the checking account?" in such a way that the real message is, "What are you trying to do, put us in the poorhouse?" Games keep people from being close and honest, and at worst they may be physically or emotionally destructive. By the way, the most common game in marriage is, "If it weren't for you" (I would be doing all the things I pretend I want to do but am afraid to try). A major goal of TA is to teach people more direct and creative ways of living, by exploring alternatives to games. Additionally, clients learn that certain games perpetuate their **life scripts.**

Question: What is a life script?

A script is a plan or drama that a person's life follows. Scripts may be "written" by parents and others. Some scripts are quite destructive. For example: "Carrying My Cross"; "Waiting for Santa Claus"; and "Rescuing Others," are all "loser scripts." Using TA, people become aware of the "plays" or "dramas" they are acting out. They can then decide which

Fig. 22-6

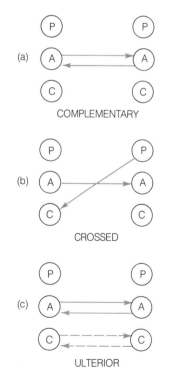

(a) COMPLEMENTARY

(b) CROSSED

(c) ULTERIOR

Table 22-1   Comparison of Psychotherapies

	Insight or action?	Directive or nondirective?	Time orientation	Individual or group?
Psychoanalysis	insight	directive	past	individual
Client-centered	insight	nondirective	past and present	individual
Rational-emotive	action	directive	present	individual
Existential	insight	both	present and future	individual
Psychodrama	insight	directive	present	group
Gestalt	insight	directive	present	group
Transactional analysis	both	directive	past and present	both
Behavior modification	action	directive	present	individual

parts are useful and which are destructive and not wanted in their lives. Ideally, in rewriting scripts, people take charge of their lives and live more freely, fully, and sanely.

Psychotherapy—An Overview

Question: How effective is psychotherapy?

Judging the outcome of therapy is tricky. Nevertheless, there is evidence that therapy is beneficial. In a survey of some 400 studies of psychotherapy and counseling, Smith and Glass (1977) found a modest but consistent positive effect for therapy compared to no treatment. Their findings, of course, are based on averages: For some people therapy was tremendously helpful; for others it was unsuccessful; overall it was effective for more people than not. Speaking more subjectively, one real success (in which a person's life is lastingly changed for the better) can be worth the frustration of several cases in which little progress is made. Psychotherapy is hard work for both therapist and client, but when it is successful there are few activities as rewarding.

Question: What do psychotherapies have in common?

The therapies we have sampled are but a few of the approaches in use. One author, writing in 1959, counted at least 36 major systems of psychotherapy (Harper, 1959). The count could easily exceed 100 today. The examples cited were selected because they represent some of the basic variations in philosophy or techniques and because

they offer ideas that may be of immediate use to you. For a summary of their major differences, see Table 22-1. To add to your understanding of psychotherapy, let us briefly summarize what all techniques have in common.

All the psychotherapies we have discussed include some combination of the following goals: insight, resolution of conflicts, an improved sense of self, a change in unacceptable patterns of behavior, better interpersonal relations, and an improved picture of oneself and the world. To accomplish these goals, psychotherapies offer:

1. A *caring relationship* between client and therapist. *Emotional rapport* based on warmth, friendship, understanding, acceptance, and empathy forms the basis for this relationship.
2. A *protected setting* in which emotional *catharsis* (release) can take place. Therapy provides a sanctuary in which the client is free to express fears, anxieties, and personal secrets without fear of rejection or loss of confidentiality.
3. All therapies to some extent offer an *explanation* or *rationale* for the suffering the client has experienced, and they propose a line of action that if followed will end this suffering.

These basic foundations of psychotherapy represent one of the more valuable lessons to be learned from this chapter. Together, they offer a useful perspective for meeting the challenge of helping a troubled friend or relative. More specific suggestions on this point will be found in the discussion that concludes the "Applications" section of this chapter.

Learning Check

1.   In psychodrama, people attempt to form meaningful wholes out of disjointed thoughts, feelings, and actions.   T or F?

2.   A T-group is a form of Gestalt therapy.   T or F?

3.   There are no dangers in participating in an encounter group.   T or F?

4. Which therapy places great emphasis on immediate awareness and on rebuilding experiences into connected wholes?

   a. psychodrama   *b.* Gestalt   *c.* TA   *d.* encounter

5. The Adult is a mature and rational decision-making part of the personality.   T or F?

6. According to TA, destructive psychological games are based on _____ transactions.

Answers: 1. F 2. F 3. F 4. b 5. T 6. ulterior

Resources Summary

● Psychotherapies may be classified as *insight* therapies, *action* therapies, *directive* therapies, *nondirective* therapies, and combinations of these. Therapies may also be conducted either individually or in groups.

● Primitive approaches to mental illness were often superstitious and misguided. *Trepanning* involved boring a hole in the skull. *Demonology,* used in the Middle Ages, attributed mental disturbance to supernatural forces and prescribed *exorcism* as the cure. In some instances, the actual cause of bizarre behavior may have been *ergot poisoning.* More humane treatment began in 1793 with the work of *Philippe Pinel* in Paris.

● Freud's *psychoanalysis* was the first formal psychotherapy. Psychoanalysis seeks a release of repressed thoughts and emotions from the unconscious. The psychoanalyst uses the techniques of *free association, dream analysis,* and *analysis of resistance* and *transference* to reveal health-producing insights. Some critics have argued that traditional psychoanalysis takes so long that patients may simply experience a *spontaneous remission* of symptoms.

● *Client-centered* therapy is nondirective and is dedicated to creation of an *atmosphere of growth. Unconditional positive regard, empathy, authenticity,* and *reflection* are combined to give the client a chance to solve his or her own problems.

● In *rational-emotive therapy* (RET) clients learn to recognize and challenge their own *irrational beliefs* and *assumptions.* In the *ABC analysis* of RET, changing B (beliefs) alters the emotional consequences (C) experienced in response to activating events (A). Rational-emotive therapy is extremely directive.

● *Existential therapies,* such as Frankl's *logotherapy,* focus on the end result of the choices one makes in life.

Clients are encouraged through *confrontation* and *encounter* to exercise *free will* and to take responsibility for their choices. The goal of existential therapy is to reestablish meaning in one's life.

● *Group therapy* may be a simple extension of individual methods or it may be based on techniques developed specifically for groups. In *psychodrama,* individuals enact roles and incidents resembling their real life problems. *Gestalt therapy* emphasizes immediate awareness and on-going thoughts and feelings. Its goal is to fill in gaps in experiences by rebuilding thinking, feeling, and acting into connected wholes.

● Although not literally psychotherapies, sensitivity and encounter groups attempt to encourage positive personality change. *Sensitivity groups* tend to be nonconfrontive, their emphasis being on self-awareness, trust, and communication. In *encounter groups* participants actively tear down facades and defenses. Communication may be intense and brutal.

● In *transactional analysis* (TA), people learn to apply the *P-A-C* (Parent-Adult-Child) analysis to their own and others' behavior. By placing the Adult in control people learn to draw on the strengths of each *ego-state.* They also learn to recognize *complementary, crossed,* and *ulterior transactions* and to avoid *games.* Another goal is the rewriting of unhealthy or self-defeating *life scripts.*

● Outcome studies of psychotherapy show that it is generally effective; there are, however, large individual differences in effectiveness. All psychotherapies offer a *caring relationship, emotional rapport,* a *protected setting, catharsis, explanations* for the client's problems, and a *line of action* to follow in alleviating them.

Applications

Seeking Professional Help—When, Where, and How?

Question: How would I know if I should seek professional help at some point in my life?

Although there is no simple answer to this question, the following guidelines may be helpful.

1. If your level of psychological discomfort (unhappiness, anxiety, or depression, for example) becomes comparable to a level of physical discomfort that would cause you to see a dentist or physician, you should consider seeing a psychologist or a psychiatrist.

2. Another sign that should influence your decision is the occurrence of significant changes in observable behavior such as the quality of your work (or school work), your rate of absenteeism, your use of drugs (including alcohol), or your relationships with others who are important to you.

3. Perhaps you have at some time urged a friend or relative to seek professional help and were then dismayed because they refused to recognize the extent of their problem. If *you* find friends or relatives making a similar suggestion, recognize that they may be seeing things more objectively than you.

4. If you have persistent or disturbing suicidal thoughts or impulses, you should seek help immediately.

Question: If I wanted to talk to a therapist, how would I find one?

Finding professional help can itself be bewildering, especially at a time when you are already under stress. Here are some tips on tracking down a therapist.

1. *The "Yellow Pages."* Psychologists are listed under "Psychologist" or in some cases under "Counseling Services." Psychiatrists are generally listed as a subheading under "Physicians." These listings will usually put you in touch with individuals in private practice.

2. *Community or county mental health centers.* Most counties and many cities in the United States now offer public mental health services. (These are listed in the phone book.) Public mental health centers usually provide counseling and therapy services directly and can make referrals to private therapists.

3. *Mental health associations.* Many cities have mental health associations organized by concerned citizens. Groups such as these usually keep listings of qualified therapists and of other services and programs in the community.

4. *Colleges and universities.* If you are a student, don't overlook counseling services offered by a student health center or special student counseling facilities.

5. *Newspaper advertisements.* Professional ethics discourage advertisements. Occasionally there are exceptions to this rule as when low-cost "outreach" clinics try to make their presence known to the public, but in the case of an advertised service one should carefully inquire into the training and qualifications of its staff.

Question: How would I know what kind of a therapist to see? How would I pick one?

The choice between a psychiatrist and a psychologist is somewhat arbitrary. Both are trained to do psychotherapy, and whereas a psychiatrist can administer somatic therapy and prescribe drugs, a psychologist can work in conjunction with a physician if such services seem indicated. Fees for psychiatrists are usually higher, averaging about $70 an hour. Psychologists average from $30 to $50 an hour.

With fees in mind, your decision may be influenced by whether or not you have health insurance that will cover the expense. If fees are a problem, keep in mind that many individual therapists charge on a sliding scale, or ability-to-pay basis and that community mental health centers almost always charge on a sliding scale. Some communities now have counseling services staffed by sympathetic paraprofessional counselors. Fees for these services are considerably lower. Group therapy is also much less expensive since the fee for the therapist's time is essentially divided among several people.

The training and professional qualifications of a therapist can usually be learned simply by asking. A reputable therapist will be glad to reveal his or her background. If you have any doubts, credentials may be checked and other helpful information can be obtained from local

Applications

branches of any of the following organizations. You can also write to the addresses listed below.

The National Association for Mental Health
1800 N. Kent St.
Arlington, Va. 22209

The American Psychiatric Association
1700 18th St. N.W.
Washington, D.C. 20009

The American Psychological Association
1200 17th St. N.W.
Washington, D.C. 20036

The American Association of Humanistic Psychology
7 Hartwood Dr.
Amherst, N.Y. 14226

The question of how to pick a particular therapist remains. The best means is to start with one short consultation with a respected psychiatrist or psychologist or with a counselor at a mental health center. This will allow the person you consult to evaluate the nature of your difficulty and recommend an appropriate type of therapy or a therapist who is likely to be helpful. As an alternative you might ask the person teaching this course for a referral.

Question: How would I know whether or not to quit or ignore a therapist?

A balanced look at psychotherapies suggests that all *techniques* are about equally successful (Frank, 1973; Gomes-Schwartz *et al.,* 1978). However, all *therapists* are not equally successful.

Far more important than the approach used are the therapist's personal qualities. The most consistently successful psychotherapists are those who are willing to use whatever method seems most helpful for a client. They are also distinguished by personal characteristics of warmth, integrity, sincerity, and empathy (Frank, 1973; Katz, 1972; Knight, 1949).

It is perhaps most accurate to say that at this stage of development, psychotherapy is an art, not a science. Since the *relationship* between a client and therapist is the therapist's most basic tool, you must trust and easily relate to a therapist for therapy to be effective. Clients who like their therapist are generally more successful in therapy

(Gomes-Schwartz *et al.,* 1978). There is always a temptation to avoid facing up to personal problems. With this in mind, you should give a therapist a fair chance and not give up too easily. But don't hesitate to change therapists or to terminate therapy if you lose confidence in the therapist or if you don't relate well to the therapist as a person.

Becoming a Community
Mental Health Resource—How to Help

Question: What can be done to help a friend or relative who has a temporary personal problem or emotional crisis?

Everyone at one time or another will be faced with the task of comforting a troubled friend. For the majority of such upsets any caring, emotionally stable, empathic person can aid effectively. But how can you best give support? As just mentioned, many observers consider the personal qualities of professional therapists more important than their specialized training. Jerome Frank (1973), Carl Rogers (1957), and others appear to be in agreement about two essential conditions for the person hoping to help in constructive personality change. These are:

1. An unconditional acceptance of the troubled person, an unshakable positive regard for him or her as a human.
2. A capacity to communicate to the person an understanding of the discomfort he or she is feeling.

We may call the second quality *empathy,* the ability to enter another person's private world, to understand feelings, and to share psychological pain. Because empathy and true caring cannot be faked, your support at times of crisis can be more valuable than anything the best-trained professional can offer. John O. Stevens (1971) has summarized:

> The way to really help someone is not to help him do anything but become more aware of his own experience—his feelings, his actions, his fantasies—and insist that he explore his own experience more deeply and take responsibility for it, no matter what that experience is.

Question: I'm still not sure exactly what is best to do when a friend wants to talk about a problem.

Several points may be kept in mind when "counseling" a friend.

Applications

Active Listening People frequently talk "at" each other without really listening. A person with problems needs to be heard. Make a sincere effort to listen to and understand the person. Let the person know you are listening through eye contact, posture, your tone of voice, and your replies.

Focus on Feelings Feelings are neither right nor wrong. By focusing on the person's feelings you can avoid making him or her defensive. Passing judgment on what is said prevents the free outpouring of emotion that is the basis for catharsis. For example, a friend confides that he has failed a test. Perhaps you know that he studies very little. If you say, "Maybe if you studied a little more you would do better," he will probably become defensive or hostile. Much more can be accomplished by saying, "You must feel very frustrated" or, simply, "How do you feel about it?"

Avoid Giving Advice It is not unreasonable to give advice when you are asked for it, but beware of the trap of the "Why don't you? Yes, but . . ." game. According to Berne (1964), this "game" follows a pattern: Someone says, "I have this problem." You say, "Why don't you do thus and so?" The person replies, "Yes, but . . ." and then gives you several reasons why your suggestion won't work. If you make a new suggestion, the reply will once again be, "Yes, but . . ." because the person either knows more about his or her personal situation than you do or because he or she has reasons for avoiding your advice. The student described above knows he needs to study. His problem is to understand why he doesn't *want* to study.

Accept the Person's Frame of Reference W. I. Thomas said, "Things perceived as real are real in their effect." Try to resist the temptation to contradict the person with your point of view. Since we all live in different psychological worlds, there is no "correct" view of a life situation. If a person feels that his point of view is understood, he will feel freer to examine it objectively and to question his perspective.

Reflect Thoughts and Feelings One of the most productive things you can do when "counseling" a friend is to give feedback by simply restating what is said. This is also a good way to encourage a person to talk. If he or she seems to be at a loss for words, restate his or her last sentence. For example:

Friend: I'm really bummed out about school. I can't get interested in any of my classes. I flunked my Spanish test, and somebody stole my notebook for psychology.
You: You're really down about school, aren't you?
Friend: Yeah, and my parents are hassling me about my grades again.
You: You're feeling pressured by your parents?
Friend: Yeah, damn.
You: It must make you angry to be pressured by them.

As simple as this sounds, it is extremely helpful to someone trying to sort out his or her feelings. Try it. If nothing else, you'll develop a reputation as a fantastic conversationalist!

Maintain Confidentiality Your efforts to help will be wasted if you fail to respect the privacy of someone who has confided in you. Put yourself in the person's place. Don't gossip.

These guidelines are not an invitation to play "junior therapist." A professional therapist is prepared to attack a serious problem from a position of experience and expertise, and formal therapy provides a protected and confidential arena in which problems can be solved. We simply urge you to recognize the role each of us plays in providing two of the greatest mental health resources available at any cost: friendship and honest communication.

Learning Check

1. Persistent emotional discomfort is a clear sign that professional psychological counseling should be sought. T or F?
2. Community mental health centers rarely offer counseling or therapy themselves; they only do referrals. T or F?
3. In many instances, a therapist's personal qualities have more of an effect on the outcome of therapy than does the type of therapy used. T or F?
4. To aid a troubled friend, you should focus on facts rather than feelings, and you should critically evaluate what the person is saying to help him or her grasp reality. T or F?
5. One danger of giving advice is the tendency for the interchange to slip into the "Yes, but . . ." game. T or F?

Answers: 1. T 2. F 3. T 4. F 5. T

=== Exploration ===

Three Therapists

Psychotherapists differ widely in personal style and choice of techniques. Following are three dialogues, each dealing with the same problem. See which one you consider most helpful.

Therapist A

C: Men are all alike.
T: In what way?
C: They're always bugging us about something or other.
T: Can you think of a specific example?
C: Well, my boyfriend made me come here.
T: Your boyfriend made you come here?
C: He says I'm depressed much of the time.
T: I am sorry to hear you are depressed.
C: It's true. I am unhappy.
T: Do you think coming here will help you not to be unhappy?
C: I need some help, that much seems certain.
T: What would it mean to you if you got some help?
C: Perhaps I could learn to get along with my mother.
T: Tell me more about your family.
C: My mother takes care of me.
T: Who else in your family takes care of you?
C: My father.
T: Your father?
C: You are like my father in some ways.
T: What resemblance do you see?
C: You are not very aggressive but I think you don't want me to notice that.
T: What makes you think I am not very aggressive?
C: You don't argue with me.
T: Why do you think I don't argue with you?
C: You are afraid of me.
T: Does it please you to believe I am afraid of you?
C: My father is afraid of everybody.
T: What else comes to mind when you think of your father?
C: Bullies.
T: Does that have anything to do with the fact that your boyfriend made you come here?

Therapist B

C: Men are all alike.
T: Do you really believe that men are all alike?
C: Well not necessarily all men, but my boyfriend and my father are always bugging me about something. My boyfriend made me come here.
T: How could he make you come here?
C: We fight a lot. He says I'm depressed too much of the time. He thought I should come see you.
T: And what do you think? Are you depressed too much of the time?
C: It's true I'm unhappy most of the time.
T: What makes you most unhappy?
C: I guess I just feel like no one cares about me, that no one really loves me.
T: Then you're trying to tell me that no one, no one at all, cares about you? And that is why you feel unhappy?
C: Yes, I think so.
T: That your boyfriend and parents *never ever* care about you and that you have no friends who care?
C: Well no, not completely. Actually I think they do care sometimes, but usually it doesn't seem like it.
T: Then if they don't seem to love you at all times it is a disaster, and the only possible response is depression, right? What I want you to see is that much of your depression is unnecessary. It is simply not realistic to expect to be loved at all times. I think you may be making yourself miserable with the ridiculous expectation that you should be loved at all times. What if no one loved you? Would you die?

Therapist C

C: Men are all alike.
T: You looked downward as you said that. Look downward again. What are you thinking?
C: They're always bugging us about something or other.
T: What are you feeling now?
C: I feel tight, tightness in my chest. I think I'm angry.

Exploration

T: You *think* you're angry!? I want you to *be* your anger.

C: I can't.

T: Say, "They're always bugging us."

C: (Softly) They're always bugging us.

T: Say it again, louder.

C: (With more conviction) They're always bugging us.

T: Louder!

C: (Shouting) They're always bugging us. Who the hell do they think they are always pushing and telling me what to do?

T: Now we see a connection between the anger you are feeling and the depression you felt earlier. Let's stay with the anger. What are you feeling now?

C: I'm thinking about my boyfriend!

Taken in order, the three dialogues illustrate: Therapist A's approach is quite general, showing no distinct use of a particular therapeutic technique; Therapist B illustrates the argumentative and confrontive qualities of rational therapy (also an emphasis on attacking irrational belief systems). Therapist C shows the emphasis Gestalt therapy places on immediate feelings and reactions, and on filling in gaps in the client's experiences.

Notice that each therapist led the client to an insight. Again, we might ask: Which therapist do you consider most helpful? If you chose Therapist A you have a surprise in store. Therapist A is *a computer*! Dialogue A is part of a "conversation" held with a computer program named ELIZA, developed by computer scientist Joseph Weizenbaum (1966).

Question: Is Weizenbaum serious about having a computer act as a therapist?

Actually, Weizenbaum opposes use of computers as therapists for real clients. But psychologist Kenneth M. Colby of the University of California at Los Angeles feels otherwise. He and other psychologists believe that computerized therapy would have the advantages of low cost, convenience, consistency, and dependability (Alexander, 1978).

Critics view experimentation with computerized therapy as "dehumanizing technology," and note that when a computer says, "I understand," it is meaningless. They also point out that computers would miss nonverbal messages contained in a glance, a gesture, laughter, or tears. On the other hand, many people find it helpful to keep a journal of their thoughts and feelings to get a clearer picture of themselves. In similar fashion, a computer "therapist" might provide a helpful sounding board for sorting out feelings and alternatives. At the very least, computer therapy might make a type of "personal education" available to large numbers of people, particularly those unable to afford traditional therapy.

Questions At this stage there are more questions than answers about computerized therapy: Are computer therapists best reserved for science fiction? Or could they provide a useful service? What does ELIZA tell us about traditional therapy? That is, when therapy of any kind "works," why does it do so? How would you feel about working with a computer therapist?

Questions for Discussion

1. What preconceptions did you have about psychotherapy? Has your understanding of therapy changed? Has your attitude changed?

2. Which of Ellis' irrational assumptions do you consider most self-defeating? Can you think of other irrational assumptions that seem to cause problems?

3. Do you agree with existential therapist Rollo May that there has been a loss of individual freedom, faith, and meaning in today's society? Why or why not?

4. Which form of psychotherapy do you find the most attractive? Why?

5. What psychological services are available in your area? Would you know how to find or make use of them? What factors would affect your decision to seek help?

6. Describe a time when you helped someone resolve a personal problem. Describe a time when you were unsuccessful in helping. What factors seemed to make the difference?

7. Do you think it would be right for a therapist to allow a person to make suicide an "existential choice" or an expression of "free will"?

8. What advantages and disadvantages would you anticipate in working with a computer therapist?

9. Which style of therapy would you expect a computer program to most closely duplicate? If a computer were programmed to provide help for a limited problem such as test anxiety would you find computer therapy more acceptable?

Suggestions for Further Reading

Axline, V. *Dibs: In Search of Self.* Houghton Mifflin, 1964.

Berne, E. *Games People Play.* Grove, 1964.

Binder, V., A. Binder, and B. Rimland. *Modern Therapies.* Prentice-Hall, 1976.

Burton, A. (ed.). *Twelve Therapists.* Jossey-Bass, 1972.

Frankl, V. *Man's Search for Meaning.* Simon and Schuster, 1970.

Freud, S. *General Introduction to Psychoanalysis.* Simon and Schuster, 1969.

Perls, F. *Gestalt Therapy Verbatim.* Real People Press, 1969.

Rogers, C. *Client-centered Therapy.* Houghton Mifflin, 1951.

Rotter, J. B. *Clinical Psychology.* 2nd ed. Prentice-Hall, 1971.

Ruitenbeck, H. M. *The New Group Therapies.* Avon, 1970.

Time Magazine. "Psychiatry on the Couch," April 2, 1979, pp. 74–82.

23

Behavior Modification

Chapter Preview

Behavior Modification and the Twilight Zone

Five times a day, for several days, Brooks Workman stopped what she was doing and vividly imagined herself opening a soft drink can. She made a special point of picturing herself bringing the can to her mouth and placing her lips on it. Just as she was about to drink, hordes of roaches poured out of the can and scurried into her mouth, writhing, twitching, and wiggling their feelers (Williams and Long, 1979).

Question: Why would anyone imagine such a thing?

Brooks Workman's behavior is not as strange as it sounds. Her goal was self-control: Brooks felt that she was drinking too many "Cokes" and wanted to reduce her consumption. The method she chose (called covert sensitization*) is but one of a large number of innovative techniques collectively termed* behavior modification.

Behavior Mod   *In the previous chapter we discussed psychotherapies based upon* insight. *The concern of this chapter is* action-oriented *approaches. Psychologists who use behavior modification (behavior therapists) feel that insight or understanding of one's problems is often unnecessary for improvement. Instead, behavior therapists try to directly alter or remove troublesome behavior—usually by applying the basic principles of operant and classical conditioning.*

   Brooks Workman didn't need to delve into her past or her emotions and conflicts; she simply wanted to break a bothersome habit. Even when serious problems are at stake, techniques like the one she used have proved helpful. Behavior modification has helped people to stop drinking, smoking, hiccoughing, stuttering, and molesting children. Behavior modification can be used to lose weight or to increase eating in the pathologically underweight. It has improved study habits, work output in factories, and speech in retarded and disturbed children, and it has increased the amount of time a psychotic patient will go without hallucinating. Also, through behavior modification, people have conquered fears of heights, snakes, public speaking, sexual intimacy, and automobiles. The list of possible applications is practically endless. It is almost certain that you will discover a useful technique for self-improvement while reading this chapter. But before we begin with some new terms, here is something to think about.

518

The Twilight Zone?   *Pretend for a moment that you work for the telephone company and that you have been sent to repair a phone. Picture a pleasant professional building, one similar to the buildings in which your own doctor and dentist are found. Inside the front door is an office bustling with quiet activity. Through the windows of side offices you see discussions taking place between clients and well-dressed therapists. You ask where the defective phone is. A secretary tells you it is in the opposite end of the building and asks you to follow her. She opens a door on your left. As you step through it, your mind reels.*

In confusion you rapidly scan your surroundings. You are in a tavern! In the dim light you see a bar and heavily padded stools. Behind the bar, a bartender polishes glasses in front of a large mirror and a row of bottles. Lighted displays advertising beer glow softly from the wall, and music flows from an unseen speaker.

Catching sight of the secretary again, you wind your way through the tables and hurry to a door on the opposite side of the room. Once again you are in an ordinary office. But over your shoulder you see the bartender close the door behind you, and the strains of an old Sinatra tune die abruptly with a click of the latch.

What's happening here? Was it a hallucination? A movie set? A modern version of Alice in Wonderland? *A hideout for the CIA? For an answer, read further.*

Survey Questions   How are learning principles applied in aversion therapy? Can behavior modification be used to treat phobias, fears, and anxieties? What role does reinforcement play in behavior modification? Is it possible to apply behavioral principles to everyday problems? What ethical questions does behavior modification raise?

Resources

Behavior Modification— Animal, Vegetable, or Mineral?

Question: In general, how does behavior modification work?

Behavior modification is based on one principal assumption: People have *learned* to be the way they are. Consequently, if they have learned responses that cause problems, then they can *unlearn* them or *relearn* more appropriate responses. Broadly speaking, **behavior modification** refers to any attempt to use the learning principles of *classical* or *operant conditioning* to change human behavior.

Question: How does classical conditioning work? I'm not sure I remember.

Classical conditioning was described in Chapter 8. It is the process of learning originally studied by the Russian physi-

ologist Ivan Pavlov. Here is a brief review of Pavlov's principles:

> A previously neutral stimulus (the *conditioned stimulus*) is followed by a stimulus (the *unconditioned stimulus*) that always produces a response (the *unconditioned response*). Eventually the conditioning stimulus begins to produce the response directly. The response is then called a *conditioned response*. Thus, for a child the sight of a hypodermic needle (CS) is followed by pain (US), which causes anxiety or emotional discomfort (UR). Eventually the sight of a hypodermic (the conditioned stimulus) may produce anxiety (a conditioned response) *before* the child feels any pain.

Question: What does classical conditioning have to do with behavior modification?

Classical conditioning can be used to associate discomfort with a bad habit. Psychologists call discomfort used in this way an *aversion*. An aversion may be used to combat an undesirable habit as it was in the case of the woman who wanted to cut down on her cola drinking. When more powerful versions of this approach are used, it is called *aversion therapy.*

Aversion Therapy—
A Little Pain Goes a Long Way

Imagine that you are eating an apple. Suddenly you discover that you have just bitten a large green worm in half. You vomit. Months pass before you can eat an apple again without feeling ill. You have experienced a *conditioned aversion* to apples.

Question: "Conditioning an aversion" was mentioned as an application of classical conditioning in behavior modification. How is a conditioned aversion used in therapy? Can you give an example of the actual procedures?

In **aversion therapy,** an individual learns to associate a strong aversion (or negative emotional response) to an

Fig. 23-1 *Aversion therapy for drinking. The sights, smells, and tastes of drinking are associated with unpleasant electrical shocks applied to the hand.*

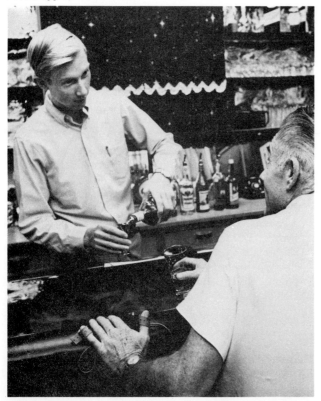

undesirable habit such as smoking, drinking, or gambling. Aversion therapy has also been used to cure hiccoughs, sneezing, stuttering (Goldiamond, 1965), vomiting (Lang and Melamed, 1969), bedwetting (Wickes, 1958), and for treatment of fetishism, transvestism, and other "maladaptive" sexual behaviors (Fuastman, 1976).

An excellent example of aversion therapy is provided by the work of Roger Vogler and his associates (1977). Dr. Vogler works with alcoholics who have been unable to stop drinking. For many patients aversion therapy is a last chance. They have often been threatened with desertion by relatives and friends, have lost their jobs, and have tried Alcoholics Anonymous, psychotherapy, detoxification, vitamin therapy, and even Antabuse therapy. (Antabuse is a drug that causes an alcoholic to become violently nauseated after he or she drinks.) Here is a typical aversion procedure:

> While drinking an alcoholic beverage, painful (although noninjurious) electric shocks are delivered to the patient's hand. From the patient's point of view, the shocks are unpredictable; he or she never knows for sure when one is due. Most of the time, however, the shocks come as the patient is beginning to take a drink of alcohol (Fig. 23-1).

This *response-contingent* (or response-connected) shock obviously takes the immediate pleasure out of drinking. It also causes the patient to develop a conditioned aversion to drinking. The sight and smell of alcohol and the motions of drinking begin to have a capacity to make the individual very uncomfortable.

Question: But can't the person tell when it is "safe" to drink and when it is not?

Transfer, or *generalization,* of aversion conditioning to the "real world" is a problem. Dr. Vogler has constructed in his office a vivid recreation of a "friendly neighborhood tavern," complete with a bar, tables, soft lights, music, and a bartender. Also provided are a "living room," a "bedroom," and a "kitchen." Patients undergo aversion therapy in a setting as much like the normal site of their drinking as possible, and carry-over of the aversion training is improved.

Actually, aversion therapy is used as a last resort, even for problems as serious as alcohol abuse. Dr. Vogler and his associates also train alcoholics to discriminate blood alcohol levels (so clients can tell how drunk they are). They teach alcoholics alternatives to drinking, and also offer education programs on alcohol abuse as well as general counseling (Vogler *et al.,* 1977). Recently, they have added an interesting twist to their aversion procedures: Alcohol abusers are videotaped as they go from sober to drunk. Later, they watch the videotaped drinking bout and see themselves with slurred speech, dropping cigarette ashes in their drinks, saying stupid and belligerent things. Most react with shame and embarrassment when they see the tapes. Apparently, few people have any idea of how unattractive they are when drunk.

To add to the videotape effect, the bartender is trained to provoke clients into becoming argumentative and obnoxious. Presumably, this is not too hard to do by the time the client is saying, "I am 'masshhhed' " (Vils, 1976). In the videotape self-confrontation held later, grossly drunken behaviors are replayed until the client says, "Okay, okay, I've seen enough." Seeing themselves as obnoxious drunks adds to the aversion people feel for drinking, and it increases their determination to quit.

Question: I'm not sure I'm comfortable with the idea of treating humans this way.

People are often disturbed (shocked?) by such methods. It must be emphasized that clients usually volunteer for aversion therapy because it helps them overcome a destructive habit. Indeed, commercial aversion programs for overeating, smoking, and alcohol abuse have attracted large numbers of willing customers. When psychologists use aversion therapy, they often back it up with supportive counseling. Also, for mild problems, such as nail-biting, a person may not have to receive shocks at all. Merely watching a trained actor (who *appears* to get shocks while biting his nails) can effectively curb the problem (Rosenthal *et al.,* 1978). Last, and most importantly, aversion therapy can be justified by its long-term benefits. As behaviorist Donald Baer puts it, "A small number of brief, painful experiences is a reasonable exchange for the interminable pain of a lifelong maladjustment" (Baer, 1971).

Learning Check

Before continuing, see if you can answer these questions. If not, review the preceding section.

1. What two types of conditioning are used in behavior modification? _____ and _____

2. Aversion therapy is used to combat what? _____

3. Shock, pain, and discomfort play what role in conditioning an aversion?

   a. conditioned stimulus   *b.* unconditioned stimulus
   c. unconditioned response   *d.* conditioned response

4. If shock is used to control drinking it must be _____-contingent.

5. A potential problem with aversion therapy is transfer of the aversion to settings outside the clinic or laboratory.   T or F?

Answers: 1. classical and operant 2. undesirable responses or destructive habits 3. b 4. response 5. T

Desensitization—Who's Afraid of a Big, Bad Hierarchy?

Assume you are a swimming instructor who wants to help a child overcome fear of the high diving board. How might you proceed? Directly forcing a terrified child off the high board could be psychologically disastrous. Obviously, a better approach would be to begin by teaching the child to dive off the edge of the pool. Then the child could be taught to dive off the low board, followed by a platform six feet above the water, and then an eight-foot platform. As a last step the child could try the high board.

This *ordered set of steps* is called a **hierarchy.** The hierarchy allows the child to undergo *adaptation.* Gradually the child adapts to the high dive and overcomes fear, much as one adapts to the cool water of a swimming pool on a hot day. When the child has overcome the fear, a psychologist would say that **desensitization** (dee-SEN-sih-tih-ZAY-

shun) has occurred. Desensitization is also based on the principle of **reciprocal inhibition,** developed by Joseph Wolpe (1974). Reciprocal inhibition means that one emotional state can prevent the occurrence of another. For instance, it is impossible to be anxious and relaxed at the same time. If we have managed to get our subject onto the high board in a relaxed state, anxiety and fear responses will be inhibited. Repeated times on the high board should cause fear in the situation to disappear. Again we would say that the person has been *desensitized.* In general, desensitization (that is, a reduction in fears) is usually brought about by gradually approaching a feared stimulus while maintaining complete relaxation.

Question: What is desensitization used for?

Desensitization is primarily used to help people unlearn or countercondition phobias or strong anxieties. Almost everyone has a phobia or two. Many people fear heights, snakes, public speaking, spiders, and so forth. Usually these cause little difficulty because the individual carefully avoids fear-producing situations. However, consider the following: a teacher with stage fright, a student with test anxiety, a salesperson who fears people, an aspiring pole-vaulter who fears heights, or a newlywed with a fear of sexual intimacy. Each may be hampered enough by fears or anxieties to seek aid.

Question: How is desensitization done?

Desensitization usually involves three steps. First, the client and the therapist *construct a hierarchy*—a list of fear-provoking situations involving the phobia and ranging from the least disturbing situation to the most disturbing one. Second, the client is taught *exercises that produce total relaxation*. Once the client is relaxed, he or she proceeds to the third step by trying to *perform the least disturbing item* on the list. For a fear of heights (acrophobia), this might be: "(1) standing on a chair." The first item is repeated until no anxiety is felt. Any change from complete relaxation is a signal to clients that they must repeat the relaxation process before continuing. Slowly clients move up the hierarchy: "(2) climb to the top of a small stepladder"; "(3) look down a flight of stairs"; and so on, until the last item is performed without fear: "(20) fly in an airplane."

Question: I understand how some fears could be desensitized by gradual approach—like the child on the high dive. But how would a therapist use desensitization to combat fear of sexual intimacy?

For a person with a fear of heights, the steps of the hierarchy might be acted out. Often, however, acting out is totally impractical. In some cases this problem can be handled by having clients observe models (live or filmed) who are performing the feared behavior (Fig. 23-2). If such **vicarious desensitization** is not practical, there is yet another alternative. Fortunately, desensitization works almost as well when a person *vividly imagines* each step in the hierarchy. If the steps can be visualized without anxiety, fear in the actual situation is reduced.

Here is a sample of the hierarchy imagined by a 24-year-old married woman to overcome the fear and disgust she felt for sexual intercourse. (Some steps are left out to shorten the list.)

   1. Dancing with and embracing husband while fully clothed.
   2. Being kissed on cheeks and forehead.
   3. Being kissed on lips.
   4. Sitting on husband's lap, both fully dressed.
   5. Husband kisses neck and ears.
   6. Husband caresses hair and face.
   •
   •
   •
  17. Having intercourse in bed in the dark.
  18. Having intercourse in the nude in a dining room or living room.
  19. Changing positions during intercourse.
  20. Having intercourse in the nude while sitting on husband's lap. (Adapted from Lazarus, 1964.)

Fig. 23-2 *Treatment of a snake phobia by vicarious desensitization. The photographs show models interacting with snakes. To overcome their own fears, phobic subjects observed the models. (Bandura et al., 1969. Photos courtesy of Albert Bandura.)*

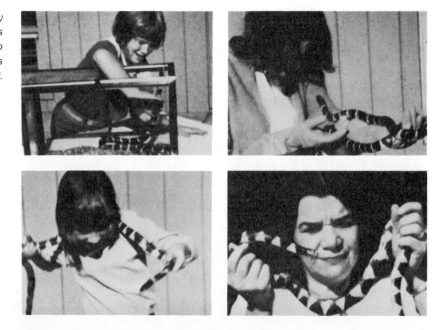

Mrs. A was able to imagine the last steps in this hierarchy without experiencing anxiety after a three-month period of desensitization. Accordingly, she and her husband reported that their sexual and marital adjustments were greatly improved.

Question: Does desensitization always take several months?

It depends, of course, on the severity of the fear or anxiety being treated. For relatively mild fears a rapid desensitization technique called *implosive therapy* may be used.

In **implosive therapy,** the client is *flooded* with anxiety-provoking images (Stampfl, 1975). For example, if you had a phobia for nonpoisonous snakes, you might be asked to imagine a great tangled knot of snakes wrapped around your body, slithering up your legs, crawling into your ears, and gnawing into your stomach. With repeated exposure in a "safe" setting such images rapidly lose their ability to unleash the flood of anxiety they cause at first. Clients are directly confronted by their fears and yet no harm comes to them. Obviously, implosive therapy must be used with discretion. Otherwise, it could be like trying to extinguish a fire with gasoline. However, for some phobias—for example, test anxiety, stage fright, and other mild fears—it is quite effective.

Learning Check

Answer these questions before reading on.

1. The ordered series of steps used in desensitization make up a _____ of feared situations.

2. What two principles underlie desensitization? _____ and _____ _____

3. When desensitization is carried out through the use of live or filmed models it is called:

    a. implosive therapy   *b.* covert desensitization
    c. flooding   *d.* vicarious desensitization

4. Three basic steps in desensitization are: construct a hierarchy, flood the person with anxiety, imagine relaxation.   T or F?

Answers: 1. hierarchy 2. adaptation and reciprocal inhibition 3. d 4. F

Operant Principles— All the World Is a . . . Skinner Box?

Question: Aversion therapy and desensitization are forms of behavior modification based on classical conditioning. Where does operant conditioning fit in?

The principles of operant conditioning have been developed by B. F. Skinner and other psychologists mostly through laboratory research with animals. The operant principles most frequently used by behavior therapists to deal with *human* behavior are:

1. *Positive reinforcement.* An action that is followed by reward will occur more frequently. If children whine and get attention, they will whine more frequently. If you get A's in your psychology class, you may become a psychology major.

2. *Nonreinforcement.* An action that is not followed by reward will occur less frequently.

3. *Extinction.* If a response is not followed by reward after it has been repeated many times, it will go away. After winning 3 times, you pull the handle on a slot machine 30 times more without a payoff. What do you do? You go away. So does the response of handle pulling (for that particular machine, at any rate).

4. *Punishment.* If a response is followed by discomfort or an undesirable effect, the response will be suppressed (but not necessarily extinguished).

5. *Shaping.* Shaping means rewarding actions that are closer and closer approximations to a desired response. If a response is complicated, it may never occur to be rewarded. If I want to reward a retarded child for saying "ball," I may begin by rewarding the child for saying anything that starts with a *b* sound.

6. *Stimulus control.* Responses tend to come under the control of the situation in which they occur. If I set my clock 10 minutes fast I can get to work on time in the morning. My departure is under the stimulus control of the clock even though I know it is fast.

7. *Time out.* A time-out procedure usually involves removing the individual from a situation in which reinforcement occurs. Time out prevents reward from following an undesirable response; it is a variation of nonreinforcement.

(For a more thorough review of operant principles return to Chapter 8.) As simple as these principles may seem, they have been used very effectively by behavior modification specialists to overcome difficulties in work, home, school, and industrial settings. Let's see how.

Nonreinforcement and Extinction— The Attention Game

An extremely overweight mental patient had a persistent and disturbing habit: She stole food from other patients. No one could persuade her to stop stealing or to diet. For the sake of her health, a behavior therapist assigned her a special table in the ward dining room. If she approached any other table, she was immediately removed from the dining room. Since her attempts to steal food went unrewarded, they rapidly disappeared. Additionally, any attempt to steal from others usually resulted in the patient's missing her own meal (Ayllon, 1963).

Question: What operant principles did the therapist in this example use?

The therapist used *nonreward* to produce *extinction*. Most frequently occurring human behaviors lead to some form of reward. An undesirable response can be eliminated by *identifying* and *removing* the rewards that maintain it. But people don't always do things for food, money, or other obvious rewards. Most of the rewards maintaining human behavior are more subtle. *Attention, approval,* and *concern* are common yet powerful reinforcers for humans (Fig. 23-3).

For instance, in a classroom we often find that misbehaving children are surrounded by others who giggle and pay attention to them. If seating is rearranged so that the disruptive children are surrounded by less responsive students, misbehavior decreases. Attention from a teacher (even scolding) can also be a reinforcer. An experiment showed that when teachers paid extra attention to classroom misbehavior, it increased. It increased even when the attention took the form of saying things such as "Sit down!" When misbehaving children were *ignored* and attention was given to children who were *not* misbehaving, misbehavior decreased (Madsen *et al.,* 1968).

Question: How are nonreward and extinction applied in therapy?

Nonreward and extinction can eliminate many problem behaviors. Frequently, difficulties center around a limited number of particularly disturbing responses. A typical strategy used in institutions is called *time out.* Time out means refusing to reward maladaptive responses, usually by refusing to play the *attention* game. Another form of time out is to remove an individual immediately from the setting in which an undesirable response occurs, so that the response will not be rewarded. For example:

Fourteen-year-old Josh periodically appeared in the nude in the activity room of a training center for disturbed juveniles. This behavior always generated a great deal of at-

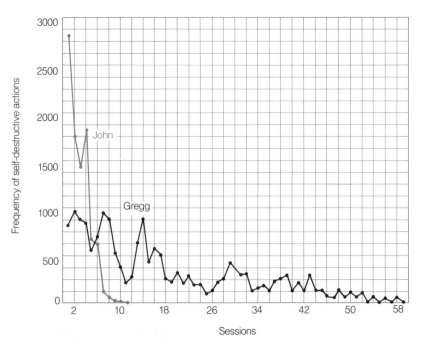

Fig. 23-3 *This graph shows extinction of self-destructive behavior in two autistic boys. Before extinction began, the boys received attention and concern from adults for injuring themselves. During extinction, self-damaging behavior was ignored. (Adapted from Lovaas and Simons, 1969.)*

tention from staff and other patients. Usually Josh was returned to his room and confined there. During this "confinement," he often missed doing his usual chores. As an experiment he was placed on time out. The next time he appeared nude, counselors and other staff members greeted him normally and then ignored him. Attention from other patients rapidly subsided. Sheepishly he returned to his room and dressed.

Reinforcement and Token Economies— Help for the "Hopeless"

This section might be called "Throwing a Lifeline to the 'Unreachable'." A distressing problem faced when dealing with severe mental illness is how to "break through" to a patient who cannot, or will not, communicate. Mental patients sometimes spend years in hospitals without noticeable improvement. Even the patient who is willing to talk about his or her problem may make little visible progress toward mental health.

Question: What can be done in such circumstances?

An approach to therapy rapidly growing in popularity is based on the use of *tokens*. **Tokens** are *symbolic* rewards that can be exchanged for real rewards. (As you may recall from Chapter 9, tokens are secondary reinforcers.)

Tokens may be printed slips of paper, plastic "poker" chips, check marks, points, or "gold stars." Whatever form they take, tokens serve as rewards because they may be exchanged for candy, food, cigarettes, recreation, or other privileges, such as private time with a therapist, outings, using the stereo record player, and so forth. Tokens are being used in mental hospitals, halfway houses for drug addicts, schools for the retarded, programs for delinquents, and ordinary classrooms. Their use is usually associated with dramatic improvements in behavior and overall adjustment.

Learning research and *everyday* experience point out the power of positive reinforcement to change behavior. If a response is followed by reward, it will occur more frequently. Using tokens, a therapist can *immediately* reward a positive response. This feature of tokens allows a therapist to use operant shaping to influence behavior directly instead of vaguely urging patients to "get themselves together."

So that incentives will have maximum impact, the therapist selects specific **target behaviors** that could or should be improved, then reinforces them with tokens. For example, an uncommunicative mental patient might initially be given a token each time he or she says a word. Next,

tokens may be given for speaking a complete sentence. Later, the patient could gradually be required to speak more frequently, then to answer questions, and eventually to carry on a short conversation in order to receive tokens. In this way, patients who have not spoken more than a few words for months or years have been returned to the world of normal communication.

Full-scale use of tokens in an institutional setting leads to the development of a **token economy.** In a token economy, patients are rewarded with tokens for a wide range of socially desirable or productive activities. They must *pay* tokens for privileges and for engaging in problem behavior (Fig. 23-4). For example, tokens are given to patients who get out of bed, dress themselves, take required medication, arrive for meals on time, and the like. Work at constructive activity, such as gardening, cooking, or custodial duties, may also earn tokens. Patients *must exchange* tokens for meals and for private rooms, movies, passes, off-ward activities, and other privileges. Sometimes tokens can be exchanged for items at a commissary or ward "store." Patients are *charged* tokens for staying in bed, disrobing in public, talking to themselves, fighting, crying, and similar target behaviors.

In a token economy program, staff members ensure that patients earn tokens easily for constructive behavior, but fine them heavily for destructive responses. This system provides the therapists with leverage. Patients are both pushed and enticed toward normality. The result can be a radical change in a patient's overall adjustment and morale. Patients have an incentive to change and are held responsible for their maladaptive habits and actions. Many "hopelessly" retarded, mentally ill, and delinquent people have been returned to a productive life by means of token economies.

Question: Wouldn't there be a problem with generalization of improvements brought about by a token economy?

Yes. As was the case with aversion therapy, lack of generalization can be a problem. To minimize it, patients are praised and given social recognition when they receive tokens. Each time a token is given the therapist says something like, "That was very good," or "You're doing so well."

By the time they are ready to leave the program, patients may be earning tokens on a weekly basis for maintaining sane, responsible, and productive behavior (Binder, 1976). The results of recent experiments suggest that the most effective token economies are those that ultimately depend on *social rewards* such as recognition and approval (Lieberman *et al.,* 1976). Such rewards are what patients will receive when they return to family, friends, and community.

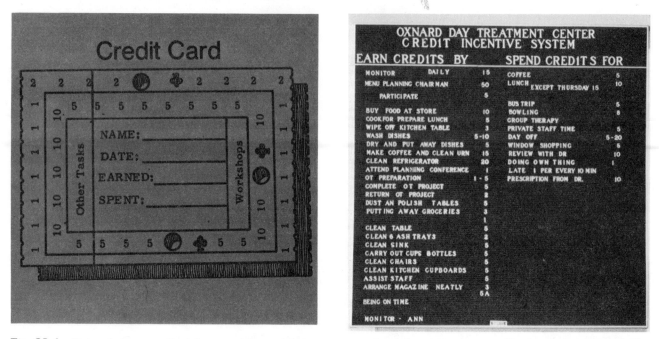

Fig. 23-4 *Pictured above are the tokens used in one token economy system; also pictured are credit values for various activities. Tokens may be exchanged for items or for privileges listed on the board. (Photographs courtesy of Dr. Robert P. Liberman.)*

Cognitive Behavior Therapy— Think Positive!

Question: How would a behavior therapist treat a problem like depression? None of the techniques described seems to apply.

As we have discussed, behavior therapists usually try to change troublesome actions. However, in recent years a new breed of therapist has appeared. **Cognitive behavior therapists,** as they are called, are interested in thoughts, as well as visible behavior. Rather than looking only at maladaptive actions, cognitive therapists try to learn what people think, believe, and feel. They then help clients change *thinking patterns* that lead to trouble (Meichenbaum, 1977).

Cognitive therapy has been especially effective in the treatment of depression. As you may recall from Chapter 13, Aron Beck believes that negative, self-defeating thoughts underlie depression. That is, depressed persons see themselves, the world, and the future in negative terms. According to Beck, this occurs because of *selective perception:* If five good things happen during the day and three bad, the depressed person will focus only on the bad. *Overgeneralization* is another thinking error underlying depression. An example would be considering yourself a total failure, or worthless, if you were to lose a job or fail a class. To complete the picture, Beck says that depressed persons

tend to *magnify* the importance of undesirable events, and they engage in *all-or-nothing thinking* (seeing events, or themselves, as completely good or bad, right or wrong, successful or a failure) (Beck *et al.,* 1979).

Question: What do cognitive behavior therapists do to alter such patterns?

Cognitive therapists make a step-by-step effort to correct negative thoughts that underlie depression or similar problems. At first clients are taught to recognize and keep track of their own thoughts. The client and therapist look especially for ideas and beliefs that cause depression, anger, avoidance, and so forth. Next, clients are asked to collect information to test their beliefs. For instance, a depressed person might list his or her activities for a week. The list can then be used to challenge the all-or-nothing thought, "I had a terrible week." With continued coaching clients make positive changes in their thinking. Such changes then affect moods, actions, and relationships.

In an alternate approach, the cognitive therapist looks for an *absence* of effective coping skills and thought patterns, not for the *presence* of self-defeating thinking (Meichenbaum, 1977). The aim in this case is to teach clients how to cope with anger, depression, shyness, stress, and similar problems. "Stress inoculation," which was described in Chapter 14, is a good example of this approach. Whatever form it takes, there is little doubt that cognitive behavior therapy is a promising and rapidly expanding specialty. As further evidence of its usefulness, two cognitive techniques (covert sensitization and thought stopping) are described in the "Applications" that follows. See what you think of them.

Learning Check

1. Behavior modification programs aimed at extinction of an undesirable behavior typically make use of what operant principles?

    a. punishment and stimulus control   *b.* punishment and shaping
    c. nonreinforcement and time out   *d.* stimulus control and time out

2. Attention can be a powerful _____ for humans.

3. Token economies depend upon use of the time-out procedure.   T or F?

4. An advantage of tokens is that they can be used to _____ _____ a desired response.

5. Tokens are used at first to change specific actions called _____ _____ .

6. Tokens basically allow the operant shaping of desired responses.   T or F?

7. According to Beck, selective perception, overgeneralization, and _____ thinking are cognitive habits that underlie depression.

Answers: 1. c   2. reinforcer   3. F   4. immediately reinforce   5. target behaviors   6. T   7. all-or-nothing

Resources Summary

● *Behavior therapists* use variations of *behavior modification,* therapeutic techniques that apply the learning principles of *operant* and *classical conditioning,* to bring about positive changes in human behavior.

● Classical conditioning, the pairing of a *conditioned stimulus (CS)* and an *unconditioned stimulus (US)* can be used to condition an *aversion* when the US causes pain or discomfort. In *aversion therapy* the sights, sounds, odors, and motions of a maladaptive response or bad habit (such as smoking or drinking) are associated with pain or other aversive events. Thus, the undesirable response becomes associated with an aversion which inhibits its occurrence.

● Classical conditioning principles also underlie *desensitization,* a technique used to overcome fears and anxieties. In desensitization, gradual *adaptation* and *reciprocal inhibition* serve to break the link between fear and particular situations. Typical steps in desensitization are: *construct a hierarchy* of feared situations, *learn* to produce *total relaxation,* and *perform items on the hierarchy* (from least to most disturbing).

● Densensitization may be carried out with real settings and situations in the environment or it may be carried out by *vivid imagination* of the fear hierarchy. Desensitization is also effective when it is administered *vicariously;* that is, when clients watch *models* perform the feared responses. In *implosive therapy* the fear hierarchy is discarded and clients are *flooded* with anxiety until their fears abate.

● Behavior modification also makes use of operant principles. The most commonly used principles are: *positive reinforcement, nonreinforcement, extinction, punishment, shaping, stimulus control,* and *time out.* Through the application of these principles, behavior modification is used to extinguish undesirable responses and to promote constructive behavior.

● Nonreward can be used to produce extinction of troublesome behaviors. Often this is done by simply *identifying* and *eliminating* reinforcers, particularly *attention* and *approval.*

● In the application of positive reinforcement and operant shaping, symbolic rewards known as *tokens* are often used. Tokens allow *immediate reinforcement* of selected *target behaviors* so that rapid shaping is possible.

● Full-scale use of tokens in an institutional setting produces a *token economy.* In a token economy, responsibilities, goods, services, and privileges are assigned values and tokens are earned and exchanged. Toward the end of a token economy program, patients are shifted to *social rewards* such as recognition and approval.

● *Cognitive behavior therapy* is a new specialty that emphasizes changing thought patterns that underlie emotional or behavioral problems. Its goals are to correct distorted thinking and/or to teach improved coping skills.

=== Applications ===

Self-Management—Applying Behavioral Principles to Yourself

''Last week I didn't even know what a 'behavior morti-fier' was and now I are one!''

''Throw out the snake oil, ladies and gentlemen, and throw away your troubles. Doctor B. Havior Modification is here to put an end to all human suffering.''

True? Well, not quite. Behavior modification is not a cure-all. Its effective use is often quite complicated and requires a great deal of experience and expertise. Also, for many problems behavior modification is a poor choice by comparison to insight therapy. Still, it does offer a straightforward solution to many problems.

It would be a serious mistake to presume that you could effectively apply the principles of behavior modification to major personal problems. As we have mentioned else-where in this book, professional help is available and should be sought when a significant problem exists. For lesser difficulties there is a good chance that you might succeed in modest attempts to apply the principles of behavior modification to yourself. Let us see how this might be done.

Applying Aversion Therapy—
Boosting Your ''Will Power''

''Have you ever decided to quit smoking cigarettes, watching television too much, eating too much, drinking too much, or driving too fast?''

''Well, one of those applies. I have decided several times to quit smoking.''

''When have you decided?''

''Usually after I am reminded of how dangerous smok-ing is—like when I heard that my uncle had died of lung cancer. He smoked constantly.''

''If you have decided to quit 'several times' I assume you haven't succeeded?''

''No, the usual pattern is for me to become upset about smoking and then to cut down for a day or two.''

''You forget the disturbing image of your uncle's death, or whatever, and start smoking again.''

''Yes, I suppose if I had an uncle die every day or so, I might actually quit!''

The use of electric shock to condition an aversion seems remote from everyday problems. However, some activities are naturally aversive if engaged in to excess. For example, a common method of using aversion therapy to reduce smoking is to have the smoker sit in a small unventilated booth and smoke three or four *cartons* of cigarettes nonstop. Even a heavy smoker comes away from such an experience with a new distaste for cigarettes and smoking. Repeating this procedure periodically can create an aversion strong enough to reduce smoking.

Question: I don't think I could actually do that myself. Besides, I don't think it would work for overeating.

Since the oversmoking procedure involves considerable discomfort, it is unlikely that one would complete it without the guidance of a therapist. However, there is an alterna-tive that can be used to help cut down on smoking as well as eating and other less naturally aversive habits.

Covert Sensitization   Obtain six 3 × 5 cards and on each write a brief description of a scene related to the habit you wish to control. The scene should be so *disturb-ing* or *disgusting* that thinking about it would temporarily make you very uncomfortable about indulging in the habit. For smoking, the cards might read:

1. I am in a doctor's office. The doctor looks at some reports and tells me I have lung cancer. He says a lung will have to be removed and sets a date for the operation.
2. I am in bed under an oxygen tent. My chest feels caved in. There is a tube in my throat. I can barely breathe.
3. I wake up in the morning and smoke a cigarette. I begin coughing up blood.
4. Other cards would continue along the same line.

For overeating the cards might read:

1. I am at the beach. I get up to go for a swim and I over-hear people whispering to each other, ''Isn't that fat dis-gusting?''
2. I am at a store buying clothes. I try on several things that are too small. The only things that fit look like rumpled sacks. Salespeople are staring at me.
3. And so forth.

Applications

The trick, of course, is to get yourself to imagine or picture vividly each of these disturbing scenes *several times* a day. Imagining the scenes can be accomplished by placing them under *stimulus control.* Simply choose something you do *frequently* each day (such as getting a cup of coffee or getting up from your chair). Next make a rule. Before you can get a cup of coffee, or get up from your chair, or whatever you have selected as a cue, you must take out your stack of cards and *vividly picture* the scene described on the top card. Imagine the scene for 30 seconds. After visualizing the top card, move it to the bottom so the cards are rotated. Make up new cards each week. This technique may sound as if you are "playing games with yourself," but it can be a great help if you want to cut down on a bad habit (Cautela, 1973). Try it!

Thought Stopping In the last few years behavior therapists have begun to realize that like more observable responses, thoughts can also cause trouble. Think of times when you have repeatedly "put yourself down" in your thoughts, or when you have been preoccupied by needless worries, fears, or other negative and upsetting thoughts. If you would like to gain control over such thoughts recent experiments show how it can be done.

The simplest thought-stopping technique makes use of mild punishment to suppress upsetting mental images and internal "talk." Simply place a large flat rubber band around your wrist. As you go through the day apply this rule: Each time you catch yourself thinking the upsetting image or thought, pull the rubber band away from your wrist and snap it. You need not make this terribly painful. Its value lies in drawing your attention to how often you form negative thoughts and in interrupting the flow of thoughts. Strong punishment is not required.

Question: It seems like this procedure might be abandoned pretty rapidly. Is there an alternative?

A second thought-stopping procedure requires only that you interrupt upsetting thoughts each time they occur. Begin by setting aside time each day during which you will deliberately think the unwanted thought. As you begin to form the thought, shout "stop!" aloud and with conviction. (Obviously you should choose a private spot for this portion of the procedure!) Repeat the thought-stopping procedure 10 to 20 times for the first two or three days.

Then switch to shouting "stop!" covertly (to yourself) rather than aloud. Thereafter, thought-stopping can be carried out throughout the day, whenever upsetting thoughts occur (adapted from Williams and Long, 1979). After several days of practice you should be able to stop unwanted thoughts whenever they occur.

Applying Desensitization Therapy— Overcoming Common Fears

You have prepared for two weeks to give a speech in a large class. As your turn approaches, your hands begin to tremble and perspire. Your heart pounds and you find it difficult to breathe. You say to your body, "Relax!" What happens? Nothing!

Relaxation The key to desensitization is relaxation. To inhibit fear, one must *learn* to relax. Here is a method for achieving deep-muscle relaxation.

Tense the muscles in your right arm until they tremble. Hold them tight for about five seconds and then let go. Allow your hand and arm to go limp and to relax completely. Repeat the procedure. Releasing tension two or three times will allow you to feel whether or not your arm muscles have relaxed. Repeat the tension-release procedure with your left arm. Compare it to your right arm. Repeat until the left arm is equally relaxed. Apply the tension-release technique to your right leg; to your left leg; to your abdomen; to your chest and shoulders. Clench and release your chin, neck, and throat. Wrinkle and release your forehead and scalp. Tighten and release your mouth and face muscles. As a last step, curl your toes and tense your feet. Then release. Practice relaxation with the tension-release method until you can achieve complete relaxation quickly (5 to 10 minutes).

After you have practiced relaxation once a day for a week or two, you will begin to be able to tell when your body (or a group of muscles) is tense. Also you will begin to be able to relax on command. Once you have learned to relax, the next step is to identify the fear you would like to control and construct a *hierarchy.*

Procedure for Constructing a Hierarchy Make a list of situations (related to the fear) that make you anxious. Try to list at least 10 situations. Some should be very

Applications

frightening and others only mildly frightening. Write a short description of each situation on a separate 3 × 5 card. Place the cards in order from the least disturbing situation to the most disturbing. Here is a sample hierarchy for a student afraid of public speaking:

1. Given an assignment to speak in class.
2. Thinking about the topic and the date the speech must be given.
3. Writing the speech; thinking about delivering the speech.
4. Watching other students speak in class the week before the speech date.
5. Rehearsing the speech alone; pretending to give it to the class.
6. Delivering the speech to my roommate; pretending my roommate is the teacher.
7. Reviewing the speech on the day it is to be presented.
8. Entering the classroom; waiting and thinking about the speech.
9. Being called; standing up; facing the audience.
10. Delivering the speech.

Using the Hierarchy When the relaxation exercises have been mastered and the hierarchy constructed, set aside time each day to work on reducing your fear. Begin by performing the relaxation exercises. When you are completely relaxed, visualize the scene on the first card (the least frightening scene). If you can *vividly picture* and imagine yourself in the first situation twice *without a noticeable increase in muscular tension,* proceed to the next card. Also, as you progress through the cards, relax yourself between each card.

Each day, stop when you reach a card that you cannot visualize without tension after three attempts. On each successive day, begin one or two cards before the one on which you stopped the previous day. Continue to work with the cards until you can visualize the last situation without experiencing tension (techniques are based on Wolpe, 1974).

Using this approach you should be able to reduce the fear or anxiety associated with things such as public speaking, entering darkened rooms, asking questions in large classes, heights, talking to members of the opposite sex, taking tests, and so forth. Even if you are unable to reduce a fear, you will have learned to place relaxation under voluntary control, and controlling unnecessary tension can increase energy and efficiency.

Applying Operant Conditioning— Improving Habits

Would you like to increase the number of hours you spend studying each week? Would you like to exercise more, attend more classes, concentrate longer, or read more books? All these activities and many others can be improved by following these rules:

1. *Choose a target behavior.* Identify the activity you want to change.
2. *Record a baseline.* Record how much time you currently spend performing the target activity.
3. *Establish goals.* Remember the principle of shaping and set realistic goals for gradual improvement on each successive week. Also, set daily goals that add up to the weekly goal.
4. *Choose reinforcers.* If you meet your daily goal, what reward will you allow yourself? Daily rewards might be watching television, eating a candy bar, socializing with friends, playing a musical instrument, or whatever you enjoy. Also establish a weekly reward. If you reach your weekly goal, what reward will you allow yourself? A movie? A dinner out? A weekend hike?
5. *Record your progress.* Keep accurate records of the amount of time spent each day on the desired activity.
6. *Reward successes.* If you meet your daily goal, collect your reward. If you fall short, be honest with yourself and skip the reward. Do the same for your weekly goal.

If you have trouble finding rewards or if you don't want to use the entire system, simply remember this: Anything *done often* can serve as reinforcement. For example, if you watch television every night and want to study more, make it a rule not to turn on the set until you have studied for an hour (or whatever length of time you choose). Then lengthen the requirement each week.

A sample of a student's plan:

1. Target behavior: number of hours spent studying for school
2. Recorded baseline: an average of 15 minutes per day for a weekly total of 1 1/4 hours
3. Goal for the first week: an increase in study time to 20 minutes per day; weekly goal of 2 hours total study time

Goal for second week: 25 minutes per day and 2 1/2 hours per week

Goal for third week: 30 minutes per day and 3 hours per week

Applications

Ultimate goal: to reach and maintain 8 hours per week study time

4. Daily reward for reaching goal: 1 hour of guitar playing in the evening; no playing if the goal is not met

Weekly reward for reaching goal: go to a movie or buy a record album

Self-Recording Even if you find it difficult to administer and withhold the rewards in your program you are likely to succeed. Simply knowing that you are reaching a desired goal can be reward enough. The key to any self-management program therefore becomes accurate record-keeping. This concept is demonstrated by an investigation in which some students in an introductory psychology course recorded study time and graphed daily and weekly study behavior. Even though no extra rewards were offered, students who recorded their study time earned better grades than those who did not (Johnson and White, 1971).

Contracting If you try the techniques discussed and have difficulty sticking with them, you may want to try *behavioral contracting*. In a behavioral contract you state a *specific* problem behavior you want to control or a goal you want to achieve. Also state the rewards you will receive, privileges you will forfeit, or punishments you must accept. The contract should be typed and signed by you and a person you are close to.

A behavioral contract can be quite motivating, especially when mild punishment is part of the agreement. Here's an example reported by Nurnberger and Zimmerman (1970): A student working on his Ph.D. had completed all requirements but his dissertation, yet for two years had not written a single page. A contract was drawn up for him in which he agreed to meet weekly deadlines on the number of pages he would complete. To make sure he would meet the deadlines, he wrote post-dated checks. These were to be forfeited if he failed to reach his goal for the week. The checks were made out to organizations he despised (the Ku Klux Klan and American Nazi Party). From the time he signed the contract, until he finished his degree, the student's work output was greatly improved.

Learning Check

1. Covert sensitization and thought-stopping combine aversion therapy and cognitive therapy.   T or F?
2. Exercises that bring about deep-muscle relaxation are an essential element in many applications of covert sensitization.   T or F?
3. Items in a desensitization hierarchy should be placed in order from the least disturbing to the most disturbing. T or F?
4. The first step in desensitization is to place the visualization of disturbing images under stimulus control.   T or F?
5. After a target behavior has been selected for reinforcement, it's a good idea to record a baseline so you can set realistic goals for change.   T or F?
6. Self-recording, even without the use of extra rewards, can bring about desired changes in target behaviors. T or F?

Answers: 1. T 2. F 3. T 4. F 5. T 6. T

Behavior Modification—To Control or Not to Control?

Obviously, if one *voluntarily* uses behavior modification to lose weight, to increase study time, to unlearn a phobia, or to face a public speaking engagement, problems of control and personal freedom are avoided. But should behavior modification be used by some people to change or control others? B. F. Skinner argues in his book *Beyond Freedom and Dignity* that everyone is already controlled by the environment and the consequences of actions. Skinner's premise is that such control might just as well be rational and orderly instead of haphazard.

Question: I have some misgivings about controlling people. Is behavior modification widely accepted by psychologists?

Behavior modification is exciting to those who have used it because it often works. It is frightening to many others for the same reason. They fear that the widespread use of behavior modification is capable of thrusting us into circumstances like those portrayed in George Orwell's book *1984* or in Stanley Kubric's movie *A Clockwork Orange.* Both depict a world in which people are controlled and molded against their will.

Traditional psychotherapists and other opponents of behavior modification claim that it is dehumanizing and that it removes the symptoms of psychological problems without dealing with their causes. Behavior modifiers counter by saying the symptom *is* the problem, and *learning* is the cause. They also argue that humanistic or insight therapists such as Carl Rogers are really controlling their clients through the subtle rewarding effects of approval and attention (Truax, 1966).

Another charge commonly leveled by critics of behavior modification is that it is cold, mechanical, and manipulative. Much to the surprise of such critics, a recent study showed that behavior therapists are rated just as "warm" and caring as traditional therapists (Staples *et al.,* 1975). And as behavior therapist Virginia Binder points out, behavior modification specialists have often worked with patients who are so "hopeless" that they have been ignored by other therapists. Behavior therapists, it would seem, are at least as humanitarian as other therapists (Binder, 1976).

Behavior Modification: Are You for or against It?

Let's say that an autistic child is mutilating himself. He bites his fingertips or repeatedly pounds his head against his knees, chews his shoulder until the bone shows, or bangs his head on the corner of a steel cabinet. Using behavior modification, psychologist Ivar Lovaas has successfully ended such actions even when other approaches have failed (see Chapter 16). The benefits of using behavior modification seem clear in this situation. But elsewhere behavior modification might be superficial or undesirable.

The use of behavior modification in public schools, prisons, mental institutions (students sometimes argue that there is no difference among these three), and other "captive" groups is more open to question. For example, prisoners at Atascadero State Hospital for the Criminally Insane and at the California Medical Facility in Vacaville have been given a drug called Anectine as part of an aversion therapy program to deal with homosexuality, chronic violence, and similar problems. Anectine paralyzes the respiratory system for up to two minutes, causing an intense feeling of suffocation. Prisoners have little choice about participation in this treatment. In many cases the "therapy" is effective, but at what cost in human terms? In the confines of a total institution, can participation in such a program really be considered a free choice?

Public concern about the possible abuses of behavior modification has not gone unrecognized by behavior therapists. Some have suggested that professional and client review boards should be set up to evaluate programs and assure protection of clients' welfare (Martin, 1975).

In general though, behavior therapists have faith in their methods. Proponents of behavior modification feel it has no peer in areas such as classroom management, work with the retarded, child discipline, treatment for obesity, phobias, sexual dysfunction, and the like. They also argue that many mental patients are serving virtual life sentences in state hospitals. In view of the demonstrated effectiveness of behavioral techniques, they consider it unethical to *withhold* treatment.

The proper place for behavior control in a free society is a complex issue. Where do you stand on the use of behavior modification?

Questions for Discussion

1. Under what conditions would you condone the use of behavior modification? When would you oppose it?

2. Based on the techniques described, would you cooperate with a therapist who wanted to employ behavior modification? Are there some techniques you find acceptable and others not?

3. Select a bad habit you would like to break or a positive behavior you would like to encourage and tell how you might use behavior modification to alter your behavior. Be explicit.

4. Some critics have charged that the use of tokens in the classroom encourages students to expect artificial rewards. Behavior theorists reply that explicit rewards are better than inconsistent rewards such as praise and attention. What are the advantages and drawbacks represented by each position?

5. How do you feel about the use of behavior modification in prisons and psychiatric hospitals? Is behavior modification any different from the involuntary administration of tranquilizers or other drugs? Why or why not?

Suggestions for Further Reading

London, P. *Behavior Control.* Perennial Library, 1971.

Rathus, S. A., and J. S. Nevid. *Behavior Therapy.* Signet, 1978.

Tharp, R., and R. Wetzel. *Behavior Modification in the Natural Environment.* Academic, 1969.

Ullman, L. P., and L. Krasner. *Case Studies in Behavior Modification.* Holt, 1965.

Vogler, R. E., and W. R. Bartz. *The Better Way to Drink.* Simon and Schuster, 1982.

Watson, D., and R. Tharp. *Self-Directed Behavior: Self-Modification for Personal Adjustment,* 3rd ed. Brooks/Cole, 1981.

Williams, R. L., and J. D. Long. *Toward a Self-Managed Life Style.* Houghton Mifflin, 1979.

Wolpe, J., and A. A. Lazarus. *Behavior Therapy Techniques.* Pergamon, 1966.

Contents

Part VII

Self
and
Others

24

Human Sexuality

=== Chapter Preview ===

That Magic Word

Sex/seks/, n 1. one of the two divisions of organisms formed on the distinction of male and female.

"Sex" has many meanings: reproduction, gender, sexual identity, recreation, intimacy, sexual behavior, and much more. Of the various meanings, the simplest would seem to be the reference to gender. What, really, could be simpler? Males are males and females are females, right? Wrong. Even something as basic as gender is complicated and many-sided.

Gender   *The complexity of gender is illustrated by the attempt (1976) of Dr. Renée Richards to enter a women's tennis tournament. You may recall from news stories that Dr. Richards is a transsexual. Formerly she was Dr. Richard Raskin, a Newport Beach, California, ophthalmologist. As a man, Richard Raskin was a modestly successful tennis player. After a sex-change operation and hormone therapy to alter gender, Dr. Richards tried to launch a new tennis career as a woman. Understandably, other women players protested. Officials finally decided to use a genetic sex test to determine if Dr. Richards could compete. She, in turn, protested this test. Genetically she would still be considered male, but psychologically she is female—she has female genitals, and she functions socially as a female (Hyde, 1979). Is Dr. Richards, then, male or female?*

You might consider the case of Renée Richards an unfair example because the transsexual seeks artificial alteration of natural gender. For most people the various indicators of gender are in agreement. Nevertheless, it is not unusual to find occasional ambiguities among the various dimensions of a person's "sex." Contrary to common belief, gender is not a simple "either-or" classification. In the first portion of this chapter we will consider some basic dimensions of "maleness" and "femaleness." An essential question we will address is, "How does one become male or female?"

Sexual Behavior   *Each of us is by nature a sexual creature, an inescapable reality that springs from the basic biology of reproduction. With this reality in mind, latter portions of this chapter discuss sexual behavior, sexual arousal and response, sexual problems, and attitudes toward sexuality. These are topics you may feel you already know a lot about. Therefore, before reading further, you may find it interesting to see if you can correctly answer the Human Sexuality Quiz. Answers follow the quiz. The reasons for the answers can be found in this chapter.*

Human Sexuality Quiz *Indicate which of the statements are true and which are false.*

1. Women are generally incapable of multiple orgasm.

2. Impotence in males is usually psychologically caused.

3. Nocturnal emissions ("wet dreams") in males are an indication of sexual disorders.

4. Male sexual potency and female pleasure in intercourse are closely related to penis size.

5. Of the various sexual dysfunctions, premature ejaculation is one of the easiest to treat.

6. Although it is less apparent, women ejaculate during orgasm.

7. For women, masturbation typically involves stimulation of the clitoris.

8. Sterilization in both men and women usually abolishes the sex drive.

9. Women have two kinds of orgasm, vaginal and clitoral.

10. Changes in sexual behavior brought about by the "sexual revolution" have had more impact on women than on men.

11. Men are more aroused by explicit erotic stimuli (such as pornographic films) than are women.

12. Maximum sexual responsiveness generally occurs later for women than it does for men.

Answers: 1. F 2. T 3. F 4. F 5. T 6. T 7. T 8. F 9. F 10. T 11. F 12. T

Survey Questions What are the basic dimensions of gender? How does one's sense of maleness or femaleness develop? How are sex roles acquired? What are the most typical patterns in human sexual behavior? To what extent do males and females differ in sexual response? Have recent changes in attitudes affected sexual behavior? What are the most common sexual adjustment problems? How are they treated?

Resources

The Development of Sex Differences

It has been said that the one thing you will never forget about a person is that person's sex. Considering the number of activities, relationships, conflicts, pressures, and choices influenced by gender, it is no wonder that we pay close attention to it. Let's begin with a few basic questions: "What does it mean to be male or female?"; "What are the dimensions of gender?"; and, "How do gender and sex role differences develop?"

Male or Female? Traditionally, the basic physical differences between males and females have been divided into *primary* and *secondary* sexual characteristics.

Primary sexual characteristics refer to the sexual and reproductive organs themselves: the penis, testes, and scrotum in males; and the ovaries, uterus, and vagina in females (Figs. 24-1 and 24-2). **Secondary sexual characteristics** appear at puberty in response to hormonal signals from the pituitary gland. In females, secondary sexual characteristics involve development of the breasts, broadening of the hips, and other changes in body shape. Males develop facial and body hair, and the voice deepens. These changes signal readiness for reproduction. Reproductive maturity is especially evident in the female **menarche** (onset of menstruation). From menarche until **menopause** (the end of regular monthly fertility cycles), women can bear children.

Question: What causes the development of sex differences?

In general terms, both primary and secondary sexual characteristics are related to the action of sex hormones in the body. (*Hormones* are chemical substances secreted by glands of the endocrine system.) The **gonads** (or sex glands) affect sexual development and behavior by secreting **estrogens** (female hormones) and **androgens** (male hormones). The gonads in the male are the testes, and in the female the ovaries. The adrenal glands (located above the kidneys) also supply sex hormones in both males and females. At puberty, adrenal secretions add to the development of secondary sexual characteristics.

Interestingly, all individuals normally produce both estrogens and androgens. It is the proportion of these substances that influences sex differences. In fact, the development of male or female anatomy is largely due to the presence or absence—before birth—of **testosterone** (one of the androgens).

Question: Then is biological sex determined by the sex hormones?

Not entirely. As suggested by our discussion in the "Chapter Preview," gender cannot be reduced to a single dimension.

Dimensions of Gender   At the very least, any designation of gender must include: (1) **genetic sex** (XX or XY chromosomes); (2) **gonadal sex** (ovaries or testes); (3) **hormonal sex** (predominance of androgens or estrogens); (4) **genital sex** (clitoris and vagina in females, penis and scrotum in males); and (5) **gender identity** (one's personal sense of maleness or femaleness) (Money and Ehrhardt, 1972).

To see why gender must be defined along several dimensions, let's follow the sequence of events involved in becoming male or female.

Fig. 24-1 *Cutaway view of internal and external male reproductive structures.*

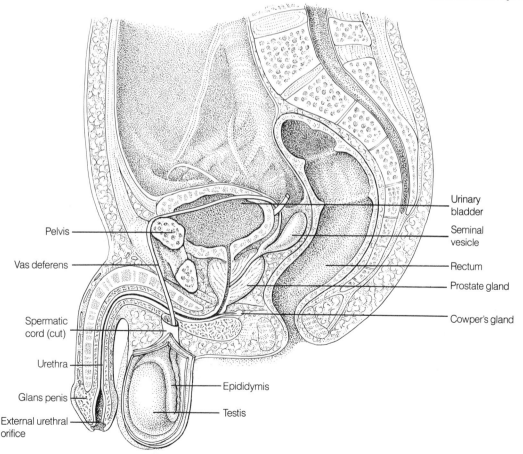

Pelvis

Vas deferens

Spermatic cord (cut)

Urethra

Glans penis

External urethral orifice

Urinary bladder

Seminal vesicle

Rectum

Prostate gland

Cowper's gland

Epididymis

Testis

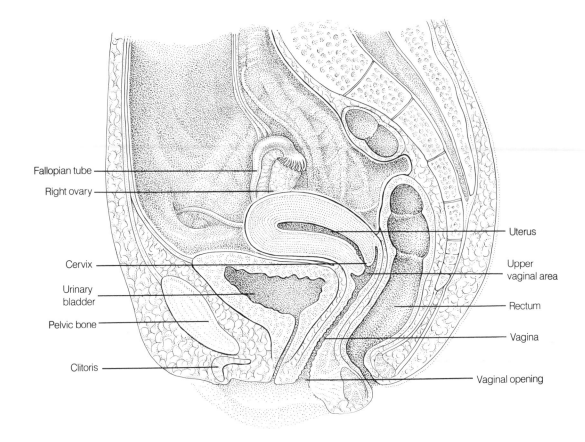

Fallopian tube

Right ovary

Cervix

Urinary
bladder

Pelvic bone

Clitoris

Uterus

Upper
vaginal area

Rectum

Vagina

Vaginal opening

Fig. 24-2 *Cutaway view of internal and external female reproductive structures.*

Gender Development   Becoming male or female starts simply enough. Genetic sex is determined at the instant of conception: two X chromosomes initiate development of a female; an X chromosome plus a Y chromosome produce a male. Genetic sex remains the same throughout life, but it alone does not determine gender. We must also consider hormonal effects before birth.

For the first six weeks of prenatal development, there is no difference between a genetically male and a genetically female embryo. However, if a Y chromosome is present, testes develop in the embryo and supply testosterone, stimulating growth of the penis and other male structures (Fig. 24-3). In the absence of testosterone, the embryo will develop female reproductive organs and genitals, regardless of genetic sex. It might be said, then, that nature's primary impulse is to make a female (Money, 1965).

Development of the embryo usually matches genetic sex, but this is not always the case. A genetic male will fail to develop male genitals if insufficient testosterone is formed during prenatal growth. Even if testosterone is present,

an inherited *androgen insensitivity* may exist, again resulting in female development.

Similarly, androgens must be either at low levels or absent for an XX embryo to develop as a female. Thus, for both genetic males and females, hormonal problems before birth may result in **hermaphroditism** (her-MAF-ro-dite-ism), which means defects in sexual development resulting in dual or ambiguous sexual anatomy. For instance, a developing female may be masculinized by exposure to *progestin* (a drug given to prevent miscarriage) or by a problem known as the *androgenital syndrome*. In the androgenital syndrome, estrogen is produced, but a genetic abnormality causes the adrenal glands to secrete excess amounts of androgen. In such cases a female child may be born with male genitals.

Question: Would such a child be reared as a male?

Some are. Usually, however, the condition is detected and corrected by surgery. If necessary, extra estrogen may be administered after birth.

Some researchers believe that, in addition to guiding physical development, the balance of sex hormones before birth may also "sex type" the brain (Diamond, 1977). Changes in the brain are then thought to alter later chances of developing masculine or feminine characteristics.

Question: Does that mean there is a physical basis for male and female traits?

In animals, clear connections exist between prenatal hormones and later emergence of male or female behaviors. However, with humans evidence suggests that most sex-linked behavior is learned (Weisstein, 1975). Be that as it may, some researchers feel that prenatal exposure to androgens or estrogens exerts a **biological biasing effect** on later psychosexual development in humans.

Question: Is there any evidence for this?

Consider women who have been exposed to androgens before birth. After birth, their hormone balance shifts to female and they are raised as girls. Does prenatal exposure to male hormones have any masculinizing effect on their psychological development? Medical psychologist John Money, who has studied many of these women, believes it does. During childhood the women were typically "tomboys" who preferred the company of boys to girls, engaged in more vigorous athletic activities than their peers, were more achievement-oriented, and were less interested in future marriage plans and romance (Money, 1977).

Question: Isn't it possible that the girls were influenced by their parents?

Yes. This explains why such research cannot be considered conclusive. The "tomboyish" qualities observed in prenatally masculinized girls may simply result from learning.

At the risk of getting entangled in the "battle of the sexes," let's consider one more idea. Some researchers feel that biology underlies male-female differences in thinking abilities. Women, they contend, are more often "left-brained," and men, "right-brained." The left brain, you may recall, is largely responsible for language and rote learning. The right brain is superior at spatial reasoning. Thus, some psychologists believe that biological differences explain why men (as a group) do better on spatial tasks and women are better at language skills. Others, however, strongly reject this theory. To them, such claims are based on shaky evidence and sexist thinking (Unger, 1979; Parlee, 1979; Fairweather, 1976). Whatever the outcome of this debate, one thing is certain: Males and females are more alike than they are different (Maccoby and Jacklin, 1974). There is no biological basis for the unequal treatment women have often faced at work, school, and elsewhere.

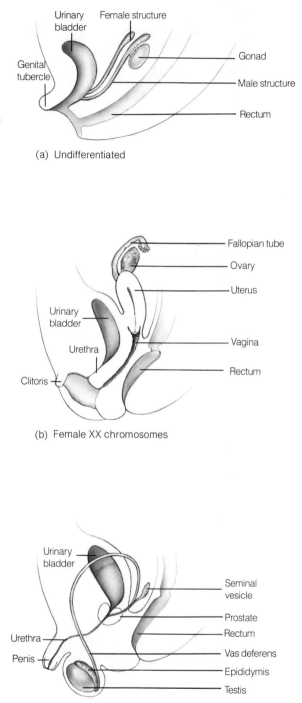

Fig. 24-3 *Prenatal development of the reproductive organs. Early development of ovaries or testes affects hormonal balance and alters sexual anatomy. (a) At first, the sex organs are the same in the human male and female. (b) When androgen is absent, female structures develop. (c) Male sex organs are produced when androgen is present.*

Gender Identity   One's personal, private sense of maleness or femaleness is referred to as *gender identity,* which can be distinguished from *sex roles.* Sex roles are observable traits, mannerisms, interests, and behaviors defined by one's culture as "male" or "female."

Gender identity appears to be a *learned* self-perception—a point emphasized by cases of hermaphroditism. If we compare two individuals having the same degree of hermaphroditism—one raised as a boy and the other as a girl—we will find that the person raised as a girl will act like and consider herself a girl, and the individual raised as a boy will act like and identify himself as a boy (Money, 1970).

Question: At what age is gender identity acquired?

Gender identity is essentially formed by three or four years of age (Money, 1977). Accordingly, children born with ambiguous gender have few problems as long as a final decision concerning their sex is made by the age of eighteen months. If the parents consistently treat the child as a boy or a girl, the child should develop a clear sense of gender. Delaying the decision can create a situation in which the child develops a gender identity at odds with his or her biological sex, or a confused sense of sexual identity.

Question: How is gender identity acquired?

Obviously, it begins with *labeling* ("It's a boy"; "It's a girl"). Thereafter it is influenced by **sex-role socialization;** that is, by the countless, subtle pressures exerted by parents, peers, and cultural institutions that urge boys to "act like boys" and girls to "act like girls." In the next section we will investigate sex roles and sex role socialization in more detail.

Sex Roles and Sex Role Socialization

In determining adult sexual behavior and sex-linked personality traits, *sex roles* are probably as important as chromosomal, genital, or hormonal sex. **Sex role** refers to the pattern of behavior encouraged and expected of individuals on the basis of gender. In our culture, boys are usually encouraged to be strong, fast, aggressive, dominant, achieving, and otherwise "male." Females have typically been expected to be sensitive, intuitive, passive, emotional, and "naturally" interested in household and child-rearing chores. The "naturalness" of such sex roles becomes questionable when they are compared with variations in different

cultures. For example, Ethel Albert (1963) has identified numerous cultures in which women do the heavy work because men are considered too weak for it. In the Soviet Union, approximately 75 percent of the medical doctors and a large proportion of the work force are women. Many more examples can be cited, but perhaps one of the most pertinent is anthropologist Margaret Mead's (1935) observations of the Tchambuli people of New Guinea.

Sex roles for the Tchambuli are a nearly perfect reversal of the American stereotypes. Tchambuli women handle the fishing and manufacturing and are expected to control the power and economic life of the community. Women also take the initiative in courting and sexual relations. Tchambuli men, on the other hand, are expected to be dependent, flirtatious, and concerned with their appearance. Art, games, and theatrics occupy most of the Tchambuli males' time, and males are particularly fond of adorning themselves with flowers and jewelry.

As the Tchambuli demonstrate, activities considered "appropriate" for males and females vary in different cultures. The arbitrary nature of sex roles is also apparent. A man is no less a man if he cooks, sews, or cares for children; a woman is no less a woman if she excels in sports, succeeds in business, or works as an auto mechanic. Still, adult personality and gender identity are closely tied to cultural definitions of "masculinity" and "femininity."

An interesting side effect of sex role socialization is the imprint left on activities having nothing to do with gender. For example, boys are superior to girls in math and visual-spatial skills. And, as previously mentioned, girls are superior to boys in language and verbal skills. There is also considerable evidence that boys are more aggressive than girls, that girls are more empathetic than boys, and so on (Maccoby and Jacklin, 1974; Block, 1979).

Question: How are such differences created?

Sex Role Socialization   Learning sex roles begins immediately after birth. Infant girls are held more gently and treated more tenderly than boys. Both parents play more roughly with their sons than with their daughters (who are presumed to be more "delicate"). Later, boys are allowed to roam over a wider area without special permission. They are also expected to run errands earlier than girls. Daughters are told that they are pretty and that "nice girls don't fight." Boys are told to be strong and that "boys don't cry." Sons are more often urged to control emotions than are daughters, and parents tolerate aggression toward other children more in boys than in girls. The toys purchased for boys and girls are strongly sex-typed:

dolls for girls; trucks and guns for boys. Even bicycles come in "boys'" and "girls'" models (Wilson *et al.,* 1977; Hoffman, 1977).

Overall, parents tend to encourage their sons to engage in **instrumental** (goal-directed) **behaviors,** to control their emotions, and to prepare for the world of work. Daughters, on the other hand, are encouraged in **expressive** (emotion-oriented) **behaviors** and, to a lesser degree, are socialized for the maternal role.

When told that they respond differently to boys and girls, parents often explain that it is because there are "natural" differences between the sexes (Wilson *et al.,* 1977). But what comes first, "natural differences" or the expectations that create them?

When quizzed about the traits they would like their children to possess, parents named for boys: hardworking, ambitious, intelligent, honest, responsible, independent, and strong-willed. For daughters they listed: kind, caring, attractive, well-mannered, having a good marriage, and being a good parent. Success and being respected in work was a far more common goal for sons than for daughters (Hoffman, 1977).

Question: Many people have become interested in the limitations imposed by stereotyped sex roles. Would such parental behavior apply to feminist mothers?

Sex roles are so pervasive that even feminists may be influenced by them. One study found that feminist women had little trouble treating their daughters in a nonstereotyped manner, but they seemed to want their sons to be "liberated but masculine." In other words, they had no anxieties when their daughters engaged in traditional "masculine" play, but they were upset if their sons played "dress up," preferred frilly clothes, imitated "female" mannerisms, or played with dolls (Van Gelder and Carmichael, 1975).

In our culture, "male" seems—for many—to be defined as "not female." That is, many parents have a vague fear of expressive and emotional behavior in male children, because to them it seems to imply effeminacy (Wilson *et al.,* 1977).

To summarize, sex role socialization in Western society prepares children for an adult world in which men are expected to be instrumental, conquering, controlling, and unemotional, and in which women are expected to be expressive, emotional, passive, and dependent. Thus, sex role socialization prepares us to be highly competent in some respects and handicapped in others. Of course, many people find traditional sex roles comfortable and desirable. It seems evident, however, that just about everyone will benefit when the more stereotyped and burdensome aspects of sex roles are laid to rest.

Learning Check

To check your progress, answer the following questions:

1. _____ sexual characteristics refer to the sexual and reproductive organs; _____ sexual characteristics refer to other bodily changes that take place at puberty.

2. All individuals normally produce both androgens and estrogens although the balance differs in males and females.   T or F?

3. The five basic dimensions of gender are: _____

   _____ .

4. In females, hermaphroditism may result from:

   a. an androgen insensitivity   *b.* excessive estrogen

   c. the androgenital syndrome   *d.* all of the above

5. For humans, the biological biasing effect of prenatal hormones can now be regarded as proven.   T or F?

6. One's private sense of maleness or femaleness is referred to as _____

7. Traditional sex role socialization encourages _____ behavior in males.

   a. instrumental   *b.* expressive   *c.* emotional   *d.* dependent

Answers: 1. Primary, secondary   2. T   3. genetic sex, gonadal sex, hormonal sex, genital sex, gender identity   4. c   5. F   6. gender identity   7. a

Sexual Behavior

Question: When does sexual behavior first appear in humans?

A capacity for sexual arousal is apparent at birth or soon after. Sexual researcher Alfred Kinsey verified instances of *orgasm* (sexual climax) in boys as young as five months old and girls as young as four months (Kinsey *et al.*, 1948, 1953). Kinsey also found that children aged two to five years spontaneously engage in manipulation and exhibition of their genitals.

Various forms of sexual behavior continue through childhood and adolescence, but as a child matures, cultural norms place greater restrictions on sexual activities. Still, 50 percent of males and 25 percent of females report having engaged in preadolescent sex play. In adulthood, norms continue to shape sexual activity along approved lines. In our culture, sex between children, incest (sex between close relatives), prostitution, homosexuality, and extramarital sex all tend to be discouraged.

As was the case with sex role behavior, it can be seen that such restrictions are somewhat arbitrary. A comparison of many cultures shows that less restriction is usually accompanied by more sexual activity of all kinds. If cultural restrictions are disregarded, it can be said that any sexual act engaged in by consenting adults is "normal" if it does not hurt anyone.

Sexual Arousal   Sexual arousal in humans is a complex phenomenon. It may, of course, be produced by direct stimulation of the body's **erogenous zones** (eh-ROJ-eh-nus: productive of pleasure or erotic desire). Human erogenous zones include the genitals, mouth, breasts, ears, anus, and to a lesser degree the surface of the body in general. It is clear, however, that more than physical contact is involved: Men undergoing urological exams and women receiving gynecological exams rarely experience any sexual arousal. Human sexual arousal obviously includes a large cognitive element. Indeed, arousal may be triggered by mere thoughts or images.

Question: Are men more easily sexually aroused than women?

On the basis of their famous questionnaire studies of sexuality, Alfred Kinsey and his colleagues (1948, 1953) concluded that men are more easily aroused than women. Men also reported more frequent arousal to visual stimuli of an explicit nature (such as pornographic movies) than did women. Women were more likely to be aroused by

movies, fiction, or poetry that emphasized romance more than sex.

Question: But haven't women's attitudes toward sex changed since 1953 when Kinsey did this study?

A later study (Mosher, 1973) suggests that women's attitudes may not be as liberalized as one might expect. Women are still more inclined to respond negatively to explicit pictures of sex than are men. Unmarried university females, who were shown fairly graphic films of intercourse, rated their *emotional reactions* more negatively than did a comparable group of male students.

Notice that the previous study tells us nothing about *physical arousal*. A more recent study made use of medical recording devices to measure sexual arousal in males and females as they were exposed to erotic tape recordings. It was found that the erotic material was equally arousing for both sexes and that adding romantic themes to the tapes did not further increase arousal for either sex (Heiman, 1977). This finding suggests that women are no less sexually aroused by erotic stimuli than are men.

If capacity for sexual arousal is measured by frequency of orgasm (brought about by masturbation or intercourse), the peak of male sexual activity is at age eighteen. Kinsey's studies (done in the early 1950s) placed the peak of female sexual activity at about thirty years of age. However, in recent years women have participated more fully in sexual activities, and at an earlier age (Hunt, 1974). The peak rate of female sexual activity still appears to occur later than that of males. However, male and female sexual behavior is becoming progressively more alike.

Question: What causes differences in sex drive?

Sex Drive   Attitudes toward sex, sexual experience, and recency of sexual release are all obviously important, but physical factors may also play a role. In males the strength of the sex drive is related to the amount of androgen secreted by the testes. When the supply of androgens dramatically increases at puberty, sex drive does likewise.

Surprisingly, androgen, which is the male hormone, may also affect the female sex drive. In addition to estrogen, a woman's body produces small amounts of androgen. Evidence from clinical studies suggests that this androgen may increase the sex drive in women just as it does in men. When women are given androgen for medical reasons, some report increased sexual desire (Carlson, 1981). Some women also report a relationship between arousal and various times during their monthly period. If such a relationship does exist, it is probably not too important since sexual activity in the human female may occur at any time during the monthly cycle (including during menstruation).

Question: Are nocturnal emissions ("wet dreams") an indication of an unusually strong sex drive? Do they ever indicate sexual disorders? Do both men and women experience nocturnal orgasms?

According to Kinsey's studies, about 85 percent of males and 35 percent of females have had sexual dreams that have resulted in orgasm. These experiences typically begin during adolescence and may continue to be a form of sexual outlet throughout adulthood. Kinsey found some reduction in the number of men experiencing nocturnal orgasms after marriage, but no change among women. Nocturnal orgasm may best be considered a completely normal (if relatively minor) form of sexual release.

Question: Does alcohol stimulate the sex drive?

In general, no. Alcohol is a *depressant*. As such, it may, in small doses, stimulate erotic desire by lowering inhibitions. This effect no doubt accounts for alcohol's reputation as an aid to seduction.[*] However, in larger doses alcohol suppresses orgasm in women and erection in men. Increasing levels of drunkenness cause a progressive decrease in sexual desire, arousal, pleasure, and performance (Malatesta *et al.,* 1979).

Question: Does removal of the testes or ovaries abolish the sex drive? Also, what happens to the sex drive in old age?

In lower animals, castration (surgical removal of the testicles) or removal of the ovaries usually completely abolishes sexual activity in *inexperienced* animals. Sexually experienced animals (particularly higher animals such as monkeys) may show little immediate change in sexual behavior. In humans, the *effects* of male and female castration vary. Initially, some individuals show a decline in sex drive, while others experience no change. However, after several years have passed, almost all subjects report a decrease in sex drive.

There is typically a natural decline in sex drive that accompanies aging and reduction in sex hormone output. However, sexual activity does not come to an unavoidable end. In some cases men and women in their nineties have continued active sex lives. The crucial factor for an extended sex life appears to be regularity and opportunity. Individuals who fairly regularly engage in intercourse after ages forty to fifty have little difficulty in later years (Masters and Johnson, 1970).

Masturbation   One of the most basic human sexual behaviors is masturbation. **Masturbation** may be defined as deliberate self-stimulation that causes sexual gratification or orgasm. Rhythmic self-stimulation has been observed in infants under one year of age. With increased maturity, masturbation in the male usually takes the form of stroking or other manipulation of the penis. Female masturbation most often centers on stimulation of the clitoris or the areas immediately surrounding it.

The following are some questions commonly asked about masturbation.

Question: In adulthood, do more men masturbate than women?

Yes. Of the women who took part in Kinsey's survey (1953), 60 percent reported that they had masturbated at some time. Of the males, 95 percent reported that they have masturbated (Kinsey *et al.,* 1948).[*]

A survey conducted in the 1970s by Morton Hunt (1974) showed almost identical rates: 94 percent for males and 63 percent for females. Hunt feels, however, that a liberalization of attitudes toward masturbation has taken place. This change is reflected in the fact that adolescents now begin masturbatory experience earlier.

Question: What purpose does masturbation serve?

Through masturbation people discover what is pleasing sexually, how to move their bodies, and what their natural rhythms and preferences are. Masturbation is therefore an important part of the psychosexual development of most adolescents. Among other things, it provides a biologically healthy substitute for sexual intercourse during a period when sexual activity is discouraged and young people are maturing emotionally (Wilson *et al.,* 1977).

Question: Is it immature for masturbation to continue after marriage?

If it is there are a large number of "immature" people around! Morton Hunt found that approximately 70 percent of married men and women masturbate at least occasionally.

Generally speaking, masturbation is a valid sexual activity at any age, and it may continue after marriage without posing any threat to a relationship. There is nothing "immature" or infantile about masturbation. As a matter of

---

[*]Humorist Ogden Nash once summarized this bit of folklore by saying "Candy is dandy, but liquor is quicker."

[*]Some cynics add ". . . and the other 5 percent lied!"

fact, masturbation may be related to sexual response in other activities. For example, 85 percent of a group of women who had masturbated before marriage reported achieving orgasm during the first year of marriage. By comparison, only about 65 percent of a group of women who did not masturbate achieved orgasm during the first year of marriage (Kinsey *et al.,* 1953).

Question: Is there any way in which masturbation can cause harm?

In the past, frightening stories about potential physical and mental ill effects abounded in the folklore surrounding masturbation. Thirty years ago, a child might be told that masturbation would cause insanity, acne, sterility, or other such nonsense. "Self-abuse," as it was often called, has enjoyed a long and unfortunate history of religious and medical condemnation.

The contemporary view is that masturbation is a normal and acceptable sexual outlet. No knowledgeable authority would deny this, and enlightened parents are well aware of it. Still, many a child has been punished or made to feel guilty for touching his or her genitals. This situation is unfortunate since there is no harm caused by masturbation itself. Typically, the only negative effects of masturbation are the fear, guilt, or anxiety that occur when an individual has learned negative attitudes toward it.

Learning Check

1. A capacity for sexual arousal is apparent at birth or soon after.   T or F?

2. Areas of the body that produce erotic pleasure are called _____ zones.

3. When exposed to erotic stimuli, men and women vary in their subjective perceptions of sexual arousal, but there appears to be no difference in their levels of physical arousal.   T or F?

4. There is some evidence to suggest that sexual activity and sex drives peak later for males than they do for females.   T or F?

5. It is possible (and normal) for sexual activity to continue to ages of 80 or 90.   T or F?

6. Males more often report having masturbated than do females.   T or F?

7. Masturbation can cause physical harm, according to the latest research reports.   T or F?

Answers: 1. T   2. erogenous   3. T   4. F   5. T   6. T   7. F

Human Sexual Response

Objective information about human sexual response has recently been expanded by the work of gynecologist William Masters and psychologist Virginia Johnson (1966, 1970). In a controversial series of experiments, interviews, and controlled observations, Masters and Johnson directly studied sexual intercourse and masturbation in nearly 700 males and females. The information they obtained has significantly improved our understanding of human sexuality.

According to Masters and Johnson, sexual response in both males and females can be divided into four phases: (1) **excitement;** (2) **plateau;** (3) **orgasm;** and (4) **resolution** (see Fig. 24-4 and Fig. 24-5).

Male Response   Sexual arousal in the male is signaled by erection of the penis during the excitement phase. There is also a significant change in heart rate, an increase in blood flow to the genitals, enlargement of the testicles, erection of the nipples, and numerous other bodily changes. If sexual stimulation ends, the excitement phase will gradually subside. Continued stimulation moves the individual into the plateau phase in which physical changes and subjective feelings of arousal become more intense. An end to stimulation during this phase will be resolved more slowly and may produce considerable frustration.

Further stimulation during the plateau phase brings about a reflex release of accumulated tension resulting in sexual climax, or orgasm. In the mature male, orgasm is accompanied by **ejaculation** (release of seminal fluid) and is followed by a short **refractory period** during which no amount of continued stimulation will produce a second orgasm. (Many men cannot even be stimulated to erection until the refractory phase has passed.) Only rarely is the male refractory period followed by a second orgasm. Orgasm is usually followed by *resolution,* a return to lower levels of sexual tension and arousal.

Female Response   Although the timing and intensity of the phases vary considerably from individual to individual,

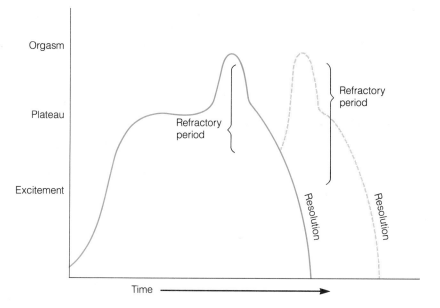

Fig. 24-4 *Male sexual response cycle. (Reproduced by permission from Frank A. Beach (ed.),* Sex and Behavior, *N.Y.: John Wiley & Sons, Inc., 1965.)*

the basic pattern of response for women is the same as that for men. During the excitement phase of arousal, a complex pattern of changes takes place to prepare the vagina for intercourse. These changes correspond to erection in the male. Also (as in the male) the nipples become erect, pulse rate changes, and the skin may become flushed. Most women go through a plateau stage comparable to that in the male, although a few follow a pattern of response that essentially skips the plateau (Fig. 24-5).

During orgasm, from 3 to 10 muscular contractions of the vagina, uterus, and related structures serve to discharge accumulated sexual tension. Contrary to the belief of some women, no form of ejaculation accompanies female orgasm. Vaginal lubrication produced during the earlier stages of arousal probably accounts for the misconception of those women who believe they have ejaculated. Both orgasm and resolution in the female usually last longer than they do in the male. After orgasm, many females return

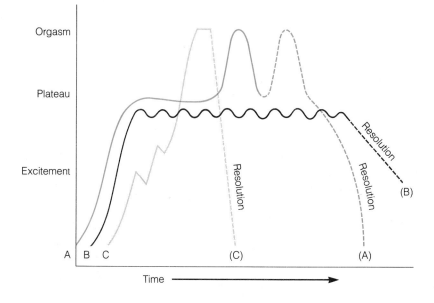

Fig. 24-5 *Female sexual response cycle. (Reproduced by permission from Frank A. Beach (ed.),* Sex and Behavior, *N.Y.: John Wiley & Sons, Inc., 1965.)*

to the plateau phase and may be stimulated to orgasm again before resolution.

Before the work of Masters and Johnson, there was considerable debate about whether a difference exists between female orgasm associated with the vagina and orgasm derived from stimulation of the clitoris. Sigmund Freud had contended in his writings that a clitoral orgasm was an "immature" form of female response. Since the clitoris is the female structure comparable to the penis, Freud felt that women whose orgasmic experiences centered on the clitoris had not fully accepted their femininity.

Masters and Johnson exploded the Freudian myth by showing that there is absolutely no difference in physical response no matter what form of stimulation produces orgasm. As a matter of fact, the vagina is quite lacking in nerve endings for touch. Most sensations during intercourse, therefore, come from stimulation of the clitoris and other external tissues. It now seems apparent that sensations from many sources are fused together into the total experience of orgasm and that for the female one of the most important sources of these sensations is the clitoris.

When women in one study were asked to express a preference for vaginal or clitoral stimulation, most said they would rather not choose, but if forced to choose, two-thirds preferred clitoral sensations (Fisher, 1973). Similarly, researcher Shere Hite has reported the results of an unscientific yet thought provoking survey of 3000 women. Among these women, only 26 percent reported regularly reaching orgasm during intercourse without separate massaging of the clitoris (Hite, 1976). Clearly, to downgrade the "clitoral orgasm" ignores the basic physiology of female sexual response.

Male and Female Responses Compared

The research of Masters and Johnson indicates that the similarities between male and female sexual responses outweigh the differences. However, the differences that do exist may have a significant effect on sexual adjustment. For example, it was found that women typically go through the sexual phases more slowly than do men. During lovemaking, from 10 to 20 minutes is often required for a woman to go from excitement to orgasm. Males may experience all four stages in as little as 4 minutes. These differences should be kept in mind by couples seeking sexual compatibility.

Question: Does that mean a couple should try to time lovemaking to promote simultaneous orgasm?

At one time the concept of simultaneous orgasm (both partners reaching sexual climax at the same time) was considered the ideal goal of lovemaking. More recently, it has been rejected as an artificial concern that may reduce satisfaction instead of enhance it. It is one thing to be aware of differences in male and female responses, and it is quite another to become preoccupied with such differences. To paraphrase one expert (Lowen, 1965):

> To govern the timing of orgasm by the response of either partner destroys the natural flow of feeling that alone guarantees mutual satisfaction. This point cannot be stressed too strongly. Inhibiting the buildup of the excitation for the sake of one partner limits the possibility of mutual satisfaction, whereas the opposite enhances that possibility.

It is more advisable to aim for the satisfaction of both partners through some combination of intercourse and manual stimulation than it is to self-consciously inhibit spontaneity.

Question: Does slower response mean that women are less sexual than men?

Definitely not. During masturbation, 70 percent of females reach orgasm in 4 minutes or less. This finding casts serious doubts on the idea that female response is actually slower. Slower female response during intercourse probably occurs because stimulation to the clitoris is less direct. It might be said that the male simply provides too little stimulation for more rapid female response, not that the female is in any way inferior.

Question: Does penis size affect female response?

Masters and Johnson found that the vagina adjusts to the size of the penis and that subjective feelings of pleasure and intensity of orgasm are not related to penis size. They also found that while individual differences exist in flaccid penis size, there tends to be much less variation in size during erection. This is why erection has been referred to as the "great equalizer." Contrary to popular belief, there is no relationship between penis size and male sexual potency.

Question: Men almost always reach orgasm during intercourse, but many women do not. Does this indicate that women are less sexually responsive?

Again, the evidence argues against any lack of female sexual responsiveness. It is true that about one woman in three does not experience orgasm during the first year of marriage. However, this does not imply lack of physical responsiveness since most of these women have reached orgasm through masturbation.

In another regard, the female is clearly more responsive. Only about 5 percent of males are capable of multiple orgasm (and then only after an unavoidable refractory period). Masters and Johnson's findings suggest that most women who regularly experience orgasm are capable of multiple orgasm. Whereas the male is almost always limited to a second orgasm at most, some women report having several orgasms in rapid succession.

Attitudes and Sexual Behavior

Question: Has there been a "sexual revolution"?

Some observers have argued that liberalized attitudes toward sexual expression and the simultaneous development of effective contraceptives have brought about a "revolution" in sexual behavior. Others believe that sexual behavior has remained essentially unchanged for the past 20 years. From this point of view, the "sexual revolution" has been mostly verbal—people are simply talking more about sex now than they were in the past (Miller and Siegal, 1972).

Attitudes An accurate description of changing sexual attitudes and behavior seems to lie somewhere between the two views just expressed. Attitudes have changed significantly in the direction of greater tolerance. Behavior has also changed but much more moderately.

Changing attitudes are graphically illustrated by the result of national polls concerning the acceptability of premarital intercourse. In a 1959 Roper Poll, 88 percent of those interviewed agreed that premarital sex is "wrong." In 1969 only 68 percent of the respondents to a Gallup Poll rejected premarital sex. By 1973 only 48 percent felt likewise. Similar changes have been observed in attitudes toward extramarital sex, homosexuality, legalized prostitution, sex education, no-fault divorce and a variety of related issues.

Question: Have changing attitudes been translated into behavior?

As we shall see in a moment, they have to some extent. Largely, however, there is greater *tolerance* for sexual behavior, especially that *engaged in by others.* For example, *Psychology Today* magazine found in a poll of its readers that 80 percent considered extramarital sex acceptable under some circumstances. But in practice, only 40 percent of married men and 36 percent of married women had actually had extramarital sexual experience (Athenasiou et al., 1970). Another survey of more conservative couples found that only 28 percent reported extramarital sexual experience (Johnson, 1970).

Question: How do such figures compare with earlier generations?

The figures cited do not allow a good comparison because they represent selected groups of people. A better indication is given by comparing Kinsey's findings from the early 1950s to Hunt's from the early 1970s. These researchers obtained very similar figures: About 50 percent of males and 20 percent of females have at least one extramarital contact during their lifetime (Kinsey, 1953; Hunt, 1974). Thus, changing attitudes have not greatly altered behavior in this area.

Question: What kinds of changes have taken place?

Behavior Premarital intercourse rates have traditionally been considered a good indication of overall sexual activity. Kinsey found that 71 percent of males and 33 percent of females had engaged in premarital intercourse by age twenty-five. Twenty years later Hunt obtained premarital intercourse rates of 97 percent for males and about 70 percent for females by age twenty-five. A more recent study found that 93 percent of women married after 1973 had engaged in premarital relations (Levin and Levin, 1975). A variety of additional studies support the idea that premarital intercourse rates have definitely increased.

A major element of the "sexual revolution" is earlier participation in sexual behavior by both sexes and a marked increase in sexual expression among females. Other studies show higher rates of intercourse in marriage for couples of all ages and a greater variety of sexual expression in marital relations (Hunt, 1974; Levin and Levin, 1975).

Question: Has a "sexual revolution" taken place, then?

A Sexual Revolution? In all, there certainly seems to be adequate evidence that sexual behavior has increased in the last 20 to 25 years. However, this trend does not seem to represent a move toward sexual promiscuity. Although it is true that sexual intercourse by unmarried couples is more freely accepted, most couples emphasize mutual commitment and a loving relationship as a requirement for sexual involvement. In this regard, premarital sex today often parallels the behavior of engaged couples 20 years ago (Simon and Gagnon, 1973).

Or, as one author has noted (Hyde, 1979), many young people today have just changed the sequence of events.

For their parents, the sequence was: fall in love, marry, begin a sexual relationship. For many, the sequence now is: fall in love, begin a sexual relationship, marry. Most women have only one premarital sexual partner whom they eventually marry. And men typically have about six premarital partners (Hyde, 1979). Overall, an image of rampant sexual behavior is not supported.

We have noted that extramarital intercourse rates seem to have changed little in the past 25 years. Thus, liberalized sexual attitudes seem not to have jeopardized the basic concept of marriage. Even premarital intercourse does not appear to represent an overthrow of traditional values and responsible behavior. The association between sexuality and love or affection remains strong for the majority of the population. Likewise, other changes in attitudes and behavior appear to reflect a greater acceptance of sexuality, rather than a true "revolution."

A more comfortable acceptance of a natural element of human relationships—sexuality—is the positive side of changing sexual attitudes and values. The negative side is represented by the plight of the individual who is not ready for, or interested in, greater sexual freedom. As one of the women who responded to Shere Hite's survey said:

> The Sexual Revolution tells me I am abnormal if I don't desire to make it with every Tom, Dick, or Jane that I see. I am only free to say yes. (Hite, 1976, cited by Hyde, 1979.)

Apparently, some individuals feel pressured into sexual behavior because it is "expected." However, pressures such as these probably come as much from the individual as from others. If a greater acceptance of human sexuality is to be constructive, it must be perceived as a general increase in personal freedom—as the right to say "no," as well as a right to choose when, where, how, and with whom one's sexuality will be expressed. As is true in other areas of human functioning, freedom must be combined with responsibility, commitment, and caring if it is to have meaning.

Learning Check

1. List the four phases of sexual response identified by Masters and Johnson: _____

2. Males typically experience _____ after ejaculation.
   a. an increased potential for orgasm   b. a short refractory period
   c. the excitement phase   d. muscular contractions of the uterus

3. The research of Masters and Johnson suggests that the similarities between male and female sexual responses outweigh the differences.   T or F?

4. During lovemaking, from 10 to 20 minutes is often required for a woman to go from excitement to orgasm, while the male may experience all four stages of sexual response in as little as 4 minutes.   T or F?

5. Simultaneous orgasm of the male and female should be the ultimate goal in lovemaking.   T or F?

6. Recent research shows there is considerable evidence that open discussion and more liberal views regarding sexual behavior are causing loose or promiscuous sexuality.   T or F?

7. Contrary to longstanding belief, it now appears that much female sexuality is focused on:
   a. the uterus   b. the urethra   c. the clitoris   d. the cervix

Answers: 1. excitement, plateau, orgasm, resolution   2. b   3. T   4. T   5. F   6. F   7. c

Resources Summary

● Physical differences between males and females can be divided into *primary sexual characteristics* (genital and reproductive organs) and *secondary sexual characteristics* (other bodily features). Reproductive maturity in females is signaled by the *menarche* (the onset of menstruation). The development of both primary and secondary sexual characteristics is influenced by *androgens* (male sex hormones) and *estrogens* (female sex hormones).
● Gender can be broken down into: *genetic sex, gonadal sex, hormonal sex, genital sex,* and *gender identity.*

● Gender development begins with genetic sex (XX or XY chromosomes). It is then influenced by prenatal hormonal influences. *Androgen insensitivity,* exposure to *progestin,* the *androgenital syndrome,* and similar problems can cause problems in the formation of the genitals. Resulting gender ambiguities are called *hermaphroditism.*

● Some researchers believe that prenatal hormones can exert a *biological biasing effect* on later psychosexual development. Most, however, place greater emphasis on learned *gender identity* and the effect of *sex roles* and *sex role socialization* on behavior. Sex role socialization in particular seems to account for most observed male/female differences.

● Sexual behavior is quite "natural," being apparent soon after birth and expressed in various ways throughout life. There appears to be little difference in sexual responsiveness between males and females.

● There is some evidence that the sex drive peaks at a later age for females than it does for males. Sex drive in both males and females may be related to bodily levels of androgen. *Nocturnal emissions* are a normal if minor form of sexual release. *Castration* may or may not influence sex drive in humans.

● *Masturbation* is a normal and completely acceptable behavior practiced by large portions of the population. For many, masturbation is an important part of sexual self-discovery. It is valid in marriage and normally has no harmful effects.

● Human sexual response can be divided into four phases: (1) *excitement;* (2) *plateau;* (3) *orgasm;* and (4) *resolution.* Both males and females may go through all four stages in 4 or 5 minutes. But during intercourse females typically take longer than this—from 10 to 20 minutes. There do not appear to be any differences between "vaginal orgasms" and "clitoral orgasms" in the female. Mutual orgasm has been abandoned by most sex counselors as the ideal in lovemaking.

● Attitudes toward sex have become more liberalized, but actual changes in sexual behavior have been rather gradual. Generally speaking, the greatest change has been in the number of people willing to talk openly about sex. The next greatest change has been a greater acceptance of female sexuality and narrowing of differences in male and female patterns of sexual behavior.

Sexual Problems

The origin of many sexual problems may be summarized in this way:

> Our competitive culture provides a constant pressure for performance. In the sexual area, this pressure concerns potency, responsiveness, and more and better orgasms as standards against which one must measure oneself. Sexual performance thus becomes a major source of personal stress. It is little wonder that counselors are finding their clients in anxiety and desperation about sexuality (Jacobs and Whiteley, 1975).

Question: What are the most common sexual problems? How are they treated?

Most people who seek sexual counseling have one or more of the following six problems (Kaplan, 1974):

A. For the male:

1. **Impotence:** inability to produce or maintain an erection.
2. **Premature ejaculation:** inability to delay or control orgasm.
3. **Retarded ejaculation:** inability to reach orgasm.

B. For the female:

1. **General sexual dysfunction:** lack of erotic response to sexual stimulation (frigidity).
2. **Orgasmic dysfunction:** inability to reach orgasm.
3. **Vaginismus:** spasm of muscles at the entrance of the vagina, preventing intercourse.

There was a time when couples and individuals endured such dysfunctions in silence. However, in recent years effective treatments have been found for each major problem. Let's briefly investigate the causes and treatments of the six barriers to sexual adjustment and fulfillment.

Male Impotence   Impotence, the inability to maintain an erection for sexual intercourse, may be an occasional or continuous problem. Males suffering from *primary impotence* have never been able to produce or maintain an erection. Those who have previously performed successfully, but then become impotent, are said to suffer from *secondary impotence.* In either case, when impotence becomes a repeated pattern it is usually very disturbing to the man and his sexual partner.

Question: How often must a man experience failure to be considered impotent?

Sex therapists Masters and Johnson (1970) feel that a problem exists when failure occurs on 25 percent or more of a man's lovemaking attempts. Repeated impotence should therefore be distinguished from an *occasional* inability to produce or maintain an erection. Fatigue, excessive consumption of alcohol, anger, and anxiety can all cause temporary impotence in healthy males.

It is important to recognize that occasional impotence is normal. In fact, overreaction to it may generate fears and doubts that will contribute to further impotence. It is particularly important at such times for the man's partner to avoid expressing anger, disappointment, or embarrassment. Patient reassurance helps prevent the establishment of a vicious cycle.

Question: What causes impotence?

For years, experts held that impotence is rarely caused by physical illness, disease, or damage. Now it is recognized that roughly 40 percent of cases are physically caused. However, even when a physical problem exists, it is almost always made worse by anxiety and other emotional factors. Also, notice that impotence is still more likely to be psychological than physical. According to Masters and Johnson (1970), primary impotence is often related to highly restrictive religious training, early sexual experience with a seductive mother, or other experiences leading to guilt, fear, and sexual inhibition. Also seen occasionally are indications of homosexual feelings the person has not come to terms with.

Secondary impotence may be related to anxiety about sex in general, guilt because of an extramarital affair, resentment or hostility toward a sexual partner, fear of ability to perform, and similar emotions and conflicts. Often the problem starts with repeated sexual failures caused by excessive consumption of alcohol or the presence of premature ejaculation. In either case, initial doubts soon become severe fears of failure—which then further inhibit sexual response.

Applications

Treatment for impotence usually begins with discussion of the fears and psychological blocks behind the problem. The man learns that he cannot consciously will an erection and that his disability is not a reflection on his manhood. To further free him of his fears (particularly that of failure), the man and his partner are usually assigned a series of exercises to perform. This technique, called **sensate focus,** directs attention to natural sensations of pleasure and builds communication skills.

In sensate focus, the couple is initially told to take turns stroking various parts of each other's bodies. They are instructed to carefully avoid any genital contact at first. Instead, they are to concentrate on giving pleasure and on signaling what is most gratifying to them. This takes the pressure to perform off the male and allows him to learn to give pleasure as a means of receiving it.

Over a period of days or weeks, the couple proceeds to more intense physical contact involving the breasts and genitals. As inhibitions are reduced and natural arousal begins to replace fear, the successful couple moves on to intercourse.

Premature Ejaculation   Masters and Johnson (1970) consider ejaculation to be premature if a man cannot delay sexual climax long enough to satisfy his partner in at least one-half of their lovemaking attempts. However, Helen Kaplan, of Cornell University Medical School, finds this definition unsatisfactory because of large variations in the time different women take to reach orgasm. Kaplan (1974) says that prematurity exists when ejaculation occurs reflexively, or when there is an inability to tolerate high levels of excitement at the plateau stage of arousal.

Question: Do many men have difficulties with premature ejaculation?

Premature ejaculation is a common problem in male sexual adjustment. Theories advanced to explain it have ranged from the idea that it may represent hostility toward the female partner (since it deprives her of satisfaction) to the suggestion that most early male sexual experiences tend to encourage rapid climax (such as those taking place in the back seat of a car and masturbation). Kaplan (1974) adds that excessive arousal and anxiety over performance are usually present, and that some men simply engage in techniques that maximize sensation and make rapid orgasm inevitable. Whatever the causes, premature ejaculation is a serious difficulty, especially in the context of long-term relationships.

Treatment for premature ejaculation is highly successful and relatively simple. The most common treatment procedure is the "squeeze technique" used by Masters and Johnson. The woman stimulates her partner manually until he signals that ejaculation is about to occur. She then firmly squeezes the tip of the penis to inhibit orgasm. When the man feels he has control, stimulation is repeated. Gradually the man acquires the ability to delay orgasm sufficiently for satisfactory intercourse. During treatment, skills are also developed between partners which provide for better communication, and a better understanding of the male's sexual response cues.

Retarded Ejaculation   Among males, an inability to reach orgasm was once considered a rare problem. But milder forms of this dysfunction have recently accounted for increasing numbers of clients seeking therapy (Kaplan, 1974). Background factors often observed are: strict religious training; fear of impregnating; lack of interest in the sexual partner; symbolic inability to give of oneself; unacknowledged homosexuality; or the recent occurrence of traumatic life events. Power and commitment struggles within relationships may be important added factors.

Treatment for retarded ejaculation consists of sensate focus, manual stimulation by the female (which is designed to orient the male to the female as a source of pleasure), and stimulation to the point of orgasm followed by immediate intromission and ejaculation. Work also focuses on resolving personal conflicts and marital difficulties underlying the problem.

Female General Sexual Dysfunction   This difficulty, commonly referred to as *frigidity,* is usually defined as a persistent inability to derive pleasure from sexual stimulation. Women who show general sexual dysfunction respond with little or no physical arousal to sexual stimulation. The problem thus appears to correspond directly to male impotence (Kaplan, 1974). As in male impotence, general female sexual dysfunction may be primary or secondary.

The causes of female general sexual dysfunction bear some similarity to those seen in male impotence. Frigidity can often be traced to frightening childhood experiences such as molestations (often by older relatives), incestuous

Applications

relations that produce lasting guilt, a harshly religious background in which sex is considered evil, or cold, unloving childhood relationships. Also common is the need to maintain control over emotions, deep-seated conflicts over being female, and extreme distrust of others, especially males (Masters and Johnson, 1970).

Question: How does treatment proceed?

Treatment at the Cornell clinic includes sensate focus, genital stimulation by the woman's partner, and "nondemanding" intercourse controlled by the woman. With success in these initial stages, full intercourse is gradually instituted. As sexual training proceeds, psychological conflicts and dynamics typically appear, and as they do, they are treated in separate counseling sessions (Kaplan, 1974).

Female Orgasmic Dysfunction The most prevalent sexual complaint among women is orgasmic dysfunction, an inability to reach orgasm during intercourse. Often it is clear in such cases that the woman is not completely unresponsive; rather, she is unresponsive in the context of a relationship—she may easily reach orgasm by masturbation, but not in intercourse.

Question: Then couldn't the woman's partner be at fault?

Sex therapists try to avoid finding fault or placing the blame. However, it is true that the male partner must be sexually adequate in terms of freedom from premature ejaculation, and that he must have a commitment to ensuring gratification of the woman. Some instances of "orgasmic dysfunction" can be traced to inadequate stimulation or faulty technique on the part of the male. Even when this is the case, sexual adjustment difficulties are best viewed as a problem the couple shares, not just as the "woman's problem" or the "man's problem."

If we focus only on the woman, the most common source of orgasmic difficulties is overcontrol of sexual response. Female orgasm requires a degree of "abandonment" to erotic feelings. It is therefore inhibited by ambivalence or hostility toward the relationship, by guilt, fears of expressing sexual needs, and by tendencies to control and intellectualize erotic feelings. The woman is unable to let go and enjoy the flow of pleasurable sensations.

In Helen Kaplan's treatment program, anorgasmic women are first trained to focus on their sexual responsiveness through masturbation or vigorous stimulation by

a partner. As the woman becomes consistently orgasmic in these circumstances, her responsiveness is gradually transferred to intercourse. Couples also typically learn alternative positions and techniques of lovemaking designed to increase clitoral stimulation. At the same time, communication between partners is stressed, especially with reference to the woman's sexual value system (expectations, motivations, preferences).

Vaginismus In the condition known as *vaginismus,* muscle spasms make intercourse impossible. Vaginismus is often accompanied by obvious fears of intercourse, and where fear is absent, high levels of anxiety are present. Vaginismus therefore appears to be a phobic response to intercourse. Predictably, causative factors include experiences of painful intercourse, rape and/or brutal and frightening sexual encounters, fear of men, misinformation about sex (belief that it is injurious), and fear of the specific male partner (Kaplan, 1974).

Treatment of vaginismus, carried out within the marital unit, is similar to what might be done for a nonsexual phobia. It includes extinction of conditioned muscle spasms by progressive relaxation of the vagina, desensitization of fears of intercourse, and masturbation or manual stimulation to associate pleasure with sexual approach by the male partner. Implosive therapy and hypnosis have also been used in some cases with success (Kaplan, 1974).

Summary Solving sexual problems can be difficult. The problems described are rarely solved without professional help (a possible exception is premature ejaculation). If a serious sexual difficulty is not resolved in a reasonable amount of time, the aid of an appropriately trained psychologist, physician, or counselor should be sought. The longer the problem is ignored, the more difficult it is to solve, but professional help is available.

Sexual Adjustment

Question: What can be done to improve sexual adjustment?

It is often useless to separate sexual adjustment from the broader context of a relationship. Conflict and unresolved anger in other areas frequently take their toll in sexual adjustment, and mutually satisfying relationships tend to carry over into sexual relations. Sex is not just a performance or a skill to be mastered like playing tennis. It is

Applications

a form of communication and an extension of a relationship. Couples with strong and open relationships can probably survive most sexual problems. A couple with a satisfactory sex life but a poor relationship rarely lasts.

Sex researchers and therapists Masters and Johnson (1970) have discussed how sexual partners can best approach disagreements about each other's sexual needs and wishes. When disagreements arise over issues such as frequency of intercourse, who initiates lovemaking, or what behavior is appropriate, Masters and Johnson believe that the rule should be "each partner must accept the other as the final authority on his or her own feelings."

Partners are urged to be *responsive* to each other's needs at an *emotional* level and to recognize that all sexual problems are *mutual*. Failures should always be shared without placing blame. Masters and Johnson feel that it is particularly important to avoid the "numbers game." That is, couples should avoid being influenced by statistics on the "average" frequency of intercourse, by stereotypes about sexual potency, and by the superhuman sexual exploits portrayed in movies and magazines.

Question: Are there any other guidelines for maintaining a healthy emotional relationship?

In a study that compared happily married couples with unhappily married couples, Navran (1967) found that in almost every regard the happily married couples showed superior *communication* skills. Many theorists agree that communication is facilitated by observing the following guidelines (after Bach and Wyden, 1969).

Avoid "Gunnysacking"   Persistent feelings, whether positive or negative, need to be expressed. Gunnysacking refers to saving up feelings and complaints. These are then "dumped" during an argument or used as ammunition in a fight. Gunnysacking is very destructive to a relationship.

Be Open about Feelings   Happy couples not only talk more, they convey more personal feelings and show greater sensitivity to their partners' feelings.

> . . . in a healthy relationship, each partner feels free to express his likes, dislikes, wants, wishes, feelings, impulses, and the other person feels free to react with like honesty to these. In such a relationship, there will be tears, laughter, sensuality, irritation, anger, fear, baby-like behavior, and so on (Jourard, 1963).

Don't Attack the Other Person's Character   Whenever possible, expressions of negative feelings should be given as statements of one's own feelings, not as statements of blame. It is far more constructive to say, "It makes me angry when you leave things around the house" than it is to say, "You're a slob!"

Don't Try to "Win" a Fight   Constructive fights are aimed at resolving shared differences, not at establishing who is right or wrong, superior or inferior.

Recognize that Anger is Appropriate   Constructive and destructive fights are not distinguished by whether or not anger is expressed. A fight is a fight, and anger is appropriate. As is the case with any other emotion in a relationship, anger should be expressed. However, constructive expression of anger requires that couples fight fair by sticking to the real issues and not "hitting below the belt."

Learning Check

1. Males suffering from primary impotence have never been able to produce or maintain an erection.   T or F?
2. According to the latest figures, most cases of impotence are caused by physical problems.   T or F?
3. Sensate focus is the most common treatment for premature ejaculation.   T or F?
4. Premature ejaculation is considered the rarest of the male sexual adjustment problems   T or F?
5. As it is for impotence, the sensate focus technique is a primary treatment mode for female general sexual dysfunction.   T or F?
6. Vaginismus appears to be a phobic response to sexual intercourse.   T or F?
7. Masters and Johnson urge sexual partners to recognize that all sexual problems are mutual, they are not just one partner's problem.   T or F?

Answers: 1. T 2. F 3. F 4. F 5. T 6. T 7. T

===== Exploration =====

Touching—Does It Always Have Sexual Implications?

The whole thing began because Sidney Jourard is a people-watcher. One day, sitting in a coffeehouse in San Juan, Puerto Rico, where he was a Peace Corps consultant, he wondered how many times the couple at the next table would touch each other in one hour. During the next two years, he did the same thing in London and Paris while studying at London's Tavistock Clinic. When he went to Gainesville, Florida, to teach in the psychology department of the University of Florida, he checked out an American couple for the one hour. The two people at the Gainesville table touched each other twice in one hour. In Paris the touch total for one hour was 110. In San Juan, 180. And in London? In London, the two people touched each other not at all.

From this information you must draw your own conclusions. The professor, back at Gainesville, Florida, teaching, being a therapist and practicing Hatha Yoga, refuses to. But his interest led him to make further surveys.

He issued booklets to his Gainesville students, 54 male and 84 female. Each booklet contained four diagrams of the body divided into 24 zones, the idea lifted (he says with a straight face) from a butcher's meatchart. He then asked his students to report, anonymously of course, which area of their bodies had been touched by mother, father, best-friend-same-sex, and best-friend-opposite-sex. Furthermore, each student was asked to show which zones of these four chums the student had touched. Time range: within the last year. The charts on this show the result (see Fig. 24-6).

Here Jourard *will* draw conclusions about "body accessibility."

"If you're out of love," says the professor, "you're out of touch."

"There isn't a great deal of body contact going on outside the strictly sexual context. It's almost as if all possible meanings of a touch are eliminated except the caress with the sexually arousing intent. . . . Most regions of a young adult's body remain untouched unless one has a close friend of the opposite sex, and that depends on the relationship going on between them."

One of our touch taboos, then, is that we equate touch with sexuality. Unless the relationship is sexual therefore, *mustn't touch.*

Jourard goes on to say that in family physical contact the daughters are "the favored ones." Her parents touch her more than they would if she were a boy. Right up into her twenties. Parents stop touching boys about the time they reach what used to be called The Age of Reason— when one can commit sin. Furthermore, a girl's mother is allowed, or allows herself (having herself once been a favored one), to give frequent touches to a girl's hair. One-half the parents get to touch her on the lips, and half manage a literal pat on the back. But—taboo, taboo— only 13 percent of the girls received a paternal pat on the bottom, and none of the girls touched or were touched by their fathers in the genital area. (Not quite the case with regard to male students and Mamma.)

Outside the Best-Friend-Opposite-Sex category very little touching goes on, but when it does happen between lovers, the professor says, "There is a virtual deluge of physical contact all over the body. . . . I suspect that the transformation from virginity or even preorgasmic existence to the experience of having a sexual climax is so radical as to be equivalent to a kind of rebirth."

For Jourard, in our maddeningly crowded world, touch may be our salvation. "I think that body contact has the function of confirming one's bodily being," he says. . . . Yet how can one learn to touch lovingly if one is not permitted to touch and be touched when young? To touch and be touched at times *other* than when making love?

"It's a blunted way of life," Jourard says. "People need physical contact to increase awareness and sensitivity to the body. But, instead, we use our relationship with others as a means to increase our status and social position. We are afraid to let others get close because then we are trapped. . . . The price we pay for this estrangement is loneliness" (H.E.F. Donohue, 1968).

Exploration

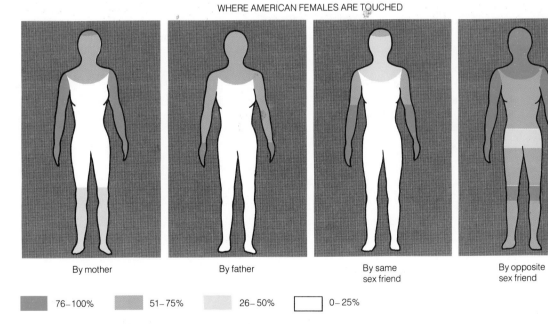

Fig. 24-6   *Results of Jourard's study of body accessibility. Figures shown are the percentages of young adults touched in each body area, during a one-year period, by the persons listed. Touching patterns are highly influenced by culture. People in other countries touch much more, or less than is customary in the United States. (After Jourard, 1966.)*

Questions for Discussion

1. Do your patterns of touching and being touched correspond to those found by Jourard?

2. In what ways does sexual contact differ from nonsexual touching? Do you feel as Jourard does that people should touch more? Why or why not?

3. Would you be jealous if your spouse or lover were touched (in a nonsexual way) by a person of the same sex? Opposite sex?

4. Do you think the "sexual revolution" will increase touching by encouraging openness or decrease it by defining more casual touching as potentially sexual?

5. Imagine that you were born as a member of the opposite sex. In what ways would your life to date have been different? (Consider relationships, self-image, clothing, recreation, interests, career plans, and so forth.)

6. In your opinion what are the advantages and disadvantages of distinctly different male/female sex roles?

7. Mentally change your male friends to females and your female friends to males. Can you separate the "human being" or "core person" from your friends' normal gender identities and sex roles? What effect does this have on your perception of others?

8. Female sexual behavior appears to be changing more rapidly than is male behavior. To what do you attribute the different rate of change?

9. Recall your own education about sexuality. In what ways and at what age would you recommend that children learn about sex?

Suggestions for Further Reading

Bach, G., and P. Wyden. *The Intimate Enemy.* Morrow, 1969.

Cherniak, D., and A. Feingold (eds.). *Birth Control Handbook.* Journal offset (Montreal), 1971.

Fisher, S. *Body Consciousness.* Prentice-Hall, 1973.

Hite, S. *The Hite Report.* Macmillan, 1976.

Hunt, M. *Sexual Behavior in the 1970s.* Playboy Press, 1974.

Hyde, J. S. *Understanding Human Sexuality.* McGraw-Hill, 1979.

Kaplan, H. S. *The New Sex Therapy.* Brunner/Mazel, 1974.

Masters, W., and V. Johnson. *Human Sexual Response.* Little, Brown, 1966.

———. *Human Sexual Inadequacy.* Little, Brown, 1970.

Tavris, C., and C. Offir. *The Longest War: Sex Differences in Perspective.* Harcourt Brace Jovanovich, 1977.

Wilson, S., B. Strong, L. M. Clarke, and T. Johns. *Human Sexuality.* West, 1977.

25

Social Psychology I

━━━━━━ Chapter Preview ━━━━━━

To live alone, one must be either an animal or a god.

Aristotle

No man is an Iland, intire of itselfe.

John Donne

The Social Animal

Your assignment, should you choose to accept it, is this: You have been given a written message and the name, address, and occupation of the person who should receive it. This "target person" lives over 1500 miles away in a city you have never visited. You are allowed to move the message through the mail, but you may send it only to a first-name acquaintance. That person is, in turn, instructed to mail the message only to one of his or her first-name acquaintances. The message is to be moved in this manner until it reaches the target person, whom the previous person must know by name.

Sound impossible? Social psychologist Stanley Milgram and his associates arranged for a number of people to try moving a message in this way. Amazingly, about one message in five made it. Even more amazing was the number of people needed to complete a chain between two strangers separated by half a continent. The average number of intermediary "links" required was about seven people! (Milgram, 1967; Korte and Milgram, 1970.)

Question: How is that possible?

Actually, the seven link average is not as astounding as it might seem. Each of us is enmeshed in a complex network of social relationships, and each person's network overlaps with many others. If you have around 1000 acquaintances (a typical number) and if each acquaintance also knows 1000 people, then you are only one step away from contact with around a million people (1000 × 1000). Actually, this number exaggerates the situation slightly since you share mutual acquaintances with many of your friends. Nevertheless, a chain of seven people creates millions of possible interconnecting acquaintances. Undeniably, humans are social animals.

Humans are born in the presence of at least one other person and are surrounded by people until death. Any doubt about our social nature can be dispelled by imagining what it would be like to be completely alone: Visualize the impact of putting this book down, walking outside, and finding the streets silent and deserted, forever. Imagine an initial period of confusion and panic followed by the lasting desolation of complete loneliness. Contrast this imagined solitude with the real-world clamor of groups, crowds, clubs, clans, families, gangs, audiences, organizations, communities, tribes, societies, and nations.

* **Social psychology** is the study of how people behave in the presence (real or implied) of others. Some of the groups just mentioned are formal and organized; others are unorganized. All influence the behavior of their members. The fascinating interplay of individual and group behavior has been the target of an immense amount of psychological study; too much, in fact, for us to cover in any detail. Therefore, this chapter and the next are "social psychology samplers." We hope you will agree that the topics selected are interesting and thought provoking.*

Survey Questions   How does group membership affect individual behavior? What are the unspoken rules governing the use of personal space? Why do people affiliate? What factors influence interpersonal attraction and romantic attraction? What have social psychologists learned about conformity, social power, obedience, and passive compliance? How does self-assertion differ from aggression? What is attribution theory?

Resources

Humans in a Social Context— People, People, Everywhere

We are born into an organized society. Established values, expectations, and behavior patterns are present when we arrive. So too is **culture,** an ongoing pattern of life that is passed from one generation to the next. Some readily visible representations of culture are language, marriage customs, concepts of ownership, and sex roles.

Groups   On a day-to-day level, the groups to which a person belongs form his or her most immediate social environment. Each person is a member of many groups: the family, teams, church groups, work groups, and so on. In each group the individual occupies a *position* in the structure of the group. **Roles** are different expected behavior patterns displayed in connection with a particular social position. There are expectations associated with playing each of the following roles: mother, teacher, employer, student. Some roles are **ascribed,** meaning they are not under the individual's control: male or female, adolescent, inmate. **Achieved** roles are those attained voluntarily, or by special effort: wife, teacher, scientist, bandleader.

Question: What effect does role playing have on behavior?

Roles allow us to anticipate the behavior of others. When a person is acting as a physician, mother, clerk, or police officer, certain behaviors are expected. In general, roles are quite useful because they streamline many of our daily interactions with others. However, roles have a negative side too. It is not unusual for a person to occupy two or more conflicting roles. Getting caught in a **role conflict** can be quite uncomfortable or frustrating. Consider, for example, the traffic court judge whose daughter is brought before him with a violation, or the teacher who must flunk a close friend's son.

  The impact of roles is dramatically illustrated by an experiment conducted by psychologist Philip Zimbardo and his students at Stanford University (described briefly in Chapter 2). In this experiment normal, healthy, male college students were paid $15 a day to serve as "inmates" and "guards" in a simulated prison. The men selected to be prisoners were "arrested" at their homes, and taken to the police station where they were searched, fingerprinted, and booked. Guards were given khaki uniforms to wear, billy clubs and whistles to maintain order, and sunglasses to conceal their emotions (Zimbardo *et al.,* 1973).

  On the second day of their "imprisonment," the prisoners staged a number of disturbances, but their rebellion was quickly suppressed by the guards. Over the next few days the guards behaved with increasing brutality and the prisoners became more traumatized, passive, and dehumanized. Four prisoners had to be released in the first four days because of reactions such as hysterical crying, confusion, and severe depression. Each day the guards tormented the prisoners with more frequent commands, insults, and demeaning tasks. After six days the experiment was halted.

What had happened? Zimbardo's interpretation is that the roles—prisoner and guard—assigned to participants were so powerful that in just a matter of days the experiment had become "reality" for those involved. Afterward, many of the guards found it hard to believe their own behavior. As one recalls, "I was surprised at myself . . . I made them call each other names and clean toilets out with their bare hands. I practically considered the prisoners cattle . . ." (Zimbardo, 1973). It would seem that the source of many destructive human relationships can be found in destructive roles.

Position in a group also determines one's **status.** In most groups higher status is associated with special privileges and respect. Status can operate very subtly to influence behavior in many situations. For example, in one interesting experiment an old Rambler and a new Chrysler Imperial were repeatedly driven through an intersection in downtown Palo Alto, California. The cars were maneuvered so that they were at the front of the line of waiting cars at the traffic signal. When the signal turned green, the test cars failed to move. Eighty-four percent of the blocked cars honked at the Rambler, but only 50 percent honked at the Imperial (Doob and Gross, 1968).

In another experiment, researchers left dimes in phone booths. When subjects entered the booths they were approached by a researcher who said, "Excuse me, I think I left a dime in this phone booth a few minutes ago. Did you find it?" Seventy-seven percent of the people returned the dime when the researcher was well-dressed, but only 38 percent returned it to poorly dressed researchers (Bickman, 1974). Perhaps the better treatment given "higher status" individuals in this and the previous example explains some of the American preoccupation with status symbols.

Question: Are there other dimensions of group membership?

Groups are made up of people who are in some way interrelated. Two very important dimensions of any group are its *structure* and *cohesiveness.* **Group structure** is the organization of roles, communication pathways, and power in the group. Organized groups such as the Army or an athletic team have a high degree of structure. Informal friendship

groups may or may not be highly structured. **Group cohesiveness** is basically an indication of the degree of attraction among group members. Cohesiveness is the basis for much of the power that groups exert over their members.

A very important aspect of the functioning of any group is its norms. **Norms** are standards of conduct that prescribe appropriate behavior in a given situation. If you have the slightest doubt about the existence of powerful group norms, Stanley Milgram suggests this test: Board a crowded bus, find a seat, and begin singing loudly in your fullest voice. Milgram's guess is that not more than one person in a hundred could actually carry out these instructions.

Question: How are norms formed?

One early investigation of pressures toward uniformity and the formation of group norms made use of a striking illusion called the **autokinetic effect.** In a completely darkened room, a stationary pinpoint of light will appear to drift or move about (it is therefore "autokinetic" or "self-moving"). Muzafer Sherif (1935) found that estimates of how far the light moves vary widely from person to person. However, when two or more people give estimates at the same time, their judgments rapidly converge. There is a similar convergence of attitudes, beliefs, and behavior among members of most groups. A good example of such convergence can be found in norms governing the use of *personal space.* Since personal space is an intriguing topic in its own right, let's take a moment to examine it.

Personal Space—Invisible Boundaries

An interesting aspect of social behavior is the effort people expend to regulate the space around their bodies. Each person has an invisible "spatial envelope" that defines his or her **personal space** and extends "I" or "me" boundaries past the skin.

Question: What effect does personal space have on behavior?

Maintaining and regulating personal space directly affects many social interactions. There are unspoken rules covering the interpersonal distance considered appropriate for formal business, casual conversation, waiting in line with strangers, and other situations. The study of rules for the personal use of space is called **proxemics** (Hall, 1974) (Fig. 25-1).

The existence of personal space and the nature of proxemics can be demonstrated by "invading" the space of

Fig. 25-1   *The use of space in public places is governed by unspoken norms, or "rules" about what is appropriate.*

another person. The next time you are talking with an acquaintance, move closer and watch the reaction. Most people show immediate signs of discomfort and step back to reestablish their original distance. Those who hold their ground turn to the side, look away, or position an arm in front of themselves as a kind of psychological barrier to intrusion. If you persistently edge toward your subjects, you should find it easy to move them several feet from their original positions.

Question: Would this technique work with a good friend?

Possibly not. Conventions governing comfortable or acceptable distances vary according to relationships as well as activities. Hall (1966) identifies four basic zones. (Listed distances apply to North American culture.)

1. Intimate Distance. For most American adults, the most private personal space extends about 18 inches out from the skin. Entry within this space is reserved for special people or circumstances. Lovemaking, comforting others, cuddling children, and massage all take place within this space. So does wrestling!

2. Personal Distance. This is the distance maintained in comfortable interaction with friends. It extends from about 1½ to 4 feet from the body. Personal distance basically keeps people within "arm's reach" of each other.

3. Social Distance. Impersonal business and casual social gatherings take place in a range of about 4 to 12 feet. This distance eliminates most possibilities of touching, and formalizes conversation by requiring greater voice projection. "Important people" in many offices use the width of their imposing desks to maintain social distance while conducting business.

4. Public Distance. When people are separated by more than 12 feet, interactions take on a decidedly formal quality. People look "flat" and the voice must be raised. Formal speeches, lectures, business meetings, and the like, are conducted at public distance.

Spatial Behavior   Violations of personal space at each distance tend to cause the "invaded" person to move away or become defensive (Dabbs, 1972). In one study, female experimental assistants sat down a foot or less from other women studying in a library. In most cases other seats were available. As the "invader" busied herself, the other student typically stopped, put an arm up, and in most cases left a few minutes later (Sommer, 1969). When it is impossible to maintain distance (for example, in a crowded elevator or a dentist's chair) privacy is most often maintained by avoiding eye contact.

The subtlety of spatial behavior is shown by a study conducted by Eric S. Knowles and his associates at the University of Wisconsin. In this study, one, two, or three individuals were seated on a bench against the wall of a long corridor. As subjects walked down the hallway, they tended to detour around the area of the bench. Interestingly, subjects made a larger detour for two bench-sitters than for one, and they gave the widest berth to three seated people. Apparently the bench-sitters' spatial bubbles *combined* to create a larger "bulge" into the hallway (Insel and Lindgren, 1977).

Territoriality   Personal space also extends to areas that become our "territory." For example, in the library, readers protect their territory by marking it with coats, handbags, books, or other personal belongings (Sommer, 1969). "Saving a place" at a theater or library also demonstrates the tendency to identify a space as "ours."

Respect for the temporary ownership of space is widespread. It is not unusual for a person to "take over" an entire table or study room by looking sufficiently annoyed when others intrude. Your own personal territory may include your room, specific seats in many of your classes, or a particular table in the cafeteria or library that "belongs" to you and your friends. Researchers have found that the more attached you are to an area, the more likely you are to announce your "ownership" with obvious **territorial markers,** such as decorations, plants, photographs, and posters. (Hansen and Altman, 1976). College dorms and business offices are prime places to observe this type of territorial marking.

Question: What purpose does territoriality serve?

The development of territorial agreements is readily understandable. Whenever two or more individuals share the same living or working quarters, some agreement is necessary concerning use of certain locations. Without the "traffic management" afforded by territoriality there would be unnecessary friction, confusion, and resentment (Insel and Lindgren, 1977). Even in communes stressing ideals of equality and sharing, it is common for members to have a sense of ownership about a room, a bed, a table, or other locations (Vander Zanden, 1977).

Learning Check

1. "Male," "female," and "adolescent" are examples of _____ roles.
2. Status refers to a set of expected behaviors associated with a social position.   T or F?
3. Research has shown that the number of first-name acquaintances needed to interconnect two widely separated strangers averages about seven people.   T or F?
4. The Stanford prison experiment demonstrated the powerful influence of the autokinetic effect on behavior.   T or F?
5. Social psychology is the study of how people behave _____.
6. If two people position themselves 5 feet apart while conversing, they are separated by a gap referred to as _____ distance.
7. Objects used to indicate the boundaries of one's personal work or living space in a particular setting are called _____.

Answers: 1. ascribed 2. F 3. F 4. F 5. in the presence of others 6. social 7. territorial markers

The Need for Affiliation—Come Together

Question: Why do people choose to associate with others?

We have already observed that the **need to affiliate** appears to be a basic human characteristic. Why? Probably because affiliation helps meet needs for approval, support, friendship, and information. We also seek company to alleviate fear or anxiety. An experiment in which college women were threatened with painful electric shock serves as an illustration.

Zilstein's Shock Shop

A man introduced as Dr. Gregor Zilstein ominously explained to arriving subjects, "We would like to give each of you a series of electric shocks. Now I feel I must be completely honest with you and tell you these shocks will hurt, they will be painful." In the room was a frightening electrical device that seemed to verify Zilstein's intentions. While waiting to be shocked, each subject was given a choice of waiting alone or with other subjects. Women frightened in this way more often chose to wait with others than did subjects told that the shock would be a mild tickle or tingle (Schachter, 1959).

Apparently, the frightened women found it comforting or reassuring to be with others. The tempting conclusion is: "Misery loves company." But this is not completely accurate. In a later experiment, women expecting to be shocked were given the option of waiting with other shock subjects, with women waiting to see their advisors, or alone. Most subjects chose to wait with other future "victims." In short, misery seems to love miserable company! In general we tend to seek the company of people in circumstances similar to our own.

Question: Is there a reason for this?

Yes. Other people provide information for evaluating one's own reactions. When a situation is threatening or unfamiliar, or when a person is in doubt, *social comparisons* serve as a guide for behavior.

Social Comparison Theory   In some cases objective standards for self-evaluation exist. If I want to know how tall I am, I simply get out a yardstick. But how do I know if I am a good athlete, guitarist, worker, parent, or friend? How do I know if my views on politics, religion, or the latest rock album are correct? The only yardstick available for such evaluations is provided by comparing myself to others. Eminent social psychologist Leon Festinger (1954) was among the first to point out that group membership fills needs for **social comparison.** When there are no objective standards, we must turn to others to evaluate our actions, feelings, opinions, or abilities. When students congregate to "compare notes" after a classroom exam, they satisfy needs for social comparison.

Festinger emphasizes that social comparisons are not made randomly, or on some ultimate scale. To illustrate, let's say we ask a student if she is a good tennis player. If she were to compare herself to a professional, the answer would be "no." But this tells little about her relative ability. In her group of tennis partners, she might be considered an excellent player. Useful personal evaluation requires comparison with people of similar backgrounds, abilities, and circumstances. On a fair scale of comparison, our tennis player knows she is good and takes pride in her skills.

In the same way, thinking of yourself as successful, talented, responsible, or fairly paid, depends entirely on whom you compare yourself to. Social comparison theory holds that a desire for self-evaluation determines what groups are joined and provides a general motive for associating with others.

Question: Don't people also affiliate out of attraction for one another?

They do, of course. The next section tells why.

Interpersonal Attraction— Social Magnetism?

"Birds of a feather flock together." "Familiarity breeds contempt." "Opposites attract." "Absence makes the heart grow fonder." Interest in what attracts people to one another has spawned an extensive folklore about what factors are important. This is understandable, since **interpersonal attraction** is the basis for most voluntary social relationships.

Question: What attracts people to each other?

Social psychologist Elliot Aronson (1969) lists several factors that determine with whom you are likely to become friends.

1. Physical Proximity. It may be difficult to admit, but our friends (or even lovers) are selected more on the basis of opportunity than we might like to believe. Nearness plays a powerful role in determining friendships. In a study of friendship patterns in a campus married-student housing complex, it was found that the closer people lived to each other, the more likely they were to be friends (Festinger *et al.,* 1950). People in love like to think they have found the "one and only" person in the universe for them. In reality they have probably found the one and only person in a five mile radius!

A main reason for proximity's effect is that it increases the *frequency of contact* between people. A variety of laboratory studies show that we are generally attracted to people with whom we have had frequent contact (Saegert *et al.,* 1973). In other words, there does seem to be a "boy-next-door" or a "girl-next-door" effect in romantic attraction, and a "folks-next-door" effect in friendship (Fig. 25-2).

2. Physical Attractiveness. As might be expected, beautiful people are consistently rated more attractive than those of average appearance. This is another example of the "halo effect" (see Chapter 18) in which it is assumed that attractive people are also intelligent, witty, honest, and so on. Being physically attractive seems to be an advantage for both males and females, but in our culture beauty has more influence on a woman's fate than on a man's. For instance, a study of dating patterns of college dormitory residents found a strong relationship between physical beauty in women and their frequency of dating. For men, looks were unrelated to dating frequency (Krebs and Adinolfi, 1975).

In later adulthood there is a tendency for beautiful women to be paired with wealthy, successful men (Elder, 1969). In other words, a double standard seems to prevail in which women are judged by physical beauty and men by how successful they are. If you view this state of affairs as rather shallow and sexist, it may be reassuring to know that beauty is a factor mainly in initial acquaintance. Later, more substantial personal qualities become important (Berscheid and Walster, 1974).

3. Competence. We are also attracted to those who are talented or competent, but there is an interesting twist to this.

Clever but Clumsy

In an experiment on attraction, college students listened to one of four tapes of a supposed candidate for the "College Quiz Bowl." On two of the tapes the person was represented as highly intelligent; on the other two he was depicted as average in ability. One of the "intelligent" and one of the "average" tapes included an incident in which the candidate clumsily spilled coffee on himself. Those listening to the tapes rated as *most* attractive the superior candidate who blundered, and as *least* attractive the student who was average and clumsy. The superior but clumsy student was more attractive than the student who was only superior (Aronson, 1969).

The upshot of this experiment seems to be that we like people who are competent, but human.

4. Similarity. Take a moment to mentally list as many of your friends as you can. What do they have in common (other than the joys of knowing you)? It is highly likely that most are close to you in age, and of the same sex and race as you are. There will be exceptions, of course. However, similarity on these three dimensions is the general rule for friendships in American culture (Huston and Levinger, 1978).

One of the most consistent findings about interpersonal attraction is that people with similar backgrounds, interests, attitudes, or beliefs are attracted to each other (Byrne, 1971). This is probably at least partially due to the reinforcing value of seeing our beliefs and attitudes affirmed by others. It shows we are "right" and reveals that they are clever people as well!

Question: How do people who are becoming friends get to know one another?

Self-Disclosure Getting to know others requires a willingness to talk about more than just the weather, sports, or subatomic nuclear physics. At some point you must begin to share private thoughts and feelings, and reveal more of your "true self." Engaging in such **self-disclosure**

Fig. 25-2 *What attracts people to each other? Proximity and frequency of contact have a surprisingly large impact.*

is a major step toward friendship. Experimental work confirms that we more often reveal ourselves to persons we like than to those we find less attractive (Chaiken and Derlega, 1974).

Disclosing oneself to others requires a degree of trust. Many people play it safe, or "close to the vest," with people they do not know well. Indeed, there are definite norms about when self-disclosure is acceptable and when it is not. Moderate self-disclosure leads to **reciprocity** (a return in kind) (Huston and Levinger, 1978). **Overdisclosure,** however, gives rise to suspicion and reduced attraction.

To illustrate, let's say you're standing in line at a market. The person in front of you starts a conversation and in a moment or two says:

> . . . This is my last stop. I'm looking forward to getting home and calling it a day. There's a good movie on TV tonight.

How would you respond? Would your reaction be different if the person said:

> . . . Lately I've been thinking about my relationships with other people. I've made several good friends during the past couple of years, but I still feel lonely a lot of the time.

What if the person said:

> . . . Lately I've been thinking about how I really feel about myself. I think that I'm pretty well adjusted, but I occasionally have some questions about my sexual adequacy.

The first statement is "safe," or low in intimacy. It reveals little about the person. It's likely that your reply would also be safe and impersonal. The second statement shows a moderate amount of self-disclosure. When subjects in an

experiment received this statement, they responded by saying something personal about themselves, such as, "I'm a grandmother but I too have been thinking of myself—where I've been—what to do—I too question my identity." In contrast, subjects responded impersonally to the last statement as they had to the first (see Fig. 25-3) (Rubin, 1975). Thus, when self-disclosure proceeds at a moderate pace, it is accompanied by growing trust and intimacy. When it is too rapid, or inappropriate, we are likely to "back off" and wonder about the person's motives.

Social Exchange Theory   Quite often, social behavior can be understood in terms of maximizing rewards while minimizing "costs" in any **social exchange.** When a relationship ceases to be attractive, people often say, "I'm not getting anything out of it any more." Actually they probably are, but their costs—in terms of effort, aggravation, or lowered self-esteem—have exceeded their rewards. According to social exchange theory, we unconsciously weigh such rewards and costs. For a relationship to last, it must be *profitable* (its rewards must exceed its costs) for both parties.

The idea that people seek comfortable or mutually beneficial relationships does not completely explain some aspects of interpersonal attraction. To complete the picture, we must also consider Aronson's gain-loss theory.

Question: I'll bite! What's gain-loss theory?

Gain-Loss Theory   This approach holds that *gains* in liking or approval are more rewarding than constant liking. The idea has been tested in this way:

Does She Like Me?

After each of seven staged "conversations," female college students were allowed to overhear another "student" (actually an actress) give her "honest opinion" of the real subject. Over the course of the experiment, some subjects heard the other "student" say consistently flattering things about them (*positive* condition). Others heard repeatedly unfavorable comments about themselves (*negative* condition). A third group heard negative evaluations at first, but these became positive by the last session (*gain* condition). After the seven conversations, subjects were interviewed to determine their liking for the other "student" (Aronson and Linder, 1965).

Question: Did the conditions have any effect on liking?

Understandably, the negative condition produced the least liking. Aronson's theory predicts that the gain condition should cause more liking than the positive condition. A look at Fig. 25-4 shows this was the case. "Winning" acceptance

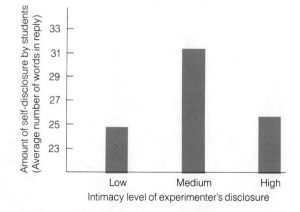

Fig. 25-3 *Self-disclosure in response to messages at three levels of intimacy. (Adapted from Rubin, 1973.)*

from another person has a positive effect on attraction. Perhaps we are attracted to those who slowly learn to like us because it shows they are discriminating in their choice of friends!

Aronson also speculates that a *loss* of liking is more punishing than consistent dislike. That is, a falling-out with a friend is more painful than the constant dislike of an enemy. Unfortunately, experimenters have been unable to consistently demonstrate loss effects (Huston and Levinger, 1978). Nevertheless, Aronson (1980) feels that losses are an important part of relationships. Gain-loss theory, he says, explains why "You always hurt the one you love." According to Aronson, a compliment from a stranger is more flattering (because it is a gain) than one from a friend or spouse (because it is expected). But the reverse is also true: An insult from a stranger represents little or no loss, but a slight by a friend or spouse is costly. It is therefore difficult to compliment, but easy to hurt, the one you love.

Question: You mention love. How does it differ from liking?

Romantic Love   One well-known newspaper columnist likes to ask of teenage romance, "Is it love or sex?" For those involved this may be an academic question, since mutual attraction is strong either way. Just the same, it may be more accurate on occasion to say, "I'm in lust," than it is to say, "I'm in love." All of which raises the question, What is love? Can it be measured? Is love distinct from intense liking? An innovative research program carried out by Zick Rubin (1973) provides some answers.

In order to study love, Rubin chose to think of it as an attitude held by one person toward another. This allowed him to develop "liking" and "love" scales (see Box 25-1) for the measurement of each "attitude." Next, he contacted dating couples through a poster that read in part:

ONLY DATING COUPLES CAN DO IT!
GAIN INSIGHT INTO YOUR RELATIONSHIP
BY PARTICIPATING IN A UNIQUE
SOCIAL-PSYCHOLOGICAL STUDY
. . . AND GET PAID FOR IT TOO!

Couples who agreed to participate were asked to complete each scale twice: once with their date in mind and once for a close friend of the same sex.

Question: What were the results?

Scores for love of partner and love of friend differed more than those for liking (see Table 25-1). In other words, dating couples liked *and* loved their partners, but mostly liked their friends. Women, however, were a little more "loving" of

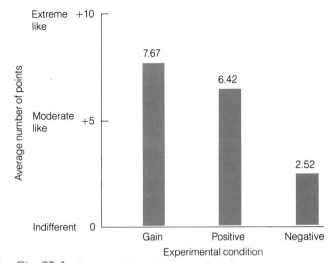

Fig. 25-4   *Reported liking for the confederate in the Aronson-Linder study. (After Aronson and Linder, 1965.)*

their friends than were men. Does this reflect real differences in the strength of male friendships and female friendships? Probably not, since it is more acceptable in our culture for women to express love for one another than it is for men.

Rubin's research helps clarify differences between love and liking, but something still seems missing. That "some-

Box 25-1   *Sample Love-Scale and Liking-Scale Items. Each scale consists of 13 items similar to those shown. Scores on these scales correspond to other indications of love and liking. (Reprinted by permission of Zick Rubin.)*

Love Scale

1. If _____ were feeling bad, my first duty would be to cheer him (her) up.
2. I feel that I can confide in _____ about virtually everything.
3. I find it easy to ignore _____'s faults.

Liking Scale

1. When I am with _____, we almost always are in the same mood.
2. I think that _____ is unusually well-adjusted.
3. I would highly recommend _____ for a responsible job.

Table 25-1   Love and Liking for Date and
Same-Sex Close Friend

Condition	Mean Scores	
	Women	Men
Love for partner	89.46	89.37
Liking for partner	88.48	84.65
Love for friend	65.27	55.07
Liking for friend	80.47	79.10

(Source: Rubin, 1970.)

thing" is probably **heightened arousal.** "Passionate" or romantic love is often associated with restlessness (in the absence of the lover), appetite loss, agitation, emotional activation, and other signs of arousal. Also, "passionate" love frequently occurs against a backdrop of danger, adversity, stress, or frustration. You may recall from a discussion in Chapter 13 that some psychologists believe heightened arousal, no matter what its cause, may be interpreted as "love" in a romantic relationship (Bersheid and Walster, 1974b). Other psychologists argue that lovers not only increase arousal for one another, they also reduce it, and are thus powerfully reinforced by being together (Kenrick and Cialdini, 1977). In any case, a variety of experiments support the idea that passionate love is associated with heightened emotional arousal (Eiser, 1980).

To conclude, let's add one more ingredient to the potent mixture of attraction, liking, and emotional arousal found in romantic love. Romantic love, in contrast to simple liking, usually involves deep **mutual absorption** of the lovers. In other words, lovers (unlike friends) attend almost exclusively to one another. It's not surprising then, that couples scoring high on Rubin's love scale spend more time gazing into each other's eyes than do couples who score low on the scale. As the song says, "Millions of people go by, but they all disappear from view—'cause I only have eyes for you" (Rubin, 1970).

Learning Check

Before reading more, check your comprehension with the following questions.

1. Women threatened with electric shock in an experiment generally chose to wait alone or with other women not taking part in the experiment.   T or F?

2. The need to affiliate is related to interest in social comparison.   T or F?

3. Social comparisons are made pretty much at random.   T or F?

4. Interpersonal attraction is increased by all but one of the following. (Which does not fit?)

   physical proximity   competence   similarity   social costs

5. High levels of self-disclosure are reciprocated in most social encounters.   T or F?

6. Women rate their friends higher on the love scale than do men.   T or F?

7. Heightened arousal appears to be a prerequisite for strong friendship.   T or F?

Answers: 1. F   2. T   3. F   4. social costs   5. F   6. T   7. F

Social Influence—Follow the Leader

Question: What is social influence?

Imagine a traffic signal brightly flashing the word WAIT. As you and a number of other pedestrians wait for it to change, a well-dressed man in a suit crosses against the light. How many people follow him? Do you think the answer would be different if the man were dressed in a denim shirt, patched pants, and scuffed shoes? One of the most heavily researched topics in social psychology concerns the effects of **social influence.** When people interact they almost always affect one another's behavior. The street-corner setting was used in a well-known experiment on social influence. As you might have guessed, more people followed the well-dressed man than the one dressed in shabby clothes (Lefkowitz *et al.*, 1955).

In another sidewalk experiment, various numbers of people were assembled on a busy New York City street.

On cue they all looked at a sixth-floor window across the street. A camera recorded the number of passersby who also stopped to stare. The larger the initial group, the more people were influenced to join in staring at the window (Milgram *et al.,* 1969).

Question: Are there different kinds of social influence?

These are only two of countless possible examples of social influence. To help organize thinking about social influence, McGuire (1969) has identified five situations in which it occurs:

1. Suggestion situations—where repeated communication is presented, often without explanation.
2. Conformity situations—where communication of differences between individual and group actions, norms, or values is made.
3. Group discussion—where, through group dynamics and social interaction, tailored arguments and counter-arguments occur.
4. Persuasive messages—where carefully considered and polished arguments are presented in one-way communication.
5. Intensive indoctrination (brainwashing)—where all of the above are used simultaneously.

Everyday behavior is highly influenced by all items on this list except number 5. Perhaps the most pervasive in their effects are conformity situations.

Conformity

When John first started working at the Fleegle Flange Factory he found it easy to process 300 flanges an hour, while those around him averaged only 200. Other workers told him to slow down and take it easy. "I get bored," he said and continued to do 300 flanges an hour. At first John had been welcomed, but now conversations broke up when he approached and other workers laughed at or ignored him when he spoke. Although he never made a conscious decision to conform, in another week John's output had slowed to 200 flanges an hour.

As mentioned earlier, all groups have shared rules of conduct called *norms*. The broadest norms, defined by society as a whole, establish "normal" or acceptable behavior in most situations. Comparing hair styles, habits of speech, dress, eating habits, and social customs in two or more cultures makes it clear that we all conform to social norms. In fact, a degree of uniformity is necessary if we are to interact comfortably. Imagine being totally unable to anticipate the actions of others. In stores, schools, and

homes this would be frustrating and disturbing. On the highways it would be lethal.

Perhaps the most basic of all group norms is (as John discovered), "Thou shalt conform!" (Suedfeld, 1966). This is equally true for the Hell's Angels, the Daughters of the American Revolution, a street-corner gang, or the board of directors of a large corporation. Groups of all kinds exert considerable pressures toward uniformity on their members. Like it or not, everyday life is filled with instances of conformity (Fig. 25-5).

Question: How strong are group pressures for conformity?

The Asch Experiment   One of the better known experiments on conformity was staged by Solomon Asch in the early 1950s. Asch's experiment is best appreciated by placing yourself in the position of a subject. Assume that you have volunteered to take part in a psychological study of perception. You are seated at a table with six other students. Your task is actually quite simple. On each trial you are shown two large cards. On one card is a single "standard" line. On the second card are three "comparison" lines of varying length (see Fig. 25-6). You are asked to select the comparison line on each card that is closest in length to the standard.

As the testing begins, each subject announces an answer for the first card. When your turn comes, you find yourself in complete agreement with the others. "This isn't hard at all," you say to yourself. For several more trials your answers correspond to those of the other group members. Then comes a shock. All six people announce that line Number 1 matches the standard, and you were about to say line Number 3 matches. Suddenly you feel alone and upset. You nervously look at the cards again as the room falls silent. Everyone seems to be staring at you as the experimenter awaits your answer. Do you yield to the group?

In this experiment the other "students" were all accomplices coached to give the wrong answer on about a third of the trials. Few real subjects suspected trickery; hence, the group pressure created was very realistic (Asch, 1956).

Question: How many people yielded to group pressure?

Subjects conformed to the group on about one-third of the critical trials. Seventy-five percent of those tested yielded at least once. The significance of these results is underscored by the fact that other people tested alone erred in less than 1 percent of their judgments. Those who yielded to group pressures were clearly denying what their eyes told them.

Question: Do you mean they actually saw things differently?

Fig. 25-5   *All groups expect a degree of conformity from their members.*

Individual Factors in Conformity Interviews with Asch's subjects showed that conformity occurred at three levels. A few subjects yielded at the **perceptual level,** having convinced themselves that they actually saw the line as reported by others. More often, yielding was *judgmental,* in that subjects felt they did not understand the task, or did not want to spoil the experiment. Subjects who wore glasses were particularly likely to yield at the **judgmental level.** The largest number of subjects were aware they were yielding, and were upset about it, but conformed in fear of being ridiculed or excluded by the group. This represents yielding at the **action level.**

Question: Are some people more susceptible to group pressures than others?

A variety of experiments have shown that people with high needs for structure or certainty are more likely to be influenced. People who are anxious, low in self-confidence, or who are concerned with the opinions or approval of others are also more susceptible.

Fig. 25-6   *Stimuli used in Solomon Asch's conformity experiments.*

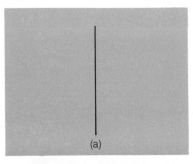

(a)

Standard line

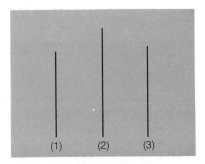

(1)   (2)   (3)

Comparison lines

Fig. 25-7 *Conformity is a subtle dimension of daily life. Notice the similarities of hair length and style, clothing, posture, body positioning, and facial expression in this foursome.*

Question: How do groups enforce norms?

Group Factors in Conformity   In most of our experiences with groups we have been rewarded with acceptance and approval for conformity, and threatened with rejection or ridicule for nonconformity. These reactions are called **group sanctions.** Negative sanctions (or punishments) for nonconformity range from laughter, staring, or social disapproval to complete rejection or formal ostracism. This is illustrated by later experiments in which Asch made up groups of six real subjects and one trained dissenter. When "Mr. Odd" announced his wrong answers, he was greeted with derisive laughter and sidelong glances.

Question: Wouldn't the effectiveness of group sanctions depend on the importance of the group?

Yes. And this is why the Asch experiments are impressive. Since these were only temporary groups, sanctions were informal and rejection had no lasting importance.

Question: What factors, besides importance of the group, affect the degree of conformity?

Earlier we described an experiment in which passersby were influenced by a group of people staring at a building.

We noted that the larger the group, the greater the number of people influenced. In Asch's face-to-face groups the size of the majority also made a difference, but a surprisingly small one. The number of conforming subjects increased dramatically as the majority was increased from two to three people. However, a majority of three produced about as much yielding as a majority of eight. Next time you want to talk someone into (or out of) something, take two friends along and see what a difference it makes!*

Even more important than the size of the majority is its **unanimity.** Having at least one person in your corner can greatly reduce pressures to conform. When Asch provided subjects with an ally (who also opposed the majority by giving the correct answer), conformity was lessened. In terms of numbers, a unanimous majority of three is more powerful than eight with one dissenting. Perhaps this accounts for the rich diversity of human attitudes, beliefs, opinions, and life-styles. If you can find at least one other person who sees things as you do (no matter how weird), you can be relatively secure in your opposition to other viewpoints (Fig. 25-7).

*Sometimes it helps if the two are large and mean-looking.

Groupthink—Agreement at Any Cost

As we have seen, conformity pressures are a normal part of social life. But what happens when people in positions of power fall prey to pressures for conformity or unanimity? To find out, Yale psychologist Irving Janis analyzed a collection of disastrous decisions made by government officials. In the early 1960s, for example, some 1400 Cuban exiles tried to land (with United States backing) on the beach at the Bay of Pigs, Cuba. Most were captured or killed in what is now recognized as a complete fiasco. How were such bright men as John F. Kennedy and his advisors taken in by the unlikely, foolish, and almost certainly disastrous plan presented to them by the C.I.A.? Janis blames the Bay of Pigs and similar fiascoes on **groupthink**—a compulsion by decision-makers to maintain each other's approval, even at the cost of critical thinking.

Question: Does Janis provide any guidelines for recognizing groupthink?

Janis and Mann (1977) list the following as major characteristics of groupthink.

Symptoms of Groupthink

1. Illusions of invulnerability. Group members become overly optimistic and think themselves immune to failure.
2. Rationalization. Warnings and contradictory information are ignored or discounted by group members who convince themselves of the correctness of their decision and views.
3. Narrowed morality. The group tends to look upon itself as the upholder of good and ignores the ethical and moral dilemmas posed by its actions.
4. Stereotyped views. The group adopts simplified and unrealistic views, particularly of rivals and enemies, who are seen as stupid, incompetent, weak, evil, etc. Such stereotypes lead to risky or unethical actions.
5. Conformity pressures. Group loyalty requires that members avoid "rocking the boat" by questioning weak arguments or sloppy thinking of others. Members who express doubts about the group's plans or illusions are subjected to strong pressures to "get in line."
6. Self-censorship. Each member withholds his or her doubts or disagreements, contributing to a false sense of solidarity and agreement.
7. Illusions of unanimity. Conformity pressures and self-censorship cause members to believe that greater agreement and unanimity exists than actually does.
8. Emergence of "mindguards." Members emerge who take it upon themselves to "protect" the group or its leader from conflicting or adverse information when it surfaces.

Janis has primarily studied major decision-making disasters such as the Bay of Pigs, Pearl Harbor (during World War II the United States military blundered badly in not detecting the coming Japanese sneak attack at Pearl Harbor), and the escalation of bombing in Vietnam and Cambodia during the 1960s. However, the concept of groupthink undoubtedly also applies to everyday groups such as school boards, therapy groups, business committees, PTAs, and the like.

Question: Is there any way to discourage groupthink?

Preventing Disaster   To prevent groupthink fiascoes, Janis suggests that group leaders should: (1) define each group member's role as that of critical evaluator; (2) avoid stating his or her own preferences in the beginning; (3) state the problem factually, and without bias; (4) invite outside colleagues to play devil's advocate or assign the devil's advocate role to a different member each meeting.

In addition, Janis suggests that there should be a "second-chance" meeting during which important decisions are reevaluated. That is, each decision should be reached twice. Janis even suggests that some decision makers might imitate the ancient Persian practice of reaching important decisions first sober and then drunk. He feels that a second-chance meeting held informally over wine or cocktails might lower inhibitions and break down any false sense of unanimity.

Personally the author is not convinced that selectively drunken leaders would be superior to leaders seduced by a desire for approval. Just the same, in an age clouded by the continuing threat of nuclear warfare and similar disasters, a solution to the problem of groupthink would be welcome. Perhaps we should form a group to work on the problem?!

Learning Check

1. The effect one person's behavior has on another is called _____.
2. Conformity is a normal aspect of social life.   T or F?
3. Subjects in Solomon Asch's conformity study yielded on about 75 percent of the critical trials.   T or F?
4. Nonconformity is punished by negative group _____.

5. Which of the following is *not* a symptom of groupthink?

    a. social distancing   *b.* self-censorship   *c.* illusions of unanimity   *d.* narrowed morality

Answers: 1. social influence **2.** T **3.** F **4.** sanctions **5.** a

Social Power—
Who Can Do What to Whom?

Here's something to think about: Whereas *strength* is a quality possessed by individuals, *power* is always social—it arises when people come together and disappears when they disperse. In trying to understand the ways in which people are able to influence each other, it is helpful to distinguish among five types of **social power** (Raven, 1974). **Reward power** lies in the ability to reward a person for complying with desired behavior. Teachers try to exert reward power over their students through the use of grades. Employers command reward power by their control of wages and bonuses. **Coercive power** is based on the ability to punish a person for failure to comply. Coercive power is the basis for most statute law, in that fines or imprisonment are used to control behavior. **Legitimate power** comes from acceptance of a person as an agent of an established social order. For example, elected leaders and supervisors have legitimate power. So does a teacher in the classroom, but outside the classroom that power would have to come from another source. **Referent power** is based on respect for or identification with a person or a group. The person "refers to" the source of referent power for direction. **Expert power** is based upon recognition that another person has knowledge or expertise necessary for achieving a goal. Allowing teachers or experts to guide behavior because you believe in their ability to produce desirable results is an example. Physicians, lawyers, psychologists, and plumbers have expert power.

A person who has power in one situation may have very little in another. In those situations where a person has power, he or she is described as an *authority*. In the next section we will investigate *obedience*. Obedience is a special type of conformity to the demands of an authority.

Obedience—
Would You Electrocute a Stranger?

The question is this: If ordered to do so, would you shock a man with a known heart condition who is screaming and asking to be released? Certainly we can assume that few people would do so. Or can we? In Nazi Germany obedient soldiers (once average citizens) helped slaughter over 9 million people. A more recent example of the same phenomenon is Lt. William Calley's massacre of helpless Vietnamese civilians at My Lai. Do such inhumane acts reflect deep character flaws? Are they the acts of heartless psychopaths or crazed killers? Or are they simply the result of obedience to authority? What are the limits of such obedience? These are questions that puzzled social psychologist Stanley Milgram (1965) when he began a provocative series of studies on obedience.

Question: How did Milgram study obedience?

As was true of the Asch experiments, Milgram's research is best appreciated by imagining yourself as a subject. Place yourself in this situation.

Milgram's Study Imagine answering a newspaper ad to take part in a "learning" experiment at Yale University. When you arrive you are immediately paid $4.50. A coin is flipped and a second subject, a pleasant-looking man in his fifties, is designated the "learner." By chance you have become the "teacher."

Your task is to read a list of word pairs to be memorized by the learner. You are to punish him with an electrical shock each time he makes a mistake. The learner is taken to an adjacent room and you watch as he is seated in an "electric chair" apparatus and electrodes are attached to his wrists. You are then escorted to your position in front of a "shock generator." On this device is a row of 30 switches labeled from 15 to 450 volts and accompanied by descriptions ranging from "Slight Shock" to "Extreme Intensity Shock" and finally "Danger Severe Shock." Your instructions are to administer a shock each time the learner makes a mistake. You are to begin with 15 volts and then move one switch (15 volts) higher for each additional mistake.

The experiment begins, and the learner soon makes his first error. You flip a switch. More mistakes. Rapidly you reach the 75-volt level. The learner moans after each shock. At 100 volts he complains he has a heart condition. At 150 volts he says he no longer wants to continue and demands release. At 300 volts he screams and says he can no longer give answers.

At some point during the experiment, you begin to protest to the experimenter. "That man has a heart condition," you say; "I'm not going to kill that man." The experimenter says, "Please continue." Another shock and another scream from the learner and you say, "You mean I've got to keep going up the scale? No, sir. I'm not going to give him 450 volts!" The experimenter says, "The experiment requires that you continue." For the remainder of the experiment the learner refuses to answer any more questions and screams with each shock (Milgram, 1965).

Question: I can't believe many people would do this. What happened?

Milgram also doubted that many people would obey his orders, and when he polled a group of psychiatrists before the experiment they predicted that less than 1 percent of those tested would obey. The astounding fact is that 65 percent of those tested obeyed completely by going all the way to the 450-volt level. Virtually no one stopped short of 300 volts ("Severe Shock") (see Fig. 25-8).

Question: Was the "learner" injured?

The time has come to reveal that the "learner" was actually an actor who turned a tape-recorder on and off in the

Fig. 25-8 *Results of Milgram's obedience experiment. Only a minority of subjects refused to provide shocks, even at the most extreme intensities. The first substantial drop in obedience occurred at the 300-volt level (Milgram, 1963).*

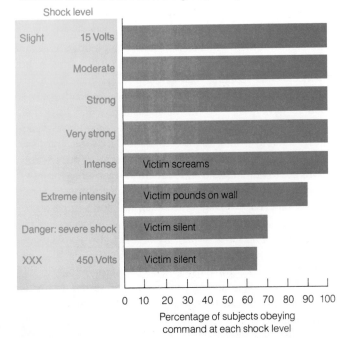

"shock room." No shocks were ever administered, but the dilemma for the "teachers" was quite real. Subjects protested, sweated, trembled, stuttered, bit their lips, and laughed nervously. Clearly they were disturbed by what they were doing, but most obeyed the experimenter's orders.

Question: Why did so many people obey?

Milgram's Follow Up   Some have suggested that the prestige of Yale University contributed to subjects' willingness to obey. Could subjects have assumed that the professor running the experiment would not really allow anyone to be hurt? To investigate this possibility, the experiment was rerun in a shabby office building in nearby Bridgeport, Connecticut. There was nothing in either the location or the experimenter's appearance to inspire confidence. Under these conditions fewer people obeyed (48 percent), but the reduction was minor.

Milgram was quite disturbed by the willingness of people to knuckle under to authority and to senselessly shock someone. In later experiments, he tried in various ways to reduce obedience. He found that distance between the "teacher" and the "learner" was of importance. When subjects were in the *same room* as the learner, only 40 percent were fully obedient. When they were *face-to-face* with the learner and required to force his hand down on a "shock plate," only 30 percent obeyed (Fig. 25-9). *Distance* from the authority also had an effect. When the experimenter delivered his orders over the phone, only 22 percent obeyed.

Milgram's research raises nagging questions about our willingness to commit antisocial or inhumane acts commanded by a "legitimate authority." The excuse so often given by war criminals—"I was only following orders"—takes on new meaning in this light. Milgram suggests that when directions come from an authority, people rationalize that they are not personally responsible for their actions.

Question: Aren't you taking an overly dim view of obedience?

Obedience to authority is obviously necessary and desirable in many circumstances. Just the same, it is probably true, as C. P. Snow (1961) has observed, "When you think of the long and gloomy history of man, you will find more hideous crimes have been committed in the name of obedience than in the name of rebellion." With this in mind, let us end this discussion on a more positive note. In one of his experiments, Milgram found that group support can greatly reduce destructive obedience. When real subjects saw two other "teachers" (both actors) resist orders and walk out of the experiment, only 10 percent continued to obey. Thus, a personal act of courage or moral fortitude by one or two members of a group may free others to disobey misguided or unjust authority.

Passive Compliance—"Little Murders"

Social scientists used to worry about our becoming a nation of sheep. As we have seen, social pressures for uniformity can be powerful. The regimentation of modern life is still cause for concern, but recently the emphasis has shifted to *passivity* rather than simple conformity.

Milgram's experiment is not the only example of excessive or unquestioning obedience. In one study conducted by Martin Orne (1962), subjects were presented with a thoroughly boring task. They were given sheets of numbers and asked to add up each pair of adjacent numbers. After finishing a sheet, subjects were directed to pick up a card upon which were instructions to tear the completed sheet into a minimum of 32 pieces, to go on to the next sheet, and then to pick up another card. The experimenter departed, commenting that he would return "eventually." Quite incredibly, many subjects worked on this meaningless task for several hours, with few outward signs of anger.

Question: Could it be that people cooperated because they didn't want to ruin the experiment?

Yes. It's possible this degree of passive compliance is limited to artificial experiments. However, researcher Thomas Moriarty (1975) has recently demonstrated passivity under more realistic conditions. Moriarty became interested in the "little murders" of daily life: the personal insults, rebuffs, and sacrifices of dignity that have become so common. Moriarty observed that many people will put up with almost anything to avoid a confrontation. He decided to put this passive, "no-hassle" attitude to experimental test.

In one experiment, two subjects (one actually an accomplice) were given a difficult test in a very small room. The two subjects were seated back-to-back and left alone to work. As soon as the experimenter left, the phoney subject turned on a portable cassette tape-player at full volume. Subjects who failed to complain were treated to 17 minutes of nerve-wracking rock music. The accomplice was instructed to turn the music off only after a third request. In

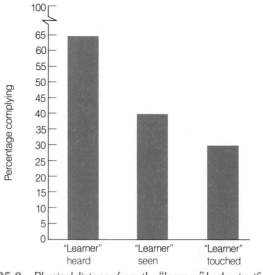

Fig. 25-9   *Physical distance from the "learner" had a significant effect on the percentage of subjects obeying orders.*

this particular experiment, 80 percent of the subjects said nothing, although they glared, cupped their ears, stopped work, and so forth. An interview later showed that most were angry or annoyed, but were afraid to tell the other "subject" to be quiet.

Again there is a possibility that the passivity observed in this study is unique to the experimental setting. However, when Moriarty and his students staged loud conversations behind theater patrons or people studying in a library, very few protested. In other naturalistic experiments, people were accosted in phone booths. The experimenter explained that he had left a ring in the booth and asked if the subject had found it. When the subject said "no," the experimenter demanded that the subject empty his pockets. Most did.

In these and similar situations, people passively accepted having their personal rights trampled, even when objecting presented no threat to their safety. Have we become, as Moriarty puts it, "a nation of willing victims?" Certainly we would hope not. Nevertheless, researchers such as Milgram and Moriarty have identified a significant social problem. We will address this problem again in the "Applications" section of this chapter.

Learning Check

1. An ability to punish others for failure to obey is the basis for:
    a. referent power   *b.* expert power   *c.* legitimate power   *d.* coercive power

2. Would you electrocute a stranger? _____

3. Obedience in Milgram's experiments was related to:
   a. distance between learner and teacher   *b.* distance between experimenter and teacher
   c. obedience of other teachers   *d.* all of the above.

4. Obedience is conformity to _____.

5. By repeating his obedience experiment in a downtown office building, Milgram demonstrated that the prestige of Yale University was the main reason for subjects' willingness to obey in the original experiment.   T or F?

6. The research of Thomas Moriarty and others has recently shifted to an interest in _____ _____ rather than obedience to authority.

Answers: 1. d   2. answer will vary   3. d   4. authority   5. F   6. passive compliance

---

Resources Summary

● Humans are social animals enmeshed in a complex network of social relationships. *Social psychology* studies humans as members of groups. Its focus is how people behave in the presence (real or implied) of others.

● *Culture* provides a broad social context for our behavior. One's *position* in groups defines a variety of *roles* to be played. Roles, which may be *achieved* or *ascribed*, are particular behavior patterns associated with social positions. When two or more contradictory roles are held, *role conflict* may occur. The Stanford prison experiment showed that destructive roles may override individual determinants of behavior.

● Positions within groups typically carry higher or lower levels of *status*. High status is associated with special privileges and respect.

● *Group structure* refers to the organization of roles, communication pathways, and power within a group. *Group cohesiveness* is basically the degree of attraction among group members. *Norms* are standards of conduct enforced (formally or informally) by groups. The *autokinetic effect* has been used to demonstrate that norms rapidly form even in temporary groups.

● The study of personal space is called *proxemics*. Four basic spatial zones around each person's body are: *intimate distance* (0–18 inches), *personal distance* (1½–4 feet), *social distance* (4–12 feet), and *public distance* (12 feet or more). An additional aspect of spatial behavior is *territoriality*, a tendency to identify certain spaces or places as one's own, especially through use of *territorial markers*.

● The *need to affiliate* is tied to additional needs for approval, support, friendship, and information. Additionally, research indicates that affiliation is related to reducing anxiety and uncertainty. *Social comparison theory* holds that we also affiliate to evaluate our actions, feelings, and abilities.

● *Interpersonal attraction* is increased by *physical proximity* (nearness), *frequent contact, physical attractiveness, competence,* and *similarity.*

● *Self-disclosure* occurs more when two people like one another. A *reciprocity norm* exists for self-disclosure: Low levels of self-disclosure are met with low levels in return, whereas moderate self-disclosure elicits more personal replies. However, *overdisclosure* tends to inhibit self-disclosure by others.

● According to *gain-loss theory,* gains in liking or approval are more rewarding than constant liking; in the same manner, a loss of liking or affection is more punishing than constant dislike. Studies of interpersonal attraction support the idea of gain effects, but loss effects generally have not been demonstrated in lab experiments.

● *Romantic love* has been studied as a special kind of attitude. Love can be distinguished from liking by the use of attitude scales. Dating couples like *and* love their partners but only like their friends. Love is also associated with *heightened arousal* and with greater *mutual absorption* between people.

● In general, *social influence* refers to alterations in behavior brought about by the behavior of others. More specifically, it pertains to the effects of *suggestion, conformity pressures, group discussion, persuasive messages,* and *intensive indoctrination.*

● Virtually everyone conforms to a variety of broad social and cultural norms. *Conformity pressures* also exist within smaller groups. The famous Asch experiments demonstrated that conformity may take place at the *perceptual level,* the *judgmental level,* or the *action level.* Various *group sanctions* encourage conformity.

● *Groupthink* refers to compulsive conformity in group decision-making. Victims of groupthink seek to maintain each other's approval, even at the cost of critical thinking.

Major symptoms of groupthink are: illusions of invulnerability, rationalization, narrowed morality, stereotyped views, conformity pressures, self-censorship, a false sense of unanimity, and the presence of "mindguards" in the group.

● Social influence is also related to five types of *social power*. The types are: *reward power, coercive power, legitimate power, referent power,* and *expert power*.

● *Obedience* to authority has been investigated in a variety of experiments, particularly those by Milgram. Obedience in Milgram's studies decreased when the victim was in the same room, when the victim and subject were face-to-face, when the authority figure was absent, and when others refused to obey.

● Recent research suggests that in addition to excessive obedience to authority, many people are surprisingly passive. Such passivity is demonstrated by *passive compliance* to unreasonable requests, and by an inability to behave assertively.

Applications

Assertiveness Training—Standing Up for Your Rights

Have you ever:

Hesitated to question an error on a restaurant bill because you were afraid of making a scene?

Backed out of asking for a raise or a change in working conditions?

Said ''yes'' when you wanted to say ''no''?

Been afraid to question a grade that seemed unfair?

Most of us have been rewarded, first as children, and later as adults, for compliant, obedient, or ''good'' behavior. Perhaps this is why so many people find it difficult to assert themselves. Or perhaps nonassertion is related to the anxiety that accompanies ''making a scene'' or feeling disliked by others. Whatever the causes, some people are so seriously inhibited that they suffer tremendous anguish in any situation requiring poise, self-confidence, or self-assertion. Fortunately for these people, behavior therapist Joseph Wolpe (and others) have pioneered a therapeutic technique called *assertiveness training.*

Question: What is done in assertiveness training?

Assertiveness training is a very direct procedure. By using group exercises, videotapes, mirrors, and staged conflicts, the behavior therapist teaches assertive behavior. People learn to practice honesty, disagreeing, questioning authority, and assertive postures and gestures. As their self-confidence improves, nonassertive clients are taken on ''field trips'' to shops and restaurants where they practice what they have learned.

Nonassertion requiring therapy is unusual. Nevertheless, many people become tense or upset in at least some situations in which they must stand up for their rights. For this reason, many people have found the techniques and exercises of assertiveness training helpful. If you have ever eaten a carbonized steak when you ordered it rare, or stood in silent rage as a clerk ignored you, the following discussion will be of interest.

Self-Assertion   The first step in assertiveness training is to convince yourself of three basic rights: You have the right to refuse, to request, and to right a wrong. Self-

assertion involves standing up for these rights by speaking out in your own behalf.

Question: Is self-assertion just getting things your own way?

Not at all. A basic distinction can be made between *self-assertion* and *aggressive* behavior. Assertion is a direct, honest expression of feelings and desires. It is not exclusively self-serving, since pent up anger can be very destructive to relationships. People who are nonassertive are usually patient to a fault. In contrast, aggression does not take into account the feelings or rights of others. Aggression is an attempt to get one's own way no matter what. Assertion techniques emphasize firmness, not attack (see Box 25-2).

The basic idea in assertiveness training is that each assertive action is practiced until it can be repeated even under stress. For example, let's say it really angers you when a store clerk waits on several people who arrived after you did. To improve your assertiveness in this situation, you would begin by *rehearsing* the dialogue, posture, and gestures you would use to confront the clerk or the other customer. Working in front of a mirror can be very helpful. If possible, you should *role play* the scene with a friend. Be sure to have your friend take the part of a really aggressive or irresponsible clerk, as well as a cooperative one. Rehearsal and role playing should also be used when you expect a possible confrontation with someone: For example, if you were going to ask for a raise, challenge a grade, or confront a landlord.

Question: Is that all there is to it?

No. Another important principle is *overlearning.* When you rehearse or role play assertive behavior, it is essential to continue practice until your responses become almost automatic. This helps prevent becoming flustered in the actual situation.

One more technique you may find useful is the *broken record.* A good way to prevent assertion from becoming aggression is to simply restate your request as many times and as many ways as necessary. As an illustration, let's

Applications

Box 25-2

Comparison of Assertive, Aggressive, and Nonassertive Behavior.
(After Alberti and Emmons, 1978.)

	Actor	**Receiver of Behavior**
Nonassertive behavior	Self-denying, inhibited, hurt, and anxious; lets others make choices; goals not achieved.	Feels sympathy, guilt, or contempt for actor; achieves goals at actor's expense
Aggressive behavior	Achieves goals at others' expense; expresses feelings, but hurts others; chooses for others or puts them down	Feels hurt, defensive, humiliated, or taken advantage of; does not meet own needs
Assertive behavior	Self-enhancing; acts in own best interests; expresses feelings; respects rights of others; goals usually achieved, self-respect is maintained	Needs are respected, and feelings are expressed; may achieve goal; self-worth maintained

say you are returning a pair of shoes to a store. After two wearings the shoes fell apart, but you bought them two months ago and no longer have a receipt. The broken record sounds something like this:

Customer: I would like to have these shoes replaced.
Clerk: Do you have a receipt?
Customer: No, but I bought them here and since they are defective I would like to have you replace them.
Clerk: I can't do that without a receipt.
Customer: I understand that, but I want them replaced.
Clerk: Well, if you'll come back this afternoon and talk to the manager . . .
Customer: I've brought these shoes in because they are defective.
Clerk: Well, I'm not authorized to replace them.
Customer: Yes, well, if you'll replace these, I'll be on my way.

Notice that the customer has not attacked the clerk or created an angry confrontation. Simple persistence is often all that is necessary for successful self-assertion.

Question: How would I respond assertively to a put-down?

Responding assertively to verbal aggression (a "put-down") is a real challenge. The tendency is to respond aggressively, which usually makes things worse. A good way to respond to a put-down is this: (1) if you are wrong admit it; (2) acknowledge the person's feelings; (3) assert yourself about the other person's aggression; (4) briskly end the interchange.

Psychologists Robert Alberti and Michael Emmons (1978) offer an example of using the four steps: Let's say you accidentally bump into someone. The person responds angrily, "Damn it! Why don't you watch where you're going! You fool, you could have hurt me!" A good response would be to say, "I'm sorry I bumped you. I didn't do it intentionally. It's obvious you're upset, but I don't like your calling me names, or yelling. I can get your point without that." Now, what if someone insults you indirectly ("I love your taste in clothes, it's so 'folksy'.")? Alberti and Emmons suggest you ask them for a clarification ("What are you trying to say?"). This will force the person to take responsibility for the aggression. It can also provide an opportunity to change the way the person interacts with you: "If you really don't like what I'm wearing, I'd like

Applications

to know it. I'm not always sure I like the things I buy, and I value your opinion."

To summarize, self-assertion is not instant poise, confidence, or self-assurance. It is a way of combating anxi-

eties associated with life in an impersonal and sometimes intimidating society. If you are interested in more information, you can consult a book entitled *Your Perfect Right* by Alberti and Emmons (Impact, 1978).

Learning Check

1. In assertiveness training, people learn techniques for getting their way in social situations and angry interchanges.   T or F?
2. Nonassertive behavior causes hurt, anxiety, and self-denial in the actor, and sympathy, guilt, or contempt in the receiver.   T or F?
3. Overlearning should be avoided when rehearsing assertive behaviors.   T or F?
4. The "broken record" must be avoided, because it is a basic nonassertive behavior.   T or F?

Answers: 1. F   2. T   3. F   4. F

Attribution Theory—Causes, Causes, Everywhere

In the last 10 years, social psychologists have become quite interested in the process of **attribution** (discussed briefly in Chapter 13). To round out our first look at social behavior, let's explore attribution a little further.

Making Attributions   Two people enter a restaurant, and order different meals. One person tastes her food and then salts it. The second salts his food before tasting it. How would you explain their behavior? In the first instance, you might assume that the *food* needed salt. If so, you have attributed the woman's actions to an **external** cause. In the second case, you might be more inclined to conclude that the man must really *like* salt. If so, you would be saying that the cause of his behavior is **internal** (McGee and Snyder, 1975).

Question: What effects do such interpretations have?

It is difficult to fully understand social behavior without considering internal and external attributions. For instance, let's say that Jim, who is in one of your classes, seems to avoid you. You see Jim at a market. Do you say hello to him? It could depend on how you have explained Jim's actions to yourself (Wegner and Vallacher, 1977). Have you assumed his avoidance is caused by shyness? Coincidence? Dislike?

Question: How do people make such judgments?

Two important factors that greatly influence attribution are the **consistency** and **distinctiveness** of a person's behavior (Kelley, 1967). If Jim has consistently avoided you, it is clear that he was not just in a bad mood on several occasions and coincidence is ruled out. Still, Jim's avoidance could mean he is shy, not that he dislikes you. This is where distinctiveness enters the picture. If Jim seems to avoid others too, you may conclude that he is shy. If his avoidance is consistently and distinctively associated with you, you will probably assume that he dislikes you. You could be wrong, of course, but your behavior toward Jim will change just the same.

To infer causes, we typically take into account the behavior of the **actor,** the **object** of the action, and the setting in which the action occurs (Kelley, 1967). Imagine for example, that someone compliments your taste in clothes. If you are at a picnic, you may attribute this compliment to what you are wearing (the "object"), unless, of course, you're wearing your worst "grubbies." If you are, you may simply assume the person (or "actor") is friendly, or tactful. However, if you are at a clothing store, and a salesperson compliments you, you will probably attribute it to the setting—not what you are wearing or the salesperson's true feelings. In making attributions, we are very sensitive to **situational demands.** When a person is quiet and polite in church, or at a funeral, it tells us little about the individual's personality. The situation demands such behavior.

When situational demands are quite strong, we tend to **discount** claims that a person's actions are internally caused. For example, you have probably discounted the sincerity of professional athletes who endorse shaving creams, hair tonics, deodorants, and the like on television. Obviously, the athletes' endorsements are well explained by the large sums of money they receive. It's not necessary to assume they actually *like* the potions they sell.

Consensus (or agreement) is another factor affecting attribution. A consensus in the behavior of a number of people implies that the behavior has an external cause. If millions of people go to see a particular movie, we tend to say *the movie* is good. If someone you know goes to see a movie six times, when others are staying away in droves, the tendency is to assume *the person* likes "that type of movie."

Actor and Observer   Let's say that at the last five parties you have attended, you've seen a woman named Pam. Based on this, you assume that Pam is very outgoing and likes to socialize. You see Pam at yet another gathering and mention that she seems to like parties. She says, "Actually, I hate these parties, but I get invited to play my tuba at them. My music teacher says I need to practice in front of an audience, so I keep attending these dumb events. Want to hear a Sousa march?"

We seldom know the real reasons for others' actions.

Exploration

This is why we tend to infer causes from circumstances. However, in doing so, we often make mistakes of the type just described. The most common error is to attribute the actions of *others* to *internal causes,* while attributing our *own* behavior to situations (*external causes*) (Kelley, 1971; Jones and Nisbett, 1971). This mistake is made so often that it is called the **fundamental attributional error** (Ross, 1977).

Psychologists have found that we consistently attribute the behavior of others to their wants, motives, and personality traits. In contrast, we tend to find external explanations for our own behavior. If your friend Jack buys a motorcycle, it's because he's a "free spirit," or "loves bikes," or is just "that kind of guy." However, if *you* buy a motorcycle, it's probably because "they're economical," "it was a good deal," or some other external reason. No doubt you chose *your* major in school because of what it has to offer; other students choose *their* majors because of the kind of people they are (Wegner and Vallacher, 1977).

Implications   As you can see, attribution theory attempts to summarize how we think about ourselves and others. It also tries to identify some of the consistent errors, or biases, in our interpretations. In addition to providing a better understanding of behavior, attribution theory has helped identify some practical problems. Let's conclude with a brief example.

Ye Old Double Standard   Attribution research has uncovered an interesting double standard for men and women. In a study by Deaux and Emswiller (1974), men and women overheard a male or female perform extremely well on a perception task. Subjects were then asked to rate whether the test-taker's success was due to his or her ability, to luck, or to some combination of the two. Both men and women attributed male success mainly to skill and women's performances mainly to luck! This was true, even though male and female performances were identical. Such attributions no doubt dog the heels of many talented and successful women.

As an interesting exercise, you may want to think about other instances in which damaging attributions are made. A good example to start with is the idea that women who are raped "deserve it," or "ask for it" because of the way they dress. There is a strong and very unfortunate tendency among judges and juries to attribute less personal responsibility to rapists if the victim is young, single, and attractive. Their attributions, of course, completely overlook the facts of rape: Studies have repeatedly shown the victim's age, appearance, and style of dress are irrelevant to the rapist, whose behavior is determined by opportunity, and a need to hurt women—any woman.

Questions for Discussion

1. Reread the experiments performed on passive compliance. What would have been an assertive response to the situations described? An aggressive response?

2. Would it be possible to be completely nonconforming (that is, to not conform to *some* group norm)?

3. How serious, in your estimation, are problems of conformity, obedience, and passivity?

4. How has physical proximity influenced your choice of friends?

5. Modern warfare allows killing to take place impersonally and at a distance. How does this relate to Milgram's experiments?

6. If a waiter or waitress wanted to use gain-loss theory to earn larger tips, how should he or she act in contact with customers?

7. People of different nationalities often have different norms for personal space. What would you expect to happen in a conversation between two people with very different proxemic habits?

8. Can you think of a personal experience in which you were subjected to group pressures similar to those in the Asch experiment? How did you feel? Did you yield?

9. In view of the Milgram obedience experiment, do you think the civil disobedience of the civil-rights and anti-war movements was justified? Why or why not?

10. If you were placed in charge of an important decision-making group, what would you do to minimize groupthink? Do you think some types of committees or groups are especially prone to groupthink? How serious a problem do you think groupthink is in the government? The military? Business? Schools? Community groups?

Suggestions for Further Reading

Aronson, E. *The Social Animal.* Freeman, 1980.

Fensterheim, H. *Don't Say Yes When You Want to Say No.* Dell, 1976.

Freedman *et al., Social Psychology.* 4th ed. Prentice-Hall, 1981.

Goffman, E. *The Presentation of Self in Everyday Life.* Doubleday, 1959.

Hall, E. T. *The Hidden Dimension.* Doubleday, 1966.

Homans, G. C. *Social Behavior: Its Elementary Forms.* Harcourt Brace Jovanovich, 1961.

Hyde, J. S. "Love." Chapter 17 in *Understanding Human Sexuality.* McGraw-Hill, 1979.

Phelps, S., and A. Austin. *The Assertive Woman.* Impact, 1978.

Rubin, Z. *Liking and Loving: An Invitation to Social Psychology.* Holt, 1973.

Zimbardo, P. G. "The Social Disease Called Shyness," *Psychology Today,* May, 1975.

26

Social Psychology II

■ Chapter Preview ■

Doomsday for the Seekers

Mrs. Keech was receiving messages from superior beings on a planet called Clarion. On their journeys to Earth, they had detected a fault in the earth's crust that would submerge the North American continent in a natural disaster of unimaginable proportions. The date of this event was to be December 21. However, Mrs. Keech and her band of followers, who called themselves the Seekers, had no fear of the impending disaster. Their plans were to assemble on December 20 when they expected to be met at midnight by a flying saucer and taken to safety in outer space.

The night of December 20 arrived, and the Seekers assembled at Mrs. Keech's house. Many had given up jobs and possessions in preparation for their departure. Expectations were high and commitment was total, but as the night wore on, midnight passed and the world continued to exist. It was a bitter and embarrassing disappointment to all concerned.

Question: Did the group break up then?

The amazing twist to this story, and the aspect that intrigued social psychologists, was that the Seekers became more convinced than ever before that they and Mrs. Keech had been right. At about 5 A.M. Mrs. Keech announced that she had received a message explaining that the Seekers had saved the world. Before the night of December 20, the group had been uninterested in convincing other people that the world was coming to an end. Now they called newspapers, magazines, and radios to explain what had happened and to convince others of their accomplishment.

How do we explain this strange turn in the behavior of Mrs. Keech's doomsday group? The answer seems to lie in the concept of cognitive dissonance. *Cognitive dissonance also helps to explain many aspects of attitude change. Watch for a discussion of cognitive dissonance in the following material.*

Survey Questions What are attitudes? How are they acquired, measured, and changed? Under what conditions is persuasion most effective? What is cognitive dissonance? What does it have to do with attitudes and behavior? Is brainwashing actually possible? How are people converted to cult membership? What causes prejudice and intergroup conflict? What can be done about these problems? How do psychologists explain human aggression? Why are bystanders so often unwilling to help in an emergency?

===== Resources =====

Attitudes—Belief + Emotion + Action

What is your attitude toward: birth control, marijuana, Republicans, higher education, Chevrolets, psychology? The answers have far-reaching effects on your behavior. The effects of attitudes are intimately woven into the way a person views the world and acts toward it. Our tastes, friendships, votes, preferences, and goals are all touched by attitudes.

Question: What specifically is an attitude?

An **attitude** is a learned predisposition to respond to people, objects, or institutions in a positive or negative way. Attitudes are one of the more heavily studied aspects of social functioning. This is because attitudes summarize past experience and *predict* or direct future actions. For example, an approach known as the **misdirected letter technique** demonstrates that actions are closely connected to attitudes:

The Luck of the Irish

During a period of civil violence in Ireland, a group of psychologists measured attitudes held toward the Irish in a sample of English households. Later, they sent wrongly addressed letters to the same households. Each letter had either an English name or an Irish name on it. The question was: Would the "Irish" letters be returned to the Post Office or thrown away? As predicted, the number of "Irish" letters returned corresponded directly to pro- or anti-Irish attitudes measured earlier (Howitt *et al.,* 1977).

"Your attitude is showing," is sometimes said. This statement seems like a simple one, but actually there are three ways in which attitudes are expressed. Most attitudes have a **belief component,** an **emotional component,** and an **action component.** Consider, as an example, your attitude toward gun control. You will have beliefs about whether or not gun control would affect rates of crime or violence. You will have emotional responses to guns, find them either attractive and desirable or threatening and destructive. And you will have a tendency to seek out or to avoid gun ownership. The action component of your attitude will probably also include support of organizations that urge or oppose gun control.

Question: How do people acquire attitudes?

Attitude Formation   Attitudes are acquired in several basic ways, sometimes through **direct contact** with the object of the attitude—such as opposing pollution when a nearby factory ruins your favorite river. Attitudes are also learned through **interaction with others** holding the same attitude—if you live in a vegetarian household, chances are you will become a vegetarian. Attitudes are also acquired through the effects of **child rearing.** For example, if both parents belong to the same political party, chances are two out of three that the child will belong to the same party as an adult (Campbell *et al.,* 1954).

In the previous chapter we discussed group forces that operate to bring about conformity. There is little doubt that many of the attitudes we hold are influenced by **group membership** (Fig. 26-1). In one classic study, for example, groups were formed to discuss the case of a juvenile delinquent. Most participants believed that what the boy needed was love, kindness, and friendship. To test group pressures on attitudes, a person who advocated severe punishment was added to each group.

Question: How did group members react to the "deviate"?

At first they directed almost all of their comments to him. But when the deviate stuck to his position, an interesting thing happened: Soon, he was almost completely excluded from conversation. And later, the deviate was strongly rejected in ratings made by other group members (Schachter, 1951). In this experiment, group pressures for conformity and the difficulty of holding deviant attitudes can be clearly seen.

Attitudes are also influenced by the **mass media.** As Marshall McLuhan puts it, we are "massaged" by the media, meaning: threatened, urged, cajoled, persuaded, and otherwise influenced. Ninety-eight percent of American homes have a television set, which is on an average of almost seven hours a day (Comstock *et al.,* 1978). The values and information thus channeled into homes exerts a powerful influence on how people perceive, think about, and react to their world. For instance, the heavy dose of violence found on television may lead viewers to develop a *"mean" world view.* That is, frequent viewers overestimate their chances of being involved in a violent incident (Roberts and Bachen, 1981). Heavy viewers are also less likely to feel that most people can be trusted (Gerbner and Gross, 1976). Of added concern are the stereotyped images of male and female roles, and racial or ethnic minorities found on "the tube."

Some attitudes are formed quite inadvertently through **chance conditioning.** Let's say, for instance, that you have

Fig. 26-1 *Attitudes are an important dimension of social behavior. They are often rooted in reference groups (see text).*

had three encounters in your lifetime with psychologists. If by chance all three were negative, you might take an unduly dim view of psychology and psychologists. In the same way, people often develop strong attitudes toward cities, restaurants, or parts of the country on the basis of one or two unusually good or bad experiences with each.

Question: Why are some attitudes acted upon while others are not?

To answer the question, let's consider an example. Assume that a person accepts that automobiles contribute to pollution, and strongly objects to smog, but continues to drive to work every day. How are such discrepancies explained? For one thing the *immediate consequences* of our actions weigh heavily on the choices we make. A person who objects to air pollution but continues to drive is responding to the immediate convenience of driving. A second factor is our expectation of how *others will evaluate* our actions (Fishbein and Ajzen, 1975). By taking this factor into account researchers have been able to accurately predict family planning choices, adolescent alcohol use, reenlistment in the National Guard, voting on a nuclear power plant initiative, and so forth (Cialdini *et al.,* 1981). Finally,

we must not overlook the effect that long-standing *habits* have on action (Triandis, 1977). Say a "male chauvinist" boss makes a vow to change his sexist attitudes toward female employees. Two months later it would not be unusual for his behavior to show the effects of habit rather than his intention to change. In short, there are often large differences between attitudes and behavior—particularly between privately held attitudes and public behavior.

Question: Can attitudes be measured?

Attitude Measurement There are a number of approaches to the measurement of attitudes. In some cases, individuals are simply asked in a straightforward manner to express attitudes toward a particular issue. For example, a person might be asked in an **open-ended interview,** "How do you feel about strip mining?" The second approach, which has been particularly useful as a measure of attitudes toward various national or ethnic groups, uses a **social distance scale.** Social distance indicates the degree to which a person would be willing to have contact with another. The person is asked to indicate his or her willingness to admit members of a particular group to various levels of social closeness ranging from "would exclude from my country" to "would admit to marriage in my family."

Use of **attitude scales** is one of the most common approaches to attitude measurement. Attitude scales consist of statements expressing various possible attitudes on a particular issue. For example, "socialized medicine would destroy the quality of health care in this country" or, "this country desperately needs a national health care program." Subjects are asked to express agreement or disagreement with each item on a five-point scale ranging from "strongly agree" to "strongly disagree." By computing scores on all items, a person can be rated in terms of overall acceptance or rejection of a particular issue.

Attitude measures, particularly as they have been used in public polls, have provided much useful information about the feelings of large segments of the population. However, it is again important to remember that expressed attitudes and behavior may differ. Publicly expressed attitudes favoring racial or sexual equality often crumble in situations involving a conflict of interest. A "racially enlightened" individual, for instance, may act quite bigoted when equal employment opportunity laws threaten a chance for employment.

Attitude Change—Or Why the "Seekers" Went Public

Although attitudes are relatively stable, they are subject to change. Some attitude change can be understood in terms of the concept of **reference groups.** A reference group is one whose values and attitudes are seen by the individual as being relevant to his or her own. Reference group membership need not be physical. It depends instead on who you identify with or care about.

In the 1930s Theodore Newcomb studied real life attitude change among students at Bennington College. Most students came from conservative homes, but Bennington was a very liberal school. Newcomb found that most students shifted significantly toward more liberal attitudes during their four years at Bennington. Those who did not change maintained parents and hometown friends as their primary reference group (typified by one student's statement, "I decided I'd rather stick to my father's ideas"). Those who did change primarily identified with the campus community. Notice that all students could count the college and their families as *membership* groups, but one or the other tended to become their reference group.

Question: What about advertising and other direct attempts to change attitudes? Are they effective?

Business corporations, politicians, and others who seek to persuade us obviously believe that attitude change can be engineered. In 1978 over 5 billion dollars was spent on television advertising in the United States alone.

Persuasion refers to any deliberate attempt to bring about attitude change by the transmission of information. Persuasion can range from the daily bombardment of media commercials to personal discussion among friends. In most cases the success or failure of attempted persuasion can be understood by considering characteristics of the **communicator,** the **message,** and the **audience** (Fig. 26-2). Let's say you have a chance to promote an issue

Fig. 26-2 *Persuasion. Would you be likely to be swayed by this person's message? Successful persuasion is related to characteristics of the communicator, the message, and the audience.*

important to you (pro or anti nuclear power, for instance) at a community gathering. Whom should you choose to .make the presentation, and how should that person present it?

Research on persuasion suggests that attitude change is encouraged when: (1) the communicator is likeable, trustworthy, an expert on the topic, and similar to the audience in some respect; (2) the message appeals to emotions, particularly to fear or anxiety; (3) the message also provides a clear course of action which will, if followed, reduce fear or anxiety; (4) the message states clear-cut conclusions; (5) both sides of the argument are presented (for a well-informed audience); (6) only one side of the argument is presented (for a poorly informed audience); (7) the persuader appears to have nothing to gain if the audience accepts the message; and (8) the message is repeated as frequently as possible (McGuire, 1969; Aronson, 1972). You should have little difficulty seeing how these principles are applied in the selling of everything from underarm deodorants to presidents.

We all know from personal observation that emotional experiences also dramatically alter attitudes. Those individuals who give up drinking after nearly dying in an automobile accident caused by their own drunkenness serve as an example. To bring about such attitude change, psychologists have experimented with creating similar experiences through role playing.

Question: For example?

Janis and Mann (1965) asked women who were known smokers to play the role of a cancer patient. A physician told each of the women that he had some "bad news": She had lung cancer and would have to undergo immediate surgery. The women played out the part by asking questions about the surgery, if it might fail, and so on. Women in the role-playing group drastically reduced their smoking. Those who listened to a tape recording of similar information showed little change.

Question: Why should role playing have more effect than hearing the same information?

Cognitive Dissonance Theory   Certainly emotional impact and realism have some effect, but part of the explanation also lies in the concept of **cognitive dissonance.**

Question: What is cognitive dissonance?

Cognitions are thoughts. Dissonance means clashing. The influential theory of cognitive dissonance (Festinger, 1957)

states that contradicting or clashing thoughts cause discomfort. We have a need for *consistency* in our thoughts and our perceptions. If individuals can be made to act in ways that are inconsistent with their attitudes, they may change their thoughts to bring them into agreement with their actions. For example, smokers are told on every pack that cigarettes may endanger their lives. They light up and smoke. How do they resolve the tension between this information and their actions? They could quit smoking, but it may be easier to convince themselves that smoking is not really so dangerous. To do this, they will seek examples of people who have lived long lives as heavy smokers, and will associate with other smokers who support this attitude. They will also avoid information concerning the link between smoking and cancer. Cognitive dissonance theory also suggests that people tend to reject new information that contradicts ideas they already hold, in a sort of "don't bother me with the facts my mind is made up" strategy.

Recall now the account of Mrs. Keech and her doomsday group. Why did their belief in Mrs. Keech's messages *increase* after the world failed to end? Why did they suddenly become interested in convincing others of the correctness of their beliefs? Cognitive dissonance explains that after publicly committing themselves to their beliefs, they had a strong need to maintain their stand. No matter what the evidence, convincing others was a way of adding additional proof that they were right.

Question: Acting contrary to one's attitudes does not always bring about change. How does cognitive dissonance account for this?

The amount of **reward,** or **justification,** for acting contrary to one's real beliefs determines the amount of dissonance created. In a now classic study, college students performed an extremely boring task consisting of turning wooden pegs on a board for an extended time. Afterward, they were asked to help lure others into the experiment by pretending it was interesting and enjoyable. Students paid $20 for lying to others did not change their own negative opinion of the task. Those who were paid only $1 later rated the experience as actually being pleasant and interesting. In other words, those paid $20 experienced no dissonance. These students could reassure themselves that anybody would lie for $20. Those paid $1 were faced with the conflicting thought, "I lied, but I had no good reason to." Rather than admit to themselves that they had lied, these students changed their attitude toward what they had done (Festinger and Carlsmith, 1959).

Learning Check

1. Attitudes have three parts, a _____ component, an _____ component, and an _____ component.

2. Which of the following is associated with attitude formation?

   a. group membership   b. chance conditioning   c. child rearing
   d. mass media   e. all of the preceding   f. a and d only

3. Because of the immediate consequences of actions, behavior contrary to one's attitudes is often enacted.   T or F?

4. Items such as, "would exclude from my country," or "would admit to marriage in my family," would be found in which attitude measure?

   a. a reference group scale   b. an attitude scale
   c. a social distance scale   d. an open-ended interview

5. In presenting a persuasive message, it is best to give both sides of the argument if the audience is already well informed on the topic.   T or F?

6. Much attitude change is related to a desire to avoid clashing or contradictory thoughts, an idea summarized by _____ _____ theory.

Answers: 1. belief, emotional, action   2. e   3. T   4. c   5. T   6. cognitive dissonance

Forced Attitude Change— Brainwashing, Confession, and Cults

Most people associate the term "brainwashing" with techniques used by the Chinese on American prisoners during the Korean War. Through various types of "thought reform," the Chinese were able to coerce approximately 16 percent of these prisoners to sign false confessions (Schein *et al.,* 1957). More recently, the mass murder/suicide at Jonestown has rekindled public interest in the subject of inducing involuntary changes in attitudes, beliefs, or personal loyalties.

Question: What is brainwashing? How does it differ from other persuasive techniques?

As we have noted, advertisers, politicians, educators, religious organizations, and others actively seek to alter attitudes and opinions. To an extent their persuasive efforts resemble brainwashing, but there is an important difference: **Brainwashing** requires a *captive* audience. If you are offended by a television commercial, you can tune it out. Prisoners in the POW camps in Korea (and later in Vietnam) were completely at the mercy of their captors. James McConnell has noted that complete control over the environment allows a degree of psychological manipulation that would be impossible in a normal setting.

Question: How does captivity facilitate persuasion?

Brainwashing McConnell identifies three techniques used for brainwashing: (1) The "target" person is isolated from other people who would support his original attitudes; (2) the "target" is made completely dependent on his captors for satisfaction of his needs; (3) the indoctrinating agent is in a position to reward the "target" for changes in attitudes or behavior.

Brainwashing typically begins with an attempt to make the "target" feel completely helpless. Physical and psychological abuse, lack of sleep, humiliation, and isolation serve to **unfreeze** former values and beliefs. **Change** comes about when exhaustion, pressure, and fear become unbearable. The prisoner reaches the breaking point and signs a false confession or cooperates to gain relief. When he does, he is suddenly rewarded with praise, privileges, food, or rest. The continued coupling of hope and fear with additional pressures for conformity then serves to **refreeze** new attitudes (Schein *et al.,* 1961).

Question: How permanent are changes caused by brainwashing?

In most cases, the dramatic alteration in attitudes brought about by brainwashing is temporary. Most "converted" prisoners who returned to the United States after the

Korean War eventually reverted to their original beliefs and repudiated their indoctrinators.

Confession   Although we tend to think of coercive persuasion as unacceptable and immoral, its use may not be restricted to brainwashing. In the United States more than 80 percent of all criminal cases are solved by confession. Most confessions come while a suspect is being interrogated by a police officer. Police interrogations are obviously quite successful. Yet everyone knows of cases in which innocent people have confessed to crimes they did not commit, and frequently we read of persons retracting confessions made during an interrogation.

Question: Why do innocent people confess to crimes they did not commit?

After studying police manuals and procedures, Philip Zimbardo (1967a) states, "I am now convinced that the secret inquisitorial techniques of our police force are sometimes more highly developed, more psychologically sophisticated, and more effective than were those of the Chinese Communists." Although many would disagree with this opinion, it is, indeed, thought provoking.

Cults   Exhorted by their leader, some 900 members of the Reverend Jim Jones' People's Temple picked up paper cups and drank purple Kool-Aide laced with the deadly poison cyanide. Psychologically, the mass suicide at Jonestown in 1978 is not so incredible as it might seem. Isolated in the jungles of Guyana, intimidated by guards, lulled with sedatives, cut off from friends and relatives, and totally accustomed to obeying rigid rules of conduct, the inhabitants of Jonestown were primed for Jones' final "loyalty test." Of greater psychological interest is the question of how people reach such a state of commitment and dependency.

Question: Why do people join groups such as the People's Temple?

Psychologist Margaret Singer (1979) has studied and aided more than 300 former cult members. Her interviews reveal that, in recruiting new members, cults make use of a powerful blend of guilt, manipulation, isolation, deception, fear, and escalating commitment. In this respect, cults employ high-pressure indoctrination techniques not unlike those used in brainwashing.

Some of those interviewed by Singer were suffering from marked psychological distress when they joined a cult. Most, however, were simply undergoing a period of mild depression, indecision, or alienation from family and friends. Cult members try to catch potential converts at a time of need, especially when a sense of belonging will be attractive to the convert (for instance, just after a romance has broken up, or when the person is struggling with exams or choice of a major, or is simply at loose ends and "on the street").

Question: How is conversion achieved?

Often it begins with intense displays of affection and understanding ("love bombing"). Next comes isolation from non-cult members and drills, disciplines, and rituals (all night meditation or continuous chanting, for instance) to wear down physical and emotional resistance, as well as to generate commitment.

At first recruits make small commitments (to stay after a meeting, for example). Then, larger commitments are encouraged (to stay an extra day, to call in sick at work, and so forth). Making a major commitment is usually the final step. The new devotee signs over a bank account or property to the group, takes up residence with the group, and so forth. Such major public commitments create a powerful cognitive dissonance effect in which it becomes virtually impossible for converts to admit that they have made a mistake.

Once in the group, members are cut off from family and friends (former reference groups), and the cult can thus control the flow and the interpretation of information to them. Members are isolated physically (by continuous activity) and psychologically from their former value systems and social structure.

Question: Why do people stay in cults?

They do so partially out of a desire for social acceptance and approval. Strong bonds develop within the group and powerful group pressures are exerted on anyone who "betrays" or questions cult doctrines. More often, however, former members mention guilt and fear as the main reasons for not leaving even when they wished they could. Most had been reduced to childlike dependency on the group for meeting all their daily needs (Singer, 1979).

Behind the "throne" from which Jim Jones ruled Jonestown was a sign bearing these words: "Those who do not remember the past are condemned to repeat it" (Fig. 26-3). If we are to take the Reverend Jones at his word, then we should remember that cults are but one example of the danger of trading independence for security. The ultimate answer to the question, "Why didn't people just walk away from Jonestown?" seems to be that, though a real door or a wall is easily broken down, mental chains are the most unbreakable bonds of all. Cults are merely the most visible indication of the extent to which we all can be influenced by sophisticated psychological coercion, and by our needs for approval from others.

Prejudice—Attitudes that Injure

Prejudice is a negative attitude or prejudgment tinged with unreasonable suspicion, fear, or hatred. Often prejudice is institutionalized and backed by social power structures. In such cases it is referred to as **racism, sexism,** or **ageism,** depending on the group discriminated against. Since sexism and ageism were discussed in earlier chapters, let's focus on racial prejudice and racism. Both racial prejudice and institutionalized racism may contribute to *discrimination.* **Discrimination** refers to behavior that prevents individuals from doing things they might reasonably expect to be able to do, such as buying a house, riding a bus, or attending a high quality school.

An indication of just how pervasive discrimination can be comes from a rather remarkable study by F. K. Heussenstamm (1971). Subjects in the study were 15 college students, all of whom had received no traffic citations in the previous year. Each subject attached a Black Panther bumper sticker to his or her car. During the next 17 days the group received a total of 33 traffic citations! The power relationship between the white establishment and black militants (at least as interpreted by individual police officers) is clear.

Question: How do prejudices develop?

Becoming Prejudiced   One theory suggests that prejudice represents a form of **scapegoating.** Scapegoating, you may recall, is a form of displaced aggression in which hostilities generated by frustration are redirected to other targets. One interesting test of this hypothesis was conducted at a summer camp for young men. Subjects were given a difficult test they were sure to fail. Additionally, completing the test caused them to miss a trip to the theater (normally the high point of their weekly entertainment). Attitudes toward Mexicans and Japanese were measured before the test and after the men had failed the test and missed the entertainment. Subjects in this study consistently rated members of these two groups lower after they had been frustrated (Miller and Bugelski, 1970).

At times, the development of prejudice (like other attitudes) can be traced to direct experiences with members of the rejected group. A child who is repeatedly bullied by members of a particular racial or ethnic group may de-

Fig. 26-3   *Aftermath of the mass suicide at Jonestown. How do cultlike groups recruit new devotees? (See text.)*

velop resentment that forms the core of a lifelong dislike for other members of the group. The tragedy in such cases is that once such an antipathy is established, it prevents accepting additional, more positive experiences which could reverse the damage.

Gordon Allport (1958) concluded that there are two important sources of prejudice. **Personal prejudice** occurs when members of another racial or ethnic group represent a threat to the individual's security or comfort. For example, members of another group may be viewed as competitors for jobs. **Group prejudice** occurs simply through the individual's adherence to *group norms.* In other words, you may have no personal reason for disliking out-group members, but you do so because you are expected to.

The Prejudiced Personality   Other research suggests that prejudice at times is a general personality characteristic.

Question: Do you mean some people are more prone to prejudice than others?

Apparently some are. Theodore Adorno and his associates (1950) have conducted extensive research on what they call the **authoritarian personality.** These researchers started out by studying anti-Semitism as a means of understanding the social climate that existed in Germany during World War II. In the process they found that people who are prejudiced against one group tend to be prejudiced against *all out-groups.*

Question: What are the characteristics of the prejudice-prone personality?

The authoritarian personality can be described as a collection of personal attitudes and values marked by rigidity, inhibition, and oversimplification. Authoritarians tend to be very **ethnocentric**—they consider only members of their own national, ethnic, or religious group acceptable. They are also overwhelmingly concerned with power, authority, and obedience. To measure these qualities, the "F" scale was created. (The "F" stands for "fascism.") This attitude scale is made up of statements such as the following—to which the authoritarian readily agrees (Adorno *et al.,* 1950):

Authoritarian Beliefs
Obedience and respect for authority are the most important virtues children should learn.
People can be divided into two distinct classes: the weak and the strong.
If people would talk less and work more, everybody would be better off.

What this country needs most, more than laws and political programs, is a few courageous, tireless, devoted leaders, in whom the people can put their faith.
Nobody ever learns anything really important except through suffering.
Every person should have complete faith in some supernatural power whose decisions are obeyed without question.
Certain religious sects that refuse to salute the flag should be forced to conform to such patriotic action, or else be abolished.

As children, authoritarians were usually severely punished and learned to fear authority (and to covet it) at an early age. Authoritarians are not happy people.

It should be readily apparent from the list of authoritarian beliefs that the "F" scale is slanted toward politically conservative authoritarians. To be fair, psychologist Milton Rokeach (1960) has noted that rigid and authoritarian personalities can be found at both ends of the political spectrum. Rokeach therefore prefers to describe rigid and intolerant thinking as **dogmatism.**

Even if we discount the obvious bigotry of the dogmatic or authoritarian personality, racial prejudice runs deep in American society. To illustrate, a recent experiment showed that liberal, white, male college students were more willing to give shocks (under laboratory conditions) to a black victim than to a white victim (Shulman, 1974). We will probe deeper into the roots of such prejudiced behavior in an upcoming discussion, but first let's stop for a Learning Check.

Learning Check

1. Brainwashing differs from other persuasive attempts in that brainwashing requires a _____.

2. Which statement about brainwashing is *false?*

   a. The target person is isolated from others.

   b. Attitude changes brought about by brainwashing are almost always permanent.

   c. The first step is unfreezing former values and beliefs.

   d. Cooperation with the indoctrinating agent is rewarded.

3. More than 80 percent of all criminal cases in the United States are solved by confession.   T or F?

4. Margaret Singer found that most former cult members had experienced a major psychological disturbance just prior to joining the cult.   T or F?

5. Which of the following is *not* a technique typically used by cults to recruit new members?

   a. "love bombing" and isolation

   b. drills and rituals to wear down resistance

   c. physical intimidation and veiled threats

   d. a succession of smaller to larger commitments

6. The authoritarian personality tends to be prejudiced against all out-groups, a quality referred to as _____.

Answers: 1. captive audience 2. b 3. T 4. F 5. c 6. ethnocentrism

Table 26-1   University Students' Characterization of Ethnic Groups, 1933 and 1967

Trait	Percent Checking Trait		Trait	Percent Checking Trait		Trait	Percent Checking Trait	
	1933	1967		1933	1967		1933	1967
Americans			**Italians**			**Jews**		
Industrious	48	23	Artistic	53	30	Shrewd	79	30
Intelligent	47	20	Impulsive	44	28	Mercenary	49	15
Materialistic	33	67	Musical	32	9	Grasping	34	17
Progressive	27	17	Imaginative	30	7	Intelligent	29	37
			Revengeful	17	0			
Germans			**Irish**			**Blacks**		
Scientific	78	47	Pugnacious	45	13	Superstitious	84	13
Stolid	44	9	Witty	38	7	Lazy	75	26
Methodical	31	21	Honest	32	17	Ignorant	38	11
Efficient	16	46	Nationalistic	21	41	Religious	24	8

Source: M. Karlins, T. L. Coffman, and G. Walters, "On the Fading of Social Stereotypes: Studies in Three Generations of College Students." *Journal of Personality and Social Psychology,* 1969, 13: 1, 1–16.

Intergroup Conflict— The Roots of Prejudice

An unfortunate by-product of the human proclivity for forming groups is that group membership often limits contact with people in other groups. Additionally, groups themselves may come into conflict. Both events tend to foster unpleasant feelings and prejudices toward the out-group. The bloody clash of opposing forces in Ireland, in South Africa, and in hometown U.S.A. are reminders that intergroup conflict is a widespread problem of modern life. Daily we read of jarring clashes between nations, communities, races, and political, religious, or ethnic groups. In many cases, intergroup conflict is accompanied by *stereotyped* images of out-group members, and by bitter prejudice.

Question: What exactly do you mean by a stereotype?

Social stereotypes are oversimplified images of people who fall into a particular category. As psychologist Gordon Allport (1958) puts it: "Given a thimbleful of facts . . . [we] rush to make generalizations as large as a tub." Stereotypes tend to simplify people into "us" and "them" categories. Actually, aside from the fact that they always oversimplify, stereotypes may be either *positive* or *negative.* Table 26-1 shows stereotyped images of various national and ethnic groups and their changes over the years (Fig. 26-4). Notice that many of the qualities listed are desirable.

Stereotypes held by the prejudiced tend to be unusually irrational. When given a list of negative statements about other groups, prejudiced individuals agree with most of them. Particularly revealing is the fact that they often agree with conflicting statements. Thus, Jews are both "pushy" and "standoffish" or blacks are "ignorant" and "sly" to the prejudiced person. In one study, prejudiced subjects even expressed negative attitudes toward two nonexistent groups, the "Piraneans" and the "Danirians." As further testimony to the irrationality of stereotypes, we may note that when a prejudiced person meets a pleasant or likable member of a rejected group, the out-group member tends to be perceived as "an exception to the rule," not as a disconfirmation of the stereotype.

Question: How do stereotypes and intergroup tensions develop?

Two experiments, both in unlikely settings and both using children as subjects, offer some insight into these problems.

An Experiment in Prejudice   What is it like to be discriminated against? Those who have never experienced discrimination probably can't imagine it. In a unique experiment, elementary school teacher Jane Elliot sought to give her pupils direct experience with prejudice.

On the first day of the experiment, Elliot announced that brown-eyed children were to sit in the back of the room

Fig. 26-4 *Racial and ethnic pride are gradually replacing stereotypes and discrimination.*

and that they could not use the drinking fountain. Blue-eyed children were given extra recess time and got to leave first for lunch. At lunch brown-eyed children were prevented from taking second helpings, because they would "just waste it." Mixing of brown-eyed and blue-eyed children was prevented, and the blue-eyed children were told they were cleaner and smarter (Peters, 1971).

At first Elliot had to maintain these imposed conditions of prejudice. She also made an effort to constantly criticize and belittle the brown-eyed children. To her surprise, the blue-eyed children rapidly joined in, and soon were out-doing her in the viciousness of their attacks. The blue-eyed children began to feel superior, and the brown-eyed children felt just plain awful. Fights broke out. Test scores of the brown-eyed children fell.

Question: How lasting were the effects of this experiment?

The effects were short-lived, because two days later the roles of the children were reversed. Before long the same destructive effects occurred again, but this time in reverse. The implications of this experiment are unmistakable. In less than one day it was possible to get children to hate each other because of their eye color and **status inequalities.** Certainly the effects of a lifetime of real racial or ethnic prejudice are infinitely more powerful and destructive.

Question: What can be done to combat prejudice?

Equal-Status Contact   Progress has been made through attempts to educate the general public about the lack of justification for prejudicial attitudes. Changing the belief component of an attitude has long been known to be one of the most direct means of changing the entire attitude. Thus, when people are made aware that minority group members share the same goals, ambitions, feelings, and frustrations as they do, intergroup relations may be improved.

However, this is not the whole answer. As we noted earlier, there is often a wide difference between attitudes and actual behavior. Until nonprejudiced behavior is engineered, changes can be quite superficial. Several lines of thought (including cognitive dissonance theory) suggest that more frequent **equal-status** interaction between groups in conflict should reduce prejudice and stereotypes.

Question: But does it?

One study suggests it does. White women who lived in integrated and segregated housing projects were compared for changes in attitude toward their black neighbors. Women in the integrated project showed a favorable shift in attitudes toward members of the other racial group. Those in the segregated project showed no change or actually became more prejudiced than before (Deutsch and Collins, 1951).

The conclusion of this particular study was that contact must be on an equal footing if it is to reduce prejudice between segregated groups. To test this idea more directly, Gerald Clore and his associates set up a unique summer camp for children. The camp was administered by one white male, one white female, one black male, and one black female. Each campsite had three black and three white campers and one black and one white counselor. Thus, blacks and whites were equally divided in number, power, privileges, and duties. Did the experience make a difference? Apparently it did: Testing showed the children had significantly more positive attitudes toward opposite-race children after the camp than they did before (Clore, 1976).

Superordinate Goals   Let us now consider a revealing study of intergroup conflict and its reduction. Muzafer Sherif and his associates conducted an ingenious experiment—also at a summer camp—with eleven-year-old boys. When they arrived at camp, the boys were separated into two groups and housed in cabins that were physically separated. At first the groups were kept apart to build up in-group friendships. Development of pride and identification with the in-group was encouraged by participation in cooperative games and activities. Soon each group had a flag, a name (the "Rattlers" and the "Eagles"), and had staked out its own territory. At this point the two groups were placed in competition with each other. After a number of clashes, disliking between the two groups bordered on hatred. Outright hostility erupted as the boys baited each other, started fights, and raided each other's cabins (Sherif *et al.*, 1961).

Question: Were they allowed to go home hating each other?

As an experiment in the reduction of intergroup conflict, and to prevent the boys from remaining enemies, various strategies were tried to reduce tensions. Having leaders from each group meet did nothing. Just getting the groups together also did little. When the groups were invited to eat together, the event became a free-for-all.

Finally, emergencies that required cooperation among members of the groups were staged at the camp. For example, the water supply was damaged in a way that required all the boys to work together to repair it. Creation of this and other **superordinate goals** served to restore relations between the two groups. As members were forced to cooperate, hostilities subsided.

"Jigsaw" Classrooms   Contrary to the hopes of many, integrating public schools often has little positive effect on racial prejudice. In fact, prejudice may be made worse, and the self-esteem of minority students frequently decreases (Aronson, 1980).

Question: If integrated schools provide equal-status contact, shouldn't prejudice be reduced?

Theoretically, yes. But in practice, minority group children often enter newly integrated schools unprepared to compete on an equal footing. Elliot Aronson and his colleagues (1978) argue that the competitive nature of schools almost guarantees that children will *not* learn to like and understand each other. In the typical classroom, children compete fiercely for the approval of the teacher. Successful students learn to feel superior and often hold unsuccessful students in contempt. This is a high-stakes game, in which only a few can win. It is clearly not a good way to reduce prejudice.

With the preceding in mind, Aronson has pioneered a

Fig. 26-5   *In a "jigsaw" classroom, children help each other prepare for tests. As they "teach" each other what they know, the children learn to cooperate and to respect the unique strengths of each individual.*

way to apply the concept of superordinate goals to ordinary classrooms. According to Aronson, such goals are effective because they make people **mutually interdependent.** Each person's needs are linked to those of others in the group, and cooperation is encouraged.

Question: How has this idea been applied?

Aronson has successfully created **"jigsaw" classrooms** that emphasize cooperation rather than competition. The term "jigsaw" refers to the pieces of a jigsaw puzzle. In Aronson's method, each child is given a "piece" of the information needed to prepare for a test.

In a typical session, children are divided into groups of five or six, and given a topic to study for a later exam. Each child is given his or her "piece" of information, and asked to learn it. For example, one child might have information on Thomas Edison's invention of the light bulb, another, facts about his invention of the telephone, and a third, information on Edison's childhood. After the children have learned their individual parts, they teach them to others in the group. Even the most competitive children quickly realize that they cannot do well without the aid of everyone in the group. Each child makes a unique and essential contribution, so the children learn to listen to, and respect, each other.

Does the jigsaw method work? Compared to children in other classrooms, children in jigsaw groups were less prejudiced, they liked their classmates more, they had more positive attitudes toward school, their grades improved, and their self-esteem increased (Aronson *et al.,* 1979). Such results are quite encouraging. As Kenneth Clark (1965) has said, "Racial prejudice . . . debases all human beings—those who are its victims, those who victimize, and in quite subtle ways, those who are merely accessories."

Aggression—
The World's Most Dangerous Animal

For a time, the City Zoo of Los Angeles, California, had on display two examples of the world's most dangerous animal—the only animal capable of destroying the earth and all other animal species. Perhaps you have already guessed which animal it was. In the cage were two college students, representing the species *Homo sapiens!*

The human capacity for aggression is staggering. It has been estimated that during the 125-year period ending with World War II, 58 million humans were killed by other humans (an average of nearly one person per minute). Murder now ranks as a major cause of death in the United

States. It is estimated that more than 1.4 million American children are subjected to physical abuse by parents each year. War, homicide, riots, family violence, assassination, rape, assault, forcible robbery, and other violent acts offer further testimony to the realities of human aggression (Fig. 26-6).

Question: What causes aggression?

The complexity of aggression has given rise to a number of potential explanations for its occurrence. Brief descriptions of some of the major possibilities follow.

Instincts   Some theorists argue that, as humans, we are naturally aggressive, having inherited a "killer instinct" from our animal ancestors. Ethologists such as Konrad Lorenz (1966, 1974) believe that aggression is a biologically rooted behavior observed in all animals, including humans. Lorenz also believes that humans lack certain innate patterns that inhibit aggression in other animal species. For example, in a dispute over territory or dominance, two wolves may growl, lunge, bare their teeth, and fiercely threaten each other. In most instances, though, neither is killed or even wounded. One wolf, recognizing the dominance of the other, will typically bare its throat in a gesture of submission. The dominant wolf could kill in an instant, but it is inhibited by the submissive gesture. In contrast, human confrontations of equal intensity almost always end in injury or homicide.

The idea that humans are "naturally" aggressive has an intuitive appeal, but many psychologists question it. Many of Lorenz's "explanations" of aggression are little more than loose comparisons between human and animal behavior. Just labeling a behavior as "instinctive" does little to explain it. More importantly, we are left with the question of why some individuals or human groups (the Arapesh, the Senoi, the Navajo, the Eskimo, and others) show little hostility or aggression.

Biology   Despite problems with the instinctive view, there is evidence that a biological basis for aggression may exist. Physiological studies have shown that there are brain areas capable of triggering or ending aggressive behavior (see Chapter 3). Also, researchers have found a relationship between aggression and such physical factors as hypoglycemia (low blood sugar), allergy, and specific brain injuries and disorders (Bolton, 1976; Bandura, 1973; Mark and Ervin, 1970). None of these conditions, however, can be considered a direct *cause* of aggression. Instead, they probably lower the threshold for aggression, making hostile behavior more likely to occur.

Fig. 26-6   *Human aggression. Violent and aggressive behavior is so commonplace, it may be viewed as entertainment. How "natural" is the aggressive behavior of these women?*

Frustration   Step on a dog's tail and you may get nipped. Frustrate a human and you may get insulted. The **frustration-aggression hypothesis** states that frustration is closely associated with aggression (Dollard *et al.*, 1939). At several points in earlier chapters we have considered examples of the link between frustration and aggression.

Question: Does frustration always produce aggression?

Although the connection is strong, a moment's thought will show that frustration does not *always* lead to aggression, and that aggression can occur in the absence of frustration. Frustration, for instance, may lead to stereotyped responding, or perhaps to a state of "learned helplessness" (see Chapters 13 and 14). Aggression in the absence of frustration might be demonstrated by sports spectators who start fights, throw bottles, tear down goal posts, and the like, after their team has *won*.

When frustration encourages aggression it probably does so by raising overall arousal levels so that we become more sensitive to *cues* for aggression (Berkowitz, 1976).

Question: What do you mean by "cues" for aggression?

Some cues, or signals, for aggression are internal (angry thoughts for instance). Many are external: Certain words, actions, and gestures of others are strongly associated with aggressive response (a raised middle finger, for instance, is an almost universal invitation to aggression).

Even inanimate objects may serve as cues for aggression. In one classic experiment subjects administered shocks to another person in a laboratory. Before doing so, they were ridiculed and shocked by the other person. Just before subjects got a chance to "return the favor," they saw either a couple of badminton rackets, or a shotgun and a revolver on a table in the testing room. In either case, the experimenter explained that someone had left the objects there, and he casually moved them aside. Subjects who glimpsed the guns gave stronger shocks to the person who had angered them than did subjects who saw the sports equipment (Berkowitz, 1968). The implication of such research seems to be that the symbols and trappings of aggression encourage aggression.

Social Learning   One of the most widely accepted explanations of aggression is also the simplest. **Social learning theory** holds that we learn to be aggressive by observing aggression in others (Bandura, 1973). According to this view, there is no instinctive human programming for fistfighting, pipe-bombing, knife-wielding, gun-loading, or other elements of violent or aggressive behavior. Hence, aggression must be learned.

Social learning theorists predict that individuals growing up in nonaggressive cultures will themselves be nonaggressive. Those raised in a culture with aggressive models and heroes will learn aggressive responses.

Considered in such terms, it is no wonder that America has become one of the most violent of the major countries of the world. It is estimated that a violent crime occurs every 54 seconds in the United States. Approximately 40 percent of the population owns firearms. Nationally, 70 percent agree that "When a boy is growing up, it is very important for him to have a few fist-fights." Eighteen percent of the population admit to having slapped or kicked another person (Stark and McEvoy, 1970). Children and adults are treated to an almost nonstop parade of aggressive models (in the media as well as in actual behavior). We are, without a doubt, an aggressive culture.

Question: What can be done about aggression?

Social learning theory implies that "aggression begets aggression." In other words, watching a prize fight, sporting event, or violent television program may increase aggression, rather than drain off aggressive urges. Thus, the spiral of aggression might be broken if we did not so often portray it, reward it, and glorify it.

Beyond this, the question remains, "How shall we tame the world's most dangerous animal?" There is no easy answer. Only a challenge of pressing importance. The solution will undoubtedly involve the best efforts of thinkers and researchers from many disciplines.

For the more immediate future, it is clear that we need more people who are willing to engage in helpful, altruistic, or *prosocial* behavior. In the "Applications" section we will examine some of the forces that operate to prevent people from helping others. Also discussed are a few glimmerings about how to encourage prosocial behavior.

Learning Check

1. Social stereotypes may be both positive and negative.   T or F?

2. The stereotypes underlying racial and ethnic prejudice tend to be irrational.   T or F?

3. Over the last 30 to 40 years there has been a marked increase in stereotyped images held by college students.   T or F?

4. Jane Elliot's classroom experiment in prejudice showed that children could be made to dislike one another

   a. by setting up group competition   *b.* by imposing status inequalities
   c. by role playing   *d.* by frustrating all the students

5. Research suggests that prejudice and intergroup conflict may be reduced by _____ _____

   interaction and _____ goals.

6. Some researchers view aggression as related to such factors as hypoglycemia, allergy, and specific brain injuries and disorders. T or F?

7. Frustration is more likely to produce aggression when cues for aggressive behavior are present.   T or F?

8. Social learning theory holds that exposure to aggression _____ aggressive behavior. (circle)

   increases   decreases   has little effect on

Answers: 1. T 2. T 3. F 4. b 5. equal status, superordinate 6. T 7. T 8. increases

Resources Summary

● *Attitudes* are learned dispositions made up of a *belief component,* an *emotional component,* and an *action component.*

● Attitudes may be formed by *direct contact, interaction with others,* and *childrearing practices.* Groups also exert pressures on attitudes held by their members. *Peer group influences,* the *mass media,* and *chance conditioning* also appear to be important in attitude formation.

● Attitudes are typically measured by use of techniques such as *open-ended interviews, social distance scales,* and *attitude scales.* Attitudes expressed in these ways do not always correspond to actual behavior.

● Attitude change is related to *reference group membership,* to deliberate *persuasion,* and to significant *personal experiences* (which may be engineered through *role playing*).

● The maintenance and change of attitudes is closely related to needs for consistency in thoughts and actions. *Cognitive dissonance theory* explains the dynamics of such needs.

● *Brainwashing* is a form of forced attitude change. It depends on control of the target person's total environment. Three steps in brainwashing are *unfreezing, changing,* and *refreezing* attitudes and beliefs.

● Many religious and quasi-religious cults recruit new members with high-pressure indoctrination techniques resembling brainwashing. Such groups attempt to catch people when they are vulnerable. Then they combine isolation, displays of affection, discipline and rituals, intimidation, and escalating commitment to bring about conversion.

● *Prejudice* is a negative attitude held toward members of various *out-groups.* One theory attributes prejudice to *scapegoating.* A second account says that prejudices may be held for personal reasons (*personal prejudice*) or simply through adherence to *group norms* (*group prejudice*).

● Prejudiced individuals tend to have an *authoritarian* or *dogmatic personality,* characterized by rigidity, inhibition, intolerance, oversimplification, and *ethnocentrism.*

● *Intergroup conflict* gives rise to hostility and the formation of *social stereotypes. Status inequalities* tend to build prejudices. *Equal-status contact* tends to reduce it. Muzafer Sherif and others have emphasized the concept of *superordinate goals* as a key to reducing intergroup conflict, be it racial, religious, ethnic, or national. On a smaller scale, *jigsaw classrooms* (which encourage cooperation through mutual interdependence) have been shown to be an effective way of combating prejudice.

● *Aggression* and violence are serious social problems and the subject of much current research. *Ethological explanations* of aggression attribute it to inherited instincts. *Biological explanations* emphasize brain mechanisms and physical factors related to thresholds for aggression. According to the *frustration-aggression hypothesis,* frustration and aggression are closely linked, especially when *aggressive cues* are present. *Social learning theory* has focused attention on the role of aggressive models in the development of aggressive behavior.

Applications

Helping—Prosocial Behavior

Late one night in March, 1964, tenants of a Queens, New York, apartment building watched and listened in horror as a young secretary named Kitty Genovese was murdered on the sidewalk outside. From the safety of their rooms, no fewer than 38 people heard the agonized screams as her assailant stabbed her, was frightened off, and returned to stab her again.

Kitty Genovese's murder took over 30 minutes, but none of her neighbors tried to help. None even so much as called the police. Perhaps it is understandable that no one wanted to "get involved." After all, it could have been a violent lovers' quarrel; or helping might have meant risking personal injury. But what prevented these people from at least calling the police?

Question: Isn't this an example of the alienation of city life?

News reports treated this incident as evidence of a breakdown in social ties caused by the impersonality of the city. While it is true that urban living can be dehumanizing, this does not fully explain the **bystander apathy** observed in this and similar emergencies. According to social psychologists Bibb Latané and John Darley (1968), failure to help is related to the *number* of people present. The more potential helpers present, the lower the chances that help will be given.

Question: Why would people be less willing to help when others are present?

In Kitty Genovese's case the answer is that everyone thought *someone else* would help. The dynamics of this effect can be illustrated with a hypothetical example: Two motorists have stalled at roadside, one on a sparsely traveled country road and the other on a busy freeway. Who gets help first?

On the freeway, where hundreds of cars pass every minute, each driver assumes someone else will help. Personal responsibility for helping is spread so thin no one takes action. On the country road, one of the first few people to arrive will probably stop, since the responsibility is clearly theirs. In general, Latané and Darley assume

that bystanders are not apathetic or uncaring; they are inhibited by the presence of others.

Bystander Intervention There are four "decision points" individuals must pass through before giving help. First they must **notice** that something is happening. Next they must **define** the event as an emergency. Then they must **take responsibility.** Finally, they must **select** a course of action. Laboratory experiments have shown that each step can be influenced by the presence of other people.

Noticing What would happen if you fainted and collapsed on the sidewalk? Would someone stop to help? Would people think you were drunk? Would they even *notice* you? Latané and Darley suggest that if the sidewalk is crowded, few people will even see you. This has nothing to do with people blocking each other's vision. Instead, it is related to widely accepted norms against staring at others in public. People in crowds carefully "keep their eyes to themselves."

Question: Is there any way to show this is a factor in bystander apathy?

As a test of this idea, students were asked to fill out a questionnaire either alone or in a room full of people. While the students worked, a thick cloud of smoke was blown into the room through a ventilator.

Most students alone in the room noticed the smoke immediately. Few of the people in groups noticed the smoke, even when it became difficult to see through it. Subjects working in groups politely kept their eyes on their papers and avoided looking at others (or the smoke). In contrast, those who were alone scanned the room from time to time.

Defining an Emergency The smoke-filled room also shows the influence others have on defining a situation as an emergency. After subjects in groups noticed the smoke, they cast sidelong glances at others in the room. Apparently they were searching for clues to help interpret

Applications

what was happening. No one wanted to overreact or make fools of themselves if there was no emergency. However, as subjects coolly surveyed the reactions of others, they were themselves being surveyed. In real emergencies, people sometimes underestimate the need for action because each is attempting to appear calm. In short, until someone acts, no one acts.

Taking Responsibility   Perhaps the most crucial step in the helping sequence is assuming responsibility. In this case, groups limit helping by causing a **diffusion of responsibility.**

Question: Is that like the unwillingness of drivers to offer help on a crowded freeway?

Exactly. It is the feeling that no one is personally responsible for helping.

This problem was demonstrated in an experiment in which students took part in a group discussion over an intercom system. Actually, there was only one real subject in each group; the others were tape-recorded confederates of the experimenter. Each subject was placed in a separate room (supposedly to maintain confidentiality), and discussions of college life were begun.

During the discussion, one of the "students" simulated an epileptic-like seizure and called out for help. In some cases, subjects thought they were alone with the seizure victim. Others believed they were members of three- or six-person groups.

Subjects who thought they were alone with the "victim" of this staged emergency reported it immediately or tried to help. Some subjects in the three-person groups failed to respond and those who did were slower. In the six-person groups, over a third of the subjects took no action at all.

People in this experiment were obviously faced with a conflict like that in many real emergencies: Should they be helpful and responsible, or should they "mind their own business"? Many were influenced toward inaction by the presence of others.

Question: People do help in some emergencies. How are these different?

It is not always clear what makes the difference. Helping behavior is a complex event, influenced by many variables.

One naturalistic experiment staged in a New York City subway gives a hint of the kinds of things that may be important. When a "victim" (actor) "passed out" in a subway car, he received more help when carrying a cane than when carrying a liquor bottle. More importantly, however, was the fact that most people were willing to help in either case. In addition, there was little evidence of a diffusion of responsibility: The number of people didn't seem to matter much (Piliavin *et al.*, 1969). These observations are encouraging, but they tell little about how to increase the incidence of helping behavior.

Question: Is there really anything that can be done?

There is evidence that people who see others helping are more likely to offer help themselves. For example, motorists were much more likely to stop to help a woman fix a tire when they had just passed another woman being helped by someone (Bryan and Test, 1967). By offering help, you make a double contribution. You will have assisted directly, and you will have encouraged others to help.

Learning Check

1. Psychologists have shown that the dehumanizing qualities of urban living explain most instances of bystander apathy.   T or F?
2. Defining an event as an emergency is the first step toward bystander intervention.   T or F?
3. People sometimes fail to define an event as an emergency because they are misled by a seeming lack of concern displayed by others.   T or F?
4. In laboratory experiments, a large number of potential helpers tends to reduce the likelihood that help will be given.   T or F?

Answers: 1. F   2. F   3. T   4. T

Exploration

Psychology and Urban Stress—Life in the Big City

Everyone has his or her own list of complaints about living in, or visiting, a large city. Traffic congestion, pollution, crime, and impersonality are urban problems that immediately come to mind. To this list psychologists have added crowding, noise, and overstimulation as significant sources of urban stress. Recent psychological research has begun to clarify the impact of each of these conditions on human functioning.

Crowding   Overpopulation ranks as one of the most serious problems facing the world today. The world's population is now well over 4 billion, and it will more than double in the next 40 years if the current rate of growth continues. Nowhere are the effects of overpopulation more evident than in the crowded buses, subways, and living quarters of our big cities. The subjective discomforts of overcrowding are familiar to most people, but is there any way to assess the effect crowding has on people? One approach is to investigate the effects of overcrowding among animals. Although the results of animal experiments cannot be considered conclusive for humans, they point to some disturbing effects.

Question: For example?

In an interesting experiment, John Calhoun (1962) let a group of laboratory rats reproduce without restriction in a confined space. Calhoun provided plenty of food, water, and nesting materials for the rats. All the rats lacked was space. At its peak the colony numbered 80 rats, yet was housed in a cage designed to comfortably hold about 50. Overcrowding in the cage was further exaggerated by actions of the two most dominant males, who staked out private territory at opposite ends of the cage, gathered harems of 8 to 10 females, and prospered. This situation forced the remaining rats into a small middle area where severe crowding resulted.

Question: What effect did crowding have on the animals?

A high incidence of pathological behavior developed in both males and females. Females abandoned nest-building and caring for their young. Pregnancies decreased and

infant mortality ran extremely high. Many of the animals became indiscriminately aggressive and went on rampaging attacks against others. Abnormal sexual behavior was rampant, with some animals displaying hypersexuality, bisexuality, homosexuality, or complete sexual passivity. Many of the animals died, apparently from stress-caused diseases. The connection between these problems and overcrowding is unmistakable.

Question: But does this apply to humans?

Many of the same pathological behaviors can be observed in crowded inner-city ghettos. It is therefore tempting to assume that violence, social disorganization, and declining birthrates as seen in these areas are directly related to crowding. However, the connection has not yet been demonstrated with humans. Nutritional, educational, income, and health care disadvantages suffered by those living in the inner city may also be to blame (Freedman, 1975). In fact, most laboratory studies using human subjects have failed to produce any serious ill effects by crowding people into small places. Most likely, this is because *crowding* is a psychological condition that is separate from *density* (the number of people in a given space).

Question: How does crowding differ from density?

Crowding refers to *subjective* feelings of being overstimulated by social inputs or by a loss of privacy. Whether high density is experienced as crowding may depend on the relationship between those involved. In an elevator, subway, or prison, high densities may be uncomfortable. In contrast, a musical concert, party, or reunion may be most pleasant at high density levels (Freedman, 1975). Thus, crowding may interact with the type of situation in which it ocurs to intensify existing stresses or pleasures. Researcher Garvin McCain and his colleagues have recently reported that there are substantial increases in death rates among prison inmates and mental hospital patients living in crowded conditions.

Overload   One unmistakable consequence of increased densities and crowding is a condition that psy-

Exploration

cniologist Stanley Milgram refers to as *overload*. Large cities tend to bombard inhabitants with continuous sensory stimulation, information, and interpersonal contact. The resulting sensory and cognitive overload can be quite stressful. Milgram (1970) believes city dwellers learn to prevent overload by engaging in only brief, superficial interpersonal contacts, by disregarding nonessential events, and by blocking off receptivity through adopting cold and unfriendly expressions. In short, many city dwellers may find that a degree of callousness is essential for survival.

Question: Is there any evidence that such strategies are actually adopted?

A fascinating recent study suggests that they are. In several large American cities and smaller nearby towns, a young child stood on a busy street corner and asked passing strangers for help, saying, "I'm lost. Can you call my house?" About 72 percent of those approached in small towns offered to help. Only about 46 percent of those asked for help in the cities aided the child. In some cities (Boston and Philadelphia) only about one-third were willing to help (Takooshian *et al.*, 1977). A decline in sensitivity to the needs of others may yet prove to be one of the more serious costs of overpopulation.

Prospect   While overcrowding ranks high among the crises that face us, it is only one of the "superordinate" problems that press for world attention. What other problems can you identify that have community-wide, nation-wide, or worldwide effects? Can these problems be used to draw humanity together? Or do they bode a threatening and uncertain future? What role will psychology and psychologists play in the alleviation of such problems? What role will psychology play in your life?

Questions for Discussion

1. Several researchers have found that women are less uncomfortable than men under crowded conditions, and that both men and women are less uncomfortable when crowded in mixed groups. Can you explain these findings?

2. You have been placed in charge of designing a college dormitory so as to minimize the effects of crowding while at the same time maintaining high density. What would you do?

3. Choose an issue you feel strongly about. State your attitudes concerning the issue. How did you come to hold your present attitudes? What types of experiences or variables influenced you?

4. If you were asked to establish a program to end conflict between students attending two rival high schools, what steps would you take?

5. What do you think are the superordinate goals facing the nation and the world? (To be truly "superordinate" a goal would have to be seen as valid by nearly everyone.) Do such goals exist? How could such a goal be converted into greater intergroup cooperation?

6. The view that humans are instinctively aggressive "naked apes" has been quite popular. To what do you attribute this popularity? Do you consider humans naturally aggressive? What evidence can you give for or against this view?

7. Describe a situation in which you did or did not offer help to someone who was, or might have been, in need. What influenced your decision? In view of what you know about helping behavior, can you explain why rape or assault victims are advised to shout "Fire!"?

8. Kenneth Clark has said, "Prejudice is a way that human beings have of betraying the fragility of their egos." What do you think Clark means? Do you agree?

9. How has the antismoking campaign of the American Cancer Society made use of cognitive dissonance to discourage smoking?

10. In what ways do magazine and television advertisements make use of the principles of persuasion? (Consider the communicator, the message, and the audience.)

Suggestions for Further Reading

Allport, G. *The Nature of Prejudice.* Doubleday, 1958.

Aronson, E. *The Social Animal.* Freeman, 1980.

Baron, R. A., and D. Byrne. *Social Psychology: Understanding Human Interaction,* 2nd ed. Allyn and Bacon, 1977.

Cohen, A. *Attitude Change and Social Influence.* Basic Books, 1964.

Festinger, L., H. W. Riecken, and S. Schachter. *When Prophecy Fails.* University of Minnesota Press, 1956.

Festinger, L. *A Theory of Cognitive Dissonance.* Stanford University Press, 1957.

Himmelfarb, S., and A. H. Eagly. *Readings in Attitude Change.* Wiley, 1974.

McGee, M. G., and M. Snyder. "Attribution and Behavior: Two Field Studies," *Journal of Personality and Social Psychology,* **32,** 1975, pp. 185–190.

Zimbardo, P. G., and E. B. Ebbesen. *Influencing Attitudes and Changing Behavior,* 2nd ed. Addison-Wesley, 1977.

Appendix: Statistics[*]

Statistics from "Heads" to "Tails"

Let's say a friend of yours invites you to try your hand at a "game of chance." He offers to flip a coin and pay you one dollar if the coin comes up "heads." If the coin shows "tails," you must pay him a dollar. He flips the coin, tails—you pay him a dollar. He flips it again: tails. Again: tails. And again: tails. And again: tails. At this point you are faced with a choice. Should you continue the game in an attempt to recoup your losses? Or should you assume the coin is biased and quit before you really get "skinned"? Taking out a pocket calculator (and the statistics book you carry with you at all times) you compute the odds of obtaining five tails in a row from an unbiased coin. The probability is 0.031 (roughly three times out of 100). If the coin really is honest, five consecutive tails is a rather rare event. Wisely, you decide the coin is probably biased and refuse to play again. (Unless, of course, your "friend" is willing to take "tails," for the next five tosses!)

Perhaps a decision could have been made in this hypothetical example without using statistics. But notice how much clearer the situation becomes when it is expressed statistically.

Statistics in Psychology From the many observations they make, psychologists try to extract and summarize meaningful information. To do so they use two major types of statistics. The first type, called **descriptive statistics,** summarizes or "boils down" numbers so they become more meaningful and more easily communicated to others. The second type, known as **inferential statistics,** is used for decision-making, for generalizing from small samples, and for drawing conclusions. As was the case in the coin-flipping example, psychologists must often base decisions on limited data. Such decisions are greatly aided by inferential statistics.

Descriptive Statistics

Together, descriptive and inferential statistics bring greater clarity and precision to psychological thought and research. To see how, let's begin by considering three basic techniques of descriptive statistics: **graphical statistics,** measures of **central tendency,** and measures of **variability.**

Graphical Statistics Table A-1 shows hypothetical scores on a test of hypnotic susceptibility administered to 100 college students.

Table A-1   Raw Scores of Hypnotic Susceptibility

55	86	52	17	61	57	84	51	16	64
22	56	25	38	35	24	54	26	37	38
52	42	59	26	21	55	40	59	25	57
91	27	38	53	19	93	25	39	52	56
66	14	18	63	59	68	12	19	62	45
47	98	88	72	50	49	96	89	71	66
50	44	71	57	90	53	41	72	56	93
57	38	55	49	87	59	36	56	48	70
33	69	50	50	60	35	67	51	50	52
11	73	46	16	67	13	71	47	25	77

---

[*]Portions of this appendix were contributed by Daniel Downey, Ph.D.

Table A-2   Frequency Distribution of Hypnotic Susceptibility Scores

Class Interval	Number of Persons in Class
0–19	10
20–39	20
40–59	40
60–79	20
80–99	10

With such disorganized data, it is difficult to form an overall "picture" of differences in hypnotic susceptibility. But by using a **frequency distribution,** large amounts of such information can be neatly organized and summarized. To make a frequency distribution, the entire range of possible scores is broken down into *classes* of equal size. Next, the number of scores falling into each class is recorded. In Table A-2 the raw data have been condensed into a fre-

quency distribution. Notice how much clearer the scores of the entire group become.

Frequency distributions are often expressed *graphically* to make them more "visual." **Histograms,** as these are called, are constructed by labeling frequencies on the *ordinate* (vertical line) and class intervals on the *abscissa* (horizontal line). Next, bars are drawn for each class interval; the height of each bar is determined by the number of scores in each class (see Fig. A-1). An alternate way of graphing scores is the more familiar **frequency polygon** (Fig. A-2). Here, points are placed at the center of each class interval to indicate the number of cases. Then, the dots are connected by straight lines.

Measures of Central Tendency   A measure of central tendency is simply a number describing a "middle score" around which other scores fall. A familiar measure of central tendency is the mean, or "average." But as we shall see in a moment, there are other types of "averages" that can be used. To illustrate each we need an example—Table A-3 shows the raw data for a hypothetical experiment in which

Fig. A-1   *Frequency histogram of hypnotic susceptibility scores contained in Table A-1.*

Fig. A-2   *Frequency polygon of hypnotic susceptibility scores contained in Table A-1.*

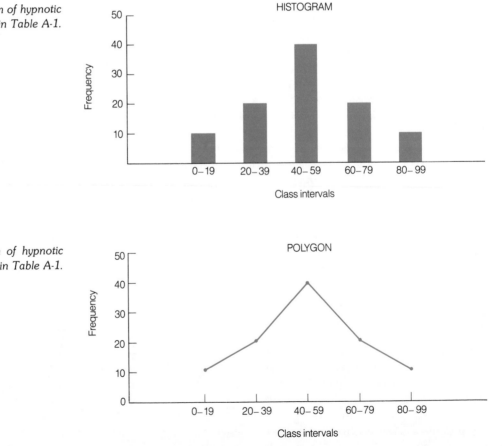

subjects were given a test of memory. Assume that one group was given a drug purported to improve memory (let's call the drug "rememberine"), while a second group received placebos. Is there a difference between memory scores of the two groups? It's difficult to tell without computing an average.

As one type of "average," the **mean** is computed by adding all the scores for each group and then dividing by the number of scores. Notice in Table A-3 that the means reveal a difference between the two groups.

The mean is sensitive to extremely high or low scores in a distribution. For this reason it is not always the best measure of central tendency. (Imagine how distorted it would be to calculate average yearly income from a small sample of people that happened to include a multimillionaire.) In such cases the *middle score* in a group of scores—called the **median**—is used instead. The median is found by arranging scores from the highest to the lowest and selecting the score that falls in the middle. Of course, if there is an even number of scores, there will be no "middle score." This problem is handled by averaging the two scores that "share" the middle spot. This procedure yields a single number to serve as the median (see bottom panel of Table A-3).

A final measure of central tendency is the **mode,** which is simply the most frequently occurring score in a distribution. If you were to take the time to count the scores in Table A-3, you would find that the mode of Group 1 is 65 and the mode of Group 2 is 60. Although it is easy to obtain, the mode can be an unreliable measure, especially in a small group of scores. The mode's advantage is that it gives the score actually obtained by the greatest number of people.

Measures of Variability Let's say a researcher discovers two drugs that lower anxiety in agitated patients. However, let's also assume that one drug consistently lowers anxiety by moderate amounts, whereas the second sometimes lowers it by large amounts, sometimes has no effect, or may even increase anxiety in some patients. Overall, there is no difference in the *average* (mean) amount of anxiety reduction, yet an important difference exists between the two drugs. As this example shows, it is not enough to simply know the average score in a distribution; usually, we would also like to know if scores are grouped closely together or scattered widely.

Measures of *variability* give a numerical value to the "spread" of scores. If you look again at the example in Table A-3, you will notice that the scores within each group vary widely. How can we show this fact?

Table A-3   Raw Scores on a Memory Test for Subjects Taking Rememberine or a Placebo

Subject	Group 1 Rememberine	Group 2 Placebo
1	65	54
2	67	60
3	73	63
4	65	33
5	58	56
6	55	60
7	70	60
8	69	31
9	60	62
10	68	61
Sum	650	540
Mean	65	54
Median	66	60

$$\text{Mean} = \frac{\Sigma X}{N} \text{ or } \frac{\text{sum of all scores, } X}{\text{number of scores}}$$

$$\text{Mean Group 1} = \frac{65 + 67 + 73 + 65 + 58 + 55 + 70 + 69 + 60 + 68}{10}$$

$$= \frac{650}{10} = 65$$

$$\text{Mean Group 2} = \frac{54 + 60 + 63 + 33 + 56 + 60 + 60 + 31 + 62 + 61}{10}$$

$$= \frac{540}{10} = 54$$

Median = the middle score or the mean of the two middle scores[*]

Median Group 1 = 55 58 60 65 **65 67** 68 69 70 73

$$= \frac{65 + 67}{2} = 66$$

Median Group 2 = 31 33 54 56 **60 60** 60 61 62 63

$$= \frac{60 + 60}{2} = 60$$

[*] ☐ indicates middle score(s).

The simplest way would be to use the **range,** which is the spread between the highest and lowest scores. In Group 1 of our experiment, the highest score is 73 and the lowest is 55; thus, the range is 18 (73 minus 55 equals 18). In Group 2, the highest score is 63, and the lowest is 31; this makes the range 32. Scores in Group 2 are more spread than those in Group 1.

A better measure of variability is the **standard deviation.** To obtain the standard deviation, the deviation (or difference) of each score from the mean is found and then

Table A-4   Computation of the Standard Deviation

| | Group 1—Mean = 65 | |
Score Mean	Deviation (d)	Deviation Squared (d²)
65 − 65 =	0	0
67 − 65 =	2	4
73 − 65 =	8	64
65 − 65 =	0	0
58 − 65 =	−7	49
55 − 65 =	−10	100
70 − 65 =	5	25
69 − 65 =	4	16
60 − 65 =	−5	25
68 − 65 =	3	9
		291

$$SD = \sqrt{\frac{\text{sum of d}^2}{n-1}} = \sqrt{\frac{291}{9}} = \sqrt{32} = 5.7$$

| | Group 2—Mean = 54 | |
Score Mean	Deviation (d)	Deviation Squared (d²)
54 − 54 =	0	0
60 − 54 =	6	36
63 − 54 =	9	81
33 − 54 =	−21	441
56 − 54 =	2	4
60 − 54 =	6	36
60 − 54 =	6	36
31 − 54 =	−23	529
62 − 54 =	8	64
61 − 54 =	7	49
		1276

$$SD = \sqrt{\frac{\text{sum of d}^2}{n-1}} = \sqrt{\frac{1276}{9}} = \sqrt{142} = 11.9$$

squared (multiplied by itself). These squared deviations are then added and averaged (the total is divided by the number of deviations minus one). Taking the square root of this average yields the standard deviation (see Table A-4). Notice again that the variability for Group 1 (5.7) is smaller than that for Group 2 (where the standard deviation is 11.9).

z-Scores   A particular advantage of the standard deviation is that it can be used to "standardize" scores in a way that gives them greater meaning. For example, John and Susan have both taken psychology midterms, but in different classes. John received a score of 118, and Susan scored 110. Who did better? It is impossible to tell without knowing what an average score was on each test, and whether John and Susan scored at the top, middle, or bottom of their classes. We would like to have one number that gives all this information. A number that does this is the **z-score.**

To convert original scores to z-scores, the mean is subtracted from the score and the resulting number is divided by the standard deviation for the group of scores from which the original came. To illustrate, Susan had a score of 110 in a class with a mean of 100 and a standard deviation of 10; her z-score is +1.0 (see Table A-5). John's score of 118 came from a class having a mean of 100 and a standard deviation of 18; thus his z-score is also +1.0 (see Table A-5). Originally it looked as if John did better on his midterm than did Susan, but we now see that, relatively speaking, their scores were equivalent. Compared to other students, each was an equal distance above average.

The Normal Curve

When chance events are recorded, we find that some outcomes have a high probability and occur very often; others have a lesser probability and occur infrequently; still others have little probability and occur rarely. As a result, the distribution (or tally) of chance events resembles a **normal curve** (see Fig. A-3). Most psychological traits or events are determined by the action of a large number of factors. Therefore, like chance events, measures of psychological variables tend to approximate a normal curve. For example, direct measurement has shown such characteristics as height, digit memory-span, and intelligence to be distributed normally. In other words, many people have average height, memory ability, and intelligence; but as we move above or below average, fewer and fewer people are found.

It is very fortunate that many psychological variables are distributed "normally," because a great deal is known about the mathematical properties of the normal curve. One property relevant to the preceding discussion is the fixed relationship between the standard deviation and the normal

Table A-5   Computation of a z-Score

$$z = \frac{X - \bar{X}}{SD} \text{ or } \frac{\text{score} - \text{mean}}{\text{standard deviation}}$$

$$\text{Susan: } z = \frac{110 - 100}{10} = \frac{+10}{10} = +1.0$$

$$\text{John: } z = \frac{118 - 100}{18} = \frac{+18}{18} = +1.0$$

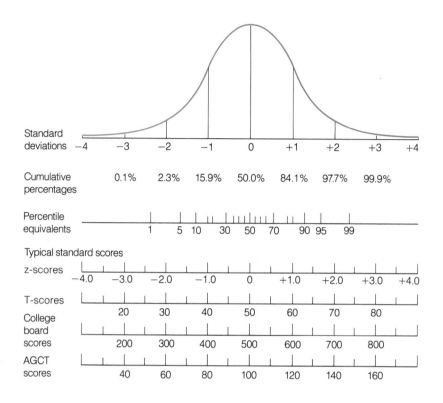

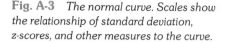

Fig. A-3 *The normal curve. Scales show the relationship of standard deviation, z-scores, and other measures to the curve.*

curve; specifically, the standard deviation measures off constant proportions of the curve above and below the mean. For example, in Fig. A-4, notice that 68 percent of all cases (IQ scores, memory scores, heights, or whatever) fall between one standard deviation above and below the mean (± 1 SD); 95 percent of all cases fall between ± 2 SD; and 99 percent of the cases can be found between ± 3 SD from the mean.

Table A-6 gives a more complete account of the relationship between z-scores and the percentage of cases found in a particular portion of the normal curve. Notice for example, that 93.3 percent of all cases fall below a z-score of $+1.5$. A z-score of 1.5 on a test (no matter what the original or "raw" score was) would be a good performance, since approximately 93 percent of all scores fall below this mark. Relationships between the standard deviation (or z-scores) and the normal curve are invariant, making possible useful comparisons between various tests or groups of scores.

Inferential Statistics

Let's say a psychologist studies the effects of isolation and loneliness on a group of monkeys. Is he or she interested only in this particular group? Usually not, since, except in rare instances, psychologists seek to discover general laws

of behavior that apply widely to human and animal species. As stated earlier, **inferential statistics** are techniques that allow us to make inferences. That is, they allow us to generalize from the behavior of small groups of subjects to that of the larger groups they represent.

Samples and Populations In any scientific investigation, we would like to observe the entire set, or **population,** of subjects, objects, or events being studied. However, this is usually impossible or impractical. Observing all Catholics, all cancer patients, or all mothers-in-law could be both im-

Fig. A-4 *Relationship between standard deviation and the normal curve.*

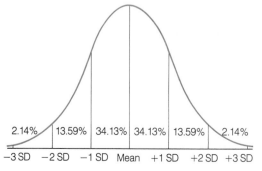

z-Score	Percentage of Area to the Left of This Value	Percentage of Area to the Right of This Value
−3.0 SD	00.1	99.9
−2.5 SD	00.6	99.4
−2.0 SD	02.3	97.7
−1.5 SD	06.7	93.3
−1.0 SD	15.9	84.1
−0.5 SD	30.9	69.1
0.0 SD	50.0	50.0
+0.5 SD	69.1	30.9
+1.0 SD	84.1	15.9
+1.5 SD	93.3	06.7
+2.0 SD	97.7	02.3
+2.5 SD	99.4	00.6
+3.0 SD	99.9	00.1

practical (since all are large populations) and impossible (since people change denominations, may be unaware of having cancer, and change their status as relatives). In such cases, **samples** or smaller cross sections of a population are selected, and observations of the sample are used to draw conclusions about the entire population.

The major requirement for any sample is that it be **representative.** That is, the sample group must truly reflect the composition and characteristics of the larger population. Referring to our hypothetical study of the effects of a drug on memory, it would be essential that the sample of 20 subjects from whom data is collected be representative of the general population. A very important aspect of representative samples is that their members are chosen at **random;** that is, each member of the population must have an equal chance of being included in the sample.

Significance of Differences Between Groups in an Experiment

In our hypothetical drug experiment, we found that the average memory score was higher for the group given the drug than it was for subjects who received no drug (the placebo group). Certainly this result is interesting, but could it have occurred by chance? If two groups were repeatedly tested (with neither receiving any drug), their average memory scores would sometimes differ. How much must two

means differ before we can consider the difference "real" (not due to chance)?

Notice that the question is similar to one discussed earlier: How many "tails" in a row must we obtain when flipping a coin before we can conclude that the coin is biased? In the case of the coin, we noted that obtaining five tails in a row is a rather rare event. Thus, it became reasonable to assume the coin was biased. Of course, it is possible to get five tails in a row when flipping an honest coin. But since this outcome is unlikely, we have good reason to suspect that something other than chance (a "loaded" coin, for instance) caused the results. Similar reasoning is used in tests of *statistical significance.*

Tests of **statistical significance** provide an estimate of how often experimental results could have occurred by chance alone. The results of a test of statistical significance are stated as a probability giving the odds that the observed difference was due to chance. In psychology, any experimental result that could have occurred by chance 5 times (or less) out of 100 (in other words, a probability of .05 or less) is considered *significant.* In the memory experiment we have used as an example, the probability is .025 ($p \leqslant .025$) that the group means would differ as they do by chance alone. This allows us to conclude with reasonable certainty that the drug actually did improve memory scores.

Correlation

Many of the statements that psychologists make about behavior do not result from the use of experimental methods. Rather, they come from keen observations and measurement of existing phenomena. A psychologist might note, for example, that the higher one's socioeconomic and educational status, the greater the variety of sexual behavior engaged in. Or that grades in high school are excellent predictors of how well an individual will do in college. Or even that as rainfall levels increase within a given metropolitan area, crime rates are drastically reduced. In these instances, we are dealing with the fact that two variables are **co-relating** (varying together in some orderly fashion).

The simplest way of visualizing a correlation is to construct a **scatter diagram.** In a scatter diagram, two measures (grades in high school and grades in college, for instance) are obtained. One measure is indicated by the X axis and the second by the Y axis. The scatter diagram plots the intersection of each pair of measurements as a single point. Many such measurement pairs give pictures like those in Fig. A-5.

Figure A-5 also shows scatter diagrams of three basic kinds of relationships between variables (or measures). Graphs *a, b,* and *c* show **positive relationships** of varying strength. As you can see, in a positive relationship, increases in the *X* measure (or score) are associated with increases on the *Y* measure (or score). An example would be finding that higher IQ scores (*X*) are associated with higher college grades (*Y*). A **zero correlation** (or relationship) is pictured in graph *d.* This might be the result of comparing subjects' hat sizes (*X*) to their college grades (*Y*). Graphs *e* and *f* both show a **negative relationship** (or correlation). Notice that as values on one measure increase, those on the second become smaller. An example might be the relationship between level of anxiety and classroom test scores: higher anxiety is correlated with lower scores.

Correlations can also be expressed as a **coefficient of correlation.** This coefficient is simply a number falling somewhere between $+1.00$ and -1.00. If the number is zero or close to zero it indicates a weak or nonexistent relationship. If the correlation is $+1.00$ a **perfect positive relationship** exists; if it is -1.00 a **perfect negative relationship** has been discovered. The most commonly used correlation coefficient is called the Pearson *r.* Calculation of the Pearson *r* is relatively simple, as shown in Table A-7. (The numbers shown are hypothetical.)

As stated in Chapter 2, correlations in psychology are rarely perfect. Most fall somewhere between zero and plus or minus one. The closer the correlation coefficient is to $+1.00$ or -1.00, the stronger the relationship. For example, identical twins are likely to have almost identical IQs, whereas parents and their children have IQs that are only generally similar. The correlation between IQs of parents and children is 0.4; that between identical twins is 0.9.

Correlations are particularly valuable for making **predictions.** If we know two measures are correlated, and we know a person's score on one measure, we can predict his or her score on the other. For example, most colleges have formulas that make use of multiple correlations to decide which prospective students have the best chances for success. Usually the formula includes such "predictors" as high school GPA, teacher ratings, and scores on the Scholastic Aptitude Test (SAT) or some equivalent. Although none of the predictors is perfectly correlated with success in college, together they correlate highly and provide a useful technique for screening applicants.

There is an interesting "trick" you can do with correlations that you may find useful. It works like this: If you *square* the correlation coefficient (multiply *r* by itself) you will get a number telling the **percent of variance** accounted for by the correlation. For example, the correlation between IQ

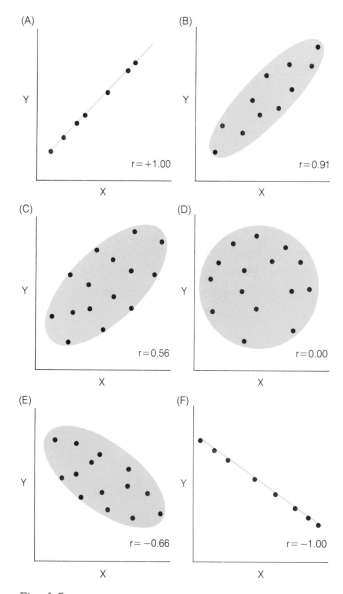

Fig. A-5 *Scatter diagrams showing various degrees of relationship for a positive, zero, and negative correlation. (Adapted from Pagano, 1981.)*

scores and college grade-point average is 0.5. Multiplying 0.5 times 0.5 gives 0.25, or 25 percent. This means that 25 percent of the variation in college grades is accounted for by knowing IQ scores. In other words, with a correlation of 0.5, college grades are "squeezed" into an oval like that in graph *c,* Fig. A-5. IQ scores take away some of the possible variation in corresponding grade-point averages. If there were no correlation between IQ and grades, grades would be completely free to vary, as shown in Fig. A-5, graph *d.*

Table A-7   IQ and Grade Point Average for Computing Pearson r

Student No.	IQ X	Grade Point Average Y	X Score Squared X^2	Y Score Squared Y^2	X Times Y XY
1	110	1.0	12,100	1.00	110.0
2	112	1.6	12,544	2.56	179.2
3	118	1.2	13,924	1.44	141.6
4	119	2.1	14,161	4.41	249.9
5	122	2.6	14,884	6.76	317.2
6	125	1.8	15,625	3.24	225.0
7	127	2.6	16,124	6.76	330.2
8	130	2.0	16,900	4.00	260.0
9	132	3.2	17,424	10.24	422.4
10	134	2.6	17,956	6.76	348.4
11	136	3.0	18,496	9.00	408.0
12	138	3.6	19,044	12.96	496.8
Total	1503	27.3	189,187	69.13	3488.7

$$r = \frac{\sum XY - \dfrac{(\sum X)(\sum Y)}{N}}{\sqrt{\left[\sum X^2 - \dfrac{(\sum X)^2}{N}\right]\left[\sum Y^2 - \dfrac{(\sum Y)^2}{N}\right]}}$$

$$= \frac{3488.7 - \dfrac{1503(27.3)}{12}}{\sqrt{\left[189,187 - \dfrac{(1503)^2}{12}\right]\left[69.13 - \dfrac{(27.3)^2}{12}\right]}}$$

$$= \frac{69.375}{81.088} = 0.856 = 0.86$$

(Adapted from Pagano, 1981.)

Along the same line, a correlation of 1.00 or −1.00 means that 100 percent of the variation in the Y measure is accounted for by knowing the X measure: If you know a person's X score, you can tell exactly what the Y score is. An example that comes close to this state of affairs is the high correlation (0.9) between the IQs of identical twins. In any group of identical twins, 81 percent of the variation in the "Y" twins' IQs is accounted for by knowing the IQs of their siblings (the "Xs").

Correlation and Causation   It is very important to recognize that the existence of a correlation between two measures does not mean that one causes the other: *Correlation does not demonstrate causation.* When a correlation exists, the best we can say is that two variables are related. Of course, this does not mean that it is impossible that two correlated variables are causally related. Rather, it means that we cannot *conclude* that a causal relationship exists on the basis of a correlation. To establish greater confidence in the existence of a causal relationship, an experiment must be performed (see Chapter 2).

Often two correlated variables are related through the influence of a third variable. For example, we might observe that the more hours students devote to studying the better their grades. Although it is tempting to conclude that more studying produces (causes) better grades, it is possible (indeed, it is probable) that grades and the amount of study time are both related to the amount of motivation or interest a student has.

The distinction between having data that indicate causality versus data that indicate a relationship of unknown origin is one that should not be forgotten. Since we rarely run experiments in daily life, the information on which we act is largely correlational. This should make us more humble and more tentative in the confidence with which we make pronouncements about human behavior.

Glossary

Absolute threshold   A point indicating the minimum amount of physical energy necessary to produce a sensation.

Accommodation   Changes in the shape of the lens of the eye that serve to focus objects at varying distances. Also the adaptation of old concepts and thinking habits to new information (Piaget).

Acetylcholine (AS-ih-til-COH-leen)   This neurotransmitter substance is released at synapses and at the neuromuscular junction (point of contact between a neuron and a muscle fiber). Acetylcholine can initiate a nerve impulse or a muscle contraction depending upon its point of release.

Achievement motivation   A need for success or the attainment of excellence.

Acromegaly (Ak-row-MEG-uh-lee)   A medical condition involving progressive enlargement of the hands, face, and feet due to excessive secretion of growth hormones by the pituitary gland.

Acuity (ah-CUE-ih-tee)   That aspect of visual perception having to do with the sharpness or resolution of images.

Acupuncture (AK-you-punk-chur)   The Chinese medical art of relieving pain and treating illness by inserting thin hair-like needles at various points on the body.

Adaptation   In general, adjustment to environmental demands. In connection with the senses, refers to a gradual decline in response to a constant stimulus.

Adaptation level   An internal or mental "medium" point that is used to judge amounts.

Addiction   Development of physical dependence on a drug such that craving and physical discomfort (withdrawal symptoms) occur in its absence.

Adrenal glands (ah-DREE-nal)   Source of adrenaline, a hormone secreted during emotional arousal. Also, a source of other important hormones.

Adrenaline (ad-REN-ah-lin)   A hormone produced by the adrenal glands similar in its effects to sympathetic nervous system activation. Adrenaline produces diffuse activation throughout the body.

Affect   Pertaining to emotion or feelings.

Affective disorders   A form of psychopathology characterized by mania or severe depression. Disorders involving extremes of emotion.

Affective psychosis   A loss of contact with reality involving extremes of emotional response such as mania, depression, or manic-depressive mood swings.

Afferent (AF-er-ent)   Carrying or conducting inward as in nerves or neurons conveying impulses toward the brain or central nervous system; opposite of *efferent*.

Afferent or **sensory nerves**   Incoming sensory fibers.

Affiliation motive   The desire to associate with other people.

Ageism   An active prejudice held on the basis of age; hence, any tendency to discriminate on the basis of age.

Age regression   Return of a hypnotized subject to a younger age.

Agnosias (ah-KNOW-zyahs)   Disturbances in perception of the meaning of sensory stimuli; hence, an inability to know; for example, an inability to recognize objects or pictures.

Alpha wave   A relatively large, slow brain-wave pattern indicating the individual is in a passive state of relaxed awareness.

Altered state of consciousness   Any non-ordinary mental state including meditation, hypnosis, and drug induced states.

Ambivalence (am-BIV-ah-lens)   Holding opposite emotions such as love and hate toward some person or object.

Amnesia   Loss of memory (partial or complete) for past events.

Amniocentesis (AM-nih-oh-SEN-teh-sis)   The extraction and analysis of amniotic fluid from the womb in the early stages of pregnancy. Used for the detection of genetic anomalies in the fetus.

Amphetamines   Class of drugs acting as central nervous system stimulants. Not known to be physically addictive but may cause strong psychological dependency.

Anal stage   In Freud's theory, the second stage of psychosexual development corresponding roughly to the period of toilent training between the second and third year.

Androgen (AN-dro-jen)   Any of a number of male sex hormones.

Androgyny (an-DROJ-ih-nee)   The condition of having both male and female behavioral traits or a balance between "masculinity" and "femininity" as they are defined by one's culture.

Anesthesia (an-es-THEES-zyah)   Loss of bodily sensations.

Anima (AN-im-ah)   In Jung's theory, an archetype representing femaleness or the female principle within the psyche. (See *archetype*.)

Animus (AN-ih-mus)   In Jung's theory, an archetype representing maleness or the male principle within the psyche. (See *archetype*.)

Anorexia nervosa (AN-or-EX-yah ner-VOH-sah)   A condition in which a person will eat, but with great reluctance, and typically not enough to sustain normal weight. A serious loss of appetite of apparent psychological origin.

Anosmia (an-NOSE-me-ah)   Loss of the sense of smell, particularly for a specific type of odor.

Anthropomorphic fallacy (AN-thro-po-MORE-fik)   The temptation to attribute human thoughts, feelings, and motives to animals.

Antidepressants   Drugs that counteract depression or despondency by elevating the individual's mood.

Antipsychotics (AN-tih-sike-OT-iks)   Drugs that alleviate psychotic symptoms, making it easier to treat psychiatric problems.

Anxiety   A feeling of painful or apprehensive uneasiness closely related to fear. Especially characterized by dread or anticipation of some unclear threat.

Anxiety disorders   A class of personal disturbances characterized by excessive and chronic anxiety states. Traditionally referred to as neurosis.

Aphasias (ah-FAZE-yahs)   Speech disturbances resulting from damage to certain areas in the temporal lobe of the brain.

Apnea (ap-NEE-uh)   To be without breath; an interruption in breathing.

Approach-avoidance conflict   Unpleasant condition in which a person is simultaneously attracted to and repelled by the same goal.

Archetype (AR-keh-type)   An original pattern, prototype, or idea on which others are modeled. In Jung's theory, archetypes are universal primordial images found in the collective unconscious.

Arousal   The overall level of excitation or activation present at any given time for a person or animal.

Assessment   Evaluation or measurement.

Astigmatism (ah-STIG-mah-tiz-im)   A defect in the shape of the cornea, lens, or the eye as a whole that causes some parts of vision to be out of focus.

Attention   Orienting toward or focusing on some stimulus.

Attitude   A predisposition having emotional, belief, and behavioral components that determines a person's reaction toward a particular social stimulus.

Autism (OT-is-im)   A severe disorder of childhood involving mutism, sensory spin-outs, sensory blocking, tantrums, lack of awareness of others, echolalia, and other difficulties.

Autokinetic effect (OT-oh-kin-ET-ik)   The apparent movement of a stationary pinpoint of light displayed in a dark room. Often occurs as a result of suggestion.

Autonomic nervous system (ANS) (OT-oh-NOM-ik)   Division of the peripheral nervous system concerned with involuntary functions of the body.

Aversive conditioning (ah-VER-siv)   Use of an unpleasant or painful stimulus to reinforce learning.

Avoidance learning   Learning procedure in which the occurrence of a particular response results in postponement or prevention of an unpleasant stimulus.

Axon (AX-on)   A thin fiber process extending from the cell body of a neuron (nerve cell). Axons normally conduct information away from the cell body.

Babinski reflex   Curling and spreading of the toes that occurs when the sole of an infant's foot is stroked.

Bait shyness   An unwillingness or hesitation on the part of animals to accept a particular food. Often caused by the presence of a taste aversion. (See *taste aversion.*)

Barbiturates   Addictive drugs that depress activity of the central nervous system. Barbiturate intoxication resembles intoxication caused by alcohol.

Behaviorism   School of psychology holding that overt observable behavior is the only worthwhile subject for psychological study.

Behavior modification   Application of principles of learning to change or eliminate maladaptive or abnormal behavior.

Beta waves (BAY-tah)   Fast, low-voltage activity of a more or less random character recorded on the EEG when an organism is alert and attending to stimuli.

Biased sampling   Selection of subjects for an experiment or public opinion poll that gives some subjects a greater chance of being included than others.

Binocular cues   Any cue for depth perception requiring two eyes.

Biofeedback   A technique allowing a subject to monitor and control his or her own internal bodily functions.

Blind spot   A portion of the retina where the optic nerve leaves the eye. No visual receptors are found at the blind spot.

Brain lesion (LEE-zhun)   Destruction of brain tissue experimentally, accidentally, or through disease.

Brainstorming   A group problem-solving technique in which ideas are offered freely, imaginatively, and initially without evaluation as to their practicality.

Brainwashing   Engineered or forced change in attitudes and beliefs.

Brightness   In perception, the brightness of a stimulus or object refers to the relative amount of light reflected from or emanating from its surface.

Carcinogen (kar-SIN-oh-jen)   Any cancer-producing substance.

Cataplexy (CAT-ah-plek-see)   A sudden loss of all muscle tone and voluntary movement in the body causing complete collapse.

Catatonic (CAT-ih-TAWN-ik)   A schizophrenic state marked by alternate periods of stupor and activity, also by mutism, and waxy flexibility (catalepsy) of the body.

Central nervous system (CNS)   The brain and spinal cord.

Character   A subjective evaluation placed upon an individual's personality, often as to its desirable and undesirable attributes.

Chemotherapy (CHEM-oh-therapy or KEY-mo-therapy)   Use of psychoactive drugs for the treatment of mental disturbances.

Chromosomes (KROE-moe-somz)   Rodlike structures within the nucleus of each cell that carry the genes. Normal human cells carry 23 pairs of chromosomes.

Circadian rhythms (SUR-kay-DEE-an)   Cyclical changes in bodily function that vary on a schedule approximating one 24-hour day.

Clairvoyance (klare-VOY-ans)   Purported form of extrasensory perception (ESP) in which objects or events are perceived without the aid of normal sensory systems.

Classical conditioning   A basic form of learning discovered by Pavlov in which existing (reflex) responses are attached to new stimuli by pairing of the stimuli with those that naturally elicit the response.

Client-centered therapy   A form of therapy designed by Rogers in which the client assumes responsibility for solving his or her own problems. The therapist's role is to clarify and assist, not to give advice.

Climacteric (kly-MAK-ter-ik)   A period or point during late middle-age in males in which a significant change in health, vigor, appearance, or potency takes place. Roughly analogous to the menopause in women.

Clinical psychologist   A psychologist who specializes in the treatment of psychological and behavioral disturbances or who does research pertaining to such disturbances.

Cloning (KLOE-ning)   The reproduction of an entire plant or organism from a single cell of the original plant or organism.

Closure   Gestalt term for the perceptual tendency to complete figures by "closing" or ignoring small gaps.

Cochlea (KOCK-lee-ah)   The snail-shaped organ of hearing in the inner ear containing the ultimate sensory receptors for audition.

Coding   Organizing information for efficient memory storage and retrieval.

Coefficient of correlation (KOE-eh-FISH-ent of KORE-eh-LAY-shun)   An index of the degree of relationship between two sets of measures or two variables. Coefficients are expressed as a number ranging from -1.00 to $+1.00$.

Cognition (cog-NISH-un)   The process of thinking, knowing, or processing information.

Cognitive (COG-nih-tiv)   Of or pertaining to thinking, knowing, understanding, or the internal processing of information.

Cognitive dissonance (COG-nih-tiv DIS-oh-nenz)   An imbalance between one's thoughts, beliefs, or attitudes, and one's behavior. According to the theory, cognitive dissonance is a tension state people are motivated to reduce.

Cognitive map   Internal images of an area (maze, city, campus, etc.) that presumably underlie an ability to choose alternate paths to the same goal.

Collective unconscious   According to Jung's theory, a portion of the psyche common to all people and housing archetypal images. (See *archetype*.)

Colostrum (ko-LOSS-trum)   The first milk secreted by women up to a few days after the delivery of a child. Colostrum is rich in antibodies to disease accumulated by the mother.

Compression   In hearing, the squeezing together of air molecules at the front of a sound wave. Collision of the compressed wave-front with the auditory apparatus sets it in motion.

Compulsion   An act the individual feels driven to repeat, often against his or her will.

Concept   A generalized idea representing a class of objects or events that are grouped together on the basis of some common feature or property characteristic of each.

Condensation   In the Freudian theory of dream interpretation, condensation is a tendency to combine images from several sources into a single complex image.

Conditioned emotional response   The conditioning of autonomic nervous system response and/or visceral response to a previously non-emotional stimulus.

Conditioned response   A learned response that becomes attached to the conditioned stimulus in classical conditioning.

Conditioned stimulus   In Pavlovian conditioning, a previously neutral stimulus that acquires the capacity to evoke a response as the result of association with an unconditioned stimulus.

Conditioning   The process of learning by association discovered by Pavlov. Also sometimes used to refer to operant learning.

Cones   Visual receptors in the eye responsible for color vision and daylight visual acuity.

Conflict   A mental or behavioral state characterized by clashing or incompatible motives, desires, goals, etc. The four most basic conflicts are approach conflicts, avoidance conflicts, approach-avoidance conflicts, and double approach-avoidance conflicts.

Congenital problems (kon-JEN-ih-tal)   A defect acquired during development in the uterus; hence, a problem existing at birth (a "birth defect"). Distinct from a *hereditary* problem (i.e., one transmitted by the genes).

Conjunctive concept (kon-JUNK-tiv)   A concept defined as having one value on one dimension *and* a second value on another dimension (e.g., red triangles). (Compare to *disjunctive* and *relational* concepts.)

Connotative meaning (KON-oh-TAY-tiv)   The subjective personal or emotional significance of a word or concept apart from its explicit and recognized meaning.

Conscience (KON-shens)   Internalized sense of right and wrong. In Freudian theory, the superego.

Consolidation (KON-sol-ih-DAY-shun)   Theoretical process by which material is solidified as a permanent memory in the brain after being learned.

Constructs   Explanatory concepts inferred from observable events but not directly observable themselves.

Contact comfort   A pleasant and reassuring feeling human and animal infants derive from touching or clinging to something soft and warm, usually the mother.

Contiguity (KON-tih-GEW-ih-tee)   In close proximity or contact; very near in time or space.

Continuous reinforcement   A schedule of reinforcement in which every response is reinforced.

Control   Eliminating, identifying, or equalizing all factors in an experiment that could affect the outcome.

Control group   A group in a psychological experiment exposed to all experimental conditions except the independent variable.

Convergence   The simultaneous turning inward of the two eyes as they focus on nearby objects.

Convergent thought   Thinking directed toward discovery of a single established correct answer. Conventional thinking.

Conversion reaction   Type of neurosis characterized by physical symptoms resulting from anxiety or stress. Anxiety that is hysterically converted into physical symptoms.

Cornea (KOR-nee-ah)   Clear outer membrane covering the eyeball.

Corpus callosum (KOR-pus cah-LO-sum)   A large nerve unit in the middle of the brain connecting the two hemispheres. Serves to transfer information from one hemisphere to the other.

Correlation (KOR-eh-LAY-shun)   The existence of a consistent (non-random) relation between two variables or measures.

Corticalization (KORE-tih-kal-ih-ZAY-shun)   The increase in the relative size and importance of the cerebral cortex observed as one ascends the biological scale from lower animals to humans.

Counselor   A mental health professional who specializes in adjustment problems not involving serious mental disorder, for example, marriage counselors, occupational counselors, or school counselors.

Cretinism (KREE-tin-ism)   A form of mental retardation resulting from a malfunction of the thyroid gland.

Critical period   A time during which a certain event must occur in an organism's life if development is to occur normally.

Dark adaptation   The process by which the eye adapts to conditions of low illumination, principally, by a shift to rod vision.

Decibel (DES-ih-bel)   A unit used to measure the loudness of sounds; ordinary speech registers around 60 decibels.

Deductive thought   A pattern of thought in which the thinker must use a general set of rules to draw a logical conclusion. (Compare to *inductive* thought.)

Defense mechanisms   Habitual and unconscious psychological devices used to reduce or avoid anxiety.

Delayed speech   A significant delay in the development of speech capacity in early childhood.

Delta waves   Large, slow, regular waves of brain activity recorded on the EEG during the deeper stages of sleep.

Delusions   False beliefs held against all evidence to the contrary. Symptomatic of some psychotic disorders.

Demonology (DEE-mon-OL-oh-gee)   In Medieval Europe, that branch of knowledge dealing with the study of demons and the treatment of those "possessed" by demons.

Dendrites (DEN-drites)   Branching projections of nerve cell bodies (neurons) that form synapses with other neurons and conduct information toward the cell body.

Denial   A defense mechanism in which we merely deny the existence of a problem or an unpleasant reality.

Denotative (de-no-TAY-tiv)   The objective dictionary meaning of a word or concept.

Dependent variable   The variable (usually a behavior) that reflects changes in the independent variable.

Depressant   A drug or chemical agent that lowers bodily or nervous system function.

Depressive neurosis (new-ROW-sis)   Prolonged and severe depression triggered by a stressful event but representing an overreaction to it.

Depressive psychosis   A form of psychosis characterized by the deepest possible despondency.

Deprivation (deh-prih-VAY-shun)   In development, the loss or withholding of normal stimulation, nutrition, comfort, love, etc. A condition of lacking.

Depth perception   The ability to see three-dimensional space and to accurately estimate distances.

Detoxification (de-TOX-ih-fih-KAY-shun)   To remove poison or the effects of poison. In the treatment of alcoholism, the physical withdrawal of the patient from alcohol.

Developmental tasks   Any of the countless personal changes that must be made throughout life for optimal development.

Difference threshold   The smallest change in a physical stimulus that can be detected by an observer.

Digit span test   A test of attention and short-term memory. Series of random digits of varying lengths are read to subjects who are then immediately asked to recall them.

Discrimination (learning)   The ability to detect differences between two or more objects or events. Often brought about by reinforcement of responses to one stimulus but not the other.

Dishabituation (DIS-ha-bit-you-AY-shun)   A reinstatement of sensory response lost or reduced by the occurrence of habituation. (See *habituation*.)

Disjunctive concept   A concept defined by the presence of at least one of a number of features, or a concept defined as having one value on one dimension *or* a different value on another dimension (e.g. blue *or* triangular). (Compare to *conjunctive* and *relational* concepts.)

Displacement   In Freudian theory, the rechanneling of energy from one target or activity to another. Often used as a defense mechanism as when aggression is displaced on someone or something other than the actual source of frustration.

Dissociative reaction (dis-SOSH-ih-tiv)   An unusual form of neurosis including amnesia, fugue, and multiple personality which allows the individual to completely separate himself from thoughts and actions he finds unacceptable.

Divergent thinking (DIE-vur-jent)   Thinking which produces many ideas or alternatives. Creative or unconventional thinking.

DNA (deoxyribonucleic acid)   Large and complex chemical molecules found in chromosomes and believed to be the substance of which genes are composed.

Dogmatism (DOG-mah-tism)   An unwarranted positiveness or certainty in matters of opinion.

Dominant gene   A gene whose influence will be expressed on every occasion in which it is present. (Compare to *recessive gene*.)

Dopamine (DOPE-ah-meen)   An important neurotransmitter found in the brain, particularly at sites within the limbic system.

Drive   The psychological representation of internal need states, for example, hunger, thirst, etc.

Drug interaction   The outcome of combining two or more drugs within the body producing effects above and beyond what would be expected from the mere addition of the effects of one to the effects of the other.

Dual personality   A form of neurotic disorder in which the person maintains two separate personalities; typically one personality is unaware of the existence of the other.

Echolalia (ek-oh-LAY-lee-ah)   A tendency, sometimes observed in autistic children, to repeat whatever is said to them.

EEG (electroencephalogram)   Record of the electrical activity of the brain made by attaching electrodes to the scalp.

Efferent (EF-er-ent)   Carrying or conducting outward as in nerves or neurons conveying impulses away from the brain or central nervous system; opposite to *afferent*.

Ego (EE-go)   In Freudian terminology, the portion of personality in conscious control of behavior. The ego reconciles the demands of the id, superego, and external reality.

Egocentric (EE-go-CENT-rik)   Being unable to take a viewpoint other than one's own.

Eidetic imagery (eye-DET-ik im-AGE-ree)   The ability to retain an image long enough to use it as a source of information. Basically, a photographic memory.

Ejaculation (EE-jac-you-LAY-shun)   The release of sperm and seminal fluid by the male at the time of orgasm.

Electra conflict (EE-lek-tra)   In Freudian theory, a conflict experienced by female children when they become attracted to their fathers and feel themselves to be in competition with their mothers.

Electroconvulsive shock (ECS) (EE-lek-tro-con-VUL-siv)   An electric shock passed directly through the brain, producing a convulsion. ECS can impair memory and produce amnesia in experimental animals. Clinically it is used in the treatment of severe depression.

Electrode   Any needle, wire, metal plate, or saltwater-filled glass tube used to apply electrical current to the body, especially to neural tissue.

Electromagnetic radiation (EE-lek-tro-mag-NET-ik)   Waves of energy produced by electric and magnetic oscillations. Radio waves, light waves, X-rays, and gamma rays are all electromagnetic waves differing only in their wavelength.

Empathy (EMP-ath-ee)   A capacity for taking another's point of view or to share their state of consciousness; to feel what another is feeling.

Empirical (em-PEER-ih-cal)   Founded upon experiment or experience; based upon direct observation.

Encopresis (en-coh-PREE-sis)   An inability to control defecation (elimination of solid wastes); hence, "soiling."

Endocrine system (EN-doe-krin)   Bodily system comprised of those glands whose secretions pass directly into the bloodstream or lymph.

Endorphins (en-DORF-ins)   A recently discovered class of brain peptides (proteins) having an apparent link to the control of pain and possibly to psychiatric disturbances.

Engrams (IN-gramz)   "Memory traces" or physical changes taking place in the brain. A general term referring to the theoretical basis for learning and memory.

Enkephalins (en-KEF-ah-lins)   Recently discovered brain peptides (proteins) having an apparent link to emotional functioning.

Enuresis (en-you-REE-sis)   An inability to control urination, particularly with reference to bed-wetting.

Episodic drive (ep-ih-SOD-ik)   A non-cyclical drive state occurring in discrete episodes associated with particular conditions (e.g., pain avoidance, specific hungers, sexual motivation).

Episodic memory (ep-ih-SOD-ik)   A hypothesized "autobiographical" subpart of memory that records life events or "episodes."

Erogenous zone (eh-ROJ-ih-nus)   Any bodily area productive of pleasurable sensations and particularly those areas producing erotic desire when stimulated.

Escape learning   Learning to make a response to escape or to terminate an aversive (painful) stimulus. Escape learning is negatively reinforced by termination of the aversive stimulus.

Estrogen (ES-tro-jen)   Any of a number of female sex hormones.

Estrus (ES-trus)   Changes in the reproductive organs and sexual drives of animals associated with a desire for mating, particularly used to refer to female animals "in heat."

Ethnocentric (ETH-no-CEN-trik) Placing one's own group or race at the center; that is, tending to reject all other groups but one's own.

Eugenics (you-GEN-iks) The science that deals with the improvement of an animal species or race.

Exorcism In Medieval Europe, the practice of expelling or driving off an "evil spirit," particularly one residing in the body of an individual who is "possessed."

Experiment A scientific technique whereby all relevant variables are manipulated, measured, or controlled so that a cause-effect relationship may be observed. Simple experiments typically include the creation of an experimental group and a control group.

Experimental group In a controlled experiment the group of subjects exposed to the independent variable or experimental manipulation.

Extinction The process of consistently not reinforcing a learned response, leading to a gradual decrease in the frequency with which the response occurs.

Extraneous variables (ex-TRAY-nee-us) Those conditions or factors to be excluded from possible influence on the outcome of a controlled experiment (i.e., variables the experimenter is not interested in).

Extrovert (EX-tro-vert) An individual whose energies and interests are directed outward, a person who seeks social contact or is out-going. (Compare to *introvert*.)

Factor analysis A statistical technique whereby multiple measures are intercorrelated. Measures that form "clusters" of correlations are assumed to represent some more general underlying factor.

Fantasy A product of the imagination determined mainly by one's motives or feelings. Fantasy may be used as an escape mechanism.

Feedback Knowledge of results relaying the effect of some action.

Figure-ground Gestaltist's observation that some aspects of a stimulus pattern appear to stand out as an object (figure) while others appear to stand in the background (ground).

Fixation The tendency to repeat wrong solutions or faulty responses as a consequence of frustration. In Freudian theory, lasting conflicts developed during a particular stage of development as a result of frustration or overindulgence during that stage.

Fixed action pattern A genetically programmed sequence of movements occurring mechanically and virtually universally in members of a particular species.

Fixed-interval schedule A schedule of reinforcement in which reinforcement is administered following a fixed period of time after the previous reinforcement. For example, every three minutes.

Fixed-ratio schedule A schedule of reinforcement in which a predetermined number of responses must be made before reinforcement is delivered. For example, one reinforcement may be delivered for *every* five responses.

Flat affect A seemingly total lack of emotional responsiveness.

Fovea (FOE-vee-ah) A small depression in the center of the retina containing the greatest concentration of cones and providing the sharpest vision.

Fraternal twins Twins conceived from two separate eggs. Fraternal twins are no more alike genetically than other siblings.

Free association A technique of psychoanalysis in which the person says anything that comes into his mind regardless of how embarrassing or unimportant it may seem.

Free-floating anxiety Feelings of dread or apprehension that cannot be traced to any particular source.

Frigidity An abnormal lack of sexual desire.

Frontal lobotomy Destruction of the frontal lobes of the brain, or separation of the frontal lobes from the remainder of the brain.

Frustration An internal emotional state resulting from interference with satisfaction of a motive or blocking of goal-directed behavior.

Fugue (fewg) A neurotic dissociative reaction characterized by taking flight and by a loss of memory for events prior to or during the act of fleeing.

Functional fixedness Rigidity in problem solving caused by an inability to see novel uses for familiar objects.

Functionalism (FUNK-shun-al-ism) School of psychology concerned with how behavior and mental abilities help people adapt to their environments.

Functional psychosis A psychosis with no apparent biological basis.

Galvanic skin response (GSR) (gal-VAN-ik) A change in the electrical resistance of the skin associated with arousal or anxiety.

General adaptation syndrome (GAS) Selye's description of a consistent pattern of reactions to prolonged stress occurring in three stages: alarm, resistance, and, finally, exhaustion.

General paresis (pah-REE-sis) An organic psychosis that results when syphilis attacks the brain.

Generalization The transfer of a learned response from one stimulus or set of circumstances to others that are in some way like the original stimulus.

Genes The carriers of hereditary characteristics found in the nucleus of every cell.

Genital stage The final stage in psychosexual development (according to Freud). Typically attained in late adolescence and representing full psychosexual maturity.

Gerontologist (JER-on-TOL-oh-jist) One who studies the effects of aging.

Gestalt (geh-SHTALT) A German word meaning form or pattern. Also, the school of psychology emphasizing the study of perception, learning, and thinking in whole units, not by analysis into parts.

Gestalt therapy A psychotherapy developed by Perls and others which emphasizes immediate experience and participation of the whole person in any activity.

Goal The object of a motivated and directed sequence of behavior.

Gonads The sex glands—testes in males and ovaries in females.

Grammar The study of classes of words and their functions and relations within sentences.

Graphology (graph-ALL-oh-jee) The legitimate study of handwriting to detect forgeries; also, the discredited notion that personality characteristics are revealed by handwriting.

Group sanctions Any rewards or punishments (real or symbolic) applied to members of a group for adherence to, or deviation from, group norms for acceptable conduct.

Group therapy Any form of psychotherapy taking advantage of the special characteristics of group interaction. Patients work out personal problems with the help of other group members and the guidance of a trained therapist.

Gustation (gus-TAY-shun) The sense of taste or the act of tasting.

Habituation (HA-bit-you-AY-shun) A decrease in the strength of a reflex caused by its repeated elicitation. Also, a decrease in sensory response to repeated presentation of a stimulus.

Hallucinations (HA-lu-sih-NAY-shuns) Experiencing imaginary sensations such as seeing, hearing, or smelling things that don't exist in the real world.

Hallucinogen (ha-lu-SIN-oh-jen) Any substance that causes hallucinations.

Halo effect The tendency to generalize a favorable or unfavorable impression to unrelated details of personality.

Hebephrenic schizophrenia (HEE-beh-FREN-ik, SKIZ-oh-FREE-nih-ah) A form of psychosis characterized by giddy, obscene, or silly behavior and including a severe disintegration of personality.

Heredity A transmission of physical and psychological characteristics from parents to offspring through genes.

Hermaphroditism (hur-MAF-roh-dite-ism) The condition of having genitals suggestive of both sexes; ambiguous genital sexuality.

Hippocampus A structure in the brain associated with the regulation of emotion and the transfer of information from short-term memory to long-term memory.

Homeostasis (HOE-me-oh-STAY-sis) Steady state of physiological equilibrium maintained by various bodily mechanisms.

Hormone A bodily chemical transported by body fluids that has an effect on physiological functioning or psychological behavior.

Hospitalism A pattern of deep depression observed in institutionalized infants; marked by weeping and sadness and a lack of normal response to other humans.

Hue That property of color represented by its classification into basic categories of red, orange, yellow, green, blue, indigo, and violet or intermediaries of these.

Humanistic Any system of thought focused specifically on human problems, potentials, or ideals.

Hydrocephaly (HI-dro-SEF-ah-lee) A type of mental retardation caused by accumulation of cerebrospinal fluid within the brain.

Hyperactivity A behavioral state characterized by short attention-span, restless movement, and impaired learning capacity. Sometimes referred to as minimal brain dysfunction (MBD).

Hyperopia (HI-per-OH-pea-ah) A visual defect causing farsightedness.

Hypnogogic images (hip-no-GAH-jik) Unusually vivid mental imagery associated with hypnosis, the period immediately preceding sleep, and other unusual states of consciousness.

Hypnosis An altered state of consciousness characterized by relaxation, focused attention, and increased susceptibility to suggestion.

Hypochondria (HI-po-KON-dree-ah) An excessive preoccupation with minor bodily problems or a neurosis characterized by complaints about illnesses which seem to be imaginary.

Hypoglycemia (HI-po-gly-SEE-me-ah) Below-normal blood sugar level.

Hypothalamus (HI-po-THAL-ah-mus) A small area at the base of the brain that regulates many aspects of motivation and emotion, particularly hunger, thirst, and sexual behavior.

Hypothesis (hi-POTH-eh-sis) The predicted outcome of an experiment or an educated guess about the relationship between variables.

Hysteria (his-TAIR-ih-ah) Wild emotional excitability sometimes associated with the presence of a neurosis.

Hysterical neurosis (his-TAIR-ih-cal new-ROW-sis) An abnormal reaction in which psychological problems are given expression as physical symptoms or disabilities. Usually expressed as paralysis or insensitivity in the absence of any actual organic disorder.

Id According to Freud, the id is the most primitive part of the personality, which supplies energy and which demands immediate gratification of needs, drives, and desires.

Identical twins Twins who develop from the same egg and who, therefore, have an identical hereditary makeup.

Identification A process in personality development in which a person becomes like an admired adult by incorporating the adult's goals and values into his or her own behavior. Also used as a defense mechanism in adulthood.

Illusion In perception, an unreal or misleading impression presented to vision or other senses. Thus, a perception that fails to give a true representation of the stimulus. (Compare to *hallucination*.)

Implicit trial and error In problem solving, the internal elimination (by covert trial and error) of wrong solutions.

Imprinting A rapid and relatively permanent type of learning occurring within a limited period of time early in life.

Incentive A goal object valued by an individual that can be employed to motivate behavior.

Independent variable In a controlled experiment the condition under investigation as a potential cause of some change in behavior; the variable manipulated (changed) by the experimenter.

Inductive thought A type of thinking in which one is given a series of specific examples and must infer from them a general rule. (Compare to *deductive* thought.)

Innate Inborn or hereditary traits.

Insanity Mental disability resulting in an inability to manage one's affairs or to be aware of the consequences of one's actions. Legally, persons declared insane may not be held fully responsible for their actions.

Insight A sudden reorganization of the elements of a problem causing the solution to become self-evident. Also refers to one's understanding of one's own behavior or motives.

Insomnia A consistent or prolonged inability to obtain sufficient sleep.

Instinct Complex unlearned behaviors that are species-specific and relatively uniform.

Instrumental conditioning Learning brought about when voluntary responses are affected by their consequences as when an animal learns its way through a maze to get food; specifically, the effects of positive and negative reinforcement, nonreinforcement, and punishment.

Intellectualization A psychological defense mechanism in which anxiety or emotion is removed from a situation by thinking or speaking of it in very formal or abstract terms.

Intelligence quotient (IQ) An index of intelligence defined as a person's mental age divided by his or her chronological age and multiplied by 100.

Interference theory The theory of forgetting that holds that previously learned materials interfere with the storage of new material or that recalling previous learning is prevented by recent learning.

Intermittent reinforcement Reinforcement occurring irregularly or unexpectedly (partial reinforcement).

Intrauterine environment (IN-tra-YOU-ter-in) The chemical and physical environment existing in the womb before birth.

Introspection (IN-tro-SPEK-shun) A psychological technique used to examine one's own conscious experience. Self-observation of one's thoughts, feelings, and sensations.

Introvert (IN-tro-vert) An individual who prefers being alone, who withdraws from social contact, or who is self-centered. (Compare *extrovert*.)

Iris Colored circular muscle of the eye that opens and closes to admit more or less light into the eye.

Isolation A psychological defense involving the separation of contradictory feelings or ideas into "logic-tight" compartments.

Just noticeable difference The amount of increase or decrease in a stimulus that can be reliably detected as a change in amount, value, or intensity.

Kinesics (kih-NEE-siks) The study of expression or communication through movements and gestures.

Kinesthesis (KIN-es-THEEZ-sis) The sense of bodily position, muscle movement, or equilibrium.

Latency (LATE-en-see) In Freudian theory, the period from age six until puberty characterized as a quiet interruption of psychosexual development.

Latent learning (LAY-tent)   Learning which occurs without obvious reinforcement and which is not apparent until reinforcement is provided.

Lateralization   Refers to the division of specific mental functions or abilities on one side of the brain or the other.

Learned helplessness   A learned inability to overcome environmental obstacles or to avoid punishment.

Learning   In general, any relatively permanent change in behavior that can be attributed to experience but not to such factors as fatigue, maturation, injury, etc.

Learning set   A readiness for learning a task or mastering a problem established by prior learning of similar tasks or solution of similar problems.

Lens   A transparent structure at the front of the eye that focuses images on the retina.

Libido (lih-BEE-doe)   In Freudian terminology, the sexual energy involved in the functioning of personality, primarily sexual in nature.

Limbic system   A collection of interconnected brain structures whose functions include smell and emotional reactions.

Linguistic determinism   Hypothesis proposed by Whorf that the language one speaks shapes perceptions of reality and influences thought.

Localization of function   The theory that particular psychological functions are represented by particular parts of the brain.

Logotherapy (LO-go-therapy)   Therapy which emphasizes the need to find meaning in life.

Long-term memory   Memory of events for relatively long periods, usually presumed to be based on permanent storage of information transferred from short-term memory.

Major tranquilizers   Drugs which in addition to having tranquilizing properties also serve as anti-psychotics by reducing hallucination, sensory distortions, and delusional thinking. (Compare to *minor tranquilizers*.)

Mandala (man-DALL-ah)   A circular design advanced to a high art form by Tibetan Buddhists. Mandalas are considered a symbolization of wholeness, balance, and totality. Mandala-type designs are observed in all cultures.

Manic   Extremely excited, hyperactive, or irritable.

Manic-depressive psychosis   A psychosis in which a person swings in mood from elation or excitement to deep depression.

Masochism (MAS-oh-kism)   Deriving sexual gratification from pain inflicted on the self by others.

Massed practice   Continuous practice without rest periods or interruption as distinct from distributed practice.

Mass media   Major channels of public communication and information flow such as radio, television, newspapers, magazines.

Masturbation   Production of orgasm by manipulation or other stimulation of the genitals other than by intercourse.

Maturation   The emergence and development of personal characteristics in an orderly sequence as a result of underlying physical growth.

Meditation   A contemplative exercise for the production of relaxation, heightened awareness, or spiritual revelation.

Menarche (MEN-ark)   The onset of menstruation; a woman's first period.

Menopause (MEN-oh-pause)   The female "change of life" signaled by the end of regular monthly menstrual periods.

Mental age   An indication of mental ability defined in terms of the average capabilities of individuals at each age; that is, mental ability apart from actual age in years.

Mescaline (MES-call-in)   A psychoactive drug derived from the peyote cactus which has properties similar to LSD.

Mesmerize   An archaic term for hypnotize.

Metabolism (meh-TAB-oh-lism)   The rate of energy production and expenditure in the body.

Microcephaly (mike-roh-CEF-ah-lee)   A type of mental retardation characterized by a very small skull which prevents normal brain development.

Microsleep   A momentary shift in brain-wave patterns to those of sleep.

Minimal brain dysfunction   A condition of brain immaturity believed by some to underlie hyperactivity in children. (See *hyperactivity*.)

Minor tranquilizers   Drugs capable of producing relaxation, a reduction of general tension or activation, and those that have an antianxiety property such as Valium. (Compare to *major tranquilizers*.)

MMPI (Minnesota Multiphasic Personality Inventory)   The most widely used self-rating personality test.

Mnemonic device (nee-MON-ik)   Any technique or strategy to assist remembering.

Model   A system of ideas and concepts designed to interrelate known facts and to provide an explanatory system.

Modeling   A type of imitation in which an individual mimics behavior performed by another person (the model).

Mongolism (Down's Syndrome)   A hereditary abnormality associated with the presence of 47 chromosomes rather than the usual 46. Characterized by a shortened life expectancy, mental retardation, and unusual physical features.

Monocular   Pertaining to the function of one eye. For example, monocular cues for depth perception are those involving the use of only one eye.

Morphemes (MORE-feems)   The smallest meaningful units in a language.

Motive   A drive or force within the organism that activates behavior or directs it toward a goal.

Motor neuron   An efferent neuron that carries motor commands from the central nervous system to muscles and glands.

Motor program   A mental representation or model of a skilled movement; similar in some ways to a computer program.

Motor skills   Learned skills having an element of physical dexterity or requiring the coordination of muscular movements.

Multiple personality   A rare form of neurosis in which an individual maintains two or more distinct personalities; classified as a dissociative reaction.

Myopia (my-OH-pea-ah)   A visual defect making it difficult to focus distant objects (nearsightedness).

Narcolepsy (NAR-co-lep-see)   A serious sleep disturbance in which the individual suffers uncontrollable sleep attacks. The urge to sleep can be sufficiently irresistible to overcome afflicted individuals when they are standing or driving.

Natural selection   Charles Darwin's theory that evolution favors the survival of those plants and animals best adjusted to the conditions under which they live (survival of the fittest).

Naturalistic observation   Observation and recording of naturally occurring behavior that is not manipulated experimentally.

Need   In motivational theory a specific state within the organism that may elicit behavior appropriate to the need (often related to the depletion of essential bodily substances or the disruption of homeostasis).

Negative practice   The deliberate repetition of an unwanted response until it becomes aversive or painful.

Negative reinforcement   Increasing the probability of a response by terminating or withdrawing an unpleasant stimulus upon completion of the response.

Negative transfer   A carry-over of skills or responses from one task to another when such carry-over impairs performance on the second task. (Compare *positive transfer*.)

Neo-Freudians (NEE-oh Freudians)   Those personality theorists who accept the broad features of Freud's psychodynamic approach but include variations and alterations of their own.

Neonate (NEE-oh-nate)   The human newborn.

Nervous system   A network of neurons that interconnects sensory receptors and effector organs to produce behavior and conscious experience.

Neurilemma (NEW-rih-LEM-ah)   A thin layer of cells wrapped around the axons of some neurons.

Neurons   Individual nerve cells that form the basic structure of the nervous system.

Neuropeptides (NEW-roh-PEP-tides)   A newly discovered class of brain chemicals consisting of simple proteins; these substances have a wide range of effects on moods and behavior.

Neurosis (new-ROW-sis)   A behavior disturbance primarily characterized by excessive anxiety, minor distortions of reality, and subjective discomfort. Neuroses appear to be psychological in origin. Typically, they do not completely prevent a person from attending school, holding a job, or maintaining relationships.

Neurotransmitter (NU-roh-transmitter)   Any one of a number of chemical substances secreted by neurons that cross the synapse and alter activity in the receiving neuron.

Night blindness   A condition in which vision becomes impaired in low levels of illumination.

Non-directive therapy   (See *Client-centered therapy.*)

Non-homeostatic   Not subject to the maintenance of homeostatic balance.

Nonsense syllable   A meaningless syllable usually consisting of a consonant, a vowel, and a consonant; used in experiments on retention and memory.

Noradrenaline (NOR-ah-DREN-ah-lin)   A neurotransmitter secreted by neurons of the sympathetic nervous system. Also produced at various locations within the brain. Increased noradrenaline output is associated with anger.

Normal curve   A bell-shaped curve having known mathematical properties. Characterized by a large number of scores in the middle tapering toward each end.

Norms   Accepted social rules for behavior to which the individual members of a group tend to conform.

NREM sleep   Sleep periods during which there is a minimum of eye movements and little or no dreaming.

Nystagmus (nis-TAG-mus)   Involuntary vibration or movement of the eyeball including tiny oscillations (physiological nystagmus) and larger reflex movements seen in the blind.

Object constancy   Tendency to perceive objects in the same way even when our view of them changes.

Object permanence   Recognition that objects continue to exist when they cannot be seen. Very young children appear to believe that objects cease to exist when they are out of sight.

Obsessions   Recurring irrational or disturbing thoughts a person cannot prevent.

Obsessive-compulsive neurosis   Extreme preoccupation with certain thoughts and compulsive performance of certain behaviors both of which occur in ritualistic or unavoidable fashion.

Oedipus conflict (ED-ih-pus)   A Freudian concept referring to a boy's sexual attachment to his mother.

Olfaction (ol-FAK-shun)   The sense of smell.

Operant conditioning (OP-er-ant)   Type of learning that occurs when an organism "operates" on the environment. The consequences of a response affect its probability of recurrence.

Operational definition   Definition of a concept or variable that specifies the operations (actions) used to measure the concept or manipulate the variable.

Optic nerve   The large nerve carrying visual impulses from each eye to the brain.

Oral stage   The Freudian stage of psychosexual development in which the individual is preoccupied with his mouth.

Organic psychosis   A psychotic disorder caused by clearly identifiable physiological or genetic factors.

Organismic valuing (or-gan-IS-mik)   The process of evaluating events on the basis of spontaneous personal reaction rather than by reference to learned systems of values.

Orgasm   A climax and release of sexual excitement.

Ovaries   Female sex organs that produce hormones and ova (eggs).

Overlearning   Practice that is continued beyond the point of mere mastery of memorized material or of a skill.

Palmistry (PALM-is-tree)   A false system wherein lines on the palms of the hands are used to identify personality traits or to predict the future.

Paradoxical sleep   A sleep pattern in which the individual produces an EEG record similar to Stage 1 sleep, or even to waking, yet remains behaviorally asleep (and typically dreaming).

Paranoia (pare-ih-NOY-yah)   A psychotic state characterized by delusions of persecution.

Paranoid schizophrenia (PARE-ih-noid SKIZ-oh-FREEN-ih-ah)   A psychosis characterized by delusions of persecution or grandeur and accompanied by severe disturbances of thought and emotion.

Parapsychology (PARE-ah-SIKE-ol-oh-jee)   The scientific study of extranormal psychological events, e.g., extrasensory perception.

Parasympathetic nervous system (PARE-ah-simp-ah-THET-ik)   A division of the autonomic nervous system associated with production of relaxation, bodily deactivation, and conservation of energy.

Partial reinforcement   Reinforcement administered only after a portion of the total responses in a particular situation (also called intermittent reinforcement).

Partial reinforcement effect   A greater resistance to extinction observed in responses acquired on a schedule of partial reinforcement (i.e., a response rewarded on only a portion of its occurrences).

Peer group   A group of people of one's own age and of equal or similar background.

Perception   The process of meaningfully organizing sensation.

Peripheral nervous system (per-IF-er-al)   All portions of the nervous system lying outside the brain and spinal cord, including sensory neurons, motor neurons, the spinal nerves, cranial nerves, skeletal nervous system, and autonomic nervous system.

Peripheral vision   Vision at the periphery (edges) of the visual field.

Persona (per-SO-nah)   In Jung's system an archetype representing the "mask" or public self presented to others.

Personality   An individual's unique and enduring traits and psychological characteristics and the dynamic relationship among them.

Personality disorder   Disturbances involving maladaptive and long-standing distortions of personality characteristics.

Personality types   Systems of personality description employing only a few categories, with each category representing a collection of related traits.

Phallic stage (FAL-ik)   The Freudian developmental stage in which the individual is preoccupied with pleasure derived from the genital organs.

Phenomenal field (fee-NOM-ih-nal)   One's complete field of subjective awareness.

Phenylketonuria (PKU) (FEE-nil-kee-toh-NER-yah)   A metabolic disorder causing the accumulation of phenylalanine in the body and leading to mental retardation.

Phi phenomenon (fie fee-NOM-en-on)   The apparent movement of two stationary lights caused when they are lighted in quick succession.

Phobia (FOE-bee-ah)   An intense and unrealistic fear of some specific object or situation.

Phonemes (FOE-neems)   The basic sounds of a language that can be distinguished from one another.

Phosphene (FOSS-feen)   A luminous visual impression caused by activation of the retina by any means, including pressure and electrical stimulation.

Photoreceptors   Sensory receptors sensitive to light and specialized for the transduction of light waves into neural impulses.

Phrenology (freh-NOL-oh-jee)   A false system that holds that the shape of the skull indicates mental faculties or personal characteristics.

Pica (PIE-kah)   A craving for unnatural foods or substances such as chalk, ashes, etc.

Pitch   Psychological experience of high or low tones corresponding to the physical dimension of frequency.

Placebo (pla-SEE-bo)   An inactive substance given in the place of a drug in psychological research or by physicians who wish to treat chronic aches and pains by suggestion.

Polygenetic   Any physical or behavioral trait influenced by three or more (often many) genes.

Polygraph   An instrument for recording several measures of bodily activity simultaneously. Commonly used to refer to the records of emotional response made by a "lie detector."

Population   An entire defined group; all members of a class or set from which a smaller sample may be drawn. (See *sample*.)

Positive reinforcement   Rewards or stimuli that increase the probability of a response they have followed.

Positive transfer   The carry-over of skills or responses from one task to another when such carry-over improves performance on the second task. (Compare to *negative transfer*.)

Precognition (PREE-kog-nish-un)   Literally, knowing beforehand; hence, any foretelling of the future or prior knowledge of events unknowable by normal means.

Prejudice   A negative attitude or prejudgment held against members of a particular group of people. Most often observed in racial or ethnic prejudice, but also frequently applied to other groups as well.

Prenatal   Events occurring before the birth of a child.

Presbyopia (prez-by-OH-pea-ah)   Farsightedness caused by aging.

Pressure   In psychological terms, pressure is said to exist when extended vigilence must be maintained, when events must be speeded up, or when a person must work at or near maximum capacity for an extended period.

Primary impotence (IM-po-tenz)   In the male, total inability to perform sexually.

Primary reinforcers   Unlearned reinforcers. Usually those that satisfy physiological needs.

Primate   A member of the family of mammals including humans, apes, and monkeys.

Proactive inhibition (pro-AK-tiv)   Forgetting that occurs when previous learning interferes with more recent learning.

Projection   Attributing to others unacceptable impulses or feelings as a means of defending against anxiety.

Projective tests   Psychological tests making use of unstructured stimuli. The subject is presumed to project his or her own thoughts and impulses onto the stimulus.

Proxemics (prox-EM-iks)   Systematic study of the human use of space, particularly interpersonal space in various social settings.

Pseudo-memories (SUE-doe memories)   False memories that a person believes to be true or accurate.

Pseudo-psychologies (SUE-do psychologies)   False or dubious systems that purport to explain behavior.

Psi events (SIE events)   Paranormal events falling outside the traditional bounds of psychology and science. Includes clairvoyance, telepathy, precognition, psychokinesis, astral projection, out-of-body experiences and the like.

Psyche (SIKE-ee)   The mind, mental life, and personality as a whole.

Psychiatrist   A medical doctor with additional training in the diagnosis and treatment of mental illness.

Psychoactive drugs (SIKE-oh-ACT-iv)   Any of a large number of substances (often quite potent) capable of altering sensation, perception, cognition, memory, or other psychological events.

Psychoanalysis (SIKE-oh-ah-NAL-ih-sis)   A Freudian approach to therapy emphasizing free association, dream interpretation, and transference.

Psychoanalyst (SIKE-oh-AN-ah-list)   A mental health professional (usually a medical doctor) trained to practice psychoanalysis.

Psychodrama (SIKE-oh-DRAH-ma)   A technique of psychotherapy in which people act out personal conflicts in the presence of other people who play supporting parts.

Psychodynamic (SIKE-oh-die-NAM-ik)   Pertaining to internal motives, unconscious forces, and other aspects of mental functioning.

Psychokinesis (SIKE-oh-kih-NEE-sis)   The ability to influence physical events by mental activity or the act of exerting mental control over inanimate objects.

Psycholinguist (SIKE-oh-LING-wist)   A psychologist who specializes in the study of language.

Psychologist   An individual highly trained in the philosophy, methods, factual knowledge, and theories of psychology. Psychologists usually possess at least a Master's degree and frequently a Doctorate in the field of psychology.

Psychology   The scientific study of behavior and conscious experience.

Psychometrics (SIKE-oh-MET-riks)   Specialty that focuses on mental measurement or psychological testing, such as personality and intelligence testing.

Psychopath (SIKE-oh-path)   An individual who appears to make no distinctions between right and wrong and who feels no guilt about destructive or antisocial behavior.

Psychopathology (SIKE-oh-pah-THOL-ih-jee)   Abnormal or maladaptive behavior. Literally, mental sickness.

Psychophysics (SIKE-oh-fiz-iks)   The study of the relationship between physical stimuli and the sensations evoked by them in a human observer.

Psychosexual stages (SIKE-oh-sexual)   In Freud's theory of personality development, the following stages: oral, anal, phallic, and genital.

Psychosis (SIKE-oh-sis)   A severe psychological disturbance characterized by loss of contact with reality, by hallucinations and delusions, and by withdrawal, and usually requiring hospitalization.

Psychosomatic illnesses (SIKE-oh-so-MAT-ik)   Disorders in which actual physical damage results from psychological stress.

Psychosurgery (SIKE-oh-surgery)   Surgical alterations of the brain designed to bring about planned behavioral or emotional changes. Psychosurgery may be performed with traditional surgical instruments or by the ablation of brain tissue through use of electrical currents and electrodes.

Psychotherapy (SIKE-oh-therapy) General term referring to any form of psychological treatment for behavioral disorders. Most often used to refer to verbal interaction between the client and a trained mental health professional.

Punishment The delivery after a response of an event or stimulus that tends to reduce the probability of that response.

Pupil The dark spot at the front of the eye through which light moves in reaching the retina.

Pupillometrics (PUE-pil-oh-MET-riks) A technique developed by Eckard Hess for the measurement of dilation and constriction of the pupils in response to various stimuli. Purportedly a measure of emotional response.

Racism Racial prejudice that has become institutional (i.e., reflected in government policy, schools, etc.) and that is enforced by the existing social power structure.

Random Haphazard and without definite pattern. Random numbers represent a series in which each digit from 0 to 9 has an equal probability of appearing in any particular position.

Randomization The use of random numbers or a random procedure (e.g., flipping a coin) to assign subjects to the experimental and control groups in an experiment or a similar situation.

Rarefaction (rare-eh-FAK-shun) In hearing, the spreading or thinning of air molecules between the crests of successive sound waves.

Rationalization Explaining away one's shortcomings in such a way as to avoid responsibility.

Rational therapy A direct and forceful therapy in which clients learn to abandon irrational and self-defeating behavior and beliefs.

Reaction formation A psychological defense mechanism in which unconscious anxiety-producing impulses are controlled by behaving in exactly the opposite way.

Recall Detailed remembering in the absence of memory cues.

Recessive gene A gene whose influence will only be expressed when it is paired with a second recessive gene (i.e., it cannot be expressed in the presence of a dominant gene). (See *dominant gene*.)

Recitation (RES-ih-TAY-shun) Repeating aloud material that is to be learned as a means for improving memory of the material.

Recognition Memory in which previously learned material is correctly identified as that which has been seen before.

Redintegration (ruh-DIN-tuh-GRAY-shun) The process of inferring or reconstructing an entire complex memory after first observing or remembering only a part of it.

Reference group Any group with which the individual identifies psychologically and uses as a standard for social comparison.

Reflex An automatic response to a stimulus, for example an eyeblink, knee jerk, or dilation of the pupil.

Regression Return to earlier behavior patterns appropriate to a child or younger person particularly as a response to stress.

Reinforcement Any stimulus that brings about learning or increases the frequency of the response. Often simply a reward.

Reinforcer Any stimulus that reliably increases the frequency or probability of responses it follows.

Relational concept A concept defined by the relationship of one or more dimensions to a second (or other) dimensions (e.g., "greater than," "above," "equal to"). (Compare to *conjunctive* and *disjunctive* concepts.)

Relearning Learning again something previously learned. Used as a measure of memory for prior learning.

Reliability An important characteristic of any test. A test that is reliable gives the same score on each administration.

Remission (reh-MISH-un) Disappearance of symptoms of a psychological disorder.

REMs An abbreviation for rapid eye movements characteristic of Stage 1 dream sleep.

REM sleep Rapid eye movement sleep corresponding to periods of dreaming.

Representative sample A sample of a larger population of subjects or observations that accurately reflects the characteristics of the population. Representative samples are frequently achieved by random selection of subjects or observations.

Repression Pushing out or barring from consciousness unwanted memories, impulses, or feelings.

Resistance Blocks that occur in psychoanalysis during free association.

Respondent conditioning Another term for classical conditioning.

Response Any muscular action, glandular activity, or other objectively identifiable aspect of behavior.

Retardation Mental capacity significantly below average; traditionally defined as an IQ score below 70.

Retention Storage or memorization of information.

Retina The photosensitive lining at the back of the eye containing rods and cones.

Retrieval Extracting stored information from memory.

Retroactive inhibition (RET-ro-AK-tiv) The interference of new learning with the memory of previously learned material.

Retrograde amnesia (RET-ro-grade) Loss of memory for events preceding a head injury or other amnesia-producing event.

Rhodopsin (row-DOP-sin) The photosensitive pigment in the rods of the retina. A chemical composed of retinene and opsin that breaks down into retinene and opsin when struck by light.

RNA (ribonucleic acid) A chemical substance similar to DNA and believed to be involved in learning and memory.

Rods Visual receptors in the retina that are responsive to low levels of illumination but that produce only black-white vision.

Role Particular type of behavior one is expected to exhibit when occupying a particular position within a group.

Sadism (SADE-izm) Deriving erotic satisfaction by the infliction of pain on another; more broadly, love of cruelty.

Sample A subset or portion of a population.

Saturation As applied to colors, saturation refers to colors that are free from the mixture of white, that are very pure, and that represent a concentrated area of the spectrum.

Savings score In testing memory by relearning, a savings score is obtained by subtracting the amount of time necessary to remaster material from the amount of time necessary to master it originally.

Scapegoating The act of causing a person or group of people to bear the blame for others or for conditions not of their making.

Schedules of reinforcement A rule for determining which response will be reinforced.

Schizoaffective disorders (SKIZ-oh-af-EK-tiv) Psychotic disorders combining elements of schizophrenia and affective disorders. (See *schizophrenia, affective disorders,* and *affective psychosis*.)

Schizophrenia (SKIZ-oh-FREE-nih-ah) A functional psychosis characterized by withdrawal from reality, apathy, and in some cases, delusions and hallucinations.

Schizotypal personality (SKIZ-oh-TYPE-al) A serious personality disorder involving withdrawal, odd behavior, and eccentric thought, but lacking the hallucinations and delusions of true schizophrenia.

Secondary elaboration   In Freudian dream theory secondary elaboration refers to a tendency to fill in gaps and missing details in the recall or retelling of dreams. Through secondary elaboration, dream accounts become more logical and organized.

Secondary impotence (IM-po-tenz)   In previously normal males, the onset of an inability to perform sexually.

Secondary reinforcement   A previously neutral stimulus that acquires reinforcement value through association with primary reinforcers.

Sedative   A drug that tends to calm, tranquilize, or to encourage sleep.

Self-actualization   The full development of personal potential, especially emotional potential.

Self-image   Total subjective perception of oneself, including an image of one's body and perceptions of one's personality, capabilities, etc.

Semantic memory   A hypothetical "mental dictionary" of basic facts and knowledge said to be a subpart of long-term memory.

Semantics   The study of meanings in language.

Sensation   The immediate response to stimulation of the sensory receptors and the transduction of environmental or internal events into neural response.

Sensory adaptation   A reduction in sensory responses to any unchanging form of stimulation.

Sensory memory   The first stage in memory storage that holds detailed and literal images of incoming information for one-half second or less.

Sensory neuron   An afferent neuron that carries sensory information toward the brain or central nervous system.

Set   A predisposition to respond in a certain way.

Sexism   Prejudice and discrimination based on gender, particularly that which is reflected in existing social power structures, but also in more subtle attitudes and actions.

Sex roles   Learned behavior that fits societal expectations concerning proper behavior for males and females.

Shaping   Gradual molding of responses to a final desired pattern by reinforcing successive approximations of it.

Short-term memory (STM)   The retention of information for brief periods without rehearsal. The first step in the creation of permanent memories.

Social comparison   Making judgments about ourselves through comparison with others.

Socialization   The process of learning to live in a particular culture by adopting socially acceptable behavior.

Sociopath   Another name for the psychopath.

Soma (SO-ma)   The body of any living cell, particularly the body of a nerve cell (neuron).

Somatic therapy (SO-ma-tik)   Any therapy directly involving bodily processes, for example, drug therapy, electroconvulsive therapy, psychosurgery, etc.

Somatoform disorders (so-MAT-oh-form)   A class of personal disturbances characterized by exaggerated bodily complaints (hypochondria) or by the presence of physical disability without apparent cause.

Somatotype (so-MAT-oh-type)   Literally, one's body type. In Sheldon's body type system, one's rating on the dimensions of endomorphy, mesomorphy, and ectomorphy.

Somesthetic (SOM-es-THET-ik)   Pertaining to sensations produced in the skin, muscles, joints, and viscera.

Somnambulism (som-NAM-bue-lism)   The formal term for sleepwalking.

Spaced practice   Learning trials or practice sessions spread over an extended period of time and including a number of rest periods.

Species   A classification comprising closely related plants or animals potentially able to breed with one another.

Species-specific behavior   Patterned behavior that is exhibited by all normal members of a particular species.

Spontaneous recovery   The sudden reappearance of a learned response after apparent extinction.

Spontaneous remission   In psychiatry or clinical psychology, the spontaneous disappearance of psychological symptoms or behavioral disturbances (e.g., clients placed on waiting lists sometimes improve at the same rate as those accepted into therapy).

Status   An individual's position in a group or social system.

Stereoscopic vision   The seeing of objects as three-dimensional and the perception of space caused chiefly by the separation of the eyes.

Stereotype   An inaccurate and rigid concept used to refer to members of an outgroup.

Stereotyped response   A rigid, repetitive, and nonproductive response made mechanically and without regard for its appropriateness.

Stimulant   A substance that produces temporary excitation of the body and/or nervous system.

Stimulus   Any physical energy that has some effect on an organism and that evokes a response.

Stimulus generalization   The tendency to make a learned response to stimuli similar to the stimulus an organism was originally conditioned to respond to.

Stress   A condition in which an organism is subjected to external conditions to which it must adjust or adapt.

Stroboscopic movement (strobe-oh-SKOP-ik)   An illusion of movement caused by the rapid presentation of a series of photographs or other representations of phases of a continuous movement. More commonly, the illusion of movement created by cartoon animation and by movie films.

Structuralism (STRUK-chur-al-ism)   An early school of thought in psychology that tried to analyze sensations and subjective experience into its basic building blocks.

Sublimation (SUB-lih-MAY-shun)   A psychological defense mechanism involving the expression of socially unacceptable impulses in a socially acceptable way. For example, converting greed into a successful business career.

Subliminal (sub-LIM-ih-nal)   Perception of a stimulus presented below the threshold for conscious recognition.

Superego (super-EE-go)   In Freud's theory of personality, the superego represents parental values and the rules of society; basically, the unit which acts as the conscience.

Superordinate goals (super-ORD-ih-nate)   Goals that exceed or override all others; goals that render other goals relatively less important.

Syllogism (SIL-oh-jis-em)   A logical format for reasoning consisting of a major and a minor premise and a conclusion.

Symbolization   In dream imagery, the tendency for images to stand for or suggest something else by reason of similarity, relationship, appearance, or unconscious association.

Sympathetic nervous system   A division of the autonomic nervous system responsible for activating the body at times of emotion or stress. The sympathetic system speeds energy consumption and prepares the body for action.

Synapse (SIN-aps)   The microscopic space over which nerve impulses travel in the junction of two neurons.

Synesthesia (sin-es-THEE-zyah)   Experiencing one sensory modality in terms of another. For example, "seeing" sounds as colors.

Synesthete (sin-es-THET)   A person who regularly experiences synesthesia.

Syntax   The study of word orderings in the formation of phrases, clauses, and sentences.

Tachistoscope (tack-IS-toh-scope)   A mechanical device capable of flashing words or pictures on a screen for very short periods of time. Used in perceptual testing, especially in studies of subliminal perception.

Taste aversion   An active dislike for a particular food frequently created when the food is associated with sickness or discomfort. (See *bait shyness*.)

Telepathy (teh-LEP-ah-thee)   A purported form of ESP in which thoughts are transferred from a sender to a receiver without direct contact.

Telodendria (tel-oh-DEN-dree-ah)   A branching network of fibers at the terminus of the axon in nerve cells. The telodendria form multiple synapses with other neurons.

Temperament   The physical foundation of personality including such things as prevailing mood, sensitivity, energy levels, etc.

Terminal decline   A significant decline in mental capacity observed before death and in some cases anticipating the occurrence of death.

Testes   The male sex organs located in the scrotum. The source of sperm and male sex hormones.

Testosterone (tes-TOS-ter-own)   Male sex hormone responsible for the development of secondary sexual characteristics.

Thanatologist (THAN-ah-TOL-oh-jist)   One who studies death and the process of dying.

Theory   A system of ideas and concepts designed to set forth and interrelate concepts and facts in a way that summarizes existing data and predicts future observations.

Timbre (TIM-ber)   The psychological aspect of sound that corresponds to the complexity of a tone.

Tinnitus (tin-NYE-tus)   A ringing or whistling sensation in the ears due to disease, injury, drugs, or unknown causes.

Tolerance   Refers to a condition in drug addiction brought about by the body's ability to withstand increased amounts of the drug. As tolerance develops, the dosage must be increased to produce the same reaction a smaller dosage once produced.

Traits (personality)   Enduring attitudes and personal qualities that an individual tends to display in most life situations.

Transactional analysis (TA)   A therapeutic technique designed to improve awareness of one's transactions (interchanges) with others.

Transduction   Changing one form of energy into another.

Transference   Refers to the tendency of a patient to transfer feelings to the therapist which correspond to feelings held toward important figures in the patient's past.

Transient situational disorder (TRAN-shent)   A psychological disturbance resembling neurosis but directly related to intense environmental stress; usually a temporary reaction.

Trepanning (TREH-pan-ing)   In modern usage any surgical procedure in which a hole is bored in the skull. Historically, the chipping or boring of holes in the skull by primitive peoples as a means of treating mental disturbances.

Trichromatic color theory (TRY-kroe-MAT-ik)   Theory of color vision, which states that there are three types of cones with maximum sensitivity to either red, green, or blue.

Unconditioned response   In classical conditioning this is the unlearned response that is innately elicited by the unconditioned stimulus. Usually a reflex response.

Unconditioned stimulus   A stimulus innately capable of eliciting a response.

Unconscious (un-KON-shus)   That part of a person's mind or personality which contains impulses and desires not directly known to the person.

Vacillation (VAS-ih-LAY-shun)   Wavering in aim or action, especially in conflict situations.

Validity   The ability of a test to measure what it purports to measure.

Variable interval schedule   A schedule of reinforcement that varies the time period between reinforcements.

Variable ratio schedule   A schedule in which the number of responses required to produce reinforcement varies.

Vestibular senses (ves-TIB-you-ler)   Concerned with balance or equilibrium, the vestibular senses are produced by the semicircular canals located close to the inner ear.

Vicarious conditioning (vie-CARE-ih-us)   The establishment of a conditioned response (often an emotional response) by observing the reactions of another to a particular stimulus.

Visual acuity   The clarity of visual perception.

White noise   An auditory stimulus made up of all audible frequencies of sound. White noise sounds like a hiss or a waterfall.

References

Aarons, L. "Sleep-Assisted Instruction." *Psychological Bulletin,* 83 (1976): 1–40.

Adams, G., M. Ghodsian and K. Richardson. "Evidence for a Low Upper Limit of Heritability of Mental Test Performance in a National Sample of Twins." *Nature,* 263 (1976): 314–316.

Adams, J. *Conceptual Blockbusting.* San Francisco: Freeman, 1974.

Adams, J. A. *Human Memory.* New York: McGraw-Hill, 1967.

_____. *Learning and Memory* (revised ed.). Homewood, Illinois: Dorsey Press, 1980.

Adler, C. S. and S. M. Adler. "Biofeedback—Psychotherapy for the Treatment of Headaches: A 5-Year Follow-Up." *Headache,* 16 (1976): 189–191.

Adorno, T. W., E. Frenkel-Brunswik, D. J. Levinson, and R. N. Sanford. *The Authoritarian Personality.* New York: Harper, 1950.

Albert, E. M. "The Roles of Women: Question of Values." In *The Potential of Women,* edited by Farber and Wilson. New York: McGraw-Hill, 1963.

Alberti, R. and M. Emmons. *Your Perfect Right.* San Luis Obispo, Calif.: Impact, 1978.

Alevizos, P. N. and E. J. Callahan. "Assessment of Psychotic Behavior." In *Handbook of Behavioral Assessment,* edited by A. R. Ciminero, K. S. Calhoun and H. E. Adams. New York: Wiley, 1977.

Alexander, G. "Terminal Therapy." *Psychology Today,* (Sept. 1978): 50–60.

Allen, B. "Winged Victory of 'Gossamer Albatross.'" *National Geographic,* 156 (1979): 642–651.

Allison, T. and H. Van Twyver. "The Evolution of Sleep." *Natural History,* (Feb. 1970), The American Museum of Natural History.

Allport, G. W. *The Nature of Prejudice.* Garden City, N.Y.: Anchor Books, Doubleday, 1958.

_____. *Pattern and Growth in Personality.* New York: Holt, 1961.

Allport, G. W. and H. S. Odbert. "Trait-Names: A Psycholexical Study." *Psychological Monographs,* No. 211 (1936).

American Medical Association, Department of Mental Health. "The Crutch that Cripples: Drug Dependence, Part I." *Today's Health,* 46, No. 9 (1968): 11–12, 70–72.

American Psychological Association. *Careers in Psychology.* Washington, D.C.: American Psychological Association, 1970.

Anand, B. K. and J. R. Brobeck. "Hypothalamic Control of Food Intake in Rats and Cats." *Yale Journal of Biological Medicine,* (1951): 123–140.

Anastasi, A. *Fields of Applied Psychology.* New York: McGraw-Hill, 1964.

Anastasi, A. and J. P. Foley, Jr. *Differential Psychology* (3rd ed.). New York: Macmillan, 1958.

Anhalt, H. S. and M. Klein. "Drug Abuse in Junior High School Populations." *American Journal of Drug and Alcohol Abuse,* 3, No. 4 (1976): 589–603.

Annett, J. "Memory for Skill." In *Applied Problems in Memory,* edited by M. M. Gruneberg and P. E. Morris. London: Academic Press, 1979.

Apfel, R. E. "Resounding Facts on Hearing Loss." *The Science Teacher,* 44, No. 8 (Nov. 1977): 31–34.

Arehart-Treichel, Joan. "The Science of Sleep." *Science News,* 111 (March 26, 1977): 203–208.

Arndt, S. and D. E. Berger. "Cognitive Mode and Asymmetry in Cerebral Functioning." *Cortex,* 14 (1978): 78–86.

Arnheim, R. *Art and Visual Perception.* Berkeley: University of California Press, 1974.

Aronson, E. "Some Antecedents of Interpersonal Attraction." In *Nebraska Symposium on Motivation,* edited by W. J. Arnold and D. Levine. Lincoln: University of Nebraska Press, 1969.

_____. *The Social Animal.* San Francisco: Freeman, 1972.

_____. *The Social Animal.* San Francisco: Freeman, 1980.

Aronson, E., C. Stephan, J. Sikes, N. Blaney and M. Snapp. *The Jigsaw Classroom.* Beverly Hills, Calif.: Sage Publications, 1978.

Aronson, E. with N. Blaney, J. Sikes, C. Stephan and M. Snapp. "Busing and Racial Tension: The Jigsaw Route to Learning and Liking." In *Personal Adjustment, Selected Readings,* edited by V. J. Derlega and L. H. Janda. Glenview, Ill.: Scott, Foresman, 1979.

Aronson, E. and D. Linder. "Gain and Loss of Esteem as Determinants of Interpersonal Attractiveness." *Journal of Experimental and Social Psychology,* 1 (1965): 156–171.

Asch, S. E. "Studies of Independence and Conformity: A Minority of One Against a Unanimous Majority." *Psychological Monographs,* 70, No. 416 (1956).

Asimov, I. *Is Anyone There?* Garden City, N.Y.: Doubleday, 1967.

Athenasiou, R., P. Shaver, and C. Tavris. "Sex." *Psychology Today,* 4, No. 2 (1970): 37–52.

Atkinson, R. C. "The Computer as a Tutor." *Psychology Today,* (Jan. 1968).

Atkinson, R. C. and R. M. Shiffrin. "The Control of Short-Term Memory." *Scientific American,* (Aug. 1971): 89–90.

Ayllon, T. "Intensive Treatment of Psychotic Behavior by Stimulus Satiation and Food Reinforcement." *Behavior Research and Therapy,* 1 (1963): 53–61.

Ayllon, T., E. Haughton, and H. B. Hughes. "Interpretation of Symptoms: Fact or Fiction?" *Behavior and Therapy,* 3 (1965): 1–7.

Azrin, N. H., R. R. Hutchinson, and R. McLaughlin. "The Opportunity for Aggression as an Operant Reinforcer during Aversive Stimulation." *Journal of Experimental Analysis of Behavior,* 8 (1965): 171–180.

Bach, G. and P. Wyden. *The Intimate Enemy.* New York: Morrow, 1969.

Back, K. W. "The Group Can Comfort But It Can't Cure." *Psychology Today,* 6, No. 7 (1972): 28–35.

Baddeley, A. D. *The Psychology of Memory.* New York: Basic Books, 1976.

Baddeley, A. D. and G. Hitch. "Working Memory." In *The Psychology of Learning and Motivation,* Vol 8, edited by G. H. Bower. New York: Academic Press, 1974.

Baer, D. M. "Let's Take Another Look at Punishment." *Psychology Today,* (Oct. 1971).

Balanovski, E. and J. G. Taylor. "Can Electromagnetism Account for Extra Sensory Phenomena?" *Nature Magazine,* (Nov. 2, 1978): 63–67.

Balswick, J. O. and C. W. Peek. "The Inexpressive Male: A Tragedy of American Society." *National Council on Family Relations,* (1971).

Baltes, P. B. and K. W. Schaie. "Aging and I.Q.: The Myth of the Twilight Years." *Psychology Today,* 7, No. 10 (1974): 35–40.

Bandura, A. "Vicarious Processes: A Case of No-Trial Learning." In *Advances in Experimental Social Psychology,* Vol. 2, edited by L. Berkowitz. New York: Academic Press, 1965, pp. 1–55.

———. *Social Learning Theory.* New York: General Learning Press, 1971.

———. *Agression: A Social Learning Analysis.* Englewood Cliffs, N.J.: Prentice-Hall, 1973.

———. "Self-Efficacy: Toward a Unifying Theory of Behavioral Change." *Psychological Review,* 84 (1977): 191–215.

Bandura, A. and T. L. Rosenthal. "Vicarious Classical Conditioning as a Function of Arousal Level." *Journal of Personality and Social Psychology,* 3 (1966): 54–62.

Bandura, A., D. Ross, and S. A. Ross. "Vicarious Reinforcement and Imitative Learning." *Journal of Abnormal and Social Psychology,* 67 (1963): 601–607.

Bandura, A. and R. Walters. *Adolescent Aggression.* New York: Ronald, 1959.

———. "Aggression." In *Child Psychology,* edited by H. W. Stevenson. Chicago: University of Chicago Press, 1963.

———. *Social Learning and Personality Development.* New York: Holt, 1963.

Barahal, H. S. "1000 Prefrontal Lobotomies: Five to Ten Year Follow-up Study." *Psychiatric Quarterly,* 32 (1958): 653–678.

Barber, T. X. "Toward a Theory of Pain: Relief of Chronic Pain by Prefrontal Leucotomy, Opiates, Placebos, and Hypnosis." *Psychological Bulletin,* 56, No. 6 (1959): 430–460.

———. "Suggested ('Hypnotic') Behavior: The Trance Paradigm Versus an Alternative Paradigm." Harding, Mass. Medfield Foundation, Report No. 103 (1970).

Barchas, J. D., G. R. Elliot, and P. A. Berger. "Biogenic Amine Hypothesis of Schizophrenia." In *The Nature of Schizophrenia: New Approaches to Research and Treatment,* edited by L. C. Wynne, R. L. Cromwell, and S. Matthysse. New York: Wiley, 1978.

Barron, F. "The Psychology of Imagination." *Scientific American,* 199, No. 3 (1958): 150–170.

Barrow, G. M. and P. A. Smith. *Aging, Ageism, and Society.* St. Paul: West, 1979.

Basedow, R. A. *The Australian Aborigine.* Adelaide, Australia: Peerce and Sons, 1925.

Basso, K. H. *Portraits of "The Whiteman": Linguistic Play and Cultural Symbols Among the Western Apache.* New York: Cambridge University Press, 1979.

Bassuk, E. L. and S. Gerson "Deinstitutionalization and Mental Health Services." *Scientific American,* 238, No. 2 (1978): 46–53.

Bateson, G., D. D. Jackson, J. Haley, and J. Weakland. "Toward a Theory of Schizophrenia." *Behavioral Science,* 1 (1956): 251–264.

Baumrind, D. "New Directions in Socialization Research." *American Psychologist,* 35 (July, 1980): 639–652.

Beach, F. A. "Behavioral Endocrinology: An Emerging Discipline." *American Scientist,* 63 (1975): 178–187.

Beck, A. T. and R. L. Greenberg. "Coping with Depression." Institute for Rational Living, 1974.

Beck, A. T., A. J. Rush, B. Shaw and G. Emery. *Cognitive Therapy of Depression: A Treatment Manual.* New York: Gilford Press, 1979.

Beck, A. T. and J. E. Young. "College Blues." *Psychology Today,* (Sept. 1978): 80–92.

Beebe, B., L. Gerstman, B. Carson, M. Dolins, A. Zigman, H. Rosensweig, K. Faughey and M. Korman. "Rhythmic Communication in the Mother-Infant Dyad." In *Interaction Rhythms, Periodicity in Communicative Behavior,* edited by M. Davis. New York: Human Sciences Press, 1982.

Beecher, H. K. *Measurement of Subjective Responses: Quantitative Effects of Drugs.* New York: Oxford University Press, 1959.

Beidler, L. M. "Dynamics of Taste Cells." In *Olfaction and Taste,* Vol. 1, edited by Y. Zotterman. New York: Macmillan, 1963.

Békésy, G. von. "The Ear." *Scientific American,* 197 (1957a): 66–78.

Bell, A. P., M. S. Weinberg and S. K. Hammersmith. *Sexual Preference.* Bloomington: Indiana University Press, 1981.

Belmont, L. and F. A. Marolla. "Birth Order, Family Size, and Intelligence." *Science,* 182 (1973): 1096–1101.

Bem, S. L. "The Measurement of Psychological Androgyny." *Journal of Consulting and Clinical Psychology,* 42 (1974): 155–162.

———. "Sex-role Adaptability: One Consequence of Psychological Androgyny." *Journal of Personality and Social Psychology,* 31 (1975a): 634–643.

———. "Psychological Androgyny." In *Beyond Sex Roles,* edited by A. G. Sargent. St. Paul: West, 1977.

———. "Androgyny vs. the Tight Little Lives of Fluffy Women and Chesty Men." *Psychology Today,* (Sept. 1975b): 58–62.

Bengelsdorf, I. S. "Alcohol, Morphine Addictions Believed Chemically Similar." *Los Angeles Times,* Part II (March 5, 1970): 7.

Bennett, W. and J. Gurin. *The Dieter's Dilemma.* Basic Books, 1982.

Bennett, W. R. "How Artificial Is Intelligence?" *American Scientist,* 65 (1977): 694.

Benson, H. "Systematic Hypertension and the Relaxation Response." *The New England Journal of Medicine,* 296 (1977): 1152–1156.

Benton, A. L. "The Neuropsychology of Facial Recognition." *American Psychologist,* 35, No. 2 (Feb. 1980): 176–186.

Bergin, A. and R. M. Suinn. "Individual Psychotherapy and Behavior Therapy." *Annual Review of Psychology,* 26 (1975): 509–556.

Berkowitz, L. "The Frustration-Aggression Hypothesis Revisited." In *Roots of Aggression: A Re-examination of the Frustration-Aggression Hypothesis,* edited by L. Berkowitz. New York: Atherton Press, 1968.

Berlyne, D. "Curiosity and Exploration." *Science,* 153 (1966): 25–33.

Berne, E. *Transactional Analysis in Psychotherapy.* New York: Grove Press, 1961.

———. *Games People Play.* New York: Grove Press, 1964.

Bernstein, I. L. "Learned Taste Aversions in Children Receiving Chemotherapy." *Science,* 200 (1978): 1302–1303.

Bersheid, E. and E. Walster. "Physical Attractiveness." In *Advances in Experimental Social Psychology,* Vol. 7, edited by L. Berkowitz. New York: Academic Press, 1974a.

———. "A Little Bit About Love." In T. L. Huston (ed.) *Foundations of Interpersonal Attraction.* New York: Academic Press, 1974b.

Bertsch, G. J. "Punishment of Consummatory and Instrumental Behavior: A Review." *Psychological Record,* 26 (1976): 13–31.

Bettelheim, B. *The Informed Heart.* New York: Free Press, 1960.

Biblow, E. "Imaginative Play and The Control of Aggressive Behavior." In *The Child's World of Make-Believe: Experimental Studies of Imaginative Play,* edited by J. L. Singer. New York: Academic Press, 1973.

Bickman, L. "Clothes Make the Person." *Psychology Today,* (April 1974).

Binder, V. "Behavior Modification: Operant Approaches to Therapy." In *Modern Therapies,* edited by V. Binder, A. Binder, and B. Rimland. Englewood Cliffs, N.J.: Prentice-Hall, 1976, pp. 150–165.

Birnbaum, I. M., E. S. Parker, J. T. Hartley and E. P. Nobel. "Alcohol and Memory: Retrieval Processes." *Journal of Verbal Learning and Verbal Behavior,* 17 (1978): 325–335.

Blanchard, E. B. and L. H. Epstein. *A Biofeedback Primer.* Reading, Mass: Addison-Wesley, 1978.

Block, J. "Socialization Influence of Personality Development in Males and Females." American Psychological Association Master Lecture, Convention of the American Psychological Association, New York City (Sept. 1979).

Bloom, B. *Stability and Change in Human Characteristics.* New York: Wiley, 1964.

Bloom, B. L. and H. J. Parad. "Professional Activity Patterns in Community Mental Health Centers." In *Community Psychology in Transition,* edited by I. Iscoe, B. L. Bloom and C. D. Spielberger. Washington, D.C.: Hemisphere, 1977.

Bloom, L. and M. Lahey. *Language Development and Language Disorders.* New York: Wiley, 1978.

Bloomer, C. M. *Principles of Visual Perception.* New York: Van Nostrand Reinhold, 1976.

Blumenthal, A. L. *The Process of Cognition.* Englewood Cliffs, N.J.: Prentice-Hall, 1977.

———. "The Founding Father We Never Knew." *Contemporary Psychology,* 24 (1979): 547–550.

Bock, F. G. "Cocarcinogenic Properties of Nicotine." In *Banbury Report,* edited by G. B. Gori and F. G. Bock. Cold Spring Harbor Laboratory, 1980.

Boker, J. R. "Immediate and Delayed Retention Effects of Interspersing Questions in Written Instructional Passages." *Journal of Educational Psychology,* 66 (1974): 96–98.

Bolles, R. C. *Learning Theory* (2nd ed.). New York: Holt, 1979.

Bolton, R. "Hostility in Fantasy: A Further Test of the Hypoglycemia-Aggression Hypothesis." *Aggressive Behavior,* 2, No. 4 (1976): 257–274.

Boneau, C. A. and J. M. Cuea. "An Overview of Psychology's Human Resources." *American Psychologist,* 29 (1974): 821–840.

Bootzin, R. *Stimulus Control of Insomnia.* Paper presented at the meeting of the American Psychological Association, Montreal (Aug. 1973).

Bornstein, M. H. "Qualities of Color Vision in Infancy." *Journal of Experimental Child Psychology,* 19 (1975): 401–419.

Bower, G. H. "How to . . . uh . . . Remember." *Psychology Today* (Oct. 1973): 63–70.

Bower, G. H. and M. C. Clark. "Narrative Stories as Mediators for Serial Learning." *Psychonomic Science,* 14 (1969): 181–182.

Bower, G. H. and F. Springston. "Pauses as Recoding Points in Letter Series." *Journal of Experimental Psychology,* 83 (1970): 421–430.

Bowerman, M. "The Acquisition of Word Meaning: An Investigation of Some Current Concepts." *Thinking* (1977).

Bowker, L. H. "The Incidence of Drug Use and Associated Factors in Two Small Towns: A Community Survey." *Bulletin on Narcotics,* 28, No. 4 (Oct.–Dec. 1976): 17–25.

Bowlby, J. *Attachment and Loss, Volume I: Attachment.* New York: Basic Books, 1969.

———. *Attachment and Loss, Volume II: Separation and Anxiety.* New York: Basic Books, 1973.

Brady, J. V. "Ulcers in Executive Monkeys." *Scientific American,* 199 (1958): 95–100.

Braginsky, B. M. and D. D. Braginsky. "Schizophrenic Patients in the Psychiatric Interview: An Experimental Study of Their Effectiveness at Manipulation." *Journal of Consulting Psychology,* 31 (1967): 543–547.

Bransford, J. D. and N. S. McCarrell. "A Sketch of Cognitive Approach to Comprehension: Some Thoughts about Understanding What It Means to Comprehend." In *Thinking: Readings In Cognitive Science,* edited by P. N. Johnson-Laird and P. C. Wason. Cambridge: Cambridge University Press, 1977.

Brazelton, T. B., B. Koslowski and M. Main. "The Origins of Reciprocity: The Early Mother-Infant Interaction." In *The Effect of the Infant on its Caregiver,* edited by M. Lewis and L. A. Rosenblum. New York: Wiley-Interscience, 1974.

Brazelton, T. B., et al. "Early Mother-Infant Reciprocity." In *Parent-Infant Interaction,* Ciba Foundation Symposium 33. Amsterdam: Associated Scientific Publishers, 1975.

Brecher, E. M. and the Editors of *Consumer Reports. Licit and Illicit Drugs.* Boston: Little, Brown, 1972.

Brecher, E. M. "Marijuana: The Health Questions." *Consumer Reports,* 40 (March 1975a): 143–149.

Breland, K. and M. Breland. "The Misbehavior of Organisms." *American Psychologist,* 16 (1961): 681–684.

Bresler, D. E. and R. Trubo. *Free Yourself from Pain,* New York: Simon and Schuster, 1979.

Bridges, K. M. B. "Emotional Development in Early Infancy." *Child Development,* 3 (1932): 324–334.

Brown, A. S. "Satisfying Relationships for Elderly and Their Patterns of Disengagement." *Gerontologist,* 14 (1974): 258–262.

Brown, B. "Perspectives on Social Stress." In *Selye's Guide to Stress Research,* vol. 1, edited by H. Selye. New York: Van Nostrand Reinhold, 1980.

Brown, R., and J. Kulik. "Flashbulb Memories." *Cognition,* 5, No. 1 (1977): 73–99.

Brown, R. and D. McNeill. "The 'Tip of the Tongue' Phenomenon." *Journal of Verbal Learning and Verbal Behavior,* 5 (1966): 325–337.

Bruch, H. "Transformation of Oral Impulses in Eating Disorders: A Conceptual Approach." *Psychiatry Quarterly,* 35 (1961): 458–481.

Bruner, J. S. *Toward a Theory of Instruction.* New York: Norton, 1968.

Bruner, J. S., *et al. Studies in Cognitive Growth.* New York: Wiley, 1966.

Bruner, J. S. and L. Postman. "On the Perception of Incongruity: A Paradigm." *Journal of Personality,* 18 (1949): 206–223.

Bryan, J. H., and M. A. Test. "Models and Helping. Naturalistic Tendencies in Aiding Behavior." *Journal of Personality and Social Psychology,* 6 (1967): 400–407.

Bryan, J. H. and N. H. Walbek. "Preaching and Practicing Generosity: Children's Actions and Reactions." *Child Development,* 41 (1970): 329–353.

Buchwald, A. "Psyching Out." *The Washington Post* (June 20, 1965).

Buckhout, R. "Eyewitness Testimony." *Scientific American,* 231 (Dec. 1974): 23–31.

Budzynski, T. H. "Biofeedback Strategies in Headache Treatment." In *Biofeedback: A Handbook for Clinicians,* edited by J. V. Basmajian. Baltimore: Williams and Wilkins, 1977.

Bursten, B. *The Manipulator.* New Haven: Yale University Press, 1973.

Burka, J. B. and L. M. Yuen. "Procrastination: Psychology and Group Treatment in a College Population." Symposium presented at the meeting of the American Psychological Association, Los Angeles, August 24, 1981.

Burtt, H. E. "An Experimental Study of Early Childhood Memory: Final Report." *Journal of General Psychology,* 58 (1941): 435–439.

Buss, A. H. *Self-consciousness and Social Anxiety.* San Francisco: Freeman, 1980.

Butler, R. "Curiosity in Monkeys." *Scientific American,* 190, No. 18 (1954): 70–75.

Butler, R. and H. F. Harlow. "Persistence of Visual Exploration in Monkeys." *Journal of Comparative Physiological Psychology,* 47 (1954): 258–263.

Butler, R. N. and M. I. Lewis. *Aging and Mental Health.* St. Louis: Mosby, 1977.

Byrne, D. *The Attraction Paradigm.* New York: Academic Press, 1971.

Cabanac, M. and P. Duclaux. "Obesity: Absence of Satiety Aversion to Sucrose." *Science,* 168 (1970): 496–497.

Calhoun, J. B. "A 'Behavioral Sink.'" In *Roots of Behavior,* edited by E. L. Bliss. New York: Harper & Row, 1962.

Cameron, P., R. Frank, M. Lifter, and P. Morrissey. "Cognitive Functionings of College Students in a General Psychology Class." Paper presented at the meeting of the American Psychological Association, San Francisco (Sept. 1968).

Campbell, A., G. Gurin, and W. E. Miller. *The Voter Decides.* New York: Harper & Row, 1954.

Campbell, C. "Transcendence Is as American as Ralph Waldo Emerson." *Psychology Today,* 7, No. 11 (1974): 37–38.

Campos, J. J., S. Hiatt, D. Ramsay, C. Henderson, and M. Svejda. "The Emergence of Fear on the Visual Cliff." In *The Development of Affect,* edited by M. Lewis and L. A. Rosenblum. New York: Plenum Press, 1978, pp. 149–182.

Canadian Government's Commission of Inquiry. *The Non-Medical Use of Drugs.* Baltimore: Penguin, 1971.

Cannon, J. T., J. C. Liebeskind, and H. Frenk. "Neural and Neurochemical Mechanisms of Pain Inhibition." In *The Psychology of Pain,* edited by R. A. Sternbach. New York: Raven Press, 1978.

Cannon, W. B. *The Wisdom of the Body.* New York: Norton, 1932.

———. "Hunger and Thirst." In *A Handbook of General Experimental Psychology,* edited by C. Murchison. Worcester, Mass: Clark University Press, 1934.

———. "'Voodoo' Death." *American Anthropologist,* 44 (1942): 169–181.

Cannon, W. B. and A. L. Washburn. "An Exploration of Hunger." *American Journal of Physiology,* 29 (1912): 441–454.

Carelli, R. "Insanity: A Legal Lever that Tips Justice Scales." Associated Press news article, *Santa Barbara News Press,* May 31, 1982.

Carew, J. V., I. Chan and C. Halfor. *Observing Intelligence in Young Children: Eight Case Studies.* Englewood Cliffs, N.J.: Prentice-Hall, 1976.

Carlson, N. R. *Physiology of Behavior* (2nd ed.). Boston: Allyn and Bacon, 1981.

Carmen, R. and W. R. Adams. *Study Skills: A Student's Guide for Survival.* New York: Wiley, 1972.

Carmichael, L., H. P. Hogan, and A. A. Walter. "An Experimental Study of the Effect of Language on the Reproduction of Visually Perceived Form." *Journal of Experimental Psychology* 15 (1932): 73–86.

Carr, R. R. and E. J. Meyers. "Marijuana and Cocaine: The Process of Change in Drug Policy." In *The Facts about "Drug Abuse."* The Drug Abuse Council. New York: The Free Press, 1980.

Carter, W. E. (ed.). *Cannabis in Costa Rica: A Study of Chronic Marihuana Use.* Philadelphia: Institute for the Study of Human Issues, 1980.

Cartwright, R. D. "Happy Endings for our Dreams." *Psychology Today,* 12 (Dec. 1978): 66–77.

———. "Sleep and Dreams, Part II." *Annual Review of Psychology,* 29 (1978): 223–252.

Cartwright, R. In *Dream Psychology and the New Biology of Dreaming,* edited by M. Kramer. Springfield, Ill.: Charles C Thomas, 1969.

Casler, L. "The Effects of Extra Tactile Stimulation on a Group of Institutionalized Infants." *Genetic Psychology Monographs* 71 (1965): 137–175.

Cattell, R. B. *The Scientific Analysis of Personality.* Baltimore: Penguin, 1965.

———. "Personality Pinned Down." *Psychology Today,* 7 (1973): 40–46.

Cautela, J. "Covert Processes and Behavior Modification." *The Journal of Nervous and Mental Disease,* 157 (1973): 27–36.

Chafetz, M. E. "Alcohol and Alcoholism." *American Scientist,* 67 (May–June 1979): 293–299.

Chaikin, A. L. and V. J. Derlega. *Self-Disclosure.* Morristown, N.J.: General Learning Press, 1974.

Challinor, M. E. *Science 80* (Dec. 1980): 27.

Chaves, J. F. and T. X. Barber. "Cognitive Strategies, Experimenter Modeling, and Expectation in the Attenuation of Pain." *Journal of Abnormal Psychology,* 83 (1974): 356–363.

Cheek, J. and A. H. Buss. "Scales of Shyness, Sociability, and Self-esteem and Correlations Among Them." Unpublished research, University of Texas, 1979. (Cited by Buss, 1980).

Cherry, L. J. "A Sociocognitive Approach to Language Development and Its Implications for Education." In *Language, Children and Society,* edited by O. K. Garnica and M. L. King. New York: Pergamon Press, 1979.

Chess, S., A. Thomas, and H. G. Birch. *Your Child Is a Person: A Psychological Approach to Parenthood without Guilt.* New York: Viking, 1965.

Chomsky, N. *Language and Mind.* New York: Harcourt, 1968.

———. *Reflections on Language.* New York: Pantheon, 1975.

Chown, S. M. and H. Heron. "Psychological Aspects of Aging in Man." *Annual Review of Psychology,* 16 (1965).

Cialdini, R. B., R. E. Petty and J. T. Cacippo. "Attitude and Attitude Change." *Annual Review of Psychology,* 32 (1981): 357–404.

Clark, K. B. *Dark Ghetto.* New York: Harper & Row, 1965.

Cleckley, H. *The Mask of Sanity* (4th ed.). St. Louis: Mosby, 1964.

Cline, V. B., R. G. Croft, and S. Courrier. "Desensitization of Children to Television Violence." *Journal of Personality and Social Psychology,* 27 (1972): 360–365.

Clore, G. L. "Interpersonal Attraction: An Overview." In *Contemporary Topics in Social Psychology.* Morristown, N.J.: General Learning Press, 1976.

Cobb, S. "Social Support as a Moderator of Life Stresses." *Psychosomatic Medicine,* 38 (1976): 300–314.

Cofer, C. N. (ed.). *The Structure of Human Memory.* San Francisco: Freeman, 1975.

Cofer, C. N. and M. H. Appley. *Motivation: Theory and Research.* New York: Wiley, 1964.

Cohen, D. *Intelligence.* New York: M. Evans, 1974.

Cohen, J. *Secondary Motivation.* Chicago: Rand McNally, 1970.

Cohen, S. *The Drug Dilemma.* New York: McGraw-Hill, 1969.

———. "Internal Opioid-Like Compounds." *Drug Abuse and Alcoholism Newsletter,* 6, No. 7 (Sept. 1977).

Coleman, J. C. "Facial Expression of Emotion." *Psychology Monthly,* No. 296 (1949).

———. *Psychology and Effective Behavior.* Glenview, Ill.: Scott, Foresman, 1969.

———. *Abnormal Psychology and Modern Life* (4th ed.). Glenview, Ill.: Scott, Foresman, 1972.

Coleman, J., J. N. Butcher, and R. C. Carson. *Abnormal Psychology and Modern Life* (6th ed.). Glenview, Ill.: Scott, Foresman, 1980.

Coleman, J. C. and C. L. Hammen. *Contemporary Psychology and Effective Behavior.* Glenview, Ill.: Scott, Foresman, 1974.

Collins, A. M. and M. R. Quillian. "Retrieval Time from Semantic Memory." *Journal of Verbal Learning and Verbal Behavior,* 8 (1969): 240–247.

Comfort, A. *A Good Age.* New York: Crown, 1976.

Comstock, G., S. Chaffee, N. Katzman, M. McCombs, and D. Roberts. *Television and Human Behavior.* New York: Columbia University Press, 1978.

Condon, W. S. and L. W. Sander. "Neonate Movement Is Synchronized with Adult Speech: Interactional Participation and Language Acquisition." *Science,* 183 (1974): 99–101.

Coopersmith, S. "Studies in Self-Esteem." *Scientific American,* 218 (1968): 96–106.

Corballis, M. C. "Laterality and Myth." *American Psychologist,* 35, No. 3 (March, 1980): 284–295.

Coren, S. and C. Porac. "Fifty Centuries of Right-Handedness: The Historical Record." *Science,* 198 (Nov. 11, 1977): 631–632.

Cornsweet, T. N. *Visual Perception.* New York: Academic Press, 1970.

Cortes, J. B. and F. M. Gatti. *Delinquency and Crime: A Biopsychological Approach.* New York: Seminar Press, 1972.

Costell, C. G. "Electroconvulsive Therapy: Is Further Investigation Necessary?" *Canadian Psychiatric Association Journal,* 21, No. 2 (March 1976): 61–67.

Cowles, J. T. "Food Tokens as Incentives for Learning by Chimpanzees." *Comparative Psychology,* Monograph, 1937, 14, No. 5, Whole No. 71.

Cox, F. D. *Human Intimacy.* St. Paul, Minn.: West, 1979.

Cox, T. *Stress.* Baltimore: University Park Press, 1978.

Craig, K. "Social Modeling Influences on Pain." In *The Psychology of Pain,* edited by R. A. Sternbach. New York: Raven Press, 1978.

Craik, F. I. M. "The Fate of Primary Items in Free Recall." *Journal of Verbal Learning and Verbal Behavior,* 9 (1970): 143–148.

Cronbach, L. *Essentials of Psychological Testing* (3rd ed.). New York: Harper & Row, 1970.

Culliton, B. J. "Psychosurgery: National Commission Issues Surprisingly Favorable Report." *Science,* 194, No. 4252 (1976): 299–301.

Cumming, E. and W. E. Henry. *Growing Old: The Process of Disengagement.* New York: Basic Books, 1961.

Dabbs, J. M. "Sex, Setting and Reactions to Crowding on Sidewalks." *Proceedings of the 80th Annual Convention of The American Psychological Association,* 7 (1972): 205–206.

Darley, J. M. and B. Latane. "Bystander Intervention in Emergencies: Diffusion of Responsibility." *Journal of Personality and Social Psychology,* 8 (1968): 377–383.

Darwin, C. *The Expression of Emotion in Man and Animals.* Chicago: University of Chicago Press, 1965. (First published, 1872.)

Davidson, R. J. and G. E. Schwartz. "The Influence of Musical Training on Patterns of EEG Asymmetry During Musical and Non-musical Self-Generation Tasks." *Psychophysiology,* 14 (1977): 58–63.

Davis, D. M. "Self-Selection of Diet by Newly Weaned Infants." *American Journal of Diseases of Children,* 36 (1928): 651–679.

Davis, J. M. "Dopamine Theory of Schizophrenia: A Two-Factor Theory." In *The Nature of Schizophrenia: New Approaches to Research and Treatment,* edited by L. C. Wynne, R. L. Cromwell, and S. Matthysse. New York: Wiley, 1978.

Davis, M., M. McKay and E. R. Eshelman. *The Relaxation and Stress Reduction Workbook.* Richmond, Calif.: New Harbinger, 1980.

Davis, R. E. "Changing Examination Answers: An Educational Myth?" *Journal of Medical Education,* 50 (1975): 685–687.

Deaux, K. and T. Emswiller. "Explanation of Successful Performance on Sex-linked Tasks: What Is Skill for the Male Is Luck for the Female." *Journal of Personality and Social Psychology,* 29 (1974): 80–85.

de Bono, E. *Lateral Thinking: Creativity Step by Step.* New York: Harper & Row, 1970.

DeCharms, R. and M. S. Muir. "Motivation: Social Approaches." *Annual Review of Psychology,* 29 (1978): 91–113.

De Chateau. In *Early Experiences and Early Behavior: Implications for Social Developments,* edited by E. C. Simmel. New York: Academic Press, 1980.

Deese, J. "Thoughts into Speech." *American Scientist,* 66 (May 1978): 314–321.

Deese, J. and S. H. Hulse. *The Psychology of Learning* (3rd ed.). New York: McGraw-Hill, 1967.

DeGood, D. E. "Cognitive Factors in Vascular Stress Responses." *Psychophysiology,* 12 (1975): 399–401.

Delgado, J. *Physical Control of the Mind.* New York: Harper & Row, 1969.

———. "ESB." *Psychology Today,* (May 1970).

Dember, W. N. and J. S. Warm. *Psychology and Perception,* 2nd ed. New York: Holt, 1979.

Dement, W. "The Effect of Dream Deprivation." *Science,* 131 (1960): 1705–1707.

———. *Some Must Watch While Some Must Sleep.* Stanford, Calif.: Stanford Alumni Association, 1972.

Dement, W. and N. Kleitman. "The Relation of Eye Movements During Sleep to Dream Activity: An Objective Method for the Study of Dreaming." *The Journal of Experimental Psychology,* 53, No. 5 (1957).

Dement, W. and E. Wolpert. "The Relation of Eye Movements, Body Mobility and External Stimuli to Dream Content." *Journal of Experimental Psychology,* 55 (1958): 543–553.

Dennenberg, V. H. "Stimulation in Infancy, Emotional Reactivity, and Exploratory Behavior." In *Neurophysiology and Emotion,* edited by D. C. Glass. New York: Russell Sage Foundation and Rockefeller University Press, 1967.

Dennis, W. and M. Dennis. "The Effects of Cradling Practices upon the Onset of Walking in Hopi Children." *Journal of Genetic Psychology,* 56 (1940): 77–86.

Depue, R. A. and S. M. Monroe. "The Unipolar-Bipolar Distinction in the Depressive Disorders." *Psychological Bulletin,* 85 (1978): 1001–1029.

Deregowski, J. B. "Pictorial Perception and Culture." *Scientific American,* (Nov. 1972): 82–88.

Deutsch, D. "Pitch Memory: An Advantage for the Left-Handed." *Science,* 199 (1978): 559–560.

Deutsch, M. and M. E. Collins. *Interracial Housing.* Minneapolis: University of Minnesota Press, 1951.

Diamond, M. "Human Sexual Development: Biological Foundations for Social Development." In *Human Sexuality in Four Perspectives,* edited by F. A. Beach. Baltimore: Johns Hopkins University Press, 1977, pp. 22–61.

Dienstbier, R. A. and P. O. Munter, "Cheating as a Function of the Labeling of Natural Arousal." *Journal of Personality and Social Psychology,* 17, No. 2 (1971): 208–213.

Dixon, J. "Jeanne Dixon Strikes Back at Scientists Who Knock Astrology." *National Star,* (Sept. 30, 1975): 5.

Dobelle, W. H., M. G. Mladejovsky, and J. P. Girvin. "Artificial Vision for the Blind: Electrical Stimulation of Visual Cortex Offers a Hope for a Functional Prosthesis." *Science,* 183 (1974): 440–444.

Dollard, J., *et al. Frustration and Aggression.* New Haven: Yale University Press, 1939.

Dollard, J. and N. E. Miller. *Personality and Psychotherapy: An Analysis in Terms of Learning, Thinking and Culture.* New York: McGraw-Hill, 1950.

Donohue, H. E. F. *Where Should You Touch?* New York: The Hearst Corporation, 1968.

Doob, A. N. and A. E. Gross. "Status of Frustrator as an Inhibitor of Horn-Honking Responses." *Journal of Social Psychology,* 76 (1968): 213–218.

Dooling, D. J. and R. Lachman. "Effects of Comprehension on Retention of Prose." *Journal of Experimental Psychology,* 88 (1971): 216–222.

Dostoevsky, F. *Crime and Punishment.* Translated by C. Garnett, New York: Collier, 1917.

Downey, D. *Personal Communication.* Tempe, Ariz.: Casales Press, 1976.

Drowatzky, J. N. *Motor Learning: Principles and Practices.* Minneapolis: Burgess, 1975.

Drug Abuse Council. *The Facts about "Drug Abuse".* New York: Free Press, 1980.

DSM-III: Diagnostic and Statistical Manual of Mental Disorders (3rd ed.). American Psychiatric Association. Washington, D.C., 1980.

Duncker, K. "On Problem Solving." *Psychological Monographs,* 58, No. 270 (1945).

Dunkle, T. "The Sound of Silence." *Science 82,* (1982): 30–33.

Durkheim, E. *Suicide: A Study in Sociology.* Translated by J. A. Spaulding and G. Simpson. New York: Free Press, 1951.

Dutton, D. G. and A. P. Aron. "Some Evidence for Heightened Sexual Attraction Under Conditions of High Anxiety." *Journal of Personality and Social Psychology,* 30 (1974): 510–517.

Ebbinghaus, H. *Memory: A Contribution to Experimental Psychology.* Translated by H. A. Ruger and C. E. Bussenius. New York: New York Teacher's College, Columbia University, 1913. (Originally published, Leipzig: Altenberg, 1885.)

Edwards, K. A. and C. Marshall. "First Impressions on Tests: Some New Findings." *Teaching of Psychology,* 4 (Dec. 1977): 193–195.

Ehara, T. H. "On the Electronic Chess Circuit." *Science 80,* (Dec. 1980): 78–79.

Ehrenberg, P. "A Last Memoir." In *What I Have Learned,* edited by N. Cousins. New York: Simon and Schuster, 1968.

Ehrlichman, H. and A. Weinberger. "Lateral Eye Movements and Hemispheric Asymmetry: A Critical Review." *Psychological Bulletin,* 85 (1978): 1080–1101.

Eibl-Eibesfeldt, I. *Ethology: The Biology of Behavior.* New York: Holt, 1970.

Einstein, D. "Results of Sanity Trials Show Weakness in System." Associated Press news article, *Santa Barbara News Press,* February 26, 1981.

Eiser, J. R. *Cognitive Social Psychology.* Maidenhead, Berkshire, England: McGraw-Hill (UK), 1980.

Ekman, P. *The Face of Man: Expressions of Universal Emotions in a New Guinea Village.* New York: Garland STPM Press, 1980.

Ekman, P. and W. V. Friesen. *Unmasking the Face.* Englewood Cliffs, N.J.: Prentice-Hall, 1975.

Elder, G. "Appearance and Education in Marriage Mobility." *American Sociological Review,* 34 (1969): 519–533.

Elkind, D. "Giant in the Nursery—Jean Piaget." *The New York Times Magazine,* (May 26, 1968).

Ellis, A. *Reason and Emotion in Psychotherapy.* New York: Lyle Stuart, 1962.

———. "The No Cop-Out Therapy." *Psychology Today,* 7, No. 2 (1973): 56–60, 62.

———. "Rational-Emotive Therapy." In *Modern Therapies,* edited by V. Binder, A. Binder, and B. Rimland. Englewood Cliffs, N.J.: Prentice-Hall, 1976, pp. 21–34.

Engel, G. "Emotional Stress and Sudden Death." *Psychology Today* (Nov. 1977): 144.

Erdelyi, M. H. "A New Look at The New Look: Perceptual Defense and Vigilance." *Psychological Review,* 81 (1974): 1–25.

Erdelyi, M. H. and A. G. Appelbaum. "Cognitive Masking: The Disruptive Effect of an Emotional Stimulus upon the Perception of Contiguous Neutral Items." *Bulletin of the Psychonomic Society,* 1 (1973): 59–61.

Erikson, E. H. *Childhood and Society* (2nd ed.). New York: Norton, 1963.

Erlenmeyer-Kimling, L. and L. F. Jarvik. "Genetics and Intelligence: A Review." *Science,* 142 (1963): 1477–1479.

Etaugh, C. "Effects of Nonmaternal Care on Children." *American Psychologist,* 35 (April 1980): 309–319.

Evarts, E. V. "Brain Mechanisms of Movement." *Scientific American,* 241, No. 3 (1979): 164–179.

Eysenck, H. J. *Sense and Nonsense in Psychology.* Harmondsworth, Middlesex, England: Penguin Books Ltd., 1957, 1958.

———. "New Ways in Psychotherapy." *Psychology Today,* (June, 1967): 40.

———. *The Intelligence Controversy.* New York: Wiley, 1981.

Fairweather, H. "Sex Differences in Cognition." *Cognition,* 4 (1976): 231–280.

Fantz, R. L. "Pattern Vision in Newborn Infants." *Science,* 140 (1963): 296–297.

Faraday, A. *Dream Power.* New York: Coward, 1972.

Farber, L. H. "Ours Is the Addicted Society." *The New York Times Magazine,* (Dec. 11, 1966).

Fast, J. *Body Language.* New York: M. Evans, 1970.

Fehr, L. "J. Piaget and S. Claus: Psychology Makes Strange Bedfellows." *Psychological Reports,* 39 (Dec. 1976): 740–742.

Feinberg, I. and V. R. Carlson. "Sleep Variables as a Function of Normal and Pathological Aging in Man." *Journal of Psychiatric Research,* 5 (1967): 107–144.

Feldman, D. H. and J. C. Bratton. "Relativity and Giftedness: Implications for Equality of Educational Opportunity." *Exceptional Children,* 38 (1972): 491–492.

Ferster, C. B. "The Autistic Child." *Psychology Today,* 2 (1968): 35–37, 61.

Ferster, C. B., J. I. Nurnberger, and E. B. Levitt. "The Control of Eating." *Journal of Mathematics,* 1 (1962): 87–109.

Festinger, L. "A Theory of Social Comparison Processes." *Human Relations,* 7 (1954): 117–140.

———. *A Theory of Cognitive Dissonance.* Stanford, Calif.: Stanford University Press, 1957.

Festinger, L. and J. M. Carlsmith. "Cognitive Consequences of Forced Compliance." *Journal of Abnormal and Social Psychology,* 58 (1959): 203–210.

Festinger, L., S. Schachter, and K. Back. *Social Pressures in Informal Groups: A Study of a Housing Project.* New York: Harper, 1950.

Fink, M. "Myths of Shock Therapy." *American Journal of Psychiatry,* 134, No. 9 (1977): 991–996.

Fishbein, M. and I Ajzen. *Belief, Attitude, Intention, and Behavior: An Introduction to Theory and Research.* Reading, Mass.: Addison-Wesley, 1975.

Fisher, S. *The Female Orgasm.* New York: Basic Books, 1973.

Fleming, J. "Field Report: The State of the Apes." *Psychology Today,* (Jan. 1974): 46.

Flint, B. M. *New Hope for Deprived Children.* Toronto: University of Toronto Press, 1978.

Foster, G. and J. Ysseldyke. "Expectancy and Halo Effects as a Result of Artificially Induced Teacher Bias." *Contemporary Educational Psychology,* 1, No. 1 (Jan. 1976): 37–45.

Frank, J. D. "The Demoralized Mind." *Psychology Today,* 6, No. 11 (1973): 22–31, 100–101.

Frankenburg, W. K. and J. B. Dodds. "The Denver Developmental Screening Test." *The Journal of Pediatrics,* 1, No. 2 (1967): 181–191.

Frankl, F. H. "Current Perspectives on ECT: A Discussion." *American Journal of Psychiatry,* 134 (1977): 1014–1019.

Frankl, V. *The Doctor and the Soul.* New York: Knopf, 1955.

Freedman, J. L. *Crowding and Behavior.* San Francisco: Freeman, 1975.

Freud, S. *The Interpretation of Dreams.* London: Hogarth, 1900.

———. *An Outline of Psychoanalysis.* New York: Norton, 1949.

Friedberg, J. "Shock Treatment, Brain Damage, and Memory Loss: A Neurological Perspective." *American Journal of Psychiatry,* 134 (1977): 1010–1014.

Friedman, M. and R. Rosenman. *Type A Behavior and Your Heart.* New York: Knopf, 1974.

Friedman, M. I. and E. M. Stricker. "The Physiological Psychology of Hunger: A Physiological Perspective." *Psychological Review,* 83 (1976): 409–431.

Frodi, A. N., M. E. Lamb, L. A. Leavitt, W. L. Donovan, C. Neff and D. Sherry. "Fathers' and Mothers' Responses to the Faces and Cries of Normal and Premature Infants." *Developmental Psychology,* 14 (1978): 190–198.

Fuastman, W. O. "Aversive Control of Maladaptive Sexual Behavior: Past Developments and Future Trends." *Psychology,* 13, No. 4 (Nov. 1976): 53–60.

Fulgosi, A. and J. P. Guilford. "Short-Term Incubation in Divergent Production." *American Journal of Psychology,* 7 (1968): 1016–1023.

Fuller, B. *Utopia or Oblivion: The Prospects for Humanity.* New York: Bantam Matrix, 1969.

Fulton, R. "Death and Dying in a Changing World." *Santa Barbara News Press,* (Jan. 21, 1979).

Gagné, R. M. and E. A. Fleishman. *Psychology and Human Performance.* New York: Holt, 1959.

Galanter, E. "Contemporary Psychophysics." In *New Directions in Psychology,* Vol. 1 New York: Holt, 1962, pp. 87–156.

Garcia, J. "Intelligence Testing: Quotients, Quotas and Quackery." In *Chicago Psychology,* edited by J. L. Martinez. New York: Academic Press, 1977.

Garcia, J., W. G. Hankins, and K. W. Rusiniak. "Behavioral Regulation of the Milieu Interne In Man and Rat." *Science,* 185 (1974): 824–831.

Gardner, H. *The Shattered Mind: The Person after Brain Damage.* New York: Knopf, 1975.

Gardner, M. "Dermo-Optical Perception: A Peek Down the Nose." *Science,* 151 (1966): 654–657.

———. "A Skeptic's View of Parapsychology." *The Humanist,* (Nov.–Dec., 1977).

Gardner, R. A. and B. T. Gardner. "Teaching Sign Language to a Chimpanzee." *Science,* 165 (1969): 664–672.

Garfield, P. *Creative Dreaming.* New York: Ballantine, 1974.

Gates, A. I. "Recitation as a Factor in Memorizing." In *The Psychology of Learning* (2nd ed.), edited by J. Deese. New York: McGraw-Hill, 1958.

Gazzaniga, M. S. and J. E. LeDoux. *The Integrated Mind.* New York: Plenum, 1978.

Geldard, F. A. *The Human Senses* (2nd ed.). New York: Wiley, 1972.

Gerbner, G. and L. Gross. "Living with Television: The Violence Profile." *Journal of Communication,* 26 (1976): 173–199.

Gersh, R. D. "Learning When Not To Shoot." *Santa Barbara News Press,* June 20, 1982.

Geschwind, N. "The Apraxias: Neural Mechanisms of Disorders of Learned Movement." *American Scientist,* 63 (1975): 188–195.

———. "Specializations of the Human Brain." *Scientific American,* 241 (Sept. 1979): 180–199.

Gesell, A., *et al. The First Five Years of Life.* New York: Harper Bros., 1940.

Gibson, E. J. and R. D. Walk. "The 'Visual Cliff.'" *Scientific American,* 202, No. 4 (1960): 67–71.

Gillam, B. "Geometrical Illusions." *American Psychologist,* 242, No. 1 (Jan. 1980): 102–111.

Ginott, H. G. *Between Parent and Child: New Solutions to Old Problems.* New York: Macmillan, 1965.

Giovannoni, J. M. and R. M. Becerra. *Defining Child Abuse.* New York: Free Press, 1979.

Girodo, M. *Shy? (You Don't Have to Be!).* New York: Pocket Books, 1978.

Glaser, R. "Adapting to Individual Differences." *Social Policy* (Sept./Oct. 1977): 27–33.

Glass, D. C. "Stress, Behavior Patterns, and Coronary Disease." *American Scientist,* 65 (1977): 177–187.

Glass, D. C. and J. E. Singer. "Behavioral Aftereffects of Unpredictable and Uncontrollable Aversive Events." *American Scientist,* 60 (1972): 457–465.

Glick, D. and W. A. Hargreaves, with J. Drues and J. Showstack. *Psychiatric Hospital Treatment for the 1980s: A Controlled Study of Short Versus Long Hospitalization.* Lexington, Mass.: Lexington Books, 1979.

Goldenson, R. M. *The Encyclopedia of Human Behavior,* Vol. 2. Garden City, N.Y.: Doubleday, 1970b.

Goldiamond, I. "Fluent and Non-Fluent Speech (Stuttering): Analysis and Operant Techniques for Control." In *Research in Behavior Modification,* edited by L. Krasner and L. P. Ullman. New York: Holt, 1965.

———. "Self-control Procedures in Personal Behavior Problems." In *Good Reading in Psychology,* edited by M. S. Gazzaniga and E. P. Lovejoy. Englewood Cliffs, N.J.: Prentice-Hall, 1971.

Goleman, D. "1,528 Little Geniuses and How They Grew." *Psychology Today* (February, 1980): 28.

———. "Staying Up: The Rebellion Against Sleep's Gentle Tyranny." *Psychology Today* (March 1982): 24–35.

Gomes-Schwartz, B., S. W. Hadley and H. H. Strupp. "Individual Psychotherapy and Behavior Therapy." *Annual Review of Psychology,* 29 (1978): 435–471.

Goodglass, H. "Disorders of Naming Following Brain Injury." *American Scientist,* 68 (Nov.–Dec. 1980): 647–655.

Gordon, T. *P.E.T. Parent Effectiveness Training: A Tested New Way to Raise Children.* New York: Wyden, 1970.

Gottesman, I. I. "Schizophrenia and Genetics: Where Are We? Are You Sure?" In *The Nature of Schizophrenia: New Approaches to Research and Treatment,* edited by L. C. Wynne, R. L. Cromwell, and S. Matthysse. New York: Wiley, 1978.

Gottesman, I. I. and J. Shield. *Schizophrenia and Genetics.* New York: Academic Press, 1972.

Gould, J. L. and C. G. Gould. "The Instinct to Learn." *Science 81* (May 1981).

Gould, L. C., *et al.* "Sequential Patterns of Multiple-Drug Use Among High School Students." *Archives of General Psychiatry,* 34, No. 2 (Feb. 1977): 216–222.

Gould, R. "Growth Toward Self-Tolerance." *Psychology Today,* (Feb. 1975).

Graubard, P. S. and H. Rosenberg. "Little Brother Is Changing You." *Psychology Today,* (March 1974).

Green, H. (Joanne Greenberg). *I Never Promised You a Rose Garden.* New York: Holt, 1964.

Greenberg, J. "The Brain and Emotions: Crossing a New Frontier." *Science News,* 112, No. 5 (July 30, 1977): 74–75.

———. "The Aging of Sleep." *Science News,* 114, No. 1 (July 1, 1978): 10–12.

Greene, D. and M. R. Lepper. "How to Turn Play into Work." *Psychology Today,* (Sept. 1974): 49.

Greenspoon, J. "The Reinforcing Effect of Two Spoken Sounds on the Frequency of Two Responses." *American Journal of Psychology,* 50 (1955): 409–416.

Greenwald, H. (Ed.) *Active Psychotherapy.* Chicago: Aldine, 1967, quoted in *Psychosources,* edited by E. Shapiro, New York: Bantam, 1973, p. 147.

Gregory, R. L. *The Intelligent Eye.* New York: McGraw-Hill, 1970.

———. *Eye and Brain: The Psychology of Seeing,* 3rd ed. New York: World University Library, 1977.

Grings, W. W. and R. A. Lockhart. "Effects of Anxiety-Lessening Instructions and Differential Set Development on the Extinction of GSR." *Journal of Experimental Psychology,* 66 (1963): 292–299.

Grinspoon, L. "Marijuana." In *Altered States of Awareness: Readings from Scientific American.* San Francisco: Freeman, 1972.

Grinspoon, L. and J. B. Bakalar. *Cocaine, A Drug and Its Social Evolution.* New York: Basic Books, 1977.

Grinspoon, L. and P. Hedblom. "Amphetamines Reconsidered." *Saturday Review,* (July 8, 1972). Special Issue.

Grobstein, P. and K. L. Chow. "Perceptive Field Development and Individual Experience." *Science,* 190 (1975): 352–358.

Guilford, J. P. "Creativity." *American Psychologist,* 5 (1950): 444–454.

———. *Personality.* New York: McGraw-Hill, 1959.

Guilleminault, C. "The Sleep Apnea Syndrome." *Medical Times* (June 1979): 59–67.

Guilleminault, C., P. Passouant, and W. C. Dement, *Narcolepsy.* New York: Spectrum, 1976.

Gustavson, C. R. and J. Garcia. "Pulling a Gag on the Wily Coyote." *Psychology Today,* (Aug. 1974): 68–72.

Gutek, B. A. "Experiences of Sexual Harassment: Results from a Representative Survey." Paper presented at symposium of the annual convention, American Psychological Association, August, 1981, Los Angeles.

Haase, W. "The Role of Socio-Economic Class in Examiner Bias." In *Mental Health of the Poor,* edited by F. Reissman, J. Cohen, and A. Pearl. New York: Free Press, 1964, pp. 241–247.

Haber, R. N. "Eidetic Images; With Biographical Sketches" *Scientific American,* 220, No. 12 (April 1969): 36–44.

———. "How We Remember What We See." *Scientific American,* (May 1970): 104–112.

———. "Eidetic Images." In *Image Object and Illusion.* San Francisco: Freeman, 1974.

———. "How We Perceive Depth from Flat Pictures." *American Scientist,* 68 (1980): 370–380.

Haefele, J. W. *Creativity and Innovation.* New York: Reinhold, 1962.

Hales, D. *The Complete Book of Sleep.* Reading, Mass.: Addison-Wesley, 1980.

Hall, C. *The Meaning of Dreams.* New York: McGraw-Hill, 1966.

———. "What People Dream About." In *The New World of Dreams: An Anthology.* edited by R. L. Woods and H. B. Greenhouse. New York: Macmillan, 1974.

Hall, E. T. *The Hidden Dimension.* Garden City, N.Y.: Doubleday, 1966.

———. *Handbook for Proxemic Research.* Washington, D.C.: Social Anthropology and Visual Communication, 1974.

Hall, G. S. *Senescence, The Last Half of Life.* New York: Appleton-Century-Crofts, 1922.

Hansel, C. E. M. *ESP and Parapsychology: A Critical Reevaluation.* Buffalo, N.Y.: Prometheus Books, 1980.

Hansen, W. B. and I. Altman. "Decorating Personal Places: A Descriptive Analysis." *Environmental Behavior,* 8 (1976): 491–505.

Hardy, A. B. *Agoraphobia: Symptoms, Causes, Treatment.* Menlo Park, Calif.: Terrap, 1976.

Hardyck, C., L. F. Petrinovich, R. Goldman. "Left Handedness and Cognitive Deficit." *Cortex,* 12 (1976): 266–278.

Hare, R. D. and D. N. Cox. "Psychophysiological Research on Psychopathy." In *The Psychopath: A Comprehensive Study of Anti-Social Disorders and Behaviors,* edited by W. H. Reid. New York: Brunner-Mazel, 1978.

Harlow, H. F. "The Formation of Learning Sets." *Psychological Review,* 56 (1949): 51–65.

———. "Learning to Love." *American Scientist,* 54 (1966): 244–272.

———. "The Young Monkeys." *Psychology Today,* 1, No. 5 (1967): 40–47.

Harlow, H. F. and M. K. Harlow. "Social Deprivation in Monkeys." *Scientific American,* 207 (1962): 136–146.

Harlow, H. F. and R. R. Zimmerman. "The Development of Affectional Responses in Infant Monkeys." *Proceedings of the American Philosophical Society,* 102 (1958): 501–509.

Harlow, J. M. "Recovery from the Passage of an Iron Bar Through the Head." *Massachusetts Medical Society,* 2 (1868): 327ff.

Harper. *Psychoanalysis and Psychotherapy.* Englewood Cliffs, N.J.: Prentice-Hall, 1959.

Harris, I. D. *The Promised Seed: A Complete Study of Eminent First and Later Sons.* New York: Free Press, 1964.

Hartmann, E. L. *The Functions of Sleep.* New Haven: Yale University Press, 1973.

———. *The Sleeping Pill.* New Haven: Yale University Press, 1978.

Hastorf, A. and H. Cantril. "They Saw a Game: A Case Study." *Journal of Abnormal and Social Psychology,* 49 (1954): 129–134.

Havighurst, R. J. "Successful Aging." *Gerontologist,* 1 (1961): 8–13.

———. "Choosing a Middle Path for the Use of Drugs with Hyperactive Children." *School Review,* 85, No. 1 (Nov. 1976): 60–77.

Hayakawa, S. I. "The Use and Misuse of Language." In *Science and Human Affairs,* edited by R. E. Farson. Palo Alto, Calif: Science and Behavior Books, 1965, pp. 95–113.

Hayes, C. *The Ape in Our House*. New York: Harper & Row, 1951.

Hayes, J. R. *Cognitive Psychology: Thinking and Creating*. Homewood, Illinois: Dorsey Press, 1978.

Hearst, E. "Psychology Across the Chess Board." In *Readings in Psychology Today*. Del Mar, Calif.: CRM, 1969, pp. 16–23.

Hebb, D. O. *Organization of Behavior*. New York: Wiley, 1949.

———. *A Textbook of Psychology* (2nd ed.). Philadelphia: Saunders, 1966.

———. "What Psychology Is About." *American Psychologist*, 29 (1974): 71–79.

Heber, R. F. *Epidemiology of Mental Retardation*. Springfield, Ill.: Charles C Thomas, 1970.

Heiman, J. R. "A Psychophysiological Exploration of Sexual Arousal Patterns in Females and Males." *Psychophysiology*, 14, No. 3 (1977): 266–274.

Heinstein, M. I. "Behavioral Correlates to Breast-Bottle Regimes Under Varying Parent-Infant Relationships." *Monographs of the Society for Research in Child Development*, 28, No. 4 (1963): 1–61.

Held, R. "Plasticity in Sensory-Motor Systems." In *Contemporary Psychology*. San Francisco: Freeman, 1971.

Heller, J. *Catch 22*. New York: Simon & Schuster, 1961.

Hellman, H. *Biology in the World of the Future*. New York: Hayden, 1971.

Helson, H. *Adaptation-Level Theory*. New York: Harper & Row, 1964.

Heron, W. "The Pathology of Boredom." *Scientific American*, 196 (1957): 52–56.

Herron, J. *Neuropsychology of Left-Handedness*. New York: Academic Press, 1980.

Hess, E. H. "Imprinting." *Science*, 130 (1959): 133–141.

———. *The Tell-Tale Eye: How Your Eyes Reveal Hidden Thoughts and Emotions*. New York: Van Nostrand Reinhold, 1975a.

———. "The Role of Pupil Size in Communication." *Scientific American*, (Nov. 1975b): 110–119.

Heussenstamm, F. K. "Bumper Stickers and the Cops." *Transaction*, 8 (1971): 32–33.

Hilgard, E. R. *The Experience of Hypnosis*. New York: Harcourt, 1968.

———. "Weapon Against Pain—Hypnosis Is No Mirage." *Psychology Today*, (Nov. 1974).

———. *Divided Consciousness*. New York: Wiley, 1977.

———. "Hypnosis and Pain." In *The Psychology of Pain*, edited by R. A. Sternbach. New York: Raven Press, 1978.

Hilgard, J. "Learning and Maturation in Preschool Children." *Journal of Genetic Psychology*, 41 (1932): 36–56.

Hilton, I. "Differences in the Behavior of Mothers Toward First and Later Born Children." *Journal of Personality and Social Psychology*, 7 (1967): 282–290.

Hite, S. *The Hite Report*. New York: Macmillan, 1976.

Hobson, J. A. and R. W. McCarley, "The Brain as a Dream State Generator: An Activation-Synthesis Hypothesis of the Dream Process." *American Journal of Psychiatry*, 134 (Dec. 1977): 1335–1348.

Hoffer, A. *Description, Diagnosis, Theory and Treatment of Schizophrenia*. Karpat, 1972.

Hoffman, L. W. "Changes in Family Roles, Socialization, and Sex Differences." *American Psychologist*, 32 (1977): 644–657.

Hoffman, M. L. "Conscience, Personality, and Socialization Techniques." *Human Development*, 13, No. 2 (1970): 90–126.

———. "Altruistic Behavior and the Parent-Child Relationship." *Journal of Personality and Social Psychology*, 31 (1975): 937–943.

Hohman, G. W. "Some Effects of Spinal Cord Lesions on Experienced Emotional Feelings." *Psychophysiology*, 3 (1966): 143–156.

Holland, M. K. *Using Psychology: Principles of Behavior and Your Life*. Boston: Little, Brown, 1975.

Holmes, T. and M. Masuda. "Psychosomatic Syndrome." *Psychology Today*, (April 1972): 71.

Holmes, T. H. and R. H. Rahe. "Social Readjustment Rating Scale." *Journal of Psychosomatic Research*, (1957).

Honzik, M. P., J. W. Macfarlane, and L. Allen. "The Stability of Mental Test Performance Between Two and Eighteen Years." *Journal of Experimental Education*, 17 (1948): 309–324.

Horn, J. M., J. C. Loehlin and L. Willerman. "Intellectual Resemblance Among Adoptive and Biological Relatives: The Texas Adoption Project." *Behavior Genetics*, 9 (1979): 177–207.

Horn, J. M., R. Plomine and R. Rosenman. "Heritability of Personality Traits in Adult Male Twins." *Behavior Genetics*, 6 (1976): 17–30.

Horner, M. S. "The Psychological Significance of Success in Competitive Achievement Situations: A Threat as Well as a Promise." In *Intrinsic Motivation: A New Direction in Education*, edited by H. I. Day, D. E. Berlyne, and D. E. Hunt. Toronto, Canada: Holt, 1971.

———. "The Motive to Avoid Success and Changing Aspirations of College Women." In *Readings on the Psychology of Women*, edited by J. Om Bardwick. New York: Harper & Row, 1972.

Horowitz, M. J. *Image Formation and Cognition*. New York: Appleton-Century-Crofts, 1970.

Horvath, F. S. "The Effect of Selected Variables on Interpretation of Polygraph Records." *Journal of Applied Psychology*, 49 (1977): 127–136.

Horwitz, W. A., C. Kestenbaum, E. Person, and L. Jarvik. "Identical Twin = 'Idiot Savants' Calendar Calculators." *The American Journal of Psychiatry*, 121 (1965): 1075–1079.

Howitt, D., G. Craven, C. Iveson, J. Kremer, J. McCabe, and T. Rolph. "The Misdirected Letter." *British Journal of Social and Clinical Psychology*, 16 (1977): 285–286.

Hsia, Y. and C. H. Graham. "Color Blindness." In *Vision and Visual Perception*, edited by C. H. Graham. New York: Wiley, 1965, pp. 395–413.

Hubel, D. H. "The Brain." *Scientific American*, 241, No. 3, (Sept. 1979): 45–53.

Hubel, D. H. and T. N. Wiesel. "Brain Mechanisms of Vision." *Scientific American*, 241 (1979): 150–162.

Huges, J. "Acquisition of a Non-vocal 'Language' by Aphasic Children." *Cognition* 3 (1974): 41–55.

Humphrey, J. A., D. Puccio, G. D. Niswander, and T. M. Casey. "An Analysis of the Sequence of Selected Events in the Lives of a Suicidal Population: A Preliminary Report." *Journal of Nervous Mental Disorders*. 154 (1972): 137–140.

Hunt, M. *Sexual Behavior in the 1970s*. Chicago: Playboy Press, 1974.

Hunter, W. S. "The Delayed Reaction in Animals and Children." *Behavior Monographs*, 2 (1913).

Hurst, M. W., C. D. Jenkins and R. M. Rose. "The Relation of Psychological Stress to Onset of Medical Illness." In *Stress and Survival: The Emotional Realities of Life-Threatening Illness*, edited by C. A. Garfield. St. Louis: Mosby, 1979.

Huston, T. L. and G. Levinger. "Interpersonal Attraction and Relationships." *Annual Review of Psychology*, 29 (1978): 115–156.

Huxley, A. "Human Potentialities." In *Science and Human Affairs*, edited by R. E. Farson. Palo Alto, Calif.: Science and Behavior Books, 1965.

———. *The Doors of Perception*. Baltimore: Penguin, 1971.

Hyde, J. S. *Understanding Human Sexuality*. New York: McGraw-Hill, 1979.

Hyman, R. "The Case Against Parapsychology." *The Humanist,* 37 (1977): 47–49.

———. "Patterns of PSI—Exposed or Imposed." *Contemporary Psychology,* 24, No. 10 (1979): 766–767.

Insel, P. M. and H. C. Lindgren. "Too Close For Comfort." *Psychology Today,* 11 (Dec. 1977): 100–106.

Isenberg, P. L. and A. F. Schatzberg. "Psychoanalytic Contribution to a Theory of Depression." In *Depression: Biology, Psychodynamics, and Treatment,* edited by J. O. Cole, A. F. Schatzberg, and S. H. Frazier. New York: Plenum Press, 1976.

Iversen, L. L. "The Chemistry of the Brain." *Scientific American,* 241, No. 3 (Sept. 1979): 134–147.

Jackson, B. "Our Prisons Are Criminal." *New York Times Magazine,* (Sept. 22, 1973): 54, 57.

Jacobs, M. and J. M. Whiteley. "Approaches to Sexual Counseling." *Counseling Psychologist,* 5 (1975): 3–8.

Jacobson, A., A. Kales, D. Lehmann, and J. R. Zweizia. "Somnambulism: All Night EEG Studies." *Science,* 148 (1965): 975–977.

Jacobson, L. E. "The Electrophysiology of Mental Activities." *American Journal of Psychology,* 44 (1932): 677–694.

James, W. *The Varieties of Religious Experience.* New York: New American Library, 1958.

Janis, I. L. *Psychological Stress.* New York: Wiley, 1958.

Janis, I. L. and L. Mann. "Effectiveness of Emotional Role-Playing in Modifying Smoking Habits and Attitudes." *Journal of Experimental Research in Personality,* 1 (1965): 84–90.

———. *Decision Making.* New York: Free Press, 1977.

Jarvik, E. M. "Ciba Found." In *Symposium of Animal Pharmacology Drug Action,* edited by H. Steinberg *et al.,* 1964.

Jarvik, L. F., C. Eisdorfer, and J. E. Blum (eds.). *Intellectual Functioning in Adults.* New York: Springer, 1973.

Jellinik, E. M. *The Disease Concept of Alcoholism.* New Haven: Hill House Press, 1960.

Jenkins, J. G. and K. M. Dallenbach. "Oblivescence During Sleep and Waking." *American Journal of Psychology,* 35 (1924): 605–612.

Jensen, A. R. "How Much Can We Boost I.Q. and Scholastic Achievement?" *Harvard Educational Review,* 39 (1969): 123.

Jerome, L. E. "Astrology: Magic or Science?" In *Objections to Astrology,* Prometheus Books, 1975.

John, E. R. *Mechanisms of Memory.* New York: Academic Press, 1967.

Johnson, J. J. "Sticking with First Responses on Multiple-Choice Exams: For Better or for Worse?" *Teaching of Psychology,* 2, No. 4 (1975).

Johnson, L., P. Naitoh, A. Lubin, and J. Moses. "Sleep Stages and Performance." In *Aspects of Human Efficiency,* edited by W. P. Colquhoun. London: English University Press, pp. 81–100.

Johnson, R. E. "Some Correlates of Extramarital Coitus." *Journal of Marriage and Family,* 32 (1970): 449–456.

Johnson, S. M. and G. White. "Self-Observation as an Agent of Behavioral Change." *Behavior Therapy,* 2 (1971): 488–497.

Jones, E. *The Life and Work of Sigmund Freud.* New York: Basic Books, 1953.

Jones, E. E. and R. E. Nisbett. "The Actor and Observer: Divergent Perceptions of the Causes of Behavior." In *Attribution: Perceiving the Causes of Behavior,* edited by E. E. Jones, D. E. Kanouse, H. H. Kelley, R. E. Nisbett, S. Valins, and B. Weiner. Morristown, N.J.: General Learning Press, 1971.

Jones, K. L. and D. W. Smith. "Recognition of the Fetal Alcohol Syndrome in Early Infancy." *Lancet,* 2 (1973): 999.

Jones, R. M. *Fantasy and Feelings in Education: A Reply to Bruner.* New York: New York University Press, 1968.

Jones, W. R. and N. R. Ellis. "Inhibitory Potential in Rotary Pursuit Acquisition." *Journal of Experimental Psychology,* 63 (1962): 534–537.

Jospe, M. *The Placebo Effect in Healing.* Lexington, Mass.: Lexington Books, 1978.

Jourard, S. M. *Personal Adjustment* (2nd ed.). New York: Macmillan, 1963.

———. "An Exploratory Study of Body-Accessibility." *British Journal of Social and Clinical Psychology,* 5 (1966): 221–231.

———. *Healthy Personality.* New York: Macmillan, 1974.

Judson, A. I. and C. N. Cofer. "Reasoning as an Associative Process: I. 'Direction' in a Simple Verbal Problem." *Psychological Reports.* 2 (1956): 469–476.

Julesz, B. *Foundations of Cyclopean Perception.* Chicago: University of Chicago Press, 1971.

———. "Experiments in the Visual Perception of Texture." *Scientific American,* 232, No. 4 (April, 1975): 34–43.

Julien, R. M. *A Primer of Drug Action* (2nd ed.). San Francisco: Freeman, 1978.

Kagan, J. *Personality Development.* New York: Harcourt, 1969.

———. *Change and Continuity in Infancy.* New York: Wiley, 1971.

———. "What Is Intelligence?" *Social Policy,* 4 (1973): 88–94.

———. "Emergent Themes in Human Development." *American Scientist,* 64 (1976): 186–196.

Kagan, J. and R. E. Klein. "Cross-Cultural Perspectives on Early Development." *American Psychologist,* 28 (1973): 947–961.

Kales, A. and J. Kales. "Recent Advances in the Diagnosis and Treatment of Sleep Disorders." In *Sleep Research and Clinical Practice,* edited by G. Usdin. New York: Brunner/Mazel, 1973.

Kamin, L. J. *The Science and Politics of I.Q.* New York: Halstead, 1974.

———. *The Intelligence Controversy.* New York: Wiley, 1981.

Kamiya, J. "Conscious Control of Brain Waves." *Psychology Today,* 1 (1968): 57–66.

Kanfer and Goldfoot. 1966, cited in Sternbach. *Pain.* New York: Academic Press, 1968.

Kanner, L. *Child Psychiatry.* Springfield, Ill.: Charles C Thomas, 1957.

Kaplan, H. S. *The New Sex Therapy.* New York: Brunner/Mazel, 1974.

Kapleau, P. *The Three Pillars of Zen.* New York: Harper & Row, 1966.

Karlins, M., T. L. Coffman, and G. Walters. "On the Fading of Social Stereotypes: Studies in Three Generations of College Students." *Journal of Personality and School Psychology,* 13 (1969): 1–16.

Kasamatsu, A. and T. Hirai. "An Electroencephalographic Study of Zen Meditation (Zazen)." *Folia Psychiatria et Neurologia Japonica,* 20 (1966): 315–336. Reprinted in Tart, *Altered States of Consciousness.*

Kastenbaum, R. and R. Aisenberg. *The Psychology of Death.* New York: Springer, 1972.

Katz, B. J. "Finding Psychiatric Help Can Be Traumatic Itself." *The National Observer,* (1972).

Kazdin, A. E. *Behavior Modification in Applied Settings.* Homewood, Ill.: Dorsey Press, 1975.

Keeffe, P. "Ice After Death." *Novus,* (Sept. 1977): 29–33.

Keller, H. *The Story of My Life.* New York: Doubleday, 1955.

Kelley, H. H. "The Warm-Cold Variable in First Impressions of Persons." *Journal of Personality,* 18 (1950): 431–439.

———. "Attribution in Social Psychology." *Nebraska Symposium on Motivation,* 15 (1967): 192–238.

———. *Attribution in Social Interaction.* Morristown, N.J.: General Learning Press, 1971.

Kellogg, L. A. and W. N. Kellogg. *The Ape and the Child.* New York: McGraw-Hill, 1933.

Kenrick, D. T. and R. B. Cialdini. "Romantic Attraction: Misattribution vs. Reinforcement Explanations." *Journal of Personality and Social Psychology,* 35 (1977): 381–391.

Kety, S. S. "Disorders of the Human Brain." *Scientific American,* 241, No. 3 (Sept. 1979): 202–214.

Keys, A., J. Brozek, A. Henschel, O. Mickelson, and H. L. Taylor. *The Biology of Human Starvation.* Minneapolis: University of Minnesota Press, 1950.

Kiell, N. (ed.). *The Psychology of Obesity: Dynamics and Treatment.* Springfield, Ill.: Charles C Thomas, 1973.

Kiester, E. "Dream World." *Human Behavior,* (Dec. 1975).

Kimble, G. A. *Hilgard and Marquis' Conditioning and Learning* (2nd ed.). New York: Appleton-Century-Crofts, 1961.

King, H. E. "Psychological Effects of Excitation in the Limbic System." In *Electrical Stimulation of the Brain,* edited by D. E. Sheer. Austin: University of Texas Press, 1961.

Kinkade, K. *A Walden Two Experiment: The First Five Years of Twin Oaks Community.* New York: Morrow, 1973.

Kinsey, A., W. Pomeroy, and C. Martin. *Sexual Behavior in the Human Male.* Philadelphia: Saunders, 1948.

———. *Sexual Behavior in the Human Female.* Philadelphia: Saunders, 1953.

Klatzky, R. L. *Human Memory Structures and Processes* (2nd ed.). San Francisco: Freeman, 1980.

Klaus, M. H. and J. H. Kennel. *Maternal-Infant Bonding.* St. Louis: Mosby, 1976.

Klausmeir, H. J. and W. Goodwin. *Learning and Human Abilities* (4th ed.). New York: Harper & Row, 1975.

Klein, R. P. and J. T. Durfee. "Infant's Reactions to Unfamiliar Adults Versus Mothers." *Child Development,* 47, No. 4 (Dec. 1976): 1194–1196.

Kleitman, N. *Sleep and Wakefulness* (2nd ed.). Chicago: University of Chicago Press, 1963.

Kleitman, N. and E. Kleitman. "Effect of Non-24-Hour Routines of Living on Oral Temperature and Heart Rate." *Journal of Applied Physiology,* 6 (1953): 283–291.

Klienke. *Self-Perception: The Psychology of Personal Awareness.* San Francisco: Freeman, 1978.

Knapp, M. L. *Nonverbal Communication in Human Interaction* (2nd ed.). New York: Holt, 1978.

Knight, R. P. "A Critique of the Present Status of the Psychotherapies." *Bulletin of the New York Academy of Medicine,* 25 (1949): 100–114.

Koestler, A. *The Act of Creation.* New York: Macmillan, 1964.

———. *The Ghost in the Machine.* New York: Macmillan, 1968.

Kohlberg, L. "The Development of Children's Orientation Toward a Moral Order: 1. Sequence in the Development of Moral Thought." *Vita Humana,* 6 (1963): 11–33.

———. "The Cognitive-Developmental Approach to Socialization." In *Handbook of Socialization Theory and Research,* edited by A. Goslin. Chicago: Rand McNally, 1969.

Köhler, I. "Experiments with Goggles." *Scientific American,* Offprint No. 465 (1962): 62–72.

Köhler, W. *The Mentality of Apes.* New York: Harcourt, 1925.

Koocher, G. P. "Bathroom Behavior and Human Dignity." *Journal of Personality and Social Psychology,* 35, No. 2 (Feb. 1977): 120–121.

Korte, C. and S. Milgram. "Acquaintance Networks Between Racial Groups." *Journal of Personality and Social Psychology,* 15 (1970): 101–108.

Kosslyn, S. M. "Information Representation in Visual Image." *Cognitive Psychology,* 7 (1975): 341–370.

Kosslyn, S. M., T. M. Ball, and B. J. Reiser. "Visual Images Preserve Metric Spatial Information: Evidence from Studies of Image Scanning." *Journal of Experimental Psychology: Human Perception and Performance,* 4 (1978): 47–60.

Koukkou, M. and D. Lehmann. "EEG and Memory Storage in Sleep Experiments with Humans." *Electroencephalography and Clinical Neurophysiology,* 25 (1968): 455–462.

Krebs, D. and A. A. Adinolfi. "Physical Attractiveness, Social Relations, and Personality Style." *Journal of Personality and Social Psychology,* 31 (1975): 245–253.

Krech, D., M. R. Rosenzweig, and E. L. Bennett. "Relations Between Brain Chemistry and Problem Solving Among Rats Raised in Enriched and Impoverished Environments." *Journal of Comparative and Physiological Psychology,* 55 (1962): 801–807.

Kripke, D. F. and R. N. Simons. "Average Sleep, Insomnia, and Sleeping Pill Use." *Sleep Research,* 5 (1976): 110.

Kristt, D. A. and B. T. Engel. "Learned Control of Blood Pressure in Patients with High Blood Pressure." *Circulation,* 51 (1975): 370–378.

Kübler-Ross, E. *Death: The Final Stage of Growth.* Englewood Cliffs, N.J.: Prentice-Hall, 1975.

La Berge, S. P. "Lucid Dreaming as a Learnable Skill: A Case Study." *Perceptual and Motor Skills,* 51 (1980): 1039–1042.

———. "Lucid Dreaming: Directing the Action as It Happens." *Psychology Today* (Jan. 1981, b): 48–57.

La Berge, S. P., L. E. Nagel, W. C. Dement and V. Zarcone. "Lucid Dreaming Verified by Volitional Communication During REM Sleep." *Perceptual and Motor Skills,* 52 (1981, a): 727–732.

Labovitz, S. and R. Hagedorn. "An Analysis of Suicide Rates among Occupational Categories." *Social Inquiry,* 41 (1971): 67–72.

Laing, R. D. *The Divided Self.* New York: Pantheon, 1970.

———. *The Politics of Experience.* New York: Pantheon, 1967.

Laird, J. D. "Self-attribution of Emotion: The Effects of Expressive Behavior on the Quality of Emotional Experience." *Journal of Personality and Social Psychology,* 29 (1974): 475–486.

Lake, A. "Get Thin, Stay Thin." *McCalls,* 100, No. 4 (1973).

Land, E. H. "The Retinex Theory of Color Vision." *Scientific American,* (Dec. 1977): 108–126.

Landis, D. "A Scan for Mental Illness." *Discover* (Oct. 1980): 26–27.

Landuet, T. K. and M. W. M. Whiting. "Infantile Stimulation and Adult Stature of Human Males." *American Anthropologist,* 66 (1964): 1007–1028.

Lang, P. J. and B. G. Melamed. "Avoidance Conditioning Therapy of an Infant with Chronic Ruminative Vomiting." *Journal of Abnormal Psychology,* 74 (1969): 1–8.

Langer, E. J. and R. P. Abelson, "A Patient by Any Other Name . . . Clinician Group Difference in Labeling Bias." *Journal of Consulting and Clinical Psychology,* 42 (1974): 4–9.

Lappé, F. M. *Diet for a Small Planet.* New York: Ballantine, 1971.

Laurendeau, M. and A. Pinard. *Causal Thinking in the Child.* New York: International Universities Press, 1962.

Lavach, J. F. and H. B. Lanier. "The Motive to Avoid Success in 7th, 8th, 9th, and 10th Grade High Achieving Girls." *The Journal of Educational Research,* 68, No. 6 (1975): 216–218.

Lazarus, A. H. "The Treatment of Chronic Frigidity by Systematic Desensitization." In *Experiments in Behavior Therapy,* edited by H. J. Eysenck. New York: Pergamon, 1964.

Lazarus, R. S. "Emotions and Adaptation: Conceptual and Empirical Relations." In *Nebraska Symposium on Motivation,* edited by W. J. Arnold. Lincoln: University of Nebraska Press, 1968.

———. "A Cognitively Oriented Psychologist Looks at Feedback." *American Psychologist,* 30 (1975): 553–561.

Leavitt, H. J. and H. Scholsberg. "The Retention of Verbal and Motor Skills." *Journal of Experimental Psychology,* 34 (1944): 404–417.

Leboyer, F. *Birth Without Violence.* New York: Knopf, 1975.

Lee, M., P. G. Zimbardo, and M. Bertholf. "Shy Murderers." *Psychology Today,* (Nov. 1977).

Leeper, R. W. "A Study of the Neglected Portion of the Field of Learning: The Development of Sensory Organization." *Pedagogical Seminary and Journal of Genetic Psychology,* 46 (1935): 41–75.

Lefkowitz, M., R. R. Blake, and J. S. Mouton. "Status Factors in Pedestrian Violation of Traffic Signals." *Journal of Abnormal and Social Psychology,* 51 (1955): 704–706.

Lester, D. "Attempted Suicide as a Hostile Act." *Journal of Psychology,* 68 (1968): 243–248.

———. "Relationship of Mental Disorder to Suicidal Behavior." *New York State Journal of Medicine,* 71 (1971b): 1503–1505.

———. *Why People Kill Themselves: A Summary of Research on Suicidal Behavior.* Springfield, Ill.: Charles C Thomas, 1972.

Lester G. and D. Lester. *Suicide: The Gamble with Death.* Englewood Cliffs, N.J.: Prentice-Hall, 1971.

Lettvin, J. Y. "Two Remarks on the Visual System of the Frog." In *Sensory Communication,* edited by W. Rosenblith. Cambridge, Mass: MIT Press, 1961.

Leveton, E. *Psychodrama for the Timid Clinician.* New York: Springer, 1977.

Levin, R. J. and A. Levin. "Sexual Pleasure: The Surprising Preference of 100,000 Women." *Redbook,* (Sept. 1975): 51.

———. "The Redbook Report on Premarital and Extramarital Sex." *Redbook,* (Oct. 1975): 38.

Levine, J. D., N. C. Gordon and H. L. Fields. "The Role of Endorphins in Placebo Analgesia." In *Advances in Pain Research and Therapy,* Vol. 3, edited by J. J. Bonica, J. C. Lielseskind, and D. Albe-Fessard. New York: Raven Press, 1979.

Levine, S. "Infantile Stimulation: A Perspective." In *Stimulation in Early Infancy,* edited by A. Ambrose. New York: Academic Press, 1969.

Levinson, D. J. with C. N. Darrow, E. B. Klein, M. H. Levinson, and B. McKee. *The Seasons of A Man's Life.* New York: Knopf, 1978.

Levitt, R. A. "Recreational Drug Use and Abuse." In *Abnormal Psychology,* edited by D. C. Rimm and J. W. Somervill. New York: Academic Press, 1977.

Levy, J. and M. Redd. "Cerebral Organization." *Science,* (1976): 337–339.

Levy, M. R. and M. W. Kahn. "Intepreter Bias on the Rorschach Test as a Function of Patients' Socioeconomic Status." *Journal of Projective Techniques and Personality Assessment,* 34 (1970): 106–112.

Lewin, K. *A Dynamic Theory of Personality.* New York: McGraw-Hill, 1935.

Lewin, R. "The Brain Through a Cat's Eyes." *Saturday Review/World,* (Oct. 5, 1974).

———. "Starved Brains." *Psychology Today,* (Sept. 1975).

Lewis, M. and J. Brooks-Gunn. *Social Cognition and the Acquisition of Self.* New York: Plenum Press, 1979.

Lieberman, D. A. "Behaviorism and the Mind: A (Limited) Call for a Return to Introspection." *American Psychologist,* 34 (April 1979): 319–333.

Lieberman, R. P., C. H. Fearn, W. Derisi, J. Roberts, and M. Carmona. "The Credit-Incentive System: Motivating the Participation of Patients in a Day Hospital." *British Journal of Clinical Psychology,* 15 (1976).

Liebert, R. M., J. M. Neale, and E. S. Davidson. *The Early Window: Effects of Television on Children and Youth.* Elmsford, N.Y.: Pergamon Press, 1973.

Liebett, R. E. "Taste Deprivation and Weight Determinants of Eating Behavior." *Journal of Personality and Social Behavior,* 10 (1968): 107–116.

Lilly, J. C. *The Center of the Cyclone.* New York: Julian Press, 1972.

Lindsay, P. H. and D. A. Norman. *Human Information Processing* (2nd ed.). New York: Academic Press, 1977.

Lindsley, D. B., J. Bowden, and H. W. Magoun. "Effect upon the EEG of Acute Injury to the Brain Stem Activating System." *EEG and Clinical Neurophysiology,* 1 (1949): 475–486.

Linton, M. "I Remember It Well." *Psychology Today* (July 1979): 81–86.

Lipinski, E. and B. G. Lipinski. "Motivational Factors in Psychedelic Drug Use by Male College Students." In *Drug Awareness,* edited by R. E. Hormon and A. M. Fox. New York: Discus Books, Avon, 1970.

Lipscomb, D. M. *Noise: The Unwanted Sounds.* Chicago, Ill.: Nelson-Hall, 1974.

Lipsett, L. "Conditioning the Rage to Live." *Psychology Today* (February 1980): 124.

Loftus, E. "Leading Questions and the Eyewitness Report." *Cognitive Psychology,* 7 (1975): 560–572.

———. "Shifting Human Color Memory." *Memory and Cognition,* 5 (1977): 696–699.

———. *Eyewitness Testimony.* Cambridge, Mass.: Harvard University Press, 1979.

———. *Memory.* Reading, Mass.: Addison-Wesley, 1980.

Loftus, E. and G. Loftus. "On the Permanence of Stored Information in the Human Brain." *American Psychologist,* 35 (May 1980): 409–420.

Loftus, E. and J. Monahan. "Trial by Data: Psychological Research as Legal Evidence." *American Psychologist,* 35, No. 3 (1980): 270–283.

Loftus, E. and J. C. Palmer. "Reconstruction of Automobile Destruction: An Example of Interaction Between Language and Memory." *Journal of Verbal Learning and Verbal Behavior,* 13 (1974): 585–589.

London, P. *Behavior Control.* New York: Harper & Row, 1971.

Lorenz, K. "Imprinting." *The Auk,* 54 (1937): 245–273.

———. *King Solomon's Ring.* New York: Time, 1962.

———. *The Eight Deadly Sins of Civilized Man.* Translated by M. Kerr-Wilson. New York: Harcourt, 1974.

Los Angeles Times. "Man Tells How Rod Ran Through Head." September 24, 1981. Part II, p. 3.

Louis, A. M. "Should You Buy Biorhythms? *Psychology Today* (April 1978): 93–96.

Lovaas, O., G. Freitag, V. Gold, and I. Kassoria. "Experimental Studies in Childhood Schizophrenia: Analysis of Self-Destructive Behavior." *Journal of Experimental Child Psychology,* 2 (1965): 67–84.

Lovaas, O., G. Freitag, M. Kinder, B. Rubenstein, B. Schaeffer, and J. Simmons. "Establishment of Social Reinforcers in Two Schizophrenic Children on the Basis of Food." *Journal of Experimental Child Psychology,* 4 (1966): 109–125.

Lovaas, O. I. and J. Q. Simmons. "Manipulation of Self-Destruction in Three Retarded Children." *Journal of Applied Behavior Analysis,* 2 (1969): 143–157.

Lowen, A. *Love and Orgasm.* New York: Macmillan, 1965.

Luce, G. G. "Current Research on Sleep and Dreams." *Health Service Publication* No. 1389, U.S. Department of Health, Education and Welfare, 1965.

———. *Body Time: Physiological Rhythms and Social Stress.* New York: Pantheon, 1971.

————. "Sleepwalking Not Related to Dreams." In *The New World of Dreams,* edited by R. L. Woods and H. B. Greenhouse. New York: Macmillan, 1974.

Luce, G. G. and E. Peper. "Mind Over Body, Mind Over Mind." *The New York Times Magazine,* (Sept. 12, 1971).

Ludwig, A. M. "Altered States of Consciousness." *Archives of General Psychiatry,* 15 (1966): 225–233.

Luria, A. R. *The Mind of a Mnemonist.* New York: Basic Books, 1968.

Lykken, D. T. "A Study of Anxiety in the Sociopathic Personality." *Journal of Abnormal and Social Psychology,* 55 (1957): 6–10.

————. "Psychology and the Lie Detector Industry." *American Psychologist,* 29 (1974): 725–739.

————. *A Tremor in the Blood, Uses and Abuses of the Lie Detector.* New York: McGraw-Hill, 1981.

Maccoby, E. E. "Sex Differences in Intellectual Functioning." In *The Development of Sex Differences,* edited by E. E. Maccoby. Stanford, Calif.: Stanford University Press, 1966.

MacFarlane, J. W., W. L. Allen, and M. P. Honzik. "A Developmental Study of the Behavioral Problems of Normal Children between 21 Months and 14 Years." *University of California Publication of Child Development,* 2, No. 169 (1954): 334.

MacKinnon, D. W. "The Nature and Nurture of Creative Talent." *American Psychologist,* 1, No. 7 (1962): 484–495.

————. "Selecting Students with Creative Potential." In *The Creative College Student: An Unmet Challenge,* edited by P. Heist. San Francisco: Jossey-Bass, 1968.

Madsen, C. H., Jr., W. C. Becher, D. R. Thomas, L. Koser, and E. Plager. "An Analysis of the Reinforcing Function of 'Sit Down' Commands." In *Readings in Educational Psychology,* edited by R. K. Parker. Boston: Allyn & Bacon, 1968.

Maier, N. R. F. *Frustration.* New York: McGraw-Hill, 1949.

Malatesta, V. J., R. H. Pollack, W. A. Wilbanks and H. E. Adams. *Journal of Sex Research,* 15 (1979): 101.

Malmo, R. B. *On Emotions, Needs, and Our Archaic Brain.* New York: Holt, 1975.

Mandell, A. J., D. S. Segal, R. T. Kuczenski, and S. Knapp. "The Search for the Schizococcus." *Psychology Today,* (Oct. 1972): 68–72.

Mandler, G. "Association and Organization: Fact, Fancies, and Theories." In *Verbal Behavior and General Behavior Theory,* edited by T. R. Dixon and D. L. Horton. Englewood Cliffs, N.J.: Prentice-Hall, 1968, pp. 109–119.

Marañon, I. "Contribution a l'étude de l'action émotive de l'adrénaline." *Franc. D'endocrinol,* 2 (1924): 301–305.

Marks, D., and R. Kammann. *The Psychology of The Psychic.* Buffalo, N.Y.: Prometheus Books, 1979.

Marks, L. "On Colored-hearing Synesthesia: Cross Modal Translations of Sensory Dimensions." *Psychological Bulletin,* 82 (1975a): 303–331.

————. "Synesthesia: The Lucky People with Mixed-Up Senses." *Psychology Today* (June 1975b): 49–52.

————. *The Unity of the Senses: Interrelations Among the Modalities.* New York: Academic Press, 1978.

Mark, V. H. and F. R. Ervin. *Violence and the Brain.* New York: Harper & Row, 1970.

Marmon, J. "Psychiatrists and Their Patients, A National Study of Private Office Practice." Joint Information Service of the American Psychiatric Association and the National Association for Mental Health. Washington, D.C., 1975.

Marmor, J., (ed.). *Homosexual Behavior: A Modern Reappraisal.* New York: Basic Books, 1980.

Marshall, G. *Affective Consequences of "Inadequately Explained" Physiological Arousal.* Unpublished doctoral dissertation, Stanford University, 1976.

Martin, B. M., T. F. Garrity, and F. R. Bowers. "The Influence of Recent Life Experience on the Health of College Freshmen." *Journal of Psychosomatic Research,* 19 (1975): 87–98.

Martin, P. J., M. L. Hunter, and J. E. Moore. "Pulling the Wool: Impression-Management among Hospitalized Schizophrenics." *Research Communications in Psychology, Psychiatry and Behavior,* 2, No. 1 (1977): 21–26.

Martin, R. *Legal Challenges to Behavior Modification.* Champaign, Ill.: Research Press, 1975.

Maslow, A. H. *Motivation and Personality.* New York: Harper, 1954.

————. "A Philosophy of Psychology: The Need for a Mature Science of Human Nature." In *Humanistic Viewpoint in Psychology,* edited by F. T. Severin. New York: McGraw-Hill, 1965, pp. 17–33.

————. "Self-Actualization and Beyond." In *Challenges of Humanistic Psychology,* edited by J. F. T. Bugental. New York: McGraw-Hill, 1967.

————. *Toward A Psychology of Being* (2nd ed.). New York: Van Nostrand, 1968.

————. *The Psychology of Science.* Chicago: Henry Regnery, 1969.

————. *Motivation and Personality* (2nd ed.). New York: Harper & Row, 1970.

————. *The Farther Reaches of Human Nature.* New York: Viking, 1971.

Masters, W. H. and V. E. Johnson. *Human Sexual Response.* Boston: Little, Brown, 1966.

————. *The Pleasure Bond: A New Look at Sexuality and Commitment.* Boston: Little, Brown, 1970.

Matossian, M. K. "Ergot and the Salem Witchcraft Affair." *American Scientist,* 70 (July–Aug., 1982): 355–357.

Matthews, L. H. and M. Knight. *The Senses of Animals.* London: Museum Press, 1963.

Maupin, E. W. "Individual Differences in Response to a Zen Meditation Exercise." *Journal of Consulting Psychology,* 29 (1965): 139–145.

Max, L. W. "Experimental Study of the Motor Theory of Consciousness: IV. Action-Current Responses in the Deaf During Awakening, Kinesthetic Imagery, and Abstract Thinking." *Journal of Comparative Psychology,* 24 (1937): 301–344.

Mayer, J. *Overweight: Causes, Cost, and Control.* Englewood Cliffs, N.J.: Prentice-Hall, 1968.

McCabe, M. S. "Reactive Psychoses and Schizophrenia with Good Prognosis." *Archives of General Psychiatry,* 33, No. 5 (May 1976): 571–576.

McCain, G. and E. M. Segal. *The Game of Science.* Belmont, Calif.: Brooks/Cole, 1969.

McCauley, E. and A. A. Ehrhardt. "Female Sexual Response: Hormonal and Behavioral Interactions." *Primary Care,* 3 (1976): 455.

McClelland, D. C. "Risk Taking in Children with High and Low Need for Achievement." In *Motives in Fantasy Action and Society,* edited by J. W. Atkinson. New York: Van Nostrand, 1958.

————. *The Achieving Society.* New York: Van Nostrand, 1961.

————. "Achievement and Entrepreneurship." *Journal of Personality and Social Psychology,* 1 (1965): 389–393.

————. "Testing for Competence Rather Than 'Intelligence.'" *American Psychologist,* 28 (1973): 1–14.

————. *Power the Inner Experience.* New York: Irvington, 1975.

McConnell, J. V. "Memory Transfer through Cannibalism in Planarians." *Journal of Neuropsychiatry,* 3, Suppl. 1 (1962): 542–548.

McGaugh, J. L. "Time-Dependent Processes in Memory Storage." In *Controversial Issues in Consolidation of the Memory Trace,* edited by J. L. McGaugh and M. J. Herz. New York: Atherton, 1970.

———. *Learning and Memory.* San Francisco: Albion, 1973.

McGee, M. G. and M. Snyder. "Attribution and Behavior: Two Field Studies." *Journal of Personality and Social Psychology,* 32 (1975): 185–190.

McGinnies, E. "Emotionality and Perceptual Defense." *Psychological Review,* 56 (1949): 244–251.

McGlothlin, W. "Drug Use and Abuse." In *Annual Review of Psychology,* edited by M. R. Rosenzweig and L. W. Porter. Palo Alto, Calif., 1975, p. 26.

McGuire, W. J. "The Nature of Attitudes and Attitude Change." In *The Handbook of Social Psychology,* Vol. 3, edited by G. Lindzey and E. Aronson. Reading, Mass.: Addison-Wesley, 1969.

McKean, K. "Anatomy of an Air Crash." *Discover,* (April 1982): 19–21.

———. "A Picture of Hinckley's Brain." *Discover,* 3 (Aug. 1982): 78–80.

McKellar, P. "The Investigation of Mental Images." In *Penguin Science Journal,* edited by S. A. Barnett and A. McLaren. Hammondsworth: Penguin, 1965.

McMahon, F. B. "A Contingent-Item Method for Constructing a Short Personality Questionnaire." *Journal of Applied Psychology,* (1964): 197–200.

———. *Abnormal Behavior, Psychology's View.* Englewood Cliffs, N.J.: Prentice-Hall, 1976.

McMullan, W. E. and J. R. Stocking. "Conceptualizing Creativity in Three Dimensions." *The Journal of Creative Behavior,* 12, No. 1, (1978): 161–167.

McMurray, G. A. "Experimental Study of a Case of Insensitivity to Pain." *Archives of Neurological Psychiatry,* 64 (1950): 650–667.

McNett, I. "Psy.D. Fills Demand for Practitioners." *APA Psychology Monitor,* 13 (Jan. 1982): 10–11.

Mead, M. *Sex and Temperament in Three Primitive Societies.* New York: Morrow, 1935.

Meeker, M. "Measuring Creativity from the Child's Point of View." *The Journal of Creative Behavior,* 12, No. 1, (1978): 52–62.

Mehrabian, A. "Significance of Posture and Position in the Communication of Attitude and Status Relationships." *Psychological Bulletin,* 71 (1969): 359–372.

Meichenbaum, D. *Cognitive Behavior Modification: An Integrative Approach.* New York: Plenum Press, 1977.

Melton, Reginald F., "Resolution of Conflicting Claims Concerning the Effect of Behavioral Objectives on Student Learning." *Review of Educational Research,* 48 (Spring 1978): 291–302.

Meltzoff, A. and M. K. Moore. "Imitation of Facial and Manual Gestures by Human Neonates." *Science,* (Oct. 7, 1977): 75–78.

Melzack, R. "Shutting the Gate on Pain." *Science Year: The World Book Science Annual.* Palo Alto, Calif.: Field, 1974.

Melzack, R. and S. G. Dennis. "Neurophysical Foundations of Pain." In *The Psychology of Pain,* edited by R. A. Sternbach. New York: Raven Press, 1978.

Melzack, R. and T. H. Scott. "The Effects of Early Experience on the Response to Pain." *Journal of Comparative and Physiological Psychology,* 50 (1957): 155–161.

Menninger, K. "Psychiatrists Use Dangerous Words." *Saturday Evening Post,* (April 25, 1964).

Menzel, E. W. "Cognitive Mapping in Chimpanzees." In *Cognitive Processes in Animal Behavior,* edited by S. H. Hulse, H. Fowler, and W. K. Honig. Hillsdale: Erlbaum, 1978.

Mercer, J. R. "Identifying the Gifted Chicano Child." In *Chicano Psychology,* edited by J. L. Martinez. New York: Academic Press, 1977.

Meyers, F. H., E. Jawetz, and A. Goldfien. *Review of Medical Pharmacology* (3rd ed.). Los Altos, Calif.: Lange Medical Publications, 1972.

Michotte, A. *The Perception of Causality.* New York: Methuen & Co., Ltd. Basic Books, 1963.

Middlemist, R. D., E. S. Knowles, and C. F. Matter. "Personal Space Invasions in the Lavatory: Suggestive Evidence for Arousal." *Journal of Personality and Social Psychology,* 33 (1976): 541–546.

Milgram, S. "Behavioral Study of Obedience." *Journal of Abnormal and Social Psychology,* 67 (1963): 371–378.

———. "Some Conditions of Obedience and Disobedience to Authority." *Human Relations,* 18 (1965): 57–76.

———. "The Small-World Problem." *Psychology Today,* (May, 1967): 61–67.

———. "The Experience of Living in the Cities: A Psychological Analysis." *Science,* 167 (March 13, 1970): 1461–1468.

———. *Obedience to Authority: An Experimental View.* New York: Harper & Row, 1974.

Milgram, S., L. Bickman, and L. Berkowitz. "Note on the Drawing Power of Crowds of Different Size." *Journal of Personality and Social Psychology,* 13 (1969): 79–82.

Miller, G. "The Magical Number Seven, Plus or Minus Two: Some Limits on Our Capacity for Processing Information." *Psychological Review,* 63 (1956): 81–87.

———. "Language and Psychology." In *New Directions in the Study of Language,* edited by E. H. Lennenberg. Cambridge, Mass.: MIT Press, 1964, pp. 89–107.

———. "On Turning Psychology Over to the Unwashed." American Psychological Association Paper, 1969.

———. *Spontaneous Apprentices: Children and Language.* Seabury Press, 1977.

———. "Giving Away Psychology in the 80's." *Psychology Today,* (January 1980): 38.

Miller, H. L. and P. S. Siegal. *Loving: A Psychological Approach.* New York: Wiley, 1972.

Miller, L. K. "The Design of Better Communities Through the Application of Behavioral Principles." In *Behavior Modification: Principles, Issues, and Applications,* edited by W. E. Craighead, A. E. Kazdin, and M. J. Mahone. Boston: Houghton Mifflin, 1976.

Miller, N. E. "The Frustration-Aggression Hypothesis." *Psychological Review,* 48 (1941): 337–342.

———. "Experimental Studies of Conflict." In *Personality and the Behavior Disorders,* Vol. I, edited by J. McV. Hunt. New York: Ronald Press, 1944, pp. 431–465.

———. "Learning of Visceral and Glandular Responses." *Science,* 163 (1969): 434–445.

Miller, N. E. and R. Bugelski. "The Influence of Frustration Imposed by the In-Group on Attitudes Expressed Toward Out-Groups." In *Social Psychology in Life,* edited by R. I. Evans and R. M. Rozelle. Boston: Allyn & Bacon, 1970.

Miller, N. E. and L. V. Di Cara. "Instrumental Learning of Heart Rate Changes in Curarized Rats: Shaping and Specificity to Discriminative Stimulus." *Journal of Comparative and Physiological Psychology,* 63 (1967): 12–19.

Miller, N. E. and B. R. Dworkin. "Visceral Learning: Recent Difficulties with Curarized Rats and Significant Problems for Human Research."

In *Cardiovascular Physiology,* edited by D. A. Obrist, *et al.* Chicago: Aldine, 1974, pp. 312–331.

Miller, W. R., R. A. Rosellini, and M. E. P. Seligman. In *Psychopathology: Experimental Models,* edited by J. D. Maser and M. E. P. Seligman. San Francisco: Freeman, 1977, pp. 104–120.

Milner, B. "Memory Disturbance After Bilateral Hippocampal Lesions." In *Cognitive Processes and the Brain,* edited by P. Milner and S. Glickman. Princton, N.J.: Van Nostrand, 1965, pp. 97–111.

Milunsky, A. *Know Your Genes.* Boston: Houghton Mifflin, 1977.

Minami, H. and K. M. Dallenbash. "The Effect of Activity upon Learning and Retention in the Cockroach." *American Journal of Psychology,* 59 (1946): 1–58.

Mischel, W. *Personality and Assessment.* New York: Wiley, 1968.

———. "Toward a Cognitive Social Learning Reconceptualization of Personality." *Psychological Review,* 80 (1973): 252–283.

Mitchell-Heggs, N., D. Kelly, and A. Richardson. "Stereotactic Limbic Leucotomy—A Follow Up at 16 Months." *British Journal of Psychiatry,* 128 (1976): 226–240.

Money, J. "Psychosexual Differentiation." In *Sex Research: New Developments,* edited by J. Money. New York: Holt, 1965, pp. 3–23.

———. "Sexual Dimorphism and Homosexual Gender Identity." *Psychological Bulletin,* 6 (1970): 425–440.

———. "Human Hermaphroditism." In *Human Sexuality in Four Perspectives,* edited by F. A. Beach. Baltimore: Johns Hopkins University Press, 1977.

Money, J. and A. Ehrhardt. *Man and Woman, Boy and Girl.* Baltimore: Johns Hopkins University Press, 1972.

Monroe, L. J. "Psychological and Physiological Differences Between Good and Poor Sleepers." *Journal of Abnormal Psychology,* 72 (1967): 255–264.

Moreno, J. L. *Who Shall Survive?* New York: Beacon House, 1953.

Moriarty, T. "A Nation of Willing Victims." *Psychology Today,* (April 1975): 43–50.

Moritz, A. P. and N. Zamchech. "Sudden and Unexpected Deaths of Young Soldiers." *American Medical Association Archives of Pathology,* 42 (1946): 459–494.

Moruzzi, G. and H. W. Magoun. "Brain Stem Reticular Formation and Activation of the EEG." *EEG and Clinical Neurophysiology,* 1 (1949): 455–473.

Moser, D. "The Nightmare of Life with Billy." *Life* (May 7, 1965).

Mosher, D. L. "Sex Differences, Sex Experience, Sex Guilt, and Explicitly Sexual Films." *Journal of Social Issues,* 29, No. 3 (1973).

Moyer, R. S. and R. H. Bayer. "Mental Comparison and the Symbolic Distance Effect." *Cognitive Psychology,* 8 (1976): 228–246.

Munn, N. L., L. D. Fernald, Jr., and P. S. Fernald. *Introduction to Psychology* (2nd ed.). Boston: Houghton Mifflin, 1969.

Murphy, L. B. and A. E. Moriarty. *Vulnerability, Coping and Growth.* New Haven: Yale University Press, 1976.

Murray, F. S. "Estimation of Performance Levels by Students in Introductory Psychology." *Teaching of Psychology,* 7 (Feb. 1980): 61–62.

Mussen, P. H., J. J. Conger, and J. Kagan. *Child Development and Personality* (3rd ed.). New York: Harper & Row, 1969.

Mussen, P. H., J. J. Conger, J. Kagan and J. Geiwitz. *Psychological Development: A Life Span Approach.* New York: Harper & Row, 1979.

Myers, A. *Experimental Psychology.* New York: Van Nostrand, 1980.

Nachman, M. "Learned Taste and Temperature Aversions Due to Lithium Chloride Sickness After Temporal Delays." *Journal of Comparative and Physiological Psychology,* 73 (1970): 22–30.

Naeye, R. L. "Sudden Infant Death." *Scientific American,* 4, No. 242 (1980): 56–62.

Nahas, G. G. *Keep Off the Grass.* Elmsford, N.Y.: Pergamon Press, 1979b.

Nahas, G. G. and W. D. M. Paton. *Marihuana, Biological Effects.* Elmsford, N.Y.: Pergamon Press, 1979a.

Naranjo, C. "Present-Centeredness: Technique, Prescription, and Ideal." In *What Is Gestalt Therapy?* edited by J. Fagan and I. L. Shepherd. New York: Harper & Row, 1970, pp. 63–97.

National Commission on Marihuana and Drug Abuse, R. P. Shafer, Chairman. *Drug Use in America: The Problem in Perspective.* Washington, D.C.: U.S. Government Printing Office, 1973.

National Institute on Drug Abuse (NIDA). *Marihuana and Health.* Princeton, N.J.: Response Analysis Corporation, 1976.

Nauta, W. J. H. and M. Feirtag. "The Organization of the Brain." *Scientific American,* (1979): 88–111.

Navran, L. "Communication and Adjustment in Marriage." *Family Process,* 6, No. 2 (1967): 173–184.

Nelson, E. "New Facts on Biorhythms." *Science Digest,* (May 1976) 71–75.

Nelson, H. and R. Jurmain. *Introduction to Physical Anthropology.* St. Paul, Minn.: West, 1979.

Nelson, R. and R. S. Crutchfield. "Mathematicians: The Creative Researcher and the Average Ph.D." *Journal of Consulting and Clinical Psychology,* 34 (1970): 250–257.

Neufeld, R. W. "The Effect of Experimentally Altered Cognitive Appraisal on Pain Tolerance." *Psychonomic Science,* 20, No. 2 (1970): 106–107.

Neugarten, B. "Grow Old Along with Me! The Best Is Yet to Be." *Psychology Today,* (Dec. 1971): 45.

Neuringer, A. J. "Superstitious Key Pecking After Three Peck-Produced Reinforcements." *Journal of the Experimental Analysis of Behavior,* 13 (1970): 127–134.

Newman, B. M. and P. R. Newman. *Infancy and Childhood, Development and Its Contexts.* New York: Wiley, 1978.

Nickerson, R. S. and M. J. Adams. "Long-term Memory for a Common Object." *Cognitive Psychology,* 11 (1979): 287–307.

Nurnberger, J. I. and J. Zimmerman. "Applied Analysis of Human Behaviors: An Alternative to Conventional Motivational Inferences and Unconscious Determination in Therapeutic Programming." *Behavior Therapy,* 1 (1970): 59–69.

O'Brien, R. M., R. W. Figlerski, S. R. Howard and J. Caggiano. "The Effects of Multi-Year, Guaranteed Contracts on the Performance of Pitchers in Major League Baseball." Paper presented at the annual meeting of the American Psychological Association, Los Angeles, August, 1981.

Olds, J. "Mapping the Mind onto the Brain." In *The Neurosciences: Paths of Discovery,* edited by F. G. Worden, J. P. Swazey and G. Adelman. Cambridge, Mass.: Colonial Press, 1975.

———. *Drives and Reinforcements: Behavioral Studies of Hypothalamic Functions.* New York: Raven Press, 1977.

Olds, J. and P. Milner. "Positive Reinforcement Produced by Electrical Stimulation of Septal Area and Other Regions of Rat Brain." *Journal of Comparative and Physiological Psychology,* 47 (1954): 419–427.

O'Leary, D. "Light-Hyperactivity Link Challenged." *Science News,* 112, No. 4 (July 23, 1977): 58.

O'Leary, V. E. and C. E. Depner. "Alternative Gender Roles Among Women: Masculine, Feminine, Androgenous." *Intellect,* (Jan. 1976): 313–315.

Orne, M. T. "On the Social Psychology of the Psychological Experiment: With Particular Reference to Demand Characteristics and Their Implications." *American Psychologist,* 17 (1962): 776–783.

Ornstein, R. E. *The Psychology of Consciousness.* San Francisco: Freeman, 1972.

Ornstein, R. E. and D. Galin. "Physiological Studies of Consciousness." In *Symposium on Consciousness,* edited by P. Lec, R. E. Ornstein, D. Galin, A. Deichman and C. Tart. New York: Viking, 1976.

Osgood, C. E. "The Nature and Measurement of Meaning." *Psychological Bulletin,* 49 (1952): 197–237.

———. "Studies on the Generality of Affective Meaning Systems." *American Psychologist,* 17 (1962): 10–28.

Oswald, I. *Sleeping and Waking: Physiology and Psychology.* New York: American Elsevier, 1962.

Overmier, J. B. and M. E. P. Seligman. "Effects of Inescapable Shock upon Subsequent Escape and Avoidance Learning." *Journal of Comparative and Physiological Psychology,* 63 (1967): 23–33.

Pagano, R. R. *Understanding Statistics.* St. Paul: West, 1981.

Page, J. D. *Psychopathology.* Chicago: Aldine, 1971.

Paivio, A. "Mental Imagery in Associative Learning and Memory." *Psychological Review,* 76 (1969): 241–263.

Palazolli, M. *Self Starvation.* New York: Jason Aronson, 1978.

Palkovitz, R. J. and R. K. Lore. "Note Taking and Note Review: Why Students Fail Questions Based on Lecture Material." *Teaching of Psychology,* 7 (Oct. 1980): 159–160.

Palmer, M. H., M. E. Lloyd and K. E. Lloyd. "An Experimental Analysis of Electricity Conservation Procedures." *Journal of Applied Behavior Analysis,* 10 (1977): 665–671.

Pappenheimer, J. R. "The Sleep Factor." *Scientific American,* (Aug. 1976).

Pardine, P., A. Napoli, M. Goodman, and M. Schure. "Physiological Correlates of Recent Life Stress Experience." Paper presented at the annual convention of the American Psychological Association, Los Angeles, August 1981.

Parke, R. D. "The Father of the Child." From *The Sciences,* (April 1979). Reprinted in *Psychology 82/83.* Guilford, Connecticut: Dushkin Publishing Group, 1982.

Parke, R. D. and D. B. Sawin. "Fathering: It's a Major Role." *Psychology Today,* (Nov. 1977).

Parkes, C. M. *Grief: The Painful Reaction to the Loss of a Loved One.* Monograph, University of California, San Diego, 1979.

Parlee, M. B. "Psychology and Women." *Journal of Women in Culture and Society,* 5 (1979): 121–133.

Parlee, M. B. and the Editors of *Psychology Today* Magazine. "The Friendship Bond." *Psychology Today,* (October 1979).

Parnes, S. J. *Creative Behavior Workbook.* New York: Scribners, 1967.

Patterson, F. "Conversations With a Gorilla." *National Geographic,* 154, No. 4 (1978): 438–465.

Pavlov, I. P. *Conditioned Reflexes.* Translated by G. V. Anrep. New York: Dover, 1927.

Pelham, W. E. "Withdrawal of a Stimulant Drug and Concurrent Behavioral Intervention in the Treatment of a Hyperactive Child." *Behavior Therapy,* 8, No. 3 (1977): 473–479.

Penfield, W. "Brain's Record of Past: A Continuous Movie Film." *Science News Letter,* (April 27, 1957): 265.

———. *The Excitable Cortex in Conscious Man.* Springfield, Ill.: Charles C Thomas, 1958.

———. *The Mystery of the Mind: A Critical Study of Consciousness and the Human Brain.* Princeton, N.J.: Princeton University Press, 1975.

Penfield, W. and L. Roberts. *Speech and Brain Mechanisms.* Princeton, N.J.: Princeton University Press, 1959.

Perin, C. T. "A Quantitative Investigation of the Delay of Reinforcement Gradient." *Journal of Experimental Psychology,* 32 (1943): 37–51.

Perkins, D. G. and F. M. Perkins. *Nailbiting and Cuticlebiting: Kicking the Habit.* Richardson, Texas: Self Control Press, 1976.

Perlmutter, F. and H. A. Silverman. "CMHC: A Structural Anachronism." *Social Work,* 17 (1972): 78–84.

Perls, F. *Gestalt Therapy Verbatim.* Lafayette, Calif.: Real People Press, 1969.

Peters, W. A. *A Class Divided.* Garden City, N.Y.: Doubleday, 1971.

Peterson, L. R. and M. J. Peterson. "Short-Term Retention of Individual Verbal Items." *Journal of Experimental Psychology,* 58 (1959): 193–198.

Phillips, J. L. *Origins of Intellect: Piaget's Theory.* San Francisco: Freeman, 1969.

Piaget, J. *The Psychology of Intelligence.* New York: Norton, 1951 (Original French, 1945).

———. *The Origins of Intelligence in Children.* New York: International University Press, 1952.

Pierrel, R. and J. G. Sherman. "Train Your Pet the Barnabus Way." *Brown Alumni Monthly,* (Feb. 1963).

Piliavin, I. M., J. Rodin, and J. A. Piliavin. "Good Samaritanism: An Underground Phenomenon?" *Journal of Personality and Social Psychology,* 13 (1969): 289–299.

Pilkonis, P. A. "The Behavioral Consequences of Shyness." *Journal of Personality,* 45 (1977): 596–611.

Pines, M. "How Three-Year-Olds Teach Themselves to Read—and Love It." *Harper's Magazine,* (May 1963): 58–64.

———. "Why Some Three-Year-Olds Get A's and Some Get C's." *The New York Times Magazine,* (July 16, 1969): 4–5, 10–17.

———. "Infants Are Smarter Than Anybody Thinks." *The New York Times Magazine,* (Nov. 29, 1970): 32–33, 110, 114–120.

———. "The Sinister Hand." *Science 80,* (Dec. 1980): 26–27.

Playboy, 16, No. 2 (1969): 46.

Plutchik, R. *Emotion.* New York: Harper & Row, 1980.

Premack, A. J. and D. Premack. "Teaching Language to an Ape." *Scientific American,* (Oct. 1972): 92–99.

Premack, D. "Reinforcement Theory." In *Nebraska Symposium on Motivation,* edited by D. Levine. Lincoln: University of Nebraska Press, 1965.

———. "The Education of S*A*R*A*H." *Psychology Today,* (Sept. 1970): 54–58.

President's Commission on Mental Health. Report to the President. Washington, D.C.: U.S. Government Printing Office, 1978.

Preston, H. J. "Diet Is Not the Cause of Hyperactivity." *Science News,* 111, No. 26 (June 25, 1977): 406–407.

Pritchard, R. M. "A Collimator Stabilizing System." *Quarterly Journal of Experimental Psychology,* 13 (1961): 181–183.

Pronko, N. H. "Are Geniuses Born or Made?" In *Panorama of Psychology.* Belmont, Calif.: Brooks/Cole, 1969, pp. 215–219.

Pueschel, S. M., C. D. Canning, A. Murphy and E. Zausmer. *Down Syndrome: Growing and Learning.* Kansas City, Mo.: Sheed Andrews & McMeel, 1978.

Pulaski, M. A. "Toys and Imaginative Play." In *The Child's World of Make-Believe: Experimental Studies of Imaginative Play,* edited by J. L. Singer. New York: Academic Press, 1973.

Rahe, R. H. "Subjects' Recent Life Changes and Their Near-Future Illness Reports." *Annals of Clinical Research,* 4 (1972). 250–265.

Rahula, W. *What the Buddha Taught.* New York: Grove Press, 1959.

Randi, J. *Flim-Flam!* New York: Lippincott and Crowell, 1980.

Raven, B. H. "The Analysis of Power and Power Preference." In J. T. Tebeschi (ed.) *Prospectus on Social Power.* Chicago: Aldine, 1974.

Reif, A. E. "The Causes of Cancer." *American Scientist,* 69, No. 4 (1981): 437–447.

Reiss, D. "Competing Hypothesis and Waring Factions: Applying Knowledge of Schizophrenia." *Schizophrenia Bulletin,* No. 8 (Spring 1974).

Rescorla, R. *Pavlovian Second-Order Conditioning: Studies in Associative Learning.* MacEachren Lectures, Halsted Press, 1980.

Resnick, R. B., R. S. Kestenbaum, and L. K. Schwartz. "Acute Systemic Effects of Cocaine in Man: A Controlled Study in Intranasal and Intravenous Routes." *Science,* 195, No. 4279 (1977): 696–698.

Rethlingshater, D. and E. D. Hinckley. "Influence of Judge's Characteristics upon the Adaptation Level." *American Journal of Psychology,* 76 (1963): 116–123.

Rhine, J. B. *New World of the Mind.* New York: Sloane, 1953.

———. Security Versus Deception in Parapsychology." *Journal of Parapsychology,* 38 (1974): 99–121.

———. "History of Experimental Studies." In *Handbook of Parapsychology,* edited by B. B. Wolman. Van Nostrand Reinhold, 1977.

Rice, B. "The New Truth Machines." *Psychology Today,* (June 1978): 61–77.

Rieger, M. G. "Pain Control Through Hypnosis." *Science News,* (Oct. 30, 1976).

Riesen, A. H. "Effects of Early Deprivation of Phobic Stimulation." In *The Biosocial Basis of Mental Retardation,* edited by S. Osler and R. Cooke. Baltimore, Md.: Johns Hopkins University Press, 1965.

Rimland, B. "Inside the Mind of the Autistic Savant." *Psychology Today,* 12 (1978): 68–80.

Rimland, B. and H. Munsinger. Letter to *Science,* 195, No. 4275 (Jan. 21, 1977): 246–247.

Rincover, A., C. D. Newsom, O. I. Lovaas and R. L. Koegel. "Some Motivational Properties of Sensory Stimulation in Psychotic Children." *Journal of Experimental Child Psychology,* 24 (1977): 312–323.

Ristow, W. "Larry P. versus IQ Tests." *The Progressive,* 42 (Nov. 1978): 48–50.

Roberts, D. F. and C. M. Bachen. "Mass Communication Effects." *Annual Review of Psychology,* 32 (1981): 307–356.

Robinson, F. P. *Effective Behavior.* New York: Harper & Row, 1941.

Robinson, H. B. and N. M. Robinson. "Mental Retardation." In *Carmichael's Manual of Child Psychology,* Vol. 2 (3rd ed.), edited by P. H. Mussen. New York: Wiley, 1970.

Rock, I. and L. Kaufman. "The Moon Illusion II." *Science,* 136 (1962): 1023–1031.

Rodin, J. "The Puzzle of Obesity." *Human Nature* (Feb. 1978).

Rogers, C. R. "The Necessary and Sufficient Conditions of Therapeutic Personality Change." *Journal of Consulting Psychology,* 21 (1957): 95–103.

———. "A Theory of Therapy, Personality, and Interpersonal Relationships, as Developed in the Client-Centered Framework." In *Psychology: A Study of a Science,* Vol. 3, edited by S. Koch. New York: McGraw-Hill, 1959.

———. *On Becoming a Person: A Therapist's View of Psychotherapy.* Boston: Houghton Mifflin, 196.

———. "Learning to Be Free." A paper given at a session on "Conformity and Diversity" in the conference on "Man and Civilization," sponsored by the University of California School of Medicine, San Francisco, Jan. 28, 1962.

Rogers, J. M. "Drug Abuse—Just What the Doctor Ordered." *Psychology Today,* (Sept. 1971): 16–24.

Rokeach, M. *The Open and Closed Mind.* New York: Basic Books, 1960.

Romanes, G. J. *Animal Intelligence.* New York: Appleton-Century-Crofts, 1912.

Rosch, E. "Classification of Real-world Objects: Origins and Representations in Cognition." In *Thinking: Reading in Cognitive Science,* edited by P. N. Johnson-Laird and P. C. Watson. Cambridge: Cambridge University Press, 1977.

Rosenhan, D. L. "On Being Sane in Insane Places." *Science,* 179 (1973): 250–258.

Rosenman, R. H., R. J. Brand, C. D. Jenkins, M. Friedman, R. Straus, and M. Wurm. "Coronary heart disease in the Western Collaborative Group Study: Final follow-up experience of 8 1/2 years." *Journal of the American Medical Association,* 233 (1975): 872–877.

Rosenthal, D. and O. W. Quinn. "Quadruplet Hallucinations: Phenotypic Variations of a Schizophrenic Genotype." *Archives of General Psychiatry,* 34, No. 7 (July 1977): 817–827.

Rosenthal, R. "Clever Hans: A Case Study of Scientific Method." Introduction to *Clever Hans: (The Horse of Mr. Von Osten),* O. Pfungst. New York: Holt, 1965.

———. *Experimenter Effects in Behavioral Research.* New York: Appleton-Century-Crofts, 1966.

———. "Interpersonal Expectations: Effects of the Experimenter's Hypothesis." In *Artifact in Behavioral Research,* edited by R. Rosenthal and R. L. Rosnow. New York: Academic Press, 1969, pp. 182–277.

———. "The Pygmalion Effect Lives." *Psychology Today,* (Sept. 1973): 56–63.

———. *Experimenter Effects in Behavioral Research.* New York: Irvington, 1976.

Rosenthal, R. and K. L. Fode. "The Effect of Experimenter Bias on the Performance of the Albino Rat." *Behavioral Science,* 8 (1963): 183–189.

Rosenthal, T. L., K. S. Linehan, J. E. Kelley, R. H. Rosenthal, D. E. Theobald and A. F. Davis. "Group Aversion by Imaginal, Vicarious and Shared Recipient-Observer Shocks." *Behavior Research and Therapy,* 16 (1978): 421–427.

Rosenthal, T. L. and R. Rosenthal. "The Vicious Cycle of Stress Reaction." Copyright, 1980, Renate and Ted Rosenthal, Stress Management Clinic, Department of Psychiatry, University of Tennessee College of Medicine, Memphis, Tenn.

Rosenthal, T. L. and G. M. White. "On the Importance of Hair in Student's Clinical Inferences." *Journal of Clinical Psychology,* 28, No. 1 (1972): 43–47.

Rosenthal, T. L. and B. J. Zimmerman. *Social Learning and Cognition.* New York: Academic Press, 1978.

Rosenzweig, M. R. "Auditory Localization." *Scientific American,* 205 (1961): 132–142.

Roskies, E. and R. Lazarus. "Coping Theory and the Teaching of Coping Skills." In *Behavioral Medicine: Changing Health Life Styles,* edited by P. Davidson and S. Davidson. New York: Brunner/Mazel, 1980.

Rosow, I. "Adjustment of the Normal Aged." In *Processes of Aging.* Vol. 2, edited by R. Williams, C. Tibbitts, and W. Donahue. New York: Atherton Press, 1963.

Ross, J. "The Resources of Binocular Perception." *Scientific American,* (March 1976): 80–86.

Ross, L. "The Intuitive Psychologist and His Shortcomings: Distortions in the Attribution Process." In *Advances in Experimental Social Psychology,* edited by L. Berkowitz. New York: Academic Press, 1977.

Ross, M., R. Karniol, and M. Rothstein. "Reward Contingency and Intrinsic Motivation in Children." *Journal of Personality and Social Psychology,* 33 (1976): 442–447.

Rothenberg, M. B. "Effects of Television Violence on Children and Youth." *Journal of the American Medical Association,* 234 (1975): 1043–1046.

Rotter, J. B. and D. J. Hochreich. *Personality.* Glenview, Ill.: Scott, Foresman, 1975.

Rubin, V. and L. Comitas (eds.) *Ganja in Jamaica.* The Hague: Mouton, 1975.

Rubin, Z. "Jokers Wild in the Lab." *Psychology Today,* (Dec. 1970).

———. "Measurement of Romantic Love." *Journal of Personality and Social Psychology,* 16 (1970): 265–273.

———. *Liking and Loving: An Invitation to Social Psychology.* New York: Holt, 1973.

———. "Disclosing Oneself to a Stranger: Reciprocity and Its Limits." *Journal of Experimental and Social Psychology,* 11 (1975): 233–260.

Rubinstein, E. A. "Television and the Young Viewer." *American Scientist,* 66 (1978): 685–693.

Rubinstein, E. A., R. M. Liebert, J. M. Neale, and R. W. Poulos. *Assessing Television's Influence on Children's Prosocial Behavior.* New York: Brookdale International Institute, 1974.

Ruch, F. L. and P. G. Zimbardo. *Psychology and Life* (8th ed.). Glenview, Ill.: Scott, Foresman, 1971.

Rudestam, K. E. "Stockholm and Los Angeles: A Cross-Cultural Study of the Communication of Suicidal Intent." *Journal of Consulting and Clinical Psychology,* 36 (1971): 82–90.

Ruff, H. A. and H. G. Birch. "Infant Visual Fixation: The Effect of Concentricity, Curvilinearity, and Number of Directions." *Journal of Experimental Child Psychology,* 17 (1974): 460–473.

Rushton, N. A. H. "Visual Pigments and Color Blindness." *Scientific American,* (March 1975): 64–74.

Saegert, S., W. Swap, and R. B. Zajonc. "Exposure, Context, and Interpersonal Attraction." *Journal of Personality and Social Psychology,* 25 (1973): 234–242.

Sage, W. "ESP and the Psychology Establishment." *Human Behavior,* (Sept.–Oct. 1972).

Sandman, C. A., J. M. George, J. D. Nolan, H. Van Riezen, and A. J. Kastin. "Enhancement of Attention in man with ACTH/MSH 4-10." *Physiology and Behavior,* 15 (1975): 427–431.

Sarason, I. G. "Test Anxiety, Attention, and the General Problem of Anxiety." In *Stress and Anxiety,* Vol. 1, edited by C. D. Spielberger and I. G. Sarason. Washington, D.C.: Hemisphere, 1975.

Savage-Rumbaugh, E. S., D. M. Rumbaugh, and S. Boysen. "Do Apes Use Language?" *American Scientist,* 68 (1980): 49–61.

Scarr, S. and R. A. Weinberg. "Intellectual Similarities Within Families of Both Adopted and Biological Children." *Intelligence,* 1 (1977): 170–191.

Scarr-Salapatek, S. "Race, Social Class, and I.Q." *Science,* 174 (1971): 1223–1228.

Scarr-Salapatek, S. and R. A. Weinberg. "When Black Children Grow Up in White Homes . . ." *Psychology Today,* (Dec. 1975).

Schachter, S. "Communication, Deviation, and Rejection." *Journal of Abnormal and Social Psychology,* 46 (1951): 190–207.

———. *Psychology of Affiliation.* Stanford, Calif.: Stanford University Press, 1959.

———. *Emotion, Obesity and Crime.* New York: Academic Press, 1971.

———. "Pharmacological and Psychological Determinants of Smoking." In *Smoking Behavior,* edited by R. E. Thornton. Edinburgh: Churchill Livingston, 1978.

Schachter, S. and L. P. Grose. "Manipulated Time and Eating Behavior." *Journal of Personality and Social Psychology,* 10 (1968): 98–106.

Schachter, S. and B. Latane. "Crime, Cognition, and Autonomic Nervous System." In *Nebraska Symposium on Motivation,* edited by D. Levine. Lincoln: University of Nebraska Press, 1969.

Schachter, S. and J. Rodin. *Obese Humans and Rats.* Potomac, Md.: Lawrence Earlbaum, 1974.

Schachter, S. and J. Singer. "Cognitive, Social and Physiological Determinants of Emotional State." *Psychological Review,* 69 (1962): 379–399.

Schachter, S. and L. Wheeler. "Epinephrine, Chlorpromazine and Amusement." *Journal of Abnormal and Social Psychology,* 65 (1962): 121–128.

Schaie, K. W. "Age Changes in Intelligence." In *Age, Learning Ability and Intelligence,* edited by R. L. Sprott. New York: Van Nostrand Reinhold, 1980.

Schally, A. V., A. J. Kastin, A. Arimura. "Hypothalamic Hormones: The Link Between Brain and Body." *American Scientist,* 65 (Nov.–Dec. 1977): 712–719.

Schank, R. and R. Abelson. *Scripts, Plans, Goals and Understanding.* Hillsdale, N.J.: Erlbaum, 1977.

Schein, E. H., W. F. Hill, A. Lubin, and H. L. Williams. "Distinguishing Characteristics of Collaborators and Resistors among American Prisoners of War." *Journal of Abnormal and Social Psychology,* 55 (1957): 197–201.

Schein, E. H., I. Schneier, and C. H. Barker. *Coercive Persuasion.* New York: Norton, 1961.

Schiff, M., M. Duyme, A. Dumaret, J. Stewart, S. Tomkiewicz, and J. Feingold. "Intellectual Status of Working-Class Children Adopted Early into Upper-Middle-Class Families." *Science,* 200 (June 30, 1978): 1503–1504.

Schless, A. P. "Life Events and Illness: A Three Year Prospective Study." *British Journal of Psychiatry,* 131 (July 1977): 26–34.

Schlosberg, H. "Three Dimensions of Emotion." *Psychological Review,* 61 (1954): 81–88.

Schmeidler, G. R. "Methods for Controlled Research on ESP and PK." In *Handbook of Parapsychology,* edited by B. B. Wolman. New York: Van Nostrand Reinhold, 1977.

Schmidt, J. A. *Help Yourself: A Guide to Self-Change.* Champaign, Ill.: Research Press, 1976.

Schneider, A. M. and B. Tarshis. *Physiological Psychology.* New York: Random House, 1975.

Schneidman, E. S. "You and Death." *Psychology Today,* 5, No. 1 (1971): 43–45, 74–80.

Schneidman, E. S., N. L. Farherow, and L. Cabista. *Some Facts about Suicide Causes and Prevention.* Washington, D.C.: U.S. Government Printing Office, (1965).

Schopler, E. "Changing Parental Involvement in Behavioral Treatment." In *Autism: A Reappraisal of Concepts and Treatment,* edited by M. Rutter and E. Schopler. New York: Plenum Press, 1978.

Schreiber, F. R. *Sybil.* Chicago: Regency, 1973.

Schultz, D. P. *Psychology in Use, An Introduction to Applied Psychology.* New York: Macmillan, 1979.

Schulz, R. *The Psychology of Death, Dying and Bereavement.* Reading, Mass.: Addison-Wesley, 1978.

Schwartz, C. J., H. C. McGill and W. R. Rogers. "Smoking and Cardiovascular Diseases." In *Banbury Report,* edited by G. B. Gori and F. G. Bock. Cold Spring Harbor Laboratory, 1980.

Science News, 112, No. 3 (July 16, 1977): 39.

Scott, E. M. and E. L. Verney. "Self-Selection and Diet. VI: The Nature of Appetites for B Vitamines." *Journal of Nutrition,* 34 (1947): 471–480.

Scott, J. P. "The Development of Social Motivation." In *Nebraska Symposium on Motivation,* edited by D. Levine. Lincoln: University of Nebraska Press, 1967, pp. 111–132.

Sears, R. R., E. E. Maccoby, and H. Levin. *Patterns of Child Rearing.* Evanston, Ill.: Row, Peterson, 1957.

Seiden, R. H. "Campus Tragedy: A Study of Student Suicide." *Journal of Abnormal Psychology,* 1 (1966): 389–399.

Seidenberg, M. S. and L. A. Petitto. "Signing Behavior in Apes: A Critical Review." *Cognition,* 7 (1979): 177–215.

Seligman, M. E. P. "For Helplessness: Can We Immunize the Weak?" In *Readings in Psychology Today* (2nd ed.). Del Mar, Calif.: CRM, 1972.

————. "Submissive Death: Giving Up on Life." *Psychology Today,* 7 (1974): 80–85.

Seligman, M. E. P., S. F. Maier, and R. L. Solomon. "Unpredictable and Uncontrollable Adverse Events." In *Aversive Conditioning and Learning,* edited by F. R. Brush. New York: Academic Press, 1971.

Selye, H. *The Stress of Life.* New York: Knopf, 1956, 1976.

————. *Stress in Health and Disease.* Boston: Butterworth, 1976.

Senden, M. V. *Space and Sight.* Translated by P. Heath. Glencoe, Ill.: Free Press, 1960.

Serbin, L. A. and K. D. O'Leary. "How Nursery Schools Teach Girls to Shut Up." *Psychology Today,* (Dec. 1975): 57–58, 102–103.

Sexual Medicine Today (April 1980): 17.

Shafer, R. P., Chairman, National Commission on Marihuana and Drug Abuse. *Marihuana: A Signal of Misunderstanding.* New York: Signet New American Library, 1972.

Shaffer, L. F. "Fear and Courage in Aerial Combat." *Journal of Consulting Psychology,* 11 (1947): 137–143.

Shaffer, L. F. and E. J. Shoben, Jr. *The Psychology of Adjustment* (2nd ed.). Boston: Houghton Mifflin, 1956.

Sheehan, J. G. and M. S. Costley. "A Reexamination of the Role of Heredity in Stuttering." *Journal of Speech and Hearing Disorders,* 42, No. 1 (Feb. 1977): 47–59.

Sheehy, G. *Passages: Predictable Crises from Adult Life.* New York: E. P. Dutton, 1976.

Sheils, M. and S. Monroe. "A Ban on I.Q. Tests?" *Newsweek,* (March 22, 1976): 49.

Sheldon, W. H. *Atlas of Men: A Guide for Somatotyping the Adult Male at All Ages.* New York: Harper, 1954.

Shepard, R. N. "Form, Formation, and Transformation of Internal Representations." In *Information Processing and Cognition: the Loyola Symposium,* edited by R. L. Solso. Hillsdale, N.J.: Erlbaum, 1975.

Sherif, M. "A Study of Some Social Factors in Perception." *Archives of Psychology,* 27, No. 187 (1935).

Sherif, M., O. J. Harvey, B. J. White, W. R. Hood, and C. W. Sherif. *Intergroup Conflict and Cooperation: The Robbers Cave Experiment.* Institute of Group Relations, University of Oklahoma, 1961.

Sherman, E. D. "Geriatrics: An Emerging Challenge to the Health Professions." *Journal of the American Geriatric Society,* 19 (1971): 199–207.

Shiffman, S. M. "Diminished Smoking, Withdrawal Symptoms, and Cessation: A Cautionary Note." In *Banbury Report,* edited by G. B. Gori and F. G. Bock. Cold Spring Harbor Laboratory, 1980.

Shiffrin, R. M. "Forgetting: Trace Erosion or Retrieval Failure? *Science,* 168 (1970): 1601–1603.

Shiffrin, R. M. and J. R. Cook. "Short-Term Forgetting of Item and Order Information." *Journal of Verbal Learning and Verbal Behavior,* 17 (1978): 189–218.

Shirley, M. M. *The First Two Years.* Institute of Child Welfare, Monograph No. 7. Minneapolis: University of Minnesota Press, 1933.

Shockley, W. "Dysgenics, Geneticity, Raceology: A Challenge to the Intellectual Responsibility of Educators." *Phi Delta Kappan,* 53, No. 5 (1972): 297–307.

Shulman, G. I. "Race, Sex and Violence: A Laboratory Test of the Sexual Threat of the Black Male Hypothesis." *American Journal of Sociology,* 79 (1974): 1260–1277.

Siegel, S., E. Hearst, N. George, and E. O'Neal. "Generalization Gradients Obtained from Individual Subjects Following Classical Conditioning." *Journal of Experimental Psychology,* 78 (1968): 171–174.

Siffre, M. "Six Months Alone in a Cave." *National Geographic,* 147, No. 3 (1975): 426–435.

Simon, W. and J. Gagnon. "Psychosexual Development." In *Human Sexuality: Contemporary Perspectives,* edited by E. S. Morrison and V. Borosage. Palo Alto, Calif.: Mayfield, 1973.

Singer, J. L. "Daydreaming and the Stream of Thought." *American Scientist,* 62 (1974): 417–425.

Singer, M. T. "Coming Out of the Cults." *Psychology Today,* (Jan. 1979): 72–82.

Singer, R. N. "Motor Skills and Learning Strategies." In *Learning Strategies,* edited by H. F. O'Neil, Jr. New York: Academic Press, 1978.

Skeels, H. M. "Adult Status of Children with Contrasting Early Life Experiences." *Monograph of the Society for Research in Child Development,* 31, No. 3 (1966).

Skinner, B. F. *The Behavior of Organisms.* Englewood Cliffs, N.J.: Prentice-Hall, 1938.

————. "Pigeons in a Pelican." *American Psychologist,* 15, (1960): 28–37.

————. *Beyond Freedom and Dignity.* New York: Bantam, 1971.

Smith, A. and O. Sugar. "Development of Above Normal Language and Intelligence 21 Years After Left Hemispherectomy." *Neurology,* 25 (1975): 813–818.

Smith, B. M. *The Polygraph in Contemporary Psychology.* San Francisco: Freeman, 1971.

Smith, E. M., H. O. Brown, J. E. P. Toman, and L. S. Goodman. "The Lack of Cerebral Effects of D-Tubo-Curarine." *Anesthesiology,* 8 (1947): 1–14.

Smith, M. L. and G. V. Glass. "Meta-Analysis of Psychotherapy Outcome Studies." *American Psychologist,* 32 (1977): 752–760.

Snow, C. E. "The Development of Conversation Between Mothers and Babies." *Journal of Child Language,* 4, No. 1 (February 1977): 1–22.

Snow, C. P. "Either-Or." *Progressive,* (Feb. 1961): 24.

Snyder, C. R. and R. J. Shenkel. "P. T. Barnum Effect." *Psychology Today,* 8, No. 10 (March 1975): 52–54.

Snyder, S. H. "The True Speed Trip: Schizophrenia." *Psychology Today,* (Jan. 1972).

Snyder, S. H. and S. R. Childers. "Opiate Receptors and Opioid Peptides." *Annual Review of Neuroscience,* 2 (1979): 35–64.

Solomon, R. C. and L. C. Wynne. "Traumatic Avoidance Learning: Acquisition in Normal Dogs." *Psychological Monographs,* 67, No. 4 (1953). (Whole No. 354).

Solomon, R. L. "The Opponent-Process Theory of Acquired Motivation." *American Psychologist,* (August 1980): 691–721.

Sommer, R. *Personal Space: The Behavioral Basis of Design.* Englewood Cliffs, N.J.: Prentice-Hall, 1969.

————. "Toward a Psychology of Natural Behavior." *APA Monitor,* (Jan. 1977).

Sostek, A. J. and R. J. Wyatt. "The Chemistry of Crankiness." *Psychology Today,* (Oct. 1981): 120.

Spence, J. T. and R. L. Helmreich. *Masculinity and Femininity: Their Psychological Dimensions, Correlates and Antecedents.* Austin: University of Texas Press, 1978.

Sperry, R. W. "The Eye and the Brain." *Scientific American,* Offprint No. 465 (1956): 48–52.

————. "The Great Cerebral Commissure." *Scientific American,* 210 (1964): 42–52.

————. "Hemisphere Disconnection and Unity in Conscious Awareness." *American Psychologist,* 23 (1968): 723–733.

Sperry, R. W. "Lateral Specialization in the Surgically Separated Hemispheres." In *The Neurosciences,* edited by F. S. Schmitt and F. G. Worden. Cambridge, Mass.: MIT Press, 1974.

Spielberger, C. D., W. D. Anton, and J. Bedell. "The Nature and Treatment of Test Anxiety." In *Emotions and Anxiety: New Concepts, Methods, and Applications,* edited by M. Zuckerman and C. D. Spielberger. Hillsdale, N.J.: Lawrence Erlbaum, 1976, pp. 317–345.

Spiesman, J. C., R. S. Lazarus, A. M. Mordkoff, and L. A. Davidson. "The Experimental Reduction of Stress Based on Ego-Defense Theory." *Journal of Abnormal and Social Psychology,* 68 (1964): 367–380.

Spitz, R. A. "Hospitalism: An Inquiry into the Genesis of Psychiatric Conditions in Early Childhood." In *The Psychoanalytic Study of the Child,* Vol. I. New York: International University Press, 1945, pp. 53–74.

Spitzer, H. F. "Studies in Retention." *Journal of Educational Psychology,* 30 (1939): 641–656.

Spotts, J. V. and F. C. Shontz. *Cocaine Users.* New York: The Free Press, 1980.

Sprott, R. L. and J. Staats. "Behavioral Studies Using Genetically-Defined Mice—a Bibliography." *Behavior Genetics,* 5 (1975): 27–82.

Stampfl, T. G. "Implosive Therapy: Staring Down Your Nightmares." *Psychology Today,* (Feb. 1975): 66–68, 72–73.

Staples, F. R., B. Sloane, K. Whipple, A. H. Cristol, and N. J. Yorkston. "Differences Between Behavior Therapists and Psychotherapists." *Archives of General Psychiatry,* 32 (1975): 1515–1522.

Stark, R. and J. McEvoy. "Middle-class Violence." *Psychology Today,* (Nov. 1970).

Staub, E., B. Tursky, and G. E. Schwartz. "Self-Control and Predictability: Their Effects on Reactions to Aversive Stimulation." *Journal of Personality and Social Psychology,* 18, No. 2 (1971): 157–162.

Stefanis, C., R. L. Dornbush and M. Fink. *Hashish: A Study of Long-Term Use.* New York: Raven Press, 1977.

Stein, M. I. *Stimulating Creativity,* Vol. 1. New York: Academic Press, 1974.

Sterman, M. B. "Effects of Sensorimotor EEG Feedback Training on Sleep and Clinical Manifestations of Epilepsy." In *Biofeedback and Behavior,* edited by J. Beatty and H. Legewie. New York: Plenum, 1977.

Stern, C. "Hereditary Factors Affecting Adoption: A Study of Adoption Practices." *Child Welfare League of America,* 2 (1956): 53.

Stern, D. "Some Interactive Functions of Rhythm Changes Between Mother and Infant." In *Interaction Rhythms, Periodicity in Communicative Behavior,* edited by M. Davis. New York: Human Sciences Press, 1982.

Stern, D., J. Jaffe, B. Beebe and S. Bennett. "Vocalizing in Unison and in Alternation: Two Modes of Communication within the Mother-Infant Dyad." In *Developmental Psycholinguistics and Communication Disorders,* edited by D. Aronson and R. Rieber. *Annals of the New York Academy of Sciences,* 253 (1975): 89–100.

Stevens, C. F. "The Neuron." *Scientific American,* 241 No. 3 (1979): 54–65.

Stevens, J. O. *Awareness: Exploring, Experimenting, Experiencing.* Lafayette, Calif.: Real People Press, 1971.

Stewart, K. "Dream Theory in Malaya." In *Altered States of Consciousness,* edited by Charles T. Tart. New York: Wiley, 1969.

Stoller, F. H. "The Long Weekend." *Psychology Today,* 1, No. 7 (1967): 28–33.

———. "Marathon Groups: Toward a Conceptual Model." In *New Perspectives on Encounter Groups,* edited by L. N. Solomon and B. Berzon. San Francisco: Jossey-Bass, 1972, pp. 171–194.

Strange, J. R. *Abnormal Psychology.* New York: McGraw-Hill, 1965.

Stratton, G. M. "Vision without Inversion of the Retinal Image." *Psychological Review,* 4 (1977): 341–360, 463–481.

Stunkard, A. *Obesity.* Philadelphia: Saunders, 1980.

Suedfeld, P. *Social Processes.* Dubuque, Iowa: Brown, 1966.

———. "The Benefits of Boredom: Sensory Deprivation Reconsidered." *American Scientist,* 63 (Jan.–Feb. 1975).

———. *Restricted Environmental Stimulation: Research and Clinical Applications.* New York: Wiley-Interscience, 1980.

Suinn, R. M. *Fundamentals of Behavior Pathology.* New York: Wiley, 1970.

———. *Fundamentals of Behavior Pathology* (2nd ed.). New York: Wiley, 1975.

Suomi, S. J. and H. F. Harlow. "Social Rehabilitation of Isolate-Reared Monkeys." *Developmental Psychology,* 6 (1972): 487–496.

Swensen, C. H. *Introduction to Interpersonal Relations.* Glenview, Ill.: Scott, Foresman, 1973.

Szasz, T. S. "Mental Illness Is a Myth." *The New York Times Magazine,* (June 12, 1966).

———. "The Crime of Commitment." *Psychology Today,* 2, No. 10 (1969): 55–57.

———. "The Ethics of Addiction." *Harpers,* (April, 1972).

Takooshian, H. S. Haber, and D. J. Lucido. "Who Wouldn't Help a Lost Child? You, Maybe." *Psychology Today,* (Feb. 1977): 67.

Tanner, J. M. "Growing Up." *Scientific American,* (Sept. 1973): 34–43.

Targ, R. and H. E. Puthoff. *Mind-Reach: Scientists Look at Psychic Ability.* London: Cape, 1977.

Tarpy, R. M. and R. E. Mayer. *Foundations of Learning and Memory.* Glenview, Ill.: Scott, Foresman, 1978.

Tart, C. T. *States of Consciousness.* New York: Dutton, 1975.

Taub, J. M. and R. J. Berger. "Acute Shifts in the Sleep-Wakefulness Cycle: Effects on Performance and Mood." *Psychosomatic Medicine,* 36 (March–April 1974): 164–173.

Taylor, C. W. "How Many Types of Giftedness Can Your Program Tolerate?" *The Journal of Creative Behavior,* 12 (First Quarter, 1978): 39–51.

Ten Danger Signals of Depression. The National Association for Mental Health, Virginia.

Terman, L. M. and M. Oden. *The Gifted Group in Mid-Life. Vol. 5, Genetic Studies of Genius.* Stanford, Calif.: Stanford University Press, 1959.

Terman, L. M. and M. A. Merrill. *Stanford-Binet Intelligence Scale.* Boston: Houghton Mifflin, 1937 (revised ed. 1960).

Terrace, H. *Nim.* New York: Knopf, 1979.

Thigpen, C. H. and H. M. Cleckley. *The Three Faces of Eve.* New York: McGraw-Hill, 1957.

Thomas, A., S. Chess, and H. G. Birch. *Temperament and Behavior Disorders in Children.* New York: New York University Press, 1968.

Thompson, R. I. *Foundations of Physiological Psychology.* New York: Harper & Row, 1967.

Thoreau, H. D. *Walden or Life in the Woods.* New York: Houghton Mifflin, 1893.

Tierney, J. "Doctor Is This Man Dangerous? *Science 82* (June 1982): 28–31.

Time, "Skinner's Utopia: Panacea, or Path to Hell?" (Sept. 20, 1971).

Time, (Jan. 8, 1973).

Time, (March 4, 1974).

Tobin, R. L. "Murder on Television and the Fourteen-Year-Old." *Saturday Review,* 55 (1972): 39–40.

Toffler, A. *Future Shock.* New York: Random House, 1970.

Tolman, E. C. and C. H. Honzik. "Introduction and Removal of Reward and Maze Performance in Rats." *University of California Publications in Psychology,* 4 (1930): 257–275.

Tolman, E. C., B. F. Ritchie, and D. Kalish. "Studies in Spatial Learning: II. Place Learning Versus Response Learning." *Journal of Experimental Psychology,* 36 (1946): 221–229.

Toman, W. "Birth Order Rules All." *Psychology Today,* (Dec. 1970).

Tresemer, D. W. *Fear of Success: An Intriguing Set of Questions.* New York: Plenum Press, 1977.

Triandis, H. C. *Interpersonal Behavior.* Monterey: Brooks/Cole, 1977.

Trotter, R. J. "Obesity and Behavior." *Science News,* (Aug. 3, 1974).

———. "The New Face of Birth." *Science News,* 108, No. 7 (1975): 106–108.

Truax, C. B. "Reinforcement and Non-Reinforcement in Rogerian Psychotherapy." *Journal of Abnormal Psychology,* 71 (1966): 1–9.

Tryon, R. C. "The Genetics of Learning Ability in Rats." *University of California Publications in Psychology,* 4 (1929): 71–89.

Tulving, E. "Episodic and Semantic Memory." In *Organization and Memory,* edited by E. Tulving and W. Donaldson. New York: Academic Press, 1972.

Turek, I. S. and T. E. Hanlon. "The Effectiveness and Safety of Electroconvulsive Therapy (ECT)." *Journal of Nervous and Mental Disease.* 164, No. 6 (1977): 419–431.

Turnbull, C. M. "Some Observations Regarding the Experiences and Behavior of the Bambuti Pygmies." *American Journal of Psychology,* 74 (1961): 304–308.

Udry, J. R. and N. M. Morris. "Human Sexual Behavior at Different Stages of the Menstrual Cycle." *Journal of Reproduction and Fertility,* 51, (1977): 419.

Ullman, L. and L. Krasner. *A Psychological Approach to Abnormal Behavior.* Englewood Cliffs, N.J.: Prentice-Hall, 1975.

Ulrich, R. E., T. J. Stachnik, and N. R. Stainton. "Student Acceptance of Generalized Personality Interpretations." *Psychological Reports,* 131 (1963): 831–834.

Underwood, B. J. "Interference and Forgetting." *Psychological Review,* 64 (1957): 49–60.

Unger, R. K. "Toward a Redefinition of Sex and Gender." *American Psychologist,* 34, No. 11 (Nov., 1979): 1085–1094.

U.S. Commission on Civil Rights. *Window Dressing on the Set: Women and Minorities in Television.* Washington, D.C.: Government Printing Office, 1977.

U.S. Department of Commerce and Bureau of the Census. *Statistical Abstract of the United States: 1978.* U.S. Government Printing Office, Washington, D.C., September 1978.

U.S. National Commission on the Causes and Prevention of Violence. *To Establish Justice to Insure Domestic Tranquility: The Final Report.* New York: Praeger, 1970.

U.S. News and World Report "Aptitude Test Scores: Grumbling Gets Louder," 86 (May 14, 1979): 76–79.

Valins, S. "Cognitive Effects of False Heart-Rate Feedback." *Journal of Personality and Social Psychology,* 4 (1966): 400–408.

———. "Emotionality and Information Concerning Internal Reactions." *Journal of Personality and Social Psychology,* 6 (1967): 458–463.

Van de Castle, R. L. *The Psychology of Dreaming.* Morristown, N.J.: General Learning Corporation, 1971.

Vander Zanden, J. W. *Social Psychology.* New York: Random House, 1977.

Van Gelder, L. and C. Carmichael. "But What About Our Sons." *Ms Magazine,* (Oct. 1975).

van Lawick-Goodall, J. *In The Shadow of Man.* New York: Houghton Mifflin, 1971.

Verhave, T. "The Pigeon as a Quality Control Inspector." *American Psychologist,* 21 (1966): 109–115.

Vigersky, R. *Anorexia Nervosa.* New York: Raven Press, 1977.

Vils, U. "Alcoholism: Tempest in a Shot Glass." *Los Angeles Times,* (Feb. 26, 1976).

Vogler, R. E., T. A. Weissbach, J. V. Compton, and G. T. Martin. "Integrated Behavior Change Techniques for Problem Drinkers in the Community." *Journal of Consulting and Clinical Psychology,* 45, No. 2 (1977): 267–279.

Waid, W. M. and Orne, M. T. "The Physiological Detection of Deception." *American Scientist,* 70 (July–Aug. 1982): 402–409.

Wall, P. D. In *Advances in Pain Research and Therapy,* Vol. 1, edited by J. J. Bonica and D. Albe-Fessard. New York: Raven Press, 1976.

Wallace, R. and H. Benson. "The Physiology of Meditation." *Scientific American,* 226 (1972): 84–90.

Wallach, M. A. and N. Kogan. *Modes of Thinking in Young Children.* New York: Holt, 1965.

Walster, E. "Passionate Love." In *Theories of Attraction and Love,* edited by B. I. Murstein. New York: Springer, 1971.

Watson, J. B. "Psychology as the Behaviorist Views It." *Psychological Review,* 20 (1913): 158–177.

———. *Bahaviorism* (revised ed.). Chicago: The University of Chicago Press, 1930.

Watson, J. B. and R. Rayner. "Conditioned Emotional Reaction." *Journal of Experimental Psychology,* 3 (1920): 1–14.

Webb, W. *Sleep the Gentle Tyrant.* Englewood Cliffs, N.J.: Prentice-Hall, 1975.

———. "Sleep and Dreams, Part I." *Annual Review of Psychology,* 29 (1978): 223–252.

Webb, W. B. and H. W. Agnew. "Are We Chronically Sleep Deprived?" *Bulletin of the Psychonomic Society,* 6, No. 1 (July 1975): 47–48.

Wechsler, D. *The Measurement and Appraisal of Adult Intelligence* (4th ed.). Baltimore: Williams and Wilkins, 1958.

Wegner, D. M. and R. R. Vallacher. *Implicit Psychology.* New York: Oxford University Press, 1977.

Weinberg, M. S. and C. J. Williams. *Male Homosexuals.* New York: Oxford University Press, 1974.

Weinland, J. D. *How to Improve Your Memory.* New York: Barnes and Noble, 1957.

Weisinger, M. "The Amazing Kreskin—It's All in the Mind." *Parade,* (July 24, 1977): 10.

Weiss, J. M. "Psychological Factors in Stress and Disease." *Scientific American,* 26 (1972): 104–113.

Weisstein, N. "Psychology Constructs the Female." In *Perspectives on Psychology,* edited by I. S. Cohen. New York: Praeger, 1975, pp. 318–331.

Weitzenhoffer, A. M. and E. R. Hilgard. *Stanford Hypnotic Susceptibility Scales Forms A and B.* Palo Alto, Calif.: Consulting Psychologists Press, 1959.

Weizenbaum, J. "ELIZA—A Computer Program for the Study of Natural Language Communication Between Man and Machine." *Communications of The Association For Computing Machinery,* 9 (Jan. 1966): 36–43.

Welch, R. B. *Perceptual Modification: Adapting to Altered Sensory Environments.* New York: Academic Press, 1978.

Wertheimer, M. *Productive Thinking.* New York: Harper & Row, 1959.

Whimbey, A., with L. S. Whimbey. *Intelligence Can Be Taught.* New York: Dutton, 1980.

White, B. L. and R. Held. "Plasticity of Sensorimotor Development in the Human Infant." In *The Causes of Behavior,* Vol. I (2nd ed.), edited by J. F. Rosenblith and W. Allinsmith. Boston: Allyn & Bacon, 1966.

White, B. L. and J. C. Watts. *Experience and Environment,* Vol. I. Englewood Cliffs, N.J.: Prentice-Hall, 1973.

White, T. "What Is a Decibel?" *Journal of Guitar Acoustics,* 4 (Sept. 1981): 31–35.

Whorf, B. L. "Science and Linguistics." *Technology Review,* 34 (1940): 229–231, 247–248.

Wicken, D. D., C. K. Allen, and F. A. Hill. "Effects of Instruction and UCS Strength on Extinction of the Conditioned GSR." *Journal of Experimental Psychology,* 66 (1963): 235–240.

Wickes, I. G. "Treatment of Persistent Enuresis with the Electric Buzzer." *Archives of Diseases in Childhood,* 33 (1958): 160–164.

Wilhelm, J. L. *The Search for Superman.* New York: Simon & Schuster, Pocket Books, 1976.

Williams, B. M. "Promise and Caution—'Hypnosis is Like A Scalpel. You Wouldn't Want it Wielded by Your Janitor.'" *Psychology Today,* (Nov. 1974).

Williams, G. J. and J. Money, (eds.). *Traumatic Abuse and Neglect of Children at Home.* Baltimore, Md.: Johns Hopkins University Press, 1980.

Williams, R. L. "The Bitch-100: A Culture-Specific Test." *Journal of Afro-American Issues,* 3 (1975): 103–116.

Williams, R. L., *et al.* "Sleep Patterns in Young Adults: An EEG Study." *Electroencephalography and Clinical Neurophysiology,* (1964): 376–381.

Williams, R. L. and J. D. Long. *Toward A Self-Managed Life Style.* Boston: Houghton Mifflin Co., 1979.

Wilson, R. R. "Perceptual Distinction of Height as a Function of Ascribed Academic Status." *Journal of Social Psychology,* 74 (1968): 97–102.

Wilson, S., B. Strong, L. M. Clarke, and J. Thomas. *Human Sexuality.* St. Paul: West, 1977.

Wing, C. W., Jr. and M. A. Wallach. *College Admissions and the Psychology of Talent.* New York: Holt, 1971.

Winget, C. and M. Kramer. *Dimensions of Dreams.* Gainesville: University Presses of Florida, 1979.

Winter, D. G. *The Power Motive.* New York: The Free Press, 1973.

Winterbottom, M. R. "The Relationship of Childhood Training in Independence to Achievement Motivation." Unpublished doctoral dissertation, Ann Arbor, Mich.: University of Michigan, 1953.

———. "The Relationship of Need for Achievement to Learning Experiences in Independence and Mastery." In *Motives in Fantasy, Action, and Society,* edited by J. W. Atkinson, Princeton, N. J.: Van Nostrand, 1958.

Wolcott, J. H., R. R. McNeekin, R. E. Burgin, and R. E. Yanowitch. "Correlation of General Aviation Accidents with the Biorhythm Theory." *Human Factors,* 19, No. 3 (June 1977): 283–293.

Wolfe, J. B. "Effectiveness of Token Rewards for Chimpanzees." *Comparative Psychology Monographs,* 12, No. 5 (1936). Whole No. 60.

Wolpe, J. *The Practice of Behavior Therapy* (2nd ed.). New York: Pergamon, 1974.

Wood, M. M. and S. T. Greenfield. "Women Managers and Fear of Success: A Study in the Field." *Sex Roles,* 2 (1976): 375–387.

Woodmansee, J. J. "The Pupil Response as a Measure of Social Attitudes." In *Attitude Measurement,* edited by G. F. Summers. Chicago: Rand McNally, 1970.

Woods, R. L. and H. B. Greenhouse. *The New World of Dreams.* New York: Macmillan, 1974.

Woolfolk, R. and F. Richardson. *Stress, Sanity and Survival.* New York: Signet, 1978.

Wulbert, M. and R. Dries. "The Relative Efficacy of Methylphenidate (Ritalin) and Behavior-Modification Techniques in the Treatment of a Hyperactive Child." *Journal of Applied Behavior Analysis,* 10, No. 1 (Spring 1977): 21–31.

Wursig, B. "Dolphins." *Scientific American,* 240, No. 3 (March 1979): 136–148.

Yalom, I. D. *Existential Psychotherapy.* New York: Basic Books, 1980.

Zajonc, R. B. "Dumber by the Dozen." *Psychology Today,* (Jan. 1975): 37–43.

Zajonc, R. B. and G. B. Markus. "Birth Order and Intellectual Development." *Psychological Review,* 82 (1975): 74–88.

Zaludek, G. M. "How to Cope with Male Menopause." *Science Digest,* (Feb. 1976): 74–79.

Zarcone, V. *et al.* "REM Deprivation and Schizophrenia." In *Recent Advances in Biological Psychiatry,* edited by J. Wortis. New York: Plenum Press, 1971.

Zigler, E. "On Growing Up, Learning and Loving." *Human Behavior,* (March 1973).

Zimbardo, P. G. "Toward a More Perfect Justice." *Psychology Today,* 1, No. 3 (1967): 44–46.

———. "On the Ethics of Intervention in Human Psychological Research: With Special Reference to the Stanford Prison Experiment." *Cognition,* 2 (1974): 243–256.

———. *Psychology and Life* (9th ed.). Glenview, Ill.: Scott, Foresman, 1975.

Zimbardo, P. G., C. Haney, and W. C. Banks. "A Pirandellian Prison." *The New York Times Magazine,* (April 8, 1973).

Zimbardo, P. G., P. A. Pilkonis and R. M. Norwood. "The Social Disease Called Shyness." In *Annual Editions, Personality and Adjustment 78/79.* Guilford, Conn.: Dushkin Publishing Group, 1978.

Zimbardo, P. G. and F. L. Ruch. *Psychology and Life.* Glenview, Ill.: Scott, Foresman, 1977.

Zinberg, N. E. "The War Over Marijuana." *Psychology Today,* (Dec. 1976): 92–98.

Zubek, J. "Sensory and Perceptual-Motor Processes." In *Sensory Deprivation: Fifteen Years of Research,* edited by J. Zubek. New York: Appleton-Century-Crofts, 1969b, pp. 207–253.

Zuckerman, M. *Manual and Research Report for the Sensation Seeking Scale (SSS).* Mimeograph, University of Delaware, Newark, Del., April 1972.

Zuckerman, M. and S. Allison. "An Objective Measure of Fear of Success: Construction and Validation." *Journal of Personality,* 40 (1976): 422–430.

Zung, W. W. K. and R. H. Green, Jr. "Seasonal Variation of Suicide and Depression." *Archives of General Psychiatry,* 30 (1974): 89–91.

Index